28th Pacific Asia Conference on Language, Information and Computing 2014

(PACLIC 28)

AA005253

Phuket, Thailand
12-14 December 2014

Editors:

Wirote Aroonmanakun
Prachya Boonkwan
Thepchai Supnithi

ISBN: 978-1-63439-928-9

Printed from e-media with permission by:

Curran Associates, Inc.
57 Morehouse Lane
Red Hook, NY 12571

Some format issues inherent in the e-media version may also appear in this print version.

Copyright© (2014) by the Association for Computational Linguistics
All rights reserved.

Printed by Curran Associates, Inc. (2015)

For permission requests, please contact the Association for Computational Linguistics at the address below.

Association for Computational Linguistics
209 N. Eighth Street
Stroudsburg, Pennsylvania 18360

Phone: 1-570-476-8006
Fax: 1-570-476-0860

acl@aclweb.org

Additional copies of this publication are available from:

Curran Associates, Inc.
57 Morehouse Lane
Red Hook, NY 12571 USA
Phone: 845-758-0400
Fax: 845-758-2634
Email: curran@proceedings.com
Web: www.proceedings.com

Table of Contents

Keynote Speeches

Invited Talks

Regular Papers

Welcome Message

Distinguished scholars and colleagues,

It is my great pleasure and honour to be here today to open the 28th Pacific Asia Conference on Language, Information and Computing which is held in Thailand for the first time.

This year's PACLIC annual meeting maintains the long-standing mission of PACLIC conferences to emphasize the synergy of theoretical analysis and processing of language, and to serve as a venue for scholars working on issues pertaining to different languages in the Pacific-Asia region to share their findings and experiences. It provides wonderful opportunities for participants to build a strong academic network, be enlightened by new insights, get entertained intellectually, and return home ready to initiate new significant contribution.

For the past years since its establishment, the PACLIC conferences have gained more and more interests and participations from linguistic researchers, as evidenced by the increasing number of papers and by the wider range of topics. Likewise, the current PACLC conference has received an overwhelming response of 151 papers from 27 countries or regions namely China, Hong Kong, Japan, Republic of Korea, Taiwan, Indonesia, Malaysia, Philippines, Thailand, Vietnam, India, Pakistan, Kazakhstan, Czech Republic, Finland, France, Germany, Ireland, Norway, Romania, Russian Federation, United Kingdom, United States, Egypt, Tunisia, New Zealand and Australia. (78.15% from 13 regions in Asia, 13.24% from 9 regions in Europe, 3.97% from the United States, 2.65% from Africa, 1.33% from New Zealand, and 0.66% from Australia). To ensure that all accepted papers meet the high quality standard of the PACLIC conference, each submission was reviewed by three reviewers. As a result, only approximately 37 % of top-notch academic papers were accepted for oral presentations and 13 % for poster sessions. From these accepted papers, 69 papers were presented and published in this proceedings.

Ladies and gentlemen, the successful conference is the result of tremendous efforts and contributions from several parties. We congratulate the Department of Linguistics, Chulalongkorn University, the National Electronics and Computer Technology Center (NECTEC) and Sirindhorn International Institute of Technology (SIIT) for their collaboration towards this significant achievement. We would like to take this opportunity to thank our keynote and invited speakers, namely Professor Mark Steedman and Professor Bonnie Webber from the University of Edinburgh, Professor Christian Matthiessen from Hong Kong Polytechnic University, Dr.Virach Sornlertlamvanich from the Technology Promotion Association (Thailand-Japan), Professor Jae-Woong Choe from Korea University, and Professor Min Zhang from Soochow University. We are overwhelmed with a sense of gratitude for the presenters and colleagues for donating your valuable time to attend and enrich this conference. We also wish to extend our sincere appreciation to the steering committee for their guidance and to the organizing team for their essential supports and dedicated works. Last but not least, we remain profoundly grateful to the sponsors: Chula Global Network, the Division of Research Development and Promotion, and the Research Affairs Division, Faculty of Arts.

It is now time to declare the 28th Pacific Asia Conference on Language, Information and Computing open. May this conference succeed in all its aims and may it stimulate broader insights into theoretical and computational linguistics for all participants and related organizations.

Conference Chair and Co-Chair

Wirote Aroonmanakun (Chulalongkorn University)

Thepchai Supnithi (National Electronics and Computer Technology Center)

Acknowledgments

PACLIC 28, the 28th Pacific Asia Conference on Language, Information and Computation, is organized by Department of Linguistics, Chulalongkorn University (CU), Language and Semantic Technology Laboratory, National Electronics and Computer Technology Center (NECTEC), and Sirindhorn International Institute of Technology (SIIT), under the auspices of PACLIC Steering Committee.

We gratefully acknowledge the support from the Chula Global Network, the Division of Research Development and Promotion, and the Research Affairs Division, Faculty of Arts.

PACLIC 28 Organizers

Steering Committee: Standing Members (in alphabetic order of surnames)

Hee-Rahk Chae, Hankuk University of Foreign Studies, Seoul

Chu-Ren Huang, The Hong Kong Polytechnic University, Hong Kong

Rachel Edita O. Roxas, National University, Manila

Maosong Sun, Tsinghua University, Beijing

Benjamin T'sou, City University of Hong Kong, Hong Kong

Kei Yoshimoto, Tohoku University, Sendai

Min Zhang, Soochow University, Suzhou

Organizer:

Department of Linguistics, Chulalongkorn University

Co-Organizers:

National Electronics and Computer Technology Center

Sirindhorn International Institute of Technology

Program Committee:

Chairs:

Aroonmanakun, Wirote (Chulalongkorn University)

Chae, Hee-Rahk (Hankuk University of Foreign Studies, Seoul)

Lai, Huei-Ling (National Chengchi University)

Supnithi, Thepchai (National Electronics and Computer Technology Center)

Yoshimoto, Kei (Tohoku University)

PC Members

Bond, Francis (Nanyang Technological University)

Boonkwan, Prachya (National Electronics and Computer Technology Center)

Chen, Doris (National Taiwan Normal University)

Chen, Kuang-Hua (National Taiwan University)

Chng, Eng-Siong (Nanyang Technological University)

Chui, Kawai (National Chengchi University, Taiwan)

Daille, Beatrice (Laboratoire d'Informatique de Nantes Atlantique)

Dellwo, Volker (University of Zurich)

Dita, Shirley (De La Salle University-Manila)

Fang, Alex Chengyu (The City University of Hong Kong)

Fu, Guohong (Heilongjiang University)

Gao, Wei (Qatar Computing Research Institute)

Gao, Helena (Nayang Technological University)

Harada, Yasunari (Waseda University)

Haruechaiyasak, Choochart (National Electronics and Computer Technology Center)

Hayashibe, Yuta (Kyoto University)

Hong, Munpyo (Sungkyunkwan University)

Hsieh, Shu-Kai (National Taiwan Normal University)

Jenks, Peter (UC Berkeley)

Ji, Donghong (Wuhan University)

Jiang, Wen Bin (Institute of Computing, CAS)

Kim, Jong-Bok (Kyung Hee University)

Kordoni, Valia (Humboldt University Berlin)

Kosawat, Krit (National Electronics and Computer Technology Center)

Kwong, Oi Yee (City University of Hong Kong)

Lai, Bong Yeung Tom (City University of Hong Kong)

Law, Paul (City University of Hong Kong)

Levow, Gina-Anne (University of Washington)

Li, Haizhou (Institute for Infocomm Research)

Liu, Jyi-Shane (National Chengchi University)

Ma, Qing (Ryukoku University)

Maekawa, Takafumi (Fuculty of Sociology, Ryukoku University)

Matsumoto, Yuji (Nara Institute of Science and Technology)

Morey, Mathieu (LPL, Université d'Aix-Marseille & LMS, Nanyang Technological University)

Natpratan, Natchanan (Kasetsart University)

Netisopakul, Ponrudee (KMAKE LAB)

Ogihara, Toshiyuki (University of Washington)

Onsuwan, Chutamanee (Thammasat University)

Okada, Makoto (Osaka Prefecture University)

Otoguro, Ryo (Faculty of Law, Waseda University)

Parinyawuttichai, Tanyaporn (Chulalongkorn University)

Park, Jong C. (KAIST)

Pittayaporn, Pittayawat (Chulalongkorn University)

Pongpairoj, Nattama (Chulalongkorn University)

Prévot, Laurent (Laboratoire Parole et Langage)

Qi, Haoliang (Heilongjiang Institute of Technology)

Qiu, Long (Institute for Infocomm Research)

Ranaivo-Malançon, Bali (MALINDO)

Ratitamkul, Theeraporn (Chulalongkorn University)

Shaikh, Samira (State University of New York - University at Albany)

Shyu, Shu-Ing (National Sun Yat-sen University)

Siegel, Melanie (Hochschule Darmstadt)

Singhapreecha, Pornsiri (Thammasat University)

Smith, Simon (Coventry University)

Sornlertlamvanich, Virach (National Electronics and Computer Technology Center)

Srioutai, Jiranthara (Chulalongkorn University)

Su, Keh-Yih (Institute of Information Science, Academia Sinica)

Suchato, Atiwong (Chulalongkorn University)

Tasanawan, Soonklang (Sirindhorn International Institute of Technology)

Thepkanjana, Kingkarn (Chulalongkorn University)

Uehara, Satoshi (Tohoku University)

Van Genabith, Josef (Dublin City University)

Villavicencio, Aline (Universidade Federal do Rio Grande do Sul)

Wang, Hsu (Yuan Ze University, Taiwan)

Wijitsopon, Raksangob (Chulalongkorn University)

Wu, Jiun-Shiung (National Chung Cheng University)

Yang, Cheng-Zen (Yuan Ze University)

Yeom, Jae-II (Hongik University)

Yokoyama, Satoru (Tohoku University)

Yu, Liang-Chih (Yuan Ze University)

Zhang, Jiajun (Institute of Automation Chinese Academy of Sciences)

Zhang, Min (Institute for Infocomm Research)

Zhao, Hai (Shanghai Jiao Tong University)

Zhou, Yu (Chinese Academy of Sciences)

Zock, Michael (CNRS-LIF)

Robust Semantics for Semantic Parsing

Mark Steedman
School of Informatics, University of Edinburgh

Abstract

The paper presents a robust semantics for NLP applications including QA, text entailment and SMT that combines a (fairly) standard treatment of logical operators such as negation and quantification (Steedman 2012) with a highly nonstandard paraphrase- and entailment--based semantics of relational terms derived from text data by machine reading (Lewis and Steedman 2013a; 2013b). I'll consider the extension of the latter component to temporal and causal entailment using text-based methods, building on Lewis and Steedman 2014.

Social Media Understanding by Word Cloud Timeline

Virach Sornlertlamvanich
Sirindhorn International Institute of Technology (SIIT), Thammasat University
Pathum Thani 12121, Thailand
virach@gmail.com

Abstract

Text from social media is significant key information to understand social movement. However, the length of the social media text is typically short and concise with a lot of absent words. Our task is to identify the proper keyword representing the message content that we are accounting for. Instead of training the model for keyword extraction directly from the Twitter messages, we propose a new method to fine-tune the model trained from some known documents containing richer context information. We conducted the experiment on Twitter messages and expressed in word cloud timeline. It shows a promising result.

1 Credits

We adopted general Thai word segmentation module to extract the words and generate the key words for a specific domain based on the texts from Wikipedia[1]. The list of key words is then used to query the related tweets through the Twitter search API[2] to collect the related tweets. In this study we propose an effective method to fine-tune the key words extracted from the document texts of Wikipedia to suit the relatively short texts from Twitter. The experiment and implementation have been conducted by Kobkrit Viriyayudhakorn.

[1] http://th.wikipedia.org/

[2] https://dev.twitter.com/docs/streaming-api

2 Introduction

Social media is a massive communication data for understanding the social behavior as well as sensing network is a massive monitoring data for observing the global environment (Gundecha and Liu, 2012). Both are the generated data that reflecting the real-time current situation of society and environment. In the rapid change of the current world, it is necessary to understand the situation and make a suitable response timely. The effect of happening or disaster nowadays has a trend to cause tremendous and pervasive damages. Since Great Hanshin earthquake in 1995, Indian Ocean earthquake and tsunami in 2004, Illinois hurricane Katrina in 2005, Arab spring a series of anti-government protests in 2011 uprising in Tunisia spread out to Yemen, Egypt, Syria, Libya and most of Arab countries, Tohoku earthquake and tsunami in 2011, Occupy Wall Street in 2011, until the recent Thailand coup d'etat in 2014, it is wondered whether we can learn something about these historical events. Focusing on social happenings, it is efficient enough to collect the social media data from the widely used social media applications such as Facebook, Twitter, Whatsapp, Line, or WeChat. Social media are actively used in most of the recent cases (Kaplan and Haenlein, 2010). If we ever view them in a proper dimension it is no doubt that we can somehow forecast, prevent, avoid the happenings by warning or influencing the communities to relief the disaster or the undesirable social situation development. In reality, social media data are vast, noisy, distributed, unstructured, and dynamic.

Copyright 2014 by Virach Sornlertlamvanich
28th Pacific Asia Conference on Language, Information and Computation pages 2–4

To study the evolution of social behavior on a happening, we analyze the time series of tweets related to the topic of the recent Thailand coup d'etat in 2014. In the 2013 survey[3], there are 12 million twitter users in Thailand with 200,000 active users/day. This means that if we can screen for the related tweets we can observe the movement of the community tie-up.

In our experiment, we estimate the topic related keywords from the target document that we can simply collected from the Internet news. Tweet is a short 140-character text, which is more likely to be a conversational text comparing to the written document, which is a kind of political news or review. There is a difference in the extracted keyword. We therefore apply a technique in GETA (Generic Engine for Transposable Association) called WAM (Word Article Matrix) to expand the set of keyword reflecting the nature of the text from Twitter (Murakami et al., 2004).

The transition of word cloud in a time series can express the social interest at the moment. From the set of related tweets, we extract keywords and express them in a word cloud manner. We then put the word cloud on the time series to create a word cloud timeline. Word cloud (Trant and Wyman, 2006; Kipp and Campbell, 2006) at each moment expresses the social interest, which significantly changes at the time of happening.

3 Keyword expansion

WAM (Word Article Matrix) is a table of weighted relation between document and keyword. Keywords in a document are counted to fill in the table.

WAM is created in Figure 1 (a) when the input documents are word segmented (in case of non-segmented language such as Thai) or lemmatized, and the corresponding keywords are counted. The matrix is used to operate dot matrix with the input of training set of tweets shown in Figure 1 (b). As a result, table of the most associated documents to the training set is obtained. The ranked documents can be cut off by setting up a threshold for the associated value as shown in Figure 1 (c). With another dot matrix in Figure 1 (d) the expanded associated keyword can be obtained with the weight. By training through the set of targeted tweets, the associated keywords in the target domain can be created. Now we can rank the keyword by its associated weight to retrieve the topic related tweets from Twitter.

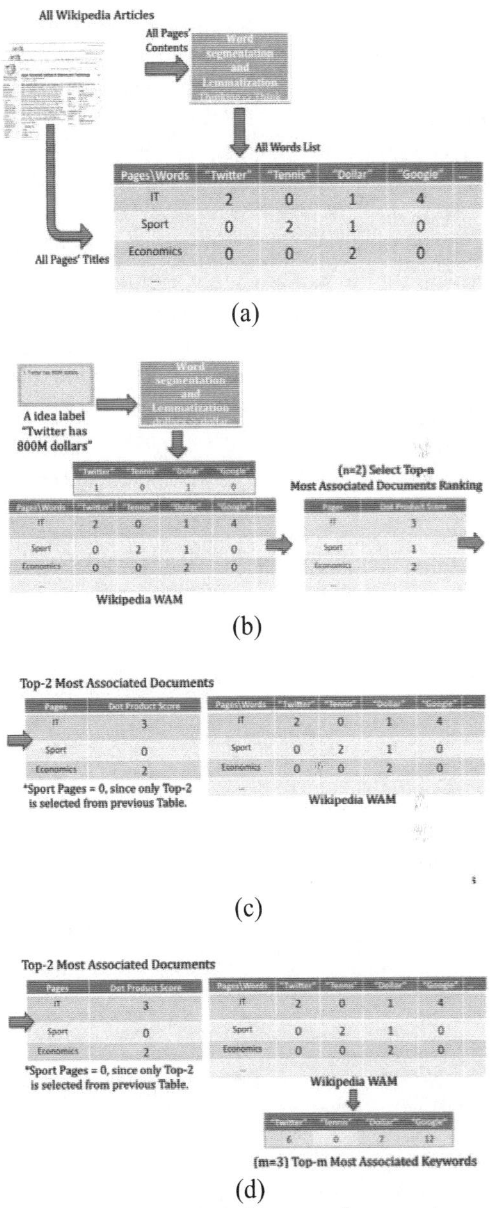

Figure 1: WAM and keyword expansion

4 Word Cloud Timeline

Figure 2 (a) shows the process in creating Twitter word cloud. A set of topic related documents are collected to create WAM. The WAM is used to expand the keyword from the initial set of tweets. The iterative operation in expanding the keyword

[3] http://www.techinasia.com/thailand-18-million-social-media-users-in-2013/

allows us to query Twitter for better coverage of the tweets. Under the constraint of 100 tweets/query and 7 days search back, we repeatedly issue the query using Twitter search API with the set of keywords (Kumar et al., 2011). As a result, 339,148 tweets centering on the date of coup d'etat on May 22, 2014 are collected. On each day the word cloud is generated to compare on hourly basis.

Investigating the happening that the National Peace Keeping Committee seized power on May 22, 2014 at 4.30 p.m., Figure 2 (b) shows the transition of word cloud around the target time. Significantly the word "coup d'etat" occur in every hour as the most focusing topic. Shortly before the moment of the announcement of seizing the power by the military, it is obvious that the Twitter community is already alert to the possibility of coup d'etat. The density of the keyword increases significantly along the climax moment. The word cloud timeline explicitly shows the critical change point of the happening. Strategic planning can be considered to handle the happening by observing the effectiveness of the timeline of the word cloud.

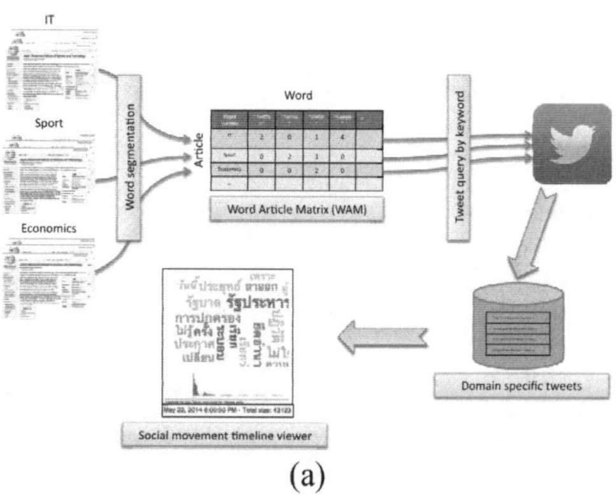

(a)

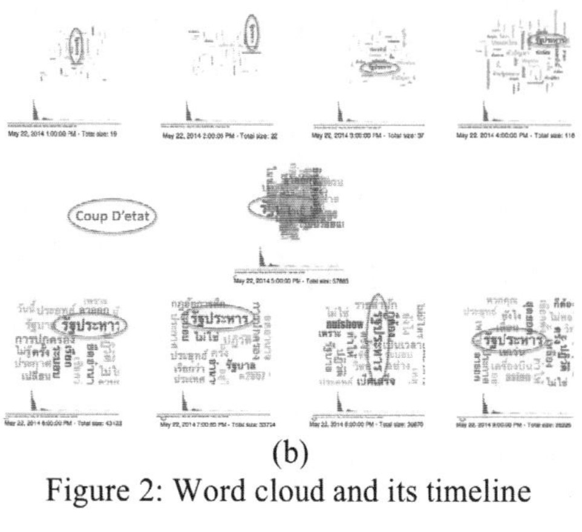

(b)

Figure 2: Word cloud and its timeline

5 Conclusion

Word cloud timeline is an effective instrument to monitor the social behavior since the community tie-up of the social media users is reliable. In the modern Internet use, the growth of social media as well as the sensing network is not ignorable. Understanding the movement of the interest in the social media community can be beneficial in the process of strategic planning or decision-making. In coming future, spatial-temporal information can be inclusively considered to create a wider dimension in monitoring the movement and the happening can be understood in a more precise manner.

Acknowledgments

Specially thanks to Kobkrit Viriyayudhakorn for experiment and implementation for this study.

References

Gundecha P., and Liu H. 2012. Mining social media: a brief introduction. Tutorials in Operations Research, Informs, 1(4).

Kaplan A. M. and Haenlein M. 2010. Users of the world, unite! The challenges and opportunities of social media. Business Horizons 53(1):59–68.

Kipp M.E.I., and Campbell D.G. 2006. Patterns and Inconsistencies in Collaborative Tagging Systems: An Examination of Tagging Practices. Proceedings of the ASIST2006.

Kumar S., Zafarani R., and Liu H. 2011. Understanding user migration patterns across social media. Twenty-Fifth International Conference on Artificial Intelligence. Association for the Advancement of Artificial Intelligence, Palo Alto, CA.

Murakami T., Hu Z., Nishioka S., Takano A., and Takeichi M. 2004. An Algebraic Interface for GETA Search Engine. Proceedings of Program and Programming Language Workshop, Japan.

Trant J., and Wyman B. 2006. Investigating social tagging and folksonomy in art museums with steve. museum. Collaborative Web Tagging Workshop at WWW2006, Edinburgh, Scotland.

Registerial cartography: context-based mapping of text types and their rhetorical-relational organization

Christian M.I.M. Matthiessen
ENGL, FH, The PolySystemic Research Group
Hong Kong Polytechnic University
christian.matthiessen@polyu.edu.hk

Abstract

This paper is concerned with one of the three types of variation inherent in language — viz. register variation, or variation in meaning according to context of use. It reports on a long-term research programme designed to map the registers that collectively make up a language using one parameter within the context of use as the starting point — the field of activity characteristic the context in which a text of a given register unfolds. I present a typology/ topology of fields of activity, and go on to show how different types of activity favour different logico-semantic relations in the global organization of texts instantiating different registers. I then also illustrate registerial variation in the lexicogrammatical realization of logico-semantic relations. The part of the long-term research I focus on here is thus concerned with registerial variation relating to the chain of realizations from context (field of activity) to semantics (logico-semantic relations), and from semantics (logico-semantic relations) to lexicogrammatical realizations (with particular attention to congruence, i.e. congruent vs. incongruent realizations). At the end of the paper, I suggest that registerial cartography is an integral part of the development of appliable linguistics, a synthesis approach to language transcending the thesis and antithesis pair of theoretical linguistics and applied linguistics.

Inherent variability of language

Language is inherently **variable**, languages are inherently variable: variability is part of the power of language — the power to adapt to socially very diverse and ever-changing contexts, at the same time contributing to the constant change. As languages evolve, they tend to remain stable because they are inherently variable, adapting to changing conditions of use; their stability is of a higher order: languages are **metastable**.

The inherent variability of languages poses a fundamental problem for any theories based on the assumption that languages are uniform and homogeneous; but it was recognized by Halliday and others in Systemic Functional Linguistics from the start of the development of the theory in the early 1960s; Halliday and others continued the Firthian tradition of conceiving of languages as **polysystemic**, as systems of systems. Firth (1935/ 1957: 29) had warned against conceiving of language in terms of unity:

> The multiplicity of social roles we have to play as members of a race, nation, class, school, club, as sons, brothers, lovers, fathers, workers, churchgoers, golfers, newspaper readers, public speakers, involves also a certain degree of linguistic specialization. Unity is the last concept that should be applied to language. Unity of language is the most fugitive of all unities whether it be historical, geographical, national, or personal. There is no such thing as *une langue une* and there has never been.

In early work, Halliday and his colleagues developed Firth's insight into language as a **system of variation** (e.g. Halliday, 1978: 156), in a sense providing a ***synthesis*** of the thesis of the unity of language and Firth's antithesis, his argument against this kind of unity (cf. Matthiessen, 1993: 222). According to this synthesis, languages are inherently variable, shading into one another just as dialects

Copyright 2014 by Christian M.I.M. Matthiessen
28th Pacific Asia Conference on Language, Information and Computation pages 5–26

do; and language is modelled as **a probabilistic system** (long before the advent of today's "probabilistic linguistics", as formulated in Bod, Hay & Jannedy, 2003, and used within "statistical natural language processing", Manning & Schütze, 1999). Thus variation can be — and has been — characterized in probabilistic terms within the overall theory of language as a probabilistic system (e.g. Halliday, 1959, 1978, 1991a,b, 1993; Nesbitt & Plum, 1988; Matthiessen, 1999, 2006, in press b).

Halliday and his colleagues originally recognized two broad kinds of variation — a familiar kind, **dialectal variation** (including sociolectal variation) and a less familiar but equally important one, **registerial variation**, drawing on Firth's notion of restricted languages (e.g. Halliday, McIntosh & Strevens, 1964; Gregory, 1967; Hasan, 1973; Ure & Ellis, 1977, and an early corpus-based investigation of Scientific English by Huddleston et al., 1968). These two varieties of language are glossed by Halliday (e.g. 1978: 35) as "variety according to the user" (dialect, or dialectal variety) and "variety according to use" (register, or diatypic variety); he writes (op cit.: 157):

> A dialect is any variety of a language that is defined by reference to the speaker: the dialect you speak is a function of who you are. In this respect, a dialect differs from the other dimension of variety in language, that of register: a register is a variety defined by reference to the social context — it is a function of what you are speaking. It seems to be typical of human cultures for a speaker to have more than one dialect, and for his dialect shifts, where they occur, to symbolize shifts in register. A 'standard' dialect is one that has achieved a distinctive status, in the form of a consensus which recognizes it as serving social functions which in some sense transcend the boundaries of dialect-speaking groups. This is often associated with writing — in many cultures the standard dialect is referred to as the 'literary [i.e. written] language' — and with formal education. Because of its special status, speakers generally find it hard to recognize that the standard dialect is at heart 'just a dialect' like any other.

To **dialect variation** and **register variation**, Halliday and his colleagues added a third kind of variation, **codal variation** ("semantic style"), based on Bernstein's notion of codes and linguistic corpus-based investigations (e.g. Hasan, 1973, 1989; Halliday, 1994). These three types of variation can be located according to two of the global dimensions of the organization of language, the **cline of instantiation** and the **hierarchy of stratification** (cf. Halliday, 1994) — represented diagrammatically here as Figure 1 (based on Matthiessen, 2007).

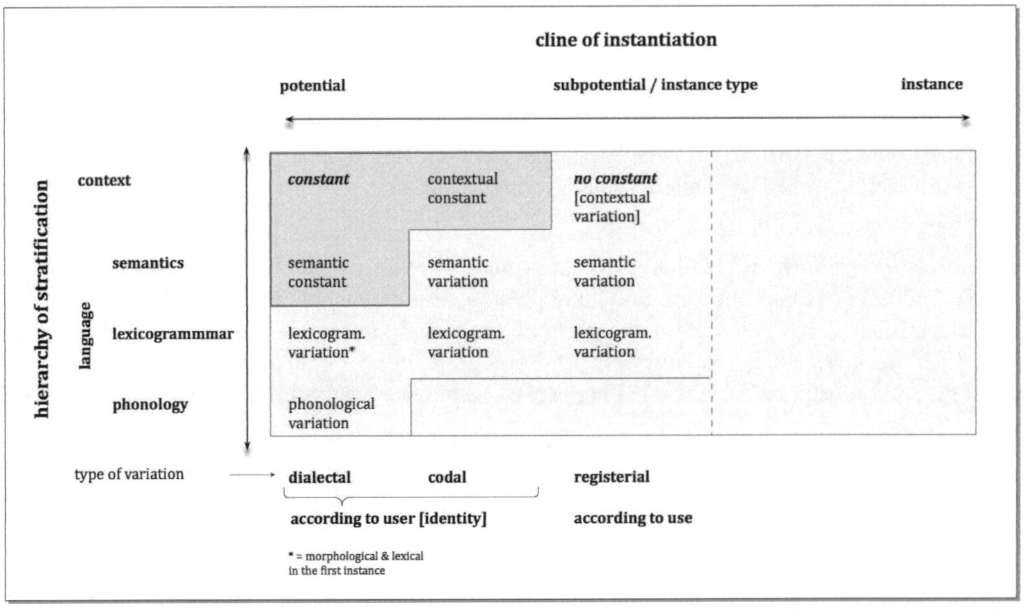

Figure 1: Locations of dialectal, codal and registerial variation along the cline of instantiation and the hierarchy of stratification — higher-level constant (if any) and primary nature of variation

The three types of variation are, in principle, distinct; but they interact in various ways, and have (as everything else in language) fuzzy boundaries — dialect variation obviously shading into language variation just as dialects shade into languages. As Halliday (1978) notes in the passage quoted above, different dialects may cover different **registerial ranges**, the standard dialect being an extreme example, as in the case of Standard English, which now embodies the registerial ranges collectively covered by English, Norman French and Latin before Standard English had evolved (cf. Halliday, 2003). Similarly, different codes are likely to embody different registerial ranges, reflecting both social hierarchy and the division of labour within a society.

Registerial variation

In this paper, among the three kinds of variation in Figure 1, I will be concerned with **registerial variation**. As shown in Figure 1, it is located **mid-region along the cline of instantiation**, between the potential pole of the overall (collective) meaning potential of a language and the instance pole of instantial acts of meaning unfolding to make up texts in context. In other words, we observe registerial variation (like any other kind of variation) as selections in texts as they unfold in their contexts of situation, and when we try to generalize these selections as recurrent patterns of selection, we find that the generalized patterns of selection are located mid-region along the cline of instantiation. In terms of stratification, it is **semantic variation** in the first instance, but it is semantic variation that co-varies with contextual variation: there is no higher-level constant, and this is precisely the notion of linguistic ***variation according to use***, i.e. according to context of use. (In this important respect, registerial variation is unlike codal variation; codal variation is also semantic variation in the first instance [cf. Hasan, 1989, 2009], but it is variation with a contextual constant — codal varieties constitute different styles of meaning in comparable contexts, different semantic strategies for pursuing comparable contextual goals.) Registers are thus **meanings at risk**, describable as **probabilistic resettings** of the general systemic probabilities of a language (Halliday, 1978) operating within particular settings of contextual variables. They are distributed among the members of a speech community in terms of its division of labour; members — individual speakers — have different **registerial repertoires**, giving them access to different institutional roles.

Languages are aggregates of registers, and they evolve through registers. Registers emerge as adaptations to new contextual pressures on languages (as documented for the evolution of scientific English by Halliday, 1988, and as can be seen in the more recent evolution of e.g. news reporting and advertising, and now of course in the evolution of technologically enabled "electronic" registers), and they may fade away as contextual conditions change: the registerial make-ups of languages keep evolving, changing the character of languages in the course of evolution (cf. Halliday, 2013: Ch. 16).

Registers and register variation have been investigated, described and theorized since the 1960s — including the original Hallidayan version (in addition to the studies cited above, see e.g. Ure, 1982; Ghadessy, 1988, 1993; Teich, 1999; Steiner, 2004; and in computational modelling, e.g. Bateman & Paris, 1991) and US American register studies (e.g. Biber, 1988, 1995; Biber & Finnegan, 1994), with new insights coming from extensive text analysis and corpus-based studies; recent overviews include Lukin et al. (2008), Matthiessen (in press a) and also the introduction to the US American work on register by Biber & Conrad (2009)[1]. Biber & Conrad provide a helpful review of terms and concepts, and differentiate "genre", "style" and "register". Interpreted in terms of a Hallidayan systemic functional model, these three are arguably simply different manifestations of register variation — different in terms of the overall stratal and metafunctional organization of language in context, but not different in terms of the fundamental notion of functional variation in language — variation according to context of use[2].

---

[1] Registers have also been studied under different names, e.g. "text type", "genre"; and in machine translation, researchers have used the term "sublanguage" (e.g. Kittredge, 1987).

[2] Biber & Conrad (2009: Section 1.1) write of "the style perspective": "The key difference from the register perspective is that the use of these features is not functionally motivated by the situational context; rather, style features reflect aesthetic preferences,

Registerial cartography

Here I will report on aspects of a long-term project I have called **registerial cartography** (e.g. Matthiessen, in press a, forthc. b) — using the metaphor of cartography since those of us involved in the project are engaged in developing comprehensive ***maps of registers*** in different languages. These maps are based, in the first instance, on a "contextual projection": we approached registers "from above" (or "top down"), moving from context to semantics in terms of the hierarchy of stratification[3], adopting a view of them based on contextual parameters (variables), in particular on the three major parameters firs proposed by Halliday, McIntosh & Strevens (1964) and developed since then — field, tenor and mode (using the terms adopted by Halliday, 1978):

- **field** (type of activity): what's going on in context — the field of activity, and the field of experience accompanying or created by the activity (also known as "subject matter", "topic", "domain");
- **tenor** (role relationships): who are taking part — the tenor of the relationship among the interactants in terms of their roles and relations (including institutional roles, status roles, contact roles, sociometric roles);
- **mode** (symbolic organization): the role played by language, other semiotic systems and social systems in context — the complementary contributions made by them in context, including channel (graphic / phonic) and medium (spoken / written).

The contextual approach to the development of maps of functional variation, of register variation, is motivated by the very nature of this type of variation: ***variation according to context of use***. However, at the same time, a central objective of the project of registerial cartography is to examine, describe and theorize registers according to Halliday's **trinocular vision** (e.g. Halliday, 1978: 130-131, 1996; Halliday & Matthiessen, 2013: 48-49), supplementing the view "from above" — from contexts, with the views "from below" — from lexicogrammar and phonology (or graphology), and "from roundabout" — from the level of semantics itself, the level at which the variation takes place in the first instance (in terms of the "meanings at risk" in different contexts). In other words, the project of registerial cartography includes centrally stratal coverage in the account of registers, from the contexts in which they operate to the linguistic strata where their semantic patterns are realized; stratal coverage thus includes a chain of inter-stratal realizations: context to semantics, semantics to lexicogrammar, and lexicogrammar to phonology or graphology (cf. Figure 6 in the Conclusion).

Of the different aspects of the registerial cartography project, I will focus in particular on the investigation of correlations between (i) fields of activity characterizing different types of context (situation types) and (ii) the choice of semantic strategies for organizing text within the register associated with a given type of context, with semantic strategy in the sense of logico-semantic relation (rhetorical relation, conjunctive relation, discourse relation).

Context: field of activity

In terms of **context**, I will present part of our typology of **fields of activity** (e.g. Matthiessen, in press a; Matthiessen & Kasyap, 2014; Matthiessen & Teruya, 2015), with types of activity differentiated in two to three steps in delicacy. The primary types are eight in number (derived from an unpublished manuscript by Jean Ure), each with subtypes as shown by means of a radial diagram in Figure 2:

---

associated with particular authors or historical periods." But "aesthetic preferences" are actually also functional, only in a different way, as was brought out by work by Mukařovský (1948) in the Prague School on the "esthetic function" of language. Cf. also Hasan (1985). For different uses of the terms "genre" and "register" in SFL, see e.g. Matthiessen (1993, in press a, forthc. b).

[3] In a sense corpus-based investigations such Biber (1988, 1995) have tended to move in "from below", using lexicogrammatical patterns that can be the basis of automated analysis in large volumes of text — though taking note of "situational factors" (e.g. Biber & Conrad, 2009). The two moves are ***complementary*** as strategies adopted to describe registers and registerial variation; and they need to be linked up through a chain of inter-stratal realizations (cf. Figure 9 below).

expounding (general classes of phenomena), **reporting** (particular instances of phenomena, typically chronicling events), **recreating** (some aspect of experience, imaginatively), **sharing** (personal values and experiences), **doing** (collaborating in, or directing, social behaviour), **enabling** (typically some course of action — some form of doing), **recommending** (some course of action or some commodity), **exploring** (assigning public value to commodities or arguing about ideas). These eight primary types of field of activity are characterized in Table 1, together with their immediate subtypes. Like all contextual and linguistics categories, fields of activity are indeterminate, and they shade into one another (see Matthiessen & Teruya, 2015).

Table 1: Primary and secondary fields of activity

primary type	nature of activity	secondary type
expounding	our experience of classes of phenomena according to a general theory (ranging from commonsense folk theories to uncommonsense scientific theories) —	either by **categorizing** (or "documenting") these phenomena (typically entities) or
		by **explaining** them (typically events or the outcomes of events);
reporting	on our experience of particular phenomena (instances of classes of phenomena), documenting them according to the principle of organization most salient to them (e.g. as a verbal time line, a verbal map or simply as a list) —	**chronicling** the flow of particular events (as in historical recounts or news reports),
		surveying particular places (as in guide books) or
		inventorying particular entities (as in catalogues);
recreating	our experience of the world imaginatively, that is, creating imaginary worlds having some direct or tenuous relation to the world of our daily lives — recreating the world imaginatively through	**narration** and/ or
		dramatization;
sharing	our personal lives, prototypically in private, thereby establishing, maintaining and negotiation personal relationships in face-to-face interaction but increasing also through social media channels (thus blurring the distinction between private and public) [sharing is a field of activity oriented towards tenor (relationships) so tenor distinctions play a significant role)] —	sharing our personal **experiences**, as in reminiscences, anecdotes and/ or
		sharing our personal **values**, as in gossip;
doing	social activities, prototypically engaging in interactive social behaviour, thereby collectively achieving some task —	either by members of one group **collaborating** with one another or
		by one person **directing** the other members of a group;
enabling	people to undertake some activity, thus very likely foreshadowing a 'doing' context —	either by **instructing** them in how to undertake the activity, as in 'how-to' manuals, or
		by **regulating** their behaviour (controlling, constraining and restricting it), as in legislation, contracts, licensing agreements;
recommending	people to undertake some activity, thus very likely	either by **advising** them

primary type	nature of activity	secondary type
	foreshadowing a 'doing' context —	(recommendation for the benefit of the addressee, as in professional consultations) or
		inducing them (promotion: recommendation for the benefit of the speaker, as in advertisements);
exploring	our communal values and positions, prototypically in public (through media channels) [exploring is a field of activity oriented towards tenor (relationships and values) so tenor distinctions play a significant role)] —	either by **reviewing** a commodity (goods-&-services), as in book reviews, or
		by **arguing** about positions and ideas, as in expositions, editorials, debates.

Figure 2: Context — the contextual parameter of field ("what's going on"): field of activity (the socio-semiotic process people are taking part in in context), primary types (inner circle) and secondary types (outer circle)

The description of field of activity diagrammed in Figure 2 and summarized in Table 1 includes two steps in delicacy — the eight primary types and their immediate subtypes; but it has of course been extended further in delicacy, and when we reach tertiary or quaternary delicacy in the differentiation of fields of activity, we can begin to relate the description to the categories of genre identified by systemic functional linguists working with Martin's (e.g. 1992) "genre model" — the genres of written language described by Martin & Veel (2008) and of spoken language described by Eggins & Slade (2005). These descriptions include the contextual structures of the genres, e.g. the structures of argumentative expositions and of explanations: see Table 2. The table contrasts sequential explanations with expositions (in the sense arguments supporting a thesis): we can specify the structure of both at the fourth step in delicacy in the description of field of activity[4]. The two types are illustrated by Text 1, a sequential explanation, and Text 2, a(n analytic) exposition; for the sake of brevity, I have selected short educational texts of around ten clause complexes (orthographic sentences; for longer examples, see Matthiessen, forthc. a). The elements of their contextual structures are indicated in bold within square brackets; their logico-semantic structures will be presented below.

Table 2: Examples of differentiation of fields of activity in delicacy to the point where contextual structures can be posited

field of activity				**contextual structure**
primary	**secondary**	**tertiary**	**quaternary**	
expounding	explaining	sequentially	temporal	Phenomenon Identification ^ Explanation Sequence
exploring	arguing	one-sided	exposition	Thesis ^ Argument$_{1-n}$ ^ Reinforcement of Thesis

Text 1: Sequential explanation from an educational resource website[5] (structural conjunctions in bold, cohesive ones in bold italics)

[0] Woodchipping

[Phenomenon Identification:]

[1] Woodchipping is a process [[used to obtain pulp and paper product from the forest]]. [2] About 10 percent of Australia's state owned forest land, **and** large areas of privately owned forest, are involved in woodchip projects.

[Explanation Sequence:]

[3.1] The woodchipping process begins [3.2] **when** the trees are cut down in a selected area of the forest [[called a coupe]]. [4.1] ***After that***, the tops and branches are cut off [4.2] **and** the logs are dragged to a log landing [4.3] **where** they are loaded onto a truck. [5.1] ***Next*** the bark of the logs is removed [5.2] **and** the logs are taken to a chipper [5.3] **which** cuts them into small pieces [[called woodchips]]. [6.1] The woodchips are ***then*** screened [6.2] to remove dirt and other impurities. [7.1] At this stage the woodchips are **either** exported to Japan in this form [7.2] **or** converted into pulp by chemicals, heat and pressure. [8.1] The pulp is ***then*** bleached [8.2] and the water content removed. [9.1] ***Finally*** it is rolled out [9.2] to make paper.

Text 2: Exposition ("analytical exposition") from an educational website[6]

[0] Cars should be banned in the city

[Thesis:]

[1] Cars should be banned in the city. [2.1] **As** we all know, [2.2] cars create pollution, [2.3] **and** cause a lot of road deaths and other accidents.

[Arguments:]

[3.1] ***Firstly***, cars, << [3.2] **as** we all know,>> contribute to most of the pollution in the world. [4] Cars emit a deadly gas [[[that causes illnesses such as bronchitis, lung cancer, || **and** 'triggers' off asthma]]]. [5] Some of these illnesses are so bad [[that people can die from them]].

---

[4] The table only serves as a simple illustration. We may need to take further steps in delicacy, e.g. in order to distinguish analytical expositions (the type in focus here) from hortatory expositions, which include a recommendation for action to be taken based on the argument. In addition, we also need to take into consideration variations due to tenor, e.g. variation according to intended readers or listeners, and to mode, e.g. variation according to medium — spoken or written.

[5] http://www.schools.nsw.edu.au/media/downloads/schoolsweb/studentsupport/programs/lrngdificulties/writespellsec5.pdf

[6] http://sman5yk.sch.id/2013-03-21-17-03-23/inggris/232-english-lesson-material-for-grade-xi-semester-1

[6] ***Secondly,*** the city is very busy. [7.1] Pedestrians wander everywhere [7.2] **and** cars commonly hit pedestrians in the city, [7.3] which causes them to die. [8] Cars today are our roads' biggest killers.

[9] ***Thirdly,*** cars are very noisy. [10.1] **If** you live in the city, [10.2] you may find it hard to sleep at night, [10.3] or concentrate on your homework, [10.4] and especially talk to someone.

[Reinforcement of Thesis:]

[11] ***In conclusion,*** cars should be banned from the city for the reasons listed.

Semantics: logico-semantic (rhetorical) relations

In terms of the **semantic strategy** used to organize texts within their contexts, I will focus on **logico-semantic relations**, or "rhetorical relations"[7], modelling them by means of a version of Rhetorical Structure Theory (RST) — an approach to the semantic organization of text in terms of rhetorical relations that Bill Mann, Sandy Thompson and I started to develop a little over three decades ago, now sometimes referred to as "classical RST" (see e.g. Mann & Thompson, 1987; Matthiessen & Thompson, 1989; Mann & Matthiessen, 1991; Mann, Matthiessen & Thompson, 1992; Taboada & Mann, 2006; and for the use of RST in computational discourse processing, see e.g. Marcu, 1997, 2000; Carlson & Marcu, 2001 [RST annotation of documents from the Penn Treebank]; and cf. Stede, 2012,). The version I use here is a "systemicized" one, i.e. a version that differs from classical RST in that it is integrated within the overall SFL framework as a logical-semantic resource — with systemic organization as primary and structural organization as secondary, derived from the systemic organization by means of realization statements (see Matthiessen, forthc. a). The system is represented informally in Figure 3; this is a description of the resources in English for organizing texts relationally.

[7] Such relations have been investigated under many names including "conjunctive relations", "discourse relations", "rhetorical predicates", "coherence relations", "interpropositional relations".

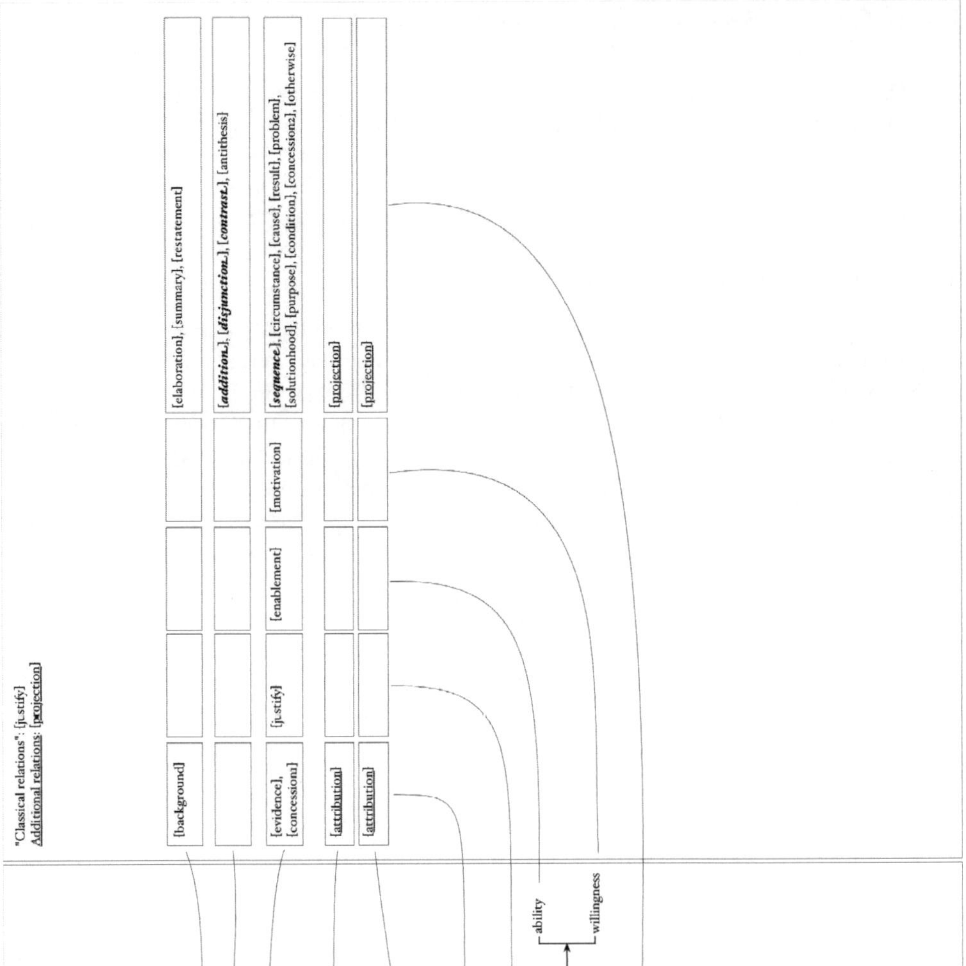

Figure 3: The semantic system of LOGICO-SEMANTIC RELATION (rhetorical relations)

The system of LOGICO-SEMANTIC RELATION in Figure 3 is composed of three simultaneous systems concerned with the nature of the logico-semantic relation used to relate one text segment to another in order to form a rhetorical nexus (i.e. a relational combination of text segments):

- The system of NUCLEARITY is the choice between relations linking the text segments as equal in status ('multi-nuclear') or as unequal, with one text segment supporting the other ('nucleus-satellite'). This distinction is part of "classical RST".
- The system of LOGICO-SEMANTIC TYPE is the choice between relations of 'projection', where one text segment sets up another as a quote or a report, and 'expansion', where one text segment elaborates, extends or enhances the other — the account of projection and expansion goes back to Halliday (1985).
- The system or orientation is the choice between linking two text segments as representations of experience ('external') or as interactional moves ('internal') — a distinction that goes back to Halliday & Hasan's (1976) description of cohesive conjunctions ("discourse markers") in English.

As can be seen from the table to the right of the system network in Figure 3, options (terms) from these three systems intersection to define sets of logico-semantic relations, including the "rhetorical relations" of classical RST. The relations can be fully differentiated if we increased the delicacy of the systems of LOGICO-SEMANTIC TYPE and ORIENTATION. For example, the relations marked by *finally* in Text 1 and *in conclusion* in Text 2 are similar in terms of LOGICO-SEMANTIC TYPE, both being enhancing relations, but different in terms of orientation: *finally* marks an 'external' relation whereas *in conclusion* marks an 'internal' one: see the logico-semantic analyses of these two texts in Figure 4 and Figure 5.

In addition to these three systems that jointly determine the nature of the relation linking the two text segments in a rhetorical nexus, there is a fourth system, the system of SYSTEMIC RECURSION. This is the choice between stopping the development of the text at the point of the current rhetorical nexus and going on to introduce a new logico-semantic relation thereby developing the text further.

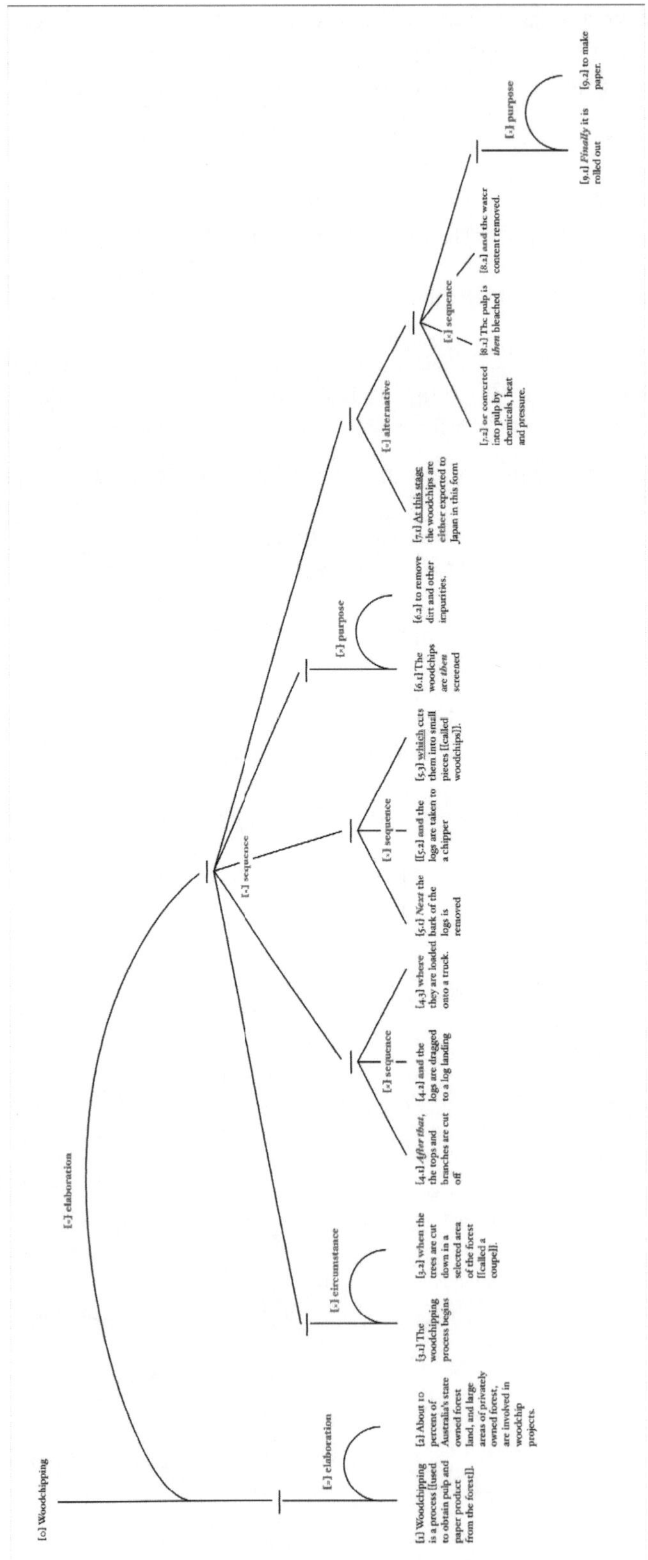

Figure 4: Logico-semantic analysis (in terms of RST) of the sequential explanation in Text 1

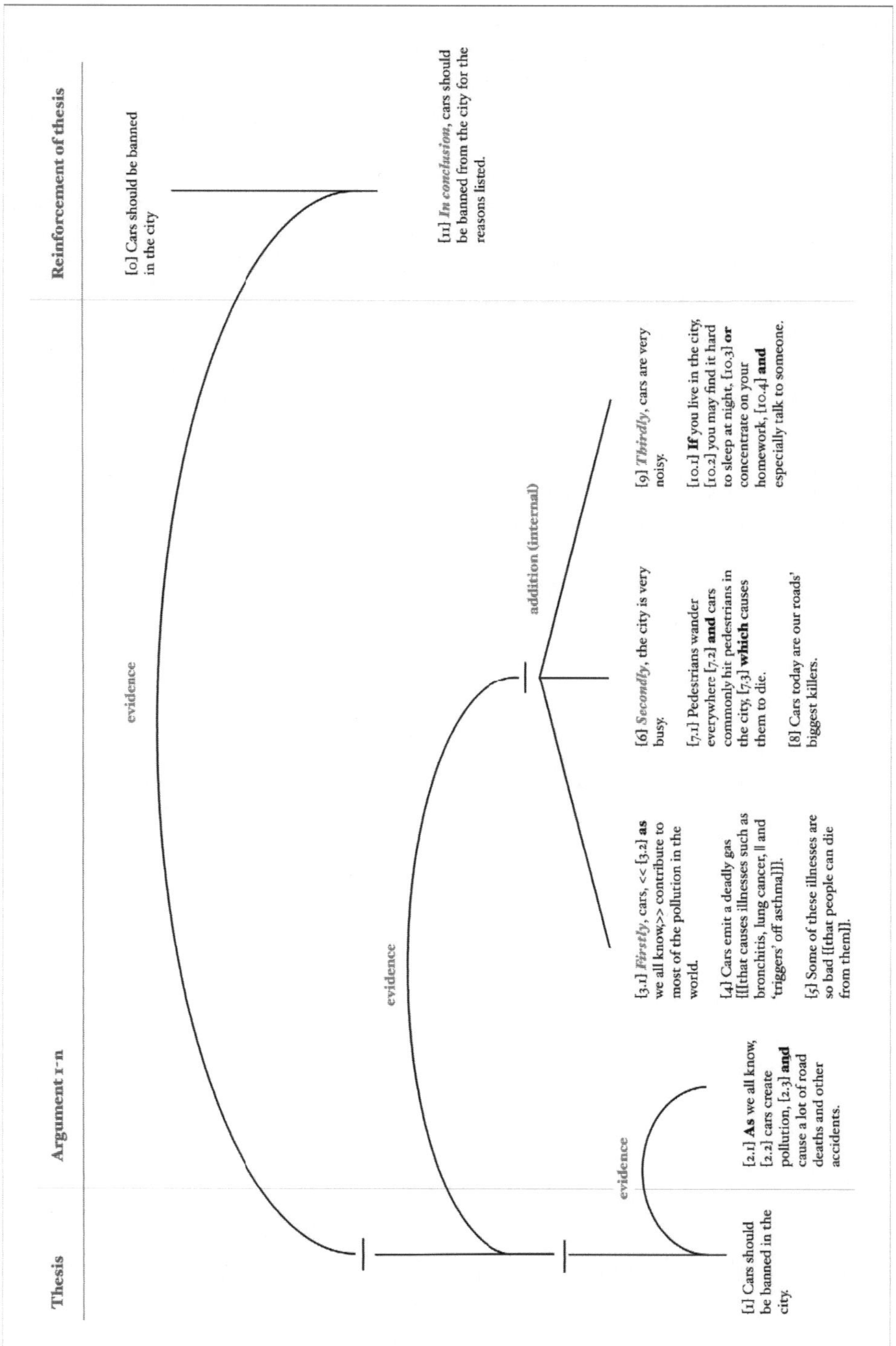

Figure 5: Logico-semantic analysis (in terms of RST) of the analytical exposition in Text 2

Fields of activity and favoured logico-semantic relations

Using the systemic description of logico-semantic relations in the organization of text set out in Figure 3, I have analysed representative samples of texts (mostly in English) from registers operating in contexts characterized by different fields of activity. These analyses show, not surprisingly, that in the ***global*** organization of texts, different logico-semantic (rhetorical) relations are favoured (i.e. are "at risk" of being selected) according to the types of the field of activity characterizing the contexts in which the texts operate (see Matthiessen, in press a, forthc. a). This correlation between field of activity and logico-semantic relation becomes discernable when we increase the delicacy in the description of fields of activity from the eight primary types to their subtypes. As we differentiate these forms of activity further, identifying secondary and tertiary types (secondary types are shown above in the outer circle in Figure 2 and identified in the rightmost of column of Table 1), we can begin to discern recurrent semantic strategies used to organize texts belonging to registers operating in contexts characterized by one type of field of activity or other, as exemplified in Figure 6[8].

For example, if the field of activity of the context is one of expounding general knowledge by categorizing phenomena in terms of classes and subclasses or wholes and parts, the context will be realized by a taxonomic report where the key semantic strategy for organizing the text is the logico-semantic (rhetorical) relation of 'elaboration'; but if the activity is one of promoting some "commodity", the context will be realized by a marketing text such as an advertisement where the key semantic strategy for organizing the text is likely to be the logico-semantic relation of 'motivation', the point being to motivate the addressee to accept whatever is being offered.

Similarly, explaining phenomena by reference to the unfolding of processes in time will favour the logico-semantic relation of 'temporal sequence' as in Text 1, whereas arguing for a position or idea will favour the logico-semantic relation of 'evidence' as in Text 2. Thus the body of Text 1, which is an elaboration of the nuclear definition of 'woodchipping', is organized externally by means of multi-nuclear relations of 'sequence', as shown in Figure 4 above. In contrast, Text 2 is organized internally by means of nucleus-satellite relations of 'evidence', as shown in Figure 5 above. The satellite segments related by 'evidence' serve to bolster the writer's nuclear claim that cars should be banned in the city. The nucleus of the whole text comes at the end — as the culmination after the arguments in favour of the position it represents. This organization of expositions and other persuasive texts is typical — the global nucleus is presented as the "macro-New" of the whole text, the main point for readers or listeners to take away from the text.

[8] As noted above and illustrated in Table 2, this is roughly where contextual or situational structures — "generic structures", "schematic structures" — such as narrative structures begin to be identified and described: see Matthiessen (forthc. b) on the link to genre types identified and described by Martin & Rose (2008).

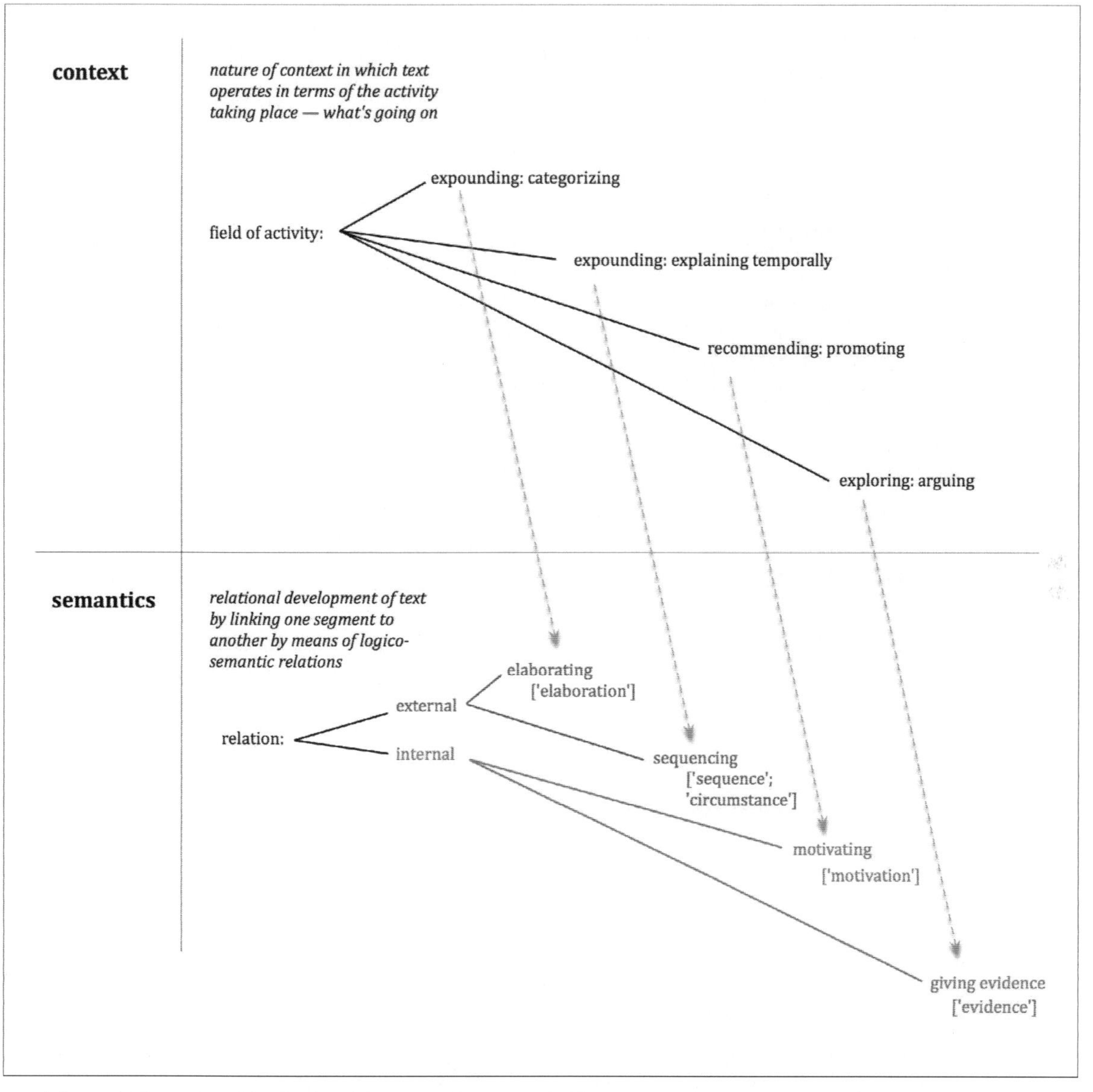

Figure 6: Examples of fields of activity (secondary types in Figure 2) with typical realizations by logico-semantic (rhetorical) relations playing role in organizing texts globally

The general principle is this: the meaning potential of a language, in this case of English, includes strategies for organizing texts by means of logico-semantic relations; and a certain subset of these will be most likely to be used (to be "at risk" of being chosen) in the global organization of texts in a context characterized by a particular type of field of activity. Different fields of activity will favour different subsets of relations. This general principle of registerial variation in the area of logico-semantic organization of text is represented diagrammatically in Figure 7. (Given a representative corpus texts from different registers that has been annotated for logico-semantic relations — cf. Carlson & Marcu, 2001, and Prasad et al., 2011, we would be able to state "favour" in probabilistic terms based on relative frequencies in the corpus.)

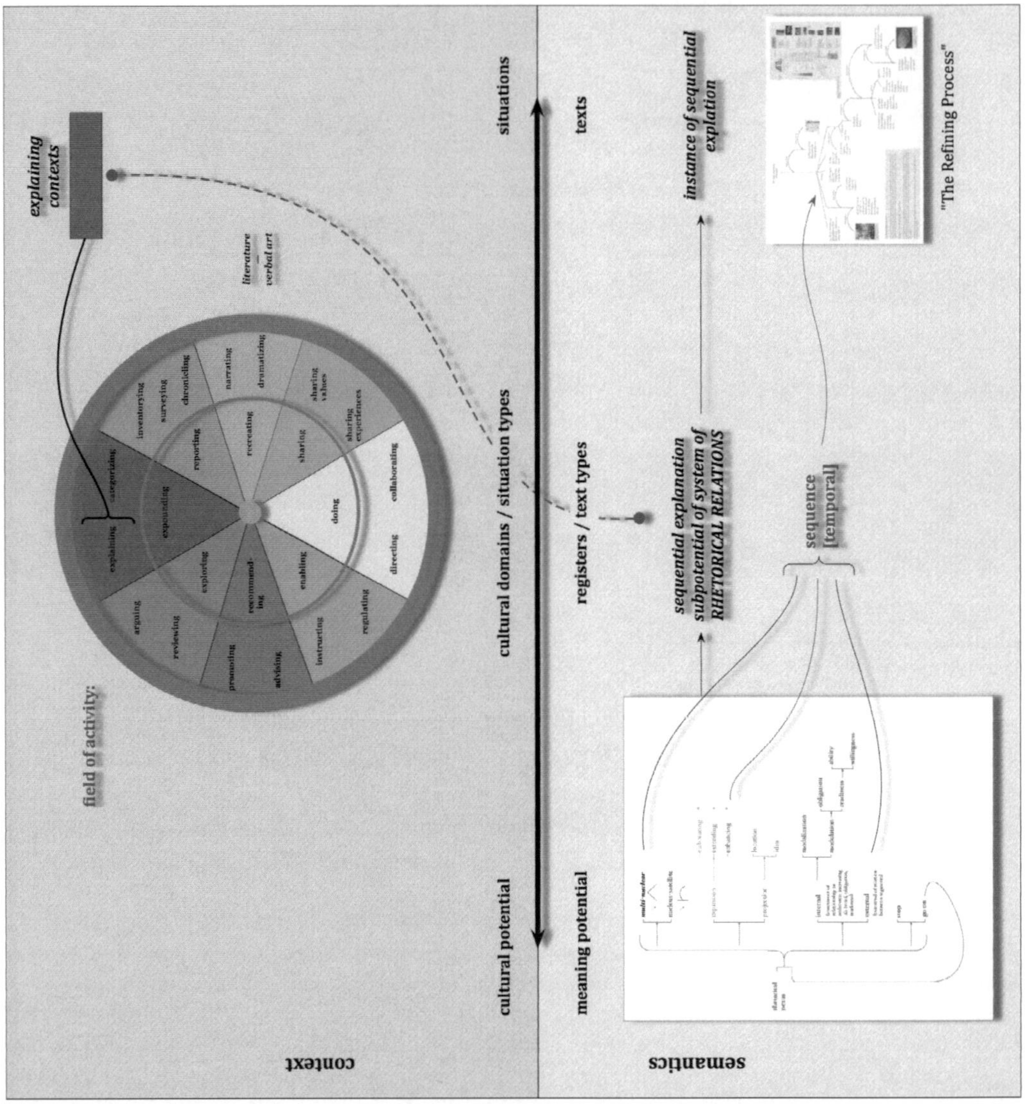

Figure 7: Registerial variation in the use of logico-semantic relations in the organization of texts belonging to different registers in accordance with the nature of the field of activity in context — exemplified by the activity of explaining by means of sequential explanations

Registerial variation in the lexicogrammatical realizations of logico-semantic relations

The logico-semantic relations favoured in the global organization of text thus vary according to the nature of the field of activity in context. By another step along the realizational chain from context to semantics and from semantics to lexicogrammar, we can also note that the **lexicogrammatical realizations** of logico-semantic relations similarly vary according to the nature of the field of activity (Matthiessen & Teruya, 2013). One interesting aspect of this variation in realization is the degree to which logico-semantic relations are realized **congruently** or **metaphorically** (incongruently). In texts of a **pragmatic** nature such as procedural texts operating in instructing enabling contexts (see the radial diagram in Figure 7), logico-semantic relations are likely to be realized congruently by conjunctions ("discourse markers"), either cohesive ones (e.g. *meanwhile*) or structural ones (e.g. *then*, *until*; *if*); but in texts of **mathetic** nature such as factorial explanations operating in expounding contexts, logico-semantic relations are likely to be realized incongruently by prepositions (e.g. *because of*), verbs (e.g. *cause*, *lead to*, *result in*) or (by yet another step) nouns (e.g. *cause*, *consequence*, *effect*), as illustrated in Figure 8.

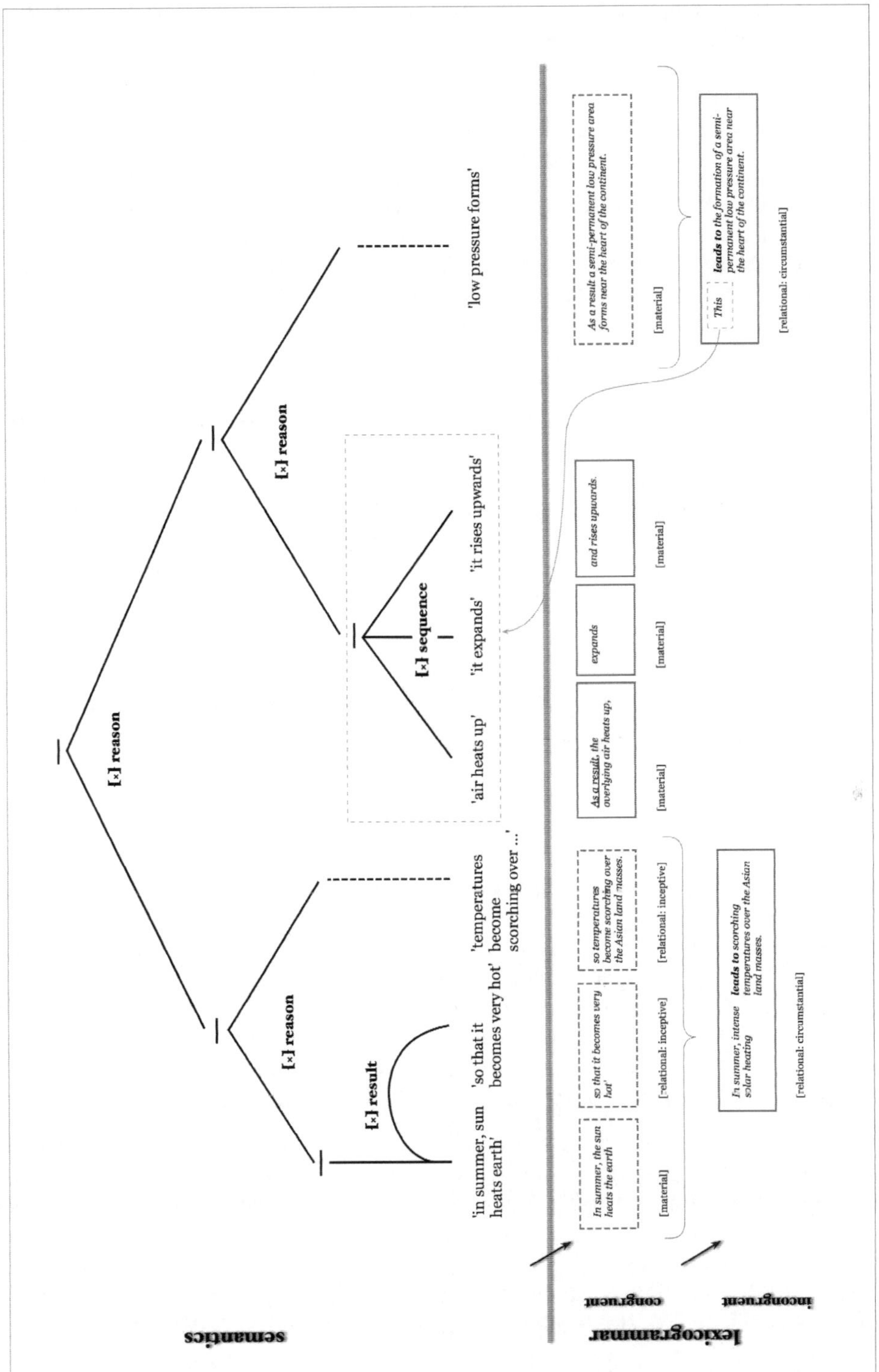

Figure 8: Congruent and incongruent realizations of logico-semantic relations in a passage from a causal explanation of monsoons

The text segment analysed in Figure 8 is an excerpt from a causal explanation of monsoons. It is organized by logico-semantic relations of 'reason', 'result' and (temporal) 'sequence', all of which are 'external' in orientation. The complex formed by relations of 'sequence' is realized congruently by a paratactic clause complex consisting of three 'material' clauses ("action" clauses). In contrast, the semantic complexes formed by means of 'reason' and 'result' are realized incongruently, by two 'circumstantial' 'relational' clauses, both of which have the causal verb *lead to* as Process. These incongruent clauses are as it were metaphoric re-codings of what would congruently be clause complexes, as indicated in Figure 8.

The metaphorical mode of realization has been investigated and discussed extensively in SFL based on Halliday (1985: Ch. 10), as in Halliday & Martin (1993), Halliday (1998), Vandenbergen, Taverniers & Ravelli (2003), Halliday & Matthiessen (2006: Ch. 6; 2013: Ch. 10), and modelled computationally as a feature of certain registers by Bateman & Paris (1991). Naturally, in addition to field of activity, other contextual parameters also play a role in shifting the realization of logico-semantic relations and rhetorical nexuses from the congruent mode to the metaphorical mode of realization; the metaphorical mode is more likely in written medium than in spoken, and, in terms of ontogenesis, more likely the further learners move into the subject-specific knowledge of secondary school (see e.g. Derewianka, 1995; Christie & Derewianka, 2008). Consequently, the realization of rhetorical nexuses is gradually "pushed down" in the lexicogrammar from cohesive sequences of clauses and clause complexes to clauses, phrases and groups. Incongruent, metaphorical realizations cover an important range of what Prasad, Joshi & Webber (2010) have identified as "alternative lexicalizations" ("AltLex") of "discourse relations" — alternative to (in our terms) congruent realizations in the form of structural and cohesive conjunctions.

Conclusion

In summary, I have reported on aspects of our research into registers — our long-term research programme of registerial cartography. In particular, I have discussed the relation between fields of activity within context, logico-semantic relations used to form rhetorical nexuses in the (global) semantic organization of text, and the mode of the lexicogrammatical realizations of these relations. This realizational chain is set out in Figure 9. The work discussed in this paper is exploratory, largely based on my manual analysis of samples of text that I have deemed to be representative of different registers. To scale up the research, one would need a registerial range of annotated corpora comparable to the discourse annotated version of the Penn Treebank (Prasad et al., 2007, 2008) and the more recent addition of the biomedical discourse relation bank (Prasad et al., 2011) — or one of the comparable corpora now becoming available for other languages, including Czech, Turkish and Hindi. With the aid of such a registerial range of corpora, or a single multi-registerial corpus, we would be able to check the patterns emerging in the exploratory work, scaling up the database to the point where statistically interesting statements can be made about the probabilistic settings of each register represented in the data — as a model, cf. Webber (2009) characterization of register varieties (in her terms, "genre distinctions") within the Penn Treebank.

The work on registerial cartography is, of course, important for its own sake: it sheds light on the essential nature of language as a system of variation — as an inherently variable, probabilistic system. In addition, there are many important areas of application where information registerial variation can lead to significant breakthroughs; these areas include education, translation, machine translation, computational discourse processing in general, multimodal studies (cf. Bateman, 2008; Matthiessen, 2009). In this way, registerial cartography is an integral part of **appliable linguistics** (cf. Halliday, 2008; Matthiessen, 2014a, 2014b).

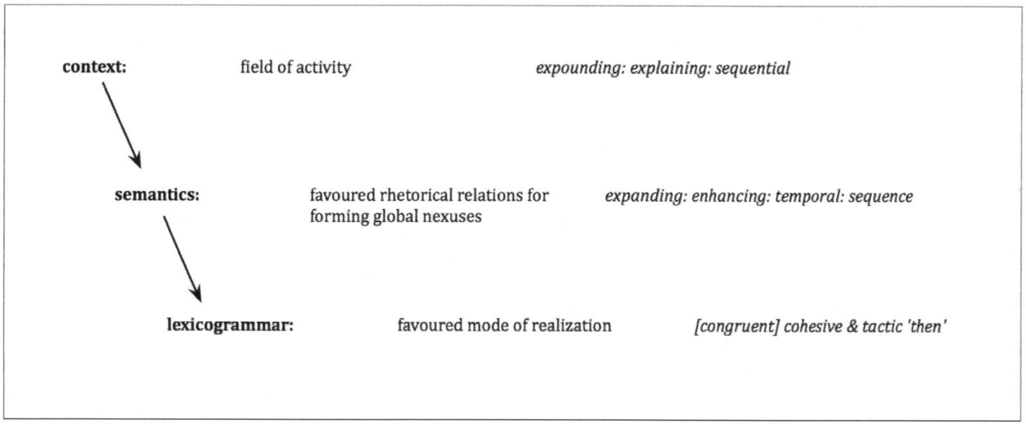

Figure 9: Stratification — the realizational chain discussed here

References

Bateman, John A. 2008. *Multimodality and genre: a foundation for the systematic analysis of multimodal documents.* London & New York: Palgrave Macmillan.

Bateman, John & Cécile Paris. 1991. "Constraining the deployment of lexicogrammatical resources during text generation: towards a computational instantiation of register theory." In Eija Ventola (ed.), *Functional and systemic linguistics: approaches and uses.* Berlin & New York: Mouton de Gruyter. 81-106.

Biber, Douglas. 1988. *Variation across speech and writing.* Cambridge: Cambridge University Press.

Biber, Douglas. 1995. *Dimensions of register variation: a cross-linguistic comparison.* Cambridge: Cambridge University Press.

Biber, Doug & Susan Conrad. 2009. *Register, genre, and style.* Cambridge: Cambridge University Press.

Biber, Douglas & Edward Finegan (eds.). 1994. *Sociolinguistic perspectives on register.* Oxford: Oxford University Press.

Bod, Rens, Jennifer Hay & Stefanie Jannedy (eds.). 2003. *Probabilistic linguistics.* Cambridge, Mass: MIT Press.

Carlson, Lynn & Daniel Marcu. 2001. *Discourse Tagging Reference Manual.* USC/ Information Sciences Institute.

Christie, Fran & Beverley Derewianka. 2008. *School discourse: Learning to write across the years of schooling.* London & New York: Continuum.

Derewianka, Beverly. 1995. *Language development in the transition from childhood to adolescence: the role of grammatical metaphor.* Macquarie University: Ph.D. thesis.

Eggins, Suzanne & Diana Slade. 2005. *Analysing casual conversation.* (First published by Cassell in 1997.) London: Equinox.

Firth, J.R. 1935. "The technique of semantics." *Transactions of the Philological Society.* Reprinted in In J.R. Firth (1957), *Papers in linguistics 1934-1951.* London: Oxford University Press. 7-33.

Ghadessy, Mohsen (ed.) 1988. *Registers of written English: situational factors and linguistic features.* London: Pinter.

Ghadessy, Mohsen (ed.). 1993. *Register analysis: theory and practice.* London & New York: Pinter.

Gregory, Michael J. 1967. "Aspects of varieties differentiation." *Journal of Linguistics* 3: 177-198.

Halliday, M.A.K. 1959. *The language of the Chinese "Secret History of the Mongols".* Oxford: Blackwell. (Publications of the Philological Society 17.) Reprinted in M.A.K. Halliday. 2006. *Studies in the Chinese language.* Volume 8 in the Collected Works of M.A.K. Halliday, edited by Jonathan J. Webster. London & New York: Continuum. 3-171.

Halliday, M.A.K. 1978. *Language as social semiotic: the social interpretation of language and meaning.* London: Edward Arnold.

Halliday, M.A.K. 1985. *An introduction to functional grammar.* London: Edward Arnold.

Halliday, M.A.K. 1988. "On the language of physical science." In Ghadessy (ed.), 162-178. Reprinted in Halliday, M.A.K. 2004. *The language of science.* Volume 5 in the Collected Works of M.A.K. Halliday. Edited by Jonathan J. Webster. London & New York: Continuum. 140-158.

Halliday, M.A.K. 1991a. "Corpus linguistics and probabilistic grammar." In Karin Aijmer & Bengt Altenberg (eds.), *English corpus linguistics: studies in honour of Jan Svartvik.* London: Longman. 30-43. Reprinted in Halliday (2005), Chapter 4: 63-75.

Halliday, M.A.K. 1991b. "Towards probabilistic interpretations." In Eija Ventola (ed.), *Trends in linguistics: functional and systemic linguistics: approaches and uses.* Berlin & New York: Mouton de Gruyter. Reprinted in Halliday (2005), Chapter 3: 42-62.

Halliday, M.A.K. 1993. "Quantitative studies and probabilities in grammar." In Michael Hoey (ed.), *Data, description, discourse: papers on the English language in honour of John McH. Sinclair.* London: Harper Collins. 1-25. Reprinted in Halliday (2005), Chapter 7: 130-156.

Halliday, M.A.K. 1994. "Language and the theory of codes." In Alan Sadovnik (ed.), *Knowledge and pedagogy: the sociology of Basil Bernstein.* Norwood, N.J.: Ablex. 124-142. Reprinted in MA.K. Halliday (2007), *Language and society.* Volume 10 in the Collected Works of M.A.K. Halliday, edited by Jonathan J. Webster. London & New York: Continuum. Chapter 8: 231-246.

Halliday, M.A.K. 1996. "On grammar and grammatics." In Ruqaiya Hasan, Carmel Cloran & David Butt (eds.), *Functional descriptions: theory into practice.* Amsterdam: Benjamins. 1-38. Reprinted in Halliday, M.A.K. 2002. *On grammar.* Volume 1 of Collected Works of M.A.K. Halliday. Edited by Jonathan Webster. London & New York: Continuum. Chapter 15: 384-417.

Halliday, M.A.K. 1998. "Things and relations: regrammaticizing experience as technical knowledge." In J.R. Martin & Robert Veel (eds.), *Reading science: critical and functional perspectives on discourses of science.* London: Routledge. 185-235.

Halliday, M.A.K. 2003. "Written language, standard language, global language." *World Englishes* 22(4): 405-418. Also in Braj B. Kachru, Yamuna Kachru & Cecil L. Nelson (eds.), 2006, *The handbook of World Englishes.* Oxford: Blackwell. 349-365.

Halliday, M.A.K. 2005. *Computational and quantitative studies.* Volume 6 in the Collected Works of M.A.K. Halliday, edited by Jonathan Webster. London & New York: Continuum.

Halliday, M.A.K. 2008. "Working with meaning: towards an appliable linguistics." In Jonathan J. Webster (ed.), *Meaning in context: implementing intelligent applications of language studies.* London & New York: Continuum. 7-23.

Halliday, M.A.K. 2013. *Halliday in the 21st century.* Volume 11 in the Collected Works of M.A.K. Halliday, edited by Jonathan J. Webster. London: Bloomsbury Academic.

Halliday, M.A.K. & Ruqaiya Hasan. 1976. *Cohesion in English.* London: Longman.

Halliday, M.A.K., Angus McIntosh & Peter Strevens. 1964. *The linguistic sciences and language teaching.* London: Longman.

Halliday, M.A.K. & J.R. Martin. 1993. *Writing science: literacy and discursive power.* London: Falmer.

Halliday, M.A.K. & Christian M.I.M. Matthiessen. 2006. *Construing experience through meaning: a language-based approach to cognition.* (First published by Cassell in 1999.) London & New York: Continuum.

Halliday, M.A.K. & Christian M.I.M Matthiessen. 2013. *Halliday's introduction to functional grammar.* Fourth Edition. London: Routledge.

Hasan, Ruqaiya. 1973. "Code, register and social dialect." In Basil Bernstein (ed.), *Class, Codes and Control: applied studies towards a sociology of language.* Volume 2. London: Routledge & Kegan Paul. 253-292.

Hasan, Ruqaiya. 1985. *Linguistics, language and verbal art.* Geelong, Vic.: Deakin University Press.

Hasan, Ruqaiya. 1989. "Semantic variation and sociolinguistics." *Australian Journal of Linguistics* 9: 221-275.

Hasan, Ruqaiya. 2009. *Semantic Variation: Meaning in Society and Sociolinguistics.* Volume Two in the Collected Works of Ruqaiya Hasan. Edited by Jonathan Webster. London: Equinox.

Huddleston, Rodney D. , Richard A. Hudson, Eugene Winter & A. Henrici. 1968. *Sentence and clause in Scientific English: final report of O.S.T.I.* Programme. University College London: Communication Research Centre.

Kittredge, Richard. 1987. "The significance of sublanguage for automatic translation." In Sergei Nirenburg (ed.), *Machine translation: theoretical and methodological issues.* Cambridge: Cambridge University Press. 59-67.

Lukin, Annabelle, Alison Moore, Maria Herke, Rebekah Wegener, Wu Canzhong. 2008. "Halliday's model of register revisited and explored." *Linguistics and the Human Sciences* 4(2): 187-243.

Mann, William C. & Christian Matthiessen. 1991. "Functions of language in two frameworks." *Word* 42(3): 231-49.

Mann, William C., Christian M.I.M. Matthiessen & Sandra A. Thompson. 1992. "Rhetorical Structure Theory and Text Analysis." USC/ISI Report. Also in William C. Mann & Sandra A. Thompson (eds.), *Discourse Description: Diverse Linguistic Analyses of a Fund Raising Text.* Amsterdam: Benjamins. 39-78.

Mann, W. & Sandra A. Thompson. 1987. *Rhetorical Structure Theory: A Framework for the Analysis of Texts.* ISI/RS-87-185.

Manning, Christopher D. & Hinrich Schütze. 1999. *Foundations of statistical natural language processing.* Cambridge, Mass.: The MIT Press.
Marcu, Daniel. 1997. *The rhetorical parsing, summarization, and generation of natural language texts.* University of Toronto: PhD thesis.
Marcu, Daniel. 2000. "The rhetorical parsing of unrestricted texts: a surface-based approach." *Computational Linguistics* 26(3): 395–448.
Martin, J.R. 1992. *English text: system and structure.* Amsterdam: Benjamins.
Martin, J.R. & David Rose. 2008. *Genre relations: mapping culture.* London & Oakville: Equinox.
Matthiessen, Christian M.I.M. 1993. "Register in the round: diversity in a unified theory of register analysis." In Mohsen Ghadessy (ed.), *Register analysis: theory and practice.* London: Pinter. 221-292.
Matthiessen, Christian M.I.M. 1999. "The system of TRANSITIVITY: an exploratory study of text-based profiles." *Functions of Language* 6(1): 1-51.
Matthiessen, Christian M.I.M. 2006. "Frequency profiles of some basic grammatical systems: an interim report." In Susan Hunston & Geoff Thompson (eds.), System and corpus: exploring connections. London: Equinox. 103-142.
Matthiessen, Christian M.I.M. 2007. "The "architecture" of language according to systemic functional theory: developments since the 1970s." In Ruqaiya Hasan, Christian M.I.M. Matthiessen & Jonathan Webster (eds.), *Continuing discourse on language.* Volume 2. London: Equinox. 505-561.
Matthiessen, Christian M.I.M. 2009. "Multisemiotic and context-based register typology: registerial variation in the complementarity of semiotic systems." Eija Ventola & Arsenio Jesús Moya Guijarro (eds.), *The world shown and the world told.* Basingstoke: Palgrave Macmillan. 11-38.
Matthiessen, Christian M.I.M. 2014a. "Appliable discourse analysis." Fang Yan & Jonathan J. Webster (eds.), *Developing Systemic Functional Linguistics: theory and application.* London: Equinox. 135-205.
Matthiessen, Christian M.I.M. 2014b. "Appliable linguistics: the potential of registerial cartography." MS of plenary given at the 3rd Forum on Applied Linguistics, the Guangdong Foreign Studies University, Guangzhou, P.R.C., 7 December 2014.
Matthiessen, Christian M.I.M. in press a. "Register in the round: registerial cartography. *Functional Linguistics* 1(2).
Matthiessen, Christian M.I.M. in press b. "Halliday's probabilistic theory of language." In Jonathan J. Webster (ed.), The Continuum Companion to M.A.K. Halliday. London & New York: Continuum.
Matthiessen, Christian M.I.M. forthc a. *Rhetorical System and Structure Theory: the semantic system of logico-semantic relations.* Book MS.
Matthiessen, Christian M.I.M. forthc b. "Modelling context and register: the long-term project of registerial cartography." Manuscript of book chapter submitted to Leila Barbara & Sara Cabral (eds.) *Teoria Sistêmico-Funcional para brasileiros* (Systemic Functional Theory for Brazilians). PPGL: Programa de Pós-Graduação em Letras. Universidade Federal de Santa Maria - UFSM: Santa Maria, Brazil.
Matthiessen, Christian M.I.M. & Abhishek Kumar Kasyap. 2014. "The construal of space in different registers: an exploratory study." *Language Sciences* 45: 1–27.
Matthiessen, Christian M.I.M. & Kazuhiro Teruya. 2013. "Grammatical realization of rhetorical relations in different registers." Paper manuscript.
Matthiessen, Christian & Kazuhiro Teruya. 2015. "Registerial hybridity: indeterminacy among fields of activity." In Donna Miller & Paul Bayley (eds.), *Permeable contexts and hybrid discourses.* London: Equinox.
Matthiessen, Christian M.I.M. & Sandra A. Thompson. 1989. "The Structure of Discourse and "Subordination"." In John Haiman & Sandra A. Thompson (eds.), *Clause Combining in Grammar and Discourse.* Amsterdam: Benjamins.
Mukařovský, Jan. 1948. "The esthetics of language." Extract from *Kapitoly z české poetiky*, translated by Paul Garvin (1964), *A Prague School reader on esthetics, literary structure and style.* Washington, D.C.: Georgetown University Press. 31-69.
Nesbitt, Christopher N. & Guenter Plum &. 1988. "Probabilities in a systemic grammar: the clause complex in English." In Robin P. Fawcett & David Young (eds.), *New developments in systemic linguistics, vol. 2: theory and application.* London: Frances Pinter. 6-39.
Prasad, Rashmi, Nikhil Dinesh, Alan Lee, Eleni Miltsakaki, Livio Robaldo, Aravind Joshi & Bonnie Webber. 2008. "The Penn Discourse TreeBank 2.0." In *Proceedings, 6th International Conference on Language Resources and Evaluation,* Marrakech, Morocco.
Prasad, Rashmi, Aravind Joshi & Bonnie Webber. 2010. "Realization of Discourse Relations by Other Means: Alternative Lexicalizations." *Coling 2010: Poster Volume*, 1023–1031.

Prasad, Rashmi, Susan McRoy, Nadya Frid, Aravind Joshi & Hong Yu. 2011. "The biomedical discourse relation bank." *BMC Bioinformatics* 12(188): 1-18.

Prasad, Rashmi, Eleni Miltsakaki, Nikhil Dinesh, Alan Lee, Aravind Joshi, Livio Robaldo & Bonnie Webber. 2007. *The Penn Discourse Treebank 2.0 Annotation Manual.* The PDTB Research Group.

Stede, Manfred. 2012. *Discourse processing.* San Rafael, CA: Morgan & Claypool Publishers.

Steiner, Erich. 2004. *Translated texts: properties, variants, evaluations.* Frankfurt.Main: Peter Lang.

Taboada, Maite & William Mann. 2006. "Rhetorical Structure Theory: Looking back and moving ahead." *Discourse Studies* 8(4): 423–459.

Teich, Elke. 1999. "System-oriented and text-oriented comparative linguistic research: cross-linguistic variation in translation." *Languages in Contrast* 2(2): 187-210.

Ure, Jean. 1982. "Introduction: approaches to the study of register range." *International Journal of the Sociology of Language* 35: 5-23.

Ure, Jean N. & Jeffrey Ellis. 1977. "Register in descriptive linguistics and linguistic sociology." In Oscar Uribe-Villegas (ed.), *Issues in Sociolinguistics.* The Hague: Mouton.

Vandenbergen, Anne-Marie, Miriam Taverniers & Louise Ravelli (eds.) 2003. *Grammatical metaphor: views from systemic functional linguistics.* Amsterdam: John Benjamins.

Webber, Bonnie. 2009. "Genre distinctions for Discourse in the Penn TreeBank." *Proceedings of the 47th Annual Meeting of the ACL and the 4th IJCNLP of the AFNLP.* 674–682.

Discourse for Machine Translation

Bonnie Webber
School of Informatics, University of Edinburgh

Abstract

Statistical Machine Translation is a modern success: Given a source language sentence, SMT finds the most probable target language sentence, based on (1) properties of the source; (2) probabilistic source--target mappings at the level of words, phrases and/or sub-structures; and (3) properties of the target language.

SMT translates individual sentences because the search space even for a single sentence can be vast. But sentences are parts of texts, and texts have properties beyond those of their individual sentences, including:

- document-wide properties, such as style, register, reading level and genre, that are visible in the frequency and distribution of words, word senses, referential forms and syntactic structures;
- patterns of topical or functional sub-structures that mean that frequencies and distributions of words, word senses, referential forms and syntactic structures will vary across a text;
- relations between clauses or between referring expressions that can be signaled explicitly or implicitly, that reflect a text's coherence;
- frequent appeal to reduced expressions that rely on context to
- efficiently convey their message.

Recognizing and deploying these properties promises to improve both fluency and accuracy in SMT -- i.e., whether the sequence of sentences in the target text conveys the same information as those in its source, in as readable a manner. This presentation describes how researchers are attempting to do this, without bringing translation to a halt.

Relating Keywords to the 'Top Ten News of the Year' in Korean Newspapers

Jae-Woong Choe
Korea University / Seoul, Korea
jchoe@korea.ac.kr

Abstract

This paper takes an in-depth look at the relationship between mechanically extracted keywords and 'Top Ten News of the Year' compiled by the news editors. A previous study that briefly touched on the topic concludes there does not seem to exist any meaningful connection between the two. In this paper, we set up a more elaborate way of comparing and connecting the two, and argue that there is a certain reasonably good converging point. The corpus we make use of for our experiment is a subset of the Trend 21 corpus which is a collection of Korean major newspapers (2000-2013). For keyword extraction, log-likelihood ratio was made use of. Extraction of collocation for each keyword was needed, for which a version of Mutual Information was utilized. Finally a detailed comparison of the top ten news with the top 100 keywords was conducted from several points of view.

1 Introduction

There is a growing use of the keyword methodology as an analytic tool to efficiently analyze texts or corpora, and we can say it now has established itself as a viable, and, importantly, objective alternative to the traditional and rather introspective method of discourse or cultural interpretation (Scott & Tribble, 2006, Bondi & Scott, 2010; Archer, 2009; Baker et al., 2013). One issue that needs to be addressed is how the new methodology relates to the introspective way of selecting keywords from a given text or corpus. Are the two supposed to be different from each other? Then why so? Or do they have to be comparable or even identical to each other? And if they do, how can we test the comparability or convergence? In this paper we raise these questions on the basis of Korean newspaper corpora and some lists of 'Top Ten News (T10N for short)' compiled, presumably introspectively, by the newspaper editors at the end of every year. Specifically we compare the top 100 keywords with T10N, and see how well they converge with each other. Some previous studies seem to suggest a tentatively negative conclusion on the issue of any systematic relationship between the introspective and quantitative keywords in general (Bondi & Scott, 2010), or between quantitative keywords and T10N (Kim & Lee, 2011).

It should be noted at the outset that each item in T10N is not a keyword per se. Though it can trivially turned into a small set of keywords on the basis of the surface description of the news item, we take the item as an abstract concept to which a set of keywords can be mapped, thus making it possible to compare the quantitatively derived keywords and the more abstract key concepts that are selected introspectively. We argue that T10N provides an interesting testing ground for the significance of the keywords extracted or the role of the 'human factor' in the selection process of T10N.

This paper briefly reviews some of the previous studies on the issue at hand in Section 2, introduces the corpora used in Section 3, provides in Section 4 two lists of T10N to be analyzed, discusses methodological issues in Section 5, and reports the results in Section 6 with related discussion, which is then followed by conclusion.

Copyright 2014 by Jae-Woong Choe
28th Pacific Asia Conference on Language, Information and Computation pages 28–37

2 Keywords: Introspection vs. Corpus

According to Stubbs (2010), there are three kinds of 'keywords', two of which are of our immediate concern in this paper: One is the 'cultural keywords', for example like the one compiled by Williams (1976/85), that are intended to capture the essence of a culture through selection of the terms or keywords that would represent some major aspects of the culture. It certainly would involve processes of understanding, interpretation, and abstraction on the part of the person that does the compiling job. In other words, they represent human interpretation and understanding of the phenomena, i.e., the culture. Let us call them 'introspective keywords', focusing on the methodology, so that they may cover not only the cultures but also other broad aspects of society. The other concept of keywords refers to the analytic tool mentioned in the previous section. They are called 'statistical keywords', which are extracted on the basis of the (relative) frequency distribution of words in the given corpora.

How are the two related to each other? Previous studies touched on the issue of the relationship between the two kinds of keywords, and suggested that they should be treated as separate kinds, little significant relationship being observed. For example, Stubbs (2010: 32) contends that they are "only loosely conceptually related, and perhaps only marginally compatible." Scott (2010: 45) also states "[i]t is perfectly true that automatic analysis works differently from human identification in the case of keyness …."

It may be true that human selection of the key words or phrases to capture the bigger picture of the society or culture is different from purely mechanical extraction of keywords from discourse. However it would also be true that the bigger picture is formed through discourse. It is mediated, communicated, and created through discourse. In other words, introspection based human keywords are not created from nothing; ideally they should reflect well the culture or society in question, and the discourse that constitutes and represents the society. Again ideally if we can get hold of the whole set of discourses which presumably reflect the culture and society as a whole, we can expect there would be a certain converging point between introspective keywords and quantitative keywords.

We will assume one of such case can be provided by news texts of a certain period of time. In particular, the top ten news summarize a year's major events which had been reported in the news articles of the year. Suppose we have fairly large corpora that reflect the social events from which we can extract keywords on the one hand, and also human interpretation of the major events in the form of T10N on the other. How would they match up with each other then?

There is one previous study that dealt with such question. Kim & Lee (2011) compared T10N of 2009 and the keywords of the same year based on the Korean major newspapers, and found out only eleven out of 100 keywords match T10N. They concluded that "[the two] are more different from each other than would be expected (2011: 178). [Translation by the author]" While the presumably introspective selection of the major news of the year need not perfectly match the keywords, it is surprising that the major news does not seem to reflect the texts of the newspapers. This paper will take a careful look at this question again, using similar but more fine-tuned sets of data and different sets of tools for keyword extraction and interpretation. We find there is an interesting and meaningful converging point between the two, and even the items that do not match well seem to shed some light on how the human interpretation process works.

3 Target and Reference Corpora

T10N are selected annually, so it is reasonable to assume that the most relevant discourse would be the whole news of the year. For this experimental study, we are going to use the same set of T10N as that in Kim & Lee (2011), but we use different subsets as the target and reference corpora. In order to explain the difference, we first need to introduce the Trend 21 Corpus from which we take a subcorpus.

The Trend 21 Corpus is a collection of newspaper articles from 2000 to 2013 (Kim et al., 2011, Choe & Lee, 2014). All the newspaper articles in four major daily newspapers published in Korea (*Chosun, Dong-a, Joongang*, and *Hankyoreh*) constitute the corpus, and new data are processed and added after the end of each year when the data are provided by respective news media. The corpus currently contains over 600 million 'ejels', or chunks between spaces in Korean which typically consist of a content word and some agglutinating particles.

For the experiment in this paper we mainly use a subset of the corpus, primarily the data that cover the four year span (2006-2009) of a newspaper, *Chosun*, referring to a larger set when necessary. Specifically, we take the news texts of 2009 of *Chosun* as the target corpus, and those of 2006-8 of the same newspaper as the reference corpus. We assumed the corpus of the previous three years as the reference would be "moderate sized (Scott, 2010:52; See also Jeon & Choe (2009))". This is different from Kim & Lee (2011) where they took all the news texts from the four major newspapers as the target and reference corpus, and then compared the results with T10N of *Chosun*. As is well known, newspapers may differ among themselves in terms of their respective stance on the social, cultural, and especially political issues (Baker et al., 2013). Thus assuming possibly different stances may influence the composition of each news texts and also the selection of T10N, we decided to compare the keywords from a particular newspaper with their own selection of T10N, thus limiting the effects of other factors to the minimum.

4 Lists of Top Ten News

There are typically two kinds of T10N compiled by each newspaper in Korea. One covers the national events, and the other international ones. *Chosun* had the following news items as their selection of T10N for the national and international major events of the year 2009, respectively.

Id	News item	Classification
cn1	Cardinal Kim and two former presidents passed away	Politics/ Death
cn2	Korea will host the G20 Summit in 2010	Foreign Affairs
cn3	Confrontation surrounding the Sejong City project and the four major river project	National Projects
cn4	The new North Korean leader Kim Jong Un, the second NK nuclear test	North Korea
cn5	The Naro space rocket launch failed	Science
cn6	Many large labor unions secede from *Minnochong* [the upper organization]	Labor
cn7	Media law passes the parliament	Media
cn8	Murderer Kang and the Nayoung case, Yongsan disaster not healed	Society
cn9	Golfer Yang wins over Tiger Woods, Kim Yu-na' golden performance, Korean Soccer qualifies for the World Cup	Sports
cn10	The [Korean rice wine] makgeolli is all the craze everywhere	Life

Table 1: National Top Ten News (*Chosun*, 2009)

Id	News item	Classification
ci1	Expanding global economic crisis, weak dollars	Economic Crisis
ci2	Swine flu caused over 10,000 deaths	Epidemic
ci3	China's formidable economic growth	China
ci4	More American troops in Afghanistan	War
ci5	Lisbon Treaty, the EU's first president elected	Europe
ci6	Hatoyama assumes power in Japan, but the US-Japan relations seem murky	Japan
ci7	Copenhagen summit failed to meet the expectation	Environment
ci8	Pop emperor Michael Jackson dies	Entertainment
ci9	US women reporters detained in North Korea	US-NK relation
ci10	Tiger Woods' infidelity scandal	Sports

Table 2: International Top Ten News (*Chosun*, 2009)

Note that the English translations of the news items provided in the above tables are not exactly the same as they appear in the newspaper but somewhat in an abbreviated and compact form, again to save the space. We also took the liberty of ignoring some metaphoric descriptions, and added some extra information so that those that are not familiar with the events may get a better grasp of them. For example, 'cn1' would be literally translated as "Kim Swu Hwan, Kim Dae Jung, Roh Moo Hyun ... Major Figures in modern history are now in history," which simply refer to the deaths of the three major players in Korean politics and society for over 40 years. We also added the "Classification" column, again as a way to help the readers, especially those that are not familiar with the events described, to comprehend the overall picture as well as the characteristics of each event.

5 Methodology

5.1 Keyword extraction

The statistical procedures typically used for keyword extraction are Dunning's Log Likelihood (LL) and chi-square (Scott & Tribble, 2006). Some authors used T-score for the calculation (Kim & Lee, 2011). The standard text tools such as *WordSmith* (Scott, 2012) and *AntConc* (Anthony, 2011) provide keyword extraction procedures like log-likelihood and chi-squared, and it is generally known that there is not much difference between the two (Rayson, 2003; Bondie & Scott, 2010). In this paper, we used a version of LL described in Rayson (2003: 50). Let us suppose we have the following contingency table.

	Target	Reference
Frequency	a	b
Corpus Size	c	d

Table 3: Contingency table

Then the log-likelihood ratio is calculated as follows, where N refers to the total value of the four cells.

$$G^2 = 2\,(a\ln a + b\ln b + c\ln c + d\ln d + N\ln N - (a+b)\ln(a+b) - (a+c)\ln(a+c) - (b+d)\ln(b+d) - (c+d)\ln(c+d))$$

The formula was implemented in a Perl script, rather than using any of the well-known tools, because the size of the data for the current study was rather huge and it was not easy, if not impossible, to handle them in the readily available tools. In order to confirm that the custom-made script works as expected, some test results were compared with those from *WordSmith* and *AntConc* on the basis of the same set of data, a Shakespearean play *Romeo and Juliet*, and there were minimal differences among the three results.

Since our concern in this paper is the topic rather than the style of the data, we limited our search to the words/morphemes that are nouns (/NNG) and proper names (/NNP), ignoring all the other categories.

5.2 Collocation extraction

For many of the extracted keywords, it was obvious which T10N item each of them belong to. But for many others, the connection was not that clear. There were several reasons for this. For one thing, a keyword may be ambiguous. For example, 지원[jiwon] in Korean may either mean 'support' or 'application', and we need to figure out in which sense the word was selected as a keyword. Another reason is that it was difficult to decide in which context a certain keyword was used. 중소기업[jungsogieop] means 'small and medium sized enterprises', and it is difficult to know whether it has anything to do with T10N or not. A third reason is that some keywords may be linked to more than one item in the T10N list. 오바마(Obama), as President of the most influential country in the world, can obviously be related to many news items. Finally there were a few keywords with baffling identities. 김정은[Kim Jung-un], apparently a personal name, was listed as a keyword, and it was not clear at first why the name cropped up as a keyword.

These problems can be solved if we take the context into consideration, of course. A widely used method is to browse the keywords in the KWIC style. But when there are so many data to be checked, a more efficient method is called for which will succinctly summarize the contextual information. One such method would be collocation, which looked good enough for our purpose so we made use of it in this study. Thus for each keyword, a set of collocation words, or more exactly a set of morphemes were gathered that co-occur in the same news item.

There are well-known collocation extraction methods like the t-test and Mutual Information. While the t-test seems to have some issues with low frequency words, Mutual Information has been considered too skewed to them, assigning a very high value, for example, to a bigram whose members occur only once in the given corpus. In this paper, we used a version of Mutual Information, called Log-Frequency based Mutual Dependency (LFMD, Thanopoulos et al., 2002), which is designed to add some frequency effect to Mutual Information. The metric is given below, which was again implemented in Perl:

$$D_{LF}(w_1w_2) = D(w_1,w_2) + \log_2 P(w_1w_2)$$

where D is:

$$D(w_1, w_2) = I(w_1, w_2) - I(w_1w_2) = \log_2 \frac{P^2(w_1w_2)}{P(w_1) \cdot P(w_2)}$$

6 Results and Discussion

Once the keywords were extracted and sorted in a descending order of their LL value, we checked each of the top 100 keywords for possible matchup with the twenty items of the national and international T10N provided in Tables 1 and 2. The collocation word list for each keyword was constantly consulted in the process. A sample of the table used for the process is provided in Appendix at the end of this paper.

6.1 Keywords that relate to the national T10N

30 out of the top 100 keywords were found to be linked to the national top 10 news. Their mutual relationship is provided in the following table, where the T10N news items and their related keywords are shown side by side. Each keyword is followed by its English gloss, and then its rank in the 100 list shown in parenthesis.

Cat: Cla.	keywords(rank)
cn1: Politics/ Death	서거/Death(22), 조문단/Condolence_delegation(74), 조문/Condolence(76), 분향소/Memorial altar(81), 국민장/National_funeral(93)
cn3: National Projects	세종시/*Sejong*_City(1), 충청/*Chungcheong*(16), 원안/First_draft(40), 대강/Major_rivers(49), 해양부/Maritime(68), 사업/Business(72), 국토/Country(99)
cn4: North Korea	오바마/*Obama*(6), 보즈워스/Bosworth(38), 김정운/Kim_Jong_Un(87), 도발/Provocation(92), 버락/*Barack*(95)
cn5: Science	나로호/*Naroho*(18), 관제/Control(23), 발사체/Projectile(55)
cn5/cn4	로켓/Rocket(15), 발사/Launch(32)
cn6: Labor	노조/Labor_union(26), 노총/Trade_unions(34), 민노총/*Minnochong*(44), 탈퇴/Withdrawal(82)
cn7: Media	미디어/Media(65)
cn8: Society	강호순/*Kang_Hosun*(66)
cn9: Sports	김연아/*Kim_Yuna*(80)
cn10: Life	막걸리/Rice_wine(19)

Table 4: National T10N and their matching keywords

It seems like each item in T10N is reasonably well represented in the top 100 keyword list. Each item, except for 'cn2', has at least one keyword that supports its selection. Half of the national T10N ('cn1', 'cn3', 'cn4', 'cn5', 'cn6'), or five out of top 6 news, are linked to at least three top 100 keywords. Top three major news given in Table 4, namely 'cn1', 'cn3', and 'cn4', have at least five matching keywords. Overall, we might be able to say that the top five items in Table 4 support rather strongly the convergence between the introspection based major news and the statistically derived keywords.

The bottom four items in Table 4 is not that well supported by the list of top 100 keywords, but still each finds a keyword in the list that can be linked. We will come back to the missing one 'cn2' in Section 6.3.

The first three names that appear as keywords for 'cn4: The new North Korean leader Kim Jong Un, the second NK nuclear test' show why collocation information is needed for proper classification. 오바마(Obama) would rather be expected to be linked to some international news, and no doubt Obama, as President of the most influential country of the world, would be featured in many international news. However, when the collocation words of the name were checked, a crucial one seems to be '핵[haek]/nuclear'. Obviously, as much as 'Obama' appeared in many other news, the name was significantly associated with the word 'nuclear' and the most noteworthy mention of the word 'nuclear' in Korea in 2009 was in the context of the North Korean nuclear test. The same applies to another name "(Steven) Bosworth" in 'cn4'. The words that collocate with it are such as '방북[bangbuk]/visiting North Korea', '회담[hoedam]/talks', '대북[daebuk]/to North Korea', and '특사[teuksa]/special envoy', clearly revealing his role as a special US envoy handling the NK nuclear issue. Finally, '김정운[Kim Jung-un]', apparently a personal name, was listed as a keyword, and even to a person that is well versed in Korean national affairs the name looked puzzling at first. Its collocation revealed the name refers to the newly emerging North Korean leader. His name was initially wrongly identified as 김정운 in the media, rather than the correct 김정은 as was later to be known through the North Korean media, befitting to the secrecy and mystery that surrounds the country.

Even with some collocation information, there were truly ambiguous cases, and thus we had to add an extra classification category 'cn5/cn4' in Table 4. The two keywords associated with the category, namely '로켓[rokes]/Rocket(15)' and '발사[balsa]/Launch(32)', when their collocated words were considered, were clearly linked either to the failed launching of the spacecraft *Naroho* in the South, and to the launching of the missile *Daephodong* in North Korea. We therefore tentatively classified it as belonging to 'cn5/cn4'.

6.2 Keywords that relate to the international T10N

The same number of keywords, namely, 30 out of the top 100 keywords was found out to be linked to the international T10N, as shown below.

Cat: Cla.	keywords(rank)
ci1: Economic Crisis	위기/Crisis(9), 회복/Recovery(10), 불황/Recession(20), 글로벌/Global(25), 금융/Finance(61), 부양책/Stimulus_package(67), 회복세/Recovery(75), 침체/Downturn(79), 신흥국/Emerging_country(91), 조정/Adjustment(96)
ci2: Epidemic	신종플루/Swine_flu(2), 플루/Flu(4), 신종/New_type(8), 백신/Vaccines(14), 접종/Vaccination(36), 확진/Confirmed(43), 타미플루/*Tamiflu*(45), 인플루엔자/Influenza(62), 감염/Infection(64), 독감/Flu(73), 바이러스/Virus(86), 의료/Medical_care(94), 환자/Patients(97)
ci6: Japan	하토야마/*Hatoyama*(11)
ci7: Environ-ment	녹색/Green(3), 저탄소/Low-carbon(46), 기후/Climate(50), 코펜하겐/*Copenhagen*(57), 온실/Greenhouse(78), 친환경/Eco-friendly(85)

Table 5: International T10N and their matching keywords

Almost all of the 30 keywords were linked only to the three international T10N items. The items 'ci1: Expanding global economic crisis, weak dollars' and 'ci2: Swine flu caused over 10,000 deaths' were the two prominent international news of the year that were amply reflected in the keywords. They were national news as well as international ones as Korea was also affected by both the economic crisis and the epidemic, and thus people in Korea were keenly following the news.

Economic crisis and the swine flu epidemic are the two pieces of news that affect the lives of the general public very much, and obviously the news media were clearly aware of them, thus dealing with them very widely and repeatedly as the related keywords show. Likewise, global warming and the subsequent climate change is one of the grave issues that largely bother the minds of the general public. Thus the 2009 United Nations Climate Change Conference, or the Copenhagen Summit was apparently covered well in the newspaper as the keywords in 'ci7: Copenhagen summit failed to meet the expectation' show in Table 5.

The other news item in the table is about Japan. Hatoyama became the first Prime Minister from the modern Democratic Party of Japan in 2009, defeating the long-governing Liberal Democratic Party. The power change in Japan, a closely related neighboring country to Korea, was an obviously newsworthy item to Koreans, and so was covered accordingly in the news media.

6.3 T10N that do not have any matching top 100 keywords

Among the national T10N news items 'cn2' was the only exception that did not have any supportive words in the top 100 keywords. The description of 'cn2' is 'Korea will host the G20 Summit in 2010' as shown in Table 1. The key phrase in the description is 'G20', but it turns out that the tagger wrongly analyzed it as 'G' and '20'.

G20 이   G/SL+20/SN+이/JKS

Since the source of the problem was located, it was possible to get the log-likelihood value for the expression "G20" separately. Had it been treated as a single unit, its LL value would be 2287.92, which means "G20" would rank as the ninth item in the top 100 keyword list (See Appendix). Every national T10N in Table 1 is supported by at least one associated keyword.

Item	O1	1%	O2	2%	LL
Word	1277	0.01	267	0.00 +	2287.92

Table 6: Log-likelihood value for 'G20'

On the other hand, as for the international T10N news items, only four of them could find their linked keywords in the top 100 keyword list, as Table 5 shows. Note that three of them, the most heavily covered ones ('ci1', 'ci2', 'ci7') in the media, concern global issues which would also affect the lives of the local general public. It is highly likely they would have made national T10N even if they were not covered by the other list.

Among the rest of the news items in Table 2, five of them deal with regional issues like China, US-led war in Afganistan, Europe, Japan, and a US-North Korean issue. The other two concern well-known popular figures like Michael Jackson the pop star and Tiger Woods the sports star. Only one of these seven items has a single related word in the top 100 keyword list. It is obvious that not particularly many news articles were written on the global scale topics in the newspaper and yet the editors felt they should be included in T10N. We will come back to this point later.

6.4 Top 100 keywords that do not belong to any of the T10N items

There were 40 keywords in the top 100 list that were left out of the national and international T10N. Four of them were included due to some other factors than the news stories themselves. For example, the use of the word '편집자[pyeonjipja]/ Editor' seems to have spiked up in 2009, but it was exclusively used as part of the editorial comments to some of the articles, rather than as part of the news stories. Many of the other keywords were used individually, having little to do with other words in the top 100 keyword list. However, there were several clusters of keywords each of which seemed to point to a particular event or topic.

cat	keywords(rank)
o_edu	사정관/Admissions_Officer(12), 교과부/MOE(28), 전형/Exams(35), 사교육/Private_tutoring(37), 입학/Admission(41), 수능/SAT(58), 성적/Grades(71), 지원/Application(77), 모집/Recruitment(90)

o_job	잡월드/Job_World(5), 취업/Job_finding(39), 일자리/Jobs(47), 비정규직/Non-regular_workers(60), 중소기업/Small_business(70)
o_housing	보금자리/Bogeumjari_ housing(27), 수도권/Metropolitan(30)
o_IT	스마트폰/Smartphone(63), 트위터/Twitter(84)

Table 7: Keyword clusters each of which points to a particular topic

The keywords in the 'o_edu' category concerns college entrance system, particularly the newly introduced one by universities in Korea that seemed to be gaining huge momentum, urged by the Ministry of Education. Education, especially the college entrance system is everybody's concern in Korea, and even a slight change in the system has huge repercussions on the society in general. Obviously, the new "Admissions Officer" system was one of the top national issues in 2009 and thus was much talked about in the media. The following chart shows that the use of the keywords '사정관[sajeonggwan]/ Admissions_Officer' and '입학[iphak]/ Admissions' greatly increased simultaneously in 2009 in the four major newspapers in Korea.

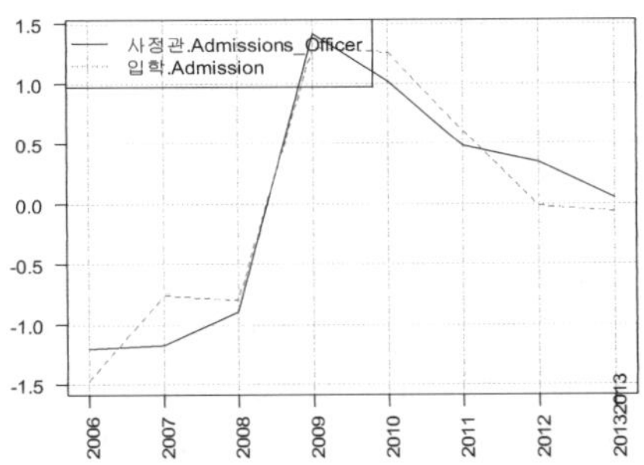

Another hot topic which is everybody's concern is unemployment or difficulty of getting a job. Growing number of the unemployed has become a social issue. It was a much talked about issue of the year again, as the keywords in the 'o_job' in Table 7 show. Incidentally, the first keyword of the category, '잡월드[jabwoldeu]/ Job_World(5)' turned out to be the name of the website created by the particular newspaper, *Chosun*, together with other institutions, as part of a social campaign to help the unemployed to find a job. Out of 1,161 occurrences of the word in the four major newspapers in 2009, the vast majority (1,151) have appeared in *Chosun*. The other two categories in Table 7, along with their keywords, again have a lot to do with everyday life of the ordinary people: a new housing project in the metropolitan area, and newly introduced popular IT items like smartphones and the twitter.

The rest of the keywords, 14 of them, seemed to deal with individual issues separately, and did not aggregate well among themselves. One thing to note before we close this section is the personal or pen names that showed unusual degree of keyness though not related to any of the T10N.

cat	keywords(rank)
p_invst	박연차/*Bakyeoncha*(13), 건호/*Geonho*(98)
p_ent	장자연/*Chang_Jayon*(48)
p_soc	미네르바/*Minerva*(100)

Table 8: Keywords of proper names

The category 'p_invst' is related to the political scandal that implicated a former president, which many believe eventually led to his suicide. The two keywords in the category refer to the principal figures in the scandal, close associates of the late president. The other two categories in Table 8 are again related some social and political scandal.

Many of the keyword clusters or keyword discussed in this section could have made the national T10N list but the editors chose otherwise.

7 Conclusion

So how well do the statistically derived keywords and the introspection based T10N converge? Based on the results of our analyses, over 60 percent of the top 100 keywords make positive contribution to the convergence. Seen from the opposite point of view, national T10N is well supported by the keywords while international T10N is markedly less so. So we can conclude that though the two do not match with each other perfectly, they converge reasonably well.

Then what is the source of the difference between them? Here we provide some speculative remarks. One thing that influences the introspection based selection or decision of T10N is a higher abstraction process involved. For example, 'cn3: National construction projects' is an abstraction over more than one separate event or project, and so are 'cn1: Politics/Death' and 'cn4: North Korea'. Secondly, the introspection based selection is likely to be influenced by the historical context. The choice of 'death' as the top national news of the year in 'cn1', rather than the second or the third or even below, would make more sense if we take it into consideration that the three people involved have left a huge impact in recent history of Korea. So it is not just their death, but in a sense the end of era in Korean political and social history that mattered in the selection.

The third factor that apparently plays a role in the selection of the T10N is the geographical balance, especially in the case of the international T10N, namely from 'ci3' to 'ci6' in Table 2, for which there were not to be found any related keywords in the top 100 list. The fourth factor is the sectional or topical balance of the newspaper (Tables 1, 2). Otherwise it is rather difficult to explain the inclusion of the last four items ('cn7' to 'cn10') in Table 4 at the expense of other events that are more prominently reflected in the linked keywords. The final factor that seems to matter is what we might call topic subsumption. Although the name '박연차/*Bakyeoncha*' and '건호/*Geonho*' appeared particularly frequently in 2009 (See Section 6.4), the event was eclipsed by a much bigger related news which was the death of the former president allegedly involved.

References

Laurence Anthony. 2011. AntConc (Version 3.2.4) [Computer Software]. Tokyo, Japan: Waseda University.

Dawn Archer. Ed. 2009. What's in a Word-list?: Investigating Word Frequency and Keyword Extraction, Ashgate.

Paul Baker, Costas Gabrielatos & Tony McEnery. 2013. Discourse Analysis and Media Attitudes: the Eepresentation of Islam in the British Press. Cambridge University Press.

Marina Bondi & Mike Scott. Ed. 2010. Keyness in Texts. John Benjamins Publishing Company.

Jae-Woong Choe, Do-Gil Lee. 2014. Trends 21 Corpus: Public Web Resources and Search Tools. Studies in Korean Culture 64. pp. 1-20. [In Korean]

Jieun Jeon & Jae-Woong Choe. 2009. A Key word Analysis of English Intensifying Adverbs in Male and Female Speech in ICE-GB. Proceedings of the 23rd PACLIC. City University of Hong Kong. pp. 210-219.

Heunggyu Kim, Beom-mo Kang, Do-Gil Lee, Eugene Chung, Ilhwan Kim. 2011. Trends 21 Corpus: A Large Annotated Korean Newspaper Corpus for Linguistic and Cultural Studies, Digital Humanities 2011, June 19-22, 2011. Stanford University.

Ilhwan Kim and Do-Gil Lee. 2011. Automatic Keyword Extraction and Analysis from the Large Scale Newspaper Corpus Based on t-score. Korean Linguistics 53. pp. 145-194. [In Korean]

Paul Rayson. 2003. Matrix: A Statistical Method and Software Tool for Linguistic Analysis through Corpus Comparison. Ph.D. thesis, Lancaster University.

Mike Scott. 2010. Problems in Investigating Keyness, or Clearing the Undergrowth and Marking out Trails.... In Bondi & Scott, 2010. pp. 43-58.

Mike Scott. 2012. WordSmith Tools version 6. Lexical Analysis Software.

Mike Scott & Christopher Tribble. 2006. Textual Patterns: Key Words and Corpus Analysis in Language Education. John Benjamins Publishing Company.

Michael Stubbs. 2010. Three Concepts of Keywords. In Bondi & Scott, 2010. pp. 21-42.

Aristomenis Thanopoulos, Nikos Fakotakis, George Kokkinakis. 2002. Comparative Evaluation of Collocation Extraction Metrics. Proceedings of the Third International Conference on Language Resources and Evaluation (LREC-2002), Las Palmas, Spain.

Raymond Williams. 1976/85. Keywords: A Vocabulary of Culture and Society. Fontana Press.

Appendix: A sample of the table used for the linking process

No	Morph/Eng	cat	cl	freq	LL	mi terms
1	세종시/ Sejong_City	NNP	n3	2718	6289.892	원안:6.351 수정:5.622 총리:3.741 충청권:3.645 정부:3.521 행정:3.436 정:3.283 정운찬:3.17 도시:3.044 문제:2.965 수정안:2.776
2	신종플루/ Swine_flu	NNG	i2	2298	5958.051	감염:4.611 환자:4.036 확진:3.994 타미플루:3.732 백신:3.471 접종:3.07 예방:2.739 독감:2.437 확산:2.242 바이러스:2.023 인플루엔자:1.938
3	녹색/Green	NNG	i7	3360	3475.75	성장:6.96 저탄소:6.219 에너지:5.153 산업:3.913 환경:3.681 친환경:3.259 사업:3.239 계획:3.15 기술:3.049 정부:2.999 추진:2.819
4	플루/Flu	NNG	i2	1185	3072.164	신종:9.552 감염:4.83 환자:3.805 인플루엔자:2.745 바이러스:2.706 감염자:2.608 백신:2.374 확진:2.073 타미플루:1.424 질병:1.199 개학:0.984
5	잡월드/ Job_World	NNP	o_job	1151	2984.009	취업:6.114 채용:5.953 기업은행:5.949 중소기업:5.947 구직자:4.945 청년:3.659 인재:3.225 사이트:2.88 일자리:2.662 조선일보:2.381 이력서:2.083
6	오바마/ Obama	NNP	n4	6809	2764.495	대통령:8.779 미국:8.015 행정부:7.894 미:7.856 버락:7.26 Obama:6.738 백악관:6.165 부시:5.716 회담:5.163 클린턴:5.017 핵:4.839
7	자전거/ Bicycles	NNG	o_trans	5081	2548.662	도로:5.841 이용:2.606 구간:1.664 공원:1.64 설치:1.627 시민:1.553 계획:1.387 조성:1.376 한강:1.248 전용:1.12 교통:1.034
8	신종/ New_type	NNG	i2	1552	2536.461	플루:9.552 감염:5.071 인플루엔자:5.043 환자:3.894 바이러스:3.47 백신:2.806 감염자:2.531 확진:2.155 독감:2.038 질병:1.899 대유행:1.68
9	위기/Crisis	NNG	i1	11859	2173.943	경제:9.897 금융:9.757 글로벌:8.092 미국:7.913 세계:7.78 말:7.735 시장:7.583 정부:7.377 이후:7.192 상황:7.119 기업:6.979
10	회복/ Recovery	NNG	i1	5174	2040.508	경기:7.848 경제:7.081 금융:6.56 위기:6.445 상승:6.118 시장:6.095 말:6 전망:5.992 이후:5.834 투자:5.7 침체:5.663
11	하토야마/ Hatoyama	NNP	i6	859	2002.735	유키오:5.55 총리:5.512 일본:3.652 자민당:3.501 일:3.383 정권:2.57 민주당:2.305 오자와:1.95 오카다:1.942 후텐마:1.661 오키나와:1.661
12	사정관/ Admissions_ Officer	NNG	o_edu	1163	1856.23	입학:8.134 전형:6.388 관제:5.97 선발:4.816 사정:4.811 면접:4.604 학생:4.215 서류:3.985 입시:3.969 대학:3.727 성적:3.423
13	박연차/ Bakyeoncha	NNP	p_invst	1164	1800.486	검찰:6.197 태광실업:6.008 수사:5.891 회장:5.15 노무현:5.119 대검:4.722 박:4.707 노:4.608 게이트:4.467 중수부:4.13 소환:4.036
14	백신/ Vaccines	NNG	i2	1460	1766.166	접종:6.082 독감:4.666 바이러스:4.212 예방:3.842 신종플루:3.471 감염:3.367 인플루엔자:3.062 신종:2.806 타미플루:2.737 플루:2.374 녹십자:2.337
15	로켓/Rocket	NNG	n5/n4	1431	1662.941	발사:7.967 우주:4.796 장거리:4.348 발사체:4.244 위성:4.191 미사일:4.188 나로호:4.001 북한:3.625 러시아:2.686 단:2.59 인공위성:2.587

Invited Talk: Word Sense Induction for Machine Translation

Min Zhang
Provincial Key Laboratory for Computer Information Processing Technology
Soochow University, Suzhou, China 215006
minzhang@suda.edu.cn

Abstract

We have witnessed the research progress of machine translation from phrase/syntax-based to semantics-based and from single sentence-based to discourse and document-based. This talk presents our work of word sense-based translation model for statistical machine translation, which is one of semantics-based SMT research at word sense level. The sense in which a word is used determines the translation of the word. The talk begins with how to build a broad-coverage sense tagger based on a nonparametric Bayesian topic model that automatically learns sense clusters for words in the source language, and then focuses on the proposed word sense-based translation model that enables the decoder to select appropriate translations for source words according to the inferred senses for these words using maximum entropy classifiers. The talk ends with experiential results and some conclusions. To the best of our knowledge, this is the first attempt to empirically verify the positive impact of lexical semantics (word sense) on translation quality.

This is a joint work with Deyi Xiong, Soochow University.

Biography

Dr. Min Zhang, a distinguished professor and Director of the Research Center of Human Language Technology at Soochow University (China), received his Bachelor degree and Ph.D. degree in computer science from Harbin Institute of Technology (China) in 1991 and 1997, respectively. He worked in Academy and Industry from 1997-2013 at Singapore and Korea. His current research interests include machine translation, natural language processing and Internet intelligence. He has co-authored more than 150 papers in leading journals and conferences, and co-authored/co-edited 12 books published by Springer, IEEE CPS and COLIPS. He is the vice president of COLIPS (2011-2013), a steering committee member of PACLIC (2011~now), an executive member of AFNLP (2013~2014), the vice-chair-elected of SIGHAN/ACL (2014), a council member of CAAI and TCCI/CCF (2014~2016), and a member of ACL, ACM and IEEE. He was the recipient of several awards in China and oversea. He has been supervising Ph.D students at National University of Singapore, Harbin Institute of Technology and Soochow University since 2005.

Setting Syntactic Parameters with Implicit Negative Evidence: The Case of Zero-derived Causatives in English

Isaac Gould
Department of Linguistics and Philosophy
Massachusetts Institute of Technology
igould@mit.edu

Abstract

In this paper, I introduce a learning challenge for various models of parameter setting in generative syntax, namely a scenario where all input to the learner underdetermines the target parameter setting. This scenario is exemplified by the case of zero-derived causatives in English, as discussed in Pylkkänen (2008). I then propose a model for parameter setting that uses a simple Bayesian learning procedure to learn from implicit negative evidence and arrive at the target parameter setting.

1 Introduction

An important question in language learnability is how to converge on a target grammar when all relevant grammars are compatible with the input. Indeed, this is a general challenge for various prominent models of parameter setting in generative syntax (e.g. Gibson and Wexler, 1994; Sakas and Fodor, 2001; and Yang, 2002). Consider a binary Parameter *P* concerning the complement of a head X^0: the complement could simply be YP (1a) or the more complex ZP containing YP (1b).

(1) a. $[_{XP}$ X [YP]]
b. $[_{XP}$ X $[_{ZP}$ Z $[_{YP}$ Y]]]

Further, suppose that the target setting for a learner is the simpler structure in (1a), but that all the input the learner receives is ambiguous as to the parametric choice in (1). In such a case, we can ask how the learner can be sure to arrive at the adult grammar of (1a). In this paper, I present a simple case study that illustrates the learning challenge in (1) with zero-derived causatives (ZDCs) in English under Pylkkänen's (2008) theory of causatives. I propose a Bayesian model for parameter setting that learns the target setting from implicit negative evidence: given repeated instances of ambiguous input, the structure in (1a) has a greater likelihood of being the correct analysis. This result is a consequence of the learning process itself, and there is thus no need to invoke some principle such as the Subset Principle (Berwick, 1986), or to resort to default values for parameter setting.

2 The Learning Challenge with Zero-derived Causatives

Pylkkänen observes that examples like (2a) are not ambiguous: only the causer John can be characterized by gumpiness, not the causee Bill. This contrasts with (2b), in which Bill's action can be characterized by grumpiness.

(2) a. John awoke Bill in a state of grumpiness.
✓John is grumpy (high reading)
✗Bill is grumpy (low reading)
b. Bill awoke in a state of grumpiness.

The question Pylkkänen asks is: if we follow Parsons (1990) in assuming that causatives involve a causing and caused eventuality, why do the PPs in (2a) unambiguously modify the causing event (and thus the state of the causer) and not the caused eventuality?[1] I call the possible adverbial interpretation in (2a) the high reading, and the impossible

[1] Thus I assume that such adverbials can modify eventualities but not nominal arguments such as the subject or object.

Copyright 2014 by Isaac Gould
28th Pacific Asia Conference on Language, Information and Computation pages 39–47

interpretation the low reading. Pylkkänen concludes that the lack of a low reading in (2a) is due to a structural property of the causatives. If we follow Pylkkänen, then with respect to learning we can ask how the learner learns this structural property such that there is no ambiguity in (2a).

Pylkkänen assumes there is a Cause-head in the syntax that introduces a causing event, which is phonologically null in ZDCs, and claims that there is parametric variation as to what the complement of the Cause-head is. This is the Cause-selection Parameter, which can account for cross-linguistic variation in causative structures.[2] For the sake of discussion, I will limit the range of complements to a binary choice, though the model could be expanded to accommodate the full range of parameter values Pylkkänen proposes. The choices the learner considers here are Root-selecting or Verb-selecting, schematic structures of which are in (3).

(3) a. *Root-selecting Cause*

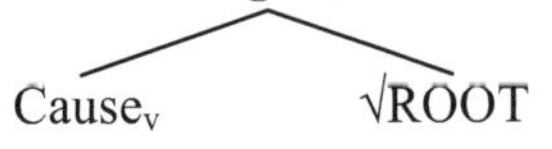

b. *Verb-selecting Cause*

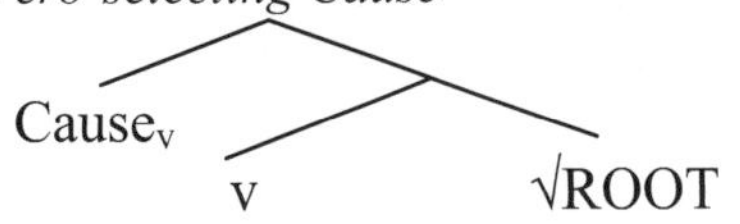

In both structures there is a category neutral lexical root that is embedded by the Cause-head. For ZDCs in English, this root could be √BREAK or √MELT and will be verbalized by a category-defining head. (See Borer, 2005 for discussion of category-neutral roots and category-defining morphology.) And in both structures, it is the head immediately above the root that verbalizes it. Before verbalization, though, the root combines with the internal argument and projects a √P. The difference in the Cause-selection Parameter in (3) can be thought of as a difference in which functional head verbalizes the √P. Is it simply a category-defining little v^0 with no apparent semantic contribution (which can also be phonologically null), or is it the Cause-head, which is a flavor of little v^0 itself? The difference might appear to be slight, but a Verb-selecting parameter setting crucially results in a more permissive grammar, allowing for more modification possibilities. Cross-linguistic variation with respect to modification possibilities is then the result of a language's choice in Cause-selection for a particular causative morpheme. Under both hypotheses, though, the external argument for English ZDCs would be in the specifier position of CauseP.

In light of the structures in (3), I return to the lack of ambiguity in (2a). According to Pylkkänen's argumentation, modifiers such as the PP in (2a) are verbal modifiers. That is, they can syntactically attach to verbal projections, but because they are not root modifiers, they cannot attach to the √P. With a Root-selecting causative, there is only one verbal attachment site, namely adjoining to CauseP in (3a). In contrast, a Verb-selecting causative provides two verbal attachment sites in (3b): adjunction to the vP of the verbalizing little v^0 and adjunction to the CauseP. The fact that Verb-selecting Cause provides more options for adjunction corresponds to a difference in interpretive possibilities for the two structures. When the Cause-head is merged in the derivation, the caused eventuality is existentially closed. Pylkkänen's argument is based on the following assumption about how event semantics are computed: when the lower caused eventuality is existentially closed, eventuality modifiers adjoined to CauseP can modify only the higher causing event introduced by the Cause-head. Thus lower modification of the caused eventuality by verbal modifiers is simply impossible in (3a), and this is an immediate consequence of the structure, given that there are no verbal projections below the Cause-head. In the structure for Verb-selecting Cause in (3b), though, modification of the lower caused eventuality is possible just in case the verbal modifier adjoins to the lower vP projection. The only way for the low reading in (2a) to be possible, then, involves adjunction to vP in (3b). But given that the low reading is not available in the causative in (2a), Pylkkänen concludes that there must be no vP projection in the structure of the ZDCs, a criterion that can be satisfied only with Root-selecting cause. Thus the simpler syntactic structure of Root-selecting cause in ZDCs derives the lack of ambiguity with verbal modifiers in (2a).

[2] Note that this parameter is relative to a particular morpheme in a language. Thus, if a language has multiple causative morphemes, each one's setting for this parameter could be different. I will discuss parameter setting only for ZDCs in English. Further, I will assume that setting this parameter for ZDCs is independent of setting any other syntactic parameters.

Turning to a learning perspective of Pylkkänen's argument, the adult grammar, which allows the high reading in (2a), can be taken to be the target state for the learner's grammar; this target state will be taken as evidence that the learner has the correct parameter setting. Pylkkänen's claim is that examples such as (2a) show that ZDCs in English are Root-selecting and thus instantiate the simpler structure in (3a). Assuming Pylkkänen is correct, the central empirical concern of this paper concerns learning a parameter setting of Root-selecting (3a) over that of Verb-selecting (3b) for these causatives in English.

The core data Pylkkänen presents for a Root-selecting setting in English ZDCs is of the sort in (2a), but the challenge for the learner is that this input underdetermines which analysis (Root or Verb-selecting) is the correct parameter setting. Consider again the example in (2a), repeated here:

(4) John awoke Bill in a state of grumpiness.

In order for a grammar to account for such an example, it must be able to generate a string-meaning pair that (among other things) (a) has a Cause-head that embeds a root and (b) has the modifier adjoin to CauseP, thereby modifying the causing event. A grammar with a parameter setting of either Root-selecting or Verb-selecting Cause is able to generate such output as is clear from the preceding discussion. Note that the same parametric ambiguity is true for the non-modified examples in (5).

(5) John awoke Bill.

To generate the example in (5), the grammar does not even need to consider which projection an adverb is adjoining to and which eventuality it is modifying – the two parameter settings are seemingly equally good at providing Cause-heads that embed lexical roots.

Recall that Pylkkänen's argument crucially involves considering the *impossibility* of the low reading (i.e. negative data),[3] a reading that a child will presumably never be exposed to in the primary linguistic data. Given that there is no clear positive evidence in favor of the Root-selecting hypothesis, we are left with the following acquisition challenge: how do children correctly choose between Root-selection and Verb-selection for the Cause-selection Parameter? Pylkkänen's argument relies on negative evidence, but how can children learn from this evidence? I note that the learner is now faced with an instantiation of the learning challenge sketched in (1).

Before proposing a learning model that addresses this challenge, and which crucially capitalizes on the fact that a learner never hears low adverbial modification, I frame the learning challenge in the context of the 'Subset Principle' (Berwick, 1986). If we consider the structural and interpretive properties of the two causative structures in (3), we see that those of Root-selecting Cause are a proper subset of those of Verb-selecting Cause. Thus (a) the core set of syntactic heads is {Cause_v, √} for Root-selecting and {Cause_v, v, √} for Verb-selecting; (b) the set of verbal adjunction positions is {CauseP} for Root-selecting and {CauseP, vP} for Verb-selecting; and (c) the set of interpretive possibilities for verbal modifiers is {high-reading} for Root-selecting and {high-reading, low-reading} for Verb-selecting. One way to state the Subset Principle would be the following: given two hypotheses X and Y such that X can be considered a proper subset of Y, do not consider Y unless forced to do so by the input. If we consider the simpler structure of Root-selecting Cause to be a subset of the more complex structure of Verb-selecting Cause, and given that both structures adequately account for the modified and non-modified data in (4) and (5), one could invoke the Subset Principle as follows. Children learning ZDCs in English only ever consider the simpler Root-selecting structure, and are never forced to consider the more complex Verb-selecting struc-

[3] Pylkkänen also claims that the absence of ZDCs that have unergative counterparts with the same root is also evidence for a Root-selecting setting. This claim is based on the assumption that such ZDCs are structurally impossible given a Root-selecting setting. This is a difficult claim to evaluate. First, it is not entirely clear in Pylkkänen's analysis why such ZDCs would be ruled out structurally. Second, the absence of such verbs is questionable. The interested reader is invited to apply the tests for unaccusativity/unergativity in Levin and Rappaport Hovav (1995) to verbs such as *graze* and *choke*. These verbs pattern as unergatives and not unaccusatives, but have ZDC forms. Nevertheless, to the extent that Pylkkänen's claim is correct, the absence of these ZDCs would constitute another form of implicit negative evidence that could be incorporated into the model. Having two kinds of implicit negative evidence (i.e. absence of low adverbial modification and of ZDCs with unergative counterparts) would presumably assist the model in the learning task.

ture (because, for example, they never hear such a causative with a low reading, which cannot be generated with the Root-selecting structure).

A similar point also holds for a default parameter setting. One could suppose that children have a default parameter setting of Root-selecting that is only switched to Verb-selecting given appropriate triggering input (such as adverbial modification of the caused eventuality).

A contribution of the learning procedure I propose is that the simpler or 'subset structure' can be learned without needing to invoke either a principle that achieves this result or a default parameter setting.

3 A Model for the Learning Challenge

The core insight of the Bayesian model proposed here is that the learner is sensitive to the *absence* of verbal modification. In the more complex Verb-selecting grammar there is a greater expectation or probability that such evidence will occur. Given that such evidence does not occur more frequently than expected under the Root-selecting grammar, the more complex grammar will leak probability, and the learning process will ultimately settle on the simpler structure, for which there is no such expectation.

I will take a learner's grammar to be a probabilistic generative model. This means the learner will take input from the primary linguistic data and try to output a string-meaning pair that matches that input as closely as possible. The way the output is generated is determined by a number of probabilistic choices. The Cause-selection Parameter can be represented as one of these choices. If these choices generate the target output, the probability distributions of these choices will be updated so as to maximize their being chosen again given similar input.

Let us consider how the model might generate input such as (5). We can base the model's learning on the rather commonplace example in (5), thereby generalizing the source of implicit negative evidence from the presumably infrequent example of the sort in (2a) that Pylkkänen discusses. I will represent the choice-points in the model as hierarchical phrase structure rules (PSRs) as in a PCFG (cf. Perfors et al., 2006). Assuming the only necessary difference between a Root and Verb-selecting grammar is the choice for the Cause-selection Parameter, this parameter can be placed on a higher tier than the other PSRs. These choice-points are all associated with priors. A schematic representation is given in (6), assuming a simplified syntax with a minimal number of PSRs. Crucially, there are PSRs for adverbial modification of CauseP and *v*P, which I assume are equally likely to be modified; these reflect the learner's expectation that any syntactic projection can be modified.

(6) a. Input: *John awoke Bill.*

b.

Root-selecting: $Prior_a$

▼

S → DP CauseP **Cause$_v$P → Cause √P** √P → √ DP	$p = 1$
Cause$_v$P → Cause$_v$P AdvP	$p = \gamma$
DP → …	…
AdvP → …	…

Verb-selecting: $(1 - Prior_a)$

▼

S → DP CauseP **Cause$_v$P → Cause vP** **vP → v √P** √P → √ DP	$p = 1$
Cause$_v$P → Cause$_v$P AdvP **vP → vP AdvP**	$p = \gamma$
DP → …	…
AdvP → …	…

A few comments on (6) are in order. The PSRs are admittedly a simplification of English syntax – I abstract away from additional functional projections such as CP and TP (i.e. S → DP CauseP), and do not fully expand some phrasal nodes (e.g. DP), or include terminal nodes (e.g. *Bill*) – but they allow the model to distill what is essential in the learning challenge. I thus abstract away from all PSRs between the two grammars other than choice of Cause-head and adverbial modification. By hypothesis, these other choices are identical across the two grammars, and abstracting away from them allows us to focus on learning the Cause-selection Parameter. In a sense then, these PSRs have been reverse-engineered to streamline the learning process here. Further, in the spirit of this simplicity, the corpus that the model learns from will contain only utterances of the form in (6a). I confine myself to such a pared-down model so as to focus on the learning challenge introduced in (1), though a scaled-up model with an enriched corpus and set of PSRs should not crucially change any fundamental issues under discussion.

We can now consider the priors for the probabilistic differences between the two grammars, namely the choice of Cause-head and adverbial modification. I assume that the priors for Root- and Verb-selecting grammars are sampled from a dirichlet distribution with initial pseudo-counts of (1, 1). For the likelihood that any verbal projection is adverbially modified, γ, we could approximate it via a frequency rate of sampled verbal projections from a corpus. So long as $0 < \gamma < 1$, the actual value of γ is immaterial; it suffices to illustrate the workings of the model to simply plug in various probabilities for this value.

Before discussing the update procedure for posterior probabilities, we can now see how the more permissive Verb-selecting grammar will leak probability given the input. The probability of generating non-modified output given the Root-selecting grammar (G_{Root}) is the joint probability of choosing the Root-selecting grammar and choosing no adverbial modification at the CauseP phrase marker, as shown in (7a).

(7) a. $p(G_{Root}) =$

$$p(\neg CausePAdvP|CauseP) * p([Cause \sqrt{P}]|CauseP) =$$

$$(1-\gamma) * (Prior_a)$$

b. $p(G_{Verb}) =$

$$p(\neg CauseP\ AdvP\ |CauseP) * p([Cause\ vP]|CauseP) * p(\neg vP\ AdvP|vP) =$$

$$(1-\gamma) * (1 - Prior_a) * (1-\gamma) =$$

$$(1-\gamma)^2 * (1 - Prior_a)$$

In contrast, the probability of generating non-modified output under the Verb-selecting grammar (G_{Verb}) is the joint probability of choosing the Verb-selecting grammar and choosing no adverbial modification at both the CauseP and vP levels (7b). Given initial pseudo-counts of (1, 1), with repeated sampling the average probability of choosing either Cause-head will be approximately equivalent; thus the probability of not having a *v*P modifier causes the Verb-selecting grammar to leak probability, resulting in the probability of the data being greater under the Root-selecting grammar. This push toward Root-selecting is amplified under the update procedure with multiple tokens of input.[4]

As an update procedure, I assume that the totals for the number of times each Cause-head is sampled while successfully generating target output are used as new pseudo-count values in the dirichlet distribution. Suppose the model runs until successfully generating target output 500 times. Next, suppose that of those 500 times, Root-selecting cause was sampled 300 times, and Verb-selecting cause 200. The new pseudo-counts will then be (300, 200). These new pseudo-counts represent revised expectations about the likelihood of each grammar generating the target output.

Finally, consider how the model learns upon receiving additional input. In the case of a second input sentence, the model will now use the updated pseudo-counts from generating output conditioned by the first input token. The model will next generate 500 times the entire corpus it has been exposed to. This means that each time that the model now chooses a grammar (based on repeated sampling of the updated dirichlet distribution), it will try to use that grammar and all subsequent choices dependent on that grammar to generate both the original first token of input and the second token as output.

Thus when the model encounters $n > 1$ tokens of input, the model will (a) take the sums of successes per grammar with $(n - 1)$ tokens of input and use these sums to update the pseudo-counts of the dirichlet distribution; then (b) generate the entire corpus of *n* tokens of input 500 times using posterior probabilities from the updated dirichlet distribution. This process repeats until only a single parameter setting is used to generate the entire corpus, at which point the model can be said to have learned that parameter setting. In this way, the model benefits from rapid and efficient learning from a small amount of input data. This rapid learning has been illustrated in numerous cognitive

[4] Note that although (7) has the effect of making the subset grammar more likely to generate target output, it is not another version of the Subset Principle. Rather (7) reflects the more general mechanisms of how a PCFG can generate output.

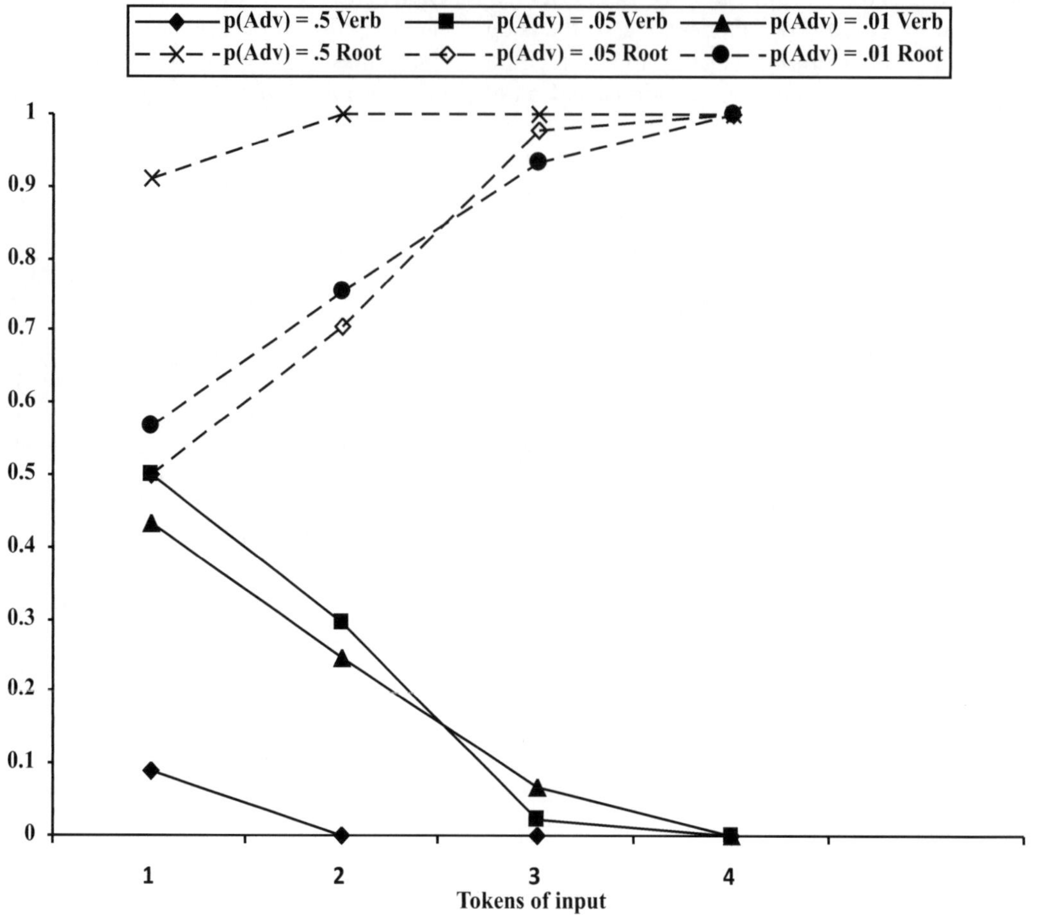

Figure 1. Average success-rate per grammar for target output

experiments outside the domain of language and has been modeled in a Bayesian framework (Kemp et al., 2007).

Indeed, sample results from running the model indicate its success at learning the target Root-selecting setting given a small input corpus. Simulations of the model were run with a simple program written in the Church language (Goodman et al., 2008). The results reported here are the average probability for each grammar being chosen given the output matching the attested input after running the model 10 times. The results are given in Figure 1 in a time-course graph showing averages for different amounts of input data, which reflect the effect of updating the priors. As the probability of a verbal projection being modified has been left as a variable, Figure 1 shows various representative values. Each graph-line shows the average success-rate of a certain grammar given a particular probability for adverbial modification of a verbal projection under that grammar. For example, *p(Adv) = .5 Verb* corresponds to a line representing the average percentage of the time the Verb-selecting setting was chosen from among the target output, given that the probability of verbal modification was .5.

What Figure 1 shows is that after only a few tokens of input, the Root-selecting grammar is overwhelmingly the more likely option. If the probability of verbal modification is .5, then the success-rate of the Root-selecting grammar is 1 after 3 tokens of input, while that of the Verb-selecting grammar is 0. This is surely an unrealistic probability to have for verbal modification, but even if we decrease it to .05 or .01 the model still settles on the Root-selecting grammar. With a smaller probability for verbal modification, it now takes the model 4 tokens of input before the success-rate of the Verb-selecting grammar reaches or approaches 0. In fact, the best that the Verb-selecting grammar does is an average success-rate of .0008 (.9992 success-rate for Root-selecting) when the probability of verbal modification is .01.

These results clearly show that the model is learning the Root-selecting grammar as the correct parameter to generate target output. Further, the model is able to learn on the basis of as few as 4 tokens of input. Going beyond the baseline model presented here, to the extent that the priors are on the right track and that the probability of verbal modification is reflective of expanded corpus results, the prediction is that expanded versions of the model will also be successful.

4 Comparison with Other Models

In this section I briefly compare the Bayesian model proposed here with three prominent models that attempt to learn correct syntactic parameter settings: Yang (2002), Gibson and Wexler (1994), and Sakas and Fodor (2001). None of these three models can guarantee convergence on the target Root-selecting setting for ZDCs. For the sake of comparison, keeping to a corpus like (6a), let us assume that in all models we have a binary parameter such as Root- or Verb-selecting cause, and that the choice of this parameter has no effect on any other parameter setting.

The core of Yang's (2002) probabilistic learning model involves increasing or decreasing a parameter's probability based on whether adopting that parameter leads to a grammar that is compatible with the input data. Thus whenever the model encounters any data containing ZDCs, it will sample a Cause-head parameter setting based on the probability distribution and test out this setting to see whether it is compatible with the input. Yang explicitly discusses how his model is not reliant on what have been called unambiguous triggers in Fodor (1998). An unambiguous trigger would be a token of input data that is compatible with only a single (relevant) parameter setting, thereby excluding all other relevant parameter settings. In the discussion on causatives above, an unambiguous trigger would be input that showed the availability of the low adverbial reading: this input is compatible only with the Verb-selecting hypothesis and not with the Root-selecting hypothesis. However, implicit in Yang's discussion is that for each non-target parameter setting there must be some input that is not compatible with it. As long as such input exists, it will result in the non-target parameters being punished, and so long as these non-target parameters are punished sufficiently, in the long run the target parameter setting will eventually prevail.

The scenario of ZDCs in English, then, is problematic for Yang's model. All the relevant parameter settings are compatible with the input, and there is thus no input data that can rule out any of the parameter settings. As Root and Verb-selecting parameter settings will have similar reward-punishment rates in this situation, all things being equal (e.g. non-biased priors), the model could converge on either setting or get stuck in a state of stasis, with neither setting's probability exhibiting asymptotic behavior (cf. discussion in Pearl, 2009). Compared to the model proposed in this paper, Yang's model is unable to learn from implicit negative evidence: unlike the Bayesian model, Yang's model does not go beyond grammar compatibility to consider the probability of the data given a particular grammar.

Similarly, in the error-driven model of Gibson and Wexler (1994), there is no guarantee that the learner will converge on the target parameter setting for ZDCs. In this model, parameter settings have weights of 1 or 0, and a parameter's value is changed only if the current vector of parameters is incompatible with the most recent token of input. In such a case, only one parameter can be changed (the Single Value Constraint). Which parameter is chosen to have its value changed is left as an open question, but there is a constraint such that whatever the new parameter vector is, the grammar represented by that new vector must now be compatible with the most recent input (the Greediness Constraint).

Consider, then, how the Gibson and Wexler model fares if the initial state, which is some random grammar or parameter vector, has a non-target parameter setting for English ZDCs. No input containing a ZDC could force the Cause-selection Parameter to change its value because both settings are compatible with that data. Further, even if this input forced the model to change its current grammar (because of non-target setting of some other parameter), the model would not change the setting of the Cause-selection Parameter because no new value for this parameter would help in the face of the latest input (the Greediness Constraint). The model would have to change the value of some other parameter and leave the Cause-selection Parameter alone (the Single Value Constraint). Thus the model will be in a local maximum: no input could push the model toward a target setting for ZDCs, and the model would remain stuck in a non-target setting. Of course, if the initial state was a Root-selecting grammar, then no input in English would push the learner from that setting, and the learner would have the target parameter setting.

Finally, the model in Sakas and Fodor (2001) crucially relies on input that contains the unambiguous triggers discussed above. In their model, as the parser builds a parse tree of the input, the parser is able to recognize at any point in the structure whether a parametric choice is underdetermined given the input data. For the case of the ZDCs discussed in this paper, the parser, upon facing the Cause-head in the parse tree, presumably would be able to determine that either a vP or √P complement is compatible with the input data. In the terms of Sakas and Fodor, the parser is faced with an ambiguity with respect to parameter selection. What the parser then does is report this ambiguity to the learning mechanism. The learning mechanism will then not use this 'ambiguous input' to learn a parameter setting. In other words, the learning mechanism will wait until an unambiguous trigger occurs in the input before setting any parameter value. Now as we have discussed, all the relevant data for zero-derived causatives in English underdetermine the correct structural analysis – it is all ambiguous input, and there is no unambiguous input. As it stands then, Sakas and Fodor's model is unable to learn the correct parameter setting when faced with the challenge of ZDCs.

Before closing this section, I note that an amendment to both Gibson and Wexler's and Sakas and Fodor's models would be able to account for the Cause-selection Parameter: a default parameter setting. The learning mechanism would only need to consider other parameter settings if pushed toward them by the input. If Root-selecting Cause was the default value, then the English zero-derived causatives would be accounted for. Only if the input data presented some evidence that is incompatible with a Root-selecting parameter setting (e.g. an utterance with the low adverbial reading) would the learning mechanism change from the default to a Verb-selecting setting. As mentioned in the introduction, though, an advantage of the model here is that no default needs to be specified.

5 Concluding remarks.

I have introduced a Bayesian model that is up to the learning challenge that Pylkkänen's theory of parameters presents us with for the case of English ZDCs in English. Given input that underdetermines that correct structural analysis, the model is able to learn from implicit negative evidence with respect to the likelihood of verbal modification and select the correct, simpler, and more restrictive parameter setting. No default value for the parameter setting was necessary, nor any principle such as the Subset Principle. The model is a simple illustration of the how the learning procedure itself in a Bayesian framework results in the correct parameter setting. Further, other prominent models of parameter setting are not capable of learning the correct parameter setting given the underdetermining nature of the data. To be sure, the model is only the simplest illustration of how this learning procedure works, and a clear direction of future research can focus on expanding its empirical scope. Now that the model has success at the most basic level we can consider scaling it up. One way to expand is to enlarge the corpus that is used as input data so that it better approximates input that a child encounters.[5] Another consideration concerns learning a Verb-selecting grammar in languages where the low reading is possible. In the absence of input with adverbials in the corpus, the model here predicts that only the Root-selecting grammar will be learned. This suggests there must another property in the input to allow for learning a Verb-selecting grammar in languages that have it; this could be a morphologically overt v^0 between CauseP and √P. Indeed, all the Verb-selecting languages discussed in Pylkkänen have such overt morphology. Such intervening morphology is impossible in Root-selecting languages, and true to their name, ZDCs in English display no such head.

[5] This could include input tokens with verbal modification, a very high proportion of which could push the learner toward the more complex Verb-selecting grammar. This is because the probability of modifying CauseP *or* *v*P given Verb-selecting is greater than that of just modifying CauseP given Root-selecting. Given a high enough proportion of the input containing verbal modifiers, this could swing the balance of data in favor of a Verb-selecting setting. It is doubtful, though, whether learner input actually contains such a high proportion.

The non-deterministic nature of the model also means there is a developmental implication for language acquisition in children: at earlier stages in the learning procedure, non-target parameter settings with likelihoods that are not too low are viable choices. Before parameter setting is finalized, then, we might expect non-target behavior from children with respect to, say, the Verb-selecting parameter setting (see Yang 2002 for discussion of this point). Is there evidence that children sometimes treat zero-derived causatives in English as being Verb-selecting before having learned that they are in fact Root-selecting? The model would lead us to expect that in initial stages of learning, the likelihood of a Verb-selecting analysis is high enough that children would incorrectly treat them as being Verb-selecting at least some of the time. Careful experimental work would be needed to test these predictions, but to the extent that they are borne out, in addition to showing how target parameter settings can be learned, an advantage of the non-deterministic framework here is its potential to model non-target behavior.

Finally, a contribution of this paper is to add to the emerging body of literature incorporating Bayesian modeling into generative linguistics. As illustrated in Pearl and Goldwater (in press), though, much of this has not looked at setting syntactic parameters. A notable exception is the line of research initiated by Regier and Gahl (2004), which attempts to learn the syntactic structure and semantics of anaphoric *one* in English. The learning issues related to anaphoric *one* differ from those of ZDCs here in at least two important ways. As Payne et al. (2013) note, (a) not all input the learner receives concerning anaphoric *one* is ambiguous, and (b) the properties that the model attempts to learn reflect only preferences in the adult grammar. The case of ZDCs, then, presents a learning model with an ideal test of the learning challenge presented in (1): categorical parameter setting in the face of entirely ambiguous evidence.

Acknowledgments

I thank the following people for their help: Adam Albright, Michael Yoshitaka Erlewine, Michelle Fullwood, Martin Hackl, Sabine Iatridou, and Tim O'Donnell. This work has been supported in part by the National Science Foundation Graduate Research Fellowship under Grant No. 1122374.

References

Berwick, Robert C. 1986. Learning from positive-only examples: The subset principle and three case studies. In R. S. Michalski, J. C. Carbonell, and T. M. Mitchell (eds.), *Machine learning: An artificial intelligence approach, Vol 2*. Los Altos: Morgan Kaufmann.

Borer, Hagit. 2005. *Structuring Sense, Vols. 1-2*. Oxford: Oxford university Press.

Fodor, Janet Dean.1998. Unambiguous Triggers *Linguistic Inquiry* 29 (1): 1-36.

Gibson, Edward and Ken Wexler. 1994. Triggers. *Linguistic Inquiry* 25 (3): 407-454.

Goodman, Noah, Vikash Mansinghka, Daiel Roy, Keith Bonawitz, and Joshua Tenenbaum. 2008. Church: A language for generative models. In *Proceedings of the 24th Conference on Uncertainty in Artificial Intelligence (UAI)*.

Kemp, Charles, Amy Perfors, and Joshua Tenenbaum. 2007. Learning overhypotheses with hierarchical Bayesian models. *Developmental Science* 10 (3): 307-321.

Levin, Beth and Malka Rappaport Hovav. 1995. *Unaccusativity*. Cambridge: MIT Press.

Parsons, Terence. 1990. *Events in the semantics of English: A study in subatomic semantics*. Cambridge: MIT Press.

Payne, John, Geoffrey Pullum, Barabara Scholz, and Eva Berlage. 2013. Anaphoric *one* and its implications. Language 89 (4): 794-829.

Pearl, Lisa. 2009. *Necessary bias in natural language learning*. PhD dissertation, The University of Maryland.

Pearl, Lisa and Sharon Goldwater. In press. Statistical learning, inductive bias, an Bayesian inference in language acquisition. In J. Lidz, W. Snyder, and C. Pater (eds.), *The Oxford Handbook of Developmental Linguistics*.

Perfors, Amy, Joshua Tenenbaum, and Terry Regier. 2006. In *Proceedings of the 28th Annual Conference of the Cognitive Science Society*.

Pylkkänen, Liina. 2008. *Introducing Arguments*. Cambridge: MIT Press.

Regier, Terry and Susanne Gahl. 2004. Learning the unlearnable: The role of missing evidence. *Cognition* 93: 147-155.

Sakas, William G. and Janet Dean Fodor. 2001. The Structural Triggers Learner. In Stefano Bartolo (ed.), *Language acquisition and learnability*, 172-233. Cambridge: Cambridge University Press.

Yang, Charles. 2002. *Knowledge and learning in natural language*. Oxford: Oxford University Press.

Pseudo-Passives as Adjectival Passives

Kwang-sup Kim
Hankuk University of Foreign Studies
English Department
81 Oedae-lo Cheoin-Gu Yongin-City
449-791 Republic of Korea
kwangsup@hufs.ac.kr

Abstract

The pseudo-passive is peculiar in that (i) the DP that appears to be the complement of a preposition undergoes passivization, and (ii) it is semantically characterized by the fact that it describes a resultant state or a characteristic of the Theme. The first peculiarity can be explained if the DP is not the complement of P but the complement of the V-P complex. However, the problem with this approach is that V and P cannot form a constituent in the corresponding active. In this paper, however, I propose that we can maintain the V-P complex approach if it is an adjectival passive. The adjectival passive describes a characteristic of the Theme, and it does not necessarily correspond to its active counterpart with regard to the internal argument structure. This suggests that the peculiarities of the pseudo-passive follow if it is an adjectival passive. This paper claims that it is indeed the case. In short, I claim that the passive morpheme in the pseudo-passive is the adjectival passive *–en*, which is empirically supported by the fact that they display the properties of adjectival passives.

1 Introduction

It is well-known that once an argument is assigned Case, it cannot undergo further A-movement. However, pseudo-passives are quite peculiar in that the DP that appears to be the complement of a preposition moves to a Case position.

(1) a. The hat was sat upon.
 b. These carpets have never been walked on.

A plausible approach to this peculiarity is to argue that in (1a) *sit upon* is a constituent, and *the hat* is the complement of *sit upon*, not *upon* (Radford 1988, Drummond & Kush 2011).

(2) the hat was [[sat upon] ~~the hat~~]]

If this approach is correct, it is predicted that *sit upon* must be a constituent in the active as well as in the passive. However, there are insurmountable pieces of evidence that it cannot be a constituent in the active (Postal 1986, Koster 1987, and Baltin and Postal 1996). For instance, the objects can be conjoined, as illustrated in (3a-b), but in the active counterpart of (1a) *the hat* cannot be conjoined, as shown in (4a-b).

(3) a. John bought a chair.
 b. John bought not a chair but a hat.

(4) a. John sat upon the chair
 b. *John sat upon not the chair but the hat.[1]

This suggests that *the hat* is not the complement of *sat upon* in (4a).

Copyright 2014 by Kwang-sup Kim
28th Pacific Asia Conference on Language, Information and Computation pages 48–56

(5) a. *John [[sat upon] not a chair but a hat].
b. John sat [$_{PP}$ upon a hat].

If we assume that (1a) is analyzed as (2), we can explain why *the hat* can undergo passivization, but *sat upon* cannot be a constituent in (4a). This puts us in a dilemma, since it is usually known that there is parallelism between the verbal passive and its active counterpart. This paper explores the possibility of resolving this dilemma by proposing that the pseudo-passive is an adjectival passive.

2 Problems with the Reanalysis Approach

There are many idiomatic expressions that contain a preposition and permit passivization. The idiom *take advantage of* is a case in point. If we assume that the idiom is simply a word, we can explain why passivization is permitted although the object appears to be the complement of the preposition *of*. This section examines whether we can extend this approach to the pseudo-passive, and then points out some potential problems.

2.1 Two Possible Ways of Generating Idioms

Sentence (6) has two corresponding passive constructions, as shown in (7a-b).

(6) John took advantage of Mary's honesty.
(7) a. Mary's honesty was taken advantage of.
b. Advantage was taken of Mary's honesty.

This puzzle can be resolved if we assume that there are two ways of deriving the idiom *take advantage of*. Let us first assume that *take advantage of* is a word, not a phrase.

(8) [$_{V}$ [$_{V}$ [$_{V}$ take] advantage] of][2]

If so, it is quite straightforward why *Mary's honesty* can be preposed in (7a). If *take advantage of* is a constituent, the preposition *of* cannot assign Case to *Mary's honesty*, and furthermore, nor can the passive morpheme *–en* assign Case to it. That is, in (9a) *Mary's honesty* occurs in a Caseless position, and it needs to move to a position where it can be assigned Case. As shown in (9b-c), the SPEC-T position is available, and so it moves to the SPEC-T.

(9) a. [en [$_{VP}$ [$_{V}$ take advantage of] Mary's honesty]]: Merger with *be* and T
b. [T [be [en [$_{VP}$ [$_{V}$ take advantage of] Mary's honesty]]]]: Raising to the SPEC-T
c. [Mary's honesty T [be [en [$_{VP}$ [$_{V}$ take advantage of] ~~Mary's honesty~~]]]]

Let us now assume that *take advantage* is a constituent, and the preposition *of* is not part of the idiom. In this case *advantage* is in a non-Case position when the VP is merged with the passive morpheme *–en*. On the other hand, *Mary's honesty* is in a Case position since it is the complement of the preposition *of*. Hence *advantage* moves to the SPEC-T position.

(10) a. [$_{VP}$ en [$_{VP}$ [$_{VP}$ take advantage] of Mary's honesty]]: Merger with *be* and T
b. [T [be [$_{VP}$ en [$_{VP}$ [$_{VP}$ take advantage] of Mary's honesty]]]]: Raising to the SPEC-T
c. [Advantage T [be [$_{VP}$ en [$_{VP}$ [$_{VP}$ take ~~advantage~~] of Mary's honesty]]]]

We have seen that the idiom *take advantage of* permits either the direct object or the prepositional object to passivize, depending on whether or not the preposition *of* is part of the idiom. There are two other types of idioms. For instance, *cast doubt on* allows only the object DP to passivize, and *lose sight of* allows only the prepositional object to passivize.

(11) a. Doubt was cast on his motives.
b. *His motives were cast doubt on.
(12) a. *Sight was lost of our goal.
b. Our goal was lost sight of.

This suggests that *cast doubt on* is a phrasal idiom, whereas *lose sight of* is a lexical idiom. In other words, *cast doubt* is a constituent, but *cast doubt on* is not, and *lose sight of* is a constituent, but *lose sight* is not.

(13) a. [$_{VP}$ cast doubt] on his motives
a'. *[$_{V}$ cast doubt on] his motives
b. [$_{V}$ lose sight of] our goal
b'. *[$_{VP}$ lose sight] of our goal

To recapitulate, the prepositional passive is permitted when the preposition is a part of a word-level idiom.

2.2 Extension to the Pseudo-Passive

With the above discussion in mind, let us attempt to account for the passives in (14a-b) while assuming that *sleep in* and *walk on* are constituents .[3]

(14) a. This bed was slept in by Napoleon.
 b. These carpets have never been walked on.

The most serious problem with this approach is that *sleep in* and *walk on* do not form constituents in actives (Postal 1986, Koster1987, and Baltin and Postal 1996). We have seen from (1-5) that *sit upon* is not a constituent in the active, but it is a constituent in the passive. There are many other examples in support of the claim that in the pseudo-passive V and P form a constituent, but in the corresponding active they do not. For instance, an adverb can intervene between V and P in the active, whereas it cannot in the pseudo-passive.

(15) a. The lawyer will go thoroughly over the contract.
 b. *The contract will be gone thoroughly over by the lawyer.
 b'. The contract will be thoroughly gone over by the lawyer.

(16) a. They spoke angrily to John.
 b. *John was spoken angrily to.
 c. John was spoken to.
 (Chomsky 1981: 123)

There are many other data that show the same point. Gapping requires a verb to be elided, as shown in (17a-b).

(17) a. Frank called Sandra and Arthur _______ Louise.
 b. Sandra was called by Frank and Louise by Arthur.

Interestingly, *talk to* cannot be a gap in the active, but it must be a gap in the pseudo-passive.

(18) a. Frank talked to Sandra and Arthur _______ *(to) Louise.
 b. Sandra was talked to by Frank and Louise (*to) Arthur.

While discussing passivization of idioms, we have assumed that if an idiom is phrasal in the active, it is also phrasal in the passive, and if it is lexical in the active, it is also lexical in the passive. In the case of pseudo-passives, however, there is no parallelism between the active and the pseudo-passive with regard to constituency. This is quite puzzling under the proposal that V and P form a constituent in the pseudo-passive. The next section is devoted to resolving this puzzle.[4]

3 Pseudo-Passive as Adjectival Passive

It is well-known that there are two-types of passives: the verbal passive and the adjectival passive. I propose that the peculiarities of the pseudo-passive can be explained if the pseudo-passive is an adjectival passive.

3.1 Contrast in Argument Structure between Verbal Passive and Adjectival Passive

There are two types of passive *en*: the verbal passive *en* and the adjectival passive *en*.[5]

(19) a. Mary was given the book.
 b. The rules are ungiven.

What is peculiar about the adjectival passive *ungiven* is that the verb *give* can have two theta-roles—Theme and Goal, but the adjective *ungiven* can assign just one theta-role.

(20) *Mary was ungiven the rules.

This follows if we assume that the adjectival passive morpheme *en* assigns a Character role, which means 'has the property x', where x is the property expressed by the adjective. Theta-roles percolate when they cannot be assigned.[6] For instance, the theta-role of *happy* can percolate when *happy* is merged with *un*.

(21) a. [$\text{happy}_{\text{(Theme)}}$]: merger with *un*
 b. [un [$\text{happy}_{\text{(Theme)}}$]]: Theta-Role Percolation

c. [un [happy$_{\cancel{\text{(Theme)}}}$]]$_{\text{(Theme)}}$

However, they cannot percolate across another theta-role due to the intervention effect. For instance, in (22c) the Theme role is not allowed to cross the Character role.[7] Instead, it is identified as the Character role: it undergoes theta-identification with Character in the sense of Higginbotham (1985). This is how a new predicate is formed in the syntax.

(22) a. [$_{\text{V}}$ give$_{\text{(Theme)}}$]: Theta-Role Percolation
b. [$_{\text{V}}$ give$_{\cancel{\text{(Theme)}}}$] $_{\text{(Theme)}}$: Merger with *en*$_{\textit{(Character)}}$
c. [$_{\text{A}}$ [$_{\text{V}}$ give$_{\text{(Theme)}}$] en$_{\text{(Character)}}$]: Theta-Identification
d. [$_{\text{A}}$ [$_{\text{V}}$ give$_{\cancel{\text{(Theme)}}}$] en$_{\cancel{\text{(Character)}}}$] $_{\text{(Character = Theme)}}$: Merger with *un* & Theta-Role Percolation
e. [un [$_{\text{A}}$ [$_{\text{V}}$ give$_{\cancel{\text{(Theme)}}}$] en$_{\cancel{\text{(Character)}}}$]$_{\cancel{\text{(Character = Theme)}}}$]$_{\text{(Character = Theme)}}$

Notice that just one theta-role can be identified as Character. Therefore, the newly-formed adjective *given* can assign just one theta role.[8,9] The main point is that the adjectival *-en* can be involved in forming a new predicate via theta-identification, and in this case only one theta-role can be realized.[10]

Before turning into the verbal passive, let us consider the nature of theta-role assignment and theta-role percolation. I propose that theta-role assignment must obey the Earliness Condition in (23).

(23) Earliness Condition: A theta-role must not be assigned late.

Let us assume that the Theme role of X percolates and is assigned to Z in (24).

(24) a. [... X$_{\text{(Theme)}}$]: Theta-Percolation
b. [... X$_{\text{(Theme)}}$]$_{\text{(Theme)}}$: Merger with Z and Theta-Role Assignment
c. [[... X$_{\text{(Theme)}}$]$_{\cancel{\text{(Theme)}}}$ Z$_{\text{(Theme)}}$]

Then, this is a violation of the Earliness Principle. It appears that given (23), there is no room for theta-role percolation. However, it is not the case. It is noteworthy that what is wrong with the derivation in (24) is not the theta-percolation in (24a-b) but with the late theta-role assignment (24b-c). If X were merged with Z, the Theme role could be assigned earlier. Hence the theta-role assignment in (24c) is in violation of the Earliness Condition. This means that once a theta-role percolates, it must not be assigned: it must be theta-identified with another theta-role; if the percolated theta-role is not assigned to an argument but identified with another theta-role, the Earliness Condition is not violated.

With the Earliness Condition in mind, let us consider the verbal passive. The verbal passive participle *given* can assign two theta-roles.

(25) Mary was given these books.

The verbal passive morpheme *-en* assigns a theta-role, but it is a theta-role for an adjunct. So it cannot be involved in theta-identification. As illustrated in (26a), let us assume that the verb *give* is merged with the verbal passive morpheme, not with DPs. Then, the theta-roles must be percolated.

(26) a. [en [$_{\text{V}}$ give$_{\text{(Goal, Theme)}}$]]: Theta-Role Percolation,
b. [en [$_{\text{V}}$ give$_{\cancel{\text{(Goal, Theme)}}}$]] $_{\text{(Goal, Theme)}}$

In accordance with the Earliness Principle in (23), the percolated theta-roles in (26b) must undergo theta-identification. However, there is no theta-role that can identify the percolated theta-roles. As a result, there is no way for the theta-roles of *give* to be discharged: that is, (26b) cannot produce a well-formed sentence. If, on the other hand, the verbal passive morpheme is merged with a VP with its theta-roles discharged, a well-formed phrase can be generated.

(27) [en [$_{\text{VP}}$ Mary give$_{\text{(Goal, Theme)}}$ these books]]

In (27) the two arguments of *give* can be syntactically realized. Now it is not surprising that the verbal passive is analogous to the active in terms of internal argument structure.

The gist of the claim is that there is parallelism in internal argument structure between the active and the verbal passive, while there is no parallelism between the active and the adjectival passive. In what follows I argue that the asymmetry between the pseudo-passive and its active counterpart arises from the fact that the pseudo-passive is an adjectival passive.

3.2 Derivation of the Pseudo-Passive

The pseudo-passive obeys some semantic constraints that the verbal passive does not. It is subject to the affectedness condition: it describes a 'resultant' state of the subject.

(28) a. The hat was sat upon.
b. *The tree was sat under.
c. John sat upon the hat.

(29) a. This bed has been slept in.
b. ??This bed has been slept beside.
c. John slept in the bed.

(30) a. The street [covered with snow] has not been walked on.
b. *The street has not been walked on.
c. We have not walked on the street.

As will be discussed in 3.3, the affected Theme is closely related with characterization. Let us first consider the contrast between (28a) and (28b). If Theme was affected by an event, it can be characterized by the event. In (28a), for instance, the sitting event can affect the shape of the hat, and consequently it can be a characteristic of the hat. On the other hand, in (28b) the sitting event cannot affect the tree, and so cannot be a property of the tree. The same point is shown by (29a-b). If someone sleeps in a bed, the event assigns a new property to the bed in the sense that it is now a used one. By contrast, when someone sleeps beside a bed, the bed is not affected and so it is not assigned a new property. This point is corroborated by (30a-b). Walking event usually does not affect a street in general, and so cannot assign a new property to the street. However, the street covered with snow will be affected if someone walks on it, and hence it is assigned a new property as a result of walking. On these grounds we can generalize that the pseudo-passive denotes a characteristic of the Theme. These considerations lead us to the conclusion that the morpheme *en* in the pseudo-passive assigns a Character role: that is, it is an adjectival passive morpheme.

With this in mind, let us attempt to derive (28a). If *sit* is merged with *upon*, the Theme role of *upon* cannot be assigned in situ, and so it undergoes percolation. If *sit upon* is merged with the Character role-assigning *en*, theta-identification takes place: the Theme role is identified as the Character role. As a result, the complex predicate $[en_{(char)}\ [_V\ sit\ upon_{(theme)}]]_{(char\,=\,theme)}$ is generated.

(31) a. $[_V$ sit upon$_{(theme)}]$: Theta-Role Percolation
b. $[_V$ sit upon~~$_{(theme)}$~~$]_{(theme)}$: Merger with en_{char}
c. $[en_{(char)}$ $[_V$ sit upon~~$_{(theme)}$~~$]_{(theme)}]$: Theta-Role Identification
d. $[en$~~$_{(char)}$~~ $[_V$ sit upon~~$_{(theme)}$~~$]$~~$_{(theme)}$~~$]_{(char\,=\,theme)}$: Merger with *this hat* and Theta-Role Assignment
e. $[[en$~~$_{(char)}$~~ $[_V$ sit upon~~$_{(theme)}$~~$]$~~$_{(theme)}$~~$]$~~$_{(char\,=\,theme)}$~~ this hat$_{(char\,=\,theme)}]$: Merger with *be* and T
f. [T [be $[[en$~~$_{(char)}$~~ $[_V$ sit upon~~$_{(theme)}$~~$]$ ~~$_{(theme)}$~~$]$~~$_{(char\,=\,theme)}$~~ this hat$_{(char\,=\,theme)}]]]$: Raising
g. [this hat$_{(char\,=\,theme)}$T [be $[[en$~~$_{(char)}$~~ $[_V$ sit upon~~$_{(theme)}$~~$]$~~$_{(theme)}$~~$]$~~$_{(char\,=\,theme)}$~~ ~~this hat~~~~$_{(char\,=\,theme)}$~~$]]]$

In this analysis *this hat* cannot be assigned Case from *upon*, since it is an argument of $[en_{(char)}\ [_V\ sit\ upon_{(theme)}]]_{(char,\ theme)}$, not an argument of *upon*. Therefore, it can undergo passivization.

The immediate question begged for in this analysis is why the verb *sit* must be merged with PP, not with P in the active. Let us suppose that it can be merged with the preposition *upon*. If so, the Theme role of *upon* percolates, and it must be identified as Agent when *sit upon* is merged with the Agent-assigning v.

(32) a. $[_V$ sit upon$_{(theme)}]$: Theta-Role Percolation
b. $[_V$ sit upon~~$_{(theme)}$~~$]_{(theme)}$: Merger with v
c. $[v_{(Agent)}$ $[_V$ sit upon~~$_{(theme)}$~~$]_{(theme)}]$

However, the Theme and the Agent cannot refer to the same object: one cannot sit upon oneself. Therefore, *sit* must be merged with a PP like *upon the hat*. Generally speaking, the non-reflexive light verb does not permit theta-identification, since it requires its own theta-role to be different from the percolated theta-role. Almost every transitive light verb is a non-reflexive light verb.[11] In short, the Character role can be theta-identified with the Theme role, whereas the Agent role cannot, which resolves the long-standing puzzle: why can V-P be a constituent in the pseudo-passive, although it cannot be a constituent in its active counterpart?

Another issue we need to address is what happens when the verbal passive morpheme *-en* is merged with *sit upon*.

(33) a. [$_V$ sit upon$_{\text{(theme)}}$]: Theta-Role Percolation
b. [$_V$ sit upon~~$_{\text{(theme)}}$~~]$_{\text{(theme)}}$: Merger with the verbal passive *en*
c. [en [$_V$ sit upon~~$_{\text{(theme)}}$~~]$_{\text{(theme)}}$]

It is quite straightforward why (33c) is ill-formed. Let us recall that the verbal passive *-en* assigns a defective theta-role—an adjunct theta role, which cannot permit theta-identification. Accordingly, there is no way for the theta-role of *upon* to be realized. The percolated Theme role in (33c) must not be assigned to an argument in accordance with the Earliness Condition. However, it cannot be theta-identified with another theta-role. Therefore, (33c) is ill-formed. To conclude, only the adjectival passive morpheme *en* can be merged with *sit upon*.

3.3 Affected Theme vs. Non-Affected Theme

According to the Earliness Principle, V can be merged with P, forming a pseudo-passive only if the percolated Theme can be identified with another theta-role. It can undergo theta-identification when the passive *–en* is adjectival and assigned a Character role. This implies that the pseudo-passive is permitted even by a verbal passive as long as the percolated thematic role can be theta-identified. This prediction is borne out. Thus far, I have claimed that the subject of the pseudo-passive is assigned a Character role by the adjectival passive morpheme *–en*. We have seen from (28-30) that the Character role is easily available when the Theme is affected, but it is not available when the Theme is not affected.[12] However, (34b) and (35b) show that the pseudo-passive is permitted if the passive describes the characteristic of the raised Theme although it is not affected,

(34) a. *Jeju City was walked around by his father.
b. Jeju City can be walked around in a day.

(35) a. *The hotel was stayed in by my sister.
b. The hotel can be stayed in by foreigners.[13]

Generally speaking, it is hard to get the reading that the sentence is about the characteristic of the subject when the Theme is not affected. In (34a) and (35a) *Jeju City* and *the hotel* cannot be affected, and hence it is not surprising that they are not grammatical. However, (34b) and (35b) are well-formed although the Theme is not affected. It seems that the Character role can be assigned by a modal such as *can*. Sentence (36b) is about the characteristic of *the book*, although (36a) is not.

(36) a. This book was read by John.
b. This book can be read in a day.

This clearly shows that modals such as *can* can assign a Character role. In fact, Diesing (1992) proposes that even T can assign a property role when it takes an individual-level VP as its complement. The main claim made here is that a percolated theta-role must undergo theta-identification, and if *can* assigns a Character role, a well-formed sentence can be generated when a theta-role percolates. If so, even the verbal passive can be a source for the pseudo-passive with the help of a modal. I propose that in (34b) and (35b) the passive morpheme is not adjectival but verbal.

(37) a. [$_V$ walk around$_{\text{(theme)}}$]: Theta-Role Percolation
b. [$_V$ walk around~~$_{\text{(theme)}}$~~]$_{\text{(theme)}}$: Merger with verbal passive-*en*
c. [en [$_V$ walk around~~$_{\text{(theme)}}$~~]$_{\text{(theme)}}$]: Theta-Role Identification
d. [en-[$_V$ walk around~~$_{\text{(theme)}}$~~]]$_{\text{(theme)}}$ Merger with *in a day* and *be* Theta-Role Assignment
d. [be [[en-[$_V$ walk around~~$_{\text{(theme)}}$~~]]$_{\text{(theme)}}$ in a day]]$_{\text{(theme)}}$: Merger with *can*
e. [can$_{\text{(char)}}$ [be [[en-[$_V$ walk around~~$_{\text{(theme)}}$~~]]$_{\text{(theme)}}$ in a day]]$_{\text{(theme)}}$: Theta-Identification
f. [can$_{\text{(char)}}$ [be [[en-[$_V$ walk around~~$_{\text{(theme)}}$~~]]$_{\text{(theme)}}$ in a day]]$_{\text{(theme)}}$]$_{\text{(Char = theme)}}$: Merger with *Jeju City* & Theta-Role Assignment
g. [Jeju City$_{\text{(Char = theme)}}$ [can$_{\text{(char)}}$ [be [[en-[$_V$ walk around~~$_{\text{(theme)}}$~~]]$_{\text{(theme)}}$ in a day]]$_{\text{(theme)}}$] ~~$_{\text{(Char = theme)}}$~~]

In fact, *walk around* is not compatible with the adjectival passive morpheme, since its Theme is not affected. So it is merged with the verbal passive and so the Theme role is percolated until it is theta-identified with the Character role of *can*.

This analysis is based on the Earliness Principle in (23), according to which a theta-role can be percolated only if it can be identified by another theta-role. In (28a), (29a), and (30a), the affected Theme undergoes Theta-Identification since the adjectival passive morpheme *–en* assigns a Character role, and in (34b) and (35b) the unaffected Theme undergoes Theta-Identification with the Character role of *can*. This claim amounts to saying that even the verbal passive can be a source for the pseuso-passive if the Character role can be assigned to the subject.

3.4 Account for the Puzzles

Now we are in a position to account for the two major puzzles revolving around the pseudo-passive: (i) why is it subject to the Characterization Condition, and (ii) why is it possible to move out of a Case position? According to the proposal advocated here, the two issues are related. The Case-related issue can be resolved if the verb *sit* can be merged with the preposition *upon*, and merger of *sit* with *upon* is permitted only when the resulting structure is merged with the adjectival passive morpheme *en* or the modal *can*, which assigns the Character role, thereby giving rise to the Characterization Condition.

Thus far, I have claimed that most pseudo-passives are adjectival passives. This is empirically supported by the fact that they display the properties of adjectival passives: (i) they can be used as a prenominal modifier, (ii) they can function as the complement of the raising verbs like *look*, (iii) they are compatible with the negative affix *un-*, and (iv) they can be modified by an adverb like *very*.

(38) a. John is the most talked about player in the game.
b. The bed looks slept in.
c. Just ten years ago this would have been unheard of.
d. Their living room is very lived in.
(Wasow 1977, (90))

(39) a. After the tornado, the fields had a marched through look.
b. Each unpaid for item will be returned.
c. You can ignore any recently gone over accounts.
d. His was not a well-looked on profession.
e. They shared an unspoken (of) passion for chocolates.
f. Filled with candy wrappers and crumpled bills, her bag always had a rummaged around in appearance.
(Bresnan 1995, (16))

(40) a. a slept-in bed
b. a much relied-upon technique
(Bruening 2011: 2)

These all support the claim that most pseudo-passives are adjectival,[14] which is confirmed by the fact that the pseudo-passive does not permit the progressive aspect.

(41) a. *This bed is being slept in.
b. *The hat is being sat upon.

Considering that the progressive aspect is compatible only with the verbal passive, we are led to the conclusion that the pseudo-passive is an adjectival passive.

However, it is worthwhile to reiterate that even the verbal passive can produce the pseudo-passive with the help of modals such as *can*, when the Theme is not affected. Precisely speaking, the pseudo-passive is an adjectival passive when its Theme is affected, and it is a verbal passive when its Theme is not affected.

4 Conclusion

Let us summarize this paper. The passive sentences in (42a-b) are peculiar, since their subject appears to originate from the complement position of a preposition.

(42) a. Mary's innocence was taken advantage of.
b. Mary beds were slept in.

This puzzle can be resolved if the preposition is a part of a bigger predicate.

(43) a. Mary's innocence was [$_{vP}$ en [$_{VP}$ [$_{V}$ take advantage of] Mary's innocence]]
b. Mary beds were [$_{vP}$ en [$_{VP}$ [$_{V}$ sleep in] many beds]].

The analysis in (43a) is plausible, since *take advantage of* can be taken to be a constituent in the corresponding active, but the one (43b) is not, since *sleep in* cannot be a constituent in the active sentence.

(44) a. John [took advantage of] Mary's innocence.
b. *John [slept in] this bed.

However, I have claimed that the analysis in (43b) is still tenable, because the passive morpheme *en* in (43b) is an adjectival *en*. The asymmetry between (43b) and (44b) does not undermine the claim that *slept in* is a constituent in the pseudo-passive, since there is no parallelism between the adjectival passive and its corresponding active in terms of the internal argument structure.

References

Anderson, Mona. 2005. Affectedness. In *the Blackwell companion to syntax*vol 1, ed. by Martin Everaert and Hen van Riemsdijk.Malden, MA.: Blackwell.
Anderson, Mona. 1979. Noun Phrase Structure. Ph.D dissertation. University of Connecticut.
Anderson, Mona. 1977. NP Pre-posing in Noun Phrases. *Proceedings of the North Eastern Linguistic Society* 8: 12-21. Amherst: Graduate Linguistics Student Association.
Baltin, Mark and Paul M. Postal.1996. More on reanalysis hypotheses. *Linguistic Inquiry* 27: 127-145.
Bresnan, Joan. 1995.Lexicality and Argument Structure. Paper presented at the Paris Syntax and Semantics Conference, 1995.
Bruening, Benjamin. 2014. Word Formation is Syntactic: Adjectival Passives in English. *Natural Language and Linguistic Theory* 32: 363-422.
Bruening, Bejamin. 2011. Pseudopassives, Expletive Passives, and Locative Inversion. Ms. University of Delaware.
Chomsky, Noam. 1995. *The Minimalist Program.* Cambridge, Mass.: MIT Press.
Chomsky, Noam. 1981. *Lectures on government and binding.* Dordrecht: Foris.
Diesing, Molly. 1992. *Indefinites.* Cambridge, Mass.: MIT Press.
Drummond, Alex & Dave Kush. 2011. Reanalysis as Raising to Object. Ms. University of Maryland.
Emonds, Joseph E. 2006.Adjectival Passives. In Martin Everaert and Henk van Riemsdijk, eds., *The Blackwell Companion to Syntax*, Oxford: Blackwell, vol. 1: 16–60.
Freidin, Robert. 1975. The analysis of passives. *Language* 51: 384-405.
Higginbotham, James 1985. On semantics. *Linguistic Inquiry* 16: 547–593.
Koster, Jan.1987. *Domain and dynasties: the radical autonomy of syntax.* Dordrecht: Foris.
Postal, Paul. M. 1986. *Studies of passive clauses.* Albany: State University of New York Press.
Radford, Andrew. 1988. *Transformational grammar: a first course.* Cambridge: Cambridge University Press.
Wasow, Thomas. 1977. Transformations and the Lexicon. In P. Culicover, A. Akmajian, and T. Wasow, eds., *Formal Syntax*, New York: Academic Press, pp. 327–360.
Williams, Edwin. 1994. *Thematic structure in syntax.* Cambridge, Mass.: MIT Press.
Williams, Edwin. 1980. Argument structure and morphology. *The Linguistic Review* 1: 81-114.

---

1 The corresponding pseudo-passive sentence is well-formed.

(i) Not the chair but the hat was sat upon.

2 Chomsky (1995) proposes that the transitive verbs like *hit* consist of the light verb v and its corresponding intransitive *hit*. In this analysis the active counterpart of (8) looks like (i).

(i) [$_{vP}$ v [$_{VP}$ [$_{V}$ [$_{V}$ take] advantage] of] Mary's honesty]

3 Radford (1988) assumes that V and P undergo reanalysis in the course of the derivation. In this paper, by contrast, I argue that V is merged with P from the start.

4 Drummond & Kush (2011) try to support the reanalysis approach by making use of raising-to-object.

[5] On the other hand, Freidin (1975) and Emonds (2006) claim that all the passive participles are adjectives.

[6] See Williams (1994) for thematic role percolation.

[7] Williams (1994) proposes that theta-percolation is blocked by a predicate that assigns an external theta-role.

[8] It is usually known that only Theme percolates (Williams 1980). However, the Goal can percolate as well.

(i) a. Untaught children
b. If the children are untaught, their ignorance and vices will in future life cost us much dearer in their consequences than it would have done in their correction by a good education. (Thomas Jefferson)

[9] Bruening (2014) observes that verbs of the *deny*-class are exceptional in that the internal argument structure is preserved in the adjectival passive: both Theme and Goal are licensed, as illustrated in (i).

(i) Victim remains denied her American nationality.

Let us recall that proposition-taking adjectives are usually raising predicates.

(ii) a. It is likely that John will come to the party.
b. John is likely to come to the party.

Verbs of the *deny*-class take a proposition as their internal argument. What is denied in (iii) is the proposition that the victim bears a relation with her American nationality.

(iii) They denied the victim her American nationality.

I propose that when the adjectival morpheme *en* is merged with a proposition-taking verb, it patterns like the proposition-taking adjectives: it is a raising morpheme in that it does not assign the Character role. The raising morpheme can maintain the argument structure of its complement. Therefore, (i) is grammatical.

[10] The possibility that the adjectival *-en* is merged with VP seems to be ruled out in (22). The *un-* is required to be merged with an X^0-level constituent, which means that *given* must be X^0. This claim amounts to saying that the adjectival –*en* can co-occur with VP if there is no negative morpheme –*un*. To put differently, it is predicted that both Theme and Goal can be realized if *given* is not attached by *un*. This prediction is borne out.

(i) She seemed given too much power.
(Bruening 2014: 33)

So I propose that when the adjectival *-en* is merged with VP, both Theme and Goal can be realized.

[11] There are few reflexive light verbs like *shave* and *wash*.
(i) John {shaved, washed}

[12] This is reminiscent of the Affectedness Condition on preposing in passive nominals (Anderson 2005, 1979, 1977).

[13] Notice that a *by*-phrase can be licensed in the pseudo-passive, as shown in (35b). This seems to support the claim that the pseudo-passive can be verbal. However, see Bruening (2014) for a claim that even the adjectival passive permits a *by*-phrase.

[14] Many linguists, including Bruening (2011), assume that the pseudo-passive is a verbal passive and sentences (32-34) are adjectival passives derived from verbal passives. However, I argue that they are well-formed, since pseudo-passives are adjectival.

Phonological Suppression of Anaphoric *Wh*-expressions in English and Korean

Park, Myung-Kwan
Department of English Linguistics, Interpretation and Translation
Dongguk University
Seoul, Korea 100-715
parkmk@dgu.edu

Abstract

This paper follows the lead of Chung (2013), examining the phonological suppression of the *wh*-expression in English and Korean. We argue that the *wh*-expression itself cannot undergo ellipsis/deletion/dropping, as it carries information focus. However, it can do so, when in anaphoricity with the preceding token of *wh*-expression, it changes into an E-type or sloppy-identity pronoun. This vehicle change from the *wh*-expression to a pronoun accompanies the loss of the *wh*-feature inherent in the *wh*-expression. In a certain structural context such as a quiz question, the interrogative [+wh] complementizer does not require the presence of a *wh*-expression, thus the expression being optionally dropped.

1. Introduction

As Chung (2013) notes, the interrogative expression in Korean corresponding to the *wh*-expression in English cannot be phonologically suppressed[1], as follows:

(1) A: na-nun chelswu-ka ecey **mwues-ul**
I-Top Chelswu-Nom yesterday what-Acc
sass-nunci molu-keyss-ta.
bought-Interr don't know
'I don't know what Chelswu bought yesterday.'
B: na-to yenghuy-ka ecey *(**mwues-ul**)
I-also Yenghuy-Nom yesterday what-Acc
sass-nunci molukeyssta.
bought-Interr don't know
'I don't know what Yenghuy bought yesterday.'

In the conversation between speakers A and B, speaker B's sentence is required to bear the interrogative expression ***mwues*** 'what', despite the fact that another token of the same expression is mentioned in the previous sentence spoken by speaker A.

Apparently, the same distribution of the *wh*-expression is found in English, as follows:

(2)A: I don't know what John bought yesterday.
B: *I don't know Bill did (~~buy **what** yesterday~~), either.
B': I don't know *(**what**) Bill did (~~buy t yesterday~~), either.

As in (2B), the *wh*-expression *what* cannot be included in the portion deleted by VP ellipsis. Nor is it phonologically suppressed after it is moved to the embedded [Spec,CP] position, as in (2B').

Chung (2013) attempts to account for the impossibility of phonologically suppressing the interrogative expression in Korean by adopting the *pro* hypothesis for the null argument. More specifically, Chung follows the line of analysis advanced by Ahn and Cho (2012), who propose that the null argument as *pro* always substitutes for NP, but not for the next higher QP projected by the functional element Q such as a quantity word or a *wh*-feature, as schematized below:

[1] We occasionally use the theory-neutral notion 'phonological(ly) suppress(ion)' to refer to such terms as (phonological) dropping, copy trace deletion, ellipsis/deletion, etc.

Copyright 2014 by Myung-Kwan Park
28th Pacific Asia Conference on Language, Information and Computation pages 57–64

(3) $[_{QP}$ $[_{NP}$ pro] Q]

Chung's analysis works fine for Korean, but his analysis squarely faces a problem when it is extended to examples like (2B) and (2B') in English, where the empty *pro* is known not to be available in grammar.

We examine this issue of why the interrogative or *wh-* expression is not phonologically suppressed. We argue that the interrogative or *wh-* expression in its own form cannot be deleted, because it carries informational focus or new information. However, it can undergo deletion when it is anaphoric with the preceding interrogative or *wh-* expression and potentially changes into a pronoun. This vehicle change from the interrogative or *wh-* expression to the corresponding pronoun results in loss of the *wh*-feature inherent in the former expression, so that the resulting pronoun necessarily fails to enter into successful Agree relation with the interrogative complementizer, inducing a derivational crash.

2. The syntax of *wh*-expression: Wisdom from English

In this section we examine the phonological suppression of the *wh*-expression in English. First of all, the *wh*-expression or relative *wh*-operator can be phonologically suppressed in relative clauses, as follows:

(4)a. We read the article [(which) Smith recommended].
b. The safe [(which) Henry keeps his money in] has been stolen. Baker (1995: 293)

In (4), the head of the chain formed by the relative pronoun or *wh*-operator *which* can be dropped. We understand this dropping of the relative pronoun along the line of analysis for the copy trace(s), as in (5):

(5) What did Stacy say [(what)$_1$ Becky bought (what)$_1$]?

In the course of the *wh*-movement, the moving *wh*-expression leaves behind its copy trace(s) along the way to its target position. The difference between the movement of the relative *wh*-operator and the regular *wh*-movement is that in the case of the former, the chain created by the relative *wh*-operator forms an 'extended' chain with the relative antecedent. This results in allowing the head of the chain created by the relative *wh*-operator to be dropped, in identity with the relative antecedent, which is now the head of the extended chain.

A question that arises is why the following sentence is ungrammatical:

(6) *Who$_1$ do you wonder $[_{CP}$ t'$_1$ $[_{TP}$ t$_1$ won the trace]]?

It is argued in Lasnik and Saito (1984) that the intermediate trace t'$_1$ cannot qualify as an operator since it does not contain the relevant feature. Their argument, however, does not seem to hold water, in light of the copy trace analysis of *wh*-movement, which dictates that the literal copy of the moving *wh*-expression occurs instead of the trace, as follows:

(6)' *Who$_1$ do you wonder $[_{CP}$ who$_1$ $[_{TP}$ who$_1$ won the trace]]?

The ill-formedness of (6)' is, in the more recent analysis (cf. Chomsky (2000), (2001a, b)), attributed to the illegitimate step of movement from the embedded to the matrix [Spec,CP] position, as the moving *wh*-expression has its featural requirement met in the embedded [Spec,CP] position, being unable to undergo further movement.

One thing to note regarding the copy trace deletion of the chain formed by the *wh*-expression or the relative *wh*-operator is that the copy trace left behind by the *wh*-expression or the relative *wh*-operator changes into a resumptive pronoun (though as well-known, the resumptive pronoun in English allegedly occurs within an island structure), as follows:

(7)a. This is the chef$_1$ that Ted inquired how *e$_1$/she$_1$ prepared the potatoes
b. The detective interrogated a man$_1$ who the prosecutor knows why the officer arrested *e$_1$/him$_1$.

The availability of a resumptive pronoun instead of a copy trace linked to the moved *wh*-expression clearly points to the fact that the copy trace is a kind of pronoun realized in anaphoricity with the head of the chain (i.e., the *wh*-expression or the relative *wh*-operator).

Not only do the *wh*-expression and the relative *wh*-operator undergo phonological suppression as part of copy trace deletion, but the *wh*-expression is also part of Sluicing or TP deletion, as follows:

(8)a. The report details what$_1$ IBM did and why [$_{TP}$ e].
b. Who$_1$ did the suspect call and when [$_{TP}$ e]?
Merchant (2001: 201)

Drawing attention to examples like (8a-b), Merchant (2001: 201-4) argue that the second conjunct clause in (8a-b) involve deletion of TP where the expression corresponding to the *wh*-expression is an E-type pronoun. In other words, the elided TP in (8a-b) is understood as the reconstructed or actually attested TP in (9a-b):

(9)a. The report details what$_1$ IBM did and why [$_{TP}$ IBM did it$_1$].
b. Who$_1$ did the suspect call and when [$_{TP}$ the suspect called him$_1$]?
Merchant (2001: 203)

This shows that the questioning *wh*-expression can be substituted for by the (E-type) pronoun. Note that the E-type pronoun as part of the full or elided clause covaries in reference with the questioning *wh*-expression. The availability of (9a-b) corresponding to (8a-b) involving ellipsis renders compelling evidence showing that the *wh*-expression is represented as a pronoun inside a portion to be deleted. The form change (or vehicle change, following Fiengo and May's (1994) and Merchant's (2001) terminology) of the *wh*-expression into a pronoun inside the portion to be deleted seems to be a reasonable option, as the whole portion to be deleted or the expressions within it are construed as discourse-given or anaphoric to the previous verbal discourse.

It seems, however, that the anaphoric substitution of the E-type pronoun for the *wh*-expression is restricted to Sluicing or TP ellipsis. The following sentences accommodate the interpretation where the *wh*-expression in the first conjunct clause and the substituting pronoun that putatively occurs in the elided VP of the second conjunct clause can be referentially distinct:

(10)a. I know when John read what, but I don't know where Bill did.
b. John asked me why Mary bought what, but John didn't ask me how Susan did.

In other words, in (10a) what John read may be referentially different from what Bill did. Note that the pronoun in the elided VP of the second conjunct clause, which is vehicle-changed from the *wh*-expression in the first conjunct clause, may be understood as a sloppy-identity pronoun.

The difference between (8a-b) and (10a-b) in regard to the interpretation of the ellipsis-internal pronoun anaphoric to the preceding *wh*-expression reminds us of the contrast between TP and VP ellipsis in regard to the ability to introduce new discourse referents by using indefinite expressions, which Chung et al. (2011) discuss. In fact, Chung et al. suggest that the contrast in question is correlated with the size of ellipsis site and the domain of existential closure that unselectively binds all indefinite expressions. Chung et al. argue that TP ellipsis involves LF reconstruction or re-use of the antecedent TP into the ellipsis site, whereas VP ellipsis involves PF deletion/unpronunciation of a vP. Departing from Chung et al., let's instead assume that both cases of ellipsis involve PF deletion. Furthermore, we take the domain of existential closure to be the smallest constituent in which all the predicate's arguments have had a chance to be introduced, presumably the position adjoined to vP. Given these assumptions, the two cases of deletion are taken to proceed in the following fashion:

(11) TP ellipsis:
[$_{CP}$ ~~[$_{TP}$ ∃ [$_{vP}$ **subject DP** [$_{VP}$ **object DP**]]~~]

(12) VP ellipsis:
[$_{CP}$ [$_{TP}$ ∃ ~~[$_{vP}$ **subject DP** [$_{VP}$ **object DP**]]~~]

TP and VP deletion differ in regard to whether the ellipsis site includes the existential closure operator (∃). The ellipsis site of the former case DOES include the existential operator as in (11). As the identity/parallelism condition on deletion demands that the indefinite expressions (including *wh*-expressions) in the ellipsis TP be identical/parallel in reference to their correlate expressions in the antecedent TP, TP ellipsis requires strict identity/parallelism. However, VP ellipsis allows looser or sloppy identity/parallelism, because the existential operator is outside of the vP to be deleted as in (12)[2].

Returning to the examples in (2), repeated below as (13), we are now in a position to account for the impossibility of phonologically suppressing the *wh*-expression in (13B) and (13B').

(13)A: I don't know what John bought yesterday.
B: *I don't know Bill did (~~buy **what** yesterday~~), either.
B': I don't know *(~~**what**~~) Bill did (~~buy t yesterday~~), either.

Recall that the portion to be deleted or the expressions within it are discourse given, so that the *wh*-expression changes into a corresponding pronoun. Otherwise, the *wh*-expression carries information focus and so cannot be subject to deletion, as stated below:

(14) The *wh*-expression carries information focus and so cannot be subject to deletion.

In Merchant's (2001) notion of e-givenness, the *wh*-expression cannot count as e-given information.

To repeat, the *wh*-expression has to change into an (E-type or sloppy-identity) pronoun to be included in the portion to be deleted. However, the resulting pronoun vehicle-changed from the *wh*-expression does not carry the *wh*-feature inherent in the *wh*-expression. This anaphoric process is a culprit for the ungrammaticality of (13B) and (13B'). For the sake of the exposition, we represented the *wh*-expression in (13B) and (13B') as undergoing deletion or dropping, but the *wh*-expression in (13B) and (13B') that undergoes deletion or dropping has to be represented as a pronoun corresponding to it. Under this circumstance, the pronoun fails to enter into successful Agree relation with the interrogative complementizer, resulting in a derivational crash (cf. Chung (2013)).

[2]The contrast between TP and VP ellipsis in terms of existential closure reminds us of the parallel difference between them in terms of voice match. Merchant (2013) argues that TP ellipsis requires voice match, whereas VP ellipsis does not. This difference follows from the fact that TP ellipsis always includes a Voice head, but VP ellipsis does not.

Leaving this section, we note that there is an additional set of examples where the *wh*-expression is phonologically suppressed. The relevant examples are as follows:

(15)a. The first emperor of the Roman empire was?
b. In ancient Rome, Nero tried to destroy the city by?
c. The Christian movement to reclaim the Iberian Peninsula was called?
d. The three most well-known teas are Darjeeling, Assam, and?
(taken from http://shrines.rpgclassics.com/psx/mml2/poktevillagequiz.shtml)

In these sentences that are used as quiz questions, the expected Subject-Aux Inversion does not apply, which indicates that the examples in (15) are assimilated to the echo *wh*-questions in (16) which are also used as quiz questions.

(16)a. Christianity became the official religion of the Roman empire **with what**?
b. 300 years ago, the first roller coaster was built **in what country**?

In this regard, it seems right to say that what is phonologically suppressed in (15a-d) is the echoic *wh*-expression as found in (16). It is also to be noted that the phonological suppression takes place only at the right edge of the sentence.

Why is it possible to drop the echoic *wh*-expression in quiz questions as in (15)? The answer to this question may be that the echoic *wh*-expression can be dropped in register-dependent contexts such as quizzes. Still the more important aspect of quiz questions using echoic *wh*-expressions is that they do not bear the interrogative complementizer (cf. Sobin (2010)). Therefore, the optional dropping of an echoic *wh*-expression in quiz questions does not result in a derivational crash.

3. Extension to Korean

In the previous section, we saw that the *wh*-expression undergoes phonological suppression as part of copy trace deletion or TP- or VP-deletion. Especially in the latter case, the *wh*-expression can be part of TP- or VP-deletion when it vehicle-changes into an (E-type or sloppy-identity) pronoun, (though in the former case, the copy trace changes into a resumptive pronoun in restricted structural contexts). However, it itself cannot be part of TP- or VP-deletion because it is inherently construed as new information.

We turn to Korean, where the *wh*-expression can be scrambled out of the embedded interrogative clause, unlike in (6) of English:

(17)a. chelswu-ka [yenghuy-ka **mwues-ul**
Chelswu-Nom Yenghuy-Nom what-Acc
sassnun-ci] alko siphehanta.
bought-Interr know want
'Chelswu wants to know what Yenghuy bought.'
b. **mwues-ul$_1$** [chelswu-ka [yenghuy-ka**mwues-ul$_1$**/**t$_1$** sassnunci] alko siphehanta].

Unlike in (6) of English, in (17b) the scrambling of the *wh*-expression proceeds to the matrix clause without entering into Agree relation with the embedded interrogative complementizer, anticipating the undoing of it to its original position in the covert syntax (cf. Saito (1989)). The copy trace left behind by the overt-syntax scrambling of the *wh*-expression undergoes copy trace deletion, in identity with the head of the chain formed by this scrambling.

The *wh*-expression can also be part of ellipsis, as follows:

(18)a. chelswu-ka **mwues-ul** sass-nunci
Chelswu-Nom what-Acc bought-Interr
alko iss-ciman,
know-Concessive -
way-i-nci-nun molukeyssta.
way-Copu-Interr-Contrast don't know.
'I know what Chelswu bought, but I don't know why.'
b. chelswu-eykey **etten mwuncey**-lul
Chelswu-to which question-Acc
phwuless-nunci mwuless-ciman,
solved-Interr asked-Concessive
ettehkey-i-nci-nun mwutci anhassta.
how-Copu-Interr-Contras ask didn't
'I asked Chelswu which question he solved, but I didn't ask how.'

In (18), either *nwues* 'what' or *ettenmwuncey* 'what question' can be part of clausal ellipsis (or Pseudosluicing, following Merchant's (1998) terminology)). Given the analysis for English, we can say that the *wh*-expressions in (19a-b) each changes into an E-type pronoun in the context of clausal ellipsis.

However, returning to the example in (1), repeated below as (19), (19B) turns out to be unacceptable, if the *wh*-expression is phonologically suppressed.

(19)A: na-nun chelswu-ka ecey **mwues-ul**
I-Top Chelswu-Nom yesterday what-Acc
sass-nunci molu-keyss-ta.
bought-Interr don't know
'I don't know what Chelswu bought yesterday.'
B: na-to yenghuy-ka ecey *(**mwues-ul**)
I-also Yenghuy-Nom yesterday what-Acc
sass-nunci molukeyssta.
bought-Interr don't know
'I don't know what Yenghuy bought yesterday.'

Continuing on extending the analysis proposed for English to Korean, we account for (19B) without the overtly-realized *wh*-expression by saying that the *wh*-expression itself cannot be phonologically suppressed haphazardly, since it carries new information. However, it can be dropped only when it changes into a discourse-old pronoun. As correctly argued by Chung (2013), *mwues-ul* 'what' can change into the empty pronoun *pro* that Korean utilizes but English does not. When this applies, however, there is no expression that the embedded interrogative complementizer can partake in legitimate Agree relation with, thus ultimately resulting in a derivational crash. By contrast, though the *wh*-expression within clausal ellipsis in the second conjunct clause of (18a-b) changes (in fact, has to change) into a pronoun, the additional *wh*-expression such as *way* 'why' and *ettehkey* 'how' steps in to successfully establish Agree relation with the interrogative complementizer.

The following example (with some slight modification) reported by Chung (2013) can be accounted for along the same line of analysis as (18):

(20) chelswu-nun **nwu-ka encey** ttenass-nunci
Chelswu-Top who-Nom when left-Interr
Cosaha-ko,
examine-Conj
yenghuy-nun (~~**nwuka**~~) **eti-lo**.
Yenghuy-Top who-Nom where-for

Ttenass-nunci cosahay-la
left-Interr examine-Imper
'Chelswu, you examine who left when, and Yenghuy, you examine who left for where.'

The difference between (18) and this example is that, on the one hand, the former contains one single *wh*-expression, but the latter contains multiple *wh*-expressions in the first conjunct clause. Unlike (19B), on the other hand, both (18) and (20) contain an additional *wh*-expression in the second conjunct clause, which participates in Agree relation with the interrogative complementizer, despite the other anaphoric argument *wh*-expression changing into a pronoun.

One thing worth noting is the referentiality of the *wh*-expression that is phonologically suppressed in the second conjunct clause of (18) and (20). It seems that there is no disagreement about the *wh*-expression that is part of clausal ellipsis in (18). It is construed as an E-type pronoun, as found in the similar structural context of (8a-b) in English. Several linguists that I consulted about (20) also claimed that the phonologically suppressed *wh*-expression in the second conjunct clause of (20) is only interpreted as an E-type pronoun. However, I concur with Chung's (2013) report that the phonologically suppressed *wh*-expression *nwu-ka* 'who' in the second conjunct clause of (20) allows for sloppy-identity interpretation. In our analysis, the *wh*-expression *nwu-ka* 'who' in the second conjunct clause of (20) changes into an empty pronoun that is construed as a sloppy-identity one in the interpretive component. Note at this point that the size of phonological suppression is critical for the interpretation of the pronoun which is vehicle changed from the *wh*-expression. In (18), the pronoun is part of clausal ellipsis, allowing for E-type interpretation. In (20), by contrast, the pronoun is a null argument, allowing for sloppy-identity interpretation in addition to E-type interpretation. As suggested above for English, the domain of existential closure and parallelism in ellipsis come into play, distinguishing the pronoun in (18) and that in (20) in terms of interpretational aspects.

Now turning to quiz questions in Korean, we note the usual instances of such questions, as follows:

(21)a. seykyey-eyse kacang kin kang-**un**?
world-in most long river-Top
'The longest river in the word is?'
b. seykyey-eyse kacang manhi phallin cha
world-in most many sold car
TOP 3-nun
TOP 3-Top
thoyothakhololla, photu F silicu, **kuliko**
Toyota Corolla, Ford F Series, and
(ikes-un)?
(this-Top)
'The 3 best-selling cars in the world are Toyota Corolla, Ford F Series, and (this)?'

To construct a quiz question, Korean utilizes the Topic marker with somewhat peculiar intonation on it, with the immediately following string of words phonologically suppressed at the right edge of the sentence. This formulaic device is extended to the non-quiz type of sentences in (22), reported by Chung (2013):

(22)A: chelswu-ka sakwa-lul swunhuy-eykey
Chelswu-Nom apple-Acc Swunhuy-to
encey cwuess-ni?
when gave-Interr
'When did Chelswu give an apple to Swunhuy?'
B: ecey
yesterday
'Yesterday.'
A: kulem, yengswu-ka sakwa-lul
then, Yengswu-Nom apple-Acc
yenghuy-eykey-nun
Yenghuy-to-Top
(~~**enceycwuessni**~~)?
when gave-Interr
'Then, Yengswu gave an apple to Yenghuy when?'

As in (22), the second sentence by speaker A has its right edge dropped immediately after the Topic marker.

It seems that the dropping of the right of the sentence does not obey such a syntactic condition as constituent-hood, allowing the embedded predicate and the matrix predicate to be phonologically suppressed, excluding the other embedded constituents.

(23)A: chelswu-ka [swunhuy-ka
Chelswu-Nom Swunhuy-Nom
nonmwun-ul manswu-eykey
article-Acc Manswu-to

encey ponayntako] malhayss-ni?
when sent said-Interr
'When did Chelswu say Swunhuy sent an article to Manswu?'
B: nayil
tomorrow
'Tomorrow.'
A: kulem, yengswu-ka [minhuy-ka
Then Yengswu-Nom Minhuy-Nom
nonmwun-ul
article-Acc
kyengswu-eykey-nun
Kyengswu-to-Top
~~(encey ponayntako)] malhayssni~~?
when sent said-Interr
'Then, Yengswu said Minhuy sent an article to Kyengswu when?'

We take the insensitivity to constituent-hood in the course of producing a quiz question to indicate that the dropping of the string of words is non-syntactic and the quiz question like (21a-b), just as in English, does not involve the interrogative complementizer, so that it does not require the presence of the *wh*-expression within it.

4. Conclusion

This paper has investigated why the *wh*-expression cannot be deleted/elided nor part of the portion to be deleted/elided. We have argued that the *wh*-expression is construed as information focus, not being able to undergo deletion, otherwise impinging on the recoverability condition on deletion/ellipsis. However, it can be substituted for by a pronoun in an anaphoric relation with the preceding token of *wh*-expression. Under this circumstance, it can be deleted/elided or part of the portion to be deleted/elided, but at the cost of losing the *wh*-feature inherent in it. Thus, if the *wh*-feature is in demand for the Agree relation with the interrogative complementizer, the pronoun that is vehicle-changed from the *wh*-expression cannot provide such a feature. In fact, this is the paradoxical situation for the *wh*-expression to be deleted/elided or part of the portion to be deleted/elided. If it remains in its form, it cannot be subject to deletion/ellipsis. If it changes into an anaphoric pronoun, the resulting pronoun ends up with losing the *wh*-feature the corresponding *wh*-expression used to have.

In passing, we have first discussed the two different types of pronouns that are vehicle-changed from *wh*-expressions: E-type pronoun and sloppy-identity pronoun. This distinction follows from the domain of existential closure and the parallelism/identity condition on deletion/ellipsis. Second, as Merchant (2001) and Chung (2013) note, when one *wh*-expression changes into an anaphoric pronoun, failing to enter into Agree relation with the interrogative complementizer, the multiple *wh*-question makes available an additional *wh*-expression, which steps in to do so instead. Third, the quiz question construction employs the echo *wh*-question strategy, thereby the interrogative complementizer in the construction not requiring for the expected Agree relation with an expression with the *wh*-feature. Thus, the dropping of the *wh*-expression in this construction does not lead to a derivational crash.

References

Ahn, Hee-Don and Sungeun Cho. 2012. On Some ellipsis phenomena in Korean. In *Proceedings of the 14th Seoul Internal Conference on Generative Grammar: Three Factors and Syntactic Theory*, ed. Bum-Sik Park, 3-33. Seoul, Korea: Hankuk Publishing Co.

Baker, Carl Lee. 1995. *English Syntax*. 2nd edition. Cambridge, MA: the MIT Press.

Chomsky, Noam. 2000. Minimalist inquiries: The framework. In *Step by Step: Essays on Minimalism in Honor of Howard Lasnik*, ed. Roger Martin, David Michaels and Juan Uriagereka, 89-155. Cambridge, MA: MIT Press.

Chomsky,Noam. 2001a. Beyond explanatory adequacy. *MIT Occasional Papers in Linguistics* 20. Cambridge, Mass.: MIT, Department of Linguistics and Philosophy, MITWPL.

Chomsky, Noam. 2001b. Derivation by phase. In *Ken Hale: A Life in Language*, ed. Michael Kenstowicz, 1-52. Cambridge, MA: the MIT Press.

Chung, Daeho. 2013. On the nature of null WH-phrases in Korean. *Linguistic Research* 30.3:473-487.

Chung, Sandra, William Ladusaw, and James McCloskey. 2011. Sluicing(:) Between structure and inference. In *Representing Language: Essays in Honor of Judith Aissen*, ed. R. Gutierrez-Bravo et al., 31-50. California Digital Library eScholarship Repository. Linguistic Research Center, UCSC.

Fiengo, Robert, and Robert May. 1994. *Indices and*

Identity. Linguistic Inquiry Monographs 24. Cambridge, MA: MIT Press.
Lasnik, Howard, and Mamoru Saito. 1984. On the nature of proper government. *Linguistic. Inquiry* 15:235-289.
Merchant, Jason. 1998. "Pseudosluicing": Elliptical Clefts in Japanese and English. In *Zas Working Papers in Linguistics*, ed. Artemis Alexiadou, N. Fuhrhop, Paul Law and U Kleinhenz, 88-112. Berlin: Zertrum Fur AllgemeineSprachwissenschaft.
Merchant, Jason. 2001. *The Syntax of Silence: Sluicing, Islands, and the Theory of Ellipsis*. Oxford: Oxford University Press.
Merchant, Jason. 2013. Voice and ellipsis. *Linguistic Inquiry* 44:77-108.
Saito, Mamoru. 1989. Scrambling as semantically vacuous A'-movement. In *Alternative Conceptions of Phrase Structure*, ed. Mark Baltin and Anthony Kroch, 182-200. Chicago: University of Chicago Press.
Sobin, Nicholas. 2010. Echo questions in the Minimalist Program. *Linguistic Inquiry* 41.1: 131-148.

Finding The Best Model Among Representative Compositional Models

Masayasu Muraoka† **Sonse Shimaoka**‡ **Kazeto Yamamoto**†
Yotaro Watanabe† **Naoaki Okazaki**†* **Kentaro Inui**†
Tohoku University†‡
Japan Science and Technology Agency (JST)*
{muraoka,kazeto,yotaro-w,okazaki,inui}
@ecei.tohoku.ac.jp†
simaokasonse@yahoo.co.jp‡

Abstract

The field of distributional-compositional semantics has yielded a range of computational models for composing the vector of a phrase from those of constituent word vectors. Existing models have various ranges of their expressiveness, recursivity, and trainability. However, these models have not been examined closely for their compositionality. We implement and compare these models under the same conditions. The experimentally obtained results demonstrate that the model using different composition matrices for different dependency relations achieved state-of-the-art performance on a dataset for two-word compositions (Mitchell and Lapata, 2010).

1 Introduction

Computing the meaning of a text has posed a challenge in NLP for many years. Based on the distributional hypothesis (Firth, 1957), the meaning of a word is typically represented as a real-valued vector, with elements representing the frequencies of words that co-occur in the context of the word in a corpus. Numerous studies have demonstrated learned word vectors from a large text corpus (Bullinaria and Levy, 2007; Collobert and Weston, 2008; Turney and Pantel, 2010; Mnih and Kavukcuoglu, 2013; Mikolov et al., 2013).

In contrast, the same approach is not scalable to a complex linguistic unit (e.g., phrase or sentence) because of the data sparseness problem: the longer the length of a phrase, the fewer times the phrase occurs in a corpus. For this reason, we cannot acquire semantic information reliably from co-occurrence statistics of a phrase. Recently, numerous studies have explored compositional semantics, in which the meaning of a phrase, clause, or sentence is computed from those of its constituents (Mitchell and Lapata, 2008; Mitchell and Lapata, 2010; Guevara, 2010; Zanzotto et al., 2010; Socher et al., 2011; Baroni et al., 2012; Socher et al., 2012; Socher et al., 2013a; Socher et al., 2014). These studies mostly address theories and methods for computing a vector of a phrase from the vectors of its constituents; the simplest but effective approach is to take the average of the two input vectors.

A simple approach such as additive and multiplicative compositions has been a strong baseline over more complex models (Blacoe and Lapata, 2012; Socher et al., 2013b). However, Erk and Padó (2008) argued the importance of syntax relations: the simple additive/multiplicative approach yields the same vector for phrases *a horse draws* and *draw a horse*, ignoring the syntactic structure by which *horse* in the former phrase is a subject whereas *horse* in the latter is the object. They formulated a generalized composition function including such a composition. However, this generalized composition is too complex to learn. These models usually do not work well for now.

As described in this paper, through a human-correlation experiment, we explore the most useful model among the representative models that have been proposed to date in terms of the semantic composition. We cast the task of learning composition matrices, which are model parameters, to minimize the errors between phrase vectors composed

Copyright 2014 by Masayasu Muraoka, Sonse Shimaoka, Kazeto Yamamoto, Yotaro Watanabe, Naoaki Okazaki, and Kentaro Inui
28th Pacific Asia Conference on Language, Information and Computation pages 65–74

by matrices and computed in a corpus. The experimentally obtained results demonstrate that the model using different composition matrices for different dependency relations achieved state-of-the-art performance for a dataset for two-word compositions (Mitchell and Lapata, 2010). Moreover, the results confirm the effectiveness of syntax-sensitive compositions.

The remainder of the paper is organized as follows. Section 2 presents a survey of the previous studies and their issues. Section 3 describes details of the methods and the training procedure. Section 4 reports and discusses the experimentally obtained results. We conclude this paper in Section 5.

2 Previous Work

In this section, we briefly overview representative methods for obtaining vector representations of word meanings. We then describe the previous work that composes the meaning of a phrase from its constituents, followed by the issues and limitations that arise in this work.

2.1 Obtaining word vectors

In distributional semantics, the meaning of a word is represented by a vector, i.e., a point in d-dimensional space. We can classify the previous studies for obtaining word vectors into two groups: approaches based on *co-occurrence statistics* and *language modeling*.

The former approach (Bullinaria and Levy, 2007; Mitchell and Lapata, 2010) counts the frequency of words co-occurring with a target word in a corpus, and refines the statistics using, for example, Pointwise Mutual Information (PMI). Vectors obtained using this method are high-dimensioned and sparse. Therefore, some methods compress vectors using a dimension reduction method such as Principal Component Analysis (PCA) and Non-negative Matrix Factorization (NMF).

The latter approach (Collobert and Weston, 2008; Mnih and Kavukcuoglu, 2013; Mikolov et al., 2013) formalizes the task of learning word vectors as a byproduct of a language model (Bengio et al., 2003), i.e., finding word vectors such that each word vector can be predicted from surrounding words. In these studies, word vectors are initialized by random values and are learned through back propagation on a neural network.

Table 1: Summary of the previous models. Vectors $\boldsymbol{u}$, $\boldsymbol{v} \in \mathbb{R}^d$ present input (word) vectors, σ is an activation function (e.g., sigmoid function and $tanh$). In general, the more parameters a model has, the greater the expressive power the model has during vector compositions.

Model	Function	Parameters
Add	$w_1\boldsymbol{u} + w_2\boldsymbol{v}$	$w_1, w_2 \in \mathbb{R}$
Fulladd	$W \begin{bmatrix} \boldsymbol{u} \\ \boldsymbol{v} \end{bmatrix}$	$W \in \mathbb{R}^{d\times 2d}$
RNN	$\sigma\left(W \begin{bmatrix} \boldsymbol{u} \\ \boldsymbol{v} \end{bmatrix}\right)$	$W \in \mathbb{R}^{d\times 2d}$
Lexfunc	$A_u\boldsymbol{v}$	$A_u \in \mathbb{R}^{d\times d}$
Relfunc	$\sigma\left(W_r \begin{bmatrix} \boldsymbol{u} \\ \boldsymbol{v} \end{bmatrix}\right)$	$W_r \in \mathbb{R}^{d\times 2d}$
Fulllex	$\sigma\left(W \begin{bmatrix} A_v\boldsymbol{u} \\ A_u\boldsymbol{v} \end{bmatrix}\right)$	$W \in \mathbb{R}^{d\times 2d}$, $A_u, A_v \in \mathbb{R}^{d\times d}$

2.2 Composing word vectors for phrases

The idea of computing a vector of a phrase from its constituents is based on the Principle of Compositionality (Frege, 1892), where the meaning of a complex unit (e.g., phrase or sentence) comprises the meanings of the constituents and the rule for combining the constituents. Equation 1 formulates this principle mathematically:

$$\boldsymbol{p} = f(\boldsymbol{u}, \boldsymbol{v}). \tag{1}$$

Here, given two input (e.g. word) vectors $\boldsymbol{u} \in \mathbb{R}^{d_1}$ and $\boldsymbol{v} \in \mathbb{R}^{d_1}$, the model f yields a phrase vector $\boldsymbol{p} \in \mathbb{R}^{d_2}$ as a composition of the input vectors. In other words, the model f is a function that computes a phrase vector $\boldsymbol{p}$ for the inputs $\boldsymbol{u}$ and $\boldsymbol{v}$. Setting $d = d_1 = d_2$ allows recursive compositions, i.e., generating phrase or sentence vectors consisting of three or more words.

Table 1 shows representative models from earlier works. The *Add* model (Mitchell and Lapata, 2008; Mitchell and Lapata, 2010) computes a linear combination of two input vectors $\boldsymbol{u}$, $\boldsymbol{v} \in \mathbb{R}^d$ with weights w_1, $w_2 \in \mathbb{R}$. This model works surprisingly well in practice despite its simplicity. The *Fulladd* model (Guevara, 2010; Zanzotto et al., 2010) extends the *Add* model, applying a linear transformation to inputs with a weight matrix $W \in \mathbb{R}^{d \times 2d}$. This model can not only scale but also rotate input vectors, unlike the *Add* model.

Regarding linear transformation with a matrix W, *Recursive Neural Network (RNN)* model (Socher et al., 2011) achieves a nonlinear transformation through the use of an activation function (e.g., sigmoid function and $tanh$). *Lexfunc* model (Baroni et al., 2012) represents a dependent word u (e.g., adjective) as a matrix A_u and composes a phrase vector with a matrix-vector product $A_u \boldsymbol{v}$. The underlying idea of representing a dependent as a matrix is that a modifier (dependent) changes some properties of a governer and that it is achieved using a matrix transforming a vector of the governer[1].

Extending *RNN*, the *Relfunc* model (Socher et al., 2013a; Socher et al., 2014) incorporates syntactical relations in compositions, which composes phrase vectors with a different weight matrix for a syntactic relation between inputs. Generalizing *Lexfunc* and *RNN*, the *Fulllex* model Socher et al. (2012) defines the meaning of each word as a tuple of a vector and matrix, where a vector represents the meaning of the word itself and a matrix provides a function to other words for compositions. In addition to these models, the *Mult* model and the *Dil* model (Mitchell and Lapata, 2008; Mitchell and Lapata, 2010) have been proposed.

Table 2 presents the benefits and shortcomings of each model. It is easy to train the *Add* model because it has only two parameters. Apparently, the *Add* model has the least expressive power using very few parameters. However, this simple model has been a strong baseline in the literature (Blacoe and Lapata, 2012). Similarly to the *Add* model, *Fulladd* uses a linear composition function; we can find a global optimum for the convex training objective. In contrast, *RNN*, *Relfunc* and *Fulllex* are neural network models using nonlinear activation functions. The nonlinearity enriches the expressive power, but it makes training difficult because the training objectives are not convex.

Regarding the performance of these models aside from *Relfunc* in the same condition, Dinu et al. (2013) concluded that *Lexfunc* performed the best among these models. According to their explanation, *Lexfunc* performs well because it considers linguistic relations between input words (e.g. modification, verb–object relation). However, *Lexfunc* cannot compose vectors recursively because of the different types of input–output representations (vector or matrix).

Table 2: Problems of representative models.

Model	Expre-ssive	Recur-sivity	Train-ing	Non-linearity
Add	NA	✓	✓	NA
Fulladd	NA	✓	✓	NA
RNN	NA	✓	✓	✓
Lexfunc	✓	NA	Depends	NA
Relfunc	✓	✓	✓	✓
Fulllex	✓	✓	NA	✓

In contrast, *RNN*, *Relfunc*, and *Fulllex* can compose vectors recursively. The recursivity is an important property because it enables comparison of a phrase vector (e.g., *football player*) with a word vector (e.g., *footballer*). However, *Fulllex* has an enormous number of parameters, representing each word as a distinct tuple of a vector and a matrix. In *RNN*, on the other hand, all compositions are computed only by a single weight matrix. Consequently, it cannot distinguish different syntax relations in compositions. Located between *RNN* and *Fulllex*, *Relfunc* can compose various types of syntax relations more precisely than *RNN* with fewer parameters than *Fulllex*.

These models have produced excellent results on many tasks such as syntax parsing or grounding between texts and images. However, no report in the literature describes an experiment examining semantic compositions directly under the same conditions. As described in this paper, we explore the best model that can perform semantic compositions well. Our experimentally obtained results show that the *Relfunc* model achieves state-of-the-art performance.

[1]For instance, we can regard *red* in the phrase *red car* as changing the property of *color* of the word *car*.

3 Details of Methods

3.1 Mathematical Expression of Models

The *Add* model in Table 1 composes two input vectors $\boldsymbol{u}$ and $\boldsymbol{v}$ simply with two parameters w_1 and w_2 (and a bias term b):

$$\boldsymbol{p} = f(\boldsymbol{u}, \boldsymbol{v}) = w_1\boldsymbol{u} + w_2\boldsymbol{v} + b\mathbf{1}. \quad (2)$$

Here, $\boldsymbol{u}$, $\boldsymbol{v}$, and $\mathbf{1}$ are d-dimensional column vectors and all elements of $\mathbf{1}$ consist of 1.

Add can only scale whereas *Fulladd* can also rotate because of a weight matrix $W \in \mathbb{R}^{d\times(2d+1)}$:

$$\boldsymbol{p} = f(\boldsymbol{u}, \boldsymbol{v}) = W \begin{bmatrix} \boldsymbol{u} \\ \boldsymbol{v} \\ b \end{bmatrix}. \quad (3)$$

Neural network models such as *RNN* in Table 1 compose a phrase vector $\boldsymbol{p}$ from two input vectors $\boldsymbol{u}$ and $\boldsymbol{v}$ using a function $f : \mathbb{R}^{(2d+1)\times 1} \longrightarrow \mathbb{R}^{d\times 1}$,

$$\boldsymbol{p} = f(\boldsymbol{u}, \boldsymbol{v}) = \sigma\left(W \begin{bmatrix} \boldsymbol{u} \\ \boldsymbol{v} \\ b \end{bmatrix}\right). \quad (4)$$

$\sigma(.)$ is an element-wise sigmoid function that yields a value for each element in the vector. In our work, we use $\tanh$ as a sigmoid function.

Socher et al. (2014) extends this model so that *Relfunc* can compose a vector depending on the relation r between two inputs. Equation 5 uses a composition matrix W_r and a bias term b_r for each relation r,

$$\boldsymbol{p} = f(\boldsymbol{u}, \boldsymbol{v}, r) = \sigma\left(W_r \begin{bmatrix} \boldsymbol{u} \\ \boldsymbol{v} \\ b_r \end{bmatrix}\right). \quad (5)$$

Here, $W_r \in \mathbb{R}^{d\times(2d+1)}$ and $b_r \in \mathbb{R}$ are parameters trained for each relation r. Introducing relation-specific matrices, Equation 5 can compose a phrase vector more precisely than *RNN* given by Equation 4. In this work, we use syntactic dependencies as relations used for compositions. We also introduce two restricted variants of *Relfunc* here.

1. Relation-specific additive model (*Relfunc-add*) has two weight parameters $w_1, w_2 \in \mathbb{R}$ for each relation r:

$$\boldsymbol{p} = \sigma\left(\begin{bmatrix} w_{1,r}I & w_{2,r}I & \begin{matrix} 1 \\ \vdots \\ 1 \end{matrix} \end{bmatrix} \begin{bmatrix} \boldsymbol{u} \\ \boldsymbol{v} \\ b_r \end{bmatrix}\right) \quad (6)$$

2. Relation-specific component-wise additive model (*Relfunc-cadd*) is modeled by diagonal elements for $\boldsymbol{u}$ and $\boldsymbol{v}$:

$$\boldsymbol{p} = \sigma\left(\begin{bmatrix} w_{1,1} & & 0 & w_{2,1} & & 0 & 1 \\ & \ddots & & & \ddots & & \vdots \\ 0 & & w_{1,d} & 0 & & w_{2,d} & 1 \end{bmatrix} \begin{bmatrix} \boldsymbol{u} \\ \boldsymbol{v} \\ b_r \end{bmatrix}\right) \quad (7)$$

These variants are used to verify the effect of non-diagonal elements of matrices W_r in the experiments.

The *Fulllex* model, the most complicated model among those in Table 1, first multiplies each input vector by the other matrix, i.e., $\boldsymbol{u}$ is multiplied by $A_v \in \mathbb{R}^{d\times d}$ and $\boldsymbol{v}$ multiplied by $A_u \in \mathbb{R}^{d\times d}$. Subsequently, *Fulllex* composes the phrase vector in the same way for *RNN* and *Relfunc*,

$$\boldsymbol{p} = f(\boldsymbol{u}, \boldsymbol{v}) = \sigma\left(W \begin{bmatrix} A_v\boldsymbol{u} \\ A_u\boldsymbol{v} \\ b \end{bmatrix}\right). \quad (8)$$

3.2 Training

We train model-specific parameters θ (e.g., for *Add*, $\theta = \langle w_1, w_2, b\rangle$, and for *Relfunc*, $\theta = \langle W_r, b_r | r\rangle$) in a supervised setting where a gold phrase vector $\boldsymbol{q}$ is given for two input vectors of constituents $\boldsymbol{u}$ and $\boldsymbol{v}$. A training set consists of T training instances $\{((\boldsymbol{u}_t, \boldsymbol{v}_t), \boldsymbol{q}_t)\}_{t=1}^{T}$. The goal of training is to find optimal parameters θ such that the parameters can compose phrase vectors of good quality. We formalize this goal as a minimization problem of the objective function defined by the square errors between composed vectors and gold vectors,

$$J(\theta) = \frac{1}{T}\sum_{t=1}^{T}\frac{1}{2}\|\boldsymbol{p}_t - \boldsymbol{q}_t\|_2^2 + \lambda\|\theta\|_1. \quad (9)$$

Here, the vector $\boldsymbol{p}_t$ presents a phrase vector composed by Equations 2 - 8 from word vectors $(\boldsymbol{u}_t, \boldsymbol{v}_t)$. Vector $\boldsymbol{q}_t$ denotes a gold phrase vector. Therefore, the first term of Equation 9 represents a least-squares problem (York, 1966) defined for vectors $\boldsymbol{p}_t$ and $\boldsymbol{q}_t$. The second term of Equation 9 presents an L_1-regularization term with a hyper-parameter λ. We employ L_1-regularization instead of L_2-regularization to make the composition model compact.

We use stochastic gradient descent and backpropagation (Rumelhart et al., 1988) to minimize the objective.

In general, a weight matrix W is updated by the following equation,

$$W' = W - \alpha \frac{\partial J(\theta)}{\partial W}, \quad (10)$$

where α is a learning rate.

Using stochastic gradient descent, we update a weight matrix W every time one training instance is processed. The gradient of the objective is

$$\frac{\partial J(\theta)}{\partial W} = \frac{\partial J(\theta)}{\partial \boldsymbol{p}_t}\frac{\partial \boldsymbol{p}_t}{\partial W} = \boldsymbol{e}_t \begin{bmatrix} \boldsymbol{u}_t \\ \boldsymbol{v}_t \\ b \end{bmatrix}^T + \lambda \frac{\partial}{\partial W}\|\theta\|_1. \quad (11)$$

Here, $\boldsymbol{e}_t$ represents a d-dimensional column vector with k-th element of

$$e_{t,k} = (p_{t,k} - q_{t,k})(1 - p_{t,k}^2). \quad (12)$$

We used $\frac{d}{dx}\tanh(x) = 1 - \tanh(x)^2$ to derive this equation.

The second term of Equation 11 is not differentiable. Following the work of Langford et al. (2008) and Tsuruoka et al. (2009), we first update the weight matrix W without consideration of the L_1 penalty. Then, we use Equation 13 to apply the L_1 regularization,

$$w'_{ij} = \begin{cases} \max(0, w_{ij} - \alpha\lambda) & \text{if } w_{ij} > 0 \\ \min(0, w_{ij} + \alpha\lambda) & \text{if } w_{ij} < 0 \\ 0 & \text{otherwise} \end{cases}, \quad (13)$$

where w_{ij} denotes the (i, j) element of W.

A neural network model such as *RNN*, *Relfunc*, and *Fulllex* is nonlinear, which means that the naive training procedure might be trapped with a local minimum. To prevent local minima, we employ some technical methods. We update the learning rate α for every iteration epoch l using the temperature of the simulated annealing algorithm (Kirkpatrick et al., 1983).

In addition, to date, the learning rate α is constant to all matrices W_r in *Relfunc*. However, the distribution of relations in the training data is highly skewed. Because the number of updates for a relation is directly proportional to the number of instances of the relation in the dataset, some matrixes are updated frequently, and some are rarely updated. Therefore, we use the diagonal variant of AdaGrad (Duchi et al., 2011; Socher et al., 2013a). This enables the learning rate to vary each matrix W_r.

4 Experiment

In this section, we explain the method for constructing vectors for words and phrases for the supervision data, followed by an explanation of some details of the training procedure. We then report experimentally obtained results.

4.1 Obtaining vectors for words and phrases as supervision data

Following the work of Dinu et al. (2013), we constructed word and phrase vectors as follows. We used a concatenation of three large corpora: PukWaC[2] (Baroni et al., 2009) (2 billion tokens), WaCkypedia_EN(Wikipedia 2009 dump) (Baroni et al., 2009) (about 800 million tokens), and ClueWeb09[3] (5 billion pages in English). The distribution of PukWaC and WaCkypedia_EN includes parse results from TreeTagger and MaltParser. We used Stanford CoreNLP[4] to parse ClueWeb09. Counting frequencies of occurrences of lemmas of content words (nouns, adjectives, verbs, and adverbs), we identified the top 10,000 most frequent words; we represent the set of these lemmas (except adverbs) as vocabulary V.

We then find the frequencies of phrases consisting only of two words in V (adjective–noun, noun–noun, verb–noun). For words in V and phrases appearing more than 1,000 times in the corpora, we build a co-occurrence matrix: each row is a vector of a target word or phrase; an element in a row represents the frequency of co-occurrences of the target word/phrase with a context word (content lemma). We regard content lemmas appearing in the same sentence within a distance of 50 words from a target word as contexts. Then we transform each element of the co-occurrence matrix into Pointwise Mutual

[2] http://wacky.sslmit.unibo.it/

[3] http://lemurproject.org/clueweb09/

[4] http://nlp.stanford.edu/software/corenlp.shtml

Information (PMI) (Evert, 2005). Finally, we compress the matrix into d dimension using Principal Component Analysis (PCA) (Roweis, 1998) with EM algorithm[5]. In this way, we obtained 10,000 word vectors and 17,433 phrase vectors.

4.2 Gold-standard data

We conducted a human-correlation experiment using the dataset[6] created in Mitchell and Lapata (2010). Each instance in the dataset is a triplet ⟨phrase1, phrase2, similarity⟩: a similarity is a semantic similarity between the phrases annotated by humans, with a value ranging from 1 (least similar) to 7 (most similar). We designate this as human-similarity. For example, the similarity between *vast amount* and *large quantity* is 7 (most similar) whereas the similarity between *hear word* and *remember name* is 1 (least similar).

For each POS pair (adjective–noun, noun–noun, verb–noun), the dataset includes 108 instances annotated by 18 human subjects (1,944 in total). We measure Spearman's ρ between the human similarity and the cosine similarity between each input pair of two phrase vectors composed using a model. Because one POS pair can include dependency relations of several types , *Relfunc* composes phrase vectors in a POS pair with several matrices. A high correlation indicates that the model can compose a phrase vector that reflects its semantic meaning.

4.3 Training

Excluding the phrases in the evaluation dataset, our training set includes 16,845 phrase types for building a training set. For each phrase p type, we include $0.001 \times \mathrm{freq}(p)$ duplicates in the training data, where $\mathrm{freq}(p)$ is the frequency of occurrences of the phrase p in the corpora. In this way, we obtained a training set consisting of $T = 175,899$ instances of phrases.

We set other hyper-parameters as described below:

- Dimension $d \in \{50, 100, 200\}$.
- Learning rate $\alpha = 1/1.1^{l-1}$. l is an epoch count.
- L_1-regularization coefficient $\lambda \in \{10^{-3}, 10^{-4}, 10^{-5}, 10^{-6}\}$.
- Convergence condition: $|J^{l-1} - J^{l}| < 10^{-6}$
- Maximum number of epochs: 100

Because models are sensitive to d and λ, we find d and λ with the highest performance with respect to each model. We observed that all models converged in 50 to 100 epochs. We prepared 31 weight matrices W_r corresponding to all types of dependency relations. A weight matrix and a weight of a bias term are initialized as ($\mathcal{N}(\mu, \sigma^2)$ denotes a normal distribution with mean μ and variance σ^2),

$$\begin{aligned} W &= 0.01[\boldsymbol{I}_{d\times d}, \boldsymbol{I}_{d\times d}, \mathbf{0}_{d\times 1}] \\ &\quad + \mathcal{N}(\mathbf{0}_{(2d+1)\times 1}, 0.001\boldsymbol{I}_{(2d+1)\times d}), \\ b &= \mathcal{N}(0.0, 0.001). \end{aligned} \tag{14}$$

We use a server running on four processors (12-core, 2.2 GHz, AMD Opteron 6174) with 256 GB main memory. Using 10 threads, approximately 7 hours were needed to train a model[7]. We use the idea of Iterative Parameter Mixture (McDonald et al., 2010) to parallelize the training process. Each thread receives a subset of the training data, and estimates parameters individually on the subset. After all threads finish an epoch for the subsets, we take the average of the parameters from all threads, and distribute it to the threads for the next epoch.

We trained models in Table 1 with the same experimental setting (the same objective, the same training set, and the same hyper-parameters) except for *Lexfunc*. This enables performance comparisons between different models. The reason for the absence of *Lexfunc* is that it requires a vector and a matrix for composition of a phrase. Two constituents for a phrase are given as vectors in our experiments. Therefore, we cannot conduct an experiment with *Lexfunc* on the same setting.

4.4 Results

Table 3 reports the correlation of similarity values with the gold-standard data. *Upper-bound* presents the mean of inter-subject correlations (between a subject and the others). *Corpus* obtains a phrase

[5] To handle a large amount of data, we implemented an online variant of PCA.

[6] http://homepages.inf.ed.ac.uk/s0453356/share

[7] We used Python modules numpy and multiprocessing for implementation of the training algorithm.

Table 3: Spearman's ρ of each POS pair, where * denotes statistical significance ($p < 0.01$) between *Relfunc* and the most competitive model among the other models: *Add-smp*.

	JJ-NN	**NN-NN**	**VB-NN**
Corpus	0.380	0.449	0.215
Add-smp	0.457	0.460	0.406
Add	0.335	0.304	0.338
Fulladd	0.359	0.359	0.366
RNN	0.364	0.360	0.367
Relfunc-add	0.440	0.455	0.388
Relfunc-cadd	0.419	0.445	0.413
Relfunc	**0.469***	**0.481***	**0.430***
Fulllex	0.322	0.160	0.222
Upper-bound	0.539	0.490	0.505

vector simply from the co-occurrence statistics in the corpora (similarly to the supervision instances). This setting corresponds to the distributional hypothesis applied to phrases without considering semantic composition. The reason for the low performance of this approach is that some phrase vectors are unavailable[8] or unreliable in the corpora because of the data sparseness problem.

Add-smp is the model in Table 1 with the weight parameter fixed: $w_1 = w_2 = 1.0$. This approach is equivalent to the simple additive baseline that adds two word vectors without training. As Table 3 shows, *Add-smp* model is a strong competitive model, beating *RNN* and *Fulladd* models. However, the *Relfunc* model outperformed all the tested models including *Add-smp* in all relations. The differences between *Relfunc* and *Add-smp* are significant ($p < 0.01$) in all relations.

Furthermore, *Relfunc* outperforms *Relfunc-add* and *Relfunc-cadd*, which are the variants of *Relfunc*. This result underscores the importance of non-diagonal elements of weight matrices.

Although we cannot compare these results directly with those reported from other studies (Dinu et al., 2013; Blacoe and Lapata, 2012) because of the different computations of Spearman's ρ[9], our results are comparable. These results demonstrate the effectiveness of using a different weight matrix for each relation of compositions.

[8]When a phrase vector is not available from the corpus, we define the similarity as zero.

[9]Reports of those studies did not describe explicitly how they computed the correlation coefficient.

Figure 1: Weight matrix of *RNN*.

4.5 What the Learned Weight Matrices Look Like

To explore why *Relfunc* outperforms *RNN*, we visualize the weight matrices learned by the two models in Figures 1 and 2. In the figures, the left side (split by the center) presents the weights for the left word. The right side presents weights for the right word. The smaller a weight value in the matrix is, the dimmer the element is visualized; the larger a weight value is, and the brighter the element is visualized.

Figure 1 visualizes the weight matrix trained by *RNN*. The diagonal elements in the left and right sides tend to be larger than the non-diagonal elements. This fact indicates that the i-th elements of input word vectors most strongly influence the i-th element of a phrase vector. The diagonal elements of the right side are brighter than those of the left side, which implies that *RNN* treats a right word as more important than a left word in semantic compositions. That implication is reasonable because the right word is usually the head of the phrase and is therefore more important. However, such is not always the case. For example, in subject–predicate constructions, the subject should be regarded as being as important as the predicate. The *RNN* model cannot manage such cases.

In contrast, *Relfunc* learns the relative importance of phrase components depending on the types of syntactic constructions. Figure 2 demonstrates how

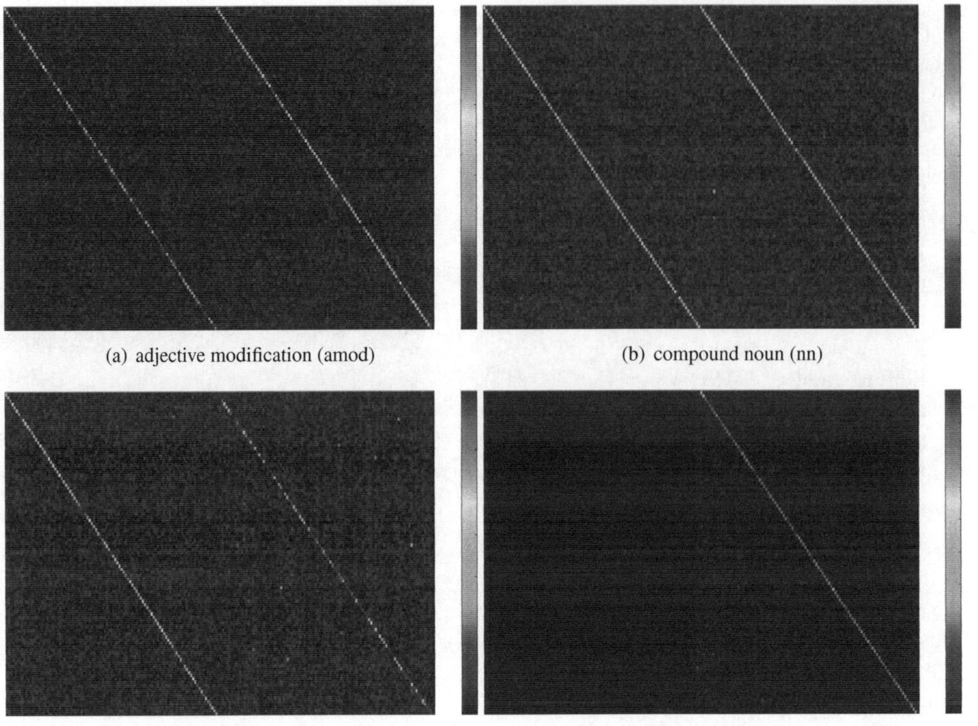

(a) adjective modification (amod) (b) compound noun (nn)

(c) subject-predicate (nsubj) (d) determiner-noun (det)

Figure 2: Weight matrices of *Relfunc*.

the weight matrices are learned differently depending on syntactic dependency relations. In the matrix for adjective modification, for example, the elements of the right diagonal tend to be larger than those of the left, which reflects a tendency by which a modified word (right word) is more important than a modifier (left word); yet, the left diagonal is assigned reasonably large weight compared with that of the *RNN* weight matrix. Different types of constructions require different weight biases. Subject–predicate constructions, for example, assign more weight on the left diagonal.

Next we examine the effects of this difference using examples. Table 4 presents examples of similarity scores assigned by human judgment (averaged human-similarity scores) and those given by three models: *Relfunc*, *Add-smp*, and *RNN*. For the first two examples, the three models estimate the similarity almost equally well. For the third example, *important part* and *significant role*, *RNN* fails to express that they are quite similar. This might be true because *RNN* assigns too much weight to head words, *part* and *role*, and loses the information given by their modifiers.

The fourth examples, *previous day* and *long period*, show the importance of learning the proper balance of weights between the left and right words. *Add-smp* overestimates the similarity between the two phrases whereas *Relfunc* and *RNN* appropriately and specifically examines the difference between the head words, *day* and *period*.

We have specifically addressed only the weights of the diagonal elements. However, it should also be noted that the non-diagonal elements play non-negligible roles as demonstrated by the performance gain between *Relfunc* and *Relfunc-cadd* (see Table 3). For further exploration of the model's behavior, more sophisticated methods of analyzing the weight matrices and word vectors must be used. That goal is left as a subject of future work.

Table 4: Examples of human-similarity and co-similarity of three models.

instance	GOLD	Relfunc	Add-smp	RNN
certain circumstance particular case	6.1	0.76	0.74	0.64
national government cold air	1.0	-0.06	-0.07	-0.02
important part significant role	6.3	0.62	0.64	0.31
previous day long period	1.8	0.36	0.52	0.32

5 Conclusion and Future Work

As presented in this paper, we described the properties of the previous methods: the expressive power, the recursivity, and the difficulty of training. To investigate the impact on these properties, we reimplemented these models and conducted a human-correlation experiment, which demonstrated the state-of-the-art performance of *Relfunc* and the usefulness of the syntactic information in composition. Moreover, learned weight matrices suggest that compositions require different calculations based on their linguistic properties. In future studies, we will extend this work to examine the goodness of models when they compose phrases consisting of three or more words. We will address this problem for tasks of paraphrase detection or entailment recognition.

Acknowledgments

This study was partly supported by Japan Society for the Promotion of Science (JSPS) KAKENHI Grant No. 23240018 and Japan Science and Technology Agency (JST).

References

Marco Baroni, Silvia Bernardini, Adriano Ferraresi, and Eros Zanchetta. 2009. The wacky wide web: a collection of very large linguistically processed web-crawled corpora. *Language Resources and Evaluation*, 43(3):209–226.

Marco Baroni, Raffaella Bernardi, Ngoc-Quynh Do, and Chung-chieh Shan. 2012. Entailment above the word level in distributional semantics. In *Proceedings of the 13th Conference of the European Chapter of the Association for Computational Linguistics (EACL '12)*, pages 23–32.

Yoshua Bengio, Réjean Ducharme, Pascal Vincent, and Christian Janvin. 2003. A neural probabilistic language model. *Journal of Machine Learning Research*, 3:1137–1155.

William Blacoe and Mirella Lapata. 2012. A comparison of vector-based representations for semantic composition. In *Proceedings of the 2012 Joint Conference on Empirical Methods in Natural Language Processing and Computational Natural Language Learning (EMNLP-CoNLL '12')*, pages 546–556.

John A. Bullinaria and Joseph P. Levy. 2007. Extracting semantic representations from word co-occurrence statistics: A computational study. *Behavior Research Methods*, 39(3):510–526.

Ronan Collobert and Jason Weston. 2008. A unified architecture for Natural Language Processing: Deep neural networks with multitask learning. In *Proceedings of the 25th International Conference on Machine Learning (ICML '08)*, pages 160–167.

Georgiana Dinu, Nghia The Pham, and Marco Baroni. 2013. General estimation and evaluation of compositional distributional semantics models. In *Proceedings of the ACL 2013 Workshop on Continuous Vector Space Models and their Compositionality (CVSC 2013)*, pages 50–58.

John Duchi, Elad Hazan, and Yoram Singer. 2011. Adaptive subgradient methods for online learning and stochastic optimization. *J. Mach. Learn. Res.*, 12:2121–2159, July.

Katrin Erk and Sebastian Padó. 2008. A structured vector space model for word meaning in context. In *Proceedings of the 2008 Conference on Empirical Methods in Natural Language Processing (EMNLP 2008)*, pages 897–906.

Stefan Evert. 2005. *The statistics of word cooccurrences: word pairs and collocations*. Ph.D. thesis, Universitt Stuttgart.

John R. Firth. 1957. *Papers in Linguistics 1934-51*. Oxford University Press.

Gottlob Frege. 1892. On sense and reference. In *Ludlow (1997)*, pages 563–584.

Emiliano Guevara. 2010. A regression model of adjective-noun compositionality in distributional semantics. In *Proceedings of the 2010 Workshop on GEometrical Models of Natural Language Semantics (GEMS '10)*, pages 33–37.

S. Kirkpatrick, C. D. Gelatt, and M. P. Vecchi. 1983. Optimization by simulated annealing. *Science*, 220(4598):671–680.

John Langford, Lihong Li, and Tong Zhang. 2008. Sparse online learning via truncated gradient. *CoRR*, abs/0806.4686.

Ryan McDonald, Keith Hall, and Gideon Mann. 2010. Distributed training strategies for the structured perceptron. In *Human Language Technologies: The 2010 Annual Conference of the North American Chapter of the Association for Computational Linguistics*, pages 456–464.

Tomas Mikolov, Ilya Sutskever, Kai Chen, Greg S Corrado, and Jeff Dean. 2013. Distributed representations of words and phrases and their compositionality. In *Advances in Neural Information Processing Systems 26 (NIPS 2013)*, pages 3111–3119.

Jeff Mitchell and Mirella Lapata. 2008. Vector-based models of semantic composition. In *Proceedings of ACL-08: HLT*, pages 236–244.

Jeff Mitchell and Mirella Lapata. 2010. Composition in distributional models of semantics. *Cognitive Science*, 34(8):1388–1429.

Andriy Mnih and Koray Kavukcuoglu. 2013. Learning word embeddings efficiently with noise-contrastive estimation. In *Advances in Neural Information Processing Systems 26 (NIPS 2013)*, pages 2265–2273.

Sam Roweis. 1998. EM algorithms for PCA and SPCA. In *Neural Information Systems 10 (NIPS'97)*, pages 626–632.

David E. Rumelhart, Geoffrey E. Hinton, and Ronald J. Williams. 1988. Neurocomputing: Foundations of research. chapter Learning Representations by Backpropagating Errors, pages 696–699. MIT Press, Cambridge, MA, USA.

Richard Socher, Cliff C. Lin, Andrew Y. Ng, and Christopher D. Manning. 2011. Parsing Natural Scenes and Natural Language with Recursive Neural Networks. In *Proceedings of the 26th International Conference on Machine Learning (ICML)*.

Richard Socher, Brody Huval, Christopher D. Manning, and Andrew Y. Ng. 2012. Semantic compositionality through recursive matrix-vector spaces. In *Proceedings of the 2012 Joint Conference on Empirical Methods in Natural Language Processing and Computational Natural Language Learning*, pages 1201–1211.

Richard Socher, John Bauer, Christopher D. Manning, and Andrew Y. Ng. 2013a. Parsing With Compositional Vector Grammars. In *ACL*.

Richard Socher, Danqi Chen, Christopher D. Manning, and Andrew Ng. 2013b. Reasoning with neural tensor networks for knowledge base completion. In *Advances in Neural Information Processing Systems 26*, pages 926–934.

Richard Socher, Andrej Karpathy, Quoc V. Le, Christopher D. Manning, and Andrew Y. Ng. 2014. Grounded compositional semantics for finding and describing images with sentences. *TACL*, 2:207–218.

Yoshimasa Tsuruoka, Jun'ichi Tsujii, and Sophia Ananiadou. 2009. Stochastic gradient descent training for l1-regularized log-linear models with cumulative penalty. In *Proceedings of the Joint Conference of the 47th Annual Meeting of the ACL and the 4th International Joint Conference on Natural Language Processing of the AFNLP: Volume 1*, ACL '09, pages 477–485. Association for Computational Linguistics.

Peter D. Turney and Patrick Pantel. 2010. From frequency to meaning: Vector space models of semantics. *Journal of Artificial Intelligence Research*, 37(1):141–188.

Derek York. 1966. Least-squares fitting of a straight line. *Canadian Journal of Physics*, 44(5):1079–1086.

Fabio Massimo Zanzotto, Ioannis Korkontzelos, Francesca Fallucchi, and Suresh Manandhar. 2010. Estimating linear models for compositional distributional semantics. In *Proceedings of the 23rd International Conference on Computational Linguistics (Coling 2010)*, pages 1263–1271.

Semantic Frame-based Statistical Approach for Topic Detection

Yung-Chun Chang[1,2] Yu-Lun Hsieh[2,3] Cen-Chieh Chen[2,3]
Chad Liu[2] Chun-Hung Lu[4] Wen-Lian Hsu[2]
[1]Department of Information Management, National Taiwan University, Taiwan
[2]Institute of Information Science, Academia Sinica, Taiwan
[3]Department of Computer Science, National Chengchi University, Taiwan
[4]Innovative Digitech-Enabled Applications & Services Institute, III, Taiwan
{changyc,morphe,can,hsu}@iis.sinica.edu.tw, [4]enricoghlu@iii.org.tw

Abstract

We propose a statistical frame-based approach (FBA) for natural language processing, and demonstrate its advantage over traditional machine learning methods by using topic detection as a case study. FBA perceives and identifies semantic knowledge in a more general manner by collecting important linguistic patterns within documents through a unique flexible matching scheme that allows word insertion, deletion and substitution (IDS) to capture linguistic structures within the text. In addition, FBA can also overcome major issues of the rule-based approach by reducing human effort through its highly automated pattern generation and summarization. Using Yahoo! Chinese news corpus containing about 140,000 news articles, we provide a comprehensive performance evaluation that demonstrates the effectiveness of FBA in detecting the topic of a document by exploiting the semantic association and the context within the text. Moreover, it outperforms common topic models like Naïve Bayes, Vector Space Model, and LDA-SVM.

1 Introduction

Due to recent technological advances, we are overwhelmed by the sheer number of documents. While keyword search systems nowadays can efficiently retrieve documents, users still have difficulty assimilating knowledge of interest from them. To promote research on this subject, the Defense Advanced Research Projects Agency (DARPA) initiated the Topic Detection and Tracking (TDT) project, with a goal of automatically detecting topics and tracking related documents from document streams such as online news feeds. In essence, a topic is associated with specific times, places, and persons (Nallapati et al., 2004). Thus, detecting the topic of a document can help readers construct the background of the topic and facilitate document comprehension, which is an active research area in information retrieval (IR).

Linguistic information provides useful features to many natural language processing (NLP) tasks, including topic detection (Nallapati, 2003). Such information is usually represented as rules or templates. The main advantages of the rule-based approach are its high precision as well as the capability of knowledge accumulation. When confronting a new domain, they can be adapted by adding rules that exploit the missing knowledge. However, only a limited number of cases can be captured by a single rule, and increasing the number of rules could create undesired conflicts. Thus, the inflexibility of rule-based systems has put their competence for NLP tasks in doubt.

On the other hand, there are several machine learning-based approaches. For instance, Nallapati et al. (2004) attempted to find characteristics of topics by clustering keywords using statistical similarity. The clusters are then connected chronologically to form a time-line of the topic. Furthermore, many previous methods treated topic detection as a supervised classification problem (Blei et al., 2003; Zhang and Wang, 2010). These approaches can achieve substantial performance without much human involvement. However, to manifest topic as-

Copyright 2014 by Yung-Chun Chang, Yu-Lun Hsieh, Cen-Chieh Chen,
Chad Liu, Chun-Hung Lu, and Wen-Lian Hsu
28th Pacific Asia Conference on Language, Information and Computation pages 75–84

sociated features, one often needs to annotate the features in documents, which is rarely done in most machine learning models (Scott and Matwin, 1999). Those models have encountered bottlenecks due to knowledge shortage, data sparseness problem, and inability to make generalizations. Once the domain is changed, the models need to be re-trained to obtain satisfactory results. Besides, fine-grained linguistic knowledge that is crucial in human understanding cannot be easily modeled, resulting in less desirable performance. One can easily find two sentences that are literally different but convey similar semantic knowledge, which could confuse most machine learning models. On the other hand, the main shortcoming of template-based or knowledge-based methods is the need of human effort to craft precise templates or rules.

In light of this, we propose a flexible frame-based approach (FBA), and use topic detection as a case study to demonstrate its advantages. FBA is a highly automated process that integrates similar knowledge and reduces the total number of patterns through pattern summarization. Furthermore, a matching mechanism allowing insertion, deletion, and substitution (IDS) of words and phrases is employed together with a statistical scoring mechanism. To create linguistic patterns with higher level of generality, we adopt the dominating set algorithm to reduce 350,000 patterns to a total of 500. Dominating set has been used extensively in network routing researches, e.g., Das and Bharghavan (1997), Du et al. (2013), and adopted in NLP related tasks such as text summarization (Shen and Li, 2010).

In the training phase, we consider keywords, context, and semantic associations to automatically generate frames. Thus, the obtained frames can be acknowledged as the essential knowledge for each topic that is comprehensible for humans. Results demonstrated that our method is more effective than the following approaches: the word vector model-based method (Li et al., 2010) and the latent Dirichlet allocation (LDA) method (Blei et al., 2003), a Bayesian networks-based topic model widely used to identify topics.

The structure of this paper is as follows. We discuss some of the previous work that apply statistical NLP methods to the topic detection problem in Section 2. Section 3 describes in detail the architecture and components of our system. Section 4 presents the performance comparison of various systems, and . Finally, we conclude our work in Section 5.

2 Related Work

Much work have been done on topic detection, or, a more general task like automatic text categorization. Most of them are concerned with the assignment of texts into a set of given categories, and rely on some measures of the importance of keywords. The weights of the features in these models are usually computed with the traditional methods such as *tf*idf* weighing, conditional probability, and generation probability. For instance, Bun and Ishizuka (2002) present the *TF*PDF* algorithm which extends the well-known VSM to avoid the collapse of important terms when they appear in many text documents. Indeed, the IDF component decreases the frequency value for a keyword when it is frequently used. Considering different newswire sources or channels, the weight of a term from a single channel is linearly proportional to the term's frequency within it, while also being exponentially proportional to the ratio of documents that contain the term in the channel itself.

Several researches have adopted machine learning-based approaches. Some formulate this task as a supervised classification problem (Blei et al., 2003; Zhang and Wang, 2010), in which a topic detection model is used to assign (i.e. classify) a topic to a document using a manually tagged training corpus. Nallapati et al. (2004) attempted to uncover characteristics of topics by clustering keywords using a statistical similarity measure into groups, each of which represents a topic. Wu et al. (2010) uses the tolerance rough set model to enrich the set of feature words into an approximated latent semantic space from which they extract hot topics by a complete-link clustering. The advantage of these methods is that they require little human involvement to acquire sizable outcome. However, they are faced with problems like data sparseness, knowledge accumulation, and the incapability to make generalizations. As we observed in the experiments, less than 1% of the keywords and semantic tags dominate the majority of the content. Thus, generalization of the surface words into a more abstract level, like the one in our approach, can substantially decrease the sparseness. Moreover, the models of such approaches need to be re-trained or re-tuned to obtain satisfactory results when applying to a different domain. Such problem can be easily tackled in our approach by including more knowledge in the knowledge base. Besides, a more comprehensive linguistic knowledge can also be encoded and utilized in the proposed system. The hierarchical nature of our semantic features is necessary for a deeper understanding of the natural language.

One of the resources that is related to the organization of human knowledge is ontology. It is the conceptualization of a domain into a human understandable and machine-readable format consisting of entities, attributes, relationships, and axioms (Tho et al., 2006). It can also be used repeatedly, making it a very powerful method for representing domain knowledge. Ontology related applications have been involved in many research fields. For instance, Alani et al. (2003) proposed the Artequakt that attempts to identify entity relationships using ontology relation declarations and lexical information to automatically extract knowledge about artists from the Web. García-Sánchez et al. (2006) proposed an ontology-based recruitment system to provide intelligent matching between employer advertisements and the curriculum vitae of the candidates. Moreover, Lee et al. (2009) used ontology to construct the knowledge of Tainan City travel and further integrated fuzzy inference with ant colony optimization to recommend a personalized travel route that effectively meets the tourist's requirements to enjoy Tainan City. Some document detection methods made use of ontology and utilized the structured information in Wikipedia to enhance their performance (Grineva et al., 2009). Other ontologies like the WordNet may be included in the proposed system to further extend the scope of its knowledge.

Our method differs from existing approaches in a number of aspects. First, the FBA mimics the perceptual behavior of humans in understanding. Second, the generated semantic frames can be represented as the domain knowledge required for detecting topics. In addition, we further consider the surrounding context and semantic associations to efficiently recognize topics. Finally, our research differs from other Chinese researches that rely on word segmentation for preprocessing by utilizing ontology for semantic class labeling.

3 System Architecture

We define the topic detection task as the following. Let $W = \{w_1, w_2, \cdots, w_m\}$ be a set of words, $D = \{d_1, d_2, \cdots, d_k\}$ be a set of documents, and $T = \{t_1, t_2, \cdots, t_n\}$ be a set of topics . Each document d is a set of words such that $d \subseteq W$. Our goal is to decide the most appropriate topic t_i for a document d_j, although one or multiple topics can be associated with each document. Our system mainly consists of three components, Semantic Class Labeling (SCL), Semantic Frame Generation (SFG), and Semantic Frame Matching (SFM), as shown in Figure 1. The SCL first uses prior knowledge of each topic to mark the semantic classes of words in the corpus. Then the SFG generates frames for each topic. These frames are stored in the topic-dependent knowledge base to provide domain-specific knowledge for our topic detection. During detection, an article is first labeled by the SCL as well. Then, the SFM applies an alignment-based algorithm which utilizes our knowledge base to calculate the similarity between each topic and the article to determine the main topic of this article. Details of these components will be explained in the following sections.

3.1 Semantic Class Labeling, SCL

First of all, the documents undergo the semantic class labeling process. Most Chinese topic detection researches rely on the error-prone word segmentation process. By contrast, our system labels words with their semantic classes, enabling us to extract representative semantic features. We adopt a novel labeling approach that utilizes various knowledge sources like dictionaries and Wikipedia. Since keywords within a topic are often considered as important information, we used the log likelihood ratio (LLR) (Manning and Schütze, 1999), an effective feature selection method, to learn a set of topic-specific keywords. Given a training dataset, LLR employs Equation (1) to calculate the likelihood of the assumption that the occurrence of a word w in topic T is not random. In (1), T denotes the set of documents of the topic in the training dataset;

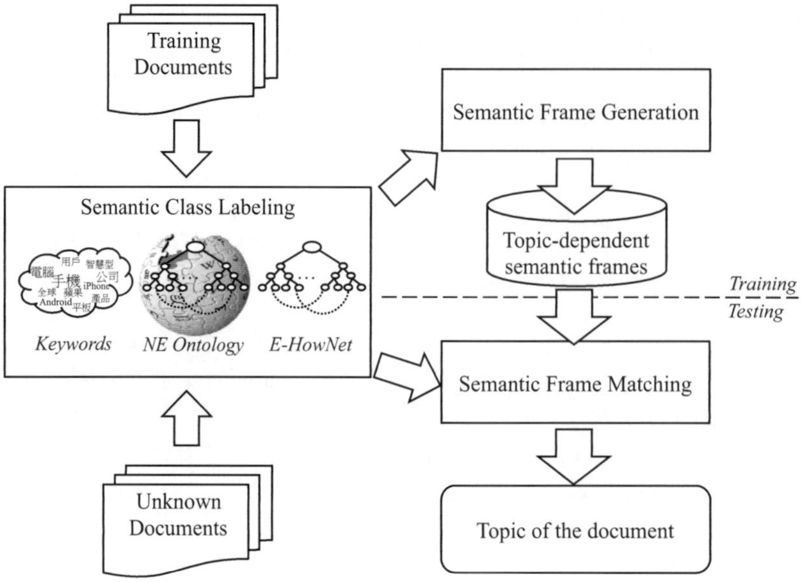

Figure 1: Architecture of our semantic frame-based topic detection system

$$-2log\left(\frac{p(w)^{N(w\wedge T)}(1-p(w))^{N(T)-N(w\wedge T)}p(w)^{N(w\wedge\neg T)}(1-p(w))^{N(\neg T)-N(w\wedge\neg T)}}{p(w|T)^{N(w\wedge T)}(1-p(w|T))^{N(T)-N(w\wedge T)}p(w|\neg T)^{N(w\wedge\neg T)}(1-p(w|\neg T))^{N(\neg T)-N(w\wedge\neg T)}}\right) \quad (1)$$

$N(T)$ and $N(\neg T)$ are the numbers of on-topic and off-topic documents, respectively; and $N(w \wedge T)$ is the number of document on-topic having w. The probabilities $p(w)$, $p(w|T)$, and $p(w| \wedge T)$ are estimated using maximum likelihood estimation. A word with a large LLR value is closely associated with the topic. We rank the words in the training dataset based on their LLR values and select the top 1,000 to compile a topic keyword list.

Recognizing named entities from text can facilitate document comprehension and improve the performance of identifying topics (Bashaddadh and Mohd, 2011). Therefore, we construct the Named Entity Ontology semi-automatically by using Wikipedia for semantic class labeling. Wikipedia category tags are used to label NEs recognized by the Stanford NER tools. We select the category tag to which the most *topic paths* are associated, and use them to represent the main semantic label of NEs in documents. Topic paths can be considered as the traversal from general categories to more specific ones. Thus, more topic paths may indicate that this category is more general. For example, Wikipedia has a page titled "勒布朗-詹姆斯(LeBron James)", and within this page, there are a number of category tags such as "邁阿密熱火隊球員(Miami Heat players)" and "美國籃球運動員(American basketball players)". For these two category tags, there are five and nine topic paths, respectively. Suppose "美國籃球運動員(American basketball players)" is the category with the most topic paths, our system will label "勒布朗-詹姆斯(LeBron James)" with the tag "[美國籃球運動員(American basketball players)]". In this way, we can transform plain NEs to a more general class, and increase the coverage of each label. In addition, we further integrated E-HowNet (Chen et al., 2005) to capture even richer semantic context. It is an extension of the HowNet (Dong et al., 2010) with the purpose of creating a structured representation of knowledge and semantics. It connects approximately 90 thousand words of the CKIP Chinese Lexical Knowledge Base and HowNet, and included extra frequent words that are specific to Traditional Chinese. It also contains a different formulation of each word to bet-

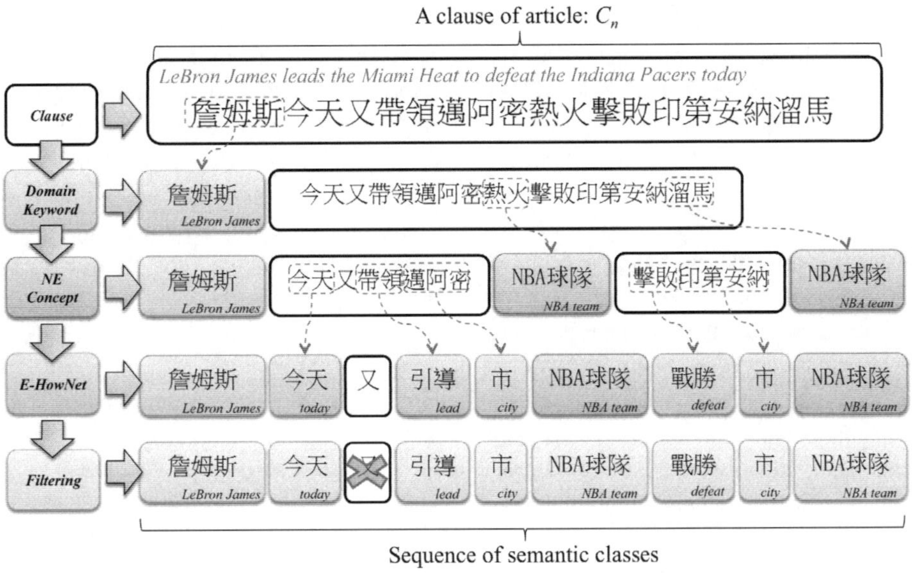

Figure 2: Semantic class labeling process

ter fit its semantic representation, as well as distinct definition of function and content words. A total of four basic semantic classes are applied, namely, object, act, attribute, and value. Furthermore, compared to the HowNet, EHowNet possesses a layered definition scheme and complex relationship formulation, and uses simpler concepts to replace *sememes* as the basic element when defining a more complex concept or relationship. To illustrate the content of the E-HowNet, let's take "手術 (Operation)" for example. It is defined as the following:

Simple Definition:
{affairs|事務: CoEvent = {開刀|HaveOperation}}
Expanded Definition:
{affairs|事務: CoEvent = {split|破開: purpose = {doctor|醫治}}}

We can see that the definitions in E-HowNet enable us to combine or dissect the meaning of words by using its semantic components. Therefore, we use it to label the remaining texts with their sense labels after all the NEs have been tagged.

To illustrate the process of SCL, consider the sentence C_n = "詹姆斯今天又帶領邁阿密熱火擊敗印第安納溜馬 (LeBron James leads the Miami Heat to defeat the Indiana Pacers again today)", as shown in Figure 2. First, "詹姆斯 (LeBron James)" is found in the keyword dictionary and tagged. Then, NEs like "熱火 (Heat)", "溜馬 (Pacers)" are found in NE ontology and tagged as "[NBA球隊 (NBA teams)]". Finally, other terms like "邁阿密 (Miami)", "今天 (today)", and "擊敗 (defeat)" are labeled with their corresponding E-HowNet senses. Evidently, the SCL can not only prevent errors caused by Chinese word segmentation, but also group the synonyms together. This enables us to generate distinctive and prominent semantic classes for a topic in the next stage.

3.2 Semantic Frame Generation, SFG

Semantic frame generation aims to automatically generate representative frames from sequences of semantic class labels and keywords. We observed that the rank-frequency distribution of semantic classes followed Zipf's law (Manning and Schütze, 1999), which was also the case for normalized frequency of semantic frames. Thus, we only used the most frequent 1,000 semantic frames ($\approx 0.5\%$) to dominate the tail of distribution. These frames can be regarded as the fundamental knowledge for a certain topic, and can be understood by computers as well as humans. Knowledge of such quality cannot be easily achieved in ordinary machine-learning models. To illustrate, consider the topic "Technology" and one of the automatically-acquired frames "[利用 (use)]-[iPhone (Tech-keyword)]-[看

(look)]-[網路術語 (Internet terminology)]". We can think of various semantically similar sentences that were covered by this frame, e.g., "使用 iPhone 來瀏覽部落格 (use iPhone to browse weblog)" or "善用 iPhone 察看電子郵件 (utilize iPhone to check email)".

The dominating set algorithm is adopted for SFG, and it has been proven that finding the dominating set on a graph is NP-hard (Garey and Johnson, 1979). Thus, several approximations have been proposed (Guha and Khuller, 1998; Kuhn and Wattenhofer, 2005; Shen and Li, 2010, i.a.). We also implemented an approximation based on the greedy algorithm. First of all, we construct a directed graph $G = \{V, E\}$, in which vertices V contains all semantic frames $\{SF_1, \cdots, SF_m\}$ in each topic, and edges E represent the dominating relations between frames. If a frame SF_x dominates SF_y, there is an edge $SF_x \rightarrow SF_y$. There are three criteria for constructing the dominating relations. First, only high frequency frames were selected for the dominators. Secondly, in general, longer frames dominate shorter frames, except for those mentioned in the following rule. Lastly, shorter frames would only be dominated if their head and tail semantic classes are identical to those of longer frames. The intermediate semantic classes could be skipped, as they can be identified as insertions and given scores based on their statistical distribution in this topic during the matching process. An illustration of a dominating frame and some dominated frames are shown in Table 1. Using dominating set to find frequent patterns on semantic graphs can help us capture the most prominent and representative frames within a topic. Afterwards, the dominating frames undergo a selection process that is similar to our keyword extraction method mentioned above. We use the LLR to discriminate semantic classes between topics. Given training data comprised of different topics, the LLR calculates the likelihood that the occurrence of a semantic class in the topic is not random. Those with a larger LLR value are considered as closely associated with the topic. Lastly, we rank the frames based on a sum of semantic classes LLR values and retain the top 100 from approx. 350,000 frames. By doing so, we can reduce the number of frames to 0.2% while keeping the most prominent and distinctive ones. Moreover, such reduction of the frames allows the execution of more sophisticated text classification algorithms, which leads to improved results. Existing algorithms cannot be executed on the original semantic class graph because the excessive execution times required makes them impractical (Baeza-Yates and Ribeiro-Neto, 2011). Therefore, selecting semantic frames closely associated with the topic would improve the performance of topic detection.

Dominating Frame:						
[player]	[team]	[person]	[player]	[news]		[speed]
Dominated Frames:						
-	[team]	-	[player]	-	[average]	[speed]
[player]	-	-	[player]	-	[attack]	[speed]
[player]	[equip]	[speed]	[player]	-	-	-
[player]	[team]	-	-	-	[attack]	[speed]
[player]	[team]	-	-	-	[attack]	[speed]
			⋮			
-	[team]	[person]	[player]	[news]	-	-
[player]	[team]	-	-	-	[average]	[speed]

Table 1: Illustration of a dominating frame and some dominated frames in the topic "Sports" generated by SFG.

3.3 Semantic Frame Matching, SFM

During matching, an unknown article is first labeled by SCL and a alignment-like algorithm (Needleman and Wunsch, 1970) is applied to determine the similarity between the article and the frames derived by SFG. It enables a single frame to match multiple semantically similar expressions. The SFM compares all sequences of semantic classes in an article to all the frames in each topic, and calculates the sum of scores for each topic. Unlike normal templates that involve mostly rigid left-right relation, we consider them as scoring criteria during frame alignment. The topic t_i with the highest sum of scores defined in (2) is considered as the winner.

$$Topic = \arg\max_{t \in Topic} Score(Document, t_i), \quad (2)$$

where

$$
\begin{aligned}
&Score(Document, t_i) \\
&= \sum_{sf_i \in SF_{topic}, sl_j \in SL_{document}} \Delta(sf_i, sl_j) \\
&+ LLR(k, t_i), \qquad (3)
\end{aligned}
$$

in which

$$\Delta(sf, sl) = \sum_i \sum_j \Delta(sf \cdot sc_i, sl \cdot sc_j), \qquad (4)$$

where sc_i and sc_j represent the ith semantic class of sf and j^{th} semantic class of sl, respectively. We use a keyword score computed from the LLR mentioned in Section 3.1, denoted as $LLR(k, t_i)$ in (3). As for scoring of the matched and unmatched components in frames, the details are as follows. If $sf \cdot sc_i$ and $sl \cdot sc_j$ are identical, we add a matched score obtained from the frequency of the semantic class in a topic times a normalizing factor $\lambda = 100$, as in (5).

$$Matched(sc) = \lambda \frac{f_{sc}}{\sum_{i=1}^{m} f_{sc_i}} \qquad (5)$$

Otherwise, the score of insertions and deletions are added. An insertion, defined as (6), can be accounted for by the inversed entropy of this class, representing the uniqueness or generality of this class among topics. And a deletion, defined as (7), is computed from the log frequency of this class in this topic. It denotes the importance of a class in a topic. The detailed algorithm is described in Algorithm 1.

$$Insertion(sc) = -\frac{1}{\sum_{i=1}^{m} P(t_i) log_2(P(t_i))} \qquad (6)$$

$$Deletion(sc) = -log \frac{f_{sc}}{\sum_{i=1}^{m} f_{sc_i}} \qquad (7)$$

Algorithm 1 Semantic Frame Matching

Input: A semantic frame $F = \{S_1, ..., S_m\}$, S: semantic class; A sequence of semantic class from a clause $C = \{s_1, ..., s_n\}$
Output: Matching score σ between F and C

$pos \leftarrow 0$;
for $i = 1$ to m **do**
    $pos \leftarrow$ current matched position in C;
    if found $s_j = S_i$ in C after pos **then**
        $\sigma \leftarrow \sigma +$ MatchedScore(S_i);
        $isMatched \leftarrow true$;
    end if
end for
if $isMatched = false$ **then**
    $\sigma \leftarrow \sigma$-(insertion or deletion) score of S_i;
end if

4 Performance Evaluation

4.1 Dataset and Experimental Settings

To the best of our knowledge, there is no official corpus for Chinese topic detection. Therefore, we compiled a news corpus for the evaluations from Yahoo! Chinese news website between the year 2010 and 2014. It contains a total of 140,000 documents with six different topics, and the number of documents of each topic is included in the parentheses, i.e., "Sports" (28,920), "Politics" (29,024), "Travel" (22,257), "Technology" (27,032), and "Education" (15,024). For each topic, 10,000 documents are selected as the training data, while the rest are used for testing. The evaluation metrics used are the precision, recall, and F_1-measure. A random baseline and three widely-used methods are also implemented and evaluated for comparison. The first is the Naïve Bayes classifier (Manning and Schütze, 1999), which is a simple probabilistic classifier based on applying Bayes' theorem with strong independence assumptions between the features (denoted as Naïve Bayes). Another is a vector space model-based method (Salton et al., 1975) that is an algebraic model for representing text documents as vectors of identifiers (denoted as VSM). The last is a probabilistic graphical model which uses the LDA model as document representation to train an SVM to classify the documents as either topic relevant or irrelevant (Blei et al., 2003) (denoted as LDA-SVM). Details of these implementations are as follows. The dictionary required by Naïve Bayes, VSM and LDA-SVM is constructed by removing stop words according to a Chinese stop word list provided by Zou et al. (2006), and retaining tokens that make up 90% of the accumulated frequency. In other words, the dictionary can cover up to 90% of the tokens in the corpus. As for unseen events, we use Laplace smoothing in Naïve Bayes and VSM, which is a common add-one smoothing method. And an LDA toolkit is used to perform the detection of LDA-SVM.

4.2 Results

A comparison of the five topic detection methods is displayed in Table 2. Our FBA system achieved the best performance on the topic "Politics", with the precision, recall, and F_1-measure scores of 78.37%, 92.12%, and 84.69%, respectively. Nevertheless, performances with high precision and low recall were found in the topics "Travel" and "Technology", as the FBA system obtained precisions over 90% with recalls only around 40%. On the contrary, the FBA system showed lower precisions of 57% and 72% and higher recalls of 95% and 93% for the topics "Sports" and "Health", respectively. Overall, the FBA system achieved an average precision of 78.17%, average recall of 69.39% and an average F_1-measure of 69.14%.

To further investigate the competence of our system, four other methods were also evaluated for comparison. As expected, the random baseline has the lowest performance among all methods with average P/R/F values around 17%. The Naïve Bayes classifier significantly outperforms the random baseline. Nevertheless, in the topics "Travel", "Technology", and "Education", this method obtained a relatively lower recall compared with others. On the other hand, VSM surpasses the overall performance of Naïve Bayes by about 20%. It is worth noting that VSM shares some of the low recall topics of the Naïve Bayes method, while acquiring the highest precision scores in three out of the six topics. For the topic "Technology", it has the best P/R/F scores of 93%, 50%, and 65%, respectively. As for the LDA-SVM, the difference is not as obvious. It achieved an improvement over the VSM's average F_1-measure by 4%. It also obtained the highest recalls among all systems in two of the six topics: "Travel" and "Education". Finally, the FBA outperforms LDA-SVM in the overall F_1-measure by 2%. In general, FBA has a higher precision while LDA-SVM has a higher recall, and FBA achieved the highest overall F_1-measure of all methods compared.

4.3 Discussion

To begin with, we provide an analysis of the difference in the average performance among different methods. The improvement in performance from the random baseline to the Naïve Bayes classifier indicates that keyword information is indispensable. The VSM benefits from weighing keywords in different topics by vectors in order to discover unique words and leave out less distinctive ones in each topic, thereby outperforming the Naïve Bayes classifier. However, since VSM considers similarity between two words as a cosine function with independent dimensions, it is difficult to represent the relations among many words.

On the other hand, when compared with the LDA-SVM method, our system has a higher precision and lower recall, resulting in a subtle increase of overall F_1-measure over the LDA-SVM. It may be attributed to the use of Chinese word segmentation tool in LDA-SVM for constructing a word dictionary as background knowledge, in addition to a probabilistic graph with weighted edge representing between-word relations. By contrast, our system relies on a NE database for semantic class labeling and frame generation, which is constrained by the scope of the data. Moreover, some keyword infor-

Topic	Random	Naïve Bayes	VSM	LDA-SVM	FBA
Sport	24.45/16.62/19.79	57.09/55.81/56.45	**94.76**/67.92/79.13	94.40/85.85/**89.92**	57.15/**95.06**/71.38
Politics	24.85/16.94/20.15	47.67/78.50/59.31	**91.86**/48.69/63.65	80.34/82.94/81.62	78.37/**92.12**/**84.69**
Travel	15.95/17.00/16.46	30.86/15.88/20.97	76.92/59.18/66.89	80.58/**62.11**/**70.16**	**91.06**/43.87/59.21
Technology	21.96/16.82/19.05	73.32/27.52/40.02	**92.87**/**50.39**/**65.33**	70.56/47.38/56.69	92.68/40.47/56.34
Health	10.28/16.26/12.59	38.43/69.65/49.53	57.49/78.92/66.31	44.41/70.56/54.51	**71.56**/**93.00**/**80.88**
Education	10.15/16.07/12.44	46.88/46.50/46.69	29.04/70.08/41.07	37.18/**82.06**/51.17	**78.19**/51.82/**62.33**
μ-Average	17.94/18.29/16.75	49.04/48.98/45.50	73.82/62.53/63.73	67.91/**71.82**/67.35	**78.17**/69.39/**69.14**

Table 2: Precision/Recall/F_1-measure(%) and micro-average of different topic detection systems. The highest numbers among all systems are in bold.

mation in the original document is discarded by the labeling process, which is retained in other keyword-based models. Potentially crucial information may be abandoned in this manner and impair the coverage of our system. Despite the slightly lower recall, our system is unique in the ability to generate and accumulate knowledge during the process. This enables us to capture essential information beyond the word-level for a topic, and generate frames that can capture the relations between them. The generated frames can describe the semantic relations within a document and assist in detecting the topic. We consider them as the foundation for a more profound understanding of topics that extends beyond the surface words.

Of the six topics, our system performed best on the topic "Politics" due to the abundant specific nouns in the articles of this topic, such as "民主黨 (Democratic Party)" or "歐巴馬 (Obama)". In addition, unique political terms like "參議員 (Senator)" and "內閣 (Cabinet)" are also common. The integration of key terms and frames contributes to the stability and uniqueness of the semantic frames of this topic, resulting in a higher overall F_1-measure. As for the topics "Sports" and "Health", we speculate that the NEs of athletes or disease names and other organizations are common among these articles. Thus, the frames in these topics are very extensive, leading to a broader coverage and higher recall. Other methods simply relying on keyword information can achieve a higher precision. Nonetheless, without long-distance information such as those encoded by frames, the recall can be limited. Regarding other topics, although the FBA can obtain the highest precision, insufficient knowledge may be the major cause of a restricted coverage. For example, the precision of the topic "Technology" is 92.68%, the highest among all topics. We believe this is due to the fact that specific technological terms, such as "iPhone" or "微軟 (Microsoft)", are predominant in these topics. Terms of such are very competent in determining the topic of these documents. However, considering the fact that novel terms are emerging frequently, we will have to integrate new knowledge into our system. Fortunately, under our framework, expanding and accumulating the knowledge base is easily done. Therefore, the advancement of our system is foreseeable.

Interestingly, it can be observed that the topics "Travel" and "Technology" generally have lower recall, regardless of the system used. This may be due to the fact that context information in these topics is hard to be captured by the current systems. Using only the word it self or word-related features is not enough. Even for a semantically-based system like the LDA-SVM or FBA, such information is still not fully encoded. Further research on the integration of richer and wider semantic context may be fruitful.

In sum, our approach can automatically generate frames that retain the benefit of knowledge-based approaches, including high precision and knowledge accumulation, while retaining considerable amount of recall. It can be continuously upgraded as more knowledge is incorporated. Hence, it has great potential in overcoming common disadvantages of other systems.

5 Concluding Remarks

This research proposes the FBA, a flexible and automatic approach to the topic detection task based on knowledge sources and automatic frame generation. It differs from popular machine learning methods as it can create an adaptable and extensible topic-dependent knowledge base, while preserving the accuracy of rule-based models. Results showed that FBA can effectively detect the topic of articles, as well as assist the user in constructing background knowledge of each topic in order to better understand the essence of them. In the future, we plan to expand this approach to include more topics, and even apply it to other applications in NLP. Also, further studies can be done on combining statistical models into different components in FBA.

Acknowledgment

This study is conducted under the NSC 102-3114-Y-307-026 "A Research on Social Influence and Decision Support Analytics" of the Institute for Information Industry which is subsidized by the National Science Council.

References

Harith Alani, Sanghee Kim, David E Millard, Mark J Weal, Wendy Hall, Paul H Lewis, and Nigel R Shadbolt. 2003. Automatic ontology-based knowledge extraction from web documents. *Intelligent Systems, IEEE*, 18(1):14–21.

R. Baeza-Yates and B. Ribeiro-Neto. 2011. *Modern Information Retrieval: The Concepts and Technology Behind Search*. Addison Wesley.

Omar Mabrook A Bashaddadh and Masnizah Mohd. 2011. Topic detection and tracking interface with named entities approach. In *Semantic Technology and Information Retrieval (STAIR), International Conference on*, pages 215–219. IEEE.

David M. Blei, Andrew Y. Ng, and Michael I. Jordan. 2003. Latent Dirichlet allocation. *Journal of Machine Learning Research*, 3:993–1022.

Khoo Khyou Bun and Mitsuru Ishizuka. 2002. Topic extraction from news archive using tf*pdf algorithm. In *Web Information Systems Engineering, International Conference on*, page 73. IEEE Computer Society.

Keh-Jiann Chen, Shu-Ling Huang, Yueh-Yin Shih, and Yi-Jun Chen. 2005. Extended-HowNet: A representational framework for concepts. In *Proc. 2nd IJCNLP*.

Bevan Das and Vaduvur Bharghavan. 1997. Routing in ad-hoc networks using minimum connected dominating sets. In *Proc. ICC'97, Towards the Knowledge Millennium.*, volume 1, pages 376–380. IEEE.

Zhendong Dong, Qiang Dong, and Changling Hao. 2010. Hownet and its computation of meaning. In *Proc. the 23rd International Conference on Computational Linguistics: Demonstrations*, pages 53–56. ACL.

Hongjie Du, Ling Ding, Weili Wu, Donghyun Kim, PanosM. Pardalos, and James Willson. 2013. Connected dominating set in wireless networks. In Panos M. Pardalos, Ding-Zhu Du, and Ronald L. Graham, editors, *Handbook of Combinatorial Optimization*, pages 783–833. Springer New York.

Francisco García-Sánchez, Rodrigo Martínez-Béjar, Leonardo Contreras, Jesualdo Tomás Fernández-Breis, and Dagoberto Castellanos-Nieves. 2006. An ontology-based intelligent system for recruitment. *Expert Systems with Applications*, 31(2):248–263.

Michael R Garey and David S Johnson. 1979. *Computers and intractability: A Guide to the Theory of NP-Completeness*. Freeman San Francisco.

Maria Grineva, Maxim Grinev, and Dmitry Lizorkin. 2009. Extracting key terms from noisy and multi-theme documents. In *Proc. the 18th International Conference on World Wide Web*, pages 661–670. ACM.

Sudipto Guha and Samir Khuller. 1998. Approximation algorithms for connected dominating sets. *Algorithmica*, 20(4):374–387.

Fabian Kuhn and Roger Wattenhofer. 2005. Constant-time distributed dominating set approximation. *Distributed Computing*, 17(4):303–310.

Chang-Shing Lee, Young-Chung Chang, and Mei-Hui Wang. 2009. Ontological recommendation multi-agent for tainan city travel. *Expert Systems with Applications*, 36(3):6740–6753.

Shengdong Li, Xueqiang Lv, Tao Wang, and Shuicai Shi. 2010. The key technology of topic detection based on K-means. In *Future Information Technology and Management Engineering (FITME), International Conference on*, volume 2, pages 387–390. IEEE.

Christopher D. Manning and Hinrich Schütze. 1999. *Foundations of statistical natural language processing*, volume 999. MIT Press.

Ramesh Nallapati, Ao Feng, Fuchun Peng, and James Allan. 2004. Event threading within news topics. In *Proc. the 13th CIKM*, pages 446–453. ACM.

Ramesh Nallapati. 2003. Semantic language models for topic detection and tracking. In *Proc. HLT-NAACL Student Research Workshop*, pages 1–6.

Saul B. Needleman and Christian D. Wunsch. 1970. A general method applicable to the search for similarities in the amino acid sequence of two proteins. *Journal of Molecular Biology*, 48(3):443–453.

Gerard Salton, Anita Wong, and Chung-Shu Yang. 1975. A vector space model for automatic indexing. *Communications of the ACM*, 18(11):613–620.

Sam Scott and Stan Matwin. 1999. Feature engineering for text classification. In *Proc. ICML-99, 16th International Conference on Machine Learning*, pages 379–388. Morgan Kaufmann Publishers.

Chao Shen and Tao Li. 2010. Multi-document summarization via the minimum dominating set. In *Proc. the 23rd International Conference on Computational Linguistics*, COLING '10, pages 984–992, Stroudsburg, PA, USA. Association for Computational Linguistics.

Quan Thanh Tho, Siu Cheung Hui, Alvis Cheuk M. Fong, and Tru Hoang Cao. 2006. Automatic fuzzy ontology generation for semantic web. *Knowledge and Data Engineering, IEEE Trans. on*, 18(6):842–856.

Yonghui Wu, Yuxin Ding, Xiaolong Wang, and Jun Xu. 2010. On-line hot topic recommendation using tolerance rough set based topic clustering. *Journal of Computers*, 5(4).

Xiaoyan Zhang and Ting Wang. 2010. Topic tracking with dynamic topic model and topic-based weighting method. *Journal of Software*, 5(5):482–489.

Feng Zou, Fu Lee Wang, Xiaotie Deng, Song Han, and Lu Sheng Wang. 2006. Automatic construction of chinese stop word list. In *Proc. the 5th WSEAS International Conference on Applied Computer Science*, pages 1010–1015.

Zero-Shot Learning of Language Models for Describing Human Actions Based on Semantic Compositionality of Actions

Hideki ASOH
National Institute of
Advanced Industrial Science and Technology
Tsukuba, Ibaraki 305-8568 Japan
h.asoh@aist.go.jp

Ichiro KOBAYASHI
Graduate School of Humanities and Sciences,
Ochanomizu University
Bunkyo-ku, Tokyo 112-8610 Japan
koba@is.ocha.ac.jp

Abstract

We propose a novel framework for zero-shot learning of topic-dependent language models, which enables the learning of language models corresponding to specific topics for which no language data is available. To realize zero-shot learning, we exploit the semantic compositionality of the target topics. Complex topics are normally composed of several elementary semantic components. We found that the language model that corresponds to a particular topic can be approximated with a linear combination of language models corresponding to elementary components of the target topics. On the basis of the findings, we propose simple methods of zero-shot learning. To confirm the effectiveness of the proposed framework, we apply the methods to the problem of generating natural language descriptions of short Kinect videos of simple human actions.

1 Introduction

Constructing topic-dependent language models is useful for many applications such as text mining, speech recognition, statistical machine translation, natural language interfaces, and textual description of images or video contents. In most methods of topic-dependent language model construction, one general model is first constructed from a large amount of language data, and then the general model is modified with a small amount of language data regarding the target topic. The technique of taking the weighted sum of language models is often used for the modification (Bacchiani and Roark, 2003; Jelinek and Mercer, 1980). However, correcting language data for all target topics is demanding and difficult. In particular, when each target topic becomes narrower and the number of target topics increases, it becomes impractical to correct language data for all topics.

In this paper, we propose a novel framework for zero-shot learning of topic-dependent language models, which enables the learning of language models corresponding to specific topics without observing language data regarding the topics on the basis of the semantic compositionality of the target topics.

In the following, we consider rather fine-grained topics such as human activities. Such detailed topics are normally composed of several elementary semantic components. For example, a human action "raising left leg in the forward direction" is considered as a topic. The action includes components such as "up (raise)", "left", "leg", and "in the forward direction". Another action "raising left hand in the side direction" shares the common elements "up" and "left" with the previous action. In this way, actions are related to each other through common components. Hence, the language models generated from natural language sentences describing those actions are also expected to be related to each other. We will show that using this kind of compositionality, we can generate language models corresponding to actions for which we do not have natural language data.

To demonstrate the effectiveness of the proposed methods, we apply the methods to the problem of generating natural language descriptions of short

Copyright 2014 by Hideki Asoh and Ichiro Kobayashi
28th Pacific Asia Conference on Language, Information and Computation pages 85–92

Kinect videos.

In summary, the original contributions of this work are as follows: 1) the problem of zero-shot learning of topic-dependent language models is newly formulated, 2) novel simple methods for zero-shot learning are proposed, and 3) the effectiveness of the methods is confirmed with real data.

The remainder of the paper is organized as follows: The problem is formalized and solutions are proposed in Section 2, Section 3 discusses related works, Section 4 presents application to the video description problem including experimental setup and results of the experiments, and Section 5 presents the conclusion and discusses future work.

2 Zero-Shot Learning of Language Models

In this section we formalize the problem of zero-shot learning of topic-dependent language models, and propose methods to solve the problem.

2.1 Problem Formalization

As described above, we are interested in the problem of learning multiple topic-dependent language models M_i $(i = 1, ..., N)$, each of which corresponds to a complex fine-grained topic such as human action x_i. When we have a language data S_i i.e. a set of sentences describing the topic x_i for all topics, we can simply calculate M_i from S_i.

The problem we will treat in this paper is estimating language models M_i corresponding to topics x_i for which we do not have language data S_i. Such estimation becomes possible on the basis of the semantic compositionality of topics. We assume that each topic is composed of several semantic components. We denote the semantic components as $y_j (j = 1, ..., K)$.

For example, in the experiments described in Section 4, we use $N = 20$ human actions such as "raising left leg in the forward direction" and "raising both hands in the side direction". Each action is composed by combining some of $K = 9$ components such as "up", "down", "front" (front direction), "side" (side direction), "hand", "leg", "right", "left", and "both".

The relation between topics and components can be described by a matrix $A = (a_{ij})$. When $a_{ij} = 1$ then the ith topic includes the jth component, and when $a_{ij} = 0$ then otherwise. In the following section, we assume that a_{ij} is known for all topics. We also assume that the number of topics N is larger than the number of components K.

As for the language model, we consider the n-gram model. An n-gram language model is normally defined by the conditional probabilities $p(w_i|w_{i-1}, ..., w_{i-n+1})$ for a word sequence $(w_{i-n+1}, ..., w_{i-1}, w_i)$. Here we use the joint probabilities $p(w_i, w_{i-1}, ..., w_{i-n+1})$ instead of the conditional probabilities because the joint probabilities are suit for the linear decomposition described below. Hence the conditional probabilities can be calculated from the joint probabilities, this does not reduce the generality and usefulness of the framework.

We denote a vector composed of the joint probability values calculated from language data S_i as ψ_i, and assume that the probability vector ψ_i for the ith topic can be approximately decomposed as the weighted sum of probability vectors ϕ_j corresponding to the jth components included in the topic as

$$\psi_i = \sum_j \frac{a_{ij}}{\sum_j a_{ij}} \phi_j + \varepsilon_i,$$

where ε_i is a vector of the noise term.

Because we consider N topics and K components, the relation can be written with matrices as

$$\Psi = \tilde{A}\Phi + E, \qquad (1)$$

where Ψ is an $N \times W$ matrix whose ith row is ψ_i and Φ is a $K \times W$ matrix whose jth row is ϕ_j, and $\tilde{A}$ is a $N \times K$ matrix whose element is $a_{ij}/\sum_j a_{ij}$. W is the dimension of the probability vector of the language model, i.e. the number of ordered word pairs appear in the language data. E is a matrix composed of noise terms. We use this linear relation for zero-shot learning.

2.2 Methods of Zero-Shot Learning

Let us assume we have language data S_i for only N' $(N' < N)$ topics. The set of topics for which we have language data is denoted by T. From the partial language data, we can compute the $N' \times W$ probability vector matrix Ψ' by the same way as the matrix Ψ. A row of Ψ' is the probability vector which corresponds to a topic in T.

If we can estimate Φ for the K components from the partial data, then we can recover the whole Ψ

using the relation of equation (1). This means that we can estimate language models ψ_i for topics for which we have no language data.

We assume that each of K components y_j is included at least once in the N' topics. Then a naive method of computing Φ is to compute the language model ϕ_j from the language data of all topics that include the jth component.

We merge the sentences regarding the topics with the jth component. Then from the merged data we compute the probability vector ϕ_j for the jth component. This method has been designated as "Method 1" in this study.

Another method of estimating Φ is to exploit the least-square estimation to estimate Φ from Ψ' as

$$\hat{\Phi} = \arg\min_{\Phi} ||\Psi' - \tilde{A}'\Phi||^2$$

where $\tilde{A}'$ is an $N' \times K$ matrix made by extracting N' rows corresponding to Ψ' from $\tilde{A}$. This optimization problem can be easily solved as

$$\hat{\Phi} = \tilde{A}'^{+}\Psi',$$

where $\tilde{A}'^{+}$ is the generalized inverse of matrix $\tilde{A}'$. Then from $\hat{\Phi}$ we can estimate the language models for topics without language data. This method has been designated as "Method 2".

3 Related Work

Zero-shot learning has recently become a popular research topic in machine learning, in particular in the domain of large scale visual object recognition and image tagging. Because the number of classes is large, it is difficult to collect true labels for the problems. Hence zero-shot learning is useful in the domain. Palatucci et al. (2009) proposed a method of zero-shot learning and applied to decoding fMRI data from subjects thinking about certain words based on the semantic representation of the target classes. They also gave theoretical analysis of the zero-shot learning framework. Lampert et al. (2009) proposed a method of visual object classification where training and test classes are disjoint. They also exploited semantic attributes of target classes. Farhadi et al. (2009) also proposed rather similar idea.

More recently, Cheng et al. (2013) applied the idea of zero-shot learning to human activity recognition task. They mapped sequence of images to category labels. Socher et al. (2013) proposed a method for zero-shot learning of object recognition using deep neural networks. Frome et al. (2014) improved the model with a larger scale dataset.

All of the previous studies treat zero-shot learning of class labels on the basis of the similarity between input information and also between semantic attribute of the classes. Our work extends the idea of zero-shot learning to language models, which have more complex structure than class labels by exploiting the semantic compositionality of complex topics. In other words, our work goes beyond the word level and treats the sentence level structure. As far as we know, this is the first work which applies the idea of zero-shot learning to topic-dependent language model learning.

The idea of linearly decomposing language models is strongly related to latent topic extraction in text mining. In the latent semantic analysis (LSA), the word frequency vector (unigram probability vector) of a document is linearly decomposed into a weighted sum of latent topic vectors (Deerwester et al., 1990). In topic extraction, the aim of the data analysis is to extract latent topics. On the contrary, in this work, the aim of zero-shot learning is to construct language models for which no language data is available.

In this paper, we assume that the latent topics (= components) are known, and we decompose the language models on the basis of the known combination of components (information of matrix A). However, we can also consider another problem setting where matrix A is unknown. In the setting, the problem is mathematically equivalent with the LSA, and singular value decomposition of the language model matrix Ψ can be used to estimate latent components and language models for the components simultaneously. Various matrix factorization algorithms such as non-negative matrix factorization (Lee and Seung, 1999; Xu et al., 2003), or other probabilistic topic extraction methods such as probabilistic latent semantic analysis (Hofmann, 1999) and latent Dirichlet allocation (Blei et al., 2003) may also be applicable.

Zero-shot learning of language models is also in-

Figure 1: An example of human action (action 11)

teresting from the viewpoint of modeling the natural language acquisition process of humans. Humans are believed to acquire language capability from a rather small amount of observations of language data. To cope with this problem of the poverty of stimuli, certain kinds of zero-shot learning may be exploited. As an example, Sugita and Tani (2005) proposes a model of language acquisition with recurrent neural networks. The robot they constructed can generate sentences describing actions that the robot has not yet experienced on the basis of the semantic compositionality of the actions.

4 Application to Video Content Description System

To demonstrate the effectiveness of the proposed methods, we applied the methods to the problem of generating natural language description of short Kinect videos.

Obtaining a huge amount of video data is becoming easier recently. Whereas we agree with the fact that fully utilization of the data has not been achieved yet. For example, to grasp the content of videos recorded by surveillance cameras, or videos of recorded meetings, we need to watch through the entire videos, which is considerably time-consuming work. If the contents of a video can be recognized and be described with natural language sentences, it will become easier to mine the content of the video data and to achieve various applications such as scene retrieval through natural language queries, etc.

On the basis of such needs, research of the learning relation between natural language and multi-media information has recently been becoming popular in the areas of both natural language processing and multi-media information processing. Many studies have been conducted to generate sentences to explain human behaviors in a video (Barbu et al., 2012; Ding et al., 2012a; Ding et al., 2012b; Kobayashi et al., 2010; Kojima et al., 2002; Rohrbach et al., 2013; Tan et al., 2011). As representative studies, Yu and Siskind (2013) propose a method that learns representations of word meanings from short video clips paired with sentences. Regneri et al. (2013) consider the problem of grounding sentences describing actions in visual information extracted from videos. Takano and Nakamura (2008, 2009) propose incremental learning of association between motion symbols and natural language. Ushiku et al. (2011, 2012) propose a method to create a caption for a still picture, by learning n-gram models for describing picture from pairs of still pictures and their explanation sentences.

Among these works, Kobayashi et al. (2013) are constructing a system for generating natural language description of short Kinect videos of several kinds of human actions. From the pairs of video data of an action taken by the Kinect and Japanese sentences describing the action, the system learns models of observed human actions and language models of the sentences. Using the two models and the correspondence between them, the system can recognizes an action in a new video of a leaned action and outputs Japanese sentences describing the action.

In the work, they assumed that they could collect natural language sentences describing all target actions and construct language models corresponding to all actions from the data. However, when the number of target actions increases, it becomes impractical to prepare natural language descriptions for all actions. Here, we apply our zero-shot learning method to learn the language models of actions for which we do not have language data.

4.1 Experimental Setup

We use $N = 20$ human actions as the target topics. We take short (less than 5 sec.) Kinect videos of

Table 1: Examples of collected sentenses

1	hidari te wo ageru. (raise left hand.)
2	hidari te wo ue ni ageru. (raise left hand upward.)
4	hidari te wo mae kara ageru. (raise left hand to the front direction)
3	hidari te wo shita kara ue ni ageru. (raise left hand upward from below.)
4	hidari te wo mae no hou kara ue ni ageru. (raise left hand upward from the front direction)

the actions, and collect several Japanese sentences that describe the actions. Figure 1 shows an example of an action ("raising both hand through the side direction"). For each action, around 15 sentences describing the action are collected. Table 1 shows some sentences describing the action of raising left hand in the front direction. The collected sentences are segmented into words and bi-gram joint probabilities $p(w_i, w_{i-1})$ are computed from the data for each action. The number of word pairs that appeared in the data is 360.

We set the number of components $K = 9$: i.e., "up", "down", "front" (front direction), "side" (side direction), "hand", "leg", "right", "left", and "both" (only for hands). The combinatorial relationship between the actions and the elements is illustrated in Figure 2. "L", "R", and "B" in the figure denotes "left", "right", and "both" respectively. The figure shows that each human action includes four components in this experiment. For example, Action 3 (ACT 3) is composed of the components "up", "front", "hand", and "left", and Action 18 (ACT 18) is composed of "down", "side", "leg", and "right".

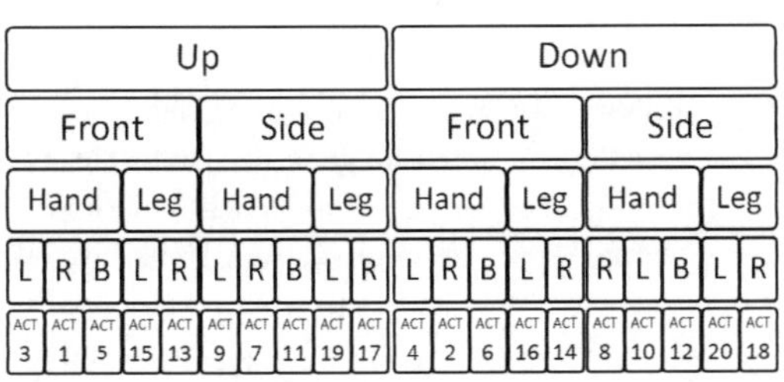

Figure 2: Combinatorial relationship between human actions and components

Table 2: Root mean squared error of the estimated values

Action	Method 1	Method 2	Training	Uniform
1	0.00353	**0.00280**	0.00387	0.00944
2	0.00320	**0.00257**	0.00354	0.00907
3	0.00338	**0.00287**	0.00365	0.00928
4	0.00358	**0.00309**	0.00389	0.00876
5	0.00275	**0.00220**	0.00336	0.00885
6	0.00322	**0.00217**	0.00387	0.00883
7	0.00373	**0.00314**	0.00404	0.00899
8	0.00318	**0.00268**	0.00348	0.00865
9	0.00353	**0.00302**	0.00381	0.00906
10	0.00335	**0.00295**	0.00365	0.00875
11	0.00344	**0.00211**	0.00411	0.00863
12	0.00330	**0.00231**	0.00394	0.00782
13	0.00380	**0.00339**	0.00419	0.00955
14	0.00311	**0.00294**	0.00350	0.00897
15	0.00339	**0.00301**	0.00378	0.00934
16	0.00315	**0.00280**	0.00359	0.00892
17	0.00346	**0.00308**	0.00385	0.00891
18	**0.00297**	0.00301	0.00330	0.00859
19	0.00361	**0.00312**	0.00398	0.00919
20	0.00351	**0.00314**	0.00389	0.00848
Mean	0.00356	**0.00282**	0.00377	0.00890

4.2 Result of Experiment

To evaluate the effectiveness of the proposed zero-shot learning methods, sentences describing one of the 20 human actions are omitted from the training data. Then we estimate Φ for components using $(M-1) \times W$ matrix Ψ' and $(M-1) \times K$ matrix A'. From the estimated $\hat{\Phi}$ we can recover the language model of the sentences omitted from the training data.

Table 1 shows the root mean squared error (RMSE) of the estimated probability values. The column "Action" denotes the target action for which the language data is omitted and the probability vector is estimated with the zero-shot learning methods. The column "Training" means that the language model is estimate using all the sentences in the training data. This is a baseline. Another baseline "Uniform" means that the estimated probability vector is uniform distribution, that is, all probability values are equal to $1/$ (# of word pairs). The minimum RMSE value for each action is shown in bold face.

Compared with the mean value of the non-zero joint probability values 0.0146, it can be said that the

Table 3: Comparisons of the top two most probable sentences

action	With language data	Without language data
1	migi te wo ageru. (raise right hand.) migi te wo ue ni ageru. (move right hand upward.)	migi te wo ageru. (raise right hand.) migi te wo ue ni ageru. (move right hand upward.)
2	migi te wo sageru. (lower right hand.) migi te wo shita ni sageru. (move right hand downward.)	migi te wo sageru. (lower right hand.) migi te wo uekara sageru. (lower right hand from upper position.)
3	hidari te wo ageru. (raise left hand.) hidari te wo ue ni ageru. (move left hand upward.)	hidari te wo ue ni ageru. (move left hand upward.) hidari te wo ageru. (raise left hand.)
5	ryou te wo ageru. (raise both hands.) ryou te wo mae kara ageru. (raise both hands in the forward direction.)	ryou te wo ue ni ageru. (move both hands upward.) ryou te wo ageru (raise both hands.)
18	migi ashi wo orosu. (lower right leg.) migi ashi wo yoko kara orosu. (lower right leg from the side direction.)	migi ashi wo sageru. (lower right leg.) migi ashi wo yoko ni sageru. (lower right leg in the side direction.)
20	hidari ashi wo orosu. (lower left leg.) hidari ashi wo yoko ni orosu. (lower left leg in the side direction.)	hidari ashi wo orosu. (lower left leg.) hidari ashi wo yoko ni orosu. (lower left leg in the side direction.)

RMSE values obtained from our two methods are small enough. The result demonstrates that Method 2 performs better than other methods for allmost all removed topics. However, in Method 2, the estimated values of ϕ_j and ψ_i do not become probabilities, that is, some values may become below zero and the sum of the values slightly differ from one. Hence, it becomes a bit difficult to interpret the values. Although this is not so serious problem in practice, this can be considered as a kind of tradeoff between the accuracy and the interpretability.

We also evaluate the RMSE values when we omit language data for more than one actions from the training data. The results strongly depend on the data which are omitted. For example, when we omit language data regarding actions 1, 2, 7, and 8, then the RMSE value of the estimated language model for Action 1 is degraded to 0.00469. However when we omit language data regarding actions 1, 3, 5, and 13, then the RMSE keeps low value 0.00223.

This difference comes from the components included in the remaining actions. The Action 1 is composed of "raise", "front", "right", "hand". When we omitted actions 1, 2, 7, and 8, no actions including components "right" and "hand" is remained in the training data. Hence this causes rather serious effect to the accuracy of the zero-shot estimation. However, when we omitted actions 1, 3, 5, and 13, all component pairs are still included in the training data. Hence this does not cause serious damage to the estimated language model.

Through the analysis of various cases, we confirmed that if the choice of omitted data is balanced to keep all semantic components remained in the training data, then the performance of zero-shot learning is not degraded so much even though language data regarding several actions are omitted.

Finally we evaluate the text generation capability of the estimated language models. Here we use the language models estimated by Method 2. We generate Japanese sentences of high likelihood value in the same way as in the work of Kobayashi et al. (2013), i.e. with the Viterbi algorithm using the language model of each action.

Table 3 contrasts the top two most probable texts generated with the bi-gram computed from the collected language data of the action and with the bi-gram estimated by the zero-shot learning using the language data of the other 19 actions. We demonstrate the results for 6 of the 20 actions. From the table, we can see that almost the same sentences are generated with the bi-gram probability vector estimated by our zero-shot learning method.

Although the actions used in the experiment are rather simple, we confirmed the possibility of zero-shot learning of effective language models. Those results show that zero-shot learning is a promising way to cope with the problem of the poverty of language data in natural language processing.

5 Conclusion and Future Work

We have proposed methods of zero-shot learning of fine-grained topic-dependent language models. Using the methods, we can learn topic-dependent language models corresponding to topics for which we do not have language data on the basis of the compositionality of the topics. We confirmed the effectiveness of the proposed methods with the task of describing short Kinect videos of human actions.

Much work remains to be done in the future. Because our experiment was conducted with a small-scale dataset, the methods should be evaluated more elaborately with larger scale datasets. The proposed zero-shot learning may be useful not only for describing videos but also for other various applications such as speech recognition, machine translation, text mining, and video retrieval. Application of the methods to such problems is an interesting topic.

In this paper, we assumed that the matrix A which denotes the relationship between actions and components is known. However, as is mentioned in the related work section, the problem setting for unknown A is also interesting. This problem is related to find the optimal elementary components to describe target topics. This is a kind of dictionary learning problem.

Finally, modeling more complex relation between multiple language models using more sophisticated probabilistic models may be an interesting research direction for natural language processing. As an example, Eisenstein et al. (2011) proposed a new way of representing multiple language models. Introducing their method of sparse additive decomposition of language models into our framework is also an interesting issue.

Acknowledgement: This work is partly supported by JSPS KAKENHI 26280096, MEXT KAKENHI 25120011, and foundation for the Fusion of Science and Technology.

References

M. Bacchiani and B. Roark. 2003. Unsupervised Language Model Adaptation. *2003 IEEE International Conference on Acoustics, Speech and Signal Processing*, Vol.1:224–227.

A. Barbu, A. Bridge, Z. Burchill, D. Coroian, S. Dickinson, S. Fidler, A. Michaux, S. Mussman, S. Narayanaswamy, D. Salvi, L. Schmidt, J. Shangguan, J. Siskind, J. Waggoner, S. Wang, J. Wei, Y. Yin, and Z. Zhang. 2012. Video In Sentences Out. *arXiv:1204.2742*.

D. M. Blei, A. Y. Ng, and M. Jordan. 2003. Latent Dirichlet Allocation. *Journal of Machine Learning Research*, 3 (4–5): 993–1022.

H.-T. Chang, M. Griss, P. Davis, J. Li, and D. You. 2013. Towards Zero-Shot Learning for Human Activity Recognition Using Semantic Attribute Sequence Model. *Proceedinsg of UbiComp'13*.

A. Farhadi, I. Endres, D. Holem, and D. Forsyth. 2009. Describing Objects by Their Attributes. *Proceedings of CVPR 2009*.

A. F. Frome, G. S. Corrado, J. Shlens, S. Bengio, J. Dean, M. A. Ranzato, and T. Mikolov. 2014. DeViSE: A Deep Visual-Semantic Embedding Model, *Proceedings of NIPS 2014*.

S. Deerwester, S. Dumais, G. W. Furnas, T. K. Landauer and R. Harshman. 1990. Indexing by Latent Semantic Analysis. *Journal of the American Society for Information Science*, 41 (6): 391–407.

D. Ding, F. Metze, S. Rawat, P. F. Schulam, and S. Burger. 2012. Generating Natural Language Summaries for Multimedia. *Proceedings of the 7th International Natural Language Generation Conference*, 128–130.

D. Ding, F. Metze, S. Rawat, P. F. Schulam, S. Burger, E. Younessian, L. Bao, M. G. Christel, and A. Hauptmann. 2012. Beyond Audio and Video Retrieval: Towards Multimedia Summarization. *Proceeding of the 2nd ACM International Conference on Multimedia Retrieval*, Article No.2.

J. Eisenstein, A. Ahmed, and E. P. Xing. 2011. Sparse Additive Generative Models of Text. *Proceedings of the 28th International Conference on Machine Learning*.

T. Hofmann. 1999. Probabilistic Latent Semantic Analysis. *Proceedings of the 15th Conference on Uncertainty in Artificial Intelligence*, 289-296.

F. Jelinek and R. L. Mercer. 1980. Interpolated Estimation of Markov Source Parameters from Sparse Data. *Proceedings of the Workshop on Pattern Recognition in Practice*.

I. Kobayashi, M. Noumi, and A. Hiyama. 2010. A Study on Verbalization of Human Behaviors in a Room. *Proceedings of the 2010 IEEE International Conference on Fuzzy Systems*.

M. Kobayashi, I. Kobayash, H. Asoh, and S. Guadarrama. 2013. A Probabilistic Approach to Text Generation of Human Motions Extracted from Kinect Videos. *Proceedings of the World Congress on Engineering and Computer Science 2013*.

A. Kojima, T. Tamura, and K. Fukunaga. 2002. Natural Language Description of Human Activities from Video Images Based on Concept Hierarchy of Actions. *International Journal of Computer Vision*, 50 (2):171–184.

C. H. Lambert, H. Nickisch, and S. Harmeling. 2009. Learning to Detect Unseen Object Classes by Between-Class Attribute Transfer. *Proceedings of CVPR 2009*.

D. D. Lee and H. S. Seung. 1999. Learning the Parts of Objects with Nonnegative Matrix Factorization. *Nature*, 401, 788–791.

M. Palatucci, D. Pomerleau, G. Hinton, and T. M. Mitchell. 2009. Zero-shot Learning with Semantic Output Codes. *Proceedings of NIPS 2009*.

M. Regneri, M. Rohrbach, D. Wetzel, S. Thater, B. Schiele, and M. Pinkal. 2013. Grounding Action Descriptions in Videos. *Proceedings of the 51st Annual Meeting of the Association for Computational Linguistics*.

M. Rohrbach, W. Qiu, I. Titov, S. Thater, M. Pinkal, and B. Schiele. 2013. Translating Video Content to Natural Language Descriptions. *Proceedings of ICCV 2013*, 433-440.

R. Socher, M. Ganjoo, C. D, Manning, and A. Y. Ng. 2013. Zero-shot learning through cross-modal transfer. *Proceedings of NIPS 2013*.

Y. Sugita and J. Tani. 2005. Learning Semantic Combinatoriality from the Interaction between Linguistic and Behavioral Processes. *Adaptive Behaviour*, 3 (1): 33–52.

W. Takano and Y. Nakamura. 2008. Integrating Whole Body Action Primitives and Natural Language for Humanoid Robots. *Proceedings of 2008 IEEE-RAS International Conference on Humanoid Robots*, 708–713.

W. Takano and Y. Nakamura. 2009. Incremental Learning of Integrated Semiotics based on Linguistic and Behavioral Symbols. *Proceedings of 2009 IEEE/RSJ International Conference on Intelligent Robots and Systems*, 1780–1785.

C. C. Tan, Y.-G. Jiang and C.-W. Ngo. 2011. Towards Textually Describing Complex Video Contents with Audio-Visual Concept Classifiers. *Proceedings of the 19th ACM international conference on Multimedia*, 655–658.

Y. Ushiku, T. Harada, and Y. Kuniyoshi. 2011. A Understanding Images with Natural Sentences. *Proceedings of the 19th Annual ACM International Conference on Multimedia*, 679–682.

Y. Ushiku, T. Harada, and Y. Kuniyoshi. 2012. Efficient Image Annotation for Automatic Sentence Generation. *Proceedings of the 20th Annual ACM International Conference on Multimedia*, 549–558.

W. Xu, X. Liu, and Y. Gong. 2003. Document Clustering based on Non-negative Matrix Factorization. *Proceedings of 26th Annual International ACM SIGIR Conference*, 267–273.

H. Yu, and J. M. Siskind. 2013. Grounded Language Learning from Video Described with Sentences. *Proceedings of the 51st Annual Meeting of the Association for Computational Linguistics*.

Partial Case-Marking in Japanese Stripping/Sluicing: A Dynamic Syntax Account

Tohru Seraku
Hankuk University of Foreign Studies
81, Oedae-ro, Cheoin-gu, Yongin-si, Gyeonggi-do
449-791, Korea
seraku@hufs.ac.kr

Abstract

This article presents novel data on partial case-marking in Japanese stripping/sluicing: only the final NP in multiple stripping/sluicing may lack a case particle. These data challenge previous works that assign radically distinct structures to stripping/sluicing depending on whether or not case-marking is involved. These case-marking patterns are reducible to incremental growth of semantic representation, formalised in Dynamic Syntax: each NP is parsed at an 'unfixed' node, and this structural uncertainty must be resolved before another unfixed node is introduced.

1 Introduction

There is a growing body of research on ellipsis in Japanese (Hiraiwa & Ishihara 2012 and references therein). Stripping is a relatively understudied type of elliptical construction (Fukaya 2007, Fukaya & Hoji 2003, Fukui & Sakai 2003, Sakai 2000; see also Hankamer & Sag 1976). As shown in (1)B, stripping consists of the NP *Mary* and the copula *da*, where case-marking of *Mary* is optional.

(1) A: *Tom-ga ringo-o tabe-ta-yo.*
T-NOM apple-ACC eat-PAST-SFP
'Tom ate apples.'
B: *Iya, Mary(-ga) da.*
no M(-NOM) COP
'No, Mary.' (= 'No, Mary ate apples.')

Japanese also allows "multiple stripping." That is, the pre-copula part may involve more than one NP:

(2) A: *Tom-ga ringo-o tabe-ta-yo.*
T-NOM apple-ACC eat-PAST-SFP
'Tom ate apples.'
B: *Iya, Mary-ga nashi-o da.*
no M-NOM pear-ACC COP
'No, Mary, pears.' (= 'No, Mary ate pears.')

The most elaborated analysis of stripping is found in Fukaya (2007), the main claim being that case-marked and case-less stripping must be structurally distinguished. According to Fukaya, movement is relevant only to case-marked stripping.[1]

What has not been noted in previous studies is that when there are multiple NPs in stripping, only the **final** NP may be case-less (see Section 4 for details). Compare (2)B with (3)B, where the final NP *nashi* (= 'pear') may be case-less, but not the non-final NP *Mary*.[2]

(3) A: *Tom-ga ringo-o tabe-ta-yo.*
T-NOM apple-ACC eat-PAST-SFP
'Tom ate apples.'
B: *Iya, Mary*(-ga) nashi da.*
no M(-NOM) pear COP
'No, Mary, pears.' (= 'No, Mary ate pears.')

[1] This non-uniform analysis is based on the observation that only case-marked stripping is sensitive to "islands" (Fukaya 2007). Seraku (2013) shows that our account captures the island-(in)sensitivity patterns of stripping by means of the 'LINK' mechanism (Cann et al. 2005).

[2] For some speakers, acceptability slightly drops with the string *Mary-ga nashi da*, but what is essential is that it is much more acceptable than the string *Mary nashi-o da* and the string *Mary nashi da*. The same type of remark also applies to the data in Sections 4 and 5.

Copyright 2014 by Tohru Seraku
28th Pacific Asia Conference on Language, Information and Computation pages 93–100

This partial case-marking phenomenon raises two problems for previous works. First, (3)B manifests case-marked and case-less stripping **at the same time**; that is, the single string contains the case-marked NP *Mary-ga* and the case-less NP *nashi*. It is thus not obvious how (3)B may be handled by the past **non-uniform** account that posits radically distinct structures depending on whether or not an NP in stripping is case-marked. Second, even if the first issue is sidestepped by stipulating a uniform syntactic structure for the two types of stripping, the question still remains of why **only** the final focus may lack a case particle.

The aim of this article is to show that the two recalcitrant puzzles are solved in a framework that directly reflects the incrementality of processing a string online, as modelled in Dynamic Syntax (DS) (Cann et al. 2005, Kempson et al. 2001, 2011).

Section 2 sets out the DS framework. Section 3 offers a unified analysis of stripping, and Section 4 deals with multiple stripping. Section 5 points out that the case-marking patterns of stripping are also found in sluicing, demonstrating that these sluicing data are amenable to our uniform analysis. Finally, Section 6 sums up the main results of this paper.

2 Dynamic Syntax (DS)

DS is a model of "competence," defined as a set of constraints on how to build an interpretation on the basis of incremental, word-by-word parsing online (Cann et al. 2005, Kempson et al 2001, 2011).[3] In the DS view of comprehension, the parser takes a string of words **left-to-right** and gradually builds an interpretation (represented as a **semantic** tree) **without** positing an independent level of syntactic structure. Syntax within DS is thus no more than a set of constraints on how to construct a semantic tree in real time.

DS semantic trees are binary-branching, where a right node is inhabited by a functor and a left node by an argument. Each node, if fully developed, is decorated with a semantic **content** and its semantic **type**. For instance, the parse of *Tom* decorates an argument node with the content *Tom'* and the type e, as in *Tom'* : e. Each node, if not fully developed, is decorated with **requirements**. The node to be decorated with *Tom'* : e is initially marked with ?e, which requires that the node will be decorated with the type e.

DS trees are progressively updated. The starting point is a root node with the requirement ?t, which requires that this node will be propositional. This initial state is defined as an **AXIOM** (see (5)). Once a root node is set out, it is subsequently updated by running **lexical** actions (triggered by the parse of a lexical item) or optionally running **general** actions.

An essential example of general actions is the introduction of an "unfixed" node, a node whose structural position is initially underspecified and will be resolved at a later point. Of note is LOCAL *ADJUNCTION, which introduces a **locally**-unfixed node decorated with the requirement **?e**.[4]

For an illustration, consider how a semantic tree is built incrementally by parsing (4) left-to-right.

(4) *Tom-ga hashi-tta.*
T-NOM run-PAST
'Tom ran.'

An initial state is the AXIOM (5), where ?t requires that this node will be decorated with a type-t (i.e. propositional) content. This is then updated to (6) by performing LOCAL *ADJUNCTION. This general action introduces an unfixed node; the positional uncertainty is expressed by a dashed line.

(5) AXIOM

?t

(6) LOCAL *ADJUNCTION

?t

?e

The unfixed node is decorated by the parse of *Tom*, triggering the actions to annotate the node with the content *Tom'* and the type e, as in (7). At this stage, the node is still unfixed, and it is the parse of the nominative case particle *ga* that fixes the structural underspecification, marking it as a subject node (i.e. the type-e node immediately dominated by the root node). The result of this resolution process is visually expressed in (8), where the dashed line has become a solid one.

[3] DS also models language production with the same machinery as used for language comprehension (Howes 2012 and references therein).

[4] Seraku (2013) argues that a type-e unfixed node is induced by LOCAL *ADJUNCTION alone in Japanese.

(7) Parsing *Tom*

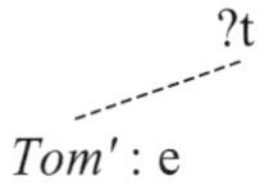

(8) Parsing *Tom-ga*

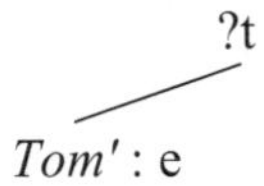

What comes next is *hashi* (= 'run'). Since Japanese is fully pro-drop, it is assumed that verbs project a propositional structure with argument slots. In the case of the intransitive verb *hashi*, it constructs a propositional structure where the subject argument is decorated with a place-holding meta-variable U.

(9) Output structure of parsing *hashi*

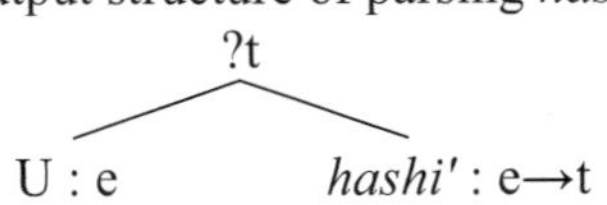

In (8), however, a subject node has already been created, and the argument slot provided by *hashi* collapses with this node. This is harmless since the argument slot is annotated with a meta-variable, a type of formula which is commensurate with any specified formula. Setting aside the tense suffix *ta* (see Cann 2011 and Seraku 2013 for a DS account of tense), the parse of *hashi* updates (8) into (10).

(10) Parsing *Tom-ga hashi*

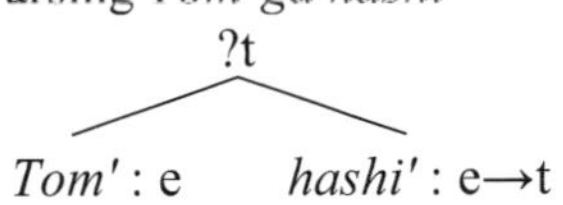

Finally, functional application and type deduction take place. This process is modelled as the general action ELIMINATION. The tree (11) is a final state, representing the interpretation of the string (4).

(11) ELIMINATION

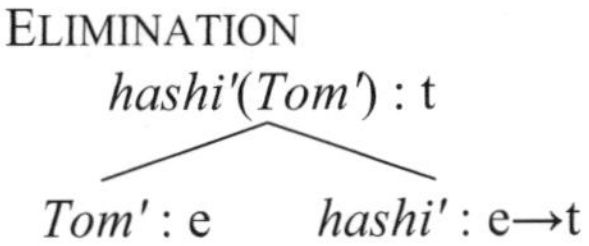

DS trees are "well-formed" iff no requirements are left in a tree, as in the tree (11). Furthermore, a string is "grammatical" iff there exists a sequence of tree updates from the AXIOM to a well-formed tree state (Cann et al. 2007).

3 A Uniform Account of Stripping

Building on Seraku's (2013) analysis of Japanese clefts, this section articulates a uniform account of case-marked and case-less stripping.

Firstly, we shall consider how the case-marked stripping (12)B (ignoring *iya* (= 'no')) is mapped onto a DS semantic tree incrementally.

(12) A: *Mary-ga hashi-tta-yo.*
M-NOM run-PAST-SFP
'Mary ran.'
B: *Iya, Tom-ga da.*
no T-NOM COP
'No, Tom.' (= 'No, Tom ran.')

Starting with the AXIOM (5), the parse of (12)B up to *Tom-ga* leads to the tree (8). The next element in (12)B is the copula *da*. Seraku (2013) argues that *da* is a **type-t** pro-form, which posits a type-t meta-variable to be replaced with a propositional content.

(13) Parsing *Tom-ga da*

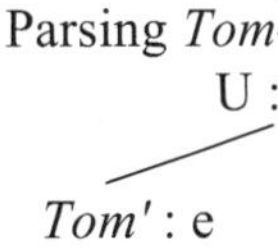

U is a type-t meta-variable. This tree state triggers the "re-use" of a previously-built type-t structure. Note that we have parsed the antecedent (12)A. In particular, when *hashi* (= 'run') was processed, a propositional structure with a subject slot was built. This is copied onto the present tree, updating (13) into (14), where the subject slot collapses with the node decorated with *Tom'* : e.

(14) Re-use of a previous structure

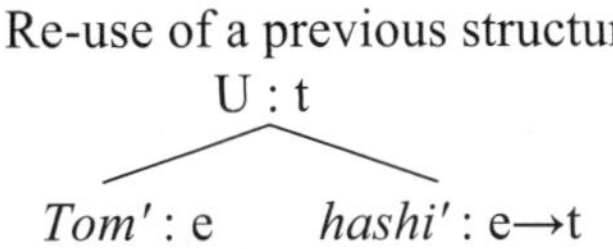

Finally, the parser runs ELIMINATION to clean up the tree, and the final state (15) correctly represents the interpretation of the stripping (12)B relative to the antecedent (12)A: 'No, Tom ran.'

(15) ELIMINATION

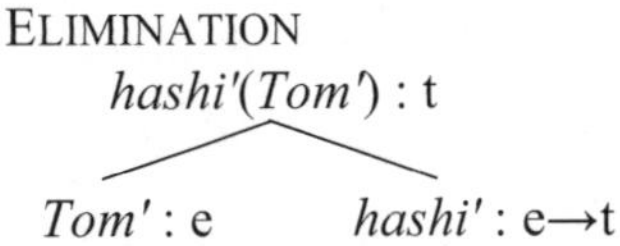

Let us turn to the case-less stripping (16)B. With the uniform nature of our account, a tree-update proceeds identically until *Tom* is parsed (see (7)).

(16) A: *Mary-ga hashi-tta-yo.*
M-NOM run-PAST-SFP
'Mary ran.'
B: *Iya, Tom da.*
no T COP
'No, Tom.' (= 'No, Tom ran.')

In (16), *Tom* is case-less, and thus the tree-update proceeds without resolving the unfixed node at this stage. The next expression is the copula *da*, which provides a type-t meta-variable, which triggers the "re-use" of the previous structure built by the parse of *hashi* in the antecedent.

(17) Re-use of a previous structure

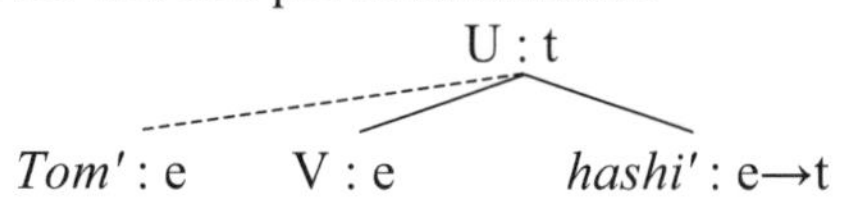

In (17), the node for *Tom* is unfixed. In general, an unfixed node may be merged with a fixed node of the same type. This structural merger is formulated as the general action UNIFICATION, which updates the tree (17) into (18).

(18) UNIFICATION

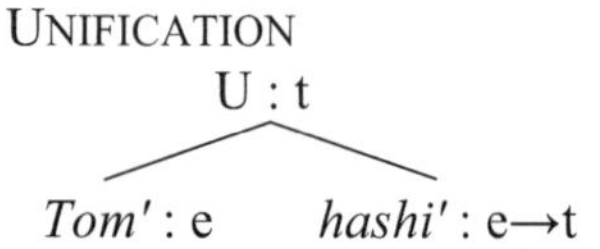

The unification process has fixed the node for *Tom* as a subject node. ELIMINATION outputs the final state (19), which is identical to (15), the tree for the case-marked stripping (12)B. This makes sure that the case-less stripping (16)B is truth-conditionally equivalent to the case-marked stripping (12)B.

(19) ELIMINATION

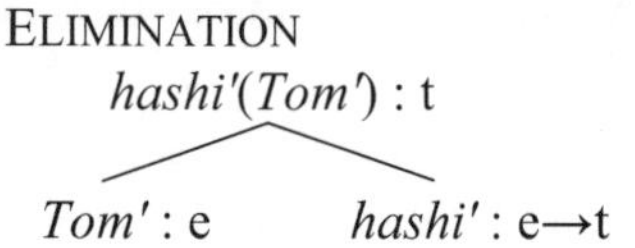

This section has developed a **uniform** account of case-marked and case-less stripping in the DS setting. The two types of stripping are mapped to **the same** tree, their difference being captured in terms of **how** a semantic tree is updated:

· In case-marked stripping, an unfixed node is fixed **lexically** by a case particle.
· In case-less stripping, it is fixed **non-lexically** by the general action UNIFICATION.

Let us close the present section by clarifying the notion of "focus." The NP in stripping is assumed to receive a focus (see Arregi 2010 and Merchant 2004). In DS, "focus" is not a primitive concept, but it emerges as an outcome of incremental tree growth (Cann et al. 2005). In stripping, the NP assigns a content value to an argument variable posited by a predicate in a presupposition clause. This saturation process evokes a focus effect as a result of incremental tree update (Seraku 2013).

4 Multiple Stripping

This section shows that our uniform treatment of stripping explains various types of data on multiple stripping data.

Within DS, each node is uniquely identified with respect to the other nodes in a tree (Blackburn & Meyer-Viol 1994). If **multiple** nodes are unfixed with respect to **the same** node, they will not be distinguishable. Thus, if supposedly distinct nodes are unfixed relative to the same node, they will lead to inconsistency in the node description.

(20) Unique-unfixed-node Constraint
If supposedly distinct nodes are unfixed with respect to the same node at a time, the node description becomes inconsistent.

This restriction is not a stipulation but a corollary of the tree logic (Blackburn & Meyer-Viol 1994). So, it plays a role in explaining linguistic puzzles cross-linguistically (Chatzikyriakidis & Kempson 2011, Gibson 2012).

Note that if two attempts to build a node with a different formula are possible only if the formulae are fully **commensurate**. In such a case, there will only be one such node. Consider UNIFICATION. In (18), the node decorated with the meta-variable V successfully merges with the node decorated with the formula *Tom'*. This is because a meta-variable is underspecified for its content and thus it is fully commensurate with any specified formula.

Based on the constraint (20), we shall address the case-marking issues of multiple stripping (see footnote 2). To being with, consider (21)B.

(21) A: *Mary-ga ringo-o tabe-ta-yo.*
M-NOM apple-ACC eat-PAST-SFP
'Mary ate apples.'
B: *Iya, Tom-ga nashi-o da.*
no T-NOM pear-ACC COP
'No, Tom, pears.' (= 'No, Tom ate pears.')

First, an unfixed node is introduced for *Tom*. This is immediately fixed by the case particle *ga*. At this point, an unfixed node is no longer in place, and an unfixed node may be once again introduced. This unfixed node is decorated by the second NP *nashi* (= 'pear') and resolved by the case particle *o*. So, the constraint (20) is not violated.

Next, consider the ungrammatical stripping data (22)B, where a case particle is dropped off *Tom* and *nashi* in (21)B.

(22) A: *Mary-ga ringo-o tabe-ta-yo.*
M-NOM apple-ACC eat-PAST-SFP
'Mary ate apples.'
B: **Iya, Tom nashi da.*
no T pear COP

In this example, an unfixed node for *Tom* cannot be resolved because (i) *Tom* is case-less and (ii) UNIFICATION cannot fire. Recall that UNIFICATION requires a **fixed type-e** node, but such a node is provided **after** the parse of the copula *da* triggers the re-use of a previous type-t structure. In short, UNIFICATION may be used for an unfixed node for the pre-copula NP alone. So, when an unfixed node is induced for the second NP *nashi*, there are two unfixed nodes relative to the same node at a time, violating the constraint (20).

Our analysis explains "partial case-marking," as illustrated in (23)B.

(23) A: *Mary-ga ringo-o tabe-ta-yo.*
M-NOM apple-ACC eat-PAST-SFP
'Mary ate apples.'
B: *Iya, Tom-ga nashi da.*
no T-NOM pear COP
'No, Tom, pears.' (= 'No, Tom ate pears.')

In this case, an unfixed node for *Tom* is resolved immediately by the nominative case particle *ga*, and an unfixed node can be safely introduced for the second NP *nashi*. This unfixed node cannot be resolved lexically since *nashi* lacks a case particle, but it can be resolved non-lexically by the general action UNIFICATION after the parse of *da*. So, there are no multiple unfixed nodes at a time, and the string is correctly predicted to be grammatical.

The analysis also predicts the ungrammaticality of (24)B, which exhibits the reversed case-marking pattern from (23)B.

(24) A: *Mary-ga ringo-o tabe-ta-yo.*
M-NOM apple-ACC eat-PAST-SFP
'Mary ate apples.'
B: **Iya, Tom nashi-o da.*
no T pear-ACC COP

These data are readily explained: an unfixed node for *Tom* cannot be fixed since (i) *Mary* is case-less and (ii) UNIFICATION cannot fire. Thus, the parser has to induce another unfixed node for the second NP *nashi*. This violates the constraint (20).

Our DS account is further corroborated by the multiple stripping with three NPs.

(25) A: *Tom-ga Mary-ni ringo-o age-ta-yo.*
T-NOM M-DAT apple-ACC give-PAST-SFP
'Tom gave apples to Mary.'
B: *Iya, Peter-ga Nancy-ni nashi-o da-yo.*
no P-NOM N-DAT pear-ACC COP-SFP
'No, Peter, to Nancy, pears.' (= 'No, Peter gave pears to Nancy.')
B':*Iya, Peter-ga Nancy-ni nashi da-yo.*
no P-NOM N-DAT pear COP-SFP

(25)B is grammatical since every unfixed node is immediately resolved by a particle. That is, there is only a single unfixed node at a time. (25)B' is also grammatical since an unfixed node for every non-final NP (i.e. *Peter*, *Nancy*) is immediately fixed by a particle, and an unfixed node for the final NP (i.e. *nashi*) is resolved by UNIFICATION after *da* is parsed. Once again, there is only a single unfixed node at a time. By contrast, the other case-marking patterns are ruled out: (i) only *Peter* is case-less, (ii) only *Nancy* is case-less, (iii) only *Peter* and *Nancy* are case-less, (iv) only *Peter* and *nashi* are case-less, (v) only *Nancy* and *nashi* are case-less, and (vi) every NP is case-less. In these cases, there are necessarily multiple unfixed nodes at a time.

Our uniform analysis explains the case-marking patterns of stripping as an outcome of incremental tree growth: an NP in stripping is processed at an unfixed node, and each unfixed node must be fixed before another unfixed node is introduced.

5 Extensions to Sluicing

There is a construction that is similar to stripping: sluicing (e.g. Hiraiwa & Ishihara 2012, Kizu 2005, Nishiyama et al. 1996, Takahashi 1996; see also Ross 1969). In this section, we note that the case-marking patterns of stripping are carried over into sluicing, and contend that our analysis of stripping is extended to various sluicing data.

In (26), the second clause exemplifies sluicing. As indicated in the parentheses, the case particle *ga* is optional, as in the case of stripping.

(26) *Paatii-de dareka-ga kyoku-o*
party-at someone-NOM song-ACC
uta-tta-ga, boku-wa [dare(-ga)-ka]
sing-PAST-but I-TOP [who(-NOM)-Q]
omoida-se-nai.
remember-can-NEG
'Someone sang a song at a party, but I cannot remember who sang a song.'

Multiple sluicing is also possible, as shown in (27). Of particular note is that in the sequence of *wh*-items, a case particle may be dropped off the final *wh*-item alone (in the present case, *nani*).

(27) *Paatii-de dareka-ga nanika-o*
party-at someone-NOM something-ACC
uta-tta-ga, boku-wa [dare(-ga)*
sing-PAST-but I-TOP [who(-NOM)
nani(-o) da-tta-ka] omoida-se-nai.
what(-ACC) COP-PAST-Q] remember-can-NEG
'Someone sang something at a party, but I cannot remember who sang what.'

The tendency in the past literature is to assign a radically different structure to sluicing depending on whether a *wh*-phrase is case-marked (Fukaya 2007, 2013; see also Takahashi 1996). Such non-uniform analyses are challenged by (27), where a single sluicing involves a case-marked *wh*-phrase and a case-less *wh*-phrase simultaneously. Further, even if it is possible to invent a new mechanism which allows case-marked and case-less *wh*-items in a single clause, it remains the mystery why only the final *wh*-phrase may be case-less.

5.1 A Uniform Account of Sluicing

Our analysis of sluicing is essentially the same as that of stripping, but there are two new ingredients. First, the content of a *wh*-phrase is a "WH-meta-variable." Unlike usual meta-variables, WH-meta-variables do not have to be saturated (Kempson et al. 2001). Second, sluicing involves the embedding of clauses; within DS, this is analysed by inducing an unfixed node of **type-t**. Building on Cann et al. (2005), Seraku (2013) claims that such an unfixed node is induced by *ADJUNCTION in Japanese.

Let us first consider (26). The parse of the pre-*ga* clause results in a propositional structure. This is associated with another, emergent propositional structure by the parse of *ga* (= 'but'). Formally, this structure pairing is instantiated as a "LINK" relation, as visually expressed by a curved arrow. (The exact LINK mechanism is not relevant to our discussion; for details, see Cann et al. 2005 and Kempson et al. 2001). In (28), the adjunct *paatii-de* (= 'at a party') is neglected for brevity, and the internal structure is schematised as a triangle.

(28) Parsing *Dareka-ga kyoku-o uta-tta-ga*

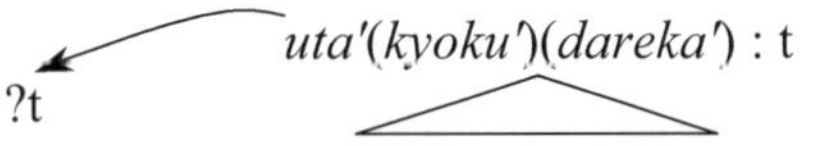

Then, the emergent propositional structure with ?t is fleshed out by the parse of the sluicing string. The parse of *boku-wa* leads to the usual structure-update: LOCAL *ADJUNCTION induces an unfixed node of type-e; this unfixed node is decorated by the matrix subject *boku* (= 'I'); finally, the node is resolved as a subject node by the topic marker *wa*.

(29) Parsing (26) up to *boku-wa*

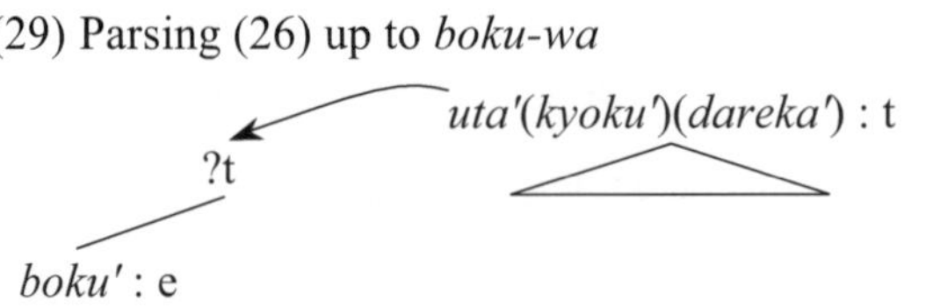

It is time to parse the *wh*-item *dare* (= 'who'). This is where the new ingredients come into place. First, *ADJUNCTION induces an unfixed node of type-t (expressed by a dotted line), allowing the parser to built an embedded propositional structure.

(30) *ADJUNCTION

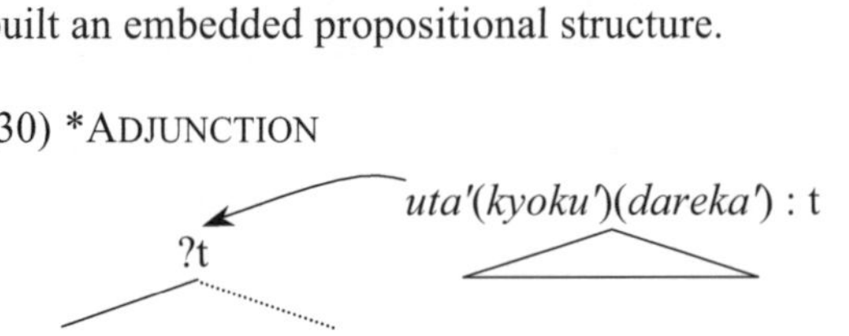

Second, LOCAL *ADJUNCTION fires to introduce an unfixed node of type-e. This node is decorated by the parse of the *wh*-phrase *dare*. As illustrated in (31), the content of *dare* is a WH-meta-variable. The unfixed node for *dare* may be resolved in two ways depending on the case-marking of *dare*.

(31) Parsing the string (26) up to *dare*

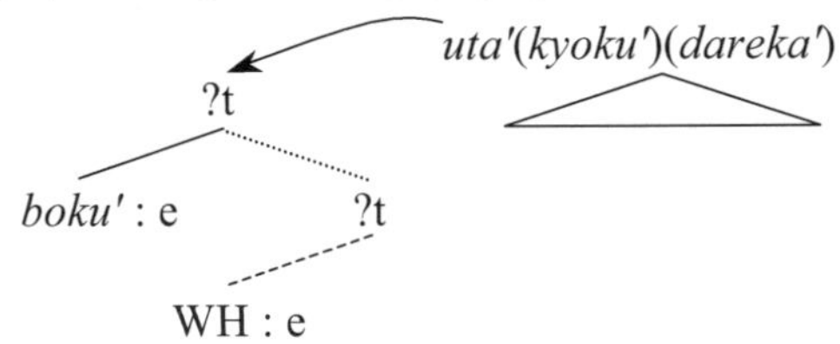

Case-marked sluicing: When *dare* is marked with the nominative case particle *ga*, the unfixed node for *dare* is immediately fixed as a subject node.

(32) Parsing the string (26) up to *dare-ga*

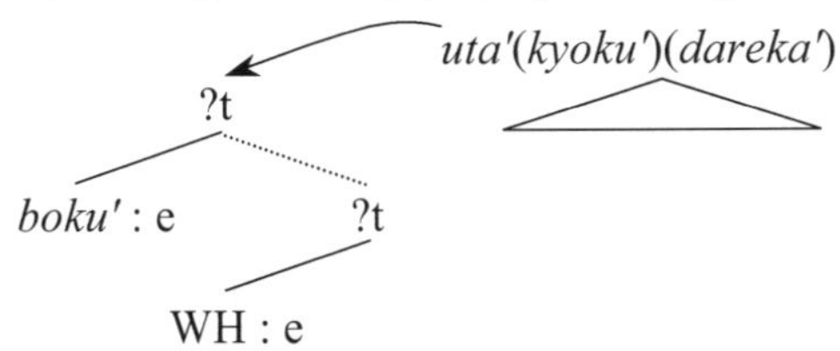

The next item *da* provides a type-t meta-variable, which triggers the re-use of the structure built by *uta* (= 'sing') in the first clause. With respect to this clause, the internal argument slot of *uta'* is saturated as *kyoku'*. As for the external argument slot, it collapses with the WH-meta-variable. Then, *omoidas-e-nai* (= 'cannot remember') fleshes out the higher ?t-decorated structure. This involves the creation of a type-t node as an internal argument. This type-t node is merged with the unfixed, lower type-t node by means of UNIFICATION. Finally, ELIMINATION is run, and the final state (33) holds, where *o-e-n'* is the content of *omoidas-e-nai*.

(33) ELIMINATION

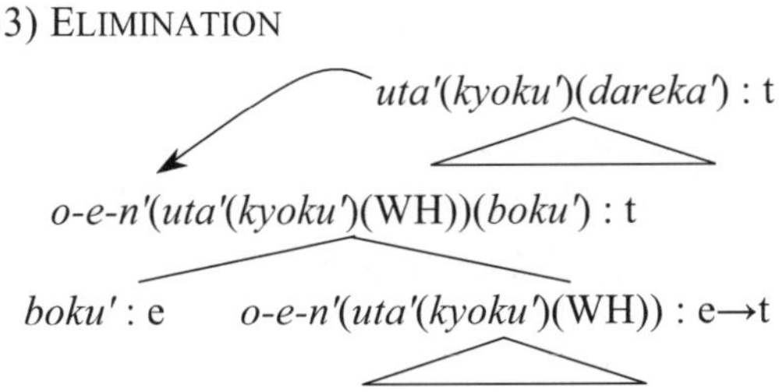

Case-less sluicing: The tree state (33) holds even when the case particle *ga* is not attached to the *wh*-phrase *dare*. That is, irrespective of case-marking, uniformity in our analysis remains intact.

To begin with, the parse of (26) up to the *wh*-phrase *dare* yields (31), repeated as (34).

(34) Parsing the string (26) up to *dare*

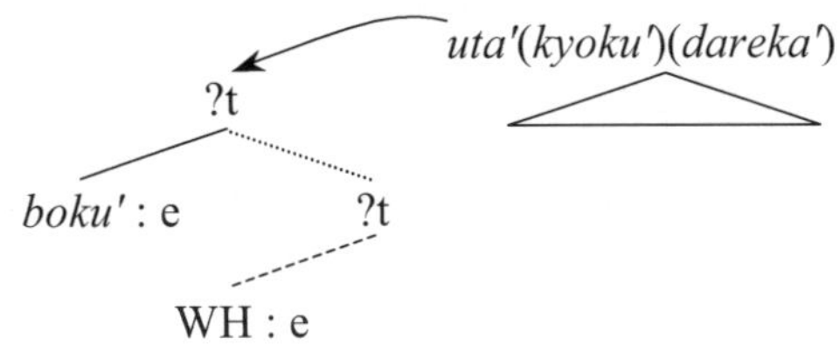

Given that a case particle is absent, the tree-update proceeds without resolving the unfixed node for *dare*. The unfixed node gets resolved as a subject node by UNIFICATION after the copula *da* is parsed. This is because *da* triggers the re-use of a previous propositional structure, where there is a fixed node of type-e, with which the unfixed node of type-e is merged. The rest of the process is as usual, and the tree update ends with the final state (33). In this way, the identical final tree state holds no matter whether case-marking is encompassed in sluicing.

There is a remaining problem for our analysis of sluicing. Unlike stripping, the copula *da* in sluicing may be omitted (Nishiyama et al. 1996). Since *da* plays an important role in our account, it must be clarified why *da* may be dropped in sluicing but not stripping. This is a residual for future work.

5.2 Multiple Sluicing

The relevant data are repeated here as (35).

(35) *Paatii-de dareka-ga nanika-o*
party-at someone-NOM something-ACC
uta-tta-ga, boku-wa [dare(-ga)*
sing-PAST-but I-TOP [who(-NOM)
nani(-o) da-tta-ka] omoida-se-nai.
what(-ACC) COP-PAST-Q] remember-can-NEG
'Someone sang something at a party, but I cannot remember who sang what.'

The case-marking patterns in (35) are explained in our account; the analysis is essentially the same as the one given in Section 4, and brief expositions would suffice. Firstly, multiple sluicing is possible as long as each *wh*-phrase has an appropriate case particle. This is because an unfixed node for each *wh*-phrase can be immediately resolved by a case particle. Second, a case particle may be dropped only if it is attached to a final *wh*-phrase. This is because UNIFICATION (i.e. the non-lexical action to resolve an unfixed node) is applicable to the final *wh*-word: (i) UNIFICATION requires a propositional structure with a fixed type-e node, (ii) such a structure is provided by the copula *da*, and (iii) *da* is parsed only after all *wh*-phrases are processed.

In a nutshell, our dynamic account integrates the two types of sluicing and predicts the distribution of case particles in terms of incremental parsing.

6 Conclusion

Our analysis of stripping and sluicing is uniform in two senses: (i) stripping/sluicing are treated by the same machinery and (ii) for each construction, no distinct structures are postulated. Further, we have revealed the partial-case-marking patterns for these ellipsis constructions, and have shown that they are amenable to our unitary account.

Acknowledgments

I greatly benefitted from discussions with Ash Asudeh, Mary Dalrymple, Ruth Kempson, Jieun Kiaer, and Lutz Marten. I would like to thank the anonymous PACLIC reviewers for their valuable comments on the earlier version of this article.

References

Arregi, K. 2010. Ellipsis in Split Questions. Natural Language and Linguistic Theory 28: 539-592.

Blackburn, P., Meyer-Viol, W. 1994. Linguistics, Logic, and Finite Trees. Bulletin of Interest Group of Pure and Applied Logics 2: 2-39.

Cann, R. 2011. Towards an Account of the Auxiliary System in English. In Kempson, R., et al. (eds.) The Dynamics of Lexical Interfaces. CSLI, Stanford.

Cann, R., Kempson, R., Marten, L. 2005. The Dynamics of Language: An Introduction. Elsevier, Oxford.

Cann, R., Kempson, R., Purver, M. 2007. Context-dependent Well-formedness. Research on Language and Computation 5: 333-358.

Chatzikyriakidis, S., Kempson, R. 2011. Standard Modern and Pontic Greek Greek Person Restrictions. Journal of Greek Linguistics 11(2): 127-66.

Fukaya, T. 2007. Sluicing and Stripping in Japanese and some Implications. Ph.D. dissertation, University of Southern California.

Fukaya, T. 2013. Island Insensitivity in Japanese and some Implications. In Merchant, J., Simpson, A. (eds.) Sluicing: Cross-linguistic perspectives. Oxford University Press, Oxford.

Fukaya, T, Hoji, H. 2003. Stripping and Sluicing in Japanese and their Implications. Bird, S. et al. (eds). Proceedings of the 18th WCCFL. Cascadilla Press, MA, Somerville.

Fukui, N., Sakai, H. 2003. The Visibility Guideline for Functional Categories. Lingua 113: 321-375.

Gibson, H. 2012. Auxiliary placement in Rangi. Ph.D. thesis, SOAS (University of London).

Hankamer, J., Sag, I. 1976. Deep and Surface Anaphora. Linguistic Inquiry 7: 391-426.

Hiraiwa, K., Ishihara, S. 2012. Syntactic Metamorphosis. Syntax 15: 142-180.

Howes, C. 2012. Coordinating in Dialogue. Ph.D. thesis, Queen Mary, University of London.

Kempson, R., Gregoromichelaki, E., Howes, C. 2011. The Dynamics of Lexical Interfaces. CSLI, Stanford.

Kempson, R., Meyer-Viol, W., Gabbay, D. 2001. Dynamic Syntax. Blackwell, Oxford.

Kizu, M. 2005. Cleft Constructions in Japanese Syntax. Palgrave, New York.

Merchant, J. 2004. Fragments and Ellipsis. Linguistics and Philosophy 27: 661-738.

Nishiyama, K., Whitman, J., Yi, E.-Y. 1996. Syntactic Movement of Overt *Wh*-Phrases in Japanese and Korean. In Akatsuka, N., et al. (eds.) Japanese/Korean Linguistics 5. CSLI, Stanford.

Ross, J. R. 1969. "Guess Who?" In Binnick, R. I. et al. (eds.) Papers from the 5th Regional Meeting of Chicago Linguistic Society. University of Chicago Press, Chicago.

Sakai, H. 2000. Predicate Ellipsis and Nominalization in Japanese. Proceedings of 2000 Seoul International Conference on Language and Computation. Korea University, Seoul.

Seraku, T. 2013. Clefts, Relatives, and Language Dynamics. D.Phil. thesis, University of Oxford.

Takahashi, D. 1994. Sluicing in Japanese. Journal of East Asian Linguistics 3, 265-300.

A Corpus-Based Quantitative Study of Nominalizations across Chinese and British Media English

Ying Liu[1], Alex Chengyu Fang[1], and Naixing Wei[2]

[1]Department of Linguistics and Translation, City University of Hong Kong, Hong Kong
yliu227-c@my.cityu.edu.hk, acfang@cityu.edu.hk
[2]School of Foreign Languages, Beihang University, Beijing, China
nxwei@buaa.edu.cn

Abstract

This paper reports on a corpus-based quantitative study of the use of nominalizations across China English and British English in two comparable media corpora. In contrast to previous corpus-based studies of nominalizations, we start by using a syntactic approach and proceed with some methodological innovations incorporating large lexical databases and syntactically annotated corpora. The data show that there are significant differences in the use of nominalizations across these two English varieties. It is hoped that this research will offer useful insights on variations in nominalization across different English varieties and also on the understanding of the two English varieties in question.

1 Introduction

Nominalization can refer to "the process of forming a noun from some other word-class (e.g. *red + ness*) or the derivation of a noun phrase from an underlying clause (e.g. *Her answering of the letter*... from *She answered the letter*)" (Crystal, 1997: 260). It has been approached by scholars from various perspectives, covering aspects of its form, meaning and use, as in the traditional grammar (e.g. Quirk et al., 1985), generative grammar (e.g. Lees, 1960; Chomsky, 1970), functional grammar (e.g. Halliday, 1994; Eggins, 2004) and cognitive grammar (e.g. Langacker, 1991). Among other things, nominalization is of close relevance to language variation studies due to its function to distinguish a nominal and compressed style from a colloquial one (e.g. Biber, 1986; Greenbaum, 1988, etc). However, in spite of numerous theoretical discussions, nominalization has only been touched upon sporadically in corpus-based studies, with notable exceptions of Biber (1986), Biber et al. (1998, 1999) and Leech et al. (2009). Due to an overwhelming word-based approach and a reliance on suffixes for identification, only a limited scope of nominalizations has been included in previous corpus-based studies. In addition, although these studies have revealed the discriminatory power of nominalization in language use with regard to spoken and written registers and genres, there are few attempts to investigate the use of nominalization across different language varieties except Leech et al. (2009).

The research to be reported on in this paper attempts to bridge the afore-said gaps. It is exploratory and descriptive in nature and attempts to examine the cross-variety quantitative differences in the use of nominalizations across China English and British English in two comparable media corpora. Our study is different from previous corpus-based studies in several important respects. First, our study is not about variations of nominalization across registers and genres, but will explore variations across different English varieties, a different level of linguistic variation. The reason why we chose China English is that previous studies (Xu, 2008, 2010) have shown that there are frequent uses of nominalization in China English. British English is chosen as the base for comparison. Second, the present study will adopt a syntactic approach to nominalizations, an approach that has not been undertaken in previous corpus-based studies. We will explain this further in Section 3. Third, there are some methodological innovations in the identification and retrieval of nominalizations in this study. We will not rely on the suffix-based

Copyright 2014 by Ying Liu, Alex Chengyu Fang, and Naixing Wei
28th Pacific Asia Conference on Language, Information and Computation pages 101–110

method. Instead, we will show how large lexical databases and syntactically annotated corpora can fruitfully complement each other in research into a syntactic feature which is not easily extracted from corpora.

The research questions that we intend to address are the following: (1) Are there any significant quantitative differences in the use of nominalizations across Chinese and British Media English? (2) In what way, if any, does Chinese Media English differ from British Media English in terms of the quantitative use of nominalizations? It is hoped that the current study will not only show whether or not these two varieties demonstrate any significant quantitative differences regarding this particular linguistic construction but also be able to suggest reasons for the differences we found.

This paper is organized as follows. We will review related work concerning corpus-based studies of nominalization in Section 2. Section 3 will describe our approach to nominalization in the present study. In Section 4, we will introduce the methodology including the corpora used and the procedures to retrieve nominalizations. Section 5 will present the quantitative findings, followed by some discussions in Section 6. Section 7 concludes this research with prospects for future work.

2 Related Work: Corpus-Based Studies of Nominalization

Most previous research of nominalization is theoretical in nature. Nominalization has so far not attracted wide-spread interests among corpus linguists. For the few previous corpus-based studies, focus has been on how its uses vary in different registers.

Chafe (1982) investigated the use of nominalizations in 9,911 words of informal spoken language (from dinner table conversations) and 12,368 words of formal written language (from academic papers). He has shown that nominalizations occur about 11 times more in the written language than in the spoken language. He further explained that such difference is due to the function of nominalization to integrate more information into fewer words which contributes to the integration and detachment of the written language in contrast to the fragmentation and involvement of the spoken language.

Biber (1986) investigated nominalizations (i.e. words ending in *-tion*, *-ment*, *-ness*, and *-ity*) in the *LOB Corpus* and the *London-Lund Corpus*. Nominalization is interpreted as having the function which "marks a highly abstract, nominal content and a highly learned style" (Biber, 1986: 395). It is found that nominalizations occur more often in written texts (e.g. official documents, academic prose, and editorial letters) but less in spoken texts (e.g. telephone and face-to-face conversations). Biber et al. (1998) have shown that the academic prose has a frequency of nominalizations (i.e. words ending in *-tion*/*-sion*, *-ment*, *-ness*, and *-ity*) almost four times larger than fiction and speech based on findings from the *Longman-Lancaster Corpus* and the *London-Lund Corpus* and concluded that nominalizations tend to occur more in more formal texts. Biber et al. (1999) investigated nominalizations (i.e. words ending in *-tion*, *-ity*, *-ism*, and *-ness*) in four registers (i.e. conversation, fiction, newspaper, and academic prose) in the *Longman Spoken and Written English Corpus*. They found that the frequency of nominalization grows sharply from conversation to fiction, newspaper language, and academic prose. They concluded that nominalization is a reliable indicator for register distinction.

Moreover, Leech et al. (2009) have examined the frequency of nominalizations ending in 12 suffixes in two different English varieties in four corpora (i.e. *LOB*, *Brown*, *FLOB* and *Frown*). They found that American English consistently uses more nominalizations across all four registers (i.e. press, general prose, learned and fiction) than British English. They therefore concluded that American English displays a more compressed style and a higher level of density of content than British English.

Despite many findings mentioned above, there are several areas where further research is necessary. First, previous empirical studies of nominalizations are overwhelmingly word-based. Yet it is clear that "nominalization is no mere substitute for a verb or an adjective. Instead, the use of a nominalized expression requires an entirely different organization of the whole sentence" (Downing and Locke, 2006: 461). This is exactly how nominalization can pack much information into a single noun phrase and contribute to the compressed and nominal style.

Second, they have been fairly limited in the

scope of nominalizations included due to the current practice of identifying nominalizations by searching suffixes. This suffix-based method seems rather random since there are usually no explanations why certain suffixes are chosen over others. Another important drawback of the suffix-based method is that nominalizations derived from verbs through conversion are left out. For example, deverbal nouns such as *increase* derived from the verb *increase* cannot be retrieved by the suffix-based method. Therefore, the existing corpus-based studies have so far only focused on nominalizations derived through suffixation although researchers are aware that nominalizations include those derived by means of both suffixation and conversion (e.g. Tyrkkö and Hiltunen, 2009; Biber and Gray, 2013).

Finally, till now, generalizations about how the uses of nominalizations vary across linguistic contexts have mostly based on their occurrences in registers and genres in British and/or American English. It is rare to find corpus-based studies of nominalizations across different English varieties.

Therefore, in the present study, we will adopt a syntactic approach and a different methodology to identify and retrieve nominalizations, and extend the scope of previous studies well beyond registers and genres to different English varieties. This will be discussed further in the following sections.

3 Our Approach: A Syntactic Approach to Nominalization

As already mentioned above, our concern will be with nominalization defined as a syntactic feature. Nominalization in this study refers to "a noun phrase such as *the quarrel over pay* which has a systematic correspondence with a clause structure and the noun head of such a phrase is normally related morphologically to a verb (i.e. a deverbal noun)" (Quirk et al., 1985:1288).

To be more specific, deverbal nouns refer to nouns that are produced by combining suffixes with verb bases (Quirk et al., 1985:1550) and nouns that are produced through the process of conversion (Quirk et al., 1985:1558). Thus, unlike previous corpus-based studies which only include nominalizations derived through suffixation, nominalizations in our study include both suffixed nominalizations (e.g. *his refusal to help*) and converted nominalizations (e.g. *the quarrel over pay*). As for the correspondence between a nominalization and a clause structure, it is stated that "the relation between a nominalization and a corresponding clause can be more or less explicit, according to how far the nominalization specifies, through modifiers and determinatives, the nominal or adverbial elements of a corresponding clause" (Quirk et al., 1985:1289). For example, sentence [1] can have the following nominalizations:

[1] *The reviewers criticized his play in a hostile manner.*
[1a] *the reviewers' hostile criticizing of his play*
[1b] *the reviewers' hostile criticism of his play*
[1c] *the reviewers' criticism of his play*
[1d] *the reviewers' criticism*
[1e] *their criticism*
[1f] *the criticism*
[1g] *criticism*

(Quirk et al., 1985:1289)

According to Quirk et al. (1985:1289), the above noun phrases are "ordered from the most explicit [1a] to the extreme of inexplicitness [1g] but each of them could occupy the function of a nominalization". We therefore will consider the correspondence between a nominalization and a clause structure as on a continuum, being explicit or implicit, and all the above constructions from [1a] to [1g] will be taken into account in this study.

With nominalizations defined as syntactic structures, we will then turn to the methodology to retrieve them from corpora in the following section.

4 Methodology

4.1 Corpora

The data for our study were drawn from two comparable corpora, namely, the *Chinese Media English Corpus* (Henceforth CMEC) and the *British Media English Corpus* (Henceforth BMEC) (Fang et al., 2012). The two media corpora, with about one million words each, are of the same design and structure and consist of about 2,000 texts sampled from three mediums, namely, newspaper, magazine and the Internet. The texts of various topics are sampled from specially allotted separate sections in the three mediums. The five categories in CMEC and BMEC are: arts and culture, business, editorial, news report, and social life. Arts and culture is largely concerned with topics of fine arts and cultural heritage. Business is about commerce, finance or economics. Editorial is "a lengthy opinion piece that provides the official view of the newspaper on particular issues" (Semino, 2009: 442) while news report is "a relatively short piece which consists of a 'factual' account of events that have occurred since the last edition of the newspaper" (Semino, 2009: 441). Social life is primarily associated with the topics of lifestyle and leisure. As can be seen, the five categories differ in various topics and so we would predict that there will be systematic differences in the uses of nominalizations.

Although the overall size of CMEC and BMEC is only about one million word tokens, the major advantage of the two corpora is the fact that they are comparable in design which allows for direct comparison between the two. The summary statistics of the two corpora is shown in Table 1.

	CMEC		*BMEC*	
Category	*Texts*	*Tokens*	*Texts*	*Tokens*
Arts&culture	451	200,464	430	205,353
Business	434	200,110	366	193,162
Editorial	371	200,456	314	196,910
News report	457	203,449	374	198,834
Social life	513	199,144	395	196,053
Total	2,226	1,003,623	1,879	990,312

Table 1. Basic Statistics of CMEC and BMEC

4.2 Retrieval of Nominalizations

In line with the definition of nominalization mentioned in Section 3, the extraction of nominalizations is operationalized in three steps as shown in Figure 1: (1) to parse the raw CMEC and BMEC; (2) to generate a list of deverbal nouns that function as the noun head of nominalizations; (3) to extract all noun phrases headed by these deverbal nouns from the parsed CMEC and BMEC.

For the first step, CMEC and BMEC have been parsed by the Stanford Parser[1] (Version 3.2.0; Klein and Manning, 2003). The Stanford parser is trained on the *Penn Treebank Corpus* (Marcus et al., 1993) and uses the Penn Treebank POS tagset (Santorini, 1990) and syntactic tagset (Santorini et al., 1991). Its parsing accuracy in terms of F1 score is reported to have reached 90.4% (Socher et al., 2013).

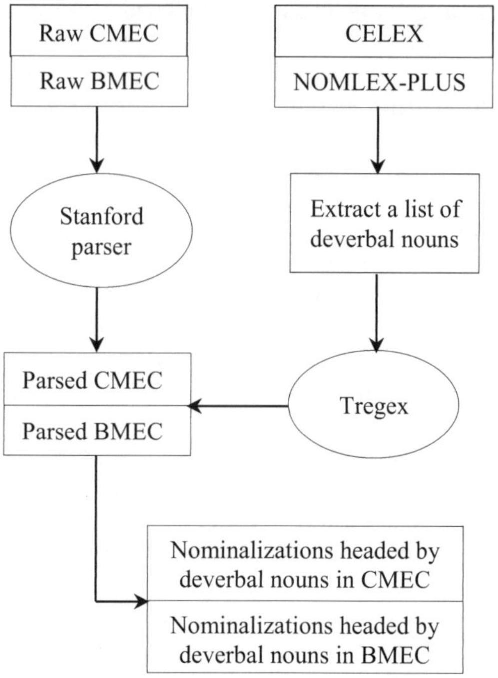

Figure 1. Flow Chart to Retrieve Nominalizations

As has been discussed in Section 2, the suffix-based method to identify nominalizations has certain drawbacks. Thus, in the second step, we adopted a wordlist method which uses lexical databases to extract deverbal nouns. Based on a survey of existing large lexical databases, CELEX and NOMLEX-PLUS which have derivational morphology information were used in this study. *CELEX English Lexical Database* (Baayen et al., 1995) consists of 52,447 lemmas[2] (or 160,595 word forms) which are extracted from *Oxford Advanced Learner's Dictionary* (1974) and *Longman Dictionary of Contemporary English* (1978). NOMLEX-PLUS (Meyers, 2007) is an extension of NOMLEX (Macleod et al., 1998), a dictionary of English deverbal nouns. In addition to NOMLEX, another source for deverbal nouns in NOMLEX-PLUS is COMLEX Syntax (Grishman et al., 1994), a dictionary annotated with rich syntactic information for nouns, adjectives and verbs. Deverbal nouns ending in *ing* in NOMLEX-PLUS were excluded in this study because their POS tagging as nouns is based on their usage in a specific corpus and their noun status is subject to

[1] See http://nlp.stanford.edu/software/lex-parser.shtml.

[2] Although CELEX-lemmas are not extracted from corpus, they cover 92% of the 17.9-million-word COBUILD corpus.

change elsewhere. In total, we extracted 5,538 deverbal noun lemmas derived by means of both suffixation and conversion from CELEX and NOMLEX-PLUS, which account for 27.64% of all noun tokens in CMEC and 29.15% in BMEC [3].

The last step was facilitated with Tregex [4] (version 3.2.0; Levy and Andrew, 2006), which is a tree query tool for matching patterns in trees. Tregex contains the main functionality of TGrep2 (Rohde, 2005) and adds a few more relations for syntactic trees such as dominance, precedence, and headship which are perfectly useful for our research purpose. We successively went through the syntactically parsed CMEC and BMEC and retrieved those nominalized structures headed by the deverbal nouns in our list.

Following the method outlined above, 66,850 nominalizations from CMEC and 65,104 nominalizations from BMEC were retrieved. The summary statistics is presented in Table 2.

Category	*#CMEC*	*#BMEC*
Arts & culture	10,938	11,295
Business	16,061	15,126
Editorial	15,220	14,061
News report	13,862	13,580
Social life	10,769	11,042
Total	66,850	65,104

Table 2. Summary Statistics of Retrieved Nominalizations from CMEC and BMEC

An example of the extracted nominalization headed by *development* from CMEC is shown in Figure 2.

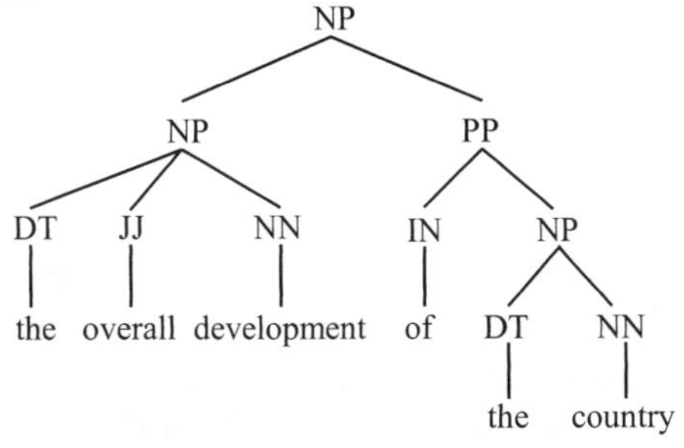

Figure 2. An Example of Retrieved Nominalizations (from c_m_ed_bjr_021.txt.prd)

[3] We admit that our deverbal noun wordlist is not a complete one. In fact, no such a complete list exists. But the deverbal noun is only one kind of nouns. Considering its coverage, we claim that nominalizations extracted in terms of our list are sufficient for our research purpose.

[4] See http://nlp.stanford.edu/software/tregex.shtml.

5 Results

5.1 Frequency and Distribution of All Nominalizations across CME and BME

Figure 3 gives a barplot representation of the mean frequencies of nominalizations across CME and BME and the five categories. Relative frequencies of nominalizations were calculated per 1,000 words in order to make comparisons of texts of diverse lengths possible. For statistical testing, we computed the relative frequency of nominalizations per 1,000 words for each text in CMEC and BMEC. Then an independent sample *t*-test was run to determine whether significant differences exist in the mean nominalization frequencies. The *t*-test results are presented in detail in Table 3.

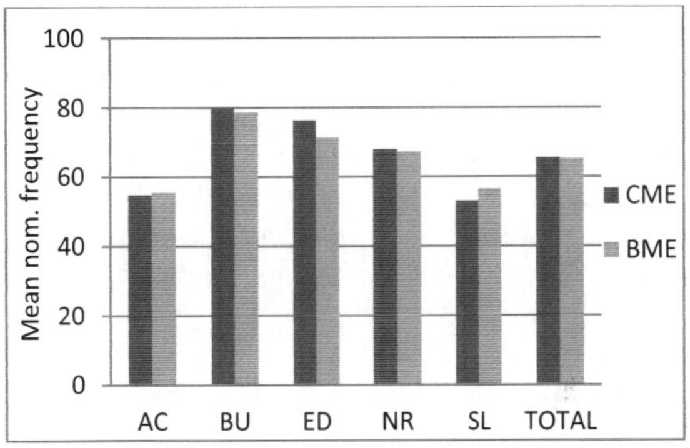

Figure 3. Barplots of Mean Nominalization Frequencies across CME and BME

As can be seen in Figure 3, the mean nominalization frequency for the overall CME (M=65.52) is a little higher than that for BME (M=65.14). But the *t*-test result shows that there is no significant difference in the uses of nominalizations in the overall CME and BME (t=0.578, p=0.563). With regard to the five categories, we can see from Figure 3 that the mean values in business (M=80.02), editorial (M=76.23), and news report (M=67.83) in CME are also higher than those in BME. However, the *t*-test result shows that only the difference in editorial is statistically significant (t=3.668, p=0.000), indicating that there are more uses of nominalizations in editorial in CME than BME. As for arts and culture and social life, the mean frequencies for BME look higher than those for

CME, but we only find statistically significant difference in social life (t=-2.964, p=0.003).

Category	*Variety*	*N. of Texts*	*Mean*	*Std. D*	*T*	*df*	*p-value*
Arts & culture	CME	451	54.71	18.39	-.634	870.583	.526
	BME	430	55.44	15.88			
Business	CME	434	80.02	23.17	1.006	780.582	.315
	BME	366	78.60	16.77			
Editorial*	CME	371	76.23	18.94	3.668	682.965	.000*
	BME	314	71.34	15.91			
News report	CME	457	67.83	22.45	.538	826.300	.591
	BME	374	67.05	19.45			
Social life*	CME	513	52.98	18.30	-2.964	906	.003*
	BME	395	56.51	17.10			
Overall corpus	CME	2226	65.52	23.11	.578	4102.285	.563
	BME	1879	65.14	19.25			

Note: * indicates a statistically significant difference ($p < 0.05$).

Table 3. Results of t-test of Mean Nominalization Frequency across CME and BME

To sum up, in terms of the mean frequencies, there are significantly more uses of nominalizations in CME in editorials, whilst BME uses significantly more nominalizations in social life than CME. Before we draw tentative conclusions, we will investigate the frequencies and distributions of suffixed nominalizations and converted nominalizations respectively.

5.2 Frequency and Distribution of Suffixed Nominalizations across CME and BME

This section shows the frequency and distribution of suffixed nominalizations (e.g. *his refusal to help*). The barplots are shown in Figure 4, and t-test results are presented in Table 4.

In terms of the overall corpus, it is observed from Figure 4 that the mean suffixed nominalization frequency for CME (M=32.58) is higher than that for BME (M=29.03). The barplot representation indicates that there are more uses of suffixed nominalizations in the overall CME than BME, and this is confirmed by the t-test result (see Table 4) which suggests that the difference in CME and BME is statistically significant (t=8.121, p=0.000). Interestingly, a higher mean score for CME can also be consistently seen in all the five categories although it is not so evident in social life. The t-test results show that there are significantly more uses of suffixed nominalizations in CME in arts and culture (t=2.903, p=0.004), business (t=5.625, p=0.000), editorial (t=7.167, p=0.000), and news report (t=3.393, p=0.001).

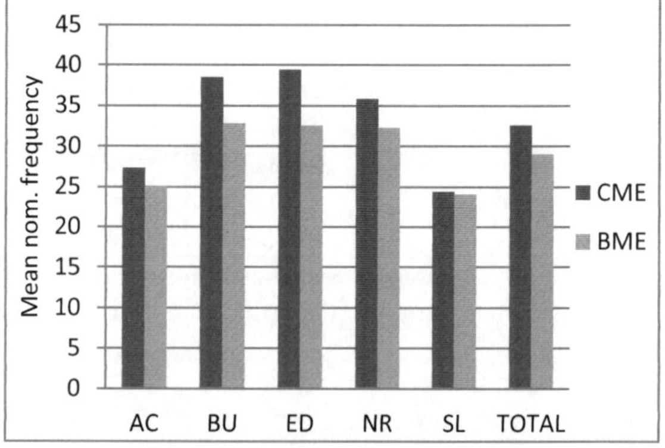

Figure 4. Barplots of Mean Suffixed Nominalization Frequencies across CME and BME

However, nominalizations are slightly more frequent but not significantly so in social life in CME (t=0.431, p=0.666). One possible interpretation is that there are few nominalizations used in social life in both CME and BME because as we previously mentioned in Section 4.1, texts in social life in CMEC and BMEC are often concerned with more casual topics such as lifestyles and leisure. We can see from Table 4 that the mean suffixed nominalization frequency in social life in CME (M=24.38) is the lowest among all the five categories (27.33 for arts and culture, 38.48 for business, 39.43 for editorial, and 35.81 for news report). The same is true for the mean frequency of suffixed nominalization in social life in BME. Therefore, the lowest frequency of suffixed nominalization in social life might have resulted in the insignificant difference in the two English varieties.

Category	*Variety*	*N. of Texts*	*Mean*	*Std. D*	*T*	*df*	*p-value*
Arts & culture*	CME	451	27.33	13.11	2.903	841.441	.004*
	BME	430	25.05	10.07			
Business*	CME	434	38.48	16.82	5.625	775.448	.000*
	BME	366	32.75	11.90			
Editorial*	CME	371	39.43	14.60	7.167	663.180	.000*
	BME	314	32.57	10.34			
News report*	CME	457	35.81	16.64	3.393	828.903	.001*
	BME	374	32.27	13.47			
Social life	CME	513	24.38	11.41	.431	906	.666
	BME	395	24.04	11.48			
Overall corpus*	CME	2226	32.58	15.81	8.121	4069.139	.000*
	BME	1879	29.03	12.16			

Note: * indicates a statistically significant difference ($p < 0.05$).

Table 4. Results of *t*-test of Mean Suffixed Nominalization Frequency across CME and BME

Previous studies (e.g. Biber, 1986; Biber et al., 1998, 1999) have shown that suffixed nominalizations tend to occur in texts which convey highly abstract information and mark a formal and nominal style. The findings that there are significantly more uses of suffixed nominalizations in CME and also in its categories (except social life) suggest that CME adopts a more formal style in media English writing than BME.

A closer observation of the data reveals that this nominal style in CME has been in use to differing extents in various categories and it is particularly more prominent in business and editorial. When we look at the distribution of suffixed nominalizations across the five categories in CME, we can see a clear descending order for their mean frequencies: editorial (M=39.43) > business (M=38.48) > news report (M=35.81) > arts and culture (M=27.33) > social life (M=24.38), but the categories in BME are not so sharply differentiated since the mean suffixed nominalization frequencies are similar for business (M=32.75), editorial (M=32.57), and news report (M=32.27). In addition, it can be seen that the more suffixed nominalizations a category in CME uses, the larger difference in the uses of nominalizations across CME and BME is. We can also find a descending order for the mean differences in CME and BME: $D_{editorial}$ (6.86 per 1,000 words) > $D_{business}$ (5.73 per 1,000 words) > $D_{news\ report}$ (3.54 per 1,000 words) > $D_{arts\ and\ culture}$ (2.28 per 1,000 words) > $D_{social\ life}$ (0.34 per 1,000 words). This suggests that differences in the two English varieties are the most salient in categories dealing with more serious topics, but smaller in those concerned with casual topics.

5.3 Frequency and Distribution of Converted Nominalizations across CME and BME

In this section, we look at the frequency and distribution of converted nominalizations (e.g. *the quarrel over pay)*. Barplots representation and *t*-test results are presented in Figure 5 and Table 5 respectively.

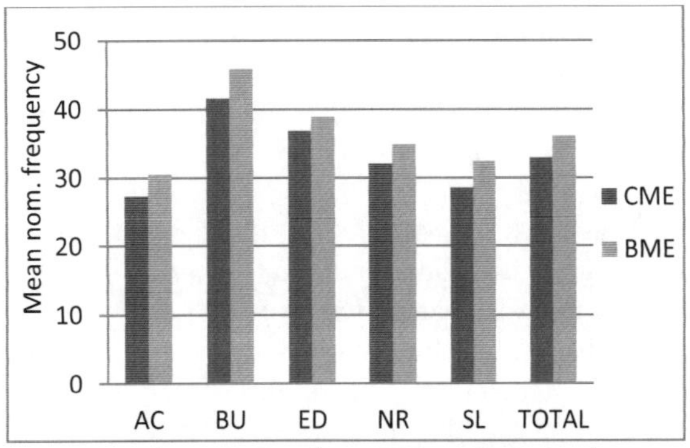

Figure 5. Barplots of Mean Converted Nominalization Frequencies across CME and BME

Figure 5 shows that the mean frequency for the overall BME (M=36.11) is higher than that for CME (M=32.95), indicating that BME has more uses of converted nominalizations. The *t*-test result confirms that this difference is statistically significant (t=-7.431, p=0.000). Furthermore, the mean values for all the five categories in BME are consistently higher than those of CME as shown in Figure 5. The *t*-test results in Table 5 confirm that all the five categories in BME use significantly more converted nominalizations than those in CME.

We have previously shown that for suffixed nominalizations, differences across CME and BME are sharper in categories dealing with more serious topics but smaller in those concerned with casual topics. However, this does not hold true for converted nominalizations. As can be seen from Table 5, the mean frequency differences in the five categories across CME and BME show a similar tendency. For example, BME has 3.01 more occurrences of nominalization per 1,000 words in arts and culture than in the case of arts and culture in CME, and it has 1.97 more occurrences of nominalization per 1,000 words in editorial than in the case of editorial in CME. Also, the mean difference in news report is 2.76 per 1,000 words, which is similar to that for arts and culture.

Category	*Variety*	*N. of Texts*	*Mean*	*Std. D*	*T*	*df*	*p-value*
Arts & culture*	CME	451	27.38	12.18	-3.716	879	.000*
	BME	430	30.39	11.87			
Business*	CME	434	41.54	17.09	-4.111	782.119	.000*
	BME	366	45.85	12.46			
Editorial*	CME	371	36.80	11.34	-2.291	683	.022*
	BME	314	38.77	11.04			
News report*	CME	457	32.02	12.84	-3.273	822.781	.001*
	BME	374	34.78	11.46			
Social life*	CME	513	28.60	12.78	-4.806	887.657	.000*
	BME	395	32.46	11.36			
Overall corpus*	CME	2226	32.95	14.40	-7.431	4088.963	.000*
	BME	1879	36.11	12.89			

Note: * indicates a statistically significant difference ($p < 0.05$).

Table 5. Results of *t*-test of Mean Converted Nominalization Frequency across CME and BME

6 Discussion

Our data provide a clear indication that there are significant quantitative differences in the uses of nominalizations across CME and BME, and such differences across the two varieties are far sharper in terms of the suffixed and converted nominalizations than in terms of nominalizations as an overall group.

With regard to suffixed nominalizations, CME uses significantly more nominalizations than BME overall and also across the five categories (except social life), indicating that CME tends to be more nominal and formal compared to BME. We also have found that this nominal style has been in use to differing extents in various categories and becomes even more evident in those dealing with more serious topics such as business. But there is no such sharp differentiation across categories in BME. Moreover, differences across CME and BME are sharper in categories dealing with more serious topics than those concerned with casual topics. According to Collins and Yao (2013), a number of quantitative differences across English varieties have a stylistic basis. We may reason that variations in the uses of nominalizations found in this study may be ascribed to the English users' particular consciousness of stylistic formality in Media English writing in China. This consciousness can be tentatively attributed to certain social factors. Unlike the status of institutionalized varieties such as Indian English, English is not an official or second language in China and not widely used in intra-national communication. CME, as an edited register of China English, is specialized in its target readership. Texts in CMEC are all sampled from the leading media in China such as *China Daily* and *Beijing Review* (Fang et al., 2012) which serve as a key source for information concerning China for overseas media as well as well-educated people at home and abroad. Moreover, it also provides learning materials for English learners in China as "many schools subscribe to *China Daily* and *Beijing Review* for their students and teaching staff" (Zhao and Campbell, 1995). Text writers in CME, mostly non-native users of English, who are aware of such informational purpose and the specialization of readership, are particularly careful with a formal style of Media English, especially in categories concerned with more serious topics.

However, British English is found to be influenced by the process of colloquialization, a stylistic shift which has brought many grammatical changes in English (Biber, 2003; Leech et al., 2009). The trend of colloquialization has made written genres more like spoken ones, and this has also manifested itself in the fewer uses of suffixed nominalizations in BME, as shown in this study.

As for the fewer uses of converted nominalizations in CME, one possible interpretation might be that English users in China are not so familiar with the usage of converted nominalizations as native speakers of English. Converted nominalization is not derived through a productive derivational rule that can be easily generalized to other word by the adding of suffixes to word bases. Instead, conversion requires a fairly large amount of lexical knowledge which non-native users of English may not have possessed, compared to native speakers of English. Another possible reason is that converted nominalizations might be associated with informality of writing and may occur more often in informal texts and less in formal texts. This is why there are fewer uses of them in the more nominal and formal CME, but more in the less formal BME.

The factors which may account for the variations in using nominalizations are of different types. What we have sketched above is only tentative and warrants further investigation.

7 Conclusions and Future Work

This paper has presented a corpus-based quantitative account of nominalizations across CME and BME. It has been observed that, for nominalization as a group, there is no significant difference in the overall CME and BME and significant differences have been found only in categories of editorial and social life. With regard to suffixed nominalizations, we have found that CME uses significantly more nominalizations than BME overall and also across the five categories (except social life), indicating a more nominal and formal style in CME. In terms of converted nominalizations, BME has significantly more uses of nominalizations overall and in all the five categories, which might have something to do with Chinese English users' ability of using converted nominalizations and the possible association between converted nominalizations and informality of writing.

Needless to say, quantitative evidence in the present study is not sufficient to describe the differences in the uses of nominalizations between China English and British English, but it nevertheless forms a practical starting-point for further research. The initial quantitative findings merit a more in-depth exploration into the uses of nominalizations in terms of the lexical patterns and syntactic structures in the future, which might offer more useful insights on variations in nominalization across different English varieties and also on the understanding of the two English varieties in question.

Acknowledgements

Research described in this paper was supported in part by grant received from the General Research Fund of the University Grant Council of the Hong Kong Special Administrative Region, China (Project no. CityU 142711) and City University of Hong Kong (Project nos. 6354005, 7004091, 9610283, 7002793, 9610226, 9041694, and 9610188).

References

Baayen, R. H, Piepenbrock, R. and Gulikers, L. (1995). *The CELEX Lexical Database (CD-ROM)*. Linguistic Data Consortium, University of Pennsylvania, Philadelphia, PA.

Biber, D. (1986). Spoken and Written Textual Dimensions in English: Resolving the Contradictory Findings. *Language*, 62(2): 384-414.

Biber, D. (2003). Compressed Noun Phrases in Newspaper Discourse: The Competing Demands of Popularization vs. Economy. In J. Aitchison and D. Lewis (Eds.). *New Media Language*. London: Routledge, pp. 169-181.

Biber, D., Conrad, S. and Reppen, R. (1998). *Corpus Linguistics: Investigating Language Structure and Language Use*. Cambridge: Cambridge University Press.

Biber, D., Johansson, S., Leech, G., Conrad, S., and Finegan, E. (1999). *The Longman Grammar of Spoken and Written English*. London: Longman.

Biber, D., and Gray, B. (2013). Nominalizing the Verb Phrase in Academic Science Writing. In B. Aarts, J. Close, G. Leech and S. Wallis (Eds.). *The Verb Phrase in English: Investigating Recent Language Change with Corpora*. Cambridge: Cambridge University Press, pp. 99-132,

Chafe, W. L. (1982). Integration and Involvement in Speaking, Writing, and Oral Literature. In D. Tannen (Ed.). *Spoken and Written Language: Exploring Orality and Literacy*. Norwood, N. J.: Ablex, pp. 35-54.

Chomsky, N. (1970). Remarks on Nominalization. In R. A. Jacobs and P. S. Rosenbaum (Eds.). *Readings in English Transformational Grammar*. Waltham, Massachusetts: Ginn, pp. 184-221.

Collins, P. and Yao, X. Y. (2013). Colloquial Features in World Englishes. *International Journal of Corpus Linguistics*, 18 (4): 479-505.

Crystal, David. (1997). *A Dictionary of Linguistics and Phonetics (Fourth Edition)*. Oxford: Blackwell Publishers Ltd.

Downing, A. and Locke, P. (2006). *English Grammar: A University Course (Second Edition)*. London: Routledge.

Eggins, Suzanne. (2004). *An Introduction to Systemic Functional Linguistics (Second Edition)*. New York/ London: Continuum.

Fang, A. C., Le, F. and Cao, J. (2012). The Design, Establish and Primary Study of a Comparable Corpus of China English. *Studies in Language and Linguistics*, 32(2): 113-127.

Greenbaum, S. (1988). Syntactic Devices for Compression in English. In J. Klegraf and D. Nehls (Eds.). *Essays on the English Language and Applied Linguistics on the Occasion of Gerhard Nickel's 60th Birthday*. Heidelberg: Julius Groos Verlag, pp. 3-10.

Grishman, R., Macleod, C., and Meyers, A. (1994). *COMLEX Syntax: Building a Computational Lexicon*. Presented at Coling 1994, Kyoto.

Halliday, M.A.K. (1994). *An Introduction to Functional Grammar (Second Edition)*. London: Edward Arnold.

Klein, D. and Manning, C. D. (2003). Accurate Unlexicalized Parsing. In *Proceedings of the 41st Meeting of the Association for Computational Linguistics*, pp. 423-430.

Langacker, R. W. (1991). *Foundations of Cognitive Grammar, Vol. 2*. Stanford: Stanford University Press.

Leech, G., Hundt, M., Mair, C., and Smith, N. (2009). *Change in Contemporary English: A Grammatical Study*. Cambridge: Cambridge University Press.

Lees, R. B. (1960). *The Grammar of English Nominalizations*. The Hague: Mouton de Gruyter.

Levy, Roger and Andrew, Galen. (2006). *Tregex and Tsurgeon: Tools for querying and manipulating tree data structures*. The 5th International Conference on Language Resources and Evaluation (LREC-2006).

Macleod, C., Grishman, R., Meyers, A., Barrett, L. and Reeves, R. (1998). NOMLEX: A Lexicon of Nominalizations. In *Proceedings of Euralex 98*.

Marcus, M., Santorini, B., and Marcinkiewicz, M. A. (1993). Building a Large Annotated Corpus of English: The Penn Treebank. *Computational Linguistics*, 19 (2): 313-220.

Meyers, A. (2007). *Those Other NomBank Dictionaries – Manual for Dictionaries that Come with NomBank*. Technical report, New York University.

Quirk, R., Greenbaum, S., Leech, G., and Svartvik, J. (1985). *A Comprehensive Grammar of the English Language*. London: Longman.

Rohde, D. L. T. (2005). *TGrep2 User Manual*. Version 1.15 edition.

Santorini, B. (1990). *Part-of-speech Tagging Guidelines for the Penn Treebank Project*. Technical report MS-CIC-90-47, Department of Computer and Information Science, University of Pennsylvania.

Santorini, B., and Marcinkiewicz, A. (1991). *Bracketing Guidelines for the Penn Treebank Project*. Unpublished manuscript, Department of Computer and Information Science, University of Pennsylvania.

Semino, Elena. (2009). Language in Newspaper. In J. Culpeper et al. (Eds.). *English Language: Description, Variation and Context*. Basingstoke: Palgrave Macmillan, pp. 439-453.

Socher, R., Bauer, J., Manning, C. D., and Ng, A. Y. (2013). Parsing with Compositional Vector Grammars. In *Proceedings of ACL*, pp. 455-465.

Tyrkkö, J. and Hiltunen, T. (2009). Frequency of Nominalization in Early Modern English Medical Writing. In A. H. Jucker, D. Schreier, and M. Hundt (Eds.) *Corpora: Pragmatics and Discourse*. Amsterdam: Rodopi, pp. 297-320.

Xu, Z. C. (2008). Analysis of Syntactic Features of Chinese English. *Asian Englishes*, 11(2): 4-31.

Xu, Z. C. (2010). *Chinese English: Features and Implications*. Hong Kong: Open University of Hong Kong Press.

Zhang, Y and Campbell, K. P. (1995). English in China. *World Englishes*, 14(3), 377-390.

Machine-Guided Solution to Mathematical Word Problems

Bussaba Amnueypornsakul
University of Illinois,
Urbana-Champaign, USA
amnueyp1@illinois.edu

Suma Bhat
University of Illinois
Urbana-Champaign, USA
spbhat2@illinois.edu

Abstract

Mathematical word problems (MWP) test critical aspects of reading comprehension in conjunction with generating a solution that agrees with the "story" in the problem. In this paper we design and construct an MWP solver in a systematic manner, as a step towards enabling comprehension in mathematics and teaching problem solving for children in the elementary grades. We do this by (a) identifying the discourse structure of MWPs that will enable comprehension in mathematics, and (b) utilizing the information in the discourse structure towards generating the solution in a systematic manner. We build a multistage software prototype that predicts the problem type, identifies the function of sentences in each problem, and extracts the necessary information from the question to generate the corresponding mathematical equation. Our prototype has an accuracy of 86% on a large corpus of MWPs of three problem types from elementary grade mathematics curriculum.

1 Introduction

Mathematical word problems (MWP) constitute an integral part of a child's elementary schooling curriculum. Solving an MWP is a complex task involving critical aspects of reading comprehension (understanding the components of the problem), and generating a solution that agrees with the 'story' in the problem. Children are trained through the process of problem solving by the use of various strategies. In this study, we formulate solving an MWP as an NLP task involving text classification, discourse processing and information extraction. Our primary goal is to guide young learners through the important steps of mathematics comprehension and problem solving of arithmetic word problems commonly encountered in the elementary grades. We take a bottom-up approach, identifying the discourse structure of the MWP and then utilizing the semantic information contained in the components of the problem to generate a solution.

In an MWP, significant background information is presented in text format. The ability to solve an MWP critically depends on the ability to detect the problem type and identify the components of the word problem as observed in studies in mathematics education and cognitive psychology (De Corte and Verschaffel, 1987; Cummins, 1991; Verschaffel et al., 2000).

Motivated by these studies, we divide the overall problem solving process into stages: *predicting the problem type*, *identification of the function of sentences* (or sentence type) in each problem, and extracting the necessary information from the question to *generate the corresponding mathematical equation*. Since classification of the problem and sentence types involves a decision based on the textual representation, the classification tasks can be viewed as automatic text categorization problems (Yang and Liu, 1999) with domain-specific feature engineering. More broadly, a knowledge of the discourse structure of an MWP provides the human solver with a critical first step for information extraction and text summarization needed for mathematics problem comprehension and solving.

A text classification perspective to MWP solu-

Copyright 2014 by Bussaba Amnueypornsakul and Suma Bhat
28th Pacific Asia Conference on Language, Information and Computation pages 111–119

tion calls for an approach different from routine text classification methods. Surface word statistics and a keyword spotting approach, that convey topicality, for instance, are insufficient to derive necessary information about problem type or document structure owing to the short document lengths of MWP. Stop word removal and stemming, two common preprocessing steps in text classification by topic, have been observed to negatively impact classification of problem types (Cetintas et al., 2009). Thus, feature engineering that *leverages* the natural language properties of word problems not only at a sentence level but also at a problem level is an important novelty in this study as we explore the usefulness of a text classification approach to solving MWPs. In addition, our study is novel in adopting the multistage approach to solving word problems automatically.

Specifically, this paper makes the following contributions.

1. Taking a text classification approach towards automatically identifying the information structure of MWPs, we show empirically that an ensemble classifier yields the best performance for identifying the problem type and for identifying the discourse structure of MWP. Not only are the performance gains over the baseline vastly substantial, but the performance gains of the solver when compared with state-of-the-art MWP solvers such as WolframAlpha (Barendse, 2012) are also substantial.

2. We demonstrate the efficacy of our software prototype to solving MWPs automatically. The multistage approach can be construed as a careful combination of inductive inference (statistical methods) and deductive inference (rule-based approach) to reflect the key aspects of mathematics comprehension in arithmetic problem solving as pointed out in psychology studies: The use of natural language to identify the discourse structure and a set of rules to derive the corresponding mathematical form (De Corte and Verschaffel, 1987; Cummins, 1991; Verschaffel et al., 2000).

2 Related Work

Prior studies attempting to solve mathematical word problems in an automatic manner fall into two primary categories: those intended to understand the cognitive aspects of problem solving in children and those intended for intelligent tutoring systems. Prototypical systems such as WORDPRO (Fletcher, 1985), SOLUTION (Dellarosa, 1985), ARITHPRO (Dellarosa, 1986) and (LeBlanc and Weber-Russell, 1996) are representations of cognitive models of human processes of mathematical word problem solving. With the exception of (LeBlanc and Weber-Russell, 1996), these operate on propositional representations of the problem text later solved in a rule-based manner.

In the realm of intelligent tutoring systems automatic MWP solvers were based on either using specific sentence structures and keywords (Bobrow, 1964), or using templates (schema) limited in scope by variety and problem types - (Supap et al., 2013) for grade-level problems in Thai and (Liguda and Pfeiffer, 2011; Liguda and Pfeiffer, 2012) for grade-level problems in German.

An early approach to automatic classification of MWP using natural language processing methods was (Cetintas et al., 2009). The study pointed out that certain problem types (such as the multiplicative compare and equal group) were characterized by their lexical content and that a blind text categorization approach via stop word removal and stemming failed to help the classification task for those problem types. Another related study (Cetintas et al., 2010), addresses sentence-level classification of sentences in MWP into relevant and irrelevant sentences to identify the information-bearing components of the problem.

A more recent study in a related area is (Matsuzaki et al., 2013), which aims at understanding the complexity of MWPs encountered by students appearing for a Japanese university entrance examination. It includes and end-to-end method of problem solving by transforming the question sentences into their logic representation to be eventually solved by an automatic solver. The problems considered are significantly more complex than grade-level arithmetic problems. A semantic parser used on the related topic of learning to solve algebra word problems is the material of (Kushman et al., 2014). In all these studies the goal was to arrive at a solution automatically without paying attention to the step-by-step approach to assisted problem solving which is what we address in this work.

Taking a view different from that of prior studies, our focus here is two-fold: first, inspired by the approach to identify the structure of scientific abstracts in (Guo et al., 2010), we would like to gain a fundamental understanding of the discourse structure of an MWP which serves as its information-bearing component; second, knowing the structure of an MWP we would like to discover the interrelation between available units of information and eventually solve the problem.

Our approach in this study is closely related to that in (Supap et al., 2013) in spirit, but instead of a top-down approach via having a static template for each problem type, we resort to constructing dynamic templates in a bottom-up fashion using information on problem types and associated discourse structure. The classification algorithm leverages natural language properties at the sentence level as well as across sentence boundaries.

For the classifiers we use a combination of a deductive learner driven by inductive learners which has been very successful in other domains such as electronic design automation tools (Chaganty et al., 2013; Liu et al., 2012). The cognitive modeling perspective to solving MWP in children renders the inductive-deductive learner combination a natural choice for our study.

3 Method

Our approach to solving an MWP is grounded in harnessing the information available in the discourse structure of the word problem. We hypothesize that classification of the problem type is a crucial first step. After knowing the problem type, we focus on the solution by identifying the components of the problem and their interrelation.

3.1 Data

MWPs have the information to solve them embedded in text rather than in an equation. While recognizing that there are several categories of word problems, we consider for our study the set of word problems considered in a cognitively guided instruction scheme (CGI).

The CGI framework aims at developing a child's mathematical thinking via intuitive strategies for problem solving (Carpenter et al., 2000). Focusing on the curriculum of the cognitively guided instruction scheme, this study aims to solve all three problem types at the elementary grade level: problems of the type *join and separate*, *compare* and *part-part-whole* involving only one mathematical operation - that of addition or subtraction.

The choice of these problem types is motivated by early developmental theories in children's arithmetic competencies that focus on word problems classified into natural classes based on their semantic structures, the relation between the sets in the problem statement.(LeBlanc and Weber-Russell, 1996).

The word problems considered here constitute the major types proposed by the CGI curriculum. The problem types are general in that they do not call for a specific arithmetic operation but we have restricted our approach to only those involving addition and subtraction. Although details of the exact proportion of these word problem types in the respective grade levels is not available, we expect word problems of the types considered here to be prevalent in grades Kindergarten to fourth grade (as evidenced from the collected corpus of sample practice problems).

Join and separate (J-S) problems have three main functional types of sentences in a question: given, change and result. A *Given sentence* is a narrative sentence where a quantity is given; a *Change sentence* indicates that there are some changes to the quantity in the *Given sentence* and the *Result sentence* is the result of the change applied to the given quantity. A sentence that is not of the above functional types is an *Unknown sentence*. When the change applied to the given quantity results in a decrease, the problem is of the *separate* kind (subtraction) and when the result is an increase in the given quantity, the problem is of the *join* kind (addition). Problems of this type are characterized by significant action language that describe changes in the possession or condition of objects. As an example consider a problem of the type *separate*:

Henry is walking dogs for money. There are 7 dogs to walk on Henry's street. Henry walked 4 of them. How many dogs does Henry have left to walk?

Note : The yellow highlight is the *given sentence*. The blue highlight is the *change sentence* and the pink highlight is the *result sentence* of the example problem. The remaining sentences are of the type *unknown sentence*.

Equation: 7 - x = 4

Part-part-whole (PPW) is the second problem type which contains two main functional types of sentences: part and whole. The *part sentence* indicates the quantity of a set, while the *whole sentence* indicates the total amount in a category that subsumes the set. Problems of this type involve static descriptions of the counts of two or more disjoint subsets and the union of those sets and do not contain significant actions. For example,

Some kids are playing in a playground. 3 boys are playing on the slide. 4 girls are playing on the merry-go-round. How many kids are there in the playground?

Note : The yellow highlight is the *part sentence*. The blue highlight is the *whole sentence*. The rest of the question is the *unknown sentence*.

Equation: 3 + 4 = x

The simplest of the three types, **compare problems** (C) involve a comparison of the counts of two sets. For example, Angela has 6 mittens. Jordan has 4 more mittens than Angela. How many mittens does Jordan have?

It is important to note that in a given problem, the missing quantity could be in the *Given*, *Change* or *Result* sentence (likewise in the *part* or the *whole* sentence). It is also crucial to remember that although the equations corresponding to the problem types are similar, our focus is not just the solution but also the steps leading to the solution. The dataset used in our study is a set of sample problems from the South Dakota Counts (Olson et al., 2008) and teacherweb.com (Ebner, 2011). A brief description of the problems of each type and their characteristics in the corpus is summarized in Table 1.

Problem type	J-S	PPW	C
No. of problems	330	164	257
No. of words/problem (mean)	25.54	22.47	21.13
No. of sentences/problem	3.42	2.72	3.06
No . of verb types (total)	99	36	46

Table 1: Corpus description of the set of problems studied.

The problems were grouped by problem type at the source. However, their sentence type annotations were not available. The problems in the dataset were manually annotated for sentence functional type (*Given*, *Change*, *Result*, *Part* and *Whole*) and sign (join or separate) by the researchers. The annotators agreed on 99.4% of the sentence function types.

Notice from Table 1 that the J-S problems constitute a majority of the problem types and that these problems are also the longest in terms of average number of words per problem. Another significant feature is the number of sentences per problem. We notice that it is 3.42 for J-S problems suggesting that there are more than 3 sentences which would be the case when just the *Given*, *Change* and *Result* sentences are present. Again, in the case of PPW sentences, we notice that the sentences are not necessarily *Part*, *Part* and *Whole*, but the 'parts' may even be relegated to the same sentence.

3.2 Models

The first stage is problem type classification. Problem type classification takes as input the entire problem divided into sentences and assigns it to one of Join-Separate, Part-Part-Whole or Compare type. Depending on the problem type, the necessary classifiers are cascaded. We divide the problem solution into a maximum of three stages depending on the problem type with a classifier for each stage, described as follows. A schematic representation of the solver is given in Figure 1.

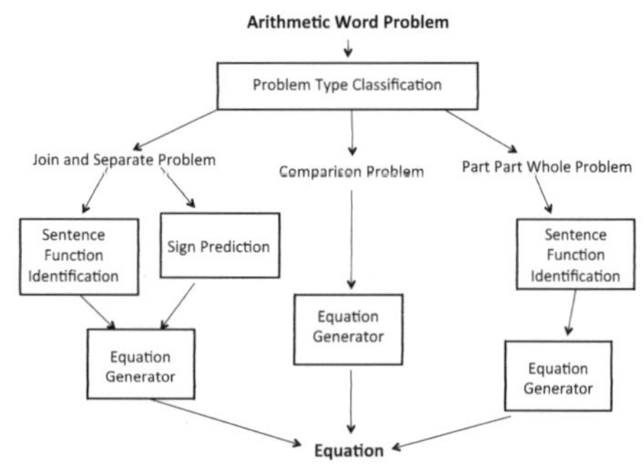

Figure 1: Flow chart for the system.

3.2.1 Join and separate problems (JS)

Join and separate problems are the most versatile of problems because the problem's discourse structure affords phrasing of its constituent sentences in many ways. The constituent sentences can either be separate, joined using a conjunction or could be formed as a complex sentence with the use of conditionals.

Figure 2 shows a step-by-step approach to solving problems of this type. First, we **classify the sentence functional type** for each sentence (whether it is Given or Change or Result sentence). Then, we perform a *sign prediction* (whether the problem calls for addition or subtraction). The pivot sentence for this task is the *Change* sentence because it indicates the direction of change of the quantity in the *Given* sentence in terms of an effective increase or decrease.The last task is to combine the results of the first two stages and generate the corresponding equation.

This problem focuses on the relationship between nouns in each sentence of the question. There are two steps to solve this problem. The first step is to identify

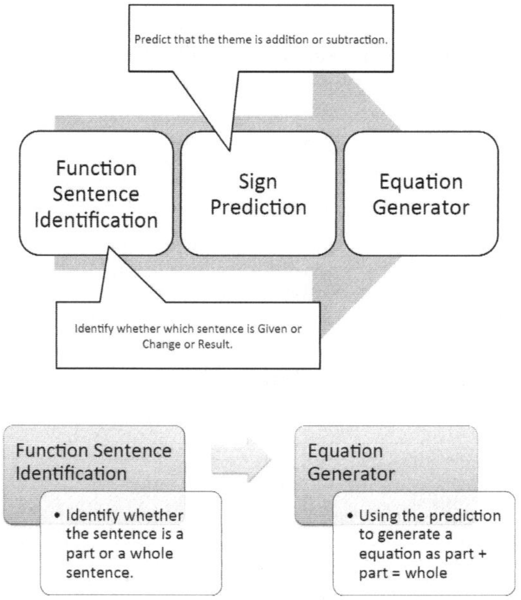

Figure 2: Top: Flow chart for Join and Separate Problem. Bottom: part part whole Problem.

whether the sentence is a *part sentence* or a *whole sentence*. We then use the information from this classification to generate the equation. The flowchart of the problem is displayed in figure 2.

3.2.2 Compare problems

Comparison problems focus on similarities or differences between sets. By nature of its type, the problem's discourse structure is limited. This means we can generate a set of rules to convert a question to its corresponding equation. Once a problem is classified as belonging to this type in the problem type identification stage, the problem is then processed by a rule-based classifier leading to its equation.

3.2.3 Equation generation

Once the component sentence types comprising the discourse structure of the problem are identified the information in each sentence is extracted. We note that the sentence type (and hence discourse structure) plays a crucial role in this stage of information extraction. We use the NLTK toolkit (Loper and Bird, 2002) to extract the numerical quantity from each sentence.

In the J-S equation generator, we construct an equation of the form (quantity in *Given*) + (quantity in *Change*) = *Result*. The quantity in the *Change* sentence bears the sign of the question (depending on whether it is addition or subtraction). If a sentence with no numerical information is classified as *Given, Change* or *Result*, we assign an **X** to that sentence and the information is excluded from the equation (a potential source of error).

The analog holds for the PPW equation generator. With its sentences classified as *Part* or *Whole* we proceed to the equation generation as follows. When the *Part* sentence has more than one numerical quantity, we assign the first number as *Part1* and the other numbers as *Part2* (or into more buckets as the case may be). Then, we arrange them into the corresponding equation as: Part1 + Part2 = Whole.

In both these equation generators, when the equation has insufficient information owing to errors from previous stages (we will defer discussing some scenarios to Section 6), a solution is not generated. The generated equation is solved using Numpy (Oliphant, 2006).

3.3 Implementation

For the tasks of problem type classification, sentence type classification and sign prediction, we use the ensemble method of inductive classifier - Random Forest. The equation generation stage is a rule-based deductive learner that combines the result of sentence type classification (and sign prediction for the J-S problems) to derive the numerical quantities needed for the equation. We use the scikit implementation of Random Forest (Pedregosa et al., 2011).

3.4 Evaluation

We evaluate the performance of the classifiers on problem type classification, sentence type, sign prediction and overall solution generation by the level of accuracy (how exact the classification is) calculated using 5-fold cross validation. In addition to evaluating a classifier's performance on each task, we also evaluate the contribution of each feature class to the classification by noting the accuracy of the classifier when that feature class is excluded.

4 Experiment

We first consider the preprocessing steps and the features considered before delving into the models by type of mathematical word problem being solved.

4.1 Preprocessing

We employed Python NLTK (Loper and Bird, 2002) to segment the problems into sentences, perform tokenization, convert words into lower case, tag the words with their Penn treebank part-of-speech tags and lemmatize all the verbs and nouns. We also obtain the dependency parse of the sentences using the Stanford parser (De Marneffe et al., 2006).

4.2 Features

We use four classes of features that we describe below.

Problem-level features:

- The features in this class are length-related and document-related. The length of the problem in number of sentences is a feature that we consider at the problem level, noticing that on an average, J-S problems tend to have more sentences per problem than those of the C type, which in turn have more sentences than those of the PPW type (refer Table 1).
- Structure that is specific for problem of type C which is the binary valued feature indicating the presence of *comparative adjective and "than"*.
- Keywords (with binary values) extracted using tf-idf constitute another type of problem-level features. To avoid overfitting, we consider only those keywords that occur at least five times in the corpus of problems. We exclude verbs and prepositions from this list. The intuition here is that keywords such as *altogether* characterize PPW problems.

Sentence-level features: Mainly used for sentence-level classification into types, the features in this class are positional, structural or semantic.

- Sentence position in the problem tends to be an indicator of the sentence type for PPW and JS problems. For instance, a majority of the JS sentences have the first sentence of the type *Given*, as a manner of discourse structure.
- Structural features essentially capture shared relationships between entities in a sentence, such as that between the subject and object in a sentence obtained in the form of dependency relations. Other structural features are verb phrase (binary valued) such as *to start with*, comparative structure such as *more than* (binary valued) and prepositions such as *on* (binary valued).

Action-related features: We observe that problems of the J-S type are characterized by significant action language that describe changes in the possession or condition of objects. Thus, we posit that the count of unique verb lemmas will serve as a discriminating feature. Consider for instance a J-S problem, *Grandma had 5 strawberries. Grandpa gave her 8 more strawberries. How many strawberries does Grandma have now?* The verb from the *Given* sentence *Grandma had 5 strawberries* has changed in the *Change* sentence *Grandpa gave her 8 more strawberries* and thus the problem has 2 verb lemmas (*have* and *give*).

Entity-related features: An example of this feature is the number of unique noun phrases. Since problems of type PPW involve static descriptions of two or more disjoint subsets in the *Part* sentence and the union of those sets (or the super category of the entities in the *Part* sentence) in the *While* sentence, a characteristic of problems of this type is the variety of noun phrases. For instance, *Jarron has 5 red triangles and 10 blue squares. How many shapes does he have altogether?* The first sentence which corresponds to *Part* sentence contains two noun phrases: *red triangles* and *blue squares*. The other sentences is *whole sentence*. It has only one noun which is *shapes*. Here red triangles and blue squares are subcategories of shapes and so the number of unique noun phrases is 3.

4.3 Parameter tuning

The hyperparameters of the Random Forest classifier were tuned as follows. The corpus of problem types and sentence types were split into a training and test set via a random 80-20 split. The parameters of the random forest classifiers at the problem type, sentence type and sign prediction stages were independently tuned by 5-fold cross validation on the training data set choosing the set that achieves the highest cross-validation accuracy.

As a result, with n as the number of total available features the problem type prediction classifier was set to have a maximum of $\sqrt{n}$ features and allowed to reach a maximum depth of 15 nodes. The sentence type classifier for J-S was set to have a maximum of n features and allowed to reach a depth of 25 nodes, whereas that for PPW had the parameters set to n and 10 respectively. The corresponding parameters for sign prediction module were $log_2 n$ and 50.

5 Experimental Results

We report results of using the inductive classification in the first few stages followed by the results of the deductive classification in the equation generation stage.

5.1 Problem type classification

The majority baseline is the proportion of the largest problem class in the corpus which is about 44% We observe that problem type classification using Random Forest yielded an accuracy of 93.47% The performance of Random Forest is justified considering that many of our features are correlated. Additionally, our data falls in the realm of the 'small n, large p' scenario where Random Forest is known to perform best. We thus use only Random Forest for classification in the following stages.

5.2 Sentence-type classification

For sentence type classification, the baseline is the majority class among sentence types since the sentences are classified independently. Thus, the baseline for J-S problems is 36.12% (majority class is *Change* sentence) and for PPW is 62.47% (majority class is *Part* sentence).

JS		PPW	
Baseline	Classifier	Baseline	Classifier
36.12%	91.55%	62.47%	92.32%

Table 2: Performance of the Random Forest classifier for sentence type classification. The improvement over the baseline is significant.

From Table 2 we notice that the ensemble classifier outperforms the baseline by a wide margin in both J-S and PPW solvers. The performance of the classifier on sentence type prediction for both types seems comparable even though one involves a 3-way classification (for J-S) and the other only two-way (for PPW).

For sign prediction, we note that the module is used only to solve problems of type J-S. Hence, the baseline is the majority class which in our case is 50% owing to the equal number of addition and subtraction problems. The accuracy of the classifier that performs sign prediction is 84.33%. This renders the sign-prediction stage a bottleneck for solving J-S problems.

JS	PPW	C	Overall
78.67%	87.33%	94.92%	85.64%

Table 3: Comparison of the accuracy of the solvers for each problem type.

5.3 Overall Solution

The overall solution is obtained by combining the result of the individual stages as per problem type to generate the corresponding equation. The accuracies of the solvers for each problem type are compared in Table 3.

We prepare a simple rule-based baseline with which we compare the results of the equation generation. First, if there is more than one numerical quantity in a sentence, they are all summed up. Any sentence without a numerical quantity is ignored and the question sentence is mapped to the variable. Second, if the number in the first sentence is larger than the number in the second sentence, the first number will be subtracted by the second number; otherwise the two numbers are added. With these two rules, we disregard the type of MWP and generate the equation. The baseline accuracy becomes 59.58% (J-S accuracy is 48%, C accuracy is 55.69%, and PPW accuracy is 87.5%). We would like to point out that a plausible reason that the baseline for PPW is higher than that of the stage-wise approach is because PPW problems' structure coincides with our rules.

This baseline is to be interpreted with some caution, however. Recalling that the purpose of the study is to guide the learner through the stages leading to generating the equation, a comparison of the results of the equation generation stage with the baseline alone is misguided. The final accuracy for solving problems of type Join-Separate is 78.67%. For problems of the PPW type, the accuracy of problem solution after the equation generation stage is 87.33% and that for the class of Compare problems is 94.92%. Based on this we remark that for the automatic solver, problems of the J-S type are the hardest to solve, and those of the Compare type are the easiest. This is justified here by noting that the sign-prediction module is a bottleneck for the J-S solver, as well as an additional classification stage compared to the other problem types.

Pooling the results of each problem type together, we arrive at the overall accuracy of our solver to be 85.64%.

5.4 Comparison with the state-of-the-art

A general purpose MWP solver is available via the publicly available WolframAlpha engine. The details of its implementation were unavailable, but we believe it to be operational from its associated blog post that elaborates its functionality and the diagrammatic solution feature of this solver) (Barendse, 2012). We compare the accuracy of our solver with that of the solver provided by WolframAlpha[1] in the absence of other published MWP solvers for arithmetic problems that we study. Since the details of the solution process employed by WolframAlpha are not available we are only able to compare the respective performances at the level of equation generation.

For the purpose of this comparison, we choose the test set (20% of our corpus) compare the accuracy of solutions produced by the solvers. While our MWP solver had an accuracy of 86% on the sample, the performance of Wolfram Alpha is remarkably poor. In particular, barely 9% of the problems were answered correctly, of which about 4% had an incorrect diagram associated with the solution. The vast majority of the MWPs are not solved and the results come back with the error "WolframAlpha doesn't understand your query". Surprisingly, the Wolfram Alpha system performed quite poorly on our dataset. Without the details of the WolframAlpha approach, we are unable to point to the advantages of our approach over that of the state-of-the-art.

5.5 Ablation Analysis

Task	Accuracy	Problem level	Sentence level	Action related	Entity related
Prob. type	93.47	77.29	92.17	75.10	81.26
Sign	84.33	61.33	60.33	61.67	65.33
JS sent	91.55	89.48	54.93	87.02	90.63
PPW sent	92.32	81.82	68.05	90.68	92.02

Table 4: Comparison of the accuracy results (in %) with different feature classes ablated for each classification task with the accuracy where no features were excluded.

Table 4 summarizes the results of the ablation study

[1]www.wolframalpha.com visited on June 01, 2014.

conducted for each task by removing each class of features. For problem type prediction, the action-related features constitute the most important set of features (most likely influenced by the predominance of J-S problems) followed by the problem-level features. The sentence level features seem to have little impact on the overall accuracy. Even though the entity-related features do not have an effect on PPW sentence type classification, it contributes substantially to question type classification (most likely by way of characterizing PPW). Sign prediction depends primarily on the sentence-level features but is about equally dependent on the other sets of features.

6 Discussion

The higher the accuracy of classification is, the better the outcome in generating equations will be. In this section, we consider some of the issues that negatively impact the classification process. The first issue involves the preprocessing steps that a MWP has to go through before passing through our analysis. This happens when the problem relates to time, money, and distance and needs quantity conversions before the arithmetic calculations (e.g. *Josie has 7 pennies and 5 nickels. How much money does she have?*). Another obvious class is when the problem requires world knowledge for its solution (e.g. *Today is October 25th. How many days are there until Halloween?*). The other case where our program fails is when a question has a complex sentence structure. e.g *How many Yodas flew away from the planet in the space shuttle if 23 Yodas stayed on the planet of 30 Yodas in all?*

Focusing on the errors of the J-S problem solver, the majority of errors result from incorrect sign prediction, explained by the fact that this module is the bottleneck in our J-S automatic solver. The overall accuracy is slightly higher than we expect because the error from sign prediction and sentence type classification overlap. It is also the case that even though the classifier misclassifies *Change* and *Given* sentences, if the sign is correctly assigned as '+', the final equation is still correct i.e. $3 + x = 4$ is the same as $x + 3 = 4$. Finally, the main source of error for problems of PPW type is that the problem type classifier misclassifies PPW to be JS, which leads to an incorrect solution. JS and PPW are very similar but they focus on different aspects. JS focuses on the dynamic action, while PPW captures the relationship between nouns in each sentence.

For problems of the Compare type, there are two sources of error. First, the rule-based classifier itself provides 94.92% because some questions need quantity conversion before being processed. For example, *Joel started the paper route at 7:05. He worked for 25 minutes. When did he finish?* The other is that the comparison problem is misclassified as J-S or PPW at the problem type classification stage. Accounting for these errors would entail working with better classifiers that handle inter-sentence semantics.

To get a feel for the model's generalizability we tested on a set of problems not of the CGI type from Dadsworksheets.com[2]. On this set of 400 addition and subtraction word problems our model yielded an overall accuracy of 87%, suggesting that our method is not restricted to solving problems of the CGI type alone. Looking ahead, we are working to solve more complicated MWPs of upper elementary grades.

It is conceivable that a multi-stage approach such as the one considered here can constitute one of the key design factors in applications involving intelligent tutoring systems for elementary mathematics education. The goal of guiding the learner to understand the steps involved in solving the problem can be met via our approach of identifying the problem types, highlighting the discourse elements (sentence types) while simultaneously helping arrive at the answer.

7 Conclusion

We present a multi-stage text-classification approach to solve arithmetic problems of elementary level automatically. Our approach recognizes the problem type, identifies the discourse structure and generates the corresponding equation to eventually solve the problem. This is in line with results from cognitive psychology studies in children learning to solve MWPs. With accuracies substantially higher than the baseline, we also observe that the performance gains of our solver compared with the state-of-the-art MWP solvers such as WolframAlpha are also substantial.

References

Peter Barendse. 2012. Solving word problems with wolfram—alpha@ONLINE, October. http://blog.wolframalpha.com/2012/10/04/solving-word-problems-with-wolframalpha/.

Daniel G. Bobrow. 1964. A question-answering system for high school algebra word problems. In *Proceedings of the October 27-29, 1964, Fall Joint Computer Conference, Part I*, AFIPS '64 (Fall, part I), pages 591–614, New York, NY, USA. ACM.

Thomas P Carpenter, Elizabeth Fennema, Megan Loef Franke, Linda Levi, and Susan B Empson. 2000. Cognitively guided instruction: A research-based teacher professional development program for elementary school mathematics. research report.

[2]http://www.dadsworksheets.com/ accessed on March 20th, 2013

Suleyman Cetintas, Luo Si, Yan Ping Xin, Dake Zhang, and Joo Young Park. 2009. Automatic text categorization of mathematical word problems. In *FLAIRS Conference*.

Suleyman Cetintas, Luo Si, Yan Ping Xin, Dake Zhang, Joo Young Park, and Ron Tzur. 2010. A joint probabilistic classification model of relevant and irrelevant sentences in mathematical word problems. *JEDM-Journal of Educational Data Mining*, 2(1):83–101.

Arun Chaganty, Akash Lal, Aditya V Nori, and Sriram K Rajamani. 2013. Combining relational learning with smt solvers using cegar. In *Computer Aided Verification*, pages 447–462. Springer.

Denise Dellarosa Cummins. 1991. Children's interpretations of arithmetic word problems. *Cognition and Instruction*, 8(3):pp. 261–289.

Erik De Corte and Lieven Verschaffel. 1987. The effect of semantic structure on first graders' strategies for solving addition and subtraction word problems. *Journal for Research in Mathematics Education*, pages 363–381.

Marie-Catherine De Marneffe, Bill MacCartney, Christopher D Manning, et al. 2006. Generating typed dependency parses from phrase structure parses. In *Proceedings of LREC*, volume 6, pages 449–454.

Denise Dellarosa. 1985. Solution: A computer simulation of childrens recall of arithmetic word problem solving. *University of Colorado Technical Report*, pages 85–148.

Denise Dellarosa. 1986. A computer simulation of children's arithmetic word-problem solving. *Behavior Research Methods*, 18:147–154, March.

Kerianne Ebner. 2011. Cognitively guided instruction (cgi) problem types @ONLINE, July.

Charles R. Fletcher. 1985. Understanding and solving arithmetic word problems: A computer simulation. *Behavior Research Methods*, 17(5):565–571.

Yufan Guo, Anna Korhonen, Maria Liakata, Ilona Silins Karolinska, Lin Sun, and Ulla Stenius. 2010. Identifying the information structure of scientific abstracts: An investigation of three different schemes. In *Proceedings of the 2010 Workshop on Biomedical Natural Language Processing*, BioNLP '10, pages 99–107, Stroudsburg, PA, USA. Association for Computational Linguistics.

Nate Kushman, Yoav Artzi, Luke Zettlemoyer, and Regina Barzilay. 2014. Learning to automatically solve algebra word problems. In *Proceedings of the 52nd Annual Meeting of the Association for Computational Linguistics (Volume 1: Long Papers)*, pages 271–281, Baltimore, Maryland, June. Association for Computational Linguistics.

Mark D LeBlanc and Sylvia Weber-Russell. 1996. Text integration and mathematical connections: a computer model of arithmetic word problem solving. *Cognitive Science*, 20(3):357–407.

Christian Liguda and Thies Pfeiffer. 2011. A question answer system for math word problems. First International Workshop on Algorithmic Intelligence.

Christian Liguda and Thies Pfeiffer. 2012. Modeling math word problems with augmented semantic networks. In Gosse Bouma, Ashwin Ittoo, Elisabeth Mtais, and Hans Wortmann, editors, *Natural Language Processing and Information Systems*, volume 7337 of *Lecture Notes in Computer Science*, pages 247–252. Springer Berlin Heidelberg.

Lingyi Liu, Chen-Hsuan Lin, and Shobha Vasudevan. 2012. Word level feature discovery to enhance quality of assertion mining. In *ICCAD*, pages 210–217.

Edward Loper and Steven Bird. 2002. Nltk: The natural language toolkit. In *Proceedings of the ACL-02 Workshop on Effective Tools and Methodologies for Teaching Natural Language Processing and Computational Linguistics - Volume 1*, ETMTNLP '02, pages 63–70, Stroudsburg, PA, USA. Association for Computational Linguistics.

Takuya Matsuzaki, Hidenao Iwane, Hirokazu Anai, and Noriko Arai. 2013. The complexity of math problems – linguistic, or computational? In *Proceedings of the Sixth International Joint Conference on Natural Language Processing*, pages 73–81, Nagoya, Japan, October. Asian Federation of Natural Language Processing.

Travis E. Oliphant, 2006. *Guide to NumPy*. Provo, UT, March.

Shawn Olson, Natalie Musser, Sue McAdaragh, Roxane Dyk, Jonath Weber, Tracy Mittleider, Lucy Atwood, and Marcia Torgrude. 2008. South dakota counts: Cgi problems created by south dakota math teacher leaders @ONLINE, January.

F. Pedregosa, G. Varoquaux, A. Gramfort, V. Michel, B. Thirion, O. Grisel, M. Blondel, P. Prettenhofer, R. Weiss, V. Dubourg, J. Vanderplas, A. Passos, D. Cournapeau, M. Brucher, M. Perrot, and E. Duchesnay. 2011. Scikit-learn: Machine learning in Python. *Journal of Machine Learning Research*, 12:2825–2830.

Wanintorn Supap, Kanlaya Naruedomkul, and Nick Cercone. 2013. Mathmaster: an alternative math word problems translation. *Computational Approaches to Assistive Technologies for People with Disabilities*, 253:109.

Lieven Verschaffel, Brian Greer, and Erik De Corte. 2000. *Making sense of word problems*. Lisse.

Yiming Yang and Xin Liu. 1999. A re-examination of text categorization methods. In *Proceedings of the 22nd annual international ACM SIGIR conference on Research and development in information retrieval*, pages 42–49. ACM.

The So-called Person Restriction of Internal State Predicates in Japanese in Contrast with Thai

Satoshi Uehara

Tohoku University
41 Kawauchi, Aoba-ku, Sendai
980-8576 JAPAN
uehara@intcul.tohoku.ac.jp

Kingkarn Thepkanjana

Chulalongkorn University
Phayathai Road, Bangkok 10330
THAILAND
kingkarn.t@chula.ac.th

Abstract

Internal state predicates or ISPs refer to internal states of sentient beings, such as emotions, sensations and thought processes. Japanese ISPs with zero pronouns exhibit the "person restriction" in that the zero form of their subjects must be first person at the utterance time. This paper examines the person restriction of ISPs in Japanese in contrast with those in Thai, which is a zero pronominal language like Japanese. It is found that the person restriction is applicable to Japanese ISPs but not to Thai ones. This paper argues that the person restriction is not adequate to account for Japanese and Thai ISPs. We propose a new constraint to account for this phenomenon, i.e., the Experiencer-Conceptualizer Identity (ECI) Constraint, which states that "The experiencer of the situation/event must be identical with the conceptualizer of that situation/event." It is argued that both languages conventionalize the ECI constraint in ISP expressions but differ in how the ECI constraint is conventionalized.

1 Introduction

Japanese is typologically known as a zero pronominal language, in which pronominal elements can take the zero form, unlike those in English. Japanese shares this characteristic with Thai even though the two languages differ drastically in morphological structure and in constituent order. Japanese is an agglutinating and head-final whereas Thai is isolating and head-initial.

Zero pronouns, or unexpressed referents, in zero pronominal languages differ from the so-called pro-drop phenomena present in languages such as Italian and Spanish, where subject arguments can be omitted, and the verbal inflections will continue to reflect the person, number and gender of the dropped arguments. Covert referents in East and Southeast Asian languages can occupy various grammatical roles and can be identified through discourse-pragmatic inference rather than through verbal morphology. Interestingly, however, internal state predicates in Japanese are known to have the so-called "person restriction", which serves to identify the person of the experiencer-subject in a way similar to the pro-drop phenomena, as we see in the following discussion. This paper closely examines the

Copyright 2014 by Satoshi Uehara and Kingkarn Thepkanjana
28th Pacific Asia Conference on Language, Information and Computation pages 120–128

internal state predicates (ISPs, henceforth) of Japanese from a contrastive perspective with those of Thai, another zero pronominal language, and makes a typological characterization of ISPs in Japanese and the "person restriction" phenomena exhibited by them.

2 Internal state predicates and the person restriction

ISPs are those predicates denoting internal states such as emotions, sensations, thought processes, etc. of sentient beings (Iwasaki 1993). It is well known that ISPs in Japanese exhibit the so-called "person restriction" when they refer to an experiencer's internal state at the time of the utterance (Kuroda 1973, Kuno 1973, Ohye 1975, Iwasaki 1993, inter alia). Kuroda was among the first researchers to discuss this restriction: he examined ISPs of Japanese, such as *atui* 'hot', *kanasii* 'sad' and *sabisii* 'lonely' and noted that the subjects of such adjectives "must be first person" (Kuroda 1973: 378). His examples are reproduced below in (1) – (3)

(1) *Watasi-wa atui* 'I am hot.'
(2) **Anata-wa atui* 'You are hot.'
(3) **John-wa atui* 'John is hot.'

Some clarifications of possible complications in the grammatical behavior of ISPs in Japanese are in order. Firstly, as Kuroda himself notes, those Japanese sentences with ISPs in (1) – (3), as well as their English translations, are ambiguous between the experiencer subject interpretation (i.e., 'I feel hot.') and the stimulus subject interpretation that the subject nominal is ascribed to have a certain property which stimulates one to have a certain feeling (i.e., 'I am a hot person.'). Furthermore, ordinary uses of sensation adjectives like *atui* 'hot' without their overt subjects includes ones in which their referents are indeterminate, rather than ambiguous (Nakamura, forthcoming). (See also Shibatani's (1990: 361) treatment of *atui* and *samui* as "zero-argument" predicates which express ambient conditions.)

Secondly, the person restriction in question holds in ordinary communicative situations, but it is often lifted in what Kuroda (1973) calls "non-reportive" style situations, such as literary work in which a story is told by a narrator who is omniscient. This makes sense: because the narrator is omniscient, she can be the "first person" in describing the internal state of any character in the story. (See Kuroda 1973 for more details, and see also Iwasaki's (1993) "literary mode" and "colloquial mode" for a similar distinction.

Thirdly, although the use of ISPs with the second person subject is rendered unacceptable by Kuroda in (2), we should point out that its unacceptability arises, at least in part, from the pragmatic infelicity of the speaker making an assertion as to the internal state of the hearer, which is readily accessible for the hearer herself, but not for the speaker. This is in fact evidenced by the fact that their use with the second person subject is rendered acceptable in interrogatives: *Anata wa atui?* 'Are you hot?', but not in declaratives as in (2). Another more relevant piece of evidence for the pragmatic factor which explains the ill-formedness of ISPs in (2) comes from the fact that the same acceptability pattern with the second person subjects holds for ISPs in Thai as well as shown in (4). However, we will demonstrate in the next section that Thai ISPs do not exhibit the "person restriction" pointed out for Japanese ISPs.

(4) a. **khun* *rɔ́ɔn*
you hot
'You are hot.'
b. *khun* *rɔ́ɔn* *mǎi?*[1]
you hot QP
'Are you hot?'

In other words, the pattern observed for the second person in (2) is not a property of the "person restriction" per se. Therefore, in order to focus on the person restriction in our discussions below, we will mainly examine the contrast in grammatical behaviors between first person and third person experiencer patterns. We shall get back to this point later in Section 3.

Lastly, let us repeat a caveat from Uehara (2006): the person restriction of ISPs is different from, and is not to be confused with, the non-canonical case-marking patterns cross-

[1] The following abbreviations are used for glosses in this paper: NOM = nominative particle, PFV = perfective aspect, POL = politeness marker, PRG = progressive aspect, QP = question particle, RES = resultative aspect, sg = singular, TOP = topic particle.

linguistically attested for ISPs as well as other predicates denoting non-canonical types of events (e.g., Croft 1991). The latter case is illustrated with Spanish examples in (5), where the experiencer role noun takes the object case, but does not exhibit the person restriction of our concern.

(5) a. *Me* *gusta* *Maria.*
'I (OBJ.) like Maria.'
b. *Le* *gusta* *Maria.*
'He/She (OBJ.) likes Maria.'

Similarly, according to Iwasaki (2002), ISPs (his "proprioceptive-state" predicates) in Thai employ the "non-canonical" [VN] order (e.g. *Pùat hu&a.* (lit. 'aches head') 'I/He/She have/has a headache.'), when "[s]ince Thai is a rather typical SVO language, the [NV] order is expected for intransitive stative verbs" (p.34). Notice that these expressions can be used for the third person experiencer as well. In Japanese, as well, ISPs constitute the "double nominative" construction, in which both experiencer- and stimulus-role nouns take nominative case-marking when both are overt: *watasi-ga mizu-ga hosii* (I-NOM water-NOM want) 'I want water.' Interesting though these phenomena are, they do not directly concern us here in our discussions on the person restriction.

3 Person restriction of ISPs in Japanese and Thai in contrast

This section examines the structure and range of the "person restriction" of ISPs in Japanese and compares them with corresponding ISPs in Thai. Let us discuss emotion predicates, such as *uresii* 'glad', *kanasii* 'sad' and *sabisii* 'lonely' in Japanese first. Such emotional lexical items belong to the lexical category of "adjectives" of the language, which, unlike adjectives in English, do not take the copula to constitute a predicate. An emotion adjective, *uresii* 'glad', in (6) below illustrates the structure and person restriction of ISPs in Japanese [parentheses indicate those constituents that can be implicit.[2]]

(6) *(watasi-wa / *kare-wa)* *uresii.*
I-TOP / he-TOP glad
'I am/ he is glad.'

(7) a. *(kare-wa) uresi-soo-da. / uresi-gat-teiru.*
he-TOP glad-seem / glad-show.the.signs.of-PRG
'He seems glad/is showing the signs of being glad.'
b. *(kare-wa)* *uresii* *yoo-da.*
he-TOP glad it.appears.that
'It appears that he is glad.'
c. *(kare-wa)* *uresii* *no-da.*[3]
he-TOP glad it.is.that
'(It is that) He is glad.'

As noted earlier and illustrated again in (6), ISPs in Japanese in their default/unmarked forms can take the first person, but not the third person, for their subject. To indicate the third person experiencer's internal states, their predicate forms must be marked with some morphemes of evidentiality. Four such morphemes are exemplified in a.-c. in (7) and they differ from one another in several ways. Structurally, for instance, *soo-da* 'seem' and *gat-teiru* 'showing the signs of' in (7a) are attached to the stem forms of the emotion adjectives and thus replace the *–i* inflectional ending of these adjectives. In contrast, *yoo-da* 'it appears that' in (7b) and *no-da* 'it is that' in (7c) are attached to the finite forms of emotion adjectives. Thus, they can be attached to the *–katta* past tense forms of emotion adjectives as well: *(kare-wa) uresi-**katta** yoo-da/no-da.* 'It appears that/It is that he was glad.'

Among such morphemes in (7), however, one important distinction in terms of the person restriction in question is the one between *soo-da*, *gat-teiru,* and *yoo-da* in (7a) and (7b), on the one hand, and *no-da* in (7c), on the other. As Kuroda 1973 and Ohye 1975 note, the attachment of the

[2] The Japanese language possesses another group of adjectival words, which are called "adjectival nouns" (Martin 1975) or "nominal adjectives" (Kuno 1973). They developed later in the history of the language than (regular, *i*-ending) adjectives. Emotion words in that category, unlike emotion adjectives, do not typically exhibit the person restriction (e.g. *suki* 'like/fond of' as in *watasi-wa/kare-wa Hanako-ga suki da* 'I like/He likes Hanako.'). However, some (e.g. Ohye 1975: 200) report some (e.g. *huan* 'worried') exhibit the same pattern as emotion adjectives, as in *watasi-wa/??kare-wa huan da.* 'I am/??He is worried.'.

[3] In colloquial speech, the *no* of *no-da* 'it is that' (and of its polite variant *no-desu*) is almost always reduced to the so-called "mora nasal" *n* to render *n-da* (and *n-desu*). Thus, in conversational discourse, the natural and more frequently attested sentence form of (c) in (7) is: *(kare wa) uresii n-da.*

former set of evidentiality morphemes to ISPs makes the third person subject possible, but in turn makes the first person subject unacceptable as in ???*watasi-wa uresi-soo-da.* 'I seem glad.' In contrast, the latter, *no-da* 'it is that', simply lifts the person restriction, thus making the third person subject, in addition to the first person subject, possible as shown in (8) (cf. (6) above).

(8) *(watasi-wa / kare-wa) uresii* *no-da.*
I-TOP / he-TOP glad it.is.that
'(It is that) I am/He is glad.'

It is beyond the scope of the current study to fully characterize semantic effects of *no-da* in Japanese, which is glossed here as 'it is that' for the lack of a better translation. Regarding its use with ISPs with the third person subject, however, Kuroda's description is worth noting here. Using the sentence *Mary-wa sabisii no-da*, where *no-da* is attached to an emotion adjective *sabisii* 'lonely' with the third person subject *Mary*, Kuroda (1973: 381) gives a simple sentence 'Mary is lonely' for its English translation and describes the semantic effects of *no-da* as follows:

> *"The speaker asserts that he knows that Mary is lonely but his knowledge is not solely or perhaps even not at all based on what he perceives of Mary. The sentence does not tell how he knows what he knows, and it can sound just like an a priori declaration–"Mary must be lonely." He might perhaps be able to judge from past experience that Mary is lonely, using circumstantial evidence of a kind that would not allow a neutral party to draw such a conclusion. Or he might even have been told by Mary that she was lonely.*" (Kuroda 1973:381) [underlining added by the authors]

The grammatical behavior as represented in (8) and the semantic effects in the above quote of emotion adjectives in the *no-da* construction in Japanese are interesting from the contrastive perspective between ISPs in Japanese and those in Thai. In terms of grammatical behaviors and functions, Japanese ISPs in the *no-da* construction, rather than those by themselves, resemble Thai ISPs.

Emotion predicates in Thai, such as *dii-cai* 'glad', *sĭa-cai* 'sad' and *rɔɔn-cai* 'worried' (See more examples in Iwasaki 2002[4]), do share the structure with emotion adjectives in Japanese in that they do not take the copula in predication, unlike their counterpart adjectives in English. The use of emotion predicates in Thai is illustrated with *dii-cai* 'glad' in (9).

(9) *(chăn / khăw)* *dii-cai*[5]
I / he glad
'I am/He is glad.'

As noted earlier, Thai and Japanese share the zero anaphoric nature (indicated with parentheses above), again departing from English. Since emotion predicates of the two languages structurally resemble each other on these two accounts, comparison of the patterns of emotion predicates in (9) and (6) brings to the fore a characteristically structural contrast between Thai and Japanese, i.e., the person restriction. Both first and third person subjects are possible for Thai emotion predicates. In contrast, Japanese emotion predicates allow only the overt and covert forms of the first person subject. Emotion predicates in Thai in (9) rather pattern with those in the *no-da* construction in (8) on all the three accounts. We will get back to these points later.

The remainder of this section examines ISPs other than emotion predicates in the two languages, namely, predicates of desire, sensation and thought processes. We will focus on the range as well as

[4] Notice here that Thai emotion predicates share a common form of [V-*cay*]. This study basically follows Iwasaki's treatment of "the [V-*cay*] expressions as [V-Suffix]" in Iwasaki (2002:49-51). See his discussion of the evidence for it. He notes that it is "a unit consisting of a verb and a suffix, the latter of which has been grammaticalized from the lexical noun meaning 'heart'" (p. 60).

[5] In neutral contexts, the first person is the preferred interpretation for the covert subject of ISPs in Thai, and the third person is a possible interpretation only in marked contexts such as below:

A: *thammay khăw hŭarɔ́ʔ daŋ yàaŋ nán*
Why he laugh loudly kind that
'Why did he laugh so loudly?'

B: *dii-cay*
glad
'(He) is glad'

However, even in such marked contexts, ISPs in Japanese cannot be used for the third person subject and require morphemes such as *no-da*, as in (8).

the types of the "person restriction" phenomena exhibited by ISPs in Japanese and find out whether the structural contrast between the two languages in terms of the person restriction prevails throughout the whole range.

Predicates of desire, which are adjectives *hosii* 'want' and *–tai* 'want to', like emotion predicates in Japanese, also exhibit the same person restriction as in (10). This is contrasted with Thai predicates of desire, which allows both the first and the third person subjects as in (11).

Japanese
(10) *(watasi-wa / *kare-wa)* *biiru-ga*
I-TOP / he-TOP beer-NOM
hosii. /nomi-tai.
want /drink-want.to
'I want/want to drink beer.'

Thai
(11) *(chǎn / khǎw)* *yàak* *dùum* *bia*
I / he want drink beer
'I/he want(s) to drink beer.'

Iwasaki (2002) reports that Thai has a wide range of pain terms, e.g. *cèp* 'pain, a general cover-term', *pùat* 'deep-seated aching, usually felt to be hot and diffuse', and *sìat* 'focused abdominal pain' (these examples and glosses are originally from Diller's 1980 list of 15 Thai pain terms), while Japanese has only one general adjective *itai* used with an array of onomatopoetic expressions, e.g. *sikusiku itai* for griping pain, *zukizuki itai* for throbbing pain, and *hirihiri itai* for tingling pain (examples and descriptions are from Iwasaki 2002: 61, footnote 4). The relevant and important point for the current study is that this general adjective *itai* in Japanese has the person restriction, so that all the pain expressions with *itai* exhibit the person restriction, as exemplified in (12), while their Thai counterpart expressions do not have the restriction, as in (13).

Japanese
(12) *(watasi-wa / *kare-wa)* *atama-ga* *itai.*
I-TOP / he-TOP head-NOM ache
'I have a headache.'

Thai
(13) *(chǎn / khǎw)* *pùat* *hǔa*
I / he painful head
'I have/ He has a headache.'

Japanese ISPs with the person restriction include the expressions of thought processes as well, such as *omou* 'think', *nozomu* 'hope', and *negau* 'wish' (see Ohye 1975). Unlike emotion adjectives, these words are verbs and denote a change of state (e.g., 'come to think', rather than a state 'think', in the case of *omou*). Therefore, the internal state of a person at the speech time, first person or third person, can be expressed as the resulting state of that thought process using the resultative aspect marker *te-iru*. For the first person subject only, however, default forms of such verbs can be used to the same effect as the person restriction exhibited by emotion adjectives (Uehara 2011). The examples with *omou* 'think' below in (14) illustrate the situation in Japanese. In contrast, the Thai word *khít* 'think' exhibits no such constraint, as in (15):

Japanese
(14) a. *(watasi-wa / *kare-wa)* *yotoo-ga*
I-TOP / he-TOP ruling.party-NOM
makeru *to* *omou.*
lose that think
'I think that the ruling party will lose (in the next election.'
b. *(watasi-wa /kare-wa)* *yotoo-ga*
I-TOP / he-TOP ruling.party-NOM
makeru *to* *omot-teiru.*
lose that think-RES
'I/He think(s) that the ruling party will lose (in the next election).'

Thai
(15) *(chǎn / khǎw)* *khít* *wâa* *phák*
I / he think that party
rátthabaan *càʔ* *phɛ́ɛ*
government will lose
'I/he think(s) that the government party will lose (in the next election).'

It should be noted furthermore that Japanese has some other verbal expressions of internal states that exhibit the person restriction in a way similar to, but still different from, the verbs of the thought processes above. These include verbs such as *tukareru* 'get tired', *odoroku* 'be surprised', *komaru* 'feel troubled' and verbal idioms such as *onaka-ga suku* (stomach-NOM get.empty) 'get hungry' and *nodo-ga kawaku* (throat-NOM get.dry) 'get thirsty' (Ohye 1975). These verbal expressions also denote the internal states of human beings, to which only the experiencer in principle has direct access. The perfect/past *–ta* forms of these verbs can indicate the internal states of the speaker only, while their resultative aspect – *te-iru* forms, just like verbs of thought processes discussed just above, can take third- as well as first-person subjects. The sentences with *tukareru* 'get tired' in (16) illustrate the situation in Japanese. In contrast, its translation equivalent in Thai, *mòt phalaŋ* (exhaust strength) 'feel physically exhausted' (as well as *mòt kamlaŋcay* (exhaust mental-energy) 'feel mentally exhausted/discouraged') exhibits no such constraint, as in (17) [slightly modified from Iwasaki 2002:43].

Japanese
(16) a. *(watasi-wa / ??kare-wa) tukare-ta.*
I-TOP / he-TOP get.tired.PFV
'I have got tired.'
b. *(watasi-wa / kare-wa) tukare-te-iru.*
I-TOP / he-TOP get-tired-RES
'I/He feel(s) tired.'

Thai
(17) *(chǎn / khǎw) mòt phalaŋ*
I / he exhaust physical.strength
'I/he feel(s) physically exhausted.'

In summary, all the data above indicate the following: 1) both languages, as zero pronominal languages, allow the experiencer subjects of ISPs to be implicit and lack person-indicating copula verbs, which are required in English and pro-drop languages such as Spanish; 2) only ISPs in Japanese exhibit the person restriction and such a restriction is not observed for corresponding ISPs in Thai; 3) All ISPs in Japanese have some parallel, but structurally more-marked, patterns that behave and function exactly like their corresponding Thai ISPs.

4. Proposed characterization of the so-called "person restriction"

Thus far the term "(first) person restriction" has been used in this study to refer to the phenomena exhibited by ISPs in Japanese. This term comes from Kuroda's characterization of the phenomena as one in which the subject of ISPs "must be first person" (Kuroda 1973: 378) and from the observations of their use in assertions as in (1) - (3). However, such characterizations of the phenomena prove to be incorrect considering the fact that, in interrogative sentences, their subjects can be second person, as noted earlier. In fact, Kuroda (ibid.) himself notes in a footnote to his characterization above that "This restriction, however, applies to declarative sentences. In interrogative sentences it is reversed" and gives a pair of examples, which are reproduced in (18) below for comparison with (1) and (2).

(18) a. *???watasi-wa atui desu ka*
I-TOP hot POL QP
'Am I hot?'
b. *anata-wa atui desu ka*
You-TOP hot POL QP
'Are you hot?'

Faced with this set of data, and taking some others to be discussed later into consideration, this study proposes to modify this popular characterization of the constraint known as the "(first) person restriction" and to term it instead as the "Experiencer-Conceptualizer Identity Constraint", which is stated below.

The Experiencer-Conceptualizer Identity (ECI) Constraint:
The experiencer of the situation/event must be identical with the conceptualizer of that situation/event.

The term "conceptualizer" is taken from the cognitive linguistic literature (e.g. Langacker 1985[6]) and is defined here as the person who conceives of a situation/event for and before making an assertion/statement about it. Thus, the conceptualizer is different from the speaker in that the latter is person-based while the former is not. The speaker can be equated with the conceptualizer only by default, i.e., in declarative sentences. Accordingly, in the interrogative sentences in (18) above, the conceptualizer is the addressee, not the speaker, because it is the addressee who takes the role of conceiving and making an assertion/judgement about the situation

[6] More recently, Langacker (2008: Sec. 13.2.3) describes in detail the conceptualizer role in a question scenario as well as in other basic speech act scenarios.

described. Thus, the sentence in (18a) is infelicitous because it violates the ECI constraint: the experiencer is the speaker while the conceptualizer is the hearer (E≠C). In contrast, the sentence in (18b) does not violate the constraint and is considered felicitous: the experiencer is the addressee and so is the conceptualizer (E=C).

This new characterization of the constraint that ISPs in Japanese exhibit has some merits over the previous, person-based one. Firstly, it clearly indicates that neither the phenomena nor the formal distinction is person-based, and that the bare/marked formal distinction of ISPs in Japanese differs in essence from the person-marking distinction of inflectional forms in the so-called pro-drop languages, such as Spanish. In Spanish, internal states are expressed with adjectives (e.g. *feliz* 'happy') + the copula verb *estar,* which inflects for person and number: *estoy* for the first person singular and *estás* for the second person singular. Obviously, the morphological person distinction persists whether the sentence is assertive or interrogative, as in (19).

(19) a. *(Yo) estoy feliz.*
(I) be.1sg happy
'(I) am happy.'
b. *¿Estás (tú) feliz?*
be.2sg (you) happy
'Are (you) happy?'

Secondly, this definition of the constraint can obviate other, rather ad-hoc, parenthetical statements/explanations to the previous person-based definition. For example, as noted and quoted above in (18), Kuroda gives an explanation for the person restriction that it is "reversed" in interrogative sentences. However, for the third person subject, it is <u>not</u> reversed and still applies even in interrogative sentences in Japanese, as shown in (20) [cf. (18) and (3)].

(20) **kare-wa atui desu ka*
He-TOP hot POL QP
'Is he hot?'

The new characterization of the constraint correctly renders the use of ISPs in the interrogative sentence in (20) ungrammatical, where the third person experiencer is not identical with the second person conceptualizer, without recourse to any additional qualification on the constraint.

Thirdly, the new characterization of the grammatical phenomena of ISPs in Japanese correctly captures their behavior in the embedded clauses as well. As noted in the previous section, the attachment of evidentiality morphemes such as *soo-da* 'seem' to ISPs makes the third person subject possible, but in turn makes the first person subject unacceptable as in (21) below.

(21) a. *(watasi-wa / *kare-wa) uresii.* (=(6))
I-TOP / he-TOP glad
'I am/ he is glad.'
b. *(kare-wa /???watasi-wa) uresi-<u>soo-da</u>.*
he-TOP / I-TOP glad-seem
'He seems /I seem glad.'

However, when the sentence (21b) above is embedded in a sentence with the third person subject, it becomes apparent that what *soo-da* precludes is not the first person, but the conceptualizer, which corresponds to the upper/main clause subject as shown in (22) below (modified from Ohye 1975:202).

(22) *Taro$_i$-wa (??zibun$_i$-/kare$_j$-/watasi-ga)*
Taro-TOP self- / he- / I-NOM
uresi-soo-da to Hanako-ni itta.
glad-seem that Hanako-to said
'Taro$_i$ told Hanako that he$_i$/he$_j$/I seemed glad.'

In the same vein, when the sentence (21a) is embedded as a reported speech in a sentence with the third person subject, the grammaticality is reversed: the subject of ISPs cannot be the speaker, but the third person, who is the upper clause subject, as in (23) below.

(23) *Taro$_i$-wa (zibun$_i$-/*kare$_j$-/*watasi-ga)*
Taro-TOP self- / he- / I-NOM
uresii to Hanako-ni itta.
glad that Hanako-to said
'Taro$_i$ told Hanako that he$_i$/he$_j$/I was glad.'

What is at issue here is not the (first) person, but the conceptualizer, who conceives and describes the internal states of some sentient being.

Finally, the ECI constraint gives natural accounts of why the phenomena in question cannot be found in the non-reportive style, but in the reportive style only, and even of exceptions to this stylistic rule as well. As noted earlier (where the default-case term "first-person" was used instead of "conceptualizer"), in omniscient narrator stories, one of the non-reportive contexts, ISPs can be used freely with third person subjects. This is because, under our new characterization of the constraint, the omniscient narrator as the conceptualizer knows the experiences of any character in the story to the effect that she can be identical with the experiencer of these internal states. In other words, it is not that the restriction is "lifted" under some condition, but rather that the ECI constraint takes effect in the case of an omniscient narrator in the literary mode. Furthermore, it should be noted that the ECI constraint takes effect (i.e., bare ISP forms can be used only when the experiencer of the internal state is identical with the conceptualizer and otherwise ISPs have to be marked with *no-da* or the like) in Japanese even in soliloquy and in writing personal diaries—contexts not in the least "reportive".

5. The ECI constraint in Japanese and Thai

We have seen that the ECI constraint is conventionalized lexically in a lot of ISPs in Japanese, whereas Thai ISPs have no such constraint.[7] Japanese also possesses a grammatical construction, namely, the *no-da* construction, which, when used with ISPs, serves to lift the ECI constraint and make them behave like their counterpart ISPs in Thai. In other words, this *no-da* morpheme has the ECI constraint-lifting function.

It should be added here that Thai also possesses a constructional expression, namely, the *caŋ* construction, which combines ISPs with the morpheme *caŋ* 'truly' and does just the opposite of the *no-da* construction in Japanese. This morpheme functions to IMPOSE the ECI constraint on ISPs which it is attached to in Thai, and make them behave exactly like bare ISPs in Japanese, as in (24).

[7] This can be characterized as a cross-linguistic difference in lexicalization patterns (Talmy 1985), and in typological studies of ISPs Japanese and Thai represent two sub-types of the zero pronominal language type.

(24) a. *(chǎn/khǎw)* *dii-cai* (= (9))
I / he glad
'I am/He is glad.'

b. *(chǎn /*khǎw)* *dii-cai* *caŋ*
I / he glad really
'I am so glad.'

The above fact gives us the overall picture of the ECI constraint phenomena in Japanese and Thai as summarized in Table 1 below with ISPs, *uresii* 'glad' in Japanese and *dii-cai* 'glad' in Thai:

	Japanese	Thai
The ECI constraint	*uresii*	*dii-cai caŋ*
No constraint	*uresii no-da*	*dii-cai*

Table 1: The ECI in Japanese and Thai

Table 1 clearly shows the contrast between Japanese and Thai regarding the ECI constraint phenomena involving ISPs. Both languages have conventionalized the ECI constraint in their expressions of internal states of sentient beings. The difference lies in which level of linguistic structure it is conventionalized. In Japanese the ECI constraint is conventionalized at the lexical level, whereas in Thai it is conventionalized at the grammatical level. That is, the two languages differ in how the ECI constraint is linguistically conventionalized.

6. Conclusion

ISPs in Japanese and the so-called "person restriction" they exhibit have been formerly examined in comparison to ISPs in languages like English, which have explicit person systems developed and/or disallow omission of personal pronouns. This paper has contrasted ISPs in Japanese with those in Thai, which belongs together with Japanese to the zero pronominal language type (with no person marking). It has thus brought to the fore typological characteristics of ISPs in Japanese, as well as the range and structural variations of the phenomena exhibited by them.

We have shown that the so-called "person restriction" is not person-based, but is based rather on the identity of the experiencer of internal states with the conceptualizer of the events, so that it should rather be termed as the Experiencer-Conceptualizer Identity Constraint. Since it is not person-based, the ECI constraint reasonably accounts for the use of ISPs in Japanese in wider contexts than the traditional "reportive" context, such as one where no interlocutor is present. We have argued that the difference between ISPs in Japanese and those in Thai lies in the patterns of lexicalization. Both languages possess expressions with the ECI constraint conventionalized. It is conventionalized or lexicalized into ISPs in Japanese, whereas Thai ISPs take a grammatical marking *caŋ* to have the similar effects. It is hoped that future studies will further reveal cross-linguistic patterns of variation in this aspect of language for a more holistic typology.

Acknowledgments

This research work is partially supported by a Grant-in-Aid for Scientific Research from the Japan Society for the Promotion of Science (No. 24520416) awarded to the first author and the Ratchadaphiseksomphot Endowment Fund of Chulalongkorn University (RES560530179-HS) awarded to the second author.

References

William Croft. 1991. *Syntactic Categories and Grammatical Relations: The Cognition Organization of Information*. University of Chicago Press, Chicago.

Anthony Diller. 1980. Cross-cultural Pain Semantics. *Pain*, 9: 9-26.

Shoichi Iwasaki. 1993. *Subjectivity in Grammar and Discourse*. John Benjamins, Amsterdam.

Shoichi Iwasaki. 2002. Proprioceptive-state Expressions in Thai. *Studies in Language*, 26(1): 33-66.

Susumu Kuno. 1973. *The Structure of the Japanese Language*. MIT Press, Cambridge.

S. Y. Kuroda. 1973. Where Epistemology, Style, and Grammar Meet: A Case Study from Japanese. In Stephen R. Anderson and Paul Kiparsky (eds.) *A Festschrift to Morris Halle*. Holt, Rinehart and Winston, Inc., New York, 377-391.

Ronald W. Langacker. 1985. Observations and Speculations on Subjectivity. In John Haiman (ed.) *Iconicity in Syntax*. John Benjamins, Amsterdam and Philadelphia, 109-150.

Ronald W. Langacker. 2008. *Cognitive Grammar: A Basic Introduction*, Oxford University Press, Oxford.

Samuel Martin. 1975. *A Reference Grammar of Japanese*. Yale University Press, New Haven.

Yoshihisa Nakamura. Forthcoming. Langacker no Shitenkouzu to (Kan-) Shukansei. [Langacker's Viewing Arrangements and (Inter-) Subjectivity.] In Nakamura and Uehara (eds.). *Langacker no (Kan-) Shukansei to sono Tenkai*. [Langacker's (Inter-) Subjectivity and Its Expansion.] Kaitakusha, Tokyo.

Saburo Ohye. 1975. *Nichieigo no Hikaku Kenkyuu: Shukansei o megutte*. [A Contrastive Study of Japanese and English: On Subjectivity.] Nan'undo, Tokyo.

Masayoshi Shibatani. 1990. *The Languages of Japan*. Cambridge University Press, Cambridge.

Leonard Talmy. 1985. Lexicalization Patterns: Semantic Structure in Lexical Forms. In Timothy Shopen (ed.) *Language Typology and Syntactic Description. Vol.3: Grammatical Categories and the Lexicon*. Cambridge University Press, Cambridge, 57-149.

Satoshi Uehara. 2006. Toward a Typology of Linguistic Subjectivity: A Cognitive and Cross-linguistic Approach to Grammaticalized Deixis. In Angeliki Athanasiadou, Costas Canakis and Bert Cornillie (eds.) *Subjectification: Various Paths to Subjectivity*. Mouton de Gruyter, Berlin, 75-117.

Satoshi Uehara. 2011. Syukansei ni Kansuru Gengo no Taisyô to Ruikei (Cross-linguistic Comparison and Linguistic Typology in terms of Subjectivity). In Harumi Sawada (ed.). *Hitsuji Imiron Kouza 5: Shukansei to Shutaisei* (Hitsuji Studies on Semantics 5: Subjectivity), Hitsujishobo, Tokyo, 69-91.

Investigation Into Using the Unicode Standard for Primitives of Unified Han Characters

Henry Larkin
Deakin University
Melbourne, Australia
henry.larkin@deakin.edu.au

Abstract

The Unicode standard identifies and provides representation of the vast majority of known characters used in today's writing systems. Many of these characters belong to the unified Han series, which encapsulates characters from writing systems used in languages such as Chinese, Japanese and Korean languages. These pictographic characters are often made up of smaller primitives, either other characters or more simplified pictography. This paper presents research findings of how the Unicode standard currently represents the primitives used in 4134 of the most common Han characters.

1 Introduction

The Unicode standard has made great strides in its ability to provide a single reference for indexing written characters in the world's languages. Several of these languages contain characters that are built up of other characters. This is especially true of the unified Han subset of the Unicode standard, which focuses on characters largely used within Japanese kanji, Chinese hanzi, and Korean hanja. These character sets are used in several languages in numerous regions in Asia. While the Unicode standard has been working towards creating a unified character set, from a research perspective there is an area of research open to explore what parts of characters might contain sub-characters (primitives), and how these primitives are represented. These primitives can be either whole characters in and of themselves, or primitive glyphs either in the form of simplified representations of actual characters, or common symbols which, by themselves, traditionally have only a vague or perhaps non-existent meaning. This is especially important to dictionary, research and language-learning projects, where the breakdown of primitives is greatly beneficial.

Some work has been done in this area before, particularly from the point of view of language learners. The work of Dr. Heisig [1][2] has made great strides in identifying common primitives within Chinese and Japanese characters. However, majority of these primitives are drawn as images and have no representation in the Unicode standard or are not referenced from the Unicode standard. Furthermore, previous research has not explored a comprehensive analysis of which primitives are used most commonly and in what positions of the character they are most commonly found. The purpose of this work is to explore the possibility of using the Unicode standard for all primitive characters.

2 Process

This research project looked at six Asian language character sets in order to investigate whether it is possible to use Unicode characters to describe the primitives that make up each character. Six language sets were considered in total.

Copyright 2014 by Henry Larkin
28th Pacific Asia Conference on Language, Information and Computation pages 129–134

- JOYO is the official kanji character set as described by the government of Japan containing 2136 characters units when including the latest updates from 2010.
- JLPT (Japanese Language Proficiency Test) is a character set used specifically for learners of Japanese. It differs from the JOYO character set in that characters are given roughly in order of those most commonly used as opposed to those that are simplest to write as would be given in a Japanese language school. The JLPT set contains 2431 characters. JLPT has five levels.
- HSK (Hanyu Shuiping Kaoshi or Chinese Proficiency Test) is the official hanzi character set of mainland China covering 2804 characters. HSK has six levels.
- TOCFL (Test of Chinese as a Foreign Language) is the character set used for learners of traditional hanzi for years in Taiwan. It contains 2815 characters over five levels.
- Taiwan School System. 2809 characters are taken for the Taiwan educational system up to grade 7. In the case of traditional characters, there are a significant number of rarely used characters that are taught in advanced levels of the Taiwan high school system. These characters will not be considered as part of this research due to their rarity. It is also worth noting that the majority of advanced characters almost always consist of a subset of whole other characters as their primitives.
- Hong Kong School System. This contains 2929 traditional hanzi characters. Note that only up to grade six is included in this research for the same reasons that the more complex characters are rare and almost always consists of whole characters as primitives.

Korean hanja was not included as it is mostly only used in older and scholarly texts, as hangul is the most common form of writing in modern-day South Korea, and this research is considering common-use han characters.

Many of these character sets overlap greatly which is why the Unicode standard spent considerable time finding ways to unify character identification (although it is worth noting that there is some consideration to be given that different regions may consider some of their characters to not be able to be unified due to different styling of their characters and different meanings given to them). In total, 4134 characters were investigated at as part of this research. For each of these characters, each character was visually broken down into primitives based on the available characters present in the Unicode standard. This was done by hand. The majority of these primitives consisted primarily of characters that already existed as whole characters. It also consisted of glyphs used either as official simplifications or similar shapes.

Three examples are included below to demonstrate the types of primitives. In the first instance, *bright*, both primitives are complete characters in their own right. In the second instance, *fathom*, the primitive on the left is an official primitive, in the sense that it has a meaning (water), that is derived from the complete character 氺. The right primitive is a whole character in its own right. In the third instance, *occupation*, the top primitive ⺍ is not an official primitive. Any records of it being an official primitive have been lost over time, or are abstract in detail. Regardless of its lack of official meaning, the primitive still has a visual representation within the Unicode standard that occurs within the character. This research considers all cases when searching for visual representations, within the Unicode standard, for representing the primitives of each Han character within the six common character sets analyzed.

1. 明, bright, l 日, r 月
2. 測, fathom, l 氵, r 則
3. 営, occupation, t ⺍, b 呂

The examples below demonstrate how this breakdown was achieved. Every character, for the purposes of this research, had an English term assigned to it for help with identification, although, this English term is not necessarily official, as different languages treat characters differently. It is worth noting, however, that in the vast majority of cases, the English term used to describe the character was somewhat similar in meaning across most data sets.

For each entry, the primitives were then defined and described relative to their position. Character positions were broken up into four main directions: *top* (t), *bottom* (b), *left* (l), *right* (r), to describe where primitives belong visually within a parent character.

名, name, t 夕, b 口
明, bright, l 日, r 月
動, move, l 重, r 力
新, new, l 亲, r 斤
製, manufacture, t 制, b 衣
災, disaster, t 巛, b 火
仙, hermit, l 亻, r 山

Two special positions were also included. These are *outer* (o) and *inner* (i). *Outer* is used to describe where a primitive occurs outside the quadrant of others. *Inner* is used to describe where a primitive occurs inside an *outer* position. An example of *outer* and *inner* positioning is given for the character *wide* seen below. In this example, there are two primitives. One that belongs in the *outer* container and one that belongs technically *inside* the container.

広, wide, o 广, i 厶

Further to this, for complex characters, it is possible that there will be more than six positions of primitives. In many cases, there are multiple primitives within a position. To support this, indentation of splitting each grid position into sub-positions using subsequent letters was defined. For example, in the case of the character used for *brain* below, there is one character positioned on the left, and then on the right, there is another pseudo character consisting of three smaller primitives. This right hand side is then divided into top and bottom by simply indicating that there is a primitive on the right and in the top quadrant of the right side and two other primitives on the right hand side in the bottom component. Furthermore, in the right bottom components, this is split further into outer and inner sections.

腦, brain, l 月, rt 巛, rbo 囗, rbi 㐅

Also note that primitives were split like this where a more complete primitive character did not exist within the Unicode standard. The primary aim was to determine if all characters could be represented by primitives in some form.

Where possible, all primitives used the most complex form possible. It is possible to represent a character, no matter how complex, using the most simple primitives, or some combination of simple and more complex and complete primitives. However, in this research, it was decided that the most detailed primitive would be used where possible. Take for example the character for wide above and the character for broaden below. *Broaden* makes use of two primitives. In this case, the right hand portion is the existing character *wide* and not the sub-components that *wide* consists of.

拡, broaden, l 扌, r 広

Furthermore, this research is focused on visual shapes entirely. So, where a character has a simplified form because of the way it is simplified visually inside another character, the simplified form is used. Table 1 below shows a sample of some of the most common characters and the simplifications.

food	食	飠	饣
water	水	氵	
going	行	彳	
gold	金	钅	
cow	牛	牜	
stream	川	巛	巜

Table 1: Example List of Official Character Simplifications

There were some instances where "official" primitives did not exist. In which case, liberties were made in selecting similar Unicode characters. A selection of which will be covered in Section 4 on Primitives with no Unicode Character. For the purposes of this research, all Unicode characters were considered as possibilities for primitives, though, in the majority of cases, the so called "official" primitives were used.

3 The Common Primitives

After all characters in the included character sets had their primitives identified and recorded, statistics were then calculated to determine information about how the primitives were being used. One of these was the common primitives in each character set. Table 2 below shows the breakdown of the common primitives and their frequency for each of the language sets investigated. Across all lists, the most common primitives are roughly the same in all cases. It is only when one gets further down the list that one starts to see new primitives that do not appears in other lists.

HK		HSK		JLPT		JOYO		TAIWAN		TOCFL	
口	249	口	219	口	147	口	152	口	238	口	242
氵	147	扌	151	木	131	氵	121	氵	137	氵	143
木	134	氵	142	氵	125	木	115	木	134	扌	140
扌	132	木	122	一	107	一	110	一	129	木	125
一	127	一	115	亻	102	亻	94	扌	127	一	120
亻	123	亻	105	土	90	土	90	亻	118	亻	116
土	104	土	87	日	86	扌	87	土	97	土	95
艹	84	日	85	扌	81	日	83	艹	91	日	83
日	83	月	78	艹	80	月	72	日	84	月	76
月	83	讠	72	言	67	言	71	月	75	言	75
言	79	艹	66	月	64	艹	69	言	74	艹	74
心	61	辶	59	辶	57	辶	54	辶	60	辶	61
辶	60	纟	57	心	54	心	53	心	58	心	59
十	58	十	52	十	49	宀	49	宀	57	宀	56
女	57	女	52	宀	49	十	46	十	56	十	54
宀	56	宀	51	阝	42	女	44	女	54	貝	53
糸	55	心	49	儿	41	田	42	糸	53	女	47
忄	53	丶	47	丷	40	阝	42	王	47	忄	47
貝	53	忄	47	女	40	丷	41	田	46	隹	46
隹	48	贝	46	糸	40	貝	40	冂	45	糸	45

Table 2: Top 20 Primitives per Character Set

Also interesting was the rapidly reducing frequency of primitive use. Figure 1 shows that the most common primitives appear far more commonly than any other character. The chart clearly shows a long tail style of frequency, where in the case of the HSK character set, only 45 primitives have an occurrence of more than 20 times with the top six primitives occurring 100 or more times. The frequency of primitive use drops off quite quickly, indicating that characters in each of these languages do have a common set of primitives. All language character sets had a very similar occurrence.

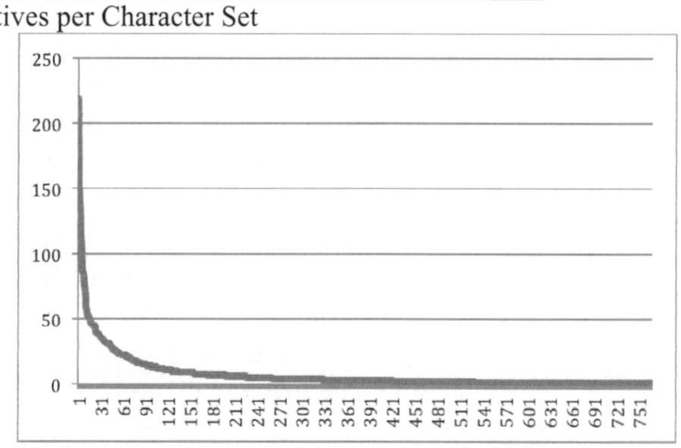

Figure 1: Frequency of Primitives in the HSK Set

It is also worth noting which position was more common in primitives. A sample of this data can be seen in Table 3 below. Each character is preceeded by a letter code to indicate its position within another character. The positions are: (l)eft, (r)ight, (t)op, (b)ottom, (i)nner, (o)uter. Across all language sets, the most common position for any primitive is the *right* side, having vastly more occurrences than its nearest competitor, the *left* side. Following this, the *top* position is the most common and the *bottom* is least common across all languages, for the four main quadrants. The *outer* and *inner* positions were quite rare. What is extremely interesting about this data is that all languages had almost identical primitive positioning. This further supports the theory that there is a very common nature among Chinese style characters in Asian languages.

What is interesting to note about primitive positions is that while the *right* position was the most common for all primitives, the most popular primitives vastly favored the *left* and sometimes the *top*. This is due to the fact that the *right* position usually contained whole characters, which were not commonly used as primitives, but the *right* position was the most common positioning.

HK		HSK		JLPT		JOYO		TAIWAN		TOCFL	
l 氵	136	l 扌	150	l 氵	117	l 氵	112	l 氵	127	l 扌	139
l 扌	131	l 氵	134	l 亻	94	l 亻	88	l 扌	125	l 氵	131
l 亻	113	l 亻	100	l 扌	80	l 扌	86	l 亻	108	l 亻	106
l 口	76	l 口	89	l 木	75	l 言	64	l 口	75	l 口	77
l 木	71	l 讠	68	t 卄	63	l 木	59	l 木	73	l 言	64
l 言	66	l 木	67	l 言	60	l 辶	52	t 卄	68	l 木	63
t 卄	63	l 辶	58	l 辶	54	t 卄	48	l 言	61	l 辶	59
l 辶	58	t 卄	55	b 心	38	l 月	40	l 辶	58	t 卄	50
l 忄	53	l 纟	53	t 宀	37	b 心	38	l 月	42	l 忄	47
b 心	43	l 月	47	l 月	33	t 宀	35	t 宀	40	b 心	42
l 月	42	l 忄	46	l 糸	33	l 忄	32	b 心	39	l 月	41
l 糸	41	b 心	45	t 一	32	l 糸	32	l 糸	39	t 宀	41
l 女	37	t 宀	42	l 忄	31	t 一	32	l 女	38	l 金	37
t 宀	35	l 钅	34	l 糹	29	l 阝	30	l 忄	37	l 糸	35
t⺮	34	t 一	34	l 阝	29	l 口	29	l 金	35	o 广	31
l 金	33	l 阝	32	l 金	27	l 土	29	t⺮	31	l 女	30
l 土	31	l 土	31	l 女	26	l 女	28	l 阝	29	l 阝	30
r 刂	31	l 女	31	l 禾	26	l 金	28	t 一	29	t⺮	29
o 广	30	r 刂	28	l 土	25	r 刂	25	o 广	28	t 一	29
t 一	29	b 口	27	o 广	25	r 頁	24	l 土	27	r 刂	28

Table 3: Top 20 Primitives in Specific Positions

4 Primitives with no Unicode Character

Seven primitives were identified which had no Unicode representation that accurately took the shape. These are shown in Table 4 below, using the closest-matching character. All but two of these characters were taken from the Japanese hiragana and katakana alphabets. The primitives ∀ and ‡ are Unicode symbols. They are not an accurate visual representation, but are the closest matching symbols found for those two commonly-used primitives.

Primitive	Examples
∀	光，单，肖
フ	场，汤
メ	风，図, 肴，哎
マ	专，矛
ス	经，轻
ム	么，云，勾
‡	牛, 泽

Table 4: Missing Primitives

It is also worth mentioning that there is a severe lacking of font support for the primitives, which can visually display the Unicode standard. This has been an issue among typeface users and designers for many years, and it is still an issue today. Even in creating this paper, several different fonts were used for displaying some of the more unique primitives.

5 Conclusion

In conclusion, this research has collated and documented the primitive breakdown of each character using Unicode primitives. The results of this research show that the Unicode standard does greatly support the identification and codifying of primitives as used in Han characters. There are only a few exceptions where character representation is not possible. Furthermore, what is interesting to note is that the most common primitives appear far more likely than any others. Also of note is that the most common positions for primitives were on the left, and also at the top. It would be interesting to see if further iterations of the Unicode standard will support the pseudo primitive characters for which there is currently no code point.

References

[1] James W. Heisig and Timothy W. Richardson. Oct 2008. Remembering Simplified Hanzi: Book 1. How Not to Forget the Meaning and Writing of Chinese Characters.

[2] James W. Heisig. Apr 2011. Remembering the Kanji: A Complete Course on How Not to Forget the Meaning and Writing of Japanese Characters.

[3] Etsuko Toyoda, Arief Muhammad Firdaus, and Chieko Kano. Identifying Useful Phonetic Components of Kanji for Learners of Japanese.

[4] James W. Heisig. 1987. Remembering the Kanji 2. Honolulu: University of Hawai'i Press.

[5] Hiroyuki Kaiho and Nomura Yukimasa. 1983. Kanji Joho Shori no Shinrigaku (The Psychology of Kanji Information Processing). Tokyo: Kyoiku Shuppan.

[6] Kano Chieko. 1993. Kanji no zoji seibun ni kan-suru ichi-kosatsu (Study on Basic Japanese Components of Kanji) (2). Bungei Gengo Kenkyu (Studies in Language and Literature) 24: 97–114.

[7] Masuda Hisashi and Saito Hirofumi. 2002. Interactive Processing of Phonological Information in Reading Japanese kanji Character Words and Their Phonetic Radicals. Brain and Language 81: 445– 453.

[8] Toshihiro Hayashi and Yoneo Yano. 1994. Kanji Laboratory: An Environmental ICAI System for Kanji Learning. IEICE Transactions on Information and Systems.

[9] Daniel Wagner and Istvan Barakonyi. 2003. Augmented Reality Kanji Learning. Proceedings of the 2nd IEEE/ACM International Symposium on Mixed and Augmented Reality.

[10] Mathieu Blondel, Kazuhiro Seki and Kuniaki Uehara 2010. Unsupervised Learning of Stroke Tagger for Online Kanji Handwriting Recognition. Pattern Recognition.

[11] Ondĺej Velek, Cheng-Lin Liu, Stefan Jaeger and Masaki Nakagawa. 2002. An Improved Approach to Generating Realistic Kanji Character Images from On-line Characters and its Benefit to Off-line Recognition Performance. Pattern Recognition.

[12] Ondĺej Velek, Cheng-Lin Liu, and Masaki Nakagawa. 2001. Generating Realistic Kanji Character Images from On-line Patterns. Document Analysis and Recognition.

[13] Jun Tsukumo. 1996. Handprinted Kanji OCR Development--What was solved in Handprinted Kanji Character Recognition? IEICE Transactions on Information and Systems

[14] Akiko Nagano and Masaharu Shimada. 2014. Morphological Theory and Orthography: Kanji as a Representation of Lexemes. Journal of Linguistics

[15] Ikumi Ota, Ryo Yamamoto, Takuya Nishimoto and Shigeki Sagayama. 2008. On-line Handwritten Kanji String Recognition Based on Grammar Description of Character Structures. Pattern Recognition

[16] Ondrej Velek and Masaki Nakagawa. 2002. The Impact of Large Training Sets on the Recognition Rate of Off-line Japanese Kanji Character Classifiers. Document Analysis Systems V.

Taking Antonymy Mask off in Vector Space

Enrico Santus
The Hong Kong Polytechnic University
Hong Kong
e.santus@connect.polyu.hk

Qin Lu
The Hong Kong Polytechnic University
Hong Kong
csluqin@comp.polyu.edu.hk

Alessandro Lenci
Università di Pisa
Pisa, Italy
alessandro.lenci@ling.unipi.it

Chu-Ren Huang
The Hong Kong Polytechnic University
Hong Kong
churen.huang@polyu.edu.hk

Abstract

Automatic detection of antonymy is an important task in Natural Language Processing (NLP) for Information Retrieval (IR), Ontology Learning (OL) and many other semantic applications. However, current unsupervised approaches to antonymy detection are still not fully effective because they cannot discriminate antonyms from synonyms. In this paper, we introduce *APAnt*, a new Average-Precision-based measure for the unsupervised discrimination of antonymy from synonymy using Distributional Semantic Models (DSMs). *APAnt* makes use of Average Precision to estimate the extent and salience of the intersection among the most descriptive contexts of two target words. Evaluation shows that the proposed method is able to distinguish antonyms and synonyms with high accuracy across different parts of speech, including nouns, adjectives and verbs. *APAnt* outperforms the *vector cosine* and a baseline model implementing the *co-occurrence hypothesis*.

1 Introduction

Antonymy is one of the fundamental relations shaping the organization of the semantic lexicon and its identification is very challenging for computational models (Mohammad et al., 2008; Deese, 1965; Deese, 1964). Yet, antonymy is essential for many Natural Language Processing (NLP) applications, such as Information Retrieval (IR), Ontology Learning (OL), Machine Translation (MT), Sentiment Analysis (SA) and Dialogue Systems (Roth and Schulte im Walde, 2014; Mohammad et al., 2013). In particular, the automatic identification of semantic opposition is a crucial component for the detection and generation of paraphrases (Marton et al., 2011), the understanding of contradictions (de Marneffe et al., 2008) and the detection of humor (Mihalcea and Strapparava, 2005).

Several existing computational lexicons and thesauri explicitly encode antonymy, together with other semantic relations. Although such resources are often used to support the above mentioned NLP tasks, hand-coded lexicons and thesauri have low coverage and many scholars have shown their limits: Mohammad et al. (2013), for example, have noticed that "more than 90% of the contrasting pairs in GRE closest-to-opposite questions are not listed as opposites in WordNet".

Copyright 2014 by Enrico Santus, Qin Lu, Alessandro Lenci and Chu-Ren Huang
28th Pacific Asia Conference on Language, Information and Computation pages 135–144

The automatic identification of semantic relations is a core task in computational semantics. Distributional Semantic Models (DSMs) have often been exploited for their well known ability to identify semantically similar lexemes using corpus-derived co-occurrences encoded as distributional vectors (Santus et al., 2014a; Baroni and Lenci, 2010; Turney and Pantel, 2010; Padó and Lapata, 2007; Sahlgren, 2006). These models are based on the *Distributional Hypothesis* (Harris, 1954) and represent lexical semantic similarity in function of distributional similarity, which can be measured by *vector cosine* (Turney and Pantel, 2010). However, these models are characterized by a major shortcoming. That is, they are not able to discriminate among different kinds of semantic relations linking distributionally similar lexemes. For instance, the nearest neighbors of *castle* in the vector space typically include hypernyms like *building*, co-hyponyms like *house*, meronyms like *brick*, antonyms like *shack*, together with other semantically related words. While impressive results have been achieved in the automatic identification of synonymy (Baroni and Lenci, 2010; Padó and Lapata, 2007), methods for the identification of hypernymy (Santus et al., 2014a; Lenci and Benotto, 2012) and antonymy (Roth and Schulte im Walde, 2014; Mohammad et al. 2013) still need much work to achieve satisfying precision and coverage (Turney, 2008; Mohammad et al., 2008). This is the reason why semi-supervised pattern-based approaches have often been preferred to purely unsupervised DSMs (Pantel and Pennacchiotti, 2006; Hearst, 1992).

In this paper, we introduce *APAnt*, a new Average-Precision-based distributional measures that is able to successfully discriminate antonyms from synonyms, outperforming *vector cosine* and a baseline system based on the *co-occurrence hypothesis,* formulated by Charles and Miller in 1989 and confirmed in other studies, such as those of Justeson and Katz (1991) and Fellbaum (1995).

Our measure is based on a distributional interpretation of the so-called *paradox of simultaneous similarity and difference between the antonyms* (Cruse, 1986). According to this paradox, antonyms are similar to synonyms in every dimension of meaning except one. Our hypothesis is that the different dimension of meaning is a salient one and it can be identified with DSMs and exploited for discriminating antonyms from synonyms.

The rest of the paper is organized as follows. Section 2 gives the definition and illustrates the various types of antonyms. Section 3 gives a brief overview of related works. Section 4 presents the proposed *APAnt* measure. Section 5 shows the performance evaluation of the proposed measure. Section 6 is the conclusion.

2 Antonymy: definition and types

People do not always agree on classifying word pairs as antonyms (Mohammed et al., 2013), confirming that antonymy identification is indeed a difficult task. This is true even for native speakers. Antonymy is in fact a complex relation and opposites can be of different types, making this class hard to define (Cruse, 1986).

Over the years, many scholars from different disciplines have tried to provide a precise definition of this semantic relation. Though, they are yet to reach any conclusive agreement. Kempson (1977) defines opposites as word pairs with a "binary incompatible relation", such that the presence of one meaning entails the absence of the other. In this sense, *giant* and *dwarf* are good opposites, while *giant* and *person* are not. Cruse (1986) points out the above-mentioned *paradox of simultaneous similarity and difference* between the antonyms, claiming that opposites are indeed similar in every dimension of meaning except in a specific one (e.g., both *giant* and *dwarf* refer to a person, with a head, two legs and two feet, but with very different size).

Mohammad et al. (2013) have used these two definitions to distinguish between (1) opposites, which are word pairs that are strongly incompatible with each other and/or are saliently different across a dimension of meaning; (2) contrasting word pairs, which have some non-zero degree of binary incompatibility and/or some non-zero difference across a dimension of meaning; (3) antonyms, which are opposites that are also gradable adjectives.

Semantic opposition is so complex that other classifications might be adopted as well (Bejar et al., 1991; Cruse, 1986). Moreover, opposites can also be sub-classified. Even though there is no agreement about the number of sub-types, we briefly mention a simple – but comprehensive –

sub-classification adopted by Mohammad et al. (2013) to exemplify the complexity of the class. In their paper, Mohammad et al. used a simple sub-classification to make their crowdsource annotation task easier to perform. This sub-classification, mostly based on Cruse (1986), includes (1) antipodals (e.g. *top-bottom*), pairs whose terms are at the opposite extremes of a specific meaning dimension; (2) complementaries (e.g. *open-shut*), pairs whose terms divide the domain in two mutual exclusive compartments; (3) disjoints (e.g. *hot-cold*), pairs whose words occupy non-overlapping regions in a specific semantic dimension; (4) gradable opposites (e.g. *long-short*), adjective- or adverb-pairs that gradually describe some semantic dimensions, such as length, speed, etc.; (5) reversibles (e.g. *rise-fall*), verb-pairs whose words respectively describe the change from A to B and the change from B to A.

Since our aim is to discriminate antonyms from synonyms, our attention is not focused on distinguishing different types of opposites. In this work, we will adopt a broad definition of antonymy, including all the previously mentioned types of opposites together with paranyms, which are a specific type of co-hyponyms (Huang et al., 2007). In fact, while co-hyponyms are simply coordinates depending from the same hypernym, paranyms are co-hyponyms partitioning a conceptual field in subfields. Different from co-hyponyms, paranyms must be very similar to each other and change only in respect to one dimension of meaning. For instance, *dry season, spring, summer*, *autumn* and *winter* are co-hyponyms, but only *spring*, *summer*, *autumn* and *winter* are paranyms.

3 Related Works

The foundation of most corpus-based research on antonymy is the *co-occurrence hypothesis*, (Lobanova, 2012). This derives from an observation by Charles and Miller (1989) that antonyms co-occur in the same sentence more often than expected by chance. This claim has found many empirical confirmations, such as by Justeson and Katz (1991) and Fellbaum (1995).

Another large part of related research has been focused on the study of lexical-syntactic constructions that can work as linguistic tests for antonymy definition and classification (Cruse, 1986). Some syntagmatic properties were also identified. Ding and Huang (2014; 2013), for example, have noticed that, unlike co-hyponyms, antonyms generally have a strongly preferred word order when they co-occur in a coordinate context (i.e. A and/or B).

Starting from these observations, computational methods for antonymy identification were implemented. Most of them rely on pattern based approaches (Schulte im Walde and Köper, 2013; Lobanova et al., 2010; Turney, 2008; Pantel and Pennacchiotti, 2006; Lin et al., 2003), which use specific patterns to distinguish antonymy-related pairs from others. Pattern based methods, however, are mostly semi-supervised. Moreover they require a large amount of data and suffer from low recall, because they can be applied only to frequent words, which are the only ones likely to occur with the selected patterns.

Lucerto et al. (2002) used the number of tokens between the target words together with some other clues (e.g. the presence/absence of conjunctions like *but*, *from*, *and*, etc.) in order to identify contrasting words. Unfortunately the method has very limited coverage.

Schwab et al. (2002) used oppositeness vectors, which were created by identifying possible opposites relying on dictionary definitions. The approach was tested only on a few word pairs and it can hardly be regarded as a general solution.

Turney (2008) proposed a supervised algorithm for the identification of several semantic relations, including synonyms and opposites. The algorithm relied on a training set of word pairs with class labels to assign the labels also to a testing set of word pairs. All word pairs were represented as vectors encoding the frequencies of co-occurrence in textual patterns extracted from a large corpus of web pages. The system achieved an accuracy of 75% against a frequency baseline of 65.4%.

Mohammad et al. (2008) proposed a method for determining what they have defined as the "degrees of antonymy". This concept, which is related to the canonicity (Jones et al., 2007), was aimed to reflect the results of psycholinguistic experiments, which show that some antonyms are perceived as 'better' (e.g. *big – small*) than others (e.g. *big – normal*). For each target word pair, they used thesaurus categories to decide whether a pair is an instance of antonymy or not. Their method then assigned the degree of antonymy using co-occurrence statistics, achieving a good precision.

Mohammad et al. (2013) used an analogical method based on a given set of contrasting words to identify and classify different kinds of opposites by hypothesizing that for every opposing pair of words, A and B, there is at least another opposing pair, C and D, such that A is similar to C and B is similar to D. Their approach outperformed other measures. But, it is not unsupervised and uses a thesaurus as knowledge.

Kim and de Marneffe (2013) exploited word vectors learned by Neural Network Language Models (NNLMs) to extract scalar relationships between adjectives (e.g., okay < good < excellent), outperforming other approaches in their indirect yes/no question answer pairs (IQAP) evaluation (de Marneffe et al., 2010).

Schulte im Walde and Köper (2013) proposed a vector space model relying on lexico-syntactic patterns to distinguish between synonymy, antonymy and hypernymy. Their approach was tested on German nouns, verbs and adjectives, achieving a precision of 59.80%, which was above the majority baselines.

More recently, Roth and Schulte im Walde (2014) proposed that discourse relations can be used as indicators for paradigmatic relations, including antonymy.

4 *APAnt*: an Average-Precision-based measure

In this work we make use of the observation that antonyms are often similar in every semantic dimension except one (Cruse, 1986). In the previous section we have shown the example of *giant* and *dwarf*, which in fact differ only with respect to *size*. This peculiarity of antonymy – called by Cruse (1986) the *paradox of simultaneous similarity and difference* – has an important distributional correlate. Antonyms, in fact, occur in similar contexts as much as synonyms do, making the DSMs models unable to discriminate them. However, according to Cruse's definition, we can expect one dimension of meaning in which the antonyms have different behaviors. That is, they occur with different contexts. We can also expect that this dimension of meaning is a salient one. For example, *size* is a salient dimension of meaning for the words *giant* and *dwarf*, and we can expect that while *giant* occurs more often with words more related to large size such as *big*, *huge*, *destroy*, etc., *dwarf* is more likely to occur in contexts more related to small size, such as *small*, *hide*, and so on. We hypothesize, therefore, that if we isolate the *N* most salient contexts for two distributionally similar lexemes and we intersect them, we can predict whether these two lexemes are antonyms or synonyms by looking at the extent and salience of this intersection: the broader and more salient the intersection, the higher the probability that the lexemes are synonyms; *vice versa* the narrower and less salient the intersection, the higher the probability that the lexemes are antonyms.

To verify this hypothesis, we select the *N* most salient contexts of the two target words (*N*=100[1]). We define the salience of a context for a specific target word by ranking the contexts through *Local Mutual Information* (LMI; Evert, 2005) and picking the first *N*, as already done by Santus et al. (2014a). Once the *N* most salient contexts for the two target words have been identified, we verify the extent and the salience of the contexts shared by both the target words. We predict that synonyms share a significantly higher number of salient contexts than antonyms.

To estimate the extent and the salience of the shared contexts, we adapt the Average Precision measure (AP; Voorhees and Harman, 1999), a common Information Retrieval (IR) evaluation metric already used by Kotlerman et al. (2010) to identify lexical entailment. In IR systems, this measure is used to evaluate the ranked documents returned for a specific query. It assigns higher values to the rankings in which most or all the relevant documents are on the top (recall), while irrelevant documents are either removed or in the bottom (precision). For our purposes, we modify this measure in order to increase the scores as a function of (1) the extent of the intersection between the *N* most relevant contexts of the two target words and (2) the maximum salience of the common contexts. To do so, we consider the common contexts as relevant documents and their maximum salience as their rank. Consequently,

[1] *N=100* is the result of an optimization of the model against the dataset. Also the following suboptimal values have been tried: 50 and 150. In all the cases, the model outperformed the baseline.

when a common context is found, the score will be increased by a value that depends on the maximum salience of the context for the two target words. For instance, in the pair *dog-cat*, if *home* is a common context, and it has salience=1 for *dog* and salience=*N*-1 for *cat*, we will consider *home* as a relevant document with rank=1.

The equation (1) below provides the formal definition of *APAnt* measure:

$$APAnt = 1/\sum_{f \epsilon F_1 \cap F_2} \frac{1}{min(rank_1(f_1), rank_2(f_2))} \quad (1)$$

where *Fx* is the set of the *N* most salient features of a term *x* and $rank_x(f_x)$ is the rank of the feature f_x in the salience ranked feature list for the term *x*. It is important to note that *APAnt* is defined as a reciprocal measure, so that higher scores are assigned to antonyms.

5 Experiments and Evaluation

The evaluation includes two parts. The first part is to examine the discrimination ability of our method through box-plot visualizations, which summarize the distributions of scores per relation. In the second part, the Average Precision measure (AP; Kotlerman et al., 2010) is used to compute the ability of our proposed measure to discriminate antonyms from synonyms for nouns, adjectives and verbs. For comparison, we compare our performance with the *vector cosine* scores and with a baseline model using co-occurrence frequency of the target pairs.

5.1 The DSM and the Dataset

In our experiments, we use a standard window-based DSM recording co-occurrences with context window of the nearest 2 content words both to the left and right of each target word. Co-occurrences are extracted from a combination of the freely available ukWaC and WaCkypedia corpora (with 1.915 billion and 820 million words, respectively) and weighted with LMI (Santus et al., 2014a).

To assess *APAnt*, we rely on a subset of English word pairs collected by Alessandro Lenci and Giulia Benotto in 2012/13 using Amazon Mechanical Turk, following the method described by Scheible and Schulte im Walde (2014). Among the criteria used for the collection, Lenci and Benotto balanced target items across word categories and took in consideration the frequency, the degree of ambiguity and the semantic classes.

Our subset contains 2.232 word pairs[2], including 1.070 antonym pairs and 1.162 synonym pairs. The antonyms include 434 noun pairs (e.g. *parody-reality*), 262 adjective pairs (e.g. *unknown-famous*) and 374 verb pairs (e.g. *try-procrastinate*). The synonyms include 409 noun pairs (e.g. *completeness-entirety*), 364 adjective pairs (e.g. *determined-focused*) and 389 verb pairs (e.g. *picture-illustrate*).

5.2 Results

5.2.1 *APAnt* Values Distribution

Figure 1 and Figure 2 show the box-plots summarizing the logarithmic distributions of *APAnt* and baseline scores for antonyms and synonyms, respectively. The logarithmic distribution is used to smooth the range of data, which would otherwise be too large and sparse for the box-plot representation. Figure 3 shows the box-plot summarizing the *vector cosine* scores. Since *vector cosine* scores range between 0 and 1, we multiplied them by ten to scale up for comparison with the other two box-plots in Figure 1 and Figure 2.

Box-plots display the median of a distribution as a horizontal line within a box extending from the first to the third quartile, with whiskers covering 1.5 of the interquartile range in each direction from the box, and outliers plotted as circles.

The box-plots in Figure 1, Figure 2 and Figure 3 include test data with all part of speech types (i.e. nouns, adjectives and verbs). The box-plots for individual parts of speech are not reported in the paper because they do not show significant differences.

[2] The sub-set includes all the pairs for which both the target words exist in the DSM.

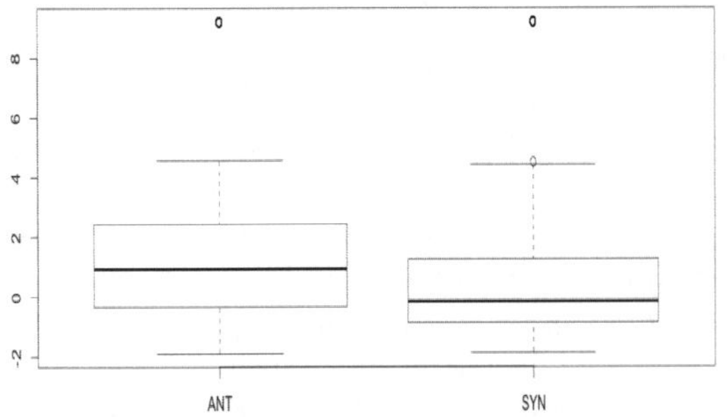

Figure 1: Logarithmic distribution of *APAnt* scores for antonym and synonym pairs (*N*=100) across nouns, adjectives and verbs.

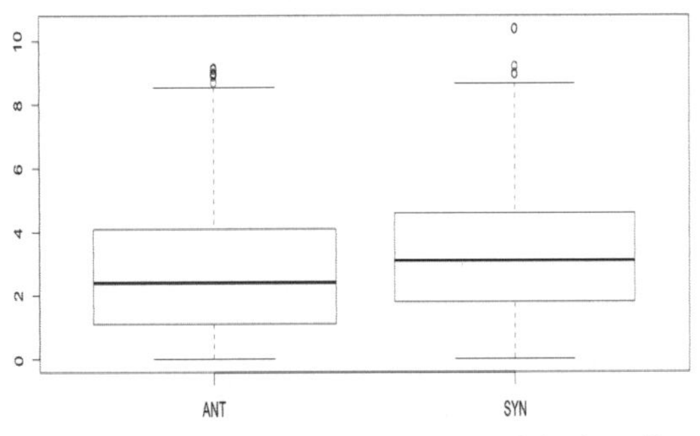

Figure 2: Logarithmic distribution of the baseline scores for antonym and synonym pairs across nouns, adjectives and verbs[3].

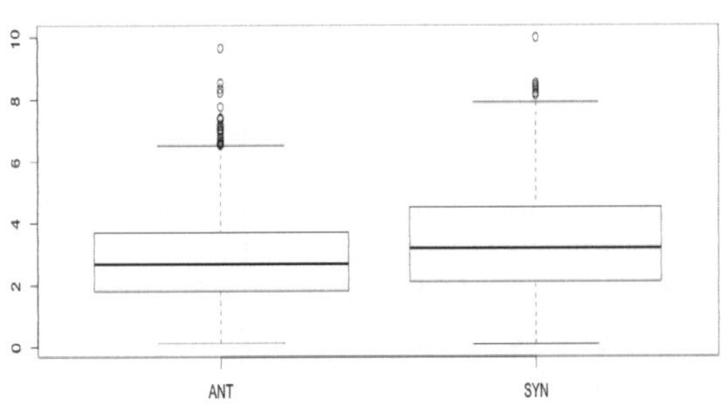

Figure 3: Distribution of the *vector cosine* scores for antonym and synonym pairs across nouns, adjectives and verbs[4].

[3] 410 pairs with co-occurrence equal to zero on a total of 2.232 have been removed to make the box-plot readable, because *log(0) = -inf*

[4] Since *vector cosine* scores range between 0 and 1, we multiplied them by ten to scale up for comparison with the other two box-plots in Figure 1 and Figure 2.

The more the boxes in in the plot overlap, the less distinctive the measure is. In Figure 2 and Figure 3, we can observe that the baseline and the *vector cosine* tend to promote synonyms on antonyms, and also that there is a large range of overlap among synonyms and antonyms distributions, showing the weakness of these two measures for discriminate antonyms from synonyms. On the other hand, in Figure 1 we can observe that *APAnt* scores are much higher for antonymy-related pairs. In terms of distribution of values, in fact, synonyms have much lower values in *APAnt*. This shows that *APAnt* is clearly more biased towards antonym, differently from the *vector cosine* or the simple co-occurrence. Moreover, results also suggest the partial inaccuracy of the *co-occurrence hypothesis*. The tendency of co-occurring is not a hallmark of antonyms, but it is a property shared by synonyms too.

5.2.2 Average Precision

Table 1 shows the second performance measure we used in our evaluation, the Average Precision (Santus et al., 2014a; Lenci and Benotto, 2012; Kotlerman et al., 2010) computed for *APAnt*, baseline and *vector cosine* scores. As already mentioned above, AP is a measure used in Information Retrieval to combine precision, relevance ranking and overall recall. The best possible score we can obtain is 1 for antonymy and 0 for synonymy, which would correspond to the perfect discrimination between antonyms and synonyms.

ALL PoS	**ANT**	**SYN**
APAnt, N=50	0.71	0.57
APAnt, N=100	**0.73**	**0.55**
APAnt, N= 150	0.72	0.55
Baseline	0.56	0.74
Cosine	0.55	0.75

Table 1: Average Precision (AP) values per relation for *APAnt* (*N=50, 100* and *150*), baseline and *vector cosine* across the parts of speech.

APAnt performs the best, compared to the reference methods, which mostly promote synonyms on antonyms. In fact, *APAnt* (*N=100*) is at the same time able (i) to better identify antonyms (+0.17 in comparison to the baseline and +0.18 over the *vector cosine*) and (ii) to better discriminate them from synonyms (-0.19 with respect to the baseline and -0.20 in comparison to the *vector cosine*). Regardless the value of *N* (either equal to 50, 100 or 150), *APAnt* clearly outperforms the baseline and the *vector cosine* by an identification improvement ranging from 26.7% (*N=50* to baseline) to 32.7% (*N=100* to *vector cosine*). These values confirm the trend shown in the box-plots of Figure 1, Figure 2 and Figure 3, proving that *APAnt* is a very effective measure to distinguish antonymy from synonymy.

Below we also list the AP values for the different parts of speech (i.e. nouns, adjectives and verbs) with the parameter *N=100*. As it can be observed, *APAnt* always outperforms the baseline. However, a slightly lower performance can be noticed in Table 3, where the AP scores for adjectives are 0.65 for both antonyms and synonyms.

NOUNS	ANT-N	SYN-N
APAnt, N=100	**0.79**	0.48
Baseline	0.53	0.77
Cosine	0.54	0.74

Table 2: Average Precision (AP) values per relation for *APAnt*, baseline and *vector cosine* on nouns.

ADJECTIVES	ANT-J	SYN-J
APAnt, N=100	**0.65**	0.65
Baseline	0.57	0.74
Cosine	0.58	0.73

Table 3: Average Precision (AP) values per relation for *APAnt*, baseline and *vector cosine* on adjectives.

VERBS	ANT-V	SYN-V
APAnt, N=100	**0.74**	0.52
Baseline	0.53	0.75
Cosine	0.52	0.77

Table 4: Average Precision (AP) values per relation for *APAnt*, baseline and *vector cosine* on verbs.

A possible explanation of this result might be that the different number of pairs per relation influences the AP values. In our dataset, in fact, we have 364 synonymy-related pairs against 262 antonym pairs for adjectives (+102 synonymy-related pairs, +39%).

To test this hypothesis, we randomly extract 262 synonymy-related pairs from the 364 that are present in our dataset and we re-calculate the AP scores for both the relations. The results can be found in Table 5.

ADJECTIVES	ANT-J	SYN-J
APAnt, N=100	**0.72**	0.60
Baseline	0.66	0.69
Cosine	0.68	0.66

Table 5: Average Precision (AP) values per relation for *APAnt*, baseline and *vector cosine* on adjectives, after extracting 262 pairs per relation.

The results in Table 5 confirm that *APAnt* works properly also for adjectives. It is in fact able to better identify antonyms (+0.06 on the baseline and +0.04 on *vector cosine*) and to better discriminate them from synonyms (-0.09 on the baseline and -0.06 on *vector cosine*). However, this is the lowest result among the three parts of speech used in our experiments.

The different results for the three parts of speech should be interpreted in relation to our hypothesis. It is in fact possible that while opposing nouns (e.g. *giant – dwarf*) share very few or none salient contexts, opposing verbs (e.g. *rise – fall*) and – even more – opposing adjectives (e.g. *hot – cold*) share some salient contexts, making the discrimination task more difficult for these parts of speech. In any case, the accuracy of our method has strongly outperformed the baseline for all the parts of speech, confirming the robustness of our hypothesis.

6 Conclusions and Ongoing Work

This paper introduces *APAnt*, a new distributional measure for the identification of antonymy based on a distributional interpretation of the *paradox of simultaneous similarity and difference between the antonyms* (preliminary results about *APAnt* were published by Santus et al., 2014b, at CLIC-IT conference).

APAnt is evaluated in a discrimination task in which both antonymy- and synonymy-related pairs are present. The evaluation has been performed on nouns, adjectives and verbs. In the task, *APAnt* has outperformed the *vector cosine* and the baseline implementing the *co-occurrence hypothesis* (Fellbaum, 1995; Justeson and Katz, 1991; Charles and Miller, 1989) for all the parts of speech, achieving good accuracy for all of them. However, its performance is higher for nouns, slightly lower for verbs and significantly lower for adjectives. These differences across parts of speech might be due to the fact that while opposing nouns share very few salient contexts, opposing verbs and – even more – opposing adjectives share some salient contexts, making the discrimination task more difficult. In all the cases, however, *APAnt* performance supports our hypothesis, according to which synonyms share a number of salient contexts that is significantly higher than the one shared by antonyms.

Moreover, following Santus et al. (2014a), we did not work with the full set of contexts of the target words, but only a subset of the *N* most salient ones. We assume, in fact, that they better describe the relevant distributional behavior of a specific term, while considering the full set would include also much noise. The *N* most salient contexts were selected after having been ranked through LMI (Evert, 2005). This method can be certainly applied for the study of other semantic relations.

Ongoing research includes the application of *APAnt* to discriminate antonymy also from other semantic relations and to automatically extract antonymy-related pairs for the population of ontologies and lexical resources. Further work can be conducted to apply *APAnt* to other languages.

Acknowledgments

This work is partially supported by HK PhD Fellowship Scheme under PF12-13656.

References

Baroni, Marco and Alessandro Lenci. 2010. Distributional Memory: A general framework for corpus-based semantics. *Computational Linguistics*, 36(4):673–721.

Bejar, Isaac I., Roger Chaffin, and Susan Embretson. 1991. *Cognitive and Psychometric Analysis of Analogical Problem Solving*. Springer-Verlag, New York.

Charles, Walter G. and George A. Miller. 1989. Contexts of antonymous adjectives. *Applied Psychology*, 10:357–375.

Cruse, David A. 1986. *Lexical Semantics*. Cambridge University Press, Cambridge.

Evert, Stefan. 2005. *The Statistics of Word Cooccurrences*. Dissertation, Stuttgart University.

de Marneffe, Marie-Catherine, Christopher D. Manning, and Christopher Potts. 2010. Was it good? It was provocative. Learning the meaning of scalar adjectives. In *Proceedings of the 48th Meeting of the Association for Computational Linguistics (ACL-10)*, pages 167–176.

de Marneffe, Marie-Catherine, Anna Rafferty, and Christopher D. Manning. 2008. Finding contradictions in text. In *Proceedings of the 46th Annual Meeting of the Association for Computational Linguistics (ACL-08)*, pages 1039–1047, Columbus, OH.

Deese, J. 1964. The Associative Structure of Some Common English Adjectives. *Journal of Verbal Learning and Verbal Behavior*, 3:347–57.

Deese J. 1965. *The Structure of Associations in Language and Thought*. Johns Hopkins University Press, Baltimore.

Ding, Jing and Chu-Ren Huang. 2014. Word Order in Chinese Opposite Compounds. Presented at the *15th Chinese Lexical Semantics Workshop*. Macau: University of Macau. 10-12 June.

Ding, Jing and Chu-Ren Huang. 2013. Markedness of Opposite. Pp. 191-195. In Pengyuan Liu and Qi Su Eds. *Chinese Lexical Semantics*. LNAI 8229. Springer, Heidelberg.

Fellbaum, Christiane. 1995. Co-occurrence and antonymy. *International Journal of Lexicography*, 8:281–303.

Harris, Zellig. 1954. Distributional structure. *Word*, 10(23):146–162.

Hearst, Marti. 1992. Automatic acquisition of hyponyms from large text corpora. In *Proceedings of the Fourteenth International Conference on Computational Linguistics*, pages 539–546, Nantes.

Huang, Chu-Ren, I-Li Su, Pei-Yi Hsiao, and Xiu-Ling Ke. 2007. Paranyms, Co-Hyponyms and Antonyms: Representing Semantic Fields with Lexical Semantic Relations. In *Proceedings of Chinese Lexical Semantics Workshop 2007*, Hong Kong Polytechnic University, May 20-23.

Jones, Steven, Carita Paradis, M. Lynne Murphy, and Caroline Willners. 2007. Googling for 'opposites': A web-based study of antonym canonicity. *Corpora*, 2(2):129–154.

Justeson, John S. and Slava M. Katz. 1991. Co-occurrences of antonymous adjectives and their contexts. *Computational Linguistics*, 17:1–19.

Kempson, Ruth M. 1977. *Semantic Theory*. Cambridge University Press, Cambridge.

Kim, Joo-Kyung and Marie-Catherine de Marneffe. 2013. Deriving Adjectival Scales from Continuous Space Word Representations. In *Proceedings of Conference on Empirical Methods in Natural Language Processing (EMNLP 2013)*, pages 1625-1630

Kotlerman, Lili, Ido Dagan, Idan Szpektor, and Maayan Zhitomirsky-Geffet. 2010. Directional Distributional Similarity for Lexical Inference. *Natural Language Engineering*, 16(4):359–389.

Lenci, Alessandro and Giulia Benotto. 2012. Identifying hypernyms in distributional semantic spaces. In *SEM 2012 – The First Joint Conference on Lexical and Computational Semantics*, 2:75–79, Montréal, Canada.

Lin, Dekang, Shaojun Zhao, Lijuan Qin, and Ming Zhou. 2003. Identifying synonyms among distributionally similar words. In *Proceedings of the 18th International Joint Conference on Artificial Intelligence (IJCAI-03)*, pages 1,492–1,493, Acapulco.

Lobanova, Anna. 2012. *The Anatomy of Antonymy: a Corpus-driven Approach*. Dissertation. University of Groningen.

Lobanova, Anna, Tom van der Kleij, and Jennifer Spenader. 2010. Defining antonymy: A corpus-based study of opposites by lexico-syntactic patterns. *International Journal of Lexicography*, 23(1):19–53.

Lucerto, Cupertino, David Pinto, and Héctor Jiménez-Salazar. 2002. An automatic method to identify antonymy. In *Workshop on Lexical Resources and the Web for Word Sense Disambiguation*, pages 105–111, Puebla.

Marton, Yuval, Ahmed El Kholy, and Nizar Habash. 2011. Filtering antonymous, trend-contrasting, and polarity-dissimilar distributional paraphrases for improving statistical machine translation. In *Proceedings of the Sixth Workshop on Statistical Machine Translation*, pages 237–249, Edinburgh.

Mihalcea, Rada and Carlo Strapparava. 2005. Making computers laugh: Investigations in automatic humor recognition. In *Proceedings of the Conference on Human Language Technology and Empirical Methods in Natural Language Processing*, pages 531–538, Vancouver.

Mohammad, Saif, Bonnie Dorr, Graeme Hirst, and Peter D. Turney. 2013. Computing lexical contrast. *Computational Linguistics*, 39(3):555–590.

Mohammad, Saif, Bonnie Dorr, and Graeme Hirst. 2008. Computing word-pair antonymy. In *Proceedings of the Conference on Empirical Methods in Natural Language Processing (EMNLP-2008)*, pages 982–991, Waikiki, HI.

Padó, Sebastian and Lapata, Mirella. 2007. Dependency-based Construction of Semantic Space Models. *Computational Linguistics*, 33(2):161–199.

Pantel, Patrick and Marco Pennacchiotti. 2006. Espresso: Leveraging generic patterns for automatically harvesting semantic relations. In *Proceedings of the 21st International Conference on Computational Linguistics and 44th Annual Meeting of the Association for Computational Linguistics*, pages 113-120, Sydney, Australia.

Roth, Michael and Sabine Schulte im Walde. 2014. Combining word patterns and discourse markers for paradigmatic relation classification. In *Proceedings of the 52nd Annual Meeting of the Association for Computational Linguistics (ACL)*, 2:524–530, Baltimore, Maryland, USA.

Sahlgren, Magnus. 2006. *The Word-Space Model: Using distributional analysis to represent syntagmatic and paradigmatic relations between words in high-dimensional vector spaces*. Ph.D. dissertation, Department of Linguistics, Stockholm University.

Santus, Enrico, Alessandro Lenci, Qin Lu, and Sabine Schulte im Walde. 2014a. Chasing Hypernyms in Vector Spaces with Entropy. In *Proceedings of the 14th Conference of the European Chapter of the Association for Computational Linguistics*, 2:38–42, Gothenburg, Sweden.

Santus, Enrico, Qin Lu, Alessandro Lenci, and Chu-Ren Huang. 2014b. Unsupervised Antonym-Synonym Discrimination in Vector Space. In *Atti della Conferenza di Linguistica Computazionale Italiana* (CLIC-IT), Pisa, Italy.

Scheible, Silke and Sabine Schulte im Walde. 2014. A Database of Paradigmatic Semantic Relation Pairs for German Nouns, Verbs, and Adjectives. In *Proceedings of the COLING Workshop on Lexical and Grammatical Resources for Language Processing*, Dublin, Ireland, August 2014.

Schulte im Walde, Sabine and Maximilian Köper. 2013. Pattern-based distinction of paradigmatic relations for German nouns, verbs, adjectives. In *Language Processing and Knowledge in the Web*, 184-198. Springer.

Schwab, Didier, Mathieu Lafourcade, and Violaine Prince. 2002. Antonymy and conceptual vectors. In *Proceedings ofthe 19th International Conference on Computational Linguistics (COLING-02)*, pages 904–910, Taipei, Taiwan.

Turney, Peter D. and Patrick Pantel. 2010. From Frequency to Meaning: Vector Space Models of Semantics. *Journal of Articial Intelligence Research*, 37:141–188.

Turney, Peter D. 2008. A uniform approach to analogies, synonyms, antonyms, and associations. In *Proceedings of the 22nd International Conference on Computational Linguistics (COLING-08)*, pages 905–912, Manchester.

Voorhees, Ellen M., and Donna K. Harman. 1999. *The Seventh Text REtrieval Conference (TREC-7)*, 7, National Institute of Standards and Technology, NIST.

Improvement of Statistical Machine Translation using Charater-Based Segmentation with Monolingual and Bilingual Information

Vipas Sutantayawalee **Peerachet Porkeaw** **Prachya Boonkwan**
Sitthaa Phaholphinyo **Thepchai Supnithi**

National Electronics and Computer Technology Center, Thailand

{vipas.sutantayawalee, peerachet.porkeaw,prachya.boonkwan, sitthaa.phaholphinyo,thepchai}@nectec.or.th

Abstract

We present a novel segmentation approach for Phrase-Based Statistical Machine Translation (PB-SMT) to languages where word boundaries are not obviously marked by using both monolingual and bilingual information and demonstrate that (1) unsegmented corpus is able to provide the nearly identical result compares to manually segmented corpus in PB-SMT task when a good heuristic character clustering algorithm is applied on it, (2) the performance of PB-SMT task has significantly increased when bilingual information are used on top of monolingual segmented result. Our technique, instead of focusing on word separation, mainly concentrate on a group of character. First, we group several characters that reside in an unsegmented corpus by employing predetermined constraints and certain heuristics algorithms. Secondly, we enhance the segmented result by incorporating the character group repacking based on alignment confidence. We evaluate the effectiveness of our method on PB-SMT task using English-Thai, English-Lao and English-Burmese language pairs and report the best improvement of 8.1% increase in BLEU score on English-Thai pair.

1 Introduction

Word segmentation is a crucial part of Statistical Machine Translation (SMT) especially for the languages where there are no explicit word boundaries such as Chinese, Japanese, and Thai. The writing systems of these languages allow each word to be written consecutively without spaces between words. The issue of word boundary ambiguities arises if word boundary is misplaced, resulting in an incorrect translation. An effective word segmentator therefore becomes a crucial pre-processing step of SMT. Word segmentators which focusing on word which focusing on word, character [1] or both [2] and [3] have been implemented to accomplish this goal.

Most of word segmentators are supervised; i.e. they require a monolingual corpus of a voluminous size. Various approaches are employed, such as dictionary-based, Hidden Markov model (HMM), support vector machine (SVM), and conditional random field (CRF). Although, a number of segementators offer promising results, certain of them might be unsuitable for SMT task due to the influence of segmentation scheme [4]. Therefore, instead of solely rely on monolingual corpus, the use of a bilingual corpus as an guideline for word segmentation in improving the performance of SMT system has become of increasing interest [4] [5].

In this paper, we propose a novel segmentation approach for Phrase-Based Statistical Machine Translation (PB-SMT) to languages where word boundaries are not obviously marked by using both monolingual and bilingual information on English-Thai, English-Burmese and English-Lao language pairs and demonstrate that (1) unsegmented corpus is able to provide the nearly identical result to manually segmented corpus in PB-SMT task when the good heuristics character clustering algorithm is applied on it, (2) the performance of PB-SMT task has significantly increased when bilingual information are used on top of monolingual segmented result. Our technique, instead of focusing on word separation, mainly concentrate on a group of character. First, we group several characters that reside in an un-

Copyright 2014 by Vipas Sutantayawalee, Peerachet Porkeaw, Prachya Boonkwan, Sitthaa Phaholphinyo and Thepchai Supnithi
28th Pacific Asia Conference on Language, Information and Computation pages 145–151

segmented monolingual corpus by employing predetermined constraints and certain heuristics algorithms. Secondly, we enhance the segmented result by incorporating the bilingual information which are character cluster alignment, CC co-occurrence frequency and alignment confidence into that result. These two tasks can be performed repeatedly.

The remainder of this paper is organized as follows. Section 2 provides some information related to our work. Section 3 describes the methodology of our approaches. Section 4 present the experiments setting. Section 5 present the experimental results and empirical analysis. Section 6 and 7 gives a conclusion and future work respectively.

2 Related Work

2.1 Thai Character Grouping

In Thai writing system, there are no explicit word boundaries as in English, and a single Thai character does not have specific meanings like Chinese, Japanese and Korean. Thai characters could be consonants, vowels and tone marks and a word can be formed by combining these characters. From our observation, we found that the average length of Thai words on BEST2010 corpus (National Electronics and Computer Technology Center, Thailand 2010) is 3.855. This makes the search space of Thai word segmentation very large.

To alleviate this issue, the notion of Thai character grouping (TCC), is introduced in [1] to reduce the search space with predetermined unambiguous constraints for cluster formation. A group of character may not be meaningful and has to combine with other consecutive group to form a word. Characters in the group cannot be separated according to the Thai orthographic rules. For example, a vowel and tone mark cannot stand alone and a tone marker is always required to be placed next to a previous character only. [6] applied TCC to word segmentation technique which yields an interesting result.

2.2 Bilingual Word Segmentation

Bilingual information has also been shown beneficial for word segmentation. Several methods use this kind of information from bilingual corpora to improve word segmentation. [5] uses an unsegmented bilingual corpus and builds a self-learned dictionary using alignment statistics between English and Chinese language pair. [4] is based on the manually segmented bilingual corpus and then try to "repack" words from existing alignment by using alignment confidence. Both approaches evaluate the performance in term of translation improvement and report the promising results of PB-SMT task.

3 Methodology

This paper aim to compare translation quality based on SMT task between the systems trained on bilingual corpus that contains both segmented source and target, and on the same bilingual corpus with segmented source but unsegmented target. First, we make use of *monolingual information* by employing several character cluster algorithms on unsegmented data. Second, we use *bilingual-guided alignment information* retrieved from alignment extraction process for improving character cluster segmentation. Then, we evaluate our performance based on translation accuracy by using BLEU metric. We want to prove that (1) the result of PB-SMT task using unsegmented corpus (unsupervised) is nearly identical result to manually segmented (supervised) data and (2) when bilingual information are also applied, the performance of PB-SMT is also improved.

3.1 Notation

Given a target $\{Thai\}$ sentence t_1^J consisting of J clusters $\{t_1, \ldots, t_j\}$, where $|t_j| \geq 1$. If $|t_j| = 1$, we call t_j as a single character S. Otherwise, we call it as a character group T. In addition, given an English sentence e_1^I consisting of I words $\{e, \ldots, e_i\}$, $A_{E\rightarrow T}$ denotes a set of English-to-Target language word alignments between e_1^I and t_1^J. In addition, since we concentrated on one-to-many alignments, $A_{E\rightarrow T}$, can be rewritten as a set of pairs a_i and $a_i = < e_i, t_j >$ noting a link between one single English *word* and several Thai *characters* that are formed to one character group T

3.2 Monolingual Information

Due to the issue mentioned in section 2.1, we apply character grouping technique (CC) on target text in order to reduce the search space. After performing CC, it will yield several character group T which can be merged together to obtain a larger unit which approaches the notion of word. However, for Thai, we do not only receive T but also S which usually has no meaning by itself. Moreover, Thai, Burmese and Lao writing rule does not allow S to stand alone in most case. Thus, we are required to develop various adapted versions of CC by using a pre-defined word list that can be grouped as a word confirmed by linguists *(orthographic insight))* to automatically pack the characters to become a new T . In addition, all of single consonants in Thai Burmese, and Lao are forced to group with either left or right cluster due to their writing rules. This decision has been made by consulting character co-occurrence statistics (*heuristic algorithm*)

Eventually, we obtain several character group alignments from the system trained on various CC approaches which effect to translation quality as shown in section 5.1

3.3 Bilingually-Guided Alignment Information

We begin with the sequence of small clusters resulting from previous character grouping process. These small T can be merged together in order to form "word" using bilingually-guided alignment information. Generally, small *consecutive* T in target side which are aligned to the same word in source data should be merged together to obtain a larger unit. Therefore, this section describes our one-to-many alignment extraction process.

For one-to-many alignment, we applied processes similar to those in phrase extraction algorithm [7] which is described as follows.

With English sentence e_1^I and a character cluster T, we apply IBM model 1-5 to extract word-to-cluster translation probability of source-to-target $P(t|e)$ and target-to-source $P(e|t)$. Next, the alignment points which have the highest probability are greedily selected from both $P(t|e)$ and $P(e|t)$. Figure 1.a and 1.b show examples of alignment points of source-to-target and target-to-source respectively. After that we selected the intersection of alignment pairs from both side. Then, additional alignment points are added according to the growing heuristic algorithm (grow additional alignment points, [8])

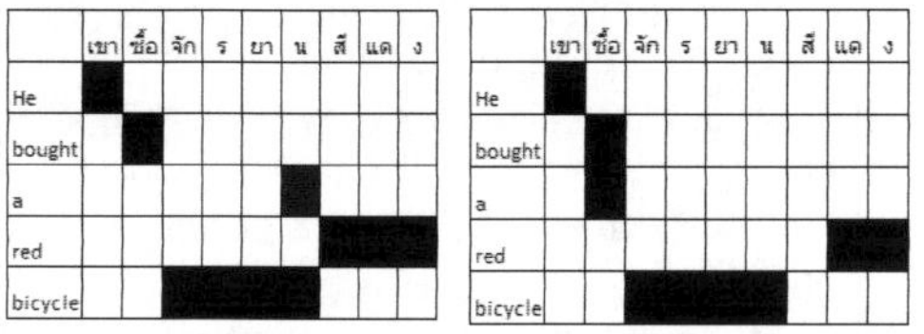

(a) (b)

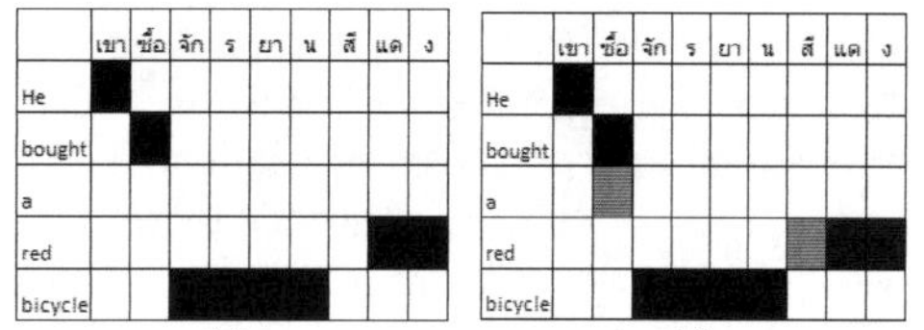

(c) (d)

Figure 1. The process of one-to-many alignment extraction (a) Source-to-Target word alignment (b) Target-to-Source word alignment (c) Intersection between (a) and (b). (d) Result of (c) after applying the growing heuristic algorithm.

Finally, we select *consecutive* T which are aligned to the same English word as candidates. From the Figure 1.d, we obtain these candidates (red, สีแดง) and (bicycle, จัก ร ยา น).

3.4 Character Group Repacking (CCR)

Although the alignment information obtained from the previous step is very helpful for the PB-SMT task. There are certain misaligned alignments that need to be corrected. As shown in Figure 2, one English word e_i is aligned with Thai characters $\{t_1, \ldots, t_j\}$ by previous step aligner but actually this word e_i must align with $\{t_1, \ldots, t_{j+2}\}$. Word repacking [4] is a one approach that can efficiently resolve this issue. However, in this paper, we slightly modified repacking technique by performing a character group repacking (CCR) instead of word. The main purpose of repacking technique is to group all small consecutive T in target side that frequently align with a single word in source data e_i. Repacking approaches uses two simple calculations which are a co-occurrence frequency ($COOC\ (e_i, t_j)$) and alignment confidence ($AC(\ a_i)$). ($COOC\ (e_i, t_j)$) is the number of times e_i and T_i co-occurrence in the bilingual corpus [4] [9] and $AC(\ a_i)$ is a measure of how often the aligner aligns e_i and t_j when they co-occur. $AC(\ a_i)$ is defined as

$$AC(a_i) \ = \ \frac{C(a_i)}{COOC\ (e_i, t_j)}$$

where $C(a_i)$ denotes the number of alignments suggested by the previous-step word aligner.

Unfortunately, due to the limited memory in our experiment machine, we cannot find $COOC\ (e_i, t_j)$) for all possible $< e_i, t_j >$ pairs. We, therefore, slightly modified the above equation by finding $C(a_i)$ first. Secondly, we begin searching $COOC\ (e_i, t_j))$ from all possible alignments in a_i instead of finding all occurrences in corpus. By applying this modification, we eliminate $< e_i, t_j >$ pairs that co-occur together but *never* align to each other by previous-step aligner ($AC(a_i)$ equals to zero) so as to reduce the search space and complexity in our algorithm. Thirdly, we choose a_i with highest $AC(a_i)$ and repack all T in target side to be a new single T unit. This process can be done repeatedly. However, we have run this task less than twice since there are few new groups of character appear after two iterations have passed.

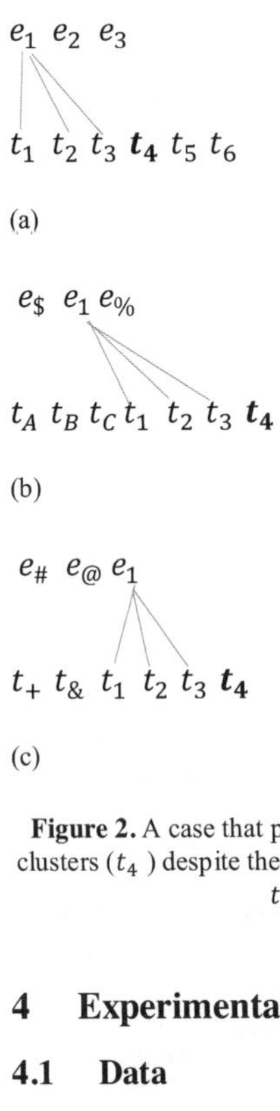

Figure 2. A case that previous aligner misaligned certain clusters (t_4) despite the fact that t_4 are often co-occur with $t_1\ t_2\ and\ t_3$

4 Experimental Setting

4.1 Data

We conduct our experiment based on two bilingual corpora. One is an English-to-Thai corpus (650K corpus) which is constructed from several sources and consists of multiple domains (e.g. news, travel, article, entertainment, computer, etc.). While another one is English-to-Multiple language corpus (20K corpus) which focuses on travel domain only and is developed from several English sentences and those sentences are manually translated to Thai, Burmese and Lao by linguists. Table 1 shows the information on these two corpora. Note that Test set #2 is manually segmented with a guideline different than test#1.

	No. of sentence pairs	
Data Set	English-to-Thai corpus	English-to-Multilanguage
Train	633,589	16,000
Dev	12,568	2,000
Test #1	3,426	2,000
Test #2	500	-

Table 1. No. of sentence pairs in each data set of bilingual corpora

4.2 Tools and Evaluation

We evaluate our system in terms of translation quality based on phrase-based SMT. Source sentences are sequence of English words while target sentences are sequences of T in Thai, Burmese and Lao. Each T 's length depends on which approach are used in the experiment.

Translation model and language model are train based on the standard phrase-based SMT. Alignments of source (English word) and target (Thai, Burmese and Lao character cluster) are extracted using GIZA++ [8] and the phrase extraction algorithm [7] is applied using Moses SMT package. We apply SRILM [10] to train the 3-gram language model of target side. We use the default parameter settings for decoding.

In testing process, we use dataset that not reside in training data. Then we compared the translation result with the reference in terms of BLEU score instead of F-score because it is cumbersome to construct a reliable gold standard since their annotation schemes are different. Therefore, we re-segment the reference data (manually segmented data) and the translation result data based on character grouping techniques. Some may concern about using character group instead of word will lead to over estimation (higher than actual) due to the BLEU score is design based on word and not based on character cluster. However, we used this BLEU score only for comparing translation quality among our experiments. Comparing to other SMT systems still require running BLEU score based on the same segmentation guideline.

5 Results and Discussion

We conducted all experiments on PB-SMT task and reported the performance of PB-SMT system based on the BLEU measure.

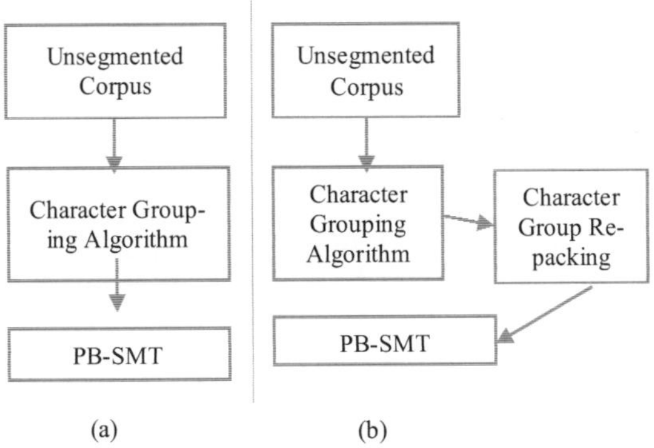

Figure 3. Experiment flows: (a) Monolingual Information (b) Bilingually-Guided Alignment Information

5.1 Monolingual Information

5.1.1 English – Thai language pair

First, we use a method proposed in Figure 3.(a) in order to receive translation results. Table 2 shows the number of Thai character clusters in 650K corpus that are decreasing over time when several different character clustering approaches are applied.

Approaches	No. of Character group (or word in original data)
CC	9,862,271
CC with orthographic insight **(CC-FN)**	8,953,437
CC with orthographic insight and heuristic algorithm **(CC-FN-B)**	6,545,617
Manually segmented corpus **(Threshold)**	5,311,648

Table 2. Number of Thai character group on 650K corpus when different character clustering approaches are applied.

Approaches	650K corpus		20K corpus
	Test #1 Without CCR	**Test #2** Without CCR	**EN-TH**
CC	37.12	36.78	47.63
CC-FN	40.23	38.36	49.21
CC-FN-B	44.69	40.45	49.21
Threshold	47.04	40.73	49.56

Table 3. The performance of SMT trained with different character grouping algorithm.

As seen from Table 3, the BLEU scores of EN-TH pair in all corpora are increasing over time and almost equal to original result on Test#2 in 650K corpus. This is because each CC tends to merge T to become larger and larger unit, which approaches the notion of word in eventually. In addition, these experiments also support the claim (1) that unsegmented corpus is able to provide the nearly identical result compares to upper bound in PB-SMT task when a good heuristic character grouping algorithm is applied on it.

However, since CC does not rely on semantic knowledge. Therefore, there are chances that certain T do not give a meaningful word resulting in incorrect translation on SMT task.

5.1.2 Preliminary experiment on low resource language (LRL)

We also conduct the experiment on LRL by choosing Lao and Burmese by imitating TCC to be Lao Character Clustering (LCC) and Burmese Character Clustering (BCC) for Lao and Burmese respectively with the same method as in section 5.1.1. However, for Lao and Burmese, we only apply simple CC without any enhanced versions of CC since our knowledge in orthographic of Burmese and Lao are limited.

Approaches	20K corpus	
	English-Lao	**English-Burmese**
CC	39.64	30.11
Upper bound	40.65	26.43

Table 4. The performance of SMT trained with different character clustering algorithm on LRL (Without CCR).

As seen in Table 4, the BLEU scores of CC are almost equal to original results. In English-Burmese pair, however, the character grouping algorithm is able to yield a better performance on upper bound data. We suspect that Burmese word segmentation guideline is still unstable resulting in misplaced word boundaries.

5.2 Bilingually-Guided Alignment Information

As mention earlier in section 3.4, we can improve the translation result by making use of alignment information from previous translation process. Therefore, we perform experiments by using a method describe in Figure 3.(b) in order to receive another translation result set. However, since the corpus size has the direct impact on translation result. We test our hypothesis on the 650K corpus only.

Approaches	Test #2		% of BLEU Improvement
	Without CCR	With CCR	
CC	36.78	38.87	5.68
CC-FN	38.36	39.09	1.90
CC-FN-B	40.45	**40.81**	0.89
Threshold	40.73	N/A	N/A

(a.) Test #1 of En-TH 650K corpus

Approaches	Test #1		% of BLEU Improve-ment.
	Without CCR	With CCR	
CC	37.12	40.13	**8.11**
CC-FN	40.23	41.90	4.15
CC-FN-B	44.69	44.43	-0.58
Threshold	47.04	N/A	N/A

(b.) Test #2 of En-TH 650K corpus

Table 5. BLEU score of each character clustering method (a and b) and the percentage of the improvement when we applied CCR to the data

As shown in Table 4 and Figure 4, when CCR have been deployed on each training dataset, the results of BLEU increase in the same manner with *Without CCR* method. It proves the claim (2) that the performance of PB-SMT task has significantly increased when bilingual information are used on top of monolingual segmented result. In addition, there are certain significant points that should be noticed. First, CCR method is able to yield maximum of 8.1 % BLEU score increase. Second, when we apply the CCR methods and reach at some point, few improvement or minor degradation is received as shown in CC-FN-B without and with CCR result.

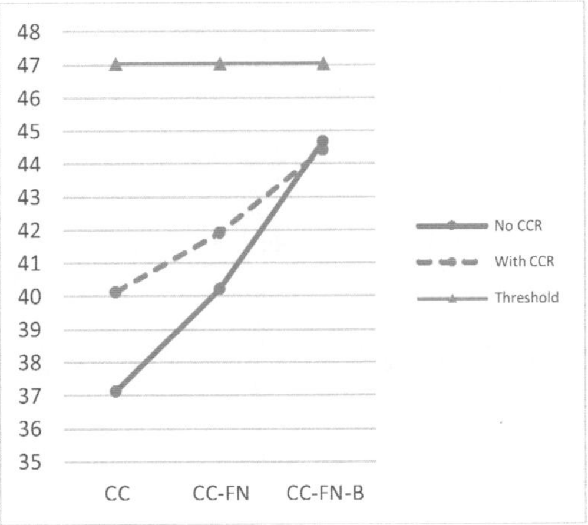

(a)

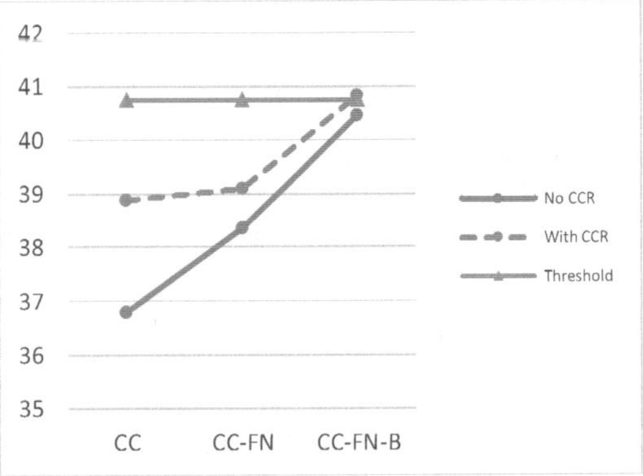

(b)

Figure 4. The BLEU score of (a) test set no.1 and (b) test set no.2

This is because the number of clusters produced by this character grouping algorithm is almost equal to number of words in threshold as shown in Table 2. However, this approach might suffer from the word boundary misplacement problem. Third, character grouping that use CC with orthographic insight and heuristic algorithm combined with CCR approach (CC-FN-B with CCR) is able to beat the threshold translation result in test set #2 for the first time.

6 Conclusion

In this paper, we introduce a new approach for performing word segmentation task for SMT. Instead of starting at word level, we focus on character group because this approach can perform on unsegmented corpus or manually segmented corpus that have multiple segmentation guideline. To begin, we apply several adapted versions of CC on unsegmented corpus. Next, we use a bilingual corpus to find alignment information for all $< e_i, t_j >$ pairs. Then, we employ character group repacking method in order to form the larger cluster of T.

We evaluate our approach on translation task based on several sources and different domain of corpus and report the result in BLEU metric. Our technique demonstrates that (1) we can achieve a dramatically improvement of BLUE as of 8.1% when we apply CC with CCR and (2) it is possible to overcome the translation result of manually segmented corpus by using CC-FN-B with CCR.

7 Future Work

There are some tasks that can be added into this approaches. Firstly, we can make use of trigram (and n-gram) statistics, maximum entropy or conditional random field on heuristic algorithm in enhanced version of CC. Secondly, we can apply our approaches on Bilinugal corpus which both source and target side are not segmented. Thirdly, we can modify CCR process to be able to re-rank the alignment confidence by using discriminative approach. Lastly, name entity recognition system can be integrated with our approach in order to improve the SMT performance.

Reference

[1] T. Teeramunkong, V. Sornlertlamvanich, T. Tanhermhong and W. Chinnan, "Character cluster based Thai information retrieval," in *IRAL '00 Proceedings of the fifth international workshop on on Information retrieval with Asian languages*, 2000.

[2] C. Kruengkrai, K. Uchimoto, J. Kazama, K. Torisawa, H. Isahara and C. Jaruskulchai, "A Word and Character-Cluster Hybrid Model for Thai Word Segmentation," in *Eighth International Symposium on Natural Lanugage Processing*, Bangkok, Thailand, 2009.

[3] Y. Liu, W. Che and T. Liu, "Enhancing Chinese Word Segmentation with Character Clustering," in *Chinese Computational Linguistics and Natural Language Processing Based on Naturally Annotated Big Data*, China, 2013.

[4] Y. Ma and A. Way, "Bilingually motivated domain-adapted word segmentation for statistical machine translation," in *Proceeding EACL '09 Proceedings of the 12th Conference of the European Chapter of the Association for Computational Linguistics, pp. 549-557*, Stroudsburg, PA, USA, 2009.

[5] J. Xu, R. Zens and H. Ney, "Do We Need Chinese Word Segmentation for Statistical Machine Translation?," *ACL SIGHAN Workshop 2004*, pp. 122-129, 2004.

[6] P. Limcharoen, C. Nattee and T. Theeramunkong, "Thai Word Segmentation based-on GLR Parsing Technique and Word N-gram Model," in *Eighth International Symposium on Natural Lanugage Processing*, Bangkok, Thailand, 2009.

[7] P. Koehn, F. J. Och and D. Marcu, "Statistical phrase-based translation," in *NAACL '03 Proceedings of the 2003 Conference of the North American Chapter of the Association for Computational Linguistics on Human Language Technology*, Stroudsburg, PA, USA, 2003.

[8] F. J. Och and H. Ney, "A systematic comparison of various statistical alignment models," *Computational Linguistics*, vol. 29, no. 1, pp. 19-51, 2003.

[9] I. D. Melamed, "Models of translational equivalence among words," *Computational Linguistics*, vol. 26, no. 2, pp. 221-249, 2000.

[10] "SRILM -- An extensible language modeling toolkit," in *Proceeding of the International Conference on Spoken Language Processing*, 2002.

Topic-based Multi-document Summarization using Differential Evolution for Combinatorial Optimization of Sentences

Haruka Shigematsu
Graduate School of Humanities and Sciences, Ochanomizu University
Bunkyo-ku, Tokyo 112-8610 Japan
shigematsu.haruka@is.ocha.ac.jp

Ichiro Kobayashi
Graduate School of Humanities and Sciences, Ochanomizu University
Bunkyo-ku, Tokyo 112-8610 Japan
koba@is.ocha.ac.jp

Abstract

This paper describes a method of multi-document summarization with evolutionary computation. In automatic document summarization, the method to make a summary by finding the best combination of important sentences in target documents is popular approach. To find the best combination of sentences, explicit solution techniques such as integer linear programming, branch and bound method, and so on are usually adopted. However, there is a problem with them in terms of calculation efficiency. So, we apply evolutionary computation, especially differential evolution which is regarded as a method having a good feature in terms of calculation cost to obtain a reasonable quasi-optimum solution in real time, to the problem of combinatorial optimization of important sentences. Moreover, we consider latent topics in deciding the importance of a sentence, and define three fitness functions to compare the results. As a result, we have confirmed that our proposed methods reduced the calculation time necessary to make a summary considerably, although precision is more worse than the method with an explicit solution technique.

1 Introduction

As a general method of automatic multi-document summarization, we often use the important sentence extraction method which obtains the most proper combination of important sentences in target documents for a summary, avoiding redundancy in the generated summary. The explicit solution techniques, e.g., integer programming, branch and bound method, for optimal combination are often used under some constraints for the best combination of sentences. They have however a problem in terms of calculation costs. In general, if the size of target data sets is huge, the problem of combinatorial optimization becomes NP-hard. On the other hand, as an optimization method to obtain quasi-optimum solution in real time, it is reported that evolutionary computation is useful for realistic solutions. In this context, we employ differential evolution (DE) known as superior to other evolutionary computation algorithms in terms of calculation costs and the accuracy of solution, and apply it to multi-document summarization. Besides, under an assumption that multiple topics are included in documents, latent topics in documents are extracted by means of latent Dirichlet allocation, we make a summary, considering the latent topics.

2 Related studies

As for document summarization using combinatorial optimization techniques, many studies employ explicit solution techniques such as branch and bound method, dynamic programming, integer linear programming, and so on (Mcdonald, 2007; Yih et al., 2007; Gillick et al., 2008; Takamura et al., 2009; Lin et al., 2010). However, the explicit solution techniques often face NP-hard, they require much calculation time for solving a problem of combinatorial optimization, though they provide optimal solution. In this context, Nishikawa et al.(2012) have proposed a method to obtain approximate solution by employing Lagrange relaxation on constraints to make a summary and to introduce it to

Copyright 2014 by Haruka Shigematsu and Ichiro Kobayashi
28th Pacific Asia Conference on Language, Information and Computation pages 152–159

the objective function of selecting best combination of important sentences, and got a good result.

On the other hand, as an optimization method to obtain approximate solution, it has been reported that evolutionary computation is useful – Petkovic et al. (2011) and Nieminen et al. (2003) have compared the ability between explicit solution techniques, and dynamic programming and genetic algorithm (GA) (Holland, 1975), and confirmed that GA is superior to the explicit techniques in terms of calculation cost. Furthermore, in the experiments in Chandrasekar et al. (2012), differential evolution (DE) (Storn et al., 1996) is superior to GA and particle swarm (Kennedy et al., 1995) in terms of the precision of solution and calculation speed.

As for document summarization using combinatorial optimization techniques, the number of the studies using evolutionary computation has been gradually increasing. Nandhini (2013) applied GA for the combinatorial optimization of sentences so that a generated summary realizes good readability, cohesion, and rich contents, and then showed that their method provided stable precision rather than other methods using explicit solution techniques. Alguliev et al. (2011) proposed a method using differential evolution to make a summary taking account of covering the whole contents of target documents and removing redundancy of the contents in a generated summary.

As for combinatorial optimization of sentences, the way of deciding an important sentences is essential. In general, the importance of a sentence is often decided by the words included in the sentence. As the way of deciding the important words, in addition to the conventional way of using tf-idf, the way of using latent information has been recently regarded as useful. To estimate latent topics in documents, latent Dirichlet allocation (LDA) (Blei et al., 2003) is often used and applied to various NLP application, e.g., clustering, summarization, information retrieval, information recommendation, etc. As for document summarization, Murray et al. (2009) and Arora et al. (2008) employed LDA to extract important sentences based on latent topics. Gao et al. (2012) have proposed a method employing LDA to make a topic-based similarity graph of sentences, and shown that the method provides high precision.

Considering these prior studies, in this study we propose a multi-document summarization method employing latent topics for deciding the importance of sentences and differential evolution for combinatorial optimization of sentences.

3 Differential evolution

Differential evolution (DE) (Storn et al., 1996) is a kind of evolutionary computation and a population-based stochastic search algorithm to solve a combinatorial optimization problem. DE has a special feature in mutation operation compared to simple GA (Holland, 1975). It performs based on differences between pairs of solutions for the purpose of deciding the orientation in search space by following the distribution of solutions in the current population. DE is regarded as a useful method for optimal solution in terms of simplicity, calculation speed and precision. The general DE algorithm is shown as follows:

Step 1. *Initialization*: N solutions are randomly generated in the initial population. $G(0) = \{P_1(0), P_2(0), \ldots, P_N(0)\}$.

Step 2. *Completion of judgment*: Complete the process if the number of generation has reached to the predefined number, g_{max}.

Step 3. *Mutation*: For each individual $P_i(g)$, three unique solutions, $P_a(g)$,$P_b(g)$,$P_c(g)$, are selected from the population $G(g)$. And then a mutation vector $Q_i(g)$ is obtained from a base vector $P_a(g)$ and a difference vector $P_b(g) - P_c(g)$ as follows:

$$Q_i(g) = P_a(g) + F(P_b(g) - P_c(g)) \quad (1)$$

Here, F is an adjustment parameter for the difference.

Step 4. *Crossover*:A parent vector $P_i(g)$ and a mutation vector $Q_i(g)$ are crossed over and a child vector $R_i(g)$ is generated.

Step 5. *Selection of solutions*: Compare a parent vector $P_i(g)$ and a child vector $R_i(g)$, the better solution is selected for the next generation. This process is adopted to all solutions in the current generation.

Step 6. Return to Step 2.

The overview of the process from step 3 to step 5 is illustrated in Figure 1.

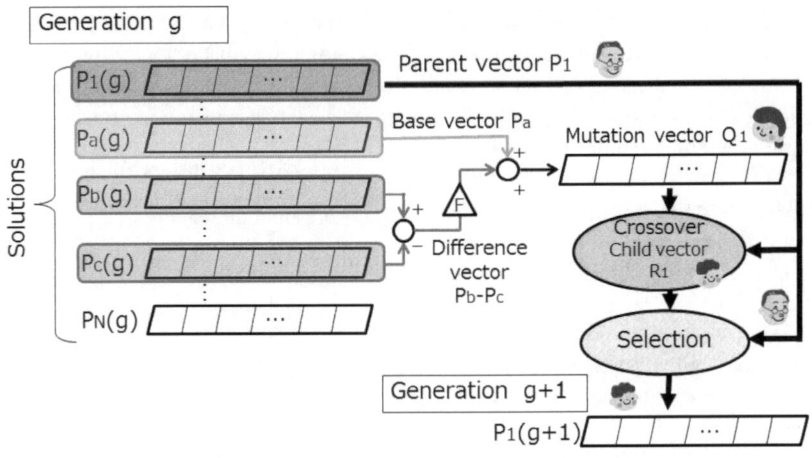

Figure 1: The DE process from step 3 to step 5

4 Document summarization using DE

Let us assume that target documents consisting of n sentences, and a summary is made by the combination of important sentences extracted from the documents. To encode the phenotype of this setting into the genotype, we employ a n-length binary vector in which 1 indicates the state of the sentence being selected and 0 is not the state. As for optimal combination of sentences uisng DE, each solution is regarded as the combination of sentences, and therefore, the best combination of sentences for a summary is found by solving the problem under some constraint such as the length of a summary, etc.

4.1 Process of document summarization using DE

A summary is made based on the best solution obtained in all generations of DE process. There are some specific processes added to general DE process for document summarization, for example, converting real number vectors into binary vectors which indicates the states of sentence selection, solution selection based on constraint on the length of a summary, etc. Each modified DE process is shown in the following.

4.1.1 Generation of the initial population

In DE process, the population $\boldsymbol{G(g)}$ consisting of N solutions is evolved in generations $g = 0, 1, \ldots, g_{max}$. Here, the i-th solution at generation g, i.e., $\boldsymbol{P_i(g)}$, is expressed as follows:

$$\boldsymbol{P_i(g)} = [p_{i,1}(g), p_{i,2}(g), \ldots, p_{i,n}(g)]$$

In general, the initial population $G(0)$ is provided by the following equation so as it should be diverse in search space.

$$p_{i,s}(0) = p_s^{min} + (p_s^{max} - p_s^{min}) \cdot rand_{i,s} \quad (2)$$

Here, p_s^{min} and p_s^{max} are the predefined minimum and the maximum values, respectively. $rand_{i,s}$ is a random value of $[0, 1]$. By equation (2), random values of $[p_s^{min}, p_s^{max}]$ are provided to $p_{i,s}(s = 1, \ldots, n)$.

4.1.2 Mutation

In general, equation (3) is used to obtain mutation vector $\boldsymbol{Q_i}$, however, there are many studies to propose other new vectors in order to obtain a better solution (Mallipeldi et al., 2007; Storn, 1996; Qin et al., 2009; Iorio et al., 2004; Ali, 2011). In our study, we adopt the equation employed by Alguliev et al.(2011) because they have got a good result for document summarization with the equation.

$$\boldsymbol{Q_i(g)} = \boldsymbol{P_a(g)} + F \cdot (\boldsymbol{P_{best}(g)} - \boldsymbol{P_b(g)}) + F \cdot (\boldsymbol{P_{best}(g)} - \boldsymbol{P_c(g)}) \quad (3)$$

$\boldsymbol{P_a(g)}$,$\boldsymbol{P_b(g)}$,$\boldsymbol{P_c(g)}$ are solutions randomly selected from the population $\boldsymbol{G(g)}$ except solution

$\boldsymbol{P_i(g)}$. $\boldsymbol{P_{best}}$ is the best solution in $\boldsymbol{G(g)}$. F is an adjustment factor, and the value of $[0.4, 1.0]$ is regarded as effective by (Storn et al., 1996).

4.1.3 Crossover

A parent vector $\boldsymbol{P_i(g)}$ and mutation vector $\boldsymbol{Q_i(g)}$ are crossed over with crossover ratio $CR(g)$, and then a child vector $\boldsymbol{R_i(g)}$ is generated. Here, each locus of a child vector $r_{i,s}(g)$ succeeds the locus of either a parent vector $p_{i,s}(g)$ or a mutation vector $q_{i,s}(g)$ under the condition shown in equation (4).

$$r_{i,s}(g) = \begin{cases} q_{i,s}(g) & (if\ rand_{i,s} \leq CR(g) or\ s = s_{rand}) \\ p_{i,s}(g) & (otherwise) \end{cases} \tag{4}$$

s_{rand} is a value randomly selected from $1, 2, \ldots, n$. By providing a chance to mutate at the s_{rand}-th locus, it prevents that a child vector becomes the same one as a parent vector.

Moreover, in general, the solution is expected to become better as generation proceeds, therefore, a child vector had better not be generated by taking over many features of a parent vector. In this context, mutation rate decreases as generation proceeds. So, mutation rate $CR(g)$ is shown in equation (5).

$$CR(g) = CR(0) \cdot sigm\left(\frac{g_{max}}{2 \cdot (g+1)}\right) \tag{5}$$

Here, $sigm(\cdot)$ is a sigmoid function and is used to decrease mutation rate as generation gets close to g_{max}. $CR(0)$ is the mutation rate given at the first generation.

4.1.4 Selection

A new solution $\boldsymbol{P_i(g+1)}$ at the next generation to generation g is selected by evaluating a parent vector $\boldsymbol{P_i(g)}$ and a child vector $\boldsymbol{R_i(g)}$. Here, in order to evaluate fitness value, a solution has to be a binary vector. So, a real-valued vector $\boldsymbol{P}$ is changed to a binary vector $\boldsymbol{P'}$ by following rule.

$$p'_{i,s}(g) = \begin{cases} 1 & (if\ 0.5 < sigm(p_{i,s}(g))) \\ 0 & (otherwise) \end{cases} \tag{6}$$

First of all, real value $p_{i,s}(g)$ is changed to the value of $[0, 1]$ through a sigmoid function. if the value is bigger than 0.5 then it is set as 1, and if not then 0. After changing real-valued vector to binary vector and obtaining fitness value, either a parent vector $\boldsymbol{P_i(g)}$ or a child vector $\boldsymbol{R_i(g)}$ is selected as a solution at next generation, i.e., $\boldsymbol{P_i(g+1)}$ by the following rules.

- If both parent and child satisfy the constraint, the one with higher fitness value is selected.
- If either a parent or a child does not satisfy the constraint the one which satisfies the constraint is selected.
- If both parent and child do not satisfy the constraint, the one which does not satisfy the constraint so much is selected.

4.2 Definition of fitness function

We define a fitness function so as it evaluates a solution $\boldsymbol{P_i}$, which includes important contents and less redundancy, as being highly regarded. Here, we propose three fitness functions, taking account of latent topics in documents.

4.2.1 Fitness function 1

We define fitness function 1 as the one which evaluates the combination of sentences including important contents of target documents as being highly regarded, considering the importance of a sentence and coverage ratio simultaneously (see, equation (7)).

$$f(\boldsymbol{P_i}) = \frac{|W_i|}{V} \sum_{s=1}^{n} b_s p'_{i,s} \tag{7}$$

Here, $|W_i|$ and V indicate the numbers of vocabularies included in a solution $\boldsymbol{P_i}$ and target documents, respectively, and $\frac{|W_i|}{V}$ indicates the coverage ratio of the vocabularies in a solution $\boldsymbol{P_i}$ to V. b_s expresses the importance of sentence s based on latent topics estimated by means of LDA, and is expressed in equation (8).

$$b_s = \sum_{t=1}^{K} b_{ts} \tag{8}$$

Here, b_{ts} expresses the importance of sentence s in each topic $t (t = 1, \ldots, K)$, therefore, it is decided by the total sum of the importance in each topic. b_{ts} is expressed in equation (9).

$$b_{ts} = \frac{\sum_{w=1}^{V} \phi_{tw} y_{sw}}{\sqrt{|W_s|}} \cdot \boldsymbol{\theta_t} \tag{9}$$

$\boldsymbol{\Phi_t}$ is the word occurrence probabilistic distribution to topics, it is represented as $\boldsymbol{\Phi_t} = \{\phi_{t1}, \ldots, \phi_{tV}\}(t = 1, \ldots, K)$. Here, ϕ_{tw} indicates the importance of word w at topic t. y_{sw} is a variable to express binary conditions to show 1 if word w is included in the sentence, and 0 if not. Moreover, considering the length of a sentence in evaluation, the total value of importance of words included in sentence s is divided by the square root of the total number of words in sentence s, i.e., $\sqrt{|W_s|}$. Here, it is regarded that the more a topic is included in documents, the more important the topic in the documents, therefore, the ratio of topic t in target documents, i.e., $\boldsymbol{\theta_t}$, is multiplied.

4.2.2 Fitness function 2

In fitness function 2, we change the way of calculating b_s defined in fitness function 1. Here, we regard that it is important if a sentence has similar topic vector to a particular topic vector of target documents (see, equation (10)).

$$b_s = \max_{t=1,2,\ldots,K} \{sim(\boldsymbol{w_{ts}}, \boldsymbol{O_t})\} \quad (10)$$

$\boldsymbol{O_t}$ represents topic t vector, i.e., $\boldsymbol{O_t} = [o_{t1}, o_{t2}, \ldots, o_{tV}], (t = 1, 2, \ldots, K)$. In other words, $\boldsymbol{O_t}$ corresponds to word distribution $\boldsymbol{\Phi_t}$ estimated by means of LDA. $\boldsymbol{w_{ts}}$ indicates sentence s vector at topic t, it is obtained by $\boldsymbol{w_{ts}} = \{o_{tj} x_{sj}\}_{j=1}^{V}$. Here, x_{sj} is the variable which indicates 1 if word j is included in sentence s, and 0 if not. $sim(\boldsymbol{a}, \boldsymbol{b})$ expresses cosine similarity between vectors $\boldsymbol{a}, \boldsymbol{b}$. The highest value of cosine similarity among K topics is regarded as the importance of sentence s.

4.2.3 Fitness function 3

In fitness function 3, the importance of a sentence is calculated with equation (10), and the total importance of solution $\boldsymbol{P_i}$ is obtained by the combination of sentences (see, the fraction of equation (11)), and the importance is divided by the total value of the similarity of any pair of sentences in target documents (see, equation (11)), taking account of the penalty of redundancy in the combination of sentences, unlike the case of fitness function 1, i.e., multiplying coverage ratio, $\frac{|W_i|}{V}$.

$$f(\boldsymbol{P_i}) = \frac{\sum_{s=1}^{n-1} \sum_{r=s+1}^{n} \left(b_s + b_r\right) p'_{i,s} p'_{i,r}}{\sum_{s=1}^{n-1} \sum_{r=s+1}^{n} sim(\boldsymbol{w_s}, \boldsymbol{w_r}) p'_{i,s} p'_{i,r}} \quad (11)$$

Here, $\boldsymbol{w_s}$ is the word vector of sentence s, i.e., $\boldsymbol{w_s} = [w_{s1}, w_{s2}, \ldots, w_{sV}]$. w_{sa} expresses importance of word a in sentence s, and it is calculated by $tf - isf$ shown in equation (12).

$$w_{s,a} = tf_{sa} \times log(\frac{n}{n_a}) \quad (12)$$

tf_{sa} expresses the ratio that word a is included in sentence s, n is the total number of sentences, and n_a is the number of sentences including word a. With $\sum_{s=1}^{n-1} \sum_{r=s+1}^{n} sim(\boldsymbol{w_s}, \boldsymbol{w_r}) p'_{i,s} p'_{i,r}$, the total sum of cosine similarity between sentences selected in solution $\boldsymbol{P_i}$ is calculated as an evaluation factor of redundancy in a generated summary.

5 Experiments and evaluations

5.1 Experimental settings

In the experiments, we use DUC04 Task2 data set. In the data set, there are 50 topic document sets. The length of a summary is the constraint on making a summary. Here, constraint is to make a summary within 665 bytes is the constraint. For each document set, a summary is generated 10 times, and averaged the precision of the 10 summaries evaluated with ROUGE-1 evaluation index (Lin et al., 2004). ROUGE-1 value is obtained for the both cases where the evaluation with and without stop words. As computation environment, we used Ubuntu 12.04.3 for OS and AMD FX(tm)-8120 1.4GHz for CPU.

We used Gibbs sampling for topic estimation with 100 iteration. The both hyper-parameters of Dirichlet prior distribution of document-topic distribution, $\boldsymbol{\alpha}$ and of topic-word distribution, $\boldsymbol{\beta}$ are all set as 0.1. To estimate the number of latent topics in the documents, we use perplexity as an index.

As for DE settings, we set the number of maximum generation as $g_{max} = 10000$, the number of solutions is $N = 50$. Besides, as the parameter used to generate the initial population, $n = 5$, and we set $p_s^{min} = -10$ and $p_x^{max} = 10$ for all the initial solutions. As for difference parameter and crossover rate, we set $F = 0.45$ and $CR(0) = 0.7$, respectively, referring to the study by Alguliev et al. (2011).

5.2 Change of the equation for the initial population

In general, we often generate the initial population randomly by following in equation (2), however, in the case of document summarization, we have confirmed that most of the solutions in the initial population generated by equation (2) do not satisfy the given constraint, i.e., the length of a summary is within 665 bytes, in preliminary experiments (see, the left figure in Figure2).

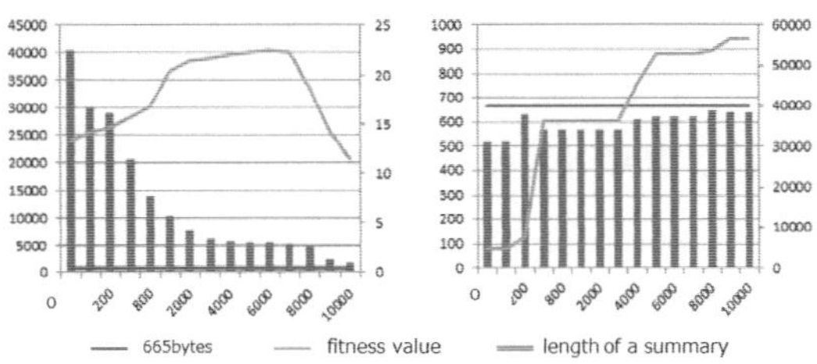

Figure 2: Operation to the generation of the initial population

If most of the solutions do not satisfy the constraint, it is difficult to obtain solutions with high fitness value satisfying the constraint, even if they are evolved. In this context, we define a new equation to generate the initial population so that the solutions satisfy the constraint at an early generation. Because of $p_s^{min} = -10$ and $p_x^{max} = 10$, the new equation for the initial population is defined as shown in equation (13).

$$p_{i,s}(0) = 10 - 20(1 - rand_{i,s})^{1/(n+1)} \quad (13)$$

With a random value, $rand_{i,s}(0 \leq rand_{i,s} \leq 1)$, the value of [-10,10] is provided to each locus of N solutions. Here, n is an adjustment parameter for occurrence probability of value of [-10,10]. The bigger n is, the closer the value is to -10. By employing equation (13), we have confirmed that solutions tend to satisfy the constraint and fitness value increases as the number of generation increases (see, the right figure of Figure 2).

5.3 Results and consideration

Table 1 shows the precision of the proposed methods and of other methods regarded as baseline methods. In the table, Topic-DE$_{fit1}$, Topic-DE$_{fit2}$, and Topic-DE$_{fit3}$ are the methods using fitness function 1, 2 and 3, respectively. As for the baseline methods, Topic-OPT adopts the same index for the importance of a sentence and coverage ratio as well as Topic-DE$_{fit1}$ and employs an explicit solution technique with CPLEX solver [1]. CLASSY (Conroy et al., 2005) is the method which provided the highest score at DUC'04.

Methods	with	without	time (sec.)
Topic-DE$_{fit1}$	0.345	0.249	458
Topic-DE$_{fit2}$	0.337	0.232	447
Topic-DE$_{fit3}$	0.287	0.145	451
Topic-OPT	0.389	0.326	9548
CLASSY	0.382	0.309	-

Table 1: Precision with DUC'04 data set

Compared the results among the three proposed methods, Topic-DE$_{fit1}$ got the highest score for both cases of with and without stop words – compared Topic-DE$_{fit1}$ with Topic-DE$_{fit2}$, in terms of deciding the importance of a sentence, we see that it is useful for calculating the importance of a sentence based on the total value of words included in the sentence rather than the value of similarity of the topic vector among all sentences. Furthermore, as for comparison between Topic-DE$_{fit2}$ and Topic-DE$_{fit3}$, in terms of removing redundancy, we see that it is useful for considering how much the combination of sentences in a generated summary covers the contents of target documents rather than the similarity among the sentences in a summary. Furthermore, compared Topic-OPT with the proposed methods, in terms of calculation time, it decreases considerably by using DE, as we see that every proposed method takes approximately 450 seconds, while Topic-OPT takes approximately 9500 seconds. On the other hand, we also see that the values of ROUGE-1 of the proposed methods are lower than that of Topic-OPT. We think the reason for the difference in precision is that the importance and

[1]http://www-01.ibm.com/software/commerce/optimization/cplex-optimizer/

coverage are obtained for each sentence in objective function in Topic-OPT, whereas in Topic-DE$_{fit1}$ those are obtained for the combination of sentences in a generated summary.

6 Conclusions

In this study, we have proposed a multi-document summarization method using differential evolution for combinatorial optimization of important sentences in a generated summary, aiming to realize the efficiency of computation for making a summary. As for the evaluation of the combination of sentences for a summary, we took two approaches: one is to evaluate the total value of the importance of sentences for each topic (i.e., fitness function 1), and the other is to evaluate the similarity of topics between a sentence vector and each topic vector of all sentences estimated by LDA (i.e., fitness function 2 and 3). From the results of the experiments, we see that the former one provides a better result, and also see that evaluating how much a generated summary covers the contents of the whole target documents provides a better result rather than evaluating the similarity among sentences in a generated summary, in terms of reducing the redundancy of the contents of a summary compared fitness function 1 with fitness function 2.

Moreover, compared the proposed methods to the methods with explicit solution techniques, though we see that calculation time was reduced by the proposed methods, precision of the proposed methods was more worse than the methods.

As future work, we will increase the number of generation in DE process to confirm whether or not precision depends on the number of generation, and devise a better fitness function for improving precision.

References

R. M. Alguliev, R. M. Aliguliyev, C. A. Mehdiyev. 2011. *Sentence selection for generic document summarization using an adaptive differential evolution algorithm.* Swarm and Evolutionary Computation 1(4), pp. 213-222.

M.M. Ali, 2011. *Differential evolution with generalized differentials,* Journal of Computational and Applied Mathematics 225 (8) pp.2205-2216.

R. Arora and B. Ravindran. 2008. *Latent Dirichlet Allocation Based Multi-Document Summarization.* Proc. of the second workshop on Analytics for noisy unstructured text data, pp. 91-97.

David M. Blei and Andrew Y. Ng and Michael I. Jordan and John Lafferty. 2003. *Latent dirichlet allocation,* Journal of Machine Learning Research,

Ying-Lang Chang and Jen-Tzung Chien. 2009. *Latent Dirichlet Learning for Document Summarization,* ICASSP, pp.1689-1692.

N. Chen and J.P. Vapnik. 2012. *Performance Comparison of GA, DE, PSO and SA Approaches in Enhancement of Total Transfer Capability using FACTS Devices.* Journal of Electrical Engineering & Technology, Vol. 7, No. 4, pp. 493-500.

John M. Conroy and Jade Goldstein Stewart and Judith D. Schlesinger, 2005. *CLASSY Query-Based Multi-Document Summarization* In Proceedings of the Document Understanding Conf. Wksp. 2005 (DUC 2005) at the Human Language Technology Conf./Conf. on Empirical Methods in Natural Language Processing (HLT/EMNLP).

Dan Gillick and Benoit Favre and Dilek Hakkani-tur, 2008. *The ICSI Summarization System at TAC 2008,*

A.Highighi and Vanderwende, 2009. *Exploring content models for multi-document summarization,* Proc. of NAACL HLT-09.

Tsutomu Hirao, Manabu Okumura, Takahiro Fukushima, and Hidetsugu Nanba, 2004. *Building TSC3 Corpus and its Evaluation (in Japanese)* The 10th Annual Conference of the Japanese Association for Natural Language Processing. pp.A10B5-02.

J.H., Holland. 1975. *Adaptation in natural and artificial systems.* An introductory analysis with applications to biology, control, and artificial intelligence, University of Michigan Press.

A. Iorio, X. Li, 2004. *Solving rotated multi-objective optimization problems using differential evolution,* Proceedings of the Australian Conference on Artificial Intelligence, Cairns, Australia, December 4.6, pp. 861-872.

J. Kennedy and R. C. Eberhart. 1995. *Particle swarm optimization.* Proc. of IEEE International Conference on Neural Networks, Vol. 1498 of Lecture Notes in Computer Science, pp. 1942-1948.

D. Gao, W. Li, Y. Ouyang, R. Zhang. 2012. *LDA-Based Topic Formation and Topic-Sentence Reinforcement for Graph-Based Multi-document Summarization.* Lecture Notes in Computer Science Volume 7675, pp 376-385.

Lin, C.-Y 2004. *ROUGE: A Package for Automatic Evaluation of Summaries,* Proc. of Workshop on Text Summarization Branches Out, Post Conference Workshop of ACL 2004, pp. 74-81,

Lin, Hui and Bilmes, Jeff, 2010. *Multi-document Summarization via Budgeted Maximization of Submodular Functions*, Human Language Technologies: The 2010 Annual Conference of the North American Chapter of the Association for Computational Linguistics, Los Angeles, California, pp. 912–920.

R. Mallipeldi, P.N. Suganthan, Q.K. Pan, M.F. Tasgetiren, 2011 *Differential evolution algorithm with ensemble of parameters and mutation strategies*, Applied SoftComputing 11 (2) pp.1679-1696.

Ryan Mcdonald. 2007. *A Study of Global Inference Algorithms in Multi-Document Summarization.* Proc. of the 29th European Conference on Information Retrieval, pp557-564.

Kenton W. Murray. 2009. *Summarization by Latent Dirichlet Allocation: Superior Sentence Extraction through Topic Modeling.* A senior thesis for Bachelors degree, Princeton University.

K. Nandhini and S. R. Balasundaram. 2013. *Use of Genetic Algorithm for Cohesive Summary Extraction to Assist Reading Difficulties.* Applied Computational Intelligence and Soft Computing Volume 2013 Article ID 945623, 11 pages.

K. Nieminen, S. Ruuth, and I. Maros. 2003. *Genetic algorithm for finding a good first integer solution for MILP.* Department of Computing, Imperial College Departmental Technical Report 2003/4, ISSN 1469-4174.

Hitoshi Nishikawa, Tsutomu Hirao, Yoshihiro Matsuo and Toshiro Makino. 2012. *Text Summarization Model based on Redundancy Constrained Knapsack Problem.* In Proc. of the 24th International Conference on Computational Linguistics (COLING), pp. 893-902.

Masaaki Nishino, Norihito Yasuda, Tsutomu Hirao, Jun Suzuki and Masaaki Nagata. 2013. *Summarization while Maximizing Multiple Objectives with Lagrangian Relaxation.* In Proc. of the 35th European Conference on Information Retrieval (ECIR), pp. 772-775.

Dusan Petkovic 2011. *Dynamic Programming Algorithm vs. Genetic Algorithm: Which is Faster?.* Research and Development in Intelligent Systems XXVII, pp 483-488.

A.K. Qin, V.L. Huang, P.N. Suganthan, 2009. *Differential evolution algorithm with strategy adaptation for global numerical optimization*, IEEE Transactions on Evolutionary Computation 13 (2) pp.398-417.

R. Storn and K. Price. 1996. *Minimizing the Real Functions of the ICEC96 Contest by Differential Evolution.* Proc. of the International Conference on Evolutionary Computation, pp. 842-844.

R. Storn 1996, *On the usage of differential evolution for function optimization*, Proceedings of the Biennial Conference of the North American Fuzzy Information Processing Society, Berkeley, USA, June 19.22, pp. 519-523.

Haruka Shigematsu and Ichiro Kobayashi, 2012. *Text Summarization based on Latent Topic Distribution*, The 26th Annual Conference of the Japanese Society for Artificial Intelligence, 4I1-R-9-1 (in Japanese)

Hiroya Takamura and Manabu Okumura 2009. *Text summarization model based on the budgeted median problem*, Proceedings of the 18th ACM conference on Information and knowledge management CIKM '09, Hong Kong, China, pp.1589–1592.

Dingding Wang, Shenghuo Zhu, Tao Li and Yihong Gong, 2009. *Multi-Document Summarization using Sentence-based Topic Models*, Proc. of the ACL-IJCNLP 2009, pp.297-300.

Yih, Wen-tau and Goodman, Joshua and Vanderwende, Lucy and Suzuki, Hisami, 2007. *Multi-document Summarization by Maximizing Informative Content-words*, Proceedings of the 20th International Joint Conference on Artifical Intelligence, IJCAI'07, pp.1776–1782.

Mapping between Lexical Tones and Musical Notes in Thai Pop Songs

Chawadon Ketkaew
Department of Linguistics, Faculty of Arts,
Chulalongkorn University,
Phayathai Road, Pathumwan,
Bangkok, 10330, Thailand
Chawadon.k@gmail.com

Pittayawat Pittayaporn
Department of Linguistics, Faculty of Arts,
Chulalongkorn University,
Phayathai Road, Pathumwan,
Bangkok, 10330, Thailand
Pittayawat.P@chula.ac.th

Abstract

The aim of this paper is to examine the parallelism between tonal transitions and musical note transitions in Thai pop songs based on the data from 30 current pop songs. The results suggest that there is a statistically significant parallelism between tonal transitions and musical note transitions. Interestingly, the results show that both contour tones, RISING and FALLING, typically pattern with HIGH with respect to the mapping between tonal transitions and note transitions. Nevertheless, when two FALLING occur consecutively, the offset of the second one is used for mapping. Our results seem to find further support for decomposability of contour tones in Thai. Furthermore, they suggest that Thai pop music composition does not strive to maximize parallel transitions but prefer to avoid opposing transitions.

1. Introduction

Pitch is an important element in both language and music. In languages, pitch is used to convey different levels of meaning, e.g. lexical, sentential, attitudinal, emotional etc. In music, pitch serves the melodic structure, whether played on instruments or sung by voice, in order to express meaning to the listener. However, pitch in language and music differs with respect to how it is treated. While pitch in language is treated as a relative difference, pitch in music is treated as an absolute difference. Given their similarity and difference, it is important for our understanding of human cognition to examine the relationship between pitch in language and music. Of crucial relevance are languages that use patterns of relative pitch to convey lexical contrast. It is a puzzle how tonal languages relate their lexical tones to musical melody, which is made up of patterns of absolute pitch played on instruments or sung.

One pertinent question is how contour tones are treated in the mapping between tone and melody. To answer this question, the Thai language is a great case study because its five tones, shown in Table 1, have been studied quite extensively both in terms of acoustics, perception, as well as phonology. However, little research has been done on the mapping between lexical tones and music in Thai, especially with respect to the treatment of contour tones.

Tone	Example	Tone value
MID	khā: 'to be stuck'	[33]
LOW	khà: 'galangal'	[21]
FALLING	khâ: 'value'	[42]
HIGH	khá: 'to trade'	[45]
RISING	khǎ: 'leg'	[24]

Table1: Thai lexical tones

Since in Thai songs syllables and musical notes are typically mapped to each other in a one to one relationship, an interesting question is how these complex tones are treated. In this paper, we examine the tone-melody mapping in current Thai pop songs. Our results indicate that, like other genres, Thai pop songs show a degree of parallelism between tonal transitions and musical note transitions. In addition, they show that both RISING and FALLING tones typically pattern with HIGH with respect to the mapping between tonal transitions and note transitions.

Copyright 2014 by Chawadon Ketkaew and Pittayawat Pittayaporn
28th Pacific Asia Conference on Language, Information and Computation pages 160–169

2. Literature review

Mapping between lexical tones and musical notes is one of the topics that have been widely studied in the past decade. While a few studies compare lexical tones to the absolute pitch of musical notes (Yung, 1983; Chao, 1956), some have investigated parallelism between tonal transitions and melodic transitions, i.e. mapping between the directions of adjacent note transitions and adjacent syllable transitions (Schellenberg, 2009; Wee, 2007;Ho, 2006;Baart, 2004; Wong and Diehl, 2002; Agawu, 1988).In our opinion, the latter method seems to be a more effective way to investigate the mapping between lexical tones and musical notes because it does not compare absolute pitch with relative pitch. Since pitch is treated as a relative difference in language but as an absolute difference in music, investigating mapping between individual tones and individual notes may miss crucial generalizations. It is thus more reasonable to examine pitch in both language and music in terms of relative pitch difference by comparing the directions between successive lexical tones and successive musical notes.

2.1 Study of tone-melody mapping in general

Most previous studies that investigated how lexical tones transitions and musical note transitions are mapped have revealed parallelism between tonal transitions and musical note transitions in languages. For example, Wong and Diehl's (2002) results on Cantonese, based on four contemporary songs, show a very high degree of parallelism between musical and lexical melodies (91.81 %).

The factors that have been reported to affect the degree of parallelism are their position within the melody. Wee (2007) suggested that the parallelism in Mandarin songs will be high in the most prominent beat in the Mandarin folk songs.

Shona, Schellenberg (2009) also examined the parallelism between speech and sung melody. Instead of using musical notes, he based his analysis on pitch tracks of the recorded songs. Despite the difference in methodology, this study still found a statistically significant number of parallel transitions.

However, cases that do not show parallelism between tonal transitions and musical note transitions do exist. For example, Agawu (1988) investigated northern Ewe songs and found that the pattern of tonal transitions did not match with sung melodies. In addition, Baart (2004) reported similar finding for Kalam Kohistani. Similarly, for mandarin pop songs, Ho (2006) suggested that there is a disagreement between tone and tune.

Interestingly, in their study of Dagaare, a two-tone language without parallelism between tones and tunes, Bodomo and Mora (2000) suggested that the degree of parallelism relies on the number of tones in each language's inventory. It predicts that in a language with a rich tonal inventory, the degree of parallelism will be high. However, studies on Kalam Kohistani (Baart, 2004) and Mandarin (Ho, 2006) disproved Bodoma and Mora's hypothesis.

Another important issue is the treatment of contour tones. Since contour tones involve dynamic changes in pitch, it is puzzling how they are mapped with musical note transitions. Ho (2006) and Wong and Diehl's (2002) studies on Cantonese pop songs suggested that the tonal endpoint of Cantonese contour tones are used as the relevant portion in mapping.

2.2 Study of tone-melody mapping in Thai

As for Thai, three important pioneering studies have revealed that Thai, like most tonal languages, is characterized by parallelism between the transition of lexical tones and the transitions between two adjacent musical notes. In other words, tonal transitions and note transitions between adjacent syllables in Thai songs typically agree in direction.

List (1961) examined the mapping between tonal transitions and musical notes in recitals and chants in Thai. The results show that the degree of parallelism between tones and sung pitch in recital reaches approximately 90 percent. In contrast, the correspondence between tones and musical notes is only approximately 60 percent in contemporary songs.

Similarly, the results of Saurman (1999) showed that the degree of parallelism between tones and tunes in classical and traditional songs is approximately 90 percent. For contemporary songs, which borrow elements of western music, the degree of mapping parallelism was between 60 to 70 percent. The parallelism was also low (42%) for western hymns translated into Thai.

Interestingly, the degree of mapping for the Thai national anthem was also only 32 percent. Not only do these studies reveal parallelism between tonal transition and sung pitch in Thai, it also shows that musical genres have an ineligible effect on the degree of parallelism.

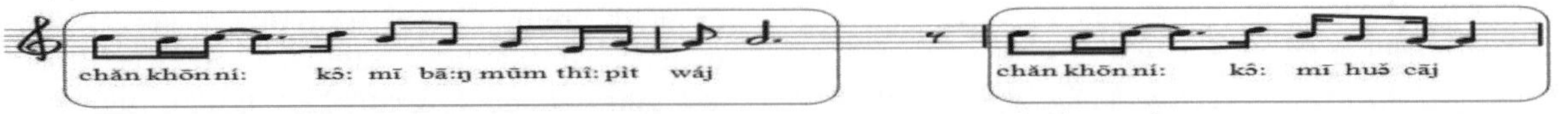

Figure 1: the sample of transcribed song using musical notation

In addition, Ho (2006) applied the idea of using the tonal endpoint in one Thai pop song and found that the tonal onset of FALLING may be the relevant part for mapping. More importantly, her study showed that the degree of parallelism is approximately 80 percent. In her observations, the mismatches are generally caused by FALLING.

In summary, the results of many studies concerning Thai songs show that there is parallelism between tonal transitions and musical note transitions. However, most studies do not systematically examine how the contour tones are treated in Thai songs. Moreover, they are based on a limited number of songs. To reach a better understanding of the mapping between tonal and note transitions, we focused on the treatment of contour tones, based on data from a relatively large corpus of Thai pop music.

3. Methods

This study examined the parallelism between tonal transitions and musical note transitions in 30 popular Thai pop songs[1]. The melody of each song was transcribed using musical notation by the researcher. Moreover, music notations in this study were then double checked by a professional musician. The lyrics were transcribed using IPA symbols such that each syllable is aligned vertically to its corresponding musical notes as exemplified in Figure 1.

Note transitions between two adjacent syllables were manually extracted from the corpus, excluding cases of one-to-many and many-to-one mapping of syllables and musical notes. To control the boundary effects, transitions across the melodic phrase boundaries were also excluded. In addition, syllables that have been described as "surface toneless" (Bennett, 1995; Luksaneeyanawin, 1983; Bee, 1975) were excluded to avoid possible noises.

By identifying such toneless syllables with Luksaneeyawin's "linking syllables", we were able to exclude all unstressed CV syllables containing /a/. For example, words like /rátt͟hàbā:n/ "government" and /thɔ̄:rámā:n/ "suffer" are typically realized as [ˌrátt͟həˈbā:n] and [ˌthɔ̄:rəˈmā:n] respectively. In these cases, /-tha-/ and /-ra-/ were not included in the analysis.

After extracting the eligible adjacent syllables, we then classified the directions of the musical note transitions into three major groups: ascending, level and descending. If the second note was higher in pitch than the first one, e.g. from note C to note D, we assigned the musical transition to the ascending category. When second note was lower than the first one, e.g. from note E to note D, we counted it as having a descending transition. Lastly, if the adjacent notes were identical in pitch, e.g. from note F to note F, we classified its note transition as a level transition. Crucially, we did not set an *a priori* assumption on how the contour tones were decomposed into sequences of H's and L's. Instead, we used the five lexical tones as primes in the analysis. Below are the 25 pairs of adjacent tones used to compare with directions of note transitions.

MID→MID	FALLING→HIGH
MID→LOW	FALLING→RISING
MID→FALLING	HIGH→MID
MID→HIGH	HIGH→LOW
MID→RISING	HIGH→FALLING
LOW→MID	HIGH→HIGH
LOW→LOW	HIGH→RISING
LOW→FALLING	RISING→MID
LOW→HIGH	RISING→LOW
LOW→RISING	RISING→FALLING
FALLING→MID	RISING→HIGH
FALLING→LOW	RISING→RISING
FALLING→FALLING	

Table2: 25 Tone pairs

[1] This data is part of a larger corpus in progress. At the end of its first phase, the corpus will consist of 100 songs covering a considerable variety in terms of composers, keys of songs and genders.

4. Treatment of contour tones

To examine how tonal transitions and note transitions are mapped, we carried out a statistical analysis to test whether the tone pairs are preferably mapped with ascending, descending, or level note transitions. The Friedman test provides a means to test whether several groups differ significantly and it is used for data that does not show normal distribution. However, the Friedman test only tells us whether there are statistically significant differences among groups. It cannot identify which pair is significantly different. Therefore, the Wilcoxon test is required to examine which pairs differ from each other significantly. In this study, the 25 tone pairs and the three directions of note transitions were the independent variables and the dependent variables respectively.

4.1 Ascending transitions

Tone pairs that occur with ascending note transitions more often than other types at a statistically significant level were classified as having ascending tonal transition.

Among the 25 pairs of tones in adjacent syllables, five, shown in Table 3, belong to this type of transition. All the tone pairs that are preferably mapped with ascending note transitions are ones whose second member is higher in pitch than the first.

Tone pairs	Musical note transition		
	Ascending	Descending	Level
MID→HIGH	136(68.7%)	37(18.7%)	25(12.2%)
MID→RISING	111(71.6%)	31(20%)	13(8.4%)
LOW→MID	186(64.8%)	38(13.2%)	63(22%)
LOW→RISING	45(81.8%)	3(5.5%)	7(12.7%)
LOW→HIGH	63(77.8%)	14(17.3%)	4(4.9%)

Table 3: Ascending transition

As expected, the results in Table 3 show that ascending note transitions were mapped with tone pairs with a higher second tone. In particular, cases of MID → HIGH were mapped with ascending transition at a statistically significant level ($p<0.001$). Similarly, tonal transitions of the types LOW → MID and LOW → HIGH were also mapped with ascending note transitions at a statistically significant level ($p<0.05$). Most importantly, both MID → RISING and LOW → RISING were mapped with ascending note transitions at a statistically significant level ($p<0.01$). This indicates that RISING behaves like HIGH with respect to tone-melody mapping. In other words, the RISING is treated as if it was HIGH.

4.2 Descending transitions

The tone pairs that were mapped with descending note transitions more often than other types at a statistically significant level were classified as having descending tonal transitions.

Tone pairs	Musical note transition		
	Ascending	Descending	Level
MID→LOW	52(15%)	229(66.4%)	64(18.6%)
FALLING→MID	130(28.8%)	244(54.1%)	77(17.1%)
FALLING→LOW	14(11.9%)	67(56.8%)	37(31.3%)
FALLING→FALLING	31(21.7%)	70(48.9%)	42(29.4%)
HIGH→MID	17(7.7%)	183(82.4%)	22(10%)
HIGH→LOW	4(6.8%)	47(79.7%)	8(13.5%)
RISING→MID	27(13.2%)	164(80%)	14(6.8%)
RISING→LOW	7(12.1%)	46(79.3%)	5(8.6%)

Table 4: Descending transition

As shown in Table 4, tone pairs in which the second tone is lower than the first one were typically matched with descending note transitions. To illustrate, cases of MID → LOW were mapped with descending note transitions at a statistically significant level ($p<0.01$). Similarly, HIGH →MID and HIGH → LOW were also mapped with descending note transitions at a statistically significant level ($p<0.01$). As expected, RISING → MID and RISING → LOW were also mapped with descending note transitions at a statistically significant level ($p<0.01$), providing further support for grouping RISING with HIGH. In addition, FALLING → MID and FALLING → LOW were also mapped with descending note transitions at a statistically significant level ($p<0.05$), suggesting that FALLING also patterns with HIGH. Most interestingly is the fact that FALLING → FALLING were mapped descending tonal transitions ($p<0.05$). If FALLING is always treated as if it was HIGH, we would expect two consecutive FALLINGs to be matched with level musical transitions. An explanation for this surprising mapping will be discussed later (see section 6).

4.3 Level transitions

Tone pairs that were frequently mapped with level note transitions than other types at a statistically significant level were classified as having a level tonal transition.

Tone pairs	Musical note transition		
	Ascending	Descending	Level
LOW→LOW	17(23%)	17(23%)	40(54%)
HIGH→HIGH	13(15.9%)	21(25.6%)	48(58.5%)

Table5: Level transition

For level musical note transitions, only two tone pairs with identical first and second member occurred with this type of transition at a statistically significant level. From Table 5, only LOW → LOW and HIGH → HIGH were mapped with level musical notes transitions at a statistically significant level ($p<0.05$). Interestingly, MID → MID does not follow the same pattern.

In summary, the results suggest that both RISING and FALLING are treated as if they were HIGH. In the case of RISING, its offset is used as a reference for tonal mapping. For FALLING, the result reveals, in contrast, that its onset is the important element in the mapping. Intriguingly, the pair FALLING → FALLING is also considered to have a descending tonal transition rather than a level transition.

5. Result of Parallelism

Based on the results in 4, tonal transitions were grouped into 3 categories according to their directions, as summarized in Table 6. Note that the RISING and FALLING are treated as if they were HIGH. One exception is FALLING→FALLING, which was classified as a descending rather than a level transition.

Ascending tonal transition	Descending tonal transition	Level tonal transition
MID→HIGH MID→RISING MID→FALLING LOW→MID LOW→FALLING LOW→HIGH LOW→RISING	MID→LOW FALLING→LOW FALLING→MID FALLING→FALLING HIGH→MID HIGH→LOW RISING→LOW RISING→MID	MID→MID LOW→LOW FALLING→HIGH FALLING→RISING HIGH→FALLING HIGH→HIGH HIGH→RISING RISING→FALLING RISING→RISING RISING→HIGH

Table6: tonal transition categories

After assigning the tonal transitions to the tone pairs, we coded the mapping between the tonal transitions and musical note transitions in terms of parallel, opposing and non-opposing. Tonal target transition which agrees with musical transition in terms of directions of pitch change was coded as parallel. We coded it as opposing if the tone transition and note transition went in opposite directions. Tonal and note transition that did not agree in direction but did not go in opposite directions, was coded as non-opposing.

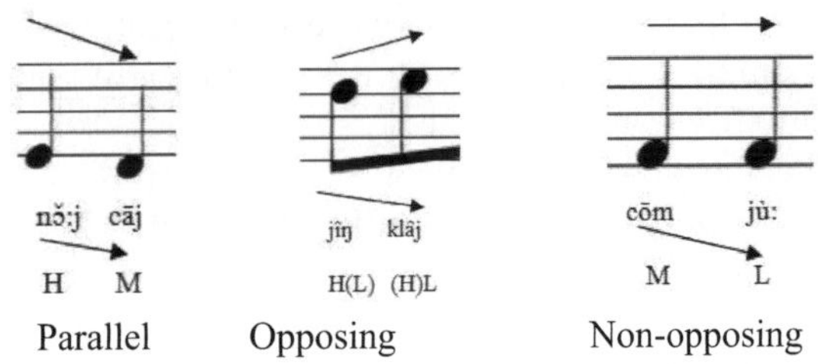

Figure 2: Example of parallel, opposing and non-opposing transitions

This analysis used the Freidman and Wilcoxon test to examine whether certain types of tonal transitions are mapped with certain types of musical note transitions. Table7 shows the percentage of parallelism between tonal transitions and note transitions.

Tonal transition	Melodic transition		
	Ascending	Descending	Level
Ascending	1091 (22.57%) (parallel)	317 (6.43%) (opposing)	230 (4.63%) (non-opposing)
Descending	415 (8.48%) (opposing)	1039 (21.49%) (parallel)	275 (5.57%) (non-opposing)
Level	426 (8.71%) (non-opposing)	483(9.9%) (non-opposing)	594 (12.22%) (parallel)

Sum of diagonal cell 55.3%

Table7: Parallelism between tonal transitions and melodic transitions

From table 7, for all 30 Thai pop songs, the total sum of mapping between tones and musical notes had 4798 transitions. Parallel mapping between tonal transitions and musical transition occurred at 55.3 percent. This was more often than opposing and non-opposing transitions at a statistically significant level ($p<0.001$). Also, 732 cases of the mapping between tonal and musical transitions were opposing (732/4798, 15.25%). Interestingly, the number of non-opposing transitions (1414/4798, 29.47%) occurred more often than opposing transitions at a statistically significant level ($p<0.001$). This seems to indicate that non-opposing transitions are acceptable in Thai pop music.

In summary, our results show that parallel transitions occur more frequently than the mapping of opposing transitions. Adjacent tones in which the second tone has a higher pitch than the previous one was mapped with an ascending melodic transition. Likewise, successive tones in which the second note is lower than the previous one were mapped with descending melodic transitions. However, tones of the same height which occurred adjacently tended to slightly map with level transitions.

6. Discussion

From our results, three issues deserve special attention: decomposability of contour tones, non-opposing mapping, and some factors that should be controlled for future study.

Firstly, this study offers further evidence in support of decomposability of Thai contour tones. In the case of RISING, our study found that the tonal offset has to be referred to in the tone-melody mapping. This suggests that RISING is composed of L followed by H rather than being an atomic unit. In the case of FALLING, our study showed that the tonal onset of FALLING in Thai normally has to be referred, confirming Ho's observation that the onset is the more important element or headship of FALLING in tone-melody mapping. Nevertheless, from our results, not only is FALLING's tonal onset important, but also its tonal offset is relevant for the mapping. To illustrate, when two FALLING occur consecutively, the offset of the second one is used for mapping. This fact also suggests that FALLING is composed of level tones (H followed by L) rather than being a unitary unit. From the phonological perspective, many phonologists, e.g. Gandour (1974a), Yip (1982) and Morén and Zsiga (2006), argue convincingly that contour tones in Thai are in fact made up of sequences of H and L. In other words, FALLING and RISING can be represented as [HL] and [LH] respectively. Therefore, our results lend further support for decomposability of contour tones in Thai.

Secondly, non-opposing transitions are acceptable in Thai pop music. As seen from a previous section, non-opposing transitions occur more often than opposing transitions at statistically significant levels. More specifically, when tone pairs with identical first and second members occur successively, although they tend to map with musical level transition, the percentage of mapping with musical ascending and descending transitions is close to that of level transitions. In other words, Thai pop music composition does not strive to maximize parallel transitions but tries to avoid opposing ones. The results should be further tested by perception studies in the future.

Finally, some additional factors should be studied in order to obtain a clearer picture of parallelism. To elaborate, the greater degree of parallelism might occur if we control for such factors as the note value and word stress. For note value, parallel transition tended to map with the note which contained the most prominent beat in the phrase of the songs. Furthermore, we observed most of FALLING was mapped with stressed grammatical words. For example, words like /mâj/ 'not', /kɔ̂/ 'also', /thî: /'REL', /yîŋ/ and /tɔ̂ŋ/'must' occurred frequently in our data and created opposing transitions. Excluding grammatical words and unstressed words might yield a lower percentage of opposing transitions. To conclude, in future studies, factors like stress, note value and grammatical word status should be also controlled for clearer results.

7. Conclusion

Based on data from a larger corpus than earlier studies, our results suggest that in Thai pop songs, like other genres, there is a statistically significant parallelism between tonal transitions and musical note transitions. They also agree with the findings by Ho (2006), who assumes that one of the two components of contour tones is taken as dominant and used as a reference in tone-melody mapping. To illustrate, both RISING and FALLING tones pattern with HIGH. Moreover, when two FALLINGs occur consecutively, the offset of the second FALLING is used for mapping. The results also provide further evidence for the decomposability of contour tones in Thai. Furthermore, the results also suggest a new way of looking at parallelism between tone transitions and musical note transitions. In particular, they suggest that the composition of Thai pop songs places more importance on avoidance of opposing transitions than achieving parallel transitions.

Acknowledgments

This research is a part of the first author's doctoral dissertation. It is supported by the Ratchadaphiseksomphot Endowment Fund of Chulalongkorn University (RES560530179-HS). Moreover, we wish to express sincere gratitude to Songphan Choemprayong for his advice on data and statistics. Many thanks are also extended to Yanin Sawanakunanon, Karntida Kerdpol, Junyawan Suwannarat, Teeranoot Siriwittayakorn, Thanasak Sirikanerat and Ponlawat Laimanoo for their help with statistics and valuable comments.

References

Agawu, V.Kofi. (1988). Tone and Tune: The Evidence for Northern Ewe Music. *Africa: Journal of the International African Institute, 58*(2), 127-146.

Baart, Joan LG. (2004). Tone and song in Kalam Kohistani (pakistan). *On Speech and Language: Studies for Sieb G. Nooteboom. Utrecht: Netherlands Graduate School of Linguistics*, 5-16.

Bee, Peter. (1975). Restricted phonology in certain Thai linker-syllables. IN J.G. Harris and J.R. Chamberlain (Ed.), *Studies in Tai Linguistics in Honor of William J. Gedney*, 17-32. Central Institute of English Language

Bennett, Fraser J. (1994). Iambicity in Thai. *Studies in the Linguistic Sciences, 24*, 39–57.

Bodomo, Adams, & Mora, Manolete. (2000). Language and Music in the Dagaare and Twi Folktakes of West Africa. *CRCG Project notes, University of Hong Kong*.

Chan, Marjorie. (1987). Tone and melody in Cantonese. *In Proceedings of the Thirteenth Annual Meeting of the Berkeley Linguistics Society*, 26-37.

Chao, Yuen Ren. (1956). Tone, intonation, singsong,chanting, recitative, tonal composition and atonalcomposition in Chinese. In M. Halle, H.G. Lunt, H. McLean and C.H. Van Schooneveld (Ed.), *For RomanJacobson: Essays on the occasion of his sixtiethbirthday, 11th October 1956* (pp. 52-59). The Hague:Monton & Co.

Gandour, Jackson. (1974). Consonant types and tone in Siamese. *Journal of Phonetics, 2*, 337-350.

Ho, Wing See Vincie. (2006, August 22-26). *The tone-melody interface of popular songs written in tone languages* Paper presented at the 9th International Conference on Music Perception and Cognition, Alma Master Studiorum University of Bologna.

List, George. (1961). Speech melody and song melody in Central Thailand. *Ethnomusicology, 5*(1), 16–32.

Luksaneeyawin, Sudaporn. (1983). *Intonation in Thai*. University of Edinburgh, Unplublished. .

Morén, Bruce, and Elizabeth Zsiga. 2006. The lexical and post-lexical phonology of Thai tones. Natural Language and Linguistic Theory 24:113–78.

Saurman, Mary Elisabeth. (1999). The agreement of Thai speech tones and melodic pitches *Notes on Anthropology, 3*(3), 15–24.

Schellenberg, Murray. (2009). *Singing in a Tone Language: Shona*. Paper presented at the Selected Proceedings of the 39th Annual Conference on African Linguistics.

Wee, Lian Hee. (2007). Unraveling the Relation between Mandarin Tones and Musical Melody. *Journal of Chinese Linguistics, 35*, 128-144.

Wong, Patrick C. M, & Diehl, Randy L. (2002). How can the lyrics of a song in a tone language be understood? *Psychology of Music, 30*(2), 202-209.

Yip, Mora. (1982). Against a Segmental Analysis of Zahao and Thai: A Laryngeal Tier Proposal. *Linguistic Analysis, 9*, 79-94.

Yung, Bell. (1989). Cantonese opera: performance as creative process. *Cambridge University Press*.

Appendix A: List of 30 songs

1. เธอยัง /thə̄: jāŋ/
2. หยุดรักยังไง/jùt rák jāŋŋāj/
3. ใจกลางความรู้สึกดีดี/cāj klā:ŋ khwā:mrú:sùk dī: dī:/
4. ใครนิยาม/khrāj nijā:m/
5. แพ้ใจ/phɛ́: cāj/
6. ผู้ป่วยความจำเสื่อม/phû puə̀j khwā:mcām sɨ̀əm/
7. อยากได้ยินว่ารักกัน/jà:k dâjjīn wâ: rákkān/
8. รักปาฏิหารย์/rák pā:tihǎ:n/
9. จะให้ฉันทำยังไง/ca hâj chǎn thām jāŋŋāj/
10. รักแท้อยู่เหนือกาลเวลา /rák thɛ́: jù:nɨ̌ə kā:nwē:lā:/
11. ไกลแค่ไหนคือใกล้/klāj kɛ̂:nǎj khɨ̄: klâj/
12. กลับมาเป็นเหมือนเดิม /klàp mā: pēn mɨ́ən də̄:m dâjmǎj/
13. หนึ่งความเหงาบนดาวเคราะห์ /nɨ̀ŋ khwā:mŋǎw bōn dā:wkhrɔ́ʔ/

14. ก้อนหินก้อนนั้น/kɔ̂:nhǐn kɔ̂:n nán/
15. คนธรรมดา/khōn thāmmadā:/
16. จำทำไม/cām thāmmāj/
17. หวานเย็น/wǎ:njēn/
18. Unlovable
19. ไม่ใกล้ไม่ไกล/mâj klâj mâj klāj/
20. อีกนานไหม/ʔì:k nā:n mǎj/
21. ยิ่งรู้จักยิ่งรักเธอ/jîŋ rú:càk jîŋ rák thə:/
22. คนแพ้ที่ไม่มีน้ำตา/khōn phɛ́:thî: mâ:j mī: námtā:/
23. น้อย/nɔ́:j/
24. ไม่บอกเธอ/mâj bɔ̀:k thə:/
25. ฉันก็รักของฉัน/chǎn kɔ rák khɔ̌:ŋ chǎn/
26. เรื่องจริงยิ่งกว่านิยาย/rɨ̂əŋ cīŋ jîŋ kwà: nijā:j/
27. เธอจะรักฉันรึเปล่าไม่รู้
/thə̄: ca rák chǎn rɨpàw mâj rú:/
28. เรือเล็กควรออกจากฝั่ง/rɨ̄ə lék khūən ʔɔ̀:k cà:k fàŋ/
29. หูทวนลม/hǔ: thūənlōm/
30. ผ่านมาแค่ให้จำ/phà:n mā: khɛ̂: hâj cām/

Appendix B: Friedman and Wilcoxon test: Tone pairs that map with musical transition

	Wilcoxon test (Ascending and Descending compared)		Wilcoxon test (Ascending and Level compared)		Wilcoxon test (Descending and Level compared)		Friedman χ^2 test (All transition types compared)	
	Z	Asymp. Sig (2 – tailed)	Z	Asymp. Sig (2 – tailed)	Z	Asymp. Sig (2 – tailed)	χ^2	Asymp. Sig
MID→HIGH	-3.369	0.000**	-3.656	0.000**	-0.806	0.420	14.000	.001**
MID→RISING	-3.515	0.000**	-4.114	0.000**	-2.150	0.032*	20.484	.000**
MID→FALLING	-1.237	0.216	-2.680	0.007**	-3.447	0.001**	11.707	.003*
LOW→MID	-3.779	0.000**	-3.081	0.002**	-0.965	0.335	7.635	.022
LOW→FALLING	-3.408	0.001**	-1.883	0.060	-0.919	0.358	10.927	.004*
LOW→HIGH	-3.301	0.001**	-3.792	0.000**	-1.977	0.048*	17.175	.000**
LOW→RISING	-3.972	0.000**	-4.165	0.000**	-1.100	0.271	36.493	.000**

Table8: Tone pairs mapped with ascending note transitions
Note: N=30, *p<0.05; **p<0.01; Based on positive ranks

	Wilcoxon test (Descending and Ascending compared)		Wilcoxon test (Descending and Level compared)		Wilcoxon test (Ascending and Level compared)		Friedman χ^2 test (All transition type compared)	
	Z	Asymp. Sig (2 – tailed)	Z	Asymp. Sig (2 – tailed)	Z	Asymp. Sig (2 – tailed)	χ^2	Asymp. Sig
MID→LOW	-4.550	0.000**	-4.524	0.000**	-0.567	0.571	37.646	.000**
FALLING→LOW	-3.513	0.000**	-2.047	0.041*	-2.674	0.007**	15.085	.001*
FALLING→MID	-3.261	0.000**	-4.056	0.000**	-1.702	0.089	24.721	.000**
FALLING→FALLING	-3.204	0.001**	-2.016	0.044*	-0.747	0.455	12.064	.002*
HIGH→MID	-4.585	0.000**	-4.514	0.000**	-0.216	0.829	42.466	.000**
HIGH→LOW	-3.665	0.000**	-3.271	0.001**	-0.702	0.483	27.000	.000**
RISING→LOW	-3.035	0.002**	-3.471	0.001**	-0.612	0.541	18.406	.000**
RISING→MID	-4.214	0.000**	-4.551	0.000**	-1.646	0.100	37.163	.000**

Table9: Tone pairs mapped with descending note transitions
Notes: N=30, *p<0.05; **p<0.01; Based on positive ranks

	Wilcoxon test (Level and Ascending compared)		Wilcoxon test (Level and Descending compared)		Wilcoxon test (Ascending and Descending compared)		Friedman χ^2 test (All transitions types compared)	
	Z	Asymp. Sig (2 – tailed)	Z	Asymp. Sig (2 – tailed)	Z	Asymp. Sig (2 – tailed)	χ^2	Asymp. Sig
MID→MID	-2.9230.003**		-0.751	0.453	-3.309	0.001*	12.463	0.002*
LOW→LOW	-2.5970.009**		-2.951	0.003**	-2.957	0.009*	7.446	0.024*
FALLING→HIGH	-		-		-		2.742	0.254
FALLING→RISING	-0.0180.986		-2.999	0.003**	-2.999	0.003**	7.600	0.022*
HIGH→FALLING	-2.2980.022*		-1.500	0.133	-4.115	0.000**	26.687	0.000**
HIGH→HIGH	-2.691	0.007**	-2.041	0.041*	-0.423	0.673	6.416	0.040*
HIGH→RISING	-		-		-		0.747	0.688
RISING→FALLING	-2.737	0.006**	-1.919	0.055	-3.244	0.001*	12.341	0.002*
RISING→RISING	-		-		-		4.056	0.132
RISING→HIGH	-		-		-		0.700	0.705

Table10: Tone pairs mapped with level note transitions
Notes: N=30, *p<0.05; **p<0.01; Based on positive ranks

Appendix C: Friedman and Wilcoxon test:

	Wilcoxon test (Parallel and opposing compared)		Wilcoxon test (Parallel and non-opposing compared)		Wilcoxon test (Opposing and non-opposing compared)		Friedman χ^2 test (All type of relation compared)	
	Z	Asymp. Sig (2 – tailed)	Z	Asymp. Sig (2 – tailed)	Z	Asymp. Sig (2 – tailed)	χ^2	Asymp. Sig
	-4.783	0.000**	-4.783	0.000**	-4.283a	0.000**	55.882	0.000**

Table11: Mapping between directions of tonal and musical transitions
Note N=30, *p<0.05; **p<0.01; Based on negative ranks

Emphasized Accent Phrase Prediction from Text for Advertisement Text-To-Speech Synthesis

Hideharu Nakajima, Hideyuki Mizuno, and Sumitaka Sakauchi
NTT Media Intelligence Labs., NTT Corporation,
1-1 Hikarino-oka, Yokosuka, Kanagawa, 239-0847 JAPAN

Abstract

Realizing expressive text-to-speech synthesis needs both text processing and the rendering of natural expressive speech. This paper focuses on the former as a front-end task in the production of synthetic speech, and investigates a novel method for predicting emphasized accent phrases from advertisement text information. For this purpose, we examine features that can be accurately extracted by text processing based on current Text-to-speech synthesis technologies. Among features, the word surface string of the main content and function words and the part-of-speech of main function words in an accent phrase are found to have higher potential on predicting whether the accent phrase should be emphasized or not through the calculation of mutual information between emphasis label and features of Japanese advertisement sentences. Experiments confirm that emphasized accent phrase prediction using support vector machine (SVM) offers encouraging accuracies for the system which requires emphasized accent phrase locations as context information to improve speech synthesis qualities.

1 Introduction

The introduction of corpus-based speech synthesis methods such as unit selection synthesis ((Hunt, et al., 1996) etc.) and Hidden Markov Model speech synthesis ((Zen, et al., 2009) etc.) makes expressive speech synthesis possible if an adequate speech database is prepared. However, the synthesized speech often fails to recreate emphasis or phrase boundary tone, even though both are key characteristics of expressive speech. The location markers of emphasis and phrase boundary tone have been confirmed useful in improving expressive speech synthesis qualities; they form part of the context information for speech synthesis (Meng, et al., 2012; Maeno, et al., 2014; Strom, et al., 2007; Yu, et al., 2010).

For establishing Text-To-Speech (TTS) synthesis for expressive speech, it is necessary to predict locations of emphasis and phrase boundary tone *from the input text*. The phrase boundary tone occurs at the phrase end, and existence/non-existence of the tone can be accurately classified, from the text to be synthesized, by using machine learning approaches (Nakajima, et al., 2013; Ross, et al., 1996). Thus, this paper focuses on the remaining target of emphasis positions. In this work, we use the word "emphasis (emphasized)" to denote portions that are perceptually more salient to the listeners in a sentence.

In human speech, emphasis can be regrouped at least into four functions based on analysis in conventional literatures as (Hovy et. al, 2013; Sridhar et. al, 2008) (bold portions show emphasized words and phrases).

1. expressing linguistic "focus": (e.g., " **Taro** did." (as an answer to "who did ...?"))
2. expressing "contrast": (e.g., "not A **but B**")
3. expressing "element of surprise": (e.g., "I heard he was sick, but he had **much energy**.")
4. disambiguating grammatical structure: clarifying parallel and dependency structure (e.g., to distinguish "{old men} and women" from "**old** {men and women}" in "old men and women")

Copyright 2014 by Hideharu Nakajima, Hideyuki Mizuno, and Sumitaka Sakauchi
28th Pacific Asia Conference on Language, Information and Computation pages 170–177

This paper focuses on items 1 to 3. For the purpose of establishing TTS for expressive speech, item 4, structural disambiguation, is hard to resolve when the text has ambiguities. On the other hand, it is not a problem when there is no ambiguity; the prosodic structure can be accurately fixed by following the clear structure.

Emphasis on location of focus, contrast, and element of surprise (items 1 to 3) are related to the novelty status of the information to be conveyed; status is normally obtained from the context. In the conversation domain, conversation history is the previous context. Consider, for example, the example of item 1. The query "who?" is answered by "Taro", which is new information to the questioner and is often focused on and emphasized in the responder's speech. In the story telling domain, the sentences before the current sentence form the context, and are the source for judging the novelty status of information in the current sentence.

In some domains, however, the previous context does not always exist, for example, as in sales pitches or advertisements in mass media services. Sales pitch sentences are composed by copywriters based on their belief of what consumers will find newsworthy and only the sentences are read aloud and broadcasted. The sentence does not include the background that copywriters considered before fixing the sales pitch. Thus, narrators, actors/actress, directors, or producers decode the sales pitch sentence to extract which portions should be emphasized when read aloud. This suggests that it is possible to predict emphasized portions from the words of the sentence being synthesized.

This paper focuses on emphasis in Japanese advertisement sentences and defines accent phrases as the prediction unit, while words have been used as the unit for predicting emphasis in the conversation domain (Hovy et. al, 2013). Exclamation marks are one of the characters indicating emphasis in written texts; they are often observed in advertisement sentences and must be a good cue for emphasis prediction. The expressive speech database, explained in Section 2, includes examples of Japanese emphasized words (in bold style) with exclamation marks ('_' denotes word delimiter and translations are indicated by parentheses):

ex.1) その_**前**_に! (**before** that!)
ex.2) **楽しめ**_る! (you can **enjoy**!)
ex.3) 110_種類_**以上**! (**more than** 110 types!)
ex.4) 水換え_**不要**! (**don't need** water exchange!)

The words immediately before exclamation marks are not always emphasized as in the Japanese word sequences of ex.1 and 2. However, the marks must have influence on emphasized words beyond their intermediate neighbors. As units longer than words might effectively include this long distance influence and accent phrases are one of the important units for Japanese speech synthesis and some studies on Japanese speech synthesis have adopted accent phrases as a unit of emphasis and confirmed improvements in speech wave generation (Maeno, et al., 2014), we adopt accent phrases as the prediction unit as well.

This paper proposes a method for predicting emphasized accent phrases from sales pitch sentences to establish expressive TTS. As far as we know, this is the first paper that proposes the emphasis prediction from Japanese sales pitch sentences and adopts accent phrases as the prediction unit. Section 2 describes the expressive speech database used in this paper. Section 3 analyzes the distributions of emphasized accent phrases in terms of linguistic expressions and their locations in both sentences and intonation phrases. Section 4 explains our method of predicting emphasized accent phrases and its experimental confirmation.

2 Expressive speech database

2.1 Target domain

This paper targets sales pitch texts for expressive speech synthesis. Given the increase of Internet-oriented advertisements, it is essential to establish technologies that can convert advertisement text to speech with emphasis in the appropriate positions to ensure that the advertisements reach the consumers.

As ambiguous and misleading messages are not suitable as advertisements, we can expect that sales pitch texts do not include ambiguities, and so we can focus research efforts on emphasis prediction. Sales pitch texts are written in Japanese and are Japanese sentences collected from advertisement pages on the Internet (Nakajima, et al., 2010). These include expressions that appear frequently in sales as "発売中 (now on sale)" and "〜円 (Yen)" and describe impressions and explanations of commercial products.

Table 1: Emphasis labels

	accent phrase base count
emphasized	853
not-emphasized	1,506
	word base count
emphasized	1,010
not-emphasized	4,727

2.2 Emphasis labels

Although human annotators can tag speech data with emphasis labels, research has showed little agreement between human annotators (Hovy et. al, 2013), and thus prediction targets cannot be fixed. As a practical solution, we asked one human subject to act as a recording director and decide emphasized accent phrases with the guideline that "labels are put at accent phrases that tend to be emphasized in commercial message conveyed through mass media."

The sales pitch database (Nakajima, et al., 2010) includes 248 utterances, which are divided into 363 texts (hereafter, sentences) by punctuation marks, and include 2,359 accent phrases as in Table 1. Emphasis labels were assigned to 853 accent phrases (36.2% of all accent phrases) as shown in Table 1. As 89% of the labels coincided with the labels set by at least one of the 3 annotators (based on listening to speech data), the labels extracted from the text are considered appropriate as emphasized labels. As reference, we also labeled emphasized words in the emphasized accent phrases as in Table 1.

2.3 Features for analysis

As this study focuses on features contributing to emphasis prediction, we added correct linguistic features as follows: *word boundaries, part-of-speech (POS), accent phrase (AP) boundaries, pause positions*. These features can be accurately extracted by text processing modules in conventional TTS. The number of POS and lemma (Fuchi, et al., 1998) were 62 and 1,571, respectively.

We also automatically extracted, from above features, *main content and function word in each accent phrase* by rules frequently used in Japanese dependency parsing studies ((Imamura, et al., 2007) etc.). We also used these features in defining the portion between pauses as "intonation phrase (IP)", and entered the following binary information:

- *whether the IP is at the sentence end or not,*

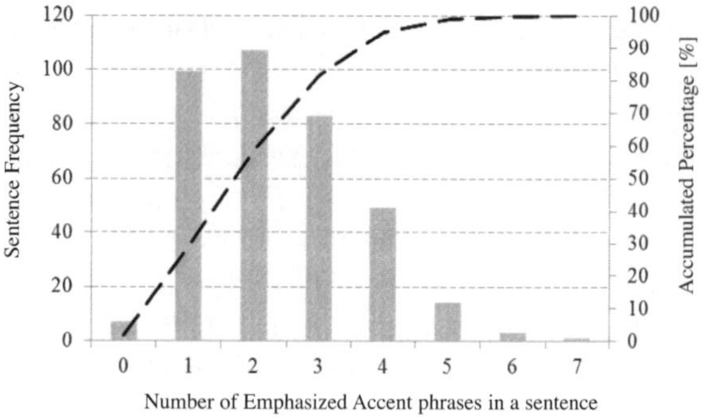

Figure 1: Sentence frequency associated with number of emphasized accent phrases in a sentence.

- *whether the AP is at the end of IP or not,*
- *existence/non-existence of exclamation marks, punctuation marks and pause at the end of the AP.*

By predetermined table look up, we also added

- *existence/non-existence of expressions on commercial products' information, evaluation, and prices in the AP*, and
- *existence/non-existence of sales-appeal words and qualifying words in the AP.*

Each word in the utterance including multiple sentences is examined if the word is mentioned in previous sentences in the utterance and

- the *existence/non-existence of words showing newness in the AP*

are added as another feature. Above features can be accurately assigned automatically because ambiguities are small. While semantic roles were used in (Hovy et. al, 2013), they are not used in our research, because automatic semantic role labeling is still immature and its accuracy remains insufficient and because our aim is to establish TTS and requires mature text processing.

3 Emphasized accent phrase distributions

As shown in Fig.1, about 70 percent of the sentences in the database have more than 2 emphasized accent phrases. Unlike conversation (Hovy et. al, 2013), sales pitch speech synthesis requires the extraction of multiple emphasized accent phrases per sentence.

With a view to identify phrase location, emphasized accent phrase distribution is summarized in Table 2. Rows differ based on whether IP is emphasized (Emphasized IP (E-IP) or Not Emphasized

Table 2: Distribution of emphasized accent phrases (IP=Intonation Phrase, AP=Accent Phrase, NE=Not Emphasized, E=Emphasized, F=Final, NF=Not Final), bold phrases in samples are emphasized accent phrases in both Japanese and translations

Location			IP ratio (%)	E-AP ratio (%)	Samples
NE-IP			21.6	0	
E-IP			78.4	100	
	NF-IP	NF-AP		26.1	… **すぐに** / 仕上げて … (… **soon** / do it up …)
		F-AP		16.5	… コレステロールが / **高めの方** … (… cholesterol / **person indicating higher** …)
	F-IP	NF-AP		20.5	**効果的に** / コリを / **ほぐして** / くれます (**effectively**/stiffness/**flexed**/will be)
		F-AP		36.8	… 乾燥肌で / **泣かないで**！ (… dry skin /**do not cry!**)

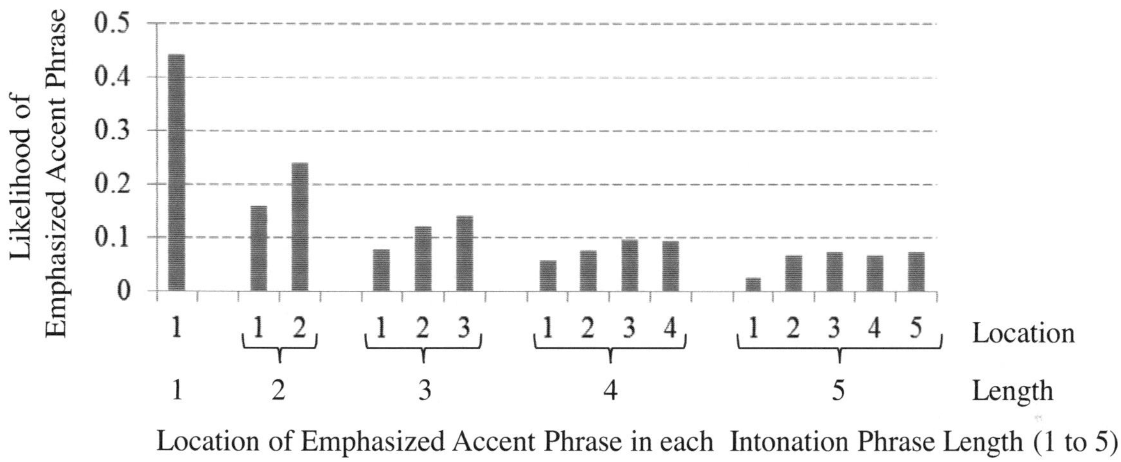

Figure 2: Likelihood of emphasized accent phrase by location in intonation phrase and its length.

IP (NE-IP)), whether IP exists at the end of sentence (Final IP (F-IP) or Not Final IP (NF-IP)), and whether AP exists at the end of IP (Final AP (F-AP) or Not Final AP (NF-AP)). Sample accent phrases are written in Japanese and divided by '/' and English translations for each accent phrase are written and divided by '/' in parentheses. The row of E-IP (Emphasized Intonation Phrase) shows that 78.4% of IPs have at least one emphasized AP.

The breakdown of E-IP lies in the four rows at the bottom of Table 2; the shares do not differ significantly (26.1, 16.5, 20.5 and 36.8 %). For detailed analysis, Fig.2 summarizes the likelihood of emphasized accent phrase by location in and length of intonation phrase whose lengths range from 1 to 5 (5 clusters correspond to length of intonation phrase). Upper number on the x axis denotes the location of emphasized accent phrase in each intonation phrase length. The larger the number is, the later in the intonation phrase does the emphasized accent phrase exist. Though later accent phrase locations showed higher likelihood of emphasized accent phrase, the likelihood values do not differ significantly. Thus, we decided to use *whether the IP is at the sentence end or not* and *whether the AP is at the end of IP or not* as location features in emphasized accent phrase distribution analysis.

We also measured the distance between two adjacent emphasized accent phrases; results are summarized in Fig. 3. 90% of emphasized accent phrases occurred within 0 to 4 accent phrases from the previous emphasized location. Thus, at most, the former

Table 3: Prediction potential

	Entropy $H(Y)$	0.94
1	Word surface string of the main content word in the AP	0.64
2	Word surface string of the main function word in the AP	0.15
3	Part-of-speech of the main function word in the AP	0.12
4	Whether the IP is at the sentence end or not	0.07
5	Existence/non-existence of exclamation marks at the end of the AP	0.07
6	Existence/non-existence of sales-appeal words in the AP	0.05
7	Existence/non-existence of expressions on commercial products' evaluation in the AP	0.05
8	Part-of-speech of the main content word in the AP	0.04
9	Whether the AP is at the end of IP or not	0.02
10	Existence/non-existence of pause at the end of the AP	0.02
11	Existence/non-existence of expressions on commercial products' information in the AP	0.01
12	Parallel structure	0.01
13	Existence/non-existence of punctuation marks at the end of the the AP	0.01
14	Existence/non-existence of expressions on commercial products' prices in the AP	0.01
15	Contrast structure	0.005
16	Existence/non-existence of words showing newness in the AP	0.001
17	Existence/non-existence of qualifying words in the AP	0.0006

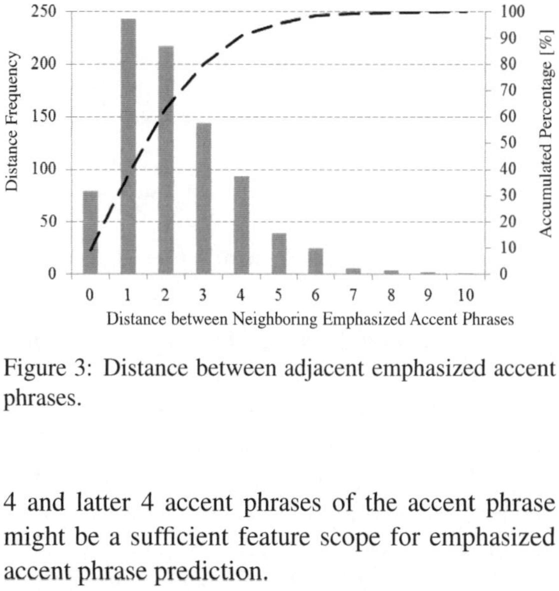

Figure 3: Distance between adjacent emphasized accent phrases.

4 and latter 4 accent phrases of the accent phrase might be a sufficient feature scope for emphasized accent phrase prediction.

To identify the promising features for emphasized accent phrase prediction, we also calculated the prediction potential of features (locations of accent phrases and linguistic expressions) based on the mutual information between those features and emphasis labels. Since the numbers of words and POS are large, we used the mutual information instead of the likelihood shown in Fig.2. When Y denotes emphasis label (emphasis or not), X each feature expression, $H(Y)$ entropy of Y, and $H(Y|X)$ is the conditional entropy of Y given X, then mutual information is calculated as $H(Y) - H(Y|X)$. The higher the mutual information value is, the greater is the contribution to emphasis prediction.

Table 3 lists prediction potentials in descending order with the first row showing entropy $H(Y)$. As the ratio of emphasized AP to not emphasized AP was almost 1 to 2, $H(Y)$ was 0.94 which is very high. Middle column in Table 3 lists the feature expressions mentioned so far and rightmost column shows mutual information values as prediction potential.

Word surface string of the main content word in the AP and *word surface string and part-of-speech of the main function word in the AP* showed higher mutual information (0.64, 0.15, 0.12, respectively) and are expected to contribute to emphasized accent phrase prediction. In the database, accent phrases accompanying exclamation marks at the end of the accent phrase are emphasized except for one sample, but too many accent phrases without the mark are emphasized, thus the mutual information was small (0.07). Though we also examined other binary features as "whether $\cdots$" and "existence/non-

Table 4: Range of parameters

Parameters	Range
dimension of polynomial kernel	1 to 4
cost of polynomial kernel	1 to 3
location index of features	-4 to 4
location index of past prediction results	-3 to -1

existence of $\cdots$" in Table 3 to confirm their contribution to prediction performance and the generality of features, their mutual information values were also small.

4 Emphasized accent phrase prediction

4.1 Prediction method

As more than 2 accent phrases are emphasized in an advertisement sentence as shown in Fig.1, we decided that the proposed method predicts multiple emphasized accent phrases in a sentence. As there are features that had few samples but whose probabilities are higher like exclamation marks, we consider emphasized accent phrase prediction as a classification problem between the existence/non-existence of emphasis. We used support vector machines (SVM) as classifiers and the features in Table 3 to establish and test the emphasized accent phrase prediction method.

4.2 Experimental conditions

The expressive speech database mentioned in section 2 were used for training and evaluating the SVM in 5-fold cross validation way. We used the polynomial kernel function of SVM and examined several parameter combinations of the kernel function (dimension and cost). Table 4 summarizes parameters and ranges. The dimension and cost are integers.

Others are indexes showing locations of accent phrases. 'i' denotes the location index of the accent phrase to be classified to emphasized or not, '-m' the location index of 'm' preceding accent phrase from i and 'n' the location index of 'n' following accent phrase from i. As we can use only past prediction results, maximum integer is '-1' for the location index of past prediction results.

For later description and discussion, F_{i-n}^{i+m} denotes the features between $(i-n)$ and $(i+m)$ locations, H_{i-n}^{i-h} the history of past prediction results between $(i-n)$ and $(i-h)$ locations, F_{i+1}^{i+m} a "future feature", F_{i-n}^{i-1} a "past feature," respectively.

Table 5: Accuracy definition ($\hat{E}$ and $\hat{N}$ are Emphasized and Not emphasized accent phrases as prediction results, E and N are Emphasized and Not emphasized accent phrases as answers,respectively, A, B, C, D are counts for each case, Accuracy is defined as $(A+D)/(A+B+C+D) \times 100$)

		Predicted results	
		$\hat{E}$	$\hat{N}$
Answers	E	A	B
	N	C	D

4.3 Evaluation measure

We used accuracy as the performance evaluation measure and evaluated the total accuracies of the proposed method using 5-fold cross validation. Accuracy is defined by the number of correctly predicted emphasis and not-emphasis ($A + D$ in Table 5) divided by the sum of the number of all 4 prediction results (in addition to the above 2 correct cases, the 2 other cases are that emphasis is erroneously classified as not-emphasis (B) and vice versa (C)): $Accuracy\ [\%] = (A+D)/(A+B+C+D) \times 100$.

4.4 Results

We examined 12 combinations of dimension (1 to 4) and cost (1 to 3) of the kernel function. Use of larger dimensions means combining more features. Better accuracies were obtained by larger dimensions than smaller dimensions. Cost values did not derive significant changes in accuracies for the same kernel dimension. Thus, we fixed dimension 4 and cost 1 and examined several scopes of features and history lengths of past prediction results.

Accuracy for test data varied from 74.1 to 77.4% under the feature scope changing from F_{i-4}^{i+4} to F_{i-1}^{i+1} and history changing from H_{i-4}^{i-1} to H_{i-1}^{i-1}. The smaller the feature scope and history length was, the better the accuracy was. As no use of future features F_{i+1}^{i+m} decreased accuracies slightly (0.2 to 0.6 points), future features somewhat contributes to prediction. No use of past prediction result H_{i-1}^{i-h} derived both slight increase (0.1 to 1.0) and decrease (0.2 to 0.3) of accuracies, but balance between recall

Table 6: Best prediction results at $F_{i-1}^{i+1} and H_{i-1}^{i-1}$ ($\hat{E}$, $\hat{N}$, E, N are the same as in Table 5)

		Predicted results		recall
		$\hat{E}$	$\hat{N}$	
Answers	E	548	305	64.2%
	N	228	1278	
precision		70.6%		
accuracy				77.4%

and precision of emphasized accent phrases became worse.

Based on these results and as we consider that both emphasized and not-emphasized cases should be correctly predicted, we chose using both future features and past prediction results. As a result, the best accuracy was 77.4% at F_{i-1}^{i+1} and H_{i-1}^{i-1} (-1 only), then recall and precision rates of emphasized accent phrase were 64.2% and 70.6%, respectively. Detailed prediction results were shown in Table 6.

As far as we know, there is no research for predicting emphasized accent phrases from Japanese advertisement text. As baseline calculations, if all the accent phrases are predicted emphasized ($\hat{E}$), accuracy is 36.2% and the recall and precision of emphasized accent phrases are 100% and 36.2%, respectively. On the other hand, if all the accent phrases are predicted non-emphasized ($\hat{N}$), accuracy is 63.8%, then both recall and precision of emphasized accent phrases are 0%. Thus, the proposed method offered 13.6 points higher accuracy than these above forced predictions.

Since Fig. 2 showed lowest likelihood of emphasized accent phrase at the top of each IP, we also examined another feature of *whether the AP is at the top of IP or not*. The feature showed smaller prediction potential 0.005 than the 9th feature in Table 3 (0.02) and did not offer prediction accuracy improvements.

5 Conclusion

This paper proposed a method for predicting which portions of an advertisement text should be emphasized; it uses only the text itself. The method uses accent phrases as the prediction unit and the features obtained by the text processing modules of current Text-to-speech synthesis systems. According to mutual information, features such as *word surface string of the main content and function word* and *part-of-speech of the main function word* offer higher prediction potential. Experiments showed the proposed method yielded encouraging accuracies for such an expressive TTS which uses emphasized accent phrase locations as a context information as (Maeno, et al., 2014). Accuracy improvement was left as a future work.

References

Takeshi Fuchi and Shin'ichiro Takagi. 1998. "Japanese morphological analyzer using word co-occurrence: JTAG" *Proceedings of Coling-ACL*, 409–413.

Dirk Hovy, Gopala Krishna Anumanchipalli, Alok Parlikar, Caroline Vaughn, Adam Lammert, Eduard Hovy, and Alan W. Black. 2013. "Analysis and Modeling of Focus in Context" *Proceedings of INTERSPEECH*, 402–406.

Andrew J. Hunt and Alan W. Black. 1996. "Unit selection in a concatenative speech synthesis system using a large speech database," *Proceedings of ICASSP*, 373–376.

Kenji Imamura, Gen'ichiro Kikui, and Norihito Yasuda. 2007. "Japanese dependency parsing using sequential labeling for semi-spoken language" *Proceedings of ACL*, 225–228.

Yu Maeno, Takashi Nose, Takao Kobayashi, Tomoki Koriyama, Yusuke Ijima, Hideharu Nakajima, Hideyuki Mizuno, and Osamu Yoshioka. 2014. "Prosodic variation enhancement using unsupervised context labeling for HMM-based expressive speech synthesis," *Speech Communication*, 57: 144–154.

Fanbo Meng, Zhiyong Wu, Helen Meng, Jia Jia and Lianhong Cai. 2012. "Hierarchical English emphatic speech synthesis based on HMM with limited training data," *Proceedings of INTERSPEECH*, Mon.P2b.09.

Hideharu Nakajima, Noboru Miyazaki, Akihiko Yoshida, Takashi Nakamura, Hideyuki Mizuno. 2010. "Creation and Analysis of a Japanese Speaking Style Parallel Database for Expressive Speech Synthesis" *Proceedings of Oriental COCOSDA*, paper id 30.

Hideharu Nakajima, Hideyuki Mizuno, Osamu Yoshioka, and Satoshi Takahashi. 2013. "Which resemblance is useful to predict phrase boundary rise labels for Japanese expressive text-to-speech synthesis, numerically-expressed stylistic or distribution-based semantic?" *Proceedings of INTERSPEECH*, 1047–1051.

Ken Ross and Mari Ostendorf. 1996. "Prediction of abstract labels for speech synthesis" *Computer Speech & Language*, 10(3): 155–185.

Virek Kumar Rangarajan Sridhar, Ani Nenkova, Shrikanth Narayanan, Dan Jurafsky. 2008. "Detecting prominence in conversational speech: pitch accent, givenness and focus" *Proceedings of Speech Prosody*, 453–456.

Volker Strom, Ani Nenkova, Robert Clark, Yolanda Vazquez-Alvarez, Jason Brenier, Simon King, and Dan Jurafsky. 2007. "Modelling prominence and emphasis improves unit-selection synthesis," *Proceedings of INTERSPEECH*, 1282–1285.

Kai Yu, François Mairesse, and Steve Young. 2010. "Word-level emphasis modelling in HMM-based speech synthesis," *Proceedings of ICASSP*, 4238–4241.

Heiga Zen, Keiichi Tokuda and Alan W. Black. 2009. "Statistical parametric speech synthesis," *Speech Communication*, 51(11): 1039–1064.

Using Tone Information in Thai Spelling Speech Recognition

Natthawut Kertkeidkachorn
[1]Department of Computer Engineering, Chulalongkorn University Bangkok, Thailand
[2]Department of Informatics The Graduate University for Advanced Studies, Tokyo, Japan
Natthawut@nii.ac.jp

Proadpran Punyabukkana
Department of Computer Engineering, Chulalongkorn University Bangkok, Thailand
Proadpran.p@chula.ac.th

Atiwong Suchato
Department of Computer Engineering, Chulalongkorn University Bangkok, Thailand
Atiwong.s@chula.ac.th

Abstract

Spelling recognition is a workaround to recognize unfamiliar words, such as proper names or unregistered words in a dictionary, which typically cause ambiguous pronunciations. In the Thai spelling task, some alphabets cannot be differentiated by only spectral cues. In such cases, tonal cues play a critical role in distinguishing those alphabets. In this paper, we therefore introduce Thai spelling speech recognition, in which a tonal score, which represents a tonal cue, is adopted in order to re-rank N-best hypotheses of the first pass search of a speech recognition system. The Hidden Conditional Random Field (HCRF)-based Thai tone recognition, which was reported as the best approach for Thai tone recognition, is selected to provide tonal scores. Experimental results indicate that our approach provides the best error rate reduction of 23.85% from the baseline system, which is a conventional Hidden Markov Model (HMM)-based speech recognition system. Besides, another finding is that exploiting tonal scores in Thai spelling speech recognition could significantly reduce the ambiguity among some alphabets.

1 Introduction

A spelling speech recognition system plays an important role in many kinds of applications, of which a domain contains unfamiliar words such as proper names. Since those words might not be pronounced straight-forwardly, an automatic speech recognition (ASR) system would have difficulty to recognize such words correctly. A practical efficient solution for handling such words in an ASR system is to pronounce them letter by letter.

Nevertheless, in tonal languages, especially Thai, a spelling recognition task is a challenging task because merely consonantal sound and vowel sound cannot perfectly distinguish Thai alphabets. For example the "ข" alphabet and the "ค" alphabet are pronounced as \k^{h}ɔ:\. Although the consonantal sound and the vowel sound of those alphabets are similar, their tones are significantly different. For the "ข" alphabet, its tonal sound is the rising tone, while the tonal sound of the "ค" alphabet is the mid tone. In Thai, tone information therefore not only expresses prosody as usual but also transmits explicit information, which characterizes lexical meanings of words (Luksaneeyanawin 1998).

In this paper, we therefore introduce a Thai spelling speech recognition employing tonal scores, which can represent tonal information, in order to re-rank N-best hypotheses according to the first pass search of an ASR system. The Hidden Conditional Random Field (HCRF)-based Thai tone recognition, which had been reported as the state of the art for Thai tone recognition

Copyright 2014 by Natthawut Kertkeidkachorn, Proadpran Punyabukkana, and Atiwong Suchato
28th Pacific Asia Conference on Language, Information and Computation pages 178–184

(Kertkeidkachorn et al. 2014), is selected to provide tonal scores.

The rest of the paper is organized as follows. In Section 2, background knowledge on Thai spelling system is introduced and related works are reviewed and discussed in the following section. Section 4 presents our Thai spelling recognition approach. Then, the HCRF-based approach for Thai tone recognition is described in the next section. Experiments and results are presented in Section 6 and experimental results are discussed in Section 7. Eventually, we conclude our work in the last section.

2 Thai Spelling

In the Thai spelling task, a sequence of Thai alphabets, which can be consonantal alphabets, vowel alphabets, tone symbols, or punctuation symbols, is pronounced. The pronunciation of consonantal alphabet has two possible variations: a consonantal alphabet and a consonantal alphabet with its extension. The alphabet extension is a word or a phrase which follows that alphabet in order to distinguish that alphabet from others. For example, the "ข" (kh-@@-z^-4) alphabet is followed by the extension word "ไข่" (kh-a-j^-1) as "ข. ไข่" (kh-@@-z^-4 kh-a-j^-1), while the extension word of the "ฃ" (kh-@@-z^-4) alphabet is "ขวด" (kh-uua-t^-1) pronounced as "ฃ. ขวด" (kh-@@-z^-4 kh-uua-t^-1). This characteristic is similar to uttering "A alpha" or "B beta" in English (NATO phonetic alphabet 2014) but occurs much more frequently. For Thai vowel alphabets and tone symbols, there are also two possible pronunciation patterns which come from the presence or the absence of indicative words, "สระ" and "ไม้", before vowel alphabets and tone symbols respectively. Punctuation marks are uttered by their actual names. In Table 1, Thai Alphabet patterns and their examples are presented.

Type	Pattern	Example
Consonantal	Base name	ก
	Base name + Extension	ก ไก่
Vowel	Base name	อา
	(s-a-z^-1 r-a-z^-1) + Base name	สระอา
Tone	Base name	เอก
	(m-a-j^4) + Base name	ไม้เอก
Punctuation	Base name	จุลภาค

Table 1: Thai Alphabet Patterns and their examples

3 Related Work

In tonal languages, tone information has been investigated and exploited in many research works in order to improve performances of ASR systems. In Chinese, Lee et al. (2002) expanded syllable lattices via recognized tone patterns to improve the performance of Cantonese large-vocabulary continuous speech recognition (LVCSR). Their results indicated that reliable tone information could improve the overall performance of Cantonese LVCRS. Later, Lei et al. (2006) then utilized tone models for improving Mandarin broadcast news speech recognition. With exploiting tone information, their experiment significantly indicated the improvement of the ASR system. Wei et al. (2008) also explored Conditional Random Field (CRF)-based tone modeling to re-rank hypotheses generated from the first pass search of an ASR system. Their results showed that tone information could really help to improve the performance of the ASR system. In Vietnamese, which is also one of tonal languages, Quang et al. (2008) succeeded in improving the performance of Vietnamese LVCSR by utilizing tone information. In Thai, Chaiwongsai et al. (2008) proposed HMM-based isolated-word speech recognition with a tone detection function. With the tone detection function, tone results were considered together with word results in order to compute the final result. Their experiment reported that the performances of Thai isolated-word speech recognition were improved. Pisarn and Theeramunkong (2006) investigated tone features and these features were incorporated into their HMM-based Thai system in order to improve Thai spelling recognition.

Based on discussed works, in tonal languages exploiting tone information to an ASR system had directly contributed to its performances. We therefore aim to exploit reliable tone information in order to improve the performance of Thai spelling recognition.

4 A Thai Spelling Recognition Approach

In our approach, Thai spelling speech recognition incorporating a tone recognizer providing tone information, which can help to recognize alphabets more accurately, is proposed as shown in Figure 1.

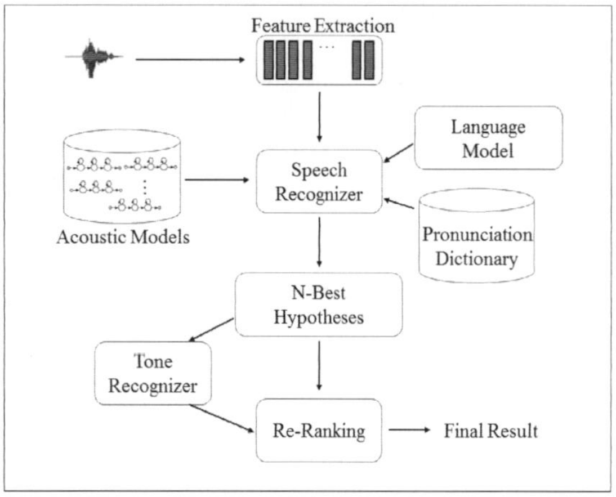

Figure 1: A Thai Spelling Recognition Approach

Acoustical feature vectors is extracted from an speech signal as an acoustic observation sequence (O) capturing spectral shapes of the signal via the feature extraction process and then these acoustical feature vectors are conveyed to the speech recognizer in order to recognize the word. With acoustical feature vectors, trained acoustic models, a language model and a pronunciation dictionary, the speech recognizer is to generate N-best hypotheses for the input speech signal. Generally, when N-best hypotheses are generated, the best hypothesis will be selected as the result. Nevertheless, in our approach the best hypothesis is not immediately decided yet. N-best hypotheses are fed to a tone recognizer in order to compute tonal scores. After that those N-best hypotheses are re-ranked according to their acoustic score ($\log(P(O/W))$), which is the probability of the acoustic observation sequence O given the hypothesis W, their language score ($\log(P(W))$), which is the probability of the hypothesis W, and their tonal score ($\log(P(T/W))$), which is the probability of the tone sequence T given the hypothesis W. The best hypothesis (W') is computed as follows:

$$W' = \arg\max_{W} (\log(P(O \mid W)) + \log(P(W)) + w \log(P(T \mid W))) \quad (1)$$

, where W is a hypothesis from N-Best hypotheses and w is a weight for the tonal score.

In our approach, we do not directly embedded tone features into the speech recognizer as reported in Pisarn and Theeramunkong's study (2006) due to the feature extraction problem. Typically fundamental frequency (F_0) movements are selected as the representation of tone information. Nonetheless, in unvoiced parts or silent parts, F_0 movements would be absent. Consequently, tone information might not be steady. Our workaround is to compute tonal scores only on voiced parts of words, which are provided by the speech recognizer, instead.

5 HCRF-Based Tone Recognition

Since our Thai spelling speech recognition approach depends on performances of Thai tone recognition, the HCRF-based Thai tone recognition (Kertkeidkachorn et al. 2014), which had been reported as the best approach for Thai tone recognition, is selected to calculate tonal scores. Given the hypothesis W, which is a sequence of syllables ($W = s_1s_2s_3...s_n$; s_i = the ith syllable of the hypothesis W), the probability of the tone sequence (T) corresponding to the hypothesis W given the hypothesis W ($P(T|W)$) is computed through the following equation:

$$\log(P(T \mid W)) = \sum_{i=1}^{n} \log(P(t_i \mid s_i)) \quad (2)$$

, where t_i is the tone of the ith syllable of the hypothesis W ($T = t_1t_2t_3...t_n$) and t_i is directly associated with s_i. Although $P(T|W)$ is a kind of measurement for the tone sequence T given the hypothesis W, its value is very small. We therefore take logarithm functions on its value and referred it as the tonal score.

Even though the HCRF-based Thai tone recognition reported by Kertkeidkachorn et al. (2014) outperformed other approaches, still, their work limited their acoustical features to F_0's values and their derivative. In the Thai tone perception study, Kertkeidkachorn et al. (2012(a)) found that spectral information could contribute to the tone perception of Thai native speakers. We therefore assumed that spectral information might contribute to the HCRF-based tone recognition as well. A preliminary experiment was conducted to prove our assumption. This preliminary experiment was conducted under the Thai tone continuous speech recognition scenario and all configurations in the preliminary experiment are also similar to Kertkeidkachorn's work (2014). Nonetheless, two further acoustical features, which were widely used in many ASR systems, were investigated by appending each of them into Kertkeidkachorn's tone feature in order to measure the improvement of the HCRF-based tone recognition. Mel-frequency Cepstral Coefficients (MFCC) and Perceptual Linear Predictive coefficients (PLP) were chosen to represent the spectral information of speech signals in the preliminary experiment. Results of the preliminary experiment are shown in Table 2.

Approach	Accuracy (%)
Kertkeidkachorn's work	71.01
Appending MFCC	74.91
Appending PLP	**75.04**

Table 2: % Accuracy results of the tone recognition in the preliminary experiment

According to the results of the preliminary experiment on the HCRF-based tone recognition, appending the PLP-based feature yields the best accuracy result. Besides, appending the PLP-based feature into tone features can provide an error rate reduction of 13.90% from what reported in Kertkeidkachorn's work (2014). We also notice that appending the MFCC-based feature gives better results than what reported in Kertkeidkachorn's work (2014) as well. The findings conform to our assumption in which spectral information could contribute to the performance of the HCRF-based Thai tone recognition as well. We therefore append the PLP-based feature into the tone feature of the HCRF-based Thai tone recognition.

6 Experiments and Results

6.1 Experimental Setting

In the experiment, the CU-MFEC corpus for Thai and English spelling speech recognition (Kertkeidkachorn et al. 2012(b)) is selected to evaluate our approach. The experiment is conducted on randomly selected speech data of 50 speakers from the alphabet with short pause set of the corpus. And, only Thai alphabets are considered in the experiment. Speech data of 40 speakers is randomized as the training data and the rest of the speech data is used as the testing data.

The speech recognizer in our approach is a traditional HMM-based speech recognizer of which models represented 135 Thai alphabets. Our models do not represent normal phoneme units because when tonal units are included, there are 375 model units which are more than 135 models of Thai alphabets. To represent speech frames, the standard 39-dimensional MFCC feature vectors are extracted at every 10 ms and each of the speech frames is windowed with 25 ms-Hamming window. Because a left to right HMM model was used to represent a context dependent Thai alphabet, of which duration is typically longer than usual phoneme duration, we also conduct another preliminary experiment to adjust a number of states of a HMM model and also fine-tune a number of appropriate Gaussian mixtures for our recognizer. Results are presented in Table 3.

No. of states	No. of Gaussian Mixtures					
	1	2	4	8	16	32
3	39.56	45.26	63.26	67.93	70.30	68.59
4	52.15	60.00	74.96	75.63	79.33	76.22
5	58.96	67.56	80.52	81.26	81.41	81.63
6	60.59	76.00	82.22	81.41	83.04	81.33
7	62.30	76.67	81.70	82.00	**84.15**	81.78
8	65.26	77.26	81.26	80.74	82.96	80.30

Table 3: % Accuracy results of the baseline varied by a number of states and a number of Gaussian mixtures

Based on results, a seven-stated HMM and 16-coponent Gaussian Mixtures with diagonal covariance matrices yields the best accuracy result at 84.15%. Therefore, this setting is set as the setting of the speech recognizer in our approach and also is referred as *baseline*.

After the first pass search of the speech recognizer, N-best hypotheses are generated. In the experiment, N is set at 135 equal to the number of Thai alphabets, so that possible hypotheses could be generated. To build the HCRF-based tone recognizer of which models represented five Thai tones, the HCRF Library (Morency et al. 2012) is used with the following setting. To represent speech frames, F_0 values, their delta and their acceleration together with the standard 39-dimensional PLP-based feature are combined as a tonal feature vector. Tonal feature vectors are extracted every 10 ms with 25-ms Hamming window. In the HCRF library, GHRF is set as the type of the model. A number of hidden states are set at 3 states due to the characteristic of Thai tones, which basically consist of three parts (Kertkeidkachorn et al. 2014), and initial weights of vectors are computed from mean and variances of each acoustic feature. The optimization method is configured as Limited-memory Broyden–Fletcher–Goldfarb–Shanno (L-BFGS) with L2 cache. Testing on the testing data, our tone recognizer provides accuracy of 87.79%. In the experiment, the parameter w for weighting a tonal score in Equation 1 is adjusted in order to find the best setting and study effects of tonal weights on Thai spelling speech recognition.

6.2 Experimental Results

Results of adjusting the tonal weight w are shown in Figure 1. Our approach obtains the best accuracy of 87.93% and also provides 23.85% relative error rate reduction from the baseline, when w is at 52.

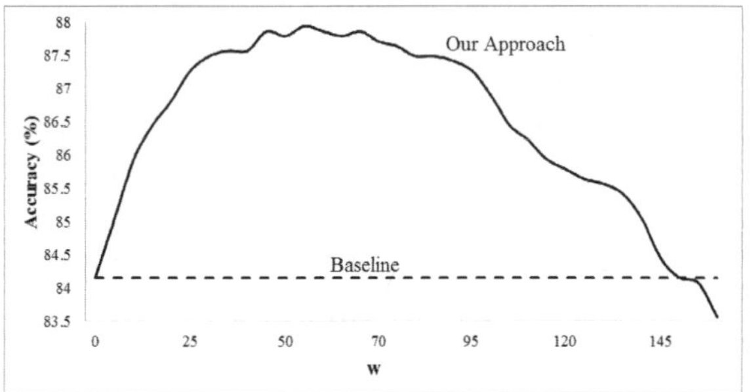

Figure 2: % Accuracy results when w parameter is adjusted

7 Discussion

In our approach, according to experimental results, adjusting the tonal weight w clearly affects the recognition accuracies of the Thai spelling task. At first, when w is increased, the recognition accuracy also tends to be increase. Nevertheless, when w becomes more than 52, the recognition performance is declined because acoustic scores and language scores are initially governed by tonal scores. Furthermore, after w is more than 150, tonal scores completely dominated results. The recognition accuracies of our approach become worse than the baseline. We therefore can conclude that tonal scores acquired from tonal cues could help improve Thai spelling speech recognition in case that the tonal weight w is set appropriately; however either acoustic scores or language scores are still far more important.

The significant testing is also conducted on experimental results to compare the recognition accuracy of Thai alphabets of the baseline with the best result of our approach, in which w is set at 52. The Mcnemar's test (Gillick and Cox 1989) is used to evaluate the statistical significance of accuracy results. The test result indicates that our approach, in which tonal cues had contributed to recognition results, statistically outperforms the baseline with p-value less than 0.01.

Paired alphabets are groups of alphabets, in which consonantal sound and vowel sound are similar but the tonal sound is different. For example, a group of the alphabets ช and ฌ pronounces as ch-@@-z^-0, while a group of the alphabet ฉ utters as ch-@@-z^-4. Without tone information, paired alphabets are difficult to differentiate their group from the other group. The error confusions between paired alphabets in the baseline and our approach are shown in Table 3. Error confusion is measured from the error that paired alphabets in the target group are misrecognized as the other group. Considering error confusion on Table 3, we found that our approach, in which tonal scores are adopted, could reduce the error confusion in any paired alphabet groups.

Paired Alphabets	Error Confusion (%)	
	Baseline	Our Approach
(ช, ฌ) - (ฉ)	3.3	0.0
(ซ) - (ษ, ศ, ส)	5.0	0.0
(พ, ภ) - (ผ)	10.0	0.0
(ฑ, ฒ, ท, ธ) - (ฐ, ถ)	11.7	0.0
(ค, ฅ, ฆ) - (ข, ฃ)	24.0	2.0
(ฮ) - (ห)	25.0	5.0
(ฟ) - (ฝ)	25.0	15.0

Table 2: Error confusion comparing between paired alphabets in the baseline and our approach

Based on our discussion, we could conclude that the tone information is necessary for improving Thai spelling speech recognition, especially in case of confusions between paired alphabets.

8 Conclusion

Recently, in tonal languages, there are many researches utilizing tone information in many kinds of ASR systems, especially where the language modeling could partly help to recognize words, such as a spelling recognition task.

This paper introduces a Thai spelling speech recognition approach, in which tonal scores acquired from the HCRF-based Thai tone recognizer, which had been reported as the state of the art for Thai tone recognition, are employed. Furthermore, this paper also explores the performance of the HCRF-based Thai tone recognizer by applying the PLP-based feature representing spectral information to improve its performance so that more reliable tone information could be provided for our approach. Experimental results evidently show that tonal scores significantly contribute to the performance of Thai spelling speech recognition, when the weight of the tonal score is adjusted properly.

Still, further factors could definitely contribute to the recognition accuracies of the Thai spelling task beyond what reported in this paper.

References

Sudaporn Luksaneeyanawin, 1998. Intonation in Thai. In Intonation Systems a Survey of Twenty Languages, Cambridge University Press, 1998, ch. 21, pp. 376–394.

Natthawut Kertkeidkachorn, Proadpran Punyabukkana and Atiwong Suchato. 2014. A Hidden Conditional Random Field-Based Approach for Thai Tone Classification, In Engineering Journal, 18(3):99-122.

NATO phonetic alphabet. 2014. In Wikipedia, The Free Encyclopedia. Retrieved 08:43, August 3, 2014, from http://en.wikipedia.org/w/index.php?title=NATO_phonetic_alphabet&oldid=618764363

Tan Lee, Wai Lau, Y. W. Wong and P. C. Ching, 2002. Using tone information in Cantonese continuous speech recognition, ACM Transactions on Asian Language Information Processing, 1(1):83-102

Xin Lei, Manhung Siu, Mei-Yuh Hwang, Mari Ostendorf and Tan Lee. 2006. Improved tone modeling for Mandarin broadcast news speech recognition, In Proc. Interspeech 2006.

Hongxiu Wei, Xinhao Wang, Hao Wu, Dingsheng Luo and Xihong Wu. 2008. Exploiting Prosodic and lexical Feature for Tone Modeling in a Conditional Random Field Framework, In Proceedings of ICASSP 2008.

Nguyen Hong Quang, Nocera Pascal, Castelli Eric and Trinh Van Loan. 2008. Using tone information for Vietnamese continuous speech recognition, In Proceedings of RIVF 2008.

Jirabhorn Chaiwongsai, Werapon Chiracharit, Kosin Chamnongthai and Yoshikazu Miyanaga. 2008. An Architecture of HMM-Based Isolated-Word Speech Recognition with Tone Detection Function, In proceedings of ISPACS 2008.

Chutima Pisarn and Thanaruk Theeramunkong 2006. Improving Thai spelling recognition with tone features, Lecture Notes in Artificial Intelligence 4139: 388-398.

Natthawut Kertkeidkachorn, Surapol Vorapatratorn, Sirinart Tangruamsub,Proadpran Punyabukkana and Atiwong Suchato 2012(a). Contribution of spectral shapes to tone perception, In Proceedings of Interspeech 2012.

Natthawut Kertkeidkachorn, Supadaech Chanjaradwichai, Teera Suri, Krerksak Likitsupin, Surapol Vorapatratorn, Pawanrat Hirankan, Worasa Limpanadusadee, Supakit Chuetanapinyo, Kitanan Pitakpawatkul, Natnarong Puangsri, Nathacha Tangsirirat, Konlawachara Trakulsuk, Proadpran Punyabukkana and Atiwong Suchato. 2012(b). The CU-MFEC corpus for Thai and English spelling speech recognition, In Proceedings of Oriental-COCOSDA 2012.

Louis-Philippe Morency, Ariadna Quattoni, C. Mario Christoudias and Sybor Wang 2012. Hidden-state

Conditional Random Field (HCRF) Library, Online at http://sourceforge.net/projects/hcrf/.

L. Gillick and S.J. Cox, 1989. Some statistical issues in the comparison of speech recognition algorithms, In Proceedings of ICASSP 1989:532-535.

Automatically Building a Corpus for Sentiment Analysis on Indonesian Tweets

Alfan Farizki Wicaksono, Clara Vania, Bayu Distiawan T., Mirna Adriani
Information Retrieval Lab.
Faculty of Computer Science, University of Indonesia
Depok, Republic of Indonesia
{alfan, c.vania, b.distiawan, mirna}@cs.ui.ac.id

Abstract

The popularity of the user generated content, such as Twitter, has made it a rich source for the sentiment analysis and opinion mining tasks. This paper presents our study in automatically building a training corpus for the sentiment analysis on Indonesian tweets. We start with a set of seed sentiment corpus and subsequently expand them using a classifier model whose parameters are estimated using the Expectation and Maximization (EM) framework. We apply our automatically built corpus to perform two tasks, namely opinion tweet extraction and tweet polarity classification using various machine learning approaches. Experiment result shows that a classifier model trained on our data, which is automatically constructed using our proposed method, outperforms the baseline system in terms of opinion tweet extraction and tweet polarity classification.

1 Introduction

There are millions of textual messages or posts generated by internet users everyday on various user generated content platfroms, such as microblogs (e.g. Twitter[1]), review websites, and internet forums. They post about their stories, experiences, current events that are happening, as well as opinions about products. As a result, the user generated content has become a rich source for mining useful information about various topics.

Twitter, one the popular microblogging platforms, is currently getting a lot of attention from internet users because it allows users to easily and instantly post their thoughts of various topics. Twitter currently has over 200 million active users and produce 400 million posts each day [2]. The posts, known as tweets, often contain useful knowledge so that many researchers focus on Twitter for conducting NLP-related research. McMinn et al. (2014) harnessed millions of tweets to develop an application for detecting, tracking, and visualizing events in real-time. Previously, Sakaki et al. (2013) also used twitter as a sensor for earthquake reporting system. They claimed that the system can detect an earthquake with high probability merely by monitoring tweets and the notification can be delivered faster than Japan Meteorology Agency announcements. Moreover, Tumasjan et al. (2010) demostrated that Twitter can also be used as a resource for political forecasting.

Due to the nature of Twitter, tweets usually express peoples personal thoughts or feelings. Therefore, tweets serve as good resources for sentiment analysis and opinion mining tasks. Many companies can benefit from tweets to know how many positive responses and/or negative responses towards their products as well as the reasons why consumers like/dislike their products. They can also leverage tweets to gain a lot of insight about their competitors. Consumers can also use information from tweets regarding the quality of a certain product. They commonly learn from peoples past experiences who have already used the product before they decide to purchase it. To realize the aforementioned

[1] http://twitter.com

[2] https://blog.twitter.com/2013/celebrating-twitter7

Copyright 2014 by Alfan Farizki Wicaksono, Clara Vania, Bayu Distiawan T., and Mirna Adriani
28th Pacific Asia Conference on Language, Information and Computation pages 185–194

ideas, many researchers have put a lot of effort to tackle one of the important tasks on Twitter sentiment analysis, that is, tweet polarity classification (Nakov et al., 2013; Hu et al., 2013; Kouloumpis et al., 2011; Agarwal et al., 2011; Pak and Paroubek, 2010). They proposed various approaches to determine whether a given tweet expresses positive or negative sentiment.

In this paper, we address the problem of sentiment analysis on Indonesian tweets. Indonesian language itself currently has more than 240 millions of speakers spread in mostly areas of south-east asia. In addition, Semiocast, a company who provides data intelligence and research on social media, has revealed that Indonesia ranked 5th in terms of Twitter accounts in July 2012 and users from Jakarta city (i.e. capital city of Indonesia) were the most active compared to the users from other big cities, such as Tokyo, London, and New York [3]. Therefore, there is absolutely a great need for natural language processing research on Indonesian tweets, especially sentiment analysis, since there would be a lot of information which is worth obtaining for many purposes. Unfortunately, Indonesian language is categorized as an under-resourced language because it still suffers from a lack of basic resources (especially labeled dataset) needed for a various language technologies.

There are two tasks addressed in this paper, namely opinion tweet extraction and tweet polarity classification. The former task is aimed at selecting all tweets comprising users' opinion towards something and the latter task is to determine the polarity type of an opinionated tweet (i.e., positive or negative tweet). To tackle the aforementioned tasks, we employ machine learning approach using training data and word features. However, a problem then appears when we do not have annotated data to train our models. Asking people to manually annotate thousands, even millions of tweets with high quality is not our choice since it is very expensive and time-consuming due to the massive scale and rapid growth of Twitter.

To overcome the aforementioned problem, we propose a method that can automatically develop training data from a pool of millions of tweets. First, we automatically construct a small set of labeled seed corpus (i.e. small collection of positive and negative tweets) that will be used for expanding the training data in the next step. Next, we expand the training data using the previously constructed seed corpus. To do that, we use the rationale that sentiment can be propagated from the labeled seed tweets to the other unlabeled tweets when they share similar word features, which means that the sentiment type of an unlabeled tweet can be revealed based on its closeness to the labeled tweets. Based on that idea, we employ a classifier model whose parameters are estimated using labeled and unlabeled tweets via Expectation and Maximization (EM) framework. In this method, we incorporate two types of dataset: the first dataset is a small set of labeled seed tweets and the second dataset is a huge set of unlabeled tweets that serve as a source for expanding the training data. Intuitively, this method allows us to propagate sentiment from labeled tweets to unlabeled tweets. Later, we show that the training data automatically constructed by our method can be used by the classifiers to effectively tackle the problem of opinion tweet extraction and tweet polarity classification.

In summary, the main contributions of this paper is two-folds: first, we present a method to automatically construct training instances for sentiment analysis on Indonesian tweets. Second, we show some significant works for sentiment analysis on Indonesian tweets which were rarely addressed before.

2 Related Works

There have been extensive works on opinion mining and sentiment analysis as described in (Pang and Lee, 2008). They presented various approaches and general challenges to develop applications that can retrieve opinion-oriented information. Moreover, Liu (2007) clearly mentions the definition of opinionated sentence as well as describes two sub-tasks required to perform sentence-level sentiment analysis, namely, subjectivity classification and sentence-level sentiment classification. However, previous researchers primarily focused on performing sentiment analysis on review data. The trends has shifted recently when social networking platform, such as Facebook and Twitter, has been growing rapidly. As

[3] http://semiocast.com/en/publications/2012_07_30_Twitter_reaches_half_a_billion_accounts_140m_in_the_US

a result, many researchers has now started to perform sentiment analysis on microblogging platform, such as twitter (Hu et al., 2013; Nakov et al., 2013; Kouloumpis et al., 2011; Pak and Paroubek, 2010). In our work, we perform two-level sentiment analysis, similar to that described in (Liu, 2007). In addition, we also perform sentiment analysis on tweets (i.e. Indonesian tweets), instead of general sentences.

Current sentiment analysis research mostly relies on manually annotated training data (Nakov et al., 2013; Agarwal et al., 2011; Jiang et al., 2011; Bermingham and Smeaton, 2010). However, employing humans for manually annotating thousands, even millions of tweets is absolutely labor-intensive, time-consuming, and very expensive due to the massive scale and rapid growth of Twitter. This becomes a significant obstacle for researchers who want to perform sentiment analysis on tweets posted in under-resourced language, such as Indonesian tweets. Limited works have been done previously on automatically collecting training data (Pak and Paroubek, 2010; Bifet and Frank, 2010; Davidov et al., 2010). Some researchers harnessed happy emoticons and sad emoticons to automatically collect training data (Pak and Paroubek, 2010; Bifet and Frank, 2010). They assumed that tweets containing happy emoticons (e.g. ":)", ":-)") have positive sentiment, and tweets containing sad emoticons (e.g. ":(", ":-(") have negative sentiment. Unfortunately, their method clearly cannot get the coverage to reach sentiment-bearing tweets as many as possible since not all sentiment-bearing tweets contain emoticons.

Limited attempts have been made to perform sentiment analysis on Indonesian tweets. Calvin and Setiawan (2014) performed tweet polarity classification limited to the tweets talking about telephone provider companies in Indonesia. Their classification method relies on a small set of domain-dependent opinionated words. Before that, Aliandu (2014) conducted research on classifying an Indonesian tweet into three classes: positive, negative, and neutral. Aliandu (2014) used the method proposed by Pak and Paroubek (2010) to collect training data, that is, emoticons for collecting sentiment-bearing tweets. Even though those researchers performed similar works to us, we have two different points. First, we use different techniques to automatically collect training data. Second, we perform two-level sentiment analysis, namely, opinion tweet extraction and tweet polarity classification. Moreover, in the experiment section, we show that our method to collect training data is better than the one proposed by Pak and Paroubek (2010). Our method also produces much larger data since we do not rely on sheer emoticon-containing tweets to collect training data.

3 Automatically Building Training Data

3.1 Data Collection

Our corpus consists of 5.3 million tweets which were collected using Twitter Streaming API between May 16th, 2013 and June 26th, 2013. As we wanted to build Indonesian sentiment corpus, we used tweet's geo-location to filter tweets posted in the area of Indonesia. We applied language filtering because based on our observation, Indonesian Twitter users also like to use English or local language in their tweets. We then divided our corpus into four disjoint datasets. Table 1 shows the overall statistics of our Twitter corpus.

Dataset	Label	#Tweets
DATASET1	Unlabeled	4,291,063
DATASET2	Unlabeled	1,000,000
DATASET3	Neutral	12,614
DATASET4	Pos, Neg, Neutral	637
Total		5,304,314

Table 1: The statistics of our Tweet collection

To collect DATASET3 (i.e. neutral or non-opinion tweets), we used the same approach as in (Pak and Paroubek, 2010). First, we selected some popular Indonesian news portal accounts from the overall corpus and then labeled them as objective. Here, we assume that tweets from news portal accounts are neutral as it usually comes from headline news. This method was actually proposed by (Pak and Paroubek, 2010). But, we also did some empirical observation and acknowledged that this method performs quite well to collect neutral tweets.

The remaining corpus which is not published by news portal accounts is then used to build seed corpus (DATASET2), development corpus (DATASET1), and gold-standard testing data

(DATASET4). In this study, DATASET2 is used to construct labeled seed corpus. The seed corpus itself contains initial data that is believed to have opinion as well as sentiment. On the other side, development corpus DATASET1 contains unlabeled tweets used to expand our seed corpus. Our testing data (DATASET4) consists of 637 tweets which were tagged manually by the human annotators. These tweets were collected using some topic words which have tendency to be discussed by a lot of people. Two annotators were asked to independently classify each tweet into three classes: positive, negative, and neutral. The agreement of the annotators reached the level of Kappa value 0.95, which is considered as a satisfactory agreement. The label of each tweet in DATASET4 is the label agreed by the two annotators. But, when they did not agree, we asked the third annotators to decide the label. It is also worth to note that our testing data comes from various domains, such as telephone operator, public transportation, famous people, technology, and films. Table 2 and 3 shows the details of DATASET4.

Sentiment Type	#Tweets
Positive	202
Negative	132
Neutral	303
Total	637

Table 2: The statistics of DATASET4

Domain	#Tweets
Telephone operators	94
Public transportations	53
Government companies	11
Figures/People	61
Technologies	12
Sports and Athletes	41
Actress	29
Films	67
Food and Restaurants	34
News	214
Others	21
Total	637

Table 3: The domains in DATASET4

We also show some examples of Tweets found in DATASET4 as follows:

- " *Telkomsel memang wokeeehhh (free internet) :)*" (Telkomsel is nice (free internet) :))
- "*Kecewa sama trans Jakarta. Manajemen blm bagus. Masa hrs nunggu lbh dr 30 menit utk naek busway.*" (really dissapointed in transjakarta. The management is not good. We waited for more than 30 minutes to get the bus on)
- "*man of steel keren bangeeeettttt :D*" (Man of steel is really cool :D)
- "*RT @detikcom: Lalin Macet, Pohon Tumbang di Perempatan Cilandak-TB Simatupang*" (RT @detikcom: Traffic jam, a tree tumbled down in the Cilandak-TB Simatupang intersection)

3.2 Building Seed Training Instances

As we explained before, our seed corpus contains initial data used for expanding the training corpus. We propose two automatic techniques to constuct the seed corpus from DATASET2:

3.2.1 Opinion Lexicon based Technique

In the first technique, we use Indonesian opinion lexicon (Vania et al., 2014) to construct our seed corpus. A tweet will be classified as positive if it contains more positive words then negative words and vice versa. If a tweet contains word with a particular sentiment but the word is preceded by a negation, the polarity of the tweet will be shifted to its opposite sentiment. Moreover, we did not consider the tweets that do not contain any words from the opinion lexicon. In total, we have collected 135,490 positive seed tweets and 99,979 negative seed tweets.

3.2.2 Clustering based Technique

The second technique was implemented by using clustering (Li and Liu, 2012). This technique has several advantages, such as we do not need to provide any resources, such as lexicon or dictionary for a particular language. Each tweet from DATASET2 will be put into three clusters, namely positive tweets, negative tweets, or neutral tweets. We use all terms and POS tags from the tweet and each term is weighted using the TF-IDF as a features. Using this approach, 194 tweets were grouped into negative tweets, 325 tweets were grouped into positive tweets, and the rest was left out.

3.3 Adding New Training Instances

After we automatically construct labeled seed corpus from `DATASET2`, we are now ready to obtain more training instances. We use `DATASET1`, which is much bigger than `DATASET2`, as a source for expanding training data. The idea is that sentiment scores of all unlabeled tweets in `DATASET2` can be revealed using propagation from labeled seed corpus. To realize that idea, we employ a classifier model whose parameters are estimated using labeled and unlabeled tweets via Expectation and Maximization (EM) framework. The well-known research done by (Nigam et al., 2000) have shown that Expectation and Maximization framework works well for expanding training data to tackle the document-level text classification problem. In our work, we also show that this framework works quite well for tweets.

EM algorithm is an iterative algorithm for finding maximum likelihood estimates or maximum a posteori estimates for models when the data is incomplete (Dempster et al., 1977). Here, our data is incomplete since the sentiment scores of unlabeled tweets are unknown. To reveal the sentiment scores of unlabeled tweets using EM algorithm, we perform several iterations. First, we train the classifier with just the labeled seed corpus. Second, we use the trained classifier to assign probabilistically-weighted labels or sentiment scores (i.e. the probability of being a positive and negative tweet) to each unlabeled tweets. Third, we trained once again the model using all tweets (i.e. both the originally and newly labeled tweets). These last two steps are iterated until the parameters of the model do not change. At each iteration, the sentiment scores of each unlabeled tweets are improved as the likelihood of the parameters is guaranteed to improve until there is no more change (Dempster et al., 1977). In addition, only tweets whose sentiment scores surpass a certain threshold will be considered as our new training instances.

Formally, we have a set of tweets $\mathcal{T}$ divided into two disjoint partitions: a set of labeled seed tweets $\mathcal{T}_l$ and a set of unlabeled tweets $\mathcal{T}_u$, such that $\mathcal{T} = \mathcal{T}_l \cup \mathcal{T}_u$. In this case, $\mathcal{T}_l$ represents seed tweets which are selected from `DATASET2` and automatically labeled using the method described in the previous section and $\mathcal{T}_u$ represents a set of all tweets in `DATASET1`. Each tweet $t_i \in \mathcal{T}$, that has length $|t_i|$, is defined as an ordered list of words $(w_1, w_2, ..., w_{|V|})$ and each word w_k is an element of the vocabulary set $V = \{w_1, w_2, ..., w_{|V|}\}$.

For the classifier in the iteration, we employ Naive Bayes classifier model. In our case, given a tweet t_i and two class label C_j, where $j \in S$ and $S = \{pos, neg\}$, the probability that each of the two component classes generated the tweet is determined using the following equation:

$$P(C_j|t_i) = \frac{P(C_j)\prod_{k=1}^{|t_i|} P(w_k|C_j)}{\sum_{j \in S} P(C_j)\prod_{k=1}^{|t_i|} P(w_k|C_j)} \quad (1)$$

The above equation holds since we assume that the probability of a word occuring within a tweet is independent of its position. Here, the collection of models parameters, denoted as θ, is the collection of word probabilities $P(w_k|C_j)$ and the class prior probabilities $P(C_j)$. Given a set of tweet data, $\mathcal{T} = \{t_1, t_2, ..., t_{|\mathcal{T}|}\}$, the Naive Bayes uses the maximum a posteori (MAP) estimation to determine the point estimate of θ, denoted by $\widehat{\theta}$. This can be done by finding θ that maximize $P(\theta|\mathcal{T}) \propto P(\mathcal{T}|\theta)P(\theta)$. This yields the following estimation formulas for each component of the parameter.

The word probabilities $P(w_k|C_j)$ are estimated using the following formula:

$$P(w_k|C_j) = \frac{1+\sum_{i=1}^{|\mathcal{T}|} N(w_k,t_i).P(C_j|t_i)}{|V|+\sum_{n=1}^{|V|}\sum_{i=1}^{|\mathcal{T}|} N(w_n,t_i).P(C_j|t_i)} \quad (2)$$

where $N(w_k, t_i)$ is the number of occurences of word w_k in tweet t_i. Similarly, the class prior probabilities $P(C_j)$ are also estimated using the same fashion.

$$P(C_j) = \frac{1 + \sum_{i=1}^{|\mathcal{T}|} P(C_j|t_i)}{|S| + |\mathcal{T}|} \quad (3)$$

In the above equation, $P(C_j|t_i), j \in \{pos, neg\}$, are sentiment scores associated with each tweet $t_i \in \mathcal{T}$, where $\sum_j P(C_j|t_i) = 1$. For the labeled seed tweets, $P(C_j|t_i)$ are rigidly assigned since the label is already known in advance:

$$P(C_j|t_i) = \begin{cases} 1 & \text{if } t_i \text{ belongs to class } C_j \\ 0 & \text{otherwise} \end{cases} \quad (4)$$

Meanwhile, for the set of unlabeled tweets T_u, $P(C_j|t_i)$ are probabilistically assigned in each iteration, so that $0 \leq P(C_j|t_i) \leq 1$. Thus, the probability of all the tweet data given the parameters, $P(\mathcal{T}|\theta)$, is determined as follows:

$$P(\mathcal{T}|\theta) = \prod_{t_i \in \mathcal{T}} \sum_j P(t_i|C_j)P(C_j) \quad (5)$$

Finally, we can compute the log-likelihood of the parameters, $logL(\theta|\mathcal{T})$, using the following equation:

$$\begin{aligned} logL(\theta|\mathcal{T}) &\approx \log P(\mathcal{T}|\theta) \\ &= \textstyle\sum_{t_i \in \mathcal{T}} \log \sum_j P(t_i|C_j)P(C_j) \end{aligned} \quad (6)$$

The last equation contains "log of sums", which is difficult for maximization process. Nigam et al. (2000) shows that the lower bound of the last equation can be found using Jensen's inequality. As a result, we can express the complete log-likelihood of the parameters, $logL_c(\theta|\mathcal{T})$, as follows:

$$\begin{aligned} & logL(\theta|\mathcal{T}) \\ & \geq logL_c(\theta|\mathcal{T}) \\ & \approx \textstyle\sum_{t_i \in \mathcal{T}} \sum_j P(C_j|t_i) \log(P(t_i|C_j)P(C_j)) \end{aligned} \quad (7)$$

The last equation is used in each iteration to check whether or not the parameters have converged. When the EM iterative procedure ends due to the convergence of the parameters, we then need to select several tweets from the set of unlabeled tweets $\mathcal{T}_u$, which are eligible for our new training instances. The criteria of selecting new training instances, denoted by $\mathcal{T}_n$, is as follows:

$$\mathcal{T}_n = \{t \in T_u | \ |P(C_{pos}|t) - P(C_{neg}|t)| \geq \epsilon\} \quad (8)$$

where ϵ is an empirical value, $0 \leq \epsilon \leq 1$. In our experiment, we set ϵ to 0.98 since we want to obtain very polarized tweets in terms of sentiment as our new training instances. In summary, the EM algorithm for expanding training data is described as follows:

- **Input:** A set of labeled seed tweets $\mathcal{T}_l$, and a large set of unlabeled tweets $\mathcal{T}_u$
- Train a Naive Bayes classifier using only the labeled seed teets $\mathcal{T}_l$. The estimated parameters, $\widehat{\theta}$, are obtained using equation 2 and 3.
- Repeat until $logL_c(\theta|\mathcal{T})$ does not change (i.e. the parameters do not change):
  - **[E-Step]** Use the current classifier, $\widehat{\theta}$, to probabilistically label all unlabeled tweets in $\mathcal{T}_u$, i.e. we use equation 1 to obtain $P(C_j|t_i)$ for all $t_i \in \mathcal{T}_u$.
  - **[M-Step]** Re-estimate the parameters of current classifier using all tweet data $\mathcal{T}_u \cup \mathcal{T}_l$ (i.e. both the originally and newly labeled tweets). Here, we once again use the equation 2 and 3.
- Select the additional training instances, $\mathcal{T}_n$, using the criteria mentioned in formula 8.
- **Output:** The expanded training data $\mathcal{T}_n \cup \mathcal{T}_l$

4 Experiments and Evaluations

4.1 Training Data Construction

After we applied our training data construction method, we collected around 2.8 millions of opinion tweets when we used opinion lexicon based technique to automatically construct labeled seed corpus. Meanwhile, when we used clustering based technique to construct labeled seed corpus, we collected around 2.4 millions of opinion tweets. We refer to the former yielded training dataset as `LEX-DATA` and the latter as `CLS-DATA`. Table 4 and 5 show the statistics of `LEX-DATA` and `CLS-DATA`, respectively.

Sentiment Type	Pos	Neg
#Seed Tweets	135,490	99,797
#Added Tweets	1,180,506	1,419,438
Total	1,315,996	1,519,235

Table 4: The statistics of `LEX-DATA`

We also automatically collected training data using the method proposed by Pak and Paroubek (2010). We used the well-known positive/negative

Sentiment Type	Pos	Neg
#Seed Tweets	325	194
#Added Tweets	1,332,741	1,160,387
Total	1,333,066	1,160,581

Table 5: The statistics of CLS-DATA

emoticons in Indonesian tweets, such as ":)", ":-)", ":(", ":-(", to capture the opinion tweets from DATASET1 and DATASET2. We refer to this training dataset as EMOTDATA, and we used it for comparison to our proposed method. Table 6 shows the detail of EMOTDATA.

Sentiment Type	Pos	Neg
#Tweets	276,970	103,740

Table 6: The statistics of EMOTDATA

4.2 Evaluation Methodology

To evaluate our automatic corpus construction method, we performed two tasks, namely opinion tweet extraction and tweet polarity classification, harnessing our constructed training data. In other words, we see whether or not a classifier model trained on our constructed training data is able to peform both the aforementioned tasks with high performance.

Task 1 - Opinion Tweet Extraction: Given a collection of tweets **T**, the task is to discover all opinion tweets in **T**. Liu (2011) defined an opinion as a positive or negative view, attitude, emotion, or appraisal about an entity or an aspect of the entity. Thus, we adapt the aforementioned definition for the opinion tweet.

Task 2 - Tweet Polarity Classification: The task is to determine whether each opinion tweet extracted from the first task is positive or negative.

To measure the performance of the classifier, we tested the classifier on our gold-standard set, i.e. DATASET4, which was manually annotated by two people. In addition, we also compared our method against the method proposed by Pak and Paroubek (2010). For the classifier, we employ two well-known classifier algorithms, namely the Naive Bayes classifier and the Maximum Entropy model (Berger et al., 1996). We use the unigrams as our features, i.e. the presence of a word and its frequency in a tweet, since unigrams provide a good coverage of the data and most likely do not suffer from the sparsity problem. Morever, Pang et al. (2002) previously had shown that unigrams serve as good features for sentiment analysis.

Before we train our classifier models, we apply data preprocessing process to all datasets. This is done because tweets usually contain many informal forms of text that can be difficult to be recognized by our classifiers. We use the following data preprocessing steps to our training data:

- Filtering: we remove URL links, Twitter user accounts (started with '@'), retweet (RT) information, and punctuation marks. All tweets are normalized to lower case and repeated characters are replaced by a single character.
- Tokenization: we split each tweet based on whitespaces.
- Normalization: we replace each abbreviation found in each tweet with its actual meaning.
- Handling negation: each negation term is attached to a word that follows it.

4.3 Evaluations on Opinion Tweet Extraction

As we mentioned previously, we see the problem of opinion tweet extraction as a binary classification problem. Thus, we assume that a tweet can be classified into two categories: an opinion tweet and non-opinion tweet. For the testing data, we use DATASET4 that consists of 303 neutral/non-opinion tweets and 334 opinion tweets (i.e. the combination of positive and negative tweets). For the training data, we only have 12,614 non-opinion tweets from DATASET3. But, we have a larger set of opinion tweets either from LEX-DATA, CLS-DATA, or EMOTDATA depending on the method we apply. To cope with this problem, we randomly selected 12,614 opinion tweets either from LEX-DATA, CLS-DATA, or EMOTDATA so that the training data is balanced. Moreover, we use the precision, recall, and F1-score as our evaluation metrics.

First, we measured the performance of the classifiers trained on the data constructed by the method proposed by Pak and Paroubek (2010). We refer to this method as BASELINE. Furthermore, the non-opinion training data consists of all tweets in DATASET3 and the opinion training data consists of 12,614 tweets randomly selected from EMOTDATA. Second, we evaluated the classifiers trained on the data constructed using our proposed method. In this case, we run experiment using the two different seed corpus construction techniques. We refer to the method that use clustering based technique (for constructing seed corpus) as CLS-METHOD and the method that use opinion lexicon as LEX-METHOD. The opinion training data was constructed in the same manner as before. This time, we used LEX-DATA and CLS-DATA to randomly select 12,614 opinion tweets for LEX-METHOD and CLS-METHOD, respectively.

Model	Prec(%)	Rec(%)	F1(%)
BASELINE			
Naive Bayes	75.47	58.98	66.21
Maxent	78.36	74.85	76.56
LEX-METHOD			
Naive Bayes	76.24	64.37	**69.80**
Maxent	81.90	79.94	**80.91**
CLS-METHOD			
Naive Bayes	73.11	46.40	56.77
Maxent	80.00	63.47	70.78

Table 7: The evaluation results for opinion Tweet extraction task

Table 7 shows the results of the experiment. We can see that the classifiers trained on EMOTDATA, which was constructed using BASELINE, actually perform quite well. Maximum Entropy model achived 76,56% in terms of F1-score, which is far from the performance score resulting from Naive Bayes model. It is worth to note that the classifiers trained on LEX-DATA outperform those trained on EMOTDATA by over 3% and 4% for Naive Bayes and Maximum Entropy model, respectively, which means that LEX-METHOD is better than BASELINE. But, the situation is different for CLS-METHOD. This is actually no surprise since LEX-METHOD uses a good prior knowledge obtained from opinion lexicon. This might also suggest that the seed corpus construction is an important aspect in our method.

4.4 Evaluations on Tweet Polarity Classification

After we extract the opinion tweets, we then classify the sentiment type of the opinion tweets into two classes: positive and negative. In the first scenario, we evaluated the classifiers trained on both positive and negative tweets from EMOTDATA since we aimed at comparing BASELINE against our proposed method. In the second scenario, we then measured the performance of the classifiers when they were trained on the data constructed by our method (i.e. LEX-METHOD and CLS-METHOD). For the testing data, both scenarios use DATASET4 that consists of 202 positive tweets and 132 negative tweets. We left the neutral/non-opinion tweets. For the training data, the first scenario uses all tweets in EMOTDATA as the training data. But, we cannot directly use all tweets in LEX-DATA or CLS-DATA for the second scenario since the size of LEX-DATA and CLS-DATA, respectively, is much bigger than EMOTDATA. As a result, due to fairness, we randomly selected 276,970 positive tweets and 103,740 negative tweets from LEX-DATA and CLS-DATA, respectively, and subsequently use them for the second scenario. Moreover, we use a classification accuracy as our metric in this experiment.

Model	Accuracy(%)
BASELINE	
Naive Bayes	74.85
Maxent	73.35
LEX-METHOD	
Naive Bayes	**81.13**
Maxent	**86.82**
CLS-METHOD	
Naive Bayes	42.81
Maxent	45.80

Table 8: The evaluation results for Tweet polarity classification task

Table 8 shows the results. We can see that the classifiers trained on LEX-DATA significantly outperform those trained on EMOTDATA by over 7% and 13% for Naive Bayes and Maximum Entropy model, respectively. Just like the previ-

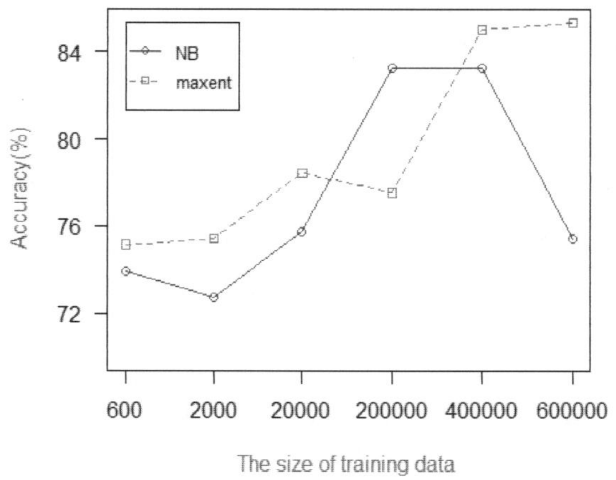

Figure 1: The effect of training data size. Here, we used the training data constructed using LEX-METHOD

ous experiment, CLS-METHOD is no better than LEX-METHOD and BASELINE. We also suggest that Maximum Entropy model is a good model for our sentiment analysis task since the results show that this model is mostly superior to Naive Bayes model.

We further investigated the effect of increasing the size of training dataset on the accuracy of the classifiers. In this case, we only examined LEX-DATA since LEX-METHOD yielded the best result before. Figures 1 shows the results. Training data of size N means that we use N/2 positive tweets and N/2 negative tweets as the training instances. As we can see, learning from large training data plays an important role in tweet polarity classification task. But, we also notice a strange case. When the size of training data is increased at the last point, the performance of Naive Bayes significantly drops. This should not be the case for Naive Bayes. We admit that the quality of our training data set is far away from perfect since it is automatically constructed. As a result, our training data set is still prone to noise disturbance and we guess that this is why the performance of Naive Bayes drops at the last point.

5 Conclusions and Future Works

We propose a method to automatically construct training instances for sentiment analysis and opinion mining on Indonesian tweets. First, we automatically build a set of labeled seed corpus using opinion lexicon based technique and clustering based technique. Second, we harness the labeled seed corpus to obtain more training instances from a huge set of unlabeled tweets by employing a classifier model whose parameters are estimated using the EM framework. For the evaluation, we test our automatically built corpus on the opinion tweet extraction and tweet polarity classification tasks.

Our experiment shows that our proposed method outperforms the baseline system which merely uses emoticons as the features for automatically building the sentiment corpus. When we tested on the opinion tweet extraction and tweet polarity classification tasks, the classifier models trained on the training data using our proposed method was able to extract opinionated tweets as well as classify tweets polarity with high performance. Moreover, we found that the seed corpus construction technique is an important aspect in our method since the evaluation shows that prior knowledge from the opinion lexicon can help building better training instances than just using clustering based technique.

In the future, this corpus can be used as one of the basic resources for sentiment analysis task, especially for Indonesian language. For the sentiment analysis task itself, it will be interesting to investigate various features beside unigram that may be useful in detecting sentiment on Indonesian Twitter messages.

References

Apoorv Agarwal, Boyi Xie, Ilia Vovsha, Owen Rambow, and Rebecca Passonneau. 2011. Sentiment analysis of twitter data. In *Proceedings of the Workshop on Languages in Social Media*, LSM '11, pages 30–38, Stroudsburg, PA, USA. Association for Computational Linguistics.

Paulina Aliandu. 2014. Sentiment analysis on indonesian tweet. In *The Proceedings of The 7th ICTS*.

Adam L. Berger, Vincent J. Della Pietra, and Stephen A. Della Pietra. 1996. A maximum entropy approach to natural language processing. *Comput. Linguist.*, 22(1):39–71, March.

Adam Bermingham and Alan F. Smeaton. 2010. Classifying sentiment in microblogs: Is brevity an advantage? In *Proceedings of the 19th ACM International Conference on Information and Knowledge Management*, CIKM '10, pages 1833–1836, New York, NY, USA. ACM.

Albert Bifet and Eibe Frank. 2010. Sentiment knowledge discovery in twitter streaming data. In *Proceedings of the 13th International Conference on Discovery Science*, DS'10, pages 1–15, Berlin, Heidelberg. Springer-Verlag.

Calvin and Johan Setiawan. 2014. Using text mining to analyze mobile phone provider service quality (case study: Social media twitter). *International Journal of Machine Learning and Computing*, 4(1), February.

Dmitry Davidov, Oren Tsur, and Ari Rappoport. 2010. Enhanced sentiment learning using twitter hashtags and smileys. In *Proceedings of the 23rd International Conference on Computational Linguistics: Posters*, COLING '10, pages 241–249, Stroudsburg, PA, USA. Association for Computational Linguistics.

A. P. Dempster, N. M. Laird, and D. B. Rubin. 1977. Maximum likelihood from incomplete data via the em algorithm. *JOURNAL OF THE ROYAL STATISTICAL SOCIETY, SERIES B*, 39(1):1–38.

Xia Hu, Lei Tang, Jiliang Tang, and Huan Liu. 2013. Exploiting social relations for sentiment analysis in microblogging. In *Proceedings of the Sixth ACM International Conference on Web Search and Data Mining*, WSDM '13, pages 537–546, New York, NY, USA. ACM.

Long Jiang, Mo Yu, Ming Zhou, Xiaohua Liu, and Tiejun Zhao. 2011. Target-dependent twitter sentiment classification. In *Proceedings of the 49th Annual Meeting of the Association for Computational Linguistics: Human Language Technologies - Volume 1*, HLT '11, pages 151–160, Stroudsburg, PA, USA. Association for Computational Linguistics.

Efthymios Kouloumpis, Theresa Wilson, and Johanna Moore. 2011. Twitter sentiment analysis: The good the bad and the omg! In Lada A. Adamic, Ricardo A. Baeza-Yates, and Scott Counts, editors, *ICWSM*. The AAAI Press.

Gang Li and Fei Liu. 2012. Application of a clustering method on sentiment analysis. *J. Inf. Sci.*, 38(2):127–139, April.

Bing Liu. 2007. *Web Data Mining: Exploring Hyperlinks, Contents, and Usage Data*. Data-Centric Systems and Applications. Springer.

Andrew J. McMinn, Daniel Tsvetkov, Tsvetan Yordanov, Andrew Patterson, Rrobi Szk, Jesus A. Rodriguez Perez, and Joemon M. Jose. 2014. An interactive interface for visualizing events on twitter. In *Proceedings of the 37th International ACM SIGIR Conference on Research & Development in Information Retrieval*, SIGIR '14, pages 1271–1272, New York, NY, USA. ACM.

Preslav Nakov, Sara Rosenthal, Zornitsa Kozareva, Veselin Stoyanov, Alan Ritter, and Theresa Wilson. 2013. Semeval-2013 task 2: Sentiment analysis in twitter. In *Second Joint Conference on Lexical and Computational Semantics (*SEM), Volume 2: Proceedings of the Seventh International Workshop on Semantic Evaluation (SemEval 2013)*, pages 312–320, Atlanta, Georgia, USA, June. Association for Computational Linguistics.

Kamal Nigam, Andrew Kachites McCallum, Sebastian Thrun, and Tom Mitchell. 2000. Text classification from labeled and unlabeled documents using em. *Mach. Learn.*, 39(2-3):103–134, May.

Alexander Pak and Patrick Paroubek. 2010. Twitter as a corpus for sentiment analysis and opinion mining. In *Proceedings of the Seventh conference on International Language Resources and Evaluation (LREC'10)*, Valletta, Malta, May. European Language Resources Association (ELRA).

Bo Pang and Lillian Lee. 2008. Opinion mining and sentiment analysis. *Found. Trends Inf. Retr.*, 2(1-2):1–135, January.

Bo Pang, Lillian Lee, and Shivakumar Vaithyanathan. 2002. Thumbs up?: Sentiment classification using machine learning techniques. In *Proceedings of the ACL-02 Conference on Empirical Methods in Natural Language Processing - Volume 10*, EMNLP '02, pages 79–86, Stroudsburg, PA, USA. Association for Computational Linguistics.

T. Sakaki, M. Okazaki, and Y. Matsuo. 2013. Tweet analysis for real-time event detection and earthquake reporting system development. *Knowledge and Data Engineering, IEEE Transactions on*, 25(4):919–931, April.

A. Tumasjan, T.O. Sprenger, P.G. Sandner, and I.M. Welpe. 2010. Predicting elections with twitter: What 140 characters reveal about political sentiment. In *Proceedings of the Fourth International AAAI Conference on Weblogs and Social Media*, pages 178–185.

Clara Vania, Mohammad Ibrahim, and Mirna Adriani. 2014. Sentiment lexicon generation for an under-resourced language. *International Journal of Computational Linguistics and Applications (IJCLA) (To Appear)*.

Automatic News Source Detection in Twitter Based on Text Segmentation

Takashi Inui **Masaki Saito*** **Mikio Yamamoto**
Graduate School of Systems and Information Engineering
University of Tsukuba
1-1-1 Tenoudai, Tsukuba, Ibaraki 305-8573, JAPAN
{inui@,masaki@mibel.,myama@}cs.tsukuba.ac.jp

Abstract

In this paper, we discuss news source detection (NSD), which involves finding additional information of a message generated in social media to understand the original message more deeply. We propose an NSD method based on the text segmentation and two extension models using web content and post times. Through the experiments using the real-world data, the proposed methods outperformed the baseline methods and exhibited an F-measure of 34.9.

1 Introduction

Recently, with the advent of social-media, it has become easy to express opinions or comment about experiences. In particular, *Twitter*[1] is a popular service used worldwide, and extremely large number of messages (*tweets*) is generated every day on it. It has been widely recognized that Twitter can potentially contain much useful information. Therefore, many researchers have conducted content analysis on Twitter (Java et al., 2006; Krishnamurthy et al., 2008; Pennacchiotti and Gurumurthy, 2011; Mehrotra et al., 2013).

Twitter can be regarded as a news feeder (Zhao et al., 2011). News content distributed by other media are often re-distributed and diffused to more people through Twitter. For example, a user *X* posted a tweet as follows.

t_{ex}: *Goal! Mario! http://example.football.com*

Many people have a chance to know the details of Mario's fantastic goal[2] through t_{ex}. Web content included in the URL *http://example.football.com* functions as an information source on t_{ex}. It can be said that tweets, such as t_{ex}, contain suitable information for news feeders. However, such cases are rare. Almost all tweets on Twitter are unsuitable due to a variety of reasons, e.g. (i) *X* did not write the information source in her stream of tweets, (ii) a tweet message and its information source (URL) were written in separate tweets, or (iii) *X* included a URL that was not related to the tweet message. In these cases, tweets do not function as the news feeders and people cannot obtain any additional information from them.

We discuss news source detection (NSD), which involves finding additional information of a message generated on social media to understand the original message more deeply. In Twitter, given a tweet t_i, the goal with NSD is to find another tweet t_j $(= t_i)$ that includes a reference to its information source on t_i. The details of NSD are described in Section 2. We propose an NSD method based on the text segmentation. It is difficult to straightforwardly resolve NSD because a search space of tweet pair combinations is exponentially large. Therefore, we simplify the NSD problem from the viewpoint of the text segmentation and provide an approximate solution. We also discuss two extension models of the proposed method using web content and post times.

*Currently, Fujitsu Limited.

[1] Twitter. https://twitter.com/

[2] Mario Götze is a German footballer who scored a goal at the final game at the FIFA Brazil World Cup.

Copyright 2014 by Takashi Inui, Masaki Saito and Mikio Yamamoto
28th Pacific Asia Conference on Language, Information and Computation pages 195–203

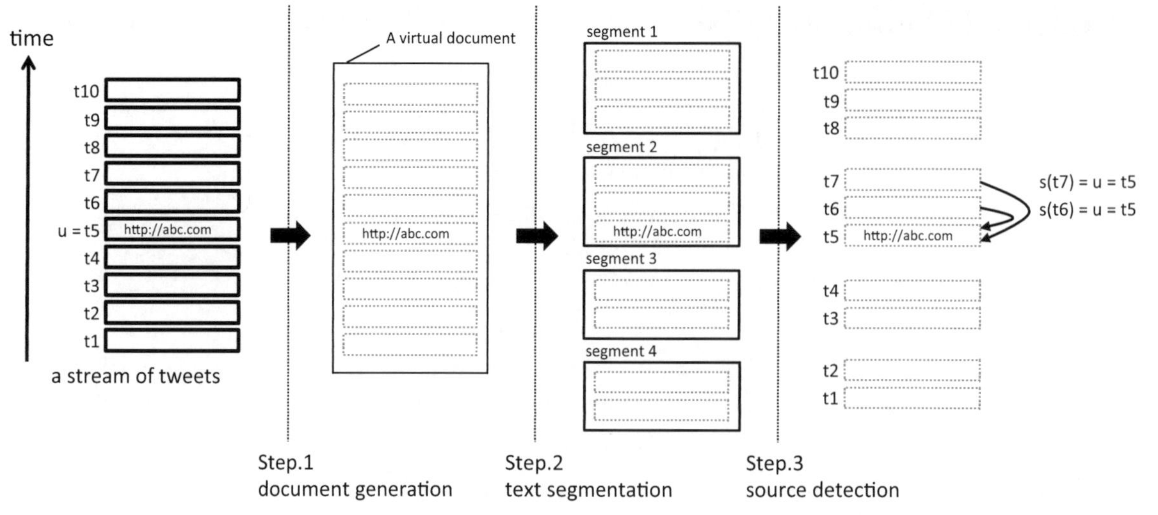

Figure 1: News source detection based on text segmentation

The rest of the paper is organized as follows. First, we define NSD and introduce some concepts and their notations for a formal description of NSD in Section 2. We then propose an NSD method that is based on the text segmentation and also discuss two extensions of the proposed method in Section 3. In Section 4, we introduce related work and discuss the differences between them. In Section 5, we describe the details of the experiments using real-world data and argue that the proposed method performs better than the baseline methods. We summarize the paper in Section 6.

2 News Source Detection

First, we introduce some concepts and their notations for a formal description of NSD.

- *target tweet* (t): a tweet for finding the information source. We call the information source especially, *news source*, hereafter.
- *source tweet* ($s(t)$): a tweet that includes a reference to the news source on t. In this paper, we only consider URL strings included in tweets as references.
- *URL tweet* (u): a tweet including a URL string.

Given a stream of tweets $T = \langle t_1, t_2, ..., t_{|T|} \rangle$ that includes at least one u, the task of NSD is to detect whether u is a source tweet on t_i for each t_i except u.

3 Proposed Methods

3.1 NSD based on Text Segmentation

We found two valuable findings in our preliminary analysis.

- A u adjacent to a t tends to be a $s(t)$ on t ($u = s(t)$).
- Two target tweets, t_i and t_j, adjacent to each other tend to have the same source tweet ($s(t_i) = s(t_j)$).

From these findings, we use *text segmentation*, which is one of the fundamental tasks in the NLP research domain. The goal with the text segmentation problem is to divide an input document into parts based on subtopics held in the input document.

We designed an algorithm to solve NSD as follows and illustrated in Figure 1.

Step.1 document generation. A stream of tweets is regarded as a virtual document.

Step.2 text segmentation. The document is divided into some segments by using a text segmentation method.

Step.3 source detection. The u is detected as a source tweet on t ($u = s(t)$) if and only if a u and t in the document belong to the same segment.

From a technical viewpoint, the text segmentation problem in Step.2 is the core part of this algorithm. We explain the details of Step.2 in the next section.

3.2 Applying TextTiling

3.2.1 TextTiling

We used a modified version of the text segmentation algorithm called TextTiling (Hearst, 1997), which is a well-known and standard text segmentation method, and is focused on adjacent sentence pairs. Suppose that s_i and s_j is an adjacent sentence pair in the input document, then, TextTiling determines whether s_i and s_j belong to the same segment or not according to a boundary score[3]. If the sentence boundary sb_{ij} between s_i and s_j has a lower boundary score than the threshold d_{th}, the sentence pair is detected as belonging to the same segment; otherwise, it is not. As a result, text segmentation in the input document is naturally done when all sentence boundaries are determined.

A boundary score d_{ij} held on the sentence boundary sb_{ij} is defined as follows:

$$d_{ij} = (ss_l - ss_{ij}) + (ss_r - ss_{ij}) \quad (1)$$

where ss_{ij} indicates a similarity score at sb_{ij} and ss_l (ss_r) indicates a similarity score at a local maximum point on the left(right)-hand side of sb_{ij}. Each similarity score ss_{ij} is defined as follows:

$$\sum_{w \in L} \frac{f(w, c_i^f) f(w, c_j^b)}{\sqrt{\sum_{w \in L} f(w, c_i^f)^2 \sum_{w \in L} f(w, c_j^b)^2}} \quad (2)$$

where c_i^f and c_j^b indicate context windows, where c_i^f indicates a forward window and c_j^b indicates a backward window (see Figure 2). The symbol L indicates a lexicon set.

The function $f(w, c_i^f)$ returns the number of occurrences of a word w in the context window c_i^f and $f(w, c_j^b)$ likewise. Intuitively, this score represents a topical coherence between c_i^f and c_j^b. The higher the ss_{ij}, the stronger the coherence.

[3] This is called the "depth" score in (Hearst, 1997).

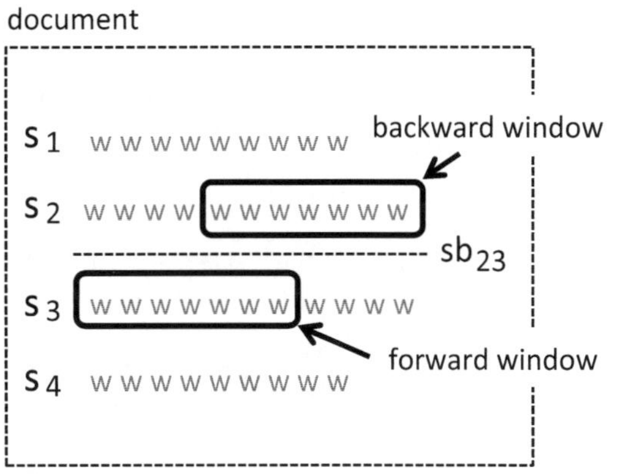

Figure 2: Backward and forward windows

Actually, d_{ij} is only measured at each local minimum point of ss_{ij} and compared with d_{th}. The d_{th} to the boundary score is defined as $d_{th} = \overline{S} - \frac{\sigma}{2}$. Here, $\overline{S}$ indicates an average value of all boundary scores and σ indicates their standard deviation.

3.2.2 Modifications

We introduce three modifications to the original TextTiling algorithm to appropriately apply it to a virtual document composed of a stream of tweets.

First, we focus on tweet boundaries instead of sentence boundaries because we want to make segments in units of tweets.

Second, we add another type of context window. The word-based window is only defined in the original algorithm. Figure 2 shows an example of the word-based window of size 7. We also use the post-based window. With the post-based window, the number of words to be included in the window varies with the length of each tweet. Therefore, we can include more meaningful context into the boundary scores.

The third is a normalization of the similarity scores. Our stream data are much shorter than those assumed in the original TextTiling algorithm. Therefore, it was frequently observed that the number of words is less than the window size at the end of the stream when using the word-based window.

We therefore prepared a normalized similarity score function to resolve this problem. The normalized score function is defined as follows.

$$\sum_{w \in L} \frac{\frac{f(w,c_i^f)}{|c_i^f|} \frac{f(w,c_j^b)}{|c_j^b|}}{\sqrt{\sum_{w \in L} \left(\frac{f(w,c_i^f)}{|c_i^f|}\right)^2 \sum_{w \in L} \left(\frac{f(w,c_j^b)}{|c_j^b|}\right)^2}} \quad (3)$$

Here, each $|c_i^f|$ and $|c_j^b|$ indicates the real number of words existing in c_i^f and c_j^b.

We call the modified algorithm described in this section **Basic** for comparing it to the extensions described in the next section.

3.3 Extension1: Web Content Concatenation (WCC)

It was found that there are many URL tweets with insufficient information to detect source tweets because they are composed of very few words. Therefore, we consider enriching URL tweets with web content referred by the URL written in them.

Suppose that $web(u)$ is web content referred by a URL written in a u. Then, we simply concatenate $web(u)$ with u and use both strings $web(u)$ and u in **Basic**. Web pages are generally composed of logical constituents such as *title*, *head*, and *body*. Some might contribute to the source detection, and some might not. We selected content in *title* and *body* as $web(u)$ in the experiments. A specific pattern rule based on HTML tags was used for extracting the main document parts from *body* in the Web pages.

We call this extension technique web content concatenation (**WCC**).

3.4 Extension2: Using Post Time (PT)

Intuitively, it seems that arbitrary tweet pairs have semantic relationships each other when they are sequentially posted in a very short span. On the other hand, it seems that they have no semantic relationships when posted in a longer span. Based on this insight, we introduce a weighted frequency function by using time span information between two tweets. Equation (4) represents the alternative weighted frequency function $f'(w, c_i^f)$, which is used in Equation (2) and Equation (3) instead of $f(w, c_i^f)$.

$$f'(w, c_i^f) = \sum_{e \in \mathcal{W}} \max\{0, 1 - \delta(e, c_i^f)\} \quad (4)$$

The set $\mathcal{W}$ indicates an instance set of w existing in c_i^f, and the symbol e indicates an element in $\mathcal{W}$. That is, $f(w, c_i^f) = |\mathcal{W}|$. The $\delta(e, c_i^f)$ is a penalty term and defined as follows:

$$\delta(e, c_i^f) = log(T(t_f^e) - T(t_b^0)). \quad (5)$$

Here, $T(t_*^*)$ indicates the time at which t_*^* was posted. The tweet t_f^e indicates a tweet in which a word instance e exists in the forward window. The tweet t_b^0 indicates a tweet in the backward window and adjacent to a tweet in the forward window. For example, when t_b^0 was posted at 09:15 and t_f^e was posted at 09:18, $\delta(e, c_i^f) = log(3) = 0.477$ because t_f^e was posted 3 minutes later from t_b^0. The $f'(w, c_j^b)$ is defined, likewise.

We call this extension technique post time (**PT**).

4 Related work

In this section, we discuss two NLP tasks related to NSD; first story detection (FSD) and document alignment (DA), then, discuss the differences between them. Figure 3 shows the outlines of the three tasks. Note that the only central phenomena are drawn in this figure. One can return to the original papers referred to the explanation below to understand the strict definition for each task.

First story detection is a subtask defined within Topic Detection and Tracking[4](Allen, 2002). The aim with FSD is detecting a news manuscript reporting a given topic for the first time from a stream of news stories. The topics given in FSD are worldwide events or disasters such as the Oklahoma City bombing and the earthquake in Kobe. Traditional techniques used in FSD are similarity-based methods. A news manuscript is detected as the *first story* when it is not similar to all past news. Petrovic et al. (2010) investigated the FSD task on Twitter. They modified the traditional FSD technique to tackle the speed and volume problems due to the tremendous updates of data generated on Twitter. They used a streaming technique based on locality sensitive hashing (Indyk and Motwani, 1998) which makes high-speed approximate calculations of similarities possible and achieves good performance.

[4]For more details, see `http://www.itl.nist.gov/iad/mig//tests/tdt/`.

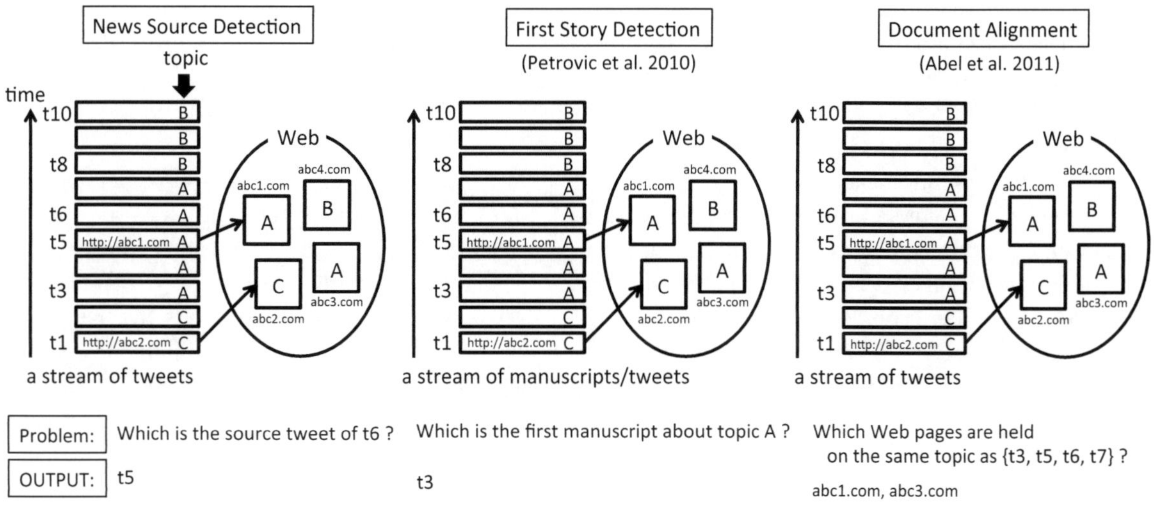

Figure 3: Differences in task definitions

Abel et al. (2011) proposed a DA method for automatically acquiring Twitter-user profiles. The goal of the user profile acquisition for a user A is to create a set of semantic entities composing text content indicating entities in the real world, such as persons and events[5], from text context A generated. For example, suppose that A's hobby is tennis and she posts something about tennis such as "French open (*event*)" and Italian tennis player "Francesca Schiavone (*person*)" on Twitter. Then A's user profile could be composed of "French open" and "Francesca Schiavone". Abel et al.(2011) adapted DA between tweets and web pages to enrich user profiles to be acquired. The aim with DA is to find all web pages aligned with the input tweets in terms of topics. In DA, all web pages are aligned with input tweets that have the same topic as the web pages. To resolve DA, they used explicit URL linkages and implicit linkages estimated using TFIDF-based similarity between tweets and web pages.

The above-mentioned research has an affinity to NSD. However, the definition of the problem(input)/output relation slightly differs in each study as shown in Figure 3. Moreover, the interest for our study was to investigate the effectiveness of the two aspects, web content and posting time of tweets, to improve NSD performance, which garnered no interest in the previous studies.

In Twitter, the *hashtag* "#" symbol is used to mark keywords or topics in a tweet. Users can mark categories of content written in tweet messages by using hashtags such as #Fashion, #Food, and #WorldCup2014. Unfortunately, they are unsuitable for NSD because categories obtained through hashtags are usually very coarse. In fact, to use hashtags for NSD, we conducted an experiment that involved the same conditions as those described in the next section and achieved a very low F-measure of 8.0.

5 Experiments

5.1 Data

We selected *SportsNavi* (`http://sports.yahoo.co.jp/`) as a news source in the experiments and crawled web pages belonging to *SportsNavi*. This site is a popular Japanese sports news sites provided by Yahoo!.

We collected 317 streams of tweets by using the TwitterAPI[6]. All tweets collected were written in Japanese. Furthermore, we required that at least one u be included for each stream of tweets. Such a tweet has a URL string referring to a web page belonging to *SportsNavi*. Of these collected stream

[5]For semantic entities, see also the OpenCalais project `http://www.opencalais.com/`.

[6]`https://dev.twitter.com/docs`

data, we focused on a set of tweet pairs $\langle u, t\rangle$ in which t exist within five tweets from u in the stream then used 3,170 $\langle u, t\rangle$ pairs as our evaluation data. The problem to be solved in the experiments was detecting whether u is the source tweet on t for each $\langle u, t\rangle$ in the evaluation data.

We asked two annotators to create a gold standard dataset. The annotators were required to independently judge whether u into $\langle u, t\rangle$ in the evaluation data is regarded as a source tweet on t. We measured the κ statistics (Cohen, 1960) to assess the reliability of the gold standard dataset. The result is that $\kappa = 0.782$. This value indicates that the data substantially agree.

5.2 Baseline methods

We adopted two baseline methods for comparison with the proposed methods. **Naive** is the most naive method and **SIM** is a customized version of the method (Abel et al., 2011) proposed to resolve DA described in Section 4.

Naive For all tweet pairs in the evaluation data, the u in $\langle u, t\rangle$ is always detected as $s(t)$ on t.

SIM This is a similarity-based method originally proposed by (Abel et al., 2011). Suppose that $\mathcal{U}$ indicates a set of URL tweets in the evaluation data and $web(u)$ indicates a web page referred from a URL written in u ($\in \mathcal{U}$). SIM focuses on each similarity between t and a web page $web(u')$ ($u' \in \mathcal{U}$) to detect whether $u = s(t)$, that is, the u in $\langle u, t\rangle$ is the $s(t)$ on t. First, given t in $\langle u, t\rangle$, u_o is selected using Equation (6).

$$u_o = \arg\max_{u' \in \mathcal{U}} sim(t, web(u')) \quad (6)$$

After that, u is detected as a source tweet on t only when $u_o = u$; otherwise, it is not. We used Equation (7) as the similarity function $sim(t, web(u'))$, which is the same setting as (Abel et al., 2011).

$$\sum_{i \in \mathcal{T}} TF(i, web(u')) * IDF(i) \quad (7)$$

where $\mathcal{T}$ is a set of words included in t, $TF(i, web(u'))$ indicates the term frequency of i in $web(u')$, and $IDF(i)$ indicates the inverse document frequency in terms of web pages in the evaluation data.

5.3 Other settings

We used the Japanese morphological analyzer *MeCab*[7] for word recognition. It is observed that each tweet in the evaluation data is composed of an average of six words.

We conducted our experiments by changing the size of the context window used in the text segmentation phase. We set up sizes from 1 to 15 for the word-based window and from 1 to 2 for the post-based window. We used only nouns as a lexicon set L.

We used Precision and Recall as evaluation measures, which are defined as

$$Precision = \frac{|X \cap Y|}{|X|} * 100,$$
$$Recall = \frac{|X \cap Y|}{|Y|} * 100.$$

The symbol X indicates a set of $\langle u, t\rangle$ instances in which the u in $\langle u, t\rangle$ is detected using a method as the source tweet on t and Y indicates a set of $\langle u, t\rangle$ instances in which the u in $\langle u, t\rangle$ is actually source tweet on t. We also used F-measure index $\frac{2*Precision*Recall}{Precision+Recall}$ as a summary of the above measures.

5.4 Experimental Results

5.4.1 Results of proposed method: Basic

We start by discussing the results of the simplest method proposed in Section 3, which we call **Basic**. We discuss the results obtained using the extended models of **Basic** in the next section.

Table 1 lists the results of **Basic**. The results from which the word-based window was used in the text segmentation are shown in the upper part of Table 1 and those from the post-based window are shown in the lower part. With the word-based window, Precision dropped when the window size was larger. Recall, on the other hand, tended to increase when the window size was larger. Similar phenomena were observed with the post-based window. The best F-measure value was 29.5, obtained when the size of

[7] https://code.google.com/p/mecab/

Table 1: Results of proposed method (**Basic**)

word-based window			
window size	Precision	Recall	F-measure
1	**100.0**	0.3	0.6
2	35.3	1.9	3.6
3	40.5	10.7	17.0
4	31.7	18.3	23.2
5	23.8	23.0	23.4
6	25.8	34.4	**29.5**
7	20.2	33.4	25.2
8	18.8	37.2	25.0
9	18.2	38.2	24.6
10	17.1	**38.8**	23.7
11	8.9	21.5	12.6
12	7.7	18.6	10.9
13	8.8	21.1	12.5
14	8.1	19.9	11.5
15	8.8	21.1	12.5
post-based window			
window size	Precision	Recall	F-measure
1	**35.2**	21.8	**26.9**
2	19.5	**29.7**	23.5

Table 2: Comparison with baseline methods

	Precision	Recall	F-measure
Naive	9.1	100.0	16.6
SIM	76.5	8.2	14.8
Basic (6)	25.8	34.4	29.5

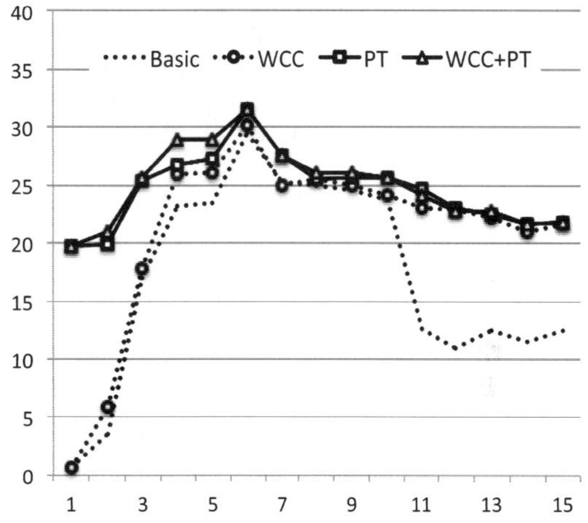

Figure 4: F-measure values from proposed methods

word-based window was 6, and 26.9, obtained when the size of the post-based window was 1.

Next, we compare **Basic** with the baseline methods. Table 2 lists the results obtained from the baseline methods. The best result obtained from **Basic** with the word-based window of size 6 is also shown in the bottom of Table 2. **Naive** naturally achieved 100% Recall while Precision was very low (9.1%). **SIM** had a contrary phenomenon to **Naive**, low Recall (8.2%) and high Precision (76.5%), since it would induce conservative decision-making by Equation (6). One can see that **Basic** achieved a well-balanced performance and higher F-measure than the baseline methods.

5.4.2 Effectiveness of extensions

We investigated the effectiveness of the two extensions, **WCC** discussed in Section 3.3 and **TP** discussed in Section 3.4. First, we discuss the results of **WCC** and then discuss those of **PT**.

Table 3 lists the results obtained from **WCC**. **WCC** outperformed **Basic** when larger windows were used. This is because **WCC** was able to make good use of word information included in both tweets and web pages. This is especially evident in the cases in which the post-based window was used. The best F-measure value was 34.7 obtained with WCC with a post-based window of size 2.

Next, Table 4 lists the results obtained from **PT**. **PT** almost totally outperformed **Basic** and also outperformed **WCC** when small windows were used. It exhibited an F-measure of 34.9 with a post-based window of size 1. This is the best performance of all experimental conditions.

5.4.3 Sensitivity to window size

We investigated the sensitivity of the proposed methods to the context window size. Figure 4 shows F-measure values obtained from the proposed methods with the word-based window. The horizontal axis indicates the size of the window and the vertical axis indicates F-measure. Each line corresponds to the result of each method. In the figure, **WCC+PT**

Table 3: Results of proposed method (**WCC**)

word-based window			
window size	Precision	Recall	F-measure
1	**100.0**	0.3	0.6
2	43.5	3.2	5.9
3	37.4	11.7	17.8
4	32.1	21.8	25.9
5	25.8	26.5	26.1
6	25.7	36.6	**30.2**
7	20.1	33.1	25.0
8	19.2	37.9	25.5
9	18.4	39.1	25.0
10	17.4	**39.7**	24.2
11	16.4	39.4	23.1
12	16.2	39.1	22.9
13	15.6	38.2	22.2
14	14.8	36.3	21.0
15	15.3	36.9	21.6
post-based window			
window size	Precision	Recall	F-measure
1	**33.1**	31.9	32.5
2	28.7	**43.8**	**34.7**

Table 4: Results of proposed method (**PT**)

word-based window			
window size	Precision	Recall	F-measure
1	**35.8**	13.6	19.7
2	31.7	14.5	19.9
3	33.2	20.5	25.3
4	29.0	24.9	26.8
5	25.0	30.0	27.3
6	26.2	39.7	**31.6**
7	21.3	39.1	27.6
8	19.0	38.8	25.5
9	18.8	40.4	25.7
10	18.4	**42.6**	25.7
11	17.4	42.3	24.7
12	16.3	39.7	23.1
13	15.9	38.5	22.5
14	15.2	37.2	21.6
15	15.5	36.9	21.8
post-based window			
window size	Precision	Recall	F-measure
1	**31.0**	**40.1**	**34.9**
2	20.2	38.8	26.6

indicates the results obtained from the method with both extension models.

One can see that all models exhibited the best performance when the window size = 6. This is intuitively supported since each tweet in the evaluation data was composed of an average of six words. One can see from Figure 5 that Precision and Recall were balanced when the window size was around 6. There seemed to be a semantic boundary seemly for NSD around 6.

It is less sensitive in the case of the **PT** extension model and the **WCC+PT** combination model. These models exhibited almost the same F-measure values. It would be reasonable and sufficient to use the **PT** extension model when it is difficult to crawl web pages.

6 Conclusion

We proposed an NSD method based on text segmentation and two extension models using web content and post times. Using the TextTiling algorithm, we achieved an F-measure of 34.9. The following issues will need to be addressed to refine our models.

- The proposed methods can provide a lightweight, approximate solution to NSD by using text segmentation. This means that it is only applicable to continuous conditions. Methods applicable to non-continuous conditions should be developed to improve performance.

- We only considered web pages referred from tweets as news sources in this paper. It would be valuable to enlarge the target of news sources to other media such as TV and radio.

References

Fabian Abel, Qi Gao, Geert-Jan Houben, and Ke Tao. 2011. Semantic enrichment of twitter posts for user profile construction on the social web. In *Proceedings*

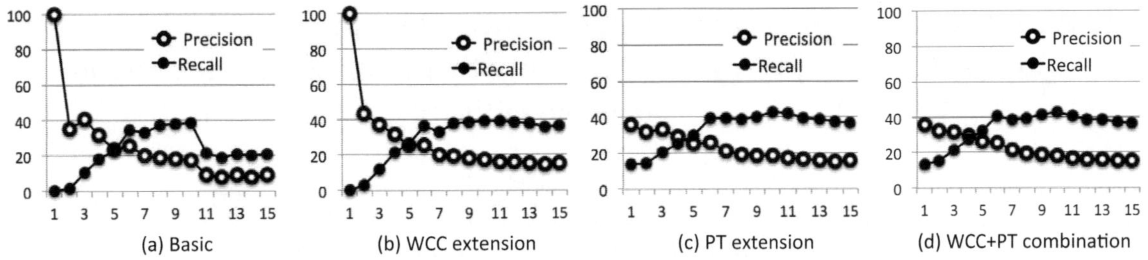

Figure 5: Precision and Recall values obtained from proposed methods

of the 8th extended semantic web conference on The semanic web, pages 375–389.

James Allen. 2002. *Topic detection and tracking: event-based information organization.* Kluwer Academic Publishers.

Jacob Cohen. 1960. A coefficient of agreement for nominal scales. *Education and Psychological Measurement*, 43(6):37–46.

Marti A. Hearst. 1997. Texttiling: Segmenting text into multi-paragraph subtopic passages. *Computational linguistics*, 23(1):33–64.

Piotr Indyk and Rajeev Motwani. 1998. Approximate nearest neighbors: towards removing the curse of dimensionality. In *Proceedings of the 13th annual ACM symposium on Theory of computing*, pages 604–613.

Akshay Java, Xiaodan Song, Tim Finin, and Belle Tseng. 2006. Why we twitter: understanding microblogging usage and communities. In *Proceedings of the 9th WebKDD and 1st SNA-KDD workshop on Web mining and social network analysis*, pages 56–65.

Balachander Krishnamurthy, Phillipa Gill, and Martin Arlitt. 2008. A few chirps about twitter. In *Proceedings of the rirst workhop on Lnline social networks*, pages 19–24.

Rishabh Mehrotra, Scott Sanner, Wray Buntine, and Lexing Xie. 2013. Improving LDA topic models for microblogs via tweet pooling and automatic labeling. In *Proceedings of the 36th international ACM SIGIR conference on Research and development in information retrieval*, pages 889–892.

Marco Pennacchiotti and Siva Gurumurthy. 2011. Investigating topic models for social media user recommendation. In *Proceedings of the 20th International World Wide Web Conference*, pages 101–102.

Sasa Petrovic, Miles Osborne, and Victor Lavrenko. 2010. Streaming first story detection with application to twitte. In *Proceedings of the 11th Annual Conference of the North American Chapter of the Association for Computational Linguistics*, pages 181–189.

Wayne Xin Zhao, Jing Jiang, Jianshu Weng, Jing He, Ee-Peng Lim, Hongfei Yan, and Xiaoming Li. 2011. Comparing twitter and traditional media using topic models. In *Proceedings of the 33rd European conference on Advances in information retrieval*, pages 338–349.

Sentiment Lexicon Interpolation and Polarity Estimation of Objective and Out-Of-Vocabulary Words to Improve Sentiment Classification on Microblogging

Yongyos Kaewpitakkun, Kiyoaki Shirai, Masnizah Mohd
Japan Advanced Institute of Science and Technology
1-1, Asahidai, Nomi City, Ishikawa, Japan 923-1292
Email: {s1320203,kshirai,masnizah}@jaist.ac.jp

Abstract

Sentiment analysis has become an important classification task because a large amount of user-generated content is published over the Internet. Sentiment lexicons have been used successfully to classify the sentiment of user review datasets. More recently, microblogging services such as Twitter have become a popular data source in the domain of sentiment analysis. However, analyzing sentiments on tweets is still difficult because tweets are very short and contain slang, informal expressions, emoticons, mistyping and many words not found in a dictionary. In addition, more than 90 percent of the words in public sentiment lexicons, such as SentiWordNet, are objective words, which are often considered less important in a classification module. In this paper, we introduce a hybrid approach that incorporates sentiment lexicons into a machine learning approach to improve sentiment classification in tweets. We automatically construct an *Add-on lexicon* that compiles the polarity scores of objective words and out-of-vocabulary (OOV) words from tweet corpora. We also introduce a novel feature weighting method by interpolating sentiment lexicon score into uni-gram vectors in the Support Vector Machine (SVM). Results of our experiment show that our method is effective and significantly improves the sentiment classification accuracy compared to a baseline uni-gram model.

1 Introduction

Sentiment analysis and opinion mining is the field of study that analyzes people's opinions, sentiments, evaluations, attitudes and emotions from written language (Liu, 2010). Recently, Twitter has become an important resource for sentiment analysis. People express their opinions and feelings using Twitter and these data can be grabbed publicly through Twitter API. There are two main approaches to sentiment analysis: lexicon-based and machine learning-based techniques. Several researchers have combined these two techniques (Kumar et al., 2012; Mudinas et al., 2012; Saif et al., 2012; Fang et al., 2011; Hung et al., 2013). This study adopts a similar approach; we seek to combine the prior polarity knowledge from the lexicon-based method and the powerful classification algorithm from the machine learning-based method. Two main motivations of this approach are discussed below.

The initial motivation is to revise the polarity of objective and out-of-vocabulary words in the public sentiment lexicon to improve Twitter sentiment classification. In the lexicon-based approach, sentiment classification is done by comparing the group of positive and negative words looked up from the public lexicon. For example, if the document contains more positive words than negative words, it will be classified as positive. Several public lexical resources such as ANEW[1], OpinionFinder[2], SentiStrength[3], SentiWordNet[4] and SenticNet[5] lexicon are available for this type of analysis. SentiWordNet or "SWN" (Esuli et al., 2010) has become one of the most fa-

[1] http://neuro.imm.dtu.dk/wiki/A_new_ANEW/
[2] http://mpqa.cs.pitt.edu/opinionfinder/
[3] http://sentistrength.wlv.ac.uk/
[4] http://sentiwordnet.isti.cnr.it/
[5] http://sentic.net/

Copyright 2014 by Yongyos Kaewpitakkun, Kiyoaki Shirai, and Masnizah Mohd
28th Pacific Asia Conference on Language, Information and Computation pages 204–213

mous and widely used sentiment lexicons because of its huge vocabulary coverage. SentiWordNet is an extended version of WordNet[6], where words and synsets in WordNet are augmented with their sentiment score. SWN 3.0 contains more than 100,000 synsets. However, more than 90% of these are classified as objective words (Hung et al., 2013); which are usually considered less important in the classification process. Furthermore, lexicon-based sentiment analysis over Twitter faces several challenges due to the short informal language used. Tweets are usually short and contain lots of slang, emoticons, abbreviations or mistyped words. Most of them are not contained in the public lexicon, which are called out-of-vocabulary (OOV) words. Both objective and OOV words may have implicit sentiment, especially in some specific domains or group of users; thus, it could be better to modify an existing public sentiment lexicon, such as SentiWordNet, by incorporating the polarity of objective and OOV words. One possible way to revise SentiWordNet is to estimate the polarity scores of sentiment unknown words based on the polarity of the sentences including them in the corpus. For example, let us suppose that the objective word "birthday" appears many more times in positive tweets than in objective or negative tweets. This word could be revised as a positive word in the sentiment lexicon. On the other hand, when the OOV word "ugh" appears many more times in negative tweets than in objective or positive tweets, it could be newly classified as a negative word. In this work, we aim to build an add-on lexicon covering the estimated polarity scores for both objective words and OOV words in the SentiWordNet.

The secondary motivation is to incorporate the prior polarity knowledge from the sentiment lexicon into powerful machine learning classifier, such as the Support Vector Machine (SVM), as extra information. Among many machine learning techniques, SVM has achieved the great performance in the sentiment classification task. The uni-gram feature has been widely and successfully used in sentiment analysis, especially in user review datasets. Since tweets are much shorter than user reviews, however, the use of only the uni-gram feature may cause a data sparseness problem. One possible way to solve this problem is to integrate the information from the sentiment lexicon to supervised algorithms as extra knowledge. Recently, some researchers incorporate information derived from a lexicon into machine learning by augmenting sentiment lexicon as extra polarity group feature to uni-gram (O'Keefe et al., 2009) or simply replacing uni-gram with a lexicon score (Hung et al., 2013). In this work, we present an alternative way to incorporate lexical information into a machine learning algorithm by interpolating a score in the sentiment lexicon into a score of uni-gram feature in vector weighting. Our experiment results show that the proposed lexicon interpolation weighting method with revised polarity estimation of objective and OOV words is effective and significantly improves the sentiment classification accuracy compared to the baseline uni-gram model.

The rest of the paper is organized as follows. Section 2 discusses related work. Section 3 describes our proposed method and framework including data pre-processing, polarity estimation technique and sentiment lexicon incorporation and feature weighting method. Section 4 describes results of the experiments and discussion. Finally, conclusions and direction for future work are discussed in Section 5.

2 Related Work

Early work on Twitter sentiment analysis used two approaches in traditional sentiment analysis on normal texts: machine learning-based and lexicon-based approaches. Recently, some studies have combined these two approaches and achieved relatively better performance in two ways. The first is to develop two classifiers based on these two approaches separately and then integrate them into one system. The second is to incorporate lexicon information directly into a machine learning classification algorithm. In the first way, Kumar et al. (2012) used a machine learning-based method to find the semantic orientation of adjectives and used a lexicon-based method to find the semantic orientation of verbs and adverbs. The overall tweet sentiment is then calculated using a linear interpolation of the results from both methods. Mudinas et al. (2012) presents concept-level sentiment analy-

[6] http://wordnet.princeton.edu/

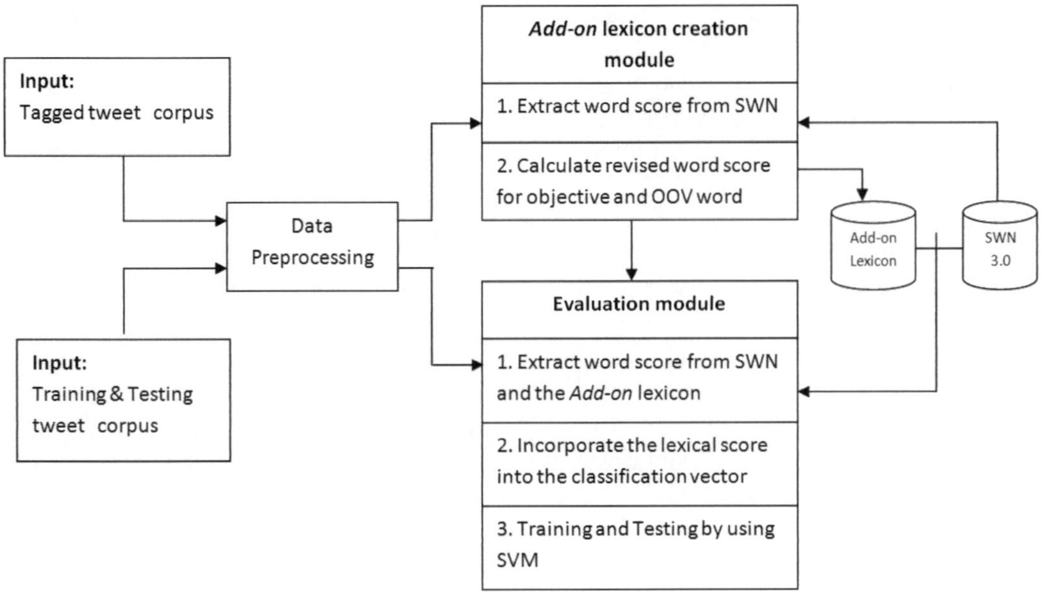

Figure 1: System framework.

sis system, which are called pSenti. Their system used a lexicon for detecting the sentiment of words and used these sentiment words as features in the machine learning-based method. Results from both lexicon and machine learning were combined together to calculate the final overall sentiment scoring. In the second way, Saif et al. (2012) utilized knowledge of not only words but also semantic concepts obtained from a lexicon as features to train a Naive Bayes classifier. Fang et al. (2011) automatically generated domain-specific sentiment lexicon and incorporated it into the SVM classifier. They applied this method for identifying sentiment classification in a product reviews. Recently, Hung et al. (2013) reported that more than 90 percent of words in SentiWordNet are objective words that are often considered useless in sentiment classification. So, they reassigned proper sentiment values and tendency of such objective words in a movie review corpus and incorporated these sentiment scores into the machine learning-based method. In this paper, we reevaluate the sentiment score of not only objective words but also out-of-vocabulary (OOV) words; which are common in tweets due to informal message used. We also propose an alternative way to incorporate the sentiment lexicon knowledge into the machine learning algorithm. We will propose sentiment interpolation weighting method that interpolates lexicon scores into uni-gram scores in the vector representation of the SVM classifier. Our method is described in detail in the next section.

3 Approach

Our two-step hybrid sentiment analysis system has been developed by combining lexicon-based and machine learning-based approaches. In the first step, the add-on lexicon has been created by reevaluating the polarity scores of objective words and out-of-vocabulary (OOV) words extracted from a specific tweet corpus. After that, the score from both the public lexicon and add-on lexicon will be incorporated into a feature vector as extra prior knowledge in four different ways that will be described in Subsection 3.3. The main advantage of our approach is the extra sentiment polarity information from both the public and add-on lexicon will be incorporated to the powerful machine learning algorithm. It can help the supervised learned classifier to identify the sentiment of tweets more precisely, even when tweets contain words that are not found in the public lexicon or less frequently appeared in the training set. The overall system framework is shown in Figure 1.

3.1 Data preprocessing

The data preprocessing process consists of part-of-speech tagging, lemmatizing, and stop word and URL removal. In the first step, tweets are POS tagged by the TweetNLP POS Tagger[7], which is trained specially from Twitter data. After that, all words are lemmatized by the Stanford lemmatizer[8]. We also reduce the number of letters that are repeated more than two times, i.e. "heellllooooo" is replaced by "heelloo". Finally, the common stop words and URL are removed because they represent neither sentiment nor semantic concept.

3.2 Add-on lexicon creation

As discussed above, SentiWordNet has become a famous and useful lexicon for sentiment analysis due to its broad coverage; however more than 90 percent of words in SentiWordNet are objective words. Moreover, lots of words in tweets are slang, informal or mistyped words that are not included in the lexicon. Based on this observation, we aim to build an add-on lexicon by compiling both objective and OOV words with their newly estimated sentiment score. Word scores are estimated based on the assumption that the polarities of words are coincident with the polarity of their associated sentences, which seems reasonable due to the short length of tweet messages. In other words, if the word frequently appears in the positive (or negative) tweets, its polarity might be positive (or negative).

In the creation of the add-on lexicon, the sentiment score of a word is calculated based on the probability that the word appears in positive or negative sentences in a sentiment tagged corpus. There are two steps. In the first step, the words from preprocessing step are extracted with their score in SentiWordNet by using Equation (1). As we will describe in Subsection 3.3, this score is used as the weight of the feature vector. In the add-on lexicon creation, SentiWordNet is just used to check if the word is an objective word ($SWNScore(w_i) = 0$) or OOV word, then objective and OOV words will be sent to the revised polarity estimation step. The revised scores for these words are calculated by Equation (2).

$$SWNScore(W_i) = SWNScore_{POS}(w_i) - SWNScore_{NEG}(w_i) \quad (1)$$

$$Score(w_i) = \begin{cases} Score_{POS}(w_i), & \\ \quad \text{if } Score_{POS}(w_i) > Score_{NEG}(w_i). & \\ (-1) \times Score_{NEG}(w_i), & \\ \quad \text{if } Score_{POS}(w_i) < Score_{NEG}(w_i). & \end{cases} \quad (2)$$

where,

$$Score_{POS}(w_i) = \frac{P(positive|w_i)}{P(positive)}$$

$$Score_{NEG}(w_i) = \frac{P(negative|w_i)}{P(negative)}$$

$$P(positive|w_i) = \frac{No.\ of\ w_i\ in\ positive\ tweets}{No.\ of\ w_i\ in\ dataset}$$

$$P(negative|w_i) = \frac{No.\ of w_i\ in\ negative\ tweets}{No.\ of\ w_i\ in\ dataset}$$

$$P(postitive) = \frac{No.\ of\ positive\ tweets}{No.\ of\ all\ tweets}$$

$$P(negative) = \frac{No.\ of\ negative\ tweets}{No.\ of\ all\ tweets}$$

In the second step, since scores in SentiWordNet are in the range of -1 to 1, we have to convert the revised word scores into the same interval. In this case, we use a Bipolar sigmoid function (Fausett, 1994) because it is continuous and returns a value from -1 to 1. The conversion formula is shown in Equation (3).

$$Score(w_i)' = sigmoid(Score(w_i)) \quad (3)$$

where, $sigmoid(x) = \frac{2}{(1+e^{-x})} - 1$

The revised polarity score may be unreliable if the frequency of the word is too low, or the difference between positive and negative tendency is not great enough. Therefore, two thresholds are introduced. Threshold 1 (T1) is the minimum number of words in the dataset and threshold 2 (T2) is the minimum difference between positive and negative word orientation scores ($Score_{POS}(w_i)$ and $Score_{NEG}(w_i)$). The objective and OOV words with their scores are added to the add-on lexicon only when equation (4) is fulfilled.

$$\begin{gathered} Frequency\ of\ w_i\ in\ dataset \geq T_1 \\ |Score_{POS}(w_i) - Score_{NEG}(w_i)| \geq T_2 \end{gathered} \quad (4)$$

3.3 Lexicon score incorporation and feature weighting methods

In this subsection, the word scores from both SentiWordNet and the add-on lexicon will be incor-

[7]http://www.ark.cs.cmu.edu/TweetNLP/

[8]http://nlp.stanford.edu/software/

porated into the SVM classification features as extra prior information in four different ways: sentiment weighting, sentiment augmentation, sentiment interpolation and sentiment interpolation plus. We start with the baseline uni-gram features, followed by our proposed sentiment lexicon incorporation method. Note that we ignore word sense disambiguation problem although the sentiment score is associated not with a word but with a synset in SWN. When SWN is consulted to obtain a sentiment score for a polysemous word, the first word sense in SWN is always chosen because it is the most representative sense of each word.

3.3.1 Uni-gram and POS Features

Uni-gram and POS features are common and widely used in the domain of sentiment analysis. There are many feature weighting schemes for the uni-gram. In this work, we use the combination of uni-gram and POS features with term presence weighting as the baseline method. As a result, the weight value of words(POSs) is 1 if they are present, otherwise 0.

3.3.2 Sentiment Weighting Features

In this method, the feature weights of uni-gram binary vectors will be simply replaced with the word sentiment scores (Equation (1) or (3)) from the lexicon. Note that the weight is set to 0 if the word does not appear in the tweet.

3.3.3 Sentiment Augmentation Features

In this method, words will be classified into 3 groups: positive, objective and negative, based on their scores in the lexicon. Then, these sentiment group features are augmented to the original uni-gram vector. There are three additional features that are the percentage of positive, objective and negative words in a tweet, where the sum of the weights of these three features would be equal to one.

3.3.4 Sentiment Interpolation Features

In this method, we proposed a new incorporation method where the word score from the lexicon will be interpolated into the original uni-gram feature weight. The weight of the new interpolated vector is shown in Equation (5). Note that uni-gram score is always 1 in our model.

Table 1: Summary of feature and weighting methods.

Methods	Feature weight value	Additional features
Uni-gram + POS	1	No
Sentiment Weighting	Lexicon score	No
Sentiment Augmentation	1	percentage of positive, objective and negative word in a tweet
Sentiment Interpolation	Equation (5)	No
Sentiment Interpolation Plus	Equation (5)	percentage of positive, objective and negative word in a tweet

$$Weight = \alpha\ Uni\text{-}gram\ score + (1-\alpha)\ Lexicon\ score \quad (5)$$

The parameter α $(0 \leq \alpha \leq 1)$ is used for controlling the influence between the uni-gram model and the sentiment lexicon model. When α is equal to 1, the weight is the fully uni-gram model, and when α is 0, the weight is the fully sentiment weighting model.

3.3.5 Sentiment Interpolation Plus Features

In this method, we combine sentiment interpolation and sentiment augmentation together. Therefore, three additional augmentation features (Subsection 3.3.3) will be added to the sentiment interpolation vector (Subsection 3.3.4) as the extra features.

The summary of all features and weight values are shown in Table 1. Please note that the weight of the feature is always 0 if it does not appear in the tweets.

4 Evaluation

In this section, we present the results of two experiments. The first experiment was conducted with Positive-Neutral-Negative classification over full datasets (3-way classification). In the second experiment, we discarded neutral tweets and conducted the experiment with Positive-Negative classification over datasets of only positive and negative tweets. The detailed results are shown in Section 4.3. In addition, we used LIBLINEAR[9] developed by Fan et al. (2008) with default setting for training the SVM classifier.

[9]http://www.csie.ntu.edu.tw/ cjlin/liblinear/

Table 2: Sanders corpus.

Subset	Used for	# Pos	# Neu	# Neg	# Total
1	Add-on lexicon creation, Training	319	1,319	345	1,983
2	Testing	109	455	114	678

Table 3: SemEval 2013 corpus.

Subset	Used for	# Pos	# Neu	# Neg	# Total
0	Development	1,297	1,401	475	3,173
1	Add-on lexicon creation, Training	2,272	3,083	884	6,239
2	Testing	372	441	187	1,000

4.1 Data set

4.1.1 Sanders Dataset

The Sanders corpus[10] consists of 5,512 tweets on four different topics (Apple, Google, Microsoft, and Twitter). Each tweet was manually labeled as positive, negative, neutral or irrelevant. After removing irrelevant and duplicate tweets, 2,661 tweets remained. Then, the dataset was randomly divided into two subsets. The first sub-dataset was used for the add-on lexicon creation part and training part, while the second was used for the testing (evaluation) part. Detailed information on this corpus is shown in Table 2. We used the Sanders dataset as a representative of small and domain-specific corpus.

4.1.2 SemEval 2013 Dataset

The SemEval 2013 corpus (Nakov et al., 2013) consists of about 15,000 tweets that were created for Twitter sentiment analysis (task 2) in the Semantic Evaluation of Systems Challenge 2013. Each tweet was manually labeled as positive, negative or neutral by Amazon Mechanical Turk workers. This dataset consists of a variety of topics. Among the full dataset, only 10,534 tweets could be downloaded, because some of them were protected or deleted. This dataset was also randomly divided into three subsets. Detailed information on this corpus is shown in Table 3. Note that the development set was used for parameter tuning. We used the SemEval 2013 dataset as a representative of a large and general corpus.

In addition, the percentages of objective words and OOV words after data preprocessing in both corpora are shown in Table 4.

4.2 Parameter optimization

As described in Subsection 3.2, in the add-on lexicon creation process, two thresholds can play an important role to control the number of revised polarity words. The objective and OOV words should not be revised if their estimated scores are not reliable enough. To investigate an optimal value for the threshold T1, we conducted a sensitivity test on the SemEval 2013 development dataset (subset 0 in Table 4). Note that the threshold T2 was set to 0.2 by the preliminary experiment. Figures 2 a and b show the accuracy of our method for various values of T1 using interpolation plus weighting method in a 3-way and a positive-negative classification, respectively. In these graphs, the horizontal axis indicates the ratio of the number of words in the add-on lexicon to that of the corpus. The results show that, in 3-way classification, the classifier achieved better performance when the numbers of revised polarity words were smaller than the case of positive-negative classification. The accuracy reached its peak with the percentage of revised polarity words set around 0.5% (in 3-way classification) and 1.2% (in positive-negative classification). We did not investigate the optimum for the threshold T1 in the Sanders corpus due to the insufficient number of tweets, but set T1 so that the percentage of the number of the add-on lexicon is the same as in the optimized value in the SemEval 2013 dataset. Based on this observation, two thresholds were set as shown in Table 5.

Table 4: Percentages of objective and OOV words in the two corpora.

Corpus	Objective words	OOV words
Sanders	26.61%	57.73%
SemEval 2013	24.01%	66.55%

4.3 Results

Table 6 and 7 show the results of the 3-way and positive-negative classification, respectively. They reveal the average of precision, recall and F1-

[10] http://www.sananalytics.com/lab/twitter-sentiment/

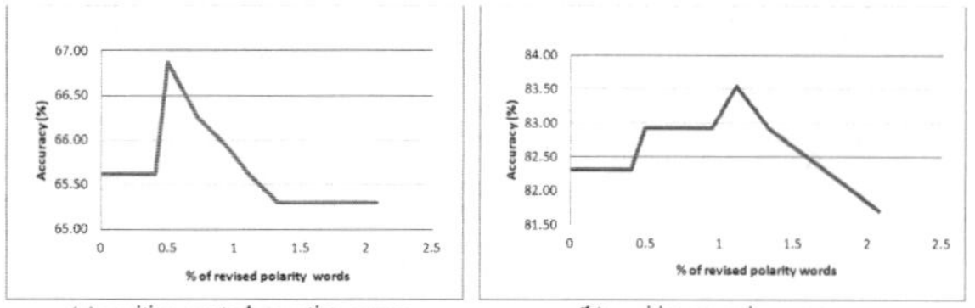

(a) positive-neutral-negative corpus (b) positive-negative corpus

Figure 2: The classification accuracy vs. number of revised polarity words on the development dataset.

Table 5: Threshold parameter setting based on % of revised words.

Corpus	Task	T1	T2	Vocab. size	*1	*2
Sanders	3-way	45	0.20	5,145	24	0.46%
	pos-neg	25	0.20	5,145	60	1.17%
SemEval 2013	3-way	60	0.20	15,366	78	0.50%
	pos-neg	35	0.20	15,366	173	1.12%

*1 = No. of revised words, *2 = % of revised words

measure over positive and negative classes as well as accuracy (Acc) for both Sanders and SemEval 2013 datasets. Five methods (including the baseline) described in Subsection 3.3 with and without the add-on lexicon are compared. In the experiment, the coefficient α in Equation (5) was initially set to 0.5 for maintaining the balance of uni-gram and lexicon score. The sensitivity of α will be investigated in Subsection 4.6.

4.4 Effect of the add-on lexicon

In this section, we compare the performance of the add-on lexicon to the original SentiWordNet lexicon. Figure 3 shows the accuracy (the average of both 3-way and positive-negative classification tasks and both datasets) of the models with original SWN and SWN plus the add-on lexicon using four different feature weighting methods. It indicates that the add-on lexicon significantly improved the accuracy in the sentiment weighting and slightly improved the accuracy in the sentiment interpolation and sentiment interpolation plus. In the case of sentiment augmentation, the accuracies were almost the same. In addition, the combination of sentiment interpolation plus the add-on lexicon achieved the highest accuracy.

When the add-on lexicon was applied, the performance improved more in positive-negative classification than in positive-neutral-negative (3-way) classification. Table 8 shows the average of both datasets of accuracy improvement in 3-way and positive-negative classification with and without the add-on lexicon when using the interpolation plus weighting method. The result shows that when the add-on lexicon was applied, the accuracy was increased about 2% compared to applying only SWN in positive-negative classification, while only 0.25% in 3-way classification. Therefore the add-on lexicon is more suitable for positive-negative sentiment classification than positive-neutral-negative sentiment classification. The reason may be that in the case of 3-way classification, some objective tweets were misclassified as subjective tweets when objective or OOV words were revised to subjective words.

Table 8: Average accuracy improvement when using SWN vs. SWN plus the add-on lexicon in 3-way and positive-negative classification.

Classification	Sentiment Interpolation	Sentiment Interpolation Plus
3-Way	+0.27%	+0.25%
Positive-Negative	+2.42%	+2.06%

Table 9 shows the performance of the add-on lexicon over the Sanders vs. SemEval 2013 corpus when using sentiment interpolation plus weighting method. It seems that the add-on lexicon performed better over the domain specific corpus (Sanders) than the general corpus (SemEval 2013). Using the add-on lexicon, the average accuracy of both 3-way and positive-negative classification tasks were improved by 1.49% on the Sanders corpus and 0.82% on the SemEval 2013 corpus.

Table 10 and Table 11 show examples of the revised positive and negative words with their POSs and scores obtained from the Sanders and SemEval 2013 corpora, respectively. It can be observed that the revised polarity words in the Sanders corpus are more domain-specific than those in the SemEval 2013 corpus since the Sanders corpus is a collection of tweets associated with only four keywords: Apple, Android, Microsoft and Twitter.

4.5 Comparison of Feature weigthing methods

Table 12 shows the comparison among four feature weighting methods and the baseline uni-gram. It reveals the average accuracy of the methods on both

Table 6: Results of 3-way classification task over the Sanders and SemEval 2013 corpora.

Methods		Sanders				SemEval 2013			
Feature	Lexicon	Precision	Recall	F1	Acc	Precision	Recall	F1	Acc
Uni-gram + POS	No	0.454	0.444	0.446	0.667	0.575	0.482	0.518	0.617
Sentiment Weighting	SWN	0.306	0.392	0.306	0.423	0.485	0.478	0.464	0.531
	+Addon	0.323	0.315	0.300	0.541	0.554	0.425	0.472	0.606
Sentiment Augmentation	SWN	0.496	0.452	0.471	0.690	0.611	0.487	0.536	0.628
	+Addon	0.485	0.452	0.466	0.684	0.620	**0.491**	0.542	0.635
Sentiment Interpolation	SWN	0.451	0.407	0.427	0.671	0.588	0.471	0.514	0.621
	+Addon	0.467	0.425	0.443	0.676	0.595	0.476	0.519	0.622
Sentiment Interpolation Plus	SWN	0.511	**0.439**	**0.471**	0.702	0.646	0.484	0.547	0.644
	+Addon	**0.522**	0.430	0.469	**0.705**	**0.650**	0.487	**0.550**	**0.646**

Table 7: Results of positive-negative classification task over the Sanders and SemEval 2013 corpora.

Methods		Sanders				SemEval 2013			
Feature	Lexicon	Precision	Recall	F1	Acc	Precision	Recall	F1	Acc
Uni-gram + POS	No	0.767	0.764	0.762	0.762	0.699	0.688	0.692	0.733
Sentiment Weighting	SWN	0.741	0.734	0.733	0.735	0.642	0.642	0.642	0.682
	+Addon	0.723	0.722	0.722	0.722	0.697	0.661	0.670	0.730
Sentiment Augmentation	SWN	0.776	0.773	0.771	0.771	0.719	0.700	0.707	0.750
	+Addon	0.765	0.763	0.762	0.762	0.725	0.712	0.717	0.755
Sentiment Interpolation	SWN	0.772	0.772	0.771	0.771	0.712	0.695	0.701	0.744
	+Addon	0.800	0.799	0.798	0.798	0.740	0.715	0.724	0.766
Sentiment Interpolation Plus	SWN	0.785	0.785	0.785	0.785	0.740	0.715	0.724	0.766
	+Addon	**0.813**	**0.812**	**0.812**	**0.812**	**0.759**	**0.728**	**0.739**	**0.780**

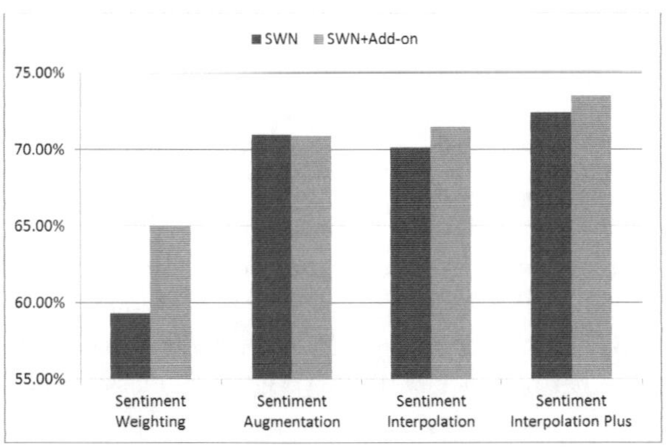

Figure 3: Average accuracy of SentiWordNet vs. SentiWordNet plus the add-on lexicon

Sanders and SemEval corpora in both 3-way classification and positive-negative classification tasks, where both SentiWordNet and the add-on lexicon are used as the sentiment lexicon. First, the accuracy of the sentiment weighting method (the score in the lexicon is used as the weight) was 4.51% worse than the uni-gram method. It may be because, unlike uni-gram weighting, the weights of objective and OOV words were set to 0 even when they appeared in the tweets. It means that the classifier loses the information about these words. Sentiment augmentation, where three lexicon scores were added to original uni-gram as extra features, improved the accuracy 1.43%. Sentiment interpolation, where lexicon scores were interpolated into uni-gram vector weights, further improved the accuracy 2.05% compared to baseline. Finally, the combination

Table 9: Performance of the add-on lexicon on the Sanders vs. SemEval 2013 corpus.

Corpus	SWN	+Add-on	Improvement
Sanders	74.34%	75.83%	1.49%
SemEval 2013	70.48%	71.30%	0.82%

Table 10: Examples of revised positive / negative words in the Sanders corpus.

Positive word	Revised score	Negative word	Revised score
#ics#OTHER	0.9223	battery#N	-0.9526
look#V	0.9211	customer#N	-0.9253
power#N	0.8926	update#N	-0.9109
:)#OTHER	0.8851	dear#OTHER	-0.9074
#android#N	0.8698	lot#N	-0.8931
help#V	0.8698	send#V	-0.8931
user#N	0.8664	#ios#OTHER	-0.8776
great#A	0.8252	service#N	-0.8049
game#N	0.8041	wait#V	-0.7434
thank#V	0.7994	ass#N	-0.7086

Table 11: Examples of revised positive / negative words in the SemEval 2013 corpus.

Positive word	Revised score	Negative word	Revised score
thank#V	0.8637	:(#OTHER	-0.9920
fun#A	0.8628	fuck#N	-0.9900
luck#N	0.8560	cancel#V	-0.9872
great#A	0.8442	damn#OTHER	-0.9864
:D#OTHER	0.8421	niggas#N	-0.9690
yay#OTHER	0.8341	die#V	-0.9554
pakistan#OTHER	0.8265	dont#V	-0.9329
:)#OTHER	0.8170	ass#N	-0.9272
yeah#OTHER	0.7999	cry#V	-0.9168
celebrate#V	0.7928	russia#OTHER	-0.9039

of sentiment interpolation and sentiment augmentation, called sentiment interpolation plus, achieved the highest accuracy among all methods with average accuracy improvement 4.08% compared to baseline uni-gram.

4.6 The sensitivity of α parameter

In the sentiment interpolation method, the α parameter in Equation (5) plays an important role for controlling the influence of uni-gram and sentiment lexicon scores. To analyze the effect of the α parameter, different values of the α parameter were applied. Note that when α is equal to 1, the vector weight becomes a fully uni-gram model (only term presence are used as feature weight) and when α is equal to 0, the vector weight value becomes a fully sentiment weighting model (only lexicon score are used as feature weight). Figures 4 a) and b) show the change of the average accuracy and F1-measure of the sentiment interpolation plus method on two datasets in the 3-way and positive-negative classification, respectively. In the positive-negative classification, the result clearly shows that the integration of uni-gram and lexicon score outperformed either uni-gram or sentiment weighting. The sentiment interpolation plus method performed well with large rage of α values (0.2 to 0.7). On the other hand, in the 3-way classification, it seems that the sentiment interpolation plus method only slightly increased the performance compared to uni-gram or sentiment weighting in most of the α values. As discussed earlier, the sentiment interpolation plus method was more suitable for the positive-negative classification than the 3-way classification task.

Table 12: Average accuracy comparison among four feature weighting methods and baseline uni-gram.

Methods	Avg. Acc	Improvement
Uni-gram + POS	69.49%	-
Sentiment Weighting	64.98%	-4.51%
Sentiment Augmentation	70.92%	1.43%
Sentiment Interpolation	**71.53%**	**2.05%**
Sentiment Interpolation Plus	**73.57%**	**4.08%**

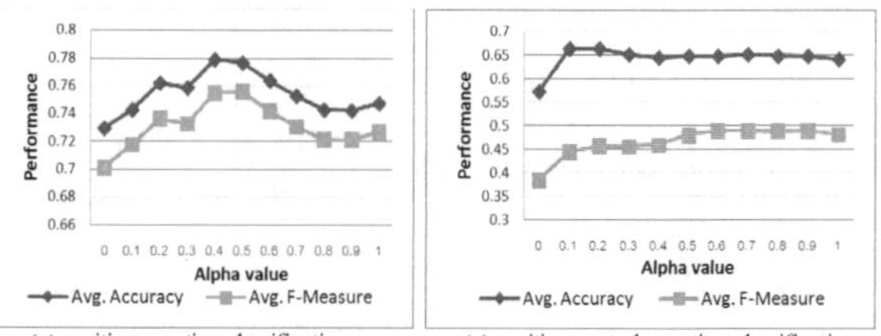

(a) positive-negative classification (a) positive-neutral-negative classification

Figure 4: Effect of the α parameter in the sentiment interpolation plus method

5 Conclusions

In this paper, we have shown an alternative hybrid method that incorporated sentiment lexicon information into the machine learning method to improve the performance of Twitter sentiment classification. There are two main contributions of this paper. First, we estimated the implicit polarity of objective and OOV words and used these words as additional information for the public sentiment lexicon. We described how we revised the polarity of objective and OOV words based on the assumption that the polarities of words are coincident with the polarity of their associated sentences, which seem reasonable due to the short length of tweets. Second, we proposed an alternative way to incorporate sentiment lexicon knowledge into a machine learning algorithm. We proposed the sentiment interpolation weighting method that interpolated lexicon score into uni-gram score in the feature vectors of SVM.

Our results indicate that the add-on lexicon improved the classification accuracy on average compared to using only the original public lexicon. The proposed sentiment interpolation weighting method performed well and the combination of sentiment interpolation and sentiment augmentation, called sentiment interpolation plus, with SentiWordNet and the add-on lexicon achieved the best performance and significantly improved the classification accuracy compared to the uni-gram model. The experiments show that the add-on lexicon performed better over the domain-specific corpus than the general corpus. In addition, our results indicate that the proposed approach was more appropriate for positive-negative classification than positive-neutral-negative (3-way) classification. Therefore, we plan to apply the subjective classification as our future work in order to filter the objective tweets before the polarity classification. Since negation words such as "not" and "less" are simply treated as uni-gram features in this work, another interesting issue is investigation on how special treatments of negation affect the polarity classification. Furthermore, we plan to find a method to reestimate the word polarity from unlabeled data or noisy label data instead of labeled data that is time consuming to create.

References

L. Barbosa and J. Feng. 2010. Robust sentiment detection on twitter from biased and noisy data. In *Proceedings of Coling*.

F. Bravo-Marquez, M. Mendoza, and B. Poblete. 2013. Combining strengths, emotions and polarities for boosting Twitter sentiment analysis. In *Proceedings of WISDOM*.

A. Esuli, S. Baccianella, and F. Sebastiani. 2010. SentiWordNet 3.0: An Enhanced Lexical Resource for Sentiment Analysis and Opinion Mining. In *Proceedings of LREC*.

R. E. Fan, K. W. Chang, C. J. Hsieh, X. R. Wang, and C. J. Lin. 2008. LIBLINEAR: A Library for Large Linear Classification. *The Journal of Machine Learning Research, volume 9*

J. Fang and B. Chen. 2011. Incorporating Lexicon Knowledge into SVM Learning to Improve Sentiment Classification. In *Proceedings of IJCNLP*.

G. Y. Fausett. 1994. *Fundamentals of Neural Networks*. Prentice Hall PTR.

A. Go, R. Bhayani, and L. Huang 2009. Twitter sentiment classification using distant supervision. *CS224N Project Report, Stanford*.

C. Hung and H. Kai Lin. 2013. Using Objective Words in SentiWordNet to Improve Word-of-Mouth Sentiment Classification. *IEEE Intelligent Systems*, volume 28.

E. Kouloumpis, T. Wilson, and J. Moore. 2011. Twitter Sentiment Analysis: The Good the Bad and the OMG!. In *Proceedings of ICWSM*.

A. Kumar and T. M. Sebastian 2012. Sentiment Analysis on Twitter *IJCSI*, volume 9.

B. Liu. 2010. Sentiment analysis and subjectivity. *Handbook of natural language processing, volume 2.*

K. L. Liu , W. J. Li, and M. Guo 2012. Emoticon Smoothed Language Models for Twitter Sentiment Analysis. In *Proceedings of AAAI*.

A. Mudinas, D. Zhang, and M. Levene 2012. Combining lexicon and learning based approaches for concept-level sentiment analysis. In *Proceedings of WISDOM*.

P. Nakov, Z. Kozareva, A. Ritter, S. Rosenthal, V. Stoyanov, and T. Wilson. 2013. Semeval-2013 task 2: Sentiment analysis in twitter. In *Proceedings of SemEval*.

T. O'Keefe and I. Koprinska 2009. Feature Selection and Weighting Methods in Sentiment Analysis. In *Proceedings of ADCS*.

A. Pak and P. Paroubek 2010. Twitter as a Corpus for Sentiment Analysis and Opinion Mining. In *Proceedings of LREC*.

H. Saif, M. Fernandez, Y. He, and H. Alani. 2012. Semantic sentiment analysis of twitter. In *Proceedings of ISWC*.

H. Saif, M. Fernandez, Y. He, and H. Alani. 2013. Evaluation Datasets for Twitter Sentiment Analysis. In *Proceedings of ESSEM*.

M. Thelwall, K. Buckley, and G. Paltoglou. 2012. Sentiment strength detection for the social web. *Journal of the American Society for Information Science and Technology, volume 9.*

How Mutual Knowledge Constrains the Choice of Anaphoric Demonstratives in Japanese and English

David Y. Oshima
Department of International Communication
Nagoya University
Furo-cho, Chikusa-ku, Nagoya
Japan 464-8601
davidyo@nagoya-u.jp

Eric McCready
Department of English
Aoyama Gakuin University
4-4-25 Shibuya, Shibuya-ku, Tokyo
Japan 150-8366
mccready@cl.aoyama.ac.jp

Abstract

It has been widely acknowledged that the choice of Japanese demonstratives (the distal *a*-series, the medial *so*-series, and the proximal *ko*-series) in their anaphoric use is regulated by the rules concerned with the interlocutors' knowledge of the referent. In cross-linguistic discussions of anaphoric demonstratives, on the other hand, the effect of the interlocutors' knowledge of the referent has not received such recognition. This paper has the following goals. First, it critically reviews Susumu Kuno's seminal analysis of Japanese anaphoric demonstratives, and presents a modified version of it. Second, it argues that the interlocutors' knowledge of the referent is relevant to the choice of the English demonstratives *this* and *that* too. Third, it provides a formal semantic analysis of anaphoric demonstratives in the two languages.

1 Introduction

Since Kuno (1973), it has been widely acknowledged in Japanese linguistics that the choice of demonstratives (the distal *a*-series, the medial *so*-series, and the proximal *ko*-series) in their anaphoric use is regulated by the rules concerned with the speaker's and the hearer's knowledge of the referent. In cross-linguistic discussions of anaphoric demonstratives (e.g., Diessel, 1999), on the other hand, the effect of the interlocutors' knowledge of the referent has not received such recognition.

The purpose of the current work is three-fold. First, it critically reviews Kuno's seminal analysis of Japanese anaphoric demonstratives, and presents a modified version of it. Second, it argues that the interlocutors' knowledge of the referent is relevant to the choice of the English demonstratives *this* and *that* too. Third, it provides a formal semantic analysis of anaphoric demonstratives in the two languages couched in the Discourse Representation Theory (DRT) framework.

It should be noted, before we proceed, that our discussion will focus on usage of anaphoric demonstratives in typical, two-agent conversations (dialogue); the question of whether and how the presented analysis can be extended to other discourse types, such as soliloquy (monologue) and nonfictional prose, will be left open. Also, our discussion will not cover the cases of demonstratives that do not refer to a specific entity (e.g., the "donkey anaphora" case, as in: *If a man is in Rhodes, that man cannot be in Athens*).

2 Distinct Uses of Demonstratives

Demonstratives in many, if not all, languages have several distinct uses. We adopt Diessel's (1999) classification and terminology, where the uses of demonstratives are first divided into the *exophoric* and *endophoric* uses, and the latter is further divided into subtypes including the *anaphoric* use.

The exophoric use is widely thought to be the most basic. Exophoric demonstratives (or expressions containing them) refer to entities present in the discourse situation.[1]

[1]For the sake of simplicity, we will say "adnominal demonstrative X refers to Y" to mean "an NP modified by X refers to Y". For example, *this* in *I read this book* will be said to refer to a book, although more precisely it is the NP *this book* that does

Copyright 2014 by David Y. Oshima and Eric McCready
28th Pacific Asia Conference on Language, Information and Computation pages 214–223

Anaphoric demonstratives, on the other hand, are coreferential with a noun phrase in the preceding discourse and keep track of the referents already introduced to the discourse (and are not present in the discourse situation), as in (1).

(1) My neighbor has a dog, and {**this/that**} dog kept me awake. (Gundel et al., 1993: 279)

Anaphoric demonstratives must be distinguished from *recognitional* and *discourse-deictic* demonstratives, two other major types of endophoric demonstratives. A recognitional demonstrative does not have an antecedent in the surrounding discourse and refers to an entity that is "discourse-new" but is identifiable for both interlocutors by virtue of their shared knowledge (e.g., *Do you still have* ***that*** *radio that your aunt gave you for your birthday?*; Diessel, 1999: 7). A discourse-deictic demonstrative refers to a proposition expressed by, or a speech act carried out by, a chunk (clause, sentence, etc.) of the surrounding discourse (e.g., *John is not here. – **That's** {false/a lie}*.)

3 Anaphoric Demonstratives in Japanese

3.1 Kuno (1973) on Anaphoric Demonstratives

Japanese has a three-term system of demonstratives, which consists of (i) the proximal *ko*-series ("close to the speaker"), (ii) the medial *so*-series ("close to the hearer and distant from the speaker"), and (iii) the distal *a*-series ("distant from both"). Each series contains several forms with different syntactic categories and meanings, e.g., pronouns *kore/sore/are* 'this/that one (insentient)', adnominal modifiers *kono/sono/ano* 'this/that', and manner adverbs *koo/soo/aa* 'in this/that way'.

There has been a vast amount of literature on anaphoric demonstratives in Japanese. Among the numerous existing studies, the chapter titled "the anaphoric use of *kore*, *sore*, and *are*" in Kuno (1973) has been one of the most influential. Regarding the contrast between the *a*-series and *so*-series, he essentially claims that the *a*-series is used to refer to an entity that both S (the speaker) and H (the hearer) know personally (know well, are acquainted with), and the *so*-series is used to refer to an entity that either S or H does not know personally (does not know well, is not acquainted with). In accordance with these generalizations, in (2) an *a*-demonstrative is chosen to refer to a person that both S and H are acquainted with, and in (3) a *so*-demonstrative is used to refer to an individual that only one of the interlocutors (i.e., A) "knows personally".[2]

(2) A: Kinoo Yamada-san-ni hajimete
yesterday Y.-Suffix-Dat for.the.first.time
aimashita. {**Ano/*sono**} hito, zuibun
meet.Pst.Plt {that$_{a}$/that$_{so}$} person quite
kawatta hito-desu-ne.
strange person-Cop.Prs.Plt-DP
'I met Yamada for the first time yesterday. That$_{a}$ man is a very strange person, isn't he?'
B: Ee, {**Ano/*sono**} hito-wa
yes {that$_{a}$/that$_{so}$} person-Top
henjin-desu-yo.
eccentric-Cop.Prs.Plt-DP
'Yes, that$_{a}$ man is an eccentric.'
(adapted from Kuno, 1973: 283–284)

(3) A: Watashi-no kinjo-ni
I-Gen neighborhood-Dat
Yamada-san-toiu hito-ga
Y.-Suffix-called person-Nom
sundeimasu. {***Ano/sono**} hito-wa
live.Ipfv.Prs.Plt {that$_{a}$/that$_{so}$} person-Top
Porsche-o motteimasu.
P.-Acc own.Ipfv.Prs.Plt
'I have a neighbor called Yamada. He$_{so}$ owns a Porsche.'
B: {***Ano/sono**} hito
{that$_{a}$/that$_{so}$} person
kanemochi-na-ndesu-ne.
wealthy-Cop.Attr-DAux.Prs.Plt-DP
'So he$_{so}$ is wealthy, I suppose?'

As for anaphoric *ko*-demonstratives, which are exemplified in (4), Kuno states that their referent must be something that S knows well but H does not, and

so.

[2]The abbreviations in glosses are: Acc = accusative, Attr = attributive, Cl= classifier, Cop = copula, Dat = dative, DAux = discourse auxiliary, DP = discourse particle, Evid = evidential particle, Inf = infinitive, Ipfv = imperfective, Loc = locative, Neg = negation, Nom = nominative, Plt = polite, Pot = potential, Prs = present, Pst = past, Top = topic, Vol = volitional. Subscript *ko*, *so*, and *a* in the glosses/translations indicate that the corresponding Japanese expression is a *ko*-, *so*-, and *a*-demonstrative, respectively.

also point out that they add an emotional overtone to the utterance.[3]

(4) Boku-no tomadachi-ni Yamada-toiu
I-Gen friend-Dat Y.-called
hito-ga iru-nda-ga,
person-Nom exist.Prs-DAux.Prs-and
{**kono/sono/*ano**} otoko-wa nakanaka-no
{this$_{ko}$/that$_{so}$/that$_{a}$} man-Top considerable
rironka-de ...
theoretician-Cop.Inf
'I have a friend by the name of Yamada, and {this$_{ko}$/that$_{so}$} man is a theoretician of some caliber, and ...'
(adapted from Kuno, 1973: 288)

3.2 Reconsideration of Kuno's Generalizations

While Kuno's analysis reviewed above captures well the way anaphoric *ko*/*so*/*a*-demonstratives contrast with each other, it leaves some room for refinements and elaborations. In the following, we address the following issues and present a modified version of Kuno's generalizations.

(5) i. It can be shown that it is not "to know well/personally", but a weaker kind of cognitive relation (between an interlocutor and a referent) that affects the choice of the Japanese anaphoric demonstratives.
ii. Kuno does not explicitly discuss cases where neither S nor H knows (well) the referent.
iii. There are cases where a *so*-demonstrative is chosen despite its referent being known (well) to both S and H.

Our discussion here will have to be brief due to space limitation; see Oshima (2014) and Oshima and McCready (in prepartion) for a fuller presentation and discussion of additional complications.[4]

The borderline between "known" and "not known": The choice of Japanese anaphoric demonstratives largely hinges on the interlocutors' knowledge of the referent. Exactly what kind of knowledge matters, however, is a question that requires careful consideration.

To begin with clear-cut cases, entities such as one's close friends, personal items that one uses day-to-day, and places that one often visits will be the central cases of referents that are "known (well)". Also, as pointed out by Kuno (1973: 285), public figures (e.g., film actors, politicians) that one knows of through public media (e.g., magazines, TV) have a good potential to be treated as, or as if they were, "known (well)", as long as the choice of anaphoric demonstratives is concerned. A referent that an interlocutor came to know through hearsay (including the other interlocutor's previous utterances), on the other hand, is not regarded as "known (well)", so that reference to it is made with a *so*-demonstrative, as in (3B) above.

According to Kuno, entities that an interlocutor had only a casual encounter with and does not know well (e.g., a person that he met briefly on the street) constitute a borderline case, and it is possible for him (or his conversation partner) to refer to them with the *so*-series.[5] This claim is hard to maintain, however, in view of data like the following:

(6) (A and B go to the cinema together. During the movie, they hear the person sitting behind them sob loudly. After leaving the theater, they talk about this person.)
A: Ushiro-no hito naiteta-yone.
back-Gen person cry.Ipfv.Pst-DP
'The person sitting behind us was sobbing, wasn't he?'
B: {**Ano/*sono**} hito-no sei-de
{that$_{a}$/that$_{so}$} person-Gen cause-by
eiga-ni shuuchuu-dekinakatta-yo.
movie-Dat concentrate-do.Pot.Neg.Pst-DP
'I couldn't concentrate on the movie because

[3]It is interesting to observe that *ko*-demonstratives of this kind have similarity with so-called "emotional-decitic" or "affective" demonstratives in English (Lakoff, 1974; e.g., *This Henry Kissinger really is something!*). A notable difference, however, is that *this* and *that* in their affective use tend not to have an explicit antecedent while an anaphoric *ko*-demonstrative needs one.

[4]The additional complications are mainly concerned with the use of an *a*-demonstrative for reference to an entity that H is not familiar with. It is observed in so-called *pseudo-soliloquy* (a type of speech that constitutes part of dialogue and yet is presented as if it were part of monologue), as well as in a discourse situation where (i) it is assumed that H is looking for an entity with some property P (e.g., a good piano instructor), and (ii) S introduces such an entity to H.

[5]See Oshima (2014: 9–10) and Oshima and McCready (in preparation) for discussion of the data which led Kuno — wrongly, in our view — to this conclusion.

of $that_a$ person.'

Unacceptability of *sono* in (6B) shows that, contra Kuno, any kind of contact involving direct perception, even if it is as casual/slight as just hearing sobbing noise, implies that the referent is in the realm of "known (well)". Henceforth, we will use the term "recognize", in place of Kuno's "know well/personally", to refer to the relation that may hold between an interlocutor and a referent and that affects the choice between the three series of Japanese anaphoric demonstratives. Along with close friends and some public figures, entities that one has had some kind of perceptual contact with belong to the domain of "recognized".

Reference to an entity that neither S nor H recognizes: Taken literally, Kuno's generalizations (with an amendment on the relevant cognitive relation) predict that the *so*-series and not the other two series can be used to refer to an entity that neither S nor H recognizes. This is because that "neither S nor H recognizes the referent" logically entails that "either S or H does not recognize the referent" (where "or" is understood to be inclusive). This prediction needs to be empirically tested, however, because the data discussed by Kuno do not preclude the possibility that the *so*-series can be used only when one of the interlocutors knows well the referent and the other does not (cf. the discussion of English *this* in §4).

Data like the following show, however, that Kuno's generalizations deal well with the situation where "neither S nor H recognizes the referent". Such a referent can be referred to with a *so*-demonstrative, but not with a *ko*- or *a*-demonstrative.

(7) (A and B are helping with the organization of an academic conference as research assistants. They were told that another research assistant would join them in the afternoon, but they are not acquainted with him.)

A: Ato-de moo hitori kuru-yone. Kono
later more one.Cl come.Prs-DP this
shigoto-wa {**sono**/***ano**/***kono**} hito-ni
task-Top {$that_{so}$/$that_a$/$this_{ko}$} person-Dat
tanomoo.
ask.Vol
'Another person will come in the afternoon, right? Let's ask $that_{so}$ person to do this task.'

B: {**Sono**/***ano**/***kono**} hito-ga
{$that_{so}$/$that_a$/$this_{ko}$} person-Nom
kuru-no-wa
come.Prs-Pro-Top
nan-ji-da-kke?
what-o'clock-Cop.Prs-DP
'What time is $that_{so}$ person supposed to come, again?'

Reference to an entity that (i) both S and H recognize but (ii) H does not know S recognizes: The use of the *so*-demonstrative in (8B) does not conform to Kuno's analysis (the use of *ano* in this place is possible, but seems to be slightly less natural than that of *sono*).

(8) (A comes to visit B's home.)

A: Ekimae-de keeki-o
station.front-Loc cake-Acc
katta-nda-kedo, sono mise-no
buy.Pst-DAux.Prs-and that shop-Gen
tenchoo-san, sugoku omoshiroi
manager-Suffix very interesting.Prs
hito-datta-yo. Sono hito, wakai
person-Cop.Pst-DP that person young.Prs
koro, Paris-de okashi zukuri-no
time P.-Loc confectionary making-Gen
shugyoo-o shita-nda-tte.
training-Acc do.Pst-DAux.Prs-Evid
'I bought some cake near the station. The manager of the cake shop was an interesting person. He told me that he received his training as a confectioner in Paris in his youth.'

B: {**Sono**/(?)**ano**} hito, watashi-no
{$that_{so}$/$that_a$} person I-Gen
osananajimi-de, ima-demo, yoku
childhood.friend-Cop.Inf now-even often
issho-ni tsuri-ni ittari
together fishing-Dat go.Representative
suru-ndesu-yo.
do.Prs-DAux.Prs.Plt-DP
'He is a childhood friend of mine. We still hang out often, and do such things as going fishing together.'

At the time (8B) is uttered, (interlocutor B knows that) the cake shop manager is recognized by both A and B, and thus, if Kuno's analysis is taken at face value, the use of the *so*-series must be blocked. Such data suggest that the choice between the three series of anaphoric demonstratives hinges not on whether (S knows that) the referent is recognized by S and H, but rather on whether it is *presupposed* (i.e., is considered a mutual knowledge of the interlocutors) in the discourse situation that the referent is recognized by both S and H.

Taking into consideration the points made above, we put forth the following generalizations:

(9) i. The *a*-series can be used only if it is presupposed that both S and H recognize the referent.
ii. The *so*-series can be used only if it is presupposed that either S or H does not recognize the referent.
iii. The *ko*-series can be used only if it is presupposed that S recognizes the referent and H does not.

The (somewhat degraded) acceptability of the *a*-demonstrative in (8B) can be accounted for in terms of *pragmatic accommodation*. Upon hearing the use of *ano hito* in (8B), interlocutor A will quickly update the common ground — the collection of mutual knowledge of the discourse participants — adding to it the information that interlocutor B recognizes the referent.

4 Anaphoric Demonstratives in English

English has a two-term system of demonstratives, consisting of proximal *this* (and *these*) and distal *that* (and *those*). These forms can be used as a pronominal (nominal head), a nominal determiner, or a degree adverb (e.g., *this big*, *that expensive*).

This and *that* used anaphorically are often interchangeable, but sometimes they are not. Lakoff (1974: 350) remarks that *this* has a more colloquial tone than *that*, and suggests that the former is not permissible in (10a) for this reason.

(10) a. John likes to kick puppies. {**That**/***this**} man's gonna get his one of these days!
b. John likes to kick puppies. {**That/this**} man has been under surveillance by the SPCA for 5 years now.

It is possible to find, however, instances of anaphoric *this* occurring in colloquial discourse.

(11) I've got a new roommate. I'll ask **this** guy if he'd be interested in buying your heap.

Gundel et al. (1993: 279) present another case, namely (12), where *that* cannot be replaced with *this*.

(12) A: Have you seen the neighbor's dog?
B: Yes, and {**that**/***this**} dog kept me awake last night.

They claim that anaphoric *this* is subject to the "speaker-activation" constraint, i.e., its referent must be something introduced to the discourse by S, as in (1) and (11), rather than by H.

An alternative way to account for the contrast between (1) and (12) is to suppose that *this* is subject to some constraint related to the interlocutors' mutual knowledge, so that it, like Japanese *so*- and *ko*-demonstratives, cannot be used to refer to an entity that (it is presupposed that) both S and H recognize (note that interlocutor A of (12), but not the hearer of (1), is assumed to recognize the dog in question).

This line of analysis seems to be applicable to the contrast between (10a) and (10b) as well. When one interprets discourse segment (10a) in isolation, it is most natural to presume that John is a mutual acquaintance of S and H. (10b), on the other hand, may be taken more easily to be an utterance where S describes some malicious person previously unknown to H.

It is furthermore possible to find evidence against the "speaker-activation"-based account. The following discourse segments show that *this* sometimes can be used to refer to a "hearer-activated" entity.

(13) A: John has a pet tortoise.
B: Oh really? How big is {**that/this**} tortoise?

(14) A: My neighbor downstairs asked me if I'd be interested in buying opium.
B: You should tell the police about {**that/this**} guy.

There are also cases where S has to choose *that*, rather than *this*, to refer to a speaker-activated entity. (10a) above is one such case, and (15) is an additional example.

(15) (Both S and H have driven Mary's Corolla several times.)
Mary decided to sell her Corolla. {**That/*this**} car is now 20 years old, and she's had it with all the maintenance problems it causes.

It seems thus that the "mutual knowledge"-based account is the more appropriate. What exactly, then, is the discourse-configurational constraint that *this* is subject to? As has been seen above with (13)/(14), unlike a *ko*-demonstrative, and like a *so*-demonstrative, *this* may be used to refer to an entity that H recognizes but S does not. *This* differs from a *so*-demonstrative, however, in that it cannot be used to refer to an entity that neither S nor H recognizes. Compare (7) with (16).

(16) (the same situation as in (7))
A: Another assistant will join us in the afternoon, right? Let's ask {**that/*this**} guy to do this task.
B: What time is {**that/*this**} guy supposed to come, again?

It can thus be concluded that the constraint on anaphoric *this* involves exclusive "or": the referent needs to be recognized by S or H, but not by both. To put it differently, *this* signals *informational asymmetry* between S and H regarding the referent. Anaphoric *that*, on the other hand, is free from any kind of constraint that has to do with the interlocutors' mutual knowledge. In more precise terms, these properties of *this*/*that* can be stated as follows:

(17) i. *This* can be used only if it is presupposed that S or H, but not both, recognizes the referent.
ii. *That* can be used whether or not it is presupposed that S and/or H recognize the referent.

From (17a,b), it follows that it is generally possible to replace anaphoric *this* with anaphoric *that*, but not vice versa.

5 Formal Analysis

This section formalizes the preceding discussion. There are many ways in which this project could be carried out; but given that our domain of inquiry is anaphoric demonstratives, it seems natural to make use of a theory of semantics formulated at the level at which discourse anaphora takes place. Consequently, in this paper, we will use Discourse Representation Theory (DRT; Kamp and Reyle, 1993; Kamp et al., 2011) as the framework for our discussion.

5.1 Preliminaries

In the interest of space, we will assume the reader's familiarity with the basic components of DRT detailed in Kamp and Reyle (1993). For a brief reminder, in DRT, each (informative) sentence in a discourse introduces *conditions* and possibly *discourse referents* into a Discourse Representation Structure (DRS) in a form specified by a construction algorithm. Discourse referents are similar to logical variables, and serve as markers for entities asserted to exist within the discourse. A DRS K can be represented set-theoretically as an ordered pair $\langle U_K, C_K \rangle$, where U_K is the set of discourse referents (the *universe* of the DRS) and C_K is the set of *conditions* that are predicated of the discourse referents. However, DRSs are usually represented using a box notation for readability. For instance, the DRS for *A wolf howled* looks as follows:

(18)

x
$wolf(x)$ $howled(x)$

In the sequel, we will use $DRef$ for the set of discourse referents and $Cond$ for the set of conditions associated with a DRS.

In addition to the above, we need three more ingredients for the purposes of this paper: (i) a model for attitude ascriptions, (ii) a model for analyzing acquaintance with the particular objects the embedding function relates to discourse referents, and (iii) a model of presupposition. The second is obviously needed in order to characterize the kind of cognitive relation we have claimed to be necessary for the use of some anaphoric demonstratives; the first is required to specify the desired notion of *establishment* of such acquaintance relations. We will now show how these elements are realized in DRT, in some detail since they will be key in our analysis. Finally, our formal analysis will treat the felicity conditions on anaphoric demonstratives in a way parallel to the treatment of other kinds of felicity conditions in the literature: as presuppositions (e.g. the treatment of ϕ-features in Kamp et al. 2011).

In recent versions of DRT, attitude ascriptions are modeled as attitudinal predicates which relate three elements: attitude holders, discourse representation structures (DRSs) K, and a function which maps (subsets of) $DRef$ directly to objects in the model, and thus have the form $Att(a, ADS, EA)$ for agent a, a so-called 'Attitude Description Set' ADS, and external anchoring function EA. The attitudinal predicate specifies that an attitude ascription is being made. The first argument is the attitude holder. The second argument, the ADS, specifies the content of the attitudes being ascribed. It consists of a set of pairs $\langle Mode, K\rangle$, where $Mode$ is an attitude specification which can be drawn from (at least) BEL(ief), DES(ire), and INT(end), and K is a DRS. It is also possible here to have conditions of the form $\langle [Anch, x], K\rangle$, which specify that x as used in K is believed by the attitude holder to be anchored to some external object. Only BEL will play a role in our analysis. Finally, EA is a function which maps some subset of the discourse referents used in the conditions in the ADS to objects external to the discourse representation, i.e., to objects whose existence is independently known, or which are taken to be so.[6]

Our final task before proceeding to the analysis proper is to give background on treatments of presupposition within DRT. There is a large literature on this topic within DRT and dynamic semantics in general, with authors proposing varied treatments, but here we will present a treatment within more or less standard DRT following van der Sandt (1992), though differing from that work in some issues of representational detail. The basic idea of DRT views of presupposition is that presuppositions are anaphoric objects which target elements already existing in DRSs by virtue of previous linguistic or nonlinguistic content. For an example of the intuition behind this approach, note that the presupposition of the possessive NP — that John has a daughter — is licensed in the discourse in (19) by virtue of the content of the first sentence.

(19) John has a daughter and a son. His daughter is going to a good university next year.

Within DRT, this can be modeled by letting presuppositional expressions introduce special DRSs of the form ∂K. Such expressions are not integrated with the rest of the DRS, instead being resolved to other preexisting elements in the DRS. The discourse in (19), for instance, gets the representation in (20). The condition $z =?$ indicates that z must be resolved to some contextual entity, if such resolution is possible.

(20)

$j\ x\ y$
$daughter(x, j)$ $son(y, j)$ $\partial\left(\begin{array}{\|l\|} \hline z \\ \hline daughter(z, j) \\ gtgu(z) \\ z =? \\ \hline \end{array}\right)$

A resolution algorithm then searches for an antecedent condition with the same content as the presuppositional DRS modulo substitution of variables.[7] After such resolution, modeled by letting the unresolved variable ? in the condition $z =?$ take on the value x, the presuppositional content is integrated; in a case like this one, where an antecedent expression exists, it is eliminated from the representation. However, if no suitable antecedent exists, the presupposed content is added to the DRS via accommodation when doing so does not result in inconsistency. This process is illustrated in the variant of the above in (21).

[6] The model theory of these conditions is complex and its full explanation is beyond the immediate requirements of this paper. Full details can be found in Kamp et al. (2011).

[7] This is a minor simplification; see van der Sandt (1992) and Beaver (1997) for a detailed discussion.

(21) John has a family. His daughter is going to a good university next year.

In the DRS representing this discourse, no condition exists of the form *daughter(y,j)* for any variable y; thus, the presupposition cannot be resolved. However, since it is plainly consistent with the rest of the discourse, it can be accommodated.

It is worth mentioning finally the case of proper names, because of their close relation to demonstratives (e.g. Kaplan, 1989), though in the present paper we will not be able to address the issue of direct reference for reasons of space. In DRT, proper names are taken to introduce discourse referents which are associated with the presupposition that the name itself holds of that referent. They are thus a species of presuppositional indefinite. The discourse referent itself must be represented at the highest level of the DRS, and so must be mapped to some object in the model; it is not allowed to scope under operators such as negation. The presence of the referent at the top level may be achieved by accommodating the presupposition if required (cf. Beaver and Zeevat, 2007).

5.2 Japanese

Let us begin by reconsidering the constraints on Japanese anaphoric demonstratives from a DRT perspective. It can be seen that the basic ingredients required for a formal analysis are (i) an anchoring function, (ii) a way to separate the anchors associated with S and H, and (iii) a way to indicate the metalinguistic beliefs of S about the anchoring functions of the S and H.

This observation can be implemented as in (23), which provides a semantics for adnominal anaphoric demonstratives *ano/sono/kono*. Here, we have treated the constraints on these expressions as presuppositional in nature. The use of an adnominal anaphoric demonstrative introduces four things to a DRS: (i) a new discourse referent x_n, (ii) a condition requiring the resolution of that referent, $x_n =?$, and two "true" presuppositions: one requiring x to satisfy the predication introduced by the nominal element, and one putting some constraint or constraints on the belief states of S and H, namely that they recognize, or do not recognize, the referent. We capture this by allowing individuals to have beliefs about each other's internal anchors and thus, indirectly, about each other's anchoring functions. In the sequel, we will use conditions of the form (22) to indicate content of this kind; (22) can be read "i believes that j takes x to be externally anchored".

(22) $Bel(i, Anch(j, x))$

The above condition abbreviates the usual DRT attitudinal representations discussed above. We can simplify this condition still further for our purposes here. In conditions of the form (22), the anchoring condition $Anch(a, x)$ indicates that a takes x to be externally anchored; the remainder indicates that the attitude holder i takes a to take x to be anchored. In all the conditions we will use below, the attitude is claimed to be jointly held by S and H, and so part of the common ground. Given that this part of the condition is constant, we will eliminate it in our analysis proper, simply writing $Anch(j, x)$.

Our semantics for the Japanese anaphoric demonstratives can then be stated as follows, with the adnominal modifiers *ano/sono/kono* used as the representative cases. In (23) and hereafter, $\{s, h\}$ represents the group of S and H, and so $Att(\{s, h\}, \dots)$ is a kind of commonly held attitude predicate. For the case of belief, the use of this argument indicates common belief of S and H (cf. van Ditmarsch et al., 2007).

(23) a. '*ano N*' introduces a condition of the form

$$\partial\left(\begin{array}{|l|}\hline x \\ \hline x =? \\ N(x) \\ Anch(\{s,h\}, x) \\ \hline\end{array}\right)$$

b. '*sono N*' introduces a condition of the form

$$\partial\left(\begin{array}{|l|}\hline x \\ \hline x =? \\ N(x) \\ \neg Anch(\{s,h\}, x) \\ \hline\end{array}\right)$$

c. '*kono N*' introduces a condition of the form

$$\partial\left(\begin{array}{|l|}\hline x \\ \hline x=? \\ N(x) \\ \neg Anch(h,x) \\ Anch(s,x) \\ \hline\end{array}\right)$$

This analysis takes the conditions on demonstratives to be essentially presuppositional. These conditions have three parts. First, a fresh discourse referent x is introduced within the DRS corresponding to the presupposition. This referent is then indicated to require an antecedent by the condition $x=?$. The core of the analysis comes in the remaining condition(s), which state the requirements on the anchoring of the variable. In (23a), the variable associated with the referent of an anaphoric demonstrative in the *a*-series is required to be jointly believed by S and H to be anchored for both of them.[8] (23b,c) are similar to the above except for the attitudinal requirement. (23b) requires that S and H do not jointly believe that they both have anchors for x, as required by the conditions on the *so*-series, and (23c) requires that S is jointly believed to have an anchor for the variable, but that H is not.

The above seems to adequately capture the conditions we have claimed to hold of the Japanese anaphoric demonstratives. It should be noted that we must assume that presupposed conditions relating to attitudes can be resolved in the structures which are used to represent attitudes in DRT. To our knowledge, this sort of case has not been discussed in the literature, mostly because metalinguistic conditions of this kind involving mutual belief have not been the focus of much work in this area. We think that this is not problematic.

5.3 English

The English case, summarized in (17) above, is substantially simpler than the Japanese one. Each of the Japanese anaphoric demonstratives had a distinct condition (or set of conditions) associated with it, but for English we find that *this*-demonstratives are relatively tightly constrained in having both negative and positive conditions (as with the *ko*-series in Japanese), but *that*-demonstratives can be used quite freely.

The task of giving a formal analysis for English thus centers on the case of *this*-demonstratives. We propose the following semantics for *this*- and *that*-demonstratives; note that we focus on the (singular) pronominal case, which differs from the adnominal case discussed above for Japanese in lacking a presupposition associated with the nominal predicate. The adnominal case (of *this/that*) is analyzed by adding such a presupposition, while the Japanese pronominal cases can be analyzed by removing the presupposition that $N(x)$ from each clause of (23). The pronominal uses also have implications for the animacy/sentience of their referents; for instance, *are/sore/kore* in general cannot denote a sentient entity, and neither can pronominal *this/that* (except when they occur as the subject of *be*, as in: *That is his assistant.*), which we model by adding a presupposition that the referent is insentient.[9]

(24) a. '*this*' introduces a condition of the form

$$\partial\left(\begin{array}{|l|}\hline x \\ \hline x=? \\ insentient(x) \\ \neg Anch(\{s,h\},x) \\ Anch(s,x) \vee Anch(h,x) \\ \hline\end{array}\right)$$

b. '*that*' introduces a new discourse referent x to $DRef$ and the conditions $x=?$ and $insentient(x)$ to $Cond$.

Given what we have done in (23) for Japanese, the analysis of *this* is rather straightforward. (24a) states that *this* behaves like a kind of combination of the Japanese *so*-series and the *ko*-series demonstratives; like the *so*-series, it indicates that the referent is not jointly anchored, but like the *ko*-series, it indicates that it is anchored for one discourse participant, though it does not indicate which one. We have treated anaphoric *that*-demonstratives as essentially ordinary pronouns lacking anchoring restrictions. Both expressions presuppose that their ref-

[8] Of course, this requirement is satisfied if the referent is jointly anchored.

[9] The interaction of animacy/sentience and the use of pronominal demonstratives is a rather intricate matter (e.g., Stirling and Huddleston 2002, 1504–1505), to which we cannot do full justice here.

erents are insentient. Note, though, that for both cases, adnominal uses require an extra specification; anaphoric demonstratives of the form *this/that N* also presuppose that $N(x)$, just as with the Japanese anaphoric demonstratives.

6 Conclusion

This paper has identified some difficulties with Kuno's (1973) analysis of the Japanese anaphoric demonstratives in the *a-*, *so-*, and *ko-*series, and presented a modified version of that analysis which accounts for a wider range of facts. This analysis was stated in terms of the interlocutors' knowledge of the referent which the demonstrative picks up; we have argued in addition that such knowledge is also relevant to the choice of the English demonstratives *this* and *that*. Finally, it has provided a formal semantic analysis of anaphoric demonstratives in the two languages stated in terms of pragmatic presuppositions on belief states, as modeled in the DRT framework. This work represents an advance on our current knowledge of anaphoric demonstratives, both in empirical and theoretical senses.

This work opens several avenues for future research. The first is the application of the current analysis to anaphoric demonstratives in other languages. We have argued that epistemic conditions on external anchoring constrain the choice of demonstratives in Japanese and English, but have not touched on other languages. The question of whether these factors also play into demonstrative use elsewhere is worthy of further investigation. Second, we have been careful to limit our analysis to the case of anaphoric demonstratives in dialogue. The constraints we have noted seem to behave in a subtly different manner in other discourse genres such as monologue or reportage; also, bound-variable uses of demonstratives also seem exempt from them, as in the case of donkey anaphora. The way(s) in which demonstratives are used across the full range of genres, and how the constraints on their use interact with constraints on other types of nominal expressions, is also a useful area for later research. Finally, it would be interesting to attempt the integration of the results of this paper with computational models of discourse generation and interpretation.

References

David Beaver. 1997. Presupposition. In *Handbook of Logic and Language*, pages 939–1008. Elsevier, Oxford.

David Beaver and Henk Zeevat. 2007. Accommodation. In Gillian Ramchand and Charles Reiss, editors, *Oxford Handbook of Linguistic Interfaces*. Oxford University Press, Oxford.

Holger Diessel. 1999. *Demonstratives: Form, Function and Grammaticalization*. John Benjamins, Amsterdam.

Hans van Ditmarsch, Wiebe van der Hoek, and Barteld Kooi. 2007. *Dynamic Epistemic Logic*. Springer, Berlin.

Jeanette Gundel, Nancy Hedberg, and Ron Zacharski. 1993. Cognitive status and the form of referring expressions in discourse. *Language*, 69:274–307.

Hans Kamp, Josef van Genabith, and Uwe Reyle. 2011. Discourse representation theory. In Dov Gabbay and Franz Guethner, editors, *Handbook of Philosophical Logic*, volume 15, pages 125–394. Springer, Berlin.

Hans Kamp and Uwe Reyle. 1993. *From Discourse to Logic*. Kluwer, Dordrecht.

David Kaplan. 1989. Demonstratives. In Joseph Almog, John Perry, and Howard Wettstein, editors, *Themes from Kaplan*, pages 481–566. Oxford University Press. Manuscript version from 1977.

Susumu Kuno. 1973. *The Structure of the Japanese Language*. MIT Press.

Robin Lakoff. 1974. Remarks on 'this' and 'that'. In *Proceedings of the Chicago Linguistics Society*, volume 10, pages 345–356.

David Y. Oshima. 2014. Nihongo shizisi no naibu shoo'oo yoohoo (bunmyaku shizi yoohoo) ni tsuite: Kuno Susumu ni yoru bunseki no saikentoo [On the endophoric use of demonstratives in japanese: A reconsideration of Susumu Kuno's analysis]. *Forum of International Development Studies*, 44:1–16.

David Y. Oshima and Eric McCready. in preparation. Anaphoric demonstratives and the interlocutors' mutual knowledge: The cases of Japanese and English. Nagoya University and Aoyama Gakuin University.

Rob van der Sandt. 1992. Presupposition projection as anaphora resolution. *Journal of Semantics*, 9:333–377.

Leslie Stirling and Rodney Huddleston. 2002. Deixis and anaphora. In Rodney Huddleston and Geoffrey K. Pullum, editors, *The Cambridge Grammar of the English Language*, pages 1449–1564. Cambridge University Press, Cambridge.

The Influence of Givenness and Heaviness on OSV in Japanese

Satoshi Imamura
Japanese Studies, University of Oxford
41 Wellington Square
Oxford, OX1 2JF
United Kingdom

Abstract

Several studies contend that the main motivation for scrambling is heaviness. In particular, Yamashita (2002) maintains that scrambling has nothing to do with givenness and that heaviness is the primary factor for scrambling. However, her conclusions count on only 19 examples and she does not distinguish VP-internal scrambling from VP-external scrambling. Thus, it is conceivable that some types of scrambling rely on givenness. In order to see if this hypothesis is on the right track, I conducted a corpus analysis of OSV order in Japanese, largely based on the quantitative approach. Consequently, it has been revealed that both givenness and heaviness have a high explanatory power for the usage of OSV order. Furthermore, there was no correlation between givenness and heaviness, showing their independent influence on OSV order. Therefore, I conclude that both givenness and heaviness are sufficient to trigger OSV order and the phenomenon cannot be fully accounted for except with reference to both. Furthemore, based on the mapping between information structure and syntactic structure, I propose that VP-external scrambling is discourse-driven while VP-internal scrambling is not.

1. Introduction

A natural language may have many kinds of options for expressing the same proposition. In Japanese, for example, the meaning of a canonical transitive sentence SOV can be expressed by a scrambled sentence OSV in which the object appears before the subject. Why do languages have many options to convey the same proposition? One explanation is that these options allow speakers to choose the way information is transmitted. They differ not in what is said about the world, but in the way it is packaged (Chafe, 1976; Lambrecht, 1996; Vallduvi and Engdahl, 1996). In other words, their differences derive from information structure, i.e. how the meaning of a sentence is conveyed. Specifically, it has long been recognized since the work of the Prague School that speakers prefer to put given information before new information. However, this description begs the question because givenness itself is not a clear-cut concept. Therefore, it is necessary to define givenness in an objective way. In this paper, givenness is defined by a quantitative approach (Givōn, 1983) and regarded as discourse-old information i.e. information mentioned in the preceding discourse. In other words, previously mentioned constituents are considered to be given information. Another explanation for variable ordering of arguments is based on heaviness. Hawkins (1994) observed that long constituents tend to be put in earlier positions than shorter ones in Japanese in order to facilitate the processing cost of heavy constituents. In this study, I am going to investigate the usages of OSV

Copyright 2014 by Satoshi Imamura
28th Pacific Asia Conference on Language, Information and Computation pages 224–233

order in terms of givenness and heaviness, mainly based on quantitative data from a Japanese corpus.

This paper is organized as follows. Section 2 surveys previous studies about Givōnian givenness and scrambling, where I will overview the basic concepts of referential distance, given-new ordering, and heaviness. Section 3 presents my corpus analysis of scrambling from the viewpoint of information structure and heaviness. Then, I will reveal that O tends to be discourse-old information in OSV. In addition, I will demonstrate that heaviness has an effect on OSV order, independent of givenness. Moreover, from the viewpoint of mapping between syntactic structure and information structure, I propose that givenness will have greater effects on VP-external scrambling than on VP-internal scrambling. In contrast, heaviness seems to have stronger effect on VP-internal scrambling than on VP-external scrambling. Section 4 is devoted to the conclusion and further studies.

2. Previous Studies

2.1. Givōnian Givenness

Givōn (1983) proposes as one quantitative approaches for calculating the topicality of referents. The metric of Referential Distance (RD) measures the gap between a referent in the current clause and its antecedent using clause boundaries as units. If there is no antecedent in the previous clauses, RD is assigned a value of 20 because without some limitation it would be infinite [1]. Hence, RD is expressed by some number of clauses from 1 to 20. What I should emphasize here is that RD is a quantitative value and has several measures to assess degrees of givenness. That is, it is possible to state that some referent is older than other referents. Let us illustrate this concept with (1).

(1) a. I met a man on the road to Philadelphia.
b. He had no face.
c. Suddenly, he said to me
d. that I would die soon.
e. Somehow I thought
f. that he told the truth.

In order to measure the RD of *he* in (1f), you need to go back to (1c). Since there are three clause boundaries between *he* in (1f) and *he* in (1c), RD for *he* in (1f) is 3. Although the same referent is once mentioned in (1a) and (1b), this has nothing to do with the RD of *he* in (1f). This is because RD is the value of the distance between the target referent and its nearest antecedent.

In this study, I will rely on RD for the purpose of calculating the givenness of scrambled objects. RD is a well recognized measurement that is easily implementable and its employment renders the results of my analysis reproducible.

2.2. Scrambling

In Japanese, it has been said that O in OSV is moved from the VP-internal position toward the sentence initial position (Miyagawa 2010; Saito, 1985, 2009). This phenomenon is called scrambling. Note that scrambling does not change the propositional meaning. What is the motivation for scrambling? One explanation is based on givenness. Kuno (1978:54) observed that word order choice in Japanese depends on given-new ordering, which means that given information is mentioned early and new information later. Applying this principle to OSV sentences, native Japanese speakers are thought to prefer OSV just in those cases where the direct object is more given than its subject. Saeki (1960) observed that NPs with demonstratives precede other constituents in general. This tendency is true of OSV. In particular,

[1] The limitation of RD is rather arbitrary. For example, Givón (1994) proposed that it should be 3 and Cooreman (1992) suggested that it should be 15 because there was no example with RD higher than 15. However, we observed sentences with RD higher than 16, so we followed the criteria of Givón (1983).

Ishii (2001) observed that when scrambled objects are modified by demonstrative *sono* 'that', the acceptability of those sentences increases, as can be seen in the difference in acceptability between (2a) and (2b). Taken together, these studies suggest that there is a correlation between scrambled object and givenness in Japanese OSV word order.

(2) a. *okane-o dare-ga nusun-da-no?
money-ACC who-NOM steal-PAST-Q
b. sono okane-o dare-ga
that money-ACC who-NOM
nusun-da-no?
steal-PAST-Q
'Who stole that money?'
(Ishii 2001: 97)

Another motivation for scrambling is the heaviness of the NP that is moved to the left. Yamashita and Chang (2001) revealed that native Japanese speakers were apt to shift long constituents to earlier positions more than short constituents in sentence production. This result is consistent with Saeki (1960), who observed that long NPs tend to precede short NPs. According to Hawkins (1994), the motivation for word order change is to facilitate the processing cost of heavy constituents.

Yamashita (2002) even insists that heaviness is more important for scrambling than referentiality is. In her written Japanese data, heaviness accounts for about 70% of the scrambled sentences while referentiality makes up about 25%. In other words, 70% of scrambled objects are long and 25% of them include a determiner or an anaphor either referring to something appearing in the preceding discourse, or inferable from it. She observed a complementary distribution between heaviness and referentiality because almost all referential constituents were light. However, her data include various types of scrambling: VP-internal, short-distance, and long-distance scrambling. Therefore, pure data are needed to examine the function of OSV in Japanese. Moreover, though Yamashita (2002) contends that heaviness is independent of referentially, it is not clear whether scrambled heavy direct objects are discourse-old information or not. The range of discourse-old information is wider than referentiality because referential NPs must have a demonstrative or anaphor such as *sono* 'that' and *sonna* 'such' but there is no such constraint for discourse-old information. Therefore, it is conceivable that scrambled direct objects in OSV are both heavy and discourse-old. If one factor strongly depends on the other, that concept is not necessary for explaining the function of OSV order. In contrast, it is possible that givenness is unrelated to heaviness. This means that both concepts are needed to explain the function of scrambling. In this study, I am going to examine whether there is an interaction between heaviness and givenness in Japanese OSV word order.

To sum up the above discussion, there are two research questions that I attempt to solve in this study. The first question is whether O in OSV is given information or not. The second question is whether both givenness and heaviness independently affect OSV word order in Japanese, or both factors work together. On the basis of Givōnian approach, I will disentangle these issues.

3. Corpus Analysis of Scrambling

3.1. Basic Predictions and Procedure

The first aim of my study is to investigate the relationship between discourse-old information and OSV word order in Japanese. In order to attain my goal, I am going to calculate the RDs of objects in OSV. If the discourse status of direct object determines whether the speaker should use OSV or not, OSV is preferred when the RD of the direct object is less than 20. The second purpose of this study is to see if there is a correlation between givenness and heaviness. If there is a strong correlation between givenness and heaviness, one factor may be derived from the other. In contrast, if there is no correlation between them, this will mean that both concepts have an influence on OSV word order independently, showing autonomy of each concept. In order to check which hypothesis is more valid, I will measure the length of scrambled objects and compare it with their RDs.

3.2. Method

3.2.1. Corpus Data

The Balanced Corpus of Contemporary Written Japanese (BCCWJ) was employed in order to assemble relevant data. BCCWJ is designed to be representative of contemporary written Japanese and thus includes 100 million words from well-balanced written materials covering books, magazines, newspapers, library books, bulletin boards, blogs, best-selling books, school textbooks, minutes of the National Diet, publicity of newsletters of local governments, laws, and poetry verses (see Maekawa et al. 2008 in detail).

3.2.2. Materials

OSV sentences were collected from BCCWJ by using *Chunagon*, which is a web interface program. In particular, the string [*o*(ACC)-noun-*ga*(NOM)] was used to extract OSV examples. The reason for using only strings with subject NPs of minimal length is that the left boundaries of NPs are not marked in the corpus. The limitation of my design is that it cannot pick out complex subjects completely. Complex subjects modified by a relative in OSV like [[noun-*ga*-verb]-noun-*ga*] were eliminated by hand in order to control the data. Thus, the scope of the OSV string includes only a simple (non-branching) noun subject.

3.2.3. Calculation of Heaviness

In order to measure the lengths of direct objects, I counted the *bunsetsu* of direct objects. *Bunsetsu* is a basic linguistic unit in Japanese Linguistics, consisting of content word(s) followed by zero or more functional words. Generally speaking, *bunsetsu* corresponds to a phrase. The reason why I chose *bunsetsu* is that the length of the subjects in my study is controlled in terms of *bunsetsu*. The *bunsetsu* of the subjects is always 1 in my data because they are a single noun plus nominative case particle *GA*. In (3), for instance, *kuruma-ga* 'car-NOM' forms a *bunsetsu* because it is a content word *kuruma* 'car' followed by a functional word *GA*. As a whole, (3) consists of four *bunsetsus*: *sono*, *kasao*, *kurumaga*, and *hanetobashita*.

(3) Sono kasa-o kuruma-ga hanetobashi-ta.
that umbrella-ACC car-NOM hit-PAST
'A car hit that umbrella.'
(BCCWJ)

3.2.4. Criterion of Given and New Information

In this study, a value along the scale of given-new is assigned according to the measurement of RD. When a constituent has its RD less than 20, it is regarded as discourse-old information. In contrast, when a constituent does not have an antecedent, it belongs to new information.

As for givenness, some kinds of inferable information are categorized into discourse-old information. In particular, bridging relations are taken into consideration. Bridging is an inference from a referent explicitly mentioned in the preceding discourse. In (4), the hearer must suppose that *ringo* 'apple' is a part of *kudamono* 'fruit'. This relation is a bridging relation. Though *ringo* 'apple' is not directly referred to in (4a), its RD is 1 because *kudamono* 'fruit' can be regarded as the antecedent.

(4) a. Taro-wa kudamono-o kat-ta
Taro-TOP fruit-ACC buy-PAST
'Taro bought fruit.'
b. Shikashi, ringo-wa kusattei-ta.
but apple-TOP be.rotten-PAST
'But the apples were rotten'

Yet, those examples which have no direct relationship with the previous discourse are not considered to be discourse-old information. In (5), both *football* and *baseball* belong to *sports*. Thus, *baseball* is indirectly connected with *football* through the concept *sports*. However, there is no direct relationship because *baseball* is not included in *football*. Therefore, baseball is not regarded as discourse-old information.

(5) a. Do you watch football?
b. Yeah. Baseball I like a lot BETTER.
(Ward and Birner 1998: 161)

3.2.5. Criterion of RD Analysis

The criterions of my analysis are mainly based on Shimojō (2005), but several modifications are added to my analysis. In the following sections, I will explain the details of these criterions.

3.2.5.1. Complex Clause
Complex clauses are divided into separate clauses based on predicates. Therefore, subordinate clauses are regarded as independent clauses. For example, the complex clause (6) is divided into three clauses because it contains the three predicates; *kumu* 'pull up', *hayaokisusu* 'get up early', and *iu* 'say'.

(6) [3 shin-iemoto-wa musuko-kara
new.head.of.school-TOP son-from
[2 ojiichan-ni sakini
grandfather-DAT in.first
kuma-re-nai-youni] [1 (S)
pull.up.PASS-NEG-so.as.to (he)
hayaoki-shina-kutya]-to
get.up.early-do-must-COMP
iwa-re-ta sooda].
tell-PASS-PAST seem
Zeniemoto-no
former-head.of.school-GEN
sekkyokusa-o mago-ga
positiveness-ACC grandson-NOM
monogatattei-te,...
give.evidence-and
'I heard that the new head of school was told by his son to get up early and pull up water from the well so as not to be preceded by his father. The grandson gave evidence of the former head of school's positive attitude...'
(BCCWJ)

In order to illustrate the process of calculation of RD, let us measure the RD of *zen-iemoto* 'the former head of school'. The first step is to check the antecedent of *zen-iemoto*. Here, it is *ojiichan* 'grandfather' because it refers to the same person that *zen-iemoto* does. The second step is to calculate the clause boundaries between the target referent *zen-iemoto* and its antecedent *ojiichan*. In this study, the linear order of arguments determines RD of a referent. Following this approach, the RD of *zen-iemoto* is 2. Here, zero subject intervenes between *zen-iemoto* and *ojiichan*.

3.2.5.2. Adjacent Predicates
V_1-*te*-V_2 form is basically categorized into the same clause, but when V_1 and V_2 have different subjects, each verb is regarded as belonging to an independent clause (Shimojō 2005: 57-8).

(7) a. kyanberu-no suupukan kat-te-ki-te
Cambell-LK soup.can buy-TE-come-and
'(I) bought a Cambell soup can (and came).'
b. dorai-no-yatsu-o tomodachi-ga
dry-LK-one-ACC friends-NOM
motte-te (S) (O) karite
have-TE (I) (it) borrow-and
'A friend had dry (basil) and (I) borrowed it' (it).'
(Shimojō 2005: 57-8)

For example, in (7a), the linked verb *kat-te-kite* 'buy-TE-come-and' share the zero subject 'I'. Thus, the V_1-*te*-V_2 form belongs to the same clause. In contrast, in (7b), V_1 and V_2 have different subjects. In other words, V_1 *motte* 'have' forms a nexus with *tomodachi* 'friend' and V_2 *karite* 'borrow' forms a nexus with the zero subject 'I'. In this case, both V_1 and V_2 are considered to constitute an independent clause because they do not share the same subject.

3.2.5.3. Back-channel feedback
Generally speaking, back-channel feedback such as *soo* 'indeed' and *un* 'yeah' are propositionally empty and are given by the hearer while speaker is holding the conversational turn (Shimojō 2005: 58). They are considered to be dependent on another clause and do not form an independent clause.

3.2.5.4. Copula
Copula expressions such as *da* and *dearu* are regarded as predicates and hence they head independent clauses.

3.2.5.5. Proposition
The method for determining RD has been developed for calculating the discourse status of a

referent (Givōn 1983, 1994). Proposition is not included in this method because it is not a referent itself but a relationship between referents. Instead of directly calculating the RD of a proposition, I count the RDs of the related referents. In my approach, the RD of the proposition is the least value of the referents pertinent to that proposition. For instance, in (8b), the scrambled object is the proposition *Hänsel-ga naka-ni hai-routosuru* 'that Hänsel is trying to come in it', which includes the referents *Hänsel* and *candy house*. Therefore, this proposition has the two related referents *Hänsel* and *candy house*. In this study, the RDs of both *Hänsel* and *candy house* are calculated. Note that the head of the scrambled object is nominalizer *no* but it is anchored by *Hänsel* and *candy house*. Thus, the RD of the scrambled object is replaced by the anchoring expression's RD and its RD is 1.

(8) a. okashinoie-ga aru-node
candy.house-NOM be-because
hutari-wa hidoku bikkurisuru
two.person-TOP very surprised
'Since there is a candy house, the two are very surprised.'

b. Hänsel-ga naka-ni
Hänsel-NOM inside-LOC
hai-routosuru-no-o Gretel-ga
come-try.to.do-NMZ-ACC Gretel-NOM
togameru
blame.for
'Gretel berates Hänsel for trying to enter.'
(BCCWJ)

3.2.5.6. Movement Verbs

Movement verbs may affect the word order choice because Saeki (1960) points out that location tends to precede subject independently of information structure. Hence, locative objects placed in the sentence initial position are eliminated from my analysis.

3.3. Results

I analyzed 3273 examples from BCCWJ. Table 1 summarizes the distributions of scrambled objects from the viewpoint of RD. This table has demonstrated that 2676 examples have an antecedent while 597 examples do not. Hence, 81.76% of objects in OSV are discourse-old information.

Table 1: Tokens of scrambled objects in terms of RD

RD	Number (%)
1	1724 (52.67%)
2	368 (11.24%)
3	194 (5.93%)
4	102 (3.12%)
5	61 (1.86%)
6	49 (1.50%)
7	34 (1.04%)
8	37 (1.13%)
9	19 (0.58%)
10	12 (0.37%)
11	14 (0.43%)
12	15 (0.46%)
13	8 (0.24%)
14	5 (0.15%)
15	5 (0.15%)
16	4 (0.12%)
17	5 (0.15%)
18	10 (0.31%)
19	10 (0.31%)
20+[2]	597 (18.24%)
Total	3273 (100%)

Table 2 is the summary of the distributions of scrambled objects in terms of *bunsetsu*. Recall that the subject in OSV is always 1 *bunsetsu* due to my design. Thus, more than one *bunsetsu* in Table 2 means the scrambled object is longer than its subject from the viewpoint of *bunsetsu*. Hence, heaviness correlates with scrambled objects in about 75.95% of examples, where the object is longer than one *bunsetsu*. However, there are many short scrambled objects in two *bunsetsu* due to the characteristics of *bunsetsu*. Although a demonstrative plus a NP constitutes two *bunsetsu*, it can be very short if the NP is short e.g. *sono-imi* 'that meaning' and *sono-hon* 'that book'. Thus, I

[2] 20+ includes the examples that have no antecedent.

counted the number of demonstratives plus NP that are short. Here, a 'short' NP means less than three characters. As a result, 149 of the two *bunsetsu* examples are short. Hence, they should be excluded from the heavy examples. Therefore, it is more appropriate to conclude that heaviness accounts for 71.40 % of the examples, which is the total ratio of 'real' heavy objects.

Table 2: The length of the objects in terms of *Bunsetsu*

Bunsetsu	Number (%)
1	787 (24.05%)
2	1028 (31.41%)
3	564 (17.23%)
4	379 (11.58%)
5	230 (7.03%)
6	109 (3.33%)
7	61 (1.86%)
8	44 (1.34%)
9	16 (0.49%)
10+[3]	55 (1.68%)
Total	3273

Next, Pearson correlation test was conducted between RD and *bunsetsu* in order to see if there is a correlation between givenness and heaviness. This analysis is based on the raw RD and *bunsetsu*. Consequently, it was revealed that there was no correlation between givenness and heaviness ($r = -.05$, $p<.01$). Thus, RD of the scrambled object is independent of its length.

3.4. Discussion

Generally speaking, the corpus analysis has demonstrated that OSV in Japanese is sensitive to discourse-old information. However, there are many counterexamples for the explanation that OSV is chosen when the scrambled object is discourse-old information. The first question I should ask is whether they are real counterexamples or not. In the following, I will point out that some counterexamples arise due to weak points in my methods. Firstly, a sequence of same-reference NPs is called an appositive phrase, and such phrases are regularly discourse-old. In my approach, the direct object in (9) is regarded as completely new information because it has no antecedent in the preceding context. However, this example can be explained by supposing that the head of the scrambled object *enmoku* 'program' is activated by *nanatsumen* 'Seven Masks'. Thus, although the RD of *enmoku* 'program' is 20, it is not completely new information. Rather, it is possible that the NP *nanatsumen* 'Seven Masks' is introduced to the discourse in order to make the scrambled object given information. Thus, this type of example is not a crucial counterexample to my hypothesis.

(9) nanatsumen nijuusuunen
Seven.Masks over.20.years
enji-rarete-inai enmoku-o
perform-PASS-NEG program-ACC
Ebizoo-ga aratana-kousoo-de
Ebizoo-NOM new-conception-with
hukkatsu-sase-ta-toiu.
revive-CAUS-PAST-seem
'I heard that Ebizoo revived with a new conception the program called Seven Masks, which had not been performed for over 20 years.'
(BCCWJ)

Secondly, let us look at scrambled 1st and 2nd persons. It has been said that interlocutors are conscious of each other (Chafe, 1987: 26; 1994:79). Thus, it is not too much to say that 1st and 2nd persons are permanently given information. In (10), the scrambled object *bokutachi-no-idokoro* 'our whereabouts' includes 1st person plural *bokutachi* 'we'. Although *bokutachi* 'we' has not been referred to in the previous discourse, it is given information because it is 1st person plural form. Hence, the scrambled direct object *bokutachi-no-idokoro* 'our whereabouts' as a whole can be regarded as given information.

(10) syainsyou-ga haitteirun-dakara,

[3] 10+ includes 10 and more than 10 *bunsetsu*.

company.ID.card-NOM have-because
sore-ga tegakari-ni-nari,
it-NOM clue-DAT-become
bokutachi-no-idokoro-o keisatsu-ga
we-GEN-whereabouts-ACC police-NOM
mitsukete-kureru-kamosirenai-yo
find-EMP-may-FP
'Since (my wallet) has my company ID card, it can be the clue to our whereabouts and police may find us.'
(BCCWJ)

Thirdly, some scrambled objects are semi-activated. Chafe (1987: 25) states that 'a semi-active concept is one that is in a person's peripheral consciousness, a concept of which a person has a background awareness, but which is not being directly focused on'. Furthermore, Chafe (1994: 86) states that a semi-active referent 'may be in the semi-active rather than new referents. It may be a referent that (a) was active at an earlier time in the discourse, (b) is directly associated with an idea that is or was active in the discourse, or (c) is associated with the nonlinguistic environment of the conversation and has for that reason been peripherally active but not directly focused on'. Note that RD can process type (a) and some parts of (b), but cannot deal with type (c). This is because RD counts on explicitly mentioned linguistic expressions. In (11), the scrambled object has no direct antecedent, but is semi-activated by non-linguistic context. *Kono-hon* 'this book' is a linguistically new referent because it has no antecedent, but it refers to the book a reader is reading now. The physical existence of 'this book' is a non-linguistic context.

(11) kono-hon-o dokusya-ga
this-book-ACC reader-NOM
tenisuru-koroniwa...
get-by.the.time
'By the time readers get this book…'
(BCCWJ)

Next, I have demonstrated that heaviness correlates with 71.4% of the scrambled objects in OSV order examples. This supports Yamashita (2002) who observed that heaviness gave an explanation of about 74% (fourteen out of nineteen) of scrambled sentences. However, it is conceivable that heaviness depends on givenness, and vice versa. If such a tendency is universal in OSV as a whole, it is economical to use only one concept in order to explain the usage of scrambling. Therefore, I checked the correlation coefficient between givenness and heaviness. Consequently, it has been revealed that there is no correlation between them. Therefore, we can conclude that givenness and heaviness independently influence word order choices in Japanese. It is necessary to take both concepts into account in order to explain the function of OSV order.

Another point is that givenness correlates with 81.76% of scrambled sentences in my data. This result is opposed to Yamashita (2002) stating that scrambling is unrelated to information structure. In her data set, only 36.8% (seven out of nineteen) of objects are given information. Recall that her data set includes all kinds of scrambling: long-distance scrambling, short-distance scrambling, and VP-internal scrambling. On the other hand, my data set contains only OSV, which constitutes short-distance scrambling. Thus, it is conceivable that the strength of givenness effects depends on scrambling types. Let us expand upon this logic. With regard to OSV order, I have shown using a corpus that givenness correlates with the scrambled object. In contrast, with regard to S-DO-IO-V order, Ferreira and Yoshita (2003) observed that there was no interaction between given-new ordering and scrambling in sentence production. In other words, givenness has no strong influence on the choice of S-DO-IO-V word order. Why is there such a difference between OSV and S-DO-IO-V? One explanation relies on the mapping between information structure and syntactic structure. Note that OSV is VP-external scrambling whereas S-DO-IO-V is VP-internal scrambling. According to Rizzi (1997), sentence-initial position is related to discourse function. He supposes that left periphery architecture (CP-zone) is used to express the interfaces between syntactic structure and information structure. As shown in (12), the left periphery consists of many kinds of discourse-related projections. Considering scrambling from the viewpoint of the left periphery, scrambled direct objects in OSV are considered to be related to information structure.

(12) Basic Structure of CP-zone and TP-zone

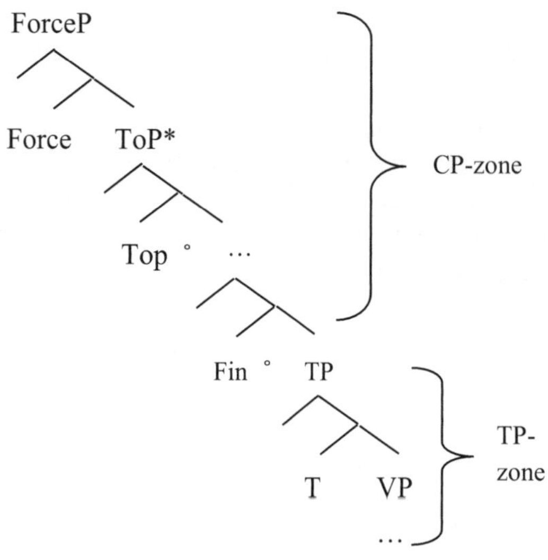

This is because sentence-initial position can have a relationship with information-related projections in the CP-zone. In particular, it may have a strong relationship with TOPIC projection, which seems to be pertinent to given information. In contrast, direct objects in S-DO-IO-V seem to be unrelated to information structure because there are no projections for information structure within the TP-zone. The TP-zone expresses only propositional meaning and information structure is not reflected in any projections within the TP-zone. In sum, givenness seems to have strong effects on OSV but have weak or no effects on S-DO-IO-V. This difference may be explained by the existence of discourse projections in the sentence-initial position. If this hypothesis is on the right track, long-distance scrambling will also be strongly influenced by information structure due to its position.

Numerous studies have shown that heaviness is an important factor for word order changes (Hawkins, 1994; Yamashita, 2002; Yamashita & Chang, 2001). The motivation for this phenomenon is to reduce processing cost, being unrelated to information structure. Hence, heaviness seems to have an influence on both VP-external and VP-internal scrambling. However, the strength of this effect may vary according to the informational status of scrambled constituents. In processing, when there are two competing factors, the strength of one factor becomes strong when the other factor is weak (Arnold et al., 2000; Trueswell and Tanenhaus, 1994). Applying this rule to heaviness and givenness, the effect of heaviness gets strong when that of givenness is weak, and vice versa. In fact, Yamashita (2002) observed that heaviness had a strong influence on VP-internal scrambling, although her data set was very small. Taken together, heaviness seems to have stronger effects on VP-internal scrambling than on VP-external scrambling. Conversely, givenness has greater effects on VP-external scrambling than on VP-internal scrambling. There might be such a complementary distribution between givenness and heaviness.

4. Conclusion

In this study, I have demonstrated that givenness has an influence on OSV order, being independent of heaviness. Specifically, it has been shown that the discourse-status of a scrambled object is important for the usage of OSV; OSV is preferable when O is discourse-old information. However, these conclusions contradict Yamashita (2002) claiming that information structure is not crucial for scrambling. This difference must derive from the data difference; her analysis includes VP-internal and VP-external scrambling while the scope of my analysis is only VP-external scrambling. Therefore, I propose that givenness has a strong effect on VP-external scrambling but a weak effect on VP-internal scrambling. The motivation for this analysis is based on Rizzi (1997)'s left periphery: sentence-initial position is related to information structure due to discourse-related projections. On the other hand, VP-internal scrambling seems to be unrelated to information structure because there are no discourse-related projections within the VP-internal zone. Moreover, since heaviness has no relationship with information structure, it seems to have effects on both VP-external and VP-internal scrambling. However, heaviness may have greater effects on VP-internal scrambling than on VP-external scrambling. In order to examine the validity of these hypotheses, further corpus data are needed. Specifically, it is necessary to check the heaviness effects and the givenness effects on S-DO-IO-V.

Acknowledgement

I am deeply grateful to Dr. Stephen Wright Horn, Einar Andreas Helgason, Dr Tohru Seraku, and Prof. Hitosi Gotoo for their help.

References

Chafe, W. (1976). Givenness, Contrastiveness, Definiteness, Subjects, Topics and Points of View. In Charles N. (ed.), *Subjects and Topic*, 25-55. New York: Academic Press.

Chafe, W. (1987). Cognitive constraints and information flow. In Tomlin, R. (ed.), *Coherence and grounding in discourse*, 21-55. Amsterdam: John Benjamins Publishing.

Chafe, W. (1994). *Discourse, consciousness and time: The flow and displacement of conscious experience in speaking and writing*. Chicago: The University of Chicago Press.

Cooreman, A. (1992). The pragmatics of word order variation in Chamorro narrative text. In Doris, P. (ed.), *Pragmatics of word order flexibility*, 243-64. Oregon: John Benjamins Publishing.

Ferreira, V. S. & Yoshita, H. (2003). Given-new ordering effects on the production of scrambled sentences in Japanese. *Journal of psycholinguistic research*, *32*: 669-692.

Givón, T. (1983) Topic continuity in discourse: An introduction. In Givón T. (ed.), *Topic Continuity in Discourse*, 5-41. Amsterdam: John Benjamins Publishing.

Givón, T. (1994) The pragamatics of de-transitive voice: Functional and typological aspects of inversion. In Givón T. (ed.) *Voice and inversion*, 3-47. Amsterdam: John Benjamins Publishing.

Hawkins, J. A. (1994). *A performance theory of order and constituency*. Cambridge: Cambridge University Press.

Ishii, Y. (2001). Presuppositional effects of scrambling reconsidered. In Inoue, K. and Hasegawa, N. (eds), *Linguistics and Interdisciplinary Research: Proceedings of the COE International Symposium. Center of Excellence in Linguistics*, 79-101. Tokyo: Kanda University of International Studies.

Kuno,S. (1978) *Danwa-no Bunpō* [Grammar of Discourse]. Tokyo: Taishūkan

Lambrecht, K. (1996) *Information structure and sentence form: Topic, focus, and the mental representations of discourse referents*. Cambridge: Cambridge University Publishing.

Maekawa, K., Yamazaki, M., Ogiso, T., Maruyama, T., Ogura, H., Kashino, W., Koizo, H., Yamaguchi, M., Tanaka, M. & Den, Y. (2008). Balanced corpus of contemporary written Japanese. *Language Resources and Evaluation*, 48: 345-71.

Miyagawa, S. (2010). *Why Agree? Why Move? Unifying Agreement-based and Discourse-configurational Languages*, Cambridge: The MIT Press.

Rizzi, L. (1997). The fine structure of the left periphery. In Haegeman, L. (ed.), *Elements of grammar*, 281-337. Dordrecht: Kluwer Academic Publisher.

Saeki, T. (1960) Gendaibun ni okeru gojun no keikou. Iwayuru hogo no baai [Tendency of Word Order in Modern Japanese- Focusing on Complements]. *Gengoseikatsu*, 111: 56-63.

Saito, M. (1985) *Some Asymmetries in Japanese and their Theoretical Implications*. Doctoral dissertation, MIT.

Saito, M. (2009) Optional A-scrambling. *Japanese/Korean Linguistics*, 16: 4-63.

Shimojō, M. (2005). *Argument encoding in Japanese conversation*. Hampshire and New York: Palgrave Macmillan.

Vallduví, E. & Elisabet Engdahl. (1996) The linguistic realization of information packaging. *Linguistics*, 34: 459-520.

Yamashita, H., & Chang, F. (2001). Long before short preference in the production of a head-final language. *Cognition*, 81: B45–B55.

Yamashita, H. (2002). Scrambled sentences in Japanese: Linguistic properties and motivations for production. *TEXT-THE HAGUE THEN AMSTERDAM THEN BERLIN*, *22*: 597-634.

Annotating article errors in Spanish learner texts: design and evaluation of an annotation scheme

María del Pilar Valverde Ibañez
Faculty of Foreign Languages
Aichi Prefectural University
1522-3 Ibaragasama, Nagakute-shi
Aichi, 480-1198, Japan
valverde@for.aichi-pu.ac.jp

Akira Ohtani
Faculty of Informatics
Osaka Gakuin University
2-36-1 Kishibe-minami, Suita-shi
Osaka, 564-8511, Japan
ohtani@ogu.ac.jp

Abstract

Annotating a corpus with error information is a challenging task. This paper describes the design, evaluation and refinement of an annotation scheme for Spanish article errors in learner data, so that future work on corpus annotation and automatic article error detection can progress. To evaluate reliability, 300 noun phrases with definite, indefinite and zero article have been tagged by four annotators. We analysed different types of disagreement, presented suggestions to increase reliability and applied the refined annotation scheme to create a gold-standard annotation.

1 Introduction

The annotation of learner texts with error information is necessary for linguistic research as well as for the development of language learning applications using natural language processing (NLP) techniques. While much efforts have concentrated on English, it is necessary to develop learner corpora and tools for other foreign languages like Spanish. This is the most commonly studied foreign language in the United States and the second most studied foreign language -after English- in many other countries. Overall, it is estimated that nearly 20 million people are studying Spanish as a foreign language (Instituto Cervantes, 2013). However, learner corpora and tools for this language are scarce (Lozano and Mendikoetxea, 2013; Nazar and Renau, 2012; del Pilar Valverde and Ohtani, 2012; Wanner et al., 2013). The goal of this paper is to define an annotation scheme that is suitable for reliable Spanish article error annotation, so that future work on corpus annotation and automatic article error detection can progress.

Automatic detection of errors has focused on function words such as articles (Izumi et al., 2004; Han et al., 2006; Felice and Pulman, 2008b; Gamon et al., 2008; Yi et al., 2008), prepositions (Felice and Pulman, 2008a) and particles (Dickinson, 2008; Oyama and Matsumoto, 2010). Function words are the most frequent words in any language, and they are also a very common source of mistakes for learners.

As for error annotation, one of the main difficulties is reliability. For some learner errors, like number and gender agreement, rules are clearly defined. Other kind of errors, like article or preposition presence and choice, are harder to annotate because native speakers differ widely with respect to what is acceptable usage. For article and noun number selection, for example, in Lee et al. (2009) raters found more than one valid construction for more than 18% of noun phrases.

To address this problem, we experiment with a preliminary annotation scheme for article errors, analyse the form disagreement among annotators takes, and refine the annotation scheme according to it. The paper is organized as follows. In section 2 we briefly summarize the linguistic properties of Spanish articles. In section 3 we explain an experiment carried out with a preliminary annotation scheme on article error annotation. In section 4 we examine the sources of disagreement among the annotators and in 5 we summarize the recommendations for reliable annotation. Section 6 presents the conclusions.

Copyright 2014 by María del Pilar Valverde Ibañez and Akira Ohtani
28th Pacific Asia Conference on Language, Information and Computation pages 234–243

2 Spanish articles

2.1 General overview

In Spanish, articles can be *definite* (as in English *the*) or *indefinite* (in English *a/an*), and their form changes according to the gender and number of the noun they complement, as shown in Table 1. [1]

	Definite		Indefinite	
	masc.	fem.	masc.	fem.
singular	*el*	*la*	*un*	*una*
plural	*los*	*las*	*unos*	*unas*

Table 1: Spanish articles

Article usage is complex because it is the result of the interaction of pragmatic, semantic, syntactic and lexical factors. Taxonomies of article use are abundant in the literature, targeted towards learners (Butt and Benjamin, 2014) or linguists (Bosque and Demonte, 1999; RAE, 2009). Basically, the main function of articles is to indicate the relationship between the nominal expressions and the entities to which the speakers refer by means of such expressions (Bosque and Demonte, 1999). For example, among other usages, we use the definite to generalize, that is, to refer to a whole class of things or people, as in (1) and to refer to something that is identifiable to the listener, as in (2). In (2), Maria's son must be identifiable for the listener either because a) Maria has only one son, or b) we have talked about him before. We use the indefinite to refer to any object of a particular class, as in (3), and we use no article when we are talking about an indefinite amount of something, as in (4) (examples from Alonso et al. (2013)).

(1) Los hijos dan muchos disgustos.
'Children cause a great deal of trouble.'

(2) El hijo de María tiene dos años.
'Maria's son is two years old.'

(3) Tener un hijo es lo mejor que te puede pasar en esta vida.
'Having a child is the best thing that can happen in life.'

(4) No tengo hijos pero tengo sobrinos.
'I do not have children but I have nephews.'

With regard to syntactic factors, for example two or more coordinated nouns should have their own article if they refer to different things: *un gato y un perro*, "a cat and dog" (*un gato y perro* suggests a cross between a cat and a dog) (Butt and Benjamin, 2014).

As for semantic factors, there are many rules which require specific knowledge. For example, place names usually have no article (*México*). For some of them the article is optional (*(el) Perú*) or depends on the context (*el México de los mexicanos*, "Mexicans' Mexico"), while the definite is obligatory for rivers, mountains, seas and oceans (*el Mediterráneo*). Other rules exist for numbers, proper nouns, names of languages, days of the week, etc.

Finally, there exist many set phrases and idioms which require definite (e.g. *con el objetivo de* 'with the objective of'), indefinite (*por una parte*, 'on the one hand') or zero article (e.g. *a corto plazo*, 'in the short run').

2.2 Difficulties for learners

Definite articles are the most frequent word in Spanish. In Davies (2005) frequency list the definite article is the most frequent *type* and the indefinite article is the 7th most frequent. In 9 billion words Spanish TenTen corpus (Jakubíček et al., 2013) the definite is also the most frequent type and the indefinite is the 6th. Approximately one out of every ten words in this corpus are articles.

Articles are also one of the most frequent grammatical errors, specially for speakers of languages that do not have articles like Chinese, Japanese, Korean or Russian. For speakers of Japanese, Fernández (1997) found 2.2 article errors per 100 words in a 4433 words sample.[2] In addition to that, this type of error diminishes as proficiency increases, but it tends to fossilize. The difficulty of the article system of Spanish may be comparable to English. McEnery et al. (2006) found that articles were the most difficult to acquire for Japanese learn-

[1] Spanish also has a definite article with neuter gender (*lo*), but its usage is quite different from the rest, so it will not be considered in this paper.

[2] The most frequent grammatical error in her sample concerns the verb (3.2 verb tense errors per 100 words), followed by prepositions (2.8 per 100 words) and articles.

ers of English, since even proficient learners had not achieved the acquisition rate of 90%. Therefore, we decided to use Japanese learners' texts to develop our annotation scheme.

3 Experiment

Annotation of learner errors is a challenging task for several reasons. First, learner sentences often contain interacting surrounding errors which can make the understanding of the meaning of the sentence quite difficult. Second, for some errors like number and gender agreement there are clear-cut rules about what is grammatical. But for other kind of errors, like article or preposition presence and choice, rules are usually not clearly defined, so in some cases more than one article choice may be acceptable. And third, in some cases more textual context or world knowledge may be needed to be able to determine the correct article usage.

As a result, inter-annotator agreement for error annotations can be relatively low. This issue has been put forward by the NLP community, that has found difficulties for evaluating error detection systems (Chodorow et al., 2012), but it has not received much attention in the learner corpus linguistic field. Several measures can be taken to address the varying number of corrections and levels of acceptability a sentence can have.

With regard to the number of possible analysis a sentence can receive, most error-annotated learner corpora permit only one tag per error. However, the "single correct construction" approach has been questioned and in recent annotation efforts there is a tendency to allow the inclusion of several alternative codes for the same item (Lüdeling et al., 2005; Boyd, 2010; Lee et al., 2012; Rozovskaya and Roth, 2010). However, it is unattainable to list all possible interpretations for every error, so this is done only "when there is doubt".

With regard to the level of confidence in the annotators' judgments, some projects include global measures of inter-annotator agreement (Rozovskaya and Roth, 2010; Lee et al., 2012) but annotated corpora do not explicitly provide confidence levels for every error. Only in some annotation experiments the annotators are asked to indicate their level of confidence for every item (as "low" or "high") (Tetreault and Chodorow, 2008).

We carry out an experiment on annotation of article errors with the following objectives:

1. Calculate inter-annotator agreement.
2. Analyse the types and sources of disagreement, to find out which are the main difficulties the annotators face when annotating article errors in learner texts.
3. Based on this experience, refine the guidelines and annotation scheme for error annotation.

3.1 Data collection

We used learners' texts written by 4th grade Japanese students of Spanish with an intermediate level of proficiency, at Aichi Prefectural University. A teacher of Spanish as a Foreign Language extracted sentences containing at least one article error from these texts, 50 sentences for each kind of article (definite, indefinite and zero article). The same number of sentences, but with at least one correct article usage, was then collected from the same texts. In every sentence only one highlighted noun phrase had to be annotated. The distribution of the resulting 300 sentences is as Table 2 shows.

	Definite	Indefinite	0 article	Total
Correct	50	50	50	150
Incorrect	50	50	50	150
Total	100	100	100	300

Table 2: Number of noun phrases and articles they contain

3.2 Preliminary annotation scheme

The 300 noun phrases were tagged by four annotators. The annotators were two experts (teachers of Spanish as a Foreign Language, who correct learners' texts on a regular basis), which we will call E1 and E2, and two non-experts (native speakers of Spanish with higher education but without experience in corpus annotation), which we will call NE1 and NE2.

They all annotated the same noun phrase in the same sentences, but presented in different orders, using a Microsoft Excel spreadsheet. Annotators were provided with the target sentence plus the preceding and the following sentence, which they could resort to if they needed more context. If the target sentence was at the beginning or end of paragraph or text in the original text, no context was provided (a "beginning or end of paragraph or text" mark was inserted instead).

They were asked to classify the noun phrase into one of the categories shown in Table 3. We are only concerned with article presence and choice, so we did not tag malformation (e.g. spelling or agreement) and order errors.

Missing (definite)	AD
Missing (indefinite)	AI
Extraneous	E
Confusion	C
Article is correct	OK
Difficult to judge	NC

Table 3: Tags

Missing article (AD, AI) A missing error occurs when the learner does not use any article but the sentence should contain one: definite, as in (5) (AD|AD|AD|AD||AD)[3] or indefinite as in (6) (AI|NC|AI|AI||AI).

(5) Originalmente el español y el portugués son categorizados en mismo grupo lingüístico, la lengua románica.
'Originally Spanish and Portuguese are categorized in the same linguistic group, the romance language.'

(6) Osu está cerca del barrio de Sakae que es centro comercial muy animado y moderno.
'Osu is near Sakae area which is a very lively and modern commercial district.'

Extraneous article (E) An extraneous article error occurs when the article used by the learner is not necessary (zero article should be used instead), as in (7) (E|E|E|E||E).

[3]For every example from the learner data, in parenthesis we indicate the tags by the four annotators, in the following order: E1|E2|NE1|NE2||gold standard. For more details about the gold standard version, see section 5.

(7) El objetivo de este trabajo es conocer cómo propagó el tomate como la verdura comestible desde el continente americano.
'The goal of this paper is to know how tomato spreaded as an edible vegetable from the American continent.'

Confusion error (C) A confusion error occurs when the learner used a definite article instead of an indefinite, or vice versa. In (8) (C|C|C|C||CA) the article should be definite because "victoria" refers to the last -unique and therefore identifiable- victory which ended the war.

(8) Franco consiguió una victoria en la Guerra Civil en 1939 y su dictadura comenzó.
'Franco pursued the victory in the Civil War in 1939 and his dictatorship began.'

Difficult to judge (NC) It was expected that the annotators would some times be unsure about the acceptability of article usage in a given sentence, or unable to determine the most likely correction.

We opted for allowing only one tag per sentence, but not forcing the annotators to mark the article usage as "right" or "wrong" and instead gave the possibility of marking sentences as "difficult to judge", as Han et al. (2006). We we wanted the annotators to correct the sentences only when they were sure about their decision, and not forcing them to make a best guess, which could lower inter-annotator agreement. Later we could look at the sentences marked as problematic, as (14), and analyse what they have in common.

4 Inter-annotator agreement

Tables 4 and 5 show the confusion matrices for expert and non-expert annotations. Observed agreement[4] is 0.79 for expert annotators and 0.76 for non-experts.

However, using observed agreement to measure reliability does not take into account agreement that is due to chance and hence is not a good measure of reliability. Therefore, an analysis using Cohen's Kappa statistic (Cohen, 1960) was performed. Perfect agreement would equate to a kappa of 1, and

[4]Defined as the number of items on which annotators agree divided by the total number of items

E1:↓ E2: →	AD	AI	C	E	NC	OK	Tot
AD	**37**	0	0	0	2	2	41
AI	0	**5**	0	0	2	0	7
C	0	0	**30**	3	2	1	36
E	0	0	3	**39**	7	1	50
NC	1	0	1	4	**5**	8	19
OK	4	0	4	7	10	**122**	147
Total	42	5	38	53	28	134	300

Table 4: Confusion matrix for E1 and E2 annotators.

NE1:↓ NE2: →	AD	AI	C	E	NC	OK	Tot
AD	**31**	2	0	1	0	10	44
AI	2	**5**	0	0	0	2	9
C	1	0	**23**	2	2	6	34
E	0	0	4	**57**	2	10	73
NC	0	0	0	1	**0**	0	1
OK	5	1	5	7	2	**119**	139
Tot	39	8	32	68	6	147	300

Table 5: Confusion matrix for NE1 and NE2 annotators.

chance agreement would equate to 0. For the whole set of sentences (300, correct or incorrect), inter-annotator agreement for experts was found to be Kappa = 0.71 ($p < 0.001$), 95% CI (0.65, 0.77), and for non-experts it was 0.68 ($p < 0.001$), 95% CI (0.62, 0.75), which indicates substantial agreement. If we exclude the 45 sentences marked as"difficult to judge" by at least one annotator, kappa is 0.85 and 0.73 respectively. If we exclude 97 sentences tagged as "correct" by the four of them, remaining only sentences where at least one annotator considers there is an error, kappa is 0.62 and 0.58. If we exclude both sentences marked as NC by at least one annotator and sentences marked as OK by four annotators (remaining only 159 sentences) kappa is 0.79 and 0.61.

In the following sections we examine different types of disagreement: disagreement due to the annotators (4.1), due to the annotation scheme (4.2) and genuine disagreement (4.3), and propose some measures to reduce it.

4.1 Disagreement due to the annotators expertise: experts vs non-experts

The difference between experts and non-experts' reliability is due to the fact that non-experts make more slips than experts, and they are also less conservative when they correct texts.

In the data we find at least five mistakes (there can be more which we cannot detect), all by non-expert annotators: in four sentences they tag for a missing article a noun phrase which already contains one article, as (9) (C|C|AD|OK||OK), and in another one they tag for an extraneous article error a noun phrase without article.

(9) En Guatemala, la gente que tiene alta enseñanza piensa que "voseo" es una norma culta.
'In Guatemala, people who have higher education think that "voseo" is an educated norm.'

To prevent this kind of mistakes, any annotation project should automatically constrain the tags the annotators can use depending on the input (e.g. if there is already an article preceding a noun phrase, do not allow the "missing" error tag). Table 6 shows the error tags a noun phrase can receive depending on the article it contains.

Error tag	Definite	Indefinite	0 article
AD			x
AI			x
C	x	x	
E	x	x	

Table 6: Error tags a noun phrase can receive depending on the type of article it contains

In addition to that, even though non-experts are supposed to be less confident about the acceptability of sentences because pointing out errors in a text is a task for which they have no previous experience, in fact they are less cautious when they correct texts. For example, in (10) (OK|OK|E|E||OK)) experts consider the article is acceptable, while non-experts classify it as an extraneous article.

(10) Segundo,ahora ya no es imprescindible usar la coca para los objetivos antiguos,como para alivia de dolor o anestesia [...].
'Second, now it is no longer necessary to use the coca for the ancient purposes, like pain relieve or anaesthetic [...].'

This bias explains why, for example, NE1 uses the tag "difficult to judge" only one time (0.3%), while E2 uses it almost once every 10 sentences (9.3%), and non-experts use the tag "extraneous article" (specially for definite articles) more frequently than experts (23.5% vs. 12.2% of times).

Principle of minimal change Part of the variability on annotators' rigour could be reduced by giving clear guidelines about the optimum level of intervention in the texts. In this regard, we advocate for following a principle of minimal change: so we should not mark as errors the sentences where the learner choice is acceptable, even if the learner choice is not the best choice, that is, the goal of the annotator should be to produce an acceptable rather than a perfect result (e.g. Hana et al. (2010)), When the input is incomprehensible and the annotator cannot make a decision, it should be left without annotation.

In relation to that, annotators should be informed about the halo effect, by which the judgement of a sentence as acceptable or unacceptable is influenced by our overall impression of previous sentences. In other words, one is more likely to find errors in a text if this text already contains other errors. Experts (teachers of a foreign language) are trained on evaluation methods and they are aware of the importance of reliability in students' evaluation. They know how external factors (e.g. the halo effect and contrast effect) can have a negative impact and what can be done to reduce it. However, non-experts lack this training and are not aware of the challenges faced to perform a fair evaluation -annotation.

4.2 Disagreement due to the annotation scheme

We find some disagreements are due to the design of the preliminary annotation scheme, specially concerning the tags "difficult to judge" (NC) and "confusion error" (C).

The tag "difficult to judge" With regard to the reliability of the 6 tags used for annotation (Table 3), "difficult to judge" is the one that causes more disagreement: most of the times (67.7%) it is used by only one of the four annotators, and it is never used by three or four annotators in the same sentence. On the contrary, the rest of tags have a much higher agreement: on average, they are used by the four annotators 63.2% of the times, by three 19.9%, by two 9.2% and by one 7.7% of times.

Therefore, this tag should at most be used to filter out problematic sentences, which annotators cannot comprehend, and not for proper annotation of sentences.

We advocate for not using this tag and instead set clear principles in the annotation guidelines specifying what the annotators should do when they are not confident about the error analysis of a sentence.

The tag "confusion error" We found there was ambiguity in the guidelines about the meaning of this tag: in principle, it refers to the confusion between definite and indefinite articles but annotators also use it to indicate the confusion between an article and another type of determiner.

Indeed, learners frequently confuse the indefinite article with the indefinite determiner *alguno* 'some', when they refer to an indefinite amount of things, as in (11) (C|C|OK|OK||CD).

(11) Los hispanos están aumentando rápidamente y la población está centrada en <u>unos estados.</u>
'Hispanics are increasing rapidly and the population is concentrated in <u>some states</u>.'

To include this kind of error in the annotation, we should break down the tag into two: confusion between definite and indefinite article (CA) and confusion between article and another type of determiner (CD).

4.3 Genuine disagreement

As explained in section 2, article presence and choice can be determined by several factors. In our data, it mainly depends on pragmatic factors (69.0% of noun phrases), followed by lexico-semantic (20.7%) and syntactic factors (10.3%).

Leaving aside sentences tagged as acceptable by four annotators, agreement is higher when the article choice depends on lexico-semantic factors ($k = 0.835$ for experts and 0.780 for non-experts) and lower with pragmatic factors (($k = 0.514$ for experts and 0.496 for non-experts). Syntactic factors seem to be in between ($k = 0.750$ for experts and 0.523 for non-experts), although their low frequency makes the figures less reliable. Therefore, more care should be paid to pragmatic distinctions.

Specifically, disagreement is more likely in noun phrases where two pragmatic interpretations (and article choices) are possible, and annotators choose one of the alternatives in an inconsistent manner (§ 4.3.1 and 4.3.2). Disagreement can also be due to a lack of the world knowledge that is needed to be able to determine the correct article usage (§ 4.3.3). As for syntactic and lexico-semantic factors (§ 4.3.4), disagreement occurs because annotators do not have a good knowledge about the existing prescriptive rules about article usage.

4.3.1 Definite article or zero article

Frequently both definite and zero article are acceptable for the same noun phrase. This happens when the noun phrase can refer to *a whole class of things or people in general* (definite article) or to *an indefinite amount of something* (zero article), as explained in 2. This distinction frequently does not change the meaning of the sentence significantly and in fact some languages with articles like English usually use the zero article in both cases.

When both pragmatic interpretations are possible for a given sentence, annotators unevenly choose one of them: some annotators tag the noun phrase for a missing article in (12) (OK|AD|AD|OK||OK) while they tag it for extraneous article in (13) (E |NC|OK|E||OK), even though in both sentences both the definite article and the zero article are acceptable, so the learner's choice should be left unchanged.

(12) Los políticos hablan en público y manifiestan sus opiniones con el objeto de conseguir votos de ciudadanos [...]
'Politicians talk in public and show their opinion with a view to get votes from the citizens [...].'

(13) Concretamente los cursos que consiguieron participantes japoneses y que ofrecen los certificados oficiales como IMEC(Instituto de Medicina China) continuarán existiendo [...].
'Specifically the courses which obtained Japanese participants and offer official certificates like IMEC (Chinese Medicine Institute) will continue existing [...].'

This distinction is specially problematic with plural nouns: in noun phrases with a plural nominal head, agreement by four annotators is less frequent (43.2%) than with singular nouns (66.7%) $\chi^2(2, N = 299) = 18.9, p < 0.001$. Therefore, more care should be paid in the annotation of plural nouns.

If the noun is singular and uncountable, we find the same ambiguous pragmatic distinction as with plural nouns, as in (14) (NC|NC|AD|E||OK), which is tagged as "difficult to judge" by some annotators and "extraneous" by others (the AD tag is a lapsus).

(14) El problema es demanda de la cocaína.
'The problem is demand of cocaine.'

In conclusion, according to the principle of minimal change, when both the definite and the zero article are acceptable, we should leave the learners' choice unchanged.

4.3.2 Indefinite article or zero article

Some times annotators agree in considering a noun phrase as unacceptable but they do not agree in the type of correction. This can happen when the learner wrongly uses a definite article, as in (15) (E|C|C|E||E/CA), and the annotators propose different corrections for it because the noun phrase can refer to *an indefinite amount of something* (zero article) or *any object of a particular class* (indefinite).

(15) En cambio, la cocaína tiene el efecto tóxico.
'On the contrary, cocaine has a toxic effect.'

Only in these cases, we allow adding two error tags (E/CA or E/CD) to the noun phrase.

4.3.3 World knowledge

In some sentences, annotators have insufficient extra-linguistic knowledge to be able to determine the right article usage. For example, in (16) (OK|E|E|E||OK) the annotator needs to know whether in Nagoya there are only nine interesting and touristy places (definite article) or there are more than nine (no article).

(16) Sale cada treinta minutos aproximadamente desde la estación de Nagoya y paran en los nueve sitios muy interesantes y turísticos, por ejemplo El castillo de Nagoya.
'It runs approximately every thirty minutes from Nagoya station and stops in nine very interesting and touristy places, for example Nagoya Castle.'

If the learner's choice is acceptable in some context, as in (16), we do not mark it as wrong. If the learner's choice is not acceptable, we tag the noun phrase as usual.

4.3.4 Syntactic and lexico-semantic rules

Unlike article usage governed by pragmatic factors, which is subject to interpretation by the annotator, for article usage determined by syntactic and lexico-semantic constraints there exist some linguistic norms about what is considered correct and incorrect.

However, native speakers -even experts- do not have a deep knowledge about these rules and some times do not follow them. For example, in (17) (AD|AD|OK|OK||OK) experts marked as error an article usage that is actually accepted, while non-experts tagged it right. It is the use of zero article between the preposition *a* ('to') and the relative pronoun *que* ('which') (RAE, 2006).

(17) [...] el capítulo 2 dice sobre el proceso del portuñol y los problemas a que el portuñol se enfrenta actualmente.
'[...] chapter 2 is about the portuñol process and the problems that the portuñol confronts nowadays.'

Therefore, to determine the acceptability of article usage, annotators should not rely only on their intuition as native speakers but also consult existing rules and recommendations published in reference dictionaries and grammars as RAE (2006) and RAE (2009).

5 Suggestions for reliable annotation

After examining the sources of disagreement in the annotation experiment, we added the following principles to the annotation scheme:

1. It is not recommended to use a tag like NC, "difficult to judge", because it has the lowest reliability. Therefore, we recommend simply not annotating the noun phrase if it impossible to determine the acceptability of the article usage. We did not find any case like that in our data from students with an intermediate level of Spanish.

2. Tags should inform us about the type of error *and* about the correction. This was true for the "add definite", "add indefinite" and "delete" tags, since we indicate which article we should add (definite or indefinite), and we know which article is deleted. The preliminary "confusion" error tag should be broken down into two tags to indicate confusion between definite and indefinite article (CA), and confusion between article and another type of determiner (CD).

3. Follow the principle of minimal change: the sentences should be acceptable rather than perfect. When more than one article choice including the learner's one is acceptable, we leave the learner's choice as correct. The pair definite article-zero article is the most interchangeable (in many sentences both are correct), so annotators should pay attention not to change the learner choice when it is correct.

4. When the learner choice is not acceptable and there are two equally good corrections, we allow double annotation. We found this mainly happens when the learner wrongly uses a definite or indefinite, and the annotators doubt between an extraneous error (zero article) and a confusion error. Only in this cases, we allow double annotation with E and CA or CD tags. There is usually no ambiguity in the appropriate correction for a missing article: annotators usually agree whether a definite or indefinite is necessary (probably for this reason the zero article has a high inter-annotator agreement.)

5. Regarding article usage governed by syntactic and lexico-semantic factors, base annotation not only on annotators' intuitions but first on the rules about article usage published by respected institutions (RAE, 2006; RAE, 2009).

6. When more world knowledge is needed to judge a sentence as correct or incorrect, we do not correct it if the learner's choice is acceptable in some context.

Following these criteria, we have revised the error tags given by the annotators for every sentence and made a decision about the most acceptable tag. The articles in the resulting gold standard set are distributed as Table 7 shows.

Tag	Definite	Indefinite	0 article	Total
AD	-	-	40	40
AI	-	-	6	6
CA	6	16	-	22
CD	0	7	-	7
E	36	18	-	54
E/CA	1	1	-	2
OK	57	58	54	169
Total	100	100	100	300

Table 7: Frequency of error tags in the gold standard per type of article (absolute frequency or %)

Despite the small size of the corpus study, some tendencies are observed in the 300 noun phrases written by Japanese learners:

1. The most frequent error regarding the definite article is extraneous use (83.7%): learners overuse it frequently probably because it is the most frequent article (and word) in Spanish.

2. When zero article is used, the most likely error is omission of the definite article (86.9%), for the same reason.

3. When learners use an indefinite article, the errors they commit are more evenly distributed. Confusion with a definite article or another type of determiner happens in 54.8% of cases and extraneous use in 42.9%.

6 Conclusions

Although article errors have been annotated in a number of small-scale studies, to date there has not been any study about article error annotation and inter-annotator agreement in Spanish learner texts. In this paper we have tested the results of an annotation scheme for article errors in a sample of learner texts written by Japanese learners. We have calculated agreement among four annotators (two experts and two non-experts) and have found kappa values between 0.85 and 0.62 for expert annotators and from 0.73 to 0.58 for non-experts, depending on the collection of sentences considered. The analysis of the disagreement among annotators has served us to find which are the main difficulties for annotators and to refine the annotation scheme according to it. Following more articulated guidelines we have revised the data to create a gold-standard.

The data used for the experiment is available to all interested researchers upon request. We hope the work presented here will facilitate future corpus annotation and development of automatic article error detection systems.

Acknowledgments

This research was partially supported by *kakenhi* (25770207 and 24500189), Grant-in-Aid for Scientific Research from the Japan Society for the Promotion of Science.

We thank the students from Aichi Prefectural University who gave their permission to use their texts for this research.

References

Rosario Alonso, Alejandro Castañeda, Pablo Martínez, Lourdes Miguel, Jenaro Ortega, and José Ruiz. 2013. *Students' Basic Grammar of Spanish*. Difusion.

Ignacio Bosque and Violeta Demonte, editors. 1999. *Descriptive Grammar of Spanish Language*. Espasa Calpe, (In Spanish: Gramática descriptiva de la lengua española).

Adriane Boyd. 2010. EAGLE: an error-annotated corpus of beginning learner German. In *Proceedings of LREC-10*, Malta.

John Butt and Carmen Benjamin. 2014. *A New Reference Grammar of Modern Spanish*. Routledge.

Martin Chodorow, Markus Dickinson, Ross Israel, and Joel Tetreault. 2012. Problems in evaluating grammatical error detection systems. In *Proceedings of COLING 2012*, pages 611–628, Mumbai, Desember.

Jacob Cohen. 1960. A coefficient of agreement for nominal scales. *Educational and Psychological Measurement*, 20(1):37–46.

Mark Davies. 2005. *A Frequency Dictionary of Spanish: Core Vocabulary for Learners (CD)*. Routledge.

María del Pilar Valverde and Akira Ohtani. 2012. Automatic detection of gender and number agreement errors in Spanish texts written by Japanese learners. In *Proceedings of the 26th PACLIC*, pages 299–307.

Markus Dickinson. 2008. Korean particle error detection via probabilistic parsing. In *Automatic Analysis of Learner Language (AALL'08)*.

Rachele De Felice and Stephen G. Pulman. 2008a. Automatic detection of preposition errors in learner writing. In *Automatic Analysis of Learner Language (AALL'08)*.

Rachele De Felice and Stephen G. Pulman. 2008b. A classifier-based approach to preposition and determiner error correction in L2 English. In *Proceedings of the COLING 2008*, pages 169–176, Manchester, UK.

Soledad Fernández. 1997. *Interlanguage and Error Analysis in the Learning of Spanish as a Foreign Language*. Edelsa, (In Spanish: Interlengua y análisis de errores en el aprendizaje del español como lengua extranjera).

Michael Gamon, Jianfeng Gao, Chris Brockett, Alex Klementiev, William B. Dolan, Dimitry Belenko, and Lucy Vanderwende. 2008. Using contextual spell checker techniques and language modelling for ESL error correction. In *Proceedings of the International Joint Conference on Natural Language Processing*, pages 449–456, Hyderabad, India.

Na-Rae Han, Martin Chodorow, and Claudia Leacock. 2006. Detecting errors in English article usage by non-native speakers. *Natural Language Engineering*, 12(2):115–129.

Jirka Hana, Alexandr Rosen, Sva, and Barbora Štindlová. 2010. Error-tagged learner corpus of Czech. In *Proceedings of the Fourth Linguistic Annotation Workshop (ACL 2010)*, pages 11–19, Uppsala, Sweden, July.

IC Instituto Cervantes. 2013. *Spanish: a Living Language. 2013 Report*. Instituto Cervantes, (In Spanish: El español: una lengua viva. Informe 2013).

Emi Izumi, Kiyotaka Uchimoto, and Hitoshi Isahara. 2004. SST speech corpus of Japanese learners' English and automatic detection of learners' errors. *International Computer Archive of Modern English Journal*, 28:31–48.

Miloš Jakubíček, Adam Kilgarriff, Vojtěch Kovář, Pavel Rychlý, and Vít Suchomel. 2013. The TenTen corpus family. In *7th International Corpus Linguistics Conference*.

John Lee, Joel Tetreault, and Martin Chodorow. 2009. Human evaluation of article and noun number usage: Influences of context and construction variability. In *Proceedings of the Third Linguistic Annotation Workshop (LAW)*, pages 60–63, Suntec, Singapore.

Sun-Hee Lee, Markus Dickinson, and Ross Israel. 2012. Developing learner corpus annotation for korean particle errors. In *Proceedings of the Sixth Linguistic Annotation Workshop, LAW VI*, pages 129–133, Stroudsburg.

Cristóbal Lozano and Amaya Mendikoetxea. 2013. Learner corpora and second language acquisition: the design and collection of CEDEL2. In Ana Díaz-Negrillo, Nicolas Ballier, and Paul Thompson, editors, *Automatic Treatment and Analysis of Learner Corpus Data*. John Benjamins, Amsterdam.

Anke Lüdeling, Maik Walter, Emil Kroymann, and Peter Adolphs. 2005. Multi-level error annotation in learner corpora. In *Proceedings of the Corpus Linguistics 2005 Conference*, Birmingham, United Kingdom, July.

Tony McEnery, Richard Xiao, and Yukio Tono. 2006. L2 acquisition of grammatical morphemes. In *Corpus-based language studies. An advanced resource book*. Routledge.

Rogelio Nazar and Irene Renau. 2012. Google books n-gram corpus used as a grammar checker. In *EACL 2012 Proceedings of the Second Workshop on Computational Linguistics and Writing (CLW 2012)*, pages 27–34.

Hiromi Oyama and Yuji Matsumoto. 2010. Automatic error detection method for Japanese case particles in Japanese language learners' writing. In *Corpus, ICT, and Language Education*, pages 235–245.

Real Academia de la Lengua Española RAE. 2006. *Diccionario panhispánico de dudas*. Real Santillana.

Real Academia de la Lengua Española RAE. 2009. *New Grammar of Spanish Language (In Spanish: Nueva gramática de la lengua española)*. Espasa Calpe.

Alla Rozovskaya and Dan Roth. 2010. Annotating ESL errors: Challenges and rewards. In *Proceedings of NAACL'10 Workshop on Innovative Use of NLP for Building Educational Applications*. University of Illinois at Urbana–Champ.

Joel Tetreault and Martin Chodorow. 2008. Native judgments of non-native usage: Experiments in preposition error detection. In *Proceedings of the Workshop on Human Judgments in Computational Linguistics at the COLING 2008*, pages 24–32.

Leo Wanner, Serge Verlinde, and Margarita Alonso. 2013. Writing assistants and automatic lexical error correction. In *Proceedings of the eLex 2013 conference*, pages 472–487.

Xing Yi, Jianfeng Gao, and William B. Dolan. 2008. A web-based English proofing system for English as a second language users. In *Proceedings of the International Joint Conference on Natural Language Processing*, pages 619–624, Hyderabad, India.

Needle in a Haystack: Reducing the Costs of Annotating Rare-Class Instances in Imbalanced Datasets

Emily K. Jamison [‡] **and Iryna Gurevych** [†‡]
[‡]Ubiquitous Knowledge Processing Lab (UKP-TUDA),
Department of Computer Science, Technische Universität Darmstadt
† Ubiquitous Knowledge Processing Lab (UKP-DIPF),
German Institute for Educational Research
http://www.ukp.tu-darmstadt.de

Abstract

Crowdsourced data annotation is noisier than annotation from trained workers. Previous work has shown that redundant annotations can eliminate the agreement gap between crowdsource workers and trained workers. Redundant annotation is usually nonproblematic because individual crowdsource judgments are inconsequentially cheap in a class-balanced dataset.

However, redundant annotation on class-imbalanced datasets requires many more labels per instance. In this paper, using three class-imbalanced corpora, we show that annotation redundancy for noise reduction is very expensive on a class-imbalanced dataset, and should be discarded for instances receiving a single common-class label. We also show that this simple technique produces annotations at approximately the same cost of a metadata-trained, supervised cascading machine classifier, or about 70% cheaper than 5-vote majority-vote aggregation.

1 Introduction

The advent of crowdsourcing as a cheap but noisy source for annotation labels has spurred the development of algorithms to maximize quality and minimize cost. Techniques can detect spammers (Oleson et al., 2011; Downs et al., 2010; Buchholz and Latorre, 2011), model worker quality and bias during label aggregation (Jung and Lease, 2012; Ipeirotis et al., 2010) and optimize obtaining more labels per instance or more labelled instances (Kumar and Lease, 2011; Sheng et al., 2008). However, much previous work for quality maximization and cost limitation assumes that the dataset to be annotated is class-balanced.

Class-imbalanced datasets, or datasets with differences in prior class probabilities, present a unique problem during corpus production: how to include enough rare-class instances in the corpus to train a machine learner? If the orginal class distribution is maintained, a corpus that is large enough for a machine learner to identify *common-class* (i.e., frequent class) instances may suffer from a lack of *rare-class* (i.e., infrequent class) instances. Yet, it can be cost-prohibitive to expand the corpus until enough rare-class instances are included.

Content-based instance targeting can be used to select instances with a high probability of being rare-class. For example, in a binary class annotation task identifying pairs of emails from the same thread, where most instances are negative, cosine text similarity between the emails can be used to identify pairs of emails that are likely to be positive, so that they could be annotated and included in the resulting class-balanced corpus (Jamison and Gurevych, 2013). However, this technique renders the corpus useless for experiments including token similarity (or ngram similarity, semantic similarity, stopword distribution similarity, keyword similarity, etc) as a feature; a machine learner would be likely to learn the very same features for classification that were used to identify the rare-class instances during corpus construction. Even worse, Mikros and Argiri (2007) showed that many features besides ngrams are significantly correlated with topic, including sentence and token length, readability measures, and word length distributions. The proposed targeted-instance corpus is unfit for experiments using sentence length similarity features, token length similarity features, etc.

Active Learning presents a similar problem of artificially limiting rare-class variety, by only identi-

Copyright 2014 by Emily K. Jamison and Iryna Gurevych
28th Pacific Asia Conference on Language, Information and Computation pages 244–253

fying other potential rare-class instances for annotation that are very similar to the rare-class instances in the seed dataset. Rare-class instances may never be selected for labelling if they are very different from those in the seed dataset.

In this paper, we explore the use of cascading machine learner and cascading rule-based techniques for rare-class instance identification during corpus production. We avoid the use of content-based targeting, to maintain rare-class diversity, and instead focus on crowdsourcing practices and metadata. To the best of our knowledge, our work is the first work to evaluate cost-effective non-content-based annotation procedures for class-imbalanced datasets. Based on experiments with three class-imbalanced corpora, we show that redundancy for noise reduction is very expensive on a class-imbalanced dataset, and should be discarded for instances receiving a single common-class label. We also show that this simple technique produces annotations at approximately the same cost of a metadata-trained machine classifier, or about 70% cheaper than 5-vote majority-vote aggregation, and requires no training data, making it suitable for seed dataset production.

2 Previous Work

The rise of crowdsourcing has introduced promising new annotation strategies for corpus development.

Crowdsourced labels are extremely cheap. In a task where workers gave judgments rating a news headline for various emotions, Snow et al. (2008) collected 7000 judgments for a total of US$2. In a computer vision image labelling task, Sorokin and Forsyth (2008) collected 3861 labels for US$59; access to equivalent data from the annotation service *ImageParsing.com*, with an existing annotated dataset of 49,357 images, would have cost at least US$1000, or US$5000 for custom annotations.

Crowdsourced labels are also of usable quality. On a behavioral testing experiment of tool-use identification, Casler et al. (2013) compared the performance of crowdsource workers, social media-recruited workers, and in-person trained workers, and found that test results among the 3 groups were almost indistinguishable. Sprouse (2011) collected syntactic acceptability judgments from 176 trained undergraduate annotators and 176 crowdsource annotators, and after removing outlier work and ineligible workers, found no difference in statistical power or judgment distribution between the two groups. Nowak and Rüger (2010) compared annotations from experts and from crowdsource workers on an image labelling task, and they found that a single annotation set consisting of majority-vote aggregation of non-expert labels is comparable in quality to the expert annotation set. Snow et al. (2008) compared labels from trained annotators and crowdsource workers on five linguistic annotation tasks. They created an aggregated *meta-labeller* by averaging the labels of subsets of n non-expert annotations. Inter-annotator agreement between the non-expert meta-labeller and the expert labels ranged from .897 to 1.0 with n=10 on four of the tasks.

Sheng et al. (2008) showed that although a machine learner can learn from noisy labels, the number of needed instances is greatly reduced, and the quality of the annotation improved, with higher quality labels. To this end, much research aims to increase annotation quality while maintaining cost.

Annotation quality can be improved by removing unconscientious workers from the task. Oleson et al. (2011) screened spammers and provided worker training by embedding auto-selected *gold instances* (instances with high confidence labels) into the annotation task. Downs et al. (2010) identified 39% of unconscientious workers with a simple two question qualifying task. Buchholz and Latorre (2011) examined cheating techniques associated with speech synthesis judgments, including workers who do not play the recordings, and found that cheating becomes more prevalent over time, if unchecked. They examined the statistical profile of cheaters and developed exclusion metrics.

Separate weighting of worker quality and bias during the aggregation of labels can produce higher quality annotations. Jung and Lease (2012) learned a worker's annotation quality from the sparse single-worker labels typical of a crowdsourcing annotation task, for improved weighting during label aggregation. In an image labelling task, Welinder and Perona (2010) estimated label uncertainty and worker ability, and derived an algorithm that seeks further labels from high quality annotators and controls the number of annotations per item to achieve a desired level of confidence, with fewer total labels. Tarasov et al. (2014) dynamically estimated annotator reliability with regression using multi-armed bandits, in a system that is flexible to annotator unavailability, no gold standard, and a variety of label types. Dawid and Skene (1979) used an EM algorithm to simultaneously estimate worker bias and aggregate labels. Ipeirotis et al. (2010) separately calculated bias and error, enabling better quality assessment of a worker.

Some research explores the decision between obtaining more labels per instance or more labelled instances. Sheng et al. (2008) evaluated machine learning performance with different corpus sizes and label qualities. They evaluated four algorithms for use in deciding between redundant labelling and more labelled instances. Kumar and Lease (2011) built on the model by Sheng et al. (2008), adding knowledge of annotator quality for faster learning.

Other work focuses on correcting labels at the instance level. Dligach and Palmer (2011) used annotation-error detection and ambiguity detection to identify instances in need of additional annotations. Hsueh et al. (2009) modelled annotator quality and ambiguity rating to select highly informative yet unambiguous training instances.

Alternatively, class imbalance can be accommodated during machine learning, by resampling and cost-sensitive learning. Das et al. (2014) used density-based clustering to identify clusters in the instance space: if the clusters exceeded a threshold of majority-class dominance, they are undersampled to increase class-balance in the dataset. Batista et al. (2004) examined the effects of sampling for class-imbalance reduction on 13 datasets and found that oversampling is generally more effective than undersampling. They evaluated oversampling techniques to produce the fewest additional classifier rules. Elkan (2001) proved that class balance can be changed to set different misclassification penalties, although he observed this is ineffective with certain classifiers such as decision trees and Bayesian classifiers, so he also provided adjustment equations for use in such cases.

One option to reduce annotation costs is the classifier cascade. The Viola-Jones cascade machine learning-based framework (Viola and Jones, 2001) has been used to cheaply classify easy instances while passing along difficult instances for more costly classification. Classification of annotations can use annotation metadata: Zaidan and Callison-Burch (2011) used metadata crowdsource features to train a system to reject bad translations in a translation generation task. Cascaded classifiers are used by Bourdev and Brandt (2005) for object detection in images and Raykar et al. (2010) to reduce the cost of obtaining expensive (in money or pain to the patient) features in a medical diagnosis setting. In this paper, we evaluate the use of metadata-based classifier cascade, as well as rule cascades, to reduce annotation costs.

3 Three Class-Imbalanced Annotation Tasks

We investigate three class-imbalanced annotation tasks; all are pairwise classification tasks that are class-imbalanced due to factorial combination of text pairs.

Pairwise Email Thread Disentanglement A pairwise email disentanglement task labels pairs of emails with whether or not the two emails come from the same email thread (a *positive* or *negative* instance). The Emails dataset[1] consists of 34 positive and 66 negative instances, and simulates a server's contents in which most pairs are negative (common class). The emails come from the Enron Email Corpus , which has no inherent header thread labelling. Annotators were shown both texts side-by-side and asked "Are these two emails from the same discussion/email thread?" Possible answers were *yes*, *can't tell*, and *no*.

Pairwise Wikipedia Discussion Turn/Edit Alignment Wikipedia editors discuss plans for *edits* in an article's *discussion* page, but there is no inherent mechanism to connect specific *discussion turns* in the discussion to the edits they describe. A corpus of matched turn/edit pairs permits investigation of relations between turns and edits. The Wiki dataset[2] consists of 750 turn/edit pairs. Additional rare-class (positive) instances were added to the corpus, resulting in 17% positive instances. Annotators were

[1] www.ukp.tu-darmstadt.de/data/text-similarity/email-disentanglement/

[2] www.ukp.tu-darmstadt.de/data/discourse-analysis/wikipedia-edit-turn-pair-corpus/

Sentence1: *Cord is strong, thick string.*
Sentence2: *A smile is the expression that you have on your face when you are pleased or amused, or when you are being friendly.*

Figure 1: Sample text pair from text similarity corpus, classified by 7 out of 10 workers as 1 on a scale of 1-5.

shown the article topic, turn and thread topic, the edit, and the edit comment, and asked, "Does the Wiki comment match the Wiki edit?" Possible answers were *yes*, *can't tell*, and *no*.

Sentence Pair Text Similarity Ratings To rate sentence similarity, annotators read 2 sentences and answered the question, "How close do these sentences come to meaning the same thing?" Annotators rated text similarity of the sentences on a scale of 1 (minimum similarity) to 5 (maximum similarity). This crowdsource dataset was produced by Bär et al. (2011). An example sentence pair is shown in Figure 1. The SentPairs dataset consists of 30 sentence pairs.

The original classification was calculated as the mean of a pair's judgments. However, on a theoretical level, it is unclear that mean, even with a deviation measure, accurately expresses annotator judgments for this task. Our experiments (see Sections 6 and 7) use mode score as the gold standard, which occasionally results in multiple instances derived from one set of ratings.

From the view of binary classification, each one of the 5 classes constitutes a rare class. For the purposes of our experiments, we treat each class in turn as the rare-class, while neighboring classes are treated as *can't tell* classes (with estimated normalization for continuum edge classes *1* and *5*), and the rest as common classes. For example, experiments treating class *4* as rare treated classes *3* and *5* as "*can't tell*" and classes *1* and *2* as common.

4 How severe is class imbalance?

The Emails and Wiki datasets consist of two texts paired in such a way that a complete dataset would consist of all possible pair combinations (Cartesian product). Although the dataset for text similarity rating does not require such pairing, it is still heavily class imbalanced.

Consider an email corpus with a set of threads T and each $t \in T$ consisting of a set of emails E_t, where rare-class instances are pairs of emails from the same thread, and common-class instances are pairs of emails from different threads. We have the following number of rare-class instances:

$$|\text{ Instances}_{\text{rare}}| = \sum_{i=1}^{|T|} \sum_{j=1}^{|E_i|-1} j$$

and number of common-class instances:

$$|\text{ Instances}_{\text{common}}| = \sum_{i=1}^{|T|} \sum_{j=1}^{|E_i|} \sum_{k=(i+1)}^{|T|} |E_k|$$

For example, in an email corpus with 2 threads of 2 emails each, 4 (67%) of pairs are common-class instances, and 2 (33%) are rare-class instances. If another email thread of two emails is added, 12 (80%) of the pairs are common-class instances, and 3 (20%) are rare-class instances.

To provide a constant value for the purposes of this work, we standardize rare-class frequency to 0.01 unless otherwise noted. This is different from our datasets' actual class imbalances, but the conclusions from our experiments in Section 7 are independent of class balance.

5 Baseline Cost

The baseline aggregation technique in our experiments (see Sections 6 and 7) is majority vote of the annotators. For example, if an instance receives at least 3 out of 5 rare-class annotations, then the baseline consensus declares it rare-class.

Emails Dataset Cost For our Emails dataset, we solicited 10 Amazon Mechnical Turk (*MTurk*)[3] annotations for each of 100 pairs of emails, at a cost of US$0.033[4] per annotation. Standard quality measures employed to reduce spam annotations included over 2000 *HIT*s (MTurk tasks) completed, 95% HIT acceptance rate, and location in the US.

Assuming 0.01 rare-class frequency[5] and 5 annotations[6], the cost of a rare-class instance is:

$$\frac{US\$0.033 \times 5 \text{ annotators}}{0.01 \text{ freq}} = US\$16.50$$

[3]www.mturk.com

[4]Including approx. 10% MTurk fees

[5]Although this paper proposes a hypothetical 0.01 rare-class frequency, the Emails and Wiki datasets have been partially balanced: the negative instances merely functioned as a distractor for annotators, and conclusions drawn from the rule cascade experiments only apply to positive instances.

[6]On this dataset, IAA was high and 10 annotations was over-redundant.

Wiki Dataset Cost For our Wiki dataset, we solicited five MTurk annotations for each of 750 turn/edit text pairs at a cost of US$0.044 per annotation. Measures for Wikipedia turn/edit pairs included 2000 HITs completed, 97% acceptance rate, age over 18, and either preapproval based on good work on pilot studies or a high score on a qualification test of sample pairs. The cost of a rare-class instance is:

$$\frac{US\$0.044 \times 5 \text{ annotators}}{0.01 \text{ freq}} = US\$22$$

SentPairs Dataset Cost The SentPairs datset consists of 30 sentence pairs, and 10 annotations per pair. The original price of Bär et al. (2011)'s sentence pairs corpus is unknown, so we estimated a cost of US$0.01 per annotation. The annotations came from Crowdflower[7]. Bär et al. (2011) used a number of quality assurance mechanisms, such as worker reliability and annotation correlation. The cost of a rare-class instance varied between classes, due to class frequency variation, from instance$_{class2}$=US$0.027 to instance$_{class5}$=US$0.227.

Finding versus Confirming a Rare-Class Instance It is cheaper to confirm a rare-class instance than to find a suspected rare-class instance in the first place. We have two types of binary decisions: finding a suspected rare-class instance ("Is the instance a true positive (*TP*) or false negative (*FN*)?") and confirming a rare-class instance as rare ("Is the instance a TP or false positive (*FP*)?"). Assuming a 0.01 rare-class frequency, 5-annotation majority-vote decision, and 0.5 FP frequency, the cost of the former is:

$$\frac{1 \text{ annotation}}{0.01 \text{ freq}} + \frac{1 \text{ annotation}}{0.99 \text{ freq}} = 101 \text{ annotations}$$

and the latter is:

$$\frac{5 \text{ annotations}}{0.5 \text{ freq}} = 10 \text{ annotations}$$

Metrics We used the following metrics for our experiment results:

TP is the number of true positives (rare-class) discovered. The fewer TP's discovered, the less likely the resulting corpus will represent the original data in an undistorted manner.

$\mathbf{P}_{rare}$ is the precision over rare instances: $\frac{TP}{TP+FP}$ Lower precision means lower confidence in the produced dataset, because the "rare" instances we found might have been misclassified.

AvgA is the average number of annotations needed for the system to label an instance common-class.

The normalized cost is the estimated cost of acquiring a rare instance: $\frac{\frac{\text{AvgA} \times \text{annoCost}}{\text{classImbalance}}}{\text{Recall}_{rare}}$

Savings is the estimated cost saved when identifying rare instances, over the baseline. Includes Standard Deviation.

6 Supervised Cascading Classifier Experiments

Previous work (Zaidan and Callison-Burch, 2011) used machine learners to predict which instances to annotate based on annotation metadata. In this section, we used crowdsourcing annotation metadata (such as time duration) as features for a cascading logistic regression classifier to choose whether or not an additional annotation is needed. In each of the five cascade rounds, an instance was classified as either *potentially rare* or *common*. Instances classified as potentially rare received another annotation and continued through the next cascade, while instances classified as common were discarded. Discarding instances before the end of the cascade can reduce the total number of needed annotations, and therefore lower the total cost. This cascade models the observation (see Section 5) that it is cheap to confirm suspected rare-class instances, but it is expensive to weed out common-class instances.

Experiments from this section will be compared in Section 7 to a rule-based cascading classifier system that, unlike this supervised system, does not need any training data.

6.1 Instances

Each experimental instance consisted of features derived from the metadata of one or more crowdsourced annotations from a pair of texts. A gold standard rare instance has >80% rare annotations.

In the first round of experiments, each instance was derived from a single annotation. In each further round, instances were only included that consisted of an instance from the previous round that had been classified *potentially rare* plus one additional annotation. All possible instances were used that could be derived from the available annotations, as long as the instance was permitted by the previous round of classification (see Figure 2). This maximized the

[7] crowdflower.com

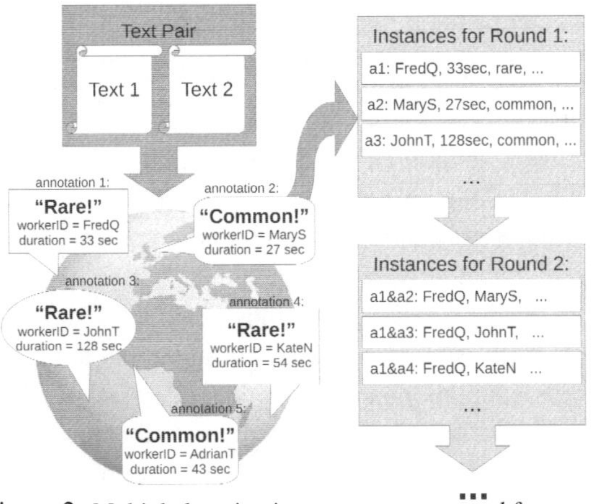

Figure 2: Multiple learning instances are generated from each original annotated text pair.

number of instances available for the experiments. K-fold cross-validation was used, but to avoid information leak, no test data was classified using a model trained on any instances generated from the same original text pairs.

Although SentPairs had 10 annotations per pair, we stopped the cascade at five iterations, because the number of rare-class instances was too small to continue. This resulted in a larger number of final instances than actual sentence pairs.

6.2 Features

Features were derived from the metadata of annotations. Features included an annotation's worker ID, estimated time duration, annotation day of the week (Emails and Wiki only), and the label (*rare*, *common*, *can't tell*), as well as all possible joins of one annotation's features (`commonANDJohnTAND30sec`). For instances representing more than a single annotation, a feature's *count* over all the annotations was also included (i.e., `common:3` for an instance including 3 *common* annotations). For reasons discussed in Section 1, we exclude features based on text content of the pair.

6.3 Results

Tables 1 and 2 show the results of our trained cascading system on Emails and Wiki, respectively; baseline is majority voting. Tables 3 and 4 show results on rare classes `1` and `5` of SentPairs (classes `2`, `3`, and `4` had too few instances to train, a disadvantage of a supervised system that is fixed by our rule-based system in Section 7); baseline is mode class voting.

features	TPs	P_{rare}	AvgA	Norm cost	Savings(%)
baseline	34	1.00	-	$16.50	-
anno	31	0.88	1.2341	$4.68	72±8
worker	0	0.0	1.0	-	-
dur	2	0.1	1.0	$16.5	0±0
day	0	0.0	1.0	-	-
worker & anno	33	0.9	1.1953	$4.38	73±7
day & anno	31	0.88	1.2347	$4.68	72±8
dur & anno	33	0.88	1.2437	$4.56	72±8
w/o anno	3	0.12	1.2577	$20.75	-26±41
w/o worker	33	0.9	1.2341	$4.53	73±8
w/o day	33	0.9	1.2098	$4.44	73±7
w/o dur	33	0.9	1.187	**$4.35**	**74**±7
all	33	0.9	1.2205	$4.48	73±8

Table 1: Email results on the trained cascade.

features	TPs	P_{rare}	AvgA	Norm cost	Savings(%)
baseline	128	1.00	-	$22.00	-
anno	35	0.93	1.7982	$20.29	08±32
worker	0	0.0	1.0	-	-
dur	0	0.0	1.0	-	-
day	0	0.0	1.0	-	-
worker & anno	126	0.99	1.6022	**$7.12**	**68±11**
day & anno	108	0.88	1.644	$8.51	61±13
dur & anno	111	0.86	1.5978	$8.08	63±12
w/o anno	4	0.12	1.0259	$11.28	49±6
w/o worker	92	0.84	1.7193	$9.46	57±15
w/o day	104	0.9	1.6639	$8.61	61±14
w/o dur	109	0.94	1.6578	$8.2	63±14
all	89	0.82	1.6717	$8.76	60±15

Table 2: Wiki results on the trained cascade.

Table 1 shows that the best feature combination for identifying rare email pairs was annotation, worker ID, and day of the week ($4.35 per rare instance, and 33/34 instances found); however, this was only marginally better than using annotation alone ($4.68, 31/34 instances found). The best feature combination resulted in a 74% cost savings over the conventional 5-annotation baseline.

Table 2 shows that the best feature combination for identifying rare wiki pairs was annotation and worker ID ($7.12, 126/128 instances found). Unlike the email experiments, this combination was remarkably more effective than annotations alone ($20.29, 35/128 instances found), and produced a 68% total cost savings.

Tables 3 and 4 show that the best feature combination for identifying rare sentence pairs for both rare classes 1 and 5 was also annotation and worker

features	TPs	P_{rare}	AvgA	Norm cost	Savings(%)
baseline	12	1.00	-	$1.50	-
anno	9	0.67	1.8663	$0.4	73±10
workerID	1	0.1	1.5426	$2.31	-54±59
dur	2	0.15	1.4759	$1.11	26±26
worker & anno	11	0.7	1.8216	**$0.39**	**74**±**9**
worker & dur	3	0.2	1.8813	$1.41	06±34
dur & anno	8	0.42	1.8783	$0.56	62±13
all	11	0.62	1.8947	$0.41	73±8

Table 3: SentPairs_{c1} results on the trained cascade.

features	TPs	P_{rare}	AvgA	Norm cost	Savings(%)
baseline	17	1.00	-	\$0.44	-
anno	14	0.72	2.4545	\$0.15	66±7
worker	14	0.63	2.7937	\$0.16	64±8
dur	10	0.52	2.7111	\$0.18	58±11
worker & anno	15	0.82	2.3478	**\$0.12**	**73±8**
worker & dur	6	0.4	2.7576	\$0.38	14±23
dur & anno	16	0.72	2.4887	\$0.14	69±10
all	17	0.82	2.4408	\$0.12	73±5

Table 4: SentPairs_{c5} results on the trained cascade.

ID (US\$0.39 and US\$0.12, respectively), which produced a 73% cost savings; for class 5, adding duration minimally decreased the standard deviation. Annotation and worker ID were only marginally better than annotation alone for class 1.

7 Rule-based Cascade Experiments

Although the meta-data-trained cascading classifier system is effective in reducing the needed number of annotations, it is not useful in the initial stage of annotation, when there is no training data. In these experiments, we evaluate a rule-based cascade in place of our previous trained classifier. The rule-based cascade functions similarly to the trained classifier cascade except that a single rule replaces each classification. Five cascades are used.

Each rule instructs when to discard an instance from further annotation. For example, `no>2` means, "if the count of *no* (i.e., common) annotations becomes greater than 2, we assume the instance is common and do not seek further confirmation from more annotations." A gold standard rare instances has >80% rare annotations.

For our rule-based experiments, we define AvgA for each instance i and for annotations a_{1_i}, a_{2_i}, ..., a_{5_i} and the probability (Pr) of five non-common-class annotations. Class c is the common class. We always need a first annotation: $\Pr(a_{1_i} \neq c) = 1$.

$$AvgA_i = \sum_{j=1}^{5} \prod_{k=1}^{j} \Pr(a_{k_i} \neq c)$$

We define $Precision_{rare}$ (P_{rare}) as the probability that instance i with 5 common[8] annotations a_{1_i}, a_{2_i}, ..., a_{5_i} is not a rare-class instance:

$$\begin{aligned} P_{rare_i} &= \Pr(\text{TP}|(a_{1\ldots5_i} = \text{rare})) \\ &= 1 - \Pr(\text{FP}|(a_{1\ldots5_i} = \text{rare})) \end{aligned}$$

Thus, we estimate the probability of seeing other FPs based on the class distribution of our annotations. This is different from our supervised cascade experiments, in which $P_{rare} = \frac{TP}{TP+FP}$.

[8]This may also include *can't tell* annotations, depending on the experiment.

7.1 Results

Table 5 shows the results of various rule systems on reducing cost on the wiki data.

While it might appear reasonable to allow one or two careless crowdsource annotations before discarding an instance, the tables show just how costly this allowance is: each permitted extra annotation (i.e., `no>1`, `no>2`, ...) must be applied systematically to each instance (because we do not know which annotations are careless and which are accurate) and can increase the average number of annotations needed to discard a common instance by over 1. The practice also decreases rare-class precision, within an *n*-annotations limit. Clearly the cheapest and most precise option is to discard an instance as soon as there is a common-class annotation.

When inherently ambiguous instances are shifted from rare to common by including *can't tell* as a common annotation, the cost of a rare Wiki instance falls from US\$7.09 (68% savings over baseline) to US\$6.10 (72% savings), and the best performing rule is `(no+ct)>0`. A rare email instance barely increases from US\$3.52 (79% savings) to US\$3.65 (78% savings). However, in both cases, TP of rare-class instances falls (Wiki: 39 instances to 22, Emails: 32 instances to 30). This does not affect overall cost, because it is already included in the equation, but the rare-class instances found may not be representative of the data.

There was not much change in precision in the Wiki dataset when *can't tell* was included as a rare annotation (such as `no>0`) or a common annotation (such as `(no+ct)>0`), so we assume that the populations of rare instances gathered are not different between the two. However, when a reduced number of TPs are produced from treating *can't tell* as a common annotation, higher annotation costs can result (such as Table 5, `no>0` cost of US\$7.09, versus `(no+ct)>0` cost of US\$10.56).

Removing ambiguous instances from the test corpus does not notably change the results (see Table 6). Ambiguous instances were those where the majority class was *can't tell*, the majority class was tied with *can't tell*, or there was a tie between common and rare classes.

Finally, the tables show that not only do the top-performing rules save money over the 5-annotations

Class = N if:	TP	P_{rare}	AvgA	NormCost	Savings(%)
baseline	128	1.00	-	$22.0	-
no > 0	39	0.95	1.61	**$7.09**	**68±16**
no > 1	39	0.85	2.86	$12.6	43±19
no > 2	39	0.73	3.81	$16.75	24±15
(no+ct) > 0	22	0.98	1.35	$10.56	52±20
(no+ct) > 1	33	0.93	2.55	$13.25	40±18
(no+ct) > 2	35	0.85	3.56	$17.44	21±15

Table 5: Wiki results: rule-based cascade. All instances included.

Class = N if:	TP	P_{rare}	AvgA	NormCost	Savings(%)
baseline	128	1.00	-	$22.0	-
no > 0	35	0.96	1.46	**$6.43**	**71±14**
no > 1	35	0.9	2.67	$11.76	47±17
no > 2	35	0.81	3.66	$16.11	27±14
(no+ct) > 0	22	0.98	1.33	$9.34	58±19
(no+ct) > 1	33	0.92	2.5	$11.66	47±17
(no+ct) > 2	35	0.85	3.49	$15.36	30±13

Table 6: Wiki results: no ambiguous instances.

baseline, they save about as much money as supervised cascade classification.

Table 7 shows results from the Emails dataset. Results largely mirrored those of the Wiki dataset, except that there was higher inter-annotator agreement on the email pairs which reduced annotation costs. We also found that, similarly to the Wiki experiments, weeding out uncertain examples did not notably change the results.

Results of the rule-based cascade on SentPairs are shown in Tables 8, 9, 10, and 11. Note there were no instances with a mode gold classification of 3. Also, there are more total rare instances than sentence pairs, because of the method used to identified a gold instance: annotations neighboring the rare class were ignored, and an instance was gold rare if the count of rare annotations was >0.8 of total annotations. Thus, an instance with the count {class1=5, class2=4, class3=1, class4=0, class5=0} counts as a gold instance of both class 1 and class 2.

The cheapest rule was no>0, which had a recall of 1.0, P_{rare} of 0.9895, and a cost savings of 80-83% (across classes 1-5) over the 10 annotators originally used in this task.

Class = N if:	TP	P_{rare}	AvgA	NormCost	Savings(%)
baseline	34	1.00	-	$16.5	-
no > 0	32	1.0	1.07	**$3.52**	**79±6**
no > 1	32	0.99	2.11	$6.95	58±7
no > 2	32	0.98	3.12	$10.31	38±6
(no+ct) > 0	30	1.0	1.04	$3.67	78±5
(no+ct) > 1	32	0.99	2.07	$6.83	59±6
(no+ct) > 2	32	0.99	3.08	$10.16	38±5

Table 7: Email results: rule-based cascade.

Class = N if:	TP	P_{rare}	AvgA	NormCost	Savings(%)
baseline	5	1.00	-	$1.5	-
no > 0	5	0.99	1.69	**$0.25**	**83±10**
no > 1	5	0.96	3.27	$0.49	67±17
no > 2	5	0.9	4.66	$0.7	53±21
(no+ct) > 0	0	1.0	1.34	-	-
(no+ct) > 1	2	0.98	2.63	$0.98	34±31
(no+ct) > 2	4	0.96	3.83	$0.72	52±19

Table 8: $SentPairs_{c1}$ results: rule-based cascade.

Class = N if:	TP	P_{rare}	AvgA	NormCost	Savings(%)
baseline	2	1.00	-	$3.75	-
no > 0	2	0.98	1.95	**$0.73**	**81±12**
no > 1	2	0.93	3.68	$1.38	63±20
no > 2	2	0.86	5.12	$1.92	49±23
(no+ct) > 0	0	1.0	1.1	-	-
(no+ct) > 1	0	1.0	2.2	-	-
(no+ct) > 2	0	1.0	3.29	-	-

Table 9: $SentPairs_{c2}$ results: rule-based cascade.

7.2 Error Analysis

A rare-class instance with many common annotations has a greater chance of being labelled common-class and thus discarded by a single crowdsource worker screening the data. What are the traits of rare-class instances at high risk of being discarded? We analyzed only Wiki text pairs, because the inter-annotator agreement was low enough to cause false negatives. The small size of SentPairs and the high inter-annotator agreement of Emails prevented analysis.

Wiki data The numbers of instances (750 total) with various crowdsource annotation distributions are shown in Table 12. The table shows annotation distributions (i.e., 302 = 3 *yes*, 0 *can't tell* and 2 *no*) for rare-class instance numbers with high and low probabilities of being missed.

We analyzed the instances from the category most likely to be missed (302) and compared it with the two categories least likely to be missed (500, 410). Of five random 302 pairs, all five appeared highly ambiguous and difficult to annotate; they were missing context that was known (or assumed to be known) by the original participants. Two of the turns state future deletion operations, and the ed-

Class = N if:	TP	P_{rare}	AvgA	NormCost	Savings(%)
baseline	16	1.00	-	$0.47	-
no > 0	16	0.99	1.98	**$0.09**	**80±9**
no > 1	16	0.96	3.83	$0.18	62±15
no > 2	16	0.9	5.47	$0.26	45±17
(no+ct) > 0	0	1.0	1.23	-	-
(no+ct) > 1	0	1.0	2.45	-	-
(no+ct) > 2	1	0.99	3.65	$2.74	-484±162

Table 10: $SentPairs_{c4}$ results: rule-based cascade.

Class = N if:	TP	P_{rare}	AvgA	NormCost	Savings(%)
baseline	17	1.00	-	$0.44	-
no > 0	17	0.99	1.96	**$0.09**	**80±10**
no > 1	17	0.95	3.77	$0.17	62±16
no > 2	17	0.89	5.37	$0.24	46±18
(no+ct) > 0	2	1.0	1.27	$0.48	-8±21
(no+ct) > 1	10	1.0	2.54	$0.19	57±8
(no+ct) > 2	13	1.0	3.8	$0.22	50±9

Table 11: SentPairs_{c5} results: rule-based cascade.

Ambiguous instances		Unambiguous instances	
Anno, *y ct n*	**# inst**	**Anno, *y ct n***	**# inst**
3 0 2	35	5 0 0	22
3 1 1	30	4 1 0	11
2 2 1	19	4 0 1	28
2 1 2	39	3 2 0	2

Table 12: Anno. distributions and instance counts.

its include deleted statements, but it is unknown if the turns were referring to these particular deleted statements or to others. In another instance, the turn argues that a contentious research question has been answered and that the user will edit the article accordingly, but it is unclear in which direction the user intended to edit the article. In another instance, the turn requests the expansion of an article section, and the edit is an added reference to that section. In the last pair, the turn gives a quote from the article and requests a source, and the edit adds a source to the quoted part of the article, but the source clearly refers to just one part of the quote.

In contrast, we found four of the five `500` and `410` pairs to be clear rare-class instances. Turns quoted text from the article that matched actions in the edits. In the fifth pair, a `500` instance, the edit was first made, then the turn was submitted complaining about the edit and asking it to be reversed. This was a failure by the annotators to follow the directions included with the task, of which types of pairs are positive instances and which are not.

8 Conclusion

Crowdsourcing is a cheap but noisy source of annotation labels, encouraging redundant labelling. However, redundant annotation on class-imbalanced datasets requires many more labels per instance. In this paper, using three class-imbalanced corpora, we have shown that annotation redundancy for noise reduction is expensive on a class-imbalanced dataset, and should be discarded for instances receiving a single common-class label. We have also shown that this simple technique, which does not require any training data, produces annotations at approximately the same cost of a metadata-trained, supervised cascading machine classifier, or about 70% cheaper than 5-vote majority-vote aggregation. We expect that future work will combine this technique for seed data creation with algorithms such as Active Learning to create corpora large enough for machine learning, at a reduced cost.

Acknowledgments

This work has been supported by the Volkswagen Foundation as part of the Lichtenberg-Professorship Program under grant No. I/82806, and by the Center for Advanced Security Research (`www.cased.de`).

References

Daniel Bär, Torsten Zesch, and Iryna Gurevych. 2011. A reflective view on text similarity. In *Proceedings of the International Conference on Recent Advances in Natural Language Processing*, pages 515–520, Hissar, Bulgaria.

Gustavo E.A.P.A. Batista, Ronaldo C. Prati, and Maria Carolina Monard. 2004. A study of the behavior of several methods for balancing machine learning training data. *ACM Sigkdd Explorations Newsletter*, 6(1):20–29.

Lubomir Bourdev and Jonathan Brandt. 2005. Robust object detection via soft cascade. In *Proceedings of the 2005 IEEE Computer Society Conference on Computer Vision and Pattern Recognition*, volume 2, pages 236–243, Washington D.C., USA.

Sabine Buchholz and Javier Latorre. 2011. Crowdsourcing preference tests, and how to detect cheating. In *Proceedings of the 12thAnnual Conference of the International Speech Communication Association (INTERSPEECH)*, pages 3053–3056, Florence, Italy.

Krista Casler, Lydia Bickel, and Elizabeth Hackett. 2013. Separate but equal? A comparison of participants and data gathered via Amazons MTurk, social media, and face-to-face behavioral testing. *Computers in Human Behavior*, 29(6):2156–2160.

Barnan Das, Narayanan C. Krishnan, and Diane J. Cook. 2014. Handling imbalanced and overlapping classes in smart environments prompting dataset. In Katsutoshi Yada, editor, *Data Mining for Service*, pages 199–219. Springer, Berlin Heidelberg.

A. P. Dawid and A. M. Skene. 1979. Maximum likelihood estimation of observer error-rates using the EM algorithm. *Applied Statistics*, 28(1):20–28.

Dmitriy Dligach and Martha Palmer. 2011. Reducing the need for double annotation. In *Proceedings of the 5th Linguistic Annotation Workshop*, pages 65–73, Stroudsburg, Pennsylvania.

Julie S. Downs, Mandy B. Holbrook, Steve Sheng, and Lorrie Faith Cranor. 2010. Are your participants gaming the system?: Screening Mechanical Turk workers. In *Proceedings of the SIGCHI Conference on Human Factors in Computing Systems*, pages 2399–2402, Atlanta, Georgia.

Charles Elkan. 2001. The foundations of cost-sensitive learning. In *Proceedings of the 17th International Joint Conference on Artificial Intelligence*, pages 973–978, San Francisco, California.

Pei-Yun Hsueh, Prem Melville, and Vikas Sindhwani. 2009. Data quality from crowdsourcing: a study of annotation selection criteria. In *Proceedings of the NAACL HLT 2009 workshop on active learning for natural language processing*, pages 27–35, Boulder, Colorado.

Panagiotis G. Ipeirotis, Foster Provost, and Jing Wang. 2010. Quality management on Amazon Mechanical Turk. In *Proceedings of the ACM SIGKDD workshop on human computation*, pages 64–67, Washington D.C., USA.

Emily K. Jamison and Iryna Gurevych. 2013. Headerless, quoteless, but not hopeless? using pairwise email classification to disentangle email threads. In *Proceedings of the International Conference Recent Advances in Natural Language Processing RANLP 2013*, pages 327–335, Hissar, Bulgaria.

Hyun Joon Jung and Matthew Lease. 2012. Improving quality of crowdsourced labels via probabilistic matrix factorization. In *Proceedings of the 4th Human Computation Workshop (HCOMP) at AAAI*, pages 101–106, Toronto, Canada.

Abhimanu Kumar and Matthew Lease. 2011. Modeling annotator accuracies for supervised learning. In *Proceedings of the Workshop on Crowdsourcing for Search and Data Mining (CSDM) at the Fourth ACM International Conference on Web Search and Data Mining (WSDM)*, pages 19–22, Hong Kong, China.

George K. Mikros and Eleni K. Argiri. 2007. Investigating topic influence in authorship attribution. In *Proceedings of the SIGIR 2007 International Workshop on Plagiarism Analysis, Authorship Identification, and Near-Duplicate Detection, PAN 2007*, Amsterdam, Netherlands. Online proceedings.

Stefanie Nowak and Stefan Rüger. 2010. How reliable are annotations via crowdsourcing: a study about inter-annotator agreement for multi-label image annotation. In *Proceedings of the international conference on Multimedia information retrieval*, pages 557–566, Philadelphia, Pennsylvania.

David Oleson, Alexander Sorokin, Greg P. Laughlin, Vaughn Hester, John Le, and Lukas Biewald. 2011. Programmatic gold: Targeted and scalable quality assurance in crowdsourcing. *Human computation*, 11:11.

Vikas C. Raykar, Balaji Krishnapuram, and Shipeng Yu. 2010. Designing efficient cascaded classifiers: tradeoff between accuracy and cost. In *Proceedings of the 16th ACM SIGKDD international conference on Knowledge discovery and data mining*, pages 853–860, New York, NY.

Victor S. Sheng, Foster Provost, and Panagiotis G. Ipeirotis. 2008. Get another label? Improving data quality and data mining using multiple, noisy labelers. In *Proceedings of the 14th ACM SIGKDD international conference on Knowledge discovery and data mining*, pages 614–622, Las Vegas, Nevada.

Rion Snow, Brendan O'Connor, Daniel Jurafsky, and Andrew Y. Ng. 2008. Cheap and fast—but is it good?: Evaluating non-expert annotations for natural language tasks. In *Proceedings of the conference on Empirical Methods in Natural Language Processing*, pages 254–263, Honolulu, Hawaii.

Alexander Sorokin and David Forsyth. 2008. Utility data annotation with Amazon Mechanical Turk. *Urbana*, 51(61):820.

Jon Sprouse. 2011. A validation of Amazon Mechanical Turk for the collection of acceptability judgments in linguistic theory. *Behavior research methods*, 43(1):155–167.

Alexey Tarasov, Sarah Jane Delany, and Brian Mac Namee. 2014. Dynamic estimation of worker reliability in crowdsourcing for regression tasks: Making it work. *Expert Systems with Applications*, 41(14):6190–6210.

Paul A. Viola and Michael J. Jones. 2001. Rapid object detection using a boosted cascade of simple features. In *2001 IEEE Computer Society Conference on Computer Vision and Pattern Recognition*, pages 511–518, Kauai, Hawaii.

Peter Welinder and Pietro Perona. 2010. Online crowdsourcing: rating annotators and obtaining cost-effective labels. In *Proceedings of IEEE Computer Society Conference on Computer Vision and Pattern Recognition Workshops*, pages 25–32, San Francisco, California.

Omar F. Zaidan and Chris Callison-Burch. 2011. Crowdsourcing translation: Professional quality from non-professionals. In *Proceedings of the 49th Annual Meeting of the Association for Computational Linguistics: Human Language Technologies*, pages 1220–1229, Portland, Oregon.

Hybrid Approach to Zero Subject Resolution for multilingual MT

- Spanish-to-Korean Cases -

Arum Park
Dept. of German Linguistics & Literature,
Sungkyunkwan University /
25-2, Sungkyunkwan-Ro, Jongno-Gu,
Seoul, Korea
remin2@skku.edu

Munpyo Hong*
Dept. of German Linguistics & Literature,
Sungkyunkwan University /
25-2, Sungkyunkwan-Ro, Jongno-Gu,
Seoul, Korea
skkhmp@skku.edu

Abstract

The current paper proposes a novel approach to Spanish zero pronoun resolution in the context of Spanish to Korean Machine Translation (MT). Spanish is one of the well-known 'pro-drop' languages so that especially a subject pronoun is often omitted, if it can be inferred from the linguistic as well as non-linguistic context. In Spanish to Korean MT the omitted subject doesn't need to be restored in many cases as Korean also allows a zero subject. However, there are some cases where the omitted subject must be identified to ensure a correct translation. To restore the omitted subject, linguistic clues can be employed, as Spanish verbs undergo morphological flections with respect to the gender and number. However, there still remain some ambiguous cases in which there are more than two possible subject candidates for the specific verb endings. In this paper, we propose a hybrid approach to resolve Spanish zero subject that integrates linguistic knowledge (morphological information) and artificial intelligence knowledge (machine learning approach). We proposed 11 linguistically motivated features for ML (Machine Learning). Our approach has been implemented with WEKA 3.6.10 and evaluated by using 10 fold cross validation method. The accuracy of the proposed method reached 83.6% while the baseline method that randomly chooses a possible subject candidate among three most frequent subject types shows only 33.3% accuracy rate.

1 Introduction

Spanish is one of the so-called pro-drop languages where certain pronouns may be omitted. In Spanish, the pronominal subject can be deleted and is called a zero subject. A zero subject is the most frequent type of anaphoric expression in Spanish.[1] Palomar et al.(2001) reported that about 65.5% of the pronouns are the zero subject pronoun in pronoun occurrences in Spanish corpus.

Spanish zero subject is one of the important issues that must be tackled in Spanish-to-Korean MT. This kind of pronoun is very important due to its high frequency in Spanish texts. In many cases its resolution is obligatory in Spanish-to-Korean MT.

Let us consider the following example. In this example, the omitted subject is represented by the symbol ø.

(1) Luis quiere que **Ø** vayamos[1st plural] a la playa.
Luis want that go to the beach

* Corresponding author
[1] Palomar et al.(2001)

Copyright 2014 by Arum Park and Munpyo Hong
28th Pacific Asia Conference on Language, Information and Computation pages 254–261

Iwuisunun wulituli haypyeney kakilul wunhanta

"Luis wants us to go to the beach."

In Spanish, the subject pronoun and the verb must agree in person and number. Even though the subject pronoun is not present in the sentence, the zero subject can be restored from the verb ending, as '-os' is a 1st person plural morpheme. This gives us clues to resolve a Spanish zero subject.

However, there is another case for which to use verb ending for Spanish zero subject resolution is not enough. In Spanish, the verb ending for the 3rd person singular subject 'él(he)', 'ella(she)' and formal 2nd person singular subject 'Usted(you)' is same and so are for the plural subjects. Also for some verbs in a specific tense like *pretérito imperfecto*, the verb endings for the 1st and 3rd person singular are identical. Even in other sentence mood, there are some verbs which conjugate in the same way. Therefore, there still exists a problem to select the one right subject among possible subjects for some verb endings. For these cases, we need to suggest another method to select the one right subject among other possible subjects.

We introduce a machine learning method to resolve the case in which morphological information is not enough to resolve Spanish zero subject. Machine learning (ML) has already been successfully used in the computational linguistics for disambiguation and classification issues. Selecting one right subject among possible candidates can also be regarded as a disambiguation issue.

In this paper we propose a hybrid approach to zero subject in Spanish, which combines linguistic knowledge and ML approach in one model. The hybrid approach can benefit from the strengths of both approaches.

The related works about anaphora resolution and their limitation are presented in Section 2. In Section 3, we suggest the method for Spanish zero subject resolution. 11 features for ML method are also proposed. In Section 4, the effect of using ML is evaluated. Finally, the conclusion is presented in Section 5.

2 Related works

A zero pronoun subject has drawn much attention for various applications in the computational linguistics. Both rule-based and machine learning approaches have been utilized for languages such as Japanese (Okumura, M. and K. Tamura., 1996), Chinese (Zhao, S. and H.T. Ng., 2007), Korean (Han, N., 2004) and Spanish (Ferrández, A. and J. Peral., 2000) for zero pronoun identification and resolution.

The current anaphora resolution approaches rely mostly on linguistic knowledge in a rule-based framework. They try to find the right antecedent for the anaphora employing constraints and preference for the resolution.

The constraints discard some of the antecedent candidates for the anaphora and tend to be absolute. Morphological information is one of the constraints. For example, pronominal anaphors and antecedents must agree in person, gender, and number (e.g. Rich, E. and S. LuperFoy., 1988; Carbonell, J.G. and R.D. Brown., 1988).

Semantic information such as semantic consistency is also used as a constraint (e.g. Wilks, Y., 1973). This constraint stipulates that if satisfied by the anaphor, the semantic consistency constraint must also be satisfied by its antecedent. Although using constraints is the surest way to remove non-anaphoric pairs, they are not always sufficient to distinguish between a set of possible candidates.

Preference is a heuristic rule and it sets priorities in the list of the antecedent candidates which are left after constraints were applied to the list. Some of the works using preference are based on the centering theory. Centering theory (e.g. Brennan et al. 1987; Dahl, D.A. and C.N. Ball., 1990; Mitkov, R., 1994; Sidner, C., 1986; Stys, M.E. and S.S. Zemke., 1995; Walker et al. 1994) is a kind of preference rule because it gives more preference to certain candidates and less to others in forward-looking center lists.

However, there seems to be some difficulty in applying the centering theory for Spanish zero subject resolution. The text type we focused on is a spoken Spanish, so that there are even no antecedents for some zero subjects in the text. Therefore, to make a list of forward-looking centers would be difficult in Spanish spoken texts.

Rello et al.(2010) dealt with ML for Spanish anaphora phenomenon but did not focus on Spanish zero subject resolution. In zero anaphora resolution, non-referential subject ellipses need to be filtered out. They present a three-fold classification of subjects as (1) explicit and

referential (2) elliptic and referential (zero pronouns) and (3) elliptic and non-referential (impersonal constructions) using ML techniques.
Unlike this work, the aim of our work lies in resolving zero pronouns, not in classifying the subject types. The focus of our work is only on the subject class (2) in Rello et al.(2010).

3 Methodology

In Spanish, morphological information such as person and number agreement is a certain constraint to discard wrong antecedent candidates. According to the result of our experiment, in about 70% of the sentence, a zero subject can be restored by consulting the verbal flection information as can be seen in (2).

(2) Ø Estudias[2nd person sing] español?
study Spanish

nenun supheyinelul kongpuhani

"Do you study Spanish?"

The rest of the sentences, about 30% are the cases where using verb ending is not enough to restore one right subject. As for some verbs, multiple subjects can be possible candidates for the zero subject as in (3)-(5).

(3) ¿Ø Podría[3rd person sing] llegar tarde?
seem come late

(ku/kunye/tangsin) nuckey ol kes kathayo

"Does(Do) he/she/you seem to come late?

(4) ¿Ø Porqué iba[1st&3rd person sing] a ir?
why be going to go

(na/ku/kunye/tangsin) oway kalyeko haysseyo

"Why were(was) I/he/she/you going to go?"

(5) Ø Está[2nd&3rd person sing] en periodo de prueba.
be for a while probation

(ne/ku/kunye/tangsin) tangpwunkan kunsiniya

"You/He/She/You were(was) placed under probation for a while."

In these cases, there still remains a problem that one right subject among possible subjects has to be selected. For the cases, we applied ML method to select the right one for the zero subject.
Using only ML method without linguistic information is not the most optimal approach to resolve zero subjects. Applying the constraint is the surest way to narrow down the list of candidate subjects. For this reason, we proposed a 'hybrid approach' to Spanish zero subject resolution, which combines linguistic knowledge with ML. Our proposal is presented in Figure 1.

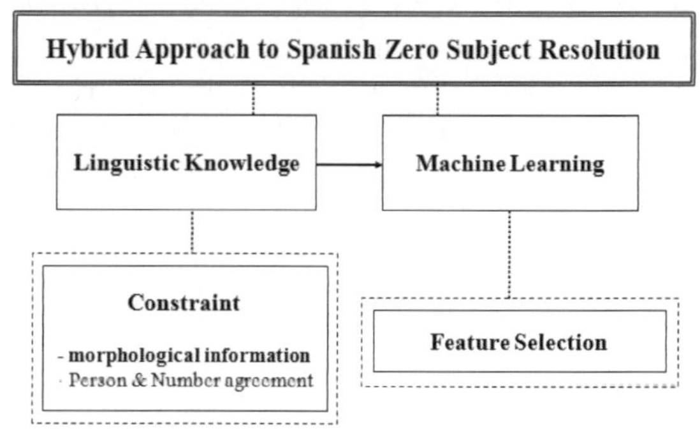

Figure 1. Hybrid approach to Spanish zero subject resolution

4 Experiments

In order to use a ML method, 11 features for Spanish zero subject resolution we introduced are presented in Table 1. The features were selected according to their linguistic as well as non-linguistic relevance to zero pronouns.

Feature Type		Feature	Value
Morpho-logical/ Syntactic	*f1*	Syntactic function of antecedent	(sub), (obj-v), (obj-p), (pos-adj), (ref-pro), (voc), (none)[2]
	f2	Person of the verb	the third person(1), the first/third person(2), the third person-indicativo/the second person-imperativo(3)
	f3	Number of the verb	singular(1), plural(2)

[2] 'none' represents the cases where there are no antecedent in the case of extra-sentential zero pronoun types.

	f4	Gender of antecedent	masculine(1), feminine(2), neutral(3)[3], (none)
Semantic	*f5*	Semantic class of antecedent	person (0), object (1), others(2), (none)
Relational	*f6*	Distance	in the same sentence(0), 1 sentence before(1) and 2 sentences before(2) and so on, (none)
Specific to Spanish	*f7*	Presence of a possessive adjective in the same sentence (same as coreferent)	false(0), possessive adjective in the first person (1), possessive adjective in the third person(2)
	f8	Presence of a reflexive pronoun in the same sentence (same as coreferent)	false(0), reflexive pronoun in the first person (1), reflexive pronoun in the third person (2)
	f9	Presence of antecedent	false(0), true(1)
	f10	mood of sentence	indicative(1), conditional(2), imperative(3), subjunctivo(4)
	f11	tense of sentence	PERFECTO(3), FUTURO IMPERFECTO(4), PRET.PERFECTO(5), PRET. PLUSCUAMPLERFECTO (6), FUTURO PERFECTO(7)

Table 1. 11 features for ML

There are features that are related to syntactic and semantic information (e.g. f1, f2, f3, f4, f5). The features can be classified according to their relevance to the linguistic levels. The first 5 features make use of the morphological, syntactic and semantic characteristics of anaphoric relations. As for f1, a subject-antecedent tends to be the most likely candidate for the anaphora resolution. This is reflected in the centering theory in the prominence hierarchy. The underlying assumption of the semantic class determination (concerning f5) is that the semantic class for a zero subject and the antecedent has to be identical.

The feature f6 is a coreference-level feature and it describes the relation between antecedents and zero subjects. McEnery et al.(1997) examined the distance of pronouns and their antecedent and concluded that the antecedents of pronouns do exhibit clear patterns of distribution.

In addition, we introduced a set of features (f7, f8, f9, f10, f11) reflecting the properties of Spanish. In Spanish, possessive adjectives and reflexive pronouns can also give some clues for the person of the antecedent because of their morphological information. Feature f7 and f8 reflect this property. As for f9, there are many extra-sentential zero subjects in Spanish spoken texts, which means they don't have any antecedents. The presence of antecedent could offer information to find zero subjects. Feature f10 and f11 are about the mood and tense of sentence.

To evaluate the ML approach, we built a corpus of 1000 sentences in which a zero subject is included and in which morphological information is not enough to restore the omitted subject.[4] The sources of the corpus were 9 movie scripts and 12 drama episodes.

Among 11 subject types in the corpus, we discarded 4 subject types whose number of frequency is less than 10, as we thought that they belong to rare cases. For this reason, only 988 sentences were tested.

There are 7 subject types in 988 sentences and the number of frequency for the subject types is presented in Table 2.

Subject type	**Frequency**
él(he)	290
ella(she)	276

[3] In Spanish, all nouns are either masculine or feminine. However, the gender of some antecedents such as 'yo(I)' and tú(you)' can vary according to their referents. In these cases, we consider that they have a 'neutral' gender.

[4] 1000 sentences are not large enough to train and to validate the classifier. However, as the building of the training corpus for Spanish zero subject resolution is time consuming and labor-intensive, the experiment was conducted with the corpus of 1000 sentences. The construction of the training corpus is still on-going.

yo(I)	275
tú(you-informal)	53
Usted(you-formal)	43
ellos(they)	32
Ustedes(you-formal plural)	19

Table 2. The number of frequency for the subject types

4.1 Experiment 1

All experiments were performed using 'WEKA' (3.6.10 version). We selected SVM (Support Vector Machine) algorithm. By performing 10-fold cross validation as a test option, the results were obtained.
Using 11 features we proposed, 83.6% for accuracy was reported. For comparison, a simple baseline would be to assume that we randomly choose one subject candidate among three most frequent subject types (él, ella, yo). The accuracy of this method would be about 33.3%. Though it might not be a quite fair comparison, the proposed method could improve the accuracy for about 50% over the baseline.

	baseline	**our method**	**remark**
Accuracy	about 33%	83.6%	about 50% improved

Table 3. The result of experiment 1

Precision, recall and f-measure for each subject type are as follows.

Subject Type	**precision (%)**	**recall (%)**	**f-measure (%)**
tú	0.962	0.943	0.952
yo	0.884	0.971	0.925
él	0.915	0.779	0.842
ella	0.774	0.917	0.839
ellos	0.558	0.906	0.69
Usted	0.2	0.023	0.042
Ustedes	0	0	0

Table 4. precision, recall and f-measure for each subject type

The values of f-measure for the subject types 'tú', 'yo', 'él', 'ella' were higher than the other subject types. We assume that the training instances for 'yo', 'él', 'ella' were relatively enough to be trained by the system (275 for 'yo', 290 for 'él', 276 for 'ella').
On the other hand, the token frequency for the subject type 'tú' was far less than the three subject types above. We assume the reason why the value of F-measure for the subject type 'tú' is the highest as follows. Feature 'f11' has a value which is for imperative sentence and in the corpus about 94.5% of imperative sentence has a subject type 'tú'. If 'f11' is eliminated, the value of F-measure dropped from 0.952% to 0.685%.
The following table shows the ranking of the features selected by using 'InfoGainAttribute Evaluator'.

Ranking	**Feature**
1	f4
2	f2
3	f10
4	f1
5	f6
6	f3
7	f11
8	f5
9	f9
10	f8
11	f7

Table 5. The ranking of 11 features

The feature 'f4' which is about the gender of the antecedent ranked top and then 'f2' which is about the person of the verb ranked second. These features might play an important role to give information about the gender and person of the zero subject.

4.2 Experiment 2

We conducted another experiment to find out the best feature combination for the zero subject resolution. The accuracy is measured by eliminating features from the lowest ranking one by one. Table 6 shows the condition of the experiment and Figure 2 its result.

ID	Condition of the experiment
1	f7 eliminated
2	f7, f8 eliminated
3	f7, f8, f9 eliminated
4	f7, f8, f9, f5 eliminated
5	f7, f8, f9, f5, f11 eliminated
6	f7, f8, f9, f5, f11, f3 eliminated
7	f7, f8, f9, f5, f11, f3, f6 eliminated
8	f7, f8, f9, f5, f11, f3, f6, f1 eliminated
9	f7, f8, f9, f5, f11, f3, f6, f1, f10 eliminated
10	f7, f8, f9, f5, f11, f3, f6, f1, f10, f2 eliminated

Table 6. Condition of experiment 2

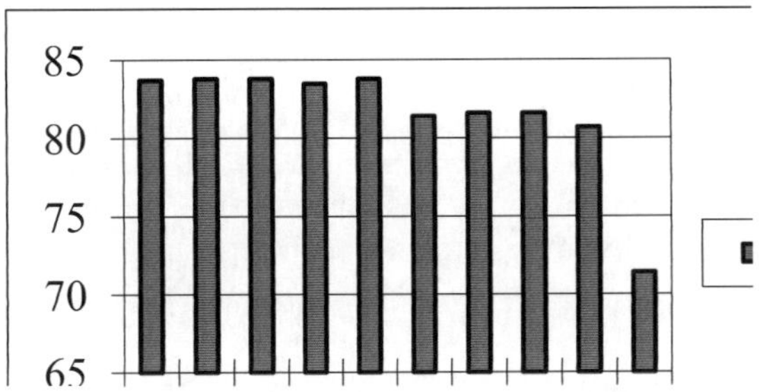

Figure 2. The result of experiment 2

There was very little difference between the accuracy when the 5 low rank features were eliminated and the accuracy when 11 features were used. If the feature 'f3' which is about number of the verb is eliminated, the accuracy decreased about 2%. In other words, the 5 low rank features may be regarded as not significant ones to classify subject types.

5 features that did not have a great influence on classifying subject types are as follows. Feature 'f7' is about presence of a possessive adjective in the same sentence and feature 'f8' is about the presence of a reflexive pronoun in the same sentence. In the corpus, there are 956 and 855 cases where the possessive adjective and the reflexive pronoun don't exist, so because of the occurrence frequency, these features might be of little importance. Feature 'f9' is about presence of antecedent and there are about 41% of sentences which don't have antecedent. Therefore, whether an antecedent exists or not may not be crucial in zero subject resolution. Feature 'f5' is about the semantic class of an antecedent and there are lots of cases where the antecedent doesn't exist as mentioned above, so this feature might also not be significant to classify subject types. 'F11' is the feature about the tense of sentence. Based on the results, the tense of sentence doesn't seem to play a significant role in zero subject resolution.

4.3 Experiment 3

We performed an experiment to identify which features contribute most to the 3 subject types, 'él', 'ella', 'yo', that showed the highest frequency in the corpus. As for the 3 subject types, the f-measure values showed little difference when the 5 lowest rank features were eliminated one by one. So we tried to eliminate the high rank features and compare the f-measure value with the case in which 11 features are used for the zero subject resolution. Table 7 presents the results of the experiment.

	f-measure (%)		
	11 features are used	**f4 eliminated**	**f2 eliminated**
él	0.842	**0.494**	0.85
ella	0.839	**0.443**	0.843
yo	0.925	0.82	**0.691**

Table 7. The result of experiment 3

These results show that as for 3rd person singular subject 'él', 'ella', when the feature 'f4' about gender of antecedent was eliminated, the value of f-measure decreased sharply. Feature 'f4' has a value to distinguish between the 3rd person masculine singular and 3rd person feminine singular subject, so it might affect to classify between the 3rd person singular subject 'él' and 'ella'.

In case of 'yo', f-measure value decreased sharper when 'f2' which is about the person of verb was eliminated than when 'f4' was removed. Feature 'f2' has a value to distinguish between the verbs which have the same verb ending in case of 1st and 3rd person, so it could be a significant feature to classify 'yo' as a right subject type.

5 Conclusion

In this paper, we proposed a hybrid approach to resolve Spanish zero in developing Spanish-to-Korean MT. It combines the linguistic knowledge and ML approach in one model. For the case in which a zero subject couldn't be resolved using verb ending, the ML method was employed. To utilize ML, 11 features were suggested for Spanish zero subject resolution. In order to identify the feasibility for our method, several experiments were conducted. The accuracy was about 83.6% which was about 50% higher than the baseline when 11 features were used for the ML.

We performed other experiments to find out the best feature combination and the specific feature to classify the subject types which showed high frequency in the corpus. As a result, we figured out 5 features which were not significant for the zero subject resolution and 2 features which played an important role to classify high frequency subject types.

Currently we are increasing the size of the training corpus to balance the various subject types. In the future we are planning to validate our model in depth with the new training corpus.

Acknowledgments

This work was supported by the IT R&D program of MSIP/KEIT. [10041807, Development of Original Software Technology for Automatic Speech Translation with Performance 90% for Tour/International Event focused on Multilingual Expansibility and based on Knowledge Learning]

References

Brennan et al. (1987) A centering approach to pronouns. In Proceedings of the 25th Annual Meeting of the ACL (ACL'87), pp. 155-162.

Carbonell, J.G. and R.D. Brown. (1988) Anaphora resolution: a multi-strategy approach, In Proceedings of the 12. International Conference on Computational Linguistics (COLING'88), Vol.I, pp. 96-101.

Dahl, D.A. and C.N. Ball. (1990) Reference resolution in PUNDIT. Research Report CAITSLS-9004. Paoli: Center for Advanced Information Technology, pp. 168-184.

Ferrández, A. and J. Peral. (2000) A computational approach to zero-pronouns in Spanish. In Proceedings of the 38th Annual Meeting of the Association from Computational Linguistics (ACL'00), Hong Kong, October, pp. 166-172.

Han, N. (2004) Korean null pronouns: classification and annotation. In Proceedings of the Workshop on Discourse Annotation. 42nd Annual Meeting of the ACL-04, pp. 33-40.

McEnery et al. (1997) Corpus annotation and reference resolution. In Proceedings of the ACL Workshop on Operational Factors in Practical, Robust Anaphora Resolution for Unrestricted Texts, pp. 67-74.

Mitkov, R. (1994) A new approach for tracking center, In Proceedings of the International Conference "New Methods in Language Processing" (NeMLaP-1), pp. 13-16.

Okumura, M. and K. Tamura. (1996) Zero pronoun resolution in Japanese discourse based on centering theory. In Proceedings of the 16th International Conference on Computational Linguistics (COLING'96), Copenhagen (Denmark), pp. 871-876.

Palomar et al. (2001) An Algorithm for Anaphora Resolution in Spanish Texts, Computational Linguistics, Vol. 27, Num. 4, pp. 545-567.

Rello et al. (2010) A machine learning method for identifying non-referential impersonal sentences and zero pronouns in Spanish. Procesamiento del Lenguaje Natural, 45, pp. 281–287.

Rich, E. and S. LuperFoy. (1988) An architecture for anaphora resolution, In Proceedings of the Second Conference on Applied Natural Language Processing (ANLP-2), pp. 18-24.

Sidner, C. (1986) Focusing in the comprehension of definite anaphora, Readings in Natural Language Processing ed. by B. Grosz, K. Jones & B. Webber. Morgan Kaufmann Publishers, pp. 363-394.

Stys, M.E. and S.S. Zemke. (1995) Incorporating discourse aspects in English – Polish MT: towards robust implementation, In Proceedings of the international conference "Recent Advances in Natural Language Processing" (RANLP'95).

Walker et al.(1994) Japanese Discourse and the Process of Centering, Computational Linguistics, Volume 20, Number 2, pp. 193-232.

Wilks, Y. (1973) Preference semantics. Stanford AI Laboratory memo AIM-206. Stanford University.

Zhao, S. and H.T. Ng. (2007) Identification and resolution of Chinese zero pronouns: a machine learning approach. In Proceedings of the 2007 Joint Conference on EMNLP/CNLL-07, pp. 541-550.

Improving Statistical Machine Translation Accuracy Using Bilingual Lexicon Extraction with Paraphrases

Chenhui Chu[1,3], **Toshiaki Nakazawa**[2], **Sadao Kurohashi**[1]
[1]Graduate School of Informatics, Kyoto University
[2]Japan Science and Technology Agency
[3]Japan Society for the Promotion of Science Research Fellow
chu@nlp.ist.i.kyoto-u.ac.jp, nakazawa@pa.jst.jp, kuro@i.kyoto-u.ac.jp

Abstract

Statistical machine translation (SMT) suffers from the *accuracy problem* that the translation pairs and their feature scores in the translation model can be inaccurate. The *accuracy problem* is caused by the quality of the unsupervised methods used for translation model learning. Previous studies propose estimating comparable features for the translation pairs in the translation model from comparable corpora, to improve the accuracy of the translation model. Comparable feature estimation is based on bilingual lexicon extraction (BLE) technology. However, BLE suffers from the data sparseness problem, which makes the comparable features inaccurate. In this paper, we propose using paraphrases to address this problem. Paraphrases are used to smooth the vectors used in comparable feature estimation with BLE. In this way, we improve the quality of comparable features, which can improve the accuracy of the translation model thus improve SMT performance. Experiments conducted on Chinese-English phrase-based SMT (PBSMT) verify the effectiveness of our proposed method.

1 Introduction

In statistical machine translation (SMT) (Brown et al., 1993), the translation model is automatically learned form parallel corpora in an unsupervised way. The translation model contains translation pairs with their features scores. SMT suffers from the *accuracy problem* that the translation model may be inaccurate, meaning that the translation pairs and their features scores may be inaccurate. The *accuracy problem* is caused by the quality of the unsupervised method used for translation model learning, which always correlates with the amount of parallel corpora. Increasing the amount of parallel corpora is a possible way to improve the accuracy, however parallel corpora remain a scarce resource for most language pairs and domains.[1] Accuracy also can be improved by filtering out the noisy translation pairs from the translation model, however meanwhile we may lose some good translation pairs, thus the coverage of the translation model may decrease. A good solution to improve the accuracy while keeping the coverage is estimating new features for the translation pairs from comparable corpora (which we call comparable features), to make the translation model more discriminative thus more accurate.

Previous studies use bilingual lexicon extraction (BLE) technology to estimate comparable features (Klementiev et al., 2012; Irvine and Callison-Burch, 2013a). They extend traditional BLE that estimates similarity for bilingual word pairs on comparable corpora, to translation pairs in the translation model of SMT. The similarity scores of the translation pairs are used as comparable features. These comparable features are combined with the original features used in SMT, which can provide additional information to distinguish good and bad translation pairs. A major problem of previous studies is that they do not deal with the data sparseness problem that BLE suffers from. BLE uses vector representations for word

[1] Scarceness of parallel corpora also leads to the low coverage of the translation model (which we call the *coverage problem* of SMT), however we do not tackle this in this paper.

Copyright 2014 by Chenhui Chu, Toshiaki Nakazawa, and Sadao Kurohashi
28th Pacific Asia Conference on Language, Information and Computation pages 262–271

pairs to compare the similarity between them. Data sparseness makes the vector representations sparse (e.g., the vector of a low frequent word tends to have many zero entries), thus they do not always reliably represent the meanings of words. Therefore, the similarity of word pairs can be inaccurate. Smoothing technology has been proposed to address the data sparseness problem for BLE. Pekar et al. (2006) smooth the vectors of words with their distributional nearest neighbors, however distributional nearest neighbors can have different meanings and thus introduce noise. Andrade et al. (2013) use synonym sets in WordNet to smooth the vectors of words, however WordNet is not available for every language. More importantly, both studies work for words, which are not suitable for comparable feature estimation. The reason is that translation pairs can also be phrases (Koehn et al., 2003) or syntactic rules (Galley et al., 2004) etc., depending on what kind of SMT models we use.

In this paper, we propose using paraphrases to address the data sparseness problem of BLE for comparable feature estimation. A paraphrase is a restatement of the meaning of a word, phrase or syntactic rule etc., therefore it is suitable for the data sparseness problem. We generate paraphrases from the parallel corpus used for translation model learning. Then, we use the paraphrases to smooth the vectors of the translation pairs in the translation model for comparable feature estimation. Smoothing is done by learning vectors that combine the vectors of the original translation pairs with the vectors of their paraphrases. The smoothed vectors can overcome the data sparseness problem, making the vectors more accurately represent the meanings of the translation pairs. In this way, we improve the quality of comparable features, which can improve the accuracy of the translation model thus improve SMT performance.

We conduct experiments on Chinese-English Phrase-based SMT (PBSMT) (Koehn et al., 2003).[2] Experimental results show that our proposed method can improve SMT performance, compared to the previous studies that estimate comparable features without dealing with the data sparseness problem of BLE (Klementiev et al., 2012; Irvine and Callison-Burch, 2013a). The results verify the effectiveness of using BLE together with paraphrases for the *accuracy problem* of SMT.

[2]Our proposed method can also be applied to other language pairs and SMT models.

2 Related Work

2.1 Bilingual Lexicon Extraction (BLE) for SMT

From the pioneering work of (Rapp, 1995), BLE from comparable corpora has been studied for a long time. BLE is based on the distributional hypothesis (Harris, 1954), stating that words with similar meaning have similar distributions across languages. Contextual similarity (Rapp, 1995), topical similarity (Vulić et al., 2011) and temporal similarity (Klementiev and Roth, 2006) can be important clues for BLE. Orthographic similarity may also be used for BLE for some similar language pairs (Koehn and Knight, 2002). Moreover, some studies try to use the combinations of different similarities for BLE (Irvine and Callison-Burch, 2013b; Chu et al., 2014). To address the data sparseness problem of BLE, smoothing technology has been proposed (Pekar et al., 2006; Andrade et al., 2013).

BLE can be used to address the *accuracy problem* of SMT, which estimates comparable features for the translation pairs in the translation model (Klementiev et al., 2012). BLE also can be used to address the *coverage problem* of SMT, which mines translations for the unknown words or phrases in the translation model from comparable corpora (Daume III and Jagarlamudi, 2011; Irvine et al., 2013). Moreover, studies have been conducted to address the *accuracy and coverage problems* of SMT simultaneously with BLE (Irvine and Callison-Burch, 2013a).

Our study focuses on addressing the *accuracy problem* of SMT with BLE. We use paraphrases to address the data sparseness problem of BLE for comparable feature estimation, which makes the comparable features more accurate.

2.2 Paraphrases for SMT

Many methods have been proposed to use paraphrases for SMT, mainly for the *coverage problem*. One method is paraphrasing unknown words or phrases in the translation model (Callison-Burch et al., 2006; Razmara et al., 2013; Marton et al., 2009).

f	e	$\phi(f\|e)$	$lex(f\|e)$	$\phi(e\|f)$	$lex(e\|f)$	Alignment
失业 人数	**unemployment figures**	0.3	0.0037	0.0769	0.0018	0-0 1-1
失业 人数	**number of unemployed**	0.1333	0.0188	0.1025	0.0041	1-0 1-1 0-2
失业 人数	. unemployment was	0.3333	0.0015	0.0256	6.8e-06	0-1 1-1 1-2
失业 人数	unemployment and bringing	1	0.0029	0.0256	5.4e-07	0-0 1-0

Table 1: An example of the *accuracy problem* in PBSMT. The correct translations of "失业 (unemployment) 人数 (number of people)" are in bold. The incorrect phrase pairs are extracted because "人数 (number of people)" is incorrectly aligned to "unemployment", and their feature scores are incorrect.

Another method is constructing a paraphrase lattice for the tuning and testing data, and performing lattice decoding (Du et al., 2010; Bar and Dershowitz, 2014). Paraphrases also can be incorporated as additional training data, which may improve both coverage and accuracy of SMT (Pal et al., 2014).

Previous studies require external data in addition to the parallel corpus used for SMT for paraphrase generation to make their methods effective. These paraphrases can be generated from external parallel corpora (Callison-Burch et al., 2006; Du et al., 2010), or monolingual corpora based on distributional similarity (Marton et al., 2009; Razmara et al., 2013; Pal et al., 2014; Bar and Dershowitz, 2014).

Our study differs from previous studies in using paraphrases for smoothing the vectors of BLE, which is used for comparable feature estimation that can improve the accuracy of SMT. Another difference is that our proposed method is effective when only using the paraphrases generated from the parallel corpus used for SMT, while previous studies require external data for paraphrase generation.

3 Accuracy Problem of Phrase-based SMT (PBSMT)

In this paper, we conduct experiments on PBSMT (Koehn et al., 2003). Here, we give a brief overview of PBSMT, and explain the *accuracy problem* of PBSMT.

In PBSMT, the translation model is represented as a phrase table, containing phrase pairs together with their feature scores.[3] The phrase pairs are extracted based on unsupervised word alignments, whose quality always correlates with the amount of the parallel corpus. Inverse and direct phrase translation probabilities $\phi(f|e)$ and $\phi(e|f)$, inverse and direct lexical weighting $lex(f|e)$ and $lex(e|f)$ are used as features for the phrase table. Phrase translation probabilities are calculated via maximum likelihood estimation, which counts how often a source phrase f is aligned to target phrase e in the parallel corpus, and vise versa. Lexical weighting is the average word translation probability calculated using internal word alignments of a phrase pair, which is used to smooth the overestimation of the phrase translation probabilities. Other typical features such as the reordering model features and the n-gram language model features are also used in PBSMT. These features are combined in a log linear model, and their weights are tuned using a small size of parallel sentences. During decoding, these features together with their tuned weights are used to produce new translations.

One problem of PBSMT is that the phrase pairs and their feature scores in the phrase table may be inaccurate. One reason for this is the quality of the word alignment. Another reason is that the translation probabilities of rare word and phrase pairs tend to be grossly overestimated. Sparseness of the parallel corpus leads to word alignment errors and overestimations, which result in inaccurate phrase pairs and feature scores. Table 1 shows an example of phrase pairs and feature scores taken from the phrase table constructed in our experiments (See Section 5 for the details of the experiments), which contains inaccurate phrase pairs.

4 Proposed Method

Figure 1 shows an overview of our proposed method. We construct a phrase table from a parallel corpus following (Koehn et al., 2003). Because this phrase table may be inaccurate, we estimate comparable features from comparable corpora following (Klementiev et al., 2012; Irvine and Callison-Burch, 2013a). These comparable features are appended to the original phrase table, to address the *accuracy*

[3] Note that in PBSMT, the definition of a phrase also includes a single word.

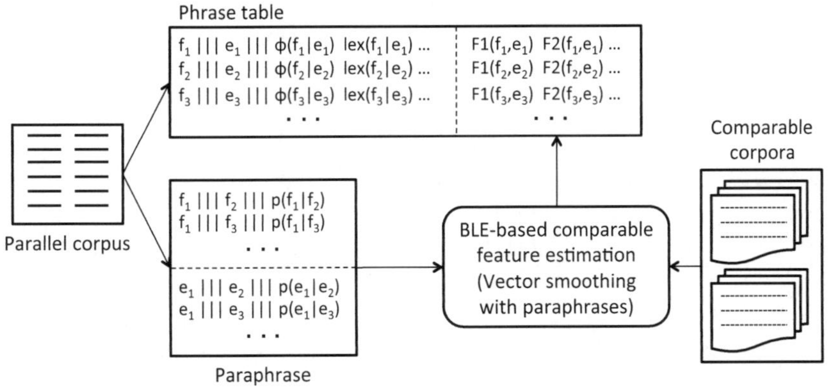

Figure 1: Overview of our proposed method.

problem of PBSMT. Comparable feature estimation is based on BLE, which suffers from the data sparseness problem. We propose using paraphrases to address this problem. We generate phrasal level paraphrases for both the source and target language from the parallel corpus. Then we use the paraphrases to smooth the vectors of the source and target phrases used for comparable feature estimation respectively. Smoothing is done by learning a vector that combines the original vector of a phrase with the vectors of its paraphrases. The smoothed vectors can represent the meanings of phrase pairs more accurately. Finally, we compute the similarity of phrase pairs based on the smoothed source and target vectors. In this way, we improve the quality of comparable features, which can improve the accuracy of the phrase table thus improve SMT performance.

Details of paraphrase generation, comparable feature estimation and vector smoothing with paraphrases will be described in Section 4.1, 4.2 and 4.3 respectively.

4.1 Paraphrase Generation

In this paper, we generate both source and target phrasal level paraphrases from the parallel corpus used for SMT[4] through bilingual pivoting (Bannard and Callison-Burch, 2005). The idea of this method is that if two source phrases f_1 and f_2 are translated to the same target phrase e, we can assume that f_1 and f_2 are a paraphrase pair. Probability of this paraphrase pair can be assigned by marginalizing over all shared target translations e in the parallel corpus, defined as follows:

$$p(f_1|f_2) = \sum_e \phi(f_1|e)\phi(e|f_2) \qquad (1)$$

where, $\phi(f_1|e)$ and $\phi(e|f_2)$ are phrase translation probability. Target paraphrases can be generated in a similar way.

Note that word alignment errors can also lead to incorrect paraphrase generation. For example, "unemployment figures" and "unemployment and bringing" in Table 1 might be generated as a paraphrase pair. However, this kind of noisy pairs can be easily pruned according to their low probabilities.

4.2 Comparable Feature Estimation

Following (Klementiev et al., 2012; Irvine and Callison-Burch, 2013a), we estimate contextual, topical and temporal similarities as comparable features. However, we do not use orthographic similarity as comparable feature, because we experiment on Chinese-English, which is not an orthographically similar language pair.

Besides phrasal features, we also estimate lexical features following (Klementiev et al., 2012; Irvine and Callison-Burch, 2013a). The lexical features are the average similarity scores of word pairs over all possible word alignments across two phrases. They are used to smooth the phrasal features, like the lexical weighting in PBSMT. However, they only can slightly alleviate the sparseness of phrasal features, because individual words also suffer from the data sparseness problem.

In the following sections, we describe the meth-

[4]Paraphrases also can be generated from external parallel corpora and monolingual corpora, however we leave it as future work.

ods to estimate contextual, topical and temporal features in detail.

Contextual feature

Contextual feature is the contextual similarity of a phrase pair. Contextual similarity is based on the distributional hypothesis on context, stating that phrases with similar meaning appear in similar contexts across languages. From the pioneering work of (Rapp, 1995), contextual similarity has been used for BLE for a long time.

In the literature, different definitions of context have been proposed for BLE, such as window-based context, sentence-based context and syntax-based context etc. In this paper, we use window-based context, and leave the comparison of using different definitions of context as future work. Given a phrase, we count all its immediate context words, with a window size of 4 (2 preceding words and 2 following words). We build a context by collecting the counts in a bag of words fashion, namely we do not distinguish the positions that the context words appear in. The number of dimensions of the constructed vector is equal to the vocabulary size. We further reweight each component in the vector by multiplying by the *IDF* score following (Garera et al., 2009; Chu et al., 2014), which is defined as follows:

$$IDF(t, D) = log\frac{|D|}{1 + |\{d \in D : t \in d\}|} \quad (2)$$

where $|D|$ is the total number of documents in the corpus, and $|\{d \in D : t \in d\}|$ denotes number of documents where the term t appears.[5] We model the source and target vectors using the method described above, and project the source vector onto the vector space of the target language using a seed dictionary. The contextual similarity of the phrase pair is the similarity of the vectors, which is computed using cosine similarity defined as follows:

$$Cos(f, e) = \frac{\sum_{k=1}^{K} F_k \times E_k}{\sqrt{\sum_{k=1}^{K}(F_k)^2} \times \sqrt{\sum_{k=1}^{K}(E_k)^2}} \quad (3)$$

where f and e are the source and target phrases, F and E are the projected source vector and target vector, K is the number of dimensions of the vectors.

Topical feature

Topical feature is the topical similarity of a phrase pair. Topical similarity uses the distributional hypothesis on topics, stating that two phrases are potential translation candidates if they are often present in the same cross-lingual topics and not observed in other cross-lingual topics (Vulić et al., 2011). Vulić et al. (2011) propose using bilingual topic model based method to estimate topical similarity. However, this method is not scalable for large data sets.

In this paper, we estimate topical feature in a scalable way following (Klementiev et al., 2012). We treat an article pair aligned by interlanguage links in Wikipedia as a topic aligned pair. For a phrase pair, we build source and target topical occurrence vectors by counting their occurrences in its corresponding language articles. The number of dimensions of the constructed vector is equal to the number of aligned article pairs, and each dimension is the number of times that the phrase appears in the corresponding article. The similarity of the phrase pair is computed as the similarity of the source and target vectors using cosine similarity (Equation 3).

Temporal feature

Temporal feature is the temporal similarity of a phrase pair. The intuition of temporal similarity is that news stories across languages tend to discuss the same world events on the same day, and the occurrences of a translated phrase pair over time tend to spike on the same dates (Klementiev and Roth, 2006; Klementiev et al., 2012).

We estimate temporal feature following (Klementiev and Roth, 2006; Klementiev et al., 2012). For a phrase pair, we build source and target temporal occurrence vectors by counting their occurrences in equally sized temporal bins, which are sorted from the set of time-stamped documents in the comparable corpus. We set the window size of a bin to 1 day. Therefore the number of dimensions of the constructed vector is equal to the number of days spanned by the corpus, and each dimension is the number of times that the phrase appears in the corresponding bin. The similarity of the phrase pair is computed as the similarity of the source and target vectors using cosine similarity (Equation 3).

4.3 Vector Smoothing with Paraphrases

Data sparseness results in sparse representations of the vectors, therefore the similarity of the phrase pair can be inaccurate. We propose using paraphrases to

[5] Since there are no document bounds in the corpus we used to estimate contextual feature, we treated every 100 sentences as one document.

Phrase	Paraphrase
tampered	being tampered
an appropriation	appropriation
11th	11th .
so many years	many years
first thing	first thing that
mass media ,	media ,

Table 2: Examples of overlaps between a phrase and its paraphrase.

smooth both the source and target vectors, to deal with the data sparseness problem. After smoothing, the vectors can more accurately represent the phrases. We compute the similarity of the phrase pair based on the smoothed source and target vectors, and use it as comparable features for PBSMT.

One problem of using paraphrases for smoothing is that a phrase and its paraphrase may overlap. Table 2 shows some examples of overlaps between a phrase and its paraphrase generated from the parallel corpus we use. The vector of the overlapped paraphrase contains overlapped information of the vector of the original phrase. Therefore, it is necessary to consider overlap when using paraphrases for vector smoothing.

There are three types of vectors (context, topical and temporal occurrence vectors) need to be smoothed. The method for smoothing context vector is different from topical and temporal occurrence vectors, because the components in context vector are different. Topical and temporal occurrence vectors can be smoothed using the same method, because the components of both vectors are occurrence information. The following sections describe the methods to smooth the context vector, and topical and temporal occurrence vectors respectively.

Context Vector Smoothing

We smooth the context vector of a phrase x with the following equation:

$$X' = \frac{f(x)}{f(x)+\sum_{j=1}^{n} f(x_j)} \cdot X + \sum_{i=1}^{n} \frac{f(x_i)}{f(x)+\sum_{j=1}^{n} f(x_j)} \cdot p(x_i|x) \cdot \begin{cases} X_i \backslash X & (x \subset x_i) \\ X_i - X & (x \supset x_i) \\ X_i & (otherwise) \end{cases} \quad (4)$$

where X' is the smoothed context vector, X is the context vector of x, n is the number of paraphrases that x has, X_i is the context vector of paraphrase x_i, $p(x_i|x)$ is the probability that x_i is a paraphrase of x. $f(x)$ is the frequency of x in the corpus, and $\frac{f(x)}{f(x)+\sum_{j=1}^{n} f(x_j)}$ is the frequency weight for x. Frequency weight is also used for the paraphrases in a similar way. The frequency weight is proposed by Andrade et al. (2013) when using synonyms to smooth the context vector of a word. They show that using the frequency information of words as weights performs better than simple summation of the vectors. For the overlap problem between x and x_i, we do the following:

- If $x \subset x_i$ namely x is contained in x_i, we use the context words that exist in X_i but do not exist in X for smoothing, which is $X_i \backslash X$;
- If $x \supset x_i$ namely x contains x_i, we remove the overlapped contextual information between X_i and X for smoothing, which is $X_i - X$;
- Otherwise, we use X_i for smoothing.

Topical and Temporal Occurrence Vectors Smoothing

We smooth the topical and temporal occurrence vectors of a phrase x with the following equation:

$$X' = X + \sum_{i=1}^{n} p(x_i|x) \cdot \begin{cases} 0 & (x \subset x_i) \\ X_i - X & (x \supset x_i) \\ X_i & (otherwise) \end{cases} \quad (5)$$

where X' is the smoothed occurrence vector, X is the occurrence vector of x, n is the number of paraphrases that x has, X_i is the occurrence vector of paraphrase x_i, $p(x_i|x)$ is the probability that x_i is a paraphrase of x. For the overlap problem between x and x_i, we do the following:

- If $x \subset x_i$, we do not use X_i for smoothing, because X already contains the occurrence information in X_i;
- If $x \supset x_i$, we remove the overlapped occurrence information between X_i and X for smoothing, which is $X_i - X$;
- Otherwise, we use X_i for smoothing.

Examples of the three types of vectors before and after smoothing are shown in Table 3.

	Before smoothing	After smoothing
Context	<rising: 2.37, economic: 0, recession: 3.94 ⋯ >	<rising: 0.03, economic: 0.06, recession: 0.04 ⋯ >
Topical	<Topic1: 0, Topic2: 1, Topic3: 0 ⋯ >	<Topic1: 0.12, Topic2: 1.27, Topic3: 0.05 ⋯ >
Temporal	<Date1: 1, Date2: 0, Date3: 6 ⋯ >	<Date1: 1.25, Date2: 0.08, Date3: 6.38 ⋯ >

Table 3: Examples of the three types of vectors for the phrase "unemployment figures" before and after smoothing.

5 Experiments

In our experiments, we compared our proposed method with (Klementiev et al., 2012). We estimated comparable features from comparable corpora using the method of (Klementiev et al., 2012) and our proposed method respectively. We appended the comparable features to the phrase table, and evaluated the two methods in the perspective of SMT performance. We conducted experiments on Chinese-English data. In all our experiments, we preprocessed the data by segmenting Chinese sentences using a segmenter proposed by Chu et al. (2012), and tokenizing English sentences.

5.1 Experimental Settings

SMT Settings

We conducted Chinese-to-English translation experiments. The parallel corpus we used is from Chinese-English NIST open MT.[6] The "NIST" column of Table 4 shows the statistics of this parallel corpus. For decoding, we used the state-of-the-art PBSMT toolkit Moses (Koehn et al., 2007) with default options, except for the phrase length limit (7→3) following (Klementiev et al., 2012). We trained a 5-gram language model on the English side of the parallel corpus using the SRILM toolkit[7] with interpolated Kneser-Ney discounting, and used it for all the experiments. We used NIST open MT 2002 and 2003 data sets for tuning and testing, containing 878 and 919 sentence pairs respectively. Note that both MT 2002 and 2003 data sets contain 4 references for each Chinese sentence. Tuning was performed by minimum error rate training (MERT) (Och, 2003), and it was re-run for every experiment.

Comparable Feature Estimation Settings

Table 4 shows the statistics of the comparable data used for comparable feature estimation. The contextual feature was estimated on the parallel corpus. We treated the two sides of the parallel corpus as independent monolingual corpora, following (Haghighi et al., 2008; Klementiev et al., 2012). Contextual feature estimation requires a seed dictionary. The seed dictionary we used is NIST Chinese-English translation lexicon Version 3.0,[8] containing 82k entries. The temporal feature was estimated on Chinese[9] and English[10] Gigaword version 5.0. We used the afp, cna and xin sections with date range 1994/05-2010/12 of the corpora. The topical feature was estimated on Chinese and English Wikipedia data. We downloaded Chinese[11] (2012/09/21) and English[12] (2012/10/01) Wikipedia database dumps. We used an open-source Python script[13] to extract and clean the text from the dumps. We aligned the articles on the same topic in Chinese-English Wikipedia via the interlanguage links.

	NIST	Gigaword	Wikipedia
# Zh articles	N/A	3.6M	248k
# En articles	N/A	4.3M	248k
# Zh sentences	991k	42.6M	2.8M
# En sentences	991k	56.9M	10.1M
# Zh tokens	26.1M	1.1B	70.5M
# En tokens	27.2M	1.3B	240.5M

Table 4: Statistics of the comparable data used for comparable feature estimation.

We estimated comparable features for the unique phrase pairs used for tuning and testing. These phrase pairs were extracted from the entire phrase table constructed from the parallel corpus, by checking all the source phrases in the tuning and testing data sets. We call these phrase pairs the filtered phrase table. Table 5 shows the statistics of the fil-

[6] LDC2007T02, LDC2002T01, LDC2003T17, LDC2004T07, HK News part of LDC2004T08, LDC2005T10 and LDC2006T04

[7] http://www.speech.sri.com/projects/srilm

[8] LDC2002L27

[9] LDC2011T13

[10] LDC2011T07

[11] http://dumps.wikimedia.org/zhwiki

[12] http://dumps.wikimedia.org/enwiki

[13] http://code.google.com/p/recommend-2011/source/browse/Ass4/WikiExtractor.py

# Phrase pairs	4,886,067
# Zh phrases	45,905
# En phrases	2,078,230
# Zh unigrams	6,719
Avg # translations	509.1
# Zh bigrams	23,029
Avg # translations	56.7
# Zh trigrams	16,157
Avg # translations	9.8

Table 5: Statistics of the filtered phrase table.

	Zh	En
# Phrases&words	46,112	2,090,345
# Phrases&words w/ paraphrases	26,718	455,099
# Unigrams w/ paraphrases	6,273	46,191
# paraphrases	39.8	21.6
# Bigrams w/ paraphrases	15,026	223,299
Avg # paraphrases	34.6	17.7
# Trigrams w/ paraphrases	5,419	185,609
# paraphrases	20.0	14.9

Table 6: Statistics the generated paraphrases for the phrases and individual words inside the phrases in the filtered phrase table.

tered phrase table. We can see that each Chinese phrase has a large number of translations on average especially for the lower order n-gram phrases, which can indicate the inaccuracy of the filtered phrase table.

Our proposed method requires paraphrases for vector smoothing. We used Joshua (Ganitkevitch et al., 2012) to generate both Chinese and English paraphrases from the parallel corpus. We kept the paraphrase pairs that satisfy $logp(x_1|x_2) > -7$ and $logp(x_2|x_1) > -7$ [14] for smoothing, where $p(x_1|x_2)$ is the probability that x_1 is a paraphrase of x_2, and $p(x_2|x_1)$ is the probability that x_2 is a paraphrase of x_1. Table 6 shows the statistics of the paraphrase generation results for the Chinese and English phrases, and individual words inside the phrases in the filtered phrase table.

Note that, for some phrase pairs, their comparable feature scores may be 0, because of data sparseness. In that case, we set their comparable features to a small positive number of $1e-07$.

[14] We also tried other pruning thresholds, and this threshold showed the best performance in the preliminary experiments.

System	+Contextual	+Topical	+Temporal	+All
Baseline	45.45			
Klementiev+	43.69	45.72	45.05	45.92
Proposed	$45.56^{\ddagger}$	$46.10^{\dagger\ddagger}$	$46.00^{\dagger\ddagger}$	**46.26**†

Table 7: BLEU-4 scores for Chinese-to-English translation experiments ("†" and "‡" denote that the result is significantly better than "Baseline" at $p < 0.01$ and "Klementiev+" at $p < 0.05$ respectively)

5.2 Results

We report results on the test set using case-insensitive BLEU-4 score and four references. Table 7 shows the results of Chinese-to-English translation experiments. "Baseline" denotes the baseline system that does not use comparable features. "Klementiev+" denotes the system that appends the comparable features estimated following (Klementiev et al., 2012) to the phrase table. "Proposed" denotes the system that uses the comparable features estimated by our proposed method. "+Contextual", "+Topical" and "+Temporal" denote the systems that append contextual, topical and temporal features respectively. "+All" denotes the system that appends all the three types of features. The significance test was performed using the bootstrap resampling method proposed by Koehn (2004).

We can see that "Klementiev+" does not always outperform "Baseline". The reason for this is that the comparable features estimated by (Klementiev et al., 2012) are inaccurate. "Proposed" performs significantly better than both "Baseline" and "Klementiev+". The reason for this is that "Proposed" deals with the data sparseness problem of BLE for comparable feature estimation, making the features more accurate thus improve the SMT performance. As for different comparable features of "Proposed", "+Contextual", "+Topical" and "+Temporal" are all helpful, and combining them can be more effective. The results verify the effectiveness of our proposed method for the *accuracy problem* of PBSMT.

We also investigated the comparable features estimated by the method of (Klementiev et al., 2012) and our proposed method. Based on our investigation, most comparable features estimated by our proposed method are more accurate than the ones estimated by the method of (Klementiev et al., 2012). Here, we give an example of the comparable fea-

f	e	con	con_lex	top	top_lex	tem	tem_lex
失业 人数	**unemployment figures**	1.4e-06	0.0408	1e-07	0.2061	0.1942	0.6832
失业 人数	**number of unemployed**	0.0144	0.0299	1e-07	0.1675	0.0236	0.6277
失业 人数	. unemployment was	0.0107	0.0701	1e-07	0.1908	0.0709	0.6981
失业 人数	unemployment and bringing	1e-07	0.0603	1e-07	0.1730	1e-07	0.6898
失业 人数	**unemployment figures**	0.0749	0.0806	0.5434	0.2629	0.4307	0.7033
失业 人数	**number of unemployed**	0.0522	0.1053	0.1907	0.2235	0.5983	0.7240
失业 人数	. unemployment was	0.0050	0.1206	0.0117	0.2336	0.0967	0.7094
失业 人数	unemployment and bringing	5.1e-05	0.0904	1e-07	0.2034	0.0073	0.7003

Table 8: Examples of comparable feature scores estimated by the method of (Klementiev et al., 2012) (above the bold line) and our proposed method (below the bold line) for the phrase pairs shown in Table 1 ("con", "top" and "tem" denote phrasal contextual, topical and temporal features respectively, "con_lex", "top_lex" and "tem_lex" denote lexical contextual, topical and temporal features respectively).

ture scores estimated for the phrase pairs shown in Table 1. Table 8 shows the comparable feature scores estimated by the method of (Klementiev et al., 2012) (above the bold line) and our proposed method (below the bold line). We can see that the method of (Klementiev et al., 2012) suffers from the data sparseness problem. Many of the feature scores are $1e-07$, and many of the feature scores for the correct translations ("unemployment figures" and "number of unemployed") are lower than the incorrect ones (". unemployment was" and "unemployment and bringing"). Our proposed method addresses the data sparseness problem by using paraphrases for vector smoothing. We can see that, after smoothing the feature scores can more accurately distinguish the good translations from the bad ones.

6 Conclusion and Future Work

In this paper, we proposed using BLE together with paraphrases to address the *accuracy problem* of SMT. The translation pairs and their feature scores in the translation model of SMT can be inaccurate, because of the quality of the unsupervised methods used for translation model learning. Estimating comparable features from comparable corpora with BLE has been proposed for the *accuracy problem* of SMT. However, BLE suffers from the data sparseness problem, which makes the comparable features inaccurate. We proposed using paraphrases to address this problem. Paraphrases were used to smooth the vectors used in comparable feature estimation with BLE. Experiments conducted on Chinese-English PBSMT verified the effectiveness of our proposed method.

As future work, firstly we plan to generate paraphrases from external parallel corpora and monolingual corpora, where as in this paper we used the paraphrases generated from the parallel corpus used for SMT. Secondly, in this paper we estimated contextual features from the parallel corpus, however in the future we plan to estimate it from comparable corpora. Finally, since our proposed method should be language independent and can be applied to other SMT models, we plan to conduct experiments on other language pairs and SMT models to verify this.

Acknowledgement

This work was supported by the Japan Society for the Promotion of Science (JSPS) Grant-in-Aid for JSPS Fellows. We also thank the anonymous reviewers for their valuable comments.

References

Daniel Andrade, Masaki Tsuchida, Takashi Onishi, and Kai Ishikawa. 2013. Translation acquisition using synonym sets. In *Proceedings of NAACL-HLT 2013*, pages 655–660.

Colin Bannard and Chris Callison-Burch. 2005. Paraphrasing with bilingual parallel corpora. In *Proceedings of ACL 2005*, pages 597–604.

Kfir Bar and Nachum Dershowitz. 2014. Inferring paraphrases for a highly inflected language from a monolingual corpus. In *Proceedings of CICLing 2014*, pages 8404:2:245–256.

Peter F. Brown, Stephen A. Della Pietra, Vincent J. Della Pietra, and Robert L. Mercer. 1993. The mathematics of statistical machine translation: Parameter estimation. *Association for Computational Linguistics*, 19(2):263–312.

Chris Callison-Burch, Philipp Koehn, and Miles Osborne. 2006. Improved statistical machine translation using paraphrases. In *Proceedings of NAACL-HLT 2006*, pages 17–24.

Chenhui Chu, Toshiaki Nakazawa, Daisuke Kawahara, and Sadao Kurohashi. 2012. Exploiting shared Chinese characters in Chinese word segmentation optimization for Chinese-Japanese machine translation. In *Proceedings of EAMT 2012*, pages 35–42.

Chenhui Chu, Toshiaki Nakazawa, and Sadao Kurohashi. 2014. Iterative bilingual lexicon extraction from comparable corpora with topical and contextual knowledge. In *Proceedings of CICLing 2014*, pages 8404:2:296–309.

Hal Daume III and Jagadeesh Jagarlamudi. 2011. Domain adaptation for machine translation by mining unseen words. In *Proceedings of ACL-HLT 2011*, pages 407–412.

Jinhua Du, Jie Jiang, and Andy Way. 2010. Facilitating translation using source language paraphrase lattices. In *Proceedings of EMNLP 2010*, pages 420–429.

Michel Galley, Mark Hopkins, Kevin Knight, and Daniel Marcu. 2004. What's in a translation rule? In Daniel Marcu Susan Dumais and Salim Roukos, editors, *Proceedings of NAACL-HLT 2004*, pages 273–280.

Juri Ganitkevitch, Yuan Cao, Jonathan Weese, Matt Post, and Chris Callison-Burch. 2012. Joshua 4.0: Packing, pro, and paraphrases. In *Proceedings of WMT 2012*, pages 283–291.

Nikesh Garera, Chris Callison-Burch, and David Yarowsky. 2009. Improving translation lexicon induction from monolingual corpora via dependency contexts and part-of-speech equivalences. In *Proceedings of CoNLL 2009*, pages 129–137.

Aria Haghighi, Percy Liang, Taylor Berg-Kirkpatrick, and Dan Klein. 2008. Learning bilingual lexicons from monolingual corpora. In *Proceedings of ACL-HLT 2008*, pages 771–779.

Zellig S. Harris. 1954. Distributional structure. *Word*, 10(23):146–162.

Ann Irvine and Chris Callison-Burch. 2013a. Combining bilingual and comparable corpora for low resource machine translation. In *Proceedings of WMT 2013*, pages 262–270.

Ann Irvine and Chris Callison-Burch. 2013b. Supervised bilingual lexicon induction with multiple monolingual signals. In *Proceedings of NAACL-HLT 2013*, pages 518–523.

Ann Irvine, Chris Quirk, and Hal Daumé III. 2013. Monolingual marginal matching for translation model adaptation. In *Proceedings of EMNLP 2013*, pages 1077–1088.

Alexandre Klementiev and Dan Roth. 2006. Weakly supervised named entity transliteration and discovery from multilingual comparable corpora. In *Proceedings of COLING-ACL 2006*, pages 817–824.

Alexandre Klementiev, Ann Irvine, Chris Callison-Burch, and David Yarowsky. 2012. Toward statistical machine translation without parallel corpora. In *Proceedings of EACL 2012*, pages 130–140.

Philipp Koehn and Kevin Knight. 2002. Learning a translation lexicon from monolingual corpora. In *Proceedings of the ACL-02 Workshop on Unsupervised Lexical Acquisition*, pages 9–16.

Philipp Koehn, Franz Josef Och, and Daniel Marcu. 2003. Statistical phrase-based translation. In *Proceedings of NAACL-HLT 2003*, NAACL '03, pages 48–54.

Philipp Koehn, Hieu Hoang, Alexandra Birch, Chris Callison-Burch, Marcello Federico, Nicola Bertoldi, Brooke Cowan, Wade Shen, Christine Moran, Richard Zens, Chris Dyer, Ondrej Bojar, Alexandra Constantin, and Evan Herbst. 2007. Moses: Open source toolkit for statistical machine translation. In *Proceedings of ACL 2007*, pages 177–180.

Philipp Koehn. 2004. Statistical significance tests for machine translation evaluation. In Dekang Lin and Dekai Wu, editors, *Proceedings of EMNLP 2004*, pages 388–395.

Yuval Marton, Chris Callison-Burch, and Philip Resnik. 2009. Improved statistical machine translation using monolingually-derived paraphrases. In *Proceedings of EMNLP 2009*, pages 381–390.

Franz Josef Och. 2003. Minimum error rate training in statistical machine translation. In *Proceedings of ACL 2003*, pages 160–167.

Santanu Pal, Pintu Lohar, and Sudip Kumar Naskar. 2014. Role of paraphrases in pb-smt. In *Proceedings of CICLing 2014*, pages 8404:2:245–256.

Viktor Pekar, Ruslan Mitkov, Dimitar Blagoev, and Andrea Mulloni. 2006. Finding translations for low-frequency words in comparable corpora. *Machine Translation*, 20(4):247–266.

Reinhard Rapp. 1995. Identifying word translations in non-parallel texts. In *Proceedings of ACL 1995*, pages 320–322.

Majid Razmara, Maryam Siahbani, Reza Haffari, and Anoop Sarkar. 2013. Graph propagation for paraphrasing out-of-vocabulary words in statistical machine translation. In *Proceedings of ACL 2013*, pages 1105–1115.

Ivan Vulić, Wim De Smet, and Marie-Francine Moens. 2011. Identifying word translations from comparable corpora using latent topic models. In *Proceedings of ACL-HLT 2011*, pages 479–484.

Incrementally Updating the SMT Reordering Model

Shachar Mirkin
Xerox Research Centre Europe
6 Chemin de Maupertuis, Meylan, France
shachar.mirkin@xrce.xerox.com

Abstract

This work is concerned with incrementally training statistical machine translation (SMT) models when new data becomes available. That, in contrast to re-training new models based on the entire accumulated data. Incremental training provides a way to perform faster, more frequent model updates, enabling keeping the SMT system up-to-date with the most recent data. Specifically, we address incrementally updating the *reordering model* (RM), a component in phrase-based machine translation that models phrase order changes between the source and the target languages, and for which incremental training has not been proposed so far. First, we show that updating the reordering model is helpful for improving translation quality. Second, we present an algorithm for updating the reordering model within the popular Moses SMT system. Our method produces the exact same model as when training the model from scratch, but doing so much faster.

1 Introduction

Parallel data for training statistical machine translation (SMT) models is being constantly generated, both by professional and by casual translators. Typically, large amounts of data are required to produce decent SMT models, yet training a model is an expensive process in terms of time and computational resources. Most often, and in particular when community effort is made to translate new content, it is desirable to keep the system up-to-date with the new data; yet, constant retraining is not feasible. The line of research concerning *incremental training* for SMT has been addressing this problem, aiming at updating the model given new parallel data, rather than retraining it.

Typical phrase-based SMT models use a log-linear combination of various features that mostly represent three sub-models: a *translation model* (TM), responsible for the selection of a target phrase for each source phrase, a *language model* (LM), addressing target language fluency, and a *reordering model* (RM). The reordering model is required since different languages exercise different syntactic ordering. For instance, adjectives in English precede the noun, while they typically follow the noun in French (*the blue sky* vs. *le ciel bleu*); in Modern Standard Arabic the verb precedes the subject, and in Japanese the verb comes last. As a result, source language phrases cannot be translated and placed in the same order in the generated translation in the target language, but phrase movements have to be considered. This is the role of the reordering model. Estimating the exact distance of movement for each phrase is too sparse; therefore, instead, the *lexicalized reordering model* (Koehn, 2009) estimates phrase movements using only a few reordering types, such as a *monotonous* order, where the order is preserved, or a *swap*, when the order of two consecutive source phrases is inverted when their translations are placed in the target side.

Most research on incremental training for SMT addresses parallel corpus alignment, the slowest step of the model training and a prerequisite of many of the following steps, including the reordering model generation. Currently, keeping the reordering model

Copyright 2014 by Shachar Mirkin
28th Pacific Asia Conference on Language, Information and Computation pages 272–281

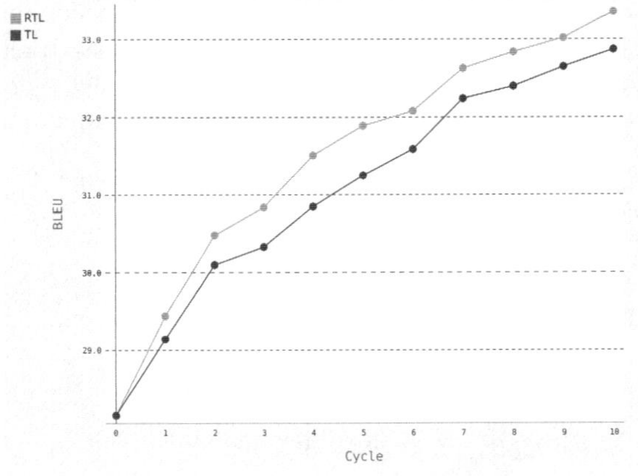

Figure 1: BLEU scores of an SMT system trained with additional data, over 10 cycles, with and without updating the reordering model. *R*, *T* and *L* denote the models that have been updated – Reordering, Translation and Language models. The exact setting of this experiment, as well as additional details, are provided in Section 6.

up-to-date requires retraining. Yet, refraining from updating this model is expected to yield inferior translation performance. An example is shown in Figure 1, comparing results with and without an updated reordering model. While not as important a component as the TM or the LM (see further results in Section 6), updating the RM does improve translation. We therefore seek to allow quick incremental updates of the RM within Moses (Koehn et al., 2007). In this paper we outline several practical options to carry out this update, and describe an implementation of one of them. In a set of experiments we show both that RM updates help improving results and that is can be carried out much quicker than reconstructing the model from scratch.

Next, we describe related work on SMT model updates (Section 2), and provide the details of the Moses reordering model and its relevant data structures (Section 3); we outline and analyze several options to perform RM updates in Section 4, and propose an method in Section 5. Section 6 includes evaluation in terms of translation performance and run-time, and Section 7 summarizes this work and suggests future research directions.

2 SMT model updates

Statistical machine translation systems rely on the availability of large parallel corpora, in particular of the target domain. Such corpora are not always available at the initial stage of the SMT model training, but are sometimes obtained during the lifetime of the system. More parallel data, especially in-domain, may become available, for instance, as users of the system *post-edit* the automatic translations. The source texts and their corrected translations then become new parallel corpora with which the system can be updated. It is then desirable to incorporate the new data into the SMT model as soon as possible. This is particularly a concern for Computer Assisted Translation (CAT) systems, where one wishes to reflect the corrections immediately to avoid repeating translation errors that have already been corrected. The straightforward way to incorporate new data into an SMT model is to retrain the model, i.e. to use all the data accumulated until that point and create the model all over again. However, such retraining may be a lengthy and computationally expensive process, leading to long lags between system updates.

Incremental training provides a principled way to incorporate new data into an existing model without retraining it. For SMT, incremental training research mainly focuses on updating the alignment probabilities from the parallel data. Rightfully so – alignment is the most time-consuming step in SMT model training, which is needed for generating both the translation and the reordering models. Once the alignment model has been updated, and the new data aligned, it is possible to create new data-structures for all sub-models which take into account the entire parallel data. Overall, model update with incremental training is typically a much faster process.

GIZA++[1] (Och and Ney, 2003) is probably the best known alignment tool, and is also the tool used in the Moses translation system. Yet, even with its multi-threaded version, MGIZA++ (Gao and Vogel, 2008), alignment remains the longest step in the SMT model generation. GIZA, like other alignment tools, is using the Expectation Maximization (EM) algorithm (Cappé and Moulines, 2009) to simultaneously learn alignment and translation probabili-

[1] `https://code.google.com/p/giza-pp/`

ties (Brown et al., 1993). Yet, EM relies on having all the data available in advance. When incremental updates to the model are required, *online EM* comes into play. Here, the model parameters may be updated every time a new data point – a sentence-pair, in our case – is introduced. This makes it feasible to perform more frequent updates, thus maintaining the model up-to-date with recent data. Several variants of online EM have been proposed (Liang and Klein, 2009), among which is *stepwise EM* used in (Levenberg et al., 2010; Levenberg, 2011) for updating the parameters of the translation and alignment models. Using IBM Model 1 (Brown et al., 1993) with HMM alignments (Vogel et al., 1996), they collect counts for translations and alignments and update them by interpolating the statistics of the old and the new data. Rather than updating the model for each data point, they do so for a set of bi-sentences, referred to as *mini-batch*. In this work we are using Incremental GIZA++,[2] an implementation of this work, updating the model multiple times with mini-batches of additional parallel data.

Force alignment (Gao et al., 2010) is a technique for aligning new data using an existing model. This enables adding the source and its translation as additional training material. It does not, however, make any updates to the model.[3]

An alternative practical approach to incrementally updating alignments, referred to as *quick updates*, was proposed in (Mirkin and Cancedda, 2013). Instead of updating the existing translation and language models, separate models are generated from smaller amounts of data (e.g. solely the new data) and combined with the previous models through a log-linear combination. This approach allows even faster updates, and in some settings yields comparable results to retraining the model.

Yet, in contrast to the translation and language models, currently Moses supports a single reordering model. Hence, while it is possible to quickly create small TMs and LMs, this is not possible for the reordering model. If its update is ignored, biphrases absent from the reordering model receive a default score, resulting with suboptimal results, as demonstrated in Section 1. Incremental updates of the reordering model have not been addressed yet and the only option currently available is to generate the reordering model from start, which might be a lengthy process. In the following sections we describe our suggestion for incremental and quick updates of this model.

3 The Moses reordering model

3.1 Reordering probability estimation

As we mentioned in Section 1, the reordering model estimates the probability of phrase movements between the source and the target. To deal with sparsity, movement is measured in the lexicalized reordering model in terms of *orientation* types, rather than exact move distance. The default orientations used in Moses are listed below, and are referred to as *msd* (Koehn, 2009):

- *mono* (*monotonous*) – the preceding target phrase is aligned to the preceding source phrase.
- *swap*: the preceding target phrase is aligned to the following source phrase.
- *discontinued* (also called *other*): the phrases did not occur consecutively, but other phrases were inserted between them.

Formally, the probability of each of the above orientation types, o, for a source phrase f and a target phrase e is denoted $p(o|f,e)$. Counting the orientation instances of each phrase pair from the word alignments, in each direction, maximum likelihood is used to estimate this probability:

$$\hat{p}(o|f,e) = \frac{count(o,f,e)}{\sum_{o'} count(o',f,e)} = \frac{count(o,f,e)}{count(f,e)} \quad (1)$$

The estimation can be smoothed by additive (Laplace) smoothing with a factor σ:

$$\hat{p}(o|f,e) = \frac{\sigma + count(o,f,e)}{\sum_{o'} \sigma + count(f,e)} \quad (2)$$

[2]https://code.google.com/p/inc-giza-pp/

[3]We have experimentally confronted Incremental GIZA with force alignment and learned that the former method outperforms the latter.

3.2 Data structures

Extracted phrases During the training of a phrase-based Moses model, phrase pairs are extracted from the word-aligned parallel data and used for training both the TM and the RM. Within the phrase extraction step, three files containing the list of phrase pairs are created. Two of them consist of the word alignments within the phrases, one in each direction (source-to-target and target-to-source); the third, the *reordering file*,[4] shows the orientation of each occurrence of the phrase pair, in either direction. Phrase pairs are alphabetically ordered in these files, and repeat if more than one instance of the phrase pair is encountered.

Figure 2 shows a few lines from a reordering file, of an English to French model, built with the *msd* (monotonous-swap-discontinued) orientations (Koehn et al., 2005)[5] Each line in the reordering file contains three parts, separated by '| | |': source phrase, target phrase, and 2 indicators of the orientation in which this instance was found, when extracting the phrases from source-to-target and from target-to-source alignments.

Reordering table The *reordering table* (RT), created from the reordering file, is the data structure representing the reordering model. It contains probability estimations for each orientation of a phrase pair in either direction. In contrast to the reordering file, in the RT, each phrase pair appears only once. Figure 3 displays a few lines from a reordering table. In Section 5 we show how these estimations are computed.

4 Updating the reordering model

In this section we describe several options to generate an updated reordering model given new data. We are specifically concerned with a multi-update scenario, where the model needs to be updated with new data repeatedly rather than only once.

4.1 Reordering model generation

Several steps must be performed before a Moses RM can be trained. The necessary steps on which the model generation depends on are listed below.

1. Corpus preparation: tokenization, lowercasing and any other preprocessing.
2. Corpus alignment in both directions, source-to-target and target-to-source.
3. Bidirectional phrase extraction.
4. Creation of the reordering file.

Note that some steps are necessary for other purposes. For instance, Step 1 is necessary for all subsequent steps, including LM training, and Steps 2 and 3 are also necessary for training the TM. In practice, the creation of the reordering file (Step 4) is done within the phrase extraction step.

From the reordering file, the reordering table is created by counting the number of occurrences of each orientation in each direction and normalizing by the total number of occurrences of the phrase pair, as in Equation 2.

4.2 Update options

We now consider several options for updating the reordering model, listing the tasks that need to be performed and analyze their complexity, where the size of a data structure is measured in terms of the number of lines it contains. We can assume that the data that was already used to train the current model (the older data) is significantly larger than the training data which we use for a single update (the newer data). This would typically be the case, for instance, with training data that is based on human feedback, as described earlier. For simplicity, we always refer below to the old data as $\mathcal{A}$ and to the new data as $\mathcal{B}$ without cycle indexes.[6] As we proceed with subsequent update cycles, $\mathcal{A}$ keeps growing, while the size of $\mathcal{B}$ does not depend on prior cycles.

We denote the set of phrase pairs instances generated from the training data – the phrase pairs in the reordering file – as $\mathcal{P}$, with subscript $\mathcal{A}$, $\mathcal{B}$ or $\mathcal{AB}$, marking whether it refers to the old, new or merged (updated) data, respectively. As mentioned, $\mathcal{B}$ is typically much smaller than $\mathcal{A}$: $|\mathcal{P}_\mathcal{B}| \ll |\mathcal{P}_\mathcal{A}|$, and the merged set is at least as large as the old one. That is, $|\mathcal{P}_{\mathcal{AB}}| \geq |\mathcal{P}_\mathcal{A}|$, and $\mathcal{P}_{\mathcal{AB}}$ is strictly larger than $\mathcal{P}_\mathcal{A}$ if any new phrase pairs are found in the new data relative to the older one.

[4]Not to be confused with the reordering *table*.

[5]More precisely, this is the *msd-bidirectional-fe* model, also referred to as *wbe-msd-bidirectional-fe-allff*.

[6]Denoting the initial "old" training data as $\mathcal{A}_0$ and the first new data as $\mathcal{B}_1$, $\mathcal{A}_i = \mathcal{A}_{i-1} \cup \mathcal{B}_i$, where $i = 1, 2, \ldots$ and '$\cup$' denotes the concatenation of the two training datasets.

```
but of course ||| mais bien sûr ||| mono mono
but of course ||| mais bien sûr ||| mono other
but of course ||| mais bien sûr ||| mono other
...
confusion between the ||| confusion entre le ||| other other
confusion between the ||| confusion parmi les ||| other mono
...
emerging ||| naissante ||| mono mono
emerging ||| naissante ||| other mono
emerging ||| naissante ||| other mono
emerging ||| naissante ||| other other
emerging ||| naissante ||| swap other
emerging ||| naissante ||| swap other
emerging ||| naissante ||| swap other
```

Figure 2: Sample lines from a Moses reordering file with *msd* orientations.

```
but of course ||| mais bien sûr ||| 0.78 0.11 0.11 0.33 0.11 0.56
...
confusion between the ||| confusion entre le ||| 0.20 0.20 0.60 0.20 0.20 0.60
confusion between the ||| confusion parmi les ||| 0.20 0.20 0.60 0.60 0.20 0.20
...
emerging ||| naissante ||| 0.18 0.41 0.41 0.41 0.06 0.53
```

Figure 3: Sample lines from a Moses reordering table generated for the *msd* orientations, with 6 feature scores for each phrase pair. The scores are probability estimations, summing to 1 for each direction. For easier display, we round the scores to 2 places after the decimal point.

In contrast to the reordering file, the reordering table contains only unique phrase pairs. We denote the set of unique phrase pairs in each data structure with the superscript (u). For example, the phrase pairs in the new RT are marked as $\mathcal{P}_{\mathcal{B}}^{(u)}$, where $|\mathcal{P}_{\mathcal{B}}^{(u)}| \leq |\mathcal{P}_{\mathcal{B}}|$. To get an intuition of the involved sizes, a reordering file created from 500,000 lines of the tokenized, lowercased Europarl corpus (Koehn, 2005) contains approximately 57M lines of non-unique phrase pairs, and the reordering table contains 33M pairs (58%); the figures for the complete Europarl corpus (1.96M lines after cleaning) are 219M for the reordering file in comparison to 107M lines for the RT (49%).[7]

The update options are listed hereunder. Using Incremental GIZA, all produce the same RT. With respect to complexity, we assume that the old reordering file and the old RT are available at no cost because they were created at previous training iterations. We also assume that phrase extraction of the new data, from which the reordering file is created, is done in any case since it is also needed for the translation model.

[7]The more data we use, especially of the same domain, the fewer new phrase pairs we expect to see; since the RT, but not the reordering file, contains only unique phrase pairs, the ratio of their sizes is expected to decrease with more data.

I. Constructing a reordering table from scratch. This is the non-incremental option to construct the reordering table. Phrase pairs are extracted from the entire data, sorted and a reordering table is constructed. This is obviously the slowest option, and the only one available to-date in Moses. All following options are incremental.

II. Merging reordering files and creating a merged reordering table. Given the reordering file from the new data, $\mathcal{B}$, we can perform a merge of two reordering files in either one of two ways: concatenate $P_{\mathcal{A}}$ and $P_{\mathcal{B}}$ and sort the concatenation, or – since both files are sorted – read the files line-by-line in parallel and merge them to a single file that is already sorted. This can be done in linear time in the size of the two reordering files, $\Theta(|\mathcal{P}_{\mathcal{A}}| + |\mathcal{P}_{\mathcal{B}}|)$. We then create a single reordering table by an additional pass over the merged reordering file. The merge of reordering files and creation of the reordering table can be collapsed into one step, requiring a single pass, but we cannot avoid creating the merged reordering file, since if we follow this option, this file will be required for the next update cycle.

III. Merging a reordering file with an existing reordering table. For this option we need to keep track of the number of occurrences of each phrase pair, since this information is lost during the creation of the reordering table. We pass through the old RT and the new reordering file at the same time, comparing their entries ($\Theta(|\mathcal{P}_{\mathcal{A}}^{(u)}| + |\mathcal{P}_{\mathcal{B}}|)$). Unique entries in the RT are copied as-is to the merged RT, and new entries are created in it for phrase pairs that appear only in the reordering file, using all the lines of the same phrase pair. Whenever we encounter a phrase pair that exists in both, we update the probability estimations of the pair in the RT, based on the accumulated counts from the two data structures.

IV. Merging two reordering tables. This options requires tracking occurrence counts as well. Here, we first create a new RT from the reordering file of the new data in $\Theta(|\mathcal{P}_{\mathcal{B}}|)$, and then merge the old and the new tables. The merge is linear in the size of the two tables, $\Theta(|\mathcal{P}_{\mathcal{A}}^{(u)}| + |\mathcal{P}_{\mathcal{B}}^{(u)}|)$. Starting with two sorted tables, the merged table we end up with is also sorted. As above, entries of unique phrase pairs are copied as-is to the merged RT, and when we encounter two lines with the same phrase pair, we update the pair's probability estimations base on the sum of its counts in the two tables. If we keep occurrence counts in the reordering tables themselves, once the merged table has been created, there is no further need to keep the reordering file. The merged RT will be sufficient for subsequent update cycles.

The fourth option may be slightly slower than the third one since it requires an additional pass through the new RT. However, any processing of $\mathcal{B}$ is fast in terms of actual runtime, due to its small size in the addressed scenario. We chose to implement the fourth option – merging of two reordering tables – due to its simplicity, and describe it in detail in Section 5.

5 Merging reordering tables

In this section we present a simple algorithm for a reordering model update via the merge of two reordering tables. As mentioned in Section 4, this update option requires keeping track of the number of occurrences of each phrase pair. We first present the format and technical details of this extension of the reordering table, and then provide the details of the suggested merge itself.

5.1 Reordering table with counts

To enable updating the table without generating it from scratch we must keep track of the number of occurrences of each phrase pair. To do it without making changes to Moses code, we add the total count of a phrase pair as an additional value following the feature scores in the reordering table. Figure 4 shows several lines of the reordering table shown earlier, now including counts.

Below is a demonstration of calculating the orientations scores in Figure 4 in the source-to-target direction, using Equation 2. In the equations below, $S(\cdot)$ is a scoring function and $C(\cdot)$ is a count function, using counts from the reordering file; f is *'emerging'* and e is *'naissante'* from Figure 4, which occur totally 7 times, out of which, the *mono* orientation occurs once in this direction, and each of *swap* and *other* occur 3 times. Each score is the result of smoothing the counts with a σ factor of 0.5 to avoid 0 probabilities. While demonstrated on the *msd* model, there is nothing that prevents applying the same approach to a different set of orientations.

$$S(mono|f,e) = \frac{\sigma + C(mono,f,e)}{3\sigma + C(f,e)} = \frac{0.5+1}{1.5+7} = 0.18 \quad (3)$$

and

$$S(swap|f,e) = \frac{\sigma + C(swap,f,e)}{3\sigma + C(f,e)} = \frac{0.5+3}{1.5+7} = 0.41 \quad (4)$$

Hence, recovering from the score the count of a specific orientation (e.g. *mono*) for a given phrase pair:

$$\begin{aligned} C(mono,f,e) &= S(mono|f,e) \times (3\sigma + C(f,e)) - \sigma \\ &= 0.18 \times (1.5+7) - 0.5 = 1 \quad (5) \end{aligned}$$

```
but of course ||| mais bien sûr ||| 0.78 0.11 0.11 0.33 0.11 0.56 3
...
confusion between the ||| confusion entre le ||| 0.20 0.20 0.60 0.20 0.20 0.60 1
confusion between the ||| confusion parmi les ||| 0.20 0.20 0.60 0.60 0.20 0.20 1
...
emerging ||| naissante ||| 0.18 0.41 0.41 0.41 0.06 0.53 7
```

Figure 4: Sample lines from a reordering table with counts.

To support RT with counts, the configuration (*ini*) file is adjusted to include 7 features instead of 6 (the number of features in the *msd* model), and its weight is set to 0. Figure 5 shows the relevant lines from a tuned configuration file, updated to support counts.

5.2 Merging RTs

Algorithm 1 presents the pseudo code of merging two reordering tables with counts, $R_{\mathcal{A}}$ and $R_{\mathcal{B}}$, into a single one, $R_{\mathcal{AB}}$. The procedure is as follows: We read the reordering tables in parallel, one line at a time, and compare the phrase pair in the old table with the one in the new one. The comparison is alphabetical, using a string made of the source phrase, the delimiter and the target phrase. When the two lines refer to different phrase pairs, we write into the merged table, $R_{\mathcal{AB}}$, the one that alphabetically precedes the other, and read the next line from that table. If they refer to the same phrase pair we merge the lines into a single one, which we write into $R_{\mathcal{AB}}$, and advance in both tables. When one table has been read completely, we write the remainder of the other one into $R_{\mathcal{AB}}$.

Merging two lines into a single one (MERGE_LINES in Algorithm 1) consists of the following steps:

1. Convert the feature scores in each line into counts, as in Equation 5.
2. Sum up the counts for each orientation, as well as the total count.
3. Convert the updated counts of the orientations into scores, as in Equations 3 and 4.

As mentioned in Section 4, the complexity of this algorithm is linear in the length of the tables, i.e. $\Theta(|\mathcal{P}_{\mathcal{A}}^{(u)}| + |\mathcal{P}_{\mathcal{B}}^{(u)}|)$. In terms of memory usage, neither table is fully loaded into memory. Instead, at any given time a single line from each table is read.

Algorithm 1 Merging reordering tables with counts

procedure MERGE_R_TABLES($R_{\mathcal{A}}$,$R_{\mathcal{B}}$)
    Read first lines of $R_{\mathcal{A}}$ and $R_{\mathcal{B}}$, $R_{\mathcal{A}}^{(1)}$, $R_{\mathcal{B}}^{(1)}$
    $i := 1; j := 1$
    while $R_{\mathcal{A}}^{(i)} \neq null$ **and** $R_{\mathcal{B}}^{(j)} \neq null$ **do**
        if $R_{\mathcal{A}}^{(i)} < R_{\mathcal{B}}^{(j)}$ **then** // Compare bi-phrases
            $R_{\mathcal{A}}^{(i)} \rightarrow R_{\mathcal{AB}}$
            $i := i + 1$
        else if $R_{\mathcal{A}}^{(i)} > R_{\mathcal{B}}^{(j)}$ **then**
            $R_{\mathcal{B}}^{(j)} \rightarrow R_{\mathcal{AB}}$
            $j := j + 1$
        else // Identical bi-phrases
            MERGE_LINES($R_{\mathcal{A}}^{(i)}, R_{\mathcal{B}}^{(j)}$) $\rightarrow R_{\mathcal{AB}}$
            $i := i + 1; j := j + 1$
        end if
    end while

    // Write the rest of the tables:
    // at least one of them is EOF
    while $R_{\mathcal{A}}^{(i)} \neq null$ **do**
        $R_{\mathcal{A}}^{(i)} \rightarrow R_{\mathcal{AB}}$
        $i := i + 1$
    end while
    while $R_{\mathcal{B}}^{(j)} \neq null$ **do**
        $R_{\mathcal{B}}^{(j)} \rightarrow R_{\mathcal{AB}}$
        $j := j + 1$
    end while
end procedure

```
LexicalReordering name=LexicalReordering0 num-features=7
type=wbe-msd-bidirectional-fe-allff input-factor=0
output-factor=0

LexicalReordering0= 0.0857977 0.0655027 0.0486593 0.115916 -0.0182552 0.0526204 0
```

Figure 5: An example Moses ini file with required changes to support RT counts.

6 Evaluation

In this section we evaluate updating the reordering model from two aspects: (i) translation performance and (ii) run-time. Specifically, we first show that updating this model helps improving translation, as reflected in the BLEU score (Papineni et al., 2002); then we show that the incremental update is faster than the complete one.

6.1 Setting

We used the IWSLT 2013 Evaluation Campaign data, of the English-French MT track.[8] The initial model was trained with 10,000 WIT3 (Cettolo et al., 2012) sentence-pairs; we use 50,000 additional ones to train updated models. The additional data is split into 10 parts of 5,000 bi-sentences, each added to the data used in the prior cycle to generate an updated model. Moses[9] is used as the phrase-based SMT system, with a configuration comprising of a single phrase table and a single LM. 5-gram language models are trained over the target-side of the training data, using SRILM (Stolcke, 2002) with modified Kneser-Ney discounting (Chen and Goodman, 1996). Mean Error Rate Training (MERT) (Och, 2003) is used for tuning the initial model using the development set of the abovementioned campaign, consisting of 887 sentence-pairs, and optimizing towards BLEU. The models are evaluated with BLEU over the campaign's test set of 1,664 bi-sentence. All datasets were tokenized, lowercased and cleaned using the standard Moses tools.

In all our experiments, we use Incremental GIZA that allows updating the alignment and translation models without aligning all the training data at every cycle. With Incremental GIZA, the alignment of the parallel data is identical in both the incremental and the complete RM generation experiments, since even though the alignment probabilities are being updated, only the new data is being aligned, while the older data is left untouched. As a result, we obtain the same phrase pairs from the new data for both RM generation methods. Given that, our algorithm produces the exact same reordering model as its generation from the entire data (up to numerical accuracy).

6.2 Translation performance

First, we demonstrate that updating the reordering table help achieving better translation quality. To that end, we compare all possible combinations of updating the three phrase-based SMT sub-models (reordering, translation and language models, denoted *R*, *T* and *L*, respectively). Figure 6, that includes a detailed view of Figure 1, shows the results of the experiments with each one of these combinations. From the figure we learn that: (i) the reordering model is the least important one of the three. This is consistent with prior work, e.g. (Mirkin and Cancedda, 2013); (ii) updating the reordering model without updating the translation model has practically no impact on results, since new phrase pairs from the new data that are not added to the phrase table cannot be used in the translation. This is reflected in the almost flat line of experiment *R*, and in the very similar results of *RL* in comparison to *L*. The slight improvement in this case may be attributed to more statistics that have been accumulated for the phrase pairs that already existed in the initial data; (iii) when the translation model is updated, adding the reordering model does help, as seen in *RTL* vs. *TL* and *RT* vs. *T*.

6.3 Run-time

We now compare the time necessary to train a reordering model from scratch (complete training) vs. using the suggested incremental update. For this experiment, we used the English-French Europarl corpus, with 1.96 million parallel sentences as $\mathcal{A}$ and 10,000 WIT3 sentence-pairs as $\mathcal{B}$. Other details of the settings did not change.

[8] Downloaded from `https://wit3.fbk.eu/mt.php?release=2013-01`.

[9] We used the version released on 14/3/2014.

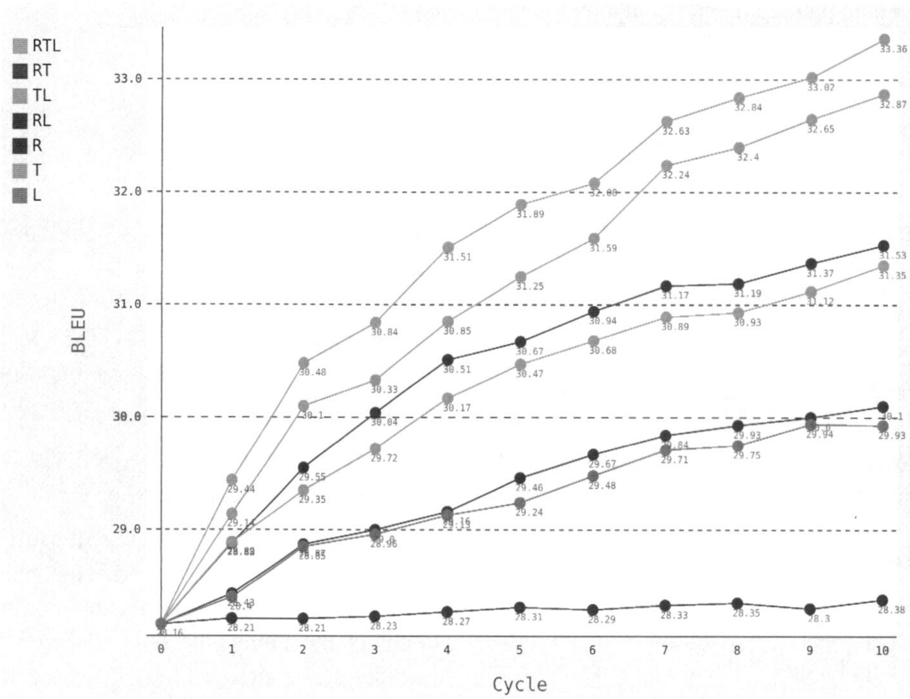

Figure 6: Translation performance (BLEU) when incrementally updating the model with additional data, over 10 update cycles, with different combinations of **R**eordering, **T**ranslation and **L**anguage models.

To objectively measure the run-time of the required steps, regardless of the computer's load at the specific time of experiment, we use the Linux command *time*, summing up the *user* and *sys* times, i.e. the total CPU-time that the process spent in user or in kernel modes. All measurements were conducted on a 64-bit Centos 6.5 Linux server, with 128 GB of RAM and 2 Intel Xeon 6-core 2.50GHz CPUs.

A complete reordering model update, when using Incremental GIZA, consists of of the following two steps:

1. Extracting phrase pairs and creating a reordering file from all the data ($\mathcal{A} \cup \mathcal{B}$)
2. Creating a reordering table from the single reordering file of $\mathcal{A} \cup \mathcal{B}$

In comparison, the incremental update requires the following steps:

1. Extracting phrase pairs and creating a reordering file from the new data ($\mathcal{B}$)
2. Creating a reordering table from the reordering file of $\mathcal{B}$
3. Merging the RTs of $\mathcal{A}$ and $\mathcal{B}$

The time required for generating the complete model in our experiment was 83.6 minutes, in comparison to 17.6 minutes for the incremental one, i.e. 4.75 times faster.

We note that $\mathcal{A}$ represents a corpus of medium size, and often the initial corpus would be much larger.[10] Concerning $\mathcal{B}$, say we plan to perform daily system updates, then a set of 10,000 sentences pairs constitutes a substantial amount of data in terms of what we can expect to obtain in a single day. Hence, the time gain in actual settings may be even larger.

7 Conclusions and future work

This work addressed the incremental update of the reordering model of a phrase-based SMT system. We showed that updating this model is useful for obtaining improved translation, even for a language

[10]For comparison, the rather popular MultiUN corpus (Eisele and Chen, 2010) consists of 13.2M parallel sentence for this language pair (`http://opus.lingfil.uu.se/MultiUN.php`, accessed on 7 August 2014).

pair such as English-French, where phrase movements are not very prominent (in comparison to English-Japanese, for example). We proposed a method for incrementally training this model within the Moses SMT system, which can be done much faster than a complete retrain. It thus supports more frequent SMT model updates to enable quickly benefiting from newly obtained data and user feedback and reflecting it in the system's translation. For future work we wish to investigate using weighted incremental updates of the reordering model, which may enable giving, for instance, more weight to in-domain vs. out-of-domain data or for preferring more recent data. Another extension of this work would be to address updating the binarized version of the reordering table, which enables using the reordering model without loading it into memory.

Acknowledgments

The research leading to these results has received funding from the European Union Seventh Framework Programme (FP7/2007-2013) under grant agreement n° 287755. We thank Philipp Koehn for a valuable discussion at the beginning of this work.

References

Peter F. Brown, Vincent J. Della Pietra, Stephen A. Della Pietra, and Robert L. Mercer. 1993. The mathematics of statistical machine translation: parameter estimation. *Computational Linguistics*, 19(2):263–311, June.

Olivier Cappé and Eric Moulines. 2009. On-line expectation–maximization algorithm for latent data models. *Journal of the Royal Statistical Society: Series B (Statistical Methodology)*, 71(3):593–613.

Mauro Cettolo, Christian Girardi, and Marcello Federico. 2012. WIT^3: Web inventory of transcribed and translated talks. In *Proceedings of EAMT*.

Stanley F. Chen and Joshua Goodman. 1996. An empirical study of smoothing techniques for language modeling. In *Proceedings of ACL*.

Andreas Eisele and Yu Chen. 2010. MultiUN: A multilingual corpus from united nation documents. In *Proceedings of LREC*.

Qin Gao and Stephan Vogel. 2008. Parallel implementations of word alignment tool. In *Proceedings of Software Engineering, Testing, and Quality Assurance for Natural Language Processing*.

Qin Gao, Nguyen Bach, and Stephan Vogel. 2010. A semi-supervised word alignment algorithm with partial manual alignments. In *Proceedings of the Joint Fifth Workshop on Statistical Machine Translation and MetricsMATR*.

Philipp Koehn, Amittai Axelrod, Alexandra Birch, Chris Callison-Burch, Miles Osborne, David Talbot, and Michael White. 2005. Edinburgh system description for the 2005 IWSLT speech translation evaluation. In *Proceedings of IWSLT*.

Philipp Koehn, Hieu Hoang, Alexandra Birch, Chris Callison-Burch, Marcello Federico, Nicola Bertoldi, Brooke Cowan, Wade Shen, Christine Moran, Richard Zens, Chris Dyer, Ondrej Bojar, Alexandra Constantin, and Evan Herbst. 2007. Moses: Open source toolkit for statistical machine translation. In *Proceedings of ACL Demo and Poster Sessions*.

Philipp Koehn. 2005. Europarl: A parallel corpus for statistical machine translation. In *Proceedings of MT Summit*.

Philipp Koehn. 2009. *Statistical machine translation*. Cambridge University Press.

Abby Levenberg, Chris Callison-Burch, and Miles Osborne. 2010. Stream-based translation models for statistical machine translation. In *Proceedings of HLT-NAACL*.

Abby Levenberg. 2011. *Stream-based Statistical Machine Translation*. Ph.D. thesis, University of Edinburgh.

Percy Liang and Dan Klein. 2009. Online EM for unsupervised models. In *Proceedings of NAACL*.

Shachar Mirkin and Nicola Cancedda. 2013. Assessing quick update methods of statistical translation models. In *Proceedings of IWSLT*.

Franz Josef Och and Hermann Ney. 2003. A systematic comparison of various statistical alignment models. *Computational linguistics*, 29(1):19–51.

Franz Josef Och. 2003. Minimum error rate training in statistical machine translation. In *Proceedings of ACL*.

Kishore Papineni, Salim Roukos, Todd Ward, and Wei-Jing Zhu. 2002. BLEU: a method for automatic evaluation of machine translation. In *Proceedings of ACL*.

Andreas Stolcke. 2002. SRILM - an extensible language modeling toolkit. In *Proceedings of Interspeech*.

Stephan Vogel, Hermann Ney, and Christoph Tillmann. 1996. HMM-based word alignment in statistical translation. In *Proceedings of COLING*.

TakeTwo: A Word Aligner based on Self Learning

Jim Chang, Jian-Cheng Wu, Jason S. Chang
Department of Computer Science
National Tsing Hua University
101, Guangfu Road, Hsinchu, Taiwan
{jim.chang.nthu, wujc86, jason.jschang}@gmail.com

Abstract

State of the art statistical machine translation systems are typically trained by symmetrizing word alignments in two translation directions. We introduce a new method that improves word alignment results, based on self learning using the initial symmetrized word alignments results. The method involves aligning words and symmetrizing alignments, generating labeled training data, and construct a classifier for predicting word-translation relation in another alignment round. In the first alignment round, we use the original *grow-diag-final-and* procedure, while in the second round, we use the classifier and a modified GDFA procedure to validate and fill in alignment links. We present a prototype system, *TakeTwo*, which applies the method to improve on GDFA. Preliminary experiments and evaluation on a hand-annotated dataset show that the method significantly increases the precision rate by a wide margin (+16%) with comparable recall rate (-3%).

1 Introduction

The first statistical machine translation (SMT) models are the IBM models, based on statistics collected over a parallel corpus of translated text. These generative IBM models break up the translation process into a number of steps. The most important step is word translation, which is modelled by the lexical translation probability, trained from a parallel corpus, typically with the Expectation Maximization (EM) algorithm (Dempster, Laird, and Rubin 1977).

However, EM word aligners are data-hungry and produce noisy links due to data sparseness. Many researchers (e.g., Gale and Church 1992, Johnson et al., 2007) have pointed out that, even with a large parallel corpus, the EM algorithms running IBM models still produces noisy links for low frequency words and non-literal translations.

Koehn, Och, and Marcu (2003) propose an improved word alignment method based on running IBM models in both translation directions for the two languages involved, and symmetrizing the results using a so-called *grow-diag-final-and* (GDFA) procedure. In a nutshell, GDFA is a heuristic greedy algorithm that starts by accepting reliable links in the intersection of the two alignments. Then, GDFA attempts to add union links neighboring intersection links. Finally, other non-neighboring links are added, subject to 1-1 alignment constraint. This progressively expanding scheme substantially enhances word alignment accuracy. However, the GDFA procedure still leaves much room for improvement, especially for low-frequency translations, non-literal translations, and sentences with extraneous/deleted translations.

Consider the following English sentence with Mandarin Chinese translation in a parallel corpus:

(1) *He made this remark after Heinonen arrived in Tehran.*

他	是	在	海諾寧	抵達	德黑蘭
ta	*shi*	*zai*	*hainuoning*	*dida*	*deheilan*
he	*is*	*when*	*Heinonen*	*arrive*	*Tehran*

後	發表	這	項	談話	。
hou	*fabiao*	*zhe*	*xiang*	*tanhua*	.
after	*deliver*	*this*	*MEASURE*	*talk*	.

See Figures 1(c) for examples of noisy and missing links, produced by *Giza++* with the GDFA sym-

Copyright 2014 by Jim Chang, Jian-Cheng Wu, and Jason S. Chang
28th Pacific Asia Conference on Language, Information and Computation pages 282–291

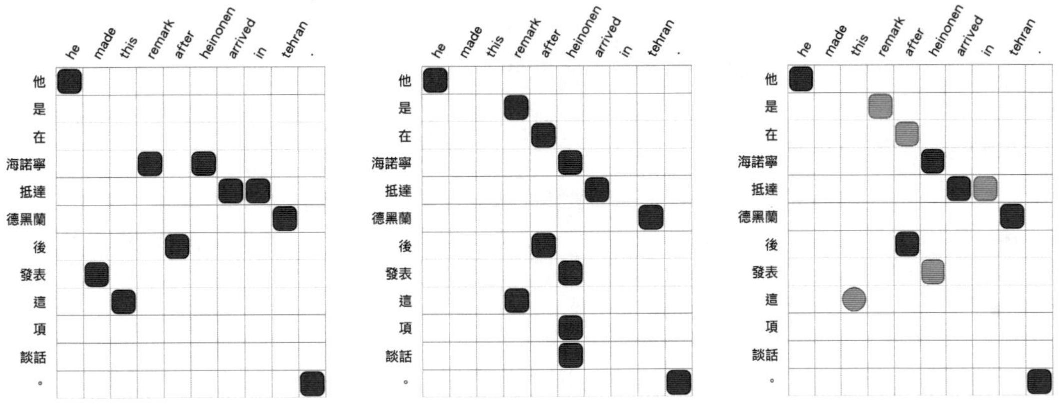

(a) (b) (c)

Figure 1: Three example alignments produced by *Giza++* for Ex. (1): **(a)** Chinese-English alignment. **(b)** English-Chinese alignment. **(c)** The symmetrized alignment of combining (a) and (b) by running the *grow-diag-final-and* procedure. Note that the dark cells (in Figure 1(c)) represent links in the intersection of two alignments, while the gray cells represent links in the rest of the union.

metrizing procedure. For Example (1), a good word alignment should include *hard-to-align* links (e.g., [*made*, 發表 (fabiao)] and [*remark*, 談話 (tanhua)] (in addition to *easy* links (e.g., [*he*, 他 (ta)] and [*arrived*, 抵達 (dita)]), and exclude invalid union links like [*remark*, 是 (shi)] and [*heinonen*, 發表 (fabiao)] (picked up by GDFA, because they are neighbors of intersection links).

In Figure 1(c), a hard-to-align link [*remark*, 談話 (tanhua)] is missed out by GDFA, because [*remark*, 談話] are not common mutual translations (*remark* is commonly translated into 評論, while [談話(tanhua)] is commonly translated to *talk*). For the same reason, the missing link [*made*, 發表 (fabiao)] is also hard to align.

Intuitively, these hard-to-align links could be identified using a classifier for predicting word-translation relation, if we have sufficient training data. Ideally, we should avoid human effort in preparing the training data. Based on the concept of *self training*, we can generate slightly imperfect training data with the most reliable links (e.g, intersection links of the two initial sets of alignments) as positive instances, and very unreliable links as negative instances (e.g., [*hienonen*, 項 (xiang)] and [*hienonen*, 談話 (tanhua)] not picked up by GDFA).

We present a new system, *TakeTwo*, that uses the concept of self training to cope with translation variants and non-literal translations, aimed at improving on GDFA. An example *TakeTwo* alignment for Example (1) is shown in Figure 2. *TakeTwo* has used predicted word-translation probability to exclude invalid links [*remark*, 是] and [heinonen, 談話], and fill in valid links [*made*, 發表] and [*remark*, 談話], leading to an improved alignment.

The rest of the paper is organized as follows. We review the related work in the next section. Then we present our method for *TakeTwo* (Section 3). To evaluate the performance of *TakeTwo*, we compare the quality of alignments produced by *TakeTwo* with those produced by *Giza++* with GDFA (Section 4 and Section 5) over a set of parallel sentences with hand-annotated word alignment.

2 Related Work

Machine translation (MT) has been an area of active research. (Dorr, 1993) summarizes various approaches to MT, while (Lopez, 2007) surveys recent work on statistical machine translation (SMT). We focus on the first part of developing an SMT system, namely, aligning words in a given parallel corpus.

The state of the art in word alignment focuses on automatically learning generative translation models via Expectation Maximization algorithm (Brown et al., 1990; Brown et al., 1993). (Och and Ney, 2003) describe Giza++, an implementation of the

Input: ... He made this remark after Heinonen arrived in Tehran.
他 是 在 海諾寧 抵達 德黑蘭 後 發表 這 項 談話 。 ...

Initial word alignments in two directions (En-Ch and Ch-En):

he(他) made this remark(是) after(在 後) heinonen(海諾寧 發表 項 談話) arrived(抵達) in tehran(德黑蘭)
他(he) 是 在 海諾寧(remark heinonen) 抵達(arrive in) 德黑蘭(tehran) 後(after) 發表(made) 這(this) 項 談話

Crosslingual relatedness:

x-sim(remark, 是) = *sim*(remark, be) = .0, *x-sim*(heinonen, 發表) = *sim*(heinonen, publish) = .0,
x-sim(made, 發表) = *sim*(make, publish) = .32, *x-sim*(remark, 談話) = *sim*(remark, talk) = .25

Output:

he(他) made(發表) this(這) remark(談話)
after(後) heinonen(海諾寧) arrived(抵達) in(抵達)
tehran(德黑蘭) . (。)

Alignment dotplot (see figure on the right)
Note that the dark cells represent links in the intersection of two alignments, while the gray cells represent links in the rest of the union

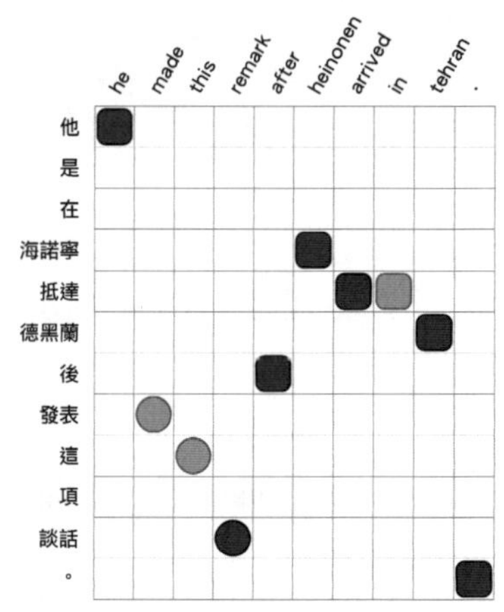

Figure 2: An example *TakeTwo* session and results

IBM models, which has since become the tool of choice for developing SMT systems.

As an alternative to the EM algorithm, researchers have been exploring various knowledge sources for word alignment, using automatically derived lexicons or handcrafted dictionaries (Gale and Church, 1991; Ker and Chang, 1997), or syntactic structure (Gildea, 2003; Cherry and Lin, 2003; Wang and Zong, 2013). There has been work on translating phrases using mixed-code web-pages (e.g., (Nagata et al., 2001; Wu and Chang, 2007)). Similarly, (Lin et al., 2008) propose a method that performs word alignment for parenthetic translation phrases to improve the performance of SMT systems.

Researchers have also studied sublexical models for machine transliteration (Knight and Graehl, 1998). More recently, (Chang et al., 2012) introduce a method for learning a CRF model to find translations and transliterations of technical terms on the Web. We use similar transliteration-based features derived from transliteration model in a different setting.

Word alignment is closely related to measuring word similarity, and especially in the form of crosslingual relatedness. Much work has been done on word similarity and crosslingual relatedness. Early research efforts have been devoted to design the knowledge-based measures, based, in particular, on WordNet (Fellbaum, 1999). Researchers have extensively investigated WordNet and other taxonomic structure in an attempt to calculate the word similarity by counting conceptual distance (Lin, 1998b). On the other hand, there has been much work on distributional word similarity, for example, (Lin,

1998a).

In the area of cross-lingual relatedness, (Michelbacher et al., 2010) present a graph-based method for building a a cross-lingual thesaurus. The method uses two monolingual corpora and a basic dictionary to build two monolingual word graphs, with nodes representing words and edges representing linguistic relations between words.

In the research area of supervised training for word alignment, (Moore, 2005) demonstrates that a discriminative model with the main feature of Log Likelihood Ratio (LLR) could result in a smaller model comparable to more complex generative EM models in alignment accuracy. (Taskar et al., 2005) independently propose a similar approach. (Liu et al., 2005) also propose a log-linear model incorporating features (alignment probability, POS correspondence and bilingual dictionary coverage).

The main difference from our current work is that previous methods use manually labeled data (typically hundreds sentences with thousands of word-translation relations) to train a word alignment model. In contrast, we take a self learning approach and automatically generate labelled training data. More specifically, We train our model based on a much larger training set (hundred of thousand of word-translation instances in partially labeled sentences) based on self learning.

Recently, some researchers have begun using syntax in word alignment, by incorporating features such as inversion transduction grammar or parse tree. Supervised (Cherry and Lin, 2006; Setiawan et al., 2010) and unsupervised (Pauls et al., 2010) methods have been proposed, showing that syntax can improve alignment performance. All these features can be used to training the classifier used in *TakeTwo*.

In a word alignment approach closer to our method, (Deng and Zhou, 2009) propose a method to optimize word alignment combination to derive a more effective phrase table. Similarly, (Nakov and Tiedemann, 2012) propose combining word-level and character-Level alignment models for improving machine translation between two closely-related languages.

In contrast to the previous research in word alignment, we present a system that automatically generates instances of word-translation relations based on self learning, with the goal of training a model to estimate translation probability for effective word alignment. We exploit the inherent crosslingual regularity in parallel corpora and use automatically annotated data for training a discriminative model.

3 The *TakeTwo* Aligner

Aligning words and translation using the EM algorithm based on generative IBM models is not effective for aligning low frequency words and nonliteral translations, especially across disparate languages. To align words and translations reliably in a given parallel corpus, a promising approach is to self-train a classifier with linguistics features, in order to impose additional requirements in combining alignments in two translation directions.

3.1 Problem Statement

We focus on producing word alignments, i.e., a set of word and translation links (word pairs), in each pair of sentences in a parallel corpus. The word alignment results can be used to estimate lexical and phrasal translation probabilities for machine translation; alternatively they can be helpful for bilingual lexicography and computer aided translation. Thus, it is crucial that we produce high-precision, broad coverage word alignments. We now formally state the problem that we are addressing.

Problem Statement: We are given a parallel corpus (E, F), and a monolingual corpus *MonoCorp*. The parallel corpus, (E, F), contains parallel sentences, (E_k, F_k), $k = 1, N$ where $E_k = e_0^k, e_1^k, ..., e_{n_k}^k$, and $F_k = f_0^k, f_1^k, ..., f_{m_k}^k$. Our goal is to produce a set of word alignments for each sentence pair (E_k, F_k). For this, we use an existing word aligner (e.g., *Giza++*) to produce two directional alignments and a symmetrized alignment:

$$\begin{gathered} E2F = (E2F_0, E2F_1, .., E2F_N) \\ F2E = (F2E_0, F2E_1, .., F2E_N) \\ \text{SYMM} = (SYMM_0, SYMM_1, .., SYMM_N). \end{gathered}$$

Each alignment A of (E_k, F_k) in *E2F*, *F2E*, and *SYMM* is represented as

$$\{(i,j) | (e_i^k, f_j^k) \text{ is an alignment link in } A\ \}.$$

We then use a post-processing stage to improve on *SYMM* based on word-translation relation, predicted based on a discrimative model derived from *E2F*,

```
Procedure Train-X-SIM(E, F, MonoCorp):

Stage 1 (Section 3.2.1)

(1)   E2F, F2E, SYMM = WordAliger(E, F)
(2)   E2F-m, F2E-m, SYMM-m = WordAligner(E, F-morph)
(3)   POSITIVES, NEGATIVES = INTERSECT(E2F, F2E), UNION(E2F, F2E) - SYMM
(4)   Return TRAIN = POSITIVES + NEGATIVES

Stage 2 (Section 3.2.2)

(1)   Tag each sentence E(k) and F(k) with parts of speech
      For all English word e, foreign word f, and morpheme m of f
(2a)      Estimate LTP, P(e|f) based on F2E
(2b)      Estimate MTP, P(e|m) based on E2F-m
(3)   Build a  transliteration model  P_translit(e|f) based on an EF name list
(4)   Build a distributional similarity model Sim(e, e') based on MonoCorp
      For each link (e, f) in training data TRAIN, augment (e, f) with features
(5a)    f1 = max(e') P(e'|f) Sim(e', e),      f3 = P_translit(e|f),
(5b)    f2 = max(m, e') P(e'|m) Sim(e', e), f4 = (pos(e), pos(f))

Stage 3  (Section 3.2.3)

(1)    Return the classifier X-SIM trained on the feature vectors
```

Figure 3: Ouline of the process to train the *TakeTwo* system.

F2E, *SYMM*, *MonoCorp*, and other linguistic resources.

In the rest of this section, we describe our solution to this problem. We describe the self-learning strategy for training a classifier for predicting word-translation relation (Section 3.2). In this section, we also describe how to enrich the training data with linguistically motivated features. Finally, we show how *TakeTwo* aligns each sentence pairs by applying the trained classifier (Section 3.3).

3.2 Learning to Predict Cross-lingual Relatedness

We attempt to generate automatically annotated word-translation instances in (E, F) to train a classifier expected to predict word-translation relation. Our learning process is shown in Figure 3.

3.2.1 ***Generating Training Instances***. In the first learning stage, we use the initial word alignments to generate positive and negative instances for training a classifier that predicts alignment links via cross-lingual relatedness. Therefore, the output of this stage is a set of (k, i, j, *Pos* or *Neg*) tuples, where *Pos* or *Neg* denotes whether (e_i^k, f_j^k) is a valid alignment link in (E_k, F_k). To produce the output, we compute $TRAIN_k$:

$$\{\ (k, i, j\ Pos) \mid (i, j) \in E2F_k \cap F2E_k\ \} \cup$$
$$\{\ (k, i, j, Neg) \mid (i, j) \in E2F_k \cup F2E_k - SYMM_k\ \}.$$

Finally, we return $(TRAIN_0, TRAIN_1, .., TRAIN_N)$ as output.

In Step (1) of the this stage, we generate two sets of word alignments (*E2F*, *F2E*) and symmetrized alignments *SYMM*. As will be described in Section 4, we used the existing tool *Giza++* to generate these three sets of alignments.

To illustrate, we show in Figure 4 sample training instances, automatically generated for an example sentence pair. As can be seen in Figure 4, we produce six positive and three negative training instances. In this case, all nine instances are correctly labeled with *Pos* or *Neg*.

To assess the feasibility of the self learning approach, we have checked the annotated instances against hand-tagged links in a small dataset. We

Pos/Neg	i	j	English	Chinese	f_1	f_2	f_3	f_4
Pos	0	0	he	他	.9	.9	.0	PRP-Nh
Pos	4	6	after	後	.9	.9	.0	IN-Ng
Pos	5	3	heinonen	海諾寧	.0	.0	.7	NNP-Nb
Neg	5	9	heinonen	項	.0	.0	.0	NNP-Nf
Neg	5	10	heinonen	談話	.0	.0	.2	NNP-Na
Neg	3	3	remark	海諾寧	.0	.0	.3	NN-Nb
Pos	6	4	arrived	抵達	.9	.9	.0	VBD-VC
Pos	8	5	tehran	德黑蘭	.9	.9	.7	NNP-Nca
Pos	9	11	.	。	.0	.0	.0	.-。

Figure 4: Example positive and negative instances generated from bidirectional alignments of Ex (1). Each instance is augmented with features involving cross-lingual lexical relatedness (f_1), morphological relatedness (f_2), transliteration (f_3), and syntactic compatibility (f_4). In order to generate lexical and syntactic features, the sentences are tagged and lemmatized : ”*He/PRP made/VBD this/DET remark/NN after/IN Heinonen/NNP arrived/VBD in Tehran/NNP ./.*”, and ”他/Nh 是/SHI 在/P 海諾寧/Nb 抵達/VC 德黑蘭/Nca 後/Ng 發表/VC 這/Nep 項/Nf 談話/Na 。/。”).

found that around 90% of positive instances are correctly labelled, while around 95% of the negative instances are correctly labelled.

3.2.2 *Generating features*. In the second stage of the learning process, we augment each training instance (k, i, j, *Pos/Neg*) generated in Section 3.2.1 with a set of features. For the sake of generality, we use a set of linguist features, involving lemmatized forms, morpholgical parts, distributional similarity, parts of speech, and transliteration model.

For this, in Step (1) of the second stage (see Figure 3), we perform tokenization and POS tagging on all sentences (E_k, F_k), k = 1, N. We tokenize F_k into words or Chinese characters, in order to perform word alignment on both word and morpheme levels. In Step (2), we estimate word translation probability and morpheme translation probability based on the initial alignment results, using both word-to-word and word-to-morpheme alignments. In Step (3), we estimate syllable-to-syllable transliteration probablity using a bilingual named entity list. In Step (4), we develop a distributional similarity model based on MonoCorp.

Finally, in Step (5), we use these models to generate a set of features for each training instance in TRAIN. The set of features we use include:

- **Cross-lingual lexical similarity.** This lexical feature is based on a simple idea: translating the foreign words f_j^k into English words e, and then measure similarity between the lemmas of e and e_i^k. Therefore, we have

$$feature_1 = \max_e P(e \mid f_j^k)\ sim\,(e, e_i^k).$$

- **Morpheme-based similarity feature.** This feature is similar to $feature_1$, but is estimated based on word part of a foreign word F_j^k aimed at handling compounds that might involves 1-to-many alignment (e.g., [*preserving water*, 節水 (jieshui)]). For this, we use the word-to-morphme and morpheme-to-word alignments to estimate lexical translation probability. Therefore, we have

$$feature_2 = \max_{e,\ m \in f_j^k} P(e \mid m) sim(e, e_i^k).$$

- **Transliteration feature.** The transliteration feature is designed to handle hard-to-align name entities appearing only once or twice in the whole corpus. Therefore, we we have

$$feature_3 = P_{translit}(f_j^k \mid e_j^k),$$

where $P_{translit}$ is a transliteration model trained on a list of bilingual named entities.

- **Syntactic feature.** We use parts of speech to capture cross-lingual regularity of words and translations on the syntactic level. For instance, an English preposition (i.e., IN) tends to align with a Chinese preposition or directional postposition (i.e., P or Ng). Therefore, we have

$$feature_4 = (pos(e_i^k), pos(f_j^k)),$$

where pos returns the part of speech of English word e_i^k or foreign word f_j^k in (E_k, F_k).

See Figure 4 for example training instances augmented with these crosslingual features.

3.2.3 *Training classifier*. In the third and final stage of training, we train a classifier on a set of positive and negative feature vectors, generated in Section 3.2.2. The output of this stage is *X-Sim*, a classifier that provides probabilistic values indicating the likelihood of word-translation relation for (e_i^k, f_j^k) with features calculated in the context of (E_k, F_k).

3.3 Run-time Word Alignment

Once the classifier *X-Sim* is trained for predicting word-translation relation, *TakeTwo* then combine the two initial sets of alignments, using *X-Sim* to improve performance using the procedure shown in Figure 5. The alignment procedure is a modified version of GDFA procedure, with four steps: INTERSECT, GROW-DIAG-SIM, FILL-IN, and FINAL-AND. We use the same INTERSECT and FINAL-AND step, while modifying GROW-DIAG by requiring crosslingual similarity. The additional step of FILL-IN aimed at adding valid links missing from both *E2F*$_k$ and *F2E*$_k$.

In Step (1), we initalize SYMM/SIM to an empty set. In Steps (2) through (5), we combine the two alignments *E2F*$_k$ and *F2E*$_k$ for each sentence pair (E_k, F_k). And Finally, in Step (6) we output the new symmetrized alignment results.

In Step (2), we start with an alignment with the links in *E2Fk* ∩ *F2E*$_k$. In Step (3), we execute the GROW-DIAG-SIM step to add additional links neighboring the intersection links. A neighboring union link (*E2Fk* ∪ *F2E*$_k$), with high predicted probabiliy, are added to the results. In Step (4), we attempt to fill in links which are probably word-translation pairs, if the link is not in conflict with the current alignment. In Step (5), we execute the FINAL-AND step the same way as in GDFA.

In Step (6), we accumulate symmetrized alignment for a sentence pair. Finally, we add the symmetrized alignment to SYMM/SIM and return SYMM/SIM as output (in Step 7).

4 Experiments and Evaluation

We evaluate our alignment systems directly. We calculate recall, precision, and F-measure.

4.1 Experimental Setting

For self learning, we ran Giza++ on the FBIS corpus with 250 thousand parallel setnences (LDC-2003E14). The training scheme is as follows: 5 iterations of Model 1, followed by 5 iterations of HMM, followed by 5 iterations of Model 3 and then 5 iterations of Model 4. The systems evaluated include:

- *TakeTwo.*
- *TakeTwo (no fill-in).*
- *Giza++: grow-diag-final-and.*
- *Giza++: intersection.*
- *Giza++: union.*

We manually aligned 300 random selected sentences with English and Chinese words as the reference answers. For simplicity, we do not distinguished between sure and uncertain alignment links as described in (Och and Ney, 2004).

For preprocessing and generating syntactic features, we used the Genia Tagger and CKIP Word Segmenter to generate tokens and parts of speech. We also used the Wikipedia Dump (English) to build distributional word similarity measure.

In order to train a classifier for word-translation relation, we used SVM classifier with the tool libsvm. We used lexical, morphological, transliteration, and syntactic features, as described in Section 3.2.2. For simplicity, we used an empirically determined values for the thresholds of similarity constraint in $TakeTwo$.

4.2 Evaluation Metrics

Each word-translation link in the test sentences produced by a word aligner was judged to be either correct or incorrect in context. Precision was calculated as the fraction of correct pairs among the pair derived, recall was calculated as the fraction all correct pairs in the reference key, and the F-measure was

```
Procedure TakeTwo(E2F, F2E, Classifier)
(1)    SYMM/SIM = empty set of word alignments

       For each word alignments, E2F(k), and F2E(k), SYMM(k)
(2)      alignment = INTERSECT(E2F(k), F2E(k))
(3)      GROW-DIAG/SIM(alignment, E2F(k), F2E(k))
(4)      FILL(alignment, E2F(k), F2E(k))
(5)      FINAL-AND(alignment, E2F(k), F2E(k))
(6)      Add alignment to SYMM/SIM

(7)    Return SYMM/SIM

neighboring = [(-1,0),(0,-1),(1,0),(0,1),(-1,-1),(-1,1),(1,-1),(1,1)]

GROW-DIAG/RF(Alignment):
  Iterate until no new points added
    For English word e = 0 ... en, foreign word f = 0 ... fm
        If ( e aligned with f )
          For each neighboring point ( e-new, f-new ):
            If ( ( e-new not aligned or f-new not aligned ) and
                 ( e-new, f-new ) in union( E2F(k), F2E(k) ) and
                 ( X-SIM ( e-new, f-new ) > threshold ) )
              Add to Alignment the link ( e-new, f-new )

FILL(alignment):
  Alignment_candidates = []
  For english word e-new = 0 ... en, foreign word f-new = 0 ... fn
    If ( ( e-new not aligned and f-new not aligned ) and
         ( X-SIM ( e-new, f-new ) > threshold ) )
      Add to Alignment_candidates the link ( e-new, f-new )
  Sort Alignment_candidates by decreasing X-SIM values
  For link (e-new, f-new) in Alignment_candidates
    If ( e-new not aligned and f-new not aligned )
      Add to Alignment the link ( e-new, f-new )

FINAL-AND(Alignment):
  For English word e-new = 0 ... en, foreign word f-new = 0 ... fn
    If ( ( e-new not aligned and f-new not aligned ) and
         ( e-new, f-new ) in alignment )
      Add to Alignment the link ( e-new, f-new )
```

Figure 5: Aligning word and translation at run-time.

calculated with equal weights for both precision and recall.

4.3 Experimental Results

In this section, we report the results of the experimental evaluation. Table 1 lists the precision, recall, and F-measure of two $TakeTwo$ variant systems, and the *Giza++* derived systems. All six systems were tested and evaluated over the test set of 300 parallel sentences sampled from FBIS.

In summary, the $TakeTwo$ with the FILL-IN step has the highest F-measure, while $TakeTwo$ without the FILL-IN step has the second highest F-measure, followed by *GIZA++* with GDFA symmetrization. Both $TakeTwo$ systems outperform the state of the art systems and gains of 6% and 3% in F-measure, with higher precision rate (+16% and +9%) with small descreases in recall rate (-3% and -1%). These results indicate that relevance feedback combined with a rich set of linguistic features are very effective in improving word alignment accuracy in a post-processing setting.

5 Conclusion and Future work

We have presented a new method for word alignment. In our work, we use self learning to generate training data for classifying word-translation relation, based on a rich set of features. The classifier is used in the second word alignment round to val-

Systems	P	R	F
TakeTwo	**.75**	**.65**	**.70**
TakeTwo w/o FILL-IN	.68	.67	.67
grow-diag-final-and (GDFA)	.59	.68	.64
intersection	.88	.46	.60
union	.47	.75	.58

Table 1: Word alignment performance of six systems compared measured by average precision rate (P), recall rate (R), and F-measure (M).

idate links in inital alignment round 'and to fill in missing links. Preliminary experiments and evaluations show our method is capable of aligning words and translations with high precision.

Many avenues exist for future research and improvement of our system. For example, Bleu score of SMT systems using the word alignment results could be used to evaluate the effectiveness of word alignment. Phrasal translations in the bilingual lexicon could be used to make many-to-many alignment decisions. In addition, natural language processing techniques such as word clustering, and cross-lingual relatedness could be attempted to improve recall. Another interesting direction to explore is training an ensemble of classifiers. Yet another direction of research would be to align word from scratch using the classifier in a beam-search algorithm.

References

Peter F Brown, John Cocke, Stephen A Della Pietra, Vincent J Della Pietra, Fredrick Jelinek, John D Lafferty, Robert L Mercer, and Paul S Roossin. 1990. A statistical approach to machine translation. *Computational linguistics*, 16(2):79–85.

Peter F Brown, Vincent J Della Pietra, Stephen A Della Pietra, and Robert L Mercer. 1993. The mathematics of statistical machine translation: Parameter estimation. *Computational linguistics*, 19(2):263–311.

Joseph Z Chang, Jason S Chang, and Jyh-Shing Roger Jang. 2012. Learning to find translations and transliterations on the web. In *Proceedings of the 50th Annual Meeting of the Association for Computational Linguistics: Short Papers-Volume 2*, pages 130–134. Association for Computational Linguistics.

Colin Cherry and Dekang Lin. 2003. A probability model to improve word alignment. In *Proceedings of the 41st Annual Meeting on Association for Computational Linguistics-Volume 1*, pages 88–95. Association for Computational Linguistics.

Colin Cherry and Dekang Lin. 2006. Soft syntactic constraints for word alignment through discriminative training. In *Proceedings of the COLING/ACL on Main conference poster sessions*, pages 105–112. Association for Computational Linguistics.

Yonggang Deng and Bowen Zhou. 2009. Optimizing word alignment combination for phrase table training. In *Proceedings of the ACL-IJCNLP 2009 Conference Short Papers*, pages 229–232. Association for Computational Linguistics.

Bonnie Jean Dorr. 1993. *Machine translation: a view from the Lexicon*. MIT press.

Christiane Fellbaum. 1999. *WordNet*. Wiley Online Library.

William A Gale and Kenneth Ward Church. 1991. Identifying word correspondences in parallel texts. In *HLT*, volume 91, pages 152–157.

Daniel Gildea. 2003. Loosely tree-based alignment for machine translation. In *Proceedings of the 41st Annual Meeting on Association for Computational Linguistics-Volume 1*, pages 80–87. Association for Computational Linguistics.

Sue J Ker and Jason S Chang. 1997. A class-based approach to word alignment. *Computational Linguistics*, 23(2):313–343.

Kevin Knight and Jonathan Graehl. 1998. Machine transliteration. *Computational Linguistics*, 24(4):599–612.

Dekang Lin, Shaojun Zhao, Benjamin Van Durme, and Marius Pasca. 2008. Mining parenthetical translations from the web by word alignment. In *ACL*, volume 8, pages 994–1002.

Dekang Lin. 1998a. Automatic retrieval and clustering of similar words. In *Proceedings of the 17th international conference on Computational linguistics-Volume 2*, pages 768–774. Association for Computational Linguistics.

Dekang Lin. 1998b. An information-theoretic definition of similarity. In *ICML*, volume 98, pages 296–304.

Yang Liu, Qun Liu, and Shouxun Lin. 2005. Log-linear models for word alignment. In *Proceedings of the 43rd Annual Meeting on Association for Computational Linguistics*, pages 459–466. Association for Computational Linguistics.

Adam Lopez. 2007. A survey of statistical machine translation. Technical report, DTIC Document.

Lukas Michelbacher, Florian Laws, Beate Dorow, Ulrich Heid, and Hinrich Schütze. 2010. Building a cross-lingual relatedness thesaurus using a graph similarity measure. In *LREC*.

Robert C Moore. 2005. A discriminative framework for bilingual word alignment. In *Proceedings of the conference on Human Language Technology and Empirical Methods in Natural Language Processing*, pages 81–88. Association for Computational Linguistics.

Masaaki Nagata, Teruka Saito, and Kenji Suzuki. 2001. Using the web as a bilingual dictionary. In *Proceedings of the workshop on Data-driven methods in machine translation-Volume 14*, pages 1–8. Association for Computational Linguistics.

Preslav Nakov and Jörg Tiedemann. 2012. Combining word-level and character-level models for machine translation between closely-related languages. In *Proceedings of the 50th Annual Meeting of the Association for Computational Linguistics: Short Papers-Volume 2*, pages 301–305. Association for Computational Linguistics.

Franz Josef Och and Hermann Ney. 2003. A systematic comparison of various statistical alignment models. *Computational linguistics*, 29(1):19–51.

Franz Josef Och and Hermann Ney. 2004. The alignment template approach to statistical machine translation. *Computational linguistics*, 30(4):417–449.

Adam Pauls, Dan Klein, David Chiang, and Kevin Knight. 2010. Unsupervised syntactic alignment with inversion transduction grammars. In *Human Language Technologies: The 2010 Annual Conference of the North American Chapter of the Association for Computational Linguistics*, pages 118–126. Association for Computational Linguistics.

Hendra Setiawan, Chris Dyer, and Philip Resnik. 2010. Discriminative word alignment with a function word reordering model. In *Proceedings of the 2010 Conference on Empirical Methods in Natural Language Processing*, pages 534–544. Association for Computational Linguistics.

Ben Taskar, Simon Lacoste-Julien, and Dan Klein. 2005. A discriminative matching approach to word alignment. In *Proceedings of the conference on Human Language Technology and Empirical Methods in Natural Language Processing*, pages 73–80. Association for Computational Linguistics.

Zhiguo Wang and Chengqing Zong. 2013. Large-scale word alignment using soft dependency cohesion constraints. *Transactions of Association for Computational Linguistics*, 1(6):291–300.

Jian-Cheng Wu and Jason S Chang. 2007. Learning to find english to chinese transliterations on the web. In *EMNLP-CoNLL*, pages 996–1004.

Frequency-influenced choice of L2 sound realization and perception: evidence from two Chinese dialects

Yizhou Lan
Department of Asian and International Studies
City University of Hong Kong
eejoe.lan@gmail.com

Abstract

The study of second language speech perception usually put L1-L2 phonological mapping as the rule of thumb in predicting learning outcome, and seldom included more fine-grained aspects such as frequency. This study examines how frequency of sounds in L1 may influence L2 segmental production and perception, with examples from English learners native to two Chinese dialects, Cantonese and Sichuanese. Although these two dialects (L1s) have very similar phonological inventory, they produce certain L2 sounds in drastic difference. Productions of English voiceless interdental fricative and central liquid in the onset position were obtained in free speech from the two dialects' speakers in vast phonological environments. Then, perception tests, including AX and oddity tasks, were done for these two groups of speakers as well. Results showed that the two English sounds were respectively realized as different sounds in Cantonese and Sichuanese L1, which was reflected by both production and perception data. Findings suggest that L2 category formation is frequency-motivated instead of markedness-motivated, and is significantly influenced by the functional load of L1 sound input. Findings further imply that a quantitative and frequency-sensitive learning model is more suitable for L2 sound acquisition.

1 Introduction

Second language speech has generally seen as function of linguistic experience. However, how experience shape the formation of phonetic category was understudied. This study addresses a case when speakers from two L1s with similar segmental layout may have different realizations of L2 categories. Although theoretic models in speech learning such were very rich in literature, such as Perceptual Assimilation Model (PAM [1]) and its another version for L2 learners (PAM-L2 [2]) as well as Speech Learning model (SLM, [3]) had addressed different L1 assimilation patterns in learning multiple L2s, few studies had found similar multiple L1s yielding different L2 learning outcomes.

PAM and SLM suggest that second language learners will either assimilate the L2 sound categories (or sequence of sounds) to L1 sound categories according to different perceptual distances. Increased exposure to L2 will thus trigger distributive learning of L2 input by forming a new intermediate category between the L1 and L2 in the learner's common phonetic space [1]. In experience-based models, the positive effect of L2 exposure will increase the chance of distributive learning because the learnability of certain L2 categories should become stable if the input of L2 categories occurs in environments with similar frequency [3].

This paper displays that similar L1 inventories may result in different learning outcomes and argues that this phenomenon is influenced by frequency in similar ways as the native language was (NLM, [5]). The two English sounds under current investigation are the voiceless interdental fricative (/θ/) and the central liquid (/r/). In a pilot study, it was found that Sichuanse speakers replace English /θ/ by /s/ but Cantonese speakers by /f/.

Copyright 2014 by Yizhou Lan
28th Pacific Asia Conference on Language, Information and Computation pages 292–298

Also, Sichuanese speakers replace English /r/ by /z/ but Cantonese by /w/.

Previous literature has pointed out that these two English phonemes are difficult for Cantonese and Sichuanese learners to produce [6-8], but the question why the two dialects of Chinese may have different realizations of the sound was not addressed.

Cantonese and Sichuanese are both southern dialects of China. Cantonese and Sichuanese share a very similar consonant inventory in the onset position. Both dialects' onsets consist of bilabial, alveolar and velar plosives (/ph, th, kh, p, t, k/), as well as labiodental and alveolar fricatives (/f, s, z/). Nasals and liquids include /m, n, ŋ/. The only difference of the two dialects is that Cantonese does not have palatalized fricatives.

In the present study, Cantonese and Sichuanese L2 production and perception were examined. Firstly, the production of /θ/ was obtained from a sentence-making task, which contains stimuli words with /θ/. Then, the spectral envelope was analyzed through fast Fourier transformation (FFT) and sent to t-test for statistics [9]. For the production of /r/, same task was administered and the analysis was made into checking the F3 and waveform of /r/ (ibid.). Then, a perception test was designed. Native speakers' production was presented to another two groups of speakers and they were required to identify from two sounds and discriminate from three sounds, which were cross-checked with the production indications. For example, both Cantonese and Sichuanese speakers listened to /f/ and /s/ tokens against /θ/ in a task, and /w/ and /z/ in another one.

2 Method

2.1 Participants

Effort was made to control all the biographical, affective and experiential factors of the two groups of participants. 8 Cantonese and 8 Sichuanese speakers, with equal numbers of males and females, were recruited. Both groups of speakers were experienced learners of English, with the age of acquisition of English (AOA) earlier than 7 years old. A group of native speakers of the Standard American English also participated in the study.

Cantonese speakers were not exposed to formal instruction of any other languages, and their parents speak any other languages other than Cantonese (including English). The situation for Sichuanese speakers is more complex. Since speaking Mandarin at school is mandatory, and those with early English AOA have all attended school, they have been exposed to Mandarin as well as Sichuanese. This has brought about a difference of these two groups of speakers. However, it cannot be eliminated due to language policy [10].

2.2 Stimuli and Procedure

We designed a production and a perception test to find out whether L2 category formation (/θ/ and /r/) is different for Cantonese and Sichuanse speakers; and we retrieved the functional load of these sounds on a small-scale corpus to see if frequency motivates the difference of categorical formation.

For the production experiment, stimuli contained experiment words (/r/ with 5 vowels and 3 syllable structures; /θ/ with 5 vowels and 4 syllable structures, with ten repetitions respectively: e.g., rit, ree, rin; θit, θee, θin) control words (/f/ /s/ /w/ /z/ with 5 vowels and 3 syllable structures, with ten repetitions; e.g., *fit, sat, wut, zot*) and filler words with other onsets (/p/, /t/, /k/ as the same structures, with five repetitions).

The experiment procedure was a semi-free speech with given stimuli. Participants were asked to make five stories with the given words, each story containing two sentences. The words were later cut out of the sentence for analysis. Most of the stimuli words were obtained after a long pause at the intonational phrase level so that phonetic environment will not influence too much of the production. For the /θ/ contrast, the spectral energy concentration was analyzed for the characterization of /s/ or /f/ contrast (here, some productions were too short and taken as /t/ tokens). Participants were not aware of the purpose of the study. They were informed that they were participating in a test testing fluency in spoken English.

As we aim to dig out the characteristics of actual vernacular form of speech instead of citation forms, we did not strictly control the number and order of occurrence of stimuli, but still controlled phonetic environment and the number of tokens. Altogether 101 usable tokens (including /s, f, θ, r, w, z/-initials) were collected from 8 Cantonese and 8 Sichuanese student participants' productions and 48 tokens from the native English participant's productions (101+48=149 tokens). The productions were cut out of the sentence and segmented as phonemes within those words. The onset parts of the productions, defined as the section from the beginning of waveform to the steady state of vowel, were examined for in spectral analysis.

The perception study was done in the same laboratory. Both an AX task and an oddity task (a variation of the ABX task) were performed. In the AX task, listeners were presented with two stimuli and they need to identify it is either /θ/ or /f/ or /s/. In the oddity task, they were given three stimuli in ABA, ABB or AAB form to distinguish. They need to decide which one is different. Theoretically the token number to be included in analysis was 27 stimuli × 5 repetitions × 2 combinations + 27 stimuli × 5 repetitions × 3 combinations = 675 tokens for each speaker. After screening, a total of 620 tokens were selected as the perception test material. Within-trial inter-stimuli interval (ISI) was set at 50ms and between-trial ISI at 200ms. All trials were randomized and added with equal numbers of fillers.

Since the relationship of frequency and category assimilation patterns was to be investigated, the third step of the current study was the extraction and comparison of functional load data from a corpus of two dialects and relating of the functional load to the empirical study (including production and production) results. Since Sichuanese does not have an established corpus to date, we used the entries of a published wordlist and annotated them with productions in Cantonese and Sichuanese, which controlled the word frequencies in these two dialects. The choices of words from *Xiandai Hanyu Changyong Zibiao* [11], a list of 2500 most commonly used Chinese characters to relate the phonological families of Chinese dialects. Word frequency was considered as a coefficient of the calculation of sound frequency count. We then examined the correlation between the assimilation pattern and functional load. It was a limitation not being able to employ more cognitive methods to establish a causal link between the two instead of a weak, correlational one, but due to technical reasons, the attempt was not realized.

3 Results

3.1 Production test

Spectral envelopes of the fricative productions were analyzed for Cantonese and Sichuanese speakers. First, the /f/ and /θ/ sounds were compared for similarity for both Cantonese and /s/ and /θ/ for Sichuanse speakers. For the /z/ and /r/ contrast, since these two sounds are easy to distinguish, sound with formant will be classified as /r/.

As the study aims not to find the criteria of identifying the fricatives but distinguishing them in shape, we are focusing on the peak of energy concentration instead of spectral moments. The average peak for Cantonese production of /f/, /s/ and /θ/ were 6754, 7259 and 6145 respectively for Cantonese speakers. For Sichuanese speakers, the figures were 6248, 7195 and 7246. Between-group variance tests show that the difference was insignificant for spectral peak. However, within the Cantonese speakers, the difference is significant for /s/ and /θ/ [$F(2, 248)=3.488$, $p<.0001$] not /f/ and /θ/ showed by an ANOVA test. The Sichuanese data was reversed, i.e. significant for /f/ [$F(2, 248)=2.125$, $p<.001$] but not for /s/. The results indicate that Cantonese speakers' production of /θ/ was similar to /f/ but different from /s/, and for Sichuanese, vice versa (see Figure 1 for an example of the Cantonese case. The energy concentrations of /θ/ overlap significantly more on /f/ than /s/).

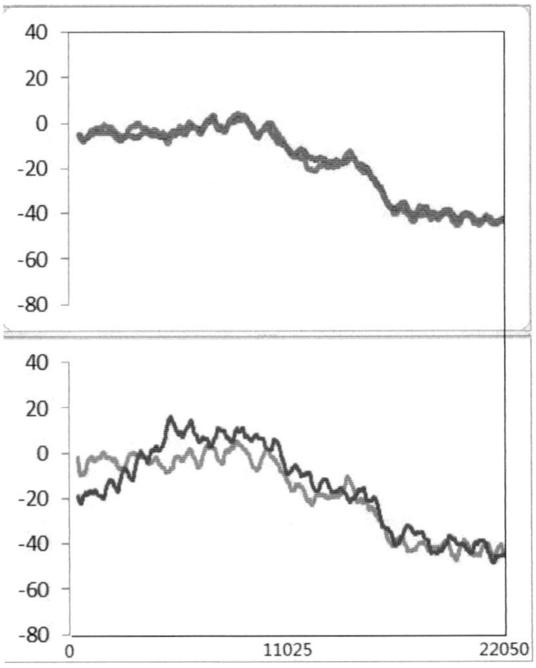

Figure 1: Comparison of sound pressure for /f/ and / θ / (upper) and /s/ and / θ / (lower) central spectrum. Measurement was done with 50ms pre-emphasis. The y-axis is in dB and y-axis in Hz.

The average duration for /s/, /f/ and /θ/ were 55, 65 and 47 ms respectively by Cantonese speaker, 53, 80 and 45 ms by Sichuanese speakers. The difference is not significant (see Figure 2).

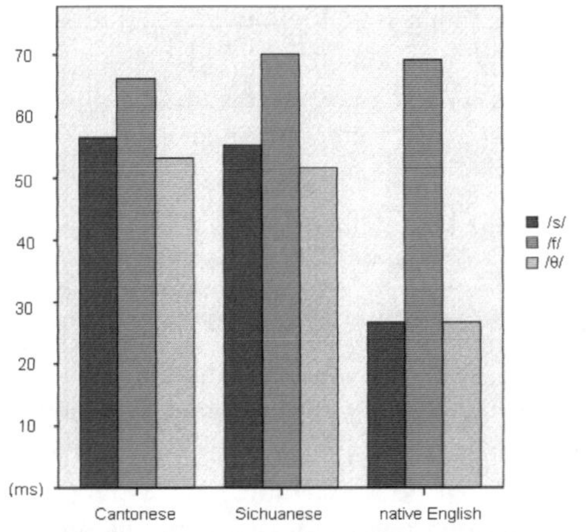

Figure 2: Duration of frication of /s, f, and θ/ by Cantonese, Sichuanese and English speakers.

However, for English speakers, the /θ/ and /f/ duration was much smaller, as 32 and 33 ms. As confirmed by previous studies (Flege and Wang, 1996), Chinese speakers of English did not distinguish fricative duration as native English speakers did, probably due to the syllable timing. Within-group variance tests shows that the difference was insignificant but significant for duration comparing between Cantonese and Sichuanese groups, [F(2, 248)=1.154, p=.248] but near-significant within groups [Cantonese: F(2, 124)=2.459, p=.065; Sichuanese F(2, 124)=3.245, p=.071] (see Figure 2).

For the /r/ contrast, the spectrogram of both Cantonese and Sichuanese speakers was examined. Formant contours and affrication was analyzed qualitatively. Only Sichuanese productions were seen of affrication indicating the presence of /z/, whereas Cantonese speech showed considerable F2 and F3 changes which could be seen as intermediate instances between /r/ and /w/. From above production data, reversed production patterns were shown for both /f/ and /s/ for /θ/ as well as /w/ and /z/ for /r/.

3.2 Perception test

Overall speaking, the identification and discrimination test result showed that the perceptual accuracy was 61.3% by the five Cantonese speakers, and 66.7% by Sichuanese speakers. For Cantonese speakers, the difference on [F(3, 617)=8.719, p<.0001], but not for English speakers [F(3, 617)=1.249, p=.576]. The effect of task was not significant. Due to such insignificance, identification and discrimination task results were computed into average and represented as /x/-/y/ accuracy rates for the ease of comparison.

For Cantonese speakers, vowel differences were not significant. Accuracy rate for /θ/ and /s/ discrimination was 85.75%, and accuracy rate for /θ/ and /f/ was 56.5%. Such a difference was significant [t=2.128, df=317, p<.0001]. Accuracy rate for /r/ and /w/ was 88.15%, /r/ and /z/ was 71.25%. The difference was near-significant [t=-0.257, df=317, p=.042].

For Sichuanese speakers, vowel differences were not significant as well. Accuracy rate for /θ/ and /s/ discrimination was 42.15%, and accuracy rate for /θ/ and /f/ was 82.45%. Such a difference was significant [t=2.719, df=317, p<.0001]. Accuracy rate for /r/ and /w/ was 67.5%, /r/ and /z/ was 78.85%. The difference was not significant [t=5.124, df=317, p<.0001] (See Figure 3).

As a random factor, individual difference within both groups did not significantly influence the perceptual accuracy.

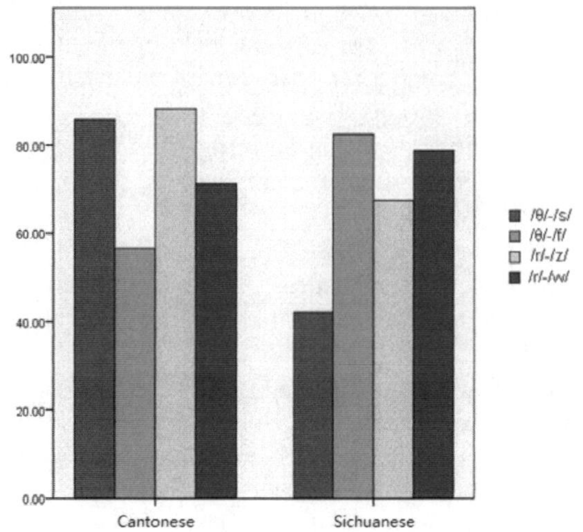

Figure 3: Comparison of mean perceptual accuracy rates of Cantonese and Sichuanese speakers.

3.3 Comparison of Frequency

The following table layouts the item under discussion, and dominantly assimilated sound as acquired from 3.1 and 3.2. For example, the dominant choice of realization and perception for Cantonese /θ/ was /f/ instead of /s/.

To investigate whether frequency was parallel to the assimilation patterns, the functional load of the two word-lists in Cantonese and Sichuanese was compared. The result summarized from the above experiment was shown in Table 1.

Item	Dominant	Item	Dominant
C /s/	/f/	C /r/	none
S /s/	/s/	S /r/	none
C /f/	/f/, /h/	C /z/	/z/
S /f/	/f/	S /z/	/z/, /r/

Table 1: Dominant sound category in Cantonese (C) and Sichuanese (S) speech.

According to its definition, functional load (FL) of two contrasting sounds is calculated as the function of frequency of a lexical entry and the frequency of the two involving sounds, which can be expressed as follows in (1):

$$FL(x,y) = \frac{H(L) - H(L_{xy})}{H(L)} \qquad (1)$$

A report showed that in American English, the functional load of /f/ and /θ/ was 1×10^{-3}, and 2×10^{-3} for /s/ and /θ/ [12]. Therefore we could see that for English, the sound /s/ is actually more frequently confused with /θ/ than /f/, and the choice by Cantonese speakers may be not reflecting the English L1 predictions. Here we could see that the functional loads for fricatives are different across the two dialects of Chinese. The functional load calculated for Cantonese and Sichuanese /s, f/ pair and /z, w/ pair was displayed in Table 2.

Sound pair	Functional load in most used Chinese characters
Cantonese /s vs. f/	0.125
Sichuanese /s vs. f/	0.750
Cantonese /z vs. w/	0.054
Sichuanese /z vs. w/	0.375

Table 2: Functional load in onset position in 2500 most used Chinese characters.

From the data, we could see that /f/ is functionally more loaded than /s/ for Cantonese speakers, and vice versa for Sichuanese speakers. On the contrary, /w/ was more functionally loaded for Sichuanese than for Cantonese.

4 General Discussion

Production results showed that the role of functional load did differ in Cantonese and Sichuanese, and the more frequent and more functionally loaded /f/ in Cantonese, compared with Sichuanese, was linked with the choice of /f/ rather than /s/ in the realization and perception of /θ/. Conversely, the Sichuanese choice also preferred the more functionally loaded one, /s/. The same patterned preference showed for /w/ and /z/ in Cantonese and Sichuanese as well.

The spectral differences in Cantonese and Sichuanese L2 English lied in spectral envelope, esp. spectral peak. However, patterns of duration of the fricatives were not significantly different amongst these two groups of speakers, maybe because this dimension of acoustic information was not distinguished by both Cantonese and Sichuanese speakers as a whole [13].

Perceptually, since it is clearly shown that the value of accuracy rates was reversed for Cantonese and Sichuanese speakers, and the inclination was especially true for the /θ/ sound. Therefore it could be drawn from the results that Cantonese and Sichuanese speakers of English have different perception of sound categories, and apply different assimilation routes to sounds.

For both Cantonese and Sichuanese learners, perception and production of these sounds were quite symmetric. It further suggested a steady tendency of difference in choice of L2 realizations for these two dialects, though their inventories were of very similar layout.

Despite the production and perception results which showed a different inclination towards /f/ and /s/ by Cantonese and Mandarin learners, such conclusion is apt to test by a question whether the difference is due to phonetic closeness as proposed by J. Jenkins. However, the design of the study confirmed that the phonetic distance of /s/-/θ/ and /f/-/θ/ acoustically is similar.

The current results shed light on the crystallization of two significant theoretic debates. The first debate involves whether L2 speech realizations are mapped on discrete phonological units, i.e., phonemes, or through more distributional processes which is influenced by the frequency of the L1. The first approach, including Optimality Theory, cannot explain the data in the current study because although OT is based on gradable constraints, it still believes that the output is the same for similar L1 phonological structures. More importantly, the difference in outputs for these two dialects is not markedness-motivated but frequency-motivated. The OT claim of tearing linguistic performance into perceptual level and representational level [14] is more complex than this frequency-based explanation.

The second debate which concerns this study is the choice of assimilation routes by L1 only or by a cluster of dynamic frequency correlates of L1 (and maybe experiences on other languages). In SLM's suggestion, assimilation is based on perceived acoustic similarity only, but the results here showed that an assimilation route can be dynamic and may be influenced by the functional load of L1. This probabilistic view is in line with the basic assumption of the NLM model [5] but slightly different from SLM in that it opposes discrete assimilation pattern projections from distance to learning outcome. A probabilistic model predicts assimilation outcomes not based on the distance, but on the instances on the input of L2 phones, and its probabilistic balance with regard to L2. In other words, L2 learning is statistical learning instead of a mere calculation of distances.

Although native English speakers perceive /s/ as a better exemplar of /θ/ compared with /f/ due to the higher functional load, Cantonese speakers prefer /f/ in a very clear-cut manner. It is implied that L1 frequency is such an important factor that can override L2 preferences, which also exists in the input in their learning. L1, in the frequency's perspective, plays a more important role than L2 even after many years of learning. This phenomenon also challenges learnability of some L2 categories, since according to SLM, the categories should receive even more influence on L1 and L2 input and establish an intermediate category provided exposure to the L2. However, as the result suggests, the preference of /f/ by Cantonese speakers cannot be eliminated and thus cannot be learned in a small time span.

Findings indicate that the mechanism for L2 categorical formation is more than a perception-production chain, and may involve statistical learning effects. When the prediction through phonological categorical assimilation and frequency-based predictions collide, the latter is favored. However, there might also be other variables stretching outside the realm of phonetics and phonology that influence the results, because the affective factors of this study were not fully controlled. Future studies should involve more specific measurements to mine out these variables.

.

Acknowledgments

The author thanks Karen Chow for data collection, and Weiping Zhong for providing word frequency measurement.

References

[1] C. T. Best, "A direct-realist view of cross-language speech perception," in Strange W [Ed.] Speech

perception and linguistic experience: Issues in cross-language research, 171–204, 1995.

[2] C. T. Best, and M. D. Tyler, "Nonnative and second-language speech perception: Commonalities and complementarities". In Munro M. J. & Bohn O.-S. [Eds.] Second language speech learning: The role of language experience in speech perception and production, 13-34, 2007.

[3] J. E. Flege, "Assessing constraints on second-language segmental production and perception," Phonetics and phonology in language comprehension and production: Differences and similarities, 319-355, 2003.

[4] B. Hayes, and C. Wilson, "A maximum entropy model of phonotactics and phonotactic learning," Linguistic Inquiry, 39(3), 379-440. 2008.

[5] P. K. Kuhl, B. T. Conboy, S. Coffey-Corina, D. Padden, M. Rivera-Gaxiola, and T. Nelson, "Phonetic learning as a pathway to language: new data and native language magnet theory expanded (NLM-e)," Philosophical Transactions of the Royal Society B: Biological Sciences, 363(1493), 979-1000, 2008.

[6] D. Rau, Chang, H. H. A., and Tarone, E. E. "Think or sink: Chinese learners' acquisition of the English voiceless interdental fricative". Language Learning, 59(3), 581-621, 2009.

[7] Hung, T. N. "Towards a phonology of Hong Kong English". Bolton, K. ed. Hong Kong English: autonomy and creativity (Vol. 1),119-140, 2002.

[8] Lee, P. W. "The study of English in China with particular reference to accent and vocabulary". Master Thesis submitted to The university of Hong Kong, 2002.

[9] R. D. Kent, and C. Read, "The acoustic analysis of speech," Thomson Learning Albany, NY, 2002.

[10] S. Evans, "The Long March to Biliteracy and Trilingualism: Language Policy in Hong Kong Education Since the Handover," Annual Review of Applied Linguistics, 33, 302-324, 2013.

[11] State Language and Letters Committee of China, "List of Commonly Used Characters in Modern Chinese, *Xiandai Hanyu Changyong Zibiao*", 1988.

[12] S. Dinoj, and N. Partha, "Quantifying the functional load of phonemic oppositions, distinctive features, and suprasegmentals", Nedergaard Thomsen, Ole [Ed.] Current trends in the theory of linguistic change. In commemoration of Eugenio Coseriu (1921-2002). Amsterdam & Philadelphia: Benjamins, 2006.

[13] W. Strange, "Automatic selective perception (ASP) of first and second language speech: A working model," Journal of Phonetics, 39(4): 456–466, 2011.

[14] J. Dekkers van der Leeuw, J. M. van de Weijer, "Optimality Theory: Phonology, Syntax, and Acquisition," OUP, 2000.

The L2 Acquisition of the Chinese Aspect Marking[1]

Suying Yang
Department of English Language and Literature
Hong Kong Baptist University
syang@hkbu.edu.hk

Abstract

By analyzing corpus data, we have shown that the tendencies of restricting perfective past marking to Accomplishments and Achievements and imperfective marking to Statives and Activities as described by the Aspect Hypothesis (Shirai, 1991; Andersen & Shirai, 1996), undesirable in the acquisition of various languages, are desirable in the acquisition of a language like Chinese, because these tendencies coincide with the natural occurrence patterns of *–le* and *–zhe*. We argue that different languages may observe the same natural language principle (Bybee's Relevance Principle) in different ways, rendering the learner tendencies desirable or undesirable in the acquisition processes. Based on our new observations, we propose some modifications to the Aspect Hypothesis.

1 Introduction

In the early nineteen seventies, researchers carried out a number of studies on first language (L1) acquisition of the tense-aspect system, and their findings show a close relationship between the use of the verbal morphology and aspectual properties of verbs/situations like [± dynamic], [± telic] and [± punctual] (Antinucci & Miller, 1976; Bloom et al., 1980; Bronckart & Sinclair, 1973; Li, 1989). Beginning L1 learners tend to restrict their use of the perfective past (simple past tense in English which indicates both past time location and perfective aspect (Smith, 1997) to telic verbs (Achievements and Accomplishments), and their use of the imperfective aspect to Activities. The same patterns have also been attested in second language (L2) acquisition (Andersen,1986, 1989, 1990; Bardovi-Harlig, 1992, 1994; Bardovi-Harlig & Bergström, 1996; Bardovi-Harlig & Reynolds, 1995; Flashner, 1989; Kaplan, 1987; Kumpf,1984; Robison, 1990; Shirai & Andersen, 1995; etc.) There widely attested developmental patterns were first referred to as the Defective Tense Hypothesis (Weist et al., 1984), and later came to be known as the Primacy of Aspect Hypothesis (Andersen, 1989; Robison 1990) or the Aspect Hypothesis (Andersen & Shrai, 1994; Robison, 1995, Shrai & Kurono, 1998). The Defective Tense Hypothesis attributes the observed patterns "to a cognitive inability of a young child to conceive of a notion of 'past event or situation'" (Andersen & Shirai, 1996, p. 560), while the Aspect Hypothesis suggests that learners primarily use verbal morphology to mark lexical aspectual distinction rather than temporal distinction. The Aspect Hypothesis as summarized in its simplest form by Andersen (2002: 79) makes the following three claims):

1) [Learners] first use past marking (e.g., English) or perfective marking (Chinese, Spanish, etc.) to achievement and accomplishment verbs, eventually extending its use to activity and [then to] stative verbs. (…)
2) In languages that encode the perfective-imperfective distinction, [a morphologically encoded] imperfective past [as in the Romance languages] appears later than perfective past, and imperfective past marking begins with

[1] The research reported here is supported by a grant (RGC/97-98/68) from the Hong Kong University Research Grant Committee.

Copyright 2014 by Suying Yang
28th Pacific Asia Conference on Language, Information and Computation pages 299–308

stative and activity verbs, then extends to accomplishment and achievement verbs.

3) In languages that have progressive aspect, progressive marking begins with activity verbs, then extends to accomplishment and achievement verbs. (Andersen & Shirai, 1996: 533).

In the following discussion, we will refer to the three claims of the Aspect Hypothesis as Claim 1, 2 and 3 respectively.

Various theories have been proposed to explain the "Primacy of Aspect" phenomena. Bickerton's (1981) Bioprogram Hypothesis suggests that some language properties, like state-process distinction and punctual-nonpunctual distinction, are bio-programmed and reflected in learners' early verbal morphology. On the other hand, Bybee's (1985) Relevance Principle emphasizes more on the relationship between meanings of inflections and meanings of verbs. She claims that "inflections are more naturally attached to a lexical item if the meaning of the inflection has direct relevance to the meaning of the lexical item" (cited in Andersen, 1991, p. 319). While applying Bybee's Relevance Principle to the emergence sequence of past marking, Andersen (1991) explains that "the gradual spread of past marking from punctual events to telic events and then to dynamic verbs and finally all verbs is in the direction of decreasing relevance to the meaning of the verb" (p. 319). Andersen's (1993) Congruence Principle advances a similar argument: "learners will use tense-aspect morphemes whose meaning is most similar to that of the verb". In addition to the Congruence Principle, Andersen & Shirai (1994) have also proposed the Distributional Bias Hypothesis which points out that in adult native speakers' language the perfective past inflections occur more often on Accomplishments and Achievements than on Statives and Activities. In other words, the input to learners exhibits, in relatively quantitative terms, similar distributional imbalance.

The Aspect Hypothesis has been the focus of much of the recent research and seems to have been well accepted (see Bardovi-Harlig (1999, 2000) for a general survey of literature on tense-aspect acquisition). The general assumption of the researchers along this line of research seems to be that the Aspect Hypothesis is true regardless of different L1s and L2s.

However, this general assumption is not unchallengeable when "there is a general lack of knowledge on the acquisition of non-Indo-European languages" (Bardovi-Harlig, 1999, p. 369). Most studies along this line of research have focused on the acquisition of a certain European language by native speakers of another European language. In other words, the L1s and the L2s involved in most studies are typologically similar languages. Only a few studies have involved non-European language speakers (Bardovi-Harlig, 1998; Bardovi-Harlig & Reynolds, 1995; Bayley, 1994; Giacalone Ramat & Banfi, 1990; Shirai, 1995) and even fewer studies have examined the L2 acquisition of a non-European language (Shrai, 1995; Shirai & Kurono, 1998).[2] Of these few studies, only two (Shirai, 1995; Shirai & Kurono,1998), as far as we know, have focused on the impact of typological differences on the Aspect Hypothesis. The others either have foci other than this or have investigated non-European language speakers and European language speakers indistinguishably. For instance, Bayley's study investigated 20 Chinese speakers learning English as a second language, but his focus was on how different factors conditioned variation in interlanguage tense marking. Bardove-Harlig & Reynolds (1995) included non-European language speakers in their studies, but the non-European language speakers were examined together with European language speakers indistinguishably, so the effect of typological differences could not be possibly observed.

It is very clear that more studies on typologically different L1s and L2s are needed to verify the Aspect Hypothesis and our study is just an endeavor in this respect. By analyzing corpus data produced by English speakers learning Chinese as a second language, we will show that the undesirable learner tendencies of under-using verbal morphology in the acquisition of various languages will become desirable in the acquisition of Chinese because different languages may observe a natural language principle (Bybee's Relevance Principle) in different ways.

2 The Special Features of the Chinese Aspectual System

[2] There are of course many studies on L1 acquisition of non-European languages.

Chinese has no tense and temporal references are made with other devices, such as lexical expressions, contexts and sentence sequencing. However, Chinese has a rich aspectual system (Li & Thompson, 1981). Quite a few aspect markers contribute to the aspectual meanings of sentences. As these markers are not grammatically obligatory and their meanings and functions are quite often elusive, there is still controversy over the exact number of them and the aspectual nature of many of them. However, the status of *-le, -guo, -zai* and *-zhe* as the most important aspect markers is unquestionable (Wang, 1985). Of these four major aspect markers, *-le* and *-zhe* show more complex relationship with aspectual properties of verb/situations, so we have chosen them as the targets of our investigation (Yang, 1995).

2.1 The Special Features of *-Le*

-Le is a prototypical perfective aspect marker providing a completion view rather than locating an event in time. This is shown by sentence (1).

(1) wo chi-le fan jiu qu kan dianying.
I eat-Perf.[3] meal then go see movie
"I will go to see a movie after I finish my meal." Or "I went to see a movie after I had finished my meal."

Depending on different contexts, this sentence can have interpretations of different temporal locations: future or past, but the relationship between the two events in either interpretation is the same: the event of eating the meal is completed before the event of going to see a movie.

-Le does not locate events in past, but its major function of providing an entirety view determines that it is mostly used to present past events. Despite the ostensible similarities between them, the Chinese *-le* displays some special properties which are not shared by the perfective past in English. The occurrence of *-le* is sensitive to various aspectual, syntactic and contextual factors.

Following Smith (1997) and Comrie (1976), we assume that aspectual meaning results from the interaction between two aspectual components: situation type (also referred to as lexical aspect) and viewpoint (also referred to as grammatical aspect), the former being realized by the verb and its arguments, while the latter being signaled by a grammatical morpheme. Whereas the English simple past, a combination of past tense and perfective viewpoint, may go with situations of all types, the occurrence of *-le* on atelic situations, namely Statives and Activities (excluding Statives that present change of state[4]) is restricted and conditional (Li & Thompson, 1981; Lu, 1986; Tsai 2008; Wu, 2005; Yang, 1995, 1999). It seems that *-le* requires an endpoint to present a situation in entirety (Yang, 2011). Telic situations, namely Achievements and Accomplishments, contain inherent endpoints (outcomes or results) by definition (Smith, 1997), and there is no problem for *-le* to occur on them.[5]

(2) Xiaojuan xie-le yi-feng xin.
Xiaojuan write-Perf. one-Cl. Letter
"Xiaojuan wrote a letter."
(Accomplishment)

On the other hand, atelic situations do not have inherent endpoints, so *-le* does not usually occur on them. However, atelic situations can become bounded temporally when temporal endpoints are provided with adverbials or made clear by contexts, and whenever this is the case, *-le* is allowed on them as shown by (4b) and (5b) with duration adverbials, and (5c) with the verb duplicated to indicate the short duration of the event.

(3) a. *Xiaojuan **ai-le** Mingming. (State)
Xiaojuan love-Perf. Mingming.
"Xiaojuan loved Mingming."
b. Xiaojuan ai Mingming **ai-le** **sannian**.
Xiaojuan love Mingming love-Perf.3 years
"Xiaojuan loved Mingming for 3 years."

To summarize, *-le* seems to require a boundary to license its presence. There are two kinds of boundaries: 1) a boundary that is inherent in a situation in the form of a result, an outcome or a change of state; and 2) a boundary that is provided by delimiting elements such as a temporal phrase (such as *sannian* "three years" in (3b); a quantity

---

[3] The following abbreviations are used: Perf. = perfective marker; Imp. = imperfective marker; Exp.=experiential perfective marker; Cl. = classifier; Mod. = modifier marker.

[4] Stative verbs in Chinese may occur in sentences that present change of states. Whenever this is the case, we have "derived non-statives", or [+telic] situations (Smith, 1994). *-Le* is possible and necessary in derived non-statives.

[5] However, there is a special kind of Achievements, the so-called [verb+completive morpheme] verb compound, in which *-le* is quite often rendered unnecessary by the completive morpheme.

phrase (such as: *yici* "once") or the verb duplication mechanism (such as: *zouzou* "walk a little" in. The first type of boundary is just what is captured by the telic feature and its function has been well documented in literature on aspect. The function of the second type of boundary to close off events temporally has also been recognized in literature (Comrie, 1976; Depraetere, 1995; Depraetere & Reed, 2000; Jackendoff, 1991; Xiao & McEnery, 2004; Yang, 1995, 1999, 2011). Despite their differences, both types of boundaries license the presence of *-le* alike.

Besides the aspectual constraints on the occurrence of *-le*, there are also some syntactic, phonological, and discoursal constraints on the occurrence of *-le*. These constraints and their effect on the acquisition of *-le* deserve discussion of a full-length paper, but as this is not the focus of the paper, we will not discuss them here.

2.2 The Special Features of *-Zhe*

-Zhe in Chinese is an imperfective marker, but it is neither the same as the imperfective aspect in Russian nor the same as the English progressive form. *-Zhe*, the Russian imperfective and the English progressive all provide a partial/imperfective view of a situation, but they represent three different subtypes of the imperfective aspect, emphasizing different meaning components of imperfectivity. The Russian imperfective simply presents a partial view of a situation and it is available for all types of situations (Smith, 1997, 231). The English progressive form emphasizes the on-goingness of process, so it occurs freely on all dynamic and durative situations (Activities and Accomplishments) but seldom occurs on Statives or Achievements, which do not involve process (Carlson, 1977; Smith, 1997; Vendler, 1967).[6] However, the major function of *-zhe* in Chinese is to provide a static view of a situation, so it usually occurs with homogeneous situations, which are more likely to be viewed as states, rather than with heterogeneous situations. Accomplishments consist of incremental processes leading to realization of results or outcomes (Dowty, 1977) and Achievements emphasize the achievement of results. Both are not homogeneous and hard to be viewed as states, so *-zhe* usually does not occur on them (Yang, 1995).[7]

(4) *Xiaojuan ying-zhe yichang bisai.
Xiaojuan win-Imp. a-Cl. Game
?"Xiaojuan is winning a game."
(Achievement)

A special type of Accomplishments indicating placement of some objects, like *gua* "hang", *fang* "place", often occur in the so-called existential sentences with *-zhe*. These sentences present existential states resulting from the placement action rather than the placement action itself, so they should be regarded as derived Statives.

(5) qiang-shang gua-zhe yi-fu hua
wall-on hang-Imp. a-Cl. painting
"A painting hangs on the wall."

Statives and Activities are both homogeneous, and in principle both types are compatible with the meanings of *-zhe*. However, as Statives are already stative by nature, there is usually no need for *-zhe* to occur on them. *-Zhe* is necessary only when the truth of a state during a particular period of time is emphasized. As stage-level Statives are more prone to change than individual-level Statives (Smith, 1994), there are more chances for *-zhe* to occur on stage-level Statives.

-Zhe may occur more freely with Activities. Activity-*zhe* clauses do not emphasize on-going process; they mainly present a static view of an Activity like (6), or an accompanying action viewed as a concomitant state like the one in (7).

(6) wo yizhi zai wu-li **zuo**-zhe
I all time at house-in sit-Imp.
"I have been sitting in the house all the time."
(Static view of an Activity)

(7) Ta **xiao**-zhe zou-le jin lai.
He/she smile-Imp. walk-Perf. in come
"He/she walked in smiling."
(An Activity viewed as a concomitant state of an action)

[6] A Stative or an Achievement takes the progressive form in special circumstances when the transitory nature of a Stative or the preliminary stage of achieving the result is emphasized.

[7] Accomplishments can occur in *zhe ... ne* structure, a very special structure that emphasizes the unavailability of the entities preoccupied in the event. Also, for some speakers, *-zhe* may be acceptable in some Accomplishments, for example: *Ta zai xie- zhe xin* "He is writng a letter." However, the several native speakers we have consulted agree that the more natural choice would be *Ta zai xie xin* without *-zhe*.

The restricted occurrence pattern of *-zhe* has also been observed by Xiao & McEnery. (2004, p. 188). Their study of native Chinese corpora data shows that *-zhe* occurs most frequently on Activities (55.46%) and stage-level Statives (26.89%). Occasionally it also occurs on individual-level Statives (15.13%). However, it is extremely rare on Accomplishments (1.68%) and never occurs on Achievements.

2.3 The Present Study

Comparing the restricted occurrence patterns of *-le* and *-zhe* and the claims of Aspect Hypothesis, we see striking coincidences: 1) the natural occurrence of *-le* chiefly on [+telic] situations corresponds to the learners' early tendency of restricting past marking to [+telic] situations as generalized in Claim 1 of the Aspect Hypothesis; 2) the native use of *-zhe* chiefly on Activities and on some Statives coincides partially with learners' early use of the imperfective past and the progressive as described in Claim 2 and Claim 3 of the Aspect Hypothesis.

Considering the differences between Chinese and English and the coincidences between the natural occurrence patterns of *-le*, *-zhe* and learners' early tendencies, immediate questions we would like to ask are: Will the Aspect Hypothesis obtain in the acquisition of Chinese? What impact will typological differences have on the generally observed acquisition tendencies? These are the questions the present study aims to answer. By answering the questions, the study will contribute to our understanding of universal language principles and the impact of typological differences on the principles.

3. Method

3.1 Data and Participants

The data for our study were taken from the 1,300,000-word L2 Chinese Learners' Interlanguage Corpus developed by the Beijing Language and Culture University (BLCU hereafter). The corpus contains essays (free production) written by students with various first language backgrounds and of different proficiency levels (Chen, 1998).

As the Corpus encodes 23 properties, including text type, L1, semester level, topic, home country, age, etc. (Chen, 1998), we could easily limit our selection of data to narrative essays and our selection of learners to those whose L1 was English. Professor Chen at the BLCU helped us extract 15 full-text narrative essays for each of our 4 proficiency levels from the corpus.

Levels	No. of essays	Total No. of sentences	Total No. of clauses	past	present	No. of characters per sentence
Beginning	15	217	323	194	129	17
Lower Inter.	15	440	756	361	395	23
Upper Inter.	15	383	765	466	299	25.6
Advanced	15	391	710	362	348	40
Total	60	1431	2554	1383	1171	N/A

Table 1: Summary of the data information

3.2 Data Processing

To obtain a clear idea how *-le* and *-zhe* should be and are actually used by the students, we tagged and sorted out the following four types of information: 1) number of situations where *-le* or -*zhe* is required; 2) number of situations where *-le* or *-zhe* is appropriately supplied; 3) number of situations where *-le* or *-zhe* is not needed but nevertheless used (over-use); and 4) number of situations where *-le* or *-zhe* is needed but not supplied (under-use).

4.Results

Before we look at each of the two aspect markers in detail, we present the overall pattern of required *–le* and *–zhe* in our data.

	Total no. of clauses	*-le* required	*-zhe* required	Total
Present	1171	2 (0.17%)	12	14
Past	1383	232 (17%)	36 (2%)	268
Total	2554	234 (9%)	48 (1.9%)	282 (11%)

Table 2: Overall pattern of required *–le* and *-zhe*.

In sharp contrast to English and many other European languages, in which tense-aspect marking is obligatory, only a small portion of the clauses in our data require the presence of one of the aspect markers.[8] Even for the 1383 clauses that present past situations, only 17% of them require the perfective marker *–le* and about 2% of them require the imperfective marker *–zhe*.

4.1 -Le and Aspectual Properties of Situations

Of the two aspect markers examined, *-le* has greater number of occurrences and the situation with *-le* is the most complicated, so we start our discussion with *-le*.

Before we look at the relationship between lexical aspect and *-le*, we will have a quick look at violations of syntactic, phonological and discoursal constraints on *-le*. We found 23 *-le*s in syntactical environments that do not allow the presence of *-le* (Beginning: 5; Lower Intermediate: 6; Upper Intermediate: 8; Advanced: 4), 5 *-le*s that violate the phonological constraints (Beginning: 1; Lower Intermediate: 1; Upper Intermediate: 2; Advanced: 1), and 7 *-le*s that affect the flow of discourse (Beginning 1; Lower Intermediate 6). As syntactic, phonological and discoursal constraints are not the focus of the present research, we will not discuss violations of them in detail here.

-Le may indicate completion or anteriority of situations of different temporal locations, but in real language use, it is mostly found in clauses that describe past time situations. Of the 1171 present/future time clauses, only 2, an Achievement and an Activity with a provided boundary, require *-le*. Students appropriately provided both of the required *-le*s. There are a few over-use cases and no cases of under-use are found in the present/future time clauses. As there is so little to say about present/future time clauses, we will focus our attention on clauses that present past time situations in the following discussion.

Before we examine the details of the relationship between situation types and *-le* at different levels, we will have a look at a brief summary to get some overall ideas.

Situation Types	Total	*-Le* Required	Appropriately. Supplied	Over-use	Under-use
Statives	475	2 (0.4%)*	2 (100%)**	10	0
Activities	195	28 (14%)	25 (89%)	9	3
Accomplishments	287	84 (30%)	75 (87%)	0	9
Achievements	305	118 (39%)	107 (90%)	0	11
Modal/Negation	121	0 (0%)	0	2	0
Total	**1383**	**232**	**209**	**21**	**23**

Table 3: Summery of the relationship between situation types and *-le*

Total = Total number of situations of that type in past time contexts.

*The percentage of *–le*s required over the total number of situations.

**The percentage of appropriately supplied *–le*s over the number of *–le*s required.

From the table, we can make the following important observations:

1) Most of the situations that require *–le* are supplied with *–le* appropriately;
2) Over-use cases are mostly found on Statives and Activities;
3) Under-use cases are mostly found on Accomplishments and Achievements. There are also a few under-use cases on Activities.

It seems that our learners do not have serious problems with appropriately supplying the marker *–le* whenever it is needed. However, there are indeed some over-use and under-use cases. To see how students develop their knowledge of *-le*, we have a breakdown of the figures at different proficiency levels in the following table.

[8] The other minor aspect markers are even rarer than these two.

Sit. / -le / Levels	*Statives*			*Activity*			*Accomplishment*			*Achievement*			*Modal /Negative*		
	RE/AS	*OV*	*UN*	*RE/AS*	*OV*	*UN*	*RE/AS*	*OV*	*UN*	*RE/AS*	*OV*	*UN*	*RE/AS*	*OV*	*UN*
Beginning	*0/0*	*1*	*0*	*9/7 (78%)*	*4*	*2*	*16/12 (75%)*	*0*	*4*	*19/14 (74%)*	*0*	*5*	*0/0*	*1*	*0*
L. Inter.	*1/1 (100%)*	*5*	*0*	*6/5 (83%)*	*1*	*1*	*17/13 (77%)*	*0*	*4*	*28/24 (86%)*	*0*	*4*	*0/0*	*1*	*0*
U. Inter.	*1/1 (100%)*	*2*	*0*	*5/5 (100%)*	*1*	*0*	*22/21 (96%)*	*0*	*1*	*43/41 (95%)*	*0*	*2*	*0/0*	*0*	*0*
Advanced	*0/0*	*2*	*0*	*8/8 (100%)*	*3*	*0*	*29/29 (100%)*	*0*	*0*	*28/28 (100%)*	*0*	*0*	*0/0*	*0*	*0*
Total	***2/2***	***10***	***0***	***28/25***	***9***	***3***	***84/75***	***0***	***9***	***118/107***	***0***	***11***	***0/0***	***2***	***0***

Table 4 *The relationship between situation types and -le at different levels*

RE=required; AS=appropriately supplied; OV=over-use cases; UN=under-use cases

From Table 4, we can make the following observations:

1). For States, only two *–le*s are required. Under-use is not likely. The over-use problem seems persistent. There are 2 over-use cases even at the highest level.

2). For Activities, increasingly high percentages of the required *le*s are appropriately supplied (78% ⇒ 85% ⇒ 100% ⇒ 100%). There are both under-use and over-use cases. In comparison, the problem of over-use is more persistent. Even at the highest level, there are 3 over-use cases.

3). For Accomplishments and Achievements, there is no over-use case for all levels, although there are some under-use cases at the Beginning, the Lower Intermediate and the Upper Intermediate levels. The rates of appropriate use steadily go up from the lower levels to higher levels.

4.2 Lexical Aspect and –Zhe

Much fewer *-zhe*s are used in our data. In all the 2554 clauses (including both past time and present/future time clauses), only 48 *-zhe*s are required. Of the 48 contexts that require *-zhe*, 45 are appropriately provided. There are only 3 cases when *-zhe* is needed but not supplied.

Sit. / -zhe / Levels	St.(1)		St.(2) (Exist.)		Act.		Accomp.		Achiev.		Total	
	AS	OV	AS	OV	AS	OV	AS	OV	AS	OV	AS	OV
Beginning	0	0	0	0	1	0	0	0	0	0	**1**	**0**
L. Inter.	1	0	3	0	5	0	0	2	0	0	**9**	**2**
U. Inter.	3	0	8	0	16	1	0	3	0	0	**27**	**4**
Advanced	3	0	1	0	4	0	0	0	0	0	**8**	**0**
Total	**7**	**0**	**12**	**0**	**26**	**1**	**0**	**5**	**0**	**0**	**45**	**6**

Table 5 Situation types and *- zhe*

From Table 5, we can see: 1) *-zhe* mostly occurs on Activities (26 out of 51 or 51%); 2) there are also quite a few occurrences of *-zhe* on Statives (7 out of 51 or 14%) and existential clauses (12 out of 51 or 24%), 3) the few over-use errors are mostly found on Accomplishments (5 out of 51 or 9.8%).

5 Discussion

5.1 Lack of Under-use of the Perfective Marker -Le on Statives and Activities

In our learners' interlanguage, *-le* is used mostly on Accomplishments and Achievements and only a few occurrences of *-le* are found on Activities and Statives. This pattern corresponds exactly to the universal learner tendency described by Claim 1 of the Aspect Hypothesis that learners tend to restrict perfective past marking to Achievements and Accomplishments. In the acquisition of English and many other languages, this tendency is undesirable because it leads to low suppliance of past marking on Statives and Activities when past marking is needed. However, most of the errors our L2 Chinese learners make with Statives and

Activities are just the opposite: using the perfective marker *-le* when it is not needed. In other words, the problem predicted by Claim 1 is UNDER-USE of the perfective marking on Statives and Activities and the L2 learners of Chinese display no UNDER-USE of the perfective marking on these situation types due to the fact that *-le* is usually NOT required on situations without boundaries. The learners even show a slight tendency of OVER-USING perfective marking on Statives and Activities as a result of transferring their L1 past marking pattern into the use of *–le*.

5.2 -Le and the Relevance Principle

The natural occurrence pattern of *-le* reflects a natural tendency in morphological attachment that has been formulated by Bybee (1985) as the Relevance Principle. The tense-aspect morphemes or markers are attached to verbs, which are classified into four aspectual classes according to their inherent semantic features: [±telic], [±puctual], and [±dynamic] (Smith, 1991). As Andersen (1991) pointed out, these features are closely related to the meanings of tense-aspect inflections or markers.

The perfective marker *-le* provides an entirety view of a situation, so it has the most direct relevance to [+punctual] and [+telic] situations (Achievements) because punctual and telic situations happen and finish in an instant and are therefore the most likely to be viewed in their entirety. Next to Achievements in degree of relevance to the entirety meaning are Accomplishments, which contain inherent natural endpoints and are also highly likely to be viewed in their entirety. Activities do not contain any natural outcomes or results, so they are not directly relevant to the meaning of the perfective viewpoint. However, Activities, no matter how long they last, do come to an end at a certain point of time. As this endpoint does not correspond to a natural result or outcome inherent in a situation, Smith (1997) uses the term "arbitrary temporal endpoint" to refer to it. When there is such an arbitrary temporal endpoint, an Activity can be viewed in its entirety too. Statives may last for an indefinite period of time until a change takes place, so they are the least relevant to the meaning of the perfective viewpoint. However, they can also be viewed in their entirety when a change takes place at a certain point of time. If we view the four aspectual classes in terms of a continuum from the most relevant to the least relevant to the perfective meaning, we can obtain a scale like the one in (16). The occurrence of *-le* is naturally restricted to the relevant classes as the two solid lines indicate.

(8) Natural occurrence pattern of the Chinese perfective *-le*

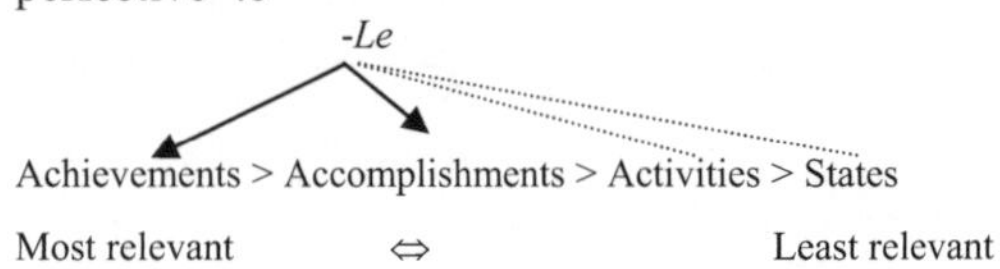

Activities and States can be made relevant to perfective marking by provided endpoints or contexts. When such is the case, the use of *-le* can be extended to Activities and Statives.

The natural occurrence pattern of *-le* seems to follow Bybee's Relevance Principle (1985) closely. If Bybee's principle is truly universal, it should be observed in other languages too. As we have mentioned, perfective meaning in English is most commonly expressed by the simple past, which may go with all types of situation to produce closed/entirety readings. How is Bybee's Relevance Principle observed in English? If we compare *–le* marked sentences in Chinese and past marked sentences in English, we cannot help but notice one big difference, that is: the English simple past indicates a past time location but *–le* does not have the function of locating a situation in time. We argue that it is this difference that leads to the differences in the occurrence patterns of *–le* and the English simple past. The past location indicated by the English simple past in fact provides an arbitrary temporal endpoint to any situation it marks. We assume that this is the reason why the perfective past can be used on verbs of all types in English:

(9) Natural occurrence pattern of the English perfective past

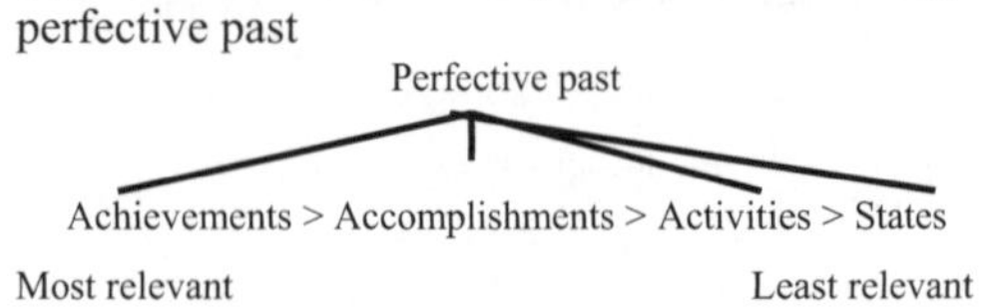

In other words, the Relevance Principle is also observed in English but in a different way.

Now, we can see that the natural occurrence pattern of *-le* in Chinese and the beginning learners' restricted use of perfective past described by Claim 1 reflect the same natural tendency predicted by Bybee's Relevance Principle. The crucial difference between the acquisition of the Chinese *-le* and the acquisition of the perfective past in English and many other European languages is: the spread of *-le* to Activities and Statives is conditional and subject to certain constraints in Chinese, but the expansion of the past perfective marking to the less relevant classes is obligatory in English and many other European languages. When obligatory spread is required in a language, the learners of this language, constrained by the Relevance Principle, will display under-use of the perfective past marking on Statives and Activities. Whereas in a language like Chinese, the spread of the perfective marking to Statives and Activities is conditional and exceptional, so L2 learners do not have much chance to under-use the perfective marking on these two types of situations. On the contrary, their L1 habit of using the perfective marking on Statives and Activities may be transferred into their use of *-le*, causing a totally different kind of errors: over-using the perfective marker.

5.3 -Zhe and the Relevance Principle

Open-ended ([-telic]) and [+durative] situations (Statives and Activities) are more likely to be viewed in part and arc thcrcforc morc rclcvant to the basic meaning of the imperfective aspect. Accomplishments are [+durative] and also have relevance. Achievements are not durative and so have the least relevance. The beginning learners' tendency of restricting simple imperfective marking to Statives and Activities is direct reflection of the relevance relationship.

What is interesting is: different subtypes of the imperfective aspect reflect the relevance relationship in different ways.

(10) Natural occurrence pattern of the Chinese imperfective *-zhe*

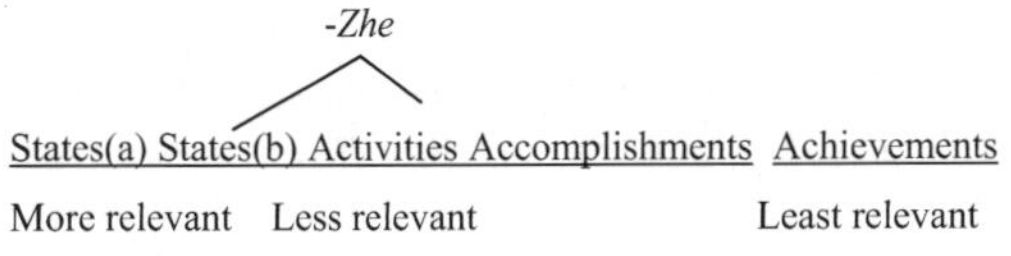

The English progressive emphasizes the on-goingness of events, so it can occur on all durative and dynamic situations, namely all Activities and Accomplishments:

(11) Natural occurrence pattern of the progressive form in English

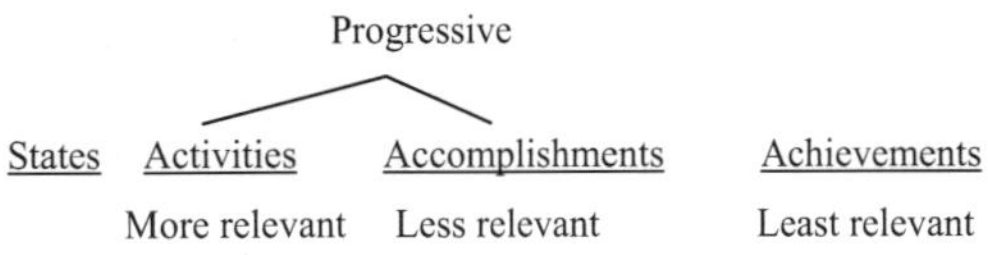

Comparing the three subtypes of the imperfective aspect, we can see that *-zhe* more strictly follows the Relevance Principle than the Russian imperfective and the English progressive.

In our data, we find that L2 Chinese learners use *-zhe* mostly on Activities and secondly on States and there are also some occurrences of the marker on Accomplishments. The learners do not extend the use of *-zhe* to Achievements.

The L2 learner's *-zhe* use pattern only partially matches the native use pattern of the marker because there is non-native use of the marker on Accomplishments and this seems to result from negative transfer of the use of the English progressive form into Chinese. The learner's use pattern is closer to the learners' early tendencies describe by Claim 2 (learners tend to restrict imperfective marking to Statives and Activities) and Claim 3 (learners tend to restrict progressive marking to Activities), with the exception of the few over-use cases on Accomplishments.

The natural occurrence pattern of *-zhe* and the learners' early tendencies of restricting the imperfective to Statives and Activities and the progressive to Activities also reflect the same natural language tendencies predicted by Bybee's Relevance Principle. The crucial difference between the acquisition of *-zhe* and the acquisition of the imperfective in Russian or the progressive in English is that the spread of *-zhe* to less relevant situations, Accomplishments and Achievements is not necessary while the expansion of the imperfective or the progressive to these two types of situations is required.

6.Conclusion

First, We have shown that a natural language principle, the Bybee's Relvevance Principle, can be observed either overtly and directly or covertly and indirectly, the occurrence pattern of the Chinese *-le* being an example of the former and the use of the English perfective past being an example of the latter. This difference may render a natural tendency (restricting perfective past marking to Accomplishments and Achievements) undesirable or desirable in the acquisition process. When it is undesirable (as in English), we observe under-use of the perfective marking on States and Activities. When it is desirable (as in Chinese), under-use is highly unlikely and we may even observe over-use of the perfective marking on Statives and Activities as a result of other factors like L1 transfer. In accordance with this finding of ours, Claim 1 of the Aspect Hypothesis can be modified into:

(13) Learners first use (perfective) past marking on Achievements and Accomplishments, eventually extending its use to Activities and Statives if the expansion is obligatory in the language being acquired.

The added "if" clause implies that languages differ in allowing or disallowing the expansion of the perfective past marking to Activities and Statives.

Second, we have also shown that different languages may have different subtypes of the imperfective viewpoint, emphasizing different meaning components of the imperfectivity (simple partial view, progressive focus, static view, etc.). The different emphases relate to the Relevance Principle in different ways. When we compare the three subtypes, we see that *-zhe* follows the Relevance Principle more closely. That is why learners' early tendencies (restricting the imperfective to Statives and Activities and the progressive to Activities) are also desirable rather than undesirable in the acquisition of *-zhe*, because it is not necessary for the use of *-zhe* to spread to Accomplishments or Achievements. In accordance with our findings, we would like to add a new claim to the original Claim 2 and Claim 3:

(14) In languages that have subcategories of the imperfective viewpoint, variations of 2 (Claim 2) and 3 (Claim 3) can be found depending on what imperfective meanings are emphasized by a particular subcategory.

Although we have made some modifications to the Aspect Hypothesis, we feel it very important to emphasize that the *-le* and *-zhe* acquisition patterns found in our study do not shake the foundation of the Aspect Hypothesis. They only show that undesirable tendencies of learners can become desirable in the acquisition of a language in which the tendencies are just what are overtly required.

Selected References

Andersen, R. W., & Shirai, Y. (1996). The primacy of aspect in first and second language acquisition: The pidgin-creole connection. In W. C. Ritchie and T. K. Bhatia (Eds.), *Handbook of second language acquisition* (pp. 527-570). San Diego, CA: Academic Press.

Bardovi-Harlig, K. & D. W. Reynolds (1995). The role of lexical aspect I the acquisition of tense and aspect. *TESOL Quarterly 29*, 107-131.

Bardovi-Harlig, K. (1998). Narrative structure and lexical aspect. *Studies in Second Language Acquisition, 20*, 471-508.

Bickerton, D. (1981). *Roots of language*. Ann Arbor, MI: Raroma.

Bybee, J. (1985). Morphology. Amsterdam and Philadelphia: John Benjamins.

Comrie, B. F. (1976). *Aspect*. Cambridge: Cambridge University Press.

Robison, R. E. (1995). The aspect hypothesis revisited: A cross-sectional study of tense and aspect marking in interlanguage. *Applied Linguistics, 16*, 344-370.

Shirai, Y. (1991). *Primacy of aspect in language acquisition: Simplified input and prototype*. Unpublished doctoral dissertation, University of California, Los Angeles.

Shirai, Y. & Andersen, R. W. (1995). The acquisition of tense-aspect morphology: A prototype account. *Language, 71*, 743-762.

Smith, Carlota A. (1997) *The Parameter of Aspect* (2nd ed.), Dordrecht: Kluwer Academic Publishers.

Vendler, Z. (1967). Verbs and times. In Z. Vendler (Ed.), *Linguistics in Philosophy*. Ithaca: Cornell University Press.

Verkuyl, H. J. (1989). Aspectual classes and aspectual compostition. *Linguistics and philosophy, 12*, 39-94.

Yang, Suying (1995). The aspectual system of Chinese. Unpublished doctoral Dissertation, University of Victoria.*linguistics* (pp. 369-386). Taipei: The Crane Publishing Co. Ltd.

Yang, Suying (2011). The parameter of temporal endpoint and the basic function of –le. Journal of East Asian Linguistics, *20*, 383-415.

Readability of Bangla News Articles for Children

Zahurul Islam and Rashedur Rahman
AG Texttechnology
Institut für Informatik
Goethe-Universität Frankfurt
zahurul@em.uni-frankfurt.de, kamol.sustcse@gmail.com

Abstract

Many news papers publish articles for children. Journalists use their experience and intuition to write these. They might not aware of readability of articles they write. There is no evaluation tool or method available to determine how appropriate these articles are for the target readers. In this paper, we evaluate difficulty of Bangla news articles that are written for children.

1 Introduction

News is the communication of selected information on current events (Shirky, 2009). This communication is shared by various mediums such as *print*, *online* and *broadcasting*. A *newspaper* is a printed publication that contains news and other informative articles. There are many *newspapers* that are also published online. Due to the rapid growth of internet use, it is very common that more people read news online nowadays than before. Newspapers try to target certain audience through different topics and stories. Children are also in their target audience. This target group is their future reader.

Nowadays children also read news online. One third of children in developed countries such as *Netherlands*, *United Kingdoms* and *Belgium* browse internet for news (De Cock, 2012; De Cock and Hautekiet, 2012). Another study by Livingstone et al. (2010) showed that one fourth of the British children between age of *nine* and *nineteen* look for news on the internet. The ratio could be similar in other developed countries where most of the citizen have access over the internet.

The number of internet users also increasing in developing countries such as Bangladesh and India. According to the English Wikipedia[1], more than *thirty three* million people in Bangladesh use internet and many of them read news online. Also the *Alexa index*[2] shows that three Bangla news sites are in the list of ten most visited websites from Bangladesh.

All newspapers contain a variety of sections. These sections are based on different news topics. Some of the them are specific to children. The news for children will vary linguistically and cognitively than news for adults. This characteristic is similar to the websites dedicated for children. De Cock and Heutekiet (2012) observed difficulties for children to navigate these websites. Readability of the texts is one of the reasons. There is no specific guideline for writing texts for this target group. Journalists use their experience and intuition while writing. However, a text that is very easy to understand for an adult reader could be very difficult for a child. This difficulty motivate children readers to skip the newspaper in future.

The readability of a text relates to how easily human readers can process and understand a text. There are many text related factors that influence the readability of a text. These factors include very simple features such as type face, font size, text vocabulary as well as complex features like grammatical conciseness, clarity, underlying semantics and lack of ambiguity. Nielsen (2010) recommended font size of 14 for young children and 12 for adults.

[1]http://en.wikipedia.org/wiki/Internet_in_Bangladesh
[2]http://en.wikipedia.org/wiki/Alexa_Internet

Copyright 2014 by Zahurul Islam and Rashedur Rahman
28th Pacific Asia Conference on Language, Information and Computation pages 309–317

Readability classification, is a task of mapping text onto a scale of readability levels. We explore the task of automatically classifying documents based on their different readability levels. As an input, this function operates on various statistics relating to different text features.

In this paper, we train a readability classification model using a corpus compiled from textbooks and features inherited from our previous works Islam et al. (2012; 2014) and features from Sinha et al. (2012). Later we use the model to classify Bangla news articles for children from different well-known news sources from Bangladesh and West Bengal.

The paper is organized as follows: Section 2 discusses related work. Section 3 describes cognitive model of children in terms of readability followed by an introduction of the training corpus and news articles in Section 4. The features used for classification are described in Section 5, and our experiments and results in Section 6 are followed by a discussion in Section 7. Finally, we present our conclusions in Section 8.

2 Related Work

Most of the text readability research works use texts for adult readers. Only few numbers of related work available that only focus on texts for children. De Belder and Moens (2010) perform a study that transfers a complex text into a simpler text so that the target text become easier to understand for children. They have focused on two types of simplification: *lexical* and *syntactic*. Two traditional readability formulas: *Flesch-Kincaid* (Kincaid et al., 1975) and *Dale-Chall* (Dale and Chall, 1948; Dale and Chall, 1995) are used to measure reading difficulty. De Cock and Heutekiet (2012) performed a usability study to analyze websites for children. The study uses texts from different websites published in *English* and *Dutch*. The usability experiment shows that *previous knowledge* of children play an important role to read and understand texts. They have used *Flesch-Kincaid* (Kincaid et al., 1975) to determine the difficulty level of English texts and a variation of the same formula for Dutch texts.

Both of the related work mentioned above use traditional readability formulas to measure text difficulty. However these traditional formulas have significant drawbacks. These formulas assume that texts do not contain noise and the sentences are always well-formed. However this is not the case always. Traditional formulas require significant sample sizes of text, they become unreliable for a text that contains less than 300 words (Kidwell et al., 2011). Si and Callan (2001), Peterson and Ostendorf (2009) and Feng et al. (2009) show that these traditional formulas are not reliable. These formulas are easy to implement, but have a basic inability to model the semantic of vocabulary usage in a context. The most important limitation is that these measures are based only on surface characteristics of texts and ignore deeper properties. They ignore important factors such as comprehensibility, syntactical complexity, discourse coherence, syntactic ambiguity, rhetorical organizations and propositional density of texts. Longer sentences are not always syntactically complex and counting the number of syllables of a single word does not show word difficulty. That is why, the validity of these traditional formulas for text comprehensibility is often suspect. Two recent works on Bangla texts use two of these traditional formulas. Das and Roychudhury (2004; 2006) show that readability measures proposed by Kincaid et al. (1975) and Gunning (1952) work well for Bangla. However, the measures were tested only for seven documents, mostly novels.

Since there are not many linguistic tools available for Bangla, researchers are exploring language independent and surface features to measure difficulty of Bangla texts. Recently, in our previous works, we proposed a readability classifier for Bangla using *information-theoretic* features (Islam et al., 2012; Islam et al., 2014). We have achieved an *F-Score* of 86.46% by combining these features with some lexical features. Sinha et al. (2012) proposed two readability models that are similar to classical readability measures for English. They conducted a user experiment to identify important structural parameters of Bangla texts. These measures are based on the average *word length* (WL), the *number of poly-syllabic words* and the *number of consonant–conjuncts*. According to their experimental results, *consonant–conjuncts* plays an important role in texts in terms of readability.

From the beginning of research on text readability, researchers proposed different measures for

English (Dale and Chall, 1948; Dale and Chall, 1995; Gunning, 1952; Kincaid et al., 1975; Senter and Smith, 1967; McLaughlin, 1969). Many commercial readability tools use traditional measures. Fitzsimmons et al. (2010) stated that the SMOG (McLaughlin, 1969) readability measure should be preferred to assess the readability of texts on health care.

Due to recent achievements in linguistic data processing, different linguistic features are now in the focus of readability studies. Islam et al. (2012) summarizes related work regarding language model-based features (Collins-Thompson and Callan, 2004; Schwarm and Ostendorf, 2005; Aluisio et al., 2010; Kate et al., 2010; Eickhoff et al., 2011), POS-related features (Pitler and Nenkova, 2008; Feng et al., 2009; Aluisio et al., 2010; Feng et al., 2010), syntactic features (Pitler and Nenkova, 2008; Barzilay and Lapata, 2008; Heilman et al., 2007; Heilman et al., 2008; Islam and Mehler, 2013), and semantic features (Feng et al., 2009; Islam and Mehler, 2013). Recently, Hancke et al. (2012) found that morphological features influence the readability of German texts.

Due to unavailability of linguistic resources for Bangla, we did not explore any of the linguistically motivated features. We have inherited features from Islam et al. (2012; 2014) and Sinha et al. (2012), these features achieve reasonable classification accuracy.

Children's reading skills is influenced by their cognitive ability. The following section describes children's cognitive model and text readability.

3 Text Readability and Children

Children start building their cognitive skills from an early age. They use their cognitive skills to perform different tasks in different environments. Kali (2009) stated that children refine their motor skills and start to be involved in different social games when they are 5 to 6 years of age. From age of 6 to 8, children start to expand their vision beyond their immediate surroundings. Children from 8 to 12 years of age acquire the ability to present different entities of the world using concepts and abstract representations. Children become more interested in social interactions in their teenage years.

Children learn to recognize alphabets prior they developed motor skills. This lead to develop their reading skills. Reading skills require two processes: *word decoding* and *comprehension*. *Word decoding* is a process of identifying a pattern of alphabets. Children must have the knowledge about these and their patterns. For example: it is impossible to recognise any word from any language without knowledge of alphabets of that language. A pattern of alphabets carry a semantic in their cognitive knowledge.

Comprehension is a process of extracting meaning from a sequence of words. The sequence of words follow an order. It could be impossible for children to understand a sentence where the order of the words is random. Therefore, *word order* plays an important role in text comprehension. Reading is different than understanding a picture, it extracts meaning from words that are separated by white spaces. The *comprehension* process is also influenced by the memory system.

The cognitive system of humans contains three different memories: *sensory memory*, *working memory* and *long-term memory* (Rayner et al., 2012). The *sensory store* contains raw, un-analyzed information very briefly. The ongoing cognitive process takes place in *working memory* and the *long-term memory* is the permanent storehouse of knowledge about the world (Kali, 2009). Older children sometimes are better where they simply retrieve a word from their memory while reading. A younger children might have to *sound out* of a novel word spelling. However they are also able to retrieve some of the familiar words. Children derive meaning of a sentence by combining words to form *propositions* then combine them get the final meaning. Some children might struggle to recognize words which make them unable to establish links between words. Children without this problem able to recognize words and derive meaning from a whole sentence. Generally, older children are better reader due to their working memory capacity where they can store more of a sentence in their memory as they are able to identify propositions in the sentence (De Beni and Palladino, 2000). Older children are able to comprehend more than younger children because of recognizing ability and more working memory (Kali, 2009). They also know more about the world and skilled to use appropriate reading strategies.

In summary, children become skilled reader as their working memories develop over time, extract propositions and combine them to understand the meaning of a sentence.

4 Data

The goal of this study is to asses difficulty of news articles that are aimed for children. The reading ability of children is very different than adult readers. The preceding section describes cognitive developments of children in terms of readability. A children who is 10 years old will have different reading capability than a children who is 15 years of old. That is why, a corpus that is categorized by the ages of children would be an ideal resource as training corpus. Duarte and Weber (2011) proposed different categories of children based on their ages. The categorized list is relevant with our study. However, our categorized list is still different than their one. The corpus is categorized as following age ranges:

- early elementary: 7 – 9 years old
- readers: 10 – 11 years old
- old children: 12 – 13 years old
- teenagers: 14 – 15 years old
- old teenagers: 16 – 18 years old
- adults: above 18 years old

In this paper, we train a model using support vector machine (SVM). This technique requires a training corpus. We compile the training corpus from textbooks that have been using for teaching in different school levels in Bangladesh. The following subsections describe the training corpus and children news articles.

4.1 Training Corpus

The training corpus targets top four age groups described above. Textbooks from grade *two* to grade *ten* are considered as sources for corpus compilation. Generally, in Bangladesh children start going to schools when they are 6 years of old and finish the grade *ten* when they are fifteen (Arends-Kuenning and Amin, 2004). In our previous studies, Islam et al. (2012; 2014), we compile the corpus from the same source. However, the latest version is more cleaned and contains more documents. It contains texts from 54 textbooks. Table 1 shows the statistics of average *document length* (DL), average *sentence length* (SL) and average word length (WL). Textbooks were written using ASCII encoding which required to be converted into Unicode. The classification distinguishes four readability classes: *very easy*, *easy*, *medium* and *difficult*. Documents of (school) grade *two*, *three* and *four* are included into the class *very easy*. Class *easy* covers texts of grade *five* and *six*. Texts of grade *seven* and *eight* were subsumed under the class *medium*. Finally, all texts of grade *nine* and *ten* are belong to the class *difficult*.

Classes	Docs	Avg. DL	Avg. SL	Avg. WL
Very easy	234	88.28	7.46	5.27
Easy	113	150.46	9.09	5.27
Medium	201	197.08	10.35	5.47
Difficult	113	251.30	12.19	5.66

Table 1: The Training Corpus.

4.2 News Articles

The goal of this paper is observing children news articles in Bangla on the basis of difficulty levels. As an Indo-Aryan language Banga is spoken in Southeast Asia, specifically in present day Bangladesh and the Indian states of West Bengal, Assam, Tripura and Andaman and on the Nicobar Islands. With nearly 250 million speakers (Karim et al., 2013), Bangla is spoken by a large speech community. However, due to lack of linguistic resources Bangla is considered as a low-resourced language.

We collected children news articles from four popular news sites from Bangladesh and one from West Bengal. The sites are: *Banglanews24*[3], *Bdnews24*[4], *Kaler kantho*[5], *Prothom alo*[6] and *Ichchhamoti*[7]. *Banglanews24*, *Bdnews24* and *Ichchhamoti* publish online only. In contrast, *Kalerkantho* and *Prothomalo* publish as printed newspapers and online. These newspapers publish weekly featured articles for children. We have collected 50 fea-

[3] www.banglanews24.com

[4] www.bangla.bdnews24.com

[5] www.kalerkantho.com

[6] www.prothomalo.com

[7] http://www.ichchhamoti.in/

tured articles from each of the sites and pre-process in similar way as the training corpus. However, the news articles are already written in Unicode and cover different topics ranges from *family*, *society*, *science* and *history* to *sports*. Table 2 shows different statistics of news articles.

News sites	Average DL	Average. SL	Average WL
Banglanews24	50.14	9.48	5.04
Bdnews24	62.66	9.82	4.91
Kaler kantho	53.08	8.90	4.89
Prothom alo	47.92	9.15	4.89
Ichchhamoti	105.50	11.86	4.66

Table 2: Statistics of news articles.

5 Feature Selection

A limited number of related works available that deal texts from Bangla. All of them are limited into traditional readability formulas, lexical and information-theoretic features. Any of features do not require any linguistic pre-processing. The following subsections describe feature selection in detail.

5.1 Lexical Features

We inherited a list of lexical features from our previous study Islam et al. (2014). Lexical features are very cheap to compute and shown useful for different text categorizing tasks. Average SL and average WL are two of most used features for readability classification. Recently, Learning (2001) showed that these are the two most reliable measures that affect readability of texts. The average SL is a quantitative measure of syntactic complexity. In most cases, the syntax of a longer sentence is difficult than the syntax of a shorter sentence. However, children of a lower grade level are not aware of syntax. A long word that contains many syllables is morphologically complex and leads to comprehension problems (Harly, 2008). Generally, most of the frequent words are shorter in length. These frequent words are more likely to be processed with a fair degree of automaticity. This automaticity increases reading speed and free-memory for higher level meaning building (Crossley et al., 2008).

Our previous study, Islam et al. (2014) also listed different *type token ratio* (TTR) formulas. The TTR indicates lexical density of texts, a higher value of it reflects the diversification of the vocabulary of a text. The diversification causes difficulties for children. In a diversified text, synonyms may be used to represent similar concepts. Children face difficulties to detect relationship between synonyms (Temnikova, 2012).

5.2 Information-Theoretic features

Nowadays, researchers exploring uncertainty based features from the field of *information theory* to measure complexity in natural languages (Febres et al., 2014). Information theory studies statistical laws of how information can be optimally coded (Cover and Thomas, 2006). The entropy rate plays an important role in human communication in general (Genzel and Charniak, 2002; Levy and Jaeger, 2007). The rate of information transmission per second in a human speech conversation is roughly constant, that is, transmitting a constant number of bits per second or maintaining a constant entropy rate. The entropy of a random variable is related to the difficulty of correctly guessing the value of the corresponding random variable. In our previous studies, Islam et al. (2012; 2014) and Islam and Mehler (2013) use different information-theoretic features for text readability classification. Our hypothesis was that the higher the entropy, the less readable the text along the feature represented by the corresponding random variable. We have inherited seven information-theoretic features from our previous studies.

5.3 Readability Models for Bangla

Recently, Sinha et al. (2012) proposed few computational models that are similar to the traditional English readability formulas. A user study was performed to evaluate their performance. We also inherited two of their best performing models:

$$Model3 = -5.23 + 1.43 * AWL + .01 * PSW \quad (1)$$

$$Model4 = 1.15 + .02 * JUK - .01 * PSW30 \quad (2)$$

In their models, they use structural parameters such as average WL, *number of jukta-akshars* (JUK) or consonant-conjuncts, *number of polysyllabic words* (PSW). The PSW30 shows that normalized value of PSW over 30 sentences.

Features	Accuracy	F-Score
Model 3	56.61%	49.13%
Model 4	56.38%	52.51%
Together	66.27%	65.67%

Table 3: Performance of Bangla readability models proposed by Sinha et al. (Sinha et al., 2012).

In this paper, we use 20 features to generate feature vectors for the classifier. The following section describes our experiments and results on training corpus and news articles.

6 Experiments and Results

In order to find the best performing training model, we use 20 features from Islam et al. (2012; 2014) and Sinha et al. (2012). Note that hundred data sets were randomly generated where 80% of the corpus was used for training and remaining 20% for evaluation. The weighted average of *Accuracy* and *F-score* is computed by considering results of all data sets. We use the SMO (Platt, 1998; Keerthi et al., 2001) classifier model implemented in WEKA (Hall et al., 2009) together with the Pearson VII function-based universal kernel PUK (Üstün et al., 2006).

6.1 Training Model

The traditional readability formulas that were proposed for English texts do not work for Bangla texts (Islam et al., 2012; Islam et al., 2014; Sinha et al., 2012). That is why, we did not explore any of the traditional formulas.

At first we build a classifier using two readability models from Sinha et al(2012). The output of these models are used as input for the readability classifier. Table 3 shows the evaluation results. The classification accuracy is little over than 66%. In our previous study Islam et al. (2014) found better classification accuracy using these features. However, the corpus is slightly different. The latest version of the corpus contains more documents for *easy* readability class. The classifier miss-classifies documents from this class mostly. The classifier labeled many of the documents from this readability class as *very easy*. Miss-classification of documents from other readability classes are also observed.

Table 4 shows the performance of features proposed in our previous study Islam et al. (2014).

Features	Accuracy	F-Score
Average SL	61.53%	55.21%
TTR (sentence)	47.32%	41.31%
TTR (document)	53.84%	52.61%
Average DW (sentence)	54.69%	55.28%
Number DW (document)	62.56%	60.12%
Avg. WL	44.63%	40.82%
Corrected TTR	59.38%	54.31%
Köhler TTR	54.61%	49.61%
Log TTR	47.49%	43.30%
Root TTR	60.76%	52.49%
Deviation TTR	52.32%	47.83%
Word prob.	60.76%	54.49%
Character prob.	50.00%	47.13%
WL prob.	51.58%	46.40%
WF prob.	52.30%	47.80%
CF prob.	60.76%	52.18%
SL and WL prob.	62.30%	59.74%
SL and DW prob.	66.92%	63.09%
18 features proposed by Islam et al. (2014)	85.60%	84.46%

Table 4: Performance of features proposed by Islam et al. (2014).

The classification accuracy also drops. The classifier also suffer to classify documents from *easy* readability class correctly. However, information-transmission based features (i.e., SL and WL prob. and SL and DW prob.) are the best performing features. Therefore, a text with higher average SL become more difficult when it contains more difficult words or more longer words.

The classification F-Score rises to 87.87 when we combine features from Islam et al. (2014) and Sinha et al. (Sinha et al., 2012).

6.2 News Articles Classification

Total 250 children news articles are collected as candidate news articles for classification. We consider the whole training corpus in order to build a training model. The training model is used to classify the candidate news articles. Among all articles, 160 articles are labeled as *very easy* and 18 articles as *easy*. Only 2 articles are labeled as *difficult* and remaining 60 articles are labeled as *medium*. Figure 1 shows classification results. More than 60% of news articles from newspapers are classified as *very easy*. However, the amount drops below 20% for the articles from *Icchamoti* children magazine. Also articles labeled as *difficult* belong to this magazine. The evaluation shows that, among all of the newspapers, news from *Banglanews24* are more suitable for children. Most of articles from that site belong to *very*

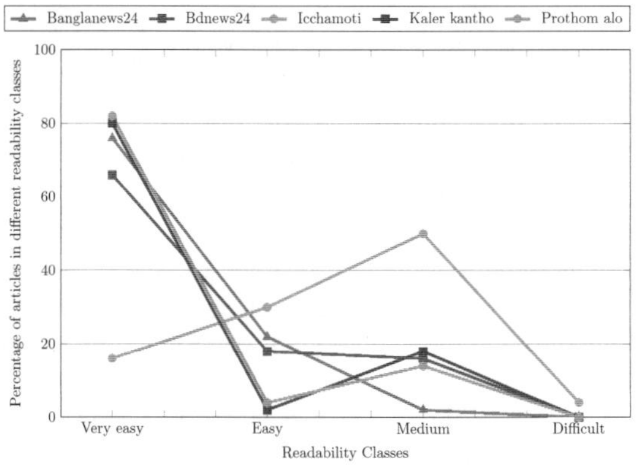

Figure 1: Classification of Bangla news articles for children.

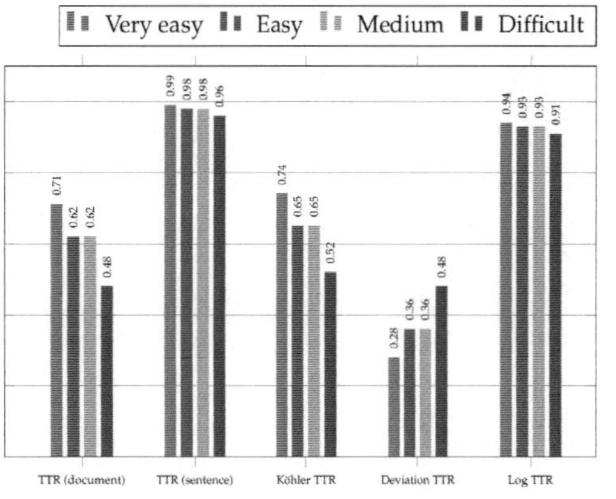

Figure 2: Observation of different TTR formulas in classified news articles.

easy and *easy* readability class.

Apart from the classification of children news articles we are also interested in behavior of different features in classified articles. The following section describes from interesting observation we notice.

7 Observation

Articles from Ichchhamoti has the lowest average WL. But, have higher values for average DW and average SL. Two of the articles from this site are labeled as *difficult*. This labeling could be influenced by average DW and average SL. Documents from training corpus have higher average WL.

Among the lexical features different TTRs have been considered to measure text difficulty (Islam et al., 2014). An article with a higher TTR value supposed to be difficult that an article with a lower TTR value (See Section 5.1). However, we observe different behavior of TTR formulas. Figure 2 shows the behaviour of different TTR formulas in classified articles. The average TTR value of articles from *very easy* readability class is higher than the average TTR value of articles from higher difficulty classes. Article length could be the reason of this irregularity. Articles from higher difficulty classes are longer and contain more words.

We also observed that some articles which have lower average SL, but labeled as *medium*. In contrast, some articles that have higher average SL, but labeled as *very easy* or *easy*. We randomly choose such articles and observe average SL. The average SL of articles belong to *medium* is 7.40 and the average SL of articles belongs to *easy* or *very easy* is 12.08. However, articles that are labeled as *medium* have higher average *word entropy* than articles that are labeled as *easy* or *very easy*. This shows that different type of features should be considered together to build a readability classifier.

8 Conclusion

In this paper, our goals was to examine the difficulty levels of news articles targeting children. Therefore we build a readability classifier that is able to classify the corresponding news articles into different difficulty levels. Children news articles are cognitively and linguistically different than articles for adult readers. A readability classifier trained on a textbooks corpus is able to classify these articles. Although linguistically motivated features could capture linguistic properties of news articles. Lexical features and features related to information density also have good predictive power to identify text difficulties. The classification results show that candidate articles are appropriate for children. This study also validate that features in our previous study Islam et al. (2014) and features proposed by Sinha et al. (Sinha et al., 2012) are useful for Bangla text readability analysis.

There are many languages in the world which lack a readability measurement tool. A readability classifier for these language could be built by using the features proposed in our previous study Islam et al.

(2014).

9 Acknowledgments

We like to thank Prof. Dr. Alexander Mehler for arranging money to travel the conference. We also like to thank the anonymous reviewers for their helpful comments. This work is funded by the LOEWE Digital-Humanities project at Goethe-University Frankfurt.

References

Ra Aluisio, Lucia Specia, Caroline Gasperin, and Carolina Scarton. 2010. Readability assessment for text simplification. In *NAACL-HLT 2010: The 5th Workshop on Innovative Use of NLP for Building Educational Applications*.

Mary Arends-Kuenning and Sajeda Amin. 2004. School incentive programs and childrens activities: The case of bangladesh. *Comparative Education Review*, 48(3):295–317.

Regina Barzilay and Mirella Lapata. 2008. Modeling local coherence: An entity-based approach. *Computational Linguistics*, 21(3):285–301.

Kevyn Collins-Thompson and James P Callan. 2004. A language modeling approach to predicting reading difficulty. In *HLT-NAACL*.

Thomas M. Cover and Joy A. Thomas. 2006. *Elements of Information Theory*. Wiley-Interscience, Hoboken.

Scott A Crossley, Jerry Greenfield, and Danielle S McNamara. 2008. Assessing text readability using cognitively based indices. *Tesol Quarterly*, 42(3):475–493.

Edgar Dale and Jeanne S. Chall. 1948. A formula for predicting readability. *Educational Research Bulletin*, 27(1):11–20+28.

Edgar Dale and Jeanne S. Chall. 1995. *Readability Revisited: The New Dale-Chall Readability formula*. Brookline Books.

Sreerupa Das and Rajkumar Roychoudhury. 2004. Testing level of readability in bangla novels of bankim chandra chattopodhay w.r.t the density of polysyllabic words. *Indian Journal of Linguistics*, 22:41–51.

Sreerupa Das and Rajkumar Roychoudhury. 2006. Readabilit modeling and comparison of one and two parametric fit: a case study in bangla. *Journal of Quantative Linguistics*, 13(1).

Jan De Belder and Marie-Francine Moens. 2010. Text simplification for children. In *Prroceedings of the SIGIR workshop on accessible search systems*, pages 19–26.

Rossana De Beni and Paola Palladino. 2000. Intrusion errors in working memory tasks: Are they related to reading comprehension ability? *Learning and Individual Differences*, 12(2):131–143.

Rozane De Cock and Eva Hautekiet. 2012. Childrens news online: Website analysis and usability study results (the united kingdom, belgium, and the netherlands). *Journalism and Mass Communication*, 2(12):1095–1105.

Rozane De Cock. 2012. Children and online news: a suboptimal relationship. quantitative and qualitative research in flanders. *E-youth: Balancing between opportunities a risks*.

Sergio Duarte Torres and Ingmar Weber. 2011. What and how children search on the web. In *Proceedings of the 20th ACM international conference on Information and knowledge management*, pages 393–402. ACM.

Carsten Eickhoff, Pavel Serdyukov, and Arjen P. de Vries. 2011. A combined topical/non-topical approach to identifying web sites for children. In *Proceedings of the fourth ACM international conference on Web search and data mining*.

Gerardo Febres, Klaus Jaffé, and Carlos Gershenson. 2014. Complexity measurement of natural and artificial languages. *Complexity*.

Lijun Feng, Noémie Elhadad, and Matt Huenerfauth. 2009. Cognitively motivated features for readability assessment. In *Proceedings of the 12th Conference of the European Chapter of the ACL*.

Lijun Feng, Martin Janche, Matt Huenerfauth, and Noémie Elhadad. 2010. A comparison of features for automatic readability assessment. In *The 23rd International Conference on Computational Linguistics (COLING)*.

PR Fitzsimmons, BD Michael, JL Hulley, and GO Scott. 2010. A readability assessment of online parkinsons disease information. *The Journal of the Royal College of Physicians of Edinburgh*, 40:292–296.

Dimitry Genzel and Eugene Charniak. 2002. Entropy rate constancy in text. In *Proceedings of the 40st Meeting of the Association for Computational Linguistics (ACL 2002)*.

Robert Gunning. 1952. *The Technique of clear writing*. McGraw-Hill; Fourh Printing Edition.

Mark Hall, Eibe Frank, Geoffrey Holmes, Bernhard Pfahringer, Peter Reutemann, and Ian H. Witten. 2009. The WEKA data mining software: an update. *ACM SIGKDD Explorations*, 11(1):10–18.

Julia Hancke, Sowmya Vajjala, and Detmar Meurers. 2012. Readability classification for german using lexical, syntactic and morphological features. In *24th International Conference on Computational Linguistics (COLING), Mumbai, India*.

Trevor A. Harly. 2008. *The Psychology of Language*. Psychology Press, Taylor and Francis Group.

Michael Heilman, Kevyn Collins-Thompson, and Maxine Eskenazi. 2007. Combining lexical and grammatical features to improve readavility measures for first and second language text. In *Proceedings of the Human Language Technology Conference*.

Michael Heilman, Kevyn Collins-Thompson, and Maxine Eskenazi. 2008. An analysis of statistical models and features for reading difficulty prediction. In *Proceedings of the Third Workshop on Innovative Use of NLP for Building Educational Applications (EANL)*.

Zahurul Islam and Alexander Mehler. 2013. Automatic readability classification of crowd-sourced data based on linguistic and information-theoretic features. In *14th International Conference on Intelligent Text Processing and Computational Linguistics*.

Zahurul Islam, Alexander Mehler, and Rasherdur Rahman. 2012. Text readability classification of textbooks of a low-resource language. In *Proceedings of the 26th Pacific Asia Conference on Language, Information, and Computation.*

Zahurul Islam, Md Rashedur Rahman, and Alexander Mehler. 2014. Readability classification of bangla texts. In *Computational Linguistics and Intelligent Text Processing*, pages 507–518. Springer.

Robert V. Kali. 2009. *Children and Their Development*. Pearson Education.

MA Karim, M Kaykobad, and M Murshed. 2013. *Technical Challenges and Design Issues in Bangla Language Processing*. IGI Global.

Rohit J. Kate, Xiaoqiang Luo, Siddharth Patwardhan, Martin Franz, Radu Florian, Raymond J. Mooney, Salim Roukos, and Chris Welty. 2010. Learning to predict readability using diverse linguistic features. In *23rd International Conference on Computational Linguistics (COLING 2010)*.

S.S. Keerthi, S. K. Shevade, C. Bhattacharyya, and K. R. K. Murthy. 2001. Improvements to Platt's SMO algorithm for SVM classifier design. *Neural Computation*, 13(3):637–649.

Paul Kidwell, Guy Lebanon, and Kevyn Collins-Thompson. 2011. Statistical estimation of word acquisition with application to readability prediction. *Journal of the American Statistical Association*, 106(493):21–30.

J. Kincaid, R. Fishburne, R. Rodegers, and B. Chissom. 1975. Derivation of new readability formulas for Navy enlisted personnel. Technical report, US Navy, Branch Report 8-75, Cheif of Naval Training.

Renaissance Learning. 2001. The ATOS readability formula for books and how it compares to other formulas. *Madison, WI: School Renaissance Institute*.

Roger Levy and T. Florian Jaeger. 2007. Speakers optimize information density through syntactic reduction. *Advances in neural information processing systems*, pages 849–856.

Sonia Livingstone, Leslie Haddon, Anke Görzig, and Kjartan Ólafsson. 2010. Risks and safety for children on the internet: the uk report. *Politics*, 6(2010):1.

G. Harry McLaughlin. 1969. SMOG grading – a new readability formula. *Journal of Reading*, 12(8):639–646.

Jakob Nielsen. 2010. Children's websites: Usability issues in designing for kids. *Jakob Nielsens Alertbox*.

Sarah E. Petersen and Mari Ostendorf. 2009. A machine learning approach to reading level assesment. *Computer Speech and Language*, 23(1):89–106.

Emily Pitler and Ani Nenkova. 2008. Revisiting readability: A unified framework for predicting text quality. In *Proceedings of the Conference on Empirical Methods in Natural Language Processing (EMNLP)*.

John C. Platt. 1998. *Fast training of support vector machines using sequential minimal optimization*. MIT Press.

Keith Rayner, Alexander Pollatsek, Jane Ashby, and Charles Clifton Jr. 2012. *Psychology of Reading*. Psychology Press.

Sarah E. Schwarm and Mari Ostendorf. 2005. Reading level assessment using support vector machines and statistical language models. In *the Proceedings of the 43rd Annual Meeting on Association for Computational Linguistics(ACL 2005)*.

R.J. Senter and E. A. Smith. 1967. Automated readability index. Technical report, Wright-Patterson Air Force Base.

Clay Shirky. 2009. *Here comes everybody: How change happens when people come together*. Penguin UK.

Luo Si and Jamie Callan. 2001. A statistical model for scientific readability. In *Tenth International Conference on Information and Knowledge Management*.

Manjira Sinha, Sakshi Sharma, Tirthankar Dasgupta, and Anupam Basu. 2012. New readability measures for bangla and hindi texts. In *COLING (Posters)*, pages 1141–1150.

Irina Temnikova. 2012. *Text Complexity and Text Simplification in the Crisis Management Domain*. Ph.D. thesis, University of Wolverhampton.

B. Üstün, W.J. Melssen, and L.M.C. Buydens. 2006. Facilitating the application of support vector regression by using a universal Pearson VII function based kernel. *Chemometrics and Intelligent Laboratory Systems*, 81(1):29–40.

Focusing on a Subset of Scripts Enhances the Learning Efficiency of Second Language Writing System

Ching-Pong Au
Community College of City University
6/F, AC2, City University of Hong Kong,
Tat Chee Avenue, Kowloon Tong, Hong Kong
chingpau@cityu.edu.hk

Yuk-Man Cheung
Hong Kong Baptist University
SCE, 2/F, Franki Centre, 320 Junction Road
Kowloon Tong, Hong Kong
cheungym@hkbu.edu.hk

Charles Chen, Jr.
The Hong Kong Polytechnic University
Hung Hom, Kowloon, Hong Kong
ctchen@polyu.edu.hk

Abstract

Memorizing the whole set of graphemes is generally accepted as the first step of learning a phonogramic language. However, it is demanding for L2 learners to familiarize the whole inventory of graphemes in advance if the language has a relatively large inventory size. We propose that learning a subset of graphemes would largely enhance the learning efficiency by reducing the memory burden. With homophony minimized, effort of acquiring vocabulary in elementary stage can be greatly reduced. In this paper, the writing system of Thai is used to illustrate the main idea. Besides, the method may also be extendable to Japanese and Korean, which grapheme inventory sizes are smaller.

1 Introduction

There is a general assumption in many language textbooks that L2 learners are able to comprehend and produce scripts of any second language just because they have acquired the reading and writing ability in their first language. However, different processes and strategies are actually involved in L1 and L2 writing systems (L1WS and L2WS) and should not be ignored by the learning material designers or the language teachers (Bassetti, 2006). English is an international language learnt globally by most people and textbooks of English are perhaps the most convenient model being imitated by textbooks of other languages for L2 learners. In the first lesson of learning a L2WS, the first thing that comes to our mind is the 26 letters. Therefore, learning how to read and write kana and hangul are expected in the first chapter of Japanese or Korean textbooks, because they function like the 26 letters of English as the most basic building blocks in the writing system (WS, hereafter).

Although it may take some time for learners to "swallow" graphemes like kana or hangul, it is not a daunting task for most people to master (at least to recognize) them well enough for general usage. However, there are also WSs which are less "learner-friendly" – Thai WS is one of them. In Hong Kong, we observed through classroom teaching that many L2 learners of Japanese or Korean can memorize kana or hangul reasonably well within weeks or even days; while L2 learners of Thai tend to give up learning to read and write for good, and confine their learning to verbal language.

In the present thesis, we propose that (1) WSs that have relatively large inventory size could be learnt more efficiently through reordering the learning sequence; (2) the usage frequencies of the basic writing units are important criteria for deciding on the learning sequence; (3) learning materials designed for L2WS adult learners should be different from those for L1WS children learners, as two groups have had different experience before they learn the target WS.

In our discussions in this paper, we would like to take learning Thai scripts as an illustration for

Copyright 2014 by Ching-Pong Au, Yuk-Man Cheung, and Charles Chen, Jr.
28th Pacific Asia Conference on Language, Information and Computation pages 318–327

the concept. In section 2, some properties of the Thai WS are compared with those of other languages. In section 3, the Thai WS (symbols for consonants, vowels and tones) will be briefly introduced and the difficulties faced by L2 learners will also be highlighted. Functional approach seems to be a more effective way for learners to acquire Thai WS. Based on the estimated usage frequencies of each consonant letter from an online dictionary, an optimized learning sequence is proposed in section 4. In the earliest steps of the sequence, beginners are recommended to restrict themselves to only a subset of consonant letters. They should not start learning the other remaining letters before they are highly familiarized with the subset in the context of basic daily life vocabularies. Each Thai consonant has a name to disambiguate the homophonic consonant letters. In section 5, we will explain why the names are burdens to foreign learners although it may be helpful to native Thai children to remember the consonant letters. In section 6, the method proposed is applied to Japanese and Korean. Finally, an overall conclusion will be drawn in section 7.

2 Comparing the Writing Systems

To measure a WS, there are 10 useful properties: inventory size, complexity, frequency, ornamentality, distinctivity, variability, phonemic load, grapheme size, grapheme load and letter utility, according to Altmann (2008). In some of the above properties, "L(etter)", "G(rapheme)" and "P(honeme)" are carefully distinguished in the definition of the properties. Letters refer to the basic writing units of a language, such as the 26 letters in English; Graphemes are the units that can minimally distinguish the meanings in writing. For example, "ph" in "phone" is a grapheme as it makes contrast with "z" in the word "zone". Phonemes are the phonological units that can minimally distinguish the meanings in speech. For example, in English, there are 24 consonant phonemes (see Altmann and Fan, 2008: 151-154 for details).

Some of the above properties are useful guidelines for us to optimize the learning path for second language learners. In this section, some properties of Thai WS are compared with those of other languages in order to see why Thai scripts are more difficult to learn than other phonogramic languages.

In terms of graphemes, Thai has a larger G-inventory size than Korean hangul and Japanese kana, than English letters. However, its G-inventory size is certainly much smaller than those of logograms such as Chinese characters or Japanese kanji.

Among the properties, grapheme load and phonemic load are the measures of how many graphemes a letter can represent and of how many phonemes a letter/grapheme can represent. However, to estimate the burden of learning L2WS, grapheme load and phonemic load are not sufficient. Phonological transparency is another parameter to examine the difficulty of a WS. The English WS is much less transparent than the Japanese kana. For example, "a" in English can represent /aː/ in "father", /æ/ in "bat", /ɔː/ in "ball", etc. and not all of them can be predicted, but Japanese kana is almost totally transparent because it is almost a one-to-one mapping system, with only a small number of exceptions (Cook and Bassetti, 2005: 7-10). With this concept, the grapheme-phoneme transparency in Thai should be quite similar to Japanese kana and Korean hangul, but much more predicable than English and the logogramic systems including Chinese character and Japanese kanji. Although Thai graphemes are as predictable as hangul and kana, the rules predicting the phonemes from the letters are far more complicated than the two. As you will see in section 3.3, not all diphthongs are direct combinations of the corresponding monophthongs and glides. Moreover, to predict tones accurately, the tone marks, open or closed syllables, types of initial consonants ("high class", "mid class" or "low class"), types of final consonants (sonorants or obstruents) and vowel lengths (long or short) all play roles as the phonic rule conditions.

3 The Writing System of Thai Language

To understand the difficulties learners face in learning Thai WS, a brief introduction will be given in this section. Thai WS consists of 44 letters for consonants, 18 symbols for vowels and 4 tone marks (For more comprehensive descriptions, see Diller, 1996).

Obviously, Thai WS have three main properties that make learning it a more difficult task than learning kana or hangul:

(1) The G-inventory size is large and many homophones are in the consonant system;
(2) Complicated phonic rules are required to predict the actual tone value of each syllable.
(3) The forms of vowels vary under different phonological conditions and not all diphthongs are direct combinations smaller units.

3.1 Inventory Size and Homophony

Due to phonological changes in history, some consonants which were distinctive in the past became homophones in the modern Thai (Smalley, 1994: 194-195; Diller, 1996). In many cases, the original written forms are still in use nowadays despite the sound changes.

	1	2	3	4	5	6	7	8	9	10
	M	M	H	H	L	L	L	L	L	L
Vel		ก	ข	ฃ	ค	ฅ	ฆ	ง		
		k	k^h	k^h	k^h	k^h	k^h	ŋ		
Pal		จ	ฉ	ศ	ช	ซ	ฌ	ญ	ย	
		tɕ	$tɕ^h$	s	$tɕ^h$	s	$tɕ^h$	j	j	
Ret	ฎ	ฏ	ฐ	ษ	ฑ		ฒ	ณ	ร	ฬ
	d	t	t^h	s	t^h		t^h	n	r	l
Den	ด	ต	ถ	ส	ท		ธ	น		ล
	d	t	t^h	s	t^h		t^h	n		l
Lab	บ	ป	ผ	ฝ	พ	ฟ	ภ	ม	ว	
	b	p	p^h	f	p^h	f	p^h	m	w	
Glo		อ		ห		ฮ				
		ʔ		h		h				

Figure 1: Consonant Letters in Thai[1]

In the consonant chart (figure 1), the IPA below each script is its actual phoneme at syllable initial position in modern Thai, but the columns represent manners of articulation and the features of aspiration and voicing in historical sense:

[1] It is controversial whether อ should be transcribed as a glottal stop, as glottal stop seems not to be contrastive with zero (See Noss 1964; Harris, 2001 for details).

- Columns 1&2: Unaspirated, unvoiced obstruents
- Columns 3&4: Aspirated, unvoiced obstruents
- Columns 5&6: Unaspirated, voiced obstruents
- Column 7: Aspirated, voiced obstruents
- Column 8: Nasals
- Column 9: Approximants (and Trills)
- Column 10: Lateral approximants

It is important to highlight that, in modern Thai, consonants in Columns 3, 5 and 7 all changed to aspirated, unvoiced stops or affricates as shown in IPA, although the columns had aspiration and/or voicing contrasts before. Consonants (fricatives in the past) in Column 6 were also devoiced.

On the other hand, in the consonant chart, different places of articulation: vel(ar), pal(atal), ret(roflex), den(tal), lab(ial) and glo(ttal) are classified into six rows. It can be easily observed that the rows 'ret' and 'den' had merged completely. All in all, a lot of homophones arise from the mergers in the dimensions of manners, places, aspiration and/or voicing. Homophony is one of the sources that make Thai WS complicated.

3.2 Complicated Phonic Rules for Tones

In figure 1, the consonants are divided into three groups. They are traditionally named "Mid class", "High class" or "Low class", based on the voicing and aspiration properties of the consonants:

- Mid class (M, hereafter) consonants include those which were historically unaspirated, unvoiced obstruents (i.e. Column 1 & 2). Consonants in Column 1 are unaspirated, voiced in modern Thai, but it was sprung from Column 2;
- High class (H, hereafter) consonants include aspirated, unvoiced obstruents (i.e. Columns 3&4);
- Low class (L, hereafter) consonants include all voiced consonants (Columns 5-10) in the past inventory, although Columns 5-7 are currently unvoiced in modern Thai.

One of the major functions of the M-H-L classification is to be part of the conditions of the phonics rules for tones. It is not surprising for voicing/aspiration correlating with tones as many similar phenomena can be found in sound changes of various Chinese dialects and other languages.

Thai language has five tones. They are called "mid-level tone", "low tone (tone 1)", "falling tone (tone 2)", "high tone (tone 3)" and "rising tone (tone 4)". The tone values are 33, 21, 41, 45, 14 respectively. (Remark: The "high", "mid" and "low" in tones and H, M, L consonants are totally two different concepts.)

Thai WS has four symbols to mark tones. They are put above the initial consonant (if a vowel occupies the place, the mark is put above the vowel). The phonic rules for tones are listed in table 1. Among the three types of consonants, the rules for M consonants are the easiest to remember: ่, ้, ๊ and ๋ are tones 1, 2, 3 and 4 respectively; "live" syllables without tone mark is tone M; dead syllables without tone mark is tone 1. The rules for H and L consonants are more complicated. (see table 1).

	"Live" Syl. w/o tone mark	"Dead" Syl. w/o tone mark	่	้	๊	๋
Mid	M	1	1	2	3	4
Low	M	2/3	2	3		
High	4	1	1	2		

Table 1: Phonic Rule for Thai Tones[2]

In Open Syllable			In Closed Syllable		
อี i:	อือ ɯ:	อู u:	อีน i:n	อืน ɯ:n	อูน u:n
เอ e:	เออ ɤ:	โอ o:	เอน e:n	เออน ɤ:n	โอน o:n
แอ ɛ:	อา a:	ออ ɔ:	แอน ɛ:n	อาน a:n	ออน ɔ:n

In Open Syllable			In Closed Syllable		
อิ i	อึ ɯ	อุ u	อิน in	อึน ɯn	อุน un
เอะ e	เออะ ɤ	โอะ o	เอ็น en	เอิน ɤn	อน on
แอะ ɛ	อะ a	เอาะ ɔ	แอ็น ɛn	อัน an	อ็อน ɔn

Figure 2: Combinations Representing Vowels

[2] A "live" syllable is one (1) with only a long vowel as rime or (2) with a nasal consonant as final, while a "dead" syllable is one (1) with only a short vowel as rime or (2) with stop consonant as final.

3.3 Inconsistency in Written Forms of Vowels and Diphthongs

In figure 2, vowels (in black) can be represented by a combination of one to three components (อ in grey is an initial consonant; น in grey is a final consonant). For long vowels (upper matrixes of figure 2), patterns in open and closed syllables are almost identical except /ɯ:/, which requires an extra อ in an open syllable. However, cases of short vowels (lower matrixes) are rather inconsistent. Non-high short vowels are completely different between open (lower, left) and closed (lower, right) syllables.

Besides, some diphthongs are irregular (figure 3), although the majority of larger units are combined with the smaller units:

(1) diphthong = monophthong + glide;
(2) triphthong = /-a/ diphthong + glide.

Diphthongs written in other combinations

ใอ	ไอ	ไอย	เอา
aj/a:j	aj	aj	aw

/-a/ Diphthongs in other symbols/combinations

เอีย	เอือ	อัว
ia	ɯa	ua

Figure 3: Irregular Combinations

4 A Usage-based Approach in Design

As Thai has a relatively large inventory size, a good learning sequence would help improving the learning efficiency. In this section, we intend to look for the optimized learning sequence by considering the usage frequencies of the consonant letters.

4.1 Measuring Usage Frequencies

In our research, the entries of the 44 Thai consonant letters in a Thai-English online dictionary (http://www.thai-language.com) were counted. Based on the numbers of entries, the consonant letters were reordered from most to least entries. Figure 4 shows the numbers of entries (in logarithmic scale, base 10), and a significant drop can be detected after the 31st letter. It is obvious that the numbers of entries in the dictionary count only the words with the letters as word initial. However, the data are still sufficient to estimate the relative usage frequencies, in order to reveal the "usefulness" of the letters for the learning material design.

4.2 Grouping and Reordering Consonants

In order to look for a desirable learning sequence, the phonological nature of the letters was examined. Learning high frequency letters in the early stage will let learners utilize the WS as early as possible. However, simply adopting the most-to-least sequence as the learning sequence would make the learning process unordered and not systematic. It would not be easy for learners to remember the letters. Therefore, besides the usage frequencies, forming phonologically-correlated subsets are also important criteria for a good learning sequence.

According to the finding in figure 4, the consonant letters can be primarily divided into two subsets based to their usage frequencies: high on the left and low on the right in figure 5. In order to seek for phonologically-correlated subsets, the information about the phonological origin of the letters in figure 1 is also extracted and listed in two tables. The first observation from the left table is that all phonemes (including the zero initial, อ) can all be found. Besides the fricatives (/f/, /s/ and /h/) and the aspirated obstruents (/k^h/, /p^h/, /t^h/ and /ts^h/), all other letters are not repeated in the left table. The repeated ones are only either H or L consonants. Comparing the repeated letters as shown in table 2, it is obvious that letters in high usage frequencies all come from Columns 3-6 in figure 1 (H3, H4, L5 and L6). Therefore, it is quite reasonable to put the three letters: ภ(24th), ศ(28th) and ธ(29th) to later stages of the learning sequence.

Consonant	Rank / MOA		
k^h	2/L5	> 12/H3	
p^h	10/L5	> 16/H3	> 24/L7
t^h	11/L5	> 22/H3	> 29/L7
ts^h	14/L5	> 25/H3	
f	26/L6	> 31/H4	
s	3/H4	> 23/L6	> 28/H4
h	8/H4	> 30/L6	

Table 2: Ranking of Corresponding Consonants

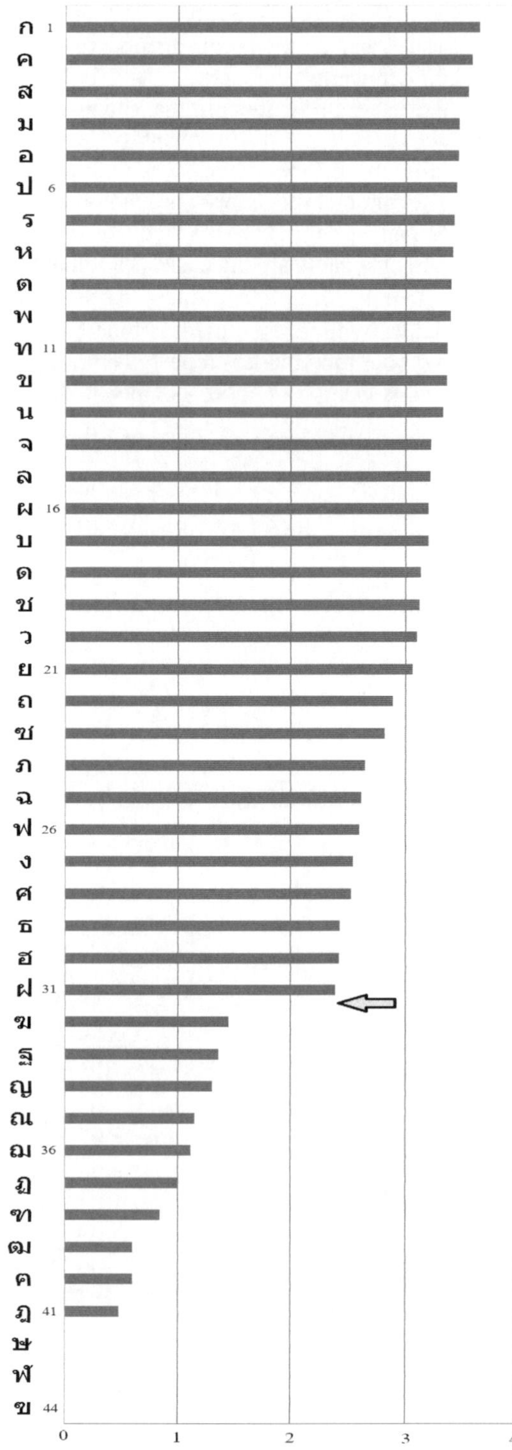

Figure 4: No. of Entries for Each Thai Consonant in a Thai-English Online Dictionary

Cons.	IPA	POA	MOA	Rank
ก	k	1_VEL	M2	1
ค	k^h	1_VEL	L5	2
ส	s	4_DEN	H4	3
ม	m	5_LAB	L8	4
อ	ʔ	6_GLO	M2	5
ป	p	5_LAB	M2	6
ร	r	3_RET	L9	7
ห	h	6_GLO	H4	8
ต	t	4_DEN	M2	9
พ	p^h	5_LAB	L5	10
ท	t^h	4_DEN	L5	11
ข	k^h	1_VEL	H3	12
น	n	4_DEN	L8	13
จ	ts	2_PAL	M2	14
ล	l	4_DEN	L10	15
ผ	p^h	5_LAB	H3	16
บ	b	5_LAB	M1	17
ด	d	4_DEN	M1	18
ช	ts^h	2_PAL	L5	19
ว	w	1_VEL	L9	20
ย	j	2_PAL	L9	21
ถ	t^h	4_DEN	H3	22
ซ	s	2_PAL	L6	23
ภ	p^h	5_LAB	L7	24
ฉ	ts^h	2_PAL	H3	25
ฟ	f	5_LAB	L6	26
ง	ŋ	1_VEL	L8	27
ศ	s	2_PAL	H4	28
ธ	t^h	4_DEN	L7	29
ฮ	h	6_GLO	L	30
ฝ	f	5_LAB	H4	31

Cons.	IPA	POA	MOA	Rank
ฆ	k^h	1_VEL	L7	32
ฐ	t^h	3_RET	H3	33
ญ	j	2_PAL	L8	34
ณ	n	3_RET	L8	35
ฌ	ts^h	2_PAL	L7	36
ฏ	t	3_RET	M2	37
ฑ	t^h	3_RET	L5	38
ฒ	t^h	3_RET	L7	39
ฅ (crossed out)	k^h	1_VEL	L6	40
ฎ	d	3_RET	M1	41
ษ	s	3_RET	H4	42
ฬ	l	3_RET	L0	43
ฃ (crossed out)	k^h	1_VEL	H4	44

Cons. : Consonant letter
IPA: IPA transcription of letters in modern Thai
POA: Place of Articulation that the letter was in the past
MOA: Manner of Articulation that the letter was in the past
Rank: Ranking of letters from highest to lowest frequency

Figure 5: Usage Frequencies of Thai Consonants

After removing ภ, ศ and ธ, we still have to choose between the two sets of homophones in the first two columns of table 2, in order to form a complete set of 21 letters, containing all contrastive phonemes. There are three reasonable choices:

(1) The set with highest frequencies regardless of their phonological properties:
2/L5, 10/L5, 11/L5, 14/L5, 26/L6, 3/H4, 8/H4;
(2) The set with all L consonants:
2/L5, 10/L5, 11/L5, 14/L5, 26/L6, 23/L6, 30/L6;
(3) The set with all H consonants:
12/H3, 16/H3, 22/H3, 25/H3, 31/H4, 3/H4, 8/H4.

As mentioned before, choice (1) may not be proper because mixing H and L consonants may cause confusion, as syllables have different tones. Between two choices with consistent consonant types, choice (2) sounds more preferable than choice (3), not only because it has a higher average ranking, but also other non-repeated letters in the left table of figure 5 belong to either M or L consonants. If we opt for choice (2), learners are only required to deal with the phonic rules for M and L consonants at the beginning stage and leave H consonants to later stages. Besides, one more advantage for choice (2) is that loanwords from English are mainly written in L and/or M consonants, although some H consonants are also occasionally used in loanwords. It is advantageous for most foreign learners to recognize the letters and gasp the first bunch of vocabularies rapidly through these déjà vu.

After deciding the earlier stages, what remains are ภ, ศ and ธ and the 13 letters in the right table of figure 5. The two /k^h/s ranked 40th and 44th are officially replaced by /k^h/s ranked 2nd and 12th respectively and are no longer in use in modern Thai. They are certainly the last step, if the learners insist to learn. A general observation from the remaining 14 is that, except /s/ ranked 28th and /j/ ranked 34th, all others belong to either "L7" or "retroflex". Although we now know the fact that rare letters are aspirated, voiced obstruents and/or retroflex consonants, it is not necessary for the learners to know them unless they are interested in the historical linguistics of Thai. As the usage frequencies are very low compared to the 28 consonant letters in the left table of figure 5, learners even do not need to border whether they are M, H or L. It seems more reasonable to memorize the entire word or phrase with the pronunciation as a whole, while learners may or may not occasionally come across a couple of them in the whole life. This process resembles people learning Chinese characters or other logogramic languages.

However, among the 14 low frequency letters, some of them are actually more useful than others, regardless of their phonological properties. Some letters may not be used in many words but they do appear in a few high frequency ones. For instance, they can be found in the following words:

(1) /k^h/ 32nd in "kill", "cloud", etc.
(2) /t^h/ 29nd in "she", "flag", etc.
(3) /p^h/ 24th in "language", "greedy", etc.
(4) /n/ 35th in "you", "Mr/Ms", "father", "mother", etc.
(5) /j/ 34th can be found in "big", "Japan", etc.
(6) /s/ 28th "country", etc.
(7) /s/ 42nd in "sorry", "language", etc.

Learners can learn these letters after they are familiarized with the 28 letters in the left table of figure 5. At this stage, taking the /n/ 35th as an example, learners can be told, "ณ is another form of น. It is only used in some specific words and the /n/ in /k^{h}un/ "you" is one of them, using ณ."

To summarize, table 3 lists our proposed learning sequence. Learning subsets 1 and 2 is similar to learning a WS of a phonogramic language with a small inventory size, while learning subsets 3, 4 and 5 is similar to learning a WS of a logogramic language.

Subset 1 (21 letters)	No homophones. All are M or L consonants	กจดตบปอ
		คชทพ/ซฟฮ /งนม/วยรล
Subset 2 (7 letters)	All are H consonants	ขฉถผ/สฝห
Subset 3 (7 letters)	Other consonants in high frequency words	ฆธภณญศษ
Subset 4 (7 letters)	Other consonants in low frequency words	ฎฏฐฑฒฌฬ
Subset 5 (2 letters)	Not used in modern Thai	ฅฃ

Table 3: Proposed Learning Sequence

4.3 Learning Sequence of Vowels

To enhance the learning efficiency, the learning sequence of vowels should also be reordered. Although it can be based on the relative usage frequencies in a similar way as the consonants, simply doing the same thing for vowels can be problematic in the considerations of pedagogy. There are two more important aspects we have to consider further.

First, besides the usage frequencies of the symbols, the simplicity of words' meanings is other important concerns. It is much easier for beginners to pick up basic words with simpler meanings at the beginning. Words with high usage frequency consonants can be easily chosen to form a list of simpler basic words. The same can be done for words with high usage frequency vowels. However, if both criteria of consonants and vowels are applied at the same time, many simple words are eliminated from the list, because words with both high frequency consonant(s) and vowel(s) are not necessarily simple in meaning. One way to deal with the problem is to take usage frequencies of consonants as the primary selection criterion for the learning sequence and those of vowels as a criterion in lower priority.

Second, the complexity of the symbols is another concern. Thai consonants and vowels are both complicated for learners, but their complications are different in nature. Contrast to vowels, the phoneme of a consonant can be represented by different homophonic graphemes and the grapheme-phoneme relationship is unpredictable phonologically. On the other hand, the vowel system is complicated because one single vowel can be represented by a combination of up to three components (e.g. /ɤ/ and /ɔ/ in open syllables are combinations of 3 components, see figure 2). Besides, a component can be used in different vowels (e.g. "เ" can be found in /e/, /eː/, /ɤ/ and /ɤː/, see figure 2). However, the grapheme-phoneme relationship of vowels is rather transparent and predictable.

With the considerations of the complexity of vowel formation, most traditional textbooks tend to introduce, first, monophthongs (long and short), then, diphthongs and finally, triphthongs. We have no objection to taking complexity as a criterion in deciding learning sequence, but we do believe that the relative usage frequency of vowels and the semantic simplicity of the words taught in beginner level should also be important criteria for ordering learning sequence. We now propose a nine-step learning sequence as follows in order to enhance the learning efficiency:

(1) All long monophthongs – Long vowels are almost same in the open and closed syllables, so the learners can acquire them without having a prior knowledge of open and closed syllables.
(2) ใ and ไ (/aj/ or /a:j/): - They are used in many high frequency grammatical words such as wh-question words, negation, modal verbs; They can only be used in open syllable.
(3) Short monophthongs /i/ and /a/ in both open and closed syllables – They are commonly found in many high frequency words; There is only one component in each of these monophthongs; They are basic building blocks of several other short vowels or diphthongs.
(4) Short monophthongs /u/ and /ɯ/ in both open and closed syllables – They are found in a few high frequency words. Although there is only symbol in each of these monophthongs, they are not used as part of other monophthongs.
(5) Other short monophthongs in closed syllables – They are quite common.
(6) Diphthongs in irregular combinations other than the two symbols in (2) – Some words are quite common but the combinations may be harder to remember due to the irregularity.
(7) Diphthongs in regular combinations – They are combinations of (1)/(3)/(4)/(5) and a glide consonant.
(8) Triphthongs in regular combinations – They are combinations of (6) and a glide consonant.
(9) Other short monophthongs in open syllables – They are rarely used in high usage frequency words.

The above list shows a reasonable learning sequence of vowels based on the three parameters:
- relative usage frequency of vowels;
- simplicity in formation of vowels; and
- simplicity in words' meanings.

Vowels with higher usage frequency, fewer components and more simple meaning words are arranged in earlier stages. As subjective judgments have been made on whether the words are appropriate for beginners, some textbook writers or course developers may find a slightly different sequence more suitable when the course is taught in different cultures or to people in various ages.

Learning basic daily life vocabularies together with the letters are very important for reinforcing the memory of orthography. Memorizing the letters in the above order alone without learning the vocabularies are not as effective. The consonant and vowel letters should be learnt in parallel so that vocabularies written in Thai scripts can also be learnt at the same time. For example, at the beginning, some consonants in subset 1 can form simple nouns with long vowels. Then, some simple nouns and verbs formed by more consonants in subset 1 and irregular /aj/s in the following lesson. Learners could "bootstrap", or initiate the acquiring process, more easily, with subsets 1 and 2 plus different vowels or diphthongs until they have learnt a couple hundreds of words. Then, they could proceed to subset 3. They could simply ignore subsets 4 and 5 until they become intermediate or advanced learners.

4.4 Tone Marks and their Phonic Rules

After settling down the consonants and vowels, the next question will be the tone marks and the phonic rules for tones. The L2 learners are recommended to learn the values of the five tones at the very beginning, even earlier than the consonant subset 1.

Instead of learning the phonic rules for tones consciously, the learners are recommended to learn only the relationship between the consonant-vowel spelling and the pronunciation of the whole word. However, the learners should be told that they must remember the tone mark as part of the spelling by heart without linking to its actual pronunciation of tone: "Just treat the tone mark of each syllable as a kind of decoration on one hand, and remember the tone of each syllable on the other hand." The process is similar to the learning of Chinese characters or Japanese kanji. When the learners are building up their lexicon of Thai gradually, the tone mark-toneme correspondence in their minds will emerge in a subconscious way without paying much effort on "calculating" tones syllable by syllable. Since each syllable lasts for several hundred milliseconds in a normal speech, it does not make sense to spend several seconds to calculate the tone of each syllable before reading the text aloud. Memorizing tones and the tone marks separately is also what native speakers do normally. They acquire the tones in their speech by heart from their L1 environment. Later on, when they learn to write, they remember the spellings by heart, although some native speakers may learn a reverse version of table 1 to predict the spellings from the sound of tone.

Some speakers tend to remember written and spoken forms separately when they learn a second language. In a recent study about Cantonese speakers learning Korean as a second language, learners could pronounce hangul spellings more accurately for words than non-words. This indicates that remembering the spoken forms by heart instead of predicting pronunciations from spellings is the main strategy the speakers use (Au and Cheung, 2014). This subconscious strategy is also applicable to people who are learning other more complicated WSs such as Thai.

5 Consonant names are burden to non-native adults

Another advantage of learning only a subset without homophones is to get rid of the names of the Thai consonant letters. Similar to English's "A for apple", "B for boy", "C for cat", Thai children learn the name of each Thai consonant letter, which composes of one consonant-vowel syllable (e.g. /tʰ/ + /ɔː/) and one noun that contains this particular consonant letter:

- ฑ /tʰɔː³³ mon³³ tʰoː³³/ (Ramayana character)
- ฒ /tʰɔː³³ pʰuː⁵¹ tʰaw⁵¹/ (old man)
- ท /tʰɔː³³ tʰa⁴⁵ haːn¹⁴/(soldier)
- ธ /tʰɔː³³ tʰoŋ³³/ (flag)

The nouns help in disambiguating homophonic consonant letters. In the above example, all four letters called /tʰɔː³³/ become distinguishable orally.

As their native language, Thai children have already learnt a certain amount of spoken forms of Thai words at home before learning the written forms in school. They can remember all letters more easily with the letters' names because they have probably acquired some, if not all, sound-meaning relationship of the words such as "old man", "soldier" and "flag". On the contrary, as the letters and the nouns are both new to the foreign learners, the names are in fact extra burdens to the L2 learners. In our proposal, when only one of the four is learnt in the subset 1, learners can simply call ท as /tʰɔː³³/. In subset 2, although there is another /tʰ/, as the tone is different, ถ can be called /tʰɔː¹⁴/ without mentioning its name. In this case, the learning of names can be postponed to later stages of the study after learners gain enough vocabularies and knowledge of Thai culture in order to know the disambiguating names of the letters.

6 Applying to learning of other languages

The concept we propose is also applicable to other languages, although their WSs may not be as complicated as Thai scripts.

Similar to table 3 for Thai WS, Japanese WS can be divided into three subsets:

- subset 1 is hiragara (e.g. あ、い), the basic set of graphemes;
- subset 2 is katakana（e.g.ア、イ), another set of graphemes used mainly for loanwords; and
- subset 3 is kanji, adopted Chinese characters.

To enhance the learning efficiency, instead of teaching both sets of kana (hiragana and katakana) at the start of a beginner course, some teachers may teach hiragana first and postpone the teaching of katakana until learners become more familiar with the hiragana through acquiring large amount of vocabularies. This is a way to reduce the interference between two sets of kana.

In the case of the WS of Korean language, although each phoneme is represented by only one consonant letter in hangul, letters with similar pronunciations and shapes can also be learnt in different stages:

- subset 1 includes ㅂ/p/, ㄷ/t/, ㄱ/k/, ㅈ/tɕ/, ㅅ/s/, ㅎ/h/, ㅁ/m/, ㄴ/n/, ㅇ/ŋ/ and ㄹ/l/;
- subset 2 is the tense consonants ㅃ/p̤/, ㄸ/t̤/, ㄲ/k̤/, ㅉ/tɕ̤/ and ㅆ/s̤/, which are formed by doubling the first five consonant letters in subset 1; and
- subset 3 is the aspirated consonants ㅍ/pʰ/, ㅌ/tʰ/, ㅋ/kʰ/ and ㅊ/tɕʰ/, which have similar shapes as the first four consonant letters in subset 1.
(Remark: The Korean letters are only transcribed phonemically. Phonetic and allophonic details are not included here)

Similarly, learning efficiency can be improved by focusing on only a subset of graphemes at the beginning. Consonants in simpler shapes (subset 1) can be learnt first, with considerable amount of simple vocabularies that are strictly formed by the first ten consonants. After having enough exposure to subset 1, learners can start learning the five tense consonants in subset 2. The phonetic contrasts of the obstruent consonants in the two subsets should also be introduced in this stage. After the learners are familiarized with the 15 consonants under the context of simple words and sentences formed by them, they can proceed to subset 3 and learn the concept of aspiration.

Although all 19 consonant graphemes are phonemically contrastive in Korean language, the three groups of obstruent consonants may not be perceptually or consciously distinctive to many non-native speakers (Au and Cheung, 2014). Therefore, allocating these "pseudo"- homophonic obstruent consonants (e.g. ㅂ, ㅃ and ㅍ) into three different subsets resembles the case of Thai shown in table 3.

In terms of usage frequencies and relatively complexity of grapheme shapes, the tense and aspirated consonants are lower, compared to the other ten consonants. Thus, it should not be difficult for course developers to gather sufficient basic sentence structures and everyday vocabularies for compiling the first few lessons without using subsets 2 and 3.

This arrangement will not only reduce the memory burden of the second language learners at the beginning stages, but also highlight the phonetic contrast among the three groups of obstruent consonants.

7 Conclusion

The present paper tries to demonstrate that the efficiency of a second language WS with a relatively large letter/grapheme inventory size (such as Thai) could be enhanced by separating the large inventory into (at least) two subsets, based on the usage frequencies. The high frequency subset(s) can be learnt early through knowing the grapheme-phoneme correspondence, while the low frequency subset(s) can be learnt in later stages in the way similar to learning a logogramic language (such as Chinese characters), by remembering the spelling and the sound individually.

Theoretically, the learning sequences proposed would improve efficiency and effectiveness of acquiring a new second language writing system, although the actual improvement needs to be substantiated by future researches on students' acceptability and performance.

References

Gabriel Altmann and Fengxiang Fan. 2008. *Analyses of Script: Properties of Characters and Writing Systems*. Mouton de Gruyter.

Ching-Pong Au and Yuk-Man Cheung. 2014. Phonological Tendencies in Korean Spoken by Hong Kong Cantonese Learners. *Proceedings of 5th ICPM*, Gwangju, South Korea, 263-266.

Benedetta Bassetti. 2006. Learning Second Language Writing systems. Centre for Languages, Linguistics and Area Studies, Guide to Good Practice. 29 Nov., 2006. https://www.llas.ac.uk/resources/gpg/2662

Vivian. J. Cook and Benedetta Bassetti. 2005. *Second Language Writing Systems*. Clevedon, UK: Multilingual Matters.

Anthony Diller 1996. Thai and Lao Writing. In P. T. Daniels and W. Bright (eds.). *The World's Writing Systems*, 457-466.

Jimmy G. Harris. 2001. States of the Glottis of Thai Voiceless Stops and Affricates. In M. R. K. Tingsabadh and A. S. Abramson (eds.), Essays in Tai Linguistics. Bangkok: Chulalongkorn University Press.

Richard B. Noss. 1964. *Thai Reference Grammar*. Washington: Foreign Service Institute.

William A. Smalley. 1994. *Linguistic Diversity and National Unity: Language Ecology in Thailand*. Chicago and London: The University of Chicago Press.

Dictionary in http://www.thai-language.com

Transition-based Knowledge Graph Embedding with Relational Mapping Properties

Miao Fan[†,*], Qiang Zhou[†], Emily Chang[‡], Thomas Fang Zheng[†,◇]
[†]CSLT, Tsinghua National Laboratory for Information Science and Technology,
Department of Computer Science and Technology, Tsinghua University, Beijing, 100084, China.
[‡]Emory University, U.S.A.
[*]fanmiao.cslt.thu@gmail.com, [◇]fzheng@tsinghua.edu.cn

Abstract

Many knowledge repositories nowadays contain billions of triplets, i.e. (head-entity, relationship, tail-entity), as relation instances. These triplets form a directed graph with entities as nodes and relationships as edges. However, this kind of symbolic and discrete storage structure makes it difficult for us to exploit the knowledge to enhance other intelligence-acquired applications (e.g. the Question-Answering System), as many AI-related algorithms prefer conducting computation on continuous data. Therefore, a series of emerging approaches have been proposed to facilitate knowledge computing via encoding the knowledge graph into a low-dimensional embedding space. **TransE** is the latest and most promising approach among them, and can achieve a higher performance with fewer parameters by modeling the relationship as a *transitional vector* from the head entity to the tail entity. Unfortunately, it is not flexible enough to tackle well with the various mapping properties of triplets, even though its authors spot the harm on performance. In this paper, we thus propose a superior model called **TransM** to leverage the structure of the knowledge graph via pre-calculating the distinct weight for each training triplet according to its *relational mapping property*. In this way, the optimal function deals with each triplet depending on its own weight. We carry out extensive experiments to compare **TransM** with the state-of-the-art method **TransE** and other prior arts. The performance of each approach is evaluated within two different application scenarios on several benchmark datasets. Results show that the model we proposed significantly outperforms the former ones with lower parameter complexity as **TransE**.

1 Introduction

Many knowledge repositories have been constructed either by experts with long-term funding (e.g. WordNet[1] and OpenCyc[2]) or by crowds with collaborative contribution (e.g. Freebase[3] and DBpedia[4]). Most of them store billions of triplets. Each triplet, abbreviated as (h, r, t), is composed by two entities (i.e the head entity h and the tail entity t), and the relationship r between them. These triplets can form a huge directed graph for each knowledge repository with millions of entities as nodes and thousands of relationships as edges.

Ideally, we can take advantages of these knowledge graphs to enhance many other intelligence-dependent systems, such as Information Retrieval Systems (Wical, 1999; Wical, 2000), Question-Answering Systems (Pazzani and Engelman, 1983; Rinaldi et al., 2003; Hermjakob et al., 2000), etc. However, the graph-based knowledge representation is some kind of rigid. More specifically, this symbolic and discrete storage structure makes it hard for us to exploit great knowledge treasures, as many AI-related algorithms prefer conducting computations on continuous data. Some recent literatures on **Language Modeling** by means of learning *distributed word representation* (Bengio et al., 2003; Huang et al., 2012; Mikolov et al., 2013), have proved that embedding each word into a low-dimensional continuous vector could achieve better performance, because the global context information for each word can be better leveraged in this way. Therefore, in-

[1]http://www.princeton.edu/wordnet
[2]http://www.cyc.com/platform/opencyc
[3]http://www.freebase.com
[4]http://wiki.dbpedia.org

Copyright 2014 by Miao Fan, Qiang Zhou, Emily Chang, and Thomas Fang Zheng
28th Pacific Asia Conference on Language, Information and Computation pages 328–337

spired by the idea of distributed representation, researchers have begun to explore approaches on embedding knowledge graphs and several canonical solutions (Bordes et al., 2011; Bordes et al., 2013b; Bordes et al., 2014a; Socher et al., 2013) have emerged recently to facilitate the knowledge computing via encoding both entities and relationships into low-dimensional continuous vectors which belong to the same embedding space.

Among prior arts, the latest **TransE** is a promising model which can achieve a higher performance than the other previously proposed approaches. Moreover, **TransE** is more efficient because the model holds fewer parameters to be decided, which makes it possible to deploy the algorithm on learning large-scale knowledge graph (e.g. Freebase[5]) embeddings. Unfortunately, it is not flexible enough to tackle well with the various relational mapping properties of triplets, even though Bordes et al. (2013b; 2013a) realize the harm on performance through splitting the dataset into different mapping-property categories, i.e. ONE-TO-ONE (*husband-to-wife*), MANY-TO-ONE (*children-to-father*), ONE-TO-MANY (*mother-to-children*), MANY-TO-MANY (*parents-to-children*). Bordes et al (2013b; 2013a) conduct experiments on each subset respectively. However, the result shows that **TransE** can only achieve less than 20% accuracy[6] when predicting the entities on the MANY-side, even though it can process ONE-TO-ONE triplets well. However, Bordes et al. (2013b) point out that there are roughly only 26.2% ONE-TO-ONE triplets. Therefore, the remainders, i.e. **73.8%** triplets with multi-mapping properties, are expected to be better processed.

In this paper, we propose a superior model named **TransM** which aims at leveraging the structure information of the knowledge graph. Precisely speaking, we keep the transition-based modeling for triplets proposed by **TransE** (Bordes et al., 2013b; Bordes et al., 2013a), i.e. $||\mathbf{h}+\mathbf{r}-\mathbf{t}||_{L_1/L_2}$. Meanwhile, our optimal function will give different respects for each training triplet via the pre-calculated weight corresponding to the relationship. Our intuition is that the *mapping property* of each triplet is decided by the relationship r, e.g. *husband-to-wife* is commonly known as ONE-TO-ONE relationship, while *parents-to-children* is naturally MANY-TO-MANY. Differing from **TransE**, **TransM** will concern more about the diverse contribution (i.e. various relational mapping properties) of each training triplet to the optimization target, i.e. minimizing the margin-based hinge loss function, so that the proposed model will be more flexible when dealing with heterogeneous mapping-properties of knowledge graphs.

We carry out extensive experiments in two different application scenarios, i.e. *link prediction* and *triplet classification*. For each task, we compare the proposed **TransM** with the state-of-the-art method **TransE** and other prior arts on several large-scale benchmark datasets. Results of both tasks demonstrate that our model significantly outperforms the others. Moreover, **TransM** has the comparable parameter complexity with **TransE**. we thus conclude that **TransM** is the most effective model so far while keeping the same efficiency with the state-of-the-art **TransE**.

2 Related Work

Almost all the related works take efforts on embedding each entity or relationship into a low-dimensional continuous space. To achieve this goal, each of them defines a distinct scoring function $f_r(h,t)$ to measure the compatibility of a given triplet (h,r,t).

Unstructured (Bordes et al., 2013b) is a naive model which just exploits the occurrence information of the head and the tail entities without considering the relationship between them. It defines a scoring function $||\mathbf{h}-\mathbf{t}||$, and obversely this model can not discriminate entity-pairs with different relationships. Therefore, **Unstructured** is commonly regarded as the baseline approach.

Distance Model (SE) (Bordes et al., 2011) uses a pair of matrix, i.e (W_{rh}, W_{rt}), to represent the relationship r. The dissimilarity[7] of a triplet (h,r,t) is calculate by the L_1 distance of $||W_{rh}\mathbf{h}-W_{rt}\mathbf{t}||$. Even though the model takes the relationships into

[5]So far, Freebase contains 1.9 billion triplets in total.

[6]Referring to the Table 4 in (Bordes et al., 2013b).

[7]Usually, $f_r(h,t)$ is a distance-measuring function and the lower dissimilarity means the higher compatibility of the triplet (h,r,t)

Model	Scoring Function	Parameter Complexity
Unstructured	$\|\|\mathbf{h}-\mathbf{t}\|\|$	$n_e d$
Distance Model (SE)	$\|\|W_{rh}\mathbf{h}-W_{rt}\mathbf{t}\|\|$; $(W_{rh}, W_{rt}) \in \mathbb{R}^{d\times d}$	$n_e d + 2n_r d^2$
Single Layer Model	$\mathbf{u}_r^T \tanh(W_{rh}\mathbf{h}+W_{rt}\mathbf{t}+\mathbf{b}_r)$; $(W_{rh}, W_{rt}) \in \mathbb{R}^{s\times d}$, $(\mathbf{u_r}, \mathbf{b}_r) \in \mathbb{R}^s$	$n_e d + 2n_r(sd+s)$
Bilinear Model	$\mathbf{h}^T W_r \mathbf{t}$; $W_r \in \mathbb{R}^{d\times d}$	$n_e d + n_r d^2$
Neural Tensor Network	$\mathbf{u}_r^T \tanh(\mathbf{h}^T W_r \mathbf{t}+W_{rh}\mathbf{h}+W_{rt}\mathbf{t}+\mathbf{b}_r)$; $W_r \in \mathbb{R}^{d\times d\times s}$, $(W_{rh}, W_{rt}) \in \mathbb{R}^{s\times d}$, $(\mathbf{u_r}, \mathbf{b}_r) \in \mathbb{R}^s$	$n_e d + n_r(sd^2+2sd+2s)$
TransE	$\|\|\mathbf{h}+\mathbf{r}-\mathbf{t}\|\|$; $\mathbf{r} \in \mathbb{R}^d$	$n_e d + n_r d$
TransM	$w_r\|\|\mathbf{h}+\mathbf{r}-\mathbf{t}\|\|$; $\mathbf{r} \in \mathbb{R}^d, w_r \in \mathbb{R}$	$n_e d + n_r d\ (+n_r)$

Table 1: The scoring function and parameter complexity analysis for each related work. For all the models, we assume that there are a total of n_e entities, n_r relations (In most cases, $n_e \gg n_r$.), and each entity is embedded into a d-dimensional vector space, i.e $\mathbf{h}, \mathbf{t} \in \mathbb{R}^d$. We also suppose that there are s slices in a tensor for the neural-network related models, i.e *Single Layer Model* and *Neural Tensor Network*.

consideration, the separating matrices, i.e. W_{rh} and W_{rt}, as pointed out by Socher et al. (Socher et al., 2013), weaken the capable of capturing correlations between entities and relationships.

Single Layer Model proposed by Socher et al. (Socher et al., 2013) aims to alleviate the shortcomings of **Distance Model** by means of the nonlinearity of a standard, single layer neural network $g(W_{rh}\mathbf{h}+W_{rt}\mathbf{t}+\mathbf{b}_r)$, where $g = tanh$. Then the linear output layer gives the score: $\mathbf{u}_r^T g(W_{rh}\mathbf{h}+W_{rt}\mathbf{t}+\mathbf{b}_r)$.

Bilinear Model (Sutskever et al., 2009; Jenatton et al., 2012) is another model that tries to fix the issue of weak entity embedding vector interaction caused by **Distance Model (SE)** (Bordes et al., 2011) with the help of a relation-specific bilinear form: $f_r(h,t) = \mathbf{h}^T W_r \mathbf{t}$.

Neural Tensor Network (NTN) (Socher et al., 2013) mixes the **Single Layer Model** and the **Bilinear Model** and gives a general function: $f_r(h,t) = \mathbf{u}_r^T g(\mathbf{h}^T W_r \mathbf{t}+W_{rh}\mathbf{h}+W_{rt}\mathbf{t}+\mathbf{b}_r)$, in which the second-order correlations are also considered into the nonlinear transformation function. This model is more expressive indeed, but the computation complexity is rather high.

TransE (Bordes et al., 2013b) is a simple but effective model which finds out that most of the relation instances in the knowledge graph are hierarchical and irreflexive (Bordes et al., 2013a). Therefore, Bordes et al. propose to embed relationship $\mathbf{r}$ as a transitional vector into the same continuous space with the entities, i.e. $\mathbf{h}$ and $\mathbf{t}$. They believe that if a triplet (h,r,t) does stand for a relation instance, then $\mathbf{h}+\mathbf{r}=\mathbf{t}$. Therefore, the scoring function of **TransE** is $||\mathbf{h}+\mathbf{r}-\mathbf{t}||$. Experiments show that **TransE** is state-of-the-art compared to the other related models. Moreover, its lower parameter complexity implies the capability of learning the embeddings for large-scale knowledge graphs. Therefore, it is a promising model which is both effective and efficient. This model works well on ONE-TO-ONE relation instances, as minimizing the global loss function will impose $\mathbf{h}+\mathbf{r}$ close to $\mathbf{t}$. However, the model will confuse about the other relation instances with multi-mapping properties, i.e MANY-TO-MANY, MANY-TO-ONE and ONE-TO-MANY, as entities locates on MANY-side will finally be trained extremely close to each other in the embedding space and also hard to be discriminated.

Therefore, we propose a superior model (**TransM**) in the next section, to give different roles to various training triplets based on their corresponding mapping properties while successively approaching the global optimal target.

Overall, Table 1 lists the scoring functions of all the works mentioned above. We furthermore analyse the parameter complexity of each prior model and conclude that **TransE** (Bordes et al., 2013b; Bordes et al., 2013a) is the most lightweight one so far.

3 TransM

In this section, we will narrate the intuition of our work at first, and then describe the proposed model **TransM** that formulates our idea. Finally, we give the detail algorithm about how to solve the proposed optimal model step by step.

3.1 Intuition

We agree with Bordes et al. (Bordes et al., 2013a; Bordes et al., 2013b) that most of the relation instances in the knowledge graph are hierarchical and irreflexive. Therefore, the relationship of each triplet (h, r, t) can be regarded as a directed transition **r** in the embedding space from the head entity **h** to the tail entity **t**. Ideally, if all the correct triplets follow the assumption that every relation instance is strictly single-mapping (i.e. ONE-TO-ONE), $\mathbf{h} + \mathbf{r}$ will equal to **t** without conflicts.

In reality, however, there are roughly only 26.2% ONE-TO-ONE triplets that are suitable to be modeled by **TransE**. On the other hand, the remainder triplets (**73.8%**) suffer as illustrated on the left hand side of Figure 1, where the tail entities $(t_1, t_2, ..., t_m)$ are all pushed into a cramped range because minimizing loss function impels every training triplet to satisfy $||\mathbf{h} + \mathbf{r} - \mathbf{t}|| = 0$, leading to $h_1 = h_2 = ... = h_m$ in the worst case. Intuitively, we expect to lose the constrain and give more flexibility to the MANY-side as shown on the right side of Figure 1.

3.2 Model

A simple way to model our intuition is to associate each training triplet with a weight which represents the degree of mapping. According to our observation, the mapping property of a triplet depends much on its relationship. For example, *husband-to-wife* is a typical ONE-TO-ONE relationship in most cases, and *parents-to-children* is a MANY-TO-MANY relationship on the other hand. Therefore, the weights are relation-specific and the new scoring function we propose for a triplet (h, r, t) is,

$$f_r(h,t) = w_{\mathbf{r}}||\mathbf{h} + \mathbf{r} - \mathbf{t}||_{L_1/L_2} \quad (1)$$

For a correct triplet (h, r, t) in the training set Δ, we expect that the score of $f_r(h,t)$ is much lower than any corrupted triplet (h', r, t') that we randomly construct[8]. $\Delta'_{(h,r,t)}$ denotes the set of corrupted triplets for the correct one (h, r, t). Moreover, we use E (i.e. $(h,t) \in E$) and R (i.e. $r \in R$) to respectively denote the set of entities and relationships in the training set Δ.

To discriminate the correct and corrupted triplets, minimizing the margin-based hinge loss function is a simple but effective optimal model

$$\mathcal{L} = \min \sum_{(h,r,t)\in\Delta} \sum_{(h',r,t')\in\Delta'_{(h,r,t)}} [\gamma + f_r(h,t) - f_r(h',t')]_+$$
$$s.t. \quad \forall e \in E, ||e||_2 = 1 \quad (2)$$

where $[\ \ ]_+$ is the hinge loss function, e.g. $[x]_+ = \max(x, 0)$, and γ is the margin. The reason that we constrain each entity located on the unit-ball is to guarantee that they can be updated in the same scale without being either wildly too large or small to satisfy the optimal target.

A simple way to measure the degree of mapping property for a relationship is to count the average number of tail entities per each distinct head entity and vice versa. We thus define h_rpt_r[9] (i.e. heads per tail) and t_rph_r[10] (i.e. tails per head) to jointly represent the mapping degree of relationship r. In this case, MANY-TO-MANY relation instances achieve much higher *hpt* and *tph* than ONE-TO-ONEs do. We would like to constrain ONE-TO-ONE instances more than MANY-TO-MANYs. Therefore, we design a formula to measure the weights as follows,

$$w_r = \frac{1}{\log(h_rpt_r + t_rph_r)} \quad (3)$$

The scoring function of **TransM** shown in Table 1 indicates that the parameter complexity of **TransM**

[8] The detail of constructing corrupted triplet is described in (Bordes et al., 2013b). Briefly speaking, the head or the tail entity (but not the both) of a gold triplet (h, r, t) is randomly replaced by other ones. In the meanwhile, we must make sure that the corrupted triplet (h', r, t') does not appear in the training set Δ.

[9] $h_rpt_r = \frac{\#(\Delta_r)}{\#(distinct(t_r))}$, where t_r represents the tail entities belonging to relationship r, and Δ_r denotes the training triplets containing the relationship r.

[10] $t_rph_r = \frac{\#(\Delta_r)}{\#(distinct(h_r))}$.

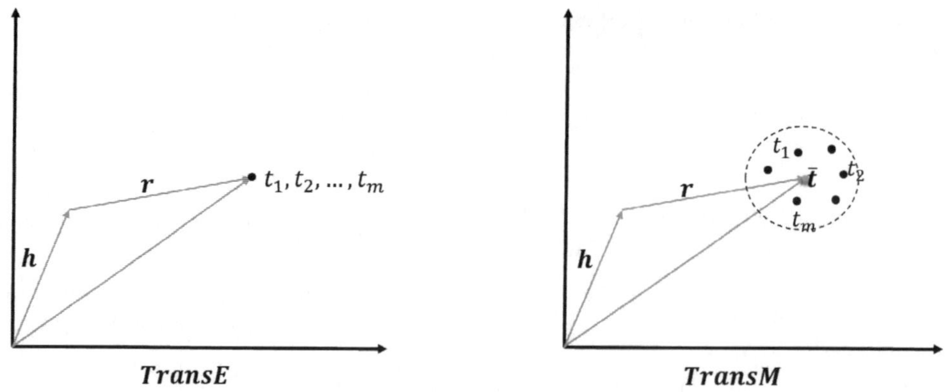

Figure 1: The differences between **TransE** and **TransM** when modeling ONE-TO-MANY relation instances, i.e. (h, r, t_1), (h, r, t_2), ..., (h, r, t_m).

is comparable with **TransE**, as the amount of entities is much larger than relationships in most cases. Moreover, as we can pre-compute the weight w_r for each relationship r, those parameters n_r can be ignored.

3.3 Algorithm

We use SGD (Stochastic Gradient Descent) to search the optimal solution in the iterative fashion. Algorithm 1 gives the pseudocodes that describe the procedure of learning **TransM**.

There are two key points we would like to clarify. First, we adopt projection method to pull back each updated entity to the uni-ball in order to satisfy the constraints in Equation (2). Second, we use the inner product ($f_r(h, t) = w_{\mathbf{r}}||\mathbf{h} + \mathbf{r} - \mathbf{t}||_2^2$) instead of L_2 norm ($f_r(h, t) = w_{\mathbf{r}}||\mathbf{h} + \mathbf{r} - \mathbf{t}||_2$) for facilitating the derivation of gradients.

Algorithm 1 Learning **TransM**

Input:

Training set $\Delta = \{(h, r, t)\}$, entity set E, relation set R and weight set W;
Dimension of embeddings d, margin γ, step size s, convergence threshold ϵ, maximum epoches n.

foreach $\mathbf{r} \in R$ **do**
  $\mathbf{r} := \text{Uniform}(\frac{-6}{\sqrt{d}}, \frac{6}{\sqrt{d}})$
  $\mathbf{r} := \text{Normalize}(\mathbf{r})$
end foreach

foreach $w_r \in W$ **do**
  Weighting$(\mathbf{r})$ according to Equation (3)
end foreach

$i := 0$
while $Rel.loss > \epsilon$ and $i < n$ **do**
  foreach $\mathbf{e} \in E$ **do**
    $\mathbf{e} := \text{Uniform}(\frac{-6}{\sqrt{d}}, \frac{6}{\sqrt{d}})$
    $\mathbf{e} := \text{Normalize}(\mathbf{e})$
  end foreach

  foreach $(h, r, t) \in \Delta$ **do**
    $(h', r, t') := \text{Sampling}(\Delta'_{(h,r,t)})$
    if $\gamma + f_r(h, t) - f_r(h', t') \geq 0$ **then**
      Updating : $\nabla_{(h,r,t,h',t')}(\gamma + f_r(h, t) - f_r(h', t'))$
    end if
  end foreach
end while

4 Experiments

Embedding the knowledge into low-dimensional space makes it much easier to conduct further AI-related computing issues, such as *link prediction* (i.e. predicting t given h and r) and *triplet classification* (i.e. to discriminate whether a triplet (h, r, t) is correct or wrong). Two latest related works (Bordes et al., 2013b; Socher et al., 2013) evaluate their model on the subsets of WordNet (**WN**) and Freebase (**FB**) data, respectively. In order to conduct solid experiments, we compare our model with many related works including state-of-the-art and baseline

DATASET	WN18	FB15K
#(ENTITIES)	40,943	14,951
#(RELATIONS)	18	1,345
#(TRAINING EX.)	141,442	483,142
#(VALIDATING EX.)	5,000	50,000
#(TESTING EX.)	5,000	59,071

Table 2: Statistics of the datasets used for link prediction task.

approaches in those two tasks. All the datasets, the source codes and the learnt embeddings for entities and relations can be downloaded from `http://1drv.ms/1nA2Vht`.

4.1 Link Prediction

One of the benefits of knowledge embedding is that we can apply simple mathematical operations to many reasoning tasks. For example, link prediction is a valuable task that contributes to completing the knowledge graph. Specifically, it aims at predicting the missing entity or the relationship given the other two elements in a fragmented triplet. For example, if we would like to tell whether the entity h has the relationship r with the entity t, we just need to calculate the distance between $\mathbf{h} + \mathbf{r}$ and $\mathbf{t}$. The closer they are, the more possibility the triplet (h, r, t) exists.

4.1.1 Benchmark Datasets

Bordes et al. (Bordes et al., 2013a; Bordes et al., 2013b) released two benchmark datasets[11] which are extracted from WordNet (**WN18**) and Freebase (**F-B15K**), respectively. Table 2 shows the statistics of these two datasets. The size of **WN18** dataset is s-maller than **FB15K**, with much fewer relationships but more entities.

4.1.2 Evaluation Protocol

For each testing triplet, the head entity is replaced by all the entities in the dictionary iteratively. The dissimilarity of each triplet candidate is firstly computed by the scoring functions, then sorted in ascending order, and finally the rank of the ground truth one is stored. This whole procedure is applied on the tail entity in the same way to gain the mean results. We use two metrics, i.e. *Mean Rank* and *Mean Hit@10* (i.e. the proportion of ground truth triplets that rank in Top-10), to measure the performance. However, those metrics are relatively raw, as the procedure above tends to bring in the false negative triplets, especially for multi-mapping relation instances. We thus filter out those triplets which appear in the training set and generate more reasonable results.

4.1.3 Experimental Results

We compare our model **TransM** with the state-of-the-art **TransE** and other models mentioned in (Bordes et al., 2013a) and (Bordes et al., 2014a) on the **WN18** and **FB15K**. We tune the parameters of each former model[12] based on the validation set and select the parameter combination which lead-s to the best performance. The results are almost the same as (Bordes et al., 2013b). We tried several parameter combinations, e.g. $d = \{20, 50, 100\}$, $\gamma = \{0.1, 1.0, 2.0, 10.0\}$ and $s = \{0.01, 0.1, 1.0\}$, for **TransM**, and finally select $d = 20$, $\gamma = 2.0$, $s = 0.01$ for **WN18** dataset; $d = 50$, $\gamma = 1.0$, $s = 0.01$ for **FB15K** dataset. Table 3 and Table 4 show the comparison between **TransM** and **TransE** on the performance of the two metrics when the s-coring function is L_1 norm and L_2 norm. Results show that **TransM** outperforms **TransE** when we choose L_1 norm. These parameter combinations are also adopted by the *Triplet Classification* task to search other parameters, which we will describe in the next section. Moreover, Table 5 demonstrates that our model **TransM** outperforms the all the prior arts (i.e. the baseline model **Unstructured** (Bordes et al., 2014a), **RESCAL** (Nickel et al., 2011), **SE** (Bordes et al., 2011), **SME (LINEAR)** (Bordes et al., 2014a), **SME (BILINEAR)** (Bordes et al., 2014a), **LFM** (Jenatton et al., 2012) and the state-of-the-art **TransE** (Bordes et al., 2013a; Bordes et al., 2013b)) by evaluating them on the two benchmark datasets (i.e. **WN18** and **FB15K**).

Moreover, we divide **FB15K** into different categories (i.e. ONE-TO-ONE, ONE-TO-MANY, MANY-TO-ONE and MANY-TO-MANY) according to the mapping properties[13] of relationships, and

[11] The datasets can be downloaded from `https://www.hds.utc.fr/everest/doku.php?id=en:transe`

[12] All the codes for the related models can be downloaded from `https://github.com/glorotxa/SME`

[13] According to (Bordes et al., 2013b), we set 1.5 as the threshold to discriminate the single and the multi mapping prop-

DATASET	WN18							
NORM	L_1				L_2			
METRIC	*MEAN RANK*		*MEAN HIT@10*		*MEAN RANK*		*MEAN HIT@10*	
	Raw	*Filter*	*Raw*	*Filter*	*Raw*	*Filter*	*Raw*	*Filter*
TransE	294.4	283.2	70.38%	80.23%	**377.1**	**366.5**	38.56%	40.15%
TransM	**292.5**	**280.8**	**75.67%**	**85.38%**	440.4	429.4	**40.55%**	**42.43%**

Table 3: The detail results of link prediction between TransM and TransE on WN18 dataset when adopting L_1 and L_2 norm for the scoring function.

DATASET	FB15K							
NORM	L_1				L_2			
METRIC	*MEAN RANK*		*MEAN HIT@10*		*MEAN RANK*		*MEAN HIT@10*	
	Raw	*Filter*	*Raw*	*Filter*	*Raw*	*Filter*	*Raw*	*Filter*
TransE	243.3	139.9	36.86%	44.33%	254.6	146.3	37.26%	44.96%
TransM	**196.8**	**93.8**	**44.64%**	**55.15%**	**217.3**	**118.4**	**41.71%**	**50.40%**

Table 4: The detail results of link prediction between TransM and TransE on FB15K dataset when adopting L_1 and L_2 norm for the scoring function.

DATASET	WN18				FB15K			
METRIC	*MEAN RANK*		*MEAN HIT@10*		*MEAN RANK*		*MEAN HIT@10*	
	Raw	*Filter*	*Raw*	*Filter*	*Raw*	*Filter*	*Raw*	*Filter*
Unstructured	315	304	35.3%	38.2%	1,074	979	4.5%	6.3%
RESCAL	1,180	1,163	37.2%	52.8%	828	683	28.4%	44.1%
SE	1,011	985	68.5%	80.5%	273	162	28.8%	39.8%
SME(LINEAR)	545	533	65.1%	74.1%	274	154	30.7%	40.8%
SME(BILINEAR)	526	509	54.7%	61.3%	284	158	31.3%	41.3%
LFM	469	456	71.4%	81.6%	283	164	26.0%	33.1%
TransE	294.4	283.2	70.4%	80.2%	243.3	139.9	36.7%	44.3%
TransM	**292.5**	**280.8**	**75.7%**	**85.4%**	**196.8**	**93.8**	**44.6%**	**55.2%**

Table 5: Link prediction results. We compared our proposed TransM with the state-of-the-art method (TransE) and other prior arts.

TASK	*Predicting head*				*Predicting tail*			
REL. Mapping	1-TO-1	1-TO-M.	M.-TO-1	M.-TO-M.	1-TO-1	1-TO-M.	M.-TO-1	M.-TO-M.
Unstructured	34.5%	2.5%	6.1%	6.6%	34.3%	4.2%	1.9%	6.6%
SE	35.6%	62.6%	17.2%	37.5%	34.9%	14.6%	68.3%	41.3%
SME (LINEAR)	35.1%	53.7%	19.0%	40.3%	32.7%	14.9%	61.6%	43.3%
SME (BILINEAR)	30.9%	69.6%	19.9%	38.6%	28.2%	13.1%	76.0%	41.8%
TransE	59.7%	77.0%	14.7%	41.1%	58.5%	18.3%	80.2%	44.7%
TransM	**76.8%**	**86.3%**	**23.1%**	**52.3%**	**76.3%**	**29.0%**	**85.9%**	**56.7%**

Table 6: The detail results of *Filter Hit@10* (in %) on FB15K categorized by different mapping properties of relationship (M. stands for MANY).

analyse the performance of **Filter Hit@10** metric on each set. Table 6 shows that **TransM** outperforms on all categories, which proves that the proposed approach can not only maintain the characteristic of modeling the ONE-TO-ONE, but also better handle the multi-mapping relation instances.

4.2 Triplet Classification

Triplet classification is another task proposed by Socher et al. (Socher et al., 2013) which focuses on searching a relation-specific distance threshold σ_r to determine whether a triplet (h, r, t) is plausible.

4.2.1 Benchmark Datasets

Similar to Bordes et al. (Bordes et al., 2013a; Bordes et al., 2013b), Socher et al.(Socher et al., 2013) also constructed two standard datasets[14] (i.e. **WN11** and **FB13**) sampled from WordNet and Freebase. However, both of the benchmark datasets contain much fewer relationships. Therefore, we build another dataset obeying the principle proposed by Socher et al. (2013) based on **FB15K** which possesses much more relations. It is emphasized that the head or the tail entity can be randomly replaced with another one to produce a negative example, but in order to build much tough validation and testing datasets, we constrain that the picked entity should once appear at the same position. For example, *(Pablo Picaso, nationality, U.S.)* is a potential negative example rather than the obvious nonsense *(Pablo Picaso, nationality, Van Gogh)*, given a positive triplet *(Pablo Picaso, nationality, Spain)*. Table 7 shows the statistics of the standard datasets that we used for evaluating models on the triplet classification task.

4.2.2 Evaluation Protocol

The decision strategy for binary classification is simple: If the dissimilarity of a testing triplet (h, r, t) computed by $f_r(h, t)$ is below the relation-specific threshold σ_r, we predict it as positive, otherwise negative. The relation-specific threshold σ_r can be searched by maximizing the classification accuracy of the validation triplets which belongs to the relation r.

DATASET	WN11	FB13	FB15K
#(ENTITIES)	38,696	75,043	14,951
#(RELATIONS)	11	13	1,345
#(TRAINING EX.)	112,581	316,232	483,142
#(VALIDATING EX.)	5,218	11,816	100,000
#(TESTING EX.)	21,088	47,466	118,142

Table 7: Statistics of the datasets used for triplet classification task.

DATASET	WN11	FB13	FB15K
Distance Model	53.0%	75.2%	-
Hadamard Model	70.0%	63.7%	-
Single Layer Model	69.9%	85.3%	-
Bilinear Model	73.8%	84.3%	-
NTN	70.4%	**87.1%**	66.7%
TransE	77.5%	67.5%	85.8%
TransM	**77.8%**	72.1%	**89.9%**

Table 8: The accuracy of triplet classification compared with the state-of-the-art method (TransE) and other prior arts.

4.2.3 Experimental Results

We use the best parameter combination settings in the Link prediction task ($d = 20$, $\gamma = 2.0$, $s = 0.01$ for **WN11** dataset; $d = 50$, $\gamma = 1.0$, $s = 0.01$ for **FB13** and **FB15K** datasets.) to generate the entity and relation embeddings, and learn the best classification threshold σ_r for each relation r. Compared with the state-of-the-art, i.e. **TransE** (Bordes et al., 2013b; Bordes et al., 2013a) and other prior arts (i.e. **Distance Model** (Bordes et al., 2011), **Hadamard Model** (Bordes et al., 2012), **Single Layer Model** (Socher et al., 2013), **Bilinear Model** (Sutskever et al., 2009; Jenatton et al., 2012) and **Neural Tensor Network (NTN)**[15] (Socher et al., 2013)), our model **TransM** still achieves better performance as shown in Table 8.

Table 8 shows the best performance of **TransM** and **TransE** when selecting L_1 norm as the distance metric of the scoring functions. To display more de-

erties, i.e. for a triplet (h, r, t), if $h_r pt_r \leq 1.5$ and $t_r ph_r \leq 1.5$ in the meanwhile, we can categorize this triplet as ONE-TO-ONE relation instance.

[14]Those datasets can be download from the website `http://www.socher.org/index.php`

[15]Socher et al. reported higher classification accuracy in (Socher et al., 2013) with word embeddings. In order to conduct a fair comparison, the accuracy of **NTN** reported in Table 6 is same with the EV (entity vectors) results in Figure 4 of (Socher et al., 2013).

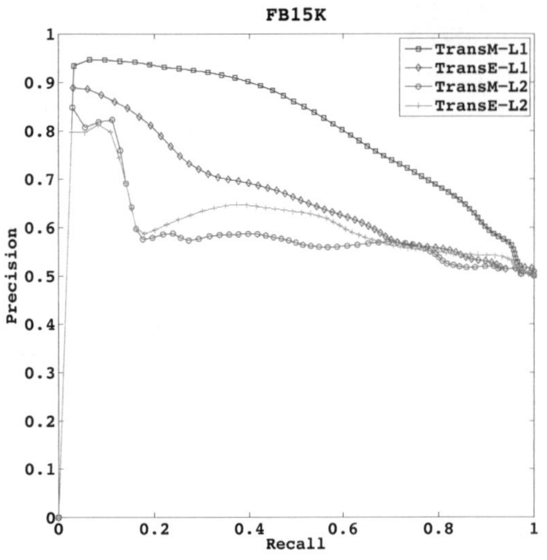

Figure 2: The Precision-Recall curves of TransE and TransM on the testing set of FB15K.

tails, we take the largest dataset as an example. We draw the Precision-Recall curves for all the positive testing triplets in the **FB15K** dataset while choosing L_1 and L_2 norm as the distance metric for the scoring functions of **TransM** and **TransE**. Figure 2 illustrates that the embeddings learned by **TransM** gain better capability of discriminating positive and negative triplets.

5 Conclusion and Future Work

TransM is a superior model that is not only expressive to represent the hierarchical and irreflexive characteristics but also flexible to adapt various mapping properties of the knowledge triplets. The results of extensive experiments on several benchmark datasets prove that our model can achieve higher performance without sacrificing efficiency. Moreover, we provide an insight that the relational mapping properties of a knowledge graph can be exploited to enhance the model.

Furthermore, we concern about two open questions in the following work:

- How to *learn* the specific weights for each triplet, so that the training examples can self-organize well with fewer conflict triplets.
- How to parallelize the algorithm without losing much performance, so that we can truly compute the world knowledge in the future.

In addition, we look forward to applying *Knowledge Graph Embedding* to reinforce some other related fields, such as *Relation Extraction* from free texts (Weston et al., 2013) and *Open Question Answering* (Bordes et al., 2014b).

6 Acknowledgments

This work is supported by National Program on Key Basic Research Project (973 Program) under Grant 2013CB329304, National Science Foundation of China (NSFC) under Grant No.61373075.

References

Yoshua Bengio, Rjean Ducharme, Pascal Vincent, and Christian Janvin. 2003. A neural probabilistic language model. *Journal of Machine Learning Research*, 3:1137–1155.

Antoine Bordes, Jason Weston, Ronan Collobert, Yoshua Bengio, et al. 2011. Learning structured embeddings of knowledge bases. In *AAAI*.

Antoine Bordes, Xavier Glorot, Jason Weston, and Yoshua Bengio. 2012. Joint learning of words and meaning representations for open-text semantic parsing. In *International Conference on Artificial Intelligence and Statistics*, pages 127–135.

Antoine Bordes, Nicolas Usunier, Alberto Garcia-Duran, Jason Weston, and Oksana Yakhnenko. 2013a. Irreflexive and hierarchical relations as translations. *arXiv preprint arXiv:1304.7158*.

Antoine Bordes, Nicolas Usunier, Alberto Garcia-Duran, Jason Weston, and Oksana Yakhnenko. 2013b. Translating embeddings for modeling multi-relational data. In *Advances in Neural Information Processing Systems*, pages 2787–2795.

Antoine Bordes, Xavier Glorot, Jason Weston, and Yoshua Bengio. 2014a. A semantic matching energy function for learning with multi-relational data. *Machine Learning*, 94(2):233–259.

Antoine Bordes, Jason Weston, and Nicolas Usunier. 2014b. Open question answering with weakly supervised embedding models. *CoRR*, abs/1404.4326.

Ulf Hermjakob, Eduard H Hovy, and Chin-Yew Lin. 2000. Knowledge-based question answering. In *Proceedings of the Sixth World Multiconference on Systems, Cybernetics, and Informatics (SCI-2002)*.

Eric Huang, Richard Socher, Christopher Manning, and Andrew Ng. 2012. Improving word representations via global context and multiple word prototypes. In *Proceedings of the 50th Annual Meeting of the Association for Computational Linguistics (Volume 1: Long Papers)*, pages 873–882, Jeju Island, Korea, July. Association for Computational Linguistics.

Rodolphe Jenatton, Nicolas Le Roux, Antoine Bordes, Guillaume Obozinski, et al. 2012. A latent factor model for highly multi-relational data. In *NIPS*, pages 3176–3184.

Tomas Mikolov, Kai Chen, Greg Corrado, and Jeffrey Dean. 2013. Efficient estimation of word representations in vector space. *arXiv preprint arXiv:1301.3781*.

Maximilian Nickel, Volker Tresp, and Hans-Peter Kriegel. 2011. A three-way model for collective learning on multi-relational data. In *Proceedings of the 28th international conference on machine learning (ICML-11)*, pages 809–816.

Michael J Pazzani and Carl Engelman. 1983. Knowledge based question answering. In *Proceedings of the first conference on Applied natural language processing*, pages 73–80. Association for Computational Linguistics.

Fabio Rinaldi, James Dowdall, Michael Hess, Diego Mollá, Rolf Schwitter, and Kaarel Kaljurand. 2003. Knowledge-based question answering. In *Knowledge-Based Intelligent Information and Engineering Systems*, pages 785–792. Springer.

Richard Socher, Danqi Chen, Christopher D Manning, and Andrew Ng. 2013. Reasoning with neural tensor networks for knowledge base completion. In *Advances in Neural Information Processing Systems*, pages 926–934.

Ilya Sutskever, Ruslan Salakhutdinov, and Joshua B Tenenbaum. 2009. Modelling relational data using bayesian clustered tensor factorization. In *NIPS*, pages 1821–1828.

Jason Weston, Antoine Bordes, Oksana Yakhnenko, and Nicolas Usunier. 2013. Connecting language and knowledge bases with embedding models for relation extraction. In *Proceedings of the 2013 Conference on Empirical Methods in Natural Language Processing*, pages 1366–1371, Seattle, Washington, USA, October. Association for Computational Linguistics.

Kelly Wical. 1999. Information presentation in a knowledge base search and retrieval system, August 17. US Patent 5,940,821.

Kelly Wical. 2000. Concept knowledge base search and retrieval system, March 14. US Patent 6,038,560.

Retrieval Term Prediction Using Deep Belief Networks

Qing Ma[†] **Ibuki Tanigawa**[†] **Masaki Murata**[‡]
[†] Department of Applied Mathematics and Informatics, Ryukoku University
[‡] Department of Information and Electronics, Tottori University
qma@math.ryukoku.ac.jp

Abstract

This paper presents a method to predict retrieval terms from relevant/surrounding words or descriptive texts in Japanese by using deep belief networks (DBN), one of two typical types of deep learning. To determine the effectiveness of using DBN for this task, we tested it along with baseline methods using example-based approaches and conventional machine learning methods, i.e., multi-layer perceptron (MLP) and support vector machines (SVM), for comparison. The data for training and testing were obtained from the Web in manual and automatic manners. Automatically created pseudo data was also used. A grid search was adopted for obtaining the optimal hyper-parameters of these machine learning methods by performing cross-validation on training data. Experimental results showed that (1) using DBN has far higher prediction precisions than using baseline methods and higher prediction precisions than using either MLP or SVM; (2) adding automatically gathered data and pseudo data to the manually gathered data as training data is an effective measure for further improving the prediction precisions; and (3) DBN is able to deal with noisier training data than MLP, i.e., the prediction precision of DBN can be improved by adding noisy training data, but that of MLP cannot be.

1 Introduction

The current Web search engines have a very high retrieval performance as long as the proper retrieval terms are given. However, many people, particularly children, seniors, and foreigners, have difficulty deciding on the proper retrieval terms for representing the retrieval objects,[1] especially with searches related to technical fields. The support systems are in place for search engine users that show suitable retrieval term candidates when some clues such as their descriptive texts or relevant/surrounding words are given by the users. For example, when the relevant/surrounding words "computer", "previous state", and "return" are given by users, "system restore" is predicted by the systems as a retrieval term candidate.

Our objective is to develop various domain-specific information retrieval support systems that can predict suitable retrieval terms from relevant/surrounding words or descriptive texts in Japanese. To our knowledge, no such studies have been done so far in Japanese. As the first step, here, we confined the retrieval terms to the computer-related field and proposed a method to predict them using machine learning methods with deep belief networks (DBN), one of two typical types of deep learning.

In recent years, deep learning/neural network techniques have attracted a great deal of attention in various fields and have been successfully applied not only in speech recognition (Li et al., 2013) and image recognition (Krizhevsky et al., 2012) tasks but also in NLP tasks including morphology & syn-

[1]For example, according to a questionnaire administered by Microsoft in 2010, about 60% of users had difficulty deciding on the proper retrieval terms. (http://www.garbagenews.net/archives/1466626.html) (http://news.mynavi.jp/news/2010/07/05/028/)

Copyright 2014 by Qing Ma, Ibuki Tanigawa, and Masaki Murata
28th Pacific Asia Conference on Language, Information and Computation pages 338–347

tax (Billingsley and Curran, 2012; Hermann and Blunsom, 2013; Luong et al., 2013; Socher et al., 2013a), semantics (Hashimoto et al., 2013; Srivastava et al., 2013; Tsubaki et al., 2013), machine translation (Auli et al., 2013; Liu et al., 2013; Kalchbrenner and Blunsom, 2013; Zou et al., 2013), text classification (Glorot et al., 2011), information retrieval (Huang et al., 2013; Salakhutdinov and Hinton, 2009), and others (Seide et al., 2011; Socher et al., 2011; Socher et al., 2013b). Moreover, a unified neural network architecture and learning algorithm has also been proposed that can be applied to various NLP tasks including part-of-speech tagging, chunking, named entity recognition, and semantic role labeling (Collobert et al., 2011).

To our knowledge, however, there have been no studies on applying deep learning to information retrieval support tasks. We therefore have two main objectives in our current study. One is to develop an effective method for predicting suitable retrieval terms and the other is to determine whether deep learning is more effective than other conventional machine learning methods, i.e., multi-layer perceptron (MLP) and support vector machines (SVM), in such NLP tasks.

The data used for experiments were obtained from the Web in both manual and automatic manners. Automatically created pseudo data was also used. A grid search was used to obtain the optimal hyperparameters of these machine learning methods by performing cross-validation on training data. Experimental results showed that (1) using DBN has a far higher prediction precision than using baseline methods and a higher prediction precision than using either MLP or SVM; (2) adding automatically gathered data and pseudo data to the manually gathered data as training data is an effective measure for further improving the prediction precision; and (3) the DBN can deal with noisier training data than the MLP, i.e., the prediction precision of DBN can be improved by adding noisy training data, but that of MLP cannot be.

2 The Corpus

For training, a corpus consisting of pairs of inputs and their responses (or correct answers) — in our case, pairs of the relevant/surrounding words or descriptive texts and retrieval terms — is needed. The responses are typically called labels in supervised learning and so here we call the retrieval terms labels. Table 1 shows examples of these pairs, where the "Relevant/surrounding words" are those extracted from descriptive texts in accordance with steps described in Subsection 2.4. In this section, we describe how the corpus is obtained and how the feature vectors of the inputs are constructed from the corpus for machine learning.

2.1 Manual and Automatic Gathering of Data

Considering that the descriptive texts of labels necessarily include their relevant/surrounding words, we gather Web pages containing these texts in both manual and automatic manners. In the manual manner, we manually select the Web pages that describe the labels. In contrast, in the automatic manner, we respectively combine five words or parts of phrases とは (*toha*, "what is"), は (*ha*, "is"), というものは (*toiumonoha*, "something like"), については (*nitsuiteha*, "about"), and の意味は (*noimiha*, "the meaning of"), on the labels to form the retrieval terms (e.g., if a label is グラフィックボード (*gurafikku boudo*, "graphic board"), then the retrieval terms are グラフィックボード とは (*gurafikku boudo toha*, "what is graphic board"), グラフィックボード は (*gurafikku boudo ha*, "graphic board is"), and etc.) and then use these terms to obtain the relevant Web pages by a Google search.

2.2 Pseudo Data

To acquire as high a generalization capability as possible, for training we use not only the small scale of manually gathered data, which is high precision, but also the large scale of automatically gathered data, which includes a certain amount of noise. In contrast to manually gathered data, automatically gathered data might have incorrect labels, i.e., labels that do not match the descriptive texts. We therefore also use pseudo data, which can be regarded as data that includes some noises and/or deficiencies added to the original data (i.e., to the descriptive texts of the manually gathered data) but with less noise than the automatically gathered data and with all the labels correct. The procedure for creating pseudo data from the manually gathered data involves (1) extracting all the different words from the

Labels (Retrieval terms)	Inputs (Descriptive texts or relevant/surrounding words; translated from Japanese)	
Graphic board	Descriptive text	Also known as: graphic card, graphic accelerator, GB, VGA. While the screen outputs the picture actually seen by the eye, the screen only displays as commanded and does not output anything if ···
	Relevant/surrounding words	screen, picture, eye, displays, as commanded, ···
	Descriptive text	A device that provides independent functions for outputting or inputting video as signals on a PC or various other types of computer ···
	Relevant/surrounding words	independent, functions, outputting, inputting, video, signals, PC, ···
Main memory	···	···

Table 1: Examples of input-label pairs in the corpus.

manually gathered data and (2) for each label, randomly adding the words that were extracted in step (1) but not included in the descriptive texts and/or deleting words that originally existed in the descriptive texts so that the newly generated data (i.e., the newly generated descriptive texts) have 10% noises and/or deficiencies added to the original data.

2.3 Testing Data

The data described in Subsections 2.1 and 2.2 are for training. The data used for testing are different to the training data and are also obtained from automatically gathered data. Since automatically gathered data may include a lot of incorrect labels that cannot be used as objective assessment data, we manually select correct ones from the automatically gathered data.

2.4 Word Extraction and Feature Vector Construction

Relevant/surrounding words are extracted from descriptive texts by steps (1)–(4) below and the inputs are represented by feature vectors in machine learning constructed by steps (1)–(6): (1) perform morphological analysis on the manually gathered data and extract all nouns, including proper nouns, verbal nouns (nouns forming verbs by adding word する (*suru*, "do")), and general nouns; (2) connect the nouns successively appearing as single words; (3) extract the words whose appearance frequency in each label is ranked in the top 50; (4) exclude the words appearing in the descriptive texts of more than two labels; (5) use the words obtained by the above steps as the vector elements with binary values, taking value 1 if a word appears and 0 if not; and (6) perform morphological analysis on all data described in Subsections 2.1, 2.2, and 2.3 and construct the feature vectors in accordance with step (5).

3 Deep Learning

Two typical approaches have been proposed for implementing deep learning: using deep belief networks (DBN) (Hinton et al., 2006; Lee et al., 2009; Bengio et al., 2007; Bengio, 2009; Bengio et al., 2013) and using stacked denoising autoencoder (SdA) (Bengio et al., 2007; Bengio, 2009; Bengio et al., 2013; Vincent et al., 2008; Vincent et al., 2010). In this work we use DBN, which has an elegant architecture and a performance more than or equal to that of SdA in many tasks.

DBN is a multiple layer neural network equipped with an unsupervised learning based on restricted Boltzmann machines (RBM) for pre-training to extract features and a supervised learning for fine-tuning to output labels. The supervised learning can be implemented with a single layer or multi-layer perceptron or others (linear regression, logistic regression, etc.).

3.1 Restricted Boltzmann Machine

RBM is a probabilistic graphical model representing the probability distribution of training data with a fast unsupervised learning.

It consists of two layers, one visible and

one hidden, that respectively have visible units $(v_1, v_2, \cdots, v_m)$ and hidden units $(h_1, h_2, \cdots, h_n)$ connected to each other between the two layers (Figure 1).

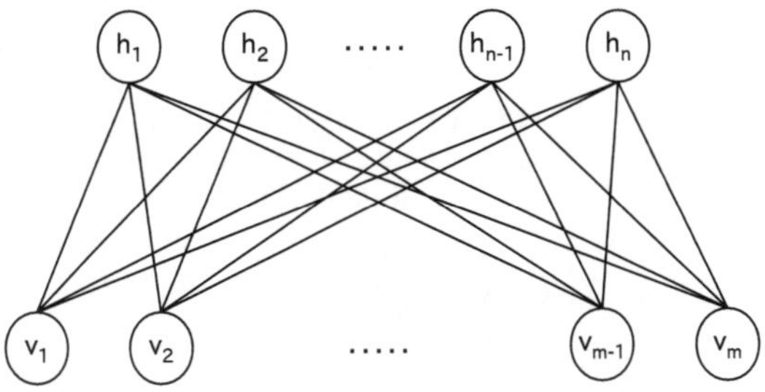

Figure 1: Restricted Boltzmann machine.

Given training data, the weights of the connections between units are modified by learning so that the behavior of the RBM stochastically fits the training data as well as possible. The learning algorithm is briefly described below.

First, sampling is performed on the basis of conditional probabilities when a piece of training data is given to the visible layer using Eqs. (1), (2), and then (1) again:

$$P(h_i^{(k)} = 1|\boldsymbol{v}^{(k)}) = \text{sigmoid}(\sum_{j=1}^{m} w_{ij}v_j^{(k)} + c_i) \quad (1)$$

and

$$P(v_j^{(k+1)} = 1|\boldsymbol{h}^{(k)}) = \text{sigmoid}(\sum_{i=1}^{n} w_{ij}h_i^{(k)} + b_j), \quad (2)$$

where k (≥ 1) is a repeat count of sampling and $\boldsymbol{v}^{(1)} = \boldsymbol{v}$ which is a piece of training data, w_{ij} is the weight of connection between units v_j and h_i, and b_j and c_i are offsets for the units v_j and h_i of the visible and hidden layers. After k repetition sampling, the weights and offsets are updated by

$$\boldsymbol{W} \leftarrow \boldsymbol{W} + \epsilon(\boldsymbol{h}^{(1)}\boldsymbol{v}^T - P(\boldsymbol{h}^{(k+1)} = 1|\boldsymbol{v}^{(k+1)})\boldsymbol{v}^{(k+1)T}), \quad (3)$$

$$\boldsymbol{b} \leftarrow \boldsymbol{b} + \epsilon(\boldsymbol{v} - \boldsymbol{v}^{(k+1)}), \quad (4)$$

$$\boldsymbol{c} \leftarrow \boldsymbol{c} + \epsilon(\boldsymbol{h}^{(1)} - P(\boldsymbol{h}^{(k+1)} = 1|\boldsymbol{v}^{(k+1)})), \quad (5)$$

where ϵ is a learning rate and the initial values of $\boldsymbol{W}$, $\boldsymbol{b}$, and $\boldsymbol{c}$ are $\boldsymbol{0}$. Sampling with a large enough repeat count is called Gibbs sampling, which is computationally expensive. A method called k-step Contrastive Divergence (CD-k) which stops sampling after k repetitions is therefore usually adopted. It is empirically known that even $k = 1$ (CD-1) often gives good results, and so we set $k = 1$ in this work.

If we assume totally e epochs are performed for learning n training data using CD-k, the procedure for learning RBM can be given as in Figure 2. As the learning progresses, the samples[2] of the visible layer $\boldsymbol{v}^{(k+1)}$ approach the training data $\boldsymbol{v}$.

```
For each of all epochs e do
    For each of all data n do
        For each repetition of CD k do
            Sample according to Eqs. (1), (2), (1)
        End for
        Update using Eqs. (3), (4), (5)
    End for
End for
```

Figure 2: Procedure for learning RBM.

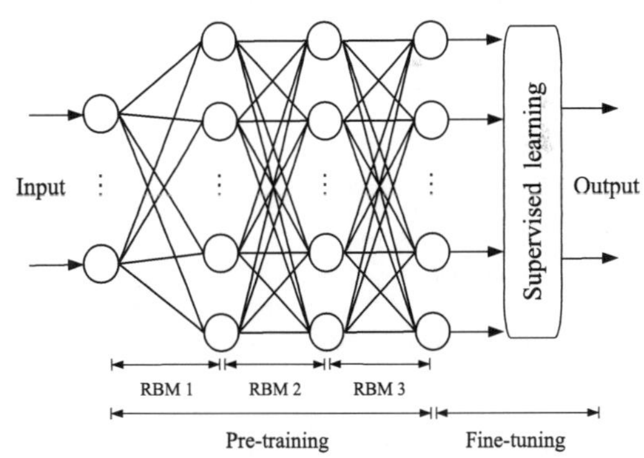

Figure 3: Example of a deep belief network.

3.2 Deep Belief Network

Figure 3 shows a DBN composed of three RBMs for pre-training and a supervised learning device for fine-tuning. Naturally the number of RBMs is changeable as needed. As shown in the figure, the hidden layers of the earlier RBMs become the visible layers of the new RBMs. Below, for simplic-

[2] By "samples" here we mean the data generated on the basis of the conditional probabilities of Eqs. (1) and (2).

ity, we consider the layers of RBMs (excluding the input layer) as hidden layers of DBN. The DBN in the figure therefore has three hidden layers, and this number is equal to the number of RBMs. Although supervised learning can be implemented by any method, in this work we use logistic regression.

The procedure for learning the DBN with three RBMs is shown in Figure 4.

1. Train RBM 1 with the training data as inputs by the **procedure for learning RBM (Figure 2)** and fix its weights and offsets.
2. Train RBM 2 with the samples of the hidden layer of RBM 1 as inputs by the **procedure for learning RBM (Figure 2)** and fix its weights and offsets.
3. Train RBM 3 with the samples of the hidden layer of RBM 2 as inputs by the **procedure for learning RBM (Figure 2)** and fix its weights and offsets.
4. Perform supervised learning with the samples of the hidden layer of RBM 3 as inputs and the labels as the desired outputs.

Figure 4: Procedure for learning DBN with three RBMs.

4 Experiments

4.1 Experimental Setup

4.1.1 Data

We formed 13 training data sets by adding different amounts of automatically gathered data and/or pseudo data to a base data set, as shown in Table 2. In the table, m300 is the base data set including 300 pieces of manually gathered data and, for example, a2400 is a data set including 2,400 automatically gathered pieces of data and m300, p2400 is a data set including 2,400 pieces of pseudo data and m300, and a2400p2400 is a data set including 2,400 pieces of automatically gathered data, 2,400 pieces of pseudo data, and m300. Altogether there were 100 pieces of testing data. The number of labels was 10; i.e., the training data listed in Table 2 and the testing data have 10 labels. The dimension of the feature vectors constructed in accordance with the steps in Subsection 2.4 was 182.

m300			
a300	a600	a1200	a2400
p300	p600	p1200	p2400
a300p300	a600p600	a1200p1200	a2400p2400

Table 2: Training data sets.

4.1.2 Hyperparameter Search

The optimal hyperparameters of the various machine learning methods used were determined by a grid search using 5-fold cross-validation on training data. The hyperparameters for the grid search are shown in Table 3. To avoid unfair bias toward the DBN during cross-validation due to the DBN having more hyperparameters than the other methods, we divided the MLP and SVM hyperparameter grids more finely than that of the DBN so that they had the same or more hyperparameter combinations than the DBN. For MLP, we also considered another case in which we used network structures, learning rates, and learning epochs completely the same as those of the DBN. In this case, the number of MLP hyperparameter combinations was quite small compared to that of the DBN. We refer to this MLP as MLP 1 and to the former MLP as MLP 2. Ultimately, the DBN and MLP 2 both had 864 hyperparameter combinations, the SVM (Linear) and SVM (RBF) had 900, and MLP 1 had 72.

4.1.3 Baselines

For comparison, in addition to MLP and SVM, we run tests on baseline methods using example-based approaches and compare the testing data of each with all the training data to determine which one had the largest number of words corresponding to the testing data. The algorithm is shown in Figure 5, where the words used for counting are those extracted from the descriptive texts in accordance with steps (1)–(4) in Subsection 2.4.

[3] As an example, the structure (hidden layers) **152-121-91** shown in the table refers to a DBN with a 182-**152-121-91**-10 structure, where 182 and 10 refer to dimensions of the input and output layers, respectively. These figures were set not in an arbitrary manner but using regular intervals in a linear form, i.e., $152 = 182 \times 5/6$, $121 = 182 \times 4/6$, and $91 = 182 \times 3/6$.

Machine learning methods	Hyperparameters	Values
DBN	structure (hidden layers)[3]	91, 137-91, 152-121-91, 273, 273-273, 273-273-273
	ϵ of pre-training	0.001, 0.01, 0.1
	ϵ of fine-tuning	0.001, 0.01, 0.1
	epoch of pre-training	500, 1000, 2000, 3000
	epoch of fine-tuning	500, 1000, 2000, 3000
MLP 1	structure (hidden layers)	91, 137-91, 152-121-91, 273, 273-273, 273-273-273
	ϵ	0.001, 0.01, 0.1
	epoch	500, 1000, 2000, 3000
MLP 2	structure (hidden layers)	91, 137-91, 152-121-91, 273, 273-273, 273-273-273
	ϵ	0.001, 0.0025, 0.005, 0.0075, 0.01, 0.025, 0.05, 0.075, 0.1
	epoch	6 divisions between 500-1000 and 10 divisions between 1200-3000 in a linear scale
SVM (Linear)	γ	900 divisions between 10^{-4}-10^4 in a logarithmic scale
SVM (RBF)	γ	30 divisions between 10^{-4}-10^4 in a logarithmic scale
	C	30 divisions between 10^{-4}-10^4 in a logarithmic scale

Table 3: Hyperparameters for grid search.

For each input **i** of testing data **do**
  For each input **j** of training data **do**
    1. Count the same words between **i** and **j**
    2. Find the **j** with the largest count and set **m=j**
  End for
  1. Let the label of **m** of training data (**r**) be the predicting result of the input **i**
  2. Compare **r** with the label of **i** of testing data and determine the correctness
End for
1. Count the correct predicting results and compute the correct rate (precision)

Figure 5: Baseline algorithm.

4.2 Results

Figure 6 compares the testing data precisions when using different training data sets with individual machine learning methods. The precisions are averages when using the top N sets of the hyperparameters in ascending order of the cross-validation errors, with N varying from 5 to 30.

As shown in the figure, both the DBN and the MLPs had the highest precisions overall and the SVMs had approximately the highest precision when using data set a2400p2400, i.e., in the case of adding the largest number of automatically gathered data and pseudo data to the manually gathered data as training data. Moreover, the DBN, MLPs, and SVM (RBF) all had higher precisions when adding the appropriate amount of automatically gathered data and pseudo data compared to the case of using only manually gathered data, but the SVM (Linear) did not have this tendency.[4] Further, the DBN and SVM (RBF) had higher precisions when adding the appropriate amount of automatically gathered data only, whereas the MLPs had higher precisions when adding the appropriate amount of pseudo data only compared to the case of using only manually gathered data. From these results, we can infer that (1) all the machine learning methods (excluding SVM (Linear)) can improve their precisions by adding automatically gathered and pseudo data as training data and that (2) the DBN and SVM (RBF) can deal with noisier data than the MLPs, as the automatically gathered data are noisier than the pseudo data.

Figure 7 compares the testing data precisions of DBN and MLPs and of DBN and SVMs when using different training data sets (i.e., the data set of Table 2) that are not distinguished from each other. As in Figure 6, the precisions are averages of using the top N sets of hyperparameters in ascending order of the cross-validation errors, with N varying from 5 to 30. We can see at a glance that the performance of the DBN was generally superior to all the other machine learning methods. We should point out that the ranges of the vertical axes of all the graphs are set to be the same and so four lines of the SVM (RBF)

[4]This is because the SVM (Linear) can only deal with data capable of linear separation.

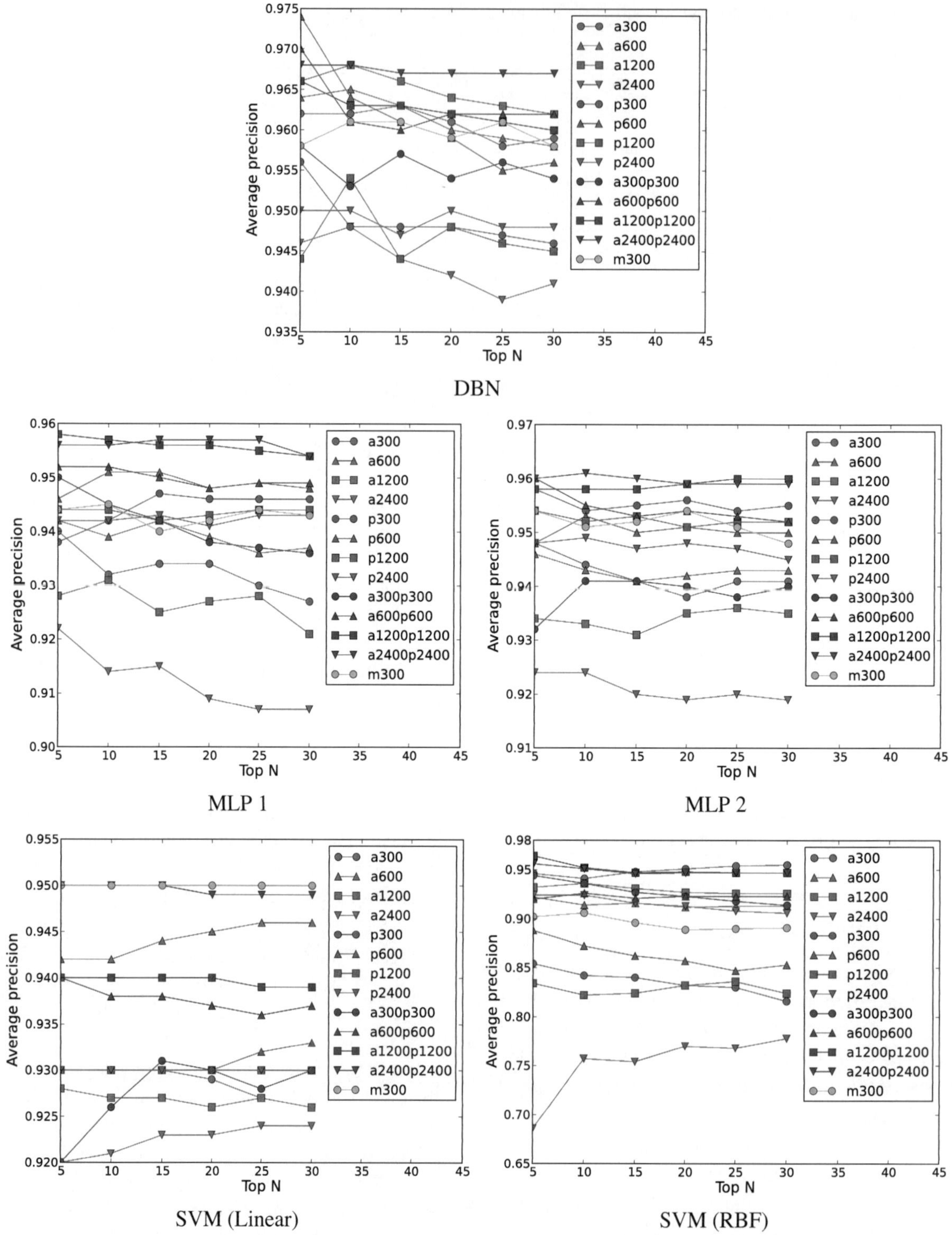

Figure 6: Average precisions of DBN, MLP, and SVM for top N varying from 5 to 30.

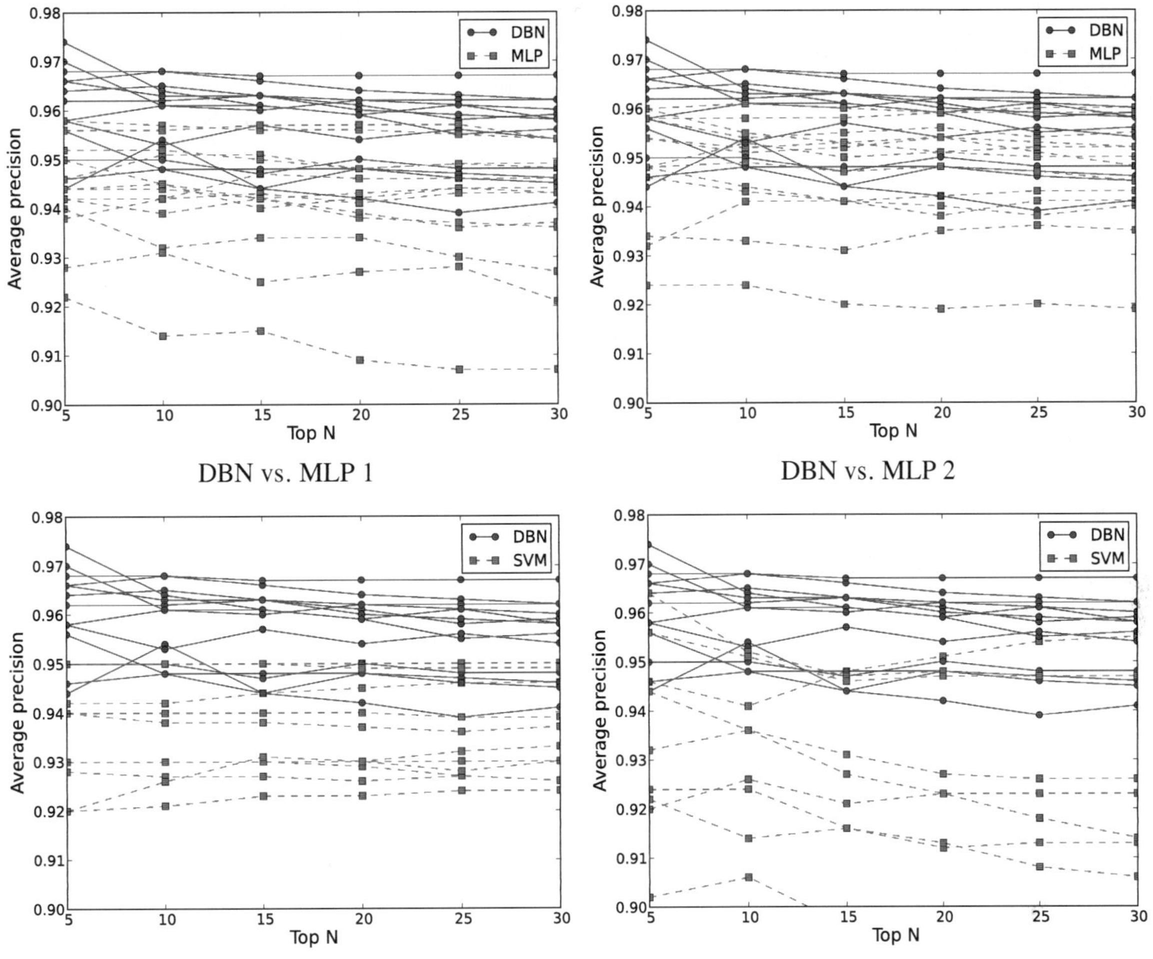

DBN vs. MLP 1

DBN vs. MLP 2

DBN vs. SVM (Linear)

DBN vs. SVM (RBF)

Figure 7: Comparison of average precisions for top N varying from 5 to 30.

are not indicated in the DBN vs. SVM (RBF) graph because their precisions were lower than 0.9. Full results, however, are shown in Figure 6.

Table 4, 5, and 6 show the precisions of the baseline method and the average precisions of the machine learning methods for the top 5 and 10 sets of hyperparameters in ascending order of the cross-validation errors, respectively, when using different data sets for training. First, in contrast to the machine learning methods, we see that adding noisy training data (i.e., adding only the automatically gathered data or adding both the automatically gathered and the pseudo data) was not useful for the baseline method to improve the prediction precisions: on the contrary, the noisy data significantly reduced the prediction precisions. Second, in almost all cases, the precisions of the baseline method were far lower than those of all machine learning methods. Finally, we see that in almost all cases, the DBN had the highest precision (the bold figures in the tables) of all the machine learning methods.

In addition, even when only using the base data set (i.e., the manually gathered data (m300)) for training, we can conclude from Figure 6 and Table 5 and 6 that, in all cases, the precision of DBN was the highest.

5 Conclusion

We proposed methods to predict retrieval terms from the relevant/surrounding words or the descriptive texts in Japanese by using deep belief networks (DBN), one of the two typical types of deep learn-

	m300	a300	a600	a1200	a2400	p300	p600
Baseline	0.850	0.500	0.320	0.390	0.370	0.850	0.840

	p1200	p2400	a300p300	a600p600	a1200p1200	a2400p2400
Baseline	0.840	0.840	0.510	0.320	0.390	0.370

Table 4: Precisions of the baseline.

	m300	a300	a600	a1200	a2400	p300	p600
MLP 1	0.944	0.940	0.942	0.928	0.922	0.938	0.946
MLP 2	0.954	0.948	0.946	0.934	0.924	**0.958**	0.948
SVM (Linear)	0.950	0.930	0.942	0.928	0.920	0.930	0.930
SVM (RBF)	0.902	0.946	0.922	0.932	0.924	0.854	0.888
DBN	**0.958**	**0.962**	**0.964**	**0.966**	**0.946**	0.956	**0.974**

	p1200	p2400	a300p300	a600p600	a1200p1200	a2400p2400
MLP 1	0.944	0.942	0.950	0.952	0.958	0.956
MLP 2	**0.954**	0.948	0.932	0.960	0.958	0.960
SVM (Linear)	0.930	0.930	0.920	0.940	0.940	0.950
SVM (RBF)	0.834	0.686	0.944	0.920	0.964	0.956
DBN	0.944	**0.950**	**0.958**	**0.970**	**0.966**	**0.968**

Table 5: Average precisions of DBN, MLP, and SVM for top 5.

	m300	a300	a600	a1200	a2400	p300	p600
MLP 1	0.945	0.932	0.939	0.931	0.914	0.942	0.951
MLP 2	0.951	0.944	0.943	0.933	0.924	**0.954**	0.953
SVM (Linear)	0.950	0.930	0.942	0.927	0.921	0.930	0.930
SVM (RBF)	0.960	0.941	0.914	0.936	0.924	0.842	0.872
DBN	**0.961**	**0.962**	**0.965**	**0.968**	**0.948**	0.948	**0.964**

	p1200	p2400	a300p300	a600p600	a1200p1200	a2400p2400
MLP 1	0.944	0.942	0.945	0.952	0.957	0.956
MLP 2	0.952	0.949	0.941	0.955	0.958	0.961
SVM (Linear)	0.930	0.930	0.926	0.938	0.940	0.950
SVM (RBF)	0.822	0.757	0.936	0.926	0.952	0.951
DBN	**0.954**	**0.950**	**0.953**	**0.961**	**0.963**	**0.968**

Table 6: Average precisions of DBN, MLP, and SVM for top 10.

ing. To determine the effectiveness of using DBN for this task, we tested it along with baseline methods using example-based approaches and conventional machine learning methods such as MLP and SVM in comparative experiments. The data for training and testing were obtained from the Web in both manual and automatic manners. We also used automatically created pseudo data. We adopted a grid search to obtain the optimal hyperparameters of these methods by performing cross-validation on the training data. Experimental results showed that (1) using DBN has far higher prediction precisions than using the baseline methods and has higher prediction precisions than using either MLP or SVM; (2) adding automatically gathered data and pseudo data to the manually gathered data as training data further improves the prediction precisions; and (3) DBN and SVM (RBF) are able to deal with more noisier training data than MLP, i.e., the prediction precision of DBN can be improved by adding noisy training data, but that of MLP cannot be.

In our future work, we plan to re-confirm the effectiveness of the proposed methods by scaling up the experimental data and then start developing various practical domain-specific systems that can predict suitable retrieval terms from the relevant/surrounding words or descriptive texts.

Acknowledgments

This work was supported by JSPS KAKENHI Grant Number 25330368.

References

M. Auli, M. Galley, C. Quirk, and G. Zweig. 2013. Joint Language and Translation Modeling with Recurrent Neural Networks. *EMNLP 2013*, 1044–1054.

Y. Bengio, P. Lamblin, D. Popovici, and H. Larochelle. 2007. Greedy Layer-wise Training of Deep Networks. 153–160. *NIPS 2006*, 153–160.

Y. Bengio. 2009. Learning Deep Architectures for AI. *Foundations and Trends in Machine Learning*, 2(1):1–127.

Y. Bengio, A. Courville, and P. Vincent. 2013. Representation Learning: A Review and New Perspectives. *IEEE Transactions on Pattern Analysis and Machine Intelligence*, 35(8):1798–1828.

R. Billingsley and J. Curran. 2012. Improvements to Training an RNN Parser. *COLING 2012*, 279–294.

R. Collobert, J. Weston, L. Bottou, M. Karlen, K. Kavukcuoglu, and P. Kuksa. 2011. Natural Language Processing (Almost) from Scratch. *Journal of Machine Learning Research*, 12:2493–2537.

X. Glorot, A. Bordes, and Y. Bengio. 2011. Domain Adaptation for Large-Scale Sentiment Classification: A Deep Learning Approach. *ICML 2011*, 513–520.

K. Hashimoto, M. Miwa, Y. Tsuruoka, and T. Chikayama. 2013. Simple Customization of Recursive Neural Networks for Semantic Relation Classification. *EMNLP 2013*, 1372–1376.

K. M. Hermann and P. Blunsom. 2013. The Role of Syntax in Vector Space Models of Compositional Semantics. *ACL 2013*, 894–904.

G. E. Hiton, S. Osindero, and Y. Teh. 2006. A Fast Learning Algorithm for Deep Belief Nets. *Neural Computation*, 18:1527–1554.

P. S. Huang, X. He, J. Gao, L. Deng, A. Acero, and L. Heck 2013. Learning deep structured semantic models for web search using clickthrough data. *CIKM 2013*, 2333–2338.

N. Kalchbrenner and P. Blunsom. 2013. Recurrent Continuous Translation Models. *EMNLP 2013*, 1700–1709.

A. Krizhevsky, I. Sutskever, and G. E. Hinton. 2012. ImageNet Classification with Deep Convolutional Neural Networks. *NIPS 2012*, 1097–1105.

H. Lee, R. Grosse, R. Ranganath, and A. Y. Ng. 2009. Convolutional Deep Belief Networks for Scalable Unsupervised Learning of Hierarchical Representations. *ICML 2009*, 609-616.

L. Li and Y. Zhao, et al. 2013. Hybrid Deep Neural Network - Hidden Markov Model (DNN-HMM) Based Speech Emotion Recognition. *ACII 2013*.

L. Liu, T. Watanabe, E. Sumita and T. Zhao. 2013. Additive Neural Networks for Statistical Machine Translation. *ACL 2013*, 791–801.

T. Luong, R. Socher, and C. Manning. 2013. Better Word Representations with Recursive Neural Networks for Morphology. *ACL 2013*, 104–113.

R. Salakhutdinov and G. E. Hinton. 2009. Semantic Hashing. *International Journal of Approximate Reasoning*, 50(7): 969-978.

F. Seide, G. Li, and D. Yu. 2011. Conversational Speech Transcription Using Context-Dependent Deep Neural Networks. *INTERSPEECH 2011*, 437-440.

R. Socher, E. H. Huang, J. Pennington, A. Y. Ng, and C. D. Manning. 2011. Dynamic Pooling and Unfolding Recursive Autoencoders for Paraphrase Detection. 801–809. *NIPS 2011*, 801–809.

R. Socher, J. Bauer, C. D. Manning, and A. Y. Ng. 2013. Parsing with Computational Vector Grammars. *ACL 2013*, 455–465.

R. Socher, A. Perelygin, J. Y. Wu, and J. Chuang. 2013. Recursive Deep Models for Semantic Compositionality Over a Sentiment Treebank. *EMNLP 2013*, 1631–1642.

S. Srivastava, D. Hovy, and E. H. Hovy. 2013. A Walk-Based Semantically Enriched Tree Kernel Over Distributed Word Representations. *EMNLP 2013*, 1411–1416.

M. Tsubaki, K. Duh, M. Shimbo, and Y. Matsumoto. 2013. Modeling and Learning Semantic Co-Compositionality through Prototype Projections and Neural Networks. *EMNLP 2013*, 130–140.

P. Vincent, H. Larochelle, Y. Bengio, and P. A. Manzagol. 2008. Extracting and Composing Robust Features with Denoising Autoencoders. *ICML 2008*, 1096–1103.

P. Vincent, H. Larochelle, I. Lajoie, Y. Bengio, and P. A. Manzagol. 2010. Stacked Denoising Autoencoders: Learning Useful Representations in a Deep Network with a Local Denoising Criterion. *Journal of Machine Learning Research*, 11:3371–3408.

W. Y. Zou, R. Socher, D. M. Cer, and C. D. Manning. 2013. Bilingual Word Embeddings for Phrase-Based Machine Translation. *EMNLP 2013*, 1393–1398.

Word-level Language Identification in Bi-lingual Code-switched Texts

Harsh Jhamtani
Adobe systems
Bangalore, India
harshjhamtani@gmail.com

Suleep Kumar Bhogi
Samsung R&D institute
Bangalore, India
suleep.kumar@gmail.com

Vaskar Raychoudhury
Dept. of Comp. Sc. & Engg.
IIT Roorkee, India
vaskar@gmail.com

Abstract

Code-switching is the practice of moving back and forth between two languages in spoken or written form of communication. In this paper, we address the problem of word-level language identification of code-switched sentences. Here, we primarily consider Hindi-English (Hinglish) code-switching, which is a popular phenomenon among urban Indian youth, though the approach is generic enough to be extended to other language pairs. Identifying word-level languages in code-switched texts is associated with two major challenges. Firstly, people often use non-standard English transliterated forms of Hindi words. Secondly, the transliterated Hindi words are often confused with English words having the same spelling. Most existing works tackle the problem of language identification using n-grams of characters. We propose some techniques to learn sequence of character(s) frequently substituted for character(s) in standard transliterated forms. We illustrate the superior performance of these techniques in identifying Hindi words corresponding to the given transliterated forms. We adopt a novel experimental model which considers the language and part-of-speech of adjoining words for word-level language identification. Our test results show that the proposed model significantly increases the accuracy over existing approaches. We achieved F1-score of 98.0% for recognizing Hindi words and 94.8% for recognizing English words.

1 Introduction

Code-switching is a popular linguistic phenomenon where the speaker alternates between two or more languages even within the same sentence. In countries like India, where there are more than 20 widely used languages, code-switching is an even more pronounced feature, mostly among urban population (Thakur et al., 2007). Hindi and English are two popular ones among these languages, with millions of people communicating through them in pure forms or using a mixture of words from both the languages (code-switched), popularly known as 'Hinglish'.

Many multi-national brands use Hinglish taglines for promoting their products in India. For example, "*Khushiyon ki* home delivery"[1] is the tag line for Domino's Pizza ™ India. Hinglish is also used for casual communication among friends, for example, "*Main* temple *ke pass hoon*" meaning "I am near the temple". There are plenty of research works focusing on analyzing texts used in popular forums, like online social groups, for applications like opinion mining, sentiment analysis, etc. However, machine analysis of Hinglish or any other code-switched text poses the following challenges.

- **Inconsistent spelling usage**: Despite the availability of the standards for transliteration (e.g., ITRANS [2]) of Devanagari script to Roman script (the Hindi language is based on Devanagari script while the English language is based on Roman script), people tend to use many inconsistent spellings for the same word. For example, the most common English transliteration for the Hindi word मैं is *mai*, as observed from our data set. But people often use *mein* or *main* as alternatives.

- **Ambiguous word usage**: The transliterated word *main*, for the Hindi

[1] http://www.dominos.co.in/blog/tag/khushiyon-ki-home-delivery/
[2] ITRANS: http://www.aczoom.com/itrans/

Copyright 2014 by Harsh Jhamtani, Suleep Kumar Bhogi, and Vaskar Raychoudhury
28th Pacific Asia Conference on Language, Information and Computation pages 348–357

word मैं could be misinterpreted by a machine to be the English word.

In order to address the afore-mentioned challenges and to enable automated analysis for code-switched languages, we need to identify the language of individual words. In case of transliterated Hindi words, we also need to find the authentic script. For example, in the sentence '*Main* temple *ke pass hoon*' the word 'main' is a non-standard transliterated form for the Hindi word मैं and 'pass' refers to the Hindi word पास and not the English word.

We propose some novel solutions to address the problem of word-level language identification in code-switched texts. Our major contributions can be summarized as below.

- We build a model to tackle the inconsistent spelling usage problem. The model learns the most common deviations from a standard transliteration scheme in English transliteration of Hindi words by identifying the erroneous character(s) that are frequently used in place of correct character(s) in standard transliterated forms.
- In addition to n-grams of characters, we use frequency of usage of a word in English and in Hindi languages as features for word-level language identification.
- We propose a technique using language and part-of-speech of neighboring words which, to the best of our knowledge, has not been applied before to solve this problem.
- We achieved F1-score of 98.0% for recognizing Hindi words and 94.8% for recognizing English words.

The rest of the paper is organized as follows. Section 2 describes the related work. Section 3 describes the data sets used. Section 4 describes the algorithms and features used. Section 5 describes the experiments conducted and their results.

2 Related Work

The socio-linguistic and grammatical aspects of code-switched texts have already been studied by many researchers. Ritchie and Bhatia (1996) and Kachru (1978) have discussed and examined different types of constraints on code-switching. Agnihotri (1998) discussed a number of examples of Hindi-English code-switching which do not comply with the constraints proposed in other literature. However, many of the constraints proposed for code switching, like the Free Morpheme Constraint (Sankoff and Poplack, 1981) and the Equivalence Constraint (Pfaff, 1979), are still widely applicable.

Automatic language identification research has focused on identifying both spoken languages as well as written texts. Language identification of speech has been studied by House and Neuburg (1977), where the authors assumed that the linguistic classes of a language are probabilistic functions of a Markov chain. Language identification of written texts has been studied at document-level as well as at word-level perspectives. Two major techniques adopted are *n-gram* (Cavnar and Trenkle, 1994) and *dictionary-lookup* (Řehůřek and Kolkus, 2009). Most of the existing research works on document-level language identification consider only mono-lingual documents (Hughes et al., 2006).

Word-level language identification in code-switched texts has received little attention so far. King and Abney (2013) have used weakly supervised methods based on n-grams of characters. However, their training data is limited to monolingual documents, which limits the capability to capture some patterns in code-switched texts. Nguyen and Dogruoz (2013) experimented with linear-chain CRFs to tackle the problem. But their contextual features are limited to bigrams of words. Our approach is more general in the sense we consider the language and POS (Part-of-speech) of the neighbouring words. So our approach will work for bigrams of words not present in training data.

Automatically identifying linguistic code-switching (**LCS**) points in code-switched texts have been studied by Joshi (1982), and Solorio and Liu (2008). Elfardy et al. (2013) tackled the problem of identifying LCS points at the word level in a given Arabic text. They used sound change rules (SCR) that model possible phonological variant of the word, along with 3-gram model for dialect identification at word-level.

Aswani and Gaizauskas (2010) proposed a bi-directional mapping from character(s) in the Devanagari script to character(s) in the Roman script for the purpose of transliteration. But they have manually come up with a limited number of mappings. Dasigi and Diab (2011) used string based similarity metrics and contextual string similarity to identify orthographic variants in Dialectal Arabic.

3 Data Sets

In this section, we describe the datasets used for our experimentation.

3.1 Data set 1: Hinglish sentences

We have a dataset of 500 Hinglish sentences containing a total of 3,287 words (CNERG[3]). Each word is labeled as Hindi (H) or English (E). Out of these, 2420 are labeled as Hindi words while the rest 867 are labeled as English words. Corresponding to each Hindi word, the authentic Devanagari script is also written. Some examples from this dataset are given below.

bangalore\E ke\H=के technical\E log\H=लोग

We have another data set of 1000 sentences of social network chats. To avoid any bias, the data set was tagged manually by three people not associated with this work. The mean Cohen's kappa coefficient of inter-annotator agreement between the sets of annotations was 0.852. There were few disagreements on the language of some named entities. An example from this dataset is given below.

Main\H=मैं main\E temple\E ke\H=के pass\H=पास hoon\H=हूँ.

Above two data sets were clubbed to form the *Data set 1*.

3.2 Data set 2: Transliteration Pairs

The data set comprises of commonly used multiple transliterated forms of Hindi words. It contains 30,823 Hindi words (Roman script) followed by the corresponding word in Devanagari script (Gupta et al., 2012). Some examples from this dataset are given below.

tera तेरा thera तेरा
teraa तेरा teraaa तेरा

3.3 Data set 3: Hindi word-frequency list

It is a Hindi word frequency list which has 117,789 Hindi words (in Devanagari script) along with their frequency computed from a large corpus (Quasthoff et al., 2006). Some examples of this dataset are as below:

लेने 2226 के 2143862

Also we generated a list standard transliteration forms of all these words using ITRANS rules. This list will be referred to as *Translated Hindi Dictionary*.

3.4 Data set 4: English word-frequency list

It is a standard dictionary of 207,824 English words along with their frequencies computed from a large news corpus.

4 Word-level Language Identification

Our model contains two classifiers. The *Classifier 1* works by combining four independent features as shown in the functional diagram Fig. 1. These features do not take into account the context of the word.

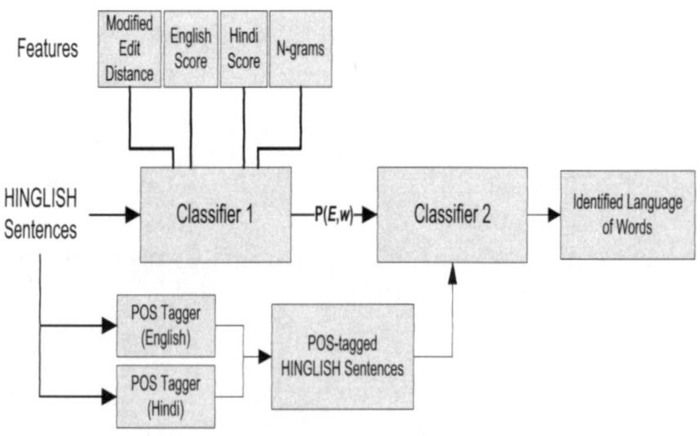

Fig 1. Functional Diagram of our Approach

The *Classifier 2* operates on the output of *Classifier 1* and the POS tagged Hinglish sentences. This classifier considers some contextual features which take into account the language and POS of neighboring words.

4.1 Using Word-level features : Classifier 1

Here, we describe the features used for *Classifier 1*. The classifier outputs the probability P with

[3] http://cse.iitkgp.ac.in/resgrp/cnerg/

which *w* is an English word, for each word *w* in a Hinglish sentence. If we call this probability P(E, w), then P(H, w) = 1- P(E, w), where P(H, w) is the probability with which *w* is a Hindi word.

4.1.1 Common Spelling Substitutions and String Similarity (Modified Edit Distance)

This feature is used to address the inconsistent spelling usage problem discussed in the Introduction section. To solve this problem, for every word we try to find the most similar word in our Transliterated Hindi Dictionary using string similarity algorithms, like 'Edit Distance' (Wagner and Fischer, 1974).

However, we observed cases in code-switching texts where this algorithm does not produce the intended outcome. For example, for the Hindi word खुशबू, the possible transliterated forms are *khushboo* and *khushbu* with the former being the standard one. With the Edit Distance algorithm applied over the two forms, we shall get a dissimilarity value of 2. The same algorithm applied over the strings *khushbu* and *khushi* (खुशी), which refer to different Hindi words, also gives the same dissimilarity value. However, for all practical purposes, *khushbu* is much closer to *khushboo* than it is to *khushi*. It is an observed fact that people often tend to substitute, 'u' in place of 'oo' while writing transliterated forms. But the Edit Distance algorithm does not capture this fact. We call this type of substitutions as *common spelling substitutions*.

To overcome this problem, we have developed a 'Modified Edit Distance' (**MED**) algorithm (Fig. 2) which considers the common spelling substitutions. The idea is similar to Weighted Edit Distance (Kurtz, 1996), but in case of MED we automate the process of deciding the corresponding *weights*. We have experimented with four different methods to learn *common spelling substitutions* using the *Transliteration Pairs* data set. Here we present the working of the four methods.

Method 1

In this method, given the standard transliterated form *w1*of a word and a non-standard form *w2* of the same word, we try to generate substitution pairs by first aligning the consonants. We add ';' at start and end of each word to act as delimiters. ';' is also to be considered as a consonant for the following procedure.

Consider a variable *i* varying from 1 to length of *w1*. For a consonant *c* at position *i* of *w1*, we try to align it with a consonant at the smallest position *j* of *w2* such that:

- j^{th} character of *w2* is same as *c*.
- No character of *w2*, at a position greater than or equal to *j*, has already been aligned.
- $|j-i|<=3$

If it is not possible to align a consonant, then it is not aligned. We define a segment to be a sequence of characters delimited by two aligned consonants (delimiting consonants inclusive). The two words will contain same number of segments. We consider two corresponding segments as substitution pairs if they do not have identical sequence of letters.

e.g. w1=;tera; , w2=;teraa;

```
; t e r a ;
| |   |   \
; t e r a a ;
```

S1 = {;t, ter, ra;}
S2 = {;t, ter, raa;}

This generates a substitution pair (ra;, raa;). Some substitution pairs generated by this method are given in Table 1.

Substitution Pair		Frequency
ra;	r;	1055
na;	n;	775

Table 1. Substitution pairs generated by Method 1

Method 2

For this method, the only difference with method 1 is in the way the segments are defined. We define a segment to be a sequence of characters delimited by two aligned consonants (delimiting consonants *exclusive*). We consider two corresponding segments as substitution pairs if they do not have identical sequence of letters.

e.g. w1=;tera; , w2=;teraa;

```
; t e r a ;
| |   |   \
; t e r a a ;
```

S1 = {e, a}, S2 = {e, aa}

This generates a substitution pair (a, aa). Some substitution pairs generated by this method are given in Table 2.

Substitution Pair		Frequency
a	aa	7764
a	ha	872

Table 2. Substitution pairs generated by Method 2

Method 3

In this method, we do *not* include any delimiter at the beginning and end of the words. Rest of the working is same as in method 2.

```
m a i n
|     |
m e i n
```

Some substitution pairs generated by this method are given in Table 3.

Substitution Pair		Frequency
a	aa	8674
om	on	1243

Table 3. Substitution pairs generated by Method 3

Method 4

In this method, we align the vowels also. Rest of the working is same as in Method 3.

For example, consider *main* (*w1*) and *mein* (*w2*) as two spelling variants of transliterated form of the Hindi word मैं. We first align 'm' of *w1* with 'm' of *w2*, 'i' of *w1* with 'i' of *w2*, and 'n' of *w1* with 'n' of *w2*.

```
m a i n
|   | |
m e i n
```

This generates the substitution pair ('a', 'e'), i.e., 'e' has been used in place of 'a' interchangeably by the user. Some substitution pairs generated by this method are given in Table 4.

Substitution Pair		Frequency
i	ee	1742
f	ph	1444

Table 4. Substitution pairs generated by Method 4

In all methods we keep some threshold *thresh* for the frequency of substitution pairs. Substitution pairs occurring less than *thresh* are not further considered. The comparison of performance of MED based on these four methods will be discussed in the section 5.7.

Let *subsList* be the list of substitution pairs. Each entry *s* in *subsList* has attributes s_x, s_y, and s_f, where (s_x, s_y) is the substitution pair and s_f is the corresponding frequency of occurrence.

Consider a substitution pair s which occurs with frequency sf in the training data. Then the cost of using the substitution is $g(s_f)$, i.e., a function of frequency sf. Here, g(f) = k / (log10(f)), where, k is a constant.

```
modifiedEditDistance (transliteration w1,
transliteration w2, list of substitutions subsList)

N← length of w1
M← length of w2
initialize all elements of matrix dp[N][M] with 0
for i ←1 to N:
  for j ←1 to M:
   if w1[i] == w2[j]:
    v1←dp[i-1][j-1]
   else:
    v1← dp[i-1][j-1] + 1// substitution of a character
    v2← 1 + dp[i-1][j]  // deletion of a character
    v3← 1 + dp[i][j-1]  // insertion of a character
    v4← infinity
    for s in subsList:
      p← length of sx
      q← length of sy
      if w1 [i-p+1 : i] = sx and w2[j-q+1 : j] =sy :
        v4← min( v4 , g(sf) + dp[i-p][j-q] )
        dp[i][j] ← min( v1, v2, v3, v4)

output: MED(w1,w2) = dp[N][M]
```

Fig 2. Pseudo code for Modified Edit Distance Algorithm

We have used logarithmic scaling as the frequencies of occurrences of the substitution pairs are very much skewed towards larger values. For every other insertion, deletion and substitution of a character, cost is 1 as is commonly used for Edit Distance. For each word *w* in test data, we try to match it against words in our *Transliterated Hindi Dictionary*. The word corresponding to the minimum cost and the minimum cost itself computed by the above algorithm are stored. The minimum cost so obtained for each word is *dissimilarityScore* for that word. The algorithm for MED is shown in Fig.2.

4.1.2 Frequency of Occurrence in English and Hindi

Here we address the ambiguous word usage problem discussed in the Introduction section. Consider that the test data contains the word 'main', which can correspond to the Hindi word मैं or the English word. If we decide its language randomly, then the expected accuracy of identifying the correct language is 50%. If we know that *main* in English language is having higher usage frequency than the word मैं in Hindi language, then the probability of the test data word 'main' being an English word increases.

Using formula (1), we compute the value corresponding to this feature and we call it English score (*eng_score*). First, we use logarithmic scaling on frequencies of occurrences of English words to do away with its skewness towards large values. Then, we normalize the word frequency values with respect to the largest frequency observed.

$M = max\ (\ log(freq(q))\ )$
$\forall word\ q \in Hindi\ Dictionary$
For a given word w in the test data,
$score(w) = log(freq(w))/M$
$eng\_score(w) = 0,\ if\ w\ not\ in\ English\ Dictionary$
$= score(w),\ otherwise\ \ ...(1)$

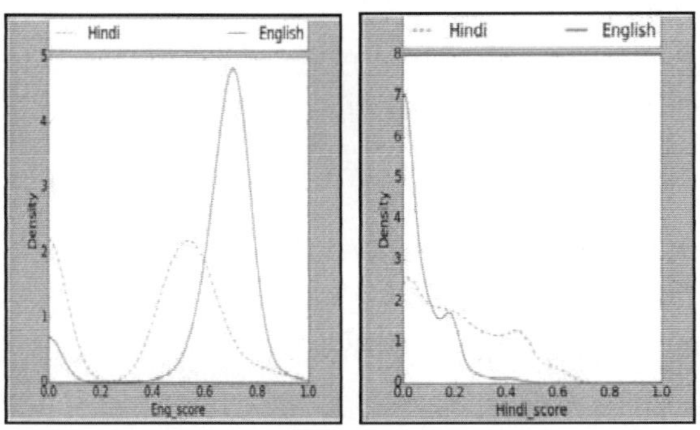

Fig 3. Density distribution plot for (a) English Score feature (b) Hindi Score feature

Similarly, we calculate the Hindi score (*hin_score*) using formula (2). However, first the MED algorithm is used to identify the closest matching Hindi word *hw* for a given word in the test data.

$M = max\ (\ log(freq(q))\ )$
$\forall word\ q \in Hindi\ Dictionary$
For a given word w in the test data,
$score(w) = log(freq(hw))/M$
$hin\_score(hw) = score(w)\ \ ...(2)$

Thus, we get English score and Hindi score for each word in the Dataset 1. The density distributions of *eng_score* and *hin_score* are shown in Fig. 3(a) and Fig. 3(b) respectively.

4.1.3 Character N-grams

This follows the idea that, in Hinglish sentences some contiguous sequences of letters occur more frequently in words of one language as compared to the words of the other language. For example, bigram 'es' frequently occurs at the end of English words (like, roses, fries), often denoting plural morphological forms. We considered bigrams and trigrams of characters for the task of word-level language identification. We used the technique of Delta TF-IDF, which has been shown to be more effective in binary classification of class imbalanced data using unigrams, bigrams, and trigrams (Martineau et al., 2009)

For any term t (n-gram of characters) in word w, the Delta TF-IDF score V is computed using formula (3).

$$V(t,w) = n(t,w) * log_2(H_t / E_t) \quad ----(3)$$

Where n (t, w) is the frequency count of term t in word w. H_t and E_t are the number of occurrences of term t in the English and Hindi dictionaries. Thus for every word w, we generate a set of feature values, with each n-gram t contributing one value.

4.2 Using Context Level Features: Classifier 2

All the previous features we have discussed focus on individual words of a code-switched sentence on a stand-alone basis, i.e., independent of the surrounding words or context. However, language usage of words in code-switched sentences may follow certain patterns, like words of a language are often surrounded by words of the same language (King and Abney, 2013). We tried to capture this context-dependence by considering the language and the POS of the surrounding words. For example, words on the two sides of conjunctions 'and', '*aur* (और)', etc. are usually of same language as the conjunction.

Our Classifier 2 operates over POS-tagged Hinglish sentences and the output from Classifier 1, i.e., P(E, w) (Refer to Fig.1.). The notations and symbols are shown in table 5, and the corresponding procedure is presented in Fig.4.

We annotated POS of each word in the training data set with POS taggers. For English, we used Stanford NLP Maxent POS tagger (Toutanova et al., 2003). In case, the word has more than one possible POS usage, we consider the most frequent POS usage. For Hindi words, we used POS tagger by Reddy and Sharoff (2011). For each word *w* in the training data, we assign an *identifier* (**id**) X_P to it, where X can take values 'E' (for English) or 'H' (for Hindi), and P is the corresponding POS of the word. For example, if 'car' is an English noun (NN), then its id will be as E_NN.

We then count the number of occurrences of various bigrams of ids' in the training data. We use these counts to calculate the conditional probability of an identifier to occur given the previous identifier e.g. $P(id_2|id_1)$ is the probability that identifier id_1 will be followed by identifier id_2.

For each word *w*, we have at most two possible candidate interpretations - Hindi word *wH* with POS as *PwH*, and English word *wE* with POS as *PwE*. *wH* is found using MED algorithm and *wE* is found using English Dictionary lookup. Now *w* refers to *wE* with probability P(E,w), and refers to *wH* with probability P(H, w) e.g. if *w* is 'main', then *wH* is मैं and *wE* is the English word *main*. Now the identifier corresponding to w_1H will be H_PRP as मैं is a Hindi personal pronoun.

Symbol	Meaning
Sentence S	A Hinglish sentence which is a sequence of words $w_1w_2w_3 \ldots w_N$
Matrix prob_pos[M][M]	Conditional probability of the current word's identifier (id) to be i, given that the identifier (id) of the previous word is j, as learnt from the training data.
Array eng_prob[N]	eng_prob[i] = $P(E,w_i)$ = Probability of the ith word in sentence to be English, as provided by *Classifier 1*.
Array hin_tag[N]	hin_tag[i] = Pw_iH = POS tag of w_iH
Array eng_tag[N]	eng_tag[i] = Pw_iE = POS tag of w_iE
Integer M	total number of identifiers possible

Table 5. Notations and Symbols for classifier 2

Consider a Hinglish sentence $S = w_1w_2w_3 \ldots w_n$. A possible interpretation can be $S_x = w_1H\ w_2H\ w_3E \ldots w_NH$. Now S has an interpretation given by S_x with probability $P(S=S_x)$ given by:

$P(S=S_x) = P(H,w_1) * P(H,w_2) * P(E,w_3)..* P(H,w_n)$

Now we define score (S_x) as follows:

$score(S_x) = P(S=S_x) * P(id_2|id_1) * P(id_3|id_2)* \ldots * P(id_N|id_{N-1})$

For a sentence S with N words, we can have a maximum of 2^N such possibilities. Now calculating the maximum score over these possibilities has optimal sub-structures, which lets us use dynamic programming. Algorithm for *Classifier 2* is presented in Fig.4. We built a similar model using trigrams of identifiers.

```
maxLikelihood (Sentence S, prob_pos[M][M],
hindi_tag[N], eng_tag[N], eng_prob[N]):
N← length of s
Initialize all elements of dp [N+1][2] with 0
dp [0][0] ← 0.5
dp [0][1] ← 0.5
for i← 1 to N:
/* dp [i][0] is the maximum score such that wi refers to
wiE when S[1,2,...i] have been considered */
/* dp [i][1] is the maximum score such that wi refers to
wiH when S[1,2,...i] have been considered */
prev_val← dp [i-1][0]  // 0 => english
v1←prev_val * eng_prob[i] * trans_prob[PwiE][Pwi-1E]
prev_val← dp[i-1][1]  // 1 => hindi
v2←prev_val *(1- eng_prob[i])*trans_prob[PwiE][Pwi-
1H]
  dp [i][0] ← max(v1,v2)
// Similar procedure to calculate dp [i][1]
```

Fig. 4. Algorithm for Classifier 2 (using identifier bigram)

Consider following cases for the first three words of the sentence '*Main* main temple *ke pass hoon*':

Case 1: Main (H_PRP) main (E_JJ) temple (E_NN)
Case 2: Main (E_JJ) main (E_JJ) temple (E_NN)
Case 3: Main (H_PRP) main (H_PRP) temple (E_NN)
Case 4: Main (E_JJ) main (H_PRP) temple (E_NN)

Case 1 is the correct case. The bigrams of identifiers corresponding to the case 1 i.e. H_PRP-E_JJ and E_JJ-E_NN occur much more frequently in the training data as compared to bigrams of other cases.

5 Experimentation and Results

In this section, we shall discuss the experiments we carried out and the results obtained. We have used 10-fold cross validation technique. We experimented with different classifiers like Decision Tree, SVM and Random Forest, provided by *Scikit Learn* (Pedregosa et al., 2011).

5.1 Experiment 1: Presence in English Dictionary

In this experiment a word is classified as belonging to English class if it is present in English Dictionary otherwise the word is classified as belonging to Hindi class.

For this experiment, we sorted the words of the English Dictionary in decreasing order of the frequency of occurrences of words. Then we considered only the top K words for the experiment. The results for different values of K are shown in Table 6.

K	HPR[4]	HRE	HF1	EPR	ERE	EF1
100	0.74	0.98	0.84	0.31	0.02	0.04
500	0.76	0.96	0.85	0.59	0.15	0.24
1000	0.79	0.95	0.86	0.69	0.28	0.40
5000	0.85	0.93	0.89	0.75	0.55	0.64
10000	0.87	0.86	0.87	0.63	0.64	0.63
ALL	0.92	0.39	0.55	0.35	0.91	0.50

Table 6. Results of Experiment 1

We observed that with an increase in the number of words in the English dictionary, more English words will be correctly identified as 'English' words, resulting in increased recall values for the 'English' class (ERE). But at the same time more Hindi words would be incorrectly marked as English, resulting in decrease in HRE.

5.2 Experiment 2: King-Abney's approach

In this experiment we run the King's (2013) n-grams and context level algorithms on our data set. The results are shown in Table 7.

	HPR	HRE	HF1	EPR	ERE	EF1
Naïve Bayes	0.66	0.83	0.74	0.39	0.20	0.27
HMM	0.75	0.91	0.83	0.59	0.29	0.39
CRF	0.76	0.96	0.85	0.76	0.28	0.41

Table 7. Results of Experiment 2

5.3 Experiment 3: Using Delta TF-IDF on n-grams of characters (Our Approach)

In this experiment we used only one of our features for classification. We have used Delta TF_IDF scores of n-grams of characters as features in our *Classifier 1*. The results of experiment 3 are presented in Table 8. The best results are obtained using Random Forest with number of trees equal to 10.

	HPR	HRE	HF1	EPR	ERE	EF1
Random Forest	0.89	0.79	0.84	0.52	0.71	0.6

Table 8. Results of Experiment 3

5.4 Experiment 4: All word-level features (Classifier 1)

In this experiment we show the results produced by our Classifier 1 i.e., only using word-level features. Results of this experiment are presented in Table 9. We can see using other features, F1 scores have significantly increased.

	HPR	HRE	HF1	EPR	ERE	EF1
Random Forest	0.95	0.98	0.97	0.94	0.85	0.89

Table 9. Results of Experiment 4

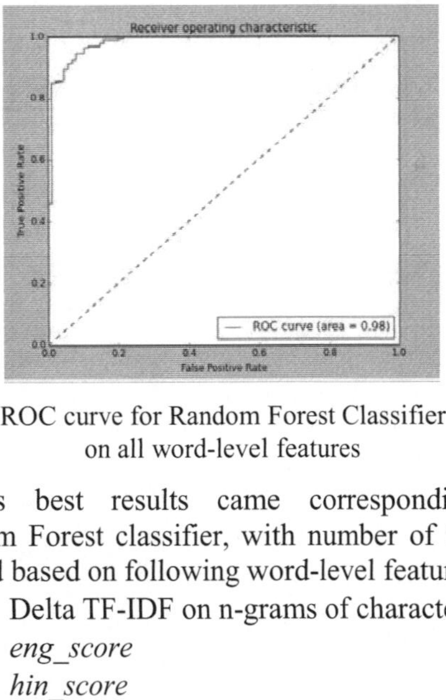

Fig.5. ROC curve for Random Forest Classifier based on all word-level features

Thus best results came corresponding to Random Forest classifier, with number of trees = 10, and based on following word-level features:

- Delta TF-IDF on n-grams of characters
- *eng_score*
- *hin_score*
- *dissimilarityScore*

The corresponding ROC curve has been shown in Fig 5. The AUC (Area Under the curve) is 0.98.

5.5 Experiment 6: Classifier 2

As input to Classifier 2, we used POS tagged Hinglish sentences and the output of Classifier 1,

[4] *HPR* = Precision for Hindi class, *HRE* = Recall for the Hindi, *HF1* = f1 score for the Hindi class
EPR = Precision for English class, *ERE* = Recall for the English class, *EF1* = f1 score for the English class

corresponding to the output from Experiment 4. We performed two experiments with Classifier 2 using bi-grams and tri-grams of identifiers. The results are shown in Table 10.

	HPR	HRE	HF1	EPR	ERE	EF1
Identifier bi-grams	0.974	0.969	0.972	0.920	0.934	0.926
Identifier tri-grams	0.983	0.977	0.980	0.941	0.955	0.948

Table 10. Results of Experiment 6

The accuracy of Classifier 2 obtained on using identifier tri-grams is more than the accuracy obtained on using identifier bi-grams. This is probably because usage of trigrams captures the context more efficiently. Moreover the improvement offered by Classifier 2 over Classifier 1 is only little. This is mainly because of the already high accuracy values of Classifier 1.

We found that the percentage of named entities in the Dataset 1 is 8.59%. We observed that the percentage of named entities in the wrongly classified words is 23.2%.

5.6 Experiment 7: Comparing four methods of creating substitution pairs

In this experiment we compare the results of previously described four methods to create substitution pairs. The results of this experiment is shown in Fig. 6. The K value which was defined in section 4.1.1 is varied to compare the results. It is observed that Method 2 gives best results among all methods discussed.

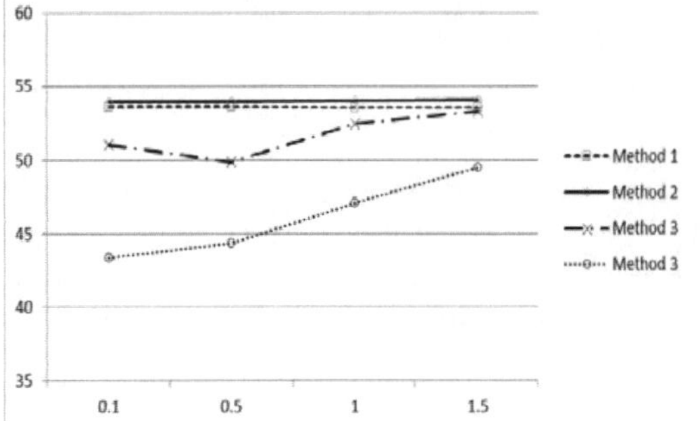

Fig 6. Graph showing comparison between four methods of creating substitution pairs

5.7 Performance of MED

To test the performance of MED algorithm in identifying correct Hindi words corresponding to given transliterated forms, we compared it with the some other well-known string matching algorithms: Damerau-Levenshtein (49.38%), Levenshtein (47.48%), Jaro-Winkler (50%), Soundex (46.23%). The accuracy of MED is 54.1%.

For each Hindi word *w* in the Hinglish data-set, we try to match it against every word in our *Transliterated Hindi Dictionary*. The word corresponding to the minimum cost is stored and later compared with the correct word. Fig.7 shows the results with a Hindi dictionary of size 117,789.

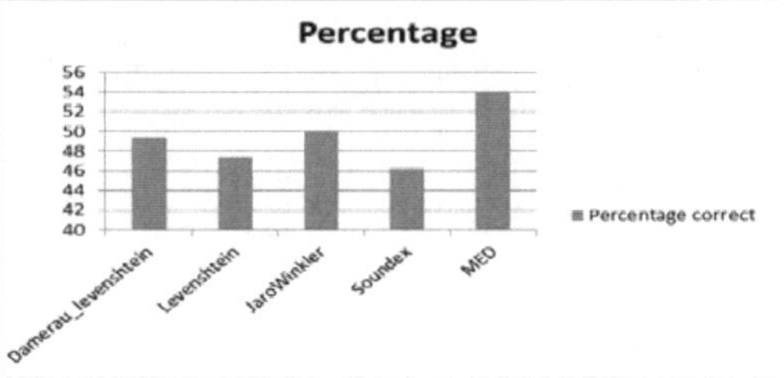

Fig 7. Performance of MED vs. other Algorithms

6 Conclusion

In this paper, we addressed the problem of word-level language identification in bilingual code-switched texts. We proposed a novel idea of utilizing the patterns in Hinglish sentences by considering the language and the POS of consecutive words. We proposed four different techniques to identify common spelling substitutions Our error analysis shows that a significant fraction of the errors made by the classifiers are actually named entities which are names of people or places, and can be considered either as Hindi or as English. In future, we would like to explore the changes of code-switching behavior from person to person. Also, we shall focus on other pairs of languages, like English-Bengali, English-Gujarati, etc. and also on word-level identification in multilingual code switched texts (i.e. having more than two languages).

7 References

Aravind K. Joshi. 1982. Processing of sentences with intra-sentential code-switching. In Proceedings of the 9th conference on Computational linguistics. Academia Praha, Volume 1: 145-150.

Arthur S. House, and Edward P. Neuburg. 1977. Toward automatic identification of the language of an utterance. I. Preliminary methodological considerations. The Journal of the Acoustical Society of America, 62: 708.

Baden Hughes, Timothu Baldwin, Steven Bird, Jeremy Nicholson, Andrew Mackinlay. 2006. Reconsidering language identification for written language resources. In Proc. International Conference on Language Resources and Evaluation: 485-488.

Ben King, and Steven P. Abney. 2013. Labeling the Languages of Words in mixed-language documents using weakly supervised methods. In Proceedings of the 2013 NAACL-HLT.

Braj B Kachru. 1978. Toward structuring code from the point of view of their usefulness in mixing: An Indian perspective. International Journal of the Sociology of Language, 16:28-46.

Carol W. Pfaff. 1979. Constraints on language mixing: intra-sentential code-switching and borrowing in Spanish/English, Language: 291-318.

David Sankoff, and Shana Poplack. 1981. A formal grammar for code - switching 1. Research on Language & Social Interaction, 14(1): 3-45.

Dong Nguyen, and A. Seza Dogruoz. 2013. Word level language identification in online multilingual communication. ACL 2013.

Fabian Pedregosa, Gael Varoquaux Alexandre Gramfort, Vincent Michel, Bertrand Thirion, Olivier Grisel, Mathieu Blondel, Peter Prettenhofer, Ron Weiss, Vincent Dubourg, Jake Vanderplas, Alexandre Passos, David Cournapeau, Matthieu Brucher, Matthieu Perrot, Édouard Duchesnay. 2011. Scikit-learn: Machine learning in Python. The Journal of Machine Learning Research, 12: 2825-2830.

Heba Elfardy, Mohamed Al-Badrashiny, and Mona Diab. 2013. Code Switch point detection in Arabic Natural Language Processing and Information Systems. Springer: 412-416.

Justin Martineau, Tim Finin, Anupam Joshi, and Shamit Patel. 2009. Improving binary classification on text problems using differential word features. In Proceedings of the 18th ACM CIKM.

Kanika Gupta, Monojit Choudhury, and Kalika Bali. 2012. Mining Hindi-English Transliteration Pairs from Online Hindi Lyrics, In Language Resources and Evaluation Conference: 2459-2465.

Kristina Toutanova, Dan Klein, Christopher D. Manning, and Yoram Singer. 2003. Feature-rich part-of-speech tagging with a cyclic dependency network. In Proceedings of the NAACL-HLT, Volume 1: 173-180.

Niraj Aswani, and Robert J. Gaizauskas. 2010. English-Hindi Transliteration using Multiple Similarity Metrics. In Language Resources and Evaluation Conference.

Pradeep Dasigi, and Mona Diab. 2011. CODACT: Towards Identifying Orthographic Variants in Dialectal Arabic. In Proceedings of the 5th International Joint Conference on Natural Language Processing.

Radim Řehůřek, and Milan Kolkus. 2009. Language identification on the web: Extending the dictionary method. In Computational Linguistics and Intelligent Text Processing.

Rama Kant Agnihotri. 1998. Mixed codes and their acceptability. Social psychological perspectives on second language learning: 191-215.

Robert A. Wagner, and Michael J. Fischer. 1974. The string-to-string correction problem. Journal of the Association for Computing Machinery (JACM), 21(1): 168-173.

Saroj Thakur, Kamlesh Dutta, and Aushima Thakur. 2007. Hinglish: Code switching, code mixing and indigenization in multilingual environment. Lingua Et Linguistica, 1.2 (2007): 109.

Siva Reddy, and Serge Sharoff. 2011. Cross language POS taggers (and other tools) for Indian languages: An experiment with Kannada using Telugu resources. Cross Lingual Information Access.

Stefan Kurtz. 1996. Approximate string searching under weighted edit distance. Proceedings of the 3rd South American Workshop on String Processing (WSP'96),

Thamar Solorio, and Yang Liu. 2008. Learning to predict code-switching points. In Proceedings of EMNLP, 973-981.

Uwe Quasthoff, Matthias Richter, and Chris Biemann. 2006. Corpus portal for search in monolingual corpora. In Proceedings of the fifth international conference on language resources and evaluation: 1799-1802.

William B. Cavnar, and John M. Trenkle. 1994. N-gram-based text categorization. Ann Arbor M, 48113(2): 161-175.

William C. Ritchie, and Tej K. Bhatia, eds. 1996. Bilingual language mixing, universal grammar, and second language acquisition. Handbook of second language acquisition: 627-688.

An Example-Based Approach to Difficult Pronoun Resolution

Canasai Kruengkrai Naoya Inoue Jun Sugiura Kentaro Inui
Graduate School of Information Sciences, Tohoku University
6-6 Aramaki Aza Aoba, Aobaku, Sendai, Miyagi 980-8579, Japan
{canasai,naoya-i,jun-s,inui}@ecei.tohoku.ac.jp

Abstract

A Winograd schema is a pair of twin sentences containing a referential ambiguity that is easy for a human to resolve but difficult for a computer. This paper explores the characteristics of world knowledge necessary for resolving such a schema. We observe that people tend to avoid ambiguous antecedents when using pronouns in writing. We present a method for automatically acquiring examples that are similar to Winograd schemas but have less ambiguity. We generate a concise search query that captures the essential parts of a given source sentence and then find the alignments of the source sentence and its retrieved examples. Our experimental results show that the existing sentences on the Web indeed contain instances of world knowledge useful for difficult pronoun resolution.

1 Introduction

Consider the following pair of sentences:[1]

(1) a. The outlaw shot the sheriff, but *he* did not shoot the deputy.

b. The outlaw shot the sheriff, but *he* shot back.

Suppose that the target pronoun is *he*, and its two candidate antecedents are *the outlaw* and *the sheriff*. The question is which of the two candidates is the correct antecedent for the target pronoun in each sentence? Most people resolve *he* to *the outlaw* in (1a) but to *the sheriff* in (1b) without noticing any ambiguity. However, for a computer program, this pronoun resolution becomes extremely difficult, requiring the use of world knowledge and the ability to reason. We refer to the pair of sentences like (1) as a *Winograd schema* (Levesque, 2011; Levesque et al., 2012). Note that the two sentences differ only in a few words and have a referential ambiguity that is resolved in opposite ways.

A previous work by Rahman and Ng (2012) showed that two sources of world knowledge, including narrative chains (Chambers and Jurafsky, 2008) and page counts returned by a search engine, are useful for resolving Winograd schemas. However, these two knowledge sources have their own weaknesses and need some heuristics to bridge the gap. Narrative chains suffer from the lack of discourse relations. For example, both sentences in (1) have a contrast relation indicated by *but*. However, narrative chains rely only on temporal relations between two events (e.g., *before* and *after*). Page counts used for estimating n-gram statistics are unstable and vary considerably over time (Lapata and Keller, 2005; Levesque et al., 2012). Therefore the answer to the question "what kind of world knowledge does a computer program need to have to resolve Winograd schemas?" (Levesque, 2013) is still unclear.

Rather than looking for new knowledge bases, we first examine whether existing sentences on the Web have sufficient evidence that could be applied to resolve Winograd schemas. If such evidence is available, we may be able to later generalize a collection of those sentences into a more abstract level of representation.

[1]The sentences are taken from the dataset created by Rahman and Ng (2012).

Copyright 2014 by Canasai Kruengkrai, Naoya Inoue, Jun Sugiura, and Kentaro Inui
28th Pacific Asia Conference on Language, Information and Computation pages 358–367

This paper explores the characteristics of world knowledge necessary for resolving Winograd schemas. We observe that people tend to avoid ambiguous antecedents when using pronouns in writing. Consider the following sentences derived from Web snippets:

(2) a. I shot Sherry, but I did not shoot Debbie.

b. Deputy Daniel Russ was working security outside the busy courthouse and was shot in the leg, but he shot back.

Both sentences in (2) have less ambiguity and are easier to be resolved. A vanilla coreference resolver can predict the coreference chains denoted by the underlined words in each sentence. Note that *he* in (2b) who shot back is the subject, while *Deputy Daniel Russ* who was shot is the object. Based on the structural similarity between (1b) and (2b), we infer that *he* in (1b) should be resolved to *the sheriff*, which is also the object. Likewise, *he* in (1a) should be resolved to *the outlaw* using the clue from (2a).

We present a method for automatically acquiring examples that are similar to Winograd schemas but have less ambiguity. First, we generate a concise search query that captures the essential parts of a given source sentence. Then, we find the alignments of the source sentence and its retrieved examples. Finally, we rank the most likely antecedent for the target pronoun using our score function.

In the following section, we discuss related work. Section 3 presents our approach. Section 4 shows our experimental results and error analysis. Section 5 concludes the paper with some directions of future research.

2 Related work

We classify the problem of pronoun resolution into two main categories: traditional anaphora and Winograd schemas.

Anaphora (or coreference) resolution has a long history in NLP. Ng (2010) and Poesio et al. (2011) provided excellent surveys of approaches to anaphora resolution. A variety of corpora and evaluation metrics also made it difficult for researchers to compare the performance of their systems. To establish benchmarking data and evaluation metrics, the CoNLL-2011 and CoNLL-2012 shared tasks mainly focused on coreference resolution (Pradhan et al., 2011; Pradhan et al., 2012).

The term "Winograd schema" was coined by Hector Levesque (2011), named after Terry Winograd who first used a pair of twin sentences to show the difficulty in natural language understanding (Winograd, 1972). Levesque proposed the Winograd Schema (WS) Challenge as an alternative to the Turing Test, which aims to test artificially intelligent systems. Unlike the Turing Test, the WS Challenge just requires systems to answer a collection of binary questions. These questions called Winograd schemas are pairs of sentences containing referential ambiguities that are easy for people to resolve but difficult for systems. A Winograd schema is designed to satisfy the following constraints (Levesque et al., 2012):

- Easily disambiguated by people;
- Not solvable by simple linguistic techniques;
- No obvious statistics over text corpora.

Levesque (2011) first provided an initial set of 19 Winograd schemas.[2] Rahman and Ng (2012) later released a relaxed version of Winograd schemas, consisting of 941 examples constructed by undergraduate students. In general, a WS sentence has main and subordinate clauses. The main clause has two candidate antecedents, and the subordinate clause has a target pronoun. The task is to resolve the target pronoun to one of the two candidate antecedents.

Shallow semantic attributes (e.g., gender and number) and grammatical relations would be useful for the traditional anaphora resolution. However, these linguistic features are not sufficient to solve the WS Challenge. Rahman and Ng (2012) proposed a ranking-based model that combines sophisticated linguistic features derived from different sources of world knowledge, such as narrative chains (Chambers and Jurafsky, 2008) and page counts returned by Google. Narrative chains are built by considering temporal relations between two events. However, the WS Challenge contains various discourse

[2] A collection of Winograd schemas has been updated and is available at: http://www.cs.nyu.edu/davise/papers/WS.html.

relations, such as explanation and contrast. Balasubramanian et al. (2013) found another issue of narrative chains in which unrelated actors are often mixed into the same chains. Lapata and Keller (2005) and Levesque et al. (2012) examined the use of page counts and found the stability issue.

The contribution of our work is the exploration of the necessary background knowledge for resolving the WS Challenge. To better understand the nature of the WS sentences, we propose to examine similar sentences having less ambiguity and develop a method for automatically acquiring those similar sentences from the Web.

3 Approach

Our goal is to acquire useful examples that are similar to the WS sentences. We try to retain lexical, syntactic, semantic, and discourse properties of the WS sentences. We represent a source sentence using the Stanford dependency (Section 3.1) and generate a search query to acquire examples from the Web (Section 3.2). We then align pairs of the source sentence and its retrieved examples (Section 3.3) and rank the most likely antecedent for the target pronoun using our score function (Section 3.4).

3.1 Dependency representation

We need to transform a sentence to a more generalized structure. The Stanford dependency (SD) representation is a practical scheme (de Marneffe et al., 2006). A dependency captures a grammatical relation holding between a head and a dependent. All dependencies for the sentence then map onto a directed graph, where words in the sentence are nodes and grammatical relations are edge labels. For example, focusing on dependencies for the candidate antecedents and the target pronoun, the sentence (1b) has the dependency structure as follows:

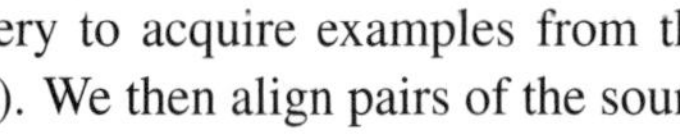

(3) The outlaw shot the sheriff, but he shot back.

In the main clause, the subject and direct object of *shot*$_3$ are *outlaw*$_2$ and *sheriff*$_5$, respectively. In the subordinate clause, the subject of *shot*$_9$ is *he*$_8$. The subscript indicates the word position in the sentence, including punctuation. Note that we only use headwords of candidate antecedents determined by using the Collins head rules (Collins, 1999). For example, the headword of the noun phrase "the sheriff" is "sheriff".

because (310)	that (16)	however (2)	until (2)
but (82)	even though (4)	as (2)	after (2)
since (69)	if (3)	then (2)	hence (1)
so (46)	although (2)	what (2)	
and (15)	when (2)	out of (2)	

Table 1: Statistics of conjunctions in Rahman's test set.

3.2 Example acquisition

We use the Google Web Search API to acquire examples from the Web. We consider Google's snippets as sentences and try to extract examples from these snippets. The question is what kind of examples would be useful for resolving difficult pronouns? Here we expect that a good example should have linguistic properties similar to a given source sentence but has less ambiguity. For example, the examples (2a) and (2b) have the similar grammatical, semantic, and discourse relations to the source sentences (1a) and (1b), but their pronouns are easier to be resolved. To retrieve such examples, our search queries should capture the essential parts of the source sentences while still being concise. In what follows, we describe our criteria on how to retain words in the source sentence when generating a search query.

Conjunction A WS sentence contains two clauses connected with a conjunction. The conjunction reflects a discourse relation between the two clauses. A line of work in cognitive science and linguistics shows that the discourse relation has a strong influence on pronoun interpretation (Hobbs, 1979; Kehler et al., 2008; Rohde and Kehler, 2013). Therefore a useful example should have the same discourse relation as the source sentence. Table 1 shows the statistics of conjunctions in Rahman's test set. The majority of discourse relations are explanation (e.g., *because* and *since*), followed by contrast (e.g., *but*).[3]

Heads of actors The two candidate antecedents and the target pronoun act certain roles in the source sentence. We capture their roles through the SD

[3]In our experiments, we used *because* as the representative word for *since* when generating the search query.

representation. For example, in (3), *outlaw*$_2$ and *sheriff*$_5$ serve as the subject and direct object of their head *shot*$_3$, while *he*$_8$ functions as the subject of its head *shot*$_9$. We then keep these two heads, *shot*$_3$ and *shot*$_9$, as well as the conjunction *but*$_7$.

In the SD representation, a word can have multiple heads. For example, consider the following sentence:

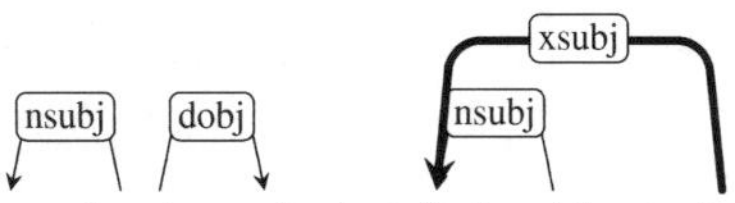

(4) Paper beats rock, but it is able to beat scissors.

The heads of *it*$_6$ are *able*$_8$ and *beat*$_{10}$, where *nsubj* and *xsubj* denote the nominal subject and the controlling subject, respectively. In the case of multiple heads, we only keep the rightmost head, *beat*$_{10}$.

Verb to be In the SD representation, a copula verb like *be* is treated as an auxiliary modifier (de Marneffe and Manning, 2008). For example, consider the following sentence, which is a twin of (4):

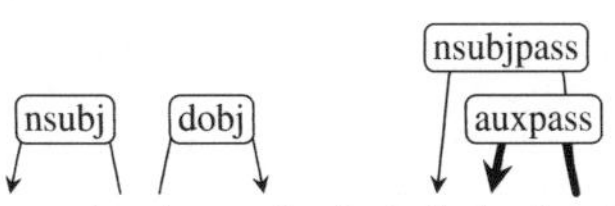

(5) Paper beats rock, but it is beaten by scissors.

Focusing on the subordinate clause, we first keep *beaten*$_8$ which is the head of *it*$_6$. The auxiliary *is*$_7$ is also important since it helps to indicate the passive form of *beaten*$_8$. Therefore we also keep the verb to be if it is the auxiliary modifier of the head.

Negation Negation is an important grammatical operation since it can invert the meaning of the clause or sentence. For example, omitting negation in (6) could make the whole sentence difficult to understand. Therefore we also keep the negation modifier of the head:

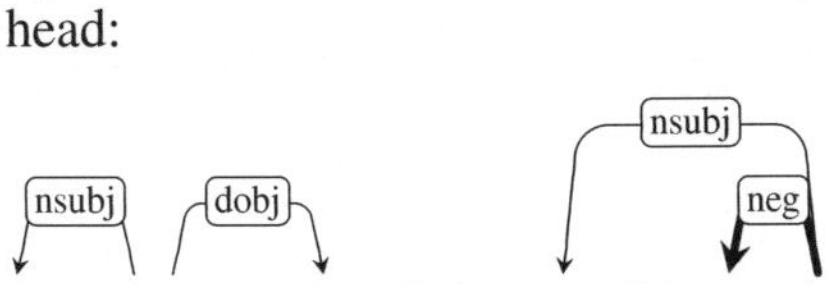

(6) The outlaw shot the sheriff, but he did not shoot the deputy.

Dependent of a light head A head of an actor could be a light verb, which is a verb that has little meaning on its own. For example, consider the following sentence:

(7) The lion bit the gazelle, because it had sharp teeth.

Based on our criteria, we first keep the heads of the actors and the conjunction, including *bit*$_3$, *because*$_7$, and *had*$_9$. However, the lemma form of *had*$_9$ is a light verb, which does not adequately explain the reason for *bit*$_3$. Therefore we also keep the dependent of the light head, *teeth*$_{11}$, to make explanation more clear. In our experiments, we defined {*be*, *do*, *have*, *make*} as a set of the light verbs. In the case of multiple dependents, we only select the rightmost one.

Phrasal verb particle A particle after a verb often provides a specific meaning to that verb. For example, "shot back" in (1b) indicates a reaction against the action of the main clause. Therefore we also keep the particle following the head.

In summary, given a source sentence, we keep the conjunction and the heads of the two candidate antecedents and the target pronoun. We then check the dependents of the heads, keeping only those that meet our criteria. We replace other words with asterisks. Multiple consecutive asterisks are combined into one. For example, we generate the search queries for (1a) and (1b) as follows:

(8) a. *"* shot * but * not shoot *"*
b. *"* shot * but * shot back"*

and for (4) and (5) as:

(9) a. *"* beats * but * is beaten by *"*
b. *"* beats * but * beat *"*

3.3 Alignment

After retrieving snippets, we analyze them using the Stanford CoreNLP (Manning et al., 2014). We use the standard pipeline, ranging from tokenization to dependency parsing. A snippet may contain several fragments or sentences, so we consider it as a short document. We then use the Berkeley coreference resolver (Durrett and Klein, 2013) for predicting coreference chains within each snippet. We consider the processed snippets as candidate examples. For example, (2a) has the following coreference chain:

Relation	Description
	subject
nsubj	nominal subject
xsubj	controlling subject
csubj	clausal subject
agent	agent
	object
dobj	direct object
iobj	indirect object
pobj	object of preposition
nsubjpass	passive nominal subject

Table 2: Generalized grammatical relations.

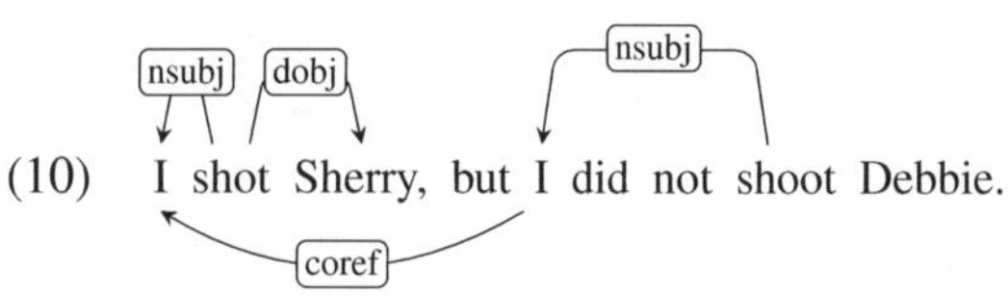

We also experimented with the Stanford coreference resolver but found that the Berkeley resolver is more robust to noisy text. We discuss the characteristics of these two resolvers in Section 4.2.

Next, we try to find alignments of a source sentence and its candidate examples. Our scheme is simple. The source sentence and the candidate example is an alignment if they satisfy the following conditions:

- The heads of the actors are synonymous.
- The grammatical roles of the heads are in the same category.

Note that the Google Web Search API expands some queries and returns results containing related words. As a result, we use the synonym instead of the exact match to increase coverage.[4] We also generalize grammatical relations to a coarser level. Here we focus on two main categories: *subject* and *object*. Table 2 shows our generalized grammatical relations.

Based on our scheme, the dependency structures (6) and (10), where their original sentences are (1a) and (2a), are a good alignment since their heads and grammatical roles match exactly. We write an analogy in the form A:B::C:D, meaning A is to B as C is to D (Turney, 2006). Therefore we derive a candidate analogy I_6:I_1::he_8:$outlaw_2$ from the alignment of (6) and (10).

Consider the following dependency structure, which corresponds to (2b):

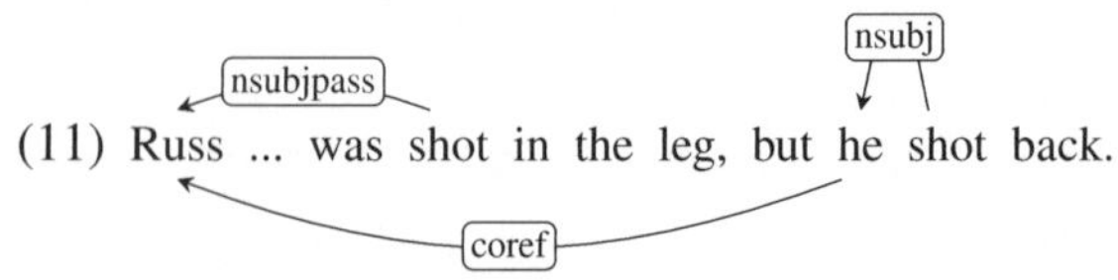

Note that we omit some words due to the limited space. Although (11) has one actor, $Russ_3$, and his grammatical role, *nsubjpass*, does not match exactly with those of the actors in (3), the dependency structures (3) and (11), where their original sentences are (1b) and (2b), are still a good alignment since the grammatical roles *nsubjpass* and *dobj* are in the same *object* category. Therefore we obtain a candidate analogy he_{19}:$Russ_3$::he_8:$sheriff_5$ from the alignment of (3) and (11).

3.4 Ranking candidate antecedents

We use candidate analogies to rank the two candidate antecedents for the target pronoun in a given source sentence. The target pronoun is resolved to a higher scoring antecedent. A simple score function is to count the number of candidate analogies of each antecedent. Note that our alignments are based on automatic processing of snippet texts, inevitably containing an amount of noise. So we would like to distinguish between acceptable and good alignments.

Let us introduce some notation. A source sentence i contains a target pronoun p_i and its two candidate antecedents $a_{i,k}$, $k \in \{1, 2\}$. An example j contains a pronoun p_j and its predicted antecedent a_j. We write $p_j{:}a_j{::}p_i{:}a_{i,k}$ for an analogy of the alignment of j and i. We define the score of a candidate antecedent $a_{i,k}$ as the sum of the scores of all candidate analogies: $\sum_j \text{score}(p_j{:}a_j{::}p_i{:}a_{i,k})$. We then apply the attributional similarity for factoring the score of each candidate analogy (Turney, 2006). Our score function becomes:

$$\text{score}(p_j{:}a_j{::}p_i{:}a_{i,k}) = \frac{1}{2}(\text{s}_a(p_j, p_i) + \text{s}_a(a_j, a_{i,k})).$$

Finally, we estimate the attributional similarity s_a by augmenting the similarity of the heads h of the

[4]We use WordNet in Natural Language Toolkit (Bird et al., 2009).

corresponding dependencies:

$$s_a(p_j, p_i) = d(p_j, p_i) + d(h(p_j), h(p_i)) ,$$

where d is the path distance similarity of two word senses available in Natural Language Toolkit (Bird et al., 2009).[5] We estimate $s_a(a_j, a_{i,k})$ using the same fashion. For example, we compute the score of the analogy I_6:I_1::he_8:$outlaw_2$ derived from the alignment of (6) and (10) as: $\frac{1}{2}(d(I_6, he_8) + d(shoot_9, shoot_{11}) + d(I_1, outlaw_2) + d(shot_2, shot_3)) = \frac{1}{2}(0.33 + 1.0 + 0.09 + 1.0) = 1.21$.

4 Experiments

4.1 Dataset and setting

We used the dataset created by Rahman and Ng (2012).[6] Their dataset can be viewed as a relaxed version of Winograd schemas since the target pronouns in some sentences could be resolved using selectional restrictions. For example, consider the following sentence: "*Lions eat zebras because they are predators*". The counts returned by Google for "*lions are predators*" are significantly higher than those of "*zebras are predators*". In other words, the system could resolve *they* to *lions* without considering the relationship between two clauses. Note that our approach does not use this kind of counting in resolving the difficult pronouns.

Our approach is a pure example-based strategy, which requires no training data. Therefore we only use Rahman's test set. In the following experiments, we only considered the test sentences where the grammatical roles of the actors are in the coarse-grained subject or object categories (Table 2), and the two candidate antecedents share the same head. For example, in (3), $outlaw_2$ and $sheriff_5$ share the same head $shot_3$. We retained 244 out of the original 564 test sentences.

Next, we generated search queries for these test sentences. Accessing the Google Web Search API is not trivial since the number of requests is limited for free use. We paused 20 seconds between each query and retrieved only top two pages (8 results per page). Therefore the maximum number of results for a given query is 16. We also tried to increase the number of retrieved pages but found that lower ranked pages tend to be irrelevant. In this stage, we obtained results for 185 (out of 244) queries and no results for 59 queries. For example, the search query "* *sued* * *because* * *was embezzling*" generated from "*Bob sued Bill because he was embezzling funds*" received no results since these terms have not explicitly co-occurred in Google's database.

After extracting examples from snippets and aligning, 155 (out of 185) test sentences could be aligned with at least one example. Some examples did not contain either coreference chains or compatible dependencies. We refer to the remaining 155 test sentences as **D1**. To ensure that each test sentence has a twin, we also generated a subset of D1 containing 120 test sentences denoted by **D2**. In the case of D2, if a system uniformly resolves the target pronoun to the subject (or object), it can achieve 50% accuracy.

4.2 Baselines and evaluation metrics

We also conducted experiments using existing coreference resolvers to see whether they could handle the difficult pronouns. We experimented with two publicly available resolvers and our baseline system:

STANFORD is the winner of the CoNLL-2011 shared task (Raghunathan et al., 2010; Lee et al., 2011). STANFORD is a rule-based system that applies precision-ordered sieves (filtering rules) to decide whether two mentions should be linked. For noun-pronoun mention pairs, STANFORD first assigns semantic attributes to the mentions. The semantic attributes include number, gender, animacy, and NER labels, which are derived from existing knowledge sources (Bergsma and Lin, 2006; Ji and Lin, 2009; Finkel et al., 2005). STANFORD links two mentions if their attributes have no disagreement.

BERKELEY is the current state-of-the-art coreference resolution system based on the mention-ranking approach (Durrett and Klein, 2013). BERKELEY learns to link two mentions using surface features that capture linguistic properties of mentions and mention pairs. BERKELEY also inherits semantic attributes from STANFORD and uses them as shallow semantic features. In

[5] Note that a word can have many senses. So we iterate over the Cartesian product of two synsets and use the maximum similarity score.

[6] http://www.hlt.utdallas.edu/~vince/data/emnlp12

System	D1			D2		
	Correct	Incorrect	No Decision	Correct	Incorrect	No Decision
STANFORD	45.16% (70/155)	45.16% (70/155)	9.68% (15/155)	46.67% (56/120))	46.67% (56/120)	6.67% (8/120)
BERKELEY$_{pre}$	49.68% (77/155)	49.68% (77/155)	0.65% (1/155)	50.00% (60/120)	50.00% (60/120)	0.00% (0/120)
BERKELEY$_{new}$	50.32% (78/155)	48.39% (75/155)	1.29% (2/155)	50.83% (61/120)	49.17% (59/120)	0.00% (0/120)
MENTRANKER	55.48% (86/155)	44.52% (69/155)	0.00% (0/155)	54.17% (65/120)	45.83% (55/120)	0.00% (0/120)
OURS	69.68% (108/155)	29.68% (46/155)	0.65% (1/155)	72.50% (87/120)	27.50% (33/120)	0.00% (0/120)

Table 3: Experimental results on the D1 and D2 test sets.

our experiments, we used the pre-trained model (BERKELEY$_{pre}$) as well as retrained a new model (BERKELEY$_{new}$) using Rahman's training set.[7]

MENTRANKER is our baseline mention ranker. We tried to replicate the ranking-based model described in Rahman and Ng (2012). We explored five features, including narrative chains,[8] Google, semantic compatibility, heuristic polarity, and lexical features. Note that some of our knowledge sources are different from those of Rahman and Ng (2012). For Google, we used the counts from the Google n-gram dataset (Brants and Franz, 2006). For semantic compatibility, instead of using BLLIP, Reuters, and English Gigaword, we extracted the features from the ClueWeb12 dataset.[9]

We provided gold mentions (the two candidate antecedents and the target pronoun) as the inputs for each baseline system in testing. Therefore the baseline systems did not need to perform mention detection. For evaluation, we followed Rahman and Ng (2012). Given a test sentence, the system could *correctly*, *incorrectly*, or *not* resolve the target pronouns.

4.3 Results

Table 3 shows our experimental results. The shallow semantic attributes used in STANFORD do not seem to be helpful for resolving the difficult pronouns. STANFORD also left many sentences unresolved. For example, consider the following sentences:

(12) a. Lions love gazelles because *they* eat them.

b. Lions love gazelles because *they* are delicious.

The two candidate antecedents (*lions* and *gazelles*) are animate and plural, which can be compatible with the target pronoun *they*.

The surface features used in BERKELEY$_{pre}$ are also not helpful for handling the difficult pronouns. Retraining BERKELEY$_{new}$ with Rahman's training set has almost no impact. Here we do not intend to indicate that STANFORD and BERKELEY are ineffective in general. We would rather say that the shallow semantic features used in the coreference literature are not sufficient for resolving the difficult pronouns. MENTRANKER exploits more sophisticated features extracted from different knowledge sources. However, MENTRANKER performs slightly better than STANFORD and BERKELEY.[10]

Our approach acquires examples from the Web and uses them to facilitate decision. For example, the following examples were retrieved and applied for resolving (12):

(13) a. I love Easter because I get to eat lots of chocolate.

b. I love them because they are delicious and the whole family likes them.

While (13a) supports resolving *they* to *lions* in (12a), (13b) helps resolving *they* to *gazelles* in (12b). Our approach correctly resolves 69.68% and 72.50% of the target pronouns in D1 and D2, respectively.

4.4 Error analysis

We manually examined errors made by our approach. We found that a common source of errors is due to automatic processing of the data, such as parsing and predicting coreference chains in snippet

[7]We parsed Rahman's training set using the Stanford CoreNLP, converted it to the CoNLL format, and retrained a new model using the 'trainOnGold' option, which yielded better results in our experiments.

[8]http://www.usna.edu/users/cs/nchamber/data/schemas/acl09

[9]http://www.lemurproject.org/clueweb12

[10]Rahman and Ng (2012) showed that narrative chains yield improved accuracy for resolving the WS Challenge. However, the improvement comes not only from narrative chains but also from other (unintentionally added) features (personal communication).

(14)	Sally gave **Kelly** a doll because *she* loved dolls. I gave you that power because I loved you and trusted you completely He gave his life a ransom, just because he loved me so
(15)	Mary gave **Sandy** her book because *she* needed it. I gave Mike Branch a call because I needed some help with a trailer loading problem I only gave $16.00, because I needed change and needed to decide to give them how much tips
(16)	The cat broke **the glass** because *it* was fragile. the glass broke because it was fragile I broke down crying because I was so fragile If the toilet broke from a light touch because it was so fragile the landlord would pay
(17)	**The cat** broke the glass because *it* was clumsy. In this story the donkey broke the manger because he was clumsy
(18)	Olga kicked **Sara** because *she* woke her up. I kicked Zayn because I woke up on the wrong side of the bed I could have kicked myself because I woke up late
(19)	**Olga** kicked Sara because *she* was drunk. he kicked her out of Homecoming dance because she was drunk in the parking lot he got kicked off because he was drunk at rehearsals
(20)	The coach told **the captain** that *he* was fired. Williams told Fox News that he was fired Wednesday by Ellen Weiss, NPR's vice president for news When I applied for unemployment benefits, I was honest and told them that I was fired

Table 4: Samples of errors made by our approach. In each row, the first line is the source sentence followed by its examples. In each source sentence, the correct antecedent is boldfaced and the target pronoun is italicized. In each example, the coreferent mentions are underlined.

texts. We also inspected some of errors based on the scores of incorrectly resolved antecedents. An incorrect antecedent with a large score gap means that most retrieved examples support the opposite antecedent to the answer. Examples of this kind of errors are shown in Table 4. In what follows, we discuss some interesting linguistic phenomena observed from the errors.

Direct and indirect objects The source sentences (14) and (15) have the same pattern. The main clause has the *subject-transfer_verb-indirect_object-direct_object* pattern, where the verb *gave* is a transfer verb. In the subordinate clause, the target pronoun interacts with *direct_object* (e.g., "she loved dolls"). In their corresponding examples, the target pronoun instead interacts with *indirect_object* (e.g., "I loved you") or has no interaction. One solution for this case is to use predefined patterns to eliminate irrelevant examples. However, the utility of such patterns is quite limited.

Selectional restrictions In the source sentence (16), the adjective *fragile* seems to co-occur more frequently with *glass* than *cat*. In the source sentence (17), the subject of the adjective *clumsy* is more likely to be an animate noun (e.g., *cat*) than an inanimate noun (e.g., *glass*). The use of selectional restrictions could be helpful for handling such cases in Rahman's dataset. Note that, in (17), our baseline coreference resolver, BERKELEY, incorrectly resolved *he* to *manger*, which is an inanimate noun.

Transitive and intransitive verbs The verb *broke* is used as a transitive verb (e.g., "the cat broke the glass") in the source sentence (16) but as an intransitive verb (e.g., "the glass broke" and "I broke down crying") in its examples. Likewise, in (18), the phrasal verb *woke up* is used in different functions. Distinguishing between the transitive and intransitive verbs could be a useful feature.

No obvious answer In the source sentence (19), the antecedent was chosen by using the background knowledge that someone who was drunk tends to do bad things. Since *Olga* was drunk, *she* should be the one who kicks other people. However, the opposite answer is possible. As in the corresponding examples, someone who was drunk can be punished by being kicked.

Semantic relation between actors The source sentence (20) was constructed by using the background knowledge that the noun *coach* has a higher status than the noun *captain* in a team environment. In other words, someone who has a higher status can fire other people. Note that the answer can be flipped if the two nouns are replaced with proper names.

5 Conclusion

We have only scratched the surface of the most fundamental question "what kind of world knowledge does a computer program need to have to pass the WS Challenge?" (Levesque, 2013). We explore the necessary background knowledge for resolving the WS Challenge. Our key observation is that people tend to avoid ambiguous antecedents when using pronouns in writing. We present a method for automatically acquiring examples that are similar to Winograd schemas but have less ambiguity. We generate a concise search query that captures the essential parts of a given source sentence and then find the alignments of the source sentence and its retrieved examples. Our experimental results show that the existing sentences on the Web indeed contain instances of world knowledge useful for difficult pronoun resolution.

Our current approach has several limitations. We only considered the WS sentences in which the actors have specific grammatical roles and share the same head. We plan to examine other sentence structures. For example, consider the following sentence: "*Lakshman asked Vivan to get him some ice cream because he was hot*". In this case, *asked* is the head of *Lakshman*, while *get* is the head of *Vivan*. We also plan to handle the WS sentences that have no obvious examples.

Our error analysis reveals that resolving the WS Challenge requires not only a wide range of world knowledge but also expressive representations that can handle the complexities of natural language. There is a line of research that tries to map natural language sentences to formal semantic representations (Kamp and Reyle, 1993; Steedman, 2000; Copestake et al., 2005; Liang et al., 2011; Banarescu et al., 2013). Exploring the usefulness of these semantic representations would be an important direction for future work.

References

Niranjan Balasubramanian, Stephen Soderland, Mausam, and Oren Etzioni. 2013. Generating coherent event schemas at scale. In *Proceedings of EMNLP*, pages 1721–1731.

Laura Banarescu, Claire Bonial, Shu Cai, Madalina Georgescu, Kira Griffitt, Ulf Hermjakob, Kevin Knight, Philipp Koehn, Martha Palmer, and Nathan Schneider. 2013. Abstract meaning representation for sembanking. In *Proceedings of Linguistic Annotation Workshop*.

Shane Bergsma and Dekang Lin. 2006. Bootstrapping path-based pronoun resolution. In *Proceedings of ACL*, pages 33–40.

Steven Bird, Edward Loper, and Ewan Klein. 2009. *Natural Language Processing with Python*. O'Reilly Media Inc.

Thorsten Brants and Alex Franz. 2006. Web 1t 5-gram version 1. https://catalog.ldc.upenn.edu/LDC2006T13.

Nathanael Chambers and Daniel Jurafsky. 2008. Unsupervised learning of narrative event chains. In *Proceedings of ACL*, pages 789–797.

Michael Collins. 1999. Head-driven statistical models for natural language parsing. *Ph.D. thesis*.

Ann Copestake, Dan Flickinger, Ivan Sag, and Carl Pollard. 2005. Minimal recursion semantics: An introduction. *Research on Language and Computation*, 3:281–332.

Marie-Catherine de Marneffe and Christopher D. Manning. 2008. Stanford dependencies manual. http://nlp.stanford.edu/software/stanford-dependencies.shtml.

Marie-Catherine de Marneffe, Bill MacCartney, and Christopher D. Manning. 2006. Generating typed dependency parses from phrase structure parses. In *Proceedings of LREC*, pages 449–454.

Greg Durrett and Dan Klein. 2013. Easy victories and uphill battles in coreference resolution. In *Proceedings of EMNLP*.

Jenny Rose Finkel, Trond Grenager, and Christopher Manning. 2005. Incorporating non-local information into information extraction systems by gibbs sampling. In *Proceedings of ACL*, pages 363–370.

Jerry R. Hobbs. 1979. Coherence and coreference. *Cognitive Science*, 3:67–90.

Heng Ji and Dekang Lin. 2009. Gender and animacy knowledge discovery from web-scale n-grams for unsupervised person mention detection. In *Proceedings of PACLIC*.

Hans Kamp and Uwe Reyle. 1993. *From Discourse to Logic: An Introduction to the Model-theoretic Semantics of Natural Language, Formal Logic and Discourse Representation Theory*. Kluwer, Dordrecht.

Andrew Kehler, Laura Kertz, Hannah Rohde, and Jeffrey L. Elman. 2008. Coherence and coreference revisited. *Journal of Semantics*, 25:1–44.

Mirella Lapata and Frank Keller. 2005. Web-based models for natural language processing. *ACM Trans. Speech Lang. Process.*, 2(1).

Heeyoung Lee, Yves Peirsman, Angel Chang, Nathanael Chambers, Mihai Surdeanu, and Dan Jurafsky. 2011. Stanford's multi-pass sieve coreference resolution system at the CoNLL-2011 shared task. In *Proceedings of CoNLL: Shared Task*, pages 28–34.

Hector Levesque, Ernest Davis, and Leora Morgenstern. 2012. The winograd schema challenge. In *Proceedings of Principles of Knowledge Representation and Reasoning*.

Hector Levesque. 2011. The winograd schema challenge. In *Commonsense*.

Hector Levesque. 2013. On our best behaviour. *IJCAI Research Excellence Award Presentation*.

Percy Liang, Michael I. Jordan, and Dan Klein. 2011. Learning dependency-based compositional semantics. In *Proceedings of ACL*, pages 590–599.

Christopher D. Manning, Mihai Surdeanu, John Bauer, Jenny Finkel, Steven J. Bethard, and David McClosky. 2014. The Stanford CoreNLP natural language processing toolkit. In *Proceedings of ACL: System Demonstrations*, pages 55–60.

Vincent Ng. 2010. Supervised noun phrase coreference research: The first fifteen years. In *Proceedings of ACL*, pages 1396–1411.

Massimo Poesio, Simone Paolo Ponzetto, and Yannick Versley. 2011. Computational models of anaphora resolution: A survey. *Linguistic Issues in Language Technology*.

Sameer Pradhan, Lance Ramshaw, Mitchell Marcus, Martha Palmer, Ralph Weischedel, and Nianwen Xue. 2011. CoNLL-2011 shared task: Modeling unrestricted coreference in ontonotes. In *Proceedings of CoNLL: Shared Task*, pages 1–27.

Sameer Pradhan, Alessandro Moschitti, Nianwen Xue, Olga Uryupina, and Yuchen Zhang. 2012. CoNLL-2012 shared task: Modeling multilingual unrestricted coreference in ontonotes. In *Proceedings of EMNLP/CoNLL: Shared Task*, pages 1–40.

Karthik Raghunathan, Heeyoung Lee, Sudarshan Rangarajan, Nathanael Chambers, Mihai Surdeanu, Dan Jurafsky, and Christopher Manning. 2010. A multi-pass sieve for coreference resolution. In *Proceedings of EMNLP*, pages 492–501.

Altaf Rahman and Vincent Ng. 2012. Resolving complex cases of definite pronouns: The winograd schema challenge. In *Proceedings of EMNLP-CoNLL*, pages 777–789.

Hannah Rohde and Andrew Kehler. 2013. A probabilistic reconciliation of coherence-driven and centering-driven theories of pronoun interpretation. *Theoretical Linguistics*, 39:1–37.

Mark Steedman. 2000. *The Syntactic Process*. MIT Press.

Peter D. Turney. 2006. Similarity of semantic relations. *Computational Linguistics*, 32(3):379–416.

Terry Winograd. 1972. *Understanding Natural Language*. Academic Press, Inc.

A Unified Analysis to Surpass Comparative and Experiential Aspect

Charles Lam
Linguistics Program, Purdue University
Beering Hall, Room 1289
West Lafayette, IN 47907
charleslam@purdue.edu

Abstract

This study compares two constructions in Cantonese which shares similar features in their syntax and semantics. Previous works observe that comparatives often appear after experiential aspect in the verbal domain historically. This study builds upon this observation and argues that the similarities between two constructions, comparatives and experientials, are of formal nature and that the similarities originate from the semantics of these constructions. This formal account means that there is a deep connection between the two constructions and therefore explains the pattern observed by typologists (Stassen, 1985; Ansaldo, 2010). The homomorphic approach also means a simpler syntax-semantics that applies to both event-denoting ('verbs') and property-denoting ('adjectives') predicates.

Keywords: *Comparatives, experiential aspect, cross-categorial behavior*

1 Introduction

English has both comparative construction (1-a) and experiential perfect (1-b) sentence, which are marked by different morphemes.

(1) a. Mary is taller than Peter. (Comparative)
b. Mary had been to England. (Experiential perfect)

Cantonese has these two constructions too, only that it uses the same morpheme *gwo3* to mark both.

(2) *Mary gou1 gwo3 Peter*
Mary tall PASS Peter
'Mary is taller than Peter.'

(3) *Mary heoi3 gwo3 jing1gwok6*
Mary go EXP England
'Mary has been to England.'
(lit: 'Mary went to England.') [1]

As a lexical verb, *gwo3* means 'to cross' or 'to surpass'. In (2), *gwo3* shows the standard of comparison (henceforth *standard* or *std*) in a comparative sentence. In (3), it shows that the event of 'going to England' has taken place at any point in the past. The correlation pattern between these two constructions, surpass-comparative (2) and experiential aspect marking (3), is reported to be common in typology literature (Ansaldo, 2010; Stassen, 1985) and is therefore not mere coincidence. The aim of this study is to provide a formal account to this well-observed correlation.

This study builds on the notion of scale structure (Kennedy & McNally, 2005) that is primarily applied to adjectives and/or property-denoting predicates. Since scale structure is non-temporal by nature, this paper posits that verbal predicates can be conceptualized and formalized as scales measured by time, i.e. a 'temporal scale'. Under this view, both comparative and experiential sentences can be treated on a par as scalar predicates specified with a degree along the scale.

[1]The transcription convention follows the Linguistics Society of Hong Kong *JyutPing* system. The numbers show the lexical tones. Abbreviations: CL: classifiers; EXP: experiential aspect; PASS: surpass comparative marker; SFP: sentence final particle

Copyright 2014 by Charles Lam
28th Pacific Asia Conference on Language, Information and Computation pages 368–377

In terms of broader implication, this study differs from the typological works in that it makes no prediction on the diachronic development. I argue that it avoids the assumption that one domain (e.g. adjectives) is more functional than another (e.g. verb), which does not appear to be well supported. Moreover, this study also suggests a deep semantic connection between comparatives and transitive verbs (represented algebraically in this study). By formulating it with semantics, this study differs from grammaticalization approaches and explains the connection between the surpass comparative and experiential marker from a formal perspective, rather than a historical one.

The remainder of this paper is organized as follows: Section 2 discusses previous work on issues related to both comparative and experiential sentences. Section 3 gives the hypothesis that *gwo3* marks the degree in relation to the predicate and it allows the morpheme to apply to both adjectival and verbal domains. The hypothesis is then tested with observations in the similarities between the two constructions in light of their syntax with question formation (section 4), specificity (section 5) and quantification *saai3* (section 6). Section 7 discusses a related comparative construction and clarifies that it is compatible with the current analysis. Section 8 discusses the implication and argues that this study demonstrates an example of homomorphism across different domains in the syntax-semantics interface.

2 Related Works

2.1 Typological Connection between Surpass and Experiential Marking

Studies on typology observe that the comparative marker SURPASS is often related to verbal use of the experiential marking across languages.

In Stassen (1985)'s survey on comparatives in over a hundred languages, he makes the generalizations that '(i)f a language has an Exceed Comparative, then its basic word order is SVO.'(Stassen, 1985, p.54)[2] Ansaldo (2010) surveys several Southern Sinitic languages (which includes Cantonese) and unrelated languages in Southeast Asia (e.g. Thai, Lao and Vietnamese) and argues with Stassen that the use of surpass comparative predicts the SVO basic word order in a language[3]. Ansaldo makes a parallel comparison between resultative verb construction (V-RVC) and comparatives in (4), where V-RVC includes the cluster of a lexical verb and *gwo3*.

(4) [V_{ADJ}-gwo3 NP_{STD}] $\approx$ [V-RVC NP_{OBJ}].

Ansaldo (2010) argues that the comparative *gwo3* is more fundamental and the aspectual use develops upon the former, contra Stassen (1985). This presents an apparent contradiction, since both theories rely on one construction being employed to extend its use to another. While acknowledging the correlations, the present study aims to show a descriptively adequate theory need not make explicit prediction on historical development to account for the cross-linguistic correlation between the two constructions. Instead of positing one grammaticalization cline for all languages, this study proposes that surpass comparative and experiential perfect are linked semantically through the common meaning of the morpheme *gwo3* and that there is not necessarily a specific order in their historical development. Hence, both grammaticalization directions are possible, and it is possible that a language has one of the two constructions without the other.

Focusing on the lexical semantics of *gwo3* and its cognates in Sinitic languages, Chappell (2001) argues for a reclassification of the experiential aspect marker to an evidential marker. By evidential, she means the 'speaker's commitment to the truth of the proposition', which means that whenever the marker is used, it shows the strength of assertion by the speaker. Her data cover eight Sinitic languages (including Cantonese) and include *gwo3* in verbal environments denoting both spatial relation (e.g. *haang1 gwo3 tiu4 kiu4* 'to go pass a bridge'[4] and temporal use, such as *heoi3 gwo3 mei5gwok3* 'went to the USA'. This extension from spatial scale to temporal scale is ubiquitous from a cross-linguistic perspective, as Chappell (2001) points out.

[2]It does not concern Stassen that Mandarin, for example, demonstrates a counterexample to his generalization, since he stresses that the generalization should not be taken as absolute universals. Also, Mandarin does have the surpass comparative, in addition to the more common *bi*-comparative and transitive comparative.

[3]Note that the prediction does not go the other way.

[4]Chappell (2001)'s examples are in Shanghainese. Cantonese examples here are adapted by the author.

Another interesting point raised by Chappell (2001) is the discontinuity effect in *gwo3*, where the verbal predicate proposition marked by *gwo3* must not be concurrent with the reference time (à la Reichenbach (1947)), as shown in (5).

(5) *jau5 jan4 hai2dou6 sik6 (gwo3) jin1*
have person at.place ingest EXP smoke
'Someone smoked here.' [5]

Without *gwo3*, the smoker in (5) would be still in sight. With *gwo3*, (5) is infelicitous if the smoking is still ongoing. It is important to note that whether the smoker is in present is not crucial. Suppose a smoker, Alan, has finished a cigarette, and Bill walks into the room and utters (5) with *gwo3*, the utterance would be felicitous. This fact about *gwo3* indicates that the progression of the event has exceeded a certain referential point, which can be measured in time.

To sum up, the co-occurrence of surpass comparative and experiential aspect is a well-attested pattern. Some researchers treat the pattern as a historical development within a language where one construction grammaticalizes and becomes another one. Some view it in light of genetic relation between languages. This study attempts to provide a formal account to the pattern without resorting to historical development. However, it is necessary to stress that the present proposal is compatible with the previous historical accounts.

2.2 Formal Generative Analysis of Chinese Comparatives

Since comparatives most often associates with adjectives[6], the generative literature argues that there is a functional projection *Degree Phrase* dominating the lexical AdjP (Cresswell, 1976; von Stechow, 1984; Kennedy & McNally, 2005).

The surpass comparative in Cantonese has not received a lot attention in the literature. Mok (1998) is the only work that discusses the construction directly. Briefly speaking, Mok adopts a VP structure and claims that whenever *gwo3* is affixed to the V^0 (spelled out by lexical adjectives), the sentence denotes a comparative. This is problematic in two ways. First, syntactic tests, such as A-not-A question formation (6), do not prove that property-denoting predicates must be verbs. Since modals like *ho2ji5* 'can' may also be used in A-not-A questions, the fact that property-denoting predicates are also found in A-not-A questions can only be interpreted that it is the main predicate.

(6) *Mary gou1 m4 gou1 gaa3 ?*
Mary tall Neg tall SFP
'Is Mary tall?'

Second, it is unclear what mechanism governs or licenses the existence of affixal *gwo3* in Mok's formulation. This is crucial in his account, because it distinguishes whether a sentence denotes a positive adjective with a measure phrase (as in 'Peter is *5 feet tall*'), or an implicit comparative, such as 'Peter is *5 feet taller*'. This study will provide some evidence supporting the affixal analysis.

Most other works on Chinese comparatives focus on Mandarin. It is generally accepted that Mandarin also has the functional Degree Phrase (DegP), dominating immediately an Adjectival Phrase (Grano & Kennedy, 2012; Xiang, 2005; Erlewine, 2007, 2012; Liu, 2010). However, most of the works listed here did not address surpass comparative, which Mandarin does have. Grano and Kennedy (2012) is the only exception. They extend their proposal for the transitive comparative to the surpass comparative, and provide the following analysis:

(7) $[\![\mu_{comp}]\!] = \lambda g_{\langle e,\langle e,d\rangle\rangle}\lambda d\lambda y\lambda x.g(y)(x) \succeq d$

Grano and Kennedy's comparative morpheme μ takes an adjective g, a degree argument d, and arguments of the comparison standard y and the subject x. Briefly speaking, what it means is that the comparative morpheme μ requires a scale-denoting predicate (i.e. the adjective), a degree compatible with that scale for felicitous measurement and two individuals to associate with the degree in question. Grano and Kennedy's order of merging these arguments reflects the steps in the standard bottom-up

[5] From Chappell (2001) and Matthews and Yip (1994). The glossing and translation are mine.

[6] Whether or not Cantonese and Mandarin have a distinct category Adjective is beyond the scope of this paper. The term 'adjective' here simply refers to property-denoting predicates, which holds for regular adjectives like 'small' and stative verbs like 'sick'. See (Paul, 2010; Francis & Matthews, 2005) for relevant discussions.

derivation, which can be directly applied to the Cantonese data. Since they deal with the transitive comparative with a measure phrase, such as '4 cm' in 'John is **4 cm** taller than Mary', they included the measure phrase as an obligatory argument, which is optional in the Cantonese surpass comparative[7]. The degree is assumed to be compatible with the scale, in order to rule out infelicitous utterances like 'John is **#4cm** heavier than Mary', where '4cm' cannot measure the scale weight.

It is also interesting that Grano and Kennedy (2012) address the parallelism between little-v and μ in Case-licensing terms. While this study does not discuss Case-licensing in Cantonese, the parallelism is argued to be an effect of the underlying common structure across the events and properties. Building on our discussion about the lexical semantics of *gwo3* in Chappell (2001) that the EXCEED meaning can extend from spatial domain to temporal domain, the next section will formulate a hypothesis as to what exactly makes it possible for *gwo3* to apply to verbs and adjectives and account for the variety of sentence types.

3 Hypothesis

This study hypothesizes:

(8) The morpheme *gwo3* has the same denotation in experiential perfect and comparatives.

More concretely, hypothesis (8) requires the following characteristics to work: First, *gwo3* is hypothesized to be an affix attached to a functional head that denotes the boundary/degree of a predicate, extending Grano and Kennedy (2012)'s μ for comparatives. We will see this with its syntax in section 4. Second, *gwo3* takes a predicate and degree as its arguments. The predicate can be either a verb or an adjective. The degree is often licensed lexically, either through an individual representing the standard of comparison, or an object of the verb[8]. This will be shown in light of the specificity constraint shown in the NP following *gwo3*.

[7]See diagram (77) of (Grano & Kennedy, 2012, p.259) for the details of the derivation.

[8]Here the term 'degree' covers not only for property-denoting predicates, but also for event-denoting predicates.

The movement analysis from Adj^0 to Deg^0 has already been argued for in previous studies (Mok, 1998; Grano & Kennedy, 2012), and is generally accepted in other studies. Since Cantonese adjectives do not form the main predicate without a degree marker like *hou2* 'very' in positive assertions (i.e. non-comparative predicates) like (9), this means that semantically they do not assert degree by themselves. Therefore the denotation of Cantonese adjectives should not include d. Also, following the general assumption DegP (see section 2), I assume that the Degree Phrase is more functional than the Adjective Phrase and thus merges later than the predicate in syntax.

(9) *Peter *(hou2) fei4*
Peter very fat
'Peter is (very) fat.'

The goal of this study is to demonstrate what allows the functional morpheme *gwo3* to show up in both experiential perfect and comparatives. The following sections will discuss the syntactic and semantic characteristics of *gwo3* to test hypothesis (8) with further details.

4 Syntactic similarities

On the surface, we see that surpass comparative (2) and postverbal aspects, which includes experiential perfect (3), share similar word order, as Ansaldo (2010) points out in (4), repeated here as (10):

(10) [V_{ADJ}-gwo3 NP_{STD}] $\approx$ [V-RVC NP_{OBJ}].

The similarity is beyond the surface order, when we look at the structural constraint with regard to question formation. It is often assumed that *gwo3* is a functional head above v (see Soh (2014) for a recent overview). However, data from A-not-A question shows the contrary. Hypothesis (8) claims that *gwo3* is an affix to a functional head and dominates the internal argument. This claim would predict that *gwo3* is not a head by itself and one should not see head movement to higher projection. Assuming that A-not-A question formation in Cantonese involves copying the head to fill a C^0 position, only head elements are expected to show up in the A-not-A sequence. In fact, we see that *gwo3* must remain between the lower copy and the internal argument:

(11) *Mary gou1 (*gwo3) m4 gou1 gwo3 Peter aa3*
Mary tall PASS Neg tall PASS Peter SFP$_Q$
'Is Mary taller than Peter?'

Crucially, *gwo3* must not be copied alone and form A-not-A:

(12) **Mary gwo3 m4 gou1 gwo3 Peter aa3*
Mary PASS Neg tall PASS Peter SFP$_Q$
'Is Mary taller than Peter?'

This indicates that *gwo3* in comparatives is not a syntactic head. The negation for experiential perfect in (13) looks slightly different, but illustrates the same point that *gwo3* should not be analyzed as a syntactic head.

(13) *Mary jau5 mou5 heoi3 gwo3 mei5gwok3 aa3*
Mary have Neg go PASS USA SFP$_Q$
'Has Mary been to the USA?'

In Cantonese, negation of eventive predicates uses a different negator *mou5*. Since *gwo3* denotes experience of an event that occurred in the past and is therefore eventive in nature, A-not-A question for *gwo3* usually has *jau5 mou5* 'have not-have', instead of the more common *V-m4-V* pattern. This, however, does not affect our analysis that *gwo3* does not undergo head movement, similar to what has been shown for comparatives.

This affix analysis of *gwo3* can be captured by (14), where *gwo3* never moves to higher head position in experiential perfect or comparatives:

(14)

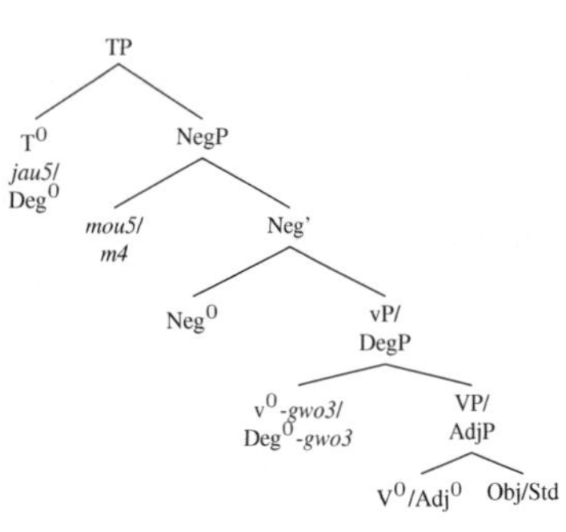

For experiential perfect (13), T^0 is filled by the base-generated *jau5* 'have', hence there is no need to raise a lower head to fill the position. The remaining vP has therefore the v^0–*gwo3*–V^0–(direct) Obj order. For comparatives[9], since the T^0 is not filled, Deg^0 moves cyclically to T^0 via Neg^0 and gives the surface order in (11). It is important to note that a head analysis of *gwo3* would wrongly predict ungrammatical sentences like (12). Therefore, structure (14) shows that *gwo3* must not be a head.

As a side note, Cantonese comparatives allows alternations like (15)[10], where *gwo3* can appear before or after the object *Peter*. Also notice the position of negator *m4*.

(15) a. *keoi5 lek1 m4 gwo3 Peter*
3sg smart Neg PASS Peter
'He is not smarter than Peter.'

b. *keoi5 lek1 Peter m4 gwo3*
3sg smart Peter Neg PASS
'He is not smarter than Peter.'

Both examples in (15) are acceptable, and they are interchangeable with only slightly different connotations[11]. However, (17) is much less acceptable than (16). This indicates that the alternation is constrained by the length of the standard of comparison NP.

(16) *keoi5 lek1 m4 gwo3 ngo5 kam6jat6 gin3dou2 go2 go3 naam4jan2*
3sg smart Neg PASS 1sg yesterday see D CL man
'He is not smarter than the man I saw yesterday.'

(17) *??keoi5 lek1 ngo5 kam6jat6 gin3dou2 go2 go3 naam4jan2 m4 gwo3*
3sg smart 1sg yesterday see D CL man Neg PASS
'He is not smarter than the man I saw yesterday.'

[9]This study assumes measure phrases to adjoin to the right in DegP, following Grano and Kennedy (2012).

[10]I thank the anonymous review who pointed out this potential problem for the analysis in (14).

[11](15-b), but not (15-a), implicates that the standard *Peter* is smart.

Structure (14) straightforwardly handles the example (15-a), with Adj^0 cyclically moves first to Deg^0 then T^0. For (15-b), one can posit that phonetically-light NPs can raise to a higher focus position, which might explain the connotation difference in footnote-11. Alternatively, one can posit a spell-out rule akin to heavy-NP shift.

The point here is that the contrast in (15) does not necessary constitute counter-examples to the affixal analysis of *gwo3* in (14). The choice between the two solutions depends largely on how one wants to accounts for the NP-shift phenomenon and is beyond the scope of the current study.

Assuming that A-not-A questions often rely on movement to spell out higher functional head positions (T^0 or C^0), the Cantonese facts above have shown that *gwo3* never undergoes head movement and should not be treated as a functional head. More importantly, this section has shown the common syntactic constraints shared by the verbal and adjectival uses that employ *gwo3* to denote a generalized degree of scales or events.

5 Specificity of Object/Standard

Beside the syntactic similarity, both uses of *gwo3* show similarity in that they require their referential arguments to be specific. Generic nouns are also allowed in the same position. This means the two constructions are also similar semantically. This section will focus on referential arguments and briefly discuss generic nouns at the end.

Mok (1998) and Tang (1996) both observe that the NP following *gwo3* must be specific. In verbal predicates (18), the NP *jat1 go3 sing4si4* 'a city' is ambiguous. (18) can either mean everyone went to a different city, or everyone went to one particular city. By switching the perfective marker *zo2* with *gwo3* in (19), the ambiguity is no longer there and the speaker must be talking about one particular city.

(18) *keoi5dei6 dou1 heoi3 zo2 jat1 go3*
3pl all go Perf one CL
sing4si4
city
'They all went to a city.' (specific or non-specific)

(19) *keoi5dei6 dou1 heoi3 gwo3 jat1 go3*
3pl all go EXP one CL
sing4si4
city
'They all went to a city.' (specific only)

The contrast can be shown by a follow-up sentence '... but not all the cities were nice'. Since 'all' pragmatically presupposes, though not logically, a plural set of cities, the follow-up is much less acceptable when it combines with (19) than with (18). This indicates that it is possible to talk about multiple cities only in (18), but not in (19). (19) appears to yield an invited inference the NP refers only to one specific city.

Comparatives show the same restriction:

(20) *keoi5dei6 dou1 gou1 gwo3 jat1 go3*
3pl all tall PASS one CL
hok6saang1
student
'They are all taller than a student.' (specific only)

Similar to the experiential perfect, one can refer back to *jat1 go3 hok6saang1* in a follow-up sentence (21). The sentence is only felicitous with the singular classifier *go3*, but not plural classifier *baan1*[12].

(21) ... *go2 {go3/*baan1} hok6saang1 gei2*
... that CL_{sg}/CL_{pl} student fairly
gou1
tall
'...that student is / *those students are fairly tall.'

This contrast indicates that *jat1 go3 hok6saang1* in (20) does not allow the free-choice any interpretation and must be specific. A thorough discussion on how to interpret these NPs after *gwo3* is beyond this study, but the data above is sufficient to show that NPs after *gwo3*, regardless of their co-occurrence with verbal or adjectival predicates, are subject to the same specificity constraint.

[12]An anonymous reviewer disagrees with the judgment that *baan1* in (21) is infelicitous. The unacceptability of (21) is based on its co-occurrence with (20), where *go2 baan1 hok6saang1* 'those students' refer back to the standard of comparison *jat1 go3 hok6saang1* in (20). In isolation without (20), I fully agree that (21) is acceptable with both classifiers.

In addition to specific referents, the NP following *gwo3* can also denote generic nouns[13].

(22) *keoi5 sik6 gwo3 wo1ngau4*
3sg eat EXP snail
'S/he has had snails/ escargot.'

(23) *keoi5 laan5 gwo3 zyu1*
3sg lazy PASS pig
'S/he is lazier than pigs.'

In these cases, the NPs 'snail' and 'pig' do not refer to specific entities. Rather, they refer to the entire kind. This shows another parallelism between verbal and adjectival uses of *gwo3*. Both cases require some sort of contextual standard: one would be considered to have tried snails if s/he had a bite or a taste (and not necessarily an entire serving); and (23) is considered true even if we do not have conclusive evidence that the person is lazier than every pig, as long as one assumes pigs in general are lazy (which is often assumed in Cantonese culture). Once the subject surpasses such a contextual standard, the *gwo3* sentences are considered true. A detailed discussion on the relation between generic nouns and contextual standard is beyond the limit of this paper. The point here is that both verbal and adjectival *gwo3* display the same pattern.

Recall that section 4 has shown *gwo3* is affixed to the v^0/Deg^0. This allows us to relate the specificity constraint imposed by *gwo3*. Based on the contrast between (18) and (19), it is clear that *gwo3* is the source of this constraint. Structurally, the head always selects a predicate and an individual, but only when this v^0/Deg^0 is affixed with *gwo3*, the individual must be specific. This supports hypothesis (8) that *gwo3* has the same effect on the selection of the NP, be it an object in experiential perfect or the standard in comparatives.

6 Quantification with *saai3*

The relation between the *gwo3*-affixed head and its internal argument can be further demonstrated by the quantification with *saai3* 'all' in example (24), where the books are construed as a known set.

(24) *keoi5dei6 tai2 (gwo3) saai3 di1 syu1*
3pl see PASS SAAI CL_{pl} book
'They read all the books.'

[13]Example (22) is suggested by an anonymous reviwer.

The occurrence of *gwo3* in (24) affects the interpretation. Without *gwo3*, (24) is true if and only if all the books are read cover to cover. If we include *gwo3*, (24) is true even if each of the books is only briefly read (while the cover-to-cover reading is still valid). It shows that *gwo3* licenses an implicit degree that is contextual[14].

Tang (1996) analyzes *saai3* as a marker of distribution. That is, *saai3* marks distributive plural sets of either events or internal arguments, but not subjects. This locality effect is supported by the contrast between unaccusative *zau2* 'leave' in (25) and unergative *haam3* 'cry' in (26). Since the surface subject with unaccusatives is raised from internal to the VP and the one with unergatives is base-generated in the subject position, the unacceptability of (26) shows that the subject of (26) is never an internal argument. Tang (1996) does not provide a syntactic representation of *saai3*. This study assumes that *saai3* is an operator at Spec-VP immediately dominated by vP, which is compatible to our V^0-to-v^0 head movement analysis.

(25) *keoi5dei6 zau2 saai3*
3pl leave SAAI
'They all left.'

(26) **keoi5dei6 haam3 saai3*
3pl cry SAAI
Intended: 'They all cried.'

The contrast in grammaticality and the distributive meaning in (25) show that the event or its internal argument is restricted under the scope of *saai3*. This observation demonstrates that the argument taken by the *gwo3*-affixed head (e.g., *saai3 di1 syu1* in (24)) must also be interpreted within the scope of this *gwo3*-affixed head. With *gwo3*, which can take an implicit degree argument, the distributive NP 'the books' is allowed to be partially read. Without *gwo3*, the verbal predicate 'read all the books' would have to be interpreted such that every single member in the set of the books must be completely read. The partial tree (27) shows that the op-

[14]The contextual reading of positive adjectives is generally assumed in the literature to handle adjectives in different scales like 'John is tall' vs. 'The Eiffel Tower is tall'.

erator *saai3* makes sure that the event or the object NP are distributive (and not collective). When the *gwo3*-affixed head then takes this distributive argument, the event is interpreted as plurality of 'reading the book' and hence the sentence denotes the situation that every member of the books has been read, but not necessarily cover to cover. In essense, the partial-reading interpretation is allowed because *gwo3* requires a degree argument, which can be implicit and does not necessarily require completion.

(27)

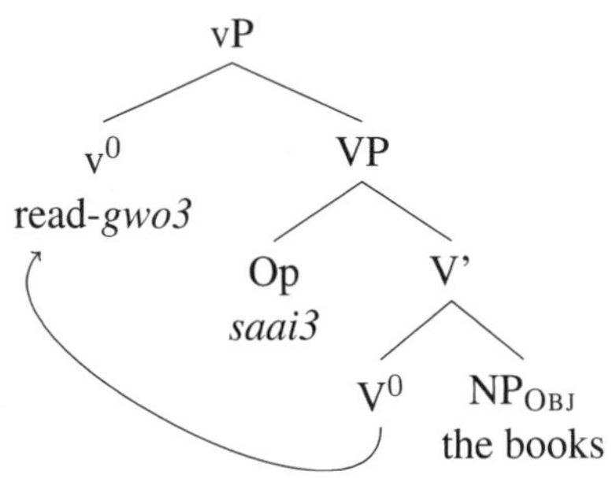

Similarly, *saai3* with surpass comparative shows distribution over the internal argument, i.e. the standard.

(28) *Mary jau5cin2 gwo3 saai3 keoi5dei6*
Mary rich PASS SAAI 3pl
'Mary is richer than *every one of them*.'

Sentence (28) describes the situation where Mary is richer than everyone in the group. Mary does not necessarily have more money than the group combined, as long as she is richer compared to each individual (the collective reading in this case happens to subsume the distributive one). This shows that the *saai3*-standard is distributive and not collective. With *saai3* forcing the distributive reading, we can see that the *gwo3*-affixed head takes each member in its argument NP separately and makes the comparison. The structure is shown in (29).

In sum, the interaction with *saai3* shows that *gwo3* takes the VP or AdjP as its argument and the internal argument must be interpreted under the scope of the *gwo3*-associated head in both verbal and adjectival domains.

(29)

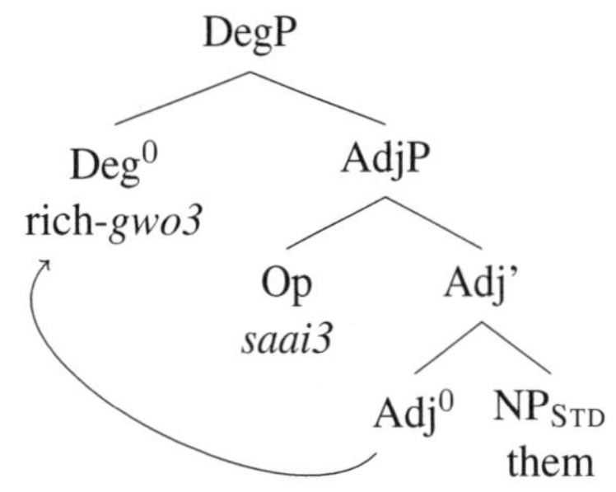

7 Bare comparatives

Cantonese has another comparative construction that does not require standard of comparison (30). This section shows that this is compatible with the current proposal and provides indirect support for the analysis of *gwo3* comparative.

(30) *Mary gou1 (Peter) (jat1) di1*
Mary tall Peter one bit
'Mary is a bit taller (than Peter).' (Standard is optional)

Notice that *(jat1) di1* '(a) bit; little' represents the measure phrase, i.e. how much Mary is taller than Peter, and the measure phrase must appear after the standard, but never before it (31), whereas a *gwo3*-comparative requires a standard (32).

(31) *Mary gou1 di1 (*Peter)*
Mary tall bit Peter
'Mary is taller.'

(32) *Mary gou1 gwo3 *(Peter)*
Mary tall PASS Peter
'Mary is taller than Peter.' (required STD)

This shows that *di* is actually a measure phrase, rather than a functional marker for comparative. On the one hand, it means that sentences like (31) are not a counterexample to the current proposal for Cantonese *gwo3* comparatives. On the other, it mean that *gwo3* is the reason why an overt standard of comparison must be overt in surpass comparatives. As a consequence, that non-*gwo3* comparatives, such as (30), do not require a specified standard of comparison, which is separate from the measure phrase, is actually expected.

8 Implications

8.1 Homomorphic theory to scalar predicates

As the data show that *gwo3* can in fact be interpreted with the same syntax and semantics in both event-denoting and property-denoting predicates, this means that the cross-categorial behaviors of *gwo3* can be explained with a homomorphic approach. That is, the semantics across categories can be structured in the same way.

In a broader sense, the current analysis shows the benefit of a simpler syntax-semantics mapping mechanism in language. With the homomorphic approach, the need for category-specific syntax-semantics is reduced, because the behaviors in different categories (V and Adj in our case) can be captured under the same syntax-semantics structure. Therefore, such an approach is desirable for any explanatory theories for human language.

The benefit of a simpler syntax-semantics is not only for theoretical simplicity. With a simpler syntax-semantics mapping, language learners' would only need one set of mapping rules, rather than multiple sets, to handle verbs and adjectives. This will in turn explain more easily why such complicated structures can be mastered by children at a young age despite its very complex structure. For this reason, such an approach will be superior to theories with category-specific syntax with regard to its explanatory power for language learnability as well.

Remaining issues with the proposal include, for instance, the literature does not handle events the same way as degrees or properties. Works on event structure or event semantics (Dowty, 1977; Parsons, 1990; Ramchand, 2008; Champollion, 2014) takes event as a variable, instead of taking a specific point in the progress of event as a variable, while the syntax-semantics of adjectives and comparatives takes degree (rather than an entire scale containing sets of degrees) as a variable, as seen in (Grano & Kennedy, 2012) and other studies. The current study cannot provide any elaborate answer to this, but would note that recent studies have found commonalities across categories in English, such as the measurement of predicates in various constructions (Wellwood, Hacquard, & Pancheva, 2012; Champollion, 2010; Krifka, 1998). Therefore, the homomorphism suggested here is not entirely novel.

8.2 'Aspects' in Cantonese

This close-up study on *gwo3* demonstrates an alternative for the analysis of (viewpoint) Aspect in the verbal domain. The literature has in general assumed that postverbal elements like *zo2*, *gwo3* and progressive *gan2* correspond to Asp(ect) head in syntax, based on the Mandarin literature (see Soh (2014) for an overview). The problem with this usual Aspect-analysis to *gwo3* is that it relies on movement to resolve the discrepancy between the theory (that the head-initial Asp^0 dominates vP) and the empirical data (that aspect markers always follow immediately after the first syllable of the verbal predicate). This study has argued that *gwo3* should be analyzed in-situ (within vP) rather than by any kind of movement (e.g., movement to Asp^0 or affix lowering). The current proposal differ substantially from Sybesma (1997, 2004) in that *gwo3* here is an affix, rather than a head. It is unclear whether the same analysis of experiential *gwo3* can be transferred to perfective *zo2* (similar to Mandarin *le*) or progressive *gan2*. This can only be left for future studies.

9 Conclusion

This study investigates the morpheme *gwo3* in two constructions: the surpass-comparative and the experiential perfect, and argues that *gwo3* should be analyzed with the same syntax and semantics, based on evidence from syntax (question formation) and semantics (specificity and quantification). The homomorphic approach of *gwo3* applies to both event-denoting ('verbs') and property-denoting ('adjectives') predicates. In a broad sense, this approach is argued to be a simpler and more explanatory theory than category-specific theories. Focusing on the study of Cantonese or other Sinitic languages, this study argues against the general Aspect analysis and suggests a non-movement account for *gwo3*, which has potential to be extended to other aspect markers.

Acknowledgments

I thank Ronnie Wilbur for constructive comments. I am also grateful to the three anonymous reviewers, who provided their critical comments.

References

Ansaldo, U. (2010). *Surpass comparatives in sinitic and beyond: typology and grammaticalization.*

Champollion, L. (2010). *Parts of a whole: Distributivity as a bridge between aspect and measurement* (Unpublished doctoral dissertation). University of Pennsylvania.

Champollion, L. (2014). *The interaction of compositional semantics and event semantics.* Retrieved from http://ling.auf.net/lingbuzz/002118

Chappell, H. (2001). The experiential perfect as an evidential marker in sinitic languages.

Cresswell, M. (1976). The semantics of degree. In B. Partee (Ed.), *Montague grammar* (pp. 261–292). Academic Press – New York.

Dowty, D. R. (1977). Toward a semantic analysis of verb aspect and the english imperfective progressive. *Linguistics and Philosophy, 1*, 45–77.

Erlewine, M. Y. (2007). A new syntax-semantics for the mandarin bi comparative. *University of Chicago MA thesis.*

Erlewine, M. Y. (2012). Share to compare: The mandarin b comparative. In *the proceedings of the 29th west coast conference on formal linguistics* (pp. 54–62).

Francis, E. J., & Matthews, S. (2005). A multi-dimensional approach to the category in cantonese. *Journal of Linguistics, 41*(02), 269-305.

Grano, T., & Kennedy, C. (2012). Mandarin transitive comparatives and the grammar of measurement. *Journal of East Asian Linguistics, 21*, 219-266. doi: DOI10.1007/s10831-012-9090-Y

Kennedy, C., & McNally, L. (2005). Scale structure, degree modification, and the semantics of gradable predicates. *Language*, 345–381.

Krifka, M. (1998). The origins of telicity. *Events and grammar, 197*, 235.

Liu, C.-M. L. (2010). Mandarin chinese as an exceed-type language. In *North american conference on chinese lingui* (p. 271).

Matthews, S., & Yip, V. (1994). *Cantonese: A comprehensive grammar.* Routledge.

Mok, S.-S. (1998). *Cantonese exceed comparatives* (Unpublished doctoral dissertation). University of California, San Diego.

Parsons, T. (1990). *Events in the semantics of English.* MIT Press.

Paul, W. (2010). Adjectives in mandarin chinese: The rehabilitation of a much ostracized category. *Adjectives: Formal analyses in syntax and semantics, ed. Patricia Cabredo Hofherr and Ora Matushansky*, 115–151.

Ramchand, G. (2008). *Verb meaning and the lexicon: A first-phase syntax.* Cambridge University Press.

Reichenbach, H. (1947). *Element of symbolic logic.* London: Macmillan.

Soh, H. L. (2014). Aspect. In C.-T. J. Huang, Y.-H. A. Li, & A. Simpson (Eds.), *The handbook of Chinese linguistics* (pp. 126–155). Wiley.

Stassen, L. (1985). *Comparison and universal grammar.* Blackwell Oxford.

von Stechow, A. (1984). Comparing semantic theories of comparison. *Journal of semantics, 3*(1), 1–77.

Sybesma, R. (1997). Why Chinese verb-le is a resultative predicate. *Journal of East Asian Linguistics, 6*(3), 215–261.

Sybesma, R. (2004). Exploring Cantonese tense. *Linguistics in the Netherlands, 21*(1), 169–180.

Tang, S.-W. (1996). A role of lexical quantifiers. *Studies in the Linguistic Sciences, 26*, 307–323.

Wellwood, A., Hacquard, V., & Pancheva, R. (2012). Measuring and comparing individuals and events. *Journal of Semantics, 29(2).*

Xiang, M. (2005). *Some topics in comparative constructions* (Unpublished doctoral dissertation). Michigan State University.

A Quantitative View of Short Utterances in Daily Conversation: A Case Study of *That's right*, *That's true* and *That's correct*

Yanjiao Li
Department of Linguistics and Translation
City University of Hong Kong
Hong Kong SAR
yanjiaoli2-c@my.cityu.edu.hk

Alex C. Fang
Department of Linguistics and Translation
City University of Hong Kong
Hong Kong SAR
acfang@cityu.edu.hk

Jing Cao
School of Foreign Languages
Zhongnan University of Economics and Law
Wuhan, P. R. China
cecilia_cao@znufe.edu.cn

Abstract

Short utterances serve a multitude of different communicative functions in interactive speech and have attracted due attention in recent research in dialogue acts. This paper presents a quantitative description of three short utterances i.e. *that's right*, *that's true*, *that's correct* and their variations based on the Switchboard Dialogue Act Corpus. Particularly, it offers an overview to account for how they are deployed by native speakers in daily conversation. At the same time, it attempts to provide a comparative account of *that's right* and *that's true*, showing that while almost 75% of them are mutually exchangeable, they nonetheless exhibit preferences in interactive speech. This insight is expected to form a useful approach towards automatic dialogue act tagging.

1 Introduction

Dialogue act (DA), defined as "communicative activity of a dialogue participant, interpreted as having a certain communicative function and semantic content" (ISO 24617-2, 2012: 2), plays a key role in the interpretation of the communicative behaviour of dialogue participants and offer valuable insight into the design of human-machine dialogue system (Bunt et al. 2010). With the goal of facilitating automatic DA tagging, this paper describes a corpus-based investigation into *that's right, that's true, that's correct* and their variations in the Switchboard Dialogue Act (SWBD) Corpus, in order to answer questions about the communicative functions they mainly perform in daily conversation. These utterances deserve our particular attention in research considering that, like other brief responses (e.g. *Oh*, *Uh huh*, *Mm*, *Okay*), they serve as important feedback to the main speaker and they usually occur as overlapping speech. They are particularly problematic to interpret because they demonstrate a drastically different functional or pragmatic meaning from the semantic meaning of the component tokens. Consider Example 1.

Example 1

sd B.54 utt1: -- {C and } I like that because [it's a, + it's] real easy to, {F uh, } follow for her, /

sd B.54 utt2: {D you know, } {F uh, } {D gosh, } [if, + if] I read straight out of the Bible to her she'd <laughter> never understand any of it. /

sd A.55 utt1: {D Well, } it's hard for me. /

ba B.56 utt1: <u>That's right <laughter>. /</u>

sw_0263_2226.utt

This is one excerpt retrieved from the targeted corpus, which will be further illustrated in section 2. A and B, two speakers, are talking about books and literature, where B is describing one of her daughter's book, "real easy to follow". The last utterance

Copyright 2014 by Yanjiao Li, Alex C. Fang, and Jing Cao
28th Pacific Asia Conference on Language, Information and Computation pages 378–386

that's right can be interpreted as serving both assessment/appreciation and agreement functions. The speaker B considers that what has been stated by A is right, not false, in which *right* is used as the evaluative adjective. Also, he implies his agreement with the interlocutor where *that's right* is used as a whole. Therefore, on the one hand, the semantic meaning of *that's right* makes it much closer to personal judgments and assessments, that is, the opinion is "right, not false". On the other hand, it is often used as a whole, indicating speaker's agreement, which goes beyond lexical meanings.

However, past studies rarely specify various usage for *that's right*, *that's true* and *that's correct* in a systematic fashion, and just sporadically describe one or two cases to illustrate one or two facets for them, without capturing a full picture of how they are used with empirical evidence. To be more exact, for the studies that do discuss usage for *that's right*, Gardner (2001) believes that *that's right* is exactly the same as *right* when responding to a preceding question, the synonym for "*that's correct*". This point has been further elaborated in that *right* is deemed "a truncated version of *that's right*" when acting as "an epistemic confirmation token", "in a sense close to one of its dictionary meanings, namely '*correct*'" (Gardner, 2004: 4). The studies indicate that *that's right*, *right*, *that's correct*, and *correct* are similar and can be alternatively used as the confirmation token oriented to a prior question. At this regard, however, Stenström (1987: 104) asserts that *that's right* is much stronger than *right* in degree of emphasis and involvement when severing as a response move to the same type initiating move. In addition, when responding to a previous declarative, *that's right* has been considered to realize the functions of seeking confirmation (Tui, 1994), showing agreement (Stenström, 1987; Tui, 1994; Gardner, 2001) as well as making assessments (Tao, 2003). Therefore, *that's right* has been considered to indicate a wide variety of intentions in interaction. With regard to *that's true,* it has received little attention, and only McCarthy (2003) makes brief description that as a syntactically independent token, *true* seems to prefer the clausal option (*that's true*) to independent occurrence (*true*). In terms of *that's correct,* it has been left largely unexamined and unspecified regarding the usage.

Considered semantic meanings of the three short utterances (i.e. *that's right*, *that's true* and *that's correct*), they largely embody in their key words *right*, *true* and *correct*. As is shown in dictionaries, the three words have similar lexical meanings and are often used to paraphrase each other. For instance, *Longman Dictionary of Contemporary English* (2009, fifth edition) defines them as follows:

Correct: having no mistakes; right (p.379)
Right: true/correct (p.1504)
True: not false, based on facts and not imagined or invented (p.1891-1892)

Thus, this paper aims to bring together the disparate findings on the uses of the three short utterances as well as their variations, attempting to depict an overview of them: how they are deployed by native speakers in daily conversation. At the same time, a comparative view has been concentrated on *that's right/true*, to seek to the circumstance in which they are mutually exchangeable and in which they are distinct. In this way, it is expected to form a useful approach towards automatic detection of DAs.

This paper is structured as follows. Section 2 briefly introduces the SWBD DA corpus, then section 3 presents how the data has been processed before statistical analysis. Section 4 is related to general figures for the three short utterances and their variations, followed by a comparative study (section 5). Section 6 draws conclusions to this paper.

2 Corpus Resource

This study uses the Switchboard Dialogue Act Corpus[1] , which comprises 1,155 transcribed telephone conversations, totaling in 223,606 utterances or 1.5 million word tokens (Fang et al., 2011). In this corpus, the segmented unit for utterances is defined as "slash-unit", which can be complete or incomplete, ranging from "a sentence" to "a smaller unit" (Meteer et al., 1995: 16). Moreover, all these segmented utterances have been annotated with DA information, such as "aa" (*accept*), "ba" (*assessment/appreciation*), etc., to denote functions of particular utterances according to the SWBD-

[1] available online www.ldc.upenn.edu

DAMSL coding scheme (Jurafsky et al., 1997). Consider Example 2[2].

Example 2
sv A.9 utt12: any jury's not going to disregard the evidence, {D you know } <laughter>. /

aa B.10 utt1: {F Uh, } that's true. /
sw_0142_2145.utt

As can be seen, the first utterance has been coded with "sv", a DA tag for *statement-opinion*, while the second one has been labeled as "aa", a code for *accept*. In the current study, investigation of various functions will be conducted based on the DA tags which have been coded for each utterance.

3 Data Pre-processing

For the benefit of the current work, *that's right*, *that's true* and *that's correct*, and their variations are retrieved from the corpus accordingly. Variations in the current study are defined with a series of factors taken into account.

- Firstly, variations of the same token share the key words and present in similar patterns, for instance, *it's true*, *this is true* and *true* are all considered as variations of *that's true*, since they contain the same key word *true* with similar patterns. Consequently, the whole utterances have similar semantic meanings.
- Secondly, cases (e.g. *it's true*) embedded with adverbs and formulaic terms are still regarded as variations, because adverbs and formulaic terms are often used to enhance or emphasize emotions or attitudes, but not to change the meaning of the whole utterance. *That's really true* and *I think that's certainly true* are cases in point, where *really* and *certainly* are adverbs, and *I think* is the formulaic term. They are used to emphasize the attitude of the speaker. Formulaic terms refer to expressions such as "*I think*" and "*I believe*", which display in the form of "I + predicate", to express the speaker's subjectivity in spoken discourse (Baumgarten and House, 2010). Also, they have been recognized as one type of "engagement", dealing with "sourcing attitudes and the play of voices around opinions in discourse" in the appraisal framework (Martin and White, 2005: 35).
- Thirdly, the negative form and interrogative form, e.g. *that's not true*, *is that true?* are excluded, since their meanings and primary functions are apparently distinct from those of *that's true*.
- Fourthly, cases subsequently followed by that-clauses or prepositional phrases are excluded from the current work either, for instance

Example 3
sv B.115 utt2: {C So } I do think it's right that they're harder on themselves, # {D you know. } # /
sw_0382_4785.utt

It's true, followed by a that-clause, is not used independently any more. Such cases are not concerned with at this moment.

- Finally, it is necessary to reconsider the independent token *right* since it is often used as acknowledging token in the literature (e.g. Gardner, 2004; 2007), different from *that's right*. As a consequence, *right* is not treated as a variant of *that's right* in this stage, which will be verified by the statistical information later.

Variations of *that's right*	**Variations of *that's true***	**Variations of *that's correct***
	True	*Correct*
Adverb + *right*	Adverb + *true*	Adverb + *correct*
That's + adverb + *right*	*That's* + adverb + *true*	
Formulaic term + *that's* + *right*	Formulaic term + *that's true*	Formulaic term + *that's correct*
Formulaic terms + *that's* + adverb + *right*	Formulaic term + *that's*+ adverb + *true*	
It's right	*It's true*	
	It's + adverb + *true*	
	Formulaic term + *it's true*	
	Formulaic term + *it's* + adverb + *true*	
	This is true	
	This is + adverb + *true*	

Table 1 Variations of *that's right/true/correct*

[2] In the Switchboard Dialogue Act Corpus, restarts and non-sentence elements also have been marked within each utterance, such as filler ({F…}), discourse marker ({D…}) and coordinating conjunction ({C…}) (Meteer et al., 1995). In Example 2, "*You know*" is coded as discourse marker and "*Uh*" as filler.

Thus, the final list can be identified as shown in Table 1, where similar patterns take one-to-one correspondence. Apparently, *that's true* has more different types of variations than the other two.

4 Descriptive Statistics

That's right, *that's true* and *that's correct* are in effect synonymous concerning the dictionary meaning, while in the corpus, they do vary regarding their frequency information.

	(1) That's right and variations	(2) That's true and variations	(3) That's correct and variations
Total	911	920	21

(1), (2) and (3) in the following will be used to stand for the three sets of utterances respectively.

Table 2 Statistical information of the three sets

It is obvious that the total occurrence of (1) and (2) are almost the same, both of which far exceed that of (3). Beyond this, a range of functions have been identified for each of them, of which "aa", "ba", "s", "na" and "b"[3] are the most significant ones, all together accounting for over 98% in each set. Table 3 sets out these functions and their relative frequencies in performing each of them.

	aa	ba	s	na	b	Total
(1)	682 75%	139 15%	30 3%	26 3%	20 2%	897 98%
(2)	659 72%	148 16%	96 10%	2 0.2%	4 0.4%	909 99%
(3)	13 62%	5 24%	1 5%	1 5%	1 5%	21 100%

aa = accept; ba = assessment/appreciation; s = statement; na = affirmative answer; b = acknowledgement/backchannel

Table 3 Top five functions of three sets

[3] In the coding scheme SWBD-DAMSL, there are very specific definitions for each of them. *Accept* (aa), one subtype of *agreement*, indicates the speaker explicitly accepts a proposal, or makes agreements with previous opinions (Jurafsky et al., 1997: 37). *Assessment/appreciation* (ba) is defined as "a backchannel/continuer which functions to express slightly more emotional involvement and support than just 'uh-huh'" (Jurafsky et al., 1997: 48). *Statement* (s) divides into *"descriptive/narrative/personal"* statements (sd) and *"other-directed opinion statements"* (sv), both with the primary purpose of making claims about the world (including answers to questions) (Allen and Core, 1997: 10). *Affirmative answer* (na) is one subclass of *answers*, which indicates affirmative answers that are not "yes" or a variant (Jurafsky et al., 1997: 50). *Acknowledgement* (b) is usually "referred to in the CA literature as a 'continuer'" (Jurafsky et al., 1997: 42).

A glance at the table establishes that these top five functions together account for a large proportion among a series of functions performed by each particular set. In particular, *accept* overwhelmingly occurs in all the three sets, followed by *assessment/appreciation*. However, set (3) displays some slight distinction from (1) and (2) in the way that its proportion of *assessment/appreciation* is around 10% higher than that of sets (1) (2), but approximately 10% lower in *accept*. In the description to follow, the major concern is to seek similarities and distinctions within each set.

4.1 *That's right* and its variations

That's right and its variations frequently occur in daily speech, which can be seen in Table 4.

Types	Freq.	Percentage
That's right	852	93.5%
That's + adverb + *right*	26	2.9%
Formulaic term + *that's* + *right*	20	2.2%
Formulaic term + *that's* + adverb + *right*	5	0.6%
It's right	4	0.4%
Adverb + *right*	4	0.4%
Total	911	100%

Table 4 Statistical information of set (1)

It is perceptible that the simple token *that's right* overwhelmingly occurs compared to a range of variations, which may be indicative of the significance of economy in casual talk. By contrast, formulaic terms and adverbs are not so often attached with *that's/it's right*, accounting for less than 3% (2.2%+0.6%) and 4% (2.9%+0.6%+0.4%) respectively, which implies that such additional emphasis of stance and attitudes is not common in daily conversation. Noticeably, *it's right* appears 4 times, and *this is right* never occurs in the corpus. Hence *that*, *it* and *this* are similar lexical items but they have their own particular preference in some circumstance: when prefacing "be + right", *that* is more often used than *it* and *this*.

Regarding a variety of functions they serve, *that's right* and its variation totally perform twelve different functions in the corpus, but the top five are extremely significant which can be seen in Table 5, together constituting over 60% in each row. Strikingly, *that's right* does exhibit some slight distinction from its variations in that *that's right* can respond to a prior question and acknowledge to what has been uttered, while its variations cannot do so.

Types	aa	ba	s	na	b	Total
That's right	642 76%	134 16%	19 2%	26 3%	20 2%	841 99%
That's + adverb + *right*	21 78%	3 15%	1 4%	0	0	25 96%
Formulaic term + *that's* + *right*	13 65%	1 5%	6 30%	0	0	20 100%
Formulaic term + *that's* + adverb + *right*	2 40%	0	1 20%	0	0	3 60%
It's right	0	1 25%	3 75%	0	0	4 100%
Adverb + *right*	4 100%	0	0	0	0	4 100%

aa = accept; ba = assessment/appreciation; s = statement; na = affirmative answer; b = acknowledgement/backchannel

Table 5 Top five functions performed by set (1)

Moreover, when formulaic terms are attached previously, the whole utterance has greater likelihood to function as *statement*. It is noted that the top three functions of *that's right* are exactly those functions analyzed and discussed in the literature, that is, agreement, assessments and affirmative answers. But with the empirical evidence, it can be further observed that agreement is much more remarkable than the other two. In addition, *it's right* is a special token in the table in that it clearly prefers *statement* to *accept*, which should not have been counted as a variant of *that's right*. Yet, considered the limited occurrence (4 times), it is not pervasive enough to determine what kind of functions it exactly serves, so it remains in this set. In the future, a larger spoken corpus will be in demand for examining such tokens.

4.2 *That's true* and its variations

Likewise, Table 6 exhibits basic frequency information of set (2). Different from set (1), *that's true* has much more variations than *that's right* in terms of types and tokens, which is illustrated by the statistics that variations of *that's true* make up 29% of set (2) while those of *that's right* just accounts for 6.5% of set (1). It needs to be noted that the symbol "*" in Table 6 means that the adverb in *that's* + adverb + *true* is able to move freely, not restricted to the middle position, such as "*probably that's true*", or "*that's true also*". This, however, has not been perceived for *that's right*.

Types	Freq.	Percentage
That's true	653	71.0%
**That's* + adverb + *true*	93	10.1%
True	59	6.4%
Adverb + *true*	13	1.4%
Formulaic term + *that's true*	36	3.9%
Formulaic term + *that's*+ adverb + *true*	11	1.2%
It's true	25	2.7%
It's + adverb + *true*	8	0.9%
Formulaic term + *it's true*	2	0.2%
Formulaic term + *it's* + adverb + *true*	1	0.1%
This is true	15	1.6%
This is + adverb + *true*	4	0.4%
Total	920	100.0%

Table 6 Statistical information of set (2)

Yet still, set (2) is consistent with set (1) in two respects. On the one hand, *that's true* occurs more frequently than *it's true* and *this is true*, which is correspondingly close to set (1). On the other hand, formulaic terms and adverbs do not show high frequency in set (2) either. *That's true*, *it's true* and *this is true* are far more frequently used than those embedded with formulaic terms or adverbs.

Types	aa	ba	s	na	b	Total
That's true	487 74%	105 16%	55 8%	0	2 0.3%	649 99%
**That's* + adverb + *true*	62 67%	15 16%	8 9%	2 2%	1 1%	88 96%
True	38 64%	18 31%	0	0	1 2%	57 97%
Adverb + *true*	10 77%	3 23%	0	0	0	13 100%
Formulaic term + *that's true*	22 61%	1 3%	13 35%	0	0	36 100%
Formulaic term + *that's* + adverb + *true*	6 55%	1 9%	3 27%	0	0	10 91%
It's true	11 44%	3 12%	11 44%	0	0	25 100%
It's + adverb + *true*	5 62.5%	0	3 37.5%	0	0	8 100%
Formulaic term + *it's true*	0	0	2 100%	0	0	2 100%
Formulaic term + *it's* + adverb + *true*	0	0	1 100%	0	0	1 100%
This is true	13 87%	2 13%	0	0	0	15 100%
This is + adverb + *true*	4 100%	0	0	0	0	4 100%

aa = accept; ba = assessment/appreciation; s = statement; na = affirmative answer; b = acknowledgement/backchannel

Table 7 Top five functions performed by set (2)

Concerning a range of functions they perform, *that's true* and its variations totally have nine different functions in the corpus, among which the top five are displayed in Table 7. Overall, the distribution here shares a large number of similarities with that of set (1) in Table 5. In particular, *accept*, *assessment/appreciation* and *statement* are considerably significant, while *affirmative answer* and *acknowledgement* are comparatively less crucial, only occurring in *that's true*, *that's* + adverb + *true* and *true*. When *that's true* is attached with formulaic terms, the likelihood to function as *accept* declines accompanying with greater proportion in *statement*. The exceptional token is *it's true*, which itself prefers both *accept* and *statement*. In this sense, *it's true* is distinguished from *that's true* which overwhelmingly deals with *accept*. By contrast, *this is true* is relatively consistent with *that's true* in primary functions they serve. Thus, in the pattern "THAT/IT/THIS + BE + TRUE", *that*, *it* and *this* indicate their particular preference as well.

4.3 *That's correct* and its variations

That's correct and its variations are used infrequently, with a total occurrence of 21 in the whole corpus. As a consequence, there are far less variations in this set. Table 8 shows the basic frequency information, and Table 9 exhibits all functions performed by these tokens.

Types	Freq.	Percentage
That's correct	13	61.9%
Formulaic term + *that's correct*	3	14.3%
Correct	4	19.0%
Adverb + *correct*	1	4.8%
Total	21	100.0%

Table 8 Statistical information of set (3)

Types	aa	ba	s	na	b	Total
That's correct	8 62%	4 31%	0	1 8%	0	13 100%
Formulaic term + *that's correct*	2 67%	0	1 33%	0	0	3 100%
Correct	2 50%	1 25%	0	0	1 25%	4 100%
Adverb + *correct*	1 100%	0	0	0	0	1 100%

aa = accept; ba = assessment/appreciation; s = statement; na = affirmative answer; b = acknowledgement/backchannel

Table 9 All functions performed by set (3)

As can be seen in Table 8, *that's correct* occurs more frequently than its variations, accounting for 62% in set (3), which is lower than that of *that's right* (93%) and *that's true* (71%). Moreover, formulaic terms and adverbs are not so frequent, either, which suggests bare tokens such as *that's correct* and *correct* are preferred by native speakers. Considered a range of functions performed Table 9, *accept* and *assessment/appreciation* are remarkable compared to *statement*, *affirmative answer* and *acknowledgement* with one occurrence for each.

To summarize, an overview of utterances in the three sets has presented with empirical evidence. Generally, they share quite a lot of similarities in terms of primary functions they serve. In addition, two points need to be further elaborated. One is that, *right* is assumed to be used in a way different from *that's right* in conversation, which is further confirmed by the evidence that 73% of *right* serve *acknowledgement* while *that's right* prefers *accept* with 76% of its total occurrence in the corpus. This can be observed in Table 10, where their top five functions have been listed respectively. Also, 16% of *that's right* can be used as *assessment/appreciation*, whereas the single *right* only occurs 11 times (0.2%) as *assessment/appreciation*. Hence, in general, *right* and *that's right* are two different cases in interactive speech.

	b	aa	na	%	fc	Total
Right	3685 73%	1154 23%	127 3%	26 0.5%	17 0.3%	5009 99%
	aa	ba	na	b	s	Total
That's right	642 76%	134 16%	26 3%	20 2%	19 2%	841 99%

aa = accept; ba = assessment/appreciation; s = statement; na = affirmative answer; b = acknowledgement/backchannel; % = abandoned utterances; fc = conversational closing

Table 10 *right* vs. *that's right*

The second point is that, *that*, *it* and *this* have their particular preference to the pattern "THAT/IT/THIS+BE+RIGHT/TRUE/CORRECT" , which can be summarized as follows.

That > Ø > it > this

It means that the ones on the left side take priority over those on the right: *that* more likely occurs than *this*, and the symbol Ø signals no pronoun occurs. This is highly consistent with Tao's finding (2003: 202) "*that* is more likely to be used as a turn initiator than *this*".

5 A Comparative Study

According to the previous statistical analysis, it is noted that *that's right*, *that's true* and *that's correct* account for quite a large proportion in each particular set. The previous observation has also shown that the total occurrence of *that's correct* is much fewer than the other two, and therefore, a comparative study will concentrate on *that's right* and *that's true*, and examine the condition where they are mutually exchangeable with each other and where they are distinct from each other. Figures 1 and 2 respectively fill out their primary functions and their preceding contexts[4]. By Figure 1, apparently *that's right* and *that's true* both exhibit considerable preference to *accept* and *assessment/appreciation* which together make up over 90% for both cases. It is meant that over 90% of their tokens perform the two same functions.

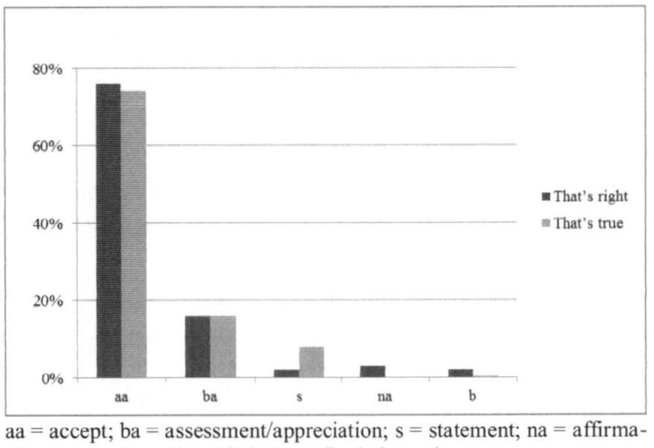

aa = accept; ba = assessment/appreciation; s = statement; na = affirmative answer; b = acknowledgement/backchannel

Figure 1 Primary functions of *that's right* and *that's true*

However, some slight difference between them can be perceived as well. *That's right* is used to perform all these five functions, while *that's true* cover four of them and cannot be not used to answer a question. At the same time, *that's true* shows far greater likelihood to serve *statement* compared to *that's right*. By contrast, *that's right* is almost ten times more likely than *that's true* to function as *acknowledgement*.

In order to see whether their previous contexts could offer useful cues to differentiate the occurrence of *that's right* and *that's true*, a specific view is taken into the previous contexts when they act as *accept* and *assessment/appreciation*, because the two functions together make up a large proportion of the total occurrence. Figure 2 depicts the salient previous context when they act as the two functions.

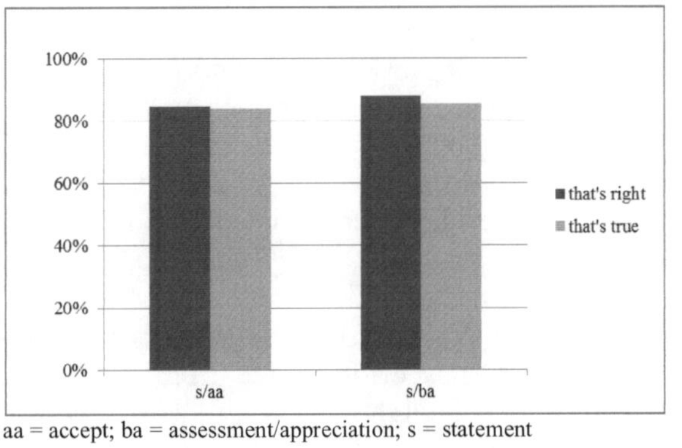

aa = accept; ba = assessment/appreciation; s = statement

Figure 2 Previous contexts of *aa* and *ba*

It is clear that *statement* is the most overwhelming previous function, accounting for over 80% previous contexts of *that's right/true* when they act as *accept* and *assessment/appreciation*. It seems that the previous contexts offer little cues to differentiate them, since both are so often preceded by *statement*. According to Figures 1 and 2, it is possible that almost 75% of *that's right/true* are mutually exchangeable since over 90% of their occurrence contributes to *accept* and *assessment/appreciation*, in which over 80% of the previous contexts are *statement*. This can be further validated by the chi-square test, which aims to test if *that's right* and *that's true* have no difference in the distribution of different functions. Table 11 shows the frequency distribution of *that's right/true* in *accept*, *assessment/appreciation* and other functions. Table 12 exhibits the result of the test.

			Functions			
			aa	ba	others	Total
Tokens	That's right	Count	642	134	76	852
		Expected count	639.1	135.3	77.6	852.0
	That's true	Count	487	105	61	653
		Expected count	489.9	103.7	59.4	653.0
Total		Count	1129	239	137	1505
		Expected count	1129.0	239.0	137.0	1505.0

aa = accept; ba = assessment/appreciation

Table 11 Tokens*functions crosstabulation

[4] The previous contexts are restricted to immediately previous utterances uttered by others.

	Value	df	Asymp. Sig. (2-sided)
Pearson Chi-Square	.130[a]	2	.937
Likelihood Ratio	.130	2	.937
N of Valid Cases	1505		

a. 0 cells (.0%) have expected count less than 5. The minimum expected count is 59.44.

Table 12 Chi-Square Tests

In Table 12, the value of pearson chi-square is 0.130, and the p-value is 0.937 which is larger than 0.05. It manifests that the difference between *that's right* and *that's true* is not significant in the distribution of primary functions according to the frequency information observed in the corpus.

In summary, the statistical analysis above demonstrates that *that's right* and *that's true* are used almost the same in interactive speech, in which nearly 75% of their total occurrence are interchangeable. This is further confirmed by the significant test which explicitly shows no significance in the distribution of primary functions, and their previous contexts supply little cues for the distinction. In some cases, however, they have their own preference and differ from each other. For instance, *that's true* has never been found to answer a previous question in the corpus, while 3% of *that's right* can perform this function. Moreover, *that's true* shows much greater likelihood to serve *statement* whereas *that's right* is almost ten times more likely than *that's true* to be *acknowledgement*. Specifically, when the preceding utterance is a statement or a question, the current utterance is more likely to serve *statement* if it is realized by *that's true*; it has greater possibility to be *acknowledgement* or *an affirmative answer* if it is realized by *that's right*. This kind of preference is expected to facilitate DA tagging.

6 Conclusions

This paper presented a quantitative investigation of three short utterances (i.e. *that's right*, *that's true*, *that's correct*) and their variations in the Switchboard Dialogue Act Corpus. Particularly, it offered an overview to account for how they are used in daily conversation with empirical evidence. By the current investigation, it has been observed that *that's right/true* and their variations much more frequently occur than *that's correct* and its variation. In terms of primary functions served in interactive speech, they consistently exhibit great preference to *accept, assessment/appreciation, statement, affirmative answer* and *acknowledgement*, among which, *accept* and *assessment/appreciation* together account for quite a large proportion. Regarding their variations, *that, it* and *this* are similar lexical items but they indicate their particular preference to this pattern "THAT/IT/THIS+BE+RIGHT/TRUE/CORRECT" . Moreover, formulaic terms and adverbs are not so frequently embedded. When formulaic terms are attached, the whole utterances have greater likelihood to be *statement.*

Also, we have specified some crucial issues for *that's right* and *that's true*, which are clearly useful to the detection of DAs. It has been discovered that almost 75% of *that's right* and *that's true* are mutually exchangeable, which has been verified by the chi-square that their difference is not significant in the distribution of primary functions. Moreover, the previous contexts offer little cues to differentiate *that's right* and *that's true*. In this sense, they are two short utterances with similar meanings and uses. But in some cases, they display their particular preference: *that's right* has fewer variations compared to *that's true*, and covers a wide range of functions in the corpus; *that's true* has never been found to answer a previous question in the corpus, while 3% of *that's right* can do that. Moreover, *that's true* shows much greater likelihood to serve *statement* whereas *that's right* is more likely to be *acknowledgement*. Such kind of empirical analysis will provide the insights and bases for automatic DA tagging. In addition, we believe that it also tells second language learners how to use these three shore utterances under specific contexts.

Acknowledgements

Research described in this paper was supported in part by grant received from the General Research Fund of the University Grant Council of the Hong Kong Special Administrative Region, China (Project no. CityU 142711) and City University of Hong Kong (Project nos. 6354005, 7004091, 9610283, 7002793, 9610226, 9041694, and 9610188).

References

Allen, J. & M. Core. 1997. DAMSL: Dialogue Act Markup in Several Layers (Draft 2.1). Technical Report, Multiparty Discourse Group, Discourse Resource Initiative, September/October 1997.

Baumgarten, N., & House, J. 2010. I think and I don't know in English as lingua franca and native English discourse. Journal of Pragmatics, 42(5), 1184-1200.

Bunt, H., Alexandersson, J., Carletta, J., Choe, J.-W., Fang, A.C., Hasida, K., Lee, K., Petukhova, V., Popescu-Belis, A., Romary, L., Soria, C. and Traum, D. 2010. Towards an ISO standard for dialogue act annotation. In Proceedings of the Seventh International Conference on Language Resources and Evaluation. Valletta, MALTA, 17-23 May 2010.

Fang, A., H. Bunt, J. Cao, and X. Liu. 2011. Relating the semantics of dialogue acts to linguistic properties: A machine learning perspective through lexical cues. In Proceedings 5th IEEE International Conference on Semantic Computing, Stanford University, Palo Alto.

Gardner, R. 2001. When Listeners Talk: Response Tokens and Listener Stance. John Benjamins Publishing

Gardner, R. 2004. Acknowledging strong ties between utterances in talk: Connections through right as a response token. In Proceedings of the 2004 Conference of the Australian Linguistic Society, pages 1–12.

Gardner, R. 2007. The Right connections: Acknowledging epistemic progression in talk. Language in Society, 36(03), 319-341.

ISO Standard 24617-2. 2012. Language resource management–Semantic annotation frame-work (SemAF), Part 2: Dialogue acts. ISO, Geneva, 2012.

Jurafsky, D., Shriberg, E. and Biasca, D. 1997. Switchboard SWBD-DAMSL shallow-discourse-function annotation coders manual, Draft 13. University of Colorado, Boulder Institute of Cognitive Science Technical Report 97-02.

M. Meteer and A. Taylor. 1995. Dysfluency annotation stylebook for the Switchboard Corpus. available online at ftp://ftp.cis.upenn.edu/pub/treebank/swbd/doc/DFL-book.ps.

Martin, J. R., & White, P. R. 2005. The language of evaluation. Basingstoke and New York: Palgrave Macmillan.

Mayor, M. (Ed.). 2009. Longman dictionary of contemporary English. Pearson Education India.

McCarthy, M. 2003. Talking back: "Small" interactional response tokens in everyday conversation. Research on Language and Social Interaction, 36(1), 33-63.

Stenström, A. B. 1987. Carry-on signals in English conversation. Corpus linguistics and beyond, 87-119.

Tao, H. 2003. Turn Initiators in Spoken English: A Corpus-Based Approach to Interaction and Grammar. Corpus Analysis: Language Structure and Language Use, (46), 187.

Tsui, A. B. 1994. English conversation. Oxford Univ Pr.

A Listenability Measuring Method for an Adaptive Computer-assisted Language Learning and Teaching System

Katsunori Kotani
Kansai Gaidai University / Osaka, Japan
kkotani@kansaigaidai.ac.jp

Shota Ueda
Ryukoku University / Shiga, Japan

Takehiko Yoshimi
Ryukoku University / Shiga, Japan

Hiroaki Nanjo
Ryukoku University / Shiga, Japan

Abstract

In teaching and learning of English as a foreign language, the Internet serves as a source of authentic listening material, enabling learners to practice English in real contexts. An adaptive computer-assisted language learning and teaching system can pick up news clips as authentic materials from the Internet according to learner listening proficiency if it is equipped with a listenability measuring method that takes into both linguistic features of a news clip and the listening proficiency. Therefore, we developed a method for measuring listening proficiency-based listenability. With our method, listenability is measured through multiple regression analysis using both learner and linguistic features as independent variables. Learner features account for learner listening proficiency, and linguistic features explain lexical, syntactic, and phonological complexities of sentences. A cross validation test showed that listenability measured with our method exhibited higher correlation ($r = 0.57$) than listenability measured with other methods using either learner features ($r = 0.43$) or other linguistic features ($r = 0.32$, $r = 0.36$). A comparison of our method with other methods showed a statistically significant difference ($p < 0.003$ after Bonferroni correction). These results suggest the effectiveness of learner and linguistic features for measuring listening proficiency-based listenability.

1 Introduction

Listening practice using authentic materials is necessary for learners of English as a foreign language (EFL) who have little or no chance to use English in their daily life because these materials let them immerse themselves in real-life settings. Since authentic materials are not usually constrained by the ease of listening comprehension or listenability (Chall & Dial 1948), teachers have to select materials according to learner listening proficiency; otherwise, too difficult or easy materials reduce the learning effect or spoil learner motivation (Hubbard 2004, Petrides 2006). An adaptive computer-assisted language learning and teaching system can pick up news clips as authentic materials from the Internet according to the listening proficiency if it is equipped with a listenability measuring method that takes into both linguistic features of a news clip and the listening proficiency. Therefore, we propose an automatic method that statistically measures listenability for EFL learners. This method is useful for learning and teaching English by showing listenability levels of authentic listening materials such as news clips. It also helps to create a computer-based self-learning environment because EFL learners can select appropriate materials with this method.

28th Pacific Asia Conference on Language, Information and Computation pages 387–394

Although listenability of authentic listening materials can be measured with readability measuring methods using lexical, syntactic, and discourse features (Flesch 1950, Graesser et al. (2004), and Shen et al 2013), our listenability measuring method uses phonological features as well as lexical and syntactic features. Phonological feature accounts for listenability in terms of speech rate and phonological modification. The natural speech rate for native speakers reduces listenability for learners because learner processing speed is slow due to the lack of automation of mental language processing. Phonological modification refers to sound change such as the elision observed in the second vowel sound of "chocolate" (Roach 2001). Phonological modification has been reported to increase listenability for native speakers, but reduce it for learners (Henricksen 1984).

In addition to linguistic features such as lexical, syntactic, and phonological, our method also uses learner features, which account for the listening proficiency. Unlike native speakers, the listening proficiency greatly differs among individuals (Saville-Troike 2006). That is, listening material can be appropriate for a learner but not for another. Therefore, it is necessary to measure listenability based not only on linguistic features but also learner features.

2 Relevant Study

Fang (1966) developed a listenability measuring method for native speakers based on a linguistic feature showing the presence of multiple-syllable words. With this method, a sentence including more multiple-syllable words is judged as more difficult. The effect from single-syllable words is suppressed because such words are assumed to be ineffective for listenability.

Unlike Fang (1966), Messerklinger (2006) took into account individual differences of background knowledge in measuring listenability for native speakers. According to Messerklinger (2006), the following features should also be taken into account in measuring listenability: speech rate, length of pause, sentence length, repairing, accent, and intensity.

Similarly to Messerklinger (2006), Kiyokawa (1990) also took into account properties of a listener. What this study focused on was not background knowledge, but the overall proficiency of EFL learners. This method measured listenability for learners at the intermediate level based on Kiyokawa's vocabulary list, which defines words that intermediate-level learners should have learnt. Words not listed in this list were regarded as difficult for intermediate-level learners. In addition, Kiyokawa (1990) used sentence length as another linguistic feature.

Although Kiyokawa's listenability method was developed for intermediate-level learners, what has not been thoroughly examined in the previous studies is the listenability for learners at different proficiency levels. Fang (1966) and Messerklinger (2006) discussed listenability for native speakers of English, assuming that listening proficiency does not differ much among native speakers. However, learners have different proficiencies; thus, individual differences of listening proficiency should be considered. Therefore, we address this remaining problem.

3 Features for Measuring Listenability

3.1 Learner Feature

Learner features must show the listening proficiency. This study uses scores of English language tests for determining the listening proficiency. The English language test used in this study was the Test of English for International Communication (TOEIC) because this test is a major English language test for university learners in the country where the experiment takes place.

Because TOEIC consists of a listening section and reading section, a learner acquires two scores. Our method uses TOEIC listening scores (the range of scores: 5-495) as a learner feature.

3.2 Linguistic Feature

Linguistic features must show the lexical, syntactic, and phonological complexity of a sentence. We used linguistic features, i.e., mean length of words, sentence length, presence of multiple-syllable words, speech rate, difficulty of words, and presence of phonological modification. The linguistic features used with our method, except phonological, which explains the presence of phonological modification, were originally used in the previous studies (Fang 1966, Kiyokawa 1990, Messerklinger 2006).

Type (Description)	Condition for phonological modification
elision (elimination of phonemes)	(i) vowel sound immediately following stressed syllable such as second "o" sound in "chocolate" (ii) consonant followed by similarly articulated sound such as (a) continuous same sound as in "unknown," (b) continuous plosive sound as in "c" sound and "t" sound of "doctor," and (c) plosive sound followed by nasal sound as in "suddenly"
reduction (weakening sound by changing vowel to schwa)	vowel sound in functional words such as personal pronouns, interrogative pronouns, auxiliaries, modals, prepositions, articles, and conjunctions
contraction (combining pair of words)	(i) pair of subject noun with (a) be-auxiliary, (b) have-auxiliary, or (c) modal (ii) pair of interrogative pronoun with (a) be-auxiliary, (b) have-auxiliary, or (c) modal (iii) pair of negative adverb "not" with (a) be-auxiliary, (b) have-auxiliary, or (c) modal
linking (connecting final sound of word with initial sound of following word)	(i) words between word starting with vowel and (a) word ending with "n" sound as in "in an hour" or (b) word ending with "r" sound as in "after all" (ii) word followed by (a) indefinite article, (b) preposition, or (c) conjunction
deduction (elimination of sounds between words)	(i) words sharing same sound between final sound of word and initial sound of following word as in "good day" (ii) words between word ending with plosive sound and word starting with plosive, affricative, fricative, nasal, or lateral sound as in "next chance"

Table 1: Condition for phonological features

The presence of phonological modification is automatically measured as follows. Because phonological modification is supposed to occur under a certain condition, it is measured as the ratio of conditions for phonological modification to the total number of words in a sentence. Table 1 summarizes the type of phonological modification, its description, and condition for phonological modification. These phonological features are extracted with the procedures shown in Table 2.

Type	Feature extraction procedure
elision	a. convert to phonetic symbol b. search conditions (i) and (ii) c. count number of words in sentence d. calculate number of identified conditions per number of words in sentence
reduction	a. parse part of speech (Schmid 1994) b. search condition c. count number of words in sentence d. calculate number of identified conditions per number of words in sentence
contraction	a. count number of apostrophes* b. calculate number of apostrophes per number of words in sentence *Contraction has written form using apostrophe such as "I've."
linking	a. convert to phonetic symbol b. search conditions (i) and (ii) c. count number of words in sentence d. calculate number of identified conditions per number of words in sentence
deduction	a. convert to phonetic symbol b. search conditions (i) and (ii) c. count number of words in sentence d. calculate number of identified conditions per number of words in sentence

Table 2: Extraction procedure for phonological features

4 Training/test Data Collection

4.1 Data Outline

To develop a listenability measuring method with multiple regression analysis, it is necessary to collect training/test data consisting of dependent and independent variables.

Dependent variables are scores for listenability of a sentence. Listenability is scored based on a five-point Likert scale of ease of listening comprehension judged by learners as 1: easy, 2: somewhat easy, 3: average, 4: somewhat difficult, or 5: difficult.

Independent variables consist of learner and linguistic features. As described in Section 3, learner features show the listening proficiency, and linguistic features show the lexical, syntactic, and phonological complexities of a sentence.

4.2 Learners

Ninety university EFL learners (males: 48 and females: 42) took part in the data collection task. They were paid for their participation. The mean age was 21.5 years (standard deviation (S.D.) 2.6). The learners were asked to submit valid TOEIC scores, taken that year or the year before. Learners were equally divided into three groups of TOEIC scores: low score group (below 475), middle score group (from 480 to 725), and high score group (above 730). That is, 30 learners were chosen for each group. TOEIC scores were used as the proficiency benchmark, because the EFL learners were recruited not only for this study but also for another study on measurement of readability (Kotani et al. 2012, 2013). The EFL learners were also confirmed for basic computer literacy such as typing with a keyboard and controlling a mouse because they needed to use a computer in the data collection task.

The mean TOEIC listening score for the 90 learners was 334.8 (S.D. 97.6). Figure 1 shows the distribution of the number of learners for TOEIC listening scores, which follows a double-peaked distribution at scores between 200 and 249 (n = 17) and scores above 450 (n = 16). The distribution was skewed due to the small number of learners below a score of 200. Kolmogorov-Smirnov test showed that the distribution did not follow the normal distribution (K=1.24, p=0.04). An investigation into the effect on measurement error due to the skewed distribution is for future study.

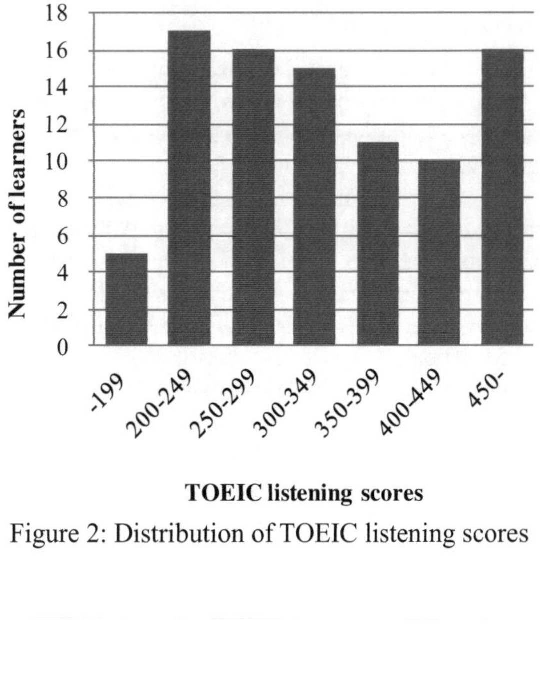

Figure 2: Distribution of TOEIC listening scores

4.3 Materials

The materials used in this study were news clips because they are often used as listening practice materials for university EFL learners. Each news clip included five multiple-choice comprehension questions to let learners work on the listening task as they would in an actual English language test. These questions were made in the format of Nation & Malcher (2007): two true questions to choose a correct description about the article; two false questions to choose an incorrect description about the article; and one content question to choose a correct brief description of the article.

The news clips were chosen from the two types of sections in the Voice of America (VOA) site (http://www.voanews.com): the special section for English learners and the editorial section. News clips in the special section were made for learners, while news clips in the editorial section were made for native speakers of English. The former news clips consisted of short, simple sentences using the 1,500 basic vocabulary of VOA, and avoiding idiomatic expressions. By contrast, the editorial section's news clips were made without any restriction on vocabulary and sentence construction as long as they were appropriate as news clips for native speakers of English. The speech rate of special section's news clips was two-thirds slower than the editorial section's news clips, which were read aloud at a natural speech rate, approximately 250 syllables per minute, according to Robb & Gillon (2007).

	Elision	Reduction	Contraction	Linking	Deduction
Mean	0.13	0.38	0.00	0.04	0.19
S.D.	0.14	0.10	0.02	0.07	0.17
Minimal	0.00	0.13	0.00	0.00	0.00
Maximal	0.63	0.75	0.17	0.40	0.75
Occurrence (n)	63	80	2	32	69

Table 3: Descriptive statistics of linguistic features for phonological modification

The linguistic features for phonological modification in the materials are summarized in Table 3. The features for phonological modification are the ratio of conditions for phonological modification as described in Section 3.2. The mean value is calculated by summing the ratio of conditions for phonological modification, and dividing the sum by the number of sentences (n = 80). Among the 80 sentences, phonological modification was observed in 63 sentences for elision, 80 sentences for reduction, 2 sentences for contraction, 32 sentences for linking, and 69 sentences for deduction.

4.4 Task

Each learner was asked to listen to the four news clips sentence-by-sentence only once, using a headphone. After listening to each sentence, the learner assigned a listenability score for the sentence from the five-point Likert scale. After listening to a news clip, the learner answered five multiple-choice comprehension questions.

Each learner used a data collecting tool, which displayed on a computer screen several icons to move on to the next sentence, and to select a choice from multiple choice items for listenability score and comprehension questions. The data collecting tool also recorded the learner's choices.

The learners were asked to complete a listening task as fast as possible during the allotted time (8 minutes for each news clip), and to stop working either when the task was completed or the experimenter and the data collecting tool alerted them of the end of the allotted time. They were prohibited to use dictionaries or any other reference books. The data collecting tool did not allow learners to return to a sentence for listening again after moving on to another sentence.

4.5 Listenability Score

Although the training/test data should consist of 7,200 instances (90 learners × 80 sentences) for a valid listenability score, 6,804 instances were used in developing our listenability measuring method. 396 instances were regarded as invalid, because no listenability score was recorded. Each instance consisted of a listenability score, a learner feature in terms of a TOEIC listening score, and linguistic features. The mean listenability score was 2.83 (S.D. 1.32).

Figure 2 shows how listenability scores distribute according to the listening proficiency level. Learners were classified into three proficiency levels based on TOEIC listening scores: 34 advanced (score range: 365-495), 40 intermediate (score range: 240-360), and 16 beginner (score range: 130-235). As expected, the distribution of listenability scores followed the proficiency levels. Advanced learners tended to judge listening as easy, intermediate learners tended to judge listening as moderate, beginner learners tended to judge listening as difficult.

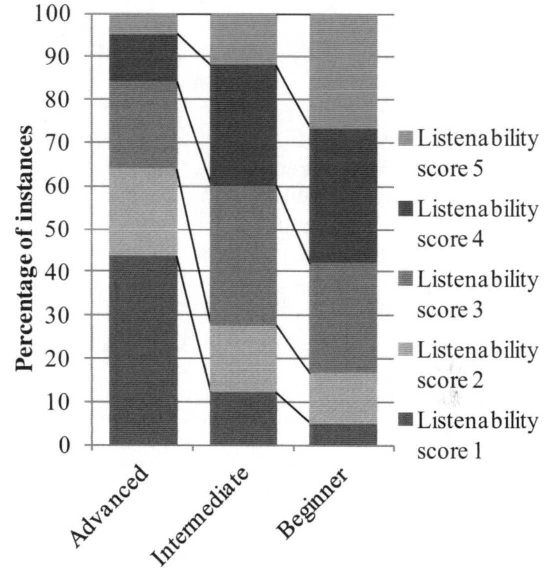

Figure 2: Distribution of listenability scores

5 Experiment

5.1 Development of Our Method

We conducted a multiple regression analysis for developing our method. The independent variables were the learner and linguistic features described in Section 3, which show the listening proficiency and lexical, syntactic, and phonological complexities of a sentence. The dependent variable was listenability scores, as described in Section 4.5.

Before carrying out the multiple regression analysis, the learner and linguistic features were examined with respect to the presence of multiple-collinearity by calculating the variance inflation factor (VIF) (Neter et al. 1996), and a multiple-collinearity of more than 10 was not found ($1.14 < VIF < 8.17$).

The linear combination of learner and linguistic features was significantly related to the listenability scores, $F(11, 6{,}792) = 292.83$, $p < 0.01$. The sample multiple correlation coefficient adjusted for the degrees of freedom was 0.57, indicating that approximately 32% of the variance of the listenability scores in the sample could be accounted for by the linear combination of learner and linguistic features. The standardized partial regression coefficients are summarized in Table 4.

Type	Feature	Standardized partial regression coefficient
learner feature	TOEIC listening score	–0.43**
linguistic feature	mean length of words	–0.08**
	sentence length	0.05
	difficulty of words	0.07*
	presence of multiple-syllable words	0.09**
	speech rate	0.25**
	elision	0.02
	reduction	0.01
	contraction	–0.10**
	linking	0.03**
	deduction	–0.06**

Table 4: Standardized partial regression coefficients
(one asterisk: $p < 0.05$, two asterisks: $p < 0.01$)

5.2 Evaluation of Our Method

Our listenability measuring method was examined in a leave-one-out cross validation test by comparing with sample methods (Method I-III) that were developed by using some of the features in our method. The features used in each method are marked in Table 5. In the cross validation test, the methods were examined n times (n = 6,804) by taking one instance as test data and n -1 instances as training data.

Each method was examined by comparing listenability scores assigned by learners and listenability scores measured with one of the methods. Spearman's correlation coefficients are also summarized in Table 5. The correlation coefficients in Table 5 were statistically significantly different from zero ($p < 0.01$). The difference in correlation coefficients between our method and the other methods was examined using the Meng-Rosenthal-Rubin method (Meng et al. 1992). The results showed that there was a statistically significant difference between our method and the other methods I-III ($p < 0.003$ after Bonferroni correction for three comparisons). Thus, our method was marked with the highest correlation. This result suggests that proficiency-based listenability is affected by both learner and linguistic features.

	Our method	Method I	Method II	Method III
TOEIC listening score	●			●
Mean length of words	●	●		
Sentence length	●	●		
Difficulty of words	●	●		
Presence of multiple syllable words	●	●		
Speech rate	●		●	
Elision	●		●	
Reduction	●		●	
Contraction	●		●	
Linking	●		●	
Deduction	●		●	
Correlation coefficient	0.57**	0.32**	0.36**	0.43**

Table 5: Feature and correlation coefficients
(two asterisks: $p < 0.01$)

Measurement errors from the cross validation test results are plotted in Figure 3. Measurement error was calculated as an absolute value of the difference between a listenability score measured with a method and a listenability score assigned by a learner. Our method had more instances in the ranges of small measurement error (0.0 and 0.1-1.0) than the other methods, as seen in Figure 3.

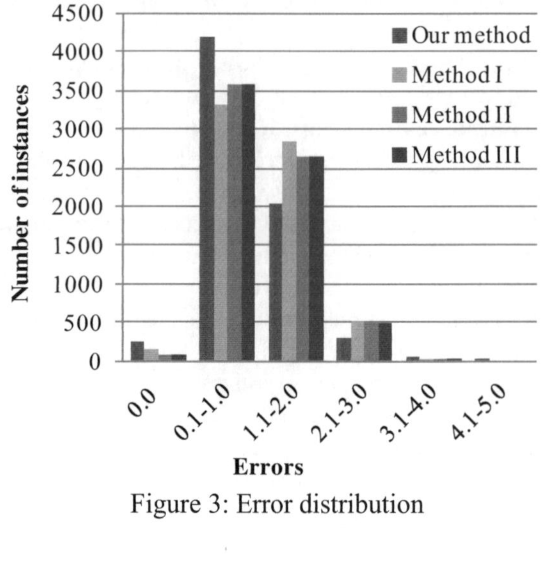

Figure 3: Error distribution

Table 6 summarizes the ratio of the number of instances with error values 0.0-1.0 to the number of instances (6,804). As expected from the results in Table 5 and Figure 3, our method had more instances with error up to 1.0 than other methods. These results also suggest the effectiveness of our method.

	Our method	Method I	Method II	Method III
Ratio	0.65	0.51	0.54	0.54

Table 6: Ratio of error up to 1.0

5.3 Discussion on Our Method

The standardized partial regression coefficients in Table 4 show that listenability mostly depends on the TOEIC listening score. This result suggests that the TOEIC listening score is useful in measuring listenability for learners.

Among the five phonological features for phonological modification, elision and reduction had no statistically significant effect, contrary to our expectation. As Henricksen (1984) suggested, it was expected that phonological modification reduces listenability for learners as seen in the positive effect from linking. However, the presence of a negative effect from contraction and deduction suggests that phonological modification can increase listenability for learners as well as native speakers.

The standardized partial regression coefficients showed the unexpected effect of sentence length. Sentence length is a well known linguistic feature for explaining syntactic complexity of a sentence and has been used for measuring listenability as well as readability. However, sentence length had no statistically significant effect on listenability. An unexpected effect was also observed in the mean length of words. Assuming that longer words convey complex meanings, word length is a primary linguistic feature for measuring readability (Flesch 1950). However, as the negative value of the standardized partial regression coefficient shows, longer words increase listenability. We believe that this divergence between readability and listenability arises from the different recognition styles. Reading requires letter recognition, while listening requires sound recognition (Rayner & Reichle 2010, Vandergrift 2011). Hence, learners may not fail in letter recognition, but fail in sound recognition. However, the learners did not fail in sound recognition probably due to longer words. These results suggest that listenability is not parallel with readability.

6 Conclusion

We proposed a method for automatically measuring listenability for EFL learners. Unlike the previous studies on listenability, our method directly takes into account the listening proficiency as well as linguistic features, which consist of mean length of words, sentence length, presence of multiple-syllable words, speech rate, difficulty of words, and presence of phonological modification (elision, reduction, contraction, linking, and deduction)

In an experiment, our method showed higher correlation between listenability scores assigned by learners and scores measured using other methods, which partially used learner and linguistic features.

With our method, linguistic features for phonological modification were extracted from transcriptions of news clips. When transcription is unavailable, our method must use automatic speech recognition. Thus, we need to examine the validity of our method when using speech recognition for future work.

Acknowledgments

This work was supported in part by Grant-in-Aid for Scientific Research (B) (22300299).

References

Chall, J. S. and Dial, H. E. 1948. Listener Understanding and Interest in Newscasts. Educational Research Bulletin. 27(6): 141–153+168.

Fang, I.E. 1966. The Easy Listening Formula. Journal of Broadcasting & Electronic Media, 11(1): 63–68.

Flesch, R. 1950. Measuring the Level of Abstraction. Journal of Applied Psychology, 34: 384–390.

Graesser, A. C., Danielle S. M., Max M. L., and Zhiqiang C. 2004.. Coh-Metrix: Analysis of Text on Cohesion and Language. Behavior Research Methods, Instruments, and Computers, 36: 193-202.

Henricksen, L. 1984. Sandhi Variation: a Filter of Input for Learners of ESL. Language Learning, 34: 103–126.

Hubbard, P. 2004. Learner Training for Effective Use of CALL. In S. Fotos and C. Browne (Eds), New Perspectives in CALL for Second Language Classrooms: 45–67, Lawrence Eribaum, Mahwah, NJ.

Kiyokawa, H. 1990. A Formula for Predicting Listenability: the Listenability of English Language Materials 2. Wayo Women's University Language and Literature, 24: 57–74.

Kotani, K., Yoshimi, T., Nanjo, H. and Isahara, H. 2012. Applicability of Readability Formulae to the Measurement of Sentence-level Readability, Proceedings of International Conference of Education, Proceedings of 5th International Conference of Education, Research and Innovation (ICERI): 6023–6031.

Kotani, K., Yoshimi, T. and Isahara, H 2013. Application of Reading Data in an Integrated Learner Corpus, Procedia–Social and Behavioral Sciences, 95: 513–521.

Meng, X.L., Rosenthal, R. and Rubin, D.B. 1992. Comparing Correlated Correlation Coefficients. Psychological Bulletin, 111(1): 172–175.

Messerklinger, J. 2006. Listenability. Center for English Language Education Journal, 14: 56–70.

Nation, P. and Malarcher, C. 2007. Reading for Speed and Fluency. Compass Publishing, Seoul, Korea.

Petrides, J. R. 2006. Attitudes and Motivation and their Impact on the Performance of Young English as a Foreign Language Learners. Journal of Language and Learning, 5(1): 1–20.

Rayner, K. and Reichle, E. D. 2010. Models of the Reading Process. Wiley Interdisciplinary Reviews: Cognitive Science, 1(6): 787–799.

Roach, P. 2001. English Phonetics and Phonology. Cambridge University Press, Cambridge.

Robb, M. P. and Gillon, G. T. 2007. Speech Rates of New Zealand English- and American English-speaking children. Advances in Speech-Language Pathology, 9(2): 1–8.

Saville-Troike, M. 2006. Introducing Second Language Acquisition. Cambridge University Press, Cambridge.

Schmid, H. 1994. Probabilistic Part-of-Speech Tagging Using Decision Trees. In Proceedings of International Conference on New Methods in Language Processing: 44–49. Manchester, UK.

Shen, W., Williams, J., Marius, T., and Salesky, E. 2013. A Language-Independent Approach to Automatic Text Difficulty Assessment for Second-Language Learners. In Proceedings of the 2nd Workshop on Predicting and Improving Text Readability for Target Reader Populations: 30–38. Sofia, Bulgaria.

Vandergrift, L. 2011. Second Language Listening: Presage, Process, Product and Pedagogy. In E. Hinkel (Ed) Handbook of Research in Second Language Teaching and Learning: 455–471. Routledge, New York.

Prosodic Differences Between Declaratives and Polar Questions in Fataluku

Tyler M. Heston
Department of Linguistics
University of Hawai'i at Mānoa
Honolulu, Hawai'i
theston@hawaii.edu

Abstract

The primary goal of the present study is to describe the basic prosodic differences between declaratives and polar questions in Fataluku, an underdocumented Papuan language spoken in the island nation of East Timor. Two robust prosodic differences between statements and questions are observed, namely, the duration of the final vowel and the intonational tune at the right margin of the sentence. Declaratives have a shorter final vowel that carries a low f0, while questions have a much longer final vowel that has a rising-falling f0 pattern. I postulate a L% boundary tone for declaratives and a L+HL% boundary tone for questions, proposing that the final syllables of questions are lengthened to accommodate the more complex sequence of final tones.

1 Introduction

Fataluku is an underdocumented language spoken by approximately 37,000 individuals in island Southeast Asia, on the far eastern tip of the nation of East Timor (Lewis et al., 2013). Fataluku is a member of the Timor-Alor-Pantar family of Papuan languages, which includes about twenty-five languages spoken on Timor and nearby islands (Klamer, 2014; Schapper et al., 2014). Relatively little has been published about any aspect of the phonology of Fataluku.

The primary goal of the present paper is to describe the intonational differences between declaratives and polar questions (also known as yes-no questions) in Fataluku. This paper is part of a larger project to describe Fataluku segmental and suprasegmental phonology. I analyze Fataluku intonation within the framework of the autosegmental-metrical (AM) theory of intonational phonology (Pierrehumbert, 1980; Ladd, 1996), which has become the standard for intonation research. In the AM model, the phonological structure of intonation is represented underlyingly as a sequence of discrete level tones, each of which is associated either with a prominent syllable (a "pitch accent") or with the edge of some prosodic constituent (a "boundary tone"). The surface intonation contour is a result of continuous interpolation between discrete level tones.

My focus here is on behavior at the right edge of an Intonational Phrase (IP) in Fataluku. The IP—the largest prosodic constituent in the AM framework—is a phrase that can stand alone and is generally accompanied by a final boundary tone and final lengthening (Jun and Fletcher, 2014). Typologically, IP-final boundary tones are rich sources of linguistic information (Lindström and Remijsen, 2005), a generalization that holds for Fataluku as well.

To lay the groundwork for the analysis of intonation, section 2 provides some background on the language, including a review of a previous study on Fataluku question intonation. After a brief discussion of methods, the results of the present study are given, describing the prosodic patterns of statements and polar questions. The discussion section proposes a phonological analysis to explain the observed prosodic differences. The paper concludes with a summary and some suggestions for future research.

Copyright 2014 by Tyler M. Heston
28th Pacific Asia Conference on Language, Information and Computation pages 395–403

2 Background

2.1 Segmental Phonology

By way of introduction, tables 1 and 2 show my present analysis of the phonemes of the Fataluku variety spoken by the participants of this project. Voiced stops are attested only in loan words.

	Bil	Lab	Dnt	Pal	Vel	Gtl
Stop	p b		t d		k g	ʔ
Affr.			t͡s			
Fric.		f v	s z			h
Nas.	m		n			
Tap			r			
Lat.			l			
Glid.				j		

Table 1: Consonant Phonemes

	Front	Central	Back
High	i		u
Mid	e		o
Low		a	

Table 2: Vowel Phonemes

The basic syllable structure of Fataluku is (C)V(V)(C). Consonant sequences are rare, especially within a morpheme. Fataluku has both long vowels and diphthongs, both of which are represented underlyingly as sequences of vowels—identical in the case of long vowels and non-identical in the case of diphthongs (Heston, 2014). The examples below are given in a phonemic practical orthography.[1]

2.2 Morphosyntax

Fataluku morphology is generally isolating. Grammatical relations are indicated primarily by word order, and grammatical information like tense, aspect and negation is coded in independent words. The basic word order is SOV, with generally left-branching constituent order. Polar questions and declaratives can be identical apart from prosody, or they can be optionally flagged with either the question marking morpheme *aa* 'Q' or the tag *ana upe* 'or not' at the end of the utterance (see examples 1–3). There is also a particle *ten* which appears in some of the polar questions collected here, but whose exact function is not yet known. No substantial differences in meaning have been found between any of the different strategies for flagging questions.

(1) Declarative/Unflagged question[2]

kinamoko a maca mahane
child NOM bat fear

'The child was afraid of the bat.'
or 'Was the child afraid of the bat?'

(2) Question flagged with *aa* 'Q'

kinamoko a maca mahane aa
child NOM bat fear Q

'Was the child afraid of the bat?'

(3) Question flagged with *ana upe* 'or not'

kinamoko a maca mahane ana upe
child NOM bat fear or not

'Was the child afraid of the bat or not?'

2.3 Suprasegmental Phonology

Some research on Fataluku suprasegmental phonology was undertaken by Ruben Stoel. He analyzes Fataluku as having lexical "tone" system in which each content word has a lexically specified high tone on either the first or the second syllable (Stoel, 2008). A full discussion of Stoel's analysis of tone lies outside the scope of this paper, although it is an interesting proposition meriting further investigation.

Stoel has also discussed question intonation in a conference presentation, the slides of which have been made available online (Stoel, 2007). Stoel (2007, p. 3) claims that "Questions have a H [high]

[1] Symbols which differ from the IPA are as follows: orthography ' = /ʔ/, c = /t͡s/, j = /z/, w = /v/, y = /j/.

[2] Glossing abbreviations are as follows: CONJ, conjunction; NOM, nominative; PST, past tense; Q, question particle; SG, singular; and VAL, valency (used to mark the morpheme -m which can be used to add additional arguments to a clause).

tone associated with the last syllable, which is absent in statements." In the example spectrogram he gives, this tone is realized as a high-falling f0 contour on the final syllable of the question. He claims that duration is also a correlate of this distinction, with the final syllables of questions lengthened and the final syllables of declaratives shortened.

Since Stoel's slides do not specify either the dialect on which his analysis is based or the number of speakers, it is not clear how generalizable these findings may be. I analyze new data from three villages in the Fataluku-speaking region, providing a more detailed description of the phonetics of polar question prosody and offering a new phonological analysis to explain the phonetic facts. I hypothesize that both the final f0 contour and the duration of the final syllable are important components of the declarative/interrogative distinction, although there may be differences between the language varieties analyzed here and the variety Stoel describes.

3 Methods

In order to test this hypothesis, six native speakers of Fataluku (five males, one female) were recorded reading broad-focus declaratives and polar questions. Speakers' ages ranged from 18 to 30 years. These speakers were from three separate villages (Lospalos, Com and Muapitin), two speakers from each.[3]

Recordings of short Fataluku sentences were made in a quiet location using a Zoom H4n or H6 solid-state digital recorder at 44.1kHz/16bit. In most cases, a headset condenser microphone (either the Shure WH30 or the Shure SM35) was used for higher-quality recordings. Since the extent of dialect variation was not known at the start of this study, speakers who were fluent in English were prompted with English sentences to translate into Fataluku, to ensure the Fataluku sentences collected were natural in each speaker's own speech variety. Speakers who were less comfortable in English were given sentences written in Fataluku to read, but they were encouraged to modify any aspects of the sentences that might be unnatural for them. No substantial difference between the elicitation strategies was observed.

To control for the effects of lexical or segmental content, there was a matching set of declaratives and interrogatives. A basic set of 12 declaratives and 12 questions was recorded 2–3 times by each speaker. Sentences with substantial disfluencies were excluded from analysis, yielding a total of 133 declaratives and 162 interrogatives. Pitch contours and durations were observed using the phonetic analysis software Praat (Boersma and Weenink, 2013). Duration was measured based on the presence of periodic vibrations and higher-level formants, as deducible from the waveform. A vowel was judged to end at the point at which regular vocalic vibrations were no longer discernible. A characteristic example of duration measurement is given in figure 1.

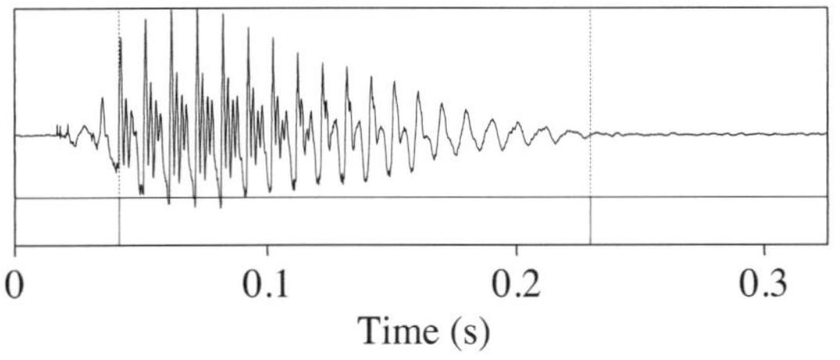

Figure 1: A characteristic duration measurement, from the final syllable of *upe* 'not'

4 Results

As hypothesized, declaratives and polar questions differ substantially in f0 and syllable duration at the right periphery of an utterance, although the basic pattern differs to a certain extent from the language variety Stoel describes. The same basic prosodic patterns were used by all six speakers, independent of gender or village. The following subsections describe the basic patterns for declaratives and polar questions.

4.1 Intonational Tune: Declaratives

Analogous to the syntax, questions and statements are very similar prosodically until the right periphery, where the primary differences are shown. Regardless of the sentence type, it is common to find a pitch peak in the first or second syllable of each

[3] I use the abbreviations Com-1, Com-2, Lp-1, etc. to uniquely refer to each speaker. The abbreviations Lp and Mp represent Lospalos and Muapitin, respectively. Com-2 represents the female speaker.

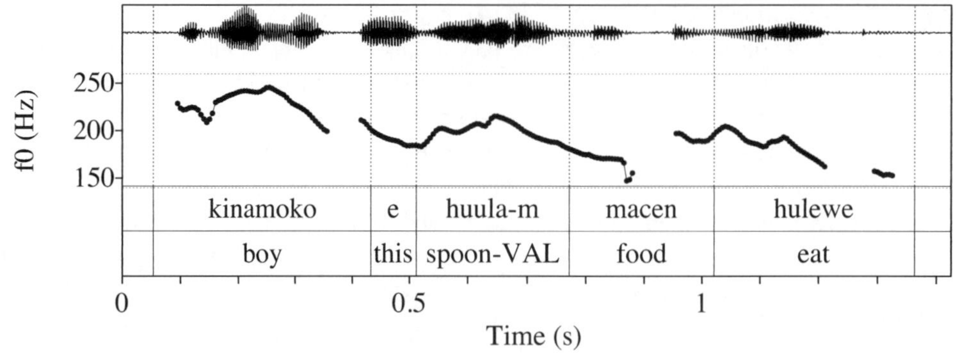

Figure 2: A basic declarative sentence (Com-2)

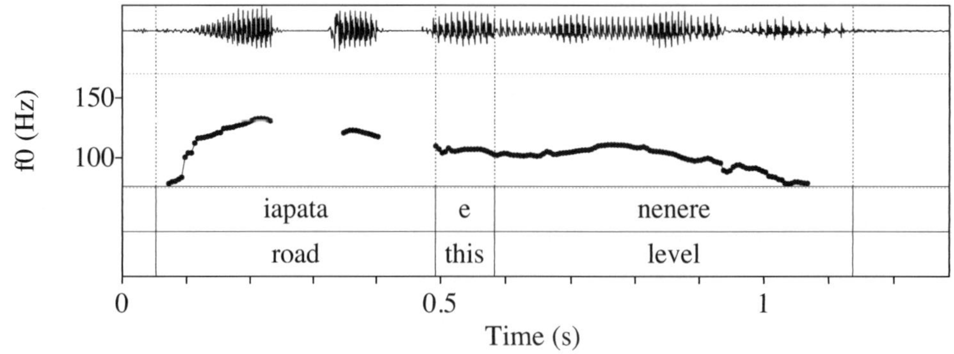

Figure 3: A basic declarative sentence (Mp-1)

word or short phrase, each generally lower than the peak preceding. These pitch peaks occur in approximately the same locations described by Stoel (2008). However, since his analysis of "tone" resembles an intonation system in some ways, I remain ambivalent about the best phonological analysis of these peaks. A more extensive analysis of Fataluku sentence intonation is the subject of ongoing research.

In declaratives, the overwhelming pattern is for the f0 to fall from earlier pitch peaks through the last several syllables of an utterance, ending on a final low.[4] The final vowel is generally quite short, and if it follows a voiceless consonant, it may be devoiced. Figures 2 and 3[5] show representative examples of declaratives.

4.2 Intonational Tune: Polar Questions

Questions are similar in intonation to declaratives until the right margin of an utterance, where polar questions are distinguished by a rising-falling pitch contour on the final syllable and a significantly lengthened final vowel. The most typical case is for the f0 to fall throughout the last few syllables, reaching a local minimum within second half of the

[4]There is an alternative prosodic pattern with rising intonation that occurred in a few of the sentences collected here, and that has been observed in narratives in contexts involving continuation. I analyze this as a distinct "continuation" contour, which I do not discuss further here.

[5]All pitch tracks were created with Praat (Boersma and Weenink, 2013), using a modified version of a Praat script developed by Pauline Welby, made available by the Department of Linguistics at the University of Victoria. Pitch ranges are optimized separately for each speaker.

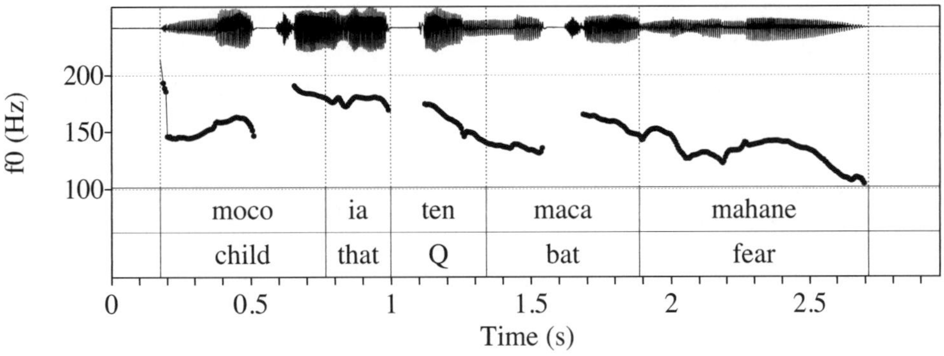

Figure 4: A polar question without *aa* 'Q' or *ana upe* 'or not' (Lp-2)

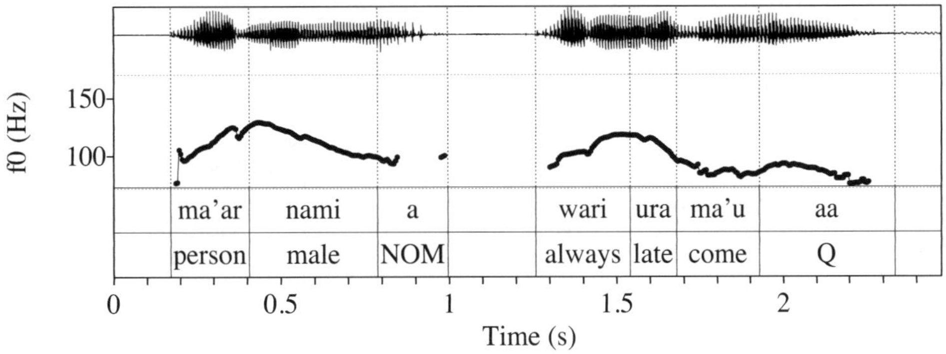

Figure 5: A polar question flagged with *aa* 'Q' (Mp-1)

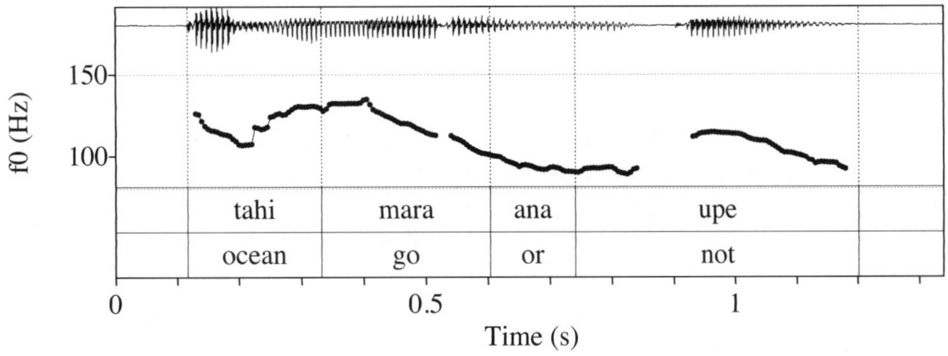

Figure 6: The latter portion of a polar question flagged with *ana upe* 'or not'. Extracted from the sentence, *Aa rahin la'a tahi mara ana upe?* 'Did you go to the beach yesterday or not?' (Lp-1)

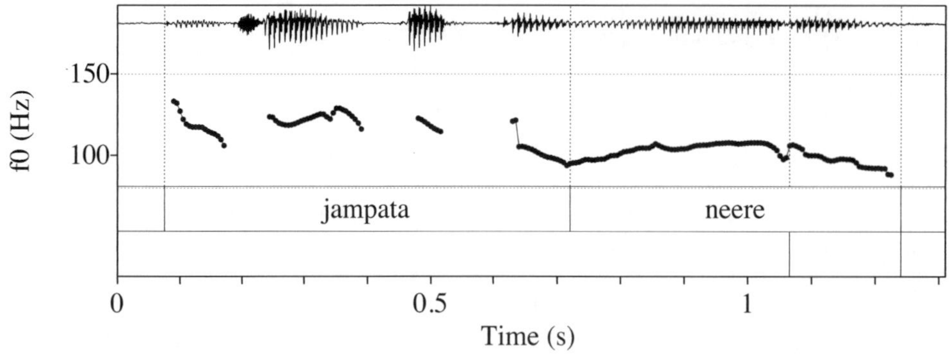

Figure 7: A declarative sentence with a pitch peak on the penultimate syllable (Lp-1)

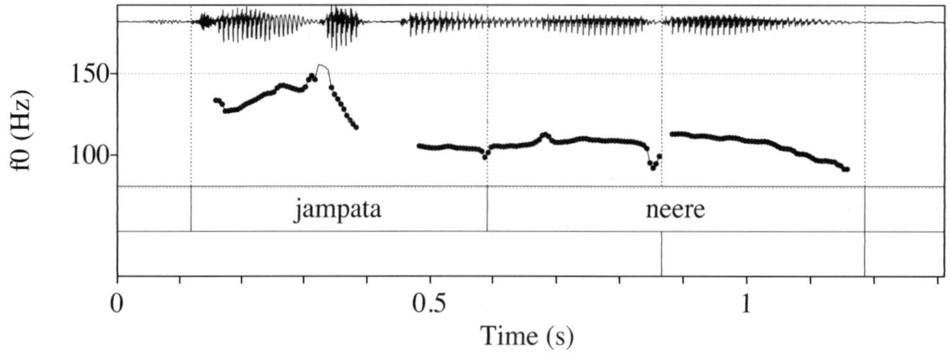

Figure 8: An unflagged interrogative with a pitch peak on the penultimate syllable (Lp-1)

penultimate syllable. The f0 then rises, peaking in the first half of the final syllable and falling to the end. In the data collected here, most speakers used a mix of syntactic strategies for flagging questions, but the same prosodic pattern occurred regardless of flagging. If the final syllable has a voiceless onset, the initial rise is obscured, since the f0 track is interrupted, but these examples show the same basic pattern of low-high-low. Figures 4–6 show several examples of this pattern.

There is also a variant of this pattern that occurs when there are other pitch peaks near the end of the utterance. In most of the sentences collected here, there are pitch peaks in the beginning of an utterance, but the last two or three syllables show a gradual decline until the boundary tone. However, there are a few examples with a pitch peak on the penultimate or prepenultimate syllable of an utterance. For instance, in the utterance *jampata neere* 'The road is level', there is a pitch peak on the first syllable of both *jampata* 'road' and *neere* 'to be level'. In the declarative condition (fig. 7), the pitch simply falls from the high on the penultimate syllable to the end, though with a steeper slope than normal. However, in the interrogative condition (fig. 8), the typical pattern is changed. There is no low on the penultimate syllable, as would typically be expected. Rather, the pitch sustains a high level throughout the first half of the final syllable before falling to the end. Although both the declarative and the interrogative involve a fall in the final syllable, they are distinguished both by their duration and by the timing of the final fall, which is substantially later in interrogatives (cf. figs. 7 and 8).

	b	$SE\ b$	95% CI	p-value
(intercept)	136.50	10.77	115.45, 157.55	$p < .0001$
Question (0=decl., 1=ques.)	146.28	13.72	119.45, 173.10	$p < .0001$
Flagging with *aa* 'Q'	21.19	9.51	2.59, 39.78	$p = .0267$
Flagging with *ana upe* 'or not'	-19.44	16.55	-51.80, 12.91	$p = .2411$

Table 3: Linear mixed-effects model of the effects of sentence type and flagging on the duration of final vowels (in ms), calculated in R (R Core Team, 2014) using the packages `nlme` (Pinheiro et al., 2014) and `lme4` (Bates et al., 2014)

4.3 Duration

Figure 9 compares the mean duration (in milliseconds) of the final vowel of declaratives with each subcategory of polar question (flagged with *aa* 'Q', flagged with *ana upe* 'or not' or syntactically unflagged). Environments were controlled as much as possible, such that each vowel came in an utterance-final open syllable. Each vowel was phonemically short (with the possible exception of *aa* 'Q', discussed below). Applying these conditions resulted in a total of 133 declaratives, 69 unflagged questions, 52 *aa*-flagged questions and 41 *upe*-flagged questions. On average, the final vowels of polar questions (274.4 ms) were 2.1 times longer than the final vowels of declaratives (132.9 ms).

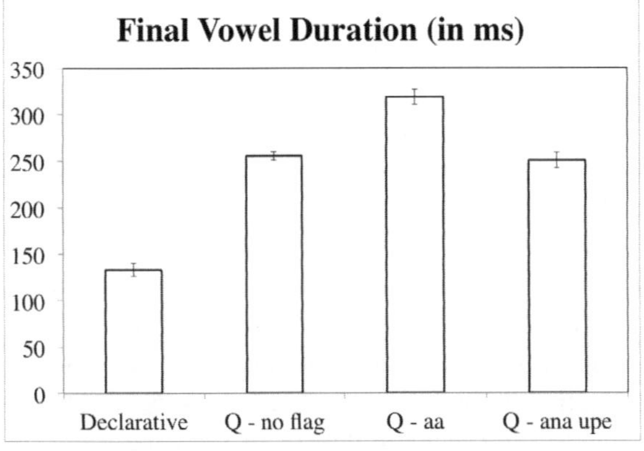

Figure 9: The mean duration (in ms) of final vowels. Error bars show standard error.

Applying a linear mixed-effects model revealed that whether an utterance is a question is a significant predictor of final vowel duration, $b = 146.28$, $t(286) = 10.66$, $p < .0001$. Morphosyntactic flagging with *aa* 'Q' was also a significant predictor of duration, $b = 21.19$, $t(286) = 2.23$, $p < .05$, although flagging with *ana upe* 'or not' had no significant effect compared to unflagged questions, $b = -19.44$, $t(286) = -1.17$, $p > .05$.

5 Discussion

The results thus show that the contrast between declaratives and polar questions is characterized by differences in the f0 contour and the duration of the final vowel. These findings are similar to the description given by Stoel, though with some differences. Stoel's only example of a question has a high-falling contour, which is much rarer in the present dataset than the typical rising-falling pattern. The lack of a preceding pitch valley may be due to undershoot, since there is a pitch peak two syllables before (which Stoel transcribes as a lexical high tone). At this point, it is not clear whether the high-falling pattern shown by Stoel is representative of the rest of his data; more examples are needed to determine whether the variety Stoel describes differs phonetically in crucial respects from the data collected here.

Stoel (2007) claims the primary phonological difference between declaratives and questions is the association of a high (H) tone with the final syllable of questions. However, as stated, this analysis does not explain the final fall present in both declaratives and questions, or the alternation between rising-falling and high-falling question contours observed here. I propose a new analysis, namely, that declaratives have have a simple low boundary tone (L%), while polar questions have a low tone on the penultimate syllable and a high-low tone on the final syllable (L+HL%). The initial low of the question contour (L+) is undershot if the penultimate or prepenultimate syllable is associated with a high tone, which explains the observed variation among questions.

Stoel's analysis also provides no apparent explanation for lengthening in questions. On the other hand, I analyze final lengthening as a phonetically motivated phonological process conditioned by the boundary tone for questions. It is phonetically difficult to realize a complex tone—such as L+HL%—in a short phonetic space because of physical limitations on the vocal tract. Prosodic lengthening gives the glottis additional time to hit each pitch target sequentially. The ability of this analysis to provide a motivation for final lengthening is an additional benefit of the complex boundary tone (L+HL%) analysis proposed here.

This lengthening is clearly prosodic, rather than a lexical feature of the morphemes *aa* 'Q' or *ana upe* 'or not', since lengthening can apply to any word in the appropriate prosodic environment. I explain the slightly greater duration of *aa* 'Q' compared to the other strategies by analyzing the morpheme as having a phonemically long vowel, which is then lengthened even further prosodically. Assessing the phonemic vowel length of this morpheme directly is difficult, since I have not found any examples of the morpheme outside of the conditioning environment for prosodic lengthening, but with this addition, the analysis of boundary tones proposed here is able to explain the observed differences in intonational tune and duration between statements and questions.

6 Conclusion

To sum up, this paper describes the differences between declaratives and polar questions in Fataluku. Syntactically, polar questions may be optionally flagged by placing the question marker *aa* 'Q' or *ana upe* 'or not' at the end of the utterance, but the main difference is found in the prosody. Declaratives are characterized by a short final vowel and a low IP-final boundary tone (L%). Polar questions—regardless of their syntactic flagging—have an intonational contour that rises from the penultimate syllable to a high fall on the final syllable (L+HL%). In order to accommodate this more complex series of final tones, the final vowel of a polar question is lengthened prosodically, becoming about twice as long as the final vowel of a declarative.

From a typological perspective, it is interesting to note that Fataluku's rising-falling intonation pattern violates the strong cross-linguistic tendency for questions to end in a high tone (e.g., Jun, 2005). While the final boundary tone does contain a high, it ends with a distinctly falling f0 contour. Another point of typological interest is the relatively short duration that is characteristic of the final syllable of a declarative, which violates a strong cross-linguistic tendency to lengthen IP-final syllables (Jun and Fletcher, 2014). It is possible that the shorter durations of declaratives are an important perceptual cue for distinguishing them from structurally identical polar questions, although the production data examined here do not make it clear what type of cues are most important for listeners.

An important direction for future research would be to examine the perceptual cues that listeners use to distinguish between declaratives and polar questions in structurally ambiguous sentences, focusing especially on the role of f0 contour and duration in perception. Another important topic is the phonological representation of the pitch peaks that occur in the first or second syllable of a prosodic phrase, whether these represent phonological tone, intonation or something else. The study of Fataluku intonation is still at its inception, and there is a great need for future research to further illuminate its prosodic structure.

Acknowledgments

I am grateful for the financial support of this project provided by the Bilinski Educational Foundation, the University of Hawai'i Arts and Sciences Advisory Council and the Department of Linguistics Endowment Fund. Much thanks are due to all of my Fataluku language consultants, for their patience and eagerness to teach me about their language. I would also like to thank Victoria Anderson, Katie Drager, Amber Camp and Bradley Rentz for their help, as well as three anonymous reviewers for their helpful suggestions. I take full responsibility for any errors.

References

Bates, Douglas, Martin Maechler, Ben Bolker and Steven Walker. 2014. lme4: Linear mixed-effects models using Eigen and S4. R package (version 1.1–7). http://CRAN.R-project.org/package=lme4

Boersma, Paul and David Weenink. 2012. Praat: doing phonetics by computer (version 5.3.32). http://www.praat.org/

Heston, Tyler M. 2014. The nature and underlying representations of long vowels and diphthongs in Fataluku. *Oceanic Linguistics* 53(2), in press.

Jun, Sun-Ah and Janet Fletcher. 2014. Methodology of studying intonation: From data collection to data analysis. In *Prosodic typology II: The phonology of intonation and phrasing*, ed. by Sun-Ah Jun, 493–519. Oxford: Oxford University Press.

Klamer, Marian. 2014. The Alor-Pantar languages: Linguistic context, history and typology. In *The Alor-Pantar languages: History and typology*, ed. by Marian Klamer, 5–53. (Studies in Diversity Linguistics 3). Berlin: Language Science Press.

Ladd, D. Robert. 1996. *Intonational phonology*. (Cambridge Studies in Linguistics 79). Cambridge: Cambridge University Press.

Lewis, M. Paul, Gary F. Simons and Charles D. Fennig, eds. 2013. Fataluku. *Ethnologue: Languages of the world*. 17th ed. Dallas: SIL International.

Lindström, Eva and Bert Remijsen. 2005. Aspects of the prosody of Kuot, a language where intonation ignores stress. *Linguistics* 43(4). 839–870.

Pierrehumbert, Janet. 1980. The phonology and phonetics of English intonation. MIT PhD Thesis. Distributed 1988, Indiana University Linguistics Club.

Pinheiro, José, Douglas Bates, Saikat DebRoy, Deepayan Sarkar and R Core Team. 2014. nlme: Linear and nonlinear mixed effects models. R package (version 3.1–117). http://CRAN.R-project.org/package=nlme

R Core Team. 2014. R: A language and environment for statistical computing. Vienna, Austria: R Foundation for Statistical Computing. http://www.R-project.org/

Schapper, Antoinette, Juliette Huber and Aone van Engelenhoven. 2014. The relatedness of Timor-Kisar and Alor-Pantar languages: A preliminary demonstration. In *The Alor-Pantar languages: History and typology*, ed. by Marian Klamer, 99–154. (Studies in Diversity Linguistics 3). Berlin: Language Science Press.

Stoel, Ruben. 2007. Question intonation in Fataluku. Presentation given at the Fifth East Nusantara Conference, Kupang, Indonesia. http://www.fataluku.com/staff/stoel/

Stoel, Ruben. 2008. Fataluku as a tone language. In *SEALS XVI: Papers from the 16th annual meeting of the Southeast Asian Linguistics Society 2006*, ed. by Paul Sidwell and Uri Tadmor, 75–84. Canberra: Pacific Linguistics.

Recognition of Sarcasm in Tweets Based on Concept Level Sentiment Analysis and Supervised Learning Approaches

Piyoros Tungthamthiti, Kiyoaki Shirai, Masnizah Mohd
Japan Advanced Institute of Science and Technology
1-1, Asahidai, Nomi City, Ishikawa, Japan 923-1292
Email: {s1320204,kshirai,masnizah}@jaist.ac.jp

Abstract

Sarcasm is a form of communication that is intended to mock or harass someone by using words with the opposite of their literal meaning. However, identification of sarcasm is somewhat difficult due to the gap between its literal and intended meaning. Recognition of sarcasm is a task that can potentially provide a lot of benefits to other areas of natural language processing. In this research, we propose a new method to identify sarcasm in tweets that focuses on several approaches: 1) sentiment analysis, 2) concept level and common-sense knowledge 3) coherence and 4) machine learning classification. We will use support vector machine (SVM) to classify sarcastic tweet based on our proposed features as well as ordinary N-grams. Our proposed classifier is an ensemble of two SVMs with two different feature sets. The results of the experiment show our method outperforms the baseline method and achieves 80% accuracy.

1 Introduction

Recognition of sarcasm is one of the most difficult tasks in natural language processing (NLP). It is a problem of determining if the actual meaning of a word is intended in a given context. Sarcasm is normally represented in a form of ironic speech in which the speakers convey an implicit message to criticize a particular person. Thus, tone of voice plays a significant role in the communication. There are many communication programs (e.g. Line, Facebook, Twitter), which allow to communicate together through only text characters. It is very difficult to determine the actual meaning by just looking at the text itself. Recognition of sarcasm prevents us from misinterpreting sentences whose meaning are opposite to their literal meaning. It is also a task that is potentially applicable for many other areas of NLP, for example, machine translation, information retrieval, information extraction and knowledge acquisition.

Twitter is an online social networking service that allows users to post and read short messages, called "tweets". However, Twitter allows users to write short messages, i.e. 140 characters per tweet. Also, users usually post a lot of tweets in complex sentence structures. Regarding to these issues, a new method is created to detect sarcasm in tweets.

Sarcasm is known as "the activity of saying or writing the opposite of what you mean, or of speaking in a way intended to make someone else feel stupid or show them that you are angry" (Macmillan, 2007). According to this definition, we can recognize sarcasm by evaluating the polarity of the sentences. In other words, a sarcastic sentence contains two or more words, which may cause conflict in sentiment polarities (both positive and negative) in a sentence, whereas a normal sentence should contain at most one polarity. Let us consider the example sentence "I love being ignored." The sentence contains both positive ("love") and negative word ("ignored") in a sentence. Therefore, it can be classified as a sarcastic sentence.

In the identification of sarcasm based on the contradiction of the polarity, unknown words in the sentiment lexicon are serious problem. To tackle it, we try to consider the related concepts for each word to identify the sentence polarity. For example, let us consider the tweet "It's Wednesday and it's freezing! It's raining! How better can this day be??" This would be classified as a normal tweet since only

Copyright 2014 by Piyoros Tungthamthiti, Kiyoaki Shirai, and Masnizah Mohd
28th Pacific Asia Conference on Language, Information and Computation pages 404–413

the word "better" is recognized as a positive word from the whole tweet. However, our approach can recognize it as a sarcastic tweet by using the concept level knowledge. That is, we can know "bad weather" is one of the related concepts of "raining" from an extra lexical resource, then we have a new concept "bad" (negative) together with the original word "better" (positive) to catch the contradiction in sentiment polarity in the sentence.

In addition, we also consider "coherence"; that is, the relationships across multiple sentences. Generally, sarcastic tweets should contain expressions which clearly show the relationships or references to some words across sentences. For example, in the tweet "And I just found out that my other pap fell and broke his hip. Awesome day thus far", the word "awesome" (positive) refers to the action "fell" and "broke" (both are negative words), that is contradiction of sentiments in the sarcastic tweet. However, when a tweet contains contradiction of sentiment polarity without coherence between them, it could be regarded as non-sarcastic tweet. For example, in the tweet "He likes dogs. She hates cats.", the word "love" (positive) and "hates" (negative) refer to the different subjects in two sentences. Although the tweet contains contradictions in sentiment polarity, the two sentences are not coherent. Therefore, it should not be classified as a sarcastic tweet. In this way, coherence is important for the recognition of sarcasm.

Finally, Support Vector Machine is used to train a classifier that judges if a tweet is sarcastic. Two SVMs will be trained with two different feature sets. One is N-gram, the other is features based on the sentiment score, coherence and punctuation. Then we will combine two SVMs, that is, more reliable judgment between two classifiers are chosen as the final result.

In this paper, we propose a new method to utilize several major modules, including 1) sentiment analysis, 2) expansion of concept level and commonsense knowledge 3) coherence identification and 4) machine learning classification. Figure 1 represents the overall process of our method. The method will try to merge our newly introduced features obtained from the module 1, 2 and 3 together with the commonly used features (e.g. N-grams) to enhance the classification performance in sarcastic tweets. Using the data consisting of 50,000 tweets, we will evaluate our results by comparing against two baseline methods derived from definition of sarcasm and supervised learning algorithm based on N-gram features.

2 Related work

Currently, there are several researches related to the recognition of sarcasm. A variety of methods have been proposed based on various kinds of techniques, including statistical models, sentiment analysis, pattern recognition, supervised or unsupervised machine learning. However, the intelligence system and computation process are not sufficient to be relied on for sarcasm recognition. It also requires the development of understanding forms of language in both psychological and linguistic aspects.

According to Stingfellow (1994) and Gibbs et al. (2007), the use of irony and sarcasm is studied to derive a definition and demonstrate some characteristics of sarcasm. Both studies agree on the similar basis that irony and sarcasm arise from the contradictory intentions represented by the opposed meaning of an ironic or sarcastic statement. These studies also discover the theories of verbal irony comprehension 1) that verbal irony requires a violation of expectations, and 2) that it requires violation of felicity conditions for speech acts. Thus, if we observe both contradictory intentions and violation of felicity conditions within a context, we can recognize a sarcastic context.

Tsur et al. (2010) present a semi-supervised learning method to classify sarcastic sentences on Twitter, Amazon and in online product reviews. The method employs two main modules: 1) semi-supervised pattern acquisition and 2) a classification algorithm. It extracts a sequence of high-frequency word (HFWs) and content words (CWs) as a pattern of a sarcastic sentence. Then, it constructs a single feature vector for each pattern. The feature value for each pattern will be calculated based on their similarities comparing to the other extracted patterns. Finally, the method will apply k-nearest neighbours (kNN)-like strategy together with the feature vector to classify the sentences. This method is based on an alternative idea which does not focus on the semantic analysis but on the sequence of HFWs and CWs as sentence

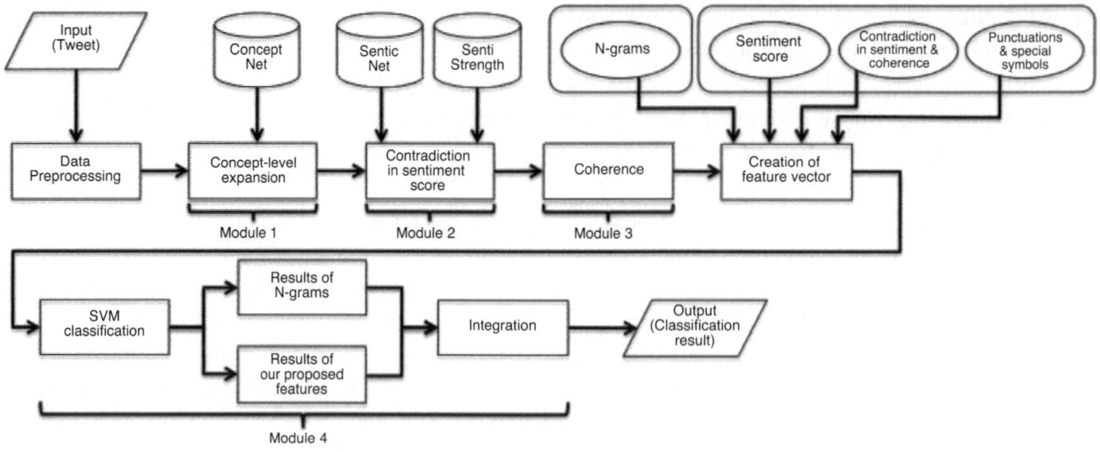

Figure 1: Flowchart of overall process of our method

patterns; this method relies on the syntactic level of natural language processing.

Ellen et al. (2013) introduce a method to identify sarcasm in tweets that arises from a contrast between a positive sentiment referring to a negative situation. In order to learn phrases corresponding to positive sentiments and negative situations, this method uses a bootstrapping algorithm that keeps iteration between two steps. The first step is learning negative situation phrases following positive sentiment, where "love" is used as an initial seed word. Then, the second step will learn positive sentiment phrases that occur near negative situation phrases. After multiple iteration processes, the obtained list of negative situations and positive sentiment phrases are used to recognize sarcasm in tweets by identifying contexts that contain a positive sentiment in close proximity (occurring nearby) to a negative situation phrase. This method relies on the assumption that many sarcastic tweets contains the following structure:

$$[+VERB\ PHRASE][-SITUATION\ PHRASE]$$

However, the method has some limitations since it cannot identify sarcasm across multiple sentences.

Coreference resolution is a task in natural language processing to identify multiple words or phrases that refer the same entity such as person, place or thing. Soon et al. (2001) introduce a machine learning approach to link coreferring noun phrases both within and across sentences. They construct a feature vector consisting of 12 features. The features include distance, antecedent pronoun, anaphor-pronoun, string matching, definite noun phrase, demonstrative noun phrase, number agreement, semantic class agreement, gender agreement, both-proper-names, alias and appositive features. Then, a classifier will be trained based on the feature vectors generated from the training documents. C5 (Quinlan, 1993; Quinlan, 2007) is used as the learning algorithm in this study. This research is the first machine-learning based system that offers performance comparable to that of state of the art non-learning based systems on MUC-6 and MUC-7 standard datasets. In this study, a simple coreference resolution method is applied to identify coherence of multiple sentences.

Language can be expressed in many different ways, such as utterance, action, signal and text. According to the definition of sarcasm, we also need to consider violation and aggressiveness of the communication. For utterance, we can easily recognize the emotion through the unsterilized tone of voice (Tepperman et al., 2006). In texts, punctuation plays a vital role in text communication to provide the reader the signals about pause, stop and change of tone of voice. Let us consider an example sentence "That is very annoying!". The exclamation mark (!) can be used to indicate a strong feeling or exaggerates something. Thelwall et at. (2012) aim to assess the sentiment lexicon (SentiStrength) in a variety of different online contexts. One part of this research discusses the usage of punctuations in various contexts. It focuses on the sentence that contains a single punctuation, repetitive punctuation marks, question marks and exclamation marks. Their result shows that punctuation plays a key role to boost the sentiment score.

The characteristic of our method is that we attempt to combine multiple approaches in both psychological and linguistic aspects to develop an innovative strategy. Our method takes various approaches into account, including sentiment analysis, concept level knowledge expansion, coherence and N-gram of words. Tweets are represented by feature vectors based on these methods. Then classifiers for sarcasm identification are trained by supervised machine learning.

3 Data

In this section, the procedures of data collection and data preprocessing will be explained.

3.1 Source

We first prepare a collection of tweets by using Twitter4J[1] as a tool to retrieve tweets data. Tweets are not just simple text data since they contain URL addresses, twitter usernames (mentions) or hashtags. For example, in the tweet "Congrats to @Kelly_clarkson on the birth of her baby GIRL! http://eonli.ne/1vgXVOU #gorgeous", "@Kelly_clarkson" is a username, "http://eonli.ne/1vgXVOU" is an URL and "#gorgeous" is a hashtag. Users can attach an URL to the tweet when they want provide more information or show an image related to the post. Twitter also contains a mention feature (e.g. @<username>), which allows the notification of other users about the tweet. Hashtags (e.g. #<texts>) are used to mark keywords or topics in a tweet. Although the usage of these meta tags is optional, they frequently appeared in a lot of tweet messages.

Two datasets are required in our study: 1) sarcastic tweets and 2) normal tweets. Different query keywords will be used for each datasets. To collect sarcastic tweets, the hashtag "#sarcasm" is used. That is, tweets with #sarcasm are retrieved via Twitter API. Normal tweets are retrieved based on randomly selected keywords from WordNet lexicon (Miller, 1995).

3.2 Preprocessing

Two kinds of preprocessing are performed on tweet datasets: 1) lemmatization and 2) usernames, URLs and hashtags removal. For lemmatization, we use the Standford Lemmatizer[2]. Usernames, URLs and hashtags are removed from tweets as they do not provide any information about the concepts or sentiments of the words and might be noise for the classification process.

4 Proposed method

Below we propose our method based on four major modules. They are the modules to generate a set of classification features or to classify a tweet if it is sarcastic.

4.1 Concept level and common-sense knowledge

Concept level and common-sense knowledge are the ability to perceive, understand and acknowledge things, which are shared through the common knowledge or facts that can be reasonably realized. In this research, we focus on the semantic analysis of tweets using the semantic network consisting of concepts of words to obtain more affective information. Let us consider an example sarcastic sentence "I love going to work on holidays." The system may misclassify it as a normal sentence due to the lack of sentiment information. From this sentence, only the word "love" has positive sentiment score, while the other words have no polarity. However, using concept level and common-sense knowledge, we can know that the word "work" would refer to a tiring or stressful situation and the word "holiday" would refer to "time for rest". Now a contradiction of the polarity in this sentence could be found since ["love" and "holiday"] and ["work"] are positive and negative words, respectively. The sentence could then, be classified as sarcastic.

In this study, we use a concept lexicon called ConceptNet[3]. ConceptNet is a semantic network

[1] http://twitter4j.org/en/index.html

[2] http://nlp.stanford.edu/software/corenlp.shtml

[3] http://conceptnet5.media.mit.edu

consisting of common-sense knowledge and concepts, represented in the form of nodes (words or short phrases) and labeled edges (relationships) between them. For example, the sentence "A dog is an animal" will be parsed into an assertion as "dog/IsA/animal". The assertion consists of two nodes ("dog" and "animal") and one edge ("IsA"). There are also other 31 different types of relationships, such as "PartOf", "UsedFor", "MadeOf", etc. ConceptNet contains more than 800,000 assertions. These assertions are ranked based on the number of votes by users. The number of votes are taken as a score to ensure the quality and the significance of each assertion.

ConceptNet will be used to expand the concepts for the words whose sentiment score is unknown. Thus, the sentiment score of the unknown words can be recognized through their generated concepts and definitions. The concept-level lexicon improves the robustness of our system in terms of calculation of the sentiment scores of tweets. The lexicon also allow the system to recognize sarcasm of the sentence at the concept level.

4.2 Contradiction in the sentiment score

As previously explained, sarcasm often occurs in a contradictory form of communication or the use of words to express something opposite to the intended meaning. In this research, we attempt to use sentiment analysis to find contradiction in sentiment polarity between words in a tweet. Two lexicons are used to check the polarities of words: SentiStrength and SenticNet.

SentiStrength is a sentiment lexicon that uses linguistic information and rules to detect sentiment strength in English text. The lexicon consists of all types of polarity words, including booster words, emotion words, negation words, question words, slang words, idioms and emoticons. SentiStrength provides positive and negative sentiment scores for each word. Both scores are integers from 1 to 5, where 1 signifies weak sentiment and 5 signifies strong sentiment. For example, the sentiment score (1,1) represents a neutral word. Basically, the overall polarity of a word is calculated by subtracting the negative sentiment score from the positive sentiment score.

SenticNet is a resource for opinion mining that aims to create a collection of commonly used common-sense concepts with positive and negative sentiment scores. The sentiment score for each word is scaled from -1 to 1, where -1 signifies strongly negative sentiment, 0 signifies neutral sentiment and 1 signifies strong positive sentiment. In this study, the score is multiplied by 5 so that it corresponds to the scores in SentiStrength.

We calculate the sentiment score of the word w, $w\_score(w)$, as shown in Equation (3). If the word is found in SentiStrength or SenticNet, the sentiment score in the lexicon is used as the $w\_score(w)$. If the word is found in both SentiStrength and SenticNet, the average of the sentiment score of both lexicons is used as the $w\_score(w)$. Otherwise, we obtain the concepts to expand the meaning of the word by choosing the top five ranked concepts from ConceptNet lexicon. Then, we take an average of the sentiment scores of the concepts as $w\_score(w)$. After we obtain the sentiment scores for all words, we will calculate the total score for positive and negative words as shown in Equation (1) and (2), respectively.

If both sum_pos_score and sum_neg_score are greater than 0, we can find contradiction of polarity in the tweet. As we will describe in 4.4.2, the total scores will also be used as weights in the feature vector in the classification process.

$$sum\_pos\_score = \sum_{pos\_w \in TW} w\_score(pos\_w) \quad (1)$$

$$sum\_neg\_score = \sum_{neg\_w \in TW} w\_score(neg\_w) \quad (2)$$

$$w\_score(w) = \begin{cases} polarity\_score(w), & \text{if } w \in SS \text{ or } SN \\ average\_polarity\_score(w), & \text{if } w \in SS \text{ and } SN \\ \frac{1}{|C|} \sum_{c \in C} polarity\_score(c), & \text{otherwise} \end{cases} \quad (3)$$

- TW refers to a tweet.
- pos_w and neg_w refers to the positive and negative words.
- w refers to a word.
- c refers to a concept of a word.
- C refers to the top five ranked concepts of a word.
- sum_pos_score and sum_neg_score are the summation of positive and negative sentiment score.
- SS refers to SentiStrength lexicon.
- SN refers to SenticNet lexicon.

4.3 Sentence coherence

Since our study focuses on contradiction in the sentiment score, coherence is another issue that we need to consider. Assume that a tweet consists of multiple sentences with sentiment contradiction. If all sentences are independent on each other, it is not obvious to say that the tweet is sarcastic. Therefore, we introduce a set of heuristic rules to identify coherence across multiple sentences.

In this study, coherence between two sentences is identified by simply checking coreference between subjects or objects of sentences. Let us suppose that sentence s_1 precedes s_2, and word w_1 and w_2 are the subject (or object) of s_1 and s_2, respectively. If w_1 is an antecedent of w_2, we regard the two sentences as coherent. We created the following five rules to check coreference between w_1 and w_2:

1. Pronoun match feature - w_1 and w_2 are identical pronouns, including reflexive pronouns, personal pronouns and possessive pronouns.
2. String match feature - w_1 and w_2 are identical. Note that stopwords are ignored in string matching.
3. Definite noun phrase feature - w_2 starts with the word "the".
4. Demonstrative noun phrase feature - w_2 starts with the "this", "that", "these" and "those".
5. Both proper names feature - w_1 and w_2 are both named entities.

Two sentences are regarded as coherent if they fulfill one of the above rules. If one pair of w_1 and w_2 satisfies our rules among all combination of w_1 and w_2 in multiple sentences in a tweet, we regard the overall tweet as coherent.

Obviously our method is too simple to identify coherence within sentences. In future, a more sophisticated method should be incorporated into our coherence identification module.

4.4 Creation of feature vector

In this section, we will explain how to represent a tweet as a feature vector to train a classifier for sarcasm identification.

4.4.1 N-grams feature

N-gram refers to a sequence of words within a tweet, where N indicates the size (number of words) of a sequence. The common used sizes of N-gram are uni-gram ($N = 1$), bi-gram ($N = 2$) and tri-gram ($N = 3$).

In our dataset, we will divide each tweet into a single word, a sequence of two words and a sequence of three words. They will be used as features. The weights of N-gram features are binary: 1 if N-gram is present in a tweet, 0 if absent.

4.4.2 Contradiction feature

As discussed earlier, contradiction in the sentiment score and coherent within multiple sentences are useful for sarcasm identification. Therefore, we introduce two new binary features, $contra$ and $contra + coher$, considering contradiction of polarity and coherence in the tweet. The feature $contra$ is activated if (1) the tweet consists of one sentence and (2) contradiction of the sentiment score is found by the method described in Subsection 4.2. $contra + coher$ is activated if (1) the tweet consists of two or more sentences, (2) contradiction of polarity is detected and (3) the tweet is judged as coherent by the method described in Subsection 4.3.

4.4.3 Sentiment feature

We also provide sentiment score features for both positive and negative sentiment phrases. In this case, we use three classes (low, $medium$ and $high$) to indicate the degree of positive and negative polarity of the tweet. After conducting a preliminary experiment to find the optimum range of sentiment scores, three positive sentiment features are defined as follows:

pos_low: activated if $sum\_pos\_score \leq -1$
pos_medium: activated if $0 \leq sum\_pos\_score \leq 1$
pos_high: activated if $sum\_pos\_score \geq 2$
neg_low, neg_medium and neg_high are defined in the same way. Note that weights of these 6 sentiment features are binary.

4.4.4 Punctuation and special symbols feature

We also consider punctuation as one of the main features in this study. Many studies have shown that punctuation has a lot of influence in text classification, especially in the area of sentiment analysis. We consider the following 7 indicators to introduce punctuation features:

P_1. Number of emoticons

P_2. Number of repetitive sequence of punctua-

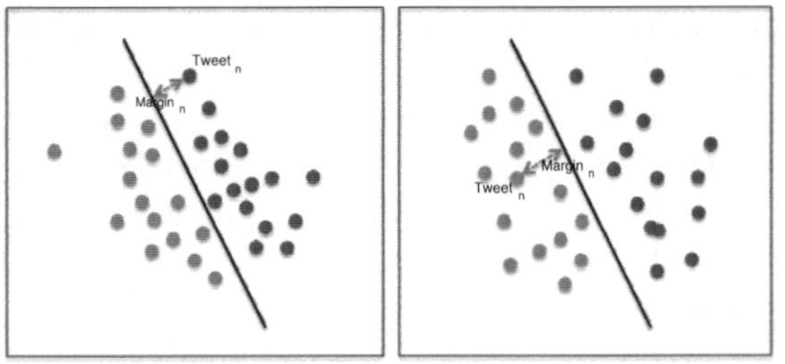

Figure 2: Example of margin based SVM classification approach

tions

P_3. Number of repetitive sequence of characters

P_4. Number of capitalized word

P_5. Number of slang and booster words[4]

P_6. Number of exclamation marks

P_7. Number of idioms[5]

We use low, $medium$ and $high$ as features to indicate the range of number of punctuation and symbols. Through our preliminary experiment to check various range of values from 0 to 7, we found the optimum range to be:

P_i_low: activated if $number = 0$

P_i_medium: activated if $1 \leq number \leq 3$

P_i_high: activated if $number \geq 4$

Thus we introduce 7 × 3 = 21 new features. Note that these features are binary.

4.5 Classification algorithm

A machine learning algorithm based on the feature vectors generated from the tweets data was used to train a classifier. The classification algorithm used is support vector machine (SVM) due to its simplicity and effectiveness in binary classification. We use the linear kernel to perform the classification task because it does not consume as much time and resources on a large amount of data as polynomial kernel.

To combine our features described from 4.4.2 to 4.4.4 with N-gram feature, we choose an approach in which two feature sets are used separately to train two different SVMs and combine them to get final decision. First, we perform the classification task twice (once for n-grams and once for our features) and obtain two sets of results. Then, we determine the final result by comparing the classification outputs of all data. For each tweet, if the judgments of two SVMs agree, it simply becomes the final result. However, if they do not agree, we need to consider the classification margin for each classifier. Figure 2 demonstrates a situation where two classifiers obtain different classification results for the same tweet. In this case, we need to compare the margin (distance between the data and separate hyperplane) of both classifiers. Usually, the higher the margin, the more reliable the output. Therefore, we take the output from the classifier with higher margin as the final result.

5 Experiment

In our experiment, we retrieved 50,000 tweets from Twitter for our datasets. 25,000 tweets were randomly selected as normal tweets, whereas the other 25,000 tweets are sarcastic tweets. Then, we classified the tweets based on variety of features, including N-grams and our proposed features. The results of the proposed method are compared against two baseline methods. The first baseline is based on the definition of sarcasm. The second baseline uses N-gram features to train an SVM classifier for sarcasm identification.

5.1 Baseline 1

Since sarcasm normally emerges in a sentence that expresses the meaning opposite to the intended meaning, we will consider tweets where both positive and negative scores (Equation (1) and (2)) are greater than 0 to be sarcastic.

5.2 Baseline 2

The other baseline is SVM trained with N-gram features. We prepare two baseline systems: one is SVM with uni-gram features, the other is SVM with uni-gram, bi-gram and tri-gram features.

5.3 Evaluation procedure

We evaluate the two proposed methods: 1) an SVM trained with our proposed feature sets, 2) a classifier combining SVMs with our proposed features and N-gram. Our proposed methods as well as Baseline 2 are evaluated by 10-fold cross validation on our

[4]SentiStrength is used as a lexicon of slang and booster words.

[5]http://www.englishcurrent.com/idioms/esl-idioms-intermediate-advanced/

tweet dataset. Recall, precision, F-measure and accuracy are measured to evaluate the performance of sarcasm identification.

6 Results and discussion

Table 1 shows the results of Baseline 1. The performance is relatively high, although Baseline 1 does not rely on supervised machine learning, but on the sentiment lexicon only. Table 2 reveals results of single SVMs with our proposed features (contradiction, sentiment and punctuation features) and Baseline 2. The accuracy of our proposed method is 63.42%, which is better than Baseline 1 but worse than Baseline 2. We found that N-gram features were still powerful for classification of sarcasm. Table 3 shows the results of the combination of two SVMs. In this table, our individual features are combined with uni-gram separately to evaluate the effectiveness of each feature. The fifth row in Table 3 is the system where coherence in a tweet is not considered[6], while the sixth row indicates the system where ConceptNet is not used for concept expansion. We can find that the combination of N-gram features and all our proposed features improve the accuracy 3% against Baseline 2 with N-grams. It indicates that several sarcastic tweets can be found by our approach but not by N-gram features. Examples of such sarcastic tweets are shown below, where polarity words are in bold:

1. I am **thrilling.** The **storm** in my area
2. A **nice** sunny day to go **pay** some **bills**.......
3. It's **brilliant** to realize when your **best** asset **screw** everything up
4. I really **enjoy** running on the treadmill. So **exhausted**!!
5. It has been **freezing** and **snowing** all week. The weather is so **gorgeous**

Although polarity words in these tweets are effective features, they do not frequently appear in the training data. SVM trained with N-gram features fails to classify them as sarcastic due to data sparseness. Our sentiment, contradiction and punctuation features are rather abstract and appear many times in the training data. Therefore, our method can classify these sarcastic tweets correctly.

[6] $contra + coher$ feature is activated even when coherence in a tweet is not confirmed.

6.1 Contribution of our proposed features

In this subsection, we further discuss the contribution of each proposed feature.

6.1.1 Punctuations and special symbols

As can be seen from Table 3, punctuations and special symbols contribute only a slight improvement. The accuracy is increased by only 0.1% when they are combined with uni-gram. This may be because punctuations and special symbols are also incorporated in uni-gram feature set, that is, our proposed feature is partially duplicated with uni-gram. Nevertheless, the feature provides some improvement to the overall result.

6.1.2 Concept level knowledge expansion

The results show that concept level knowledge expansion can enhance the quality of the sentiment score features from 75.48% to 76.35%. Tweets are unstructured and context free data. There are a lot of unknown words and slang that are very difficult to handle. From this reason, concept level and common sense knowledge can be applied to improve our method.

6.1.3 Effectiveness of coherent identification

As explained in 4.4.2, coherence in the tweet is required to be considered in order to detect contradiction of polarity more precisely. Next we will discuss the contribution of coherence feature. The accuracy decreased by 1% (from 76.35% to 75.48%) when coherence is ignored as shown in Table 3. It is clear that contradiction in the sentiment score with coherence feature has an impact on the improvement of the result. Let us consider a non-sarcastic tweet in our dataset "My gf's mac failed three times and I had to reboot twice. Windows are WAY simpler." Suppose that we ignore coherence when constructing the feature vector. This tweet would be misclassified as a sarcastic tweet since it contains contradiction in the sentiment score of both positive ("simpler") and negative ("fail") words in two different sentences. However, when coherence in the tweet is checked, our method will recognize that the words "My gf's mac", "I" and "Windows" are not related to each other. In other words, coherence does not exist within the tweet. Now it can be correctly classified as a non-sarcastic tweet. As shown in this example,

Table 1: The result of contradiction in sentiment score approach

Methods	Recall	Precision	F-measure	Accuracy
Contradiction in sentiment score (Baseline 1)	0.55	0.56	0.56	57.14%

Table 2: The result of SVM classification based on various features

Methods	Recall	Precision	F-measure	Accuracy
Our proposed features	0.64	0.63	0.63	63.42%
Uni-gram features (Baseline 2)	0.72	0.73	0.73	73.81%
Uni-gram, bi-gram and tri-gram features (Baseline 2)	**0.76**	**0.76**	**0.76**	**76.40%**

Table 3: The result of marjority vote and margin based SVM classification

Methods	Recall	Precision	F-measure	Accuracy
uni-gram and contradiction	0.72	0.72	0.72	72.83%
uni-gram and sentiment score	0.75	0.75	0.75	75.64%
uni-gram and punctuations + special symbols	0.72	0.73	0.73	73.91%
uni-gram and our proposed features without coherence	0.75	0.75	0.75	75.72%
uni-gram and our proposed features without concept level knowledge generation	0.74	0.75	0.75	75.48%
uni-gram and all our proposed features	0.76	0.77	0.76	76.35%
uni-gram, bi-gram, tri-gram and all our proposed features	**0.79**	**0.78**	**0.79**	**79.43%**

contradiction of polarity in an incoherent tweet does not indicate sarcasm.

6.2 Limitation of our approaches

There are some limitations in our method. First, there are a lot of ambiguous words in concept knowledge expansion, which may lead to misclassification of sarcastic tweets. Inappropriate concept expansion causes erroneous detection of contradiction in the sentiment score. For example, the sentence "I love when its raining." contains a positive sentiment word "love" and also negative situation word "rain" whose concept is "bad weather". However, it is not always true that the word "rain" refers to a negative situation. It may cause misclassification. Second, in our dataset, some normal sentences retrieved by random sampling are actually sarcastic although there is no hashtag "#sarcasm". It is rather difficult to prevent it. It means that our collection of tweets is noisy data. Finally, there are a lot of sarcastic sentences, which provide absolutely no clues. An illustrative example is "I feel great #sarcasm". Without "#sarcasm" hashtag, there is no way that we can realize it as a sarcastic tweet.

7 Conclusion

In this research, we present a new method for recognition of sarcasm in tweets. The method is based on a variety of approaches, including sentiment analysis, concept level knowledge expansion, coherence of sentences and machine learning classification. Sentiment scores of words are used as features for the classification. We also use the common-sense concept to find the sentiment score for the word with unknown sentiment score. Then, we consider coherence in a tweet to ensure that the tweets with contradiction in the sentiment score have dependent relationships across multiple sentences. Finally, we construct the feature vector to train an SVM classifier based on our proposed features. N-gram and our proposed features are used to train separate classifiers, then a more reliable judgment between them is chosen as the final result.

We compared our results against two strong baselines. One of them is derived based on the definition of sarcasm and the other is SVM trained with N-gram features. The results show that our method has the greatest accuracy, when we combine our proposed features with N-gram. Although the model with the proposed features achieves only 63.42% accuracy, the results clearly show that our features can help to classify some tweets that the model using only N-gram features cannot identify.

Even for human, it is not easy to identify sarcasm in tweets because sarcasm often depends on common-sense knowledge associated with the context of tweets. It makes automatic identification of sarcasm difficult. We think that about 80% accuracy could be considered a satisfying result.

7.1 Future work

For the future work, we plan to improve the efficiency of our method based on three major issues: 1) coherence and 2) word sense disambiguation 3) evaluation using real data.

In this research, we have provided some heuristic rules to determine coherence within multiple sentences. Coherence may have a lot of influence in the classification, however, the improvement by coherence scheme was not so great in our experiment. We should investigate a better way to identify and incorporate the coherence feature in our model.

Word sense disambiguation is another issue that we need to consider. In our method, we always expand five concepts for each word, that does not exist in SentiStrength or SenticNet lexicon. However, some expanded concepts may be irrelevant with the context of the tweet. Therefore, if we can obtain only the suitable concepts for each word, the performance of our method might increase.

Finally, we tested our system on balanced datasets, where the number of sarcastic and non-sarcastic tweets are equal. However, this situation rarely occurs in a real situation, since the number of non-sarcastic tweets may be much higher than the number of sarcastic tweets. We also need to evaluate our method on an unbalanced dataset and a real dataset.

References

Ellen R., Ashequl Q., Prafulla S., Lalindra S., Gilbert D. S., Gilbert N., Ruihong H. 2013 Sarcasm as Contrast between a Positive Sentiment and Negative Situation *Proceedings of the Conference on Empirical Methods on Natural Language Processing (EMNLP)*, pages 704–714, Seattle, Washington

Gibbs, R. W., Colston, H. L. 2007 *Irony in Language and Thought: A Cognitive Science Reader* Lawrence Erlbaum Associates, eds. 2007.

Macmillan, E. D. 2007. *Macmillan English Dictionary*, Macmillan Education, 2 edition.

Miller A. G. 1995 WordNet: A Lexical Database for English *Communications of the ACM*, Vol. 38, No. 11: 39-41.

Quinlan, R. J. 1993. *C4.5: Programs for machine learning*, Morgan Kaufmann San Francisco, CA

Quinlan, R. J. 2007. *C5* Available: http://rulequest.com

Soon W. M., Ng H. T, Lim D. C. Y. 2001 A Machine Learning Approach to Coreference Resolution of Noun Phrases *Computational Linguistics*, pages 521–544, Cambridge, MA, USA

Stringfellow, F. J. 1994. *The Meaning of Irony* NewYork: State University of NY.

Tepperman, J., Traum, D., Narayanan, S. 2006 Sarcasm Recognition for Spoken Dialogue Systems *Interspeech 2006*, Pittsburgh, PA, USA

Thelwall, M., Buckley, K., Paltoglou, G. 2012 Sentiment Strength Detection For The Social Web *Journal of the American society for information science and technology*, 63(1):163–173

Tsur O., Davidov D. 2010 Icwsm - a great catchy name: Semi-supervised recognition of sarcastic sentences in product reviews *In International AAAI Conference on Weblogs and Social*

Tsur O., Davidov D., Rappoport A. 2010 Semi-supervised Recognition of Sarcastic Sentences in Twitter and Amazon *Proceedings of the Fourteenth Conference on Computational Natural Language Learning*, pages 107–116, Uppsala, Sweden

CHULA TTS: A Modularized Text-To-Speech Framework

Natthawut Kertkeidkachorn
[1]Department of Computer Engineering
Faculty of Engineering, Chulalongkorn University Bangkok, Thailand
[2]Department of Informatics
The Graduate University for Advanced Studies, Tokyo, Japan
Natthawut@nii.ac.jp

Supadaech Chanjaradwichai
Department of Computer Engineering
Faculty of Engineering, Chulalongkorn University Bangkok, Thailand
Supadaech.C@student.chula.ac.th

Proadpran Punyabukkana
Department of Computer Engineering
Faculty of Engineering, Chulalongkorn University Bangkok, Thailand
Proadpran.p@chula.ac.th

Atiwong Suchato
Department of Computer Engineering
Faculty of Engineering, Chulalongkorn University Bangkok, Thailand
Atiwong.s@chula.ac.th

Abstract

Spoken and written languages evolve constantly through their everyday usages. Combining with practical expectation for automatically generating synthetic speech suitable for various domains of context, such a reason makes Text-to-Speech (TTS) systems of living languages require characteristics that allow extensible handlers for new language phenomena or customized to the nature of the domains in which TTS systems are deployed. ChulaTTS was designed and implemented with a modularized concept. Its framework lets components of typical TTS systems work together and their combinations are customized using simple human-readable configurations. Under .NET development framework, new text processing and signal synthesis components can be built while existing components can simply be wrapped in .NET dynamic-link libraries exposing expected methods governed by a predefined programming interface. A case of ChulaTTS implementation and sample applications were also discussed in this paper.

1 Introduction

A Text-to-Speech (TTS) system is a system which artificially produces human speech by converting a target text into its corresponding acoustic signal. TTS systems are crucial components to many kinds of computer applications, particularly applications in assistive technology, E.g. applications for assisting the visually-impaired to access information on the Internet (Chirathivat et al. 2007), applications for automatically producing digital talking books (DTB) (Punyabukkana et al. 2012), and etc.,

Over the past decades, several TTS systems had been developed to fulfill applications on various computing platforms including mobile devices (Chinathimatmongkhon et al. 2008). Given specific domains, some applications of TTS systems require the systems to produce word pronunciations or generating speech signals that sound more natural to the listeners than ones generated with systems designed for texts of more general domains. For example, an application to read text from a social media web site might need a TTS system that performs a normalization of wordplays rather than attempting to pronounce them straightforwardly according to their exact spellings. While such a TTS system produced more

Copyright 2014 by Natthawut Kertkeidkachorn, Supadaech Chanjaradwichai, Proadpran Punyabukkana, and Atiwong Suchato
28th Pacific Asia Conference on Language, Information and Computation pages 414–421

naturally-sounded speech utterances (Hirankan et al. 2014), the normalization process might degrade a TTS's performance on a domain involving more formal texts where wordplays are scarce. For a TTS system aiming for expressive speech utterances, with multiple handlers, each of which is responsible for handling a different expression, the system could produce better results as well as easier handler development. A TTS system that allows interoperation of components, such as Grapheme-To-Phoneme (G2P) or signal generation components, deploying different speech and text processing algorithms without re-compiling of the system is obviously desirable. Still, many TTS systems were not designed with such abilities.

In this paper, we therefore reported our recent attempt on designing and implementing a modularized TTS framework, namely ChulaTTS. The goal of the design of ChulaTTS was to allow a TTS system to incorporate multiple speech and text processing components and allow them to work together with minimal development efforts. Components with similar classes of functionality must interoperate despite the differences in their underlying algorithms or the differences in phonetic units primitive to each of the components. With that goal in mind, ChulaTTS is suitable for conducting speech synthesis experiments to observe the performance of newly-developed algorithms in a complete TTS system conveniently. Furthermore, ChulaTTS can be easily configured into a TTS system expected to handle special phenomena appearing in the domain that it is deployed.

The rest of the paper was organized as follows. Related works were reviewed and discussed in the Section 2. In Section 3, we reported the design of our modularized TTS framework, and described the details of an implementation of a TTS system based on the modularized framework in Section 4. Section 5 discussed real applications of ChulaTTS systems. Finally, we concluded the paper in the last section.

2 Literature Review

In order to allow a TTS system to incorporate extensible handlers, several TTS frameworks (Orhan et al. 2008; Malcangi and Grew 2009; Wua et al. 2009) had been introduced. Orhan (2008) presented the Turkish syllable-based concatenation TTS framework. In their work, linguistic rules on Turkish were designed for handling exceptional cases such as special characters or symbols in Turkish. Although their framework installed the handler to provide a choice for applications, its choice was very limited to normal text and some special characters. Consequently, when a language had been evolved, the framework could not be extensible to support that evolution. Malcangi (2009) therefore introduced the rule-based TTS framework for mixed-languages, which allowed linguists to define multiple rule-based handlers to cope with various kinds of text. Even though their framework could be extensible to support the evolution of languages by simply adding a new rule-based handler, the new handler might cause ambiguity in the selecting handler process, in which an input text might follow conditions of many handlers, especially when handlers were become more and more. For this reason, the framework was not flexible to directly install new handlers, since we might have to modify the existing handlers in order to avoid ambiguity among handlers. Later, Wua (2009) proposed a unified framework for a multilingual TTS system. Their framework was designed to support extensible handlers of a TTS system by using a speech synthesis markup language (SSML) specification in which the mark-up tag provided a name of a particular method which should process the value in the mark-up. Unlike Malcangi's framework, the SSML markup clearly identified a handler which had to operate in order to avoid unclear situation in the handler selection. By following the SSML specification the framework could properly allow extensible handlers without causing any trouble to existing handlers. Still, some parts of their framework did not allow extensible handlers such as their waveform production.

Considering many related works above, we found that the aim of TTS frameworks was to enable ability to install extensible handlers. Still, there were many limitations to incorporate and extend new handlers in such frameworks. Our recent attempt therefore was to design and implement the modularized TTS framework, which supported extensible handlers in any stages of TTS systems without troubling other existing handlers.

3 The Modularized Framework

Typically, TTS systems have a common architecture similar to the illustration shown in Figure 1. This architecture consisted of two parts: the text analysis part and the speech synthesis part. An input text is fed into a text analysis block to generate its sequence of phonetic representation comprising phoneme and prosody annotation and then the sequence is passed to the speech synthesis block in order to generate real signal associated with the sequence of phonetic representation. Algorithms implemented in each processing step usually vary from system to system. According to the architecture in Figure 1, there are components whose underlying algorithms could be varied or allowing options in applying different algorithms to different portions of the text input. These components involve how the input texts are processed in order to obtain both underlying phonetic sequences and their suprasegmental information such as prosodic information governing how each phonetic unit in the sequence should be uttered and how speech signal should be generated. Typically, algorithms used for each component in a TTS system are predetermined and developed as an entire system.

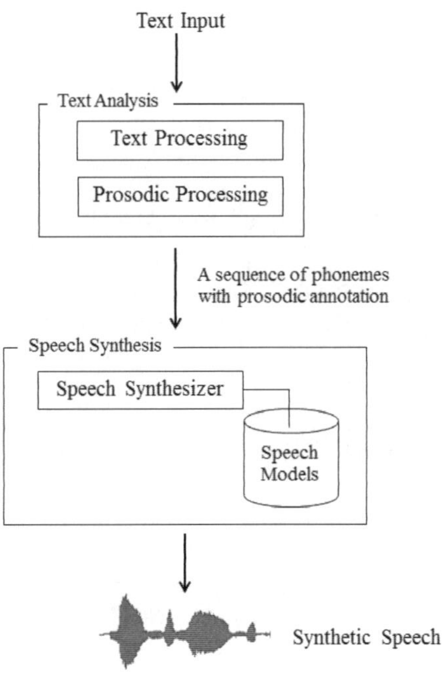

Figure 1. An architecture of a typical TTS system

Contrary to the architecture of a typical TTS system, we proposed a modularized TTS framework called ChulaTTS in which implementation of different text and speech signal processing are considered modules that can interoperate with one another. The aim of the framework is to provide flexibility in experimenting with different algorithms that could affect only a part of the whole system as well as to enable interoperability of multiple modules responsible for similar tasks of the TTS process. The latter makes a TTS system extensible when a new module is introduced and incorporated among existing ones in the system. Programming-wise, neither shuffling modules of a system nor adding additional modules to the system requires re-compiling of the source code of any modules already deployed in the system. To build a functional TTS system with the ChulaTTS framework, ones implement the TTS system by exposing components involving in the TTS process in the forms of modules consistent with the framework's specification and configuring the framework to utilize them.

Before elaborating on the classes of module in ChulaTTS, let's consider the typical architecture in Figure 1. Based on the architecture, if multiple processors were to simply process the input texts in parallel, there would be situations when ambiguities arisen from the different processors produced inconsistent results in some parts of the input. Some decision making components could be introduced to handle such inconsistent parts. In the ChulaTTS framework, we adopted multiple (or single) segment taggers that independently tagged each segment of the input with different algorithms as well as different sets of tags. A tag selector was deployed to determine how all the tagged segments be processed later on in the TTS process. With the mentioned segment tagging part, the overall architecture of the ChulaTTS framework is shown in Figure 2. The architecture is divided into three stages: 1) Segment tagging, 2) Text analyzer, and 3) Speech synthesizer. The details of the tasks to be performed in each of the three stages, classes of modules and their contractual (programming) interfaces, software implementation requirements, and how the resulting TTS system is configured are elaborated in Section 3.1 to Section 3.5.

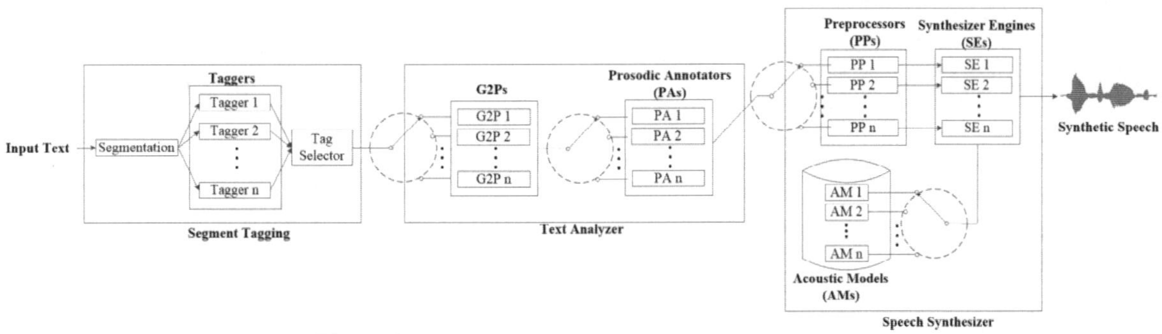

Figure 2. The Modularized Text-To-Speech Framework

3.1 Segment Tagging Stage

Segment Tagging in ChulaTTS is dedicated to segmenting an input text into smaller pieces of text, each of which with a proposed tag. Segment tags identify which modules process the tagged segments in later stages of the TTS process. Three steps are performed in this segment tagging stage: 1) Segmentation step, 2) Segment tagging step, and 3) Tag selector step.

Segmentation: The segmentation step inserts word or phrase boundaries into the input text string. Portions of texts located between adjacent boundaries are called “segments”, each of which will then be marked with a tag in the next step. In an implementation of the ChulaTTS framework, one segmentation module can be selected via the corresponding configuration. All modules performing as a segmentation module must provide at least one segmentation function that receives the input text in the form of a string of characters and returns its corresponding sequence of segments.

Segment tagging: The segment tagging assigns an appropriate tag to each segment. Modules performing this step can have their own set of tags and conduct the tagging independently from other modules. An implementation without alternative algorithms for steps of the TTS process needs only a single tagger. Figure 3 depicts a conceptual example of the need for the later steps of the TTS process to heterogeneously handle different parts of input text motivates the inclusion of segment tagging. In the figure, segment tags can be used to process and synthesize speech with different personalities or expressions.

	Professor McGonagall gasped. "Lily and James... I can't believe it... I didn't want to believe it... Oh, Albus..."	
Segment	Professor McGonagall gasped.	"Lily and James... I can't believe it... I didn't want to believe it... Oh, Albus..."
G2P Tag	Narrator	Conversation
Prosodic Tag	Normal	Emotion
Synthesizer Tag	Narrator	Emotion
Model Tag	Narrator	Female

	Dumbledore reached out and patted her on the shoulder. "I know... I know..." he said heavily.		
Segment	Dumbledore reached out and patted her on the shoulder.	"I know... I know..."	he said heavily.
G2P Tag	Narrator	Conversation	Narrator
Prosodic Tag	Normal	Normal	Normal
Synthesizer Tag	Narrator	Normal	Narrator
Model Tag	Narrator	Old Male	Narrator

Figure 3. Conceptual examples of tags for the later stages[1]

All modules performing as a segment tagging module must provide at least one tagging function that receives a sequence of segments and provides a single tag for each of the input segment.

Tag selector: In cases of conflicting segment tags due to multiple segment tagging modules, this step decides on which of the conflicting tags should be kept and used as parameters in selecting modules in the later steps of the TTS process. A single tag selector module capable of handling all tags produced by all active segment tagging modules is required in a ChulaTTS implementation. The tag selector modules provide at least one function returning a sequence of tagged segments.

3.2 Text Analyzer Stage

The text analyzer stage is for producing a sequence of phonetic units with prosodic parameters. It consists of two steps: 1) G2P conversion, and 2) Prosodic annotation. The first step produces

[1] The example text from Harry Potter and the Sorcerer's Stone

phonetic units from the input sequence of segments. One or more G2P conversion module can be deployed in a single ChulaTTS implementation providing that they cover all possible tags in the implementation. Each segment tag must be associated with a G2P module while each G2P module can handle multiple segment tags. Segments are fed to G2P modules according to the implementation configuration. For a segment, the G2P module responsible for the segment produces a sequence of corresponding phonetic units, each of which can be declared by the module itself. Different phonetic units must use unique symbols. Phonetic units with similar symbols are considered the same type of units regardless of which modules handle the G2P conversion.

Prosodic annotator modules are deployed in the prosodic annotation step. Different modules are activated based on the segment tag according to the configuration of the implementation. Similarly to the phoneme units, prosodic markers produced by the modules must be supported in the Speech Synthesizer stage of the implementation.

3.3 Speech Synthesizer Stage

The role of this stage is to generate synthetic speech signals based on the phonetic representation and the prosodic parameters provided by the Text Analyzer stage. This stage involves three configurable parts: 1) Pre-processing, 2) Synthesizer Engine, and 3) Acoustic Models. A pair of Synthesizer Engine module and its corresponding Pre-processing module, responsible for adjusting the format of the phonetic representation and prosodic parameters so that they are consistent with the input interface of the Synthesizer Engine, must be configured to handle all segments tagged with a segment tag, while Acoustic Models can also be selected by the configuration, providing that their phonetic units and file formats are supported by the associated Synthesizer Engine module. All modules performing as a Synthesizer Engine module must provide at least one signal synthesis function that generates a waveform file that will be treated as the final synthesized speech by the ChulaTTS framework.

3.4 Module Development

An option that we chose in order to maximize interoperability of modules and, at the same time, avoid steep learning curves for researchers who wish to evaluate algorithms in ChulaTTS is to adhere to the .NET development framework on Windows platform for module development. The framework was written in C# and all classes of modules (described in Section 3.1 to Section 3.3) to be integrated to an implementation of the framework are expected to be in the form of .NET Dynamic-Link Library (DLL) exposing functions whose signatures are consistent with the contractual interface defined by the framework according to their module classes. New modules can be developed using any .NET targeted programming languages while existing executables can be wrapped inside .NET

3.5 Implementation Configurations

Configuring the ChulaTTS implementation is performed by modifying three key configuration files: Segment Tagging configuration which determines how the framework should execute steps in the three stages listed in Section 3. Configuration files are all in plain text format read by the framework at run-time. In each configuration file, the name of the DLL file together with the name of the function residing in that DLL file associated with its corresponding step in the TTS process must be specified in a pre-defined format. The framework checks for the consistency of these functions with their corresponding contractual interface defined by the framework.

The next section reports an example case of the implementation of the ChulaTTS framework. The case showed a sample scenario in which a newly developed algorithm was evaluated via subjective tests in a complete TTS system using the ChulaTTS framework.

4 Implementation

4.1 System Implementation

We put ChulaTTS framework to the test by implementing a complete TTS system called ChulaTTS. ChulaTTS inherently employ .NET framework and C#, where all handlers are implemented and compiled as DLL.

Segment Tagging Implementation: To identify segments in ChulaTTS, we consider all white spaces in input text and break them into segments. We use single Tagger handler that was implemented by using regular expression to determine the tags for each segment. The four available tags are (1) Thai, (2) English, (3) Number, and (4) Symbol. Table 1 shows example of segments and their corresponding tags. Because ChulaTTS only uses one tagger handler, naturally, there is no confusing tag. Thus, tag selector was not executed in this case.

Segment	Results of Tagging
สวัสดี[2]	<1>สวัสดี</1>
Hello	<2>Hello</2>
2014	<3>2014</3>
น่ารักจุงเบยยยย[3]55[4]	<1>น่ารักจุงเบยยยย</1> <3>55</3>
ขอบคุณ[5]:)	<1>ขอบคุณ</1> <4>:)</4>

Table 1. The example of segments and tags

Text Analyzer Implementation: Four G2P handlers; G2P1, G2P2, G2P3, and G2P4, corresponding to the four tags were developed for ChulaTTS. The G2P1 handler was responsible for parsing Thai text into phonemes. It employed TLEX (Haruechaiyasak and Kongyoung 2009) to extract Thai words from each segment. Then, the phonemes were generated by looking a Thai dictionary. In addition, because Thai is a tonal language, tone marker was also supplied for each and every word. G2P2 handler employed an English dictionary to produce phonemes. Moreover, with the situation of out-of-vocabulary, the resulting phonemes would be the spelling pronunciation. G2P3 handler was to convert numbers into the right pronunciation using Thai rule-based technique for numbers. Finally, G2P4 handler was used for converting symbols to pronunciation using dictionary-based method. In this implementation, prosodic annotator, namely tone parameter, were embedded in all four GSP handlers.

[2] 'Hello' in Thai
[3] 'So cute' in Thai
[4] Pronounced as 'haha' in Thai
[5] 'Thank you' in Thai

Speech Synthesizer Implementation: In Speech Synthesizer, an acoustical model was implemented. One male speaker spoke 600 utterance sentences randomly selected from the T-Sync speech corpus (Hansakunbuntheung et al. 2003), in order to construct a speech corpus for training the acoustical model. The recording process was conducted in the sound proof chamber with the sampling rate of 16,000 Hz. After the recording process, a transcriber manually added short pause marks into the transcriptions and force align phoneme and recorded audio. In the ChulaTTS-based system, HTS (PukiWiki 2013) was selected as the synthesizer engine handler, and use it to train our acoustical model. Furthermore, we also developed a preprocessor handler to transform the results from text analyzer block into the format compatible to that of the HTS engine.

4.2 System Testing

To learn about the performance of ChulaTTS, a subjective test was conducted, using five-scaled Mean Opinion Score (MOS) approach (Orhan and Görmez 2008; Zeki et al. 2010). Six participants were recruited in order to perceive a set of stimuli synthesized from randomly selected text from BEST corpus (Nectec 2009), in which each stimulus was randomly presented and played from the same handset. Each participant was asked to listen to 30 stimuli and score each utterance on a five-scale basis, excellent (5), good (4), fair (3), poor (2) and bad (1). The overall MOS was 3.64.

4.3 System Improvement

Since ChulaTTS framework provides the ability to add extensible handlers to cope with new tasks, we implemented a new handler to evaluate how users may opt to prefer the new system. We used the implementation of ChulaTTS system described above as baseline. Curious how social media played its role in TTS, we extended our baseline by implementing a Tagger handler which could tag wordplay following the algorithm reported by (Hirankan et al. 2014).We defined tag of wordplay as "5". An example of Tagging results between baseline system and the extended system were shown in Table 2. We also implemented a new G2P handler, G2P5, which corresponded to tag "5" to handle wordplay as the technique introduced by (Hirankan et al. 2014).

Systems	Results of Tagging
Baseline	<1>น่ารักจุงเบยยยย</1> <3>55</3>
Extended	<5>น่ารักจุงเบยยยย</5> <3>55</3>

Table 2. The example of tagging chunks of "น่ารักจุงเบยยยย55"

To understand the performances of both the baseline and the extended systems, another subjective test was conducted. Eight users were recruited to give the opinion on the stimuli produced from both systems. All stimuli were synthesized from randomly selected text on Facebook. Each user was asked to compare ten stimuli produced from the two systems. We use ten-scaled MOS and asked the users to rate the quality of the sound. Score of five signifies indifference between the two systems. Scores less than five means the user prefers sounds generated from the baseline system, the lower the number, the more confidence the user have with the baseline system. On the contrary, Scores greater than five shows that the users prefer the extended system, the higher the score, the more confidence. The score of comparing performances was at 7.19, which indicated higher preference of the extended system.

5 Applications

ChulaTTS system has been implemented in two applications: Chula DAISY (Punyabukkana et al. 2012), an audio book generation system; and Chula FungPloen (Limpanadusadee et al. 2012), a universal listening device. Since ChulaTTS employs .NET framework, applying it to applications built on .NET framework was a simple task, regardless of the difference in domains.

Since Chula DAISY aimed to handle Thai book contents, the domain of the application was generally Thai well-written text. Consequently, a standard Thai G2P handler and a standard Thai synthesizer engine handler were sufficient Punyabukkana et al. 2012). However, For Chula Fungploen, the domain of input text became more sophisticated because the task in Chula Fungploen largely dealt with text appeared on the internet. For this reason, only the standard Thai G2P, and the Thai synthesizer engine handler were insufficient. Without ChulaTTS framework, one would have to implement another TTS system to fit each task. However, with the nature of ChulaTTS framework, it allowed flexibility to enhance new handlers to support this task without the redesign of the system. In Chula Fungploen, there were needs to cope with non-Thai text, especially numbers, symbols and English texts. The number tagger handler, the symbol tagger handler, the English tagger handler, the number G2P handler, the symbol G2P handler, the English G2P handler and the English synthesizer engine handler were simply installed into the existing TTS system. By adding those new handlers, Chula TTS was able to support the task of Chula Fungploen as reported in (Limpanadusadee et al. 2012). This scenario clearly demonstrated the extensibility of Chula TTS framework, which implies time savings as well as extra efforts.

6 Conclusion

Conventional TTS development cycle can be improved with the proposed ChulaTTS framework, which provides extensibility and flexibility for implementing a TTS system in a modular fashion. ChulaTTS framework comprises three parts, Segment Tagging, Text Analyzer, and Speech Synthesizer. This paper describes not only the framework itself, but also the sample of a real-world implementation scenario that proved to be effective.

References

Jirasak Chirathivat, Jakkrapong. Nakdej, Proadpran Punyabukkana and Atiwong Suchato. 2007. Internet explorer smart toolbar for the blind, In Proceedings of i-CREATe 2007: 195-200.

Proadpran Punyabukkana, Surapol Vorapatratorn, Nat Lertwongkhanakool, Pawanrat Hirankan, Natthawut Kertkeidkachorn and Atiwong Suchato. 2012. ChulaDAISY: an automated DAISY audio book generation, In Proceedings of i-CREATe 2012.

Nipon Chinathimatmongkhon, Atiwong Suchato and Proadpran Punyabukkana. 2008. Implementing Thai text-to-speech synthesis for hand-held devices, In Proceedings of ECTI-CON 2008.

Pawanrat Hirankan, Atiwong Suchato and Proadpran Punyabukkana. 2014 Detection of wordplay generated by reproduction of letters in social media texts, In Proceedings of JCSSE 2014.

Zeynep Orhan and Zeliha Görmez, The framework of the Turkish syllable-based concatenative text-to-speech system with exceptional case handling. 2008. In WSEAS Transactions on Computers, 7(10):1525-1534.

Mario Malcangi and Philip Grew. 20009 "A framework for mixed-language text-to-speech synthesis, In Proceedings of CIMMACS 2009: 151-154.

Zhiyong Wua, Guangqi Caoa, Helen Menga and Lianhong Caib. 2009. A unified framework for multilingual text-to-speech synthesis with SSML specification as interface, In Tsinghua Science and Technology, 14(4): 623-630.

PukiWiki. HMM-based Speech Synthesis System (HTS) http://hts.sp.nitech.ac.jp/ 2013.

Choochart Haruechaiyasak and Sarawoot Kongyoung, 2009. TLex: Thai Lexeme Analyzer Based on the Conditional Random Fields, In Proceedings of 8th International Symposium on Natural Language Processing 2009.

Chatchawarn Hansakunbuntheung, Virongrong Tesprasit and Virach Sornlertlamvanich. 2003. Thai tagged speech corpus for speech synthesis, In processing of O-COCOSDA 2003: 97-104.

Mustafa Zeki, Othman O. Khalifa and A. W. Naji. 2010. Development of an Arabic text-to-speech system, In Proceedings of ICCCE 2010: 1-5

Nectec. 2009. BEST 2009 : Thai Word Segmentation Software Contest", http://thailang.nectec.or.th/best/

Worasa Limpanadusadee, Varayut Lerdkanlayanawat, Surada Lerkpatomsak, Proadpran Punyabukkana and Atiwong Suchato, 2012. Chula-FungPloen: assistive software for listening to online contents, In Proceedings of i-CREATe 2012.

Modeling Structural Topic Transitions for Automatic Lyrics Generation

Kento Watanabe[1], **Yuichiroh Matsubayashi**[1], **Kentaro Inui**[1], and **Masataka Goto**[2]

[1]Graduate School of Information Sciences Tohoku University, JAPAN
[2]National Institute of Advanced Industrial Science and Technology (AIST), JAPAN
[1]{kento.w, y-matsu, inui}@ecei.tohoku.ac.jp
[2]m.goto@aist.go.jp

Abstract

By adopting recent advances in music creation technologies, such as digital audio workstations and singing voice synthesizers, people can now create songs in their personal computers. Computers can also assist in creating lyrics or generating them automatically, although this aspect has been less thoroughly researched and is limited to rhyme and meter. This study focuses on the structural relations in Japanese lyrics. We present novel generation models that capture the topic transitions between units peculiar to the lyrics, such as verse/chorus and line. These transitions are modeled by a Hidden Markov Model (HMM) for representing topics and topic transitions.

To verify that our models generate context-suitable lyrics, we evaluate the models using a log probability of lyrics generation and fill-in-the-blanks-type test. The results show that the language model is far more effective than HMM-based models, but the HMM-based approach successfully captures the inter-verse/chorus and inter-line relations. In the result of experimental evaluation, our approach captures the inter-verse/chorus and inter-line relations.

1 Introduction

Recent music creation technologies such as digital audio workstations and singing voice synthesizers (Kenmochi and Oshita, 2007) have become immensely popular among enthusiasts of automatically created or vocally synthesized music. These technologies assist individuals with their musical creativity and thereby have promoted automatic song generation. To date, many individual and group musical amateurs have created songs and commercial activities. To satisfy the demand for composer-supportive automatic composition systems and services, various systems, including Orpheus (Fukayama et al., 2012), have been developed. Furthermore, as musical composition becomes easier, there is a growing need for automatic lyrics generation.

However, lyrics generation has yet to be thoroughly explored in the natural language processing field. While several works have tackled lyrics generation based on lyric-specific characteristics, current methods are limited to local contexts, such as single sentences, which cannot capture the overall structure of the generated lyrics (Barbieri et al., 2012; Ramakrishnan A et al., 2009; Reddy and Knight, 2011; Wu et al., 2013; Greene et al., 2010).

The contribution of our study is twofold: (1) To more comprehensively understand lyrics generation, we examine the characteristics or rules by which people identify Japanese lyrics writing and survey some previous methods. (2) Based on the survey, we construct three generation models as an initial step toward our aim. We focus on two types of information that are essential for lyrics creation: a language model for lyrics and topic transitions for passages.

Experiments revealed that the language model is far more effective than models capturing topic transitions. However, by capturing the topic transitions, we achieve consistency among the topics.

Copyright 2014 by Kento Watanabe, Yuichiroh Matsubayashi, Kentaro Inui, and Masataka Goto
28th Pacific Asia Conference on Language, Information and Computation pages 422–431

2 Related Work

Previous studies have attempted to reproduce characteristics specific to song lyrics, such as syntax, rhythm, rhyme, and the relation between melody and text. Barbieri et al. (2012) adopted a Markov process to create lyrics satisfying the structural constraints of rhyme and meter. They also ensured syntactical correctness by a part-of-speech template and computed the semantic relatedness between a target concept and the generated verse/chorus by a Wikipedia link-based measure. Our model extends Barbieri et al.'s approach to capture not only the semantic relatedness but also the verse-chorus transitions.

Ramakrishnan A et al. (2009) generated melodic lyrics in a phonetic language (in their case, Tamil). First, they labeled an input melody with appropriate syllable categories using conditional random fields and then filled the syllable pattern with words. Reddy and Knight (2011) developed a language-independent model based on a Markov process that finds the rhyme schemes in poetry and the model stanza dependency within a poem. However, rhyme transition in their model is used to generate a stanza; the overall flow of the poem is not captured.

Some researchers have generated lyrics using statistical machine translation. Wu et al. (2013) applied stochastic transduction grammar induction algorithms to generate a fluent rhyming response to the hip hop challenges allowing various patterns of meter. Using a finite-state transducer, Greene et al. (2010) assigned a syllable-stress pattern to every word in each line, subject to metrical constraints. Moreover, they generated English love poetry and translated Italian poetry into English following a user-defined rhythmic scheme.

Although these works capture lyric-specific characteristics to some extent, the structural relations are limited to lines or local word contexts. To the best of our knowledge, no existing method accounts for the semantic relations among large structures, such as verses and choruses.

Inter-text structural relations are frequently considered in text summarization and conversation modeling. The summarization technique of Barzilay and Lee (2004) captures topic transitions in the text span by a hidden Markov model (HMM), referred to as a *content model*. Using HMM and a large amount of tweet data, Ritter et al. (2010) and Higashinaka et al. (2011) modeled the transition of speech acts in an unsupervised manner.

3 Survey on Lyric Writing Techniques

To create a comprehensive model for lyrics generation, we first investigated the characteristics or rules by which people proceed with lyrics writing in general. We surveyed five textbooks on Japanese lyrics writing (Endo, 2005; Takada, 2007; Aku, 2009; Ueda, 2010; Taguchi, 2012) and identified the common features as follows.

3.1 Consistency of Entire Lyrics

The lyrics preferably follow a consistent theme. Authors usually desire to convey a message in their lyrics, and they reflect their theme in their lyric topics. Frequently, the theme is indirectly expressed through a concrete story composed of who, what, when, where, and why information. Each lyric should be consistent in writing style, such as the point of view (first or third person), gender, and date.

3.2 Lyrics and Melody

Lyrics and melody are mutually dependent and influence each other during the creation process. Which comes first depends on the situation. If developing the melody first, the writer must concentrate on achieving a suitable melody through rhythm, phonetic length, and lyrical structure. They should also match the word intonation and accents to the melody to ensure that their lyrics can be both sung and heard.

Most songs contain some common melodies. However, listeners may experience dissonance when simultaneously hearing upbeat and downbeat melodies. Thus, the writer needs to share the tone and atmosphere of his/her lyrics in the same melody.

3.3 Musical Structure of the Lyrics

The structural units of lyrics are verse, bridge, and chorus. Each unit repeatedly appears and shares the same musical phrases. Consequently, rhythm and meter are common to shared among the same type of units. In addition, same-type units are often created as semantically similar topics, such as scene and emotion, or contrastive topics, such as different seasons and feelings.

In general, each unit plays a typical role in the storyline. For example, verses often describe a concrete scene or complementary topic that emphasizes a message in the following chorus. Furthermore, the lines of a single verse/chorus may relay a suitable order of topic transitions. In the example as follows, the first and second lines collectively describe a concrete scene. This description is followed by the protagonist's reaction to the scene in the third and fourth lines.

Example of relations between lines

(On the way home, it began to snow.)
帰り道 降り始めた雪 ———————— Scene
(It is touching your shoulder and melting.)
あなたの肩に 触れて 溶けてゆく—— Scene
(Time flies. Today went by fast, too.)
今日もまた あっという間だね—— Sentiment
(The weekend with you is almost over.)
あなたとの週末 終わってしまうの – Sentiment

Excerpt from "Everlasting" by Mayo Okamoto

3.4 Balance of Contents

Emotion and scene are often combined in a verse/chorus. For instance, if a verse/chorus expresses emotions alone, such as "I love you" and "I want you", the lyrics are insufficiently balanced to convey the theme. To ensure that their lyrics are easily understood and arouse empathy in listeners, writers should adopt lead-in scenes such as "The road has been long" and "Reflections in a pool". Similarly, maintaining the balance between *subjective* and *objective*, *concrete* and *abstract*, *positive* and *negative*, and *universal* and *novel* will prevent egocentricity in the lyrics.

3.5 Figure of Speech

Lyrical content is frequently emphasized by figures of speech such as rhyme, metaphor, double meaning, double negatives, interrogatives, onomatopoeia, inversion, repetition, and rewording. The grammatical patterns of the lyrical sentence construction markedly differ from those in the general text.

4 Lyrics Generation Task

As noted in the previous section, songwriters incorporate various features, such as theme, structure, and the lyrics-melody relation, into their lyrics, some of which are decided in advance. These predetermined features provide natural inputs to a lyrics generation task.

Figure 1: Example of a mora composed of musical notes. Japanese writers usually compose lyrics in such a manner that they can be easily sung by the singer. For example, the melody sequence "A-A-B" corresponds to "sa-ku-ra" (meaning "cherry blossom").

Some previously defined lyrics generation tasks account of the structural features and lyric-melody relation by inputting rhyme and meter. In our approach, the melody is replaced by the *mora* length of each phrase. In phonology, a mora specifies the period of a sound unit. For example, in Japanese, the mora length of the phrase *"帰り道, (ka-e-ri-mi-chi)" (On the way home)* is 5, whereas that of *"降り始めた雪, (fu-ri-ha-ji-me-ta-yu-ki)" (it began to snow)* is 8. In a Japanese song, a mora often corresponds to a musical note as shown in Figure 1.

In summary, if the input is provided as $M^{line} = [M_0^{phrase}, M_1^{phrase}] = [5, 8]$, the task generates lyrics such as *"帰り道 降り始めた雪" (On the way home, it began to snow)*.

Now, consider that the input includes partially composed lyrics. In this scenario, the system partially supports lyrical writer. For example, if the writer has completed a verse but is unsure of the chorus, the system can generate a chorus that is consistent with the completed verse. The experiments reported in Section 6 confirm that our models correctly capture the suitable topic transitions.

Our lyrics generation task is formally depicted in Figure 2. The task accepts the inputs as follows: (1) previously written parts of the target lyrics including an unwritten line and (2) sequences of mora length $M^{line} = [M_0^{phrase}, M_1^{phrase}, ...]$, each corresponding to the mora length of a line to be generated. The

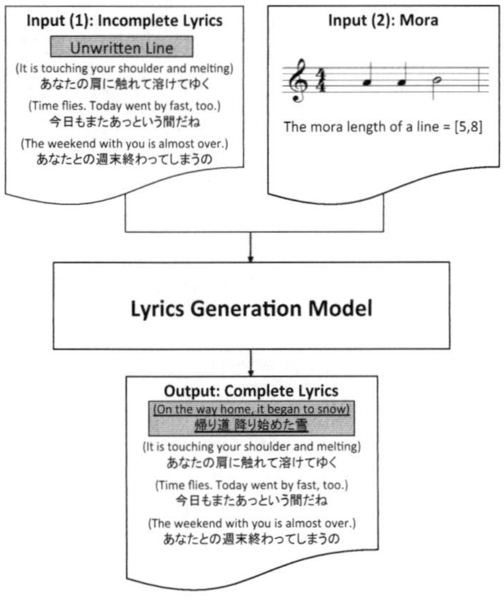

Figure 2: Lyrics Generation Task.

output of our lyrics generation task is a line that satisfies the restriction of the input mora.

5 Proposed Method

This section introduces the three generation models that capture some of the features introduced in previous sections.

In the models, (1) we utilize an n-gram language model assuming that lyrics are characterized by fluent, easily sung word orderings. In our models, the n-gram model is conditioned by the appropriate mora length.

Also, (2) we use a state-transition model assuming that the line and verse/chorus are generated from a consistent, context-dependent word set. Recall from Subsection 3.3 that each line and verse/chorus are often created as semantically related topics, and that topic transitions between lines and verses/choruses follow an appropriate order. We expand the content model (Barzilay and Lee, 2004) which originally estimates the topic transitions in documents using a hidden Markov model by assuming that each sentence has its hidden state representing its topic, to capture the inter-verse/chorus and inter-line relations.

Using these two components, we create three models illustrated in Figure 3: Although the model (a) employs a tri-gram model, the models (b) and (c) employ a bi-gram model to avoid data-sparsity due to the additional conditional parameter, the hidden state. We explain the details of each model in the next section.

5.1 Lyrics Generation Model

The inputs of the lyrics generation model are demonstrated in Figure 4. The positions of the verse/chorus, line, phrase, and word that should be generated are defined by i, j, k, and l, respectively. The mora lengths of the line that should be generated is assigned into the variable $M_{i,j}^{line}$. In Figure 4, the second line in the second verse/chorus should be generated, and the mora length of this line is given as input. We assigned **Line**$_i$ and **Verse** to the previously written lines and verses/choruses of the target lyrics including an unwritten line. These inputs were applied to the three generation models as shown in Figure 3.

(a) The first proposed model is the tri-gram language model $P(w_l|w_{l-1}, w_{l-2}, m_l)$ with mora restrictions (Equation 1), which assumes that a word is generated from its predecessors to satisfy the condition of fluent, easily sung lyrics. Note that m_l in this model is the mora length of the word and not the phrase; therefore, the model output is a sequence of the mora word lengths. For example, if the input is a mora length of the phrase $M_{i,j,k}^{phrase} = 7$, the model should first generate a sequence of the mora word lengths $[m_0, m_1, m_2, m_3] = [3, 1, 2, 1]$, followed by a word sequence $[w_0, w_1, w_2, w_3] =$ [“あなた (a-na-ta)”, “の (no)”, “肩 (ka-ta)”, “に (ni)” $(your\ shoulder)$]. Therefore, we specified that a sequence of words with the mora length **m** is generated with some probability $P(\mathbf{m}|M_{i,j,k}^{phrase})$. Thus, we have $\mathbf{m} = [m_0, ..., m_l, ...]$.

$$P(Line_{i,j}|M_{i,j}^{line}) = \prod_{k=0}^{|M_{i,j}^{line}|} P(\mathbf{m}|M_{i,j,k}^{phrase}) \prod_{l=0}^{|\mathbf{m}|} P(w_l|w_{l-1}, w_{l-2}, m_l) \quad (1)$$

(b), (c) The second and third proposed models is implemented for generating a consistent lyric. In generating a consistent lyric as described in Subsection 3.3, the topic transitions between lines and verses/choruses must be estimated. In this

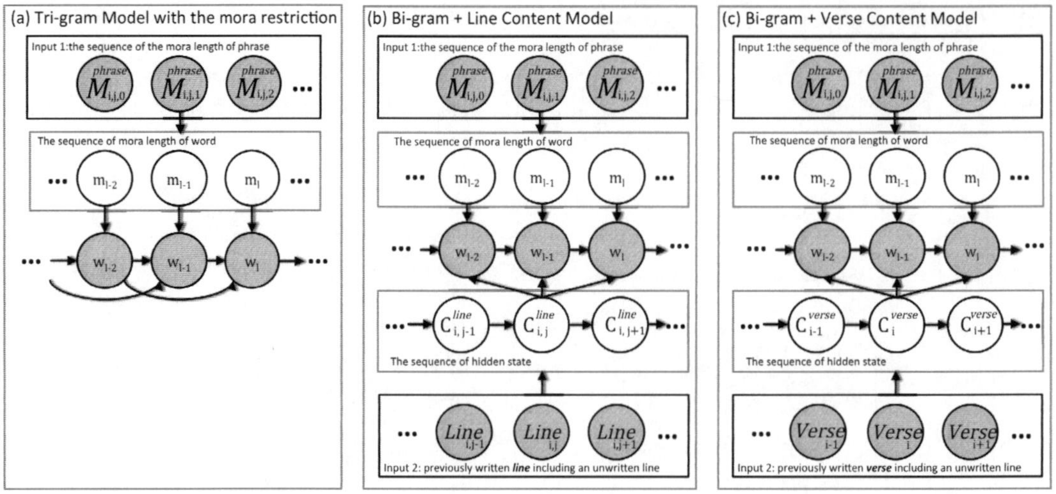

Figure 3: Lyrics generation model: (a) The n-gram language model generates a word given the line's mora length $M^{line}_{i,j} = [M^{phrase}_{i,j,0}, M^{phrase}_{i,j,1}, ...]$. The sequence of the mora lengths of the word $[m_0, m_1, ...]$ is generated from $M^{phrase}_{i,j,k}$. (b), (c) Based on the content model (Barzilay and Lee, 2004), the generation model captures the relations between lines and verses/choruses. The transition sequence of the hidden state $[C^{line}_{i,0}, ..., C^{line}_{i,j}, ...]$ or $[C^{verse}_{0}, ..., C^{verse}_{i}, ...]$ is estimated by specifying the context (already composed lines or already composed verses/choruses) and applying the Viterbi algorithm. Finally, the words are generated from each hidden state $C^{line}_{i,j}$ and C^{verse}_{i}, the mora length of the word m_l, and the previous word w_{l-1}.

study, the hidden state transitions between lines and verses/choruses in Japanese lyrics were learned by a content model (Barzilay and Lee, 2004). The features of the content model were bag-of-word-unigram containing the top 5,000 words in the training set, determined in a preliminary experiment. The hyper parameter in the content model training was set to 0.01. Next, we obtained the sequence of hidden states $\mathbf{C}^{line}_{i} = [C^{line}_{i,0}, ..., C^{line}_{i,j}, ...]$ and $\mathbf{C}^{verse} = [C^{verse}_{0}, ..., C^{verse}_{i}, ...]$; these are the topic transitions obtained by the Viterbi algorithm given the preferably written parts $\mathbf{Line}_i = [Line_{i,0}, ..., Line_{i,j}, ...]$ and $\mathbf{Verse} = [Verse_0, ..., Verse_i, ...]$ including an unwritten line. Finally, we specify the word generation probabilities $P(w_l|w_{l-1}, C^{verse}_{i}, m_l)$ and $P(w_l|w_{l-1}, C^{line}_{i,j}, m_l)$ to generate a word belonging to the hidden state C^{verse}_{i} and $C^{line}_{i,j}$ (Equations 2 and 3). In this study, a fluent, easily sung lyric has been generated from the previous word w_{l-1}, the mora length m_l of the word, and the hidden state C^{verse}_{i} or $C^{line}_{i,j}$. In contrast, the algorithms of Barzilay and Lee (2004), Ritter et al. (2010), and Higashinaka et al. (2011) use only the hidden state.

$$P(Line_{i,j}|C^{line}_{i,j}, M^{line}_{i,j}) = \prod_{k=0}^{|M^{line}_{i,j}|} P(\mathbf{m}|M^{phrase}_{i,j,k}) \prod_{l=0}^{|\mathbf{m}|} P(w_l|w_{l-1}, C^{line}_{i,j}, m_l) \quad (2)$$

$$P(Line_{i,j}|C^{verse}_{i}, M^{line}_{i,j}) = \prod_{k=0}^{|M^{line}_{i,j}|} P(\mathbf{m}|M^{phrase}_{i,j,k}) \prod_{l=0}^{|\mathbf{m}|} P(w_l|w_{l-1}, C^{verse}_{i}, m_l) \quad (3)$$

Although it appears that this method is restricted to the hidden state estimation for only one unwritten line, it is possible to extend this method for multipul unwritten lines by repeatedly applying the Viterbi algorithm after generating one line.

5.2 Model Estimation

Our generation model is estimated by maximum likelihood (Equations 4 and 5). The $count(*, w)$ returns the number of the occurrences of the word

The position of verse/chorus that should be generated: $i = 1$
The position of line that should be generated: $j = 1$
The position of phrase that should be generated: k
The position of word that should be generated: l
The mora length of line: $M_{1,1}^{line} = [M_{1,1,0}^{phrase}, M_{1,1,1}^{phrase}, M_{1,1,2}^{phrase}] = [7, 3, 5]$
The previously written lines including an unwritten line: **Line**$_1 = [Line_{1,0}, Line_{1,1}, Line_{1,2}, Line_{1,3}]$
$Line_{1,0}$ ="帰り道 降り始めた雪" (On the way home, it began to snow.)
$Line_{1,1}$ =Unwritten Line
$Line_{1,2}$ ="今日もまた あっという間だね" (Time flies. Today went by fast, too.)
$Line_{1,3}$ ="あなたとの週末 終わってしまうの" (The weekend with you is almost over.)
The previously written verses/choruses including an unwritten line: **Verse** $= [Verse_0, Verse_1, Verse_2]$
$Verse_0$ ="何も言わず そっと 肩を抱き寄せて, ..." (Please hug me softly, ...)
$Verse_1$ = **Line**$_1 = [Line_{1,0}, Line_{1,1}, Line_{1,2}, Line_{1,3}]$
$Verse_2$ ="5 分だけ, あと 10 分だけ, ..." (Just 5 minutes, just 10minutes, ...)

Excerpt from "Everlasting" by Mayo Okamoto

Figure 4: Example of the model input.

w (or a hidden state), and the W_{m_l} is the word set with the mora length m_l. To avoid the word sparseness problem, these probabilities are smoothed by Good-Turing discounting using SRILM (a toolkit for building and applying statistical language models) (Stolcke, 2002).

$$P_{ML}(w_l|w_{l-1}, w_{l-2}, m_l) = \frac{count(w_{l-2}, w_{l-1}, w_l)}{\sum_{w \in W_{m_l}} count(w_{l-2}, w_{l-1}, w)} \quad (4)$$

$$P_{ML}(w_l|C, w_{l-1}, m_l) = \frac{count(C, w_{l-1}, w_l)}{\sum_{w \in W_{m_l}} count(C, w_{l-1}, w)} \quad (5)$$

The generated sequence of the mora word lengths is simply estimated by maximum likelihood (Equation 6).

$$P(\mathbf{m}|M_{i,j,k}^{phrase}) = \frac{count(\mathbf{m})}{\sum_{\mathbf{m} \in M_{i,j,k}^{phrase}} count(\mathbf{m})} \quad (6)$$

6 Experiments

6.1 Evaluation Measure

The evaluation measure is another open problem in lyrics generation. Barbieri et al. (2012) and Wu et al. (2013) evaluated the generated lyrics by human annotation. However, because manual evaluations are expensive and time consuming, they are limited to a small number of test instances. Furthermore, the evaluation measures of an artistic quality strongly depend on the individuals; therefore, to achieve an evaluation measure of an adequate quality, copious annotation is required.

We evaluated our generation model by two different measures: log probability of the original line and fill-in-the-blanks-type testing. In the log-probability measure, we assumed that among all possible lines, the original line is generated with the highest probability. To calculate the log probability, the topic transition $[C_0, C_1, ...]$ was predetermined by providing the lines or verses/choruses and applying the Viterbi algorithm. The log probability, $log(P(Line))$ of generating each line was then calculated as the logarithm of Equations 1, 2, and 3.

The fill-in-the-blanks-type test evaluates whether the correct line, selected from two candidates, is inserted into a given hidden line. One of the candidates is a correct answer randomly selected from the original song. The other candidate is an incorrect answer with the same mora length as the line from the original song but is randomly selected from another song. The candidate scoring the highest

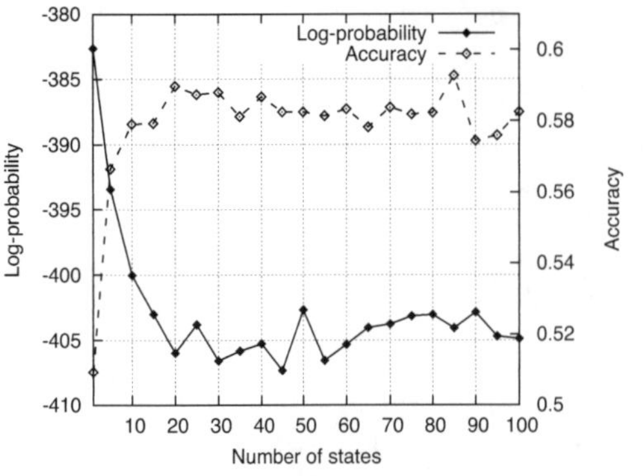

Figure 5: Log probability of whole lyrics generation (black circles) and the accuracy of a fill-in-the-blanks-type test evaluated on the development set, with the content model restricted to verses and choruses (gray diamonds).

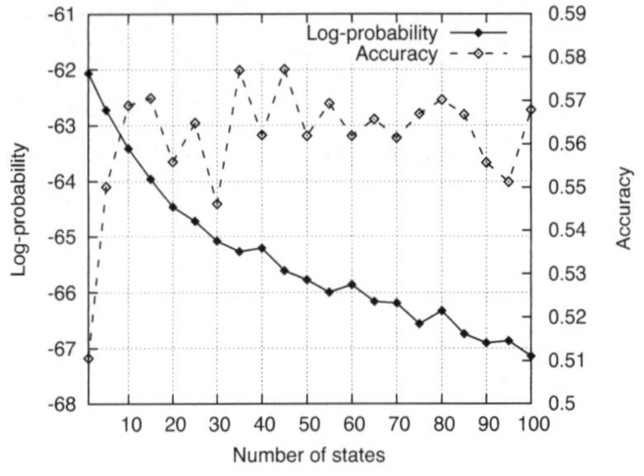

Figure 6: Log probability of verse/chorus generation (black circles) and the accuracy of a fill-in-the-blanks-type test evaluated on the development set, with the content model operated in the line mode (gray diamonds).

log probability is predicted as the correct answer. This measure checks whether the proposed model correctly captures topic transitions in each line or verse/chorus.

6.2 Dataset

The experiments were performed on Japanese popular music lyrics covering various genres, such as *Enka* [1] and *1970s pop*. Because our algorithm has limited capacity for calculating the mora length, foreign language songs were excluded in advance. The dataset contains 24,000 songs, 136,703 verses/choruses, 411,583 lines, and 61,118 words. We allocated 20,000 songs to the training set and reserved 2,000 songs each for development and testing.

6.3 Number of Hidden States

Prior to evaluation, the numbers of the hidden states in the two content models needed to be strategically selected to optimize the accuracy of the fill-in-the-blanks-type test on the development set. Figures 5 and 6 show the average log probabilities and accuracies of the fill-in-the-blanks-type test when applying this test to each content model. Note that the log probability shown in Figure 5 is $log(P(Lyrics))$, calculated as the sum of the logarithm of Equation 2 over the entire lyrics. Similarly, the log probability shown in Figure 6 is the $log(P(verse/chorus))$, calculated as the sum of the logarithm of Equation 3 in an entire verse or chorus.

In each case, the log probability decreases as the number of states increases because the bi-gram counts face data sparsity. However, the accuracy of the fill-in-the-blanks-type test monotonically increases and almost saturates at 10 states. Consequently, we specified 10 states in each content model.

6.4 Evaluation

Table 1 lists the average log probability, $log(P(Line))$, of line generation in each model, evaluated on the development and test data. Although the content models partially include a bi-gram language model, the tri-gram model yielded the best performance. This result indicates the superior effectiveness of line generation by the language model than by the contents models.

Nonetheless, the content models capture a suitable order of lines. The average accuracy of the fill-in-the-blanks-type test is tabulated in Table 2. In this task, the counter-candidate line is randomly selected from another song and thus almost grammatical in construct. The main clue for accurate selection is a semantic relation between the topics. In this situation, the accuracy of the tri-gram model is equiva-

[1] *Enka* is a genre of a Japanese traditional ballad.

Model	Dev	Test
Tri-gram Model	-28.28	-29.02
Content model for Line	-38.36	-38.89
Content model for Verse	-33.03	-33.84

Table 1: Log probability of line generation.

Model	Dev	Test
Tri-gram Model	50.80%	47.97%
Content model for Line	56.89%	56.14%
Content model for Verse	57.91%	56.69%

Table 2: Accuracy of the fill-in-the-blanks-type test.

lent to the chance rate. On the other hand, both content models significantly improve the performance of lyrics generation.

We also qualitatively analyzed the obtained hidden states and their transitions in the content models. Table 3 illustrates the state transition table in the verse/chorus mode with 10 states. To clarify the discussion, we manually assigned easy-to-understand labels to the states and representative words to each hidden state (see Table 4).

Our content model in the verse/chorus mode concurrently learns two types of hidden states (Table 3). The first type corresponds to specific music genres; the second corresponds to specific tendencies of word appearances. The model successfully captures music genres with particular stylistic and vocabulary characteristics, such as *1970s pop*, *Enka*, and *modern songs*. Once a current state shifts into one of these states, it rarely shifts to another state. This indicates that the model generates suitable words that consistently fit the target genre.

Secondly, some states successfully capture the topics where the transition probabilities between them have some tendency; state transition probabilities are not random but instead biased against semantically related contents. As seen in Table 3, this type embraces five states, namely, *Scene*, *Memory*, *Sorrow & Love*, *Dream & Future*, and *Life & World*. In these topics, (1) the self-transition is the most likely one. (2) The transition probability from *START* to *Scene* is relatively high, and the transition probability from *Scene* to *END* is relatively low compared with the ones from others to *END*. (3)

Interpretation	Representative words
Scene	town (*machi*), room (*heya*), city (*tokai*), sunset (*yuuhi*), run (*hashiru*),
Memory	remember (*wasurenai*), memory (*omoide*), met (*deatta*), nostalgic (*natsukasii*),
Sorrow & Love	love (*koi*), express (*iu*), cry (*naku*), affections, sentiment, mind (*kimochi*),
Life & World	live (*ikiru*), future (*mirai*), bravery (*yuuki*), destination (*yukusaki*), reality (*genjitsu*),
Dream & Future	dream (*yume*), future (*mirai*), new (*atarashii*), world (*world*), one (*hitotsu*),
1970s pop	lie (*uso*), romance (*romansu*), rose (*bara*) lullaby (*rarabai*), kiss (*kuchiduke*),
Enka *traditional ballads*	human life (*jinsei*), harbor (*minato*), sake (*sake*), old home (*kokyou*),
Modern Song	paradise (*paradaisu*), cute (*kawaii*), drama (*dorama*), dance (*danse*),

Table 4: Representative Words in each Semantic Class.

The transition probabilities from *Memory* are almost even except for the self-transition and the transition to specific music genres (*1970s pop*, *Enka*, and *Modern song*). Therefore, *Memory* tends to play the role of an intermediate content in a lyrics. (4) The transition probability from *Sorrow & Love*, *Life & World*, and *Dream & Future* to *END* is relatively high. Thus the last verse/chorus in whole lyrics tends to become these three states. (5) *Life & World* and *Dream & Future* are strongly correlated. This indicates that the words representing hopes and bright futures tend to appear side by side.

7 Conclusion and Future Works

In this study, we presented content models for automatic lyrics generation that capture topic transitions in individual lines or verses/choruses. The content models are less capable of computing original line probabilities than the tri-gram model but better capture the inter-verse/chorus and inter-line relations. Currently, each model is separately constructed but the result suggested that combining these models would improve topic consistency. A multi-modal approach combining musical and lyrics information is also worthy of consideration. Some previous researchers have generated lyrics from musical information (Mihalcea and Strapparava, 2012; Hannah Davis, 2014). Musical information other than mora (such as rhyme, rhythm, melody, and chord) will be incorporated in the next version of our structured model.

		State after transition								
		END	Scene	Memory	Sorrow & Love	Life & World	Dream & Future	1970s pop	Enka	Modern Song
State before transition	START		**26.6%**	11.3%	2.4%	9.0%	**11.5%**	10.3%	**17.4%**	10.3%
	Scene	9.0%	**37.7%**	**12.9%**	3.7%	7.6%	9.7%	**10.8%**	1.2%	5.0%
	Memory	9.1%	**11.6%**	**38.1%**	**12.6%**	10.2%	11.0%	5.0%	0.3%	1.1%
	Sorrow & Love	**25.1%**	5.1%	12.5%	**32.1%**	6.1%	**13.2%**	4.6%	0.1%	0.5%
	Life & World	**14.0%**	5.1%	6.3%	4.5%	**49.2%**	**13.5%**	1.3%	0.2%	5.0%
	Dream & Future	**18.5%**	5.5%	6.9%	7.0%	**11.9%**	**45.5%**	2.5%	0.5%	0.7%
	1970s pop	**16.1%**	**10.5%**	3.6%	4.9%	2.0%	4.5%	**52.0%**	1.3%	2.9%
	Enka	**28.8%**	0.9%	0.3%	0.0%	0.4%	0.8%	**1.4%**	**65.5%**	1.3%
	Modern	**12.7%**	6.5%	1.2%	0.6%	**8.1%**	1.2%	3.9%	1.4%	**62.1%**

Table 3: Transition table between the hidden states of a verse/chorus. The vertical axis represents the hidden states before transition. The horizontal axis represents the hidden states after transition. Each cell contains the transition probabilities between the hidden states. The top three transition probabilities are shown in bold. To simplify the table, we omit hidden states that are erroneously reached from the start state.

References

Yu Aku. 2009. *Sakushi Nyumon (Introduction to Writing the Lyrics)*. Iwanami Shoten.

Gabriele Barbieri, Franois Pachet, Pierre Roy, and Mirko Degli Esposti. 2012. Markov constraints for generating lyrics with style. In Luc De Raedt, Christian Bessire, Didier Dubois, Patrick Doherty, Paolo Frasconi, Fredrik Heintz, and Peter J. F. Lucas, editors, *ECAI*, volume 242 of *Frontiers in Artificial Intelligence and Applications*, pages 115–120. IOS Press.

Regina Barzilay and Lillian Lee. 2004. Catching the drift: Probabilistic content models, with applications to generation and summarization. In *Proceedings of HLT-NAACL*, pages 113–120.

Kozo Endo. 2005. *Sakushi Hon (Bool for Writing the Lyrics)*. Shinko-Music Entertainment.

Satoru Fukayama, Daisuke Saito, and Shigeki Sagayama. 2012. Assistance for novice users on creating songs for japanese lyrics. In *in Proceedings of the International Computer Music Association 2012*.

Erica Greene, Tugba Bodrumlu, and Kevin Knight. 2010. Automatic analysis of rhythmic poetry with applications to generation and translation. In *Proceedings of the 2010 Conference on Empirical Methods in Natural Language Processing*, EMNLP '10, pages 524–533, Stroudsburg, PA, USA. Association for Computational Linguistics.

Saif M. Mohammand Hannah Davis. 2014. Generating music from literature. pages 1–10. Workshop on Computational Linguistics for Literature.

Ryuichiro Higashinaka, Noriaki Kawamae, Kugatsu Sadamitsu, Yasuhiro Minami, Toyomi Meguro, Kohji Dohsaka, and Hirohito Inagaki. 2011. Building a conversational model from two-tweets. In *Workshop on Automatic Speech Recognition and Understanding*, pages 330–335.

Hideki Kenmochi and Hayato Oshita. 2007. Vocaloid — commercial singing synthesizer based on sample concatenation. In *in Proceedings of Interspeech 2007*, pages 4009–4010.

Rada Mihalcea and Carlo Strapparava. 2012. Lyrics, music, and emotions. In *Proceedings of the 2012 Joint Conference on Empirical Methods in Natural Language Processing and Computational Natural Language Learning*, EMNLP-CoNLL '12, pages 590–599, Stroudsburg, PA, USA. Association for Computational Linguistics.

Ananth Ramakrishnan A, Sankar Kuppan, and Sobha Lalitha Devi. 2009. Automatic generation of tamil lyrics for melodies. In *Proceedings of the Workshop on Computational Approaches to Linguistic Creativity*, CALC '09, pages 40–46, Stroudsburg, PA, USA. Association for Computational Linguistics.

Sravana Reddy and Kevin Knight. 2011. Unsupervised discovery of rhyme schemes. In *ACL (Short Papers)'11*, pages 77–82. Association for Computational Linguistics.

Alan Ritter, Colin Cherry, and Bill Dolan. 2010. Unsupervised modeling of twitter conversations. In *Human Language Technologies: The 2010 Annual Conference of the North American Chapter of the Association for Computational Linguistics*, HLT '10, pages 172–180, Stroudsburg, PA, USA. Association for Computational Linguistics.

Andreas Stolcke. 2002. Srilm - an extensible language modeling toolkit. pages 901–904.

Shun Taguchi. 2012. *Omoidori Ni Sakushi Ga Dekiru Hon (Book tha You Can Write the Lyrics)*. Rittor-Music.

Motoki Takada. 2007. *Sakushi No Kotsu Ga Wakaru (You Understand the How to Write the Lyrics).* Chuo Art Publishing.

Tatsuji Ueda. 2010. *Yoku Wakaru Sakushi No Kyoukasho (The Textbook of the Lyrics).* Ymaha Music Media.

Dekai Wu, Karteek Addanki, Markus Saers, and Meriem Beloucif. 2013. Learning to freestyle: Hip hop challenge-response induction via transduction rule segmentation. In *Proceedings of the 2013 Conference on Empirical Methods in Natural Language Processing*, pages 102–112, Seattle, Washington, USA, October. Association for Computational Linguistics.

Influence of Information Structure on Word Order Change and Topic Marker *WA* in Japanese

Satoshi Imamura[1] **Yohei Sato**[2] **Masatoshi Koizumi**[2]

[1] Japanese Studies, University of Oxford
41 Wellington Square
Oxford, OX1 2JF
United Kingdom

[2] Department of Linguistics
Tohoku University
27-1 Kawauchi, Aoba-ku, Sendai
Japan

Abstract

The purpose of this study is to investigate the influence of given-new ordering on word order change and topic marker *WA*, using a self-paced reading task. The results demonstrated that $O_{ACC}S_{NOM}V$ is sensitive to given-new information, but $S_{NOM}O_{ACC}V$, $S_{TOP}O_{ACC}V$, and $O_{TOP}S_{NOM}V$ are not. This fact can be explained by the Markedness Principle for Discourse Rule Violation (Kuno, 1987: 212): both $S_{NOM}O_{ACC}V$ and $S_{TOP}O_{ACC}V$ are not penalized even when they violate given-new ordering because they are unmarked options, $O_{ACC}S_{NOM}V$ is penalized when it violates given-new ordering because it is a marked option, and $O_{TOP}S_{NOM}V$ is penalized even when given-new ordering is preserved because it requires more contrastive contexts (McGloin, 1990:113). Another point is that topic marker *WA* is not responsive to the given-new distinction. This suggests that the usage of *WA* does not rely on anaphoricity in general. Note that there are two usages of *WA*: thematic topic needs to be previously mentioned while contrastive topic does not require anaphoricity. Taken together, we can conclude that the essence of *WA* is not thematic topic but contrastive topic.

1. Introduction

In Japanese, a relatively free word order language, various word orders share the basic meaning of a sentence. Hence, OSV can convey the same meaning as SOV does. Moreover, Japanese is equipped with topic marker *WA*, which can be attached to both subject and object. Therefore, there are choices between topic marker and case marker: S_{NOM} vs S_{TOP} and O_{ACC} vs. O_{TOP}. As a result, when they use transitive sentences, Japanese need to select an option regarding word order and marker: SOV or OSV, and case marker or topic marker. What factor, then, determines the choice among them? One factor is givenness. Since Prague School, it has been shown that word order changes follow given-new ordering i.e. given information comes first and new information comes later. In addition, research on Japanese has demonstrated that nominative case marker *GA* usually marks new information and topic marker *WA* prefers given information. Therefore, based on a self-paced reading task, we will study the relationship among word order, topic and case marker, and given-new ordering.

In section 2, we will overview previous studies about scrambling, *GA*/*WA* distinction, and topicalization. Section 3 provides our experiment and discusses the results of the sentence

Copyright 2014 by Satoshi Imamura, Yohei Sato, and Masatoshi Koizumi
28th Pacific Asia Conference on Language, Information and Computation pages 432–441

comprehension task. Section 4 is devoted to the conclusion.

2. Previous Studies

2.1. Scrambling

Theoretically, it has been assumed in general that $O_{ACC}S_{NOM}V$ is derived by moving the direct object to the sentence initial position in Japanese (Miyagawa, 2001, 2003, 2010; Saito, 1985, 2009; Saito and Hoji 1983). Thus, this operation is called 'scrambling'. What we should emphasize here is that scrambling does not change grammatical relations between constituents. For example, both (1a) and (1b) convey the same proposition *John pushed Ken.*

(1) a. John-ga　Ken-o　oshi-ta.
　　John-NOM　Ken-ACC　push-PAST
　　'John pushed Ken.'
　b. Ken-o　John-ga　oshi-ta.
　　Ken-ACC　John-NOM　push-PAST
　　'John pushed Ken'

In processing, numerous studies have reported that scrambling incurs a larger processing cost compared to canonical word order. Rösler et al. (1998) and Weyerts et al. (2002) provide examples from German, Frazier and Flores d' Arcais (1989) from Dutch, and Sekerina (2003) from Russian. In sentence comprehension, in Japanese, it has been reported that the reaction times for scrambled sentences were longer than those for canonically ordered ones (Chujo, 1983; Koizumi and Tamaoka, 2010; Miyamoto and Takahashi, 2002; Tamaoka et al. 2005). All these studies support the claim that scrambling is more difficult to process than canonical sentences.

However, there are cases where native speakers select scrambled word orders. When do they prefer non-canonical word orders to canonical word order? One factor is given-new ordering, which means given information is mentioned early and new information later. In order to meet this requirement, OSV may be chosen. To put it more concretely, Kuno (1978:54) argues that native Japanese speakers use OSV when the direct object is given information (Kuno 1978: 54). In Finnish, Kaiser and Trueswell (2004) conducted a self-paced reading task and reported that OgivenVSnew is read faster than OnewVSgiven. This fact supports the proposal that scrambling is chosen in order to preserve given-new ordering.

In sum, given-new ordering seems to be a crucial factor for the usage of scrambling.

2.2. *GA*/ *WA* distinction

Traditionally, it has long been noted that nominative case *GA* correlates with new information and topic marker *WA* is related to given information in general (see e.g. Kuno, 1972, 1973; Mikami, 1963; Ono, 1973). In particular, Kuno (1972: 277) illustrates the usage of *GA* and *WA* by citing (2). He points out that only the *WA*-marked subject *sono-gōtō* "the robber" is acceptable in (2b) because it has already been mentioned in (2a). If it were attached with *GA*, it would be unacceptable because *GA* marks new information although *sono-gōtō* "the robber" is given information.

(2) a . gōtō-ga　boku-no-ie-ni
　　robber-NOM　I-GEN-house-into
　　hait-ta
　　enter-PAST
　　'A robber broke into my house.'
　b. sono-gōtō　*ga/wa
　　the-robber　NOM/TOP
　　boku-ni-pisutoru-o　tsukitsukete
　　I-to-gun-ACC　point
　　kane-o　da-se-to　it-ta.
　　money-ACC　give-IMP-QT　say-PAST
　　'The robber, pointing a pistol at me,
　　said, "give me money". '

Yet, Kuno (1972:270) points out that *WA* is not necessarily anaphoric (i.e. previously mentioned) when it has a contrastive meaning. In other words, contrastive *WA* can be both given information and new information. In fact, Miyagawa (1987: 186) observed that thematic *WA* cannot follow a *wh*-phrase as in (3a) but contrastive *WA* can be attached to a *wh*-phrase as in (3b). Note that *wh*-phrases generally require new information and are not anaphoric because they have no specific referents. Thus, *wh*-phrases cannot be accompanied with thematic *WA*, which usually requires an anaphoric antecedent. However, there is no such constraint for contrastive *WA*.

(3) a. *dare-wa ki-ta-no?
who-TOP come-PAST-Q
'* Speaking of whom, did he/she/they come?'
b. dare-wa ki-te, dare-wa
who-TOP come-GER who-TOP
ko-nakat-tano?
come-do not-PAST-Q
'Who came, and who didin't?'

Summing up, generally speaking, nominative case marker *GA* is used for new information and topic marker *WA* is appropriate for given information. However, contrastive *WA* is an exception to this observation.

2.3. Topicalization

In Japanese, topicalized constituents are accompanied with topic marker *WA*. Kuno (1973: 357) points out that when *WA* follows a non-subject noun phrase, it tends to be interpreted as contrastive. Moreover, McGloin (1990) maintains that topicalized objects are apt to have only a contrastive meaning unless they have not been mentioned in the preceding discourse. For instance, (4b) needs more specific contexts than (4a) does. In other words, native Japanese speakers feel that the topicalized object, *sono-ringo* "the apple", in (4b) should be interpreted as contrastive while there is no such constraint for the accusative object in (4a).

(4) a. John-wa sono-ringo-o tabeta
John-TOP the-apple-ACC ate
'John ate the apple.'
b. Sono-ringo-wa John-ga tabeta
the-apple-TOP John-NOM ate
'The apple, John ate.'

To summarize, $O_{TOP}SV$ in Japanese is likely to have a contrastive meaning.

3. Experiment

3.1. Prediction

This experiment is intended to examine the interaction between information structure and syntactic structure. It has been shown that preposed objects and topic marker *WA* prefer given information. Therefore, given-new ordering is expected to mitigate the processing cost of $S_{TOP}OV$, $O_{ACC}SV$, and $O_{TOP}SV$. On the other hand, it is predicted to have a negative influence on the processing of $S_{NOM}OV$ because nominative subject *GA* is incompatible with given information.

3.2. Method

3.2.1. Participants

Sixty-four Japanese graduate and undergraduate students (28 males and 36 females) at Tohoku University participated in the experiment. Their average age was 21.5 years.

3.2.2. Materials

Ninety-six sets of four two-sentence passages such as (5) were used for the sentence correctness decision task (see the appendix for two-sentence passages used for S_{NOM}/given O_{ACC}/new V condition). Each passage consisted of a context sentence and a target sentence. The former were all existential sentences, and the latter were all transitive sentences. Subjects in the context sentences (e.g., *Sato* in (5a)) were reused in the immediately following target sentences. The phrases were given information in the target sentences, with the result that either the subject or the object in the target sentences was given information. On the other hand, NPs that were not used in context sentences (e.g., *Suzuki* in (5b)) were new information in the target sentences.

(5) a. Kōen-ni Sato-ga iru.
park-LOC Sato-NOM be.PRS
'There is Sato at the park.'
b. Sato-ga Suzuki-o ot-ta.
Sato-NOM Suzuki-ACC chase-PAST
'Sato chased Suzuki.'

This experiment was a 2×2×2 factorial design, with the informational factor (given-new/new-given), syntactic factor (SOV/OSV), and morphological factor (case marker/topic marker). Hence, there were eight experimental conditions, as shown in (6).

(6) Experimental Conditions:
a. S_{NOM}/given O_{ACC}/new V
b. S_{NOM}/new O_{ACC}/given V
c. S_{TOP}/given O_{ACC}/new V
d. S_{TOP}/new O_{ACC}/given V
e. O_{ACC}/given S_{NOM}/new V
f. O_{ACC}/new S_{NOM}/given V
g. O_{TOP}/given S_{NOM}/new V
h. O_{TOP}/new S_{NOM}/given V

The sets of two-sentence passages such as (5) were shuffled in Latin Square Design and divided into eight lists of 120 two-sentence passages, which included 48 correct, 48 incorrect, and 24 filler two-sentence passages. An example of a correct two-sentence passage is shown in (5). (7a) illustrates an incorrect two-sentence passage and (7c) demonstrates a filler one. Note that (7a) is semantically unacceptable because *noboru* 'climb' is incompatible with *Mizuno*. This is why it is an incorrect two-sentence passage. On the other hand, the filler example shown in (7b) is acceptable. However, filler examples differ from correct examples in their sentence structure. For example, (7b) includes a copula sentence and a negative sentence.

(7) a. Incorrect Two-Sentence Passage
Umibe-ni Mizuno-ga iru.
beach-LOC Mizuno-NOM be.PRS
Mizuno-wa Takano-ga nobot-ta.
Mizuno-TOP Takano-NOM climb-PAST
'There is Mizuno at the beach. * Takano climbed Mizuno.'
b. Filler Two-Sentence Passage
pro Hokkaido-ni shucchō-da.
(I) Hokkaido-LOC business.trip-COP
pro samui-basho-niwa iki-taku-nai
(I) cold-place-to go-want-NEG
'I will go on a business trip to Hokkaido. I would not like to go to a cold place.'

Participants were asked to complete two lists. Only the reaction times and error rates for correct sentences were analyzed. The lexical material of the sentences was controlled for length and frequency. In addition, no lexical words were used in more than one two-sentence passage in order to prevent interference from familiarity.

3.2.3. Procedure

This experiment was conducted by using E-Prime (Psychology Software Tools, Inc.) with an external mouse for participants' use in responding. Stimuli were presented to the participants in random order in the center of the computer screen. After a fixation mark (+) appeared in the center of the screen for 2000ms, an existential sentence appeared on the screen as context until participants pushed the left button. Next, a transitive sentence was presented as a target sentence and participants were asked to indicate whether it was semantically acceptable or unacceptable by pressing the left mouse button for "yes" or the right mouse button for "no. Participants were instructed to respond as quickly and accurately as possible. The reaction times were registered from the point of transitive sentence presentation on the screen to the point when participants clicked the mouse to answer. Error rates for target sentences were also registered.

Seven two-sentence practice passages were given to participants prior to the commencement of the actual trial.

3.2.4. Data Analysis

Analyses of variances (ANOVAs) were conducted on reaction times and error rates for target sentences (48 correct sentences), using subject (*F1*) and item (*F2*) variables. There were three factors for our analysis: an informational factor (given-new /new-given), a syntactic factor (SOV/OSV), and a morphological factor (case marker *O* or *GA*/topic marker *WA*). Only correctly judged target sentences were used in the analyses of reaction times. First, extremes among sentence correctness decision times (less than 500 ms and longer than 5000 ms) were recorded as missing values. Second, reaction times outside of 2.5 standard deviations at both the high and low ranges were replaced by boundaries indicated by 2.5 standard deviations from the individual means of participants in each category.

3.3. Results

3.3.1. Question Accuracy

The error rates for correctness decision of target sentences are shown in table 1.

Table 1 Error rates (%) for target sentences

Sentence type	M	SD
S_{NOM}/given O_{ACC}/new	5.86%	10.25%
S_{NOM}/new O_{ACC}/given	5.99%	12.01%
S_{TOP}/given O_{ACC}/new	5.60%	11.70%
S_{TOP}/new O_{ACC}/given	6.64%	13.04%
O_{ACC}/given S_{NOM}/new	8.85%	13.68%
O_{ACC}/new S_{NOM}/given	13.67%	18.63%
O_{TOP}/given S_{NOM}/new	23.57%	28.19%
O_{TOP}/new S_{NOM}/given	25.39%	27.11%

There was a significant main effect of both the syntactic factor ($F_1(1, 63) = 54.79, p < .001$; $F_2(1, 11) = 100.22, p < .001$) and the morphological factor ($F_1(1, 63) = 33.27$ $p <. 001$; $F_2(1, 11) = 54.40, p < .001$). The informational factor was marginally significant ($F_1(1, 63) = 7.62, p < .01$; $F_2(1, 11) = 3.64, p = .08$). In addition, there was a significant interaction between the syntactic factor and the morphological factor ($F_1(1, 63) = 38.42, p < .001$; $F_2(1, 22) = 50.48, p < .001$). Planned comparison showed that the effect of the morphological factor to be significant in OSV ($F_1(1, 126) = 71.13, p < .001$; $F_2(1, 22) = 104.81, p < .001$) but not in SOV ($F_1(1, 126) = 0.01$, *n.s.*; $F_2(1, 22) = 0.02$, *n.s.*). The main effect of syntactic factor was significant both in case marked condition ($F_1(1, 126) = 7.76, p < .01$; $F_2(1, 22) = 12.57, p < .005$) and topic marked condition ($F_1(1, 126) = 91.96, p < .001$; $F_2(1, 22) = 150.40, p < .001$).

3.3.2. Reaction Times

The reaction times for correctness decisions are demonstrated in table 2.

Table 2 Reaction times for target sentences

Sentence Type	M	SD
S_{NOM}/given O_{ACC}/new	1688	515
S_{NOM}/new O_{ACC}/given	1822	565
S_{TOP}/given O_{ACC}/new	1705	515
S_{TOP}/new O_{ACC}/given	1748	558
O_{ACC}/given S_{NOM}/new	1899	633
O_{ACC}/new S_{NOM}/given	2141	865
O_{TOP}/given S_{NOM}/new	2155	917
O_{TOP}/new S_{NOM}/given	2193	807

The results showed a significant effect for the syntactic factor ($F_1(1, 63) = 80.59, p < .001$; $F_2(1, 11) = 153.04, p < .001$). This indicates that OSV was processed slower than SOV. The main effects of the informational factor ($F_1(1, 63) = 22.11, p < .001$; $F_2(1, 11) = 2.52$, *n.s.*) and the morphological factor ($F_1(1, 63) = 4.69, p < .05$; $F_2 = 1.96$, *n.s.*) were observed for participant analysis but not for item analysis. There was a significant interaction between the informational factor and the morphological factor ($F_1(1, 63) = 9.72, p < .01$; $F_2(1, 11) = 14.34, p < .01$). This interaction was marginally significant in SOV ($F_1(1, 63) = 3.94, p = .051$; $F_2(1, 11) = 3.28, p = .09$) and was significant in OSV ($F_1(1, 63) = 4.39, p < .05$; $F_2(1, 11) = 10.90, p < .01$). Furthermore, the main effect of the informational factor was significant in $O_{ACC}S_{NOM}V$ ($F_1(1, 126) = 16.34, p < .001$; $F_2(1, 22) = 6.68, p < .05$) though it was not in $O_{TOP}S_{NOM}V$ ($F_1(1, 126) = 0.40$, *n.s.*; $F_2(1, 22) = 0.45$, *n.s.*). Moreover, the syntactic factor and the morphological factor were found to interact ($F_1(1, 63)) = 11.71, p < .005$; $F_2(1, 11) = 23.81, p < .001$). Planned comparison revealed the effect of the morphological factor to be significant in OSV ($F_1(1, 126) = 12.29, p < .001$; $F_2(1, 22) = 11.58, p < .005$) but not in SOV ($F_1(1, 126) = 0.47$, *n.s.*; $F_2(1, 22) = 0.78$, *n.s.*). The effect of the syntactic factor was significant both in the case marked condition ($F_1(1, 126) = 30.63, p < .001$; $F_2(1, 22) = 58.50, p < .001$) and in the topic marked condition ($F_1(1, 126) = 87.57, p < .001$; $F_2(1, 22) = 169.42, p < .001$).

3.4. Discussion

3.4.1. SOV and OSV

The results of reaction times showed the interaction between three factors: informational, syntactic, and morphological. First, there was an interaction between the informational factor and the morphological factor. This was caused by the fact that given-new ordering facilitated the processing cost of O_{ACC} S_{NOM} V, but not the cost of S_{NOM} O_{ACC} V, S_{TOP} O_{ACC} V, and O_{TOP} S_{NOM} V. In other words, only scrambled sentences were affected by give-new ordering. This is compatible with Kaiser and Trueswell (2004) in that scrambled sentences were processed easier in an appropriate context (given-new condition) than in an inappropriate context (new-given condition). Moreover, this supports previous studies stating that $O_{ACC}S_{NOM}V$ is selected when the direct object is older than the subject (Kuno, 1978). However, even in given-new condition, the processing cost of the scrambled word order was higher than that of the canonical counterpart. Namely, information structure could not override the cost related to scrambling. This indicates that some parts of the processing cost derive from syntactic complexity and they are robust enough for pragmatic factors to be unable to erase.

Second, an interaction between the syntactic factor and the morphological factor was observed. The cause of this interaction was due to a significant difference between $O_{ACC}S_{NOM}V$ and $O_{TOP}S_{NOM}V$ but not between $S_{NOM}O_{ACC}V$ and $S_{TOP}O_{ACC}V$. To put it more concretely, $O_{TOP}S_{NOM}V$ was processed slower than $O_{ACC}S_{NOM}V$. However, in the new-given condition, there was no difference in reaction time between $O_{ACC}S_{NOM}V$ and $O_{TOP}S_{NOM}V$, although, in the given-new condition, there was. This means that information structure mitigated the processing cost of scrambling while it was useless for processing topicalization. This data indicates that given-new ordering is not an important factor for the usage of topicalization in Japanese. Then, what are the appropriate contexts for topicalization? It has been said that topicalized objects tend to have a contrastive meaning (Kuno, 1973; McGloin, 1990). Taking this fact into consideration, a discourse context to make topicalized object contrastive is needed.

To summarize the results, focusing on the information structure, the given-new distinction has influence on $O_{ACC}S_{NOM}V$, but not on SOV and $O_{TOP}S_{NOM}V$. Why did such differences occur? One explanation is the markedness principle for discourse-rule violations (Kuno, 1987:212), which is formally defined in (8).

(8) Markedness Principle for Discourse-Rule Violations: Sentences that involve marked (or intentional) violations of discourse principles are unacceptable. On the other hand, sentences that involve unmarked (or unintentional) violations of discourse principles go unpenalized and are acceptable.

This coincides with previous studies that claim the marked pattern to occur only in the licensing context, whereas the unmarked pattern is contextually unrestricted (Aissen, 1992; Birner and Ward 2009; Kuno, 1995). Specifically, Birner and Ward (2009) point out that canonical word order can be used in a wide range of contexts while non-canonical word orders can be permitted only in a specific context. Applying this rule to Japanese, canonical word order SOV is an unmarked option and thus can violate discourse principles. On the other hand, OSV is a marked option and hence cannot violate discourse principles.

Let us explain the results of our experiment based on (8). First, $S_{NOM}O_{ACC}V$ and $S_{TOP}O_{ACC}V$ are not sensitive to one of the discourse principles, given-new ordering. Even when they violate given-new ordering, they are not penalized because both options are unmarked. In the new-given condition, the reaction times were not slowed down and the error rates did not become higher than in the given-new condition. In other words, SOV was not penalized even in an inappropriate context. Although given-new ordering is preferred for SOV, it is not required and violating it is not penalized. Second, $O_{ACC}S_{NOM}V$ is sensitive to given-new ordering. Scrambling is a marked option and it is penalized when it violates given-new ordering. Indeed, $O_{ACC}A_{NOM}V$ was processed slower in the new-given condition than in the given-new condition. In other words, $O_{ACC}S_{NOM}V$ was penalized in the new-given condition and this is why it was processed slower than in the given-new condition. Third, $O_{TOP}S_{NOM}V$ is not responsive to given-new ordering. Neither in reaction times nor in error rates was there any difference between the given-new condition and the new-given condition. Apparently, this seems to be in contradiction with (8) because $O_{TOP}S_{NOM}V$ does not seem to be penalized in the new-given condition although it is a marked option. However, note that the reaction time for $O_{TOP}S_{NOM}V$ was very slow even in the given-new condition. In fact, in reaction times, given-new ordered $O_{TOP}S_{NOM}V$ was as slow as new-given ordered $O_{ACC}S_{NOM}V$. This means that $O_{TOP}S_{NOM}V$ was penalized even in the given-new condition. The $O_{TOP}S_{NOM}V$ construction needs a contrastive context. In fact, the error rates for $O_{TOP}S_{NOM}V$ are higher than for the other constructions. This indicates that discourse contexts provided in our experiment were not supportive for interpreting $O_{TOP}S_{NOM}V$. Therefore, we can conclude that $O_{TOP}S_{NOM}V$ was penalized even when a give-new context was provided because it demands a more specific context.

In sum, the markedness principle for discourse-rule violations and contrastiveness is the key to explaining the results of our experiment.

3.4.2. Topic Marker *WA*

Information structure had no influence on *WA*-marked conditions: $S_{TOP}O_{ACC}V$ and $O_{TOP}S_{NOM}V$. This result is surprising because numerous studies have insisted that topic marker *WA* prefers given information (Mikami, 1963; Kuno, 1972, 1973; Ono, 1973). Why was no preference for given information with topic marker *WA* observed? One explanation is to suppose that the essence of *WA* is not thematic topic but contrastive topic. Kuno (1972:270) observed that thematic topic must have an anaphoric antecedent while there is no such constraint for contrastive topic. What we should emphasize here is that contrastive topic is not sensitive to given information. Whether *WA*-marked constituents are given or new is not crucial for contrastive topic *WA*. Therefore, in our experiment, participants seem to have considered topic marker *WA* to have a contrastive meaning in $S_{TOP}O_{ACC}V$ and $O_{TOP}S_{NOM}V$ and thus there was no difference in reaction time between the given-new condition and the new-given condition in $S_{TOP}O_{ACC}V$ and $O_{TOP}S_{NOM}V$. Our assumption agrees with Clancy and Downing (1987) who state that it is the contrastive usage of *WA* which is basic. According to their study, 75% of *WA*s are used in contrastive context. In recent study, Shimojo (2005:179) observed that the contrastive usage accounts for 82% of *WA* in spoken Japanese. Furthermore, Makino (1982) and Yoshimoto (1982) claim that thematic topic *WA* is merely a special case of the contrastive use of *WA*. According to Yoshimoto, picking out one prominent entity is the primary function of *WA*. He contends that there is no need to distinguish thematic topic *WA* from contrastive topic *WA*.

Yet, there is a possibility that participants interpreted *WA*-marked NPs as contrastive topic in our experiment because of our design. Miyagawa (1987:205) points out that a contrastive interpretation can arise from dividing the set into two or more parts. This kind of contrastive interpretation is called set-contrastive. His definition of set-contrast is formally defined in (8).

(8) Set-contrastive:
Partitioning of a set into two or more subsets, the member(s) of one subset being associated with a property that can be contrasted with the property explicitly or implicitly associated with the member(s) of the other subset(s).

Our design may have met the condition for set-contrastive. Note that proper nouns are employed in transitive sentences in our experiment. This means that the subject and object form a superset of human beings. To put it the other way round, subjects and objects seem to divide the super-set of human beings into sub-sets of proper nouns. In such a situation, it is easy to find a contrastive relationship between subject and object (p.c. Dr. Stephen Wright Horn). Because of this reason, participants might have considered *WA*-marked NPs to have a contrastive meaning. If this is on the right track, participants will regard *WA*-marked NPs as thematic topics when they are given a context appropriate for thematic topics. However, this conclusion may be refuted by the data of topicalization ($O_{TOP}S_{NOM}V$). Remember that topicalization seems to require contrastive context and that appropriate contexts facilitate processing of marked constructions like scrambling. Hence, if a contrastive relationship arose because of the superset, the processing cost of topicalization would be mitigated. However, topicalization showed the slowest reaction time and the highest error rate of all conditions. If topicalization was processed easier because of the superset, the reaction time would be as fast as scrambling in the given-new condition, but there was no such tendency. Moreover, the highest error rates mean that the superset relation for our experiment was not enough to allow topicalization. Thus, it is unlikely that participants regarded *WA*-marked NPs as thematic topics because of our design. We conclude that participants were insensitive to the given-new distinction when they processed *WA*-marked NPs because the basic function of *WA* is not thematic topic but contrastive topic.

4. Conclusion

We conducted a sentence comprehension experiment to see if there is an influence of given-new ordering on scrambling, topicalization, and topic marker *WA*. The results have revealed that the processing cost of scrambling was mitigated in given-new condition. However, the processing of topicalization and topic marker *WA* was not facilitated by given-new ordering. Our explanation based on (8) is shown in (9).

(9) Hypothesis based on Markedness Principle for Discourse-Rule Violations: $S_{NOM}O_{ACC}V$ and $S_{TOP}O_{ACC}V$ are not penalized when they violate given-new ordering because they are unmarked options. $O_{ACC}S_{NOM}V$ is penalized when it violates given-new ordering because it is a marked option. $O_{TOP}S_{NOM}V$ is penalized even when it conforms to given-new ordering because it is a marked option and hence needs more contrastive context.

Moreover, it has been demonstrated that topic marker *WA* is not sensitive to given-new ordering. This indicates that anaphoricity is not necessary for noun phrases to be marked by *WA*. Note that thematic topic is not allowed in a non-anaphoric context while contrastive topic can be used both in anaphoric contexts and in non-anaphoric contexts. This fact means that the basic usage of *WA* is based on contrastive topic.

Acknowledgments

We are grateful to Dr. Stephen Wright Horn and Einar Andreas Helgason. Without their help, we could not have completed this paper. They supported us and proofread the earlier versions of this paper.

References

Aissen, J. L. (1992). Topic and Focus in Mayan. *Language*, 68: 43–80.

Birner, B. J. & Ward, G. (2009). Information structure and syntactic structure. *Language and Linguistics Compass*, 3: 1167-87.

Chujo, K. (1983). Nihongo tanbun-no rikai katei — Bunrikai sutoratejii no sougo kankei [The Interrelationships among Strategies for Sentence Comprehension]. *Japanese Journal of Psychology*, 54: 250–6.

Clancy, P. & Downing, P. (1987). The use of *wa* as a cohesion marker in Japanese oral narratives. In Hinds, J. et al. (eds), *Perspectives on topicalization: The case of Japanese wa*, 3-56. Amsterdam: John Benjamins.

Frazier, L. & Flores d'Arcais, G. B. (1989). Filler-driven Parsing: A Study of Gap-filling in Dutch. *Journal of Memory and Language*, 28: 331–44.

Koizumi, M. & Tamaoka, K. (2010). Psycholinguistic evidence for the VP-internal subject position in Japanese. *Linguistic Inquiry*, 41: 663-80.

Kaiser, E. & Trueswell, J.C. (2004). The Role of Discourse Context in the Processing of a Flexible Word-order Language. *Cognition*, 94: 113–47.

Kuno, S. (1972). Functional sentence perspective: A case study from Japanese and English. *Linguistic Inquiry*, 3: 269-320.

Kuno, S. (1973). *The Structure of the Japanese Language*. Cambridge, Mass: MIT Press.

Kuno, S. (1978). *Danwa-no Bunpō* [Grammar of Discourse]. Tokyo: Taishūkan.

Kuno, S. (1987). *Functional Syntax: Anaphora, Discourse and Empathy*. The University of Chicago Press.

Kuno, S. (1995). Null elements in parallel structures in Japanese. In Mazuka, R. and Nagai, N. (eds), *Japanese Sentence Processing*, 209-33. Hillsdale, NJ: Erbaum.

Makino, S. (1982). Japanese grammar and functional grammar. *Lingua*, 57: 125-73.

McGloin, N. H. (1990). The Pragmatics of Object Topicalization in Japanese. In Kamada, O. and Jacobsen, W. M. (eds), *On Japanese and How to teach it: in Honor of Seiich Makino*, 111-20. Tokyo: Japan Times.

Mikami, A. (1963). *Nihongo no ronri - wa to ga* [Logic of the Japanese Language]. Tokyo: Kuroshio Shuppan.

Miyagawa, S. (1987). *WA* and the Wh phrase. In Hinds, J. et al. (eds), *Perspectives on topicalization: The case of Japanese wa*, 185-217. Amsterdam: John Benjamins.

Miyagawa, S. (2001). The EPP, scrambling, and *wh*-in-situ. *Current Studies in LInguistics Series*, 36: 293-338.

Miyagawa, S. (2003). *A movement scrambling and options without optionality*. In Karimi, S. (ed), Word order and scrambling, 177-200. Blackwell Publishers.

Miyagawa, S. (2010). *Why Agree? Why Move? Unifying Agreement-based and Discourse-configurational Languages*, Cambridge: The MIT Press.

Miyamoto, E. T. & Takahashi, S. (2002). Sources of Difficulty in Processing Scrambling in Japanese. In Nakayama, M. (ed.), *Sentence Processing in East Asian Languages*, 167–88. Stanford, CA: CSLI.

Ono, H. (1973). Japanese Grammar. Tokyo: The Hokuseido Press.

Rösler, F., Pechmann, T., Streb, J., Röder, B., & Hennighausen, E. (1998). Parsing of Sentences in a Language with Varying Word Order: Word-by-word Variations of Processing Demands are Revealed by Event-related Brain Potentials. *Journal of Memory and Language*, 38: 150–76.

Saito, M. (1985). *Some Asymmetries in Japanese and their Theoretical Implications*. Doctoral dissertation, MIT.

Saito, M. (2009). Optional A-scrambling. *Japanese/Korean Linguistics*, 16: 44-63.

Saito, M. & Hoji, H. (1983). Weak cross over and move α in Japanese. *Natural Language and Linguistic Theory*, 1: 245-259.

Sekerina, I. (2003). Scrambling and Processing: Dependencies, Complexity and Constraints. In Karimi, S. (ed.), *Scrambling and Word Order*, 301-24. Malden, MA: Blackwell.

Shimojo. M. (2005). *Argument Encoding in Japanese Conversation*. Hampshire and New York: Palgrave Macmillan.

Tamaoka, K.， Sakai, H., Kawahara, J., Miyaoka, Y., Lim, H., & Koizumi, M. (2005). Priority Information Used for the Processing of Japanese Sentences: Thematic Roles, Case Particles or Grammatical Functions? *Journal of Psycholinguistic Research*, 34: 281–332.

Weyerts, H., Penke, M., Münte, T. F., Heinze, H. & Clahsen, H. (2002). Word Order in Sentence Processing: An Experimental Study of Verb Placement in German. *Journal of Psycholinguistic Research*, 31: 211–68.

Yoshimoto, K. (1982). *Wa* and *ga*. *Gengo Kenkyu*, 81: 1-17.

Appendix: List of the Sentence Pairs

1. 公園に佐藤がいる。	佐藤が鈴木を褒めた。
2. 学校に伊藤がいる。	伊藤を田中が許した。
3. 窓際に加藤がいる。	加藤は吉田を押した。
4. 会社に木村がいる。	木村は山田が叱った。
5. 校庭に清水がいる。	清水が池田を蹴った。
6. 会議室に小川がいる。	小川を前田が責めた。
7. 居酒屋に藤田がいる。	藤田は岡田を称えた。
8. 大学に石井がいる。	石井は後藤が呼んだ。
9. 食堂に青木がいる。	青木が藤井を騙した。
10. 研究室に太田がいる。	太田を福田が認めた。
11. 台所に三浦がいる。	三浦は松田を守った。
12. 病院に原田がいる。	原田は中野が支えた。
13. 美術館に田村がいる。	田村が金子を探した。
14. 海辺に上田がいる。	上田を石田が助けた。
15. 喫茶店に森田がいる。	森田は柴田を待った。
16. 教室に工藤がいる。	工藤は酒井が叩いた。
17. 八百屋に内田がいる。	内田が高木を追った。
18. 薬局に高木がいる。	高木を大野が襲った。
19. 銀行に今井がいる。	今井は河野を脅した。
20. 郵便局に武田がいる。	武田は須藤が救った。
21. 博物館に村田がいる。	村田が上野を雇った。
22. コンビニに小山がいる。	小山を増田が睨んだ。
23. 駐車場に平野がいる。	平野は松井を殺した。
24. 空港に松尾がいる。	松尾は野口が殴った。
25. 消防署に吉田がいる。	加藤を吉田が褒めた。
26. 交番に山田がいる。	木村は山田を許した。
27. 入口に池田がいる。	清水は池田が押した。
28. 図書館に前田がいる。	小川が前田を叱った。
29. 体育館に岡田がいる。	藤田を岡田が蹴った。
30. 本屋に後藤がいる。	石井は後藤を責めた。
31. 地下室に藤井がいる。	青木は藤井が称えた。
32. 玄関に福田がいる。	太田が福田を呼んだ。
33. 広場に松田がいる。	三浦を松田が騙した。
34. 野球場に中野がいる。	原田は中野を認めた。
35. 三階に金子がいる。	田村は金子が守った。
36. 屋上に石田がいる。	上田が石田を支えた。
37. 木陰に柴田がいる。	森田を柴田が探した。
38. 救急車に酒井がいる。	工藤は酒井を助けた。
39. 改札に高木がいる。	内田は高木が待った。
40. 正門に大野がいる。	高田が大野を叩いた。
41. バス停に河野がいる。	今井を河野が追った。
42. デパートに須藤がいる。	武田は須藤を襲った。
43. 階段に上野がいる。	村田は上野が脅した。
44. トイレに増田がいる。	小山が増田を救った。
45. 事務所に松井がいる。	平野を松井が雇った。
46. ベンチに野口がいる。	松尾は野口を睨んだ。
47. 日なたに鈴木がいる。	佐藤は鈴木が殺した。
48. 駐輪場に田中がいる。	伊藤が田中を殴った。

On the Functional Differences between the Discourse Particles *Ne* and *Yone* in Japanese

David Y. Oshima
Department of International Communication, Nagoya University
Furo-cho, Chikusa-ku, Nagoya, Japan 464-8601
davidyo@nagoya-u.jp

Abstract

The Japanese discourse particles (sentence-final particles) *ne* and *yone* both have the functions that can be roughly characterized as the ⟨shared information⟩ use and the ⟨call for confirmation⟩ use. In the literature, an adequate descriptive analysis has not been obtained as to how the choice between the two particles is made. This paper aims to clarify discourse conditions under which *ne* and *yone* can be felicitously used.

1 Introduction

The Japanese discourse particles (also called sentence-final particles) *ne* and *yone* each have a variety of functions, and both have the functions that can be roughly characterized as the ⟨shared information⟩ (SI) use and the ⟨call for confirmation⟩ (CFC) use. The semantic effect of *ne*/*yone* in their SI use is comparable to that of English reversed polarity tag interrogatives[1] with a falling tone (e.g. *He was here, wasn't he*↘); that is, it conveys that S (the speaker) assumes that H (the hearer) has been aware that the propositional content (e.g., Ito's having been sullen in (1)) holds. The semantic effect of *ne*/*yone* in their CFC use is comparable to that of English reversed polarity tag interrogatives with a rising tone (e.g. *He was here, wasn't he*↗); that is, it serves to form a polar question with expectation of the positive answer (e.g., "Yes, I am Arai." in (2)).[2]

(1) Ito-san, saikin nanka kigen
I.-Suffix recently somehow mood
warui-{**ne**/**yone**}.
bad.Prs-{*ne*/*yone*}
'Ito has been kind of sullen these days, hasn't he↘' (shared information)

(2) Sumimasen, Arai-san desu-{**ne**/**yone**}?
excuse.me A.-Suffix Cop.Prs.Plt-{*ne*/*yone*}
'Excuse me, you are Mr. Arai, right?' (call for confirmation)

Some scholars treat *yone* as a sequence of the two discourse particles *yo* and *ne*.[3] I treat it as a single particle, however, based on the consideration that it is hard to compositionally derive the functions of *yone* from those of *yo* and *ne*. It should also be noted that, under the "sequence-of-two-particles" analysis, the different intonational properties of *ne* and *yone* cannot be easily explained (see Section 2).

In the existing literature (e.g., Takubo and Kinsui 1997, Miyazaki et al. 2002, Izuhara 2003, Nihongo Kijutsu Bunpo Kenkyukai 2003, Ohso 2005, McCready 2009), a satisfactory description has not been obtained as to how the choice between the two particles is made. This paper aims to clarify discourse conditions under which *ne* and *yone* can be felicitously used. Section 2 illustrates, as a preliminary, intonational contrasts between the two parti-

[1] See Huddleston and Pullum (2002:891–895) for a general description of English tag interrogatives.

[2] The abbreviations used in glosses are: Acc = accusative, Attr = attributive, Ben = benefactive auxiliary, Cl = classifier, Cond = conditional, Cop = copula, Dat = dative, DAux = discourse auxiliary, DP = discourse particle, Gen = genitive, Ger = gerund, Hon = honorific, Imp = imperative, Inf = infinitive, Ipfv = imperfective auxiliary, Loc = locative, Neg = negation, Nom = nominative, Plt = polite, Pot = potential, Pro = pronoun, Prs = present, Pst = past, Top = topic, Vol = volitional.

[3] See Oshima (2013, 2014) for semantic discussion of *yo*.

Copyright 2014 by David Y. Oshima
28th Pacific Asia Conference on Language, Information and Computation pages 442–451

cles in their SI and CFC uses, to which relatively scarce attention has been paid in previous studies. Section 3 discusses the discourse-functional differences between *ne* and *yone* in their SI use. Section 4 discusses the discourse-functional differences between *ne* and *yone* in their CFC use. Section 5 presents a summary and concludes the paper.

Two points are worth noting before we proceed. First, the functions of *ne* and *yone* are not limited to the aforementioned two. There are many other, especially if one takes into consideration cases where they occur in environments other than at the end of a bare declarative[4] (e.g., at the end of an imperative, as in *Kite-(yo)ne!* 'Come!'). It is beyond the scope of the current work to discuss how the SI/CFC uses are related to the other uses. Second, the discussion in this work on the contrast between *ne* and *yone* by and large carries over to that between *na* and *yona*. *Na* and *yona* are discourse particles that have largely overlapping functions and distributions as (but tend to carry a more masculine and casual tone than) *ne*/*yone* and share the SI/CFC uses. The reason why this work draws on data with *ne*/*yone* is that they are more dominant in standard Japanese as far as the SI/CFC uses are concerned.

2 Intonational Properties of *Ne* and *Yone*

Ne and *yone* in the two uses illustrated above contrast as to compatibility with different intonation types. The current work adopts the four-way distinction of intonations: (i) the question-rise contour (annotated with "LH%" by Venditti 2005), (ii) the insisting-rise contour (Venditti's "H%"), (iii) the flat contour (considered as "the absence of boundary pitch movement" by Venditti), and (iv) the rise-fall contour (Venditti's "HL%"). Throughout the paper, I use the arrow symbols ↗, ↑, ↘ and ↑↓ to represent the question-rise, insisting-rise, flat and rise-fall contours, respectively (a similar notational convention is used in Kori 1997).[5] Also, shorthand like "*ne*↑" will be used to represent "*ne* accompanied by the insisting-rise contour", etc.

[4] A bare declarative refers to a declarative without a discourse particle or a discourse auxiliary (e.g., *noda*).

[5] ↗ and ↘ are also used to represent the rising and falling intonations in English, without assuming that they are phonetically identical or similar to the question-rise and flat intonations in Japanese.

The question-rise contour is more concave (scooped) than the insisting rise contour. The question-rise contour is typically (though not always) used in questions, as in (3a). The insisting-rise contour adds an emotive and childish tone to the utterance when it occurs on a bare declarative,[6] and is exemplified in (3b). The flat contour is the unmarked intonation for declaratives, and is exemplified in (3c).

(3) a. Mieru↗
see.Pot.Prs
'Can (you) see (it)?'
b. Mieru↑
see.Pot.Prs
'(I) can see (it)!'
c. Mieru↘
see.Pot.Prs
'(I) can see (it).'

The rise-fall contour consists of a rise and a fall following it, and is often accompanied by lengthening of the final vowel. The rise-fall contour is not used on a root declarative without a discourse particle, so that *Mieru*↑↓ sounds unnatural as an independent utterance. The rise-fall may occur sentence-medially, however, indicating that the utterance has not yet finished, as in (4).[7]

(4) Mieru↑↓ toki-mo↑↓ atta↘
see.Pot.Prs time-also exist.Pst
'There were also, um, times when, um, (I) could see (it).'

Figure 1 illustrates actual tokens of *mieru* with the question-rise, insisting-rise, flat, and fall-rise contours.

(5) shows with which intonational contours *ne*/*yone* in their SI/CFC uses can be combined:

(5) SI: ϕ-ne{↑/↑↓/↘}, ϕ-yone↑
CFC: ϕ-ne↗, ϕ-yone↑↓

Ne in its SI use may be accompanied by the insisting-rise contour, the rise-fall contour, or the flat contour. *Ne* with the rise-fall or flat contour conveys

[6] Utterances ending with *ne*↑ or *yone*↑, however, do not necessarily convey an emotive or childish tone.

[7] The rise-fall contour is also used on a sentence fragment, as in *Hayaku*↑↓ 'Do it already!' (lit. 'Fast.').

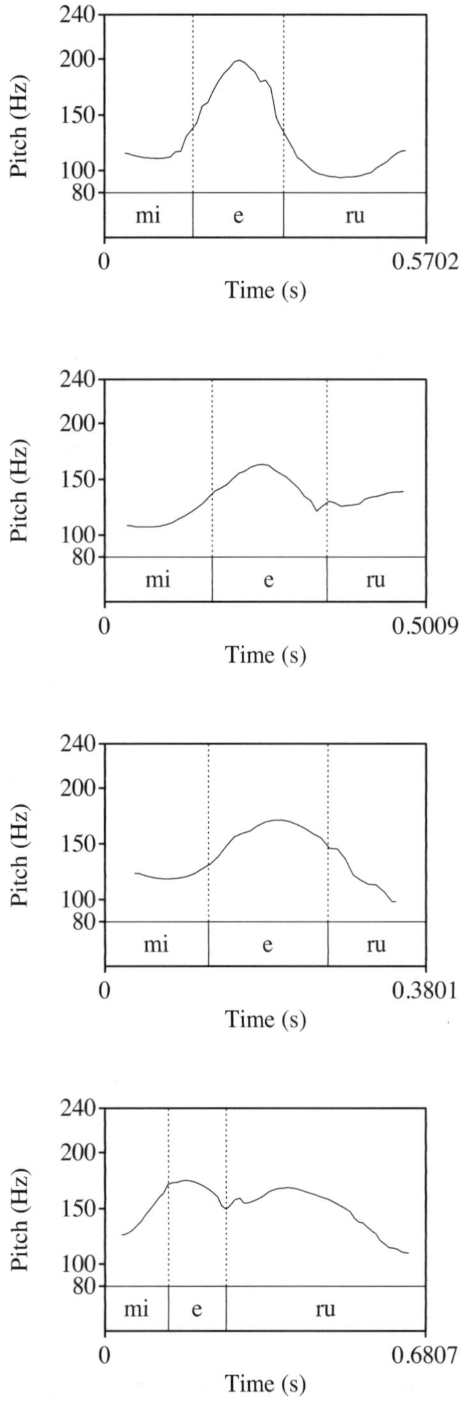

Figure 1: "Mieru↗", "Mieru↑", "Mieru↘", and "Mieru↑↓ . . ."

an added emotional tone in comparison to *ne* with the insisting-rise contour (Oshima 2013). Also, *ne* with the flat contour appears to be stylistically more constrained than *ne* with the insisting-rise or rise-fall contour (Inukai 2001). *Ne* in its CFC use is accompanied by the question-rise. *Yone* in its SI and CFC uses are accompanied by the insisting rise and the rise-fall contour, respectively (see Oshima 2013 for further discussion of the correlation between intonation types and the the functions of discourse particles).

Pitch trackings of actual tokens of (6a–d) are presented in Figure 2.

(6) a. Mieru-**ne**↑
see.Pot.Prs-*ne*
'(We) can see (it), can't (we)↘'

b. Mieru-**yone**↑
see.Pot.Prs-*yone*
'(We) can see (it), can't (we)↘'

c. Mieru-**ne**↗
see.Pot.Prs-*ne*
'(You) can see (it), can't (you)↗'

d. Mieru-**yone**↑↓
see.Pot.Prs-*yone*
'(You) can see (it), can't (you)↗'

3 The ⟨Shared Information⟩ Use

This section discusses how *ne* and *yone* in their SI use contrast with each other in their discourse-conditional distribution.

The primary factor that conditions the choice between *ne* and *yone* in their SI use is whether the propositional content is information (belief) that S acquired in the discourse situation, or in other words, "on the spot" (what is called "newly-learned information" in Akatsuka 1985). When this discourse condition holds, the choice of *ne* is compulsory and the use of *yone* is blocked.

(7) (S and H have been working in a room without a window. Coming out of the room, they see that, to their surprise, it is raining.)

a. A, ame-ga futte-ru-**ne**{↑/↑↓/↘}
oh rain-Nom fall.Ger-Ipfv.Prs-*ne*
'Oh, it is raining.'

b. #A, ame-ga futte-ru-**yone**↑
oh rain-Nom fall.Ger-Ipfv.Prs-*yone*

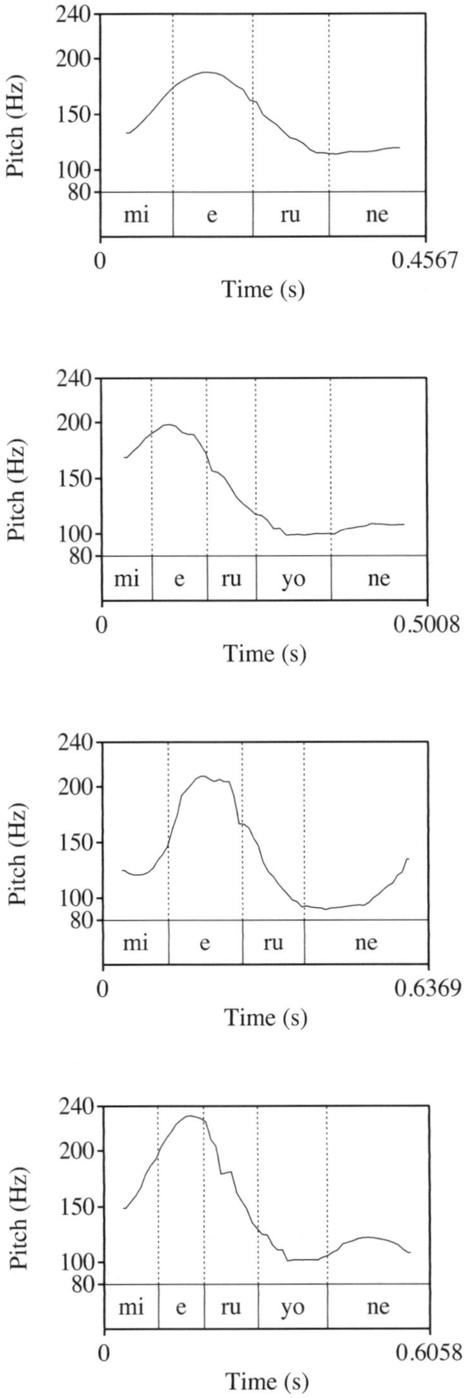

Figure 2: "Mieru-{ne/yone}(?)" (in the order of (6a–d))

(8) (S was invited to H's home for the first time. Looking out on the garden, S notices that there is a pine tree.)

a. Matsu-no ki-ga arimasu-**ne**{↑/↑↓/↘}
pine-Gen tree-Nom exist.Prs.Plt-*ne*
'You have a pine tree.'

b. #Matsu-no ki-ga arimasu-**yone**↑
pine-Gen tree-Nom exist.Prs.Plt-*yone*

When the condition that the propositional content is added to S's belief store on the spot does *not* hold, *yone* is chosen as a general rule, but there are cases where the choice of *ne* is still possible. First, in an utterance (whose propositional content is assumed to be known by H and) whose purpose is to bring up a new discourse topic, not only *yone* but also *ne* can be used.

(9) (S and H live on the same floor of the student dormitory. There was thunder last night.)
Kinoo-no kaminari
yesterday-Gen thunder
sugokatta-{a. **ne**↑/b. **yone**↑}
extraordinary.Pst-{a. *ne*/b. *yone*}
'The thunder last night was extraordinary, wasn't it↘'

(10) (S and H are graduate students studying at the same department.)
Iwata-sensei, kinoo-no konshinkai-no
I.-professor yesterday-Gen party-Gen
toki, nanka fukigen
time somehow sullen
datta-{a. **ne**↑/b. **yone**↑}
Cop.Pst-{a. *ne*/b. *yone*}
'Prof. Iwata was kind of sullen at the party yesterday, wasn't he↘'

(11) is a naturally occurring discourse segment in a novel; here, *ne*↑ can be replaced with *yone*↑ without leading to unnaturalness. Throughout the paper, examples that are adapted from naturally occurring texts (novels), including (11), are marked with the dagger symbol (†) at the end, and their sources are provided in Appendix A. Also, for ease of presentation, some long examples are presented in the form of: (i) the preceding context, (ii) the key segment, and (iii) the following context, where original

Japanese texts and/or glosses are omitted from (i) and (iii).

(11) (The interlocutors are talking about how Murasaki Shikibu, an author in the classical period, came to be named so.)

(i) Hagi said, "Yeah. People like Akiko Yosano advocate such a view too, but some say that people around her called her after [the character in her novel] Murasaki no Ue, who was very popular then, and some others say that the direct reason was that, as written in *Murasaki Shikibu Nikki*, Fujiwara no Kinto said to her [jokingly], 'My, is young Murasaki around here?'. I think these are the major theories out there". Then, he said,

(ii) "Tokorode, Omiya-kun-ga shinda-**ne**↑
by.the.way O.-Suffix-Nom die.Pst-*ne*
Kimi-wa naka-ga
you-Top relation-Nom
yokatta-ndaroo?"
good.Pst-DAux.Presumptive
'By the way, Omiya died, right? You were close to him, weren't you?'

(iii) Takako said, unflinchingly, "Yes, everyone in the seminar class says he was killed by somebody. I want to find out the culprit, no matter what it takes". She wanted to ask him about his alibi, even though she would risk offending him by doing so.†

Another environment in which the use of *ne* is allowed is an utterance where S echoes part (or the whole) of the immediately preceding utterance by H with a tone of sympathy.

(12) (in reply to (9a) or (9b))
Sugokatta-**ne**{↑/↑↓/↘}
extraordinary.Pst-*ne*
'It was extraordinary, indeed.'

(13) (in reply to (10a) or (10b))
Fukigen datta-**ne**{↑/↑↓/↘}
sullen Cop.Pst-*ne*
'He was sullen, indeed.'

(14) (A and B work at the same office. One day, on his way to work, A notices that there was a new ramen noodles restaurant in front of the nearby station. After getting to the office, he reports this to B.)

A: Ekimae-ni atarashii
station.front-Dat new.Prs
raamen-ya-ga
ramen-shop-Nom
dekite-ta-yo.
come.to.exist.Ger-Ipfv.Pst-DP
'There is a new ramen noodles restaurant in front of the station.'

B: Dekite-ta-**ne**{↑/↑↓/↘} Kaeri-ni
come.to.exist.Ger-Ipfv.Pst-*ne* return-Dat
yotte-miyoo-ka?
stop.by.Ger-try.Vol-DP
'I know. Shall we try it after work?'

In the contexts of (12)–(14), it is also possible to use *yone*↑↓.

When none of the conditions discussed above that license the use of *ne* is met, *yone* must be chosen, or at least is strongly preferred (note that *ne* is acceptable in (15A) because it can easily be interpreted as an utterance to bring up a new discourse topic).

(15) A: Ekimae-no raamen-ya-san
station.front-Gen ramen-shop-Suffix
kekkoo oishii-{**ne**↑/**yone**↑}
quite tasty.Prs-{*ne*/*yone*}
'The ramen noodles restaurant in front of the station serves tasty food, doesn't it↘'

B: Un, sore-ni nedan-mo
yes and price-also
yasui-{??**ne**↑/**yone**↑}
cheap.Prs-{*ne*/*yone*}
'Yeah, and it is cheap too, isn't it↘'

B': Un, demo nedan-ga chotto
yes but price-Nom a.little
takai-{??**ne**↑/**yone**↑}
expensive.Prs-{*ne*/*yone*}
'Yeah, but it is a little expensive, isn't it↘'

(16) A: Yappari densha-de iku
on.second.thought train-Loc go.Prs
koto-ni shiyoo.
matter-Dat do.Vol
'On second thought, let's go by train.'

B: Ii-yo. Densha nara
good.Prs-DP train Cop.Cond

juutai-no shinpai-ga nakute
traffic.jam-Gen worry-Nom not.exist.Ger
ii-{??**ne**↑/**yone**↑}
good.Prs-{*ne*/*yone*}
'Okay. (As you know) a good thing about going by train is that we don't need to worry about traffic congestion.'

(17) A: Sakki terebi-de Akan-ko-no
a.while.ago TV-Loc A.-lake-Gen
dokyumentarii-o yatte-te,
documentary-Acc do.Ger-Ipfv.Ger
Kushiro-ni ryokoo shita toki-no
K.-ni trip do.Pst time-Gen
koto-o omoidashita-yo.
matter-Acc recall.Pst-DP
'A documentary about Lake Akan was on TV a while ago, and it reminded me of our trip to Kushiro.'
B: Ano toki-wa samukatta-{??**ne**↑/**yone**↑}
that time-Top cold.Pst-{*ne*/*yone*}
'It was cold then, wasn't it↘'

4 The ⟨Call for Confirmation⟩ Use

This section discusses how *ne* and *yone* in their CFC use contrast with each other in their discourse-conditional distribution.

When S asks for confirmation or clarification about the content of what H has just said, *ne* must be chosen. (In (20), which is a naturally occurring example, it would be unnatural to replace *ne* with *yone*.)

(18) A: Kono shorui-no copii-o onegai
this document-Gen copy-Acc favor
dekiru-kana? 20-bu hitsuyoo
do.Pot.Prs-DP 20-Cl need
na-nda.
Cop.Attr-DAux.Prs
'Can I ask you to photocopy this document? I need 20 copies.'
B: 20-bu desu-{**ne**↗/#**yone**↑↓}
20-Cl Cop.Prs.Plt-{*ne*/*yone*}
Wakarimashita.
understand.Pst.Plt
'You need 20 copies. I got it.'

(19) (A is handing B paper bags with sandwiches in them.)
A: Shiro-ga biifu de, chairo-ga
white-Nom beef Cop.Inf brown-Nom
yasai desu.
vegetable Cop.Prs.Plt
'The white ones are the beef (sandwiches) and the brown ones are the vegetable (sandwiches).'
B: Shiroi fukuro-ga biifu
white.Prs bag-Nom beef
da-{**ne**↗/#**yone**↑↓}
Cop.Prs-{*ne*/*yone*}
'(Let me make sure.) The white bags are the beef.'

(20) (An experienced cop is giving advice on investigation to a younger cop.)
(i) "There is another thing to pay attention to. This often explains an unnatural death in an apartment, like the one we investigated this morning. In an old apartment, you should carefully check any hot-water heaters."
(ii) "Fukanzen nenshoo desu-**ne**↗"
incomplete combustion Cop.Prs.Plt-*ne*
'You are talking about incomplete combustion, right?'
(iii)"That's right. [...]"†

This type of utterance needs to have a nominal predicate, or the discourse auxiliary *noda*.

(21) A: Ashita-wa Maeda-san-ga
tomorrow-Top M.-Suffix-Nom
kimasu.
come.Prs.Plt
'Maeda will come tomorrow.'
B: #Maeda-san-ga kimasu-{**ne**↗/**yone**↑↓}
M.-Suffix-Nom come.Prs.Plt-{*ne*/*yone*}
(Maeda will come.)
B': Maeda-san desu-{**ne**↗/#**yone**↑↓}
M.-Suffix Cop.Prs.Plt-{*ne*/*yone*}
'It is Maeda (who will come, I got it).'
B": Maeda-san-ga
M.-Suffix-Nom
kuru-ndesu-{**ne**↗/#**yone**↑↓}
come.Prs-DAux.Prs.Plt-{*ne*/*yone*}
'Maeda will come(, I got it).'

Also, when S checks whether H understood what he has just said (e.g., instructions, directions, S's planned action), *ne* must be chosen.[8]

(22) Kono ranpu-ga tsuite-iru toki-ni
this lamp-Nom be.lit.Ger-Ipfv.Prs time-Dat
dengen-o kiru-to, koshoo-no
power.source-Acc cut.Prs-if trouble-Gen
gen'in-ni narimasu.
cause-Dat become.Prs.Plt
Wakarimashita-{**ne**↗/#**yone**↑↓}
understand.Pst.Plt-*ne*/*yone*
'If you shut off the power when this lamp is on, that may cause a breakdown. Okay?'

(23) Saiten-ga sunda tooan-wa
grading-Nom finish.Pst answer.sheet-Top
kono hako-ni irete-kure.
this box-Dat put.Ger-Ben.Imp
Ii-{**ne**↗/#**yone**↑↓}
good.Prs-*ne*/*yone*
'After grading the answer sheets, please place them in this box. Okay?'

(24) (The driver of a van starts the engine and says to the passengers:)
Jaa shuppatsu shimasu-yo. Ii
then start do.Prs.Plt-DP good.Prs
desu-{**ne**↗/#**yone**↑↓}
Cop.Prs.Plt-*ne*/*yone*
'We are leaving, then. Okay?'

In environments where neither of these discourse conditions that block the use of *yone* is met, the availability of *ne* is quite limited. To illustrate, in the contexts of (25)–(27), the choice of *ne* would be unnatural.

[8] When the purpose of the utterance is to confirm that H agrees to comply with S's request, or that H approves S's action, on the other hand, *yone* can be used and often is the preferred option.

(i) Kono shigoto-wa suiyoobi-made-ni shiagete-kure.
this work-Top Wednesday-by-Dat finish.Ger-Ben.Imp
Ii-**yone**↑↓
good.Prs-*yone*
'Please finish this work by Wednesday. You can do it, can't you↗'

(ii) Kuruma kariru-yo. Ii-**yone**↑↓
car borrow.Prs-DP good.Prs-{*ne*/*yone*}
'I'll use your car. You don't mind, do you↗'

(25) (A and B are friends. They are at a restaurant. A looks out of the window and sees a man standing at some distance who looks like a mutual friend of theirs. A asks B:)
Nee, asoko-ni iru-no Ueda-kun
hey there-Dat exist.Prs-Pro U.-Suffix
da-{#**ne**↗/**yone**↑↓}
Cop.Prs-{*ne*/*yone*}
'Hey, the guy over there is Ueda, isn't he↗'

(26) (A and B are roommates. A wants to use soy sauce for cooking, but cannot find it. A asks B:)
Nee, shooyu mada
hey soy.sauce still
nokotte-ta-{#**ne**↗/**yone**↑↓}
remain.Ger-Ipfv.Pst-*ne*/*yone*
'Hey, we have some soy sauce left, don't we↗'

(27) (A and B are going to leave the office where they work together. A asks B:)
Ekimae-no hon'ya-tte mada
in.front.of.station-Gen bookstore-Top still
aite-ru-{#**ne**↗/**yone**↑↓}
open.Ger-Ipfv.Pst-*ne*/*yone*
'The bookstore in front of the station is still open, isn't it↗'

There are, however, two more types of contexts where the use of *ne* is possible. The first is cases where the truth of the propositional content is a prerequisite for the speech act that S plans to perform subsequently. In (28), the truth of the proposition that B will be free in the evening is part of the preparatory conditions, in Searle's (1975) sense, for A's speech act of inviting B to the movies.

(28) (A and B are college students and roommates.)
A: Kadai moo owatta?
assignment already finish.Pst
'Have you finished your homework?'
B: Un, sakki-ne.
yes a.while.ago-*ne*
'Yes, I finished it a while ago.'
A: Jaa yoru-wa hima
then evening-Top free
da-{**ne**↗/**yone**↑↓}
Cop.Prs-*ne*/*yone*

'Then you are free in the evening, aren't you↗'

B: Un. Dooshite?
yes why
'Yes, I am. Why did you ask?'

A: Eiga-no ken-o 2-mai
film-Gen ticket-Acc 2-Cl
moratta-nda. Issho-ni ikanai?
receive.Pst-DAux.Prs together go.Neg.Prs
'Someone gave me two movie tickets. Do you want to come with me?'

The occurrences of *ne* in (29)–(31), adapted from novel texts, are of the same kind; in these cases, the truth of the propositional content to be confirmed with *ne* is a prerequisite for the representational speech act (i.e., statement) that S plans to perform subsequently.

(29) (Two friends are talking about the circumstances of a certain criminal case.)

(i) "Is that right? Then, I must ask you to tell me about the alibis for everyone who was related to the [murder] case."

(ii) "Aribai-wa-ne, minna pat-to
alibi-Top-*ne* everyone spectacularly
shinai-nda. Heitaro-no
do.Neg.Prs-DAux.Prs H.-Gen
aribai-wa hanashita-**ne**↗
alibi-Top tell.Pst-*ne*
'Speaking of alibis, none of them had a strong one. I've told you about Heitaro's alibi, haven't I↗'

(iii) Nobody other than him has a clear alibi. To start with, his mother Yasue was apparently saying that she was out in Ginza [...]"†

(30) (i) "That tower too has been there since before the war, and it imitates [the building known as] Juunikai, but I heard that the real Juunikai was very close to here."
"Where was it?"
The proprietor walked to the center of the road.

(ii) "Kono toori-zoi-no zutto saki
this street-along-Gen far ahead
desu. Hora, asoko-ni
Cop.Prs.Plt hey there-Dat
kooban-ga miemasu-**ne**↗
police.box-Nom see.Pot.Plt-*ne*
'It was along this street, at a far distance from here. Look, you can see a police box over there, right?'

(iii) They say Juunikai and [the pond known as] Hyootan-ike were in the area beyond it, where there now is a bowling alley."†

(31) (i) "Now, explain to me about your scheme to remove Nobuko [from her position as the president]?"

(ii) "Haa ... Kore-o hanashitara,
hmm this-Acc tell.Cond
shachoo-ni
president-Dat
torinashite-moraemasu-**ne**↗"
intercede.Ger-Ben.Pot.Prs.Plt-*ne*
'Hmm ... Will you intercede with the president [= Nobuko] on behalf of me if I tell you about it?'

(iii) What a pathetic guy! Resisting temptation to kick him hard, Junko made him a promise, saying, "Okay, fine."†

In (29)–(31), *ne* can be felicitously replaced with *yone*. It appears that in contexts where either *ne*↗ or *yone*↑↓ can be used, the former tends to sound more casual (less formal) than the latter.[9]

Another kind of context where the choice of *ne* is possible is situations where S considers himself to carry the role of a "questioner", i.e., an interlocutor who is expected primarily to ask questions and gather information from the other interlocutor; typical examples of a questioner are a police detective questioning a suspect or a witness, and a journalist interviewing a celebrity. Two naturally occurring examples are presented below; in these discourse segments too, it is not unnatural to replace *ne* with *yone*.

(32) (i) He [= Detective Jimbo] quietly got off the car and passed through the gate of the ryotei [(Japanese-style luxurious restaurant)]. When he entered the entrance hall, a hostess in her sixties came out to greet

[9] In Nihongo Kijutsu Bunpo Kenkyukai (2013:268), it is pointed out that *ne* in its CFC use is, in comparison to *yone*, often inappropriate in a conversation with somebody who is socially superior.

him.
"You are meeting somebody, I suppose."
"I am not a customer."
Jimbo flashed his police ID card. The hostess' round-cheeked face became strained.

(ii) "Sukoshi mae-ni Kamiume-ga
a.little before-Dat K.-Nom
kita-**ne**↗"
come.Pst-*ne*
'Kamiume came a while ago, didn't he↗'

(iii) "Um, yes."
"Which room is he in, and with whom?"
"I cannot answer that kind of question. Unless you have a search warrant, I mean."†

(33) (i) Luckily, the assistant professor Hirose was just about to go home but was still in the room. He was talking fast about something with a young man who looked like an assistant, but stopped the conversation when he caught sight of me.
"Are you Professor Hirose? Could I have a moment of your time?"
I gave him my business card.
The young man left his seat and moved to the other side of a partitioning screen, so that he will not stand in the way.
"How may I help you?" [. . .]

(ii) "Kinoo, Tozai Hoteru-ni
yesterday T. hotel-Dat
ikaremashita-**ne**↗
go.Pst.Hon.Plt-*ne*"
'You went to Tozai Hotel yesterday, didn't you↗'

(iii) I immediately cut to the chase.
". . ."
As the way I asked the question was abrupt, Hirose carefully refrained from replying and patiently waited for my next word.†

(34a) sounds at least as natural as (34b) – at least in fictional writing like detective stories – as an utterance made by a police detective to somebody who he wants to question.

(34) Watanabe Ken-san
W. K.-Suffix
desu-{a. **ne**↗/b. **yone**↑↓}
Cop.Prs.Plt-{*ne*/*yone*}
'You are Mr. Ken Watanabe, right?'

On the other hand, in a situation where one finds an actor or a professional sports player on the street and addresses him to ask for his autograph, (34a) would be unnatural while (34b) would be fine. This contrast can be attributed to the difference in the situational role that S assigns to himself. In the former situation, he would naturally consider himself a "questioner"; in the latter situation, he would not.

5 Summary and Conclusion

This paper discussed how the Japanese discourse particles *ne* and *yone* contrast in their discourse-conditional distribution, focusing on two major uses shared by them.

The principles based on which the choice between *ne* and *yone* in their ⟨shared information⟩ use is made can be summarized as follows:

(35) a. The choice of *ne* is compulsory (the choice of *yone* is blocked) when the condition holds that the propositional content of the utterance has been added to S's belief store in the discourse situation. (relevant examples: (7), (8))

b. When the condition in (a) does not hold, either *ne* or *yone* can be used in an utterance (i) whose purpose is to bring up a new topic or (ii) where part (or the whole) of the immediately preceding utterance by H is repeated with a tone of sympathy. (relevant examples: (9)–(14))

c. In an utterance that does not meet none of the conditions described above, *yone* must be chosen, or at least is strongly preferred. (relevant examples: (15)–(17))

The principles based on which the choice between *ne* and *yone* in their ⟨call for confirmation⟩ use is made can be summarized as follows:

(36) a. The choice of *ne* is compulsory (the choice of *yone* is blocked) in an utterance (i) (which is with a nominal predicate or the

discourse auxiliary *noda* and) where S asks for confirmation or clarification about the content of the immediately preceding utterance by H or (ii) where S checks if H understood what he has just said. (relevant examples: (18)–(24))

b. When neither of the conditions in (a) holds, either *ne* or *yone* can be used (i) if the propositional content to be confirmed constitutes part of the preparatory conditions for S's subsequent speech act or (ii) S considers himself to carry the role of a "questioner" in the discourse situation. (relevant examples: (28)–(34))

c. In an utterance that does not meet none of the conditions described above, *yone* must be chosen. (relevant examples: (25)–(27))

While the licensing conditions of *ne* and *yone* are rather complicated, the general pattern behind their contrasts seems to be as follows: the more tightly bound to the discourse situation the propositional content is, the more likely *ne* rather than *yone* is chosen. It is an interesting question how the described division of labor between the two particles arose historically. I leave this issue open for future research.

Appendix A. The Sources of the Examples Adapted from Naturally Occurring Texts

(11) Balanced Corpus of Contemporary Written Japanese (BCCWJ; Sample ID: LBb9_00147). Originally from *Murasaki Shikibu Satsujin Jiken* by Misa Yamamura, published by Chuokoron-sha in 1987; **(20)** *Chi-no Wadachi* by Hideo Aiba, published by Gentosha in 2013; **(29)** *Senseijutsu Satsujin Jiken* by Soji Shimada, published by Kodansha in 1981; **(30)** *Kakei Toshi* by Soji Shimada, published by Kodansha in 1986; **(31)** *Onna Shachō-ni Kanpai!* by Jiro Akagawa, published by Shinchosha in 1982; **(32)** BCCWJ (Sample ID: PB49_00605). Originally from *Hijō Rensa* by Hideo Minami, published by Tokuma Shoten in 1987; **(33)** BCCWJ (Sample ID: LBj9_00004). Originally from *Iesu Kirisuto no Nazo* by Sakae Saito, published by Kobunsha in 1995.

References

Akatsuka, Noriko. 1985. *Conditionals and the epistemic scale*. *Language* 61(3):625–639.

Huddleston, Rodney and Geoffrey K. Pullum. 2002. *The Cambridge Grammar of the English Language*. Cambridge University Press, Cambridge.

Inukai, Takashi. 2001. Hikuku mijikaku tsuku shūjoshi "ne". Onsei Bunpo Kenkyukai (ed.) *Bunpō to Onsei*. Kurosio Publishers, Tokyo. pp.17–29.

Izuhara, Eiko. 2003. Shūjoshi "yo" "yone" "ne" saikō. *The Journal of Aichi Gakuin University: Humanities & Sciences* 51(2):1–15.

Kori, Shiro. 1997. Nihongo no intonēshon: Kata to kinō. Kunihiro, Tetsuya, Hajime Hirose, and Morio Kono (eds.) *Akusento, Intonēshon, Rizumu to Pōzu*. Sanseido, Tokyo. pp.169–202.

Miyazaki, Kazuhito, Taro Adachi, Harumi Noda, and Shino Takanashi. 2002. *Modaritī*. Kurosio Publishers, Tokyo.

Nihongo Kijutsu Bunpo Kenkyukai. 2003. *Gendai Nihongo Bunpō*, vol. 4. Kurosio Publishers, Tokyo.

Ohso, Mieko. 2005. Shūjoshi "yo" "yone" "ne" saikō: Zatsudan kōpasu ni motozuku kōsatsu. Kamada, Osamu, Yukiko Hatasa, Mayumi Oka, Michio Tsutsui, and Fumiko Nazikian (eds.) *Gengo Kyōiku no Shintenkai: Makino Seiichi Kyōju Koki Kinen Ronshū*. Hituzi Syobo, Tokyo. pp.3–15.

Oshima, David Y. 2013. Nihongo ni okeru intonēshongata to shūjoshi kinō no sōkan ni tsuite. *Forum of International Development Studies*, 43:47–63.

Oshima, David Y. 2014. On the functions of the Japanese discourse particle *yo* in declaratives. McCready, Eric, Katsuhiko Yabushita, and Kei Yoshimoto (eds.) *Formal Approaches to Semantics and Pragmatics*. Springer, Heidelberg. pp.251–271.

McCready, Eric. 2009. Particles: Dynamics vs. utility. Takubo, Yukinori et al. (eds.) *Japanese/Korean Linguistics*, vol. 16. CSLI Publications, Stanford. pp.466–481.

Searle, John R. 1975. Indirect speech acts. Cole, Peter and Jerry L. Morgan (eds.) *Syntax and Semantics*, vol. 3: *Speech Acts*. Academic Press, New York. pp.64–83.

Takubo, Yukinori and Satoshi Kinsui. 1997. Discourse management in terms of mental spaces. *Journal of Pragmatics* 28(6):741–758.

Venditti, Jennifer J. 2005. The J_ToBI model of Japanese intonation. Jun, Sun-Ah (ed.) *Prosodic Typology: The Phonology of Intonation and Phrasing*. Oxford University Press, Oxford. pp.172–200.

The Centre and Periphery of Discourse Connectives

Magdaléna Rysová
Charles University in Prague
Faculty of Arts
magdalena.rysova@post.cz

Kateřina Rysová
Charles University in Prague
Faculty of Mathematics and Physics
rysova@ufal.mff.cuni.cz

Abstract

The paper tries to contribute to the general definition of discourse connectives. It examines connectives in broader sense, i.e. all language expressions that have an ability to express discourse relations within a text (e.g. both conjunctions like *but*, *and*, *or* and expressions like *the condition for this is*, *due to this situation* etc.). The paper tries to classify connectives from different perspectives and to divide them into several groups to specify their similarities and differences. We try to discuss various attributes an expression must have to be a connective. We understand discourse connectives as a set of expressions with a center and periphery and we focus here mainly on the periphery – i.e. on description of the secondary connectives (like *the reason is simple*, *this means that...* etc.) because it is not much investigated but a very current theme of discourse analysis.

1 Introduction

Discourse connectives are generally understood as explicit indicators of discourse relations within a text. However, there is not any shared and generally accepted definition of them. Therefore, various authors dealing with discourse studies try to give a list of connectives for the given language and to describe their common features.

In this paper, we want to contribute to this general discussion (as well as to the terminology issue) and to bring new perspectives from which we may look at discourse connectives. We also want to present general principles according to which we may draw boundaries among such a wide and heterogeneous group of expressions.

Our general observations are made on the basis of the large corpus study enabled by the annotated corpus Prague Dependency Treebank. Our research is carried out on Czech newspaper texts but we believe that our general principles may be used also for other languages.

2 Discourse Connectives – General Discussion

As said above, discourse connectives are hardly definable expressions, which is seen already in the fact that there are many different terms used for these expressions – cf. *discourse connectives* (Blakemore, 2002), *discourse operators* (Redeker, 1991), *discourse markers* (Schiffrin, 1987), *pragmatic connectives* (van Dijk, 1979) etc. We use the term *discourse connectives* following the Czech traditional terminology.

The variability in terminology points at the fact that discourse connectives are studied from different perspectives – e.g. from the syntactical, lexical, phonetic or pragmatic point of view. Since there is a chaos in terminology as well as in the definition of discourse connectives, we want to bring some new observations of this theme based on a large corpus study.

3 Discourse Connectives in the Prague Dependency Treebank

Our research on discourse connectives in Czech was carried out on the data of the Prague Dependency Treebank (PDT) – a manually annotated corpus of about 50 thousand sentences from newspaper texts containing, among others, annotation of discourse relations.

3.1 The First Annotation of Discourse Connectives in Czech

The first annotation of discourse relations in Czech was carried out in 2012. It was done on the data of the Prague Dependency Treebank 2.5 (Bejček et al., 2012) and was published independently as the

Copyright 2014 by Magdaléna Rysová and Kateřina Rysová
28th Pacific Asia Conference on Language, Information and Computation pages 452–459

Prague Discourse Treebank 1.0 (Poláková et al., 2012).

The annotation was limited to explicit discourse connectives in narrow sense, i.e. connectives were understood only as expressions from selected parts of speech, especially conjunctions[1] (*ale 'but'*, *nebo 'or'*, *přesto 'yet'* etc.) and some types of particles (*jenom 'only'*, *také 'too'* etc.). We will call these expressions **primary connectives**, as their primary function is to connect two units of a text and not to have some semantic role of a sentence element within the sentence.

Following the theory and terminology of the Pennsylvanian corpus Penn Discourse Treebank, the Prague Dependency Treebank understands connectives as expressions opening positions for two units of a text – in other words, connectives connect two textual pieces called arguments. During the first annotation of the primary connectives in PDT, there were annotated only such connectives whose arguments were verbal – i.e. represented mainly by two propositions or clauses – cf. an example from PDT:

(1) *Pro 600 zaměstnanců muselo nové vedení sehnat práci.*
Proto se manažeři rozjeli za zakázkami nejen po republice, ale i do zahraničí.

'The new leadership had to find a job for 600 employees.
Therefore, the managers started to look for contracts not only around the country but also abroad.'

In the Example 1, there is a discourse connective *proto 'therefore'* expressing a discourse relation of reason and result between two verbal (here propositional) arguments *the new leadership had to find...* and *the managers started to look...*

[1] There is often a discrepancy between the parts of speech like conjunctions, particles and adverbs. We define **conjunctions** (following the traditional Czech grammar) as synsemantic words with primary connecting function (like *but*, *or*, *therefore*, *however*, *and* etc.), structuring **particles** as synsemantic words expressing a relation of a speaker to the structure of a text (like *only*, *too* etc.) and **adverbs** as autosemantic words functioning as sentence elements expressing circumstances of events (like *subsequently*, *previously* etc.). Due to the often discrepancy of these parts of speech, the boundaries among connectives should not be stated strictly on the basis of the part-of-speech membership.

The first discourse annotation of the Prague Dependency Treebank includes both inter- and intra-sentential discourse relations and has been carried out partially manually and automatically[2]. The annotation of implicit discourse relations (i.e. without explicit connectives) and relations expressed by other means than primary connectives (e.g. by expressions like *that is the reason why*) has not been included here.

3.2 The Extended Annotation of Discourse Connectives in Czech

Apart from the annotation of primary connectives, we decided to annotate also discourse relations in Czech expressed by other means, i.e. by structures like *rozdílem bylo 'the difference is'*, *to bylo způsobeno tím 'this was caused by...'*, *jedinou podmínkou bylo 'the only condition was'* etc. – cf. an example from PDT where the expression *z tohoto důvodu 'from this reason'* expresses a discourse relation of reason and result:

(2) *Jak vyplynulo z vyšetřování, oba muži si přepadení vymysleli.*
Z tohoto důvodu byli v těchto dnech z ČR vypovězeni.

'The investigation revealed that the two men have lied about the attack.
From this reason, they were expelled from the Czech Republic these days.'

The group of these connective structures is very wide and heterogeneous.

1) One subgroup of them are **open collocations** (grammatically free) containing mainly nouns (*příčina 'cause'*, *důvod 'reason'*, *podmínka 'condition'* etc.), verbs (*odůvodnit 'to give reasons'*, *vysvětlit 'to explain'*, *znamenat 'to mean'* etc.) and secondary prepositions[3] (*díky 'thanks to'*, *vzhledem k 'with respect to'* etc.). Moreover, the individual connective "key words" occur in different structures – cf. the word *příčina 'cause'* form structures like *příčinou bylo... 'the cause was...'*, *vidět příčinu v tom... 'to see the cause*

[2] The automatic annotation has been checked by human annotators.

[3] The term *secondary prepositions* is used for prepositions that arose from another part of speech originally.

in...', *hledat příčinu v tom... 'to seek the cause in...*'.

2) Other types of these connective structures are **fixed phrases** (both grammatically and lexically restricted) that are fully frozen (like *o to více* '*what's more*') or that enable only a slight modification – cf. *stručně/jednoduše/prostě řečeno* '*shortly/simply/generally speaking*' etc. (more details to characteristics of these structures in Rysová, 2012).

As we can see, there is a wide range of structures that have a connecting discourse function within a text. Since they are not connectives from their nature (as conjunctions or structuring particles), but only in the form of certain collocations (whether free or fixed), we use for all of these connective structures a term **secondary connectives** (some authors use the term alternative lexicalizations of discourse connectives, shortly AltLexes – cf. Prasad et al., 2010).

This extended discourse annotation of secondary connectives in the Prague Dependency Treebank is manual, but the detection of some structures was done automatically (cf. Rysová and Mírovský, 2014). The annotation contains both inter- and intra-sentential discourse relations.

The aim of the next part is to compare and contrast these two annotations (i.e. of primary and secondary connectives) and then to draw some general observations that resulted from the practical data annotations.

4 Results and Evaluation

As said in section 3.1, the annotation of primary connectives contains only discourse relation between two verbal arguments (i.e. represented mostly by two propositions or clauses). Altogether, the Prague Dependency Treebank contains 20,255 of such expressions (measured on whole data).

The annotation of secondary connectives has been finished right now and we bring the first complex results of it (although we are aware that the numbers of tokens may slightly change, as the data are now being checked and corrected).

When preparing the annotation principles, we realized that it is not possible to strictly follow the principles stated for primary connectives. Secondary connectives form a very heterogeneous group of connective structures that behave differently than primary connectives in some cases. Therefore, we could adopt only a part of the old principles and we had to create some new for the specific structures. We will now present all these principles, i.e. which both overlap and differ from the principles for primary connectives.

Some of the secondary connectives are fully replaceable by the primary ones, as they may also connect two units of a text realized by verbal arguments – see Example 2 where the structure *z tohoto důvodu* '*from this reason*' expresses a discourse relation between two propositions. It is here replaceable by the primary connective *proto* '*therefore*' and the meaning remains practically the same. Altogether, the Prague Dependency Treebank contains 924 of such types of relations.

During the data annotation, we found also such secondary connectives that allow nominalization of the second argument; in other words, they are followed not by a verbal clause but by a nominal phrase. See Example 3 from PDT:

(3) *Privatizované mlékárny se však zatím mezi sebou nedokázaly domluvit.*
<u>Důsledkem je</u> nekompromisní konkurenční <u>boj</u>, který tlačí ceny výrobků až takřka k nulové rentabilitě zpracovatelů.

'*The privatized dairies have so far failed to agree among themselves.*
<u>The consequence is</u> a rigorous <u>competition</u> that pushes up the price of products to almost zero profitability of processors.'

In this example, the connective structure *důsledkem je* '*the consequence is*' is followed by a nominal phrase *boj* '*competition*' (not by its verbal representation *that they rigorously compete*). These connectives have mostly a similar structure – *důvodem je* '*the reason is*', *důsledkem je* '*the consequence is*', *příčinou je* '*the cause is*', *podmínkou je* '*the condition is*'etc.

The difference between *the consequence is a rigorous competition* and *the consequence is that they rigorously compete* is only syntactic, not semantic so we decided to include these cases into our annotation. (However, we distinguish between annotation of verbal and nominal arguments technically, so they may be automatically detected for possible further investigation). It appeared that nominalization of the second argument is a feature of written rather than spoken language.

This is the first case when the annotations of primary and secondary connectives differ, i.e. in the nature of discourse arguments. However, the restriction on verbal arguments for primary connectives is clear, as we cannot say, for example, **a proto boj* '**therefore the competition*'. In this respect, it is clearly visible the heterogeneity of secondary connectives and their bigger flexibility.

Altogether, the Prague Dependency Treebank contains 237 of these relations, i.e. relations expressed by secondary connectives followed by a nominalized argument.

4.1 The Universality Principle

During the annotation, we observed also another interesting phenomenon. In the data, the individual connective key words (like *reason*, *due to*, *because of*, *condition* etc.) occurred in different structures with respect to their connective status. We saw a difference between combinations like *kvůli tomu* '*because of this*', *kvůli této skutečnosti* '*because of this situation*', *kvůli tomuto nárůstu* '*because of this increase*' or *kvůli jejich pomoci* '*because of their help*'. All of these combinations containing the preposition *kvůli* '*because of*' refer to the preceding context and express a discourse relation of reason and result. However, we feel that there is a difference between them concerning the fact whether the structure is context dependent (as, for example, *because of this increase*) or not (as *because of this*). In other words, *because of this increase* may be used only in a limited set of contexts (in texts about *increasing*), but *because of this* is context independent – *this* is a deictic word so it may be embedded to any context and it will find there its semantic relations. Other words like *increase* or *help* do not have this ability, i.e. to adapt their meaning to context. Therefore, we decided to annotate these structures differently according to this contextual in/dependency that we called **universality principle**.

The universality principle evaluates connective structures from the fact whether they have a universal status of connectives, i.e. whether they function as indicators of certain discourse relation universally or occasionally. In other words, we tried to answer – if we have several different contexts with, e.g., the relation of reason and result – whether the given connective structure (with an ability to express this type of relation) fits into each of them (and is therefore universal) or not.

In this respect, we evaluated *kvůli tomu* '*because of this*' as a universal secondary connective whereas *kvůli tomuto zvýšení* '*because of this increase*' as a non-universal connecting phrase.

We decided to state the boundary of connectives right here, i.e. according to the universal or non-universal status of expressions. In this respect, connectives function as universal indicators of given discourse relations (whether primary /like *and*, *but*, *or*/ or secondary /like *that is the reason why*, *due to this*, *the condition of this is*, *in spite of this* etc./). We decided that we will not include the non-universal structures in discourse connectives – because even though they express certain discourse relation, they contain too much other lexical items occurring in the connective structure only occasionally. Therefore, we will call these structures (like *because of this increase*, *the reason of his late arrival is* etc.) non-universal connecting phrases, not connectives.

In the Prague Dependency Treebank, we annotated 79 non-universal connecting phrases between two verbal arguments and 72 non-universal connecting phrases followed by nominal arguments. See the Table 1 depicting the annotation of secondary connectives and other connecting phrases in the Prague Dependency Treebank (where the abbreviation VP means verbal phrase and NP nominal phrase).

	VP_VP	VP_NP	**TOTAL**
Universal Secondary Connectives	924	237	**1,161**
Non-universal Connecting Phrases	79	72	**151**
TOTAL	1,003	309	**1,312**

Table 1: Extended Discourse Annotation in PDT

The Table 1 demonstrates that PDT contains 1,161 occurrences of universal secondary connectives (i.e. 88 % within the total number) and 151 occurrences of non-universal connecting phrases (i.e. 12 %). So there are obvious fixing tendencies concerning the form and gaining a universal status of connectives.

5 General Observations – the Centre and Periphery of Discourse Connectives

In current stage, the discourse annotation in the Prague Dependency Treebank contains altogether 21,416 of discourse relations – 20,255 expressed by primary connectives and 1,161 by secondary connectives. We may see that relations of secondary connectives form 5 % of the total number. Therefore, the primary connectives may be viewed as a centre of all connecting expressions and the secondary as its periphery.

5.1 Primary Connectives

Based on the large data annotation, we would like to contribute to the general discussion on discourse connectives, especially on their definition. Although our research has been carried out on Czech, we believe that our statements may be used also for other languages.

As we discussed above, we understand connectives as a large and heterogeneous group of expressions with its center and periphery. The center is formed by expressions we called primary connectives.

The primary connectives are synsemantic words that do not function as sentence elements (i.e. they do not play a role of a subject, object, adverbial etc.), they are mostly one-word expressions, lexically frozen. Therefore, they mostly do not allow modification (i.e. it is not possible to say, e.g., **generally and*, **simply but* etc. with some exceptions like *simply/mainly/generally because*).

As they do not affect the syntax of the sentence, the primary connectives may be also omitted without any syntactical changes in most cases – see Example 1 from PDT where the primary connective *therefore* may be simply omitted from the sentence without any changes and the discourse relation is maintained (i.e. remains implicit).

We use the term primary connectives also because of the frequency. As said in the section 5, the primary connectives occur in 95 % of all discourse relations expressed explicitly (i.e. by some language expression, not implicitly).

5.2 Secondary Connectives

Secondary connectives are much more heterogeneous group than primary connectives – concerning the part-of-speech perspective as well as the syntactic, semantic and lexical point of view.

Secondary connectives occur in the sentence mainly as structures with some basic or key word – these words are from different parts of speech, the most numerous are nouns (like *cause*, *reason*, *condition*, *explication*, *justification*, *exception*, *contrast*, *difference* etc.), verbs (like *to give reasons*, *to explain*, *to mean*, *to be related to*, *to specify*, *to continue*, *to contrast*, *to precede*, *to follow* etc.) and secondary prepositions (like *because of*, *due to*, *despite*, *except for* etc.) .

Secondary connectives are structures containing autosemantic words (in contrast to synsemantic conjunctions or particles as primary connectives) and they are integrated (as a whole) into clause structure as sentence elements (e.g. *because of this* as an adverbial of reason) or they function as clause modifiers (like e.g. *shortly speaking*).

Some secondary connectives function as one sentence element (like *due to this fact* as an adverbial of reason) or their individual parts have a role of a sentence element on their own (cf. the structures like *this is the cause* where *this* is a subject, *is* is a predicate, *cause* is an object etc.). This is one of the phenomena in which the secondary connectives differ from the primary ones to a large and significant extent.

All secondary connectives also contain (implicitly or explicitly) the reference to the previous context. In this respect, the secondary connectives may be divided into three groups – they 1) may express the reference in the surface (like *the result /of this/ is*); 2) must express the reference in the surface due to valency (*this means that...*) or 3) cannot express the reference in the surface (e.g. it is impossible to say **this generally speaking*, although *speaking* indicates implicitly that it was spoken about something in the preceding context). For more details, see Rysová (2012 and 2014).

Another very interesting thing is that some secondary connectives may be even syntactically higher than the second argument of the discourse relation. There are examples like *I cannot go for a trip tomorrow*. The reason is that *I am ill* etc. In these structures, the second discourse argument *I am ill* (syntactically a nominal content subordinate clause) is dependent on the connective structure *the reason is* (syntactically the main clause). This is a phenomenon that can never occur to primary connectives – in case of the primary connective (*I cannot go for a trip tomorrow* because *I am ill*), the second argument would be syntactically dependent on the first one. This is one of the phenomena making secondary connectives unique and original structures among the whole class of discourse connectives.

Most of the secondary connectives (apart from the lexically restricted phrases) are modifiable. So we may say *the main/only/first/important... reason is*.

Some secondary connectives have even a form of a separate sentence like *The reason is simple/easy*. etc. – see Example 4 from PDT:

(4) *S vašimi akciemi se musí obchodovat na burze, ale Wall Street vám nabízí cenu z RMS.*
Důvod je vcelku jednoduchý.
V RMS je cena většiny akcií nižší než na burze.

'You must trade with your shares on the stock market, but the Wall Street offers you a price of RMS.
The reason is quite simple.
In RMS, the price of most stocks is lower than on the stock market.'

In this respect, the secondary connectives demonstrate another big difference from the primary ones – they may stay alone, outside the discourse arguments, i.e. outside the two units of a text they connect. So it is interesting that some secondary connectives show a big deal of independency, as they may form syntactically and semantically complete textual units.

The secondary connectives in the form of whole separate sentences may be replaceable by primary connectives, but only in some cases – when the suitable primary connective allows the same modification as appears in the connective sentence – cf. *The reason is simple*. may be substituted by the modified primary connective *simply because*. In case of more complex modification, the substitution is only partial – some of the lexical meaning is lost. Cf. the PDT example *Další důvod je složitější a je v podstatě filozofický 'Another reason is more complex and in essence philosophical'* that cannot be fully replaced by the primary connective, as we cannot say **philosophically because*. Therefore, the substitution by primary connectives is very limited in these cases.

The secondary connectives form altogether 5 % of all discourse relations (expressed explicitly) in the Prague Dependency Treebank, so their frequency in the texts is much lower than in case of the primary connectives. This could be another reason why to call them secondary. On the other hand, although they seem to be peripheral as a whole group because of their lower frequency, they enrich the discourse by various structures and behaviour the primary connectives can never do. Therefore, due to their idiosyncrasy in behaviour, they occupy a special and unique place in discourse and the term secondary does not mean less important – we established the opposition of primary and secondary connectives mainly due to their peculiarities and different behaviour.

For the structured difference between the primary and secondary connectives see Table 2.

5.3 Permeability of Borderline between Primary and Secondary Connectives

Within the secondary connectives, we may observe several subclasses of expressions being closer or farther to primary ones. Some of the secondary connectives may even cross the borderline and become primary, as we will demonstrate in this section.

One large group of the secondary connectives are structures containing prepositions (like *because of*, *due to*, *in spite of*, *despite*, *except for* etc.) that obligatory combine with some anaphoric autosemantic words to become discourse connectives – cf. it is impossible to say **due to, I did it* but only *due to this, I did it*.

Primary Connectives	Secondary Connectives
synsemantics	structures with autosemantic words
lexically frozen (grammaticalized)	open or fixed collocations (non-grammaticalized)
non-modifiable (with exceptions)	modifiable (with exceptions)
mainly one-word	mainly multiword
universal	universal
not sentence elements	sentence elements, clause modifiers or separate sentences
	convey anaphoric reference to the 1st argument
	uniqueness of some structures:
	a) syntactically higher than the 2nd argument
	b) form of a separate sentence
	c) nominalization of the 2nd argument

Table 2: Characteristic of Primary and Secondary Connectives

The secondary prepositions may combine with various nouns and pronouns (cf. examples like *because of this*, *because of this situation*, *because of this increase* or *because of their help*). Some of these variants are context dependent (as *because of their help*), some are universal (*because of this*).

The universal connecting structures are prepositions in combination especially with an anaphoric pronoun *this* and are very close to the primary connectives.

Primary connectives are lexically frozen, grammaticalized expressions that have also not been primary connectives from their origin. We will demonstrate this on examples of primary connectives that historically consisted of two words and later became grammaticalized as one-word connectives. A typical example is the primary connective *therefore* that arose from the connection of *there* and a preposition *fore* (an Old English and Middle English collateral form of the preposition *for*) meaning *in consequence of that*. The same historical process may be seen in case of the foreign counterparts of *therefore* – like Czech connective *proto* (a connection of the preposition *pro* '*for*' and the pronoun *to* '*this*'), Dutch *daarfoor*, German *dafür* or Danish *derfor*.[4] So we may see that this process is not language specific but that it happened similarly in more languages. Since this process is generally common in language, there is a possibility that it might occur again.

Therefore, today's similar combinations of prepositions and anaphoric pronouns like *due to this*, *despite this* (in Czech *kvůli tomu*, *navzdory tomu*) etc. functioning as universal secondary connectives might be grammaticalized as well and might cross the borderline toward the primary connectives in the future.

In this respect, we understand the borderline between primary and secondary connectives as being permeable, i.e. that some structures from the secondary connectives may undergo changes that would fix them to expressions with the primary connecting function.

6 Conclusion

In the paper, we introduced the annotations of discourse relations in the Prague Dependency Treebank, especially the annotation principles for expressions like *hlavní podmínkou je* '*the main condition is*', *to je důvod, proč* '*that is the reason why*' etc. signaling relations within a text.

On the large data analysis, we tried to contribute to the general discussion on discourse connectives and especially on their definition. We suggest a division of connectives on primary and secondary. Primary connectives are mainly one-word expressions, lexically frozen that are not integrated into the clause structure as sentence elements and whose primary function is to connect two pieces of a text. The primary connectives form 95 % of all explicitly expressed discourse relations in PDT and therefore we consider them the center of all connective expressions.

The secondary connectives function as connectives mainly in various structures or combinations, they may be integrated into clause structure as sentence elements (like *because of this*), function as sentence modifiers (like *simply*

[4] Other similar examples in English are, e.g., *thereafter*, *thereupon* etc.

speaking) or may even form a separate sentence (*the reason is simple*). All of them contain autosemantic words, most often nouns (*reason*, *cause*, *explanation*...), or verbs (*to explain*, *to result*, *to continue*...). The secondary connectives function as connectives universally (like *because of this*), which makes them closer to primary connectives (like *therefore*, *thereafter*). Other connecting structures are contextually dependent (like *because of this increase*). These non-universal phrases are on the very edge of the connecting elements and they have very little chance to be grammaticalized. Therefore, we do not count them among connectives.

Although the secondary connectives are not as frequent as the primary ones and in this respect, they could be viewed as the periphery within all connectives, they enriched the discourse annotation of Czech in PDT by 1,161 of new relations. Moreover, some of them behave differently than the primary connectives (e.g., they may form a separate sentence or stay syntactically higher than the second argument). Because of this idiosyncrasy, they have a unique place within other expressions structuring discourse.

Acknowledgments

This paper was supported by the project "Discourse Relations within a Text" solved at the Faculty of Arts, Charles University in Prague from the funding of the Specific university research for the year 2014.
The authors acknowledge support from the Czech Science Foundation (project n. P406/12/0658) and from the Ministry of Education, Youth and Sports of the Czech Republic (project n. LM2010013 LINDAT/CLARIN and n. LH14011).
The authors gratefully thank to Jiří Mírovský from the Charles University in Prague for his kind measuring the figures on the PDT data for this paper.

References

Eduard Bejček et al. 2012. Prague Dependency Treebank 2.5 – a revisited version of PDT 2.0. In: *Proceedings of Coling 2012*, Bombay, India, pp. 231–246.

Diane Blakemore. 2002. *Relevance and Linguistic Meaning. The Semantics of Discourse Markers*. Cambridge, Cambridge University Press.

Teuen A. van Dijk. 1979. Pragmatic Connectives. In: *Journal of Pragmatics 3*. North-Holland Publishing Company, pp. 447–456.

Lucie Poláková et al. 2012. *Prague Discourse Treebank 1.0*. Data/software, ÚFAL MFF UK, Prague, Czech Republic.

Rashmi Prasad, Aravind Joshi, Bonnie Weber. 2010. Realization of Discourse Relations by Other Means: Alternative Lexicalizations. In: *Proceedings of Coling 2010*, Tsinghua University Press, Beijing, China, pp. 1023–1031.

Gisela Redeker. 1991. Linguistic markers of discourse structure. In: *Linguistics 29(6)*, pp. 1139-1172.

Magdaléna Rysová. 2012. Alternative Lexicalizations of Discourse Connectives in Czech. In: *Proceedings of the 8th International Conference on Language Resources and Evaluation (LREC 2012)*, European Language Resources Association, Istanbul, Turkey, ISBN 978-2-9517408-7-7, pp. 2800–2807. WWW: http://lrec.elra.info/proceedings/lrec2012/pdf/420_Paper.pdf

Magdaléna Rysová. 2014. Verbs of Saying with a Textual Connecting Function in the Prague Discourse Treebank. In: *Proceedings of the Ninth International Conference on Language Resources and Evaluation (LREC'14)*, European Language Resources Association, Reykjavik, Iceland, ISBN 978-2-9517408-8-4, pp. 930–935. WWW: http://www.lrec-conf.org/proceedings/lrec2014/pdf/79_Paper.pdf

Magdaléna Rysová, Jiří Mírovský. 2014. Use of Coreference in Automatic Searching for Multiword Discourse Markers in the Prague Dependency Treebank. In: *Proceedings of The 8th Linguistic Annotation Workshop (LAW-VIII)*. Dublin, Ireland, ISBN 978-1-941643-29-7, pp. 11–19. WWW: http://www.aclweb.org/anthology/W14-4902

Deborah Schiffrin. 1994. *Approaches to Discourse*. Malden (MA), Blackwell. ISNB 0-631-16623-8.

Toward a Discourse Theory for Annotating Causal Relations in Japanese

Kimi Kaneko
Ochanomizu University
kaneko.kimi@is.ocha.ac.jp

Daisuke Bekki
Ochanomizu University
National Institute of Informatics
CREST, JST
bekki@is.ocha.ac.jp

Abstract

We present a revised discourse theory based on segmented discourse representation theory and provide a method for building a Japanese corpus suitable for causal relation extraction. This extends and refines the framework proposed in Kaneko and Bekki (2014), and we evaluate our corpus and compare it with that work.

1 Introduction

In recent years, considerable attention has been paid to deep semantic processing. Many studies, including Bethard et al. (2008), Inui et al. (2007), Inui et al. (2003), and Riaz and Girju (2013), have recently been conducted on deep semantic processing, and causal relation extraction (hereinafter, CRE) is one of the specific tasks of deep semantic processing. Research on CRE is still progressing, and there are many obstacles that must be overcome.

In Inui et al. (2003), cause and effect pairs were acquired from Japanese texts by using keywords such as "node" and "kara". In (1), for example, the antecedent *ame-ga hut-ta* ("it rained") denotes an event taken as a cause, and the consequent *mizutamari-ga dekita* ("puddles emerged") denotes an event taken as an effect.

(1) Ame-ga hut-ta-<u>node</u>
rain-NOM fall-past-<u>*because*</u>
mizutamari-ga deki-ta.
puddles-NOM emerge-past
'Because it rained, puddles emerged.'

However, antecedents do not always denote causes or reasons for consequents, as illustrated by the following example.

(2) Kesa kubi-ga
this.morning neck-NOM
itakat-ta-<u>*node*</u>
have.a.pain-past-<u>*because*</u>
netigae-ta-no daroo.
strain.my.neck-past-attr may.
'Because I had a pain in my neck this morning, I might have strained my neck while sleeping.'

In example (2), the antecedent *kesa kubi-ga itakat-ta* ("I had a pain in my neck this morning") is not taken as the cause of the consequent *netigae-ta* ("I strained my neck while sleeping") but as the basis for the judgment expressed by the consequent. In this example, the consequent denotes the cause, and the antecedent denotes its effect. For a computer to automatically recognize causal relations in text, it is important to distinguish cases like (2) from cases like (1). However, existing studies have not dealt with these kinds of problems.

To solve such problems, Kaneko and Bekki (2014) (henceforth K&B) analyzed the information necessary for acquiring more accurate cause–effect knowledge and proposed a method for creating a Japanese corpus suitable for CRE. However, as is explained below, some problems remain: first, the coverage of discourse relations is not sufficient; second, annotating at two levels (i.e. fact and epistemic levels) is sometimes redundant.

Copyright 2014 by Kimi Kaneko and Daisuke Bekki
28th Pacific Asia Conference on Language, Information and Computation pages 460–469

We try to solve these remaining problems in K&B; toward that end, we propose a new method for building a Japanese corpus for causal relation extraction. In addition, we evaluate the validity of our method in terms of agreement and frequency, and analyze the results.

2 Previous Studies

In this section, we introduce some of the previous studies on annotation of temporal, causal, and other relations, as well as some linguistic analyses of temporal, causal and discourse relations.

Bethard et al. (2008) generated English data sets annotated with temporal and causal relations and analyzed interactions between the relations. In addition, these specialized data sets were evaluated in terms of inter-annotators agreement and accuracy. Relations were classified into two causal categories (CAUSAL, NO-REL) and three temporal categories (BEFORE, AFTER, NO-REL). With regard to the evaluation, they pointed out that the classification was coarse and that reanalysis with finer relations would be necessary. Moreover, they reported that some event pairs have ambiguous temporal relations. For (3), for example, it was difficult for most annotators to judge which event of "was ahead from the start" and "don't need to invite in competitive allies" precedes the other and how much the events temporally overlap.

(3) IBM established its standard to try to stop falling behind upstart Apple Computer, but NEC [$_{EVENT}$ *was*] ahead from the start and didn't [$_{EVENT}$ *need*] to invite in competitive allies.[1]

Inui et al. (2005) characterized causal expressions in Japanese text and built a Japanese corpus with tagged causal relations. However, usages such as that illustrated in (2) and interactions between temporal relations and causal relations were not analyzed.

Asher and Lascaridas (2003)'s segmented discourse representation theory (SDRT) is a formal discourse theory that accounts for cases in which discourse relations (rhetorical relations) interact with the truth-conditional meanings of sentences. Some of the discourse relations in SDRT have constraints on temporal and causal relations, so that we can calculate semantic contents that interact with them by means of sequences of logical reasoning. Consequently, we can build a corpus for CRE in which we have considered the influences of discourse and temporal relations by annotating not only causal relations but also discourse relations in SDRT into text. As examples of theories of discourse relations, we mention especially rhetorical structure theory (RST) (Mann and Thompson, 1987) and cross-document structure theory (CST) (Radev, 2000). One of the problems that they equally share is the inability to exhibit sequences of reasoning based on nonverbal information for specifying discourse relations. To solve this problem, exhibiting a process of sequences of reasoning should be possible.

K&B reframed SDRT by distinguishing between discourse relations, temporal relations, and causal relations, and annotated Japanese texts with these three types of relations. These relations are assigned at two levels: the fact level, which describes the fact that is actually occurring in the real world, and the epistemic level, which describes what the speaker recognizes as the fact. Example (1) is annotated as in (4).

(4) Fact-level: [**Precedence(π1,π3), Explanation(π1,π3), CAUSE(π1,π3)**],
Epistemic-level: [**Precedence(π2,π4), Explanation(π2,π4), CAUSE(π2,π4)**],
$_{\pi2\pi1}$Ame-ga hut-ta-*node*,
$_{\pi4\pi3}$ mizutamari-ga dekita.

According to K&B, discourse relations and causal relations impose some restrictions on the interpretation of temporal relations. For example, the relation CAUSE(A,B) imposes the temporal relation Precedence(A,B). In (4), CAUSE(π1,π3) imposes the temporal constraint Precedence(π1,π3) at the fact level; at the same time, CAUSE(π2,π4) imposes

[1] This sentence was extracted from Bethard et al. (2008).

Precedence($\pi 2,\pi 4$) at the epistemic level. In the following example, by contrast, the causal and temporal relations at the fact level that hold between the main clause and the subordinate clause are reversed at the epistemic level.

(5) Fact-level: [**Precedence($\pi 3,\pi 1$), Explanation($\pi 1,\pi 3$), CAUSE($\pi 3,\pi 1$)**],
Epistemic-level: [**Precedence($\pi 2,\pi 4$), Explanation($\pi 2,\pi 4$), CAUSE($\pi 2,\pi 4$)**],
$_{\pi 2 \pi 1}$Kesa kubi-ga itakat-ta -*node*,
$_{\pi 4 \pi 3}$netigae-ta-no-daroo.

Note that by distinguishing the two levels, the temporal constraints that discourse and causal relations impose are kept consistent. In (5), the temporal constraints Precedence($\pi 3,\pi 1$) and Precedence($\pi 2,\pi 4$) hold at different levels, so no contradiction arises here. In this way, K&B can handle examples, like (5), that involve an apparent mismatch between causal and temporal relations.

However, it is not clear whether this approach would also be effective for a large-scale corpus because the data sets built by K&B are relatively small. In this study, we follow the approach of K&B and attempt to build a Japanese corpus tagged with discourse relations for CRE. In the course of doing so, we have discovered that the theory of K&B has the following problems.

- The coverage of discourse relations is sometimes insufficient. The balanced corpus of contemporary written Japanese (BCCWJ) (Maekawa, 2008) is designed as a corpus that contains texts of various styles, and further annotation has revealed that the set of discourse relations in K&B covers only some parts of the possible relations.
- Annotating both fact- and epistemic-level information for every pair of segments is redundant. As mentioned above, the distinction between fact- and epistemic-level information plays an important role in K&B, but in most cases the information will coincide.
- Judging the temporal relation between the events is not an easy task; however, the "Narration" family can only be further classified by means of the temporal relations. We can highlight the difficulty by the following simple example (6).

(6) a. Nippon-no natu-wa atui.
Japan-GEN summer-TOP be.hot
Ippou-de, Nippon-no
on.the.other.hand Japan-GEN
huyu-wa samui.
winter-TOP be.cold
'The summer is hot in Japan. On the other hand, the winter is cold in Japan.'

b. Fact-level: [**Narration($\pi 1,\pi 3$)?, Overlap($\pi 1,\pi 3$)?**][2],
Epistemic-level: [**Narration($\pi 2,\pi 4$)?, Overlap($\pi 2,\pi 4$)?**],
$_{\pi 2 \pi 1}$Nippon-no natu-wa atui.
$_{\pi 4}$Ippoo-de, $_{\pi 3}$Nippon-no huyu-wa samui.

One may tag this sentence pair with the "Narration" label, which actually includes different kinds of narrative relations, such as "Background" and "Parallel" relations, depending on the temporal relation between them. However, both sentences of example (6) are generic, which means there is no temporal order between the things described. In other words, we can decide neither which fact occurred earlier nor which fact was recognized earlier.

One may additionally tag this sentence with the "Overlap" label described in K&B, but it is apparent that the times spanned by "summer" never overlap those spanned by "winter," contradictory to what the "Overlap" label means. Because of this, the descriptive power of the label set described in K&B is insufficient, and so we have to reconsider the label system.

This study aims to rearrange K&B's theory on the basis of further reflections on SDRT as a means to rebuild an exhaustive theory of discourse relations for CRE. First, we propose

[2]In K&B, pairs of sentences are not tagged with causal relations when there is no causal relation.

a new annotation scheme to solve the above-mentioned problems. Second, we focus on the first problem and annotate sentences with this new setting. Finally, we evaluate and analyze our annotation scheme and the data set.

3 Method

We extended and refined K&B and developed a new method for annotating the relation between the following segment pairs in discourse.

1. A discourse and a subsequent sentence
2. A main clause and its subordinate clause
   (a) when the predicate of subordinate clause is in continuation form or "te"-form)
   (b) when two clauses are connected by causal suffixes (e.g. "node", "kara")

3.1 Causal Relation

We distinguish two different kinds of 'causal' relations and annotate them separately. **Explanation** is a discourse relation, which is a relation between two linguistic expressions, and **Cause** is a causal relation between two propositions.[3]

As a discourse relation, **Explanation** is a relation between two adjacent segments: in other words, it is a grammatical relation between two constituents. In contrast, **Cause** is a relation between facts and not restricted to two adjacent segments. **Cause**(A,B) is the only causal relation that we adopt, as shown in Table 1. We use the tag only when there exists a causal relation between a pair of propositions A and B; in other cases, no annotation is used.

The distinction between these two relations is essential because, on one hand, the causality may not be expressed linguistically and, on the other hand, a linguistically claimed causal relation does not ensure actual causality.

As an example of the former case, consider (7), where John's putting the banana peel is in reality a possible cause of Bill's tumbling even though it is not linguistically marked. The discourse relation between the two sentences here is **Narration**, which specifies only a temporal relation between them (as consecutive events).

(7) John-ga bananaokawa-wo
John-NOM banana.peel-ACC
yuka-ni oi-ta. Bill-ga
the.floor-LOC put-past Bill-NOM
koron-da.
tumble-past
'John put a banana peel on the floor. Then, Bill tumbled.'

The latter case is exemplified by (8), where the speaker claims that John's rain-making ritual caused the rain, by using a causal discourse relation, although nobody can tell whether it is in fact so.

(8) John-ga amagoi-wo
John-NOM rain.making.ritual-ACC
si-ta-node ame-ga fut-ta
do-past-*cause* rain-NOM fall-past
noda.
epistemic.modal-pres
'Because John performed a rain-making ritual, it rained.'

3.2 Without a Fact/Epistemic Level Distinction

Unlike K&B, we abolish the distinction between the factual and epistemic levels. We distinguish only whether a given segment is propositional or modal (including the segment with the causal suffix "node" and the epistemic modal suffix "noda": the former roughly corresponds to the fact level, and the latter to the epistemic level).

This decision substantially simplifies and reduces the work of annotators. However, the distinction between fact and epistemic levels is one of the core ideas in K&B used to avoid temporal contradiction, which we described in Section 1. Therefore, we have to show how our simplified setting is still free from that contradiction.

As examples, the result of annotating (1) and (2) are shown in (9) and (10), respectively.

[3] A "proposition" in this paper is a tensed predicate (e.g. "fall," "have a pain," and "strain" in (1)(2)) whose eventuality is either an event or a state, along with its arguments and modifiers.

Level	Description
Cause(A,B)	The proposition A is a cause of the proposition B.

Table 1: Causal relation

(9) [**Explanation(π2,π3), Cause(π1,π3)**]
$_{\pi 2 \pi 1}$Ame-ga hut-ta-*node*,
$_{\pi 3}$mizutamari-ga dekita.

a". Temporal relation:
Precedence(π1,π3), Precedence(π2,π3)

(10) [**Explanation(π2,π4), Cause(π3,π1)**]
$_{\pi 2 \pi 1}$Kesa kubi-ga itakat-ta -*node*,
$_{\pi 4 \pi 3}$netigae-ta-no-daroo.

a". Temporal relation:
Precedence(π3,π1), Precedence(π2,π4)

Both **Cause**(A,B) and **Explanation**(A,B) require that a temporal relation Precedence(A,B) holds[4] since a cause must precede its effect (otherwise, it is not a cause–effect relation). The issue is determining whether these two relations impose contradictory temporal relations.

In (10), the antecedent part π2 of the conditional has the causal suffix "node", which embeds a propositional part π1, and the consequent part π4 has the modal suffix *daroo*, which also embeds a propositional part π3.

Because **Explanation** is a discourse relation, it is a relation between a pair of adjacent segments π2 and π4. As a result, it is a relation between two modal expressions, stating that "Realizing that I had a pain in my neck caused me to infer that I strained my neck," which is as expected. The temporal requirement Precedence(π2,π4) is that realization of a pain precedes the inference of the strain, which is also as expected.

In contrast, **Cause**(π3,π1) in (10) is a causal relation between the propositions π3 and π1, namely, straining the neck is a cause of the pain. Here, the temporal requirement is Precedence(π3,π1), which states that the strain must precede the pain.

[4]For the sake of brevity, we do not discuss the details of temporal relations in this paper.

In this way, two different precedence relations, one at the fact level and the other at the epistemic level, can be properly treated in this setting, without introducing fact and epistemic levels to every segment.

3.3 Discourse Relations

In addition to **Explanation**, we have the set of discourse relations, based on SDRT and K&B, shown in Table 2. It is also shown in Table 3 how discourse relations in our method correspond to those in K&B and those in SDRT. As Table 3 displays, discourse relations in our study integrate the temporal relations and discourse relations of K&B.

Moreover, a procedure to identify discourse relations in our method is shown below.

Procedure:

1. First, judge the logical relation between the pair A and B to determine whether it is conjunctive, disjunctive, or conditional (by the standard truth-conditional tests):
   (a) If it is disjunctive, tag it with the **Alternation** label.
   (b) If it is conditional, tag it with the **Consequence** label.
   (c) If it is conjunctive, proceed to 2.
2. Judge whether the relation is adversative or contrastive:
   (a) If it is adversative, proceed to 3.
   (b) If it is contrastive, especially when expressions such as "*sikasi*", "*tokoroga*" appear, tag it with the **Contrast** label.
3. (a) If B describes an event that is a part of the whole event described by A, then tag the relation with the **Elaboration** label.

[5]Temp_rel(A,B) $\equiv$ Precedence(A,B) $\vee$ Overlap(A,B) $\vee$ Subsumption(A,B)

Label	Description
Alternation(A,B)	"A or B": logical disjunction ($A \lor B$).
Consequence(A,B)	"If A then B": logical implication ($A \rightarrow B$).
Contrast(A,B)	"A but B": B contrasts with A.
Elaboration(A,B)	B describes a part of A in detail.
Explanation(A,B)	A is a cause and B is its effect.
Commentary(A,B)	The content of A is summarized or complemented by B.
Instance(A,B)	"A, for example, B',' where B describes an instance of A.
Addition(A,B)	The description of the state B is added to the description of the state A.
Parallel(A,B)	The two events A and B overlap.
Narration(A,B)	The occurrence of the event B is subsequent to that of A.
Introduction(A,B)	B introduces a new reference point that is independent from that of A.
Background(A,B)	B describes the background situation of the event A.

Table 2: Discourse relation list

Ours	SDRT	K&B
Cause(A,B)	Explanation(A,B)	CAUSE(A,B)
Alternation(A,B)	Alternation(A,B)	Alternation(A,B)
Consequence(A,B)	Consequence(A,B)	Consequence(A,B)
Contrast(A,B)	Contrast(A,B)	Contrast(A,B)
Elaboration(A,B)	Elaboration(A,B)	Elaboration(A,B)
Explanation(A,B)	Result(A,B)	Explanation(A,B)
Commentary(A,B)	Commentary(A,B)	Commentary(A,B)
Instance(A,B)	–	–
Addition(A,B)	Parallel(A,B)	Narration(A,B)∧Overlap (A,B)
Parallel(A,B)		Parallel(A,B)
Narration(A,B)	Narration(A,B)	Narration(A,B)∧Precedence (A,B)
Introduction(A,B)	Narration(A,B)	Narration(A,B)∧Temp_rel(A,B)[5]
Background(A,B)	Background(A,B)	Narration(A,B)∧Subsumption (A,B)

Table 3: Correspondence among K&B, SDRT, and our method

(b) If A describes the basis of the judgment B, particularly indicated when an expression such as "*dakara*", "*sitagatte*", or "*yueni*" appears, tag the relation with the **Explanation** label.

(c) If B is a summary, a restatement, or a complementary remark of A, especially when expressions such as "*tumari*" and "*yoosuruni*" appear, then tag the relation with the **Commentary** label.

(d) If A is a universal or generic sentence and B is an instance of A, then tag the relation with the **Instance** label.

(e) Otherwise, proceed to 4.

4. Judge whether the eventualities of A and B are events or states, and the reference points (in the sense of tense) of A and B:

(a) If both A and B are states, then tag the relation with the **Addition** label.

(b) If both A and B are events and they take place in the same time span (and overlap), then tag the relation with the **Parallel** label.

(c) If B is an event and B happens successively to A, then tag the relation with the **Narration** label. Specifically, do so when B's reference point is just after A's reference point.

(d) If A is a state, B is an event, and B introduces a reference point that is independent of A's reference point, then tag the relation with the **Introduction** label.

(e) If A is an event, B is a state, and B's reference point is the same as A's, then tag the relation with **Background** label.

The whole decision process is depicted by Figure 1.

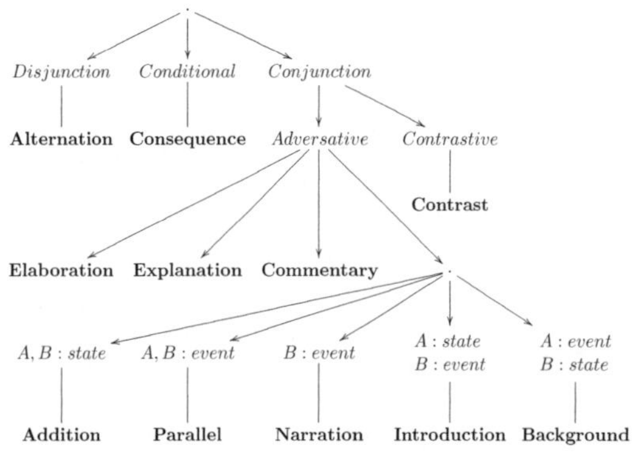

Figure 1: Decision tree for discourse relations

3.4 Comparison with Kaneko and Bekki (2014)

We compare our approach to that of K&B.

First, we refined the set of discourse relations in K&B by adding new discourse relations, as necessitated by the cases that K&B's set of discourse relation does not cover.

Second, we proposed a decision procedure in Figure 1 for classifying a discourse relation. We consider this as a substantial advance since the previous criteria for identifying discourse relations in K&B are vague and we believe that we could make them clearer.

Third, we abolished the distinction between the fact and epistemic levels, which makes our annotation far simpler than that of K&B, while still enabling us to deal with the cases, such as (2), in which the temporal precedence relations at the fact and epistemic levels seem to contradict, as discussed in Section 3.

4 Results

We applied our method to 128 sentences from BCCWJ (Maekawa, 2008). The labels were assigned to the sentences by two annotators. During labeling, we used the labels presented in Section 3. Our method was developed on the basis of 73 sentences, and by using the 73 sentences and the other 55 sentences, we evaluated the inter-annotators agreement and kappa coefficient as well as the number of annotations and compared the results with those of K&B. The agreement for 128 sentences was 0.67 and was computed as follows (the kappa coefficient was 0.57).

$$Agreement \quad = \quad Identical\ labels/Total\ labels$$

K&B reported an agreement rate of 0.68, although they computed the agreement by using annotated segment data, which means the results are not directly comparable to ours. Nevertheless, the close values suggest that our method is comparable to that in K&B's study in terms of agreement.

Analyzing more segments in actual text and improving our method could lead to further improvement in terms of agreement.

An average of 20 and 11 sentences were tagged per hour in our study and K&B's study, respectively. This indicates that the complexity of our method is not much different from that in K&B.

Table 4 shows the distribution of labels into segments in K&B and into sentences in our study. **Background**, **Addition**, **Parallel**, **Introduction** and **Instance** were newly added in our study. "Narration" in K&B covers **Back-**

Label	**K&B**			**Ours (sentences)**
	Total	Fact	Epistemic	Total
Precedence	25	14	11	–
Overlap	7	4	3	–
Subsumption	61	29	32	–
Total	**94**	**47**	**47**	–
CAUSE	14	8	6	6
Total	**14**	**8**	**6**	**6**
Alternation	–	–	–	–
Consequence	6	3	3	–
Explanation	14	7	7	9
Contrast	2	1	1	6
Commentary	–	–	–	6
Narration	66	33	33	52
Background	–	–	–	1
Addition	–	–	–	17
Parallel	–	–	–	0
Introduction	–	–	–	8
Elaboration	4	2	2	23
Instance	–	–	–	6
Total	**94**	**47**	**47**	**128**

Table 4: Distribution of labels to segments in our study for the BCCWJ (italicized labels are newly added).

ground, **Addition**, and **Parallel**. "Elaboration" in K&B and SDRT includes **Instance**. While **Narration** was the most frequently used label, and so it was biased greatly in K&B, the frequency of each relation in our study is more balanced than that in K&B. Thus, the classification in our study is more appropriate for performing machine learning. However, whether our method is truly more appropriate than K&B should be judged by annotating segments with our relations and comparing those results with K&B.

We can see from Table 4 that **Narration** was still the most frequently used label, and some labels, such as **Alternation**, never appeared. As a result, we can assume that frequent relations will be distinct from non-frequent relations. So far, all relations are either frequent or non-frequent, although a larger data set should be analyzed to confirm this.

5 Discussion

We analyzed errors in this annotation exercise. First, under the current version of our annotation guideline, some judgments inevitably remain ambiguous. We explain when and why this happens, in a mini-discourse example shown in Fig.2 (p.10). The annotators do not agree with the results of annotations for $\pi 4$ in the sentence (14): their results range over **Addition**($\pi 1$,$\pi 4$) (or **Addition**($\pi 2$,$\pi 4$)), **Commentary**($\pi 1$,$\pi 4$), and **Narration**($\pi 3$,$\pi 4$). The problem is that this case may be actually ambiguous among these three cases, and none of the choices alone adequately explains the discourse relation.

The **Addition** label here breaks the continuous structure from $\pi 1$ to $\pi 4$ by skipping $\pi 3$ and directly connects to $\pi 1$ or $\pi 2$, which is due to the restriction that its first argument must be a state but $\pi 3$ is an event. However, this choice does not correctly capture the structure of the discourse, in which the sequence of sentences $\pi 1$ to $\pi 4$ seem to incrementally add information to the discourse.

The **Commentary** label currently covers several heterogeneous cases: (1) the case that the second argument is a summary of the first argument, (2) the case that the second argument is a restatement of the first argument, and (3) the case that the second argument adds some supplementary comments (such as footnotes). Now, the third case applies to $\pi 4$; however, this is not distinguishable from the **Addition** label. It is necessary to separate the different uses of this label.

The **Narration** label, which has a restriction that the second argument must be a state, is reasonable if we assume that the verb with the aspect "teiru" (a perfect suffix) in $\pi 4$ denotes an event. However, the reference time of $\pi 3$ is in the year 2004 while that of $\pi 4$ is a speech time, which is a bit too long of a time span to consider $\pi 3$ and $\pi 4$ to be sequential.

Second, there are problems in annotating non-assertive sentences, such as interjections, exclamatory sentences, and rhetorical questions. They appear not only in dialogue but also in monologue, which causes difficulty in making a judgment about their discourse relation to previous sentences.

At present, we treat interjections such as "Ooops!" as if they are ellipses: for example, we may regard its full form as "I cried out ooops!", and judge their relations accordingly.

The cases of rhetorical questions such as "how do I know it?", as in 15, can be treated in the same way; for example, here we regard it as an elliptical form of the full form "I wonder how I know it."

(15) Dare-demo sorekurai-wa
everyone-NOM to.such.extent-ACC
taiken-siteiru daroo to
experience-perf may that
souzou-siteiru noda-ga,
imagine-prog I.know-but
doudaroo.
how.do.I.know
'I imagine that everyone may have experienced such things, but how do I know?'

However, it should be further investigated whether this method can be applied to all cases in a uniform and principled manner.

6 Conclusions

We proposed a method for discourse annotation based on a discourse theory that revises and extends that of K&B as a means of building a more precise Japanese corpus for CRE. We have annotated 128 sentences in BCCWJ with discourse relations and causal relations, and compared the annotations of 128 of these sentences with the annotations in K&B in terms of agreement, kappa coefficient, frequencies, and time needed for decomposition. We reported and analyzed the results and discussed some problems of our method. For future work, we intend to address the problems we described in Sections 4 and 5 by the further refinement of our discourse theory.

Acknowledgments

Our sincere thanks to Koji Mineshima and Maika Utsugi for many helpful discussions, and to the anonymous reviewers of PACLIC28 for insightful comments. This research is partially supported by JST, CREST and Data Centric Science Research Commons.

References

Asher N. and Lascaridas A. 2003. *Logics of Conversation: Studies in Natural Language Processing.* Cambridge University Press, Cambridge, UK.

Bethard S., Corvey W. and Kilingenstein S. 2008. *Building a Corpus of Temporal Causal Structure.* LREC 2008, Marrakech, Morocco.

Inui T., Inui K. and Matsumoto Y. 2005. *Acquiring Causal Knowledge from Text Using the Connective Marker Tame.* ACM Transactions on Asian Language Information Processing (ACM-TALIP), Vol.4, Issue 4, Special Issue on Recent Advances in Information Processing and Access for Japanese, 435–474.

Inui T., Inui K. and Matsumoto Y. 2003. *What Kinds and Amounts of Causal Knowledge Can Be Aquired from Text by Using Connective Markers as Clues.* The 6th International Conference on Discovery Science (DS-2003), 180–193.

Inui T., Takamura H. and Okumura M. 2007. *Latent Variable Models for Causal Knowledge Acquisition. Alexander Gelbukh(Ed.), Computational Linguistics and Intelligent Text Processing, Lecture Notes in Computer Science,* 4393:85–96.

Kaneko K. and Bekki D. 2014. *Building a Japanese Corpus of Temporal-Causal-Discourse Structures Based on SDRT for Extracting Causal Relations.* EACL-2014 Workshop on Computational Approaches to Causality in Language, 33–39.

Maekawa K. 2008. *Balanced Corpus of Contemporary Written Japanese.* In Proceedings of the 6th Workshop on Asian Language Resources (ALR), 101–102.

Mann W. C. and Thompson S. 1987. *Rhetorical Structure Theory: A Theory of Text Organization.* ISI Reprint Series, ISI/RS-87-190, 1–82.

Radev D.R. 2000. *A common theory of information fusion from multiple text sources step one: cross-document structure.* In SIGDIAL '00 Proceedings of the 1st SIGdial workshop on Discourse and dialogue, Volume 10, 74–83.

Riaz M. and Girju R. 2013. *Toward a Better Understanding of Causality between Verbal Events:Extraction and Analysis of the Causal Power of Verb-Verb Associations.* In Proceedings of the SIGDIAL 2013 Conference, Metz, France 21–30.

(11) π1:Bunkatyoo-bunkakooryuusi-zigyou-wa, nipponbunka-ni
Agency.for.Cultural.Affairs's.cultural.ambassador.project-TOP Japanese.culture-DAT
tazusawaru hitobito-ni "Bunkakooryuusi"-tosite nipponbunka-wo
be.concerned.with-attr people-DAT as."cultural.ambassadors" Japanese.culture-ACC
hiromete-moraukoto-wo mokuteki-tosite 2003-nendo-kara hazimeta zigyou-desu.
to.make.promote-ACC aim.for-cont from.year.2003 start-attr be.project-past

'The cultural ambassador project of the Agency for Cultural Affairs is a project that started in the year 2003 with the aim of appointing people who are concerned with Japanese culture to promote Japanese culture, as "cultural ambassadors." '

(12) π2:"Bunkakooryuusi"-no-katudoo-niwa, (i)"kaigaihaken-gata",
"cultural.ambassador"'s.activity-TOP "overseas.dispatching-type"
(ii)"gentitaizaisya-gata", (iii)"rainitigeizyutuka-gata"-no 3tu-no-ruikei-ga aru.
"immigrant-type" "visiting.artist-type" 3.types-NOM exist-pres

'There are three types of "cultural ambassador" activities: (i) "the overseas dispatching type," (ii) "the immigrant type," and (iii) "the visiting artist type".'

(13) π3:2004-nendo-wa, "kaigaihaken-gata"-bunkakooryuusi-tosite 11-mei,
In.year.2004-TOP as."overseas.dispatching-type"-cultural.ambassador 11-people
"gentitaizaisya-gata"-bunkakooryuusi-tosite 4-mei,
as."immigrant-type"-cultural.ambassador 4-people
"rainitigeizyutuka-gata"-tosite 4-kumi-no simei-wo
as."visiting.artist-type"-cultural-ambassador" 4-teams-ACC appoint-ACC
okonai-masi-ta.
execute-polite-past

'In the year 2004, the Agency for Cultural Affairs appointed 11 people as "overseas dispatching type" cultural ambassadors, 4 people as "immigrant type" cultural ambassadors, and 4 teams as "the type of artist who visits Japan" cultural ambassadors".'

(14) π4:Nipponbunka-ni nazimino-usukat-ta kuni ya tiiki-deno nipponbunnka-no
Japanese.culture-DAT unfamiliar.with-past country and area-LOC Japanese.culture-ACC
syoukai-wo okonatte-i-masu.
introduce-ACC execute-prog-polite

'Cultural ambassadors are introducing Japanese culture in countries and areas that were unfamiliar with Japanese culture.'

Figure 2: Example sentences and annotations

On-line Summarization of Time-series Documents using a Graph-based Algorithm

Satoko Suzuki
Graduate School of Humanities and Sciences, Ochanomizu University
2-1-1 Otsuka Bunkyo-ku Tokyo,Japan
suzuki.satoko@is.ocha.ac.jp

Ichiro Kobayashi
Graduate School of Humanities and Sciences, Ochanomizu University
2-1-1 Otsuka Bunkyo-ku Tokyo,Japan
koba@is.ocha.ac.jp

Abstract

As enormous amount of electronic documents on the Web have been increasing, the necessity of automatic summarization has also been increasing to help people grasp the essential points of the documents. Many summarization techniques dealing with single document and multi-documents have been studied. However, due to the increase of the documents which report the change of topics along a timeline, called time-series documents, in recent years, a summarization technique which generates a summary of time-series documents, called timeline summarization, has been actively studied as an area of automatic summarization. There are different difficulties in summarizing time-series documents from other type of automatic summarization. The basic approach for timeline summarization is to extract sentences which describe major events in object documents in chronological order to generate a timeline summary.

However, unlike the prior studies of timeline summarization, we particularly focus on on-line summarization of time-series documents and propose an on-line graph-based timeline summarization method. With our proposed method, a summary of time-series documents can be generated at any point of time when it is required. We conduct experiments to investigate the ability of our proposed method, evaluate the results with ROUGE metrics, and show our proposed method produces a better summary compared to other representative summarization methods.

1 Introduction

The automatic summarization techniques have been required due to increasing the amount of electronic documents. The object documents handled by automatic summarization are diverse from newspaper and academic articles to the documents used in social network services such as Weblog, Twitter, etc. Depending on object documents, an appropriate summarization technique is applied. Due to the increase of electronic documents updated day by day, in recent years, new techniques which summarize time-series documents, called timeline summarization, have been actively studied. There are different difficulties in summarizing time-series documents from other type of automatic summarization, because as for timeline summarization we have to summarize current information taking account of the information from the past. Besides, we have to decide the important information which should be included in a summary, tracking the change of topics. The basic approach for timeline summarization is to extract sentences which describe major events in object documents in chronological order to generate a timeline summary.

In this study we paticularly focus on the development of an on-line method to summarize time-series documents. To achieve this, we have to deal with various problems, for example, how to combine the current information with the information from the past in order to recompile object information to be summarized, how to track topics, how to rank important information, etc. To deal with these problems, we employ graph structure to represent sentence re-

Copyright 2014 by Satoko Suzuki and Ichiro Kobayashi
28th Pacific Asia Conference on Language, Information and Computation pages 470–478

lation and apply graph-based algorithm to extract important information from the graph — here, the graph is evolved along a timeline by combining the current and past information, and then it represents object information to be summarized. In our proposed method, a summary can be generated at any point of time by request.

The structure of this paper is as follows. Related studies are summarizsed in section 2. In section 3, we show our proposed method. In section 4, we explain the experiments based on our proposed method and discuss the results. Finally, we conclude this study in section 5.

2 Related Studies

As an application of automatic summarization, summarization of time-series document, called timeline summarization, has recently been actively studied. At an early stage of the development of the technique, Allan et al. (2001) have proposed several summarization methods for time-series documents and built evaluation corpus for the method. Chieu et al. (2004) have proposed a framework for making a timeline of events occurrence. They extract events, which correspond to important sentences, relevant to a query from documents and place such events along a timeline. Yan et al. (2011a) have also proposed a method to extract important sentences to make a timeline summary expanding the graph-based sentence ranking algorithm used for multi-document summarization, and proposed a summarization method, called Evolutionary Trans-Temporal Summarization (ETTS), which extracts sentences from different points of time in a particular period, and they have also proposed a method to optimize the function for the combination of important factors such as relevance, coverage, coherence and variety of words in a generated summary (Yan et al., 2011b). Tran et al. (2013a) have employed support vector machine based ranking algorithm to rank sentences with 28 features and selected sentences with high ranking score for a timeline summary. They have reported that their method outperforms other representative timeline summarization methods, e.g., (Yan et al., 2011a) and the reason for that is because they leverage some latent factors under supervision of human timelines.

As the studies using graph representation for the relation among sentences, Erkan et al. (2004) have introduced the PageRank algorithm to rank sentences in the order of high centrality and then extracted the sentences with high ranking score as important sentences which are expected to be included in a summary. Yan et al. (2012) have introduced hierarchical graph structure to represent both textual and semantic relation among sentences. Moreover, Li et al. (2013) have proposed a method called Evolutionary Hierarchical Dirichlet Process(EHDP) to consider the development of topics along a timeline. In their method, they have introduced a nonparametric Bayesian topic model to represent latent information among sentences — in their method, coverage and coherence are mainly considered for extracting sentences for a summary.

As the studies to focus on the topic development along a timeline, Zhao et al. (2013) have focused on the attention attracted to topics of interest – they call it social attention – to make a timeline summary which reflects user's interest. Hu et al. (2014) have explored the interactions of storylines in a news topic. They have especially focused on the coherence between news articles and discovered storyline interactions for timeline summarization.

Unlike the prior studies mentioned above, we focus on on-line summarization for time-series documents. The information reported in time-series documents such as news paper articles is updated day by day, and we often need a summary for the information which has so far been reported. Therefore, in this study we aim to propose an on-line summarization of time-series documents with a graph-based algorithm. By our method, a summary can be generated at any point of time when it is required.

3 On-line graph-based timeline summarization

Figure 1 illustrates an overview of our proposed method.

The basic framework for our proposed method is that a summary can be generated at any point of time when it is required, with the sentences which are both passed over from the past articles and the articles of that day. In each day, a graph representing the relation among sentences is constructed and

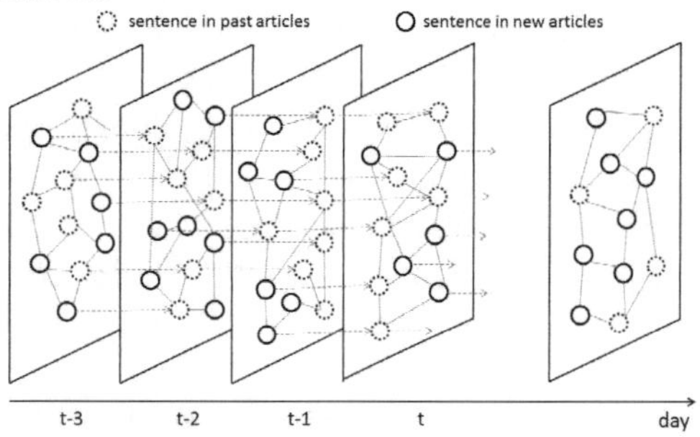

Figure 1: Overview of our proposed method

LexRank algorithm (Erkan et al., 2004) is applied to the graph to rank the sentences, which correspond to the nodes in the graph, based on the the centrality of the sentences in the graph. Based on the ranking score, a particular number of top sentences are selected and recompiled as a new object documents to be summarized, and then a summary is generated with the constraint on summary length. The summary candidate sentences are passed over to the next day as the sentences from past articles, and then a new graph consisting of both sentences from past and that day is reconstructed and the same procedure is applied to the updated graph. Like this, a series of the procedures is repeatedly applied to the summary candidate sentences in each day, and a summary of time-series documents is generated at any point of time when it is required.

The algorithm of our proposed method is shown in Algorithm 1.

Algorithm 1 ranking algorithm

```
Input: D_t, ε, l
S = { }
ε ← threshold
for t = 0 to T do
    S' ← S + D_t
    ranking S' with LexRank
    if length of S' > ε then
        S ← top ε sentences of S'
    else
        S ← S'
    end if
end for
return top l sentences of S
```

In Algorithm 1, D_t, ϵ, and l are provided as input values. Here,D_t is a set of documents provided at time t=$\{0,\ldots,T\}$, ϵ is the threshold of graph size, and l is the number of sentences included in a summary. $\boldsymbol{S}$ is a set of sentence candidates which are expected to be included in a generated summary. As mentioned above, as for the ranking algorithm for sentences, we employ LexRank algorithm proposed in (Erkan et al., 2004) – the detail procedure is shown in Algorithm 2.

Here, the similarity between two sentence vectors is defined as in equation (1).

$$\text{idf-modified-cosine}(x, y) = \frac{\sum_{w\in x,y} tf_{w,x} tf_{w,y} (idf_w)^2}{\sqrt{\sum_{x_i\in x}(tf_{x_i,x} idf_{x_i})^2} \times \sqrt{\sum_{y_i\in y}(tf_{y_i,y} idf_{y_i})^2}} \quad (1)$$

In the above equation, $tf_{w,s}$ indicates the frequency of word w in sentence s. x and y indicate sentences and x_i and y_i indicate words in x and y, respectively. idf_i is defined equation (2).

$$idf_i = \log \frac{N_d}{n_i} \quad (2)$$

N_d is the total number of the documents in $\boldsymbol{S}'$, and n_i is the number of documents in which word i occurs.

The score of node u is calculated based on equation (3).

$$p(u) = \frac{d}{N} + (1-d) \sum_{v\in adj[u]} \frac{p(v)}{deg(v)} \quad (3)$$

Here, N indicates the number of nodes in a graph, $adj[u]$ is a set of nodes adjoining sentence u. d is the damping factor to estimate the similarity between noncontiguous nodes with a particular rate. The generated graph shall be an unweighted graph whose edges are pruned by threshold t. Correspondingly, as a summarization method using a weighted graph, Continuous LexRank (Cont.LexRank) has been proposed (Erkan et al., 2004). In the method, edges are not pruned by threshold, but the similarity between the objective node and other nodes are accounted when calculating the score of the node. Therefore,

Algorithm 2 LexRank

```
Input: An array S of n sentences, cosine threshold t output: An array L of LexRank scores
Array CosineMatrix[n][n];
Array Degree[n];
Array L[n];
for i ← 1 to n do
   for j ← 1 to n do
     CosineMatrix[i][j] = idf-modified-cosine(S[i],S[j]);
     if CosineMatrix[i][j] > t then
       CosineMatrix[i][j] = 1;
       Degree[i]++;
     end
     else
       CosineMatrix[i][j] = 0;
     end
   end
end
for i ← 1 to n do
   for j ← 1 to n do
     CosineMatrix[i][j] = CosineMatrix[i][j]/Degree[i];
   end
end
L = PowerMthod(CosineMatrix,n,ε);
return L;
```

equation (3) which is used for calculating the socre of a node is enhanced as shown in equation (4).

$$p(u) = \frac{d}{N} + (1-d) \times \sum_{v \in adj[u]} \frac{\text{idf-modified-cosine}(u,v)}{\sum_{z \in adj[v]} \text{idf-modified-cosine}(z,v)} p(v) \quad (4)$$

In our proposed method, we limit the size of a graph. If the size of a graph, i.e., the number of sentences, exceeds the predefined threshold, it will be reduced to the size of the threshold. Then the sentences represented in the graph are ranked by LexRank algorithm and are extracted according to the raking score for a summary. In generating a summary, we use MMR-MD (Maximal Marginal Relevance-Multi Documents) proposed in (Goldstein et al., 2000) to avoid redundancy in a summary. This index works to avoid extracting similar sentences in a summary by providing penalty corresponding to the similarity between a newly extracted sentence and the already extracted sentences. It is often used for query-based summarization. In our method, it is required to extract the sentences which have high ranking score and are not similar to the already extracted sentences as a part of a summary. Therefore, we modify MMR-MD as shown in equation (5). We call our modified MMR-MD MMR' hereafter.

$$\text{MMR'} \equiv \arg\max_{s_i \in S \backslash S'} \Big[\lambda score(s_i) - (1-\lambda) \max_{s_j \in S'} sim(s_i, s_j) \times \eta\Big] \quad (5)$$

S	:	A set of summary candidate sentences
S'	:	A set of already extracted sentences as summary S
s_i	:	A sentence in $S \backslash S'$
λ	:	Weighting parameter
η	:	Adjustment coefficient

As for the calculation of similarity between sentences, we use cosine similarity. In order to adjust the weighting balance between ranking score, i.e., $score(s_i)$, and penalty score, i.e., $sim(s_i, s_j)$, we have introduced λ as an weighting parameter, besides introduced η as an adjustment coefficient for balancing exponential order between the two terms in the equation.

4 Experiment

4.1 Data

As the data for experiments, we use the data set for timeline summarization used in (Tran et al., 2013a; Tran et al., 2013b). This data set consists of the newspaper articles about 9 topics and is collected from multiple news resources. The referential summary manually generated by humans is prepared for each topic. Table 1 shows the detail about the data set used in the experiments.

Table 1: Data set used in the experiments

Topic	News sources	Num. of documents	Total num. of sentences
H1N1	Guardian	76	2630
H1N1	Reuters	207	4769

H1N1 is the topic about influenza. Guardian and Reuters are the names of news agency.

4.2 Evaluation metrics

The proposed methods are evaluated based on the comparison between the referential summary and a generated summary. We employ ROUGE (Lin et al., 2004) — in particular, we employ ROUGE-1, ROUGE-2, and ROUGE-L, as metrics to evaluate our method. Here, ROUGE-1 and ROUGE-2 are metrics based on unigram and bigram matching between the referential summary and a generated summary, respectively. ROUGE-L is metrics based on the longest common subsequence part between a referential summary and a generated summary. We calculate recall, precision, and F-score in each metrics.

Equation (6), (7), and (8) show the recall, precision, and F-score of N-gram in ROUGE metrics.

$$\text{ROUGE-N-R} = \frac{\sum_{S \in RS} \sum_{N-gram \in S} \text{Count}_{match}(\text{N-gram})}{\sum_{S \in RS} \sum_{N-gram \in S} \text{Count}(\text{N-gram})} \quad (6)$$

$$\text{ROUGE-N-P} = \frac{\sum_{S \in CS} \sum_{N-gram \in S} \text{Count}_{match}(\text{N-gram})}{\sum_{S \in CS} \sum_{N-gram \in S} \text{Count}(\text{N-gram})} \quad (7)$$

$$\text{ROUGE-N-F} = \frac{2 \times \text{ROUGE-N-P} \times \text{ROUGE-N-R}}{\text{ROUGE-N-P} + \text{ROUGE-N-R}} \quad (8)$$

Here, R, P, F stand for recall, precision, and F-score, respectively. S indicates a summary, RS indicates a referential summary, and CS indicates a candidate summary. Count(N-gram) is the number of N-gram in a summary and Count_{match}(N-gram) is the maximum number of N-grams which are common to both referential summary and generated summary. We evaluated the result in two cases: i.e., with and without stop words by introducing stemming processing.

As the baseline to compare the ability between the proposed method and other methods, we prepare two summaries: one is generated by randomly selecting sentences and the other is generated by Cont.LexRank algorithm. Hereafter, we call Cont.LexRank "LexRank". In terms of the lenght of a generated summary, we adopted the same length as that of the referential summary of each topic. Moreover, as pre-processing, stop words, e.g., 'a', 'the', etc., are removed and stemming processing is adopted for all object documents. We employed Porter's algorithm (Porter, 1980) for stemming.

4.3 Result and discussion

The experiment result of each data evaluated with ROUGE metrics is shown from Table 2 to Table 5. Table 2 and 4 are the results in the case of using stop words when evaluating by ROUGE, and Table 3 and 5 are the results in the case of without stop words. Here, MMR' was not introduced in the above results. In the tables, R1, R2, and RL stand for ROUGE-1, ROUGE-2, and ROUGE-L, respectively. R1-R indicates the value of recall in ROUGE-1. The results shown in the tables are represented in the form of being rounded off to three decimal place. The best score in each metrics is expressed in bold fonts.

Looking at the results, `random` gets the lowest score at any evaluation metrics. On the other hand, the proposed method gets close scores or higher

Table 2: H1N1 Guardian

Methods	R1-R	R1-P	R1-F	R2-R	R2-P	R2-F	RL-R	RL-P	RL-F
random	0.386	0.389	0.415	0.067	0.069	0.072	0.360	0.367	0.388
LexRank	**0.602**	0.389	0.472	**0.187**	**0.121**	**0.147**	**0.566**	0.365	0.444
our method	0.593	**0.403**	**0.476**	0.172	0.116	0.138	0.562	**0.383**	**0.451**

R1: ROUGE-1, R2:ROUGE-2, RL: ROUGE-L, -R: Recall, -P: Precision, -F: F-score

Table 3: H1N1 Guardian without stop words

Methods	R1-R	R1-P	R1-F	R2-R	R2-P	R2-F	RL-R	RL-P	RL-F
random	0.197	0.223	0.212	0.022	0.024	0.023	0.197	0.218	0.207
LexRank	**0.465**	0.305	0.368	0.127	0.083	0.101	**0.446**	0.292	0.353
our method	0.453	**0.311**	**0.369**	**0.130**	**0.089**	**0.106**	0.441	**0.303**	**0.359**

Table 4: H1N1 Reuters

Methods	R1-R	R1-P	R1-F	R2-R	R2-P	R2-F	RL-R	RL-P	RL-F
random	0.415	0.253	0.317	0.030	0.020	0.024	0.394	0.237	0.297
LexRank	0.609	0.245	0.349	**0.150**	0.060	0.086	0.576	0.232	0.330
our method	**0.641**	**0.255**	**0.358**	0.147	**0.063**	**0.088**	**0.603**	**0.241**	**0.34**

Table 5: H1N1 Reuters without stop words

Methods	R1-R	R1-P	R1-F	R2-R	R2-P	R2-F	RL-R	RL-P	RL-F
random	0.175	0.120	0.142	0.005	0.004	0.005	0.170	0.116	0.138
LexRank	0.454	0.196	0.273	**0.083**	**0.036**	**0.050**	0.443	0.191	0.267
our method	**0.495**	**0.205**	**0.284**	0.078	**0.036**	0.049	**0.474**	**0.200**	**0.274**

scores than LexRank. As for the results shown in Table 3, i.e., H1N1 Guardian without stop words, the proposed method gets higher scores than LexRank at most evaluation metrics. However, as for the results shown in Table 4, i.e., H1N1 Reuters, the proposed method gets higher scores at many metrics than LexRank when evaluating the result with stop words. However, both methods produce similar results.

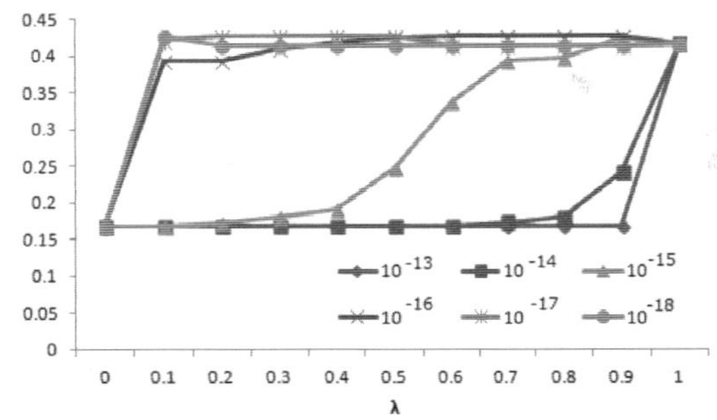

Figure 2: ROUGE-1/Recall(without stop words)

Introducing MMR'

We conducted an experiment to investigate the influence on the accuracy of summarization results by introducing MMR'. We used the articles of H1N1 of Guardian and set the graph size as 2000. For evaluation, we employed ROUGE-1 whose result is considered as being close to the sense of humans (Lin et al., 2004). The results of the experiment obtained by changing the value of an adjustment coefficient η are shown from Figure 2 to 4.

The figures show the results in the case of without stop words. The vertical axis shows ROUGE-1 value, and the horisontal axis shows the value of the weighting parameter λ. Each line in the figures show the value of η. Figure 2, 3, and 4 show the changes of recall, precision and F-score by ROUGE-1 evaluation, respectively. Looking at the results, at any metrics, when $\eta = 10^{-15}$, the value chages gently, if η is larger than 10^{-15}, the penalty term influences

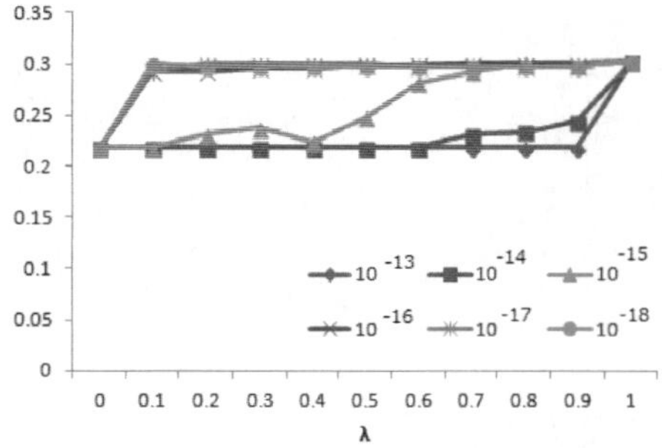

Figure 3: ROUGE-1/Precision(without stop words)

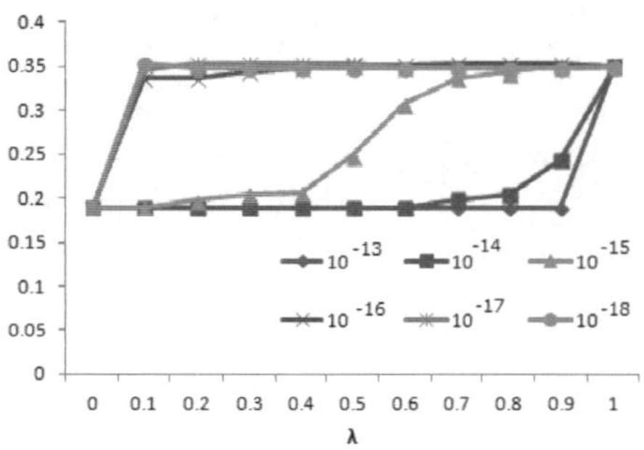

Figure 4: ROUGE-1/F-score(without stopword)

the result, and if η is smaller, the ranking score influences the result. As a result, even though we can find some parts where the accuracy is higher if we put weight on the penalty term rather than the ranking score term, the difference is a little. So, we have not been able to confirm that MMR' works to raise the accuracy in this experiment.

4.4 Supplementary experiment

Each sentence is represented as a sentence vector constructed with the words included in itself and the frequency of those words. When making a sentence or document vector, we usually remove stop words from the vector because the stop word do not represent the contents of the documents. As well as this, the word which do not appear in documents are hardly to represent the contents of the documents. Based on this, we have conducted experiments on removing such words from the object documents to be summarized and investigated the summarization result. As object documents, we used the articles about H1N1 of Guardian from which low frequency words are removed, and we set the graph size 2000 as experimental settings. Figures 5 and 6 show the results, that is, ROUGE-1 values of recall, precision and F-score in the cases of with and without stop words, respectively.

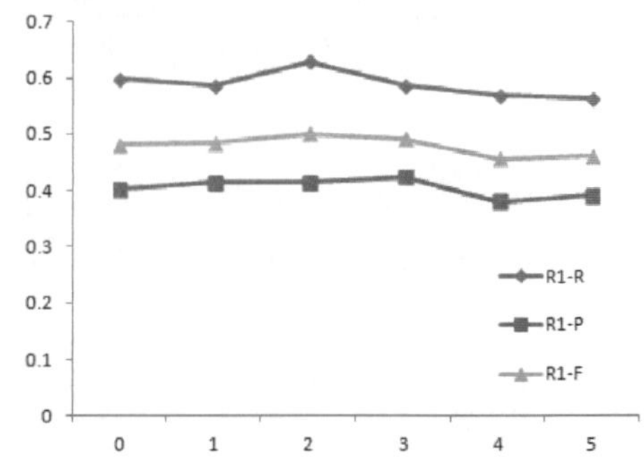

Figure 5: ROUGE without low frequency words (with stop words)

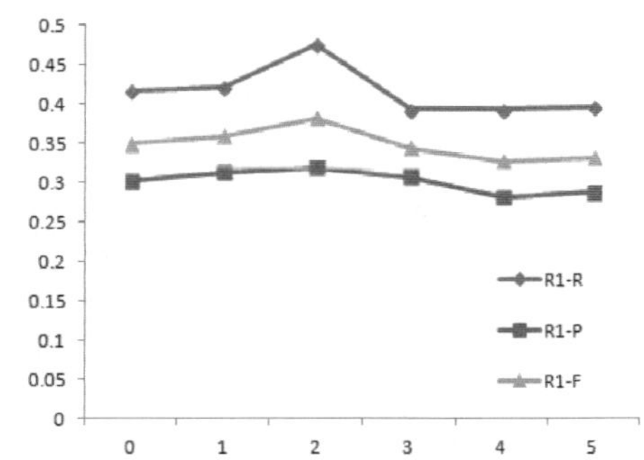

Figure 6: ROUGE without low frequency words (without stop words)

In the figures, the horizontal axis indicates the frequency for the words which are removed from the object documents — for example, 3 indicates the case where the words appearing less than three times in object documents are removed from the documents and a summary is generated with the recompiled documents. The vertical axis indicates evaluation value — for evaluation we employ ROUGE-1 value. Each line in the figure indicates each metrics. We see from the figures that the summary generated in the case of removing the words which appear less than twice or three times in the documents gets highly evaluated. Furthermore, in the case that a summary is generated by removing the words which appear less than twice from objective documents, the accuracy is better than the case without any pre-processing. Compared with other methods, the result is summarized in Table 6. Here, the case of removing the words whose frequency is less than twice is shown in the table. The best score is expressed in bold fonts.

Table 6: Comparison with other methods (ROUGE-1)

Methods	with			without		
	R1-R	R1-P	R1-F	R1-R	R1-P	R1-F
random	0.386	0.389	0.415	0.197	0.223	0.212
LexRank	0.602	0.389	0.472	0.465	0.305	0.368
our method	0.593	0.403	0.476	0.453	0.311	0.369
cut2	**0.629**	**0.415**	**0.500**	**0.475**	**0.319**	**0.382**

Making a comparison among all methods, the result indicates that the best summary is generated by our proposed method with recompiled documents removing the words appearing less than twice from the original documents. From this result, removing low frequency words from the objective documents to be summarized can be regarded as useful pre-processing to make sentence vectors which reflect the contents of the document.

5 Conclusions

In this study, we have proposed a graph-based online automatic summarization for time-series documents. The algorithm of our proposed method can deal with the renewal of the object documents to be summarized over time, and generate a summary of the documents at any time when it is required. Furthermore, by providing the limit on the size of a graph, it is not necessary to take account of irrelevant sentences for a summary. To evaluate the proposed method, we conduct an experiment to compare the proposed method with the other two methods, i.e., the method of randomly extracting sentences to make a summary and LexRank. We employ ROUGE as evaluation metrics. As a result, the proposed method gets close or higher accuracy than LexRank. Moreover, we have introduced an index to avoid redundancy in a summary by modifying MMR-MD — with the modified index, we provide a penalty for selecting a similar sentence to the already extracted sentences. As the result of the experiments using MMR', we have confirmed that MMR' works to raise the accuracy in some cases, however, have not yet confirmed its usefulness as a whole. Furthermore, we assume that the low frequency words are not regarded as important to represent the contents of documents as well as stop words, therefore, we conducted a supplementary experiment on considering word frequency in object documents to be summarized. As the result of the experiment, we have confirmed that the acuuracy gets better than any other methods if we remove the words which do not appear less than twice in object documents and generate a summary. By this fact, we can say that removing low frequency words leads to making sentence vectors which reflect the contents of documents, and it works well as a pre-processing for generating a summary.

As future work, as the first issue, we like to consider how to decide the initial value for the importance of a sentence in a graph — it is expected to be decided based on the ranking score at the previous time so as it will be useful for generating a summary at the current time. As the second issue, we will investigate more about the possibility of introducing MMR'. In this paper, we have not yet confirmed that the usefulness of MMR'. However, we think that providing a penalty for similarity of sentences should work to generate a summary, so we like to propose a better metrics which works well in the proposed algorithm. As the third issue, we could not use enough data in the experiments in this study, so, we will use more data to confirm the proposed method is useful. Finally, we will compare the proposed method with the other timeline summarization methods.

Acknowledgements: This work is partly supported by Kayamori Foundation of Information Science Advancement.

References

James Allan, Rahul Gupta, and Vikas Khandelwal. 2001. *Temporal Summaries of News Topics*. In Proceedings of the 24th annual international ACM SIGIR conference on Research and development in information retrieval, pp. 10-18.

Hai Leong Chieu and Yoong Keok Lee. 2004. *Query Based Event Extraction along a Timeline*. In Proceedings of the 27th annual international ACM SIGIR conference on Research and development in information retrieval, pp. 425-432.

Gunes Erkan and Dragomir R. Radev. 2004. *LexRank: Graph-based Lexical Centrality as Salience in Text Summarization*. Journal of Artificial Intelligence Research, Vol. 22, No. 1, pp. 457-479.

Jade Goldstein, Vibhu Mittal, Jaime Carbonell, and Mark Kantrowitzt. 2000. *Multi-Document Summarization By Sentence Extraction*. In Proceedings of the 2000 NAACL-ANLP Workshop on Automatic Summarization, Vol. 4, pp. 40-48.

Po Hu, Min-Lie Huang, and Xiao-Yan Zhu. 2014. *Exploring the Interactions of Storyline from Informative News Events*. Journal of Computer Science and Technology, Vol. 29, No. 3, pp.502-518.

Hongyan Jing. 2000. *Sentence Reduction for Automatic Text Summarization*. In Proceedings of the Sixth Conference on Applied Natural Language Processing, pp. 310–315, Association for Computational Linguistics.

Kevin Knight and Daniel Marcu. 2002. *Summarization Beyond Sentence Extraction: A Probabilistic Approach to Sentence Compression*, Journal of Artificial Intelligence, Vol. 139, No.1, pp. 91-107, Elsevier Science Publishers Ltd.

Jiwai Li and Sujian Li. 2013. *Evolutionary Hierarchical Dirichlet Process for Timeline Summarization*. In Proceedings of the 51st Annual Meeting of the Association for Computational Linguistics, Vou. 2, pp. 556-560.

Chin-Yew. Lin. 2004. *ROUGE: a Package for Automatic Evaluation of Summaries*. In Proceedings of the Workshop on Text Summarization Branches Out, pp. 74-81.

Ryan McDonald. 2007. *A study of global inference algorithms in multi-document summarization*. In Proceedings of the 29th European conference on IR research, pp. 557-564.

Rada Mihalcea and Paul Tarau. 2004. *TextRank: Bringing order into texts*. In Proceedings of EMNLP-03 and the 2004 Conference on Empirical Methods in Natural Language Proceeding.

M.F. Porter. 1980. *An algorithm for suffix Stripping*. Program, Vol. 14 No.3,pp.130-137.

Dragomir R. Radev, Hongyan Jing, Malgorzata Stys, and Daniel Tam. 2004. *Centroid-based summarization of multiple documents*. Information Processing and Management: an International Journal, Vol.40, No 6, pp. 919-938.

Giang Binh Tran, Tuan A. Tran, Nam-Khanh Tran, Mohammad Alrifai, and Nattiya Kanhabua. 2013. *Leveraging Learning To Rank in an Optimization Framework for Timeline Summarization*. SIGIR 2013 Workshop on Time-aware Information Access.

Giang Binh Tran, Mohammad Alrifai, and Dat Quoc Nguyen. 2013. *Predicting Relevant News Events for Timeline Summaries*. In Proceedings of the 22nd international conference on World Wide Web Companion, pp. 91-92.International World Wide Web Conferences Steering Committee.

Dingding Wang, Li Zeng, Tao Li, and Yi Deng. 2009. *Evolutionary Document Summarization for Disaster Management* In Proceedings of the 32nd international ACM SIGIR conference on Research and development in information retrieval, pp. 680-681.

Rui Yan, Liang Kong, Congrui Huang, Xiaojun Wan, Xiaoming Li, and Yan Zhang. 2011a. *Evolutionary Timeline Summarization: a Balanced Optimization Framework via Iterative Substitution*. In Proceedings of the 34th international ACM SIGIR conference on Research and development in Information Retrieval, pp. 745-754.

Rui Yan, Congrui Huang, Xiaojun Wan, Jahna Otterbacher, Xiaoming Li, and Yan Zhang. 2011b. *Timeline Generation Evolutionary Trans-Temporal Summarization*. In Proceedings of the Conference on Empirical Method in Natural Language Processing, pp. 433-443.

Rui Yan, Xiaojun Wan, Yan Zhang, and Xiaoming Li. 2012. *Hierarchical Graph Summarization: Leveraging Hybrid Information through Visible and Invisible Linkage*. 16th Pacific-Asia Conference, PAKDD 2012, pp. 97-108.

Wayne Xin Zhao, Yanwei Guo, Rui Yan, Yulan He, and Xiaoming Li. 2013. *Timeline generation with social attention*. In Proceedings of the 36th international ACM SIGIR conference on Research and development in information retrieval, pp. 1061-1064.

Adjacency Pair Recognition in Wikipedia Discussions using Lexical Pairs

Emily K. Jamison ‡ **and Iryna Gurevych** †‡
‡Ubiquitous Knowledge Processing Lab (UKP-TUDA),
Department of Computer Science, Technische Universität Darmstadt
† Ubiquitous Knowledge Processing Lab (UKP-DIPF),
German Institute for Educational Research
http://www.ukp.tu-darmstadt.de

Abstract

Adjacency pair recognition, a necessary component of discussion thread reconstruction, is the task of recognizing reply-to relations between pairs of discussion turns. Previously, dialogue act classification and metadata-based features have been shown useful in adjacency pair recognition. However, for certain forums such as Wikipedia discussions, metadata is not available, and existing dialogue act typologies are inapplicable. In this work, we show that adjacency pair recognition can be performed using lexical pair features, without a dialogue act typology or metadata, and that this is robust to controlling for topic bias of the discussions.

1 Introduction

A growing cache of online information is contained inside user-posted forum discussions. Thread structure of the discussion is useful in extracting information from threads: Wang et al. (2013) use thread structure to improve IR over threads, and Cong et al. (2008) use thread structure to extract question-answer pairs from forums. However, as Seo et al. (2009) point out, thread structure is unavailable in many forums, partly due to the popularity of forum software phpBB[1] and vBulletin[2], whose default view is non-threaded.

Thread reconstruction provides thread structure to forum discussions whose original thread structure is nonexistant or malformed, by sorting and reordering turns into a directed graph of *adjacency* (reply-to) relations. Pairs of adjacent turns (*adjacency pairs*) were first identified by Sacks et al.

[1]http://www.phpbb.com/
[2]http://www.vbulletin.com/

Turn1: *This article has been gutted. I deleted a lot of the cruft that had taken over, but a lot of former material is missing.[...]*
> **Turn2:** *Good; the further this nest of doctrinaire obscurities is gutted, the better.*
> **Turn3:** *Wait, you changed it to say that English doesn't have a future tense or you're citing that as an error (which it would naturally be)? For what it matters, [...]*
>> **Turn4:** *English doesn't have a future tense. It indicates the future with a modal (will) used with the present-tense inflection of the verb. [...]*

Figure 1: Excerpt from the EWDC discussion *Grammatical Tense:gutted.*

(1974) as the structural foundation of a discussion, and recognition of adjacency pairs is a critical step in thread reconstruction (Balali et al., 2014; Wang et al., 2008; Aumayr et al., 2011).

Figure 1 shows an excerpt from Ferschke's (2014) English Wikipedia Discussions Corpus. Thread structure is indicated by tab indents. Turn pairs *(1,2)*, *(1,3)*, and *(3,4)* are adjacency pairs; pairs *(2,3)* and *(1,4)* are not. Adjacency pair recognition is the classification of a pair of turns as adjacent or nonadjacent.

Although most previous work on thread reconstruction takes advantage of metadata such as user id, timestamp, and quoted material (Aumayr et al., 2011; Wang et al., 2011a), metadata is unreliable in some forums, such as Wikipedia Discussion page forums, where metadata and user contribution is difficult to align (Ferschke et al., 2012). Wang et al. (2011b) find that joint prediction of dialogue act labels and adjacency pair recognition improves accuracy when compared to separate classification; dialogue act classification does not require metadata. However, existing dialogue act typologies are unapplicable for some forums (see Section 2.2).

In this paper, we perform adjacency pair recognition on pairs of turns extracted from the English

Copyright 2014 by Emily K. Jamison and Iryna Gurevych
28th Pacific Asia Conference on Language, Information and Computation pages 479–488

Wikipedia Discussions Corpus (*EWDC*). We use lexical pair features, which require neither metadata nor development of a dialogue act typology appropriate for Wikipedia discussions. We perform two sets of supervised learner experiments. First, we use lexical pairs for adjacency pair recognition in K-fold Cross Validation (*CV*) setting. Then we show how this permits topic bias, inflating results. Second, we repeat our first set of experiments, but in a special CV setting that removes topic bias. We find that lexical pairs outperform a cosine similarity baseline and a most frequent class baseline both without and with controlling for topic bias, and also exceed the performance of lexical strings of stopwords and discourse connectives on the task.

2 Background

Adjacency pairs were proposed as a theoretical foundation of discourse structure by Sacks et al. (1974), who observed that conversations are structured in a manner where the current speaker uses structural techniques to select the next speaker, and this structure is the adjacency pair: a pair of adjacent discussion turns, each from different speakers, and the relation between them.

2.1 Adjacency Pair Typologies

Previous work on adjacency pair recognition has found adjancency pair typologies to be useful (Wang et al., 2011b). Early work on adjacency pair typologies labelled adjacency pairs by adjacency relation function. Schegloff and Sacks (1973) proposed initial sequences (e.g., greeting exchanges), preclosings, pre-topic closing offerings, and ending sequences (i.e., terminal exchanges). Other adjacency pair typologies consist of pairs of dialogue act labels. Based on their work with transcripts of phone conversations, Sacks et al. (1974) suggested a few types of adjacency pairs: greeting-greeting, invitation-acceptance/decline, complaint-denial, compliment-rejection, challenge-rejection, request-grant, offer-accept/reject, question-answer. In transcribed phone dialogues on topics of appointment scheduling, travel planning, and remote PC maintenance, Midgley et al. (2009) identified adjacency pair labels as frequently co-occurring pairs of dialog acts, including suggest-accept, bye-bye, request/clarify-clarify, suggest-reject, etc.

2.2 Discussion Structure Variation

Much adjacency pair descriptive work was based on transcriptions of phone conversations. Sacks et al. (1974) were discussing phone conversations when they observed that a speaker can select the next speaker by the use of adjacency pairs, and the subsequent speaker is obligated to give a response appropriate to and limited by the adjacency pair, such as answering a question. In a phone conversation, the participant set is fixed, and rules of the conversation permit the speaker to address other participants directly, and obligate a response.

However, in other types of discussion, such as forum discussions, this is not the case. For example, in QA-style forums such as CNET (Kim et al., 2010), a user posts a question, and anyone in the community may respond; the user cannot select a certain participant as the next speaker. Wikipedia discussions vary even further from phone conversations: many threads are initiated by users interested in determining community opinion on a topic, who avoid asking direct questions. Wikipedia turns that might have required direct replies from a particular participant in a speaker-selecting (*SS*) phone conversation, are formulated to reduce or remove obligation of response in this non-speaker-selecting context. Some examples are below; NSS turns are actual turns from the EWDC.

Rephrasing a user-directed command as a general statement:

SS turn: "Please don't edit this article, because you don't understand the concepts."

NSS turn: "Sorry, but anyone who argues that a language doesn't express tense [...] obviously doesn't understand the concept of tense enough to be editing an article on it."

Obtaining opinions by describing past user action instead of questioning:

SS turn: "Which parts of this article should we delete?"

NSS turn: "This article has been gutted. I deleted a lot [...]."

Using a proposal instead of a question:

SS turn: "Should we rename this article?"

NSS turn: "I propose renaming this article to [...]"

Following questions with statements that deflect need for the question to be answered:

NSS turn: "Wait, you changed it to say that English doesn't have a future tense or you're citing that as an error (which it would naturally be)? For what it matters, even with the changes, this entire article needs a rewrite from scratch because so much of it is wrong."

Avoiding questions to introduce a new topic:

SS turn: "Have you heard of Flickr?"

NSS turn: "I don't know whether you know about Flickr or not, but theres a bunch of creative commons licensed images here some better and some worse than the article which you might find useful[...]".

Anticipating responses:

NSS turn: "What are the image names? :Image:Palazzo Monac.jpg has a problem, it's licensed with "no derivative works" which won't work on Commons.[...] If you meant other ones, let me know their names, ok?"

As seen above, Wikipedia discussions have different dialogue structure than phone conversations. Because of the different dialogue structure, existing adjacency pair typologies developed for phone conversations are not appropriate for Wikipedia discussions. As it would require much effort to develop an appropriate adjacency-pair typology for Wikipedia discussions, our research investigates the cheaper alternative of using lexical pairs to recognize adjacency pairs.

3 Related Work

To the best of our knowledge, our work is the first work that uses lexical pairs to recognize adjacency pairs.

3.1 Adjacency Pair Recognition

Most previous work on thread reconstruction has, in addition to using metadata-based features, used word similarity, such as cosine similarity or semantic lexical chaining, between turn pairs for adjacency pair recognition or thread structure graph construction. Wang and Rosé (2010) trained a ranking classifier to identify "initiation-response" pairs consisting of quoted material and the responding text in Usenet `alt.politics.usa` messages, based on text similarity features (cosine, LSA). Aumayr et al. (2011) reconstructed discussion thread graphs using cosine similarity between pairs of turns, as well as reply distance, time difference, quotes, and thread length. They first learned a pairwise classification model over a class-balanced set of turn pairs, and then used the predicted classifications to construct graphs of the thread structure of discussions from the Irish forum site `Boards.ie`. Wang et al. (2011a) also reconstructed thread graphs using cosine similarity in addition to features based on turn position, timestamps, and authorship, using forum discussions from Apple Discussion, Google Earth, and CNET. Wang et al. (2008) reconstructed discussion threads of player chats from the educational legislative game *LegSim*, using TF-IDF vector space model similarity between pairs of turns to build the graphs. Balali et al. (2014) included a feature of TF-IDF vector-space model of text similarity between a turn and a combined text of all comments, a feature of text similarity between pairs of turns, and an authorship language model similarity feature, to learn a pairwise ranking classifier, and then constructed graphs of the thread structures of news forum discussions. Wang et al. (2011c) evaluated the use of WordNet, Roget's Thesaurus, and WORDSPACE SemanticVector lexical chainers for detecting semantic similarity between two turns and their titles, to identify thread-linking structure. Wang et al. (2011b) used a dependency parser, based on unweighted cosine similarity of titles and turn contents, as well as authorship and structural features, to learn a model for joint classification of Dialogue Acts and "inter-post links" between posts in the CNET forum dataset.

3.2 Lexical Pairs

We use lexical pairs as features for adjacency pair recognition. Although not previously been used for this task, lexical pairs have been helpful for other discourse structure tasks such as recognising discourse relations. Marcu and Echihabi (2002) used lexical pairs from all words, nouns, verbs, and cue-phrases, to recognise discourse relations. A binary relation/non-relation classifier achieves 0.64 to 0.76 accuracy against a 0.50 baseline, over approx. 1M instances. Lin et al. (2009) performed discourse relation recognition using lexical pairs as well as constituent and dependency information of relations in the Penn Discourse Treebank. They achieved 0.328 accuracy against a 0.261 most frequent class baseline, using 13,366 instances. Pitler et al. (2009) performed binary discourse relation prediction using lexical pairs, verb information, and linguistically-motivated features, and achieve improvements of up to 0.60-0.62 accuracy, compared with a 0.50 baseline, on datasets sized 1,460 to 12,712 instances from the Penn Discourse Treebank. Biran and McKeown (2013) aggregated lexical pairs as clusters, to combat the feature sparsity problem. While improvements are modest, lexical pairs are helpful in these discourse tasks where useful linguistically-motivated features have proven elusive.

4 Dataset

Our dataset[3] consists of discussion turn pairs from Ferschke's (2014) English Wikipedia Discussions Corpus (EWDC). Discussion pages provide a forum for users to discuss edits to a Wikipedia article.

We derived a class-balanced dataset of 2684[4] pairs of adjacent and non-adjacent discussion turn pairs from the EWDC. The pairs came from 550 discussions within 83 Wikipedia articles. The average number of discussions per article was 6.6. The average number of extracted pairs per discussion was 4.9. The average turn contained 81$\pm$95 tokens (standard deviation) and 4$\pm$4 sentences. To reduce noise, usernames and time stamps have been replaced with generic strings.

4.1 Indentation Reliability

Adjacency is indicated in the EWDC by the user via tab indent, as can be seen in Figure 1.

Incorrect indentation (i.e., indentation that implies a reply-to relation with the wrong post) is quite common in longer discussions in the EWDC. In an analysis of 5 random threads longer than 10 turns each, shown in Table 1, we found that 29 of 74 total turns, or 39%$\pm$14pp of an average thread, had indentation that misidentified the turn to which they were a reply. We also found that the misindentation existed in both directions: an approximately equal

Discussion	# Turns	% Misind.	R	L	P(pos)
Grammatical_tense	20	.50	8	7	10/10
Hurricane_Iniki:1	15	.2	2	4	2/3
Hurricane_Iniki:2	13	.46	11	4	5/7
Possessive_adjective	13	.23	1	5	9/10
Prince's_Palace_of_Monaco	13	.54	9	9	6/6
Average	14.8	.39	6.2	5.8	.89

Table 1: Analysis of wrong indentation in 5 discussions, showing misindentation rate, the sum of how many tabs to the left or right are needed to fix the misindented response turn, and P of extracted positive pairs.

number of tabs and tab deletions were needed in each article to correct the misindented turns.

To minimize the number of turn pairs with incorrect indentation extracted from the corpus, we extracted our positive and negative pairs as follows: An adjacent pair is defined as a pair of turns in which one turn appears directly below the other in the text, and the latter turn is indented once beyond the previous turn. A non-adjacent pair is defined as a pair of turns in which the latter turn has fewer indents than the previous turn. Our extraction method yields 32 true positives and 4 false positives (precision = 0.89) in the 5 discussions. Analysis of 20 different pairs in Section 7.2 yielded 0.90 class-averaged precision.

5 Human Performance

We annotated a subset of out data, to determine a human upper bound for adjacency pair recognition. Two annotators classified 128 potential adjacency pairs (23 positive, 105 negative) in 4 threads with an average length of 6 turns. The annotators could see all other turns in the conversation, unordered, along with the pair in question. This pairwise binary classification scenario matches the pairwise binary classification in the experiments in Sections 7 and 9. Each pair was decided independently of other pairs. Cohen's kappa agreement (Cohen, 1960) between the annotators was 0.63.

We noticed a common pattern of disagreement in two particular situations. When an "I agree" turn referred back to an adjacency pair in which one turn elaborated on the other, it was difficult for an annotator to determine which member of the original adjacency pair was the parent of the "I agree" comment. In a different situation, sometimes a participant contributed a substantially off-topic post that spawned a new discussion. It was difficult for the annotators to determine whether the off-topic post

[3] www.ukp.tu-darmstadt.de/data/wikidiscourse

[4] Lexical pairs use a large feature space, and dataset size was constrained by computational feasability.

was a vague response to an existing post, or whether the off-topic post was truly the beginning of a brand-new discussion, albeit using the same original discussion thread.

6 Features

We use three types of features for adjacency pair recognition: *lexical pairs*, *structural context information*, and *pair symmetry*.[5]

Lexical pairs. A lexical pair feature consists of a pair of ngrams with one ngram taken from the first document and one ngram taken from the second document. An ngram is a string of consecutive tokens of length n in a text. Following Marcu and Echihabi (2002), we find a relation (in our case, adjacency) that holds between two text spans, N_1, N_2, is determined by the ngram pairs in the cartesian product defined over the words in the two text spans $(n_i, n_j) \in N_1 \times N_2$.

The goal of using lexical pairs is to identify word pairs indicative of adjacency, such as (*why, because*) and (*?, yes*). These pairs cannot be identified using text similarity techniques used in previous work (Wang and Rosé, 2010).

In addition to lexical pairs created from document ngrams, lexical pairs were created from a list of 50 stopwords (Stamatatos, 2011), Penn Discourse Treebank discourse connectives (Prasad et al., 2008), and a particularly effective combination of just 3 stopwords: *and, as, for*. Other variables included the parameter ngram n, and removed stopwords, which skipped unallowed words in the text.

Structural context information. Some of our feature groups include structural context information of the discussion turn codified as lexical items in the lexical pair string. We include sentence boundaries (SB), commas (CA), and sentence location (i.e., sentence occurs in first quarter, last quarter, or middle of the discussion turn). A sample lexical string representing text from the beginning of a turn is below.

Text: *No, that is correct.*
Lexical string: `no-that-is-correct`
with struct.: `no-CA-that-is-correct-SBBEGIN`

Pair symmetry. Our dataset of discussion turn pairs retains the original order from the discussion. This permits us to detect order-sensitive features such as *(why, because)* and not *(because, why)*, in which the ngram from Turn1 always occurs on the left-hand side of the feature name. Adjacency pairs, by definition, are nonsymmetrical. To confirm this property, in some of our feature groups, we extract a reverse-ordered feature for each standard feature. An example with symmetrical and non-symmetrical features is shown below.

Turn1: *Why ?*
Turn2: *Because .*
Non-Sym features: `(why, because)`
Sym features: `(why, because), (because, why)`

7 Experiments without Topic Bias Control

In our first set of experiments, we perform adjacency pair recognition without topic bias control ("non-TBC"). We use the SVM classifier SMO (Hall et al., 2009) in the DKPro TC framework (Daxenberger et al., 2014) for pairwise classification[6] and 5-fold[7] cross-validation (*CV*), in which all instances are randomly assigned to CV folds. These experiments do not control for any topic bias in the data. Previous work (Wang and Rosé, 2010) has structured adjacency pair recognition as a ranking task, with the classifier choosing between one correct and one incorrect response to a given turn. In our experiments, we use pairwise binary classification, because the high indentation error rate and our EWDC instance selection method did not yield enough matched turn pairs for ranking. Feature parameters (such as top k ngrams, string lengths, and feature combinations) were tuned using CV on a development subset of 552 pairs, while the final results reflect experiments on the remaining dataset of 2684 pairs. Results are shown as F-measure

[5] Because our goal is adjacency pair recognition based on text content features, we do not use indentation offset as a feature.

[6] Although discourse turns are sequential, we classify individual pairs. Future work may investigate this as a sequence labelling task.

[7] Although 10-fold CV is more common in many NLP experiments, we use 5-fold cross validation (*CV*) in Section 7 to make our results directly comparable with results in Section 9.

for class c=adjacent, nonadjacent): $F1_c = \frac{2 \cdot P_c \cdot R_c}{P_c + R_c}$, and Accuracy=$\frac{TP+TN}{TP+FP+TN+FN}$. The most frequent class (MFC) baseline chooses the most frequent class observed in the training data, as calculated directly from the experiment. The cosine similarity (CosineSim) baseline is an SVM classifier trained over cosine similarity scores of the turn pairs. The Human Upper Bound shows agreement from Section 5 and reflects a natural limit on task performance.

7.1 Results

Table 2 shows our feature combinations and results. All experiment combinations were $p \leq 0.05$ significantly different (McNemar, 1947) from the CosineSim and MFC baselines. The highest performing feature combination was pair unigrams with stopwords removed (pair1grams+noSW), which had higher accuracy (.68±.02) than all other feature combinations, including pair1grams that included stopwords (.64±.01), and all of the stopword feature sets. Stopword removal increases the system performance for our task, which is unexpected because in other work on different discourse relation tasks, the removal of stopwords from lexical pairs has hurt system performance (Blair-Goldensohn et al., 2007; Marcu and Echihabi, 2002; Biran and McKeown, 2013).

Longer ngrams did not increase performance: pair2grams (.57±.03) significantly underperformed pair1grams (.64±.01).

We examined the performance curve using various n numbers of most frequent lexical pairs as features on a subset of our corpus (1,380 instances). We found that there was no sharp benefit from a few particularly useful pairs, but that performance continued to increase as n approached 5000.

We found that the classifier performs better when the model learns turn pair order, and the reduced data sparsity from using symmetrical features was not valuable (Stopwords+SB+noSym, .62 ±.01 versus Stopwords+SB+Sym, .55 ±.02). We found that including sentence boundaries was helpful (Stopwords+SB+noSym, .60 ±.01 versus Stopwords+noSB+noSym, .62 ±.01, significance p=0.05), but that commas and sentence location information were not useful (Stopwords+SB+CA+SL+noSym, .61±.01).

Despite their connections with discourse structure, discourse connectives (DiscConn+SB+noSym, .61±.01) failed to outperform stopwords (Stopwords+SB+noSym, .62 ±.01). This may be due to the rarity of discourse connectives in the discussion turns: Turn pairs have an average of 9.0±8.6 (or 6.5±6.3 if *and* is removed from the list) discourse connectives combined, and 118 different discourse connectives are used.

7.2 Error Analysis

We examined five pairs each of *true positives* (TP), *false negatives* (FN), *false positives* (FP), and *true negatives* (TN), one set of four from each fold of the best performing system, pair1grams+noSW. Generally, turns from instances classified negative appeared to be shorter in number of sentences than instances classified positive (shown by pairs of texts: TN (3.2±2.2 and 3.0±3.4); FN (3.0±2.2 and 2.2±1.1); versus, TP (4.8±4.7 and 4.4±3.6); FP (7.6±10.3 and 5.2±2.8)). Two of the 20 had incorrect gold classification based on misindentation.

FP's. One instance is misindented. Four of the five FP's appear to require extensive linguistic analysis to properly determine their non-adjacency. For example, one second turn begins, " 'Linking' just distracts from, but does not solve, the main issue", but linking is not discussed in the earlier turn. To solve this, a system may need to determine keywords, match quotations, or summarize the content of the first turn, to determine whether 'linking' is discussed. In another example, the turns can be respectively summarized as, "here is a reference" and "we need to collectively do X." This pair of summaries is never adjacent. Another FP instance cannot be adjacent to any turn, because it states a fact and concludes "This fact seems to contradict the article, doesn't it?" In the final FP instance, both turns express agreement; they start with "Fair enough." and "Right." respectively. This pattern of sequential positive sentiment among adjacency pairs in this dataset is very rare.

FN's. Among FN's, one pair appears nonsensically unrelated and unsolvable, another is misindented, while another requires difficult-even-for-humans coreference resolution. The other two FN's need extensive linguistic analysis. In the first in-

Name	Words	NGram Length	Context	Symmetry	removed words	F1+	F1-	Acc
Chance								.50
MFC						.44	.54	.49±.01
CosineSim						.62	.49	.56±.01
Human Upper Bound						.70	.93	.89
Stopwords+SB+NoSym	stopwords	1-3	SB	-	-	.61	.63	.62±.01
Stopwords+SB+Sym	stopwords	1-3	SB	Sym	-	.54	.56	.55±.02
Stopwords+noSB+noSym	stopwords	1-3	-	-	-	.57	.63	.60±.01
Stopwords+SB+CA+SL+noSym	stopwords	1-3	SB,CA,SL	-	-	.60	.63	.61±.01
DiscConn+SB+noSym	disc. conn.'s	1-3	SB	-	-	.60	.63	.61±.01
And-as-for	"and", "as", "for"	1-3	-	Sym	-	.63	.39	.54±.03
Pair1grams	all words	1	-	-	-	.62	.66	.64±.01
Pair2grams	all words	2	-	-	-	.60	.53	.57±.03
Pair1ngrams+noDC	all words	1	-	-	disc. conn.'s	.64	.66	.65±.02
pair1ngrams+noSW	all words	1	-	-	stopwords	.66	.70	**.68±.02**

Table 2: Non-TBC adjacency pair recognition feature set descriptions and results. F_1 results are shown by adjacent (+) and nonadjacent (-) classes. Accuracy is shown with cross-validation fold standard deviation. `Human Upper Bound` is calculated on a different dataset, which was also derived from the EWDC.

stance, the first turn begins, "In languages with dynamic scoping, this is not the case,[...]," and the other turn replies, "I'll readily admit that I have little experience with dynamic scoping[...]" This may be solvable with centering theoretic approaches (Guinaudeau and Strube, 2013), which probabilistically model the argument position of multiple sequential mentions of an entity such as "dynamic scoping". The second instance consists of a deep disagreement between the two authors, in which they discuss a number of keywords and topic specific terms, disagree with each other, and make conclusions. This instance may need a combination of a centering theoretic approach, opinion mining, and topic modeling to solve.

7.3 Feature Analysis

We examined the top-ranked features from our most accurate system, `pair1grams+noSW` (accuracy = .66±.01), as determined by Information Gain ranking. Of the five lists of features produced during each of the 5 folds of CV, 12 of the top 20 features were in common between all 5 lists, and 11 of these 12 features contained an ngram referencing "aspirin": (*acid*, *asa* (an abbreviation for acetylsalicylic acid, the generic name for *aspirin*), *aspirin*, *acetylsalicylic*, *name*, *generic*). We explain the likely cause of the topicality in feature importance in Section 8, and run a second set of experiments to control topic bias in Section 9.

8 Topic Bias and Control

In Section 7, we showed that lexical pairs are useful for adjacency pair recognition with random CV fold assignment. However, it is possible that the system's good performance was due not to the lexical pairs, but to information leakage of learning a topic model on instances extracted from a single discussion.

Topic bias is the problem of a machine learner inadvertently learning "hints" from the topics in the texts that would not exist in another experiment addressing the same task. Consider a sample dataset which contains 16 adjacent and 0 nonadjacent pairs from an article on *Aspirin*, and 7 adjacent and 9 nonadjacent pairs from an article on *Wales*. A model trained on this corpus will probably find lexical pair features such as (*?*, *yes*) and (*why*, *because*) to be highly predictive. But, lexical pairs containing topic-sensitive words such as *aspirin* and *generic* may also be highly predictive. Such a model is recognizing adjacency by topic. To remove this topic bias, instances from a single article should never occur simultaneously in training and evaluation datasets.

Topic bias is a pervasive problem. Mikros and Argiri (2007) have shown that many features besides ngrams are significantly correlated with topic, including sentence and token length, readability measures, and word length distributions. Topic-controlled corpora have been used for authorship identification (Koppel and Schler, 2003), genre detection (Finn and Kushmerick, 2003), and Wikipedia quality flaw prediction (Ferschke et al., 2013).

The class distribution by discussion in our dataset is shown in Figure 2; imbalance is shown by the percentage of positive pairs minus the percentage of negative pairs. Only 39 of 550 discussions contributed an approximately equal number of positive

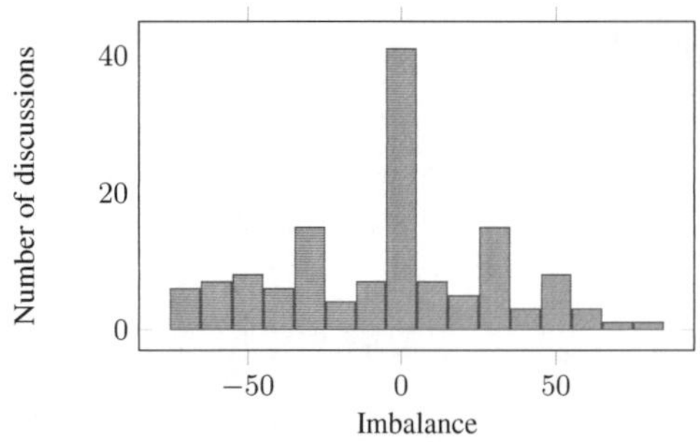

Figure 2: Class imbalance by discussion, in percent. -20 means a discussion is 20 percentile points more negative instances than positive; i.e., if there are 10 instances, 4 positive and 6 negative, then the discussion is a -20 discussion.

Feature	Acc w/o TBC	Acc w TBC
MFC	.49±.01	.44±.04
CosineSim	.56±.01	.54±.06
Nonpair1grams	.67±.02	.49±.03
Stopwords+SB+noSym	.62±.01	.51±.01
Stopwords+SB+Sym	.55±.02	.51±.01
Stopwords+noSB+noSym	.60±.01	.53±.02
Stopwords+SB+CA+SL+noSym	.61±.01	.52±.02
DiscConn+SB+noSym	.61±.01	.51±.02
And-as-for	.54±.03	.49±.03
Pair1grams	.64±.01	**.56±.03**
Pair2grams	.57±.03	.52±.03
Pair1ngrams+noDC	.65±.02	**.56±.03**
Pair1ngrams+noSW	**.68±.02**	.52±.03

Table 3: Adjacency pair recognition, without and with topic bias control.

and negative instances. 12 discussions contributed only negative instances, and 321 discussions contributed only positive instances[8]. Of discussions with some instances from each class, a whopping 43 of 137 discussions contributed a set of instances that was class imbalanced by 40 percentage points or more. As a result, a classifier will perform above chance if it assumes all instances from one discussion have the same class.

9 Experiments with Topic Bias Control

In our second set of experiments, we performed adjacency pair recognition while controlling for topic bias. To control topic bias, instances from any discussion in a single Wikipedia article are never split across a training and test set. When the cross-validation folds are created, instead of randomly assigning each *instance* to a fold, we assign each *set* of instances from an entire article to a fold. With this technique, any topic bias learned by the classifer will fail to benefit the classifier during the evaluation. We did not use stratified cross-validation, due to the computational complexity of constructing folds of variable-sized threads containing variable class-balance.

We compare against the actual MFC baseline, as seen by the classifier in the experiment. The classifier will perform at this baseline if lexical pairs are not useful for the task. We also compare against cosine similarity, similarly to our previous experiments. The *nonpair 1grams* baseline uses an SVM classifier trained over 5000 individual unigrams from the turn pairs.

9.1 Results

The results of our topic bias controlled experiments are shown in Table 3. As entropy decreases with more folds, to avoid exaggerating the reduced entropy effect, 5-fold cross-validation is used. All other experiment parameters are as in Section 7.

All experiment combinations were $p \leq 0.05$ significantly different (McNemar, 1947) from the `CosineSim` and `MFC` baselines, except `Stopwords+SB+CA+SL+noSym`, and all were significantly different from the Nonpair1grams baseline. Absolute classifier performance in the topic bias control paradigm drops significantly when compared with results from the non-topic-bias-control paradigm. This indicates that the classifier was relying on topic models for adjacency pair recognition. Not only is the classifier unable to use its learned topic model on the test dataset, but the process of learning topic modeling reduced the learning non-topic-model feature patterns. Even the feature group `And-as-for` drops, illustrating how topic can also be modelled with stopword distribution, even though the stopwords have no apparent semantic connection to the topic.

The benefit of pair ngrams is shown by the significant divergence of performance of `Nonpair 1grams` and `Pair1grams` in the topic bias control paradigm (.49±.03 versus .56±.03, respectively).

However, several feature sets are still significantly effective for adjacency pair recognition. (`Pair1grams`, `Pair1grams+noDC` perform well above the `MFC` baseline, cosine similarity

[8]Many of these discussions may have consisted of only 2 turns.

baseline, and `Nonpair 1grams` baseline. They also outperform the stopword and the discourse connectives feature sets. The shorter ngrams of `Pair1grams` continue to outperform the bigrams in `Pair2grams`, similarly to the experiments without TBC.

Performance of feature sets exceeding the `MFC` baseline indicates that lexical pair features are informative independently of topic bias.

10 Conclusion

Adjacency pair recognition, the task of discovering reply-to relations between pairs of discussion turns, is a necessary component of discussion thread reconstruction. In this paper, we have evaluated the use of lexical pairs for adjacency pair recognition, and we have shown that they are helpful, outperforming cosine similarity. We have further shown that this benefit is robust to topic bias control.

Our error analysis raises intriguing questions for future research, showing that a number of forms of deeper linguistic analysis, such as keyword extraction, turn summarization, and centering theoretic analysis may be necessary to reduce the current error rate in metadata-less adjacency pair recognition.

Acknowledgments

This work has been supported by the Volkswagen Foundation as part of the Lichtenberg-Professorship Program under grant No. I/82806, and by the Center for Advanced Security Research (`www.cased.de`).

References

Erik Aumayr, Jeffrey Chan, and Conor Hayes. 2011. Reconstruction of threaded conversations in online discussion forums. In *Proceedings of the International Conference on Weblogs and Social Media*, pages 26–33, Barcelona, Spain.

A. Balali, H. Faili, and M. Asadpour. 2014. A supervised approach to predict the hierarchical structure of conversation threads for comments. *The Scientific World Journal*, 2014:1–23.

Or Biran and Kathleen McKeown. 2013. Aggregated word pair features for implicit discourse relation disambiguation. In *Proceedings of the 51st Annual Meeting of the Association for Computational Linguistics*, pages 69–73, Sofia, Bulgaria.

Sasha Blair-Goldensohn, Kathleen McKeown, and Owen Rambow. 2007. Building and refining rhetorical-semantic relation models. In *Human Language Technologies 2007: The Conference of the North American Chapter of the Association for Computational Linguistics*, pages 428–435, Rochester, New York.

Jacob Cohen. 1960. A coefficient of agreement for nominal scales. *Educational and Psychological Measurement*, 20(1):37–46.

Gao Cong, Long Wang, Chin-Yew Lin, Young-In Song, and Yueheng Sun. 2008. Finding question-answer pairs from online forums. In *Proceedings of the 31st annual international ACM SIGIR conference on Research and development in information retrieval*, pages 467–474, Singapore.

Johannes Daxenberger, Oliver Ferschke, Iryna Gurevych, and Torsten Zesch. 2014. DKPro TC: A Java-based framework for supervised learning experiments on textual data. In *Proceedings of 52nd Annual Meeting of the Association for Computational Linguistics: System Demonstrations*, pages 61–66, Baltimore, Maryland.

Oliver Ferschke, Iryna Gurevych, and Yevgen Chebotar. 2012. Behind the article: Recognizing dialog acts in Wikipedia talk pages. In *Proceedings of the 13th Conference of the European Chapter of the Association for Computational Linguistics*, pages 777–786, Avignon, France.

Oliver Ferschke, Iryna Gurevych, and Marc Rittberger. 2013. The impact of topic bias on quality flaw prediction in Wikipedia. In *Proceedings of the 51st Annual Meeting of the Association for Computational Linguistics*, pages 721–730, Sofia, Bulgaria.

Oliver Ferschke. 2014. *The Quality of Content in Open Online Collaboration Platforms: Approaches to NLP-supported Information Quality Management in Wikipedia*. Ph.D. thesis, Technical University of Darmstadt, Darmstadt, Germany.

Aidan Finn and Nicholas Kushmerick. 2003. Learning to classify documents according to genre. In *IJCAI-03 Workshop on Computational Approaches to Style Analysis and Synthesis*, Acapulco, Mexico. Electronic proceedings.

Camille Guinaudeau and Michael Strube. 2013. Graph-based local coherence modeling. In *Proceedings of the 51st Annual Meeting of the Association for Computational Linguistics (Volume 1: Long Papers)*, pages 93–103, Sofia, Bulgaria, August.

Mark Hall, Eibe Frank, Geoffrey Holmes, Bernhard Pfahringer, Peter Reutemann, and Ian H Witten. 2009. The weka data mining software: an update. *ACM SIGKDD explorations newsletter*, 11(1):10–18.

Su Nam Kim, Li Wang, and Timothy Baldwin. 2010. Tagging and linking web forum posts. In *Proceedings of the Fourteenth Conference on Computational*

Natural Language Learning, pages 192–202, Uppsala, Sweden.

Moshe Koppel and Jonathan Schler. 2003. Exploiting stylistic idiosyncrasies for authorship attribution. In *IJCAI03 Workshop on Computational Approaches to Style Analysis and Synthesis*, pages 69–72, Acapulco, Mexico.

Ziheng Lin, Min-Yen Kan, and Hwee Tou Ng. 2009. Recognizing implicit discourse relations in the Penn Discourse Treebank. In *Proceedings of the 2009 Conference on Empirical Methods in Natural Language Processing*, pages 343–351, Singapore.

Daniel Marcu and Abdessamad Echihabi. 2002. An unsupervised approach to recognizing discourse relations. In *Proceedings of 40th Annual Meeting of the Association for Computational Linguistics*, pages 368–375, Philadelphia, Pennsylvania.

Quinn McNemar. 1947. Note on the sampling error of the difference between correlated proportions or percentages. *Psychometrika*, 12(2):153–157.

T. Daniel Midgley, Shelly Harrison, and Cara MacNish. 2009. Empirical verification of adjacency pairs using dialogue segmentation. In *Proceedings of the 7th SIGdial Workshop on Discourse and Dialogue*, pages 104–108, London, UK.

George K. Mikros and Eleni K. Argiri. 2007. Investigating topic influence in authorship attribution. In *Proceedings of the SIGIR 2007 International Workshop on Plagiarism Analysis, Authorship Identification, and Near-Duplicate Detection, PAN 2007*, Amsterdam, Netherlands. Electronic proceedings.

Emily Pitler, Annie Louis, and Ani Nenkova. 2009. Automatic sense prediction for implicit discourse relations in text. In *Proceedings of the Joint Conference of the 47th Annual Meeting of the ACL and the 4th International Joint Conference on Natural Language Processing of the AFNLP*, pages 683–691, Suntec, Singapore.

Rashmi Prasad, Nikhil Dinesh, Alan Lee, Eleni Miltsakaki, Livio Robaldo, Aravind Joshi, and Bonnie Webber. 2008. The Penn Discourse TreeBank 2.0. In *Proceedings of the Sixth International Conference on Language Resources and Evaluation (LREC'08)*, pages 2961–2968, Marrakech, Morocco.

Harvey Sacks, Emanuel A. Schegloff, and Gail Jefferson. 1974. A simplest systematics for the organization of turn-taking for conversation. *Language*, pages 696–735.

Emanuel A. Schegloff and Harvey Sacks. 1973. Opening up closings. *Semiotica*, 8(4):289–327.

Jangwon Seo, W. Bruce Croft, and David A. Smith. 2009. Online community search using thread structure. In *Proceedings of the 18th ACM conference on Information and knowledge management*, pages 1907–1910, Hong Kong, China.

Efstathios Stamatatos. 2011. Plagiarism detection using stopword n-grams. *Journal of the American Society for Information Science and Technology*, 62(12):2512–2527.

Yi-Chia Wang and Carolyn P. Rosé. 2010. Making conversational structure explicit: identification of initiation-response pairs within online discussions. In *Human Language Technologies: The 2010 Annual Conference of the North American Chapter of the Association for Computational Linguistics*, pages 673–676, Los Angeles, California.

Yi-Chia Wang, Mahesh Joshi, William W Cohen, and Carolyn Penstein Rosé. 2008. Recovering implicit thread structure in newsgroup style conversations. In *Proceedings of the International Conference on Weblogs and Social Media*, pages 152–160, Seattle, Washington.

Hongning Wang, Chi Wang, ChengXiang Zhai, and Jiawei Han. 2011a. Learning online discussion structures by conditional random fields. In *Proceedings of the 34th international ACM SIGIR conference on Research and development in Information Retrieval*, pages 435–444, Beijing, China.

Li Wang, Marco Lui, Su Nam Kim, Joakim Nivre, and Timothy Baldwin. 2011b. Predicting thread discourse structure over technical web forums. In *Proceedings of the Conference on Empirical Methods in Natural Language Processing*, pages 13–25, Edinburgh, UK.

Li Wang, Diana McCarthy, and Timothy Baldwin. 2011c. Predicting thread linking structure by lexical chaining. In *Australasian Language Technology Association Workshop 2011*, page 76, Canberra, Australia.

Li Wang, Su Nam Kim, and Timothy Baldwin. 2013. The utility of discourse structure in forum thread retrieval. In *Information Retrieval Technology*, pages 284–295. Springer.

A Hierarchical Word Sequence Language Model

Xiaoyi Wu
Nara Institute of Science and Technology
Computational Linguistics Laboratory
8916-5 Takayama, Ikoma, Nara Japan
xiaoyi-w@is.naist.jp

Yuji Matsumoto
Nara Institute of Science and Technology
Computational Linguistics Laboratory
8916-5 Takayama, Ikoma, Nara Japan
matsu@is.naist.jp

Abstract

Most language models used for natural language processing are continuous. However, the assumption of such kind of models is too simple to cope with data sparsity problem. Although many useful smoothing techniques are developed to estimate these unseen sequences, it is still important to make full use of contextual information in training data. In this paper, we propose a hierarchical word sequence language model to relieve the data sparsity problem. Experiments verified the effectiveness of our model.

1 Introduction

Most language models used for natural language processing, such as n-gram approach proposed by Shannon (1948), are continuous. However, the assumption that a word depends upon the preceding n-1 words is too simple to cope with data sparsity problem.

Thus, a number of useful smoothing techniques such as back-off (Katz,1987), Kneser-Ney (Kneser & Ney,1995), modified Kneser-Ney (Chen & Goodman,1999) have been developed to estimate the probabilities of unseen sequences. Yet even with 30 years worth of newswire text, more than one third of all trigrams are unseen (Allison et al., 2005). It is still important to make full use of contextual information hidden in training data.

D. Guthrie. et. al. (2006) proposed using skip-gram (Huang et. al., 1993) to overcome the data sparsity problem. The skip-gram model using discontinuous sequences to model languages has truly helped to decrease the unseen sequences, but we should not neglect the fact that it also brings the greatly increase of processing time and redundant contexts. D. Guthrie. et. al. (2006) examined the coverage of skip-gram, but didn't analyze the efficiency of them, which will be discussed in section 4.3 and section 4.4 in this paper.

Taking into account of the balance between coverage and usage, we present a hierarchical word sequence model to relieve the data sparsity problem. Differing from other hierarchical language models, such as hierarchical phrase-based model (Chiang, 2007) used in SMT systems, our model is essentially a n-gram language model whose modeling assumption is determined by tree structures.

We introduce our main idea in Section 2. In Section 3, we propose the hierarchical word sequence model. We show the effectiveness of this model by several experiments in Section 4 and conclude in Section 5.

2 Basic Ideas

Data sparsity is caused by the low frequency word combinations and unknown word combinations, which are inevitably increased by the assumption that a word depends upon the preceding n-1 words.

For instance, given two sentences A = 'I hit the tennis ball' and B = 'I hit the ball', suppose that A is in the training data and B is in the test data, then the bigram (the, ball) and trigram (hit, the, ball) will not be learned by normal n-gram models.

Skip-gram models relieve this problem by skipping some words so that bigram (the, ball) and trigram (hit, the, ball) can be learned. But suppose that

Copyright 2014 by Xiaoyi Wu and Yuji Matsumoto
28th Pacific Asia Conference on Language, Information and Computation pages 489–494

Models	Trained Bigrams	Tested Bigrams
bigram model	(the, ball), (a, naughty), (naughty, boy)	(the, tennis), (tennis, ball), (a, boy)
skip-bigram model	(the, ball), (a, naughty), (naughty, boy), **(a, boy)**	(the, tennis), (tennis, ball), **(a, boy)**
proposed model	**(the, ball)**, **(a, boy)**, (boy, naughty)	(ball, tennis), **(the, ball)**, **(a, boy)**

Table 1: An example of bigrams trained and tested by three different kinds of models. The bolded bigrams occur in both training data and test data.

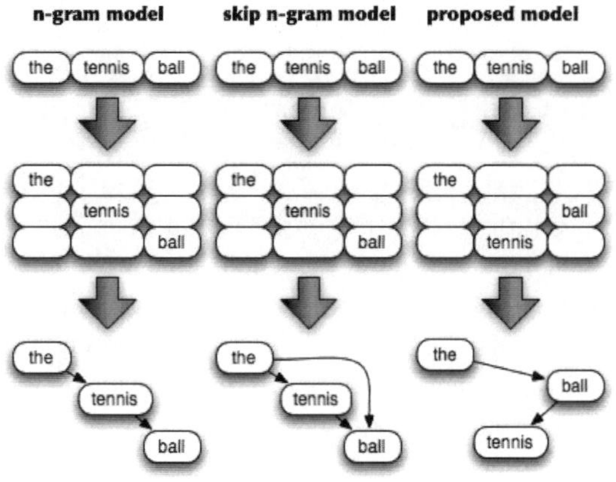

Figure 1: The assumptions of three different models

B is in the training data and A is in the test data, then the bigrams (the, tennis), (tennis, ball) and trigrams (hit, the, tennis), (the, tennis, ball) cannot be learned too. Besides, the skipping is actually a partial enumeration of word combinations, which come along with lots of modeling redundancy.

Since 'tennis ball' is a specification of pattern '... ball', it is more appropriate to consider that 'tennis' depends upon 'ball' rather than its preceding word 'the'. Similarly, 'the ball' can be considered as a specification of pattern 'the ...'. Based on such an assumption, we propose to reorder the dependent sequence as 'the→ball→tennis' instead of the original one ('the→tennis→ball'), and consequently, the bigrams are trained and tested as (the, ball), (ball, tennis), which is quite different from the traditional sequential way as shown in Figure 1.

To reveal the advantages of this idea, suppose we have {'the ball', 'a naughty boy'} in the training data and {'the tennis ball', 'a boy'} in the test data. Table 1 shows what we will have in the bigram model and the skip-bigram model, and what we hope to have in our proposed model. As shown in this table, our model learns pairs of words that hopefully have direct dependencies. Besides, without enumeration, proposed model can keep size of trained grams as small as normal n-gram model.

Although we also change the word sequence of test data in a different way, it is still appropriate to compare it with n-gram models for two reasons. First, the word sequence of training data and test data are reordered by the same assumption that a word depends upon its schematic pattern as we described above, just as the n-gram model assume that every word of test data depends upon its preceding words. Second, the number of total tested bigrams is still the same as that of n-gram models. For each word of test data, we only make a different assumption about what the dependent words should be.

Since these dependent words can be determined if we parse 'the tennis ball' into an intermediate structure as shown in Figure 1, the only remaining problem is how to achieve such kind of structure from any sequence. Although similar structures can be achieved by applying dependency parsers, the accuracy of word dependency parsing is highly language-dependent. It is expected for us to figure out a method that can be applied to any language as easily as normal n-gram models.

Intuitively, the more frequently a word is used, the more probable it becomes part of a useful pattern. We establish our method based on such a heuristic rule in the following section.

3 Method

As we discussed previously, we assume that a word depends upon its schematic pattern, and also assume that such a pattern consists of relatively high frequency words.

Based on these two assumptions, first, we calculate all the uni-grams of training data and sort them into a ranking list by frequency as shown in Table 2.

According to this ranking list, for each sentence in

Word	Frequecy
,	2501
the	2040
.	1950
of	1149
to	1087
a	1014
and	847
in	753
's	465
...	...

Table 2: An example of frequency ranking list

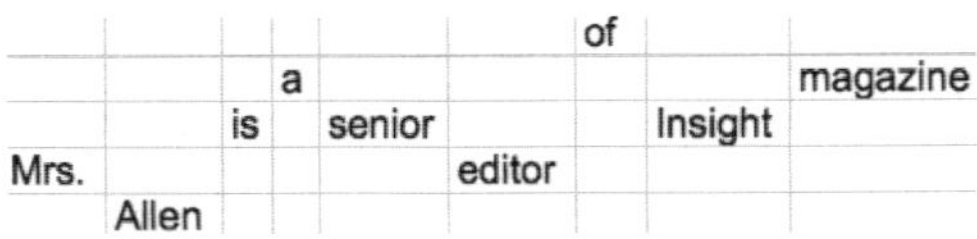

Figure 2: An example of divided sentence

training data, we find the most frequently used word [1] and use it to divide this sentence into 2 parts. For instance, in the sentence 'Mrs. Allen is a senior editor of insight magazine', 'of' is the most frequently used word in Table 2, then we use 'of' to divide this sentence into 'Mrs. Allen is a senior editor' and 'insight magazine', recursively, for each part, we divide it into two shorter parts (or one if there are not remaining subsequences on both sides). Finally, the result is represented as a matrix in Figure 2.

Alternatively, this matrix is also represented in a binary tree as shown in Figure 3.

[1]If this word appears multiple times in this sentence, then select the first one.

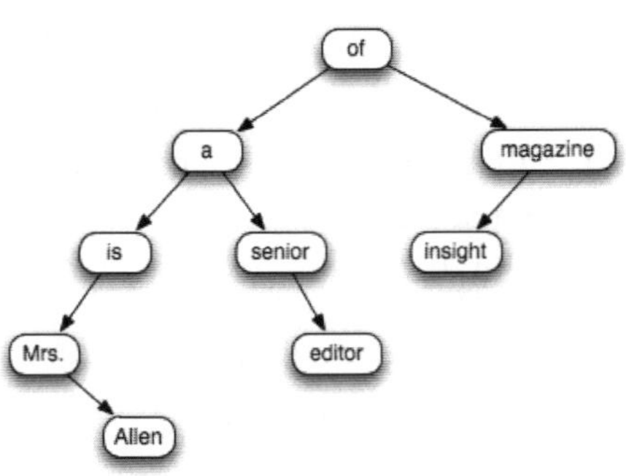

Figure 3: An example of binary tree

In this binary tree, each node (word) is generated from its parent nodes, which can be considered as a schematic pattern of this node. For instance, in Figure 3, the node 'Mrs.' is generated from the path 'of→a→is', which means that the word 'Mrs.' is generated from the pattern '... is a ... of ...' in the original sentence.

Assuming that each node in this tree depends on the preceding n-1 parent nodes, then a special n-gram model can be trained. We define this kind of model as a **hierarchical word sequence n-gram language model** (abbreviated as **hws-n-gram model**). For instance, the hws-2-grams of Figure 3 are {($[2], of), (of, a), (a, is), (is, Mrs.), (Mrs., Allen), (a, senior), (senior, editor), (of, magazine), (magazine, insight)}, while the hws-3-grams are {($, $, of), ($, of, a), (of, a, is), (a, is, Mrs.), (is, Mrs. Allen), (of, a, senior), (a, senior, editor), ($, of, magazine), (of, magazine, insight)}.

4 Experiments

4.1 Setting

To test the performance on out-of-domain data, we use two different corpora **British National Corpus** and **English Gigaword Corpus** to perform experiments.

British National Corpus is a balanced synchronic text corpus consisting of English sentences with 100 million word tokens of written and spoken language from a wide range of sources. We use the entire BNC corpus as training data.

English Gigaword Corpus consists of over 1.7 billion words of English newswire from four distinct international sources. We use 100,000 words of wpb_eng file (Washington Post/Bloomberg Newswire Service) as test data.

As preprocessing of training and test data, all words were converted to lowercase and all numbers were replaced with a special tag, <NUM>.

4.2 Perplexity

This experiment evaluates the performance of the proposed model based on perplexity.

We compared our model with normal n-gram models and skip-n-gram models by applying additive smoothing (as Equation 1), Kneser-Ney (Kneser

[2]'$' represents the beginning of a sentence.

Model+Smoothing	Perplexity
2gram+ADD	1634.22
2gram+KN	1034.543
2gram+MKN	999.213
1skip-2gram+ADD	1096.116
2skip-2gram+ADD	972.283
3skip-2gram+ADD	884.781
hws-2gram+ADD	**865.795**
3gram+ADD	9556.827
3gram+KN	973.766
3gram+MKN	**912.076**
1skip-3gram+ADD	6568.764
2skip-3gram+ADD	4444.833
3skip-3gram+ADD	3460.362
hws-3gram+ADD	1284.708

Table 3: Perplexity values of normal n-gram models, skip-n-gram models and proposed model by applying different smoothing methods

& Ney,1995) and modified Kneser-Ney (Chen & Goodman,1999) as smoothing method separately.

$$P(w_i|w_{i-n+1}^{i-1}) = \frac{C(w_{i-n+1}^{i}) + \alpha}{C(w_{i-n+1}^{i-1}) + \alpha V}^{3} \quad (1)$$

The results are shown in Table 3, since the grams of our model is trained in a special way, it's not appropriate to directly incorporate lower order models to higher ones, and consequently, we cannot directly apply Kneser-ney Smoothing on our model[4]. Yet even though with additive smoothing, our bigram model outperforms normal bigram model with Modified Kneser-Ney Smoothing. Thus, if we can figure out an appropriate way to incorporate it to our trigram model, it is highly possible that ours outperforms normal trigram models as well.

4.3 Coverage and Usage

This experiment illustrates the coverage and usage of our model compared to those of normal n-gram model and skip-n-gram model. We trained on the entire BNC corpus (100 million words) and measured the coverage on 100,000 words of newswire from the Gigaword corpus.

[3]V stands for vocabulary size, and smoothing parameter α ($0.0001 \leq \alpha \leq 1.0$) is determined by golden section search (Kiefer,1953).

[4]Neither can skip-n-gram model.

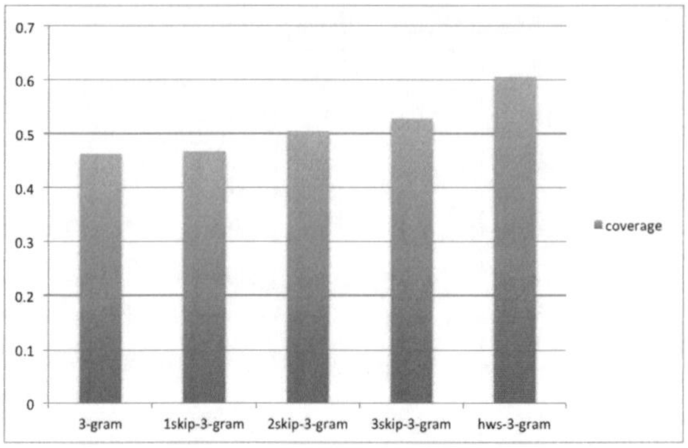

Figure 4: The coverage of 3-grams

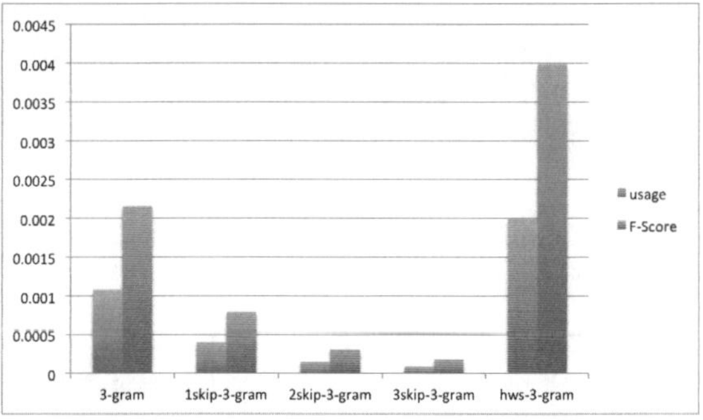

Figure 5: The usage and F-Score of 3-grams

We list all trigrams of test data to examine how many of them actually occurred in trained model and how many trigrams of trained model actually are used in test data.

We define the grams of training data as TR, and unique grams of test data as TE, then we calculate coverage by Equation 2.

$$coverage = \frac{|TR \bigcap TE|}{|TE|} \quad (2)$$

We also use Equation 3 to estimate how much redundancy contained in a model and Equation 4 as a balanced measure.

$$usage = \frac{|TR \bigcap TE|}{|TR|} \quad (3)$$

$$FScore = \frac{2 \times coverage \times usage}{coverage + usage} \quad (4)$$

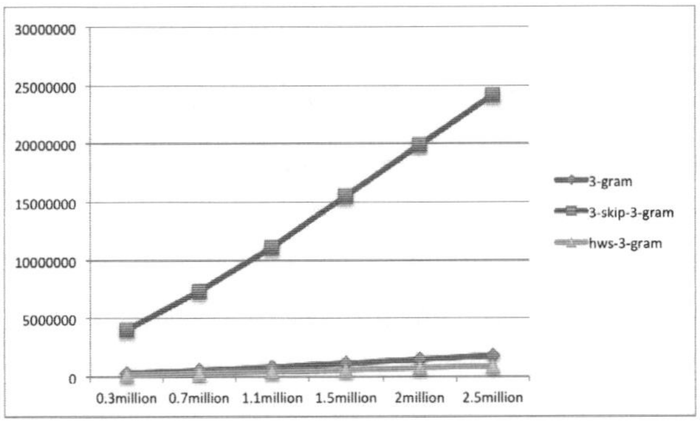

Figure 6: The growth of trained grams with the addition of training data size

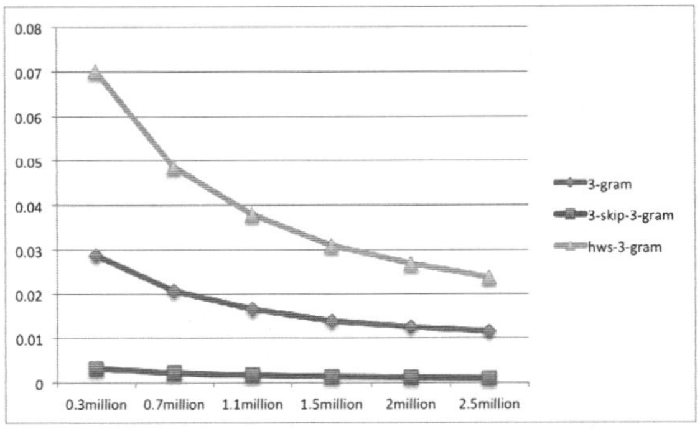

Figure 7: The decreasing of usage with the addition of training data size

The results of coverage are shown in Figure 4. Even though skip-gram model use a partial enumeration of word combinations to expand trained grams, proposed model still outperforms 3skip-3-gram model by 7.3 percent.

Figure 5 shows the results of usage and F-score. Apparently, there is much less modeling redundancy in our model, and as a result, ours keeps better balance between coverage and usage than the other ones.

4.4 Length of Trained Grams and Training Data Size

This experiment examines the relation between length of trained grams and training data size. We use exactly the same test data (100,000 words of Gigaword corpus) as above. But for training data, we use different portions of different sizes of BNC corpus. We gradually increase the amount of training data to examine how it affects these trained grams.

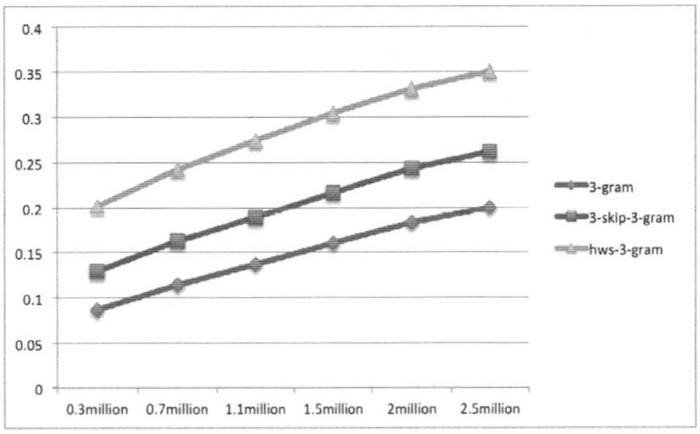

Figure 8: The increasing of coverage with the addition of training data size

Intuitively, the length of trained grams will be increased with the addition of corpus size. As shown in Figure 6, in comparison with normal 3-gram model and hws-3-gram model, the grams learned by 3-skip-3-gram grow very fast, which means the cost of producing and storing them is quite considerable.

Consequently, the growth of grams comes along with modeling redundancy, appearing as the decreasing of usage. As shown in Figure 7, though hws-3-gram is decreasing, it is still more efficient (with higher usage) than the other two models.

Of course, the inefficiency of 3-skip-3-gram would be worth if it resulted in higher coverage. But as shown in Figure 8, all the three kinds of models increase at almost the same speed, and proposed model still hold the lead.

5 Conclusions and Future Work

In this paper, we proposed a hierarchical word sequence language model to make full use of contextual information and relieve the data sparsity problem.

Proposed model has a good performance on decreasing perplexity, which also keeps better balance between coverage and usage than normal n-gram model and skip-n-gram model. Besides, the cost of storing our model is more economical than other models.

In this paper, we only used additive smoothing as the smoothing method for our model, the performance can be further improved if we incorporate lower order models to higher ones. Besides that, if we use certain criteria to filter schematic patterns trained by our model, some useful sentence patterns can be extracted, which is also a promising future study.

References

B. Allison, D. Guthrie, et. al. 2005. *Quantifying the Likelihood of Unseen Events: A further look at the data Sparsity problem.* Awaiting publication.

C. E. Shannon. 1948. *A Mathematical Theory of Communication. The Bell System Technical Journal*, 27: 379-423.

D. Chiang. 2007. *Hierarchical Phrase-based Translation. Computational Linguistics*, Vol33, No.2, 201–228.

D. Guthrie, B. Alliso, et. al. 2006. *A Closer Look at Skipgram Modelling. Proceedings of the 5th international Conference on Language Resources and Evaluation*, 2006: 1-4.

J. Kiefer. 1953. *Sequential minimax search for a maximum. Proceedings of the American Mathematical Society*, 1953, 4(3): 502-506.

R. Kneser, H. Ney. 1995. *Improved backing-off for m-gram language modeling. Acoustics, Speech, and Signal Processing, 1995. ICASSP-95., 1995 International Conference on. IEEE*, 1995, 1: 181-184.

S. F. Chen, J. Goodman. 1999. *An empirical study of smoothing techniques for language modeling. Computer Speech & Language*, 1999, 13(4): 359-393.

S. Katz. 1987. *Estimation of probabilities from sparse data for the language model component of a speech recognizer. Acoustics, Speech and Signal Processing, IEEE Transactions on*, 1987, 35(3): 400-401.

X. Huang, F. Alleva, H. W. Hon, et al. 1993. *The SPHINX-II speech recognition system: an overview. Computer Speech & Language*, 1993, 7(2): 137-148.

An Analysis of Radicals-based Features in Subjectivity Classification on Simplified Chinese Sentences

Ge Xu
Minjiang University
xuge@pku.edu.cn

Chu-Ren Huang
Hong Kong Polytechnic University
Churen.huang@poly.edu.hk

Abstract

Chinese radicals are linguistic elements smaller than Chinese characters[1]. Normally, a radical is a semantic category and almost all characters contain radicals or are radicals themselves. In subjectivity classification on sentences, we can use radicals to represent characters, which reduce the scale of word space while keep the subjectivity information.

In this paper, we manually labeled a character set to build a high-quality radical-character mapping, and then the mapping is used to generalize character-based features with radicals. In experiments, we at first evaluated the performance when directly generalizing characters with radicals, and then offer a hypothesis that can reduce noises.

Experiments show that this approach based on our hypothesis can reduce feature space while keep or improve the performance, which is especially useful when the training samples are scarce.

keyword: sentiment analysis, subjectivity classification, radical, Chinese character

1 Introduction

In sentiment analysis, an important task is subjectivity classification on sentences, which means classify sentences as subjective or objective. This step's performance greatly affects the following processing that is related with polarity or emotion etc. Here

1. 邻近的永乐国小大部分的教室也被列为危楼。 Most classrooms of Yongle elementary school nearby are also classified as dangerous buildings.
2. 寄读生涯孩子累家长烦。 Boarding school life makes students tired and their parents irritable.

we offer two sentences from NTCIR6 training corpus for subjectivity classification.

For the first sentence, although 危(dangerous) is a sentiment character, it is used to modify building, so the semantic emphasis of 危楼(dangerous building) is building, and also 危楼(dangerous building) is somewhat known as a term, so normally is regarded as objective, thus the whole sentence is labeled as objective.

For the second sentence, the subjectivity mainly comes from 累(tired) and 烦(irritable). These two characters are also with different level of subjectivity. "tired" is a physical experience, compared with 烦(irritable), it is somewhat "objective". But 烦(irritable) can surely make the sentence subjective. If we take a further step, we can see that 烦(irritable) has a Chinese radical 火(fire), which can derive concepts of sentiment from linguistic perspective.

In real system, to label subjectivity sentences is of high cost especially when high quality is required. As we know, the size of common Chinese characters is around several thousands, while the size of radicals in Chinese is only around several hundreds, if we use the radicals to generalize character, it may overcome to some extent the sparseness problem

[1]We use the terminology "character" for "Chinese character" in this paper.

Copyright 2014 by Ge Xu and Chu-Ren Huang
28th Pacific Asia Conference on Language, Information and Computation pages 495–502

when training model and reduce the time and space required.

2 Related work

Sentiment classification on texts has been studied by many researchers, such as (Goldberg and Zhu, 2006; Pang and Lee, 2005) etc. Normally, machine learning-based methods dominate the filed, and much emphasis is put on polarity instead of subjectivity. Furthermore, compared with English, subjectivity classification on Chinese is relatively few. In the following, we pay more attention to work on Chinese, subjectivity and Chinese radicals.

Yao and Peng (2007) used 7 features to describe a text, which include "if a personal pronoun occurs in the sentence?", "if interjection occurs in the sentence?", etc. A SVM-based method offered the best performance (F-value 0.938) in their experiments. The work used a small corpus which includes 359 texts (191 subjective and 168 objective).

Li et al. (2006) made a detail comparison between words and character-bigrams when they are used to represent features in text classification, and concluded that Chinese character bigrams are better than words in feature representation for text classification. In our experiments, we followed some experimental configuration in (Li et al., 2006) and put more emphasis on evaluating the performance of subjectivity classification using radical representation

Qiu et al. (2009) presented an approach to guess word's sense by its components(characters), they used the LC(lexical compositionality) principle: "The words formed by similar constituents in the same mode fall into the same semantic category". When we use radicals to generalize characters, we are following the similar principle. If two characters share the same radical, they may fall into the same semantic category.

Huang et al. (2008) presented a qualia structure to analyze how characters derived from radicals, they classified the derived concepts of character radicals into 7 categories, expanded from the original four qualia aspects of Formal, Constitutive, Agentive, and Telic. This structure is useful when we label radicals for subjectivity classification, because characters derived by similar path may have similar concept, and when we use radicals to generalize characters, we can choose an accurate semantic category (finer than a radical) to avoid semantic roughness. For example, a frequent radical, such as 人(human), can derive many characters. In these characters, some are persons with certain identification，such as 仙(fairy),侠(swordsman) and 佛(Buddha); some are descriptive such as 仁(benevolent),俊(handsome) and 傻(stupid). Other possible concepts derived from 人(human) is not listed due to space limit. Considering this, we have to define finer semantic categories for the radical 人(human); Otherwise, different concepts will be grouped together, making the generalization in feature construction error-prone.

3 The basics of radicals

Chinese characters have a history of over 5000 years. They evolved from pictographs to nowadays characters after all sorts of unification and simplification. Basically, there are four ways to create a character: pictographs(象形) , ideographs(指示), logical aggregates(会意), phonograms(形声).

1. pictographs(象形): Character is similar with the entity in the world. Examples include 伞 for "umbrella", and 木 for "tree".

2. ideograph(指示): For instance, 刀 is "knife", and placing an indicator in the knife makes 刃, an ideograph for "blade". Other common examples are 上(up) and 下 (down).

3. logical aggregates(会意)：For instance, 木 (tree) is a pictograph of a tree, and putting two 木 together makes 林 , meaning forest. The difference between ideograph and logical aggregates lies in that the indicator for ideograph is normally not a radical, much more like a stroke of a Chinese character; while logical aggregate characters contain at least two radicals.

4. phonograms(形声)：It is also titled semantic-phonetic compounds, or phono-semantic compounds. According to (Xu, 121), approximately 82 percent of characters are classified into this category, and also the largest group of characters in modern Chinese. A phonogram character includes two parts: a pictograph,

which indicates the semantics of the character, and a phonetic part, which is a character itself and indicate how the phonogram character is pronounced. For example, 榕(banyan tree) contains two parts: 木(tree) and 容(pronounced as róng), 木 indicates that 榕 is a kind of tree, and 容 indicates that 榕 is pronounced as róng.

Roughly speaking, in Chinese, radicals are the minimum semantic units[2]. Normally, a character is composed of radical(s) or a radical itself. Let us check how four types of character-formations (pictograph,ideograph,logical aggregate,phonogram) are related with radicals.

1. For pictograph characters, normally they are radicals, such as 木(tree),鱼(fish),鹿(deer), 田(cropland) etc.

2. For ideograph characters, normally they are based on a pictograph, and add some stroke(s).

3. For logical aggregate characters, they contain two or more radicals.

4. For any phonogram character, one of two parts in the character is a radical and indicates the semantics of the character.

So we can see that radicals are closely related with character, we can know the rough semantic of a character by its radical(s). If the given NLP task required a semantic granularity coarser than radical-level, we can use radicals to assistant the task without sacrificing accuracy.

In "ShuoWenJieZi"(Xu, 121), all Chinese characters are classified as derived from 540 radicals. Nowadays, many of 540 radicals have been deprecated or are seldom used, so the size of common and active radicals is around 200. In (Zhou and Huang, 2005), ranked by how many characters a radical can derive, the top 20 radicals can cover 4425 of 9353 characters in (Xu, 121). Such radicals are closely related with human life, such as 水(water),艸(grass),木(tree), 手(hand),心(heart),言(speak) etc. When a radical can derive many characters, normally the semantics is derived into several categories, we will give more details in section 4.2 how we process this issue.

Of cause, there exists some case that radicals fail to indicate the semantics of characters. For example, 笨(stupid) contains two radicals: 竹(bamboo) above and 本(base) at the bottom which contains the radical 木(tree). Perhaps due to complicated evolution, it is hard to connect the semantics with either of the two radicals. By experience, such phenomenon is scarce, accounting for only a small portion in all Chinese characters. So in most cases, for a character, we can relate it to a radical which indicate its semantics.

[2]In our paper, we do not define radical strictly as in some linguistic literature As long as a element in character can be used to represent semantics and indivisible, we accept it as a radical

4 Radical labeling on a Chinese character set

For subjectivity classification on Chinese sentences in our experiments, we manually created a radical-character mapping. For this task, two problems have to be considered:

- Choosing a Chinese character set
- Design a labeling schema

Furthermore, another important problem should be noticed. The corpus and the character set we used in experiments is simplified Chinese. However, in order to obtain high-quality radical-character mapping, we used traditional Chinese character to analyze radicals. For example, 云(cloud) is the simplified character of 雲(cloud) which has the radical 雨(rain),and we think that 云(cloud) has the radical 雨(rain) although this radical has been omitted after Chinese character simplification.

4.1 Choosing a Chinese character set

We have four choices for a Chinese character set, see table 1 for more details.

Note that, apart from "ShuoWenJieZi" character set which is traditional Chinese, other three character sets should use traditional Chinese character as a bridge to identify radicals in characters. In our experiments, we choose the first level character set of GB2312, which complies with national regulation of P.R.China and includes frequent (compared with the second level character set) Chinese characters which can cover most of Chinese conversation. We do not

Table 1: Introduction of available Chinese character sets

1	XinHua Dictionary. The newest version contains 11200+ entries (characters). This dictionary accompanies almost every Chinese people from primary school, and each Chinese character in this dictionary is listed with all its senses.
2	GB2312 character set. The first level contains 3755 characters, and the second level contains 3008 characters. This Chinese character set complies with national regulation, which makes it easy to introduce and deliver. Most important of all, the first level is frequent Chinese character, which is naturally proper when processing big corpus and for obtaining comprehensive performance.
3	The character set in ShuoWenJieZi. It has 9353 characters. This dictionary is edited by radicals. But it suffers two several problems: This book's author didn't know oracle bone inscriptions, so many radical explanation is wrong; Many characters in this dictionary are deprecated.
4	Chinese character set from a given corpus. The size varies and although this is the minimum cost when develop a system on text processing, this set is too specific and is limited when transferred to other applications.

choose the character set in XinHua dictionary because it is a bit too large for one annotator to label.

4.2 Labeling schema

At first, we collected from internet all sorts of radical resources. We only consider those resources which list all Chinese characters sharing one radical in one line, and the first Chinese character is normally the radical. A clip of the finally collected radical resources is shown in figure 1.

Based on this resource, we will use the following labeling schema:

1. The first Chinese character should represent its original semantics of the radical that derives the characters in the line. For example, lot of Chinese characters with the radical 月(moon) is in fact related with 肉(meat), and 月(moon) is the pictograph of meat; so we put the 肉(meat) at the first of the line, which looks like:"肉肌肉肝肛肚肪肩股肢胚胎胃脆......". The processing can make it more readable and understandable when we use radicals to replaces Chinese characters.

2. If some radical is only used for looking up in a dictionary, it is omitted. For example, a lot of Chinese characters are arranged in the line started with 一(one), "一亅丂丏丈上下且......", but in terms of semantics, 一(one) has little relationship with other Chinese character. So we omit the whole line.

3. If a Chinese character contains more than one radicals, choose the radical more similar in semantics with the character. For example, 娶(marry a woman) can be related to two parts, 取(fetch)and 女(female). Furthermore, 取(fetch) can be analyzed as 耳(ear) and 又(again), and 又(again) is the pictograph of 手(hand). So, in a more general level, 娶(marry a woman) contain the abstract semantics of the behavior of 手(hand), so the radical for 娶(marry a woman) should be 手(hand). In another situation, although a character contains more than one radical, but none is closely semantics-related. For example, 笨(stupid) includes two radicals 竹(bamboo) and 木(tree), but neither has the same semantic category with 笨(stupid), so we tend to regard such character as an independent character.

4. Since our main task is subjectivity classification, we require that each line is subjective or objective. For example, many characters share the radical 女(female), some characters are ob-

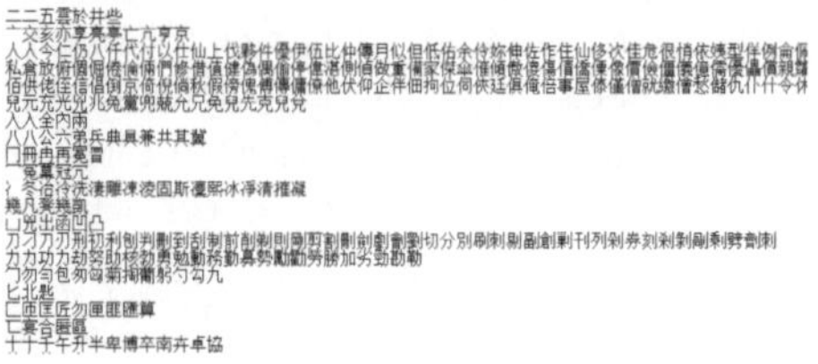

Figure 1: Collected radical resources

jective, they are mainly all sorts of female relatives such as “姐姑妈姨婆奶妹”; and some are subjective, such as “奴奸妒妓婀妙娟娥”.You also may note that the subjective ones contain both positive ones(婀妙娟娥) and negative ones(奴奸妒妓), since we do not distinguish polarities in our classification, we put both in one line.

5. Some radicals can derive too many character, and such radicals are normally closely related with human life, such as 人(human),口(mouth) and 手(hand) etc. In this situation, the radicals must be further divided.

In (Huang et al., 2008), the authors use Pustejovsky's Qualia Structures base and observe the analysis on the definitions in “ShuoWenJieZi”, and then classify the derived concepts of character radicals into 7 categories , expanded from the original four qualia aspects of Formal, Constitutive, Agentive, and Telic, as shown in table 2.

We would refer to this schema in our labeling practicing while adjust and modify according to actual conditions.

4.3 Labeling practice

The labeling costs the first author approximately half a day with the help of a electrical dictionary[3]. Some radicals are easy to label. For example, all characters contain radical 父(father) are 父爸爹爺, which are fathers or grandfathers.

Once the size of the characters that a radical derived become large, it can derive different semantic categories. We used the Qualia Structures mentioned in (Huang et al., 2008) to create finer categories for a radicals. Several cases are listed as following:

1. Constitutive:鳞鳃鳔(various parts of a fish)

2. Formal-vision:鱼鲤鲸鲍......(various types of fishes)

3. Descriptive:鲜(delicious)

The above is for the radical 鱼(fish).

[3]http://cn.bing.com/dict/

Table 2: Seven categories of derived concepts from radicals

Formal	This category can be further divided into 5 small categories: "sense," "characteristic," "proper names," and "atypical." The "sense" categories can be further divided into 5 small categories: "vision," "hearing," "smelling," and "taste."
Constitutive	This category can be further divided into 3 small categories: "part,""member," and "group."
Telic	Concepts related to function or usage
Participant	Words are classified into this category when the definition in 'ShuoWenJieZi' mentions the participant involved.
Participating	According to different events, concepts are divided into 6 small categories:"action," "state," "purpose," "function," "tool," and "others."
Descriptive	This category can be further divided into two categories: "active" and "state."
Agentive	The relationship between the radical and its meaning cluster coming from production or giving birth are classified in to agentive.

1. Constitutive:木 杈 本 末 林 根 梢 森 树 枝 果(various parts of a tree)

2. Formal-vision: 柳 栗 桑 桐 梨 棉 梅 枣 棕......(various types of tree)

3. Telic/Agentive:梗 柯 柄 框 案 梁 梳 棋 棚......(various types of components made by wood, various wood buildings)

The above is for the radical 木(tree).

1. Constitutive:叶 苗 蕊 蒂 茎 芯 藤 菁 苞 芽 茸(various parts of grass)

2. Formal-vision: 草 艾 芭 芥 芹 芝 茶 荔......(various types of grass)

3. Descriptive:芬 芳 苦 茂 茫 芜 萧 菲 苍 蔼 萌(various characteristics of grass)

The above is for the radical 艸(grass).

The first-level character set of GB2312 contains 3755 characters, and some characters will be removed according to labeling schema in section 4.2, so the size of the final character set is smaller than 3755.

5 Experiment

In this section, we aim to evaluate how the generalization affects the subjectivity classification on Chinese simplified sentences when we use radicals to generalize characters.

5.1 The corpus

The NTCIR (NII-NACSIS Test Collection for Information Retrieval) workshops have been organized since 1999. In the sixth NTCIR Workshop (NTCIR6 for short), five subtasks are set in the evaluation, one of which is mandatory, which is to decide whether each sentence expresses an opinion or not. In another word, the subtask is a binary subjectivity classification on all sentences. The pilot task has tracks in three languages: Chinese, English, and Japanese. In this paper, we use its Chinese corpus for our experiments.

In our paper, the lenient evaluation metric is adopted, where two of the three annotators must agree for a value to be included in the gold standard. There are around 9000 sentences in the corpus, in which subjective sentences account for 60% roughly.

We use ICTCLAS[4] package to perform word segmentation and POS tagging, during which Specification for Corpus Processing at Peking University in (Shiwen Yu, 2003) is adopted.

5.2 Results of experiments

We used Weka[5] package for our experiments. According to research work on Chinese text classification(Li et al., 2006), SVM with linear kernel is a good classifier for such task, so we do not evaluate how various classifiers affect the performance, and put more emphasis on how feature are represented. Four-fold cross-validation is chosen.

Table 3: Comparison of different feature representations

Key_Dataset	Accuracy
radical_unigram	73.171%
radical_unibigram	75.033%
radical_bigram	75.303%
char_unigram	73.420%
char_unibigram	76.028%
char_bigram	76.050%
word_unigram	73.398%
word_unibigram	**76.548%**
word_bigram	74.026%
wordRadical_unigram	73.074%
wordRadical_unibigram	76.255%
wordRadical_bigram	73.745%
pos_unigram	73.117%
pos_unibigram	76.504%
pos_bigram	73.540%
posRadical_unigram	72.911%
posRadical_unibigram	76.310%
posRadical_bigram	73.788%

In the table 3, "unigram","bigram","unibigram" mean three types of n-gram; "char" means that a sentence is seen as sequence of characters, and "radical" means that each char is generalized to a radical or is kept if it contains no radical; "word" means we

[4]http://www.ictclas.cn
[5]http://www.cs.waikato.ac.nz/ml/weka/

see a sentence as a sequence of words after using word segmentation tools, and "wordRadical" means to generalize characters in words; 'pos' and "posRadical" are the POS version of "word" and "wordRadical".

According to table 3, for a char, a word and a word with tag, directly generalizing them by radicals will decrease the performance a little. Such phenomenon can be explained as that some noise will be incurred when generalize words or character-bigrams by radicals. For example, when using radicals, 抨击(denounce),提拔(promote),投掷(throw) are all generalized to 手手， because the three words are composed of two characters containing 手(hand). However, we know that these three words are of different semantic categories, of different subjectivity and even of different polarity.

A way to reduce such noise is based on a hypothesis in the next section.

5.3 A Radical-based Representation

Hypothesis: For two character bigrams, if they share a character in the same position and the other two character have the same radical, these two bigrams are in the same semantic category.

For example, 袜子(sock),袄子(a short Chinese-style coat),袖子(sleeve) have the same character 子(suffix for thing) in second position, and the first character 袜袄袖 are all derived from radical 衣(cloth). So, under our hypothesis, 袜子(sock),袄子(a short Chinese-style coat),袖子(sleeve) should fall into same semantic class, namely 'cloth'. Other examples are listed in table 4.

Of cause, there are counterexamples. When checking the corpus, we find that 应该(should) and 应试(take an examination) start by the same character 应(response) and the second character share the radical 言(speak). However, 应该(should) contain subjectivity to some extent, but 应试(take an examination) is an objective word. Such error comes from that derivation complexity of characters. The original meaning of 该(should) is a promise, but nowadays the meaning of 'promise' has been seldom used, and almost have no connection with 言(speak). Such error suggested that we should pay much attention on character's present usage when labeling radicals since most corpora given are not ancient.

We design an experiment to investigate how the hypothesis works and analyze the experimental results. Since 'unigram+bigram' performance best in table 4, it is used as default setting. The experimental result is shown in table 5.

Table 4: Examples of hypothesis

梨花,杨花,杏花,樱花,棉花,梅花	the first characters all share a 木(tree) radical, the second character is the same. Each word is a kind of flower.
说话，讲话，训话，谈话	the first characters all share a 木(tree) radical, the second character is the same. Each word is a kind of speaking.
老爹，老爸，老爷，老父	the second characters all share a 父(father) radical, the first character is the same. Each word is "father" or "grandfather".

Table 5: Comparison on hypothesis and other generalizations

word	76.5476%
wordRadical	76.2554%
wordRadical_Hypothesis	**76.7424%**
pos	76.5043%
posRadical	76.3095%
posRadical_Hypothesis	76.6667%

"wordRadical_Hypothesis" and "posRadical_Hypothesis" mean processing the corpus using the hypothesis on "word" and "word with pos" representation respectively. Briefly speaking, based on the hypothesis, we at first find all the groups with same semantics, which means all words in a group should share one character and the other characters should contain the same radical. We can iterate this process from 2 character words to 3 characters, and so on. Finally, we got a set of groups, each group contain a set of words which belong to the same semantic category according to our hypothesis. In generalizing features, we use the first word in a group to label all the words in the group when processing the corpus.

The results show that such hypothesis can improve the performance by a small margin. At first, the improvement is due to using the hypothesis, so some noises are removed. "posRadical_Hypothesis"is especially useful when part-of-speech tag can be used to reduce the generalization noise. For example, 下流(obscene) and 下海(go to sea, or go into business) is in the same group based on hypothesis, but they belong to different semantic categories and have different subjectivity. When POS is considered, 下流(obscene) is an adjective while 下海(go to sea, or go into business) is a verb, so they can be divided into different categories, which helps to reduce the noise when generalizing.

The improvement is not obvious enough because the words in groups is relatively small compared to the whole word space. In our experiments, there are 18099 words (without POS tag) in the corpus, but only 486 groups. Furthermore, most of the groups contain only two words or normally low-frequency words, so the impact is limited. Such a problem is supposed to be improved by labeling a bigger character set and by using other generalization strategies.

6 Conclusion and Future work

In this paper, we evaluate how subjectivity classification on Chinese sentences performs when radicals are used to generalize characters, and offer a hypothesis that can be used to find groups with the same semantic categories. All words in a group belong to the same semantic category, so the group ID can be used to label any word in it without decreasing the classification performance. Although the improvement on performance is not obvious enough, by manual checking the group, we find the quality is very high (which to some extent explains the amount of groups and amount of the words in groups are not very large.), which can guarantee that the improvement, although not obvious, is steady.

In the future, we will pay attention to two problems:1) label a larger character set with higher quality;2) explore new ways that can utilize radicals to obtain better performance.

Acknowledgements

References

Andrew B. Goldberg and Jerry Zhu. 2006. Seeing stars when there aren't many stars: Graph-based semi-supervised learning for sentiment categorization. In *TextGraphs: HLT/NAACL Workshop on Graph-based Algorithms for Natural Language Processing*.

Chu-Ren Huang, Ya-Jun Yang, and Sheng-Yi Chen. 2008. An ontology of chinese radicals: Concept derivation and knowledge representation based on the semantic symbols of the four hoofed-mammals. In *Proceedings of the 22nd Pacific Asia Conference on Language, Information and Computation*, pages 189–196, The University of the Philippines Visayas Cebu College, Cebu City, Philippines, November. De La Salle University, Manila, Philippines.

Jingyang Li, Maosong Sun, and Xian Zhang. 2006. A comparison and semi-quantitative analysis of words and character-bigrams as features in chinese text categorization. In *ACL*.

Bo Pang and Lillian Lee. 2005. Seeing stars: Exploiting class relationships for sentiment categorization with respect to rating scales. In *Proceedings of the Association for Computational Linguistics (ACL)*, pages 115–124.

Likun Qiu, Kai Zhao, and Changjian Hu. 2009. A hybrid model for sense guessing of chinese unknown words. In *PACLIC*, pages 464–473.

Bin Swen Bao-Bao Chang Shiwen Yu, Huiming Duan. 2003. Specification for corpus processing at peking university: Word segmentation, pos tagging and phonetic notation. *Journal of Chinese Language and Computing*, 13.

Shen Xu. 121. 說文解字*ShuoWenJieZi*.

Tianfang Yao and Siwei Peng. 2007. 汉语主客观文本分类方法的研究. In 第三届全国信息检索与内容安全学术会议.

Yamin Zhou and Chu-Ren Huang. 2005. Construction of a knowledge structure based chinese radicals. In *The Sixth Chinese Lexical Semantics Workshop. Xiamen.*

A Semantics for Honorifics with Reference to Thai

Eric McCready
Aoyama Gakuin University
Department of English and American Literature
4-4-25 Shibuya, Shibuya-ku Tokyo 150-8366
JAPAN
mccready@cl.aoyama.ac.jp

Abstract

This paper proposes a general framework for the semantics of honorific expressions, including honorific pronouns, morphology, and discourse particles. Such expressions are claimed to indicate a level of politeness which must be compatible with a level of formality fixed by the discourse context together with sociolinguistic factors, and, with their use, to change the range of formality the context specifies. Specific honorifics are taken to introduce expressive content of a kind modeled by real-numbered intervals. This general picture is exemplified with the honorific system of Thai.

1 Introduction

The phenomena of honorification and politeness register have received extensive attention in linguistics, both from formal and informal perspectives. Most of this work has focused on three general topics. First, from a formal perspective, researchers have been concerned with the way in which semantic composition with honorific expressions takes place, and with the kinds of denotations which they have; some main results of these investigations will be summarized later in this paper.[1] A second line of research is found within the sociolinguistic tradition (and also within discourse analysis), and looks at ways in which speakers use politeness expressions to indicate aspects of their social identities and further their general societal goals (Brown and Levinson, 1987; Watts, 2003). Finally, there is a tradition which attempts to situate the use of politeness, including honorifics, within a general theory of rational linguistic behavior; this work begins with Brown and Levinson (1987) and continues to game-theoretic accounts like that of van Rooy (2003).

Given the amount of research done in this area, it is no surprise that significant results have been obtained. However, a problematic feature of the literature is that the three strands of research mentioned above do not engage extensively with each other. Research on honorific meanings tends not to consider observations made within discourse analysis; game-theoretic accounts try to predict rational honorific use without a serious semantics for honorific content. A theory which can bring the various aspects of politeness together seems necessary, especially given the current interest in honorification in formal circles, and further is essential for the automatic generation of appropriate speech in computational pragmatics. The aim of the present paper is to propose a theory of the requisite sort. That said, space limitations preclude doing more than laying the formal groundwork needed; modeling substantial sociolinguistic observations and tying the result to game-theoretic calculation is left for future work.

The paper is structured as follows. I will take the system of politeness marking found in Thai as the empirical domain of the analysis. This system is introduced in §2, though this introduction is necessarily non-exhaustive for reasons of space. Some lessons are drawn here for formal theories of polite-

[1] Work on syntactic aspects of honorification is closely related (Niinuma, 2003), but since morphological affixes with honorific meanings will not be my focus here, I will not consider this aspect of honorification further in the present paper.

Copyright 2014 byEric McCready
28th Pacific Asia Conference on Language, Information and Computation pages 503–512

Low		Mid		High
wá,wóoy		*há, há?*		*khá,khráp*

Figure 1: Formality of Thai particles.

ness. I then turn in §3 to past analyses of honorification, showing that they propose denotations that do not perfectly track intuitions about honorific content. My own proposal, an extension and modification of that of (Potts and Kawahara, 2004), is given in §4, and applied to the Thai system in §5. §6 concludes and indicates some directions for future work.

2 Honorification and politeness in Thai

The empirical focus of this paper is Thai. This language has a number of means for indicating politeness. The present paper will not attempt an exhaustive treatment, but will focus on politeness-marking pragmatic particle and pronominal forms. My aim is to show how the different levels of politeness/honorification marked by these terms come together to determine a general level of formality in speech, which is one of the core phenomena which a theory of honorific meanings must consider. My development closely follows that of Iwasaki and Ingkaphirom Horie (1995; Iwasaki and Ingkaphirom (2005) and adopts their description of the levels of politeness indicated by each form.[2]

2.1 Particles

Thai marks speech levels directly using pragmatic particles.[3] Essentially three speech levels are marked: casual speech, formal speech, and a mid-level gray area in between, as shown in Figure 1. With particles, as elsewhere in the domain of honorific expressions, Thai makes a distinction between female and male speech; *khá* is used by women, and *khráp* by men. Both of these particles appear in a range of phonological variants: for instance, the tone of *khá* may vary depending on the clause type the particle appears in, and *khráp* may lose its rhoticity as conversations become less formal.

From these particles, we can already see a need to separate utterances into at least three levels of formality: formal, mid-level, and casual. The simplest theory of honorific meanings might take the particles to directly indicate one of these speech levels. However, the particles can combine with other terms with honorific content, and need not match them perfectly in register, as will be shown in the next section. This means that a theory which marks speech levels directly will fail as it will result in inconsistency in such cases. The facts are more complex.

2.2 Pronouns

Thai has a large number of first and second person pronouns which mark various levels of politeness. These pronouns can be separated into casual, mid-level, and formal pronouns, as indicated in Figures 2 and 3. Within these general classes, the pronouns differ in their precise degree of formality: for instance, within the category of formal pronouns, *kraphǒm* is more formal than the simpler *phǒm*. As with particles, male and female speakers use a partly distinct set of pronouns: thus, ordinarily men use *phǒm* in formal contexts and women use *kháw*.[4]

The simple analysis discussed in §2.1 would predict that, for example, the politeness-marking particle *khráp* is incompatible with pronouns in other levels such as the mid-level formal pronoun *raw*, for the information carried by *khráp* – roughly, that the level of formality is high – is inconsistent with that of *raw* – that the formality level is neither high nor low. Still, Iwasaki and Ingkaphirom Horie (1995) observe that " signs within the same level, as well as those in the contiguous levels in the domains of [particles] and pronominals, are often mixed to create the level and shade of speech formality that participants wish" (p. 528). We would also expect that, assuming that information about discourse levels is consistent, no changes are possible in formality level

[2]There appears to be some variance between native speakers in how these levels are perceived. I put this issue aside, and also do not discuss certain other means of indicating politeness such as other forms of address, as well as the pure honorific speech used in addressing royalty and monks of some ranks. These will be addressed within the current system in a later paper.

[3]For formal work on the topic of particles, see e.g. (McCready, 2008; Davis, 2009).

[4]While this does not mean that use of the other gender's pronouns is necessarily infelicitous, it is the case that special implicatures are produced when a form usually used by the other gender is selected.A useful question here is whether such restrictions correspond to presuppositions or e.g. conventional implicatures. In §5 I will treat them as conventionally implicated. Some useful discussion is in (Sudo, 2012) and (McCready, 2012a).

Low	*kuu* < *kháw*
Mid	*raw* < *chán*
High	*dichán* < *phǒm* < *kraphǒm*

Figure 2: Formality of Thai 1P pronouns.

Low	*mung*
Mid	*raw, tua, naaj, thEE*
High	*khun*

Figure 3: Formality of Thai 2P pronouns.

within a particular conversational exchange; but this is well-known to be false, not only for Thai but for many other languages that mark formality with lexical forms (Kikuchi, 1997; McCready et al., 2013; Asher and McCready, 2013). Something more complex is therefore required.

The facts about pronominals also make it clear that a simple separation into three levels will not be sufficient. Within each level of formality, various gradations can be found, which should carry over to the general politeness of a given discourse move; for instance, the combination *kraphǒm–khun–khráp* should be judged more formal than *phǒm–khun–khráp* even though both of the first person pronouns used are relatively formal. This observation suggests that the range of politeness must be continuous, rather than discrete, something that should be reflected in the honorific content.

2.3 Summary

Thai has several means of indicating formality and deference via the conventional meaning of lexical items. Here, I have focused on particles and pronominal forms.We have seen that combining such forms can lead to different levels of formality, and that not all elements selected must be drawn from the same level. From a formal perspective, then, the question is how to determine the general formality of an utterance from its component parts, and how to integrate the result with a general picture of how formality and honorification works in language and of how different levels of formality are judged appropriate in general. The rest of this paper is devoted to addressing these questions.

3 Earlier work

There has been significant work on honorification within semantics in the past few years. Most of this work has concentrated on composition: how honorific meaning enters into the compositional calculation of sentential meanings, and how it interacts with semantic operators.The main conclusion of this line of research is that honorific meanings are best construed as expressive (Potts and Kawahara, 2004; Sells and Kim, 2007; Horn, 2007; McCready, 2010). The main reasons for thinking so is that honorific meanings do not interact with operators like negation, and appear to resist non-expressive paraphrasing.[5] However, most of this work does not attempt to seriously propose denotations for honorific meanings, instead using dummy expressions like $\lambda x[honor(s,x)]$ to indicate honorification, and showing how these expressions play out in composition (where s denotes the agent of the utterance). The sole exception is Potts and Kawahara (2004), which will be the focus of this section. As we will see, this work gives an excellent starting point for a full semantics of honorifics.

The compositional semantics given by Potts and Kawahara is set within type theory. It begins with the proposal of a new expressive type ε, which denotes relations between individuals and attitudes. These attitudes are expressed by real-number intervals, $I \sqsubseteq [-1,1]$, which indicate positive (> 0) and negative (< 0) attitudes in the obvious way, which relate two individuals, and thus have the form aIb. These intervals are used to model the meanings of both honorifics and expressive adjectives like *damn*. The combinatorics of the ε-types follow the usual Pottsian rules for composition, which ensures that they are independent of operators.[6]

Potts and Kawahara provide the following sample denotation for a Japanese subject honorific. Subject honorifics are taken to denote functions from individuals to expressive types, and to state that the speaker s has a highly positive attitude toward x, as indicated by the closeness of the interval to 1, and by its specificity. This, of course, is not quite

[5]Detailed argumentation can be found in the works cited in the main text.

[6]For extensive discussion of these rules and their problems in this context, see (Potts, 2005; McCready, 2010; Watanabe et al., 2014).

right; on this semantics, emotive attitudes and honorification are conflated, so that the subject honorific has a meaning close to the positive interpretation of *damn* (or even the stronger *fucking*) (cf. (McCready, 2012b)). But it is clear that speakers can use politeness markers without having any kind of emotive attitude at all, or even when they have a negative one.

(1) $[\![SH]\!] = \lambda x.s[0.8, 1]x : \langle e, \varepsilon \rangle$

Definitions of this kind have the drawback of only indicating an attitude toward a specific individual. The facts about Thai honorifics are a bit more complex: they seem to jointly indicate the speaker's level with respect to a particular individual, and also indicate the speaker's assumptions about the formality of the context of speech. When honorifics are used, they change the context; the speaker indicates a particular level of formality (perhaps with respect to some individual, as in (1) above). This point is neglected by Potts and Kawahara (2004), but Potts (2007) models it by assuming that discourse contexts contain a set c_I of indices of the sort above. This set can be updated by a newly introduced index aIb in two ways: (i) if c_I does not contain any index of the form $aI'b$, then $c'_I = c_I \cup \{aIb\}$, and (ii) if it does contain such an index of the form $aI'b$, then aIb replaces $aI'b$, where it is also required that $I' \sqsubseteq I$. This last clause is problematic in that it certainly seems possible to indicate altered attitudes as opposed to simply further specifying existing ones.

A fully adequate semantics for honorifics and politeness markers must satisfy the following criteria. Given the force of the above arguments that honorific meaning is expressive, the proposed meanings must be expressive in nature, both in denotation and in terms of the means by which they compose with other content; they must, of course, also yield the intuitively correct meanings. Further, the result of semantic composition must be able to support analysis of the rational use of honorifics and politeness markers in communication. The proposals of Potts and Kawahara (2004) and their followers do not appear to fully satisfy these criteria, for they equate honorific content with emotive attitudes, which is intuitively odd, and further seems to give wrong results when input to game-theoretic analysis. Still, the notion of scales of politeness and the general notion of expressivity at play seem highly useful; I will take them as a starting point for my proposal, which is given in the next section.

4 Denotations and domains for honorifics

To give a semantics for honorifics it is first necessary to decide the domain of meanings over which they operate, and the kinds of effects which they have.

Iwasaki and Ingkaphirom Horie (1995) propose that politeness behavior in Thai operates along three dimensions: psychological distance, social distance, and formality. Psychological distance is the perceived interpersonal closeness of the discourse participants. Social distance is determined by the societal roles of the participants. Formality is determined by the situation of utterance together with the purposes and topic of the conversation. These three dimensions are obviously not completely independent, but for the purposes of the present paper I will treat them separately. The exact manner in which they interact is an empirical question too complex to address here.

These considerations prompt the use of denotations for honorific expressions which reference these three dimensions. I will thus take the domain associated with the semantics of honorifics to be a 3-tuple of intervals of the form [0,1].

(2) **Politeness domains.**
$\mathcal{D}_\varepsilon =_{df} \langle P, S, F \rangle, X \in [0, 1]$ for $X \in \{P, S, F\}$.

This essentially follows Potts (2007) but differs in two respects: (i) I assume a multidimensional domain for honorifics, and (ii) these dimensions, while real-numbered intervals as in Potts's work, inhabit the space between 0 and 1, as I take it that it does not make sense to have a negative degree of (e.g.) social distance. These two differences entail that honorific denotations are distinct from what is found in the emotive domain of e.g. expressive adjectives, which was shown to be desirable in the previous section.

How is one to determine which level of speech to use? Here, the three factors above come into play. Iwasaki and Ingkaphirom Horie (1995) indicate a number of different ways in which the appropriate speech register can be determined for a particular utterance. The simplest are what they call 'preset' registers, which are completely determined by a social situation. These can be separated into classes

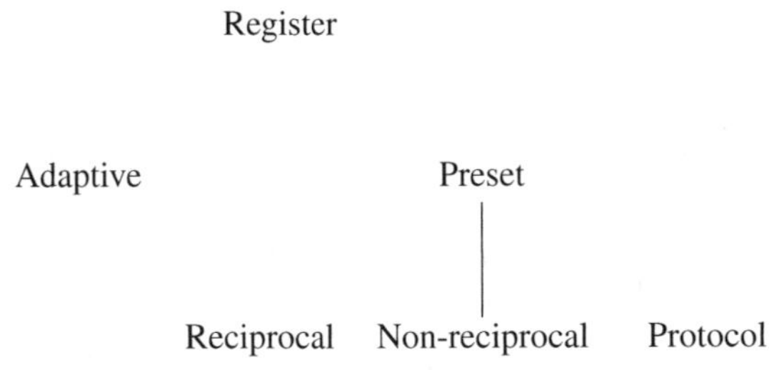

Figure 4: Types of register (I&IH 1995).

as in Figure 4. Here, reciprocal registers are those in which both participants have roughly the same status, so it is appropriate for them to use the same forms, as when close friends meet in an informal setting; non-reciprocal registers are those in which such is not the case, as the interaction of a boss and her employee. Protocol registers arise in formal situations in which a particular register – ordinarily a formal one – is required. Finally, adaptive registers are those in which the proper degree of politeness must be negotiated among the discourse participants.

To analyze register, I will make use of the notion of discourse context. In semantics and pragmatics, contexts are often taken to be sets of worlds or other elements, as with the sets of attitudes utilized by Potts (2007) and discussed above. For honorifics, I will take contexts to simply indicate the formality of the current discourse situation. Situations can be distinguished in terms of formality at an extremely fine-grained level, so they should be analyzed using continuous techniques; I take this to mean that they too should be viewed as subintervals of [0,1]. The exact range of a given context is determined by the three factors mentioned above. So contexts C have the form $\langle P, S, F\rangle$, where each of these elements is a subinterval of [0,1]; but it does not seem to be the case that honorifics directly reference these factors in general. My use of a formal first person pronoun may relate to psychological or social distance, or to the formality of the speech situation.[7] Given this observation, it seems that honorifics need to reference only a single range of values, so a single range must be derived from the context. This can be done as follows, yielding a notion of 'global register' $\mathcal{R}$. Here, $min(C) =_{df} min(\pi_1(C)) + min(\pi_2(C)) + min(\pi_3(C))$, and $max(C)$ is the corresponding function for the upper bounds of the intervals in C, where min and max are functions picking out the upper and lower bounds of intervals $[i, j]$, respectively.

(3) **Global register.**
$\mathcal{R} =_{df} \left[\frac{min(C)}{3}, \frac{max(C)}{3}\right]$, for $C = \langle P, S, F\rangle$.

Thus the appropriate level of formality for a discourse context is derived from the interpersonal and social distances of a context and its formality, and is itself a subinterval of [0,1]. Here I have given all the same weight; whether this formula needs to be made more complex is an empirical question, and likely differs from culture to culture. It is simple to adjust if such is required.

With the above, the discourse context specifies an interval corresponding to a formality level. But how should this tie to the use of the honorifics themselves? In §2, expressions with honorific content – particles and pronouns – were separated into three general levels of politeness: low, mid, and high. I will therefore define intervals corresponding to those, as follows.

(4) a. High $\sqsubseteq [.6, 1)$
b. Mid $\subseteq [.3, .7]$
c. Low $\sqsubseteq [0, .4]$

Note that the categories overlap: High and Mid share [.6,.7] and Mid and Low share [.3,.4]. The reason is that these forms are compatible: it is possible to use High and Mid forms together, and the same is true for Low and Mid forms. However, doing so indicates a relatively specific degree of formality. The use of Mid and High forms together means that, while the speaker does not take the context to be an extremely formal one, it is still relatively formal. This suggests that honorific use ought to be tied closely to speaker assumptions about the nature of the discourse context, which appears correct.

Now we are ready to consider the denotations and discourse effects of the honorifics themselves. I will take honorifics to denote subintervals of $\mathcal{R}$, higher

[7]This may not hold for all politeness expressions, but I will assume it in this paper for simplicity. If it is false, for instance for certain kinds of honorifics which may directly reference the formality of a context without regard for the other elements, we need only allow honorifics to reference one or the other element of a discourse context as defined here.

intervals for more formal expressions, and lower intervals for less formal ones. The context will determine whether a given expression is appropriate or not. Since these denotations are expressive, appropriateness cannot be stated in terms of truth, but rather must involve conditions of use. I follow Gutzmann (2012) in taking use-conditional judgements to involve two values, '$\surd$' and '$\times$', indicating appropriateness and inappropriateness respectively.

(5) **Appropriateness for honorifics.**

$$\text{Utter(S) in } C = \begin{cases} \surd \text{ if } Hon(S) \sqcap \mathcal{R} \neq \emptyset \\ \times \text{ else} \end{cases}$$

The above says that an utterance of a given sentence is honorific-appropriate if its honorific level is compatible with the global register. This seems right, but requires the derivation of a sentence's honorific level. Recall that the use of multiple honorific expressions in a sentence gives a different result from using a single one; this means that honorific levels must be fairly nuanced, but still derivable from the honorific levels of the expressions involved. However, since denotations are expressive, we need not worry about interactions with semantic operators (Potts, 2007). Thus it will be sufficient to take the average of all expressions used in the sentence, with the proviso that their denotations also be compatible (in order to rule out illicit combinations). This last condition serves to implement an observation made by (Iwasaki and Ingkaphirom Horie, 1995), according to whom high and low-level items cannot be used together, though combinations of high- and mid-level items are possible, as are combinations of and mid- and low-level items. This is predicted in the present theory, as only adjacent speech levels have non-empty intersections.[8] (6) defines the honorific level of a sentence with n honorifics.

(6) **Honorific level of a sentence.**

$$Hon(S) = \left[\frac{min(1)+\cdots+min(n)}{n}, \frac{max(1)+\cdots+max(n)}{n}\right]$$
if $Hon_1 \sqcap \cdots \sqcap Hon_n \neq \varnothing$, else 0.

[8]Interestingly, Thai behaves differently from Japanese in this respect; in Japanese, such things are common, though they have special discourse effects (Asher and McCready, 2013). I have to leave the reason for this difference for future work. I should also note that combining nonadjacent levels is possible for particles in at least the case of *wá* together with *khráp/khá*, which is interpreted as an attempt to curse or be aggressive toward someone while still being polite (U. Tawilapakul, p.c.).

The above seems a reasonable characterization of how the appropriateness of a given honorific will be determined. If the context is formal, use of an extremely informal pronoun will be inappropriate; in the context of casual speech among friends over drinks, extremely formal pronouns will sound very unnatural. I will give more detail in section 5 in conjunction with the semantics of particular honorific items in Thai.

This proposal also is able to account for changes in honorific use over the lifespan of a conversation or long-term social interaction. It is well known that, in many social situations, one tends to begin speaking formally and then move to informal speech. This is reflected in the use of honorifics: often, formal pronouns and other markers are initially used, and then at some point speakers jointly move to the use of informal markers.[9] In the present context, it corresponds quite simply to a change in the parameters comprising C: as the measure P of interpersonal distance becomes smaller, a corresponding diminishment of the value of $\mathcal{R}$ occurs, given sufficiently low values for F and S (i.e. a context which does not automatically specify formal speech). Honorific use thus depends on external, social, parameters in the expected manner.

One issue has been left unaddressed. While ordinarily changes in speech level are determined by the external context (or so the model above has it), it is also the case that the use of honorifics can impact the formality level of the discourse continuation. Specifically, there are points at which it is obvious that the speech level should be changed; but sometimes the use of an informal form causes a switch to an informal level, although if the informal form had not been used, the level would not have changed. This is a kind of performative effect and should be captured by the semantics. However, at present the semantics simply assumes that the level of the honorifics is checked against the context, and makes no provision for honorific-induced context change.

In the present theory, this observation can be

[9]This situation has been analyzed by (McCready et al., 2013) for the binary *tu-vous* distinction on second person pronouns common in European languages, and for a Japanese honorific pronouns by (Asher and McCready, 2013), using the tools of infinitely repeated games and topological analysis of strategy complexity.

made more concrete. Suppose that a sentence S with politeness level $Hon(S)$ is used in context C with register $\mathcal{R}$. Then two cases arise. In the first, $Hon(S) \sqcap \mathcal{R} \neq \emptyset$. In such a situation, S is deemed appropriate. The discussion so far has focused on case 1. In case 2, $Hon(S) \sqcap \mathcal{R} = \emptyset$. Here, use of S is inappropriate. But the use of S can also serve as a proposal to modify the context to one in which S would be appropriate after all. In essence, the use of S aims to move $\mathcal{R}$ upward or downward in a way that makes $Hon(S)$ an appropriate honorific level.

How should this process be modeled in the formal theory? One option is to allow honorifics to modify the context directly and dynamically via their use. For instance, a use of *khráp* could be taken to preemptively change the context to a formal one, irrespective of what it was formerly. However, this view would seem to obviate the analysis so far, in that the definition in (5) would become obsolete; since the use of *khráp* would change the context to one in which *khráp* was appropriate, we no longer have any means to model inappropriate use of honorific elements.[10] Instead of allowing such extreme changes, I will model honorifics as proposals to change the context in an incremental manner, if they were originally inappropriate.

The basic idea is to take honorifics to, as before, denote subintervals of [0,1], which are checked for compatibility with the register currently specified by the context. However, the performative character of honorifics functions as a proposal to change the register to one compatible with the honorific level. Thus, use of a formal particle like *khráp* proposes raising the level of formality, and a particle indexing casual speech like *wóoy* proposes lowering the register. But this register shift cannot be completely unrestricted, as discussed in the previous paragraph. It should be tied to the current formality of the context. I propose the following shift, where $C[(S)]_H$ signifies 'honorific update' of the current register with the honorific content of a sentence, C' is the register arrived at after such update.

(7) **Dynamic registers.** $C[(S)]_H = C'$, where

$$C' = \begin{cases} C \text{ if } C \sqsubseteq Hon(S) \\ \left[\frac{min(C)+Hon(S)}{4}, \frac{max(C)+Hon(S)}{4}\right] \text{ else} \end{cases}.$$

[10]Of course, external constraints could be placed on the update mechanism, but this seems inelegant.

This formula simply averages the honorific content of the current with the elements of the current context unless the honorific content is less specific than the current context. Note that this generalizes the proposal of (Potts, 2007), who allows only restriction to subintervals in the emotive case. In case of change, each of the four elements are given equal say in the ultimate register. This is the simplest option, which can of course be weighted as required by empirical observation, as with (3). Note that this is a proposal, which can be rejected by the hearer, just as with other update operations (Stalnaker, 1978; McCready, 2014). The result of this operation is used to check the appropriateness of an utterance via (5). Some detailed derivations will be provided in §5.

With all this in place, we can provide a semantics for the Thai honorifics discussed in section 2.

5 Semantics for Thai honorifics

The aim of this section is to provide a semantics for the Thai politeness particles, first person pronouns, and second person pronouns. In this paper, I will not examine the details of semantic composition with these terms, or provide detailed sentential derivations. However, I will outline lexical entries for them which can be used in semantic derivations.

From the perspective of composition, the particles are the simplest case. They can be subdivided into categories along two dimensions: the degree of formality they introduce (cf. Figure 1), and whether their use indicates the gender of the speaker. As for the second dimension, *khráp* and *khá* are interchangeable in terms of formality but indicate masculinity and femininity respectively, while the informal particles are generally taken to be masculine in quality. This last, however, appears to be defeasible: like the Japanese *zo* and *ze*, these particles indicate aggression or forcefulness, qualities generally taken in Japanese and Thai society to be masculine; these particles are indeed sometimes used by women, which is not the case for e.g. *khráp*. I thus take the gender implications of *wá* and *wóoy* to be conversational implicatures (Grice, 1975). With these assumptions, we arrive at the following lexical entries. Here t^s is an expressive type somewhat more general than Potts's (2007) ε, and s_c denotes the speaker of the current context (Kaplan, 1989).[11] I have capped the register associated with $[\![khráp]\!]$ at 0.9 due to the existence of the even more formal masculine particle *khrápphǒm*.

(8) **Semantics of Thai politeness particles:**

a. $[\![khráp]\!] = (Hon = [.6,.9] \wedge masc(s_c)) : t^s$
b. $[\![khá]\!] = (Hon = [.6,1) \wedge fem(s_c)) : t^s$
c. $[\![há]\!] = (Hon = [.3,.7]) : t^s$
d. $[\![wá]\!] = (Hon = [0,.4]) : t^s$

The pronominals are more complex, as they are instances of what McCready (2010) calls *mixed content*. Mixed content bearers are expressions which introduce both expressive and ordinary truth-conditional content. Clearly, the pronouns are expressive, as they encode politeness (and also gender); equally clearly, they have at-issue content, for they participate in composition by providing discourse referents and arguments for verbs. We thus must use mixed types to give their denotations; mixed types are formed by forming ordered pairs of standard at-issue types σ^a and types for expressive content σ^s, which correspond to mixed terms in the meaning language formed with the operator '♦'.

In this setting, first person and second person pronouns have denotations of the following kind. Here a_c denotes the addressee of the current context.

(9) **Semantics of Thai first person pronouns:**

a. $[\![kraphǒm]\!] = s_c \blacklozenge (Hon = [.8,1) \wedge masc(s_c)) : e^a \times t^s$
b. $[\![phǒm]\!] = s_c \blacklozenge (Hon = [.6,.9] \wedge masc(s_c)) : e^a \times t^s$
c. $[\![chán]\!] = s_c \blacklozenge (Hon = [.3,.7]) : e^a \times t^s$
d. $[\![kháw]\!] = s_c \blacklozenge (Hon = [0,.3] \wedge fem(s_c)) : e^a \times t^s$

(10) **Semantics of Thai second person pronouns:**

a. $[\![khun]\!] = a_c \blacklozenge (Hon = [.6,1)) : e^a \times t^s$
b. $[\![tua]\!] = a_c \blacklozenge (Hon = [.3,.7] \wedge fem(s_c)) : e^a \times t^s$
c. $[[mɯŋ]] = a_c \blacklozenge (Hon = [0,.4]) : e^a \times t^s$

Let us work through several examples. The first, a naturally occurring example, is taken from (Iwasaki and Ingkaphirom Horie, 1995) and is made by a male speaker in a formal context.[12] The expressions with honorific content are in boldface.

(11) **phǒm** kˆɔ mây sâap ná **kháp**
1P.M.Hon FP Neg know PP PolP.M

'I don't know either.'

In this example, the politeness markers used are *phǒm* and *kháp*, which both mark formal speech. I have taken the former to indicate $Hon = [.6,.9]$ and the latter to also indicate $Hon = [.6,.9]$. Thus, the two together yield $Hon(S) = [.6,.9]$ given the formula for calculating the politeness of a sentence in (6). As indicated above, the context in which this sentence was used was a formal one (a communication between parent and teacher), which can be somewhat arbitrarily assigned the register value [.6,.8]. Since the intervals [.6,.9] and [.6,.8] overlap, the sentence is predicted to be appropriate, which is correct. Further, use of this sentence will have an effect on the register value via the formula in (7); in the absence of detailed information about C, we can duplicate the $\mathcal{R}$ value three times for the input to (7), giving the result in (12). Thus, the use of the rather polite forms in (11) brings up the contextual level slightly, as expected given that the speaker in this exchange indicates a willingness or even desire to be highly polite.

(12) $\mathcal{R}' = \left[\frac{.6+.6+.6+.6}{4}, \frac{.8+.8+.8+.9}{4}\right] = [.6,.825]$

The second example, taken from (Iwasaki and Ingkaphirom, 2005), mixes distinct speech levels. The first person pronoun *chán* is a mid-level marker, but the particle used, *wá*, marks casual speech. Note that this example is produced by a female speaker, showing that *wá* is not directly tied to masculinity.

[11]It is open to question whether one ought to use ε-types or simple conventionally implicated truth values; Geurts (2007) brings the distinction into question. One could also ask whether the correct type is t^s or the shunting-type version t^s is to be preferred given that the former option is chosen; here, I have chosen the latter option for consistency with the system needed for the mixed types used for the pronominals. I do not think the difference matters much otherwise for the purposes of this paper.

[12]Here *ná* is a pragmatic particle of the kind studied by (McCready, 2008; Davis, 2009) and *kɔ̂* is a focus particle.

(13) **chán** kɔ̂ é, lɯ̌ man pen lekhǎa dûay **wá**
I LP Exc or 3P Cop secretary also PolP

'I was wondering 'Huh? Is she also his secretary?'

The first person pronoun has content *Hon* = [.3, .7]; the particle indicates that *Hon* = [0, .4]. (6) requires the two to be averaged together, yielding [.15,.55]. This sentence is therefore compatible with both casual and mid-level situations given the setting of speech levels in (4). When used in an informal setting, it will raise the contextual level slightly, but when used in a mid-level setting, it will lower it, given the dynamic operation in (7).

The final example involves multiple sentences. Consider the following short discourse, also from (Iwasaki and Ingkaphirom, 2005). The setting is a casual exchange between male friends.

(14) a. A: pen ŋay **mɯŋ**
Cop how 2P.Inf
'What's up?'

b. B: yɛ̂ɛ **wà**
terrible PolP
'It's terrible!'

A and B both use items appropriate only in contexts with low formality. Both *mɯŋ* and *wá* indicate that *Hon* = [0, .4]; but, given that the speakers are already good friends, it is highly likely that the level of formality of the discourse context already does not contain anything as high as 0.4 anyway. Given that, (7) requies the contextual level of politeness to be kept at its more specific current level.

6 Conclusion and extensions

The denotations of honorific expressions are a long-standing yet mostly unaddressed problem in linguistic theory. This paper has proposed a solution using tools from formal semantics and pragmatics. According to it, honorifics have a dual function. They indicate a degree of politeness, which is checked against the external context for appropriateness. Simultaneously, if the level of formality in the external context is distinct from the degree the honorific indicates, the honorific works as a proposal to shift the context to a new degree consistent with the linguistic expression. This theory builds closely on the work of Potts and Kawahara (2004), but improves on it in both theoretical and empirical respects.

There are many avenues for future work. The most obvious is empirical. The range of expressions treated can be extended even within Thai; I have not considered other sorts of terms which can be used to mark levels of formality, such as language used specifically for the royal family, or the various non-pronominal ways in which people can be addressed (nicknames, kinship terms, etc.). It will also be useful to consider other languages. Japanese has a highly articulated system of honorification which shares some characteristics with the Thai system, but also has extensive honorific verbal morphology which Thai lacks (Kikuchi, 1997). Another obvious language to consider is Javanese, which is well-known for having an extensive system of expression which carry honorific information.

Many other formal extensions are likely to be necessary. One is already brought out by example (14): different agents must be associated with different levels of formality. As things stand, the context is taken to indicate a single range of possible values for politeness expressions, but I have already mentioned that every agent need not speak at the same level of formality; in fact, one of the most common situations in honorific use involves non-reciprocal uses where the social roles of the agents are asymmetric, as with teacher and student, or boss and employee (cf. Figure 1). Every conversation should therefore make use of at least two distinct contextual representations, something already expected from formal pragmatic work on context (Gunlogson, 2003). Still more will be required when conversations involve more agents; ultimately, it is likely that contexts as described here must be lifted to context sets, where each agent is associated with a distinct context, and such contexts represent each agent separately.

At the beginning of the paper, I indicated that one motivation for this project is to bring game-theoretic tools to bear on the analysis of honorification; this is another issue for future work. An interesting question here is the way in which manipulation of honorific parameters helps agents to achieve their goals, especially in terms of the analysis of face threats (Brown and Levinson, 1987). For the present analysis to help here, it must be clarified how the parameters referenced by honorifics contribute to decision-making and the satisfaction of requests through the expression of factors like closeness and deference. There is a great deal of work to be done here, but it is likely that existing sociolinguistic analysis can be of significant help in this area.

A final area of extension is the analysis of discourse-level politeness strategies as studied by (McCready et al., 2013; Asher and McCready, 2013). This line of work uses the topological analysis of infinite games to help understand the complexity of available politeness strategies. This work is useful but up to now has lacked formal underpinnings for the (intuitively correct) strategies it considers, a gap which the present work can rectify. However, it remains to be seen how compatible the continuous operations used by the present approach will be with the analysis of infinite games, where the move from a finite (even countable) alphabet to an uncountable one substantially increases the complexity of the resulting topology.

References

Nicholas Asher and Eric McCready. 2013. Discourse-level politeness and implicature. In *Proceedings of LENLS10*. JSAI.

Penelope Brown and Stephen Levinson. 1987. *Politeness: Some Universals in Language Usage*. Cambridge University Press.

Christopher Davis. 2009. Decisions, dynamics and the Japanese particle *yo*. *Journal of Semantics*, 26:329–366.

Bart Geurts. 2007. Really fucking brilliant. *Theoretical Linguistics*, 33:209–214.

H. Paul Grice. 1975. Logic and conversation. In Peter Cole and Jerry Morgan, editors, *Syntax and Semantics III: Speech Acts*, pages 41–58. Academic Press, New York.

Christine Gunlogson. 2003. *True to Form: Rising and Falling Declaratives as Questions in English*. Outstanding Dissertations in Linguistics. Routledge, New York.

Daniel Gutzmann. 2012. *Use-Conditional Meaning: Studies in Multidimensional Semantics*. Ph.D. thesis, Universität Frankfurt.

Laurence Horn. 2007. Toward a Fregean pragmatics: Voraussetzung, Nebengedanke, Andeutung. In Istvan Kecskes and Laurence Horn, editors, *Explorations in Pragmatics*, pages 39–69. Mouton de Gruyter, Berlin.

Shoichi Iwasaki and Preeya Ingkaphirom Horie. 1995. Creating speech register in Thai conversation. *Language in Society*, 29:519–554.

Shoichi Iwasaki and Preeya Ingkaphirom. 2005. *A Reference Grammar of Thai*. Cambridge University Press.

David Kaplan. 1989. Demonstratives. In Joseph Almog, John Perry, and Howard Wettstein, editors, *Themes from Kaplan*, pages 481–566. Oxford University Press. Manuscript version from 1977.

Yasuto Kikuchi. 1997. *Keigo [Honorifics]*. Kodansha.

Eric McCready, Nicholas Asher, and Soumya Paul. 2013. Winning strategies in politeness. In Yoichi Motomura, Alastair Butler, and Daisuke Bekki, editors, *New Frontiers in Artificial Intelligence*, volume 7856 of *Lecture Notes in Computer Science*, pages 87–95. Springer Berlin Heidelberg.

Eric McCready. 2008. What man does. *Linguistics and Philosophy*, 31:671–724.

Eric McCready. 2010. Varieties of conventional implicature. *Semantics and Pragmatics*, 3:1–57.

Eric McCready. 2012a. Classification without assertion. In Matthew Tucker, Anie Thompson, Oliver Northup, and Ryan Bennett, editors, *Proceedings of FAJL 5*, MITWPL, pages 141–154. MIT.

Eric McCready. 2012b. Emotive equilibria. *Linguistics and Philosophy*, 35:243–283.

Eric McCready. 2014. Reliability in pragmatics. To appear Oxford University Press.

Fumikazu Niinuma. 2003. *The Syntax of Honorification*. Ph.D. thesis, University of Connecticut.

Christopher Potts and Shigeto Kawahara. 2004. Japanese honorifics as emotive definite descriptions. In *Proceedings of SALT XIV*.

Christopher Potts. 2005. *The Logic of Conventional Implicatures*. Oxford University Press. Revised version of 2003 UCSC dissertation.

Christopher Potts. 2007. The expressive dimension. *Theoretical Linguistics*, 33:165–198.

Peter Sells and Jong-Bok Kim. 2007. Korean honorification: A kind of expressive meaning. *Journal of East Asian Linguistics*, 16:303–336.

R.C. Stalnaker. 1978. Assertion. In P. Cole, editor, *Syntax and Semantics*, pages 315–322. Academic Press.

Yasutada Sudo. 2012. *On the Semantics of Phi Features on Pronouns*. Ph.D. thesis, MIT.

Robert van Rooy. 2003. Being polite is a handicap: towards a game theoretical analysis of polite linguistic behavior. In *TARK*, pages 45–58.

Narumi Watanabe, Eric McCready, and Daisuke Bekki. 2014. Japanese honorification: Compositionality and expressivity. Paper presented at FAJL 7.

Richard Watts. 2003. *Politeness*. Cambridge University Press.

Disunity in Cohesion: How Purpose Affects Methods and Results When Analyzing Lexical Cohesion

Stuart G. Towns **Richard Watson Todd**
Department of Applied Linguistics
King Mongkut's University of Technology Thonburi
Bangkok, Thailand
sgtowns@gmail.com iricttodd@kmutt.ac.th

Abstract

Lexical Cohesion is a commonly studied linguistic feature as it is easily identified from the surface of a text. However, the purposes for studying lexical cohesion are varied, and each purpose requires different methods. This study analyzes two short movie review texts for four different research purposes using lexical cohesion: text evaluation, text segmentation, text summarization, and text criticism. The analysis shows that these four different purposes produce very different results concerning the lexical cohesion of the two texts, suggesting that the apparently straightforward construct of lexical cohesion is actually complex.

1 Introduction

The purposes of text analysis research can be divided into two main categories: applications and descriptions. The difference between these two areas is that applications produce results that are useful to end users who are outside of the field of linguistics, while descriptions of language are used internally by the linguistic community (Sinclair, 2004a). Many text analysis applications created for those outside of linguistics use automated tools, and therefore they focus on features that can be identified and analyzed with computers. One linguistic feature that can be analyzed to varying degrees of success using computers is lexical cohesion, since lexical cohesion can be found in the surface features of text. The analysis of lexical cohesion has been used in many text analysis applications, such as discourse analysis (Morris & Hirst, 1991), automatic text summarization (Barzilay & Elhadad, 1999), text segmentation (Stokes, Carthy, & Smeaton, 2004), word sense disambiguation (Okumura & Honda, 1994), and evaluation of machine translations (Wong & Kit, 2012).

Lexical cohesion was defined by Halliday and Hasan (1976, p. 274) as "the cohesive effect achieved by the selection of vocabulary" and is one of five types of cohesion (the other four being reference, substitution, ellipsis, and conjunction). A cohesive text is held together by explicit relationships found in the lexis and grammar of the text. These lexico-grammatical relationships are called cohesive ties as they connect one sentence to another. Multiple ties can, in turn, be combined into longer lexical chains which can span large portions of the text.

Current technology can identify lexical cohesion ties and lexical chains of ties with varying degrees of accuracy. Some cohesive ties are very easy to identify, such as the exact repetition of a lexical unit in an adjacent sentence, while others can be more difficult to correctly identify, such as the relationship of a pronoun to a noun in a previous sentence. Hoey (1991) outlined six types of lexical cohesion which are ordered by ease of identification from easiest to most difficult, along with some examples in Table 1.

As stated earlier, lexical cohesion has been used in text analysis research for many different

Copyright 2014 by Stuart G. Towns and Richard Watson Todd
28th Pacific Asia Conference on Language, Information and Computation pages 513–521

Lexical Cohesion Type	Definition	Examples (Hoey, 1991)
Simple repetition	Repetition of a word (singular or plural)	bear/bear, bear/bears
Complex Repetition	Repetition of two lexical items with a common stem, but different parts of speech	historical/history, quoted/quotation
Simple Paraphrase	Where a lexical item can replace another lexical item without a change in meaning	volume/book, writings/works
Complex Paraphrase	Antonymy, or the presence (or absence) of two links creating a third link	hot/cold, writer/writings/author, teacher/(teaching)/instruction
Semantic Association	Superordinate, Hyponymic, Co-reference	bears/animals, scientists/biologists
Non-lexical repetition	Personal and demonstrative pronouns	he, she, it, they, this, that, these, those

Table 1: Hoey's (1991) six types of lexical cohesion

purposes. This paper will look at four main purposes: text evaluation, text segmentation, text summarization, and text criticism. The first three of these can be analyzed using automated computerized tools, while the fourth is a qualitative analysis that is beyond the capabilities of today's computers.

These four purposes can be described as follows. The first purpose, text evaluation, especially of student writing, has often focused on the lexical cohesion of the text as a marker of the quality of the text, with the assumption being that features such as referential cohesion correlate with human evaluations of high quality text (Weston, Crossley, & McNamara, 2010). The second purpose, text segmentation, finds breaks in the text where there are no lexical chains. The lack of lexical chains in a span of text shows that the topic might have changed (Şimon, Gravier, & Sébillot, 2013). The third purpose, text summarization, tries to identify the important topics in the text in order to create a summary of the text. Lexical cohesion aids this task by showing which topics are repeated throughout the text (Barzilay & Elhadad, 1999). The fourth purpose, text criticism, looks at the lexical cohesion in a text and attempts to understand the meaning behind the lexical choices, for example to find metaphors in political speeches that support the speaker's public image (Klebanov, Diermeier, & Beigman, 2008).

A key issue for lexical cohesion analysis is that the unit on which the analysis is conducted differs depending on the purpose of the research. Each of the four purposes discussed in this paper investigate a different unit. For the first purpose, a text evaluation is an evaluation of the cohesiveness of the text as a whole, and therefore should be based on the entire text. This can be done, for example, by computing the average cohesion between all of the sentences in the text. Text segmentation is an attempt to segment the whole text into smaller units and therefore the analysis must be based on units that are smaller than the whole text, such as measuring the lexical cohesion between individual adjacent pairs of sentences. Text summarization is focused on the lexical items of the text in order to find the important concepts, so the cohesive lexical items take priority over the whole text itself. Text criticism is not only looking at the lexical choices made by the writer or speaker but also at the potential meaning behind these choices. Therefore, the unit of investigation can vary in length as needed.

Even though all of these purposes are using lexical cohesion as the subject of research, the results of the research may be very different. The purpose of this paper, then, is to illustrate how different purposes require different methods, and how these methods can lead to very different results depending on the operationalization of lexical cohesion, whether it is lexical cohesion of a text as a whole, lexical cohesion between adjacent sentences, lexical cohesion chains, or lexical cohesion created through nearby items in the same semantic sets.

2 Methodology

The texts to be used for the lexical cohesion analyses in this study will be movie reviews. Eight movie reviews of Wes Anderson's *Moonrise Kingdom* were downloaded from the Internet. Four of the reviews were written by Pulitzer Prize movie reviewers while four were written by amateur movie review bloggers. These eight movie reviews were analyzed using Coh-Metrix, an automated web-based tool which was originally created to automatically analyze text for cohesion and readability (Graesser, McNamara, Louwerse, & Cai, 2004). It was found that two of the reviews, one written by a Pulitzer Prize winner and one written by a blogger, showed very similar high scores relative to the other six reviews on the Coh-Metrix indices for lexical cohesion, or what Coh-Metrix calls referential cohesion.

This study will analyze these two texts for the four research purposes mentioned above: text evaluation, text segmentation, text summarization, and text criticism. The text written by the blogger will be labeled Text 1 and the text written by the Pulitzer Prize winner will be labeled Text 2. Text 1 has 324 words and 14 sentences while Text 2 has 758 words and 19 sentences (for the full texts, see Luke, 2012 for Text 1 and Hornaday, 2012 for Text 2.)

Since each of the four research purposes focuses on a different aspect of the text, each one has its own methodology. For text evaluation, which looks at the cohesion of the text as a whole as a measure of the quality of the text, the first analysis tool that will be used is Coh-Metrix. The eight lexical cohesion indices in Coh-Metrix represent averages across the text of the scores of the lexical cohesion between pairs of sentences. A binary score of either 1 for cohesion or 0 for no cohesion is found for every pair of adjacent sentences as well as for every sentence compared to every other sentence in the text, and is then averaged to give one number for each index.

Another way to analyze the cohesion of the text as a whole is to consider the lexical cohesion chains. Averages can be computed for the whole text for metrics such as the number of lexical chains, chain length, and chain density (defined here as the number of lexical items in the chain divided by the number of sentences in the chain).

For text segmentation, it is desirable for the results to show where the text has topic breaks. Therefore, a unit smaller than the entire text should be analyzed. As in the first analysis, lexical cohesion will be identified in pairs of adjacent sentences, but it will be done using a moving window approach (Stokes, Carthy, & Smeaton, 2004) where the individual scores for sentence-pair lexical cohesion are computed. A topic break occurs when a sentence pair does not have any shared lexical cohesive items. The text will then be divided into segments at these topic breaks. The length of the segments and the number of segments will be compared between the two texts to find out if there are any differences between the lexical cohesion in each.

For text summarization, the analysis is attempting to find the important topics in the text. These important topics will occur frequently in lexical cohesion chains running through the text. Therefore, the analysis will focus on the lexical items that can combine to form topics by looking at the number of lexical items inside each chain and the length of the chain. The chains will be mapped to show how much of the text they cover, as well as the location of the lexical items inside the chains. The patterns created by the lexical cohesion chains can then be compared between the two texts.

Coh-Metrix Lexical Cohesion (Referential Cohesion) Indices	Text 1	Text 2	Avg of 6
Noun Overlap, Adjacent Sentences, Binary, Mean	.385	.500	.215
Noun Overlap, All Sentences, Binary, Mean	.294	.370	.194
Stem Overlap, Adjacent Sentences, Binary, Mean	.615	.611	.275
Stem Overlap, All Sentences, Binary, Mean	.435	.437	.241
Argument Overlap, Adjacent Sentences, Binary, Mean	.846	.667	.452
Argument Overlap, All Sentences, Binary, Mean	.529	.548	.383
Content Word Overlap, Adjacent Sentences, Proportional, Mean	.067	.047	.066
Content Word Overlap, All Sentences, Proportional, Mean	.046	.039	.048

Table 2: Referential cohesion results from Coh-Metrix for Text 1 and Text 2

For text criticism, the purpose is to understand the meaning behind the important words in the text. This requires a qualitative analysis of the lexical cohesion chains as well as the words that are collocated with these chains.

Throughout this paper so far, and in many other studies, there has been no distinction made between the terms “text” and “corpus”. However, mentioning this potential distinction might be helpful to describe the difference between the first three methods (text evaluation, text segmentation, and text summarization), and the fourth (text criticism). Viewing data as a corpus (as was done for the first three methods) implies that automated tools will be used to observe the data. The researcher must choose the appropriate tool or must create their own tool depending on the type of information that is desired. Viewing the data as a text, on the other hand, means that the analysis will be done in a similar fashion to a human reading the text (Sinclair, 2004b). The first three analyses view the movie review data as a corpus, and have used automated tools to analyze the data. The fourth analysis will take a more human approach, viewing the data as a text to be read and understood. In this fourth analysis, the words themselves are not as important as the implied meaning behind the words in the mind of the reader.

3 Results

The first research purpose that will be considered is text evaluation. For this purpose, texts in their entirety are analyzed to find an overall lexical cohesion score. This analysis was done using Coh-Metrix on all eight original movie review texts. It was found that two of the texts, which are labeled in this study as Text 1 and Text 2, had similar, high cohesion scores for many of the Coh-Metrix indices compared to the other six texts. For example, for the Coh-Metrix index “Stem Overlap, all sentences, binary, mean”, Text 1 scored .435 and Text 2 scored a very similar .437. The average of the other six texts was much lower at .241. The results from the Coh-Metrix analysis for Text 1, Text 2, and the average of the other six texts are found in Table 2.

Another way to measure the cohesion of the text as a whole is to investigate the lexical cohesion chains that are in the text. There are several metrics related to lexical chains that can be found, as seen in Table 3. These numbers, in contrast to the ones in Table 2, show some major differences between the two texts. Text 2 has 36% more sentences than Text 1, but three times more lexical chains. This means that, on average, there are more cohesive lexical items in each sentence in Text 2.

In addition, the lexical chains in Text 2 are on average longer and less dense than the ones in Text 1. This means that the cohesive ties are more likely to span longer distances in Text 2 than in Text 1.

The lexical chain patterns also show a lot of difference between the two texts. Half of the lexical chains in Text 1 are two-sentence chains with just one cohesive tie. Text 2 on the other hand, has several chains with one tie that span four sentences.

	Text 1	**Text 2**
Text length	14 sentences	19 sentences
# of Lexical Chains	7	22
Avg. Chain Length	4.0 sentences	6.0 sentences
Longest Chain	13 sentences	18 sentences
Avg. Chain Density	81%	44%
Most common pattern	2-sentence chains with 1 tie (100% density)	4-sentence chains with 1 tie (25% density)

Table 3: Whole-text cohesion chain metrics

The second research purpose considered was text segmentation. To segment the text, lexical cohesion can be used to find topic breaks. Wherever there is no cohesion between adjacent sentences, it may be a signal that the topic of the text has changed. By analyzing the two texts using a two-sentence moving window, it can be seen that the two texts would be segmented very differently.

The segmentation of Text 1 is straightforward. It can be divided into three segments, as seen in Table 4. Segment 1 covers sentences 1-5, Segment 2 covers sentences 6-10, and Segment 3 covers the remaining sentences 11-14. The segmentation of Text 2 is more complicated. It can be divided into five segments. The first segment covers

Sentence			
1	film	words	Anderson
2	medium	words	he
3	film		he
4	M.K.		
5	it		
6	start	story	
7	start	story	Anderson
8	M.K.		Anderson
9	M.K.	summer	Anderson
10		summer	
11	film		
12	it		
13	film		
14	film		

Sentence			
1	house		
2	house	created	Anderson
3	artisanal	create	Anderson
4	damp canvas		
5			
6		house	
7	Hayward	house	
8	Hayward		
9	Sam,Suzy	M.K.	
10	Sam,Suzy	M.K.	adults
11	Suzy		grown-ups
12	players		
13	plays		
14	play	film	
15	solemnity	films	Anderson
16	solemnity		Anderson
17			Anderson
18			Anderson
19			

Table 4: Two-sentence moving window cohesion showing text segmentation

sentences 1-4. Then, sentence pairs 4-5, and 5-6 do not have any lexical cohesion, which means that there is a sentence-long break between the first two segments. The next three segments of sentences 6-11 and 12-18 are straightforward. The last sentence does not have any lexical cohesion with the sentence before it, so it is counted as the fifth segment.

The third research purpose was text summarization. To accomplish this, lexical cohesion chains can be analyzed to find the important topics in the text. The methodology here is different than what was done for text segmentation above in that the focus is on words rather than sentences. These lexical cohesion chains can span multiple sentences, and the lexical items do not necessarily have to be in adjacent sentences. Looking at the lexical cohesion chains that were analyzed for the first research purpose of text evaluation, the frequency of the lexical cohesive units within the chains can be seen in Tables 5 and 6. Text 1 has 7 lexical cohesion chains and Text 2 has 22 lexical cohesion chains.

The lexical chains that appear in a text can point to the important topics of the text. There are two ways that a summarization might be done. If the desired result is simply a noun phrase (i.e., a single short topic for the whole text), then the most frequent lexical items in the longest chains might form this phrase. Both Text 1 and Text 2 have similar items at the top of the most frequent lists, so the noun phrase summary might be something like *Anderson's film Moonrise Kingdom*.

Lexical Items in Text 1	**# of lexical items**	**Chain Length (# of ties)**
film/MK/it/medium	11	13
Anderson/he	6	8
words	2	2
start	2	2
story	2	2
summer	2	2
world	2	4

Table 5: Chain frequency and length for Text 1

Lexical Items in Text 2	**# of lexical items**	**Chain Length (# of ties)**
film/MK	11	18
Anderson/his	6	16
Suzy/Hayward	6	11
house	4	6
play/played/plays	4	4
audience/viewers	3	15
scout	3	10
Sam	3	8
opens/opening	3	5
young love	2	10
camera	2	7
story	2	5
Fantastic Mr Fox	2	4
friend	2	4
Khaki	2	4
kid	2	4
rain/rainy	2	4
Rushmore	2	3
scene/sequence	2	2
solemn/solemnity	2	1
artisan/canvas	2	1
create	2	1

Table 6: Chain frequency and length for Text 2

If, however, the desired summary is longer than one phrase, then additional, less frequent cohesive items can be used. In Text 1, lexical chains at the end of the text refer to the movie as a *world* that has a *summer* motif. A summary of Text 2, on the other hand, might cover many more topics, such as focusing on the two main characters, *Suzy* and *Sam* as well as characters who the various actors *play*. The *house* in the *rain* in the *opening sequence* of the film is also important in this text. Longer summaries would then be very different for the two texts.

Another type of analysis with these lexical chains can be done by mapping them to see what kinds of patterns are created. Figures 1 and 2 show a lexical chain mapping, with the location of the lexical units shown with an "X". This analysis is a graphical representation of the chains, and it can be seen that the long, dense chains in both Text 1 and Text 2 such as *film/Moonrise Kingdom and Anderson/he* play an important role in the cohesion of both of the entire texts. However, differences are also apparent in these two texts. In Text 1, the minor lexical chains for *words*, *start* and *story*, and *summer* and *world* do not connect to each other. In Text 2, on the other hand, chains such as *Suzy*, *Sam*, *play*, and *story* act as connections between different sets of cohesive items. Even the short, dense lexical chains in Text 2 connect to each other, such as *house*, *create*, *artisanal* in sentences 1-4.

In addition, in Text 2, half of the lexical chains (11 out of 22) are represented in the final four sentences of the text, regardless of when they were first introduced. These chains include *Moonrise Kingdom*, *audience*, *Anderson*, *young love*, *Suzy*,

	Text 1: Sentences 1-14													
film/MK/it/medium	X	X	X	X	X			X	X		X	X	X	X
Anderson/he	X	X	X		X			X	X					
words	X	X												
start						X	X							
story						X	X							
summer									X	X				
world									X			X		

Figure 1: Lexical chain map of Text 1

	Text 2: Sentences 1-19																		
film/MK	X	X	X					X	X		X			X	X	X		X	X
audience/viewers	X		X													X			
camera	X							X											
house	X	X				X	X												
rain/rainy	X				X														
opens/opening	X			X		X													
Anderson/his		X	X		X										X	X	X	X	
create		X	X																
Artisanal/canvas			X	X															
scene/sequence				X		X													
young love						X										X			
Suzy/Hayward						X	X	X	X	X							X		
Sam									X	X							X		
friend									X				X						
kid									X				X						
Khaki									X				X						
scout									X				X						X
play/plays/played										X		X	X	X					
story												X					X		
solemn/solemnity															X	X			
Rushmore															X			X	
Fantastic Mr Fox															X				X

Figure 2: Lexical chain map of Text 2

Sam, scout, story, solemnity. These terms might also be important in an extended summary of the text. By graphing the locations of the chains as was done in Figure 2, the grouping of these words at the end of the text is clear.

The fourth and final research purpose was text criticism. Whereas the first three purposes were studied using automatable methods, text criticism requires a qualitative methodology where the interpretation of the lexical cohesion in the text would be impossible using a computer. In this methodology, the most frequent cohesive items are not necessarily the focus of the analysis. Instead, the items are first organized semantically into categories such as "movie description" or "characters and actors".

For example, in Text 1, the two cohesive words in Text 1 that describe an aspect of the movie are *summer* and *world*. These two words appear in close proximity to one another at the end of the text. They paint a picture of a sunny, carefree atmosphere of "summers when kids played outside", "summer games", and "grand adventures".

In contrast, Text 2 presents a much more serious interpretation of the same movie. When *summer* is mentioned in Text 2, it is not as a reiterated cohesive item signifying playfulness, but instead as the name of the house seen in the opening credits -- *Summer's End.* As Text 2 describes the house, words such as *autumnal* and *September* are found nearby, adding to the atmosphere of changing seasons.

So while Text 1 focuses on the childlike freedom that summer brings, Text 2 instead describes the movie as the end of summer, a time of change where life becomes more serious. This can be seen in cohesive units in Text 2 such as *rain* and *solemn*. Other phrases collocated with *solemn* add to the atmosphere such as "death, abandonment" and the movie's "earnest adolescent protagonists". Through the cohesive items in Text 2, it can be seen that the protagonists are going through a change from the playful summer days of youth as they leave the comfort and protection of their families (as symbolized by the cohesive links highlighting the *house* in the *rain* in the *opening sequence*) and entering an adult world of "burgeoning sexuality" and "reckless passions".

In this way, it can be seen that the lexical cohesion of these two texts are used very differently. Text 1 leaves the reader with a positive feeling of a summertime childhood, while Text 2 is a much more serious take on the rite of passage from the fun of childhood to the somberness of adulthood.

4 Conclusion

This paper has discussed four different purposes for analyzing lexical cohesion in text: text evaluation, text segmentation, text summarization, and text criticism. These purposes require different methods, and each method delivers different results. For these two particular texts, two of the methods show that the lexical cohesion characteristics of the texts are the same. Some of the indices of Coh-Metrix (such as Stem Overlap of both adjacent and all sentences) give very similar results for the two texts. The Coh-Metrix results could be interpreted to show that both texts are highly cohesive compared to other similar texts. Likewise, a noun-phrase summary based on the most frequent and lengthy cohesive chains also gives the same results for Text 1 and Text 2: "Anderson's film Moonrise Kingdom".

However, all of the other methods show that the lexical cohesion characteristics of these two texts are very different. When doing a text evaluation by looking at metrics for the entire text, it was shown that Text 2 has more lexical chains. These chains are also longer, and less dense than Text 1. A moving window analysis for the purpose of text segmentation showed that the writers cover different topics in the different segments. Using lexical cohesion for text summarization gives twice as many cohesive lexical chains for Text 2 than for Text 1, meaning that a richer summary can be created for Text 2. A graphical representation of these lexical chains also showed large differences in the ways that the lexical chains helped to tie the different parts of the text together. And finally, the qualitative interpretation of the text from the reader's perspective shows that Text 1 focuses on a happy summer motif of children's games, while Text 2 has a somber autumn feel that addresses a coming of age story.

These results point to the conclusion that although lexical cohesion appears to be a fairly straightforward concept, different purposes for using it in research can produce wildly different methods and results. This implies that lexical cohesion may not be a single construct; rather, it could comprise a cluster of several constructs, suggesting that it is a far more complex issue than it first appears. Researchers should keep these differences in mind as they decide what perspective to take when analyzing lexical cohesion in text.

References

Barzilay, Regina & Elhadad, Michael. (1999). Using lexical chains for text summarization. *Advances in automatic text summarization*, 111-121.

Graesser, Arthur C., McNamara, Danielle S., Louwerse, Max M., & Cai, Zhiqiang. (2004). Coh-metrix: Analysis of text on cohesion and language. *Behavior Research Methods, Instruments, & Computers*, 36(2), 193-202.

Hoey, Michael. (1991). *Patterns of lexis in text*. Oxford: Oxford University Press

Hornaday, Ann (June 1, 2012). Adolescent love among eccentrics. Retrieved Nov 17, 2013 from http://www.washingtonpost.com/gog/movies/moonrise-kingdom,1221101.html

Klebanov, Beata B., Diermeier, Daniel, & Beigman, Eyal. (2008). Lexical cohesion analysis of political speech. *Political Analysis*, 16(4), 447-463.

Morris, Jane, & Hirst, Graeme. (1991). Lexical cohesion computed by thesaural relations as an indicator of the structure of text. *Computational linguistics*, 17(1), 21-48.

Okumura, Manabu & Honda, Takeo. (1994). Word sense disambiguation and text segmentation based on lexical cohesion. In *Proceedings of the 15th conference on Computational linguistics-Volume 2* (pp. 755-761).

Luke. (October 21, 2012). Moonrise Kingdom. Retrieved September 29, 2013 from http://canetoadwarrior.blogspot.com/2012/10/moonrise-kingdom.html

Şimon, Anca, Gravier, Guillaume, & Sébillot, Pascale. (2013). Leveraging lexical cohesion and disruption for topic segmentation. In *Proceedings of International Conference on Empirical Methods in Natural Language Processing*, EMNLP 2013.

Sinclair, John. (2004a). Intuition and annotation–the discussion continues. *Language and Computers*, 49(1), 39-59.

Sinclair, John. (2004b). *Trust the text: Language, corpus and discourse*. London: Routledge.

Stokes, Nicola, Carthy, Joe, & Smeaton, Alan F. (2004). SeLeCT: a lexical cohesion based news story segmentation system. *AI Communications*, 17(1), 3-12.

Weston, Jennifer L., Crossley, Scott A., & McNamara, Danielle S. (2010). Towards a computational assessment of freewriting quality. In *Proceedings of the 23rd International Florida Artificial Intelligence Research Society (FLAIRS) conference*, 283-288.

Wong, Billy T.M., & Kit, Chunyu. (2012). Extending machine translation evaluation metrics with lexical cohesion to document level. In *Proceedings of the 2012 Joint Conference on Empirical Methods in Natural Language Processing and Computational Natural Language Learning*, 1060-1068.

Topics are conditionals: A case study from exhaustification over questions

Yurie Hara
Department of Linguistics and Translation, City University of Hong Kong
83 Tat Chee Avenue Kowloon, Hong Kong SAR
y.hara@cityu.edu.hk

Abstract

This paper argues in favor of Haiman's (1978) idea that conditionals and topics are analogous. The evidence comes from exhaustification over topicalized questions, which have the same semantics as conditional questions (Isaacs & Rawlins, 2008).

1 Introduction

Similarities between conditionals and topics are identified by many linguists (Haiman, 1978, 1993; Collins, 1998; Bittner, 2001; Bhatt & Pancheva, 2006; Ebert et al., 2008). Some languages use an identical morpheme to mark topics and conditionals. In Japanese, for instance, a conditional suffix *nara* is used for both conditional and topic constructions. When *nara* follows a clause as in (1-a), the clause serves as an antecedent of a conditional sentence. When *nara* attaches to a NP as in (1-b), the NP is the topic of the sentence.

(1) a. Taro-ga kuru nara, paatii-wa
Taro-nom come if party-top
tanosiku naru.
fun become
'If Taro comes, the party will be fun.'

b. Taro-nara kaeri-mas-ita.
Taro-if go.home-pol-past
'As for Taro, he went home.'

This paper offers another piece of evidence for the virtual identity of topics and conditionals. In particular, I argue that topics have the same semantics as conditional antecedents in that both serve as context-shifters. In dynamic semantics, conditionals are defined in terms of a two-step (Stalnaker, 1968; Karttunen, 1974; Heim, 1982) or three-step (Kaufmann, 2000; Isaacs & Rawlins, 2008) update procedure:

(2) $c+$ 'if P, Q' $= (c \cap P \cap Q) \cup (c \cap \overline{P})$, where a context c and propositions P and Q are sets of possible worlds.

(3)
1. A derived context is created by updating the speech context with the antecedent of the conditional ($c \cap P$).
2. The derived context is updated with the consequent ($c \cap P \cap Q$).
3. The original context learns the effects of the second step.

To illustrate briefly, in (4-a), the initial context is assertively updated by the antecedent 'Max comes', that is, the worlds that make the proposition false are deleted. The derived context is then assertively updated by the consequent 'we'll play poker'. Finally, the worlds removed in the second step are also removed from the original context.

(4) a. If Max comes, we'll play poker.

b. There's food in the fridge, if you're hungry. (Haiman, 1978, 564)

The idea of *context-shifting* nature of conditionals might be clearer with so-called *biscuit conditionals* like (4-b). In (4-b), the antecedent 'if you're hungry' shifts the context so that the assertive update of the consequent 'There's food in the fridge' becomes relevant or optimal (Franke, 2007, 2009).

Copyright 2014 by Yurie Hara
28th Pacific Asia Conference on Language, Information and Computation pages 522–531

Just like English *if*-clauses, the Japanese Topic-marking *wa* serves to shift the context. Let us take the following ambiguous English sentence which can be a sign at an airport:

(5) Dogs must be carried. (Wasow et al., 2005)

The Japanese translations of (5) are not ambiguous. The assertion of the non-*wa*-marked (6-a) could be about a general situation at an airport, thus the sentence is pragmatically implausible because it expresses a requirement that everyone at the airport has to be a dog-carrier. In contrast, the phrase *inu-wa* in (6-b) restricts the context of the assertion to cases where there is a dog, thus the sentence can be a plausible sign at the airport.

(6) a. inu-o kakae nakerebanaranai.
dog-ACC carry must
'You must carry a dog.'
b. inu-wa kakae nakerebanaranai.
dog-TOP carry must
'As for dogs, you must carry them.'≈'If there is a dog, you must carry it.'

As can be seen from the paraphrase in (6-b), the topic-marking encodes the meaning similar to the conditional antecedent.

This paper further supports the idea that topics have the same semantics as conditionals by analyzing topic-marked interrogatives. An incompatibility arises between an interrogative and the Japanese *dake-wa* 'only-TOP' construction.[1] Observe the following pair:

(7) a. John-dake-wa ki-masi-ta.
John-only-TOP come-Hon-Past.
'Only as for John, he came.'
(I don't make assertions about other individuals; only>assertion)
b. *John-dake-wa nani-o
John-only-TOP what-ACC
kai-masi-ta-ka?
buy-HON-PAST-Q
Intended: 'Only as for John, I ask: What did he buy?'
(I don't make questions about other individuals; only>question)

As a focus particle, *dake* 'only' generates a set of alternatives. When *dake* is combined with the topic *wa* , the exhausification by *dake* takes place at speech act level. Thus, the declarative construction marked with *dake-wa* as in (7-a) denotes exhaustification over assertion acts. That is, only the assertion of the prejacent proposition is executed and the rest of the alternative assertions are cancelled. In contrast, a parallel operation is not possible for interrogatives as shown in (7-b). I argue that the ungrammaticality of (7-b) is due to the violation of *Inquistive Constraint* (Isaacs & Rawlins, 2008), which dictates that any outstanding issue must be resolved before the conversation proceeds. Isaacs & Rawlins (2008) analyze conditional sentences with interrogative consequents (conditional questions) like (19) using a dynamic semantics for conditionals and a partition semantics of questions.

(8) If the party is at Emma's place, will it be fun?

Given the dynamic semantics of conditionals introduced above, a conditional question creates an issue on the derived context. If the topic-marking also creates a derived context, it also creates an issue on the derived context. In case of exhaustification, however, dues to the focus particle, alternative question acts are created and cancelled, thus many of the issues raised are abandoned, which violates Inquistive Constraint.

2 Topics as Conditionals and Exhaustification over speech acts

This section presents the data central to the current paper in detail. In particular, the *dake-wa* 'only-TOPIC' construction is incompatible with question acts. To see this, let us start with the *wa*-marked declaratives like (9).

(9) John-wa kita.
John-TOP came
'John came.'

[1] Some linguists treat the use of *wa* in (7-a) as contrastive rather than topical (Kuno, 1973; Hara, 2006). I assume that the contrastive use of *wa* is obtained when there is a focus-marking on the NP to which *wa* attaches. Due to the focus particle *dake*, *John* in (7-a) is indeed focus-marked. Thus, I take *wa* in (7-a) is an instance of contrastive topic.

As we have seen in (6), the *wa*-phrase restricts the context for the speech act of the utterance, just like English *if*-clauses.[2] Thus, I propose that the Japanese topic-marker *wa* marks Austinian topics (Austin, 1950). That is, the topic-marked element denotes what an utterance is about.[3]

I adopt the claim by Cinque (1999); Krifka (2001); Speas & Tenny (2003); Speas (2004); Tenny (2006) that there are syntactic representations for speech acts such as ASSERT, QUEST, etc., and propose that the *wa*-phrase is base-generated at the Spec position of Speech Act Phrase (SAP). In (10-a), *John* is nominative-marked, i.e., a subject, hence it is inside a TP, which is in turn in the scope of ASSERT. In contrast, according to Austin's (1950) idea of topic, the *wa*-marked phrase takes scope over the entire speech act. In implementing this scope relation, I propose that the *wa*-marked phrase is base-generated and adjoined to the Speech Act Phrase (SAP). In the subject position of TP, there is a little *pro* co-indexed with the *wa*-marked phrase. The structure of (9) is depicted in (10-b) .

(10) a.

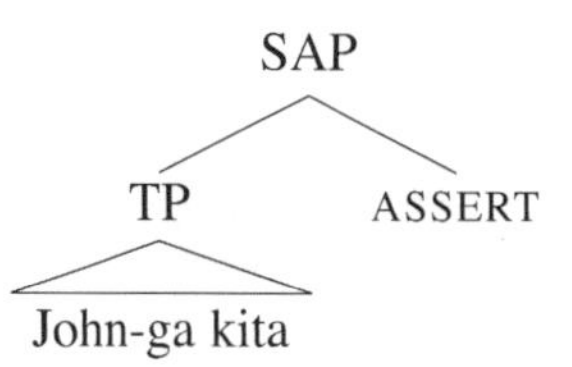

b.

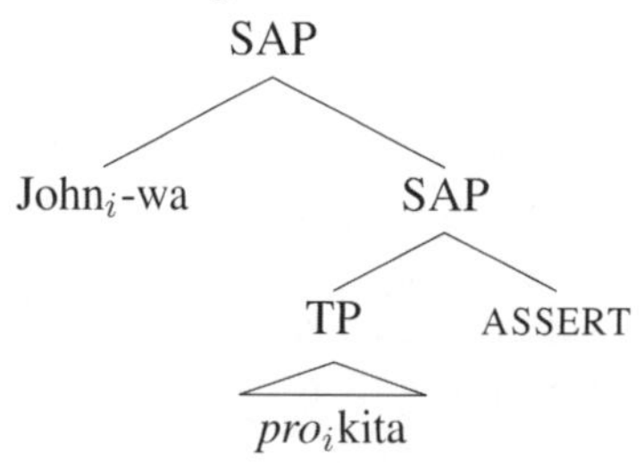

Wa-marked declaratives can be rendered into interrogatives without any problem as in (11).[4]

(11) John-wa ki-masi-ta-ka?
John-TOP come-HON-PAST-Q
'As for John, did he come?'

[2]It is suggestive that *wa* is argued to be etymologically related to Old Japanese *ba* 'place, situation' (Martin, 1975).

[3]See also Jäger (2001), who shows that the descriptive material of the topic contributes to the restrictive clause of adverbs of quantification.

[4]Honorific forms are added in order to make the examples pragmatically more natural.

Intuitively, the topic phrase restricts the context for the subsequent question. This is similar to the function of an English *if*-clause. Isaacs & Rawlins (2008) discuss English conditional questions. The issue raised by the consequent question in (12) is relevant only in the hypothetical context created by the antecedent. The questioner is not interested in whether the party will be fun if the party is not at Emma's place.

(12) If the party is at Emma's place, will it be fun?

Put another way, the issue does not have to deal with the cases where the party is not at Emma's place. Section 3 presents how Isaacs & Rawlins (2008) implement this intuition of question at the hypothetical context.

In summary, the function of the *wa*-marked phrase is a context-shifter just like the English *if*-clause in dynamic semantics. Both items create hypothetical contexts for subsequent speech acts.

Now, consider what happens when the topic-marked phrase is further modified by the exhaustive focus particle *dake*. First, let us consider a non-*wa*-marked *dake* sentence as in (13).

(13) John-dake-ga kita.
John-only-NOM came.
'Only John came.' (Others didn't come; assertion>only)

Just like English *only*, the *dake* sentence involves a focus structure and gives rise to two entailments, 'John came' and 'Other alternative individuals didn't come'. Thus, *dake* generates a set of alternatives in the sense of Rooth (1985, 1995) and expresses that the alternative propositions are false (see also Horn, 1969):

(14) $[\![$**John-dake-ga kita**$]\!] = 1$ iff

a. John came; and

b. $\forall p[[p \in C \wedge p \neq \textbf{came}(j)] \rightarrow p = 0]$, where C is a contextually given set of propositions and C is the subset of the Rooth's (1992) focus value of "[John]$_F$ came", i.e., $C \in [\![\textbf{[John]}_F\textbf{kita}]\!]^f$

In other words, the exhaustification by *dake* happens at the level of the propositional content.

In (15), due to *wa*-marking on the subject, *dake* takes scope over the restriction of the assertion.

(15) John-dake-wa kita.
John-only-TOP came.
'Only as for John, he came.' (I don't make assertions about other individuals; only>assertion)

Hence, *dake* generates alternative temporary contexts, 'if we are speaking of John', 'if we are speaking of Mary', etc., and the exhaustive component of *dake* conveys that the speaker is restricting her assertion to the proposition 'John came' with the discourse topic 'John':

(16) The utterance of 'John-dake-wa kita' is felicitous iff

a. S asserts 'John came'; and
b. $\forall p[[p \in C \wedge p \neq \textbf{came}(j)] \rightarrow [S$ does not assert $p\,]]$.

In other words, the truth-condition of (15) is the same as that of *John-ga kita* and *John-wa kita*, namely 'John came'. The difference is the speaker's intention in the discourse. That is, in (15), the speaker is indicating that she is willing to make assertions only about John and the alternative speech acts about other individuals are cancelled.

We are now ready to look at the main puzzle of the current paper: The *dake-wa* construction is illicit with an interrogative, as in (17).

(17) *John-dake-wa nani-o
John-only-TOP what-ACC
kai-masi-ta-ka?
buy-HON-PAST-Q

The empirical pattern is schematically represented in (18), where d stands for a discourse individual and P stands for a predicate.

(18) a. d is the x such that [ASSERT $P(x)$]
b. ASSERT $[P(d)]$
c. d is the x such that [quest $P(x)$]
d. QUEST $[P(d)]$
e. d is the only x such that, [ASSERT $P(x)$]
f. QUEST [d is the only x such that $P(x)$]
g. *d is the only x such that [QUEST $P(x)$]
h. QUEST [d is the only x such that $P(x)$]

Given the discussion above, the ungrammaticality of (17) suggests that it is an illicit act to cancel the alternative question acts. A *wa*-marking alone shifts the current context in a minimal way, thus it is easy to query into the shifted context. However, *dake-wa*, the topicalized focus particle, creates multiple contexts and multiple issues. The exhaustification meaning of *dake* cancels alternative question acts. Thus, many of the issues raised in those contexts would remain unresolved. This would yield a defective context since an issue raised by questioning must be something assumed to be immediately resolvable. I claim that this immediacy is one of the fundamental features of questionhood.

The rest of the paper is devoted to formally motivate this asymmetry between assertions and questions. More specifically, cancelling question acts is prohibited because it would result in a violation of Isaacs and Rawlins's (2008) *Inquisitive Constraint*, which dictates that any outstanding issue must be resolved before the conversation proceeds. In order to understand this principle, the next section presents Isaacs and Rawlins's (2008) analysis on conditional questions.

3 Conditional Questions and Inquisitive Constraint

Isaacs & Rawlins (2008) analyze conditional sentences with interrogative consequents (conditional questions) like (19) using a dynamic semantics for conditionals and a partition semantics of questions.

(19) If the party is at Emma's place, will it be fun?

In analyzing conditional questions, Isaacs & Rawlins (2008) argue that questions affect the current context whereas assertions can affect the entire stack of contexts. Employing Kaufmann's (2000) temporary contexts for conditionals and stack-based account of modal subordination, Isaacs and Rawlins suggest that information conveyed by assertions can percolate down the stack while issues raised by questions cannot.

3.1 Partition Semantics for Questions

Following Hamblin and others (Hamblin, 1958, 1973; Karttunen, 1977; Kratzer & Shimoyama, 2002), Isaacs and Rawlins assume that the meaning of a question is the set of possible answers to the question. In terms of partition semantics, possible answers correspond to blocks in a partition of the set of possible worlds.[5] To implement this approach to questions in a dynamic semantics, Isaacs and Rawlins adopt Groenendijk's (1999) analysis of questions, which defines the *context set* as an equivalence relation on worlds. That is, the context set is a set of pairs of worlds specifying a relation that is symmetric, transitive, and reflexive:

(20) **Definition:** context
A context c is an equivalence relation on the set of possible worlds W. (Groenendijk, 1999)

In a standard model of assertion (Stalnaker, 1968), where the context set is a set of worlds, an assertive update removes worlds which make the assertive content false. In the current framework, the context set is a set of world-pairs, hence an assertive update amounts to deleting all pairs which contain a member which makes the assertive content false.

(21) Assertive update ($\oplus$) on contexts: For some context (set) c and clause ϕ:
$c \oplus \phi = \{\langle w_1, w_2\rangle \in c \,|\, [\![\phi]\!]^{w_1,c} = [\![\phi]\!]^{w_2,c} = 1\}$
(Isaacs and Rawlins' (2008) reformulation of Groenendijk (1999))

In contrast, a question does not remove worlds but disconnects worlds and thereby partitions the context into blocks. That is, a question ϕ? removes pairs that contain worlds, each of which resolves the question in a different way, i.e., assigns a different truth value to ϕ. If both worlds in the pair give the same answer to ϕ?, the pair is kept, i.e., the worlds are still connected.

(22) Inquisitive update ($\oslash$) on contexts: For some context (set) c and clause ϕ:
$c \oslash \phi = \{\langle w_1, w_2\rangle \in c \,|\, [\![\phi]\!]^{w_1,c} = [\![\phi]\!]^{w_2,c}\}$
(Isaacs and Rawlins' (2008) reformulation of Groenendijk (1999))

3.2 Stack-based Model for Conditionals

Given the dynamic view of assertive and inquisitive updates, conditionals are characterized using a three-step update procedure as introduced in (2) in Section 1.

In implementing these steps, Isaacs and Rawlins employ Kaufmann's (2000) model of temporary contexts. Let us illustrate how Isaacs and Rawlins's theory derives the meaning of (19), repeated here as (23).

(23) If the party is at Emma's place, will it be fun?

In Kaufmann's (2000) system, utterances are treated as operations over macro-contexts, where a macro-context is a stack of contexts in Kaufmann (2000) and Isaacs & Rawlins (2008):

(24) **Definition:** macro-context
a. $\langle\rangle$ is a macro-context.
b. If c is a (Stalnakerian) context and s is a macro-context, then $\langle c, s\rangle$ is a macro-context.
c. Nothing else is a macro-context.
d. If s is a macro-context, then s_n is the nth context (counting from 0 at the top) and $|s|$ is its size (excluding its final empty element).
(Isaacs & Rawlins, 2008, (43); p. 291)

Suppose that the initial input macro-context s ($= \langle c, \langle\rangle\rangle$) for some context c is defined as in (25) and that the facts of the worlds are as follows: the party is not at Emma's place in w_1, w_2, and the party is at Emma's place in w_3, w_4; the party is fun in w_1, w_3, and the party is not fun in w_2, w_4.[6] At the initial stage, the conversational agent is ignorant about these issues. That is, the agent has no pre-existing commitments about facts or issues. Reflecting this state of the context, all the worlds are connected and thereby treated as equivalent.

[5] By definition, the blocks in a partition of the set are mutually exclusive and collectively exhaust the set being partitioned. This property of a question becomes crucial in Section 3.3.

[6] Tense is ignored for simplicity.

(25) $s = \langle c, \langle\rangle\rangle =$

$$\boxed{s_0: \; c} \models s_0: \left\{ \begin{array}{cccc} \langle w_1, w_1\rangle & \langle w_2, w_1\rangle & \langle w_3, w_1\rangle & \langle w_4, w_1\rangle \\ \langle w_1, w_2\rangle & \langle w_2, w_2\rangle & \langle w_3, w_2\rangle & \langle w_4, w_2\rangle \\ \langle w_1, w_3\rangle & \langle w_2, w_3\rangle & \langle w_3, w_3\rangle & \langle w_4, w_3\rangle \\ \langle w_1, w_4\rangle & \langle w_2, w_4\rangle & \langle w_3, w_4\rangle & \langle w_4, w_4\rangle \end{array} \right\}$$

In interpreting the antecedent of the conditional in (23), a temporary context is created by making a copy of the initial context c. More precisely, a temporary context is pushed onto the stack:

(26) **Definition:** push operator
For any macro-context s and context c:
$\text{push}(s, c) =_{\text{def}} \langle c, s\rangle$
(Isaacs & Rawlins, 2008, (44); p. 292)

The temporary context is assertive-updated according to (21). In a nutshell, the function of the 'if'-clause is defined as the macro-context change potential (MCCP) which creates a temporary context which is assertive-updated by the propositional content of the clause, as in (27):[7]

(27) **Definition:** MCCP of an 'if'-claus
For any macro-context s and 'if'-clause [if ϕ]:
$s+$ if $\phi =_{\text{def}} \text{push}(s, s_0 \oplus \phi)$
Admittance condition: 'If ϕ' is admissible in a macro-context s iff $s_0 \oplus \phi \neq \emptyset$ (adapted from Isaacs & Rawlins, 2008, (54); p. 297)

That is, all pairs which contain a member that makes the assertion false, i.e., w_1 and w_2, are removed from the temporary context, as in (28).

(28) $s' = s$+[If [the party is at Emma's place]]=

s'_0:	$\left\{ \begin{array}{cc} \langle w_3, w_3\rangle & \langle w_4, w_3\rangle \\ \langle w_3, w_4\rangle & \langle w_4, w_4\rangle \end{array} \right\}$
s'_1	c

In interpreting the question in the consequent, the derived context is partitioned into two blocks (rendering it into an inquisitive context).

(29) **Definition:** Inquisitive update on macro-contexts
For any macro-context $\langle c, s'\rangle$ where c is the top member, and s' is a stack, and clause ϕ:
$\langle c, s'\rangle$ + [Question ϕ] $=_{\text{def}} \langle c \oslash \phi, s'\rangle$
(Isaacs & Rawlins, 2008, (49); p. 294)

Remember that the party is fun in w_3, and the party is not fun in w_4. Since w_3 and w_4 resolve the question in different ways, the two worlds are disconnected. In other words, the pairs that connect the two worlds are removed as in (30), and the temporary context is partitioned into two cells. The pairs which resolve the question as *yes* are in bold.

(30) $s'' = s'$+[will the party be fun?]=

s''_0:	$\left\{ \begin{array}{cc} \boldsymbol{\langle w_3, w_3\rangle} & \\ & \langle w_4, w_4\rangle \end{array} \right\}$
s''_1	c

According to Isaacs and Rawlins, a *yes*-answer is an assertive update removing all the pairs that make the assertion (answer) false in the temporary context. This assertive update by the answer affects not only the temporary context but also other members in the stack. As illustrated in (31), the update removes pairs which contain worlds where the antecedent is true and the consequent is false (w_4: the party is at Emma's place and the party is boring.).

(31) $s''' = s''$+yes=

s'''_0:	{ $\boldsymbol{\langle w_3, w_3\rangle}$ ~~$\langle w_4, w_4\rangle$~~ }
s'''_1:	{ $\langle w_1, w_1\rangle$ $\langle w_2, w_1\rangle$ $\langle w_3, w_1\rangle$ ~~$\langle w_4, w_1\rangle$~~ $\langle w_1, w_2\rangle$ $\langle w_2, w_2\rangle$ $\langle w_3, w_3\rangle$ ~~$\langle w_4, w_3\rangle$~~ $\langle w_1, w_3\rangle$ $\langle w_2, w_3\rangle$ $\langle w_3, w_3\rangle$ ~~$\langle w_4, w_3\rangle$~~ ~~$\langle w_1, w_4\rangle$~~ ~~$\langle w_2, w_4\rangle$~~ ~~$\langle w_3, w_4\rangle$~~ ~~$\langle w_4, w_4\rangle$~~ }

After the question is resolved and the temporary context is no longer inquisitive, the temporary context can be popped off the stack according to (32) as illustrated in (33).[8]

(32) **Definition:** pop operator
For any macro-context $\langle c, s'\rangle$:
$\text{pop}(\langle c, s'\rangle) =_{\text{def}} \langle c, s'\rangle$ if $s' = \langle\rangle$, s' otherwise
(Isaacs & Rawlins, 2008, (45); p. 292)

(33) $s'''' = \text{pop}(s''')$=

s''''_0:	$\left\{ \begin{array}{ccc} \langle w_1, w_1\rangle & \langle w_2, w_1\rangle & \langle w_3, w_1\rangle \\ \langle w_1, w_2\rangle & \langle w_2, w_2\rangle & \langle w_3, w_3\rangle \\ \langle w_1, w_3\rangle & \langle w_2, w_3\rangle & \langle w_3, w_3\rangle \end{array} \right\}$

In general, derived contexts are discarded after the interpretation of *declarative* conditionals. Subsequent utterances do not refer back to the temporary contexts. In contrast, Isaacs and Rawlins propose that derived contexts are not discarded after the interpretation of *interrogative* conditionals, since the

[7]The admittance condition encodes the presupposition that the propositional content of the antecedent is possible, which is often assumed since Stalnaker (1968).

[8]The definition in (32) itself does not determine when the pop operation applies. The Inquisitive Constraint (34) bans a pop operation on a stack with an inquisitive context.

derived contexts are still inquisitive. This requirement is formulated as the *Inquisitive Constraint*:

(34) **Inquisitive Constraint**
A macro-context may not be popped if the top element is inquisitive.
(Isaacs and Rawlins' (2008) (49); p. 294)

Accordingly, information introduced by assertions percolates down the stack but issues raised by questions do not. Because this point made by Isaacs and Rawlins is particularly relevant to the current paper, I will expand on this idea in the next section.

3.3 Exclusivity and Exhaustivity in Questions

Why do issues, i.e., inquisitive contexts, not percolate down the stack? In other words, why do questions not affect the other members of the stack? According to Isaacs and Rawlins, percolating issues would result either in abandoning exhaustivity or in abandoning mutual exclusivity. Recall that issues are partitions of the context set. In mathematics, "a partition of a set S is a collection of mutually disjoint, non-empty subsets of S whose union is S" (Joshi, 1989):

(35) A set P is a partition of a set S iff:
a. $\emptyset \notin P$
b. $\bigcup P = S$ (exhaustivity)
c. $[X \in P \,\&\, Y \in P \,\&\, X \neq Y] \rightarrow X \cap Y = \emptyset$ (mutual exclusivity)

Since an issue or a set of possible answers is defined as a partition, an issue is by definition required to be collectively exhaustive and mutually exclusive.

Going back to the issue raised by a conditional question, a derived context created by a conditional is a context where some of the worlds in the initial context have been removed. Hence, if an issue percolated, we would have to do something extra to the worlds which were not included in the derived context in order to maintain exhaustivity and mutual exclusivity. Pairs in s_1 which contain worlds that are not partitioned in s_1 are in blue in the table. Pairs which resolve the question as *yes* are in bold.

(36)

s_0:	$\left\{ \begin{array}{llll} \langle \mathbf{w_3, w_3} \rangle & & & \\ & \langle w_4, w_4 \rangle & & \end{array} \right\}$
s_1:	$\left\{ \begin{array}{llll} \langle w_1, w_1 \rangle & \langle w_2, w_1 \rangle & \langle w_3, w_1 \rangle & \langle w_4, w_1 \rangle \\ \langle w_1, w_2 \rangle & \langle w_2, w_2 \rangle & \langle w_3, w_2 \rangle & \langle w_4, w_2 \rangle \\ \langle w_1, w_3 \rangle & \langle w_2, w_3 \rangle & \langle \mathbf{w_3, w_3} \rangle & \\ \langle w_1, w_4 \rangle & \langle w_2, w_4 \rangle & & \langle w_4, w_4 \rangle \end{array} \right\}$

If these extra world pairs are added to both blocks of the partition specified in the derived context, then the resulting relation does not obey mutual exclusivity, as illustrated in (37).[9]

(37) Mutual exclusivity abandoned in the main context:

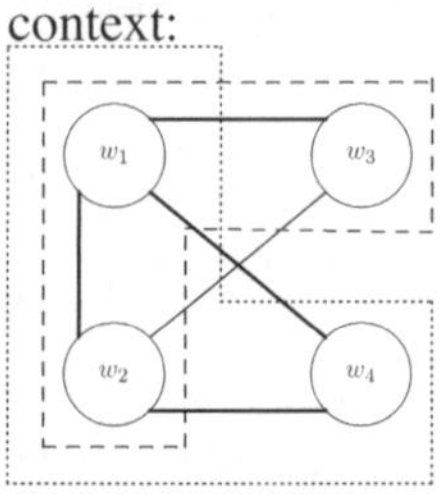

On the other hand, if we put those worlds in no block, as in (38), we end up abandoning exhaustivity.

(38) Exhaustivity abandoned in the main context:

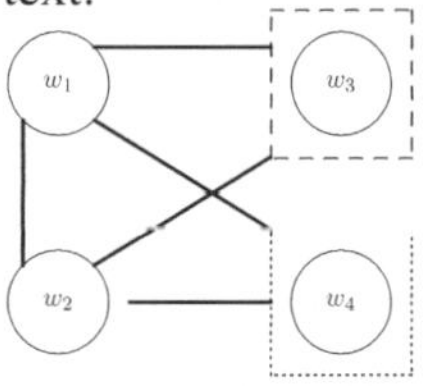

Since questions must obey exhaustivity and mutual exclusivity (Hamblin, 1958; Groenendijk & Stokhof, 1997), issues cannot percolate. Questions can only partition the top-most context. Furthermore, assuming that percolation precedes the pop operation, an inquisitive (i.e., partitioned) context can never be popped without being resolved, as stated in the Inquisitive Constraint, repeated here as (39):

(39) **Inquisitive constraint**
A macro-context may not be popped if the

[9] In recent work in inquisitive semantics by Groenendijk and his colleagues (Groenendijk, 2007; Sano, 2009; Ciardelli & Roelofsen, To appear), mutual exclusivity is not treated as a principal property of questionhood. Isaacs and Rawlins also give an alternative inquisitive update operation which allows issues to percolate immediately, in which mutual exclusivity is not strictly enforced. Furthermore, according to Isaacs and Rawlins, the alternative version gives a simpler analysis for embedded conditional questions. However, even if issues percolate down the stack, the topmost context must be exclusive and exhaustive. Furthermore, the inquisitive constraint (34) must be maintained.

top element is inquisitive.
(Isaacs and Rawlins' (2008) (49); p. 294)

In short, Isaacs and Rawlins argue that only the topmost context in the stack can be partitioned, and issues raised by questions must be resolved before the context is popped.

4 Deriving the asymmetry

We are now ready to derive the asymmetry between *dake-wa* assertions and questions. The topic phrase, understood as an antecedent of a conditional, creates a temporary context. If it is further modified by *dake*, temporary contexts are multiplied.

In implementing this proposal, I introduce the notion of multi-stack, as in (40). A multi-stack is a sequence of stacks. The context can be rendered into a multi-stack by using the n-copy operator (41) when necessary, i.e., when multiple speech act updates are performed on multiple contexts. This n-copy operation can be understood as playing the role of the F-feature in Rooth (1985, 1992). Like F-feature, it generates a set of Hamblin alternatives, A. When the alternative set takes scope over a speech act operator, a multi-stack S is created ($|S| = |A|$) and each member of the alternative set creates a hypothetical context on top of each stack in S.

(40) **Definition:** multi-stack
$S := \langle s^{(0)}, s^{(1)}, s^{(2)}, ...s^{(n)}\rangle$ is a multi-stack, where $s^{(i)}$ is a macro-context and $|s^{(0)}| = ... = |s^{(n)}|$.

(41) **Definition:** n-copy operator
For any macro-context s:
$n\text{-copy}(s) =_{\text{def}} \langle s^{(0)}, ..., s^{(n-1)}\rangle$, where $s = s^{(0)} = ... = s^{(n-1)}$

Let us first consider the grammatical *dake-wa* assertion like (15), repeated here as (42).

(42) John-dake-wa kita.
John-only-TOP came.
'Only as for John, he came.'
(I don't make assertions about other individuals; only>assertion)

When the F-feature of the *dake-wa* phrase is processed, the interpreter realizes that multiple stacks will be created. In other words, a topic-marked F-feature denotes a macro-context change potential which creates a multi-stack and performs an update over the created multi-stack:

(43) **Definition:** MCCP of a 'd_0 F-wa, ACT$(P(d_0))$'
For a macro-context s and a topicalized construction [[d_0 F-wa] ACT$(P(d_0))$]:
$s+$ [[d_0 F-wa] ACT$(P(d_0))$] $=_{\text{def}}$
$\langle s^{(0)}+$[if we are talking about d_0]+ACT$(P(d_0))$,
$s^{(1)}$ + [if we are talking about d_1]+ACT$(P(d_1))\rangle$,
where $\langle s^{(0)}, s^{(1)}\rangle$ =2-copy(s)
and $d_0, d_1 \in \text{Alt}(d_0)$.

(44) $S' = s$ +[[d_0 F-wa] $P(d_0)$] =

	$s'^{(0)}$	$s'^{(1)}$
S'_0:	$\left\{\begin{matrix} \langle w_1, w_1\rangle & \cancel{\langle w_2, w_1\rangle} \\ \cancel{\langle w_1, w_2\rangle} & \cancel{\langle w_2, w_2\rangle} \end{matrix}\right\}$	$\left\{\begin{matrix} \cancel{\langle w_1, w_1\rangle} & \cancel{\langle w_2, w_1\rangle} \\ \cancel{\langle w_1, w_2\rangle} & \langle w_2, w_2\rangle \end{matrix}\right\}$
S'_1:	$\left\{\begin{matrix} \langle w_1, w_1\rangle & \cancel{\langle w_2, w_1\rangle} & \langle w_3, w_1\rangle \\ \cancel{\langle w_1, w_2\rangle} & \cancel{\langle w_2, w_2\rangle} & \cancel{\langle w_3, w_2\rangle} \\ \langle w_1, w_3\rangle & \cancel{\langle w_2, w_3\rangle} & \langle w_3, w_3\rangle \end{matrix}\right\}$	$\left\{\begin{matrix} \cancel{\langle w_1, w_1\rangle} & \cancel{\langle w_2, w_1\rangle} & \cancel{\langle w_3, w_1\rangle} \\ \cancel{\langle w_1, w_2\rangle} & \langle w_2, w_2\rangle & \cancel{\langle w_3, w_2\rangle} \\ \cancel{\langle w_1, w_3\rangle} & \langle w_2, w_3\rangle & \langle w_3, w_3\rangle \end{matrix}\right\}$

After the percolation, i.e., the assertive update on macro-contexts, the temporary contexts are popped from the entire multi-stack. I now define MSpop, an operator which performs the pop operation on each member of the multi-stack. Since no temporary contexts are inquisitive in (44), all of them can be popped off without violating Inquisitive Constraint.

(45) **Definition:** multi-stack pop
For any multi-stack S:
$\text{MSpop}(S) =_{\text{def}}$
$\langle \text{pop}(s^{(0)}), ..., \text{pop}(s^{(n)})\rangle$.

Now, in the current example, the topic phrase also contains the exhaustive particle *dake*; therefore, it cancels all the alternative assertion acts except for the foreground one, i.e., ASSERT('John came'). I define the cancel operator to characterize the wide-scope exhaustification of *dake-wa*:

(46) **Definition:** cancel operator
For a multi-stack S: cancel(S) is defined if $\forall s \in S.|s| = 1$.
If defined, $\text{cancel}(S) =_{\text{def}} s^{(0)}$

Crucially, this cancel operation can be executed only when there is no hypothetical context, i.e., after MSpop is executed.

Turning to the case of *dake-wa* with a question

like (47), *dake* creates multiple alternative temporary contexts that the upcoming speech act will apply to, as we saw in (42). In the current case, however, the act is a question (i.e., an inquisitive update), creating a partition over those multiple contexts, as depicted in (48).

(47) *John-dake-wa shinbun-o
John-only-TOP newspaper-ACC
kai-mashi-ta-ka?
buy-HON-PAST-Q

(48) $S' = s + [d\ \text{F-wa}]\ \text{QUEST}(P(d))\ ]=$

	$s'(0)$	$s'(1)$
S'_0:	$\left\{ \begin{matrix} \langle w_1, w_1 \rangle & \\ & \langle w_2, w_2 \rangle \end{matrix} \right\}$	$\left\{ \begin{matrix} \langle w_1, w_1 \rangle & \\ & \langle w_2, w_2 \rangle \end{matrix} \right\}$
S'_1:	$\left\{ \begin{matrix} \langle w_1, w_1 \rangle & \langle w_2, w_1 \rangle & \langle w_3, w_1 \rangle \\ \langle w_1, w_2 \rangle & \langle w_2, w_2 \rangle & \langle w_3, w_2 \rangle \\ \langle w_1, w_3 \rangle & \langle w_2, w_3 \rangle & \langle w_3, w_3 \rangle \end{matrix} \right\}$	$\left\{ \begin{matrix} \langle w_1, w_1 \rangle & \langle w_2, w_1 \rangle & \langle w_3, w_1 \rangle \\ \langle w_1, w_2 \rangle & \langle w_2, w_2 \rangle & \langle w_3, w_2 \rangle \\ \langle w_1, w_3 \rangle & \langle w_2, w_3 \rangle & \langle w_3, w_3 \rangle \end{matrix} \right\}$

Moreover, the exhaustive particle *dake* attempts to cancel the alternative question acts except for the foreground question, 'As for John, did he buy a newspaper?'. However, the cancel operation fails here. As defined in (46), in order to perform $\text{cancel}(S)$, each member of the multi-stack S must have no temporary contexts. In turn, MSpop must have been performed beforehand. However, due to the Inquisitive Constraint, no inquisitive contexts can be popped. Since the inquisitive contexts are never resolved, and can never be popped off the stack, the discourse fails to proceed. As a result, a question modified by the *dake-wa* construction is illicit. The questioner cannot perform the act of questioning while ignoring the issues that the questioner herself raised at the same time.

5 Conclusion

Topics are analyzed as context-shifter for the subsequent updates, analogously to antecedents of conditionals in dynamic semantics. Thus, topicalized questions have an analogous semantics to conditional questions. Question acts render the hypothetical contexts created by topics or conditional antecedents into inquisitive ones. This line of analysis also correctly derives the asymmetry between assertions and questions with respect to wide-scope exhaustification. Alternative assertion acts can be cancelled, while alternative question acts cannot, since the latter would force popping of inquisitive contexts, which is prohibited by Inquisitive Constraint.

References

Austin, J. L. 1950. Truth. *Aristotelian Society Supp.* 24. 111–129.

Bhatt, R. & R. Pancheva. 2006. Conditionals. In M. Everaert, H.V. Riemsdijk, R. Goedemans & B. Hollebrandse (eds.), *The Blackwell companion to syntax*, vol. I, 638–687. Hoboken: Blackwell.

Bittner, Maria. 2001. Topical referents for individuals and possibilities. In R. Hastings, B. Jackson & Z. Zvolenszky (eds.), *Proceedings from SALT 11*, 36–55.

Ciardelli, Ivano & Floris Roelofsen. To appear. Inquisitive logic. *Journal of Philosophical Logic* .

Cinque, G. 1999. *Adverbs and Functional Heads: A cross-linguistic perspective*. Oxford University Press.

Collins, Chris. 1998. A note on extraction from conditionals. In Niken Adisasmito-Smith & Toby Doeleman (eds.), *Cornell Working Papers in Linguistics*, vol. 16, Ithaca: Cornell University.

Ebert, Christian, Cornelia Endriss & Stefan Hinterwimmer. 2008. Topics as speech acts: An analysis of conditionals. In Natasha Abner & Jason Bishop (eds.), *Proceedings of the 27th West Coast Conference on Formal Linguistics*, 132–140. Somerville, MA: Cascadilla Proceedings Project.

Franke, Michael. 2007. The pragmatics of biscuit conditionals. In Maria Aloni, Paul Dekker & Floris Roelofson (eds.), *Proceedings of the 16th Amsterdam Colloquium*, 91–96.

Franke, Michael. 2009. *Signal to Act: Game Theory in Pragmatics*: Universiteit van Amsterdam dissertation.

Groenendijk, Jeroen. 1999. The logic of interrogation. In Tanya Matthews & Devon Strolovitch (eds.), *Proceedings of SALT IX*, 109–126. Ithaca, NY: Cornell University.

Groenendijk, Jeroen. 2007. Inquisitive semantics: Two possibilities for disjunction. In P. Bosch, D. Gabelaia & J. Lang (eds.), *Seventh International Tbilisi Symposium on Language, Logic, and Computation*, Springer-Verlag.

Groenendijk, Jeroen & Martin Stokhof. 1997. Questions. In J. van Benthem & A. ter Meulen (eds.), *Handbook of Logic and Language*, chap. 19, 1055–1124. Elsevier.

Haiman, John. 1978. Conditionals are topics. *Language* 54. 565–589.

Haiman, John. 1993. Conditionals. In Joachim Jacobs, Arnim von Stechow, Wolfgang Sternefeld & Theo Vennemann (eds.), *Syntax: An International Handbook of Contemporary Research*, Berlin: de Gruyter.

Hamblin, C. L. 1973. Questions in Montague English. *Foundations of Language* 10. 41–53.

Hamblin, C.L. 1958. Questions. *Australasian Journal of Philosophy* 36. 159–168.

Hara, Yurie. 2006. *Japanese Discourse Items at Interfaces*. Newark, DE: University of Delaware dissertation.

Heim, Irene. 1982. *The Semantics of Definite and Indefinite Noun Phrases*: University of Massachussets, Amherst dissertation. [Distributed by GLSA].

Horn, L. 1969. A presuppositional analysis of only and even'. In *Papers from the Fifth Regional Meeting of the Chicago Linguistics Society*, 98–107.

Isaacs, James & Kyle Rawlins. 2008. Conditional questions. *Journal of Semantics* 25. 269–319.

Jäger, G. 2001. Topic-Comment Structure and the contrast between stage level and individual level predicates. *Journal of Semantics* 18. 83–126.

Joshi, K.D. 1989. *Foundations Of Discrete Mathematics*. Wiley.

Karttunen, L. 1977. Syntax and semantics of questions. *Linguistics and Philosophy* 1. 3–44.

Karttunen, Lauri. 1974. Presupposition and linguistic context. *Theoretical Linguistics* 1(1/2). 182–194.

Kaufmann, Stefan. 2000. Dynamic context management. In S. Kaufmann M. Faller & M. Pauly (eds.), *Formalizing the Dynamics of Information*, Stanford, CA: CSLI.

Kratzer, Angelika & Junko Shimoyama. 2002. Indeterminate pronouns: The view from Japanese. In Y. Otsu (ed.), *Proceedings of the 3rd Tokyo conference on psycholinguistics*, 1–25. Hitsuji Syobo.

Krifka, Manfred. 2001. Quantifying into question acts. *Natural Language Semantics* 9. 1–40.

Kuno, Susumu. 1973. *The Structure of the Japanese Language*. Cambridge, Mass: MIT Press.

Martin, S. 1975. *A reference grammar of Japanese*. New Haven: Yale University Press.

Rooth, Mats. 1992. A Theory of Focus Interpretation. *Natural Language Semantics* 1(1). 75–116.

Rooth, Mats. 1995. Indefinites, adverbs of quantification and focus semantics. In Gregory N. Carlson & Francis Jeffry Pelletier (eds.), *The Generic Book*, Chicago: Chicago University Press.

Rooth, Matts. 1985. *Association with Focus*: University of Massachusetts at Amherst dissertation.

Sano, Katsuhiko. 2009. Sound and complete tree-sequent calculus for inquisitive logic. In H. Ono, M. Kanazawa & R. de Queiroz (eds.), *Workshop on Logic, Language, Information, and Computation*, 365–378. LNAI 5514.

Speas, Margaret. 2004. Evidentiality, Logophoricity and the Syntactic Representation of PragmaticFeatures. *Lingua* 114. 255–276.

Speas, Peggy & Carol Tenny. 2003. Configurational properties of point of view roles. In A DiSciullo (ed.), *Asymmetry in Grammar*, 315–343. Amsterdam: John Benjamins.

Stalnaker, Robert. 1968. A theory of conditionals. In N. Resher (ed.), *Studies in Logical Theory*, Oxford: Blackwell.

Tenny, Carol. 2006. Evidentiality, Experiencers, and the Syntax of Sentience in Japanese. *Journal of East Asian Linguistics* 15(3). 245–288.

Wasow, Thomas, Amy Perfors & David Beaver. 2005. The puzzle of ambiguity. In O. Orgun & P. Sells (eds.), *Morphology and The Web of Grammar: Essays in Memory of Steven G. Lapointe*, CSLI Publications.

Detecting the Untranslatable Colloquial Expressions of Japanese Verbs in Cross-Language Instant Messaging

Yuchang Cheng[1], Masaru Fuji[1], Tomoki Nagase[1], Minoru Uegaki[2], Isaac Okada[2]
[1]Speech & Language Technologies lab.,
Media Processing Systems Laboratories, Fujitsu Laboratories Limited., Kawasaki, Japan
[2]System Engineering Knowledge Improvement div.,
System Engineering Technology Unit, Fujitsu Limited., Tokyo, Japan
[1]{cheng.yuchang, fuji.masaru, nagase.tomoki}@jp.fujitsu.com,
[2]{uegaki.minoru, isaac-okada}@jp.fujitsu.com

Abstract

Using instant messenger in real time communication is widespread worldwide. However, in the communication of using cross-language (Japanese - other languages) instant messaging, the use of colloquial expressions usually degrades the efficiency of communication. The contributions of our research can be split into two parts: (1) we analyzed the in-house conversation logs of business correspondence to obtain the cause of the failure of translation in cross-language instant messaging conversations; (2) we proposed an automatic system to detect the untranslatable colloquial expressions of Japanese verbs that are the most significant cause of the failure of Japanese-Chinese (and Japanese-English) machine translation in instant message conversation.

1 Introduction

In recent years, using instant messenger in real-time communication has become common worldwide, and there have been advances in the use of machine translation for efficient communications in multi-lingual conversation. There are an increasing number of global enterprises that use instant messenger for real-time business correspondence. The users of instant messenger can use machine translation service to overcome the language barrier with foreign language speakers in real-time business correspondence. However, the unnecessary conversation arising from the discrepancy of intention increases when the quality of the machine translation is insufficient.

Recently, it has been concluded that the current technology of natural language processing can achieve a high level of accuracy only in processing standard linguistic expressions such as newspaper articles. However, non-canonical linguistic expressions are frequently used in instant message conversation. We believe that the translation quality of instant message conversation decreases due to the use of non-canonical language expressions.

In our research, we first analyzed a log of instant message conversation. The conversation log is in Japanese and it is collected from our in-house business correspondence. We observed the attributes in the conversation and calculated the appearance probability of the attributes. In order to observe the effect that the attributes have on the quality of machine translation, we translated the Japanese utterance[1] in the conversation log into English using Japanese-English translation software.

We found that the attribute "the colloquial expressions of Japanese verbs" is an important factor that causes machine translation quality to decrease. In Japanese, the string expression of a verb composes of two parts. One is the stem, which explains the core concept of the verb, and the other is a terminal expression that explains other information of the verb (such as voice type and tense/aspect). For example, the verb "買った(bought)" consists of the stem "買(buy)" and the termination "った(past tense)". The colloquial expressions of a verb usually occur as a non-canonical termination. Therefore the verb cannot be processed correctly because the termination is untranslatable. If verbs with the colloquial expressions cannot be processed correctly, the machine translation result will become impossible to understand. Therefore, to deal with collo-

[1] In this research, the "utterance" indicates the text that instant messaging users input into the massager.

Copyright 2014 by Yuchang Cheng, Masaru Fuji, Tomoki Nagase, Minoru Uegaki, and Isaac Okada
28th Pacific Asia Conference on Language, Information and Computation pages 532–541

quial expressions, the verb is an important task for improving the quality of the translation in instant message conversation.

Automatic correction of colloquial verbs involves two steps: (1) detecting the colloquial expressions that cause machine translation failure; (2) replacing the colloquial expressions with corresponding formal expressions. Step (2) is difficult because the proofreading system should recognize the user's intention. Step (1) is a relatively easy task because the system only needs to detect the expressions that cause the degrading of the translation quality. In this paper, we proposed a method of detecting Japanese colloquial verbs that will cause the degrading of translation quality.

Detection of Japanese colloquial verbs involves two steps, namely detecting and inspecting the verb, which includes a stem and a terminal expression. First, the system will detect the range of the verb. Because the word order in Japanese is SOV and the length of the instant message is short, the verb is usually placed at the end of the sentence. Second, the system confirms whether the terminal expression of the verb will degrade the translation quality.

In Section 2, we describe related works that deal with the machine translation used in the instant message conversation. In Section 3, we describe an analysis of a log of instant message conversation that involves business correspondence. Section 4 describes our proposed method for detecting the colloquial expressions of Japanese verbs. Section 5 describes the experiment of our proposed method.

2 Related Works

Along with the rapid increase in the use of instant messaging, there are many pieces of research that deal with this topic from different angles. In (Yang, 2011), they introduced the design of the cross-language instant messaging with existing machine translation services.

Komine, Kinukawa, and Nakagawa (2002) discussed the feature that brought the influence to the accuracy of a Japanese-English translation in the Japanese chat conversation of the instant message. They explained that the colloquial expressions usually occur in Japanese chat conversation and the colloquial expressions are difficult to translate.

	Japanese conversations
The number of users	587
The number of conversations	2000
The total number of utterances	22715
The average number of the utterances in one conversation	11.3
The average length of the utterances	19.5 (characters)
The average response time between utterances	40.7 (sec.)

Table 1: Outline of our in-house conversation log

These observations are similar to ours, as we discuss in Section 3.

Saito, Sadamitsu, Asano, and Matsuo (2013) explained that twitter and other micro-blogging data are written in an informal style, so there are many types of non-standard tokens such as abbreviations and phonetic substitutions. They proposed a method for simultaneous morphological analysis and normalization using derivational patterns. Their method used a surface collection, which is expensive to collect. Also, their method was unable to deal with new non-standard tokens that are not included in the collection.

The research that is most related to our mention is (Miyabe & Yoshino, 2010; Miyabe, Yoshino, & Shigenobu, 2009). In (Miyabe et al., 2009), Translation correction plays an important role in multilingual communication using machine translation; it can be used to create messages that include very few translation mistakes. Miyabe and Yoshino (2010) explained the use of back translation for cross-language instant messaging. In their observation, using back translation for detecting the untranslatable text can improve the efficiency of cross-language communication. However, the observations are based on manual simulation. In contrast, our research proposed a procedure for detecting the untranslatable colloquial expressions automatically.

3 Analyzing the Log of Instant Message Conversation in Business Correspondence

It is necessary to analyze a monolingual instant message conversation that does not use machine translation in order to verify the influence of machine translation on the instant message conversation. In this section, we describe the log of the in-

Meanings of attributes	Appearance probability of the attributes	Acceptability in J-C translation	Acceptability in J-E translation
Using face marks	7%	4.29	4.33
Colloquial expression of Japanese verbs	8%	2.65	2.41
Other colloquial expressions	23%	3.58	3.26
Using named entities	16%	3.50	3.62
Incomplete utterances	12%	3.36	3.10
Omitted subject	3%	3.30	3.0
URL, source code, file path	2%	4.16	3.81
Using background knowledge	16%	3.52	3.62
Average (all utterances)		3.62	3.43

Table 2: Distribution and acceptability of the attributes in Japanese instant message conversation

stant message conversations of in-house business correspondence.

In this research, we adopted the communication application "Lync[2]" as the instant messenger. Table 1 shows the outline of our conversation log. The log of the instant message conversation acquired in this paper includes the content of the utterances and thc transmission time, where 587 users used Lync in Japanese communications. The record period is three months and it includes 22,715 utterances.

Because the conversations are collected from in-house business correspondence, the definition of the boundary of a "conversation" is unclear. The users do not intentionally specify the beginning and the end of the conversations. We cannot divide the chunk of utterances as independent conversations. However, it is necessary to define the boundary of a "conversation" clearly in order to analyze the intention behind the conversation. We decided to define the "conversation" based on the time period between two utterances. We defined the verge of the conversation as the time of the utterance's transmission progressed ten minutes from the last utterance, and the log of conversations was divided to 2000 conversations.

In Table 1, the average number of the utterances in one conversation is 11.3. This means that when using instant messenger for the business correspondence, the users finished the business by the utterances of about five round trips. Moreover, the average length of the utterances is 19.5 (Japanese) characters. This result shows that the instant message sentences are shorter than other kinds of texts, such as news articles and the papers (Komine et al., 2002). We can also consider that the short sentences (instant message utterances) include simple structures. This means that we can analyze the influence of the factors that affect the machine translation quality easily and clearly.

Next, we analyzed the attributes of the instant message utterances in the conversation log, and we observed the effect that the attributes had on the quality of machine translation. In our research, we adopted the "acceptability" criterion for judging the quality of the machine translation (Goto, Chow, Lu, Sumita, & Tsou, 2013). We defined the quality of machine translation ranging 1 to 5, which corresponds to the acceptability from "F" to "AA".

We executed the machine translation in Japanese-Chinese and Japanese-English. In this experiment, we adopted the commercial translation software "J-Beijing 7[3]" and "ATLAS V14[4]" for the J-C and J-E translation. We can obtain the attributes that affect the quality of the machine translation in different language pairs. Table 2 shows the analysis results. Because there are many attributes that we observed in the analysis, Table 2 lists the major attributes that affect the machine translation quality. The column "Meanings of attributes" shows the observed attributes and descriptions thereof, and the column "Appearance probability of the attributes" shows the appearance probability of the corresponding attribute. The columns "Acceptability in J-C translation" and "Acceptability in J-E translation" show the acceptability in Japanese-

[2] Microsoft™ http://products.office.com/en/lync/

[3] KODENSHA™ http://www.kodensha.jp/

[4] FUJITSU ™ http://www.fujitsu.com/global/products/software/packaged-software/translation/atlas/

Chinese/English translation. The last row in Table 2 shows the average acceptability of all utterances in J-C and J-E translation.

It should be noted that the probability of occurrence of the attributes is independent in different attributes. It is possible that an utterance includes several attributes simultaneously. For example, the utterance "あのう、食べたらいかんぜよ (Uh…you should not eat that)" includes the interjection "あのう(Uh….)" and the colloquial[5] expression "いかんぜよ (you should not do…)" and we defined these expressions as the attributes "Other colloquial expressions" and "Colloquial expressions of Japanese verbs". The length of the string of utterances is not long, so most utterances include fewer than two different attributes.

The attribute with the maximum appearance probability is "Other colloquial expressions". Because the utterances of the attribute "Other colloquial expressions" includes various types of colloquial expressions (excepting the colloquial expressions of verbs), it is difficult to divide this attribute and to consider the measures for deal with various types of colloquial expressions. According to the results of translation acceptability, the translation quality of the utterances that has the attribute "Other colloquial expressions" is not significantly worse than the average acceptability of all utterances. Similarly, the acceptability of the attribute "Using named entities" and the attribute "Using background knowledge" are also not significantly worse than the average acceptability of all utterances. This means that these attributes (with high appearance probability) do not affect the translation quality in a significant way.

However, although the appearance probability of the attribute "Colloquial expressions of Japanese verbs" is 8%, which is less than the attribute "Other colloquial expressions" and the attribute "Using named entities", the acceptability of the utterances with this attribute (J-C:2.65, J-E:2.41) is significantly worse than the average acceptability (J-C:3.62, J-E:3.43). Similarly, compared to other attributes, the acceptability of the attribute "Colloquial expressions of Japanese verbs" is significantly worse than others.

[5] In our research, we didn't subdivide the types of colloquial expressions. The dialectal expressions (such as "いかんぜよ") are regarded to a type of colloquial expressions.

This observation means that if the utterance with the attribute "Colloquial expressions of Japanese verbs" appears, the translation quality will decrease. Moreover, because the average number of the utterances in one conversation is 11.3 (see Table 1), almost all conversations include at least one utterance with the attribute "Colloquial expressions of Japanese verbs". If an utterance with worse translation quality appears, the users will perhaps misunderstand each other. The effort to iron out misunderstandings is necessary. Therefore, the following conversation would be used for ironing out misunderstanding and the business correspondence would be suspended temporarily.

The suspending of the business correspondence using cross-language instant messaging is undesirable. In order to use cross-language instant messaging efficiently, we think that the important task is to deal with the colloquial expressions of Japanese verbs that degrade the translation quality. In the next section, we describe our proposed method for detecting the colloquial expressions of Japanese verbs.

4 Proposed Method - Using Back Translation to Detect the Colloquial Expressions of Japanese Verbs

4.1 The Proposed Method for Detecting the Colloquial Expressions of Japanese Verbs

In explaining our proposal, we used a metaphor to explain the concept of our idea: A personal computer cannot work well and we do not know which part of the PC is broken. To detect the broken part in the PC, we can replace a part of the PC randomly, such as the power supply, and then observe the operation of the PC. If the PC works better than it did when using the former power supply, we can declare that the former power supply is broken. If the PC works similarly to when using the former power supply, the former power supply is not broken.

The motivation of our proposed method is that using formal termination to replace the colloquial expressions of Japanese verbs can obtain a better translation result. According to the discussion in Section 3, the important feature that causes translation quality to decrease is the utilization of the colloquial expressions of Japanese verbs. The colloquial expressions of Japanese verbs usually occur in the termination of the verbs. If the expressions

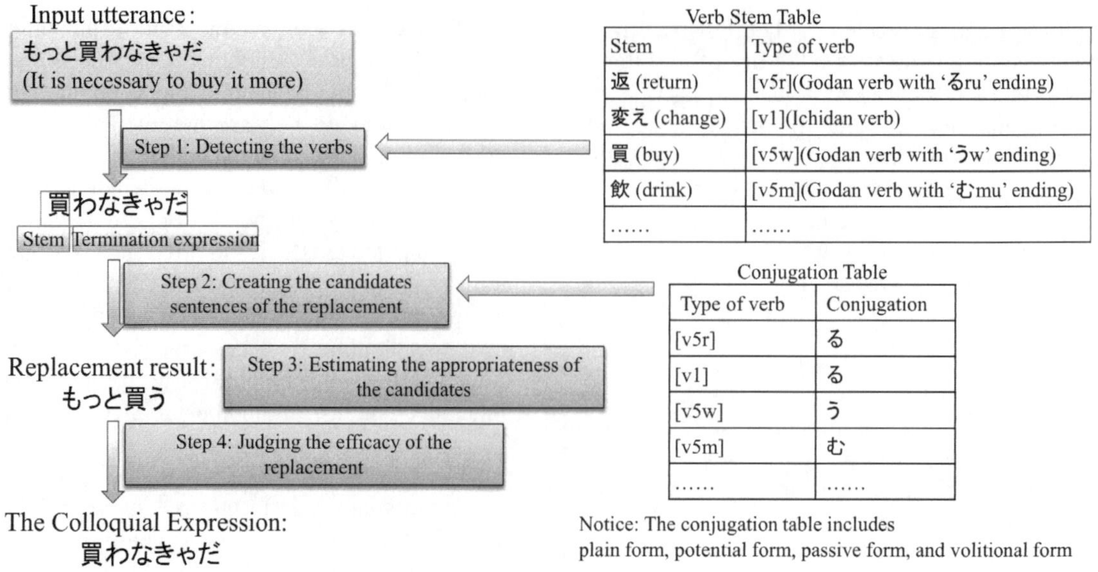

Figure 1: The process of the proposed method
The input utterance "もっと買わなきゃだ (It is necessary to buy it more)" is processed by the four steps and then the untranslatable colloquial expression "買わなきゃだ" is detected.

are untranslatable, the translation process cannot obtain an understandable result. However, using a formal termination of the verb to replace the colloquial expressions can obtain an understandable translation.

For example, the colloquial expression "買わねぇよ" (I don't buy it) cannot be translated into English by using a machine translation application because the termination "わねぇよ (do not)" is an untranslatable expression. If we replace the termination "わねぇよ (do not)" with "ない (do not)", the replaced sentence "買わない (I don't buy it)" can be translated.

Therefore, if a Japanese sentence that has worse translation quality obtains better translation quality remarkably after the replacement, we conclude that the replacement has fixed the untranslatable expressions. Figure 1 shows an example of detecting the untranslatable expressions by means of our idea. The input utterance "もっと買わなきゃだ (It is necessary to buy it more)" is processed by the four steps and then the untranslatable colloquial expression "買わなきゃだ" is detected.

Referring to Figure 1, our proposed method includes the following four steps:

Step 1: Detecting the verbs (comprising a stem and a termination expression)

First, the system detects untranslatable expressions that are extracted by referring to the verb stem table. The input utterance is analyzed into a sequence of morphemes. The verb stem table includes the stem of verbs and the type of verbs. The system detects the stem of verbs from the morpheme sequence and extracts the terminal expression that follows the stem. Because the terminal expression of a verb usually consists of the Japanese "Hiragana" characters, the system extracts the "Hiragana" characters that follow the stem as the terminal expressions.

In Figure 1, the system extracted the stem "買 (buy)" and the terminal expression (Hiragana characters) "わなきゃだ", which is an untranslatable colloquial expression.

Step 2: Creating the candidate sentences for replacement

In step 2, the system creates new utterances by replacing the suspect part of the original utterance. Refer to our idea; the system is not sure that the suspect part is untranslatable. Therefore, the system replaces the suspect expressions with the "correct" expressions. In Figure 1, the system refers to the conjugation table to replace the suspect expressions. The conjugation table is created from the Japanese textbook and the table describes the simple expressions of the verbs. The system used the conjugation table to replace the suspect expres-

Original Sentence	Back Translation Sentence
もっと買う (Let's buy it more.)	それはそれをさらに買います。 (It buys it more .)

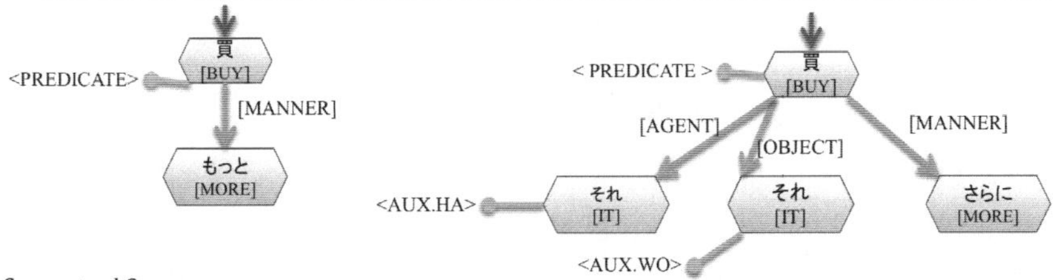

$$\begin{aligned} &Full\ Conceptual\ Score \\ &\quad = The\ Total\ Score\ of\ Both\ Original\ Sentence\ and\ Back\ Translation\ Sentence \\ &\quad = 2 \times 50 + 4 \times 20 + 4 \times 10 + 4 \times 5 = 240 \\ &Different\ Conceptual\ Score \\ &\quad = The\ Different\ Between\ Original\ Sentence\ and\ Back\ Translation\ Sentence \\ &\quad = 2 \times 20 + 2 \times 10 + 2 \times 5 = 70 \end{aligned}$$

$$Simularity = \frac{Full\ Concept\ Score\ - Different\ Concept\ Score}{Full\ Concept\ Score} = \frac{240 - 70}{240} = 0.71$$

Graphic	Meaning	Score
それ [IT]	Concept nodes	20
[MANNER]	Relation of node pair	10
<GA>	Node attributes	5
買 [BUY]	Root concept node	50

Figure 2: An example of calculating the similarity between the original sentence and the back translation sentence

sions "わなきゃだ" with the simple expression "う" according to the type of the verb, which is "v5w".

Step 3: Estimating the appropriateness of the candidates

After the process in step 2, the system had two candidates - the suspect verb expression "買わなきゃだ" and the simple verb expression "買う". Next, the system estimates the appropriateness of the candidates. The system calculates the similarity between the original sentence and the back translation sentence in each candidate. The system analyzed the concept structures of the original sentence and the back translation sentence of each candidate. Then the system compared the concept structure of the original sentence and the back translation sentence and calculated the similarity as the appropriateness of the candidates. Further detail will be described in Section 4.2. The result of the estimation in this step is that the appropriateness of the candidate "もっと買わなきゃだ" is 0.1 and the appropriateness of the candidate "もっと買う" is 0.71.

Step 4: Judging the efficacy of the replacement

In step 4, the system compared the appropriateness of the candidates and judged the efficacy of the replacement. If the appropriateness has increased tangibly after replacement, the system will judge that the replacement is efficient. The system will output the result of the judgment to indicate the untranslatable colloquial expressions. In Figure 1, the system judged that the replacement of the suspect expression "わなきゃだ" is efficient, and therefore the suspect expression "わなきゃだ" is untranslatable. More details are described in Section 4.3.

4.2 The Similarity between the Original Sentence and the Back Translation Sentence

In step 3 of the proposed method, we adopted the similarity between the original sentence and the back translation sentence for judging the efficacy of the replacement.

"Back translation" is the process of translating a sentence that has already been translated into a foreign language back to the original language (Miyabe et al., 2009) . Using back translation to check the quality of the machine translation is generally used by the users that do not understand the target language. Because the high-quality translation is correct semantically and grammatically, the translation result can be translated to the original language while maintaining a high level of quality. We considered that the system could compare the original sentence with the back translation sentence to judge the quality of translation.

The system uses conceptual structures to compare the original sentence and the back translation sentence. The conceptual structures can explain the semantics of the sentence while avoiding the effect

Case 1 (The untranslatable utterance): the verb in the original sentence includes the stem "買" (buy) and the termination "**わなきゃだ**" (should to do something)

Original (a)	もっと買**わなきゃだ** (It is necessary to buy it more.)
Translation (b)	..purchase.. [wanakyada] .. More
Back Translation (c)	購買wanakyada

The similarity of (a) and (c) : 0.1

Replacement: [わなきゃだ] -> [う]

Original (d)	もっと買**う**
Translation (e)	It does buy it more.
Back Translation (f)	それはそれをさらに買います

The similarity of (d) and (f) : 0.71

Case 2 (The translatable utterance): the verb in the original sentence includes the stem "買" (buy) and the termination "**おう**" (want to do something)

Original (g)	もっと買**おう** (Let's buy it more)
Translation (h)	It does buy it more.
Back Translation (i)	それはそれをさらに買います

The similarity of (g) and (i) : 0.71

Replacement: [おう] -> [う]

Original (j)	もっと買**う**
Translation (k)	It does buy it more.
Back Translation (l)	それはそれをさらに買います

The similarity of (j) and (l) : 0.71

Figure 3: The effect of replacing the verb termination
The difference of the similarity between the left part (before the replacement) and the right part (after the replacement) is 0.61 in Case 1 and 0 in Case 2. The replacement of Case 1 has greater impact than the replacement of Case 2.

of the variant expressions and the effect of the word order. For example, although the sentence "昨日(yesterday)私(I)はリンゴ(apple)を食べた(ate) (I ate the apple yesterday)" and the sentence "僕(I)は昨日(yesterday)林檎(apple)を食った(ate) (I ate the apple yesterday)" have different word order and use variant expressions, these sentences have similar conceptual structures and are translated into the similar English sentence "I ate the apple yesterday".

Figure 2 describes how to calculate the similarity between the original sentence and the back translation sentence. The system first obtains the back translation "それはそれをさらに買います (It buys it more)" of the original sentence "もっと買う (Let's buy it more)" by using a machine translation system. Then the system analyzes the conceptual structure of these sentences. The table on the lower-right side of Figure 2 explains the graphics that are used in this example. A hexagon is the concept node and it includes the surface string and the concept (shown in the square bracket). A hexagon with a blue arrow shows the root concept of the sentence. The arrows show the relations between nodes. The parenthesis shows the grammatical features of the node.

The right column of the table in Figure 2 shows the score of a node, node relation, root node, and features. We defined the scores heuristically. We assigned a high score to the root node because the root node is the core concept of the sentence. Also, the concept node has a higher score than the node relation because the concept node represents the meaning of the sentence.

The expressions for calculating the similarity are shown at the bottom of Figure 2. We calculated the full conceptual score of the two sentences and the different conceptual score and then calculated the similarity. The full conceptual score is the sum of the score of all root nodes, concept nodes, node relations and grammatical features. In this example, the full conceptual score is 240. The different score is the score sum of the different part of the sentences. As the node "それ (it)" in the back translation sentence did not occur in the original sentence, it is regarded as a different part. In this example, the different conceptual score is 70. Finally, we calculated the similarity using the expressions and the similarity of this example is 0.7.

4.3 Judging the Untranslatable Colloquial Expressions of Japanese Verbs

In step 3, the system estimates the appropriateness of the candidates by calculating the similarity of the original sentence and the back translation sentence. In step 4, the system judges the untranslatable colloquial expressions by comparing the appropriateness of the candidates.

Figure 3 shows an example that describes the judgment mechanism. The example includes two cases: the untranslatable utterance "もっと買わなきゃだ (It is necessary to buy it more)" and the translatable utterance "もっと買おう (Let's buy it more)". Using the process in step 3, the system obtained the difference of the similarity in Case 1 (0.71 – 0.1 = 0.61) and the difference of the similarity in (0.71 – 0.71). In Case 1, the difference of similarity (0.61) can be seen as having tangibly increased the translation quality after replacing the suspect terminal expressions. Therefore, we concluded that the original colloquial expressions "わなきゃだ" is untranslatable. Alternatively, the difference of similarity in Case 2 (0.0) can be seen as having not changed the translation quality after replacing the suspect terminal expressions. Therefore, the original expression is translatable.

There are several calculation expressions and methods for the judgment. In this example, we used the simplest calculation to judge the untranslatable colloquial expressions. However, we can also adopt other factors for judging it accurately, such as comparing the conceptual structures. To minimize computational complexity, we used a heretical threshold to judge the untranslatable colloquial expressions of Japanese verbs.

	Utterances
Automatically detected untranslatable colloquial expression	2229
All utterances in our conversation log	14394

Table 3: The number of total utterances and the number of automatically detected untranslatable colloquial expression

Explain	The average acceptability
The detected untranslatable expression (2229 utterances) BEFORE manual correct	3.03
The detected untranslatable expression (2229 utterances) AFTER manual correct	3.46
The total conversation (14394 utterances) BEFORE manual correct	3.41
The total conversation (14394 utterances) AFTER manual correct	3.48

Table 4: The average acceptability in J-C translation before / after correcting the detected colloquial expression

Acceptability	Utterances	%
Increased	752	33.7%
Similar	1163	52.2%
Decreased	60	2.7%
Manually uncorrected	254	11.4%
Total	2229	

Table 5: The transition of the acceptability in J-C translation by correcting the utterances according to the judgment of the proposed system
The row "Total" means the number of automatically detected untranslatable colloquial expression.

5 Experiments

The automatic correction of colloquial verbs involves two steps: (1) detecting the colloquial expressions that cause machine translation failure; and (2) replacing the colloquial expressions with corresponding formal expressions. Out of the two steps, we have implemented and have given full discussion on detection step (1), while correction step (2) is yet to be implemented in our future works.

In order to estimate the effectiveness of detection module (1) used in the entire automatic correction flow, we firstly applied detection module (1) to Japanese-Chinese translation, and then we manually corrected the detected colloquial expressions. Since the user of translation cannot differentiate between translatable and untranslatable expressions, we have decided to manually correct all the machine detected expressions.

Table 3 shows the experiment data and the result of the automatic detection. Our system obtained the J-C back translation and the detected results are the untranslatable expressions in Japanese-Chinese translation. We used the proposed system to process the conversation log of the in-house business correspondence that we described in Section 3. The conversation log includes 22,715 Japanese utterances but there are a lot of duplicates. We deleted these duplicate utterances, and the remaining conversation logs include 14,394 utterances. The proposed system detected 2,229 untranslatable utterances (see the row "Automatically detected untranslatable colloquial expressions"). We believe that the users of instant messaging do not like the excess detection. Therefore we tune the system to reduce the excess detection and to require higher precession more than the recall.

Table 4 shows the average acceptability before / after the manual correction in J-C translation. We considered the average acceptability of the automatic detected colloquial expressions (2,229) and all utterances in our conversation log (14,394). The average acceptability of automatically detected colloquial expressions increased from 3.03 to 3.46. The average acceptability of the total utterances increased from 3.41 to 3.48. Although the quality didn't increase dramatically, these results show that our system detected the untranslatable utterances effectively and helped users to increase the translation quality.

It should be noted that the system detected the untranslatable utterances. Therefore the translation quality of the detected utterances (3.03) is worse than the quality of all utterances (3.41). We can also claim that our system could be used for automatically evaluating the translation quality of the conversation.

Table 5 shows the number of the utterances that the acceptability increases / decreases / is similar. In this research, we manually corrected the untranslatable colloquial expressions that the system detected. In the manual correction, our operators try to "TRUST" the automatic detection and they tried to rewrite the untranslatable colloquial expressions with simple and synonymous expressions. If it is impossible to rewrite the expressions, the operators may decide not to correct the expressions. There are 254 (11.4%) utterances that the operators cannot correct any more. This result shows that the operators recognized the automatic detection.

After the manual correction process, we used the J-C translation application to translate the original utterances and the manual correction results. Then we evaluated the acceptability of these translation results. In our experiment results (see Table 5), 752 (33.7%) utterances are corrected and have their acceptability increased (see the row "Increased"). The acceptability did not change in 1,163 (52.2%) utterances, and the acceptability decreased in 60 (2.7%) utterances. This results show that the automatic detection can help the users to deduce the untranslatable utterances and our system achieved our expectation – detecting the untranslatable colloquial expressions in high precision and low degradation. We think that our system can be put into use.

6 The efficiency of communication

For the practical application of our system, the system is not only evaluated in the quality of translation, but also to be evaluated in the efficiency of communication. However, we didn't establish the method for evaluating the efficiency of communication.

The difficulty in evaluating the effect of our proposed method is that we cannot define the criteria of the success and the effectiveness of a cross-language instant messaging conversation. It can be considered that the number of the utterances in a conversation is useful information. If the conversation includes few utterances, it could be said that the instant massager users enjoy efficient communication. If the translation results cannot be understood, the users are forced to suspend the conveying of their intention and try to explain their intention to understand the unclear utterances (untranslatable utterances). This sort of communication will increase the number of utterances.

Table 6 and Table 7 show examples of cross-language instant messaging conversations. Table 6 has the correct translation results; therefore the users (user A and B) finished their intention transmission. In Table 7, the Japanese user (A) used the untranslatable colloquial expression "もっと買わなきゃだ" and the user (B) could not understand the intention of user A. Users A and B discussed the unclear translation (see the shaded row of Table 7). After the discussion, users A and B cleared up the misunderstanding. However, the number of the utterances increased in Table 7. Although there is only one untranslatable utterance "もっと買わなきゃだ" in Table 7[6], we thought that the effectiveness of the conversion of Table 7 is worse than Table 6.

Our system can detect the untranslatable colloquial expressions in Table 7 but does not detect the other utterances. Referring to our experiment, only one sentence will be counted as successful detection and the variation of the average acceptability is small. Therefore, the real effectiveness of our system is to reduce the non-effective utterance (see the shaded row in Table 7) but it cannot be evaluated fairly in this experiment.

7 Conclusion and future direction

In this research, we analyzed the in-house conversation logs of business correspondence to obtain the cause of the failure of translation in cross-language instant messaging conversations. Then

[6] In Table 6, the other utterances are translated correctly.

we proposed a method for automatically detecting the untranslatable colloquial expressions of Japanese verbs that are the most significant cause of the failure of Japanese-Chinese (and Japanese-English) machine translation in instant message conversation. The experiments result shows that our system can improve the average acceptability of all utterances from 3.41 to 3.48. The results of automatic detection can help users to reduce the untranslatable utterances with high precision. We also explained that the utterance unit criteria could not evaluate the effectiveness of our system. Therefore, one future direction is to create a criterion for evaluating the effectiveness of the conversation.

Another direction is to improve the calculation of the similarity of the original sentence and the back translation sentence. We used a simple method to evaluate the similarity but there are several related works that deal with the similarity of two graphs or tree structures. These methods can provide more credibility to the similarity of the original sentence and the back translation sentence.

Speaker (translation direction)	User (A)'s view (Japanese)	User (B)'s view (English)
A (J->E)	冷蔵庫にコーラがない。もっと買わないといけない	There is no cola in the refrigerator. It is necessary to buy it more.
B (E->A)	より多くのコーラも買いたいと思います。	I want to buy more cola, too.
A (J->E)	一緒に買いに行こう	Let's go for purchase together.

Table 6: Example of conversation without non-effective utterance

Speaker (translation direction)	User (A)'s view (Japanese)	User (B)'s view (English)
A (J->E)	冷蔵庫にコーラがない。***もっと買わなきゃだ***	There is no cola in the refrigerator. *More... purchase... [wanakyada]*
B (E->J)	「さらに。」「購入します」。? あなたは、より多くのコーラを買いたいと言っていましたか?	"More… purchase..."? Did you mean that you want to buy more cola?
A (J->E)	そうです、私はコーラをもっと買いたい	It is so, and I want to buy cola more.
B (E->J)	より多くのコーラも買いたいと思います。	I want to buy more cola, too.
A (J->E)	一緒に買いに行こう	Let's go for purchase together.

Table 7: Example of conversation with non-effective utterance
The translation direction "A (J->E)" means that the user (A)'s utterance is in Japanese and is translated to English

References

Goto, Isao, Chow, Ka Po, Lu, Bin, Sumita, Eiichiro, & Tsou, Benjamin K. (2013). *Overview of the patent machine translation task at the NTCIR-10 workshop.* Paper presented at the Proceedings of the 10th NTCIR Workshop Meeting on Evaluation of Information Access Technologies: Information Retrieval, Question Answering and Cross-Lingual Information Access, NTCIR-10.

Komine, Hisashi, Kinukawa, Hiroshi, & Nakagawa, Hiroshi. (2002). *Sentence Extraction based on Document Frequency and Text Length.* Paper presented at the IPSJ SIG Notes.

Miyabe, Mai, & Yoshino, Takashi. (2010). *Influence of detecting inaccurate messages in real-time remote text-based communication via machine translation.* Paper presented at the Proceedings of the 3rd international conference on Intercultural collaboration, Copenhagen, Denmark.

Miyabe, Mai, Yoshino, Takashi, & Shigenobu, Tomohiro. (2009). *Effects of undertaking translation repair using back translation.* Paper presented at the Proceedings of the 2009 international workshop on Intercultural collaboration, Palo Alto, California, USA.

Saito, Itsumi, Sadamitsu, Kugatsu, Asano, Hisako, & Matsuo, Yoshihiro. (2013). *Extracting Derivational Patterns based on the Alignment of a Standard Form and its Variant towards the Japanese Morphological Analysis for Noisy Text.* Paper presented at the IPSJ SIG Notes.

Yang, Che-Yu. (2011). *Cross-Language Instant Messaging with Automatic Translation.* Paper presented at the Ubi-Media Computing (U-Media), 2011 4th International Conference on.

A Keyword-based Monolingual Sentence Aligner in Text Simplification

[1]Chung-Chi Huang [2]Maxine Eskenazi [3]Mei-Hua Chen [4]Ping-Che Yang
[1,2]Language Technologies Institute, CMU, United States
[3]Hua Fan University, Taipei, Taiwan
[4]Institute for Information Industry, Taipei, Taiwan
{[1]u901571,[3]chen.meihua}@gmail.com,[2]max+@cs.cmu.edu,[4]maciaclark@iii.org.tw

Abstract

We introduce a method for learning to align sentences in monolingual parallel articles for text simplification. In our approach, word keyness is integrated to prefer aligning essential words in sentences. The method involves estimating word keyness based on TF*IDF and semantic PageRank, and word nodes' parts-of-speech and degrees of reference. At run-time, the keyword analyses are used as word weights in sentence similarity measure. And a global dynamic programming goes through sentence similarities further weighted by aligned content-word ratios and positions of aligned words to determine the optimal candidates of parallel sentences. We present a prototype sentence aligner, *KEA*, that applies the method to monolingual parallel articles. Evaluation shows that *KEA* pays more attention to key words during sentence aligning and outperforms the current state-of-the-art in alignment accuracy and f-measure. Our pilot study also indicates that language learners benefit from our sentence-aligned parallel articles in reading comprehension test.

1 Introduction

Many articles are posted on the Web every day, and an increasing number of educational websites specifically provide articles for audiences with different needs. For example, NewsInLevels (www.newsinlevels.com) and BreakingNewsEnglish (www.breakingnewsenglish.com) select news articles and provide versions with different readability for language learners. Simple Wikipedia (simple.wikipedia.org) and EasierEnglishWiki (eewiki.newint.org) contain articles easier to read with simpler vocabulary and syntactic structure than English Wikipedia and New Internationalist for people with low literacy. And SoundReading (www.soundreading.com) even has audio recording for those with learning disabilities such as dyslexia.

Language learning websites such as NewsInLevels and EasierEnglishWiki typically simplify original articles into easier ones and present the original and easier articles as pairs to non-native speakers, children, or lay people. However, language learners may want to compare the article pairs conveying the same information at sentence level, and most text simplification systems build on top of original and simplified sentence pairs. Unfortunately, current monolingual sentence alignment methods treat article sentences as bags of words, equally weight words, and align sentences with high word-overlap ratios. These article pairs could be sentence aligned more accurately if a system distinguished words of different importance and leveraged their importance levels in articles while aligning.

Consider the original-simplified article pair in Figure 1. The best sentence alignment methods are probably not the ones with equal word weights (i.e., weights are the same with "*the*" and "*gorilla*" and the same with "*everything*" and "*project*"). A

Copyright 2014 by Chung-Chi Huang, Maxine Eskenazi, Mei-Hua Chen, and Ping-Che Yang
28th Pacific Asia Conference on Language, Information and Computation pages 542–550

Original article:
(1) An army of gorillas came to the River Thames! (2) They aren't real animals, but statues dressed up as people. (3) There are 20 life-sized, individually decorated gorillas, including Elvis and Spiderman. (4) They are here to bring people's attention to the problems of gorillas. (5) There are very few gorillas in the wild and their number decreases every year. (6) People destroy their homes and kill them. (7) But not everything is lost. (8) There are a lot of excellent projects, which can help gorillas. (9) These statues are one of such projects. (10) The show will finish on 22 September.

Simplified article:
(s1) There are gorillas in London. (s2) They are not animals. (s3) They are big statues. (s4) There are 20 gorillas in London. (s5) They have different clothes. (s6) There is Elvis or Spiderman. (s7) People made them. (s8) They want to show problems of gorillas. (s9) A lot of gorillas die every year. (s10) People take their homes. (s11) They kill them too. (s12) But there are a lot of projects. (s13) These projects can help gorillas. (s14) The statues are one of these projects. (s15) The show will finish on 22 September.

Words' keyness scores:
gorilla:0.15; September:0.13; project:0.10; statue:0.09; Spiderman: 0.08; Elvis: 0.06; 22: 0.06; home:0.06; people:0.05; problem:0.05; animal: 0.04; show: 0.04 …

Sentence pairs:
(1,s1), (2,s2), (2,s3), (3,s4), (3,s6), (4,s8), (5,s9), (6,s10), (6,s11), (8,s12), (8,s13), (9,s14), (10,s15)

Figure 1. An example *KEA* sentence alignment for an article pair.

good aligning approach might take into account the words' significance in the pair. Intuitively, word significance can be evaluated by keyword extraction methods and by leveraging word significance, sentence aligners can be biased towards aligning sentences with more words that are more essential.

We present a new system, *KEA* (keyword extraction based sentence aligner), that automatically learns to align sentences, considering word keyness, of monolingual parallel articles. That is, *KEA* aligns texts in the same language at sentence level that are "translation" of each other with different readability. An example *KEA* sentence alignment for an article pair is shown in Figure 1. *KEA* has determined the keyness scores of the words in the article pair. *KEA* learns these scores automatically during training by using TF*IDF and PageRank with semantic information (see details in Section 2). Both are famous keyword extraction methods.

At run-time, *KEA* starts with a pair of monolingual parallel articles. *KEA* then computes similarity scores among sentences in the original and simplified article based on words' keyness scores from TF*IDF and PageRank. Cosine similarity is adopted to evaluate sentence-wise similarity with the help of alignment ratio of content words and differences of relative aligned word positions. Based on sentence-level similarity, *KEA* employs global dynamic programming with deletion and insertion operation to generate the optimal sentence alignment for the pair. In our prototype, *KEA* returns sentence pairs for evaluation and language learning directly (see Figure 1); alternatively, the sentence pairs returned by *KEA* can be used as input to a text simplification system.

2 The KEA System

Submitting monolingual parallel articles to sentence aligners counting word overlaps often does not work very well. Such aligners typically assign equal weights to words. Unfortunately, some words (e.g., content words) are more important than others (e.g., function words) and aligners should pay more attention to topic/key words while sentence aligning. To align monolingual parallel articles at sentence level, a promising approach is to automatically integrate words' keyness that reflects the significance of words in the articles.

2.1 Problem Statement

We focus on the first step of automated text simplification: aligning monolingual parallel articles at sentence level. These sentence pairs are then returned as the output of the system. The returned sentences pairs can be examined for alignment accuracy, used for language learning, or passed on to sophisticated text simplification models (e.g., (Zhu et al., 2010) and (Woodsend and Lapata, 2011)). Thus, it is crucial that the aligned sentences be accurate. At the same time, the set of identified sentence pairs cannot be so small that it bores the user or hurts the performance of the subsequent (typically data intensive) simplification models. Therefore, our goal is to return a reasonable-sized set of parallel sentences that, at the same time, must contain correct sentence mappings of the parallel articles. We now formally state the problem that we are addressing.

Problem Statement: We are given a monolingual parallel article pair, specifically, an original article Art_o and its simplified counterpart Art_s. Our goal is to retrieve a set of sentence pairs that are likely to be the parallel sentences between Art_o and Art_s. For this, we transform Art_o and Art_s into a set of sentences, $Sent_{o,1}, \ldots, Sent_{o,m}, Sent_{s,1}, \ldots, Sent_{s,n}$, and calculate keyness scores for words within such that the sentences are aligned considering word importance and the candidate set of sentence pairs are likely to contain parallel sentences in Art_o and Art_s.

In the rest of this section, we describe our solution to this problem. First, we define a strategy for distinguishing words of different importance in the parallel articles and assigning them keyness socres accordingly (Section 2.2). This strategy relies on TF*IDF and PageRank. In this section, we also describe how we extend PageRank to semantic one using semantic information such as keyword preference model, and words' parts-of-speech and degrees of reference in the articles. Finally, we show how *KEA* applies global dynamic programming to align sentences at run-time by leveraging keyness scores for words, and sentence-level ratios of aligned content words and aligned word positions (Section 2.3).

(1) Estimate word keyness based on TF*IDF
(2) Estimate word keyness based on semantic PageRank
(3) Combine word keyness from TF*IDF and PageRank
(4) Output the resulting word keyness

Figure 2. Outline of the process used to train the *KEA* system.

2.2 Word Keyness Estimation

We attempt to evaluate significance levels for words that are expected to reflect their keyness in parallel articles. Our learning process is shown in Figure 2.

In the first stage, we estimate words' keyness in the article pair (Art_o, Art_s) based on TF*IDF. As inspired by (Nelken and Shieber, 2006), we view sentences in both Art_o and Art_s as documents, and define the sentence-based TF to indicate the existence of a word in an article sentence and the sentence-based IDF to be the reciprocal of the sentential appearance of a word. The TF*IDF keyness of a word w in sentence $Sent$ is $\text{tfidf}(w|Sent)=\text{TF}(w|Sent)\times\text{IDF}(w|\{Sent\})$ where $\text{TF}(w|Sent)$ is active and set to 1 if $Sent$ contains w (0 otherwise) and $\{Sent\}$ represents the set of the article sentences in Art_o and Art_s. Take the words "*gorillas*" and "*of*" of sentence 1 in Figure 1 for example. "*gorillas*" is in 5 original sentences and 5 simplified ones, while "*of*" has 4 sentential occurrences in Art_o and 4 in Art_s. Thus, tfidf("*gorillas*"|sentence 1) is $1\times1/(5+5)=0.1$ and tfidf("*of*"|sentence 1) is $1\times1/(4+4)=0.125$.

As one can speculate, TF*IDF penalizes frequent content words (e.g., "*gorillas*" assigned 0.1 compared to "*of*" assigned 0.125), but frequent content words are more likely to be key words and should receive more attention during sentence aligning. Therefore, we also turn to PageRank, a famous keyword extraction algorithm, to infer word significance and give better share of weights for essential words.

In the second stage of the learning algorithm (Step (2) in Figure 2), we estimate words' keyness in Art_o and Art_s based on PageRank, or specifically semantically motivated PageRank. Figure 3 shows the algorithm for deriving keyness scores for article words.

In Step (1) of the algorithm, we view the original article Art_o and its simplified counterpart Art_s as a whole, following the sentence-wise TF*IDF. Then we construct PageRank word graph for the article pair. The graph is represented by a v-by-v matrix **EW** where v is the vocabulary size. **EW** stores normalized edge weights for word w_i and w_j (Step (3) and (4)). Note that the graph is directional (pointing from w_i to w_j) and that edge weights are associated with words' co-occurrence counts satisfying window size *WS*.

```
procedure EstimateKeyness(Art_o,Art_s,KwPrefs,m,λ)
(1) Concatenate Art_o with Art_s into Content
//Construct word graph for PageRank
(2) EW_v×v=0_v×v
    for each sentence st in Content
      for each word pair w_i, w_j in st where i<j and j-i≤WS
        if not IsContWord(w_i) and IsContWord(w_j)
(3a)       EW[i,j]+=1×m
        esle
(3b)       EW[i,j]+=1
(4) normalize each row of EW to sum to 1
//Iterate for PageRank
(5) set NS_v×v to a diagonal matrix with
          NS[i,i]=RD(w_i|Art_o,Art_s)
(6) set KP_1×v to [KwPrefs(w_1),...,KwPrefs(w_v)]
(7) initialize KY_1×v to [1/v,1/ v, ...,1/v]
    repeat
(8a) KY'=λ×KY×EW×NS + (1-λ)×KP
(8b) normalize KY' to sum to 1
(8c) update KY with KY' after the check of KY and KY'
    until maxIter or avgDifference(KY,KY')≤smallDiff
    return KY
```

Figure 3. Evaluating word keyness via semantic PageRank.

In this paper, we exploit semantic features of word nodes to make PageRank semantically aware. Three types of semantic information are used. First, we weight edges according to the parts-of-speech of the connecting word nodes via edge multiplier $m>1$. The weighting mechanism concerns content words and function words. If a word is a function word and its connecting outbound word is a content word (i.e., nouns, verbs, adjectives and adverbs), their edge weight is conceptually enlarged m times (Step (3a)), 1 otherwise (Step (3b)). The goal of this multiplier is to differentiate edges and increase the edge weights from function words to content words, which in turn propagates function words' PageRank scores more to content words and leads to content words' gains in importance.

The second semantic feature takes node's significance into account (Step (5)). Intuitively, if a word node is mentioned in Art_o as frequently as in Art_s, it is more likely to be an essential word, whereas if the degrees of reference of a word in Art_o and Art_s differ a lot, the word may not be as important. In our PageRank keyness estimation, a word node's reference distribution (i.e., *RD*) between Art_o and Art_s comes into play and is defined sentence-wise as

$$RD(w|Art_o, Art_s) = \frac{2 \times \min\left(|\{Sent: Sent \in Art_o \cap w \text{ in } Sent\}|, |\{Sent: Sent \in Art_s \cap w \text{ in } Sent\}|\right)}{|\{Sent: Sent \in Art_o \cap w \text{ in } Sent\}| + |\{Sent: Sent \in Art_s \cap w \text{ in } Sent\}|}$$

where the numbers of sentences in Art_o and in Art_s containing the word w are leveraged. Take the word "*gorillas*" and "*army*" in Figure 1 for instance. "*gorillas*" occurs in Art_o as often as in Art_s while "*army*" only occurs in Art_o. As far as word keyness in sentence alignment concerns, "*gorillas*" is a much more significant word than "*army*", reflected by *RD*("*gorillas*")=1 being larger than *RD*("*army*").

We exploit the keyword preference model (i.e., **KP**) as the third semantic feature to distinguish words that tend to be keywords (Step (6)). TF*IDF scores of Step (1) in Figure 2 are used for this purpose and denoted by *KwPrefs*.

After Step (6) of Figure 3 sets the one-by-v matrix **KP**, Step (7) initializes the matrix **KY** of PageRank scores or, in our case, word keyness scores. Then, we re-distribute words' keyness scores until the number of iterations or the average score differences of two consecutive iterations reach their respective limits. In each iteration, a word's keyness score is the linear combination of its keyword preference score and the sum of the propagation of its inbound words' previous PageRank scores. And the sum of the propagation is further weighted by the word's degree of reference. Specifically, for the word w_j in *Content*, its PageRank score is computed as

$$\mathbf{KY'}[1,j]=\lambda\times\left(\sum_{i \in v}\mathbf{KY}[1,i]\times\mathbf{EW}[i,j]\times\mathbf{NS}[j,j]\right)+(1-\lambda)\times\mathbf{KP}[1,j]$$

where λ is referred as damping factor and usually set to 0.85. After the iterative process stops, the algorithm returns the scores as PageRank-based word keyness estimation.

In the final stage of training (Step (3) in Figure 2), we combine word keyness scores from TF*IDF and semantic PageRank. Note that to gather solid word statistics all article sentences are lemmatized and shallowly parsed with part-of-speech information. Example word keyness scores are shown in Figure 1. Notice that the word "*gorillas*" clearly gains more attention in terms of significance in the articles, compared to its TF*IDF estimation alone.

2.3 Run-Time Sentence Alignment

Once the keyness scores for words are automatically learned, they are stored for run-time query. *KEA* then aligns sentences of given monolingual parallel articles using the procedure in Figure 4. We first segment the original article Art_o and its simplified counterpart Art_s into sentences (Step (1)). And we employ a global dynamic programming with deletion and insertion operation to identify the parallel sentences between the monolingual article pair that are translations of each other with different readability or targeted for different groups of audience (from Steps (2) to (6)).

```
procedure AlignSentences(Art_o,Art_s,KY,x,N)
(1a) Segment Art_o into sentences Sent_o,1,..., Sent_o,m
(1b) Segment Art_s into sentences Sent_s,1,..., Sent_s,n
//initialization for dynamic programming
(2)  initialize DP_(m+1)×(n+1)=0_(m+1)×(n+1)
//recurrence for dynamic programming
     for 1 ≤ i ≤m
      for 1≤ j ≤n
(3a)   (W_o,CW_o)=findWordAndContentWord(Sent_o,i)
(3b)   (W_s,CW_s)=findWordAndContentWord(Sent_s,j)
(3c)   CosSim=findCosSimBasedOnWP(W_o,W_s,KY)
(3d)   AlignedRatio_cw=findCWAlignedRatio(CW_o,CW_s)
(3e)   DP[i+1,j+1]=CosSim × AlignedRatio_cw
                +max{DP[i,j],DP[i+1,j],DP[i,j+1]}
//backtracking for dynamic programming
(4) AG_m×n=backtrack(DP)
//deletion operation for the global dynamic programming
     for any i where |{j|AG[i,j]==1}|>1
(5a)   AG[i,j]=0 if Sent_s,j is not in Sent_o,i's top x similar
     for any j where |{i|AG[i,j]==1}|>1
(5b)   AG[i,j]=0 if Sent_o,i is not in Sent_s,j's top x similar
//insertion operation for the global dynamic programming
     for any (Sent_o,i,Sent_s,j) in the top N similar
(6)    AG[i,j]=1 if CosSim(Sent_o,i,Sent_s,j) > threshold
     return {(i,j)|AG[i,j]==1}
```

Figure 4. Aligning sentences at run-time.

The algorithm initializes a $(m+1)$-by-$(n+1)$ matrix **DP** to store the optimal sentence alignment score. Specifically, $\mathbf{DP}[i+1,j+1]$ records the best score for aligning sentences between $Sent_{o,1},\ldots,Sent_{o,i}$ and $Sent_{s,1},\ldots,Sent_{s,j}$ (Step 2) where $1 \leq i \leq m$, the number of the sentences in Art_o, and $1 \leq j \leq n$, the number of the sentences in Art_s. Step (3a) and Step (3b) finds the word vector $\mathbf{W}_o=\{w_o\}$ of sentence $Sent_o$ and $\mathbf{W}_s=\{w_s\}$ of $Sent_s$ respectively. The word vectors are then used to estimate cosine-based sentence similarity:

$$CosSim(Sent_o, Sent_s) = \frac{\sum_{w \in \{w_o\} \cap \{w_s\}} \mathrm{KY}^2[w]}{\sqrt{\sum_{w_o} \mathrm{KY}^2[w_o] \times \sum_{w_s} \mathrm{KY}^2[w_s]}}$$

The cosine similarity is equipped with the knowledge of word keyness (i.e., **KY**) learned from the articles as in Section 2.2. Compared to the frequent sentence re-structuring and re-ordering, re-ordering of words in sentences seldom happens in simplification. In other words, words in the original sentences will be translated or simplified in order. As a result, word vectors contain words' relative positions in sentences, $posi(w)/|Sent|$ where absolute word positions are divided by sentential word lengths. And words' keyness scores are weighted by (1-*diff*) to consider the effort or travel distance needed to align words in sentences where *diff* is the absolute difference of the aligned words' relative word positions. Take the second sentence "*They aren't real animals, but statues dressed up as people.*" in the original article and the seventh sentence "*People made them.*" in the simplified in Figure 1 for example. The keyness of their common word "*people*" will be penalized by $(1-|11/12-1/4|)$ since long-distance word alignment should be discouraged. Note that Step (3c) implements this word position functionality to encourage short-distance word alignment and punctuations should re-set the absolute word position to accommodate splits of article sentences.

Intuitively, mapping content words in sentences is more important than mapping non-content words. Therefore, Step (3e) further weights sentence-level cosine similarity using the aligning ratio of content words in sentences, $AlignedRatio_{cw}$, computed as $2 \times |\mathbf{CW}_o \cap \mathbf{CW}_s| / (|\mathbf{CW}_o| + |\mathbf{CW}_s|)$ where the size of the common content words is divided by the sum of the size of the individual sentential content-word set. To allow for word changes, sentences' *CosSim* will only be penalized by $AlignedRatio_{cw}$ if their aligned content word ratio is below certain degree, which discourages the alignment of these sentences. Otherwise, *CosSim* will be left as it is.

Following (Gale and Church (1991)) and (Nelken and Shieber, 2006), Step (3e) computes the optimal alignment score for aligning $Sent_{o,1},\ldots,Sent_{o,i}$ and $Sent_{s,1},\ldots,Sent_{s,j}$ in global alignment dynamic programming. The optimal score is recursively hypothesized to come from **DP**[*i*,*j*], **DP**[*i*+1,*j*], and **DP**[*i*,*j*+1]. Step (4) backtracks and returns an **AG** matrix where **AG**[*i*,*j*] is on if the best sentence aligning result contains $Sent_{o,i}$ and $Sent_{s,j}$ pair.

Subsequently, we prune the complete path by discarding sentence pair ($Sent_{o,i}$,$Sent_{s,j}$) whenever $Sent_{o,i}$ (or $Sent_{s,j}$) has multiple alignments and $Sent_{s,j}$ (or $Sent_{o,i}$) is not in $Sent_{o,i}$'s (or $Sent_{s,j}$'s) top *x* similar sentences in Step (5a) (or Step (5b)). *x* is used to control the one-to-many and many-to-one alignments. For instance, if *x* is set to two, the algorithm only allows each original sentence to be split to two simplified sentences and vice versa.

On the other hand, since the gaps and re-orderings between sentence alignments are more prominent in monolingual setting than in bilingual, Step (6) is to recover some of the missing aligning points in the optimal complete path and acts as a straightforward insertion operation. It activates **AG**[*i*,*j*] if ($Sent_{o,i}$,$Sent_{s,j}$) is one of the *N* most similar sentence pairs among the $m \times n$ sentence pairs and its similarity exceeds a certain threshold.

Once the complete path has been constrained to 1-to-*x* and *x*-to-1 purer alignments and expanded by high-confident alignments, the aligning points are returned as the final result produced by the *KEA* system. An example sentence alignment for monolingual parallel articles on our working prototype is shown in Figure 1.

3 Experiments

KEA was designed to identify sentences that are likely to be parallel in monolingual article pairs. As such, *KEA* will be evaluated over alignment accuracy at sentence level. Since the goal of *KEA* is to leverage word significance in sentence alignment, different estimation strategies for word keyness will be compared. In this section, we first examine the parallel level of English Wikipedia and Simple English Wikipedia, the original-simplified article pairs commonly used by text simplification community (Section 3.1). Section 3.2 presents the details of training *KEA* for the evaluation. Finally, we report system performance with different settings concerning keyness estimation for words, aligned content word ratios in sentences, and offsets of relative aligned word positions in Section 3.3. Section 3.3 also shows the results of our pilot study as to the effect of our sentence-aligned parallel articles on language learning.

3.1 English and Simple Wikipedia

This section examines the parallel level of English Wikipedia (EW) and Simple English Wikipedia (SEW), a common article source for training simplification model (e.g., Zhu et al., 2010 and Woodsend and Lapata, 2011). We manage to see if articles on SEW are written based on their counterparts on EW and to see if articles on EW and SEW are actually translations of each other with different target audiences in mind where SEW with basic vocabulary and grammar aims for lay people.

With language links and image files from Wikipedia, we were able to find 183K article pairs between EW and SEW in October, 2013. To see their parallel-ity, we randomly chose 10 pairs and hand aligned them at sentence level. Table 1 summarizes the alignment result.

	# sent on EW (# sent aligned)	# sent on SEW (# sent aligned)
article pair 1	136(1)	2(1)
article pair 2	145(1)	7(1)
article pair 3	86(2)	16(2)
article pair 4	180(2)	6(3)
article pair 5	166(2)	12(4)
article pair 6	242(16)	53(16)
article pair 7	8(1)	4(1)
article pair 8	2(2)	2(2)
article pair 9	160(1)	3(1)
article pair 10	70(1)	1(1)

Table 1. Alignment results of the sampled EW and SEW article pairs.

In Table 1 we list the numbers of sentences in articles on EW and SEW and enclose in parentheses the number of sentences that are manually aligned to its SEW or EW counterparts. We observe that (1) the numbers of sentences of the EW and SEW article pairs vary a lot; (2) only a handful of sentences in EW articles are aligned to, or kept in, SEW sentences; (3) most of time, alignments happen only at the first few article sentences except for the identical EW and SEW articles in article pair 8 and the much more parallel article pair 6. Surprisingly, these article pairs may not be as parallel as one may think, and SEW articles are typically written on their own without referring to or seldom based on their EW counterparts.

Since our goal is to find sentence pairs in parallel articles which differ in readability, using English Wikipedia and Simple English Wikipedia may not be a good idea. Fortunately, there are monolingual *parallel* article pairs on the Web.

3.2 Training KEA

Based on the findings in Section 3.1, we collected (original) articles and their direct simplified counterparts, i.e., parallel articles, on the Web. English articles on websites NewsInLevels, BreakingNewsEnglish, and EasierEnglishWiki made up of our monolingual parallel corpus. These sites publish parallel news articles on daily or monthly basis and our current collection contains 607K words on the original side and 510K words on simplified.

100 article pairs were set aside and manually aligned for sentence alignment evaluation. This test set had 1,098 original and 1,285 simplified sentences. Specifically, there were 17K words in the testing original articles while there were 14K words in the simplified. Note that both training and testing article pairs were lemmatized and part-of-speech tagged by GENIA tagger from Tsujii lab (Tsuruoka and Tsujii, 2005).

3.3 Evaluation Results

In this section, we examine the effectiveness of *KEA*'s keyword-based weighting for aligning words, content-word alignment ratio, and offsets of relative aligning word positions, in monolingual sentence alignment (See Table 2).

	Precision	F-measure
KEA	85	83.9
KEA-WP	84.7	83.8
KEA-CW	83.4	83.1
TF*IDF	80	81.4

Table 2. Alignment performance (%).

Applied on monolingual parallel corpora, *KEA* with full capability outperforms the current state-of-the-art TF*IDF (Nelken and Shieber, 2006). Specifically, *KEA* further improves precision and f-measure relatively by 6.25% and 3%. Figure 5 shows a testing article pair's sentence alignment results done by TF*IDF and *KEA*. As we can see, although TF*IDF is a straightforward context-sensitive approach, it does not handle well with the two-word alignment between original sentence 1 and simplified sentence 1 (i.e., aligned words are "*mobile*" and "*phone*") and the two-word alignment between original sentence 3 and simplified sentence 2 (i.e., aligned words are "*they*" and "*with*"). By assigning keyword-based weights to words, *KEA* better distinguishes the importance of aligning "*mobile*" and "*phone*", and that of "*they*" and "*with*", in sentence pairs, and successfully identifies the alignment of (1,s1) and discards the alignment of (3,s2).

Original article:
(1) Mobile phones don't always work perfectly. (2) They can have a bad signal or a dying battery and they can make us very angry. (3) In Finland 12 years ago, they came up with a new idea. (4) They started to throw their phones as far as possible not only to make themselves feel better but also in the name of sports. (5) People from all over the world met for this year's event and one man from Finland threw his mobile phone 101 metres. (6) He was the winner. (7) He didn't practise much before the event. (8) He spent the day before in the pub.

Simplified article:
(s1) Mobile phones have sometimes problems. (s2) They have a bad signal or a bad battery and we are not happy with them. (s3) In Finland 12 years ago, they had a new idea. (s4) They started to throw their mobile phones. (s5) They tried to throw the phones very far. (s6) People from many countries met this year again. (s7) They threw the mobile phones again. (s8) The best man was from Finland. (s9) He threw his mobile phone 101 metres. (s10) He didn't train for this moment because he was in the pub.

(a) Alignments by TF*IDF: (2,s2), (3,s2), (3,s3), (4,s4), (4,s5), (5,s6), (5,s9), (7,s10), (8,s10)

(b) Alignments by *KEA*: (1,s1), (2,s2), (3,s3), (4,s4), (4,s5), (5,s6), (5,s9), (7,s10), (8,s10)

Figure 5. Alignment results of a testing article pair done by (a) TF*IDF (b) *KEA*.

In addition, Table 2 indicates that differences of relative positions of aligned words (i.e., *KEA* minus WP) and percentages of aligned content words with flexibility of vocabulary change (i.e., *KEA* minus CW) both plays a role in aligning sentences. Content-word alignment ratio, clearly, is a much more important feature in boosting alignment accuracy.

A pilot study, on the other hand, was conducted to see if monolingual parallel articles aligned at sentence level can help readers understand original articles better than given article pairs with different readability. In this study, an English professor was asked to set multiple-choice reading comprehension exam paper for two of our testing article pairs. And a class of 16 college students learning English as a second language participated and was divided into two groups: one reading original articles and their simplified counterparts (i.e., control group) and the other reading the sentence-aligned article pairs (i.e., experimental group). Promisingly, our sentence alignment information helps the language learners. The experimental group outperforms the control relatively by 27.5% (51% vs. 40%) in reading comprehension test. Also, post-experiment survey indicates 85% of the participants found our sentence-aligned article pairs helpful in understanding the original or difficult articles.

Overall, we are modest to say that *KEA* can extract parallel sentences from monolingual articles more accurately than the current state-of-the-art, by identifying key words for alignment, and that *KEA* can yield original-to-simplified sentence pairs that are beneficial to language learners in article understanding or language learning.

4 Related Work

Sentence alignment has been regarded as an important first step for bilingual translation or monolingual translation/simplification. In our work we address an aspect of monolingual sentence alignment. More specifically, we focus on the first part of text simplification (Siddharthan, 2010; Zhu et al., 2010; Woodsend and Lapata, 2011; Biran et al., 2011), namely monolingual sentence alignment (MSA) on parallel articles.

The research in MSA starts in summarization. For example, Marcu (1999) leverages cosine measure to estimate sentence similarity while Jing (2002) uses Hidden Markov Model for sentence and summary matching. Hatzivassiloglou et al's SimFinder (1999; 2001), on the other hand, exploits word overlap and matching nouns to align sentences in multi-document summary.

Recent work has been using context information in MSA. Barzilay and Elhadad (2003) exploit inter-document topical sub-structures in Encyclopedia entries. Nelken and Shieber (2006) describe how to use sentence-based TF*IDF to weight aligned words. And their work has been suggested as the current state-of-the-art monolingual sentence aligner (Nelken and Shieber, 2006; Zhu et al., 2010).

In contrast to the previous research, we consider word keyness in aligning words during sentence alignment. The famous keyword extraction algorithm, PageRank (Mihalcea and Tarau, 2004; Padmanabhan et al., 2005; Liu et al., 2010; Zhao et al., 2011), is used to weight words and to favor the aligning of essential words in sentences. Word keyness, weighted by ratios of aligned content words and offsets of aligned relative word positions, is integrated into a global dynamic programming to identify parallel sentences in monolingual articles.

5 Summary and Future Work

We have introduced a method for learning to differentiate key words in sentence alignment on monolingual parallel articles, the very first step for text simplification. The method involves estimating word keyness based on TF*IDF and semantic PageRank, weighting keyword-based sentence-level cosine similarity via percentages of content word alignment and differences of relative positions of aligned word, and identifying parallel sentences using a global dynamic programming with deletion and insertion operations. We have implemented and evaluated the method as applied to monolingual sentence alignment and language learning. In the evaluation, we have shown that the method outperforms the current state-of-the-art in both alignment accuracy and f-measure, and that language learners benefit from our sentence-aligned monolingual parallel articles in reading comprehension test.

Many avenues exist for future research and improvement of our system. For example, we would like to see if we can boost simplification systems' performance using our better-aligned parallel sentences. And we would like to examine the possibility of employing such keyword concept to determine articles' good simplified versions. Yet another interesting direction to explore is to fully examine the possibility of using our aligned original and simplified sentence pairs for educational purposes.

Acknowledgement

This study is conducted under the "Online and Offline integrated Smart Commerce Platform (1/4)" of the Institute for Information Industry which is subsidized by the Ministry of Economy Affairs of the Republic of China.

References

Regina Barzilay and Noemie Elhadad. 2003. Sentence alignment for monolingual comparable corpora. In *Proceedings of the EMNLP*.

Or Biran, Samuel Brody, and Noemie Elhadad. 2011. Putting it simply: a context-aware approach to lexical simplification. In *Proceedings of the ACL*, pages 496-501.

William Gale and Kenneth Church. 1991. A program for aligning sentences in bilingual corpora. In *Proceedings of the ACL*.

Vasileios Hatzivassiloglou, Judith Klavans, and Eleazar Eskin. 1999. Detecting text similarity over short passages: exploring linguistic feature combinations via machine learning. In *Proceedings of the EMNLP*.

Vasileios Hatzivassiloglou, Judith Klavans, Melissa Holcombe, Regina Barzilay, Min-Yen Kan, and Kathleen McKeown. 2001. SIMFINDER: a flexible clustering tool for summarization. In *Proceedings of the Workshop on Automatic Summarization*, pages 41-49.

Hongyan Jing. 2002. Using hidden Markov modeling to decompose human-written summaries. *Computational Linguistics*, 28(4):527-543.

Zhiyuan Liu, Wenyi Huang, Yabin Zheng, and Maosong Sun. 2010. Automatic keyphrase extraction via topic decomposition. In *Proceedings of the EMNLP*, pages 366-376.

Daniel Marcu. 1999. The automatic construction of large-scale corpora for summarization research. In *Proceedings of the SIGIR*.

Rada Mihalcea and Paul Tarau. 2004. TextRank: Bringing orders into texts. In *Proceedings of the EMNLP*, pages 404-411.

Rani Nelken and Stuart M. Shieber. 2006. Towards robust context-sensitive sentence alignment for monolingual corpora. In *Proceedings of the EACL*, pages 161-168.

Divya Padmanabhan, Prasanna Desikan, Jaideep Srivastava, and Kashif Riaz. 2005. WICER: a weighted inter-cluster edge ranking for clustered graphs. In *Proceedings of the IEEE/WIC/ACM WI*, pages 522-528.

Advaith Siddharthan. 2010. Complex lexico-syntactic reformulation of sentences using typed dependency representations. In *Proceedings of the INLG*, pages 125-133.

Yoshimasa Tsuruoka and Jun'ichi Tsujii. 2005. Bidirectional inference with the easiest-first strategy for tagging sequence data. In *Proceedings of the EMNLP*, pages 467-474.

Kristian Woodsend and Mirella Lapata. 2011. Learning to simplify sentences with quasi-synchronous grammar and integer programming. In *Proceedings of the EMNLP*, pages 409-420.

Wayne Xin Zhao, Jing Jiang, Jing He, Yang Song, Palakorn Achananuparp, Ee-Peng Lim, and Xiaoming Li. 2011. Topical keyword extraction from Twitter. In *Proceedings of the ACL*, pages 379-388.

Zhemin Zhu, Delphine Bernhard, and Iryna Gurevych. 2010. A monolingual tree-based translation model for sentence simplification. In *Proceedings of the Coling*, pages 1353-1361.

Automatic Detection of Comma Splices

John Lee, Chak Yan Yeung
Halliday Centre for Intelligent Applications of Language Studies
Department of Linguistics and Translation
City University of Hong Kong
jsylee@cityu.edu.hk
chak.yeung@my.cityu.edu.hk

Martin Chodorow
Department of Psychology
Hunter College
City University of New York
martin.chodorow@hunter.cuny.edu

Abstract

In English text, independent clauses should be demarcated with full-stops (periods), or linked together with conjunctions. Non-native speakers are often prone to linking them improperly with commas instead of conjunctions, producing comma splices. This paper describes a method to detect comma splices using Conditional Random Fields (CRF), with features derived from parse tree patterns. In experiments, our model achieved an average of 0.91 precision and 0.28 recall in detecting comma splices, significantly outperforming both a baseline model using only local features and a widely used commercial grammar checker.

1 Introduction

English text consists of a sequence of clauses linked and separated by punctuation and conjunctions. To separate two independent clauses, one uses a full-stop (period); to link together two related clauses, one typically uses a semicolon or a comma with an appropriate conjunction, which can be either coordinate ("and", "but", "or") or subordinate ("because", "so"). For example, to link the two related clauses "it was raining" and "we stayed home", one may use a comma and the conjunction "so", yielding the complex sentence "It was raining, so we stayed home". When a comma is used instead of a full-stop, or when it is used without a conjunction (e.g., "It was raining, we stayed home"), the result is a comma splice[1].

Our use of the term comma splice also includes improper linking of verb phrases. This occurs when a comma is used without a conjunction (e.g., "We stayed home, watched TV."); without a relative pronoun (e.g., "The boy chased after the rat, fled into the sewer"); or with the wrong verb form (e.g., "Waterborne pathogens are the pathogenic microorganisms, includes bacteria"). Comma splices are not only considered poor writing style, but they also compromise the readability of a text.

Although native speakers have been found to commit a substantial number of common splice errors (Connors and Lunsford, 1988; Lunsford and Lunsford, 2008), non-native speakers appear to be especially prone to producing them, possibly due to interference from syntactic differences in L1 (Tseng and Liou, 2006; Bennui, 2008; Rahimi, 2009). This may be especially true for L1s where comma splices are frequently found and are not considered mistakes, such as in Chinese (Lin, 2002). Comma splices are one of the errors addressed in the 2014 CoNLL Shared Task on Grammatical Error Correction (Ng et al., 2014). They are annotated in many learner corpora, including the NUS Corpus of Learner English (Dahlmeier et al., 2013) and the EF-Cambridge Open Language Database (Geertzen et al., 2013).

This paper addresses the task of detecting comma splices. We report human agreement in detecting these errors and propose a CRF model to automatically detect them. Our best model, which uses features derived from parse trees produced by the Stanford parser (Klein and Manning, 2003), significantly outperforms both a baseline that does not consider

[1] Note that a list of noun phrases with a missing conjunction (e.g., "I like apples, oranges.") is not a comma splice.

Copyright 2014 by John Lee, Chak Yan Yeung, and Martin Chodorow
28th Pacific Asia Conference on Language, Information and Computation pages 551–560

syntactic information and a widely used commercial grammar checker.

Recently, there has been much effort in developing writing assistance systems that can automatically correct errors in text written by non-native speakers. Such systems focus mostly on word or phrase-level errors, such as the misuse of articles (Han et al., 2006), prepositions (Tetreault et al., 2010) and verbs (Tajiri et al., 2012). Although these errors do involve long-distance grammatical constructions, this paper is the first report of a research effort to address the improper linking of clauses, a sentence-level error.

Our ultimate goal, after detecting a comma splice, is to automatically correct it. We will, however, not treat the correction task here because it concerns a host of other issues, such as automatic analysis of style, to choose between splitting the comma splice into two sentences ("It was raining. We stayed home.") and conjoining them ("It was raining, so we stayed home"), as well as inference of discourse relations (Marcu and Echihabi, 2002), to choose an appropriate conjunction (e.g., use of "so" rather than "because" in the above example).

The rest of the paper is organized as follows. After reviewing previous research in related areas (section 2), we describe our approach for comma splice detection (section 3). We then describe our datasets, report on human agreement and experimental results (section 4), followed by our conclusions (section 5).

2 Previous work

A comma splice may be the result of a misuse of punctuation (comma instead of full-stop), a misuse of verb form (finite instead of participle), or a missing conjunction. Hence, our work can draw on previous research on detecting and correcting punctuation, verb and conjunction errors.

Automatic punctuation restoration had originally been applied on output of automatic speech recognition systems (Stolcke and Shriberg, 1996; Huang and Zweig, 2002), but has more recently been expanded to written text (Gravano et al., 2009; Baldwin and Joseph, 2009). These techniques can be used to detect fused sentences, which result "when a writer puts no mark of punctuation and no coordinating conjunction between independent clauses" (Hacker and Sommers, 2011), a phenomenon also common to ESL writers but distinct from comma splices.

A more related task is the correction of comma usage, an error type that ranks first in ESL writing (Donahue, 2001). The task of inserting missing commas and deleting unnecessary ones has been approached as a sequence labelling problem (Israel et al., 2012), where each space between words was considered by a CRF model to determine whether a comma should be present. Features such as POS, bi-grams, and distances to the nearest conjunctions were effective and these will form the basis of our baseline model. The comma errors addressed in Israel et al. (2012), however, are distinct from ours. Instead of adding in missing commas or deleting unnecessary ones, our focus is on the improper linking of clauses that manifests as wrongly used commas, which cannot be fixed by simply removing them.

Work by Lee and Seneff (2008) on correcting the misuse of verb forms is relevant to detecting comma splice errors that involve participles. They found that verb form errors result in predictable irregularities in parse trees which can be used as cues for error detection. We follow their approach of using parse tree patterns, but will incorporate these patterns in a machine learning framework rather than a rule-based system.

We are not aware of any previous work on detecting or restoring missing conjunctions, but this task is implicitly or explicitly performed by four existing systems that give feedback about comma splices. The Criterion Online Writing Service (Burstein et al., 2004) identifies errors, including comma splices, in student essays and suggests possible corrections. Grammarly[2] scans a paragraph of text and suggests "punctuation between clauses" when comma splices are detected. WhiteSmoke[3] underlines the problematic comma and suggests that it should be replaced with either a full-stop or a semi-colon. The grammar checker embedded in Microsoft Word, perhaps the most widely used system, also gives feedback about comma splices. To the best of our knowledge, the first three do not explicitly consider parse tree patterns; we will evaluate our approach against the

[2]www.grammarly.com
[3]www.whitesmoke.com

fourth.

In addition to these four, a number of writing assistance systems have also been built for the two *Helping Our Own* shared tasks (Dale and Kilgarriff, 2011; Dale et al., 2012) and two *CoNLL* shared tasks (Ng et al., 2013; Ng et al., 2014). Run-on sentences and comma splices were among the 28 error types introduced in the CoNLL-2014 shared task (Ng et al., 2014). Among teams that tackled individual error types, none addressd run-on sentences and comma splices. Among teams that attempted to correct all error types, many obtained good results for word- and phrase-level errors, but none achieved any recall for run-on errors and comma splices.

3 Approach

We cast comma splice detection as a sequence labeling task, using a linear-chain CRF as our model. Each comma in a sentence is to be tagged as `T[rue]` (it is a comma splice) or `F[alse]` (it is not). Consider the sentence "Then, he chased after the rat, fled into the sewer, and died." It should be labeled as `FTF`, since only the second comma constitutes a comma splice (the relative pronoun "which" should follow the comma). In our datasets, consecutive comma splices are relatively uncommon; this preference can be captured by transition features in the linear-chain CRF.

Table 1 shows our list of features. The baseline features replicate those in (Israel et al., 2012); there are then four "clause features" indicating linguistics characteristics of the neighboring clauses[4], but without considering syntactic parse trees; finally, there are five features derived from parse tree patterns.

3.1 Baseline features

Our baseline features include the first word in the clause preceding the comma and the two words to the left and right of the comma, together with their POS and a combined feature with both the word and its POS. We also include the word and POS bigrams of the tokens to the left and right of the comma. In addition, there are four distance features: the number of tokens in the clauses preceding and following the comma, and the distances from the comma to the nearest conjunction to its left and right. All of these can be obtained without syntactic parsing.

3.2 Clause features

We identified four additional features that help prevent the system from flagging the commas around non-restrictive clauses as comma splices (e.g., "The powder diffractometer, Siemens D500, was used in this experiment."; and "The insurance industry, however, is now suffering."), thereby reducing the number of false positives. These features include the number of nouns/pronouns in the clauses preceding and following the comma, and two binary features that indicate whether the clauses contain any verbs. We selected these features because the addition of non-restrictive clauses in the middle of the sentences often results in segments of words without verbs or nouns.

3.3 Parse features

When a sentence contains two or more improperly joined clauses, its parse tree will be "disturbed" because the missing linkage prevents the parser from properly processing the clauses after the first comma. We identified several parse patterns that are characteristic of comma splices, as shown in Table 2.

A comma splice may consist of two improperly joined clauses (e.g., "It was raining, we stayed home"), which tend to produce a parse tree with an S, followed by the comma, an NP and a VP to its right (Pattern S+NP+VP)[5]. Three or more improperly joined clauses (e.g., "The pink shirt is $20, black skirt is $18, dark pant is $15.") tend to result in a parse tree with multiple S siblings (Pattern S+S). A comma splice may also involve improperly joined VPs (e.g., "It can help salesperson to promote up-sales and cross sales, provide better services."), which tend to produce a parse tree with two VP siblings immediately below another VP (Pattern VP+VP). In addition, two binary features for partial pattern matches are included: whether there is an S in the clause to the left of the comma, and whether

[4]We use the term 'clause' here to refer to all words between the comma and the nearest comma to its left or right.

[5]This pattern also appears when the first half of the sentence is a participial phrase that modifies the rest of the sentence. The pattern is therefore ignored if the sentence begins with either a present participle or a past participle.

there is an NP followed by a VP in the clause to the right.

Accurate extraction of parse features depends on the quality of the parse trees, but non-native errors in the sentence often cause the parser to produce unexpected tree patterns (Foster et al., 2008), hence causing noise in the parse tree features. In general, parsers perform better on shorter sentences. To reduce this kind of interference, therefore, we remove those parts of the sentence that cannot contain comma splices.

Unlike the task of sentence compression for summarization (Knight and Marcu, 2000; Filippova and Strube, 2008), we do not need to preserve important words or the meaning of the original sentence. Rather, we aim to preserve the phrases in the sentence that can potentially result in comma splices and strip away the rest so that the parser has the best chance to produce the expected parse patterns.

Specifically, using the parse tree of the original sentence, we remove (1) introductory phrases at the beginning of a sentence, which include transition phrases such as "for example", as well as prepositional phrases and adverbials[6]; (2) clauses that are properly connected to the rest of the sentence by a coordinate conjunction; (3) subordinate clauses that are properly connected to the rest of a sentence by subordinate conjunctions or relative pronouns; and (4) dialogue tags such as "he claimed" or "he argued"[7]. The simplified sentence is then re-parsed before feature extraction.

4 Experiments

We first describe our datasets (sections 4.1 and 4.2) and report on the human agreement on comma splices (section 4.3), and then we discuss our experimental results (section 4.4).

4.1 Training Set

We automatically produced training data from the Penn Treebank (Marcus et al., 1993). While in-domain training data is likely to yield better performance, we chose to use only general-domain training data in our experiments so as to provide a realistic estimate of system performance on arbitrary learner text.

Similar to (Foster and Andersen, 2009), we artificially introduced comma splices into the text by removing conjunctions and relative pronouns to the right of commas. To ensure that the generated sen-

Feature	Example
Baseline features	
Left words	raining, was
Left POS	VBG, VBD
Left combo	raining_VBG, was_VBD
Right words	we, stayed
Right POS	PRP, VBD
Right combo	we_PRP, stayed_VBD
First word in left clause	it
First POS in left clause	PRP
First combo in left clause	it_PRP
Left word bigram	was_raining
Right word bigram	we_stayed
Left POS bigram	VBD_VBG
Right POS bigram	PRP_VBD
# tokens in left clause	3
# tokens in right clause	3
Distance to nearest left conjunction	-
Distance to nearest right conjunction	-
Clause features	
# nouns/pronouns in left clause	1
# nouns/pronouns in right clause	2
has verb in left clause	yes
has verb in right clause	yes
Parse features	
Pattern S+S	no
Pattern S+NP+VP	yes
Pattern VP+VP	no
S in left clause	yes
NP and VP in right clause	yes

Table 1: List of features. Example values for each feature are drawn from the comma of the sentence "It was raining, we stayed home".

[6]The list of phrases are taken from http://www.msu.edu/user/jdowell/135/transw.html

[7]We used a list of 292 verbs that are the hyponyms of the words "express" and "convey" in WordNet 3.0 (Miller, 1995).

Feature	Pattern	Example
Pattern S+NP+VP	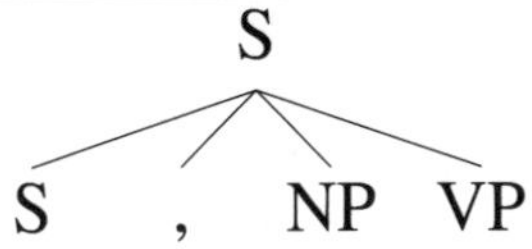	^{S}[It was raining], ^{NP}[we] ^{VP}[stayed home.]
Pattern S+S	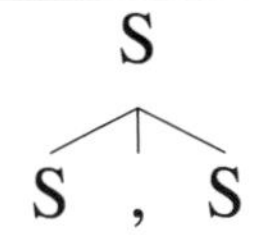	^{S}[The pink shirt is \$20], ^{S}[black skirt is \$18], ^{S}[dark pant is \$15].
Pattern VP+VP	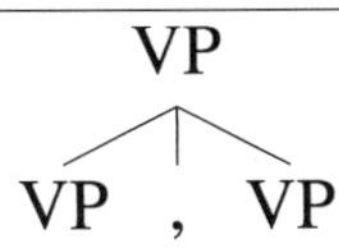	It can help salesperson ^{VP}[to ^{VP}[promote up-sales and cross sales] , ^{VP}[provide better services]].

Table 2: Parse tree patterns distinctive of comma splices, illustrated with examples.

tence is a comma splice, we need to ensure that the removed conjunction or relative pronoun was serving as the link between two clauses or verb phrases. For this purpose, we manually identified several parse patterns. In the parse tree, a conjunction and the elements that it joins together are always on the same level — the level of coordination (Bies et al., 1995). We looked to the right of the conjunctions in the trees and only removed those that were followed by either an "S" or a "VP". Relative clauses are adjoined to the head noun phrase, and both the relative pronoun and the clause are put inside the SBAR level. We removed only those relative pronouns that were followed by either an "S" or a "VP" and with an "SBAR" parent, which in turn had an "NP" parent. For example, the "and" was removed in the sentence "Mr. Katzenstein would have learned something, and it's possible Mr. Morita would have too.", and the relative pronoun "which" was removed in the sentence "Cray Research is transferring about $53 million in assets, primarily those related to the Cray-3 development, which has been a drain on Cray Research 's earnings.".

Another way to create a comma splice is to fuse two sentences together and replace the full-stop of the first sentence with a comma. However, comma splices introduced with this method do not reflect well the actual mistakes that English learners make, especially in terms of lexical features. For example, we observed that it is more common for comma splices to occur before pronouns than before proper nouns in the students' writing, but it would not be the case for the sentences created with this method. Therefore, we did not include comma splices introduced by fusing sentences together.

Out of 13159 instances of commas, this method yielded 2775 comma splices.

4.2 Test Sets

Although run-on sentences and comma splices were among the 28 error types introduced in the CoNLL-2014 shared task (Ng et al., 2014), the test set used in the task only contained about 26 such errors, and is therefore too small for our purpose. We evaluated our system on two test sets[8]: the learner corpus at City University of Hong Kong (Lee and Webster, 2012) (henceforth, the "CityU Set") and the EF-Cambridge Open Language Database (Geertzen et al., 2013) (henceforth, the "Cambridge Set").

CityU Set. The learner corpus at City University of Hong Kong consists of academic writing by university students, most of whom are native speakers of Chinese. Three of the error categories in this corpus are concerned with comma splices — "new sentence", "conjunction missing" and "missing relative pronoun". We randomly selected 550 sentences that are marked with one of these three categories: 215 with "new sentences", 215 with "conjunction missing", and 120 with "missing relative pronoun". Not every sentence marked with these categories is

[8]In another potential source of data, the NUCLE corpus (Dahlmeier et al., 2013), the annotation for comma splices is non-exhaustive, and would require additional human annotation to measure precision.

a comma splice since the error tags cover other error types as well, e.g., fused sentences, missing conjunctions for NPs, missing complementizer "that", etc. Human annotation (section 4.3) is therefore necessary to tell these apart. We also randomly selected 300 sentences from the corpus that are not marked with any of the three categories, with the sole constraint that their average length be similar to those of the marked sentences. Among the 1247 commas in these sentences, 235 were marked by at least one of the annotators as comma splices. Among sentences with comma splices, most contain only one; only about 10% contain two or more.

Cambridge Set. The Cambridge Set consists of writing submitted by language learners to an online school of EF Education First. The database has been partially error-annotated and the error category "New sentence" covers most comma splices. We used the writing by Chinese students, totaling 1.3 million words. Unfortunately, the annotation for run-on errors is not exhaustive, so human annotation was needed.

We selected a subset of 400 sentences marked with the "New sentence" error in the corpus and 400 unmarked sentences for annotation. This subset contains 2206 commas, of which 951 were marked as comma splices by one of the human annotators.

4.3 Human agreement

We asked two annotators, one a native speaker of English and the other a near-native speaker, to identify comma splices in 850 sentences drawn from the CityU Set. We first measured the agreement between the annotators on whether a sentence contained a comma splice, without regard to the location. The kappa was 0.90. Next, we investigated how often the annotators agreed on the location of the comma splice. Using one annotator as the gold standard, the precision is 91% and the recall is 92%. Most disagreements involve two consecutive commas enclosing a subordinate phrase, e.g., the phrase headed by "because" in the sentence "The most time consuming part is to purchase components, because most of the components were not sold in Hong Kong, it was need to purchase them in Mainland China". One annotator, attaching the "because" phrase to the preceding clause, identified the first comma as a comma splice; the other annotator, attaching the "because" phrase to the following clause, identified the second comma as a comma splice.

On the Cambridge Set, we measured the agreement between the annotator and original annotations in the corpus. Using the original annotations as the gold standard, the recall of the annotator is 0.91. Most disagreements involve the treatment of informal language. For example, the annotator considered it acceptable to use a comma in the sentence "I can cook dinner for you, please buy something for me." while the original annotation changed the comma to a full-stop.

4.4 Baselines

We evaluated two baseline systems in our experiments. First, we trained a CRF model on the Penn Treebank (section 4.1) with the baseline features. We computed a second baseline using the grammar checker in Microsoft Word 2013. We configured Microsoft Word's grammar checker to capture all error types and inspected each comma that the checker marked as a mistake, then compared the commas it flagged with our results. Two of Word's error types are relevant to our experiment: "Comma splice" and "Comma use". In the first case, the grammar checker would flag the comma as "Comma splice" and suggest that it be replaced with a semi-colon. In the second case, the grammar check would highlight the clauses before and after the comma, and suggest that an "and" should be added after it.

4.5 Results

We used CRF++ (Kudo, 2005) in our experiments. In our CRF model with the full feature set (Table 1), the parse features were extracted both from the sentences and from the output of the Stanford parser (Klein and Manning, 2003). Following (Israel et al., 2012), we used a filter that required the classifier to be at least 90% confident in a positive decision before flagging the comma as a comma splice. We adopted the evaluation metric used in the CoNLL-2014 shared task, $F_{0.5}$, which emphasize precision twice as much as recall because it is important to minimize false alarms for language learners[9].

[9] $F_{0.5}$ is calculated by $F_{0.5} = (1 + 0.5^2) \times R \times P / (R + 0.5^2 \times P)$ for recall R and precision P.

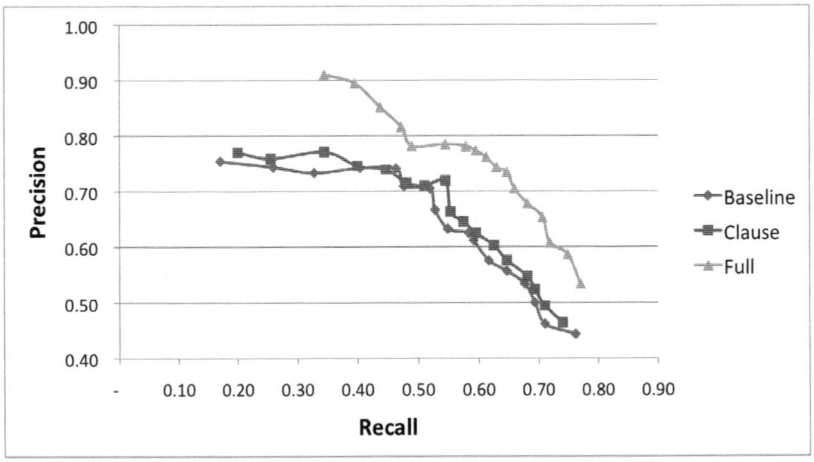

Figure 1: The precisions and recalls of the baseline, clause, and full system on the CityU Set when the probability threshold was decreased from 0.9 to 0.1 with a 0.05 interval.

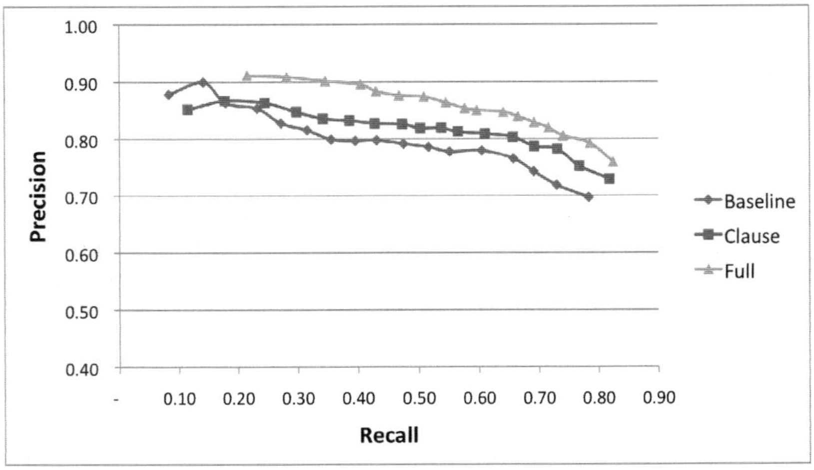

Figure 2: The precisions and recalls of the baseline, clause, and full system on the Cambridge Set when the probability threshold was decreased from 0.9 to 0.1 with a 0.05 interval.

On cross-validation of the training set, our baseline system achieved 0.82 precision, 0.29 recall and an F-measure of 0.60. The inclusion of clause features yielded 0.78 precision, 0.30 recall and an F-measure of 0.59 while the full system yielded 0.87 precision, 0.45 recall and an F-measure of 0.73.

The results for the test sets are shown in Table 3. On the CityU Set, our baseline system achieved 0.75 precision, 0.17 recall and an $F_{0.5}$ of 0.45; it performed better on the Cambridge Set, at 0.88 precision, 0.08 recall and an $F_{0.5}$ of 0.30. The Microsoft Word grammar checker achieved similar results as the baseline system on the CityU set, but outperformed it on the Cambridge Set, at 0.90 precision, 0.13 recall and $F_{0.5}$ of 0.41.

The clause features improved upon the baseline system in recall on both sets, at 0.20 for the CityU Set and 0.11 for the Cambridge Set. In terms of precision, they improved performance on the CityU set (0.77), but were unhelpful for the Cambridge set (0.85).

The full system improved upon the two baselines and the clause system in both precision and recall, performing at 0.91 precision, 0.34 recall and an $F_{0.5}$ of 0.69 for the CityU set; and slightly lower, at 0.91 precision, 0.22 recall and an $F_{0.5}$ of 0.55, for the Cambridge set. All these improvements are statistically significant[10].

On both test sets, many of the errors were due to sentences with non-standard vocabulary and real-word spelling errors. such as misspelling "maybe" as "may be", or "besides" as "beside". Both phenomena can yield an unexpected parse tree, causing a missed parse pattern.

For the CityU set, performance was hurt by the structurally more complicated sentences. The system failed to flag comma splices that involve three or more clauses, i.e., "S_1, S_2, S_3", where both "S_1, S_2" and "S_2, S_3" would form perfectly correct sentences (e.g., "The most time consuming part is to purchase components, because most of the components were not sold in Hong Kong, it was need to purchase them in Mainland China").

Performance on the Cambridge Set was helped by shorter and structurally simpler sentences, which resulted in more accurate parsing, but was hurt by the presence of many consecutive comma splices (e.g., "He is student, he is always wearing school uniform, my name is Songlin.") and unconventional use of conjunctions such as beginning a sentence with "but", which are rare in the training data. The Cambridge Set also contained plenty of informal sentences, for which the rules concerning the use of commas are less rigid. For example, while the system marked the sentence "Hi granny, my name is Winky." as a comma splice, the annotators did not because using a comma in this situation is commonly acceptable.

→ Corpus	CityU Set	Cambridge Set
↓ System	P/R/$F_{0.5}$	P/R/$F_{0.5}$
Full	0.91/0.34/0.69	0.91/0.22/0.55
Clause	0.77/0.20/0.49	0.85/0.11/0.37
Baseline	0.75/0.17/0.45	0.88/0.08/0.30
MS Word	0.74/0.15/0.41	0.90/0.13/0.41

Table 3: Precision, recall and F-measure for comma splice detection. "Baseline" refers to the CRF model trained only on the baseline features (Table 1). "Clause" refers to the CRF model that uses both baseline features and clause features. "Full" uses the full feature set. "MS Word" refers to the grammar checker embedded in Microsoft Word 2013.

[10]At $p <= 0.05$ by McNemar's test.

4.6 Precision-Recall Trade-off

The precision-recall balance can be adjusted based on the probability threshold above which a comma is flagged as a comma splice. Figures 1 and 2 show the degree to which precision can be traded off for recall by using different thresholds. For example, when a threshold of 0.65 was used, the precision of the full system on the CityU set dropped to 0.79 while recall rose to above 0.5.

On both test sets, the precision and recall of the full system are consistently higher than the baseline and clause systems. The drop in precision for the CityU set is steeper than that of the Cambridge set. This may be because the sentences in the CityU set are generally more complicated than those in the Cambridge set. In order for the system to perform with a high precision, a greater degree of recall has to be sacrificed.

5 Conclusion

We have introduced a new task — detection of comma splices, a common mistake made by non-native speakers in English writing — and have shown a high level of agreement among human annotators.

We have also applied a CRF model to comma splice detection. Our best system uses parse tree-based features and achieved an average of 0.91 precision and 0.28 recall. It significantly outperformed a baseline system that does not consider syntactic features, and a widely used commercial grammar checker.

In future work, we aim to further raise detection accuracy by improving parser robustness, and to tackle the task of suggesting repairs for comma splices.

Acknowledgments

The work described in this paper was supported by a Strategic Research Grant (Project No. 7008166) from City University of Hong Kong.

References

Timothy Baldwin and Manuel Paul Anil Kumar Joseph. 2009. Restoring Punctuation and Casing in English

Text. *Proc. Australasian Conference on Artificial Intelligence.*

Pairote Bennui. 2008. A study of L1 interference in the writing of Thai EFL students. *Malaysian Journal of ELT Research* 4:72–102.

Ann Bies, Mark Ferguson, Karen Katz, and Robert MacIntyre. 1995. Bracketing guidelines for Treebank II style Penn Treebank project. *Technical Report*, University of Pennsylvania.

Jill Burstein, Martin Chodorow, and Claudia Leacock. 2004. Automated Essay Evaluation: the Criterion Online Writing Service. *AI Magazine*.

Robert Connors and Andrea Lunsford. 1988. Frequency of Formal Errors in Current College Writing, or Ma and Pa Kettle do Research. *College Composition and Communication* 39(4).

Daniel Dahlmeier, Hwee Tou Ng, and Siew Mei Wu. 2013. Building a Large Annotated Corpus of Learner English: The NUS Corpus of Learner English. *Proc. 8th Workshop on Innovative Use of NLP for Building Educational Applications.*

Robert Dale and Adam Kilgarriff. 2011. Helping Our Own: The HOO 2011 pilot shared task. *Proc. 13th European Workshop on Natural Language Generation*, p.242–249.

Robert Dale, Ilya Anisimoff, and George Narroway. 2012. HOO 2012: A report on the preposition and determiner error correction shared task. *Proc. 7th Workshop on the Innovative Use of NLP for Building Educational Applications*, pages 54–62.

Steven Donahue. 2001. Formal errors: Mainstream and ESL students. Presented at the *2001 Conference of Two-Year College Association (TYCA).*

Katja Filippova and Michael Strube. 2008. Dependency tree based sentence compression. *Proc. Fifth International Natural Language Generation Conference* pp. 25–32.

Jennifer Foster, Joachim Wagner, and Josef van Genabith. 2008. Adapting a WSJ-trained parser to grammatically noisy text. *Proc. ACL.*

Jennifer Foster and Oistein E. Andersen. 2009. GenERRate: generating errors for use in grammatical error detection. *Proc. Fourth Workshop on Innovative Use of NLP for Building Educational Applications.*

Jeroen Geertzen, Theodora Alexopoulou, and Anna Korhonen. 2013. Automatic linguistic annotation of large scale L2 databases: The EF-Cambridge Open Language Database (EFCAMDAT). *Proc. 31st Second Language Research Forum (SLRF).*

Agustin Gravano, Martin Jansche, and Martin Bachiani. 2009. Restoring Punctuation and Capitalization in Transcribed Speech. *Proc. IEEE International Conference on Acoustics, Speech and Signal Processing (ICASSP).*

D. Hacker and N. Sommers. 2011. *Rules for writers.* Macmillan.

Na-Rae Han, Martin Chodorow, and Claudia Leacock. 2006. Detecting Errors in English Article Usage by Non-Native Speakers. *Natural Language Engineering*, 12(2).

Jing Huang and Geoffrey Zweig. 2002. Maximum entropy model for punctuation annotation from speech. *Proc. ICSLP* p. 917–920.

Dan Klein and Christopher D. Manning. 2003. Accurate Unlexicalized Parsing. *Proc. ACL.*

Kevin Knight and Daniel Marcu. 2000. Statistics-based summarization-step one: Sentence compression. *Proc. National Conference on Artificial Intelligence* pp. 703–710.

Ross Israel, Joel Tetreault and Martin Chodorow. 2012. Correcting Comma Errors in Learner Essays, and Restoring Commas in Newswire Text. *Proc. NAACL.*

Taku Kudo. 2005. CRF++: Yet another CRF toolkit. Obtained from http://crfpp.sourceforge.net.

John Lee and Stephanie Seneff. 2008. Correcting Misuse of Verb Forms. *Proc. ACL.*

John Lee and Jonathan Webster. 2012. A Corpus of Textual Revisions in Second Language Writing. *Proc. ACL.*

F. Y. Lin. 2002. Preferred structures in Chinese-English translation. Master's thesis, National Changhua University of Education, Taiwan.

Andrea A. Lunsford and Karen J. Lunsford. 2008. Mistakes are a Fact of Life: A National Comparative Study. *College Composition and Communication* 59(4):781–806.

Daniel Marcu and Abdessamad Echihabi. 2002. An Unsupervised Approach to Recognizing Discourse Relations. *Proc. ACL.*

George A. Miller. 1995. WordNet: A Lexical Database for English. *Communications of the ACM* 38(11):39–41.

Mitchell Marcus, Mary Ann Marcinkiewicz, and Beatrice Santorini. 1993. Building a large annotated corpus of English: the Penn Treebank. *Computational Linguistics* 19(2).

Hwee Tou Ng, Siew Mei Wu, Wu, Y., Hadiwinoto, C., and Tetreault, J. 2013. The CoNLL-2013 shared task on grammatical error correction. *Proc. CoNLL: Shared Task.*

Hwee Tou Ng, Siew Mei Wu, Ted Briscoe, Christian Hadiwinoto, Raymond Hendy Susanto, and Christopher Bryant. 2014. The CoNLL-2014 Shared Task on Grammatical Error Correction. *Proc. CoNLL: Shared Task.*

Mohammad Rahimi. 2009. The role of teacher's corrective feedback in improving Iranian EFL learners' writing accuracy over time: is learner's mother tongue relevant? *Reading and Writing*, 22(2):219–243.

Andreas Stolcke and Elizabeth Shriberg. 1996. Automatic linguistic segmentation of conversational speech. *Proc. Fourth International Conference on Spoken Language Processing (ICSLP).*

Toshikazu Tajiri, Mamoru Komachi, and Yuji Matsumoto. 2012. Tense and aspect error correction for ESL learners using global context. *Proc. ACL.*

Joel Tetreault, Jennifer Foster, and Martin Chodorow. 2010. Using Parse Features for Preposition Selection and Error Detection. *Proc. ACL.*

Yen-Chu Tseng and Hsien-Chin Liou. 2006. The effects of online conjunction materials on college EFL students' writing. *System*, 34(2):270–283.

Predicting the use of BA construction in Mandarin Chinese discourse: A modeling study with two verbs

Yao Yao
Hong Kong Polytechnic University
Department of Chinese and Bilingual Studies
Hong Kong
ctyaoyao@polyu.edu.hk

Abstract

This paper investigates the use of BA construction in Mandarin Chinese discourse with two frequently-occurring Chinese verbs 放 fàng ("v. to put") and 拿 ná ("v. to take"). Previous literature suggests that the use of BA construction is influenced by a number of factors, including semantic meaning of the verb phrase and prominence and weight of the object NP. However, what is unclear is how these factors work together in conditioning word order variation (BA vs. SVO) in real context, especially regarding the effects of object NP prominence and weight and their interaction. In this study, we explore this issue by building corpus-based statistical models for predicting the use of BA construction in context. Our results show that for both verbs 放 fàng and 拿 ná, the use of BA construction is sensitive to the prominence (especially givenness) and weight of the object NP as well as structural parallelism, while no interaction effects were found. Furthermore, the weight effects are in opposite directions in the two models, raising new questions regarding the nature of heavy NP shift and revealing a great degree of cross-verb differences in word order variation.

1 Introduction

One of the most well-documented syntactic structure in Mandarin Chinese, the BA construction features an SOV word order with a preposed object noun phrase. An example of BA construction is shown in (a), with a corresponding sentence in canonical SVO word order shown in (b).

(a)	我	把	饭	吃完	了。
	I	BA	rice	eat-finish	ASP
	I ate the rice.				

(b)	我	吃完	了	饭。
	I	eat-finish	ASP	rice
	I ate the rice.			

A voluminous body of literature has been devoted to the study of the structural properties and historical development, as well as the semantic conditions for appropriately using BA construction. However, few studies have looked at the use of BA construction in context (see Liu 2007 for an exception). As Sun and Givón (1985) pointed out, the canonical SVO word order was used overwhelmingly in natural context, even in cases where the conditions for using BA construction were met. How to account for the variation between BA construction and canonical SVO in context then? Is there any general rule that can predict the use of BA construction in context or is the variation completely random and unpredictable? These are the questions that motivate the current research.

In this study, we model the use of BA construction and the alternative SVO construction in naturally produced discourse, using data from a large-scale Chinese corpus. The overarching goal of this research is to gain a comprehensive picture on the actual use of BA construction and

Copyright 2014 by Yao Yao
28th Pacific Asia Conference on Language, Information and Computation pages 561–567

to unveil the mechanism of interactions between form, meaning, and context.

There are two lines of previous work that are relevant for this research: The first line concerns the linguistic properties of BA construction and the second line statistical modeling of syntactic variation. We will briefly review previous works along these two lines in the following section.

2 Background literature

2.1 Previous work on the use of BA construction

Numerous studies have examined when it is acceptable to use BA construction. The most well-acknowledged conditions include high prominence of object NP (i.e. definite, specific, or generic) and disposal meaning of the sentence verb (Li and Thompson 1974, 1975, 1981, Xu 1995). It is for this reason that the use of BA construction is often associated with notions of topic (Givón 1978, Tsao 1987, etc) and verb transitivity (Hopper and Thompson 1980, Liu 1999, Sun 1995, Thompson 1973). However, although these conditions seem to promote the use of BA construction, it is not clear how effective they are. As Sun and Givón (1985) has shown, BA construction could hardly compete with canonical SVO word order in real usage, even when these conditions were met. A more recent study by Liu (2007) examined the use of BA construction (and other types of object preposing) in context. From a corpus of about 400,000 characters, Liu collected 456 "structurally interchangeable" sentences which, regardless of their surface word order, could be expressed in the alternative word order without changing the meaning. Based on this dataset, Liu found a significant interaction of information status and weight on object preposing. If the object NP carried old information, it was more likely to be preposed if it was short; contrarily, if the object NP carried new information, it was more likely to be preposed if it was long. In other words, the general tendency was for a preposed NP to be either discourse-old + short or discourse-new + long, and for a postverbal NP to be the opposite. However, Liu's study only considered information status and weight but not any other syntactic, semantic or discourse properties (e.g. structural parallelism). Furthermore, Liu's study did not distinguish sentences with different verbs, which may lead to two potential problems. First, since the use of verbs in natural context is highly unbalanced, it is possible that the general tendency seen in the overall dataset was in fact driven by only a few high-frequency verbs. Second, the distribution of verbs may very well vary across sentence types (BA vs. SVO), therefore, it is possible that the observed pattern reflects more of verb-specific idiosyncrasies regarding word order as opposed to other factors (such as information status and weight).

What we see as lacking in the current literature is a study of BA vs. SVO variation in natural context that (1) considers all related factors and (2) provides sufficient control for verb type. The current study used data from a well-annotated 10-million-word Chinese corpus. As a result, our dataset was big enough to allow a wide range of predictor factors to be considered and sentences of different verbs to be modeled separately. Before we introduce the modeling detail of the current study, we will first review some major relevant works on statistical modeling of word order variation in both Chinese and English and briefly introduce what previous works have found to be significant predictors for surface word order.

2.2 Previous work on statistical modeling of syntactic variation

Using corpus data and statistical modeling methods, Bresnan and colleagues (Bresnan 2007, Bresnan et al. 2007, Bresnan and Ford 2010, Tily et al. 2009, Wolk et al. 2011, etc) have successfully modeled English dative variation (e.g. *I gave John a book* vs. *I gave John a book*) and genitive variation (e.g. *John's book* vs. *the book of John*). The models showed that both variation phenomena were sensitive to a wide range of properties pertaining to different sentence components (e.g. semantic type of the verb, NP accessibility, pronominality, definiteness, syntactic complexity, etc) and context (e.g. presence of parallel structures). After being trained with large corpus datasets, model accuracy reached over 90% when predicting the surface dative/genitive form in unseen sentences. Bresnan et al.'s research has been extended to other varieties of English (e.g. Australian English; Bresnan and Ford, 2010) as well as historical English (Wolk et al. 2011).

Similar modeling techniques have been applied in the investigation of syntactic variation in Chinese, too (e.g. Yao and Liu 2010, Starr under review). Yao and Liu (2010) examined Chinese dative variation in written texts. Two statistical models were constructed to investigate the three-way contrast among Chinese dative constructions (PREVERBAL: 我把书送给小王; POSTVERBAL DATIVE: 我送书给小王; POSTVERBAL DOUBLE OBJECT: 我送小王书). The models were overall quite successful in predicting surface form (accuracy > 87%). However, in the model for preverbal-postverbal variation, in contrast with the proposal in Liu (2007), Yao and Liu (2010) did not find a significant interaction between information status and weight on object preposing. Instead their results suggested a weak weight effect, as heavy direct object NPs were slightly more likely to be preposed than light direct object NPs. The discrepancy between Yao and Liu (2010) and Liu (2007) provides another motivation for reexamining the word order variation regarding BA and SVO constructions.

3 Methods

3.1 Data

This study uses data from the Academia Sinica Balanced Corpus of Modern Chinese (Version 5.0; *Sinica 5.0* for short; (Chen et al., 1996)), which contains about 10 million words of text (both spoken and written) and has been tagged with part of speech. To compile a dataset, we first created an initial list of BA sentences by locating instances of the BA markers (either 把 bǎ or 将 jiāng tagged as preposition) in the corpus. The initial list contained more than 11 thousand BA sentences of over 1600 different verbs, among which the five most frequent verbs were 放 *fàng* "v. to put", 当 *dāng* "v. to consider as", 带 *dài* "v. to bring", 送 *sòng* "v. to give", 拿 *ná* "v. to take". In this study, we chose to focus on 放 *fàng* and 拿 *ná* because (1) 带 (dài) and 送 (sòng) are both typical transfer verbs and are therefore involved in the complex three-way variation of dative constructions; (2) preliminary corpus analysis suggests that the verb 当 (dāng) is predominantly used in BA construction with little variation in word order.

The next step was to construct a comparable set of SVO sentences of the two target verbs (放 *fàng* and 拿 *ná*). Since the key was to find structurally interchangeable sentences, we narrowed the scope of search to sentences that not only contained a target verb but also an aspect marker (e.g. 了, 过, 着) or verb complement (e.g. 上, 下, 来, 去, 回, 完) that has been used in at least one BA sentence with the same target verb and an explicit object noun phrase (NP). As pointed out in previous studies, an important condition for using BA construction is the disposal meaning of the sentence, which is often expressed by aspect markers and verb complements in Mandarin Chinese (for examples, the verb 吃 "v. to eat" in (a) and (b) is followed by a complement 完 "finish"). In fact, sentences with bare verbs were nearly extinct in the BA sentence set of the current study.

Both the BA sentence set and the SVO sentence set of the two target verbs were manually checked and pruned for false hits, corpus errors and verb+aspect/complement combinations with non-alternating word order. Furthermore, since the verb 放 *fàng* can also mean "v. to release" and "v. to emit (light, electricity, etc.)", we further restricted the 放 *fàng* sentences to only those with the basic meaning "v. to put". The final dataset for 放 *fàng* includes 688 BA sentences and 320 SVO sentences, and the final dataset for 拿 *ná* includes 261 BA sentences and 727 SVO sentences.

3.2 Statistical models

All sentence tokens in the dataset were annotated for 16 properties: genre (`Genre`), language mode (`Mode`), adverbial phrase before the target verb (`AdvP_before`), another verb phrase before the target verb (VP_before), another verb phrase after the target verb (VP_after), target verb phrase embedded in a relative clause (RelClause), target verb phrase embedded in an adverbial phrase (AdvClause), target verb phrase is nominalized (Nominalization), a BA construction is used in previous context (BA_before), a BA construction is used in following context (BA_after), object of the target verb is mentioned in previous context (ObjMentioned_before), object of the target verb is mentioned in following context (ObjMentioned_after), object of the target verb contains a demonstrative pronoun 这 *zhé* "this" or 那 *nà* "that" (ObjDemonstrative), object of the target verb is animate (ObjAnimacy), object of the target verb is a pronoun (ObjPronoun), length of object NP (ObjLen).

Apart from Genre and Mode, which were already annotated in the corpus, all other properties were annotated manually by a trained linguist. Previous and following contexts were defined as 10 sentences (delimited by comma, full stop, exclamation mark or question mark) before or after the target verb phrase. ObjLen was counted by the number of Chinese characters or syllables, in case the object NP contained foreign words (e.g. code-switching). Since raw ObjLen was always greater than 1 and resembled a Zipfian-like distribution in our dataset, we centered and log-transformed ObjLen before entering in the models.

Word order variation in sentences of 放 *fàng* and 拿 *ná* were modeled separately in two generalized mixed-effects regression models. The two models had highly similar model structures. Both models contained a binary variable SurfaceWordOrder (BA=1; SVO=0) as the outcome variable, the set of annotated features described above as fixed effects and verb+aspect/complement as random effects, to control for individual differences of aspect markers and verb complements regarding surface word order. Since previous studies suggested that object NP weight might have a non-linear effect on word order variation and may work in interaction with information status, we also included a quadratic term of ObjLen as well as the interaction of ObjLen (both linear and quadratic terms) and ObjMentioned_before in the models. Table 1 shows a complete list of model terms.

Fixed-effect predictor	Variable type
Genre	Categorical
Mode	Categorical
AdvP_before	Boolean
VP_before	Boolean
VP_after	Boolean
RelClause	Boolean
AdvClause	Boolean
Nominalization	Boolean
BA_before	Boolean
BA_after	Boolean
ObjMentioned_before	Boolean
ObjMentioned_after	Boolean
ObjDemonstrative	Boolean
ObjAnimacy	Boolean
ObjPronoun	Boolean
centered(log(ObjLen))	Numeric
centered(log($ObjLen^2$))	Numeric

Table 1: Fixed-effects predictors in the initial models

After the initial construction, both models were submitted backward elimination where non-significant predictors (i.e. predictors whose elimination did not significantly affect model fit) were eliminated from the model, in order to avoid spurious effects due to the inclusion of non-significant predictor variables. Only results from the final models are reported in this paper. All models were constructed with the lmer() function in the lme4 package (Bates and Maechler, 2011) of R (R Development Core Team, 2008).

4 Results

4.1 Modeling results of 放 *fàng*

The final model of 放 *fàng* contained 7 significant fixed-effect predictors. Table 2 below shows the model parameters. For simplicity, we only report the coefficient (β) of each term and the associated p value (i.e. $p(>|z|)$).

As shown in Table 2, everything else being equal, a verb phrase with 放 *fàng* is more likely

Predictor	β	p
(Intercept)	-0.27	.74
RelClause =T	-2.34	< .001
BA_after=T	0.81	.006
ObjMentioned_before =T	1.31	< .001
ObjMentioned_after=T	0.78	.015
ObjDemonstrative=T	1.22	.059
center(log(ObjLen))	-0.44	.031
center(log(ObjLen))^2	0.65	.0019

Table 2: Summary of fixed effects in the final model of 放 *fàng*.

to be used in a BA construction (than a SVO construction) when (1) the target verb is *not* used in a relative clause; (2) a BA construction is used in the following context; (3) the object NP is mentioned in the surrounding context (either before or after the current sentence); (4) the object NP contains a demonstrative (marginally significant); (5) the object NP is short. Overall the model correctly predicts (635+277)/1008 = 90.5% of the use of BA construction in context, a significant improvement compared with the baseline accuracy at (635+53)/1008 = 68.3%. Table 3 below shows the number of correct and incorrect predictions.

	Surface BA	Surface SVO
Predicted BA	635	43
Predicted SVO	53	277

Table 3: 放 *fàng* sentence counts by surface word order and predicted word order.

All the above effects were in the expected directions except for maybe the weight effects. As suggested in previous literature, the use of BA construction is promoted when the object NP is highly prominent, which is the case when the object NP contains a demonstrative - an explicit marker for definiteness in Mandarin Chinese - and when the NP is given in previous context or repeated in the following context (i.e. likely to be a discourse topic). Meanwhile, language users are also more likely to produce a BA construction when at least one BA construction has been produced in the near context, suggesting an influence of structural parallelism in word order variation. The effect of relativization might be due to elevated processing difficulty associated with BA construction in relative clause.

What is intriguing is the effect of object NP weight. The model of 放 *fàng* shows that object weight has a negative effect on the use of BA construction. The longer the object is, the **less** likely to observe a BA construction. Furthermore, the magnitude (i.e. the steepness) of this negative effect reduces as ObjLen increases, as suggested by the positive coefficient of the quadratic term ObjLen^2. But the model found no significant interaction between ObjMentioned_before and ObjLen or ObjLen^2.

4.2 Modeling results of 拿 *ná*

Results of the final model of 拿 *ná* sentences are shown in Table 4. Everything else being equal, a verb phrase with 拿 *ná* is more likely to be expressed in a BA construction (than a SVO construction) when (1) the target VP is used in an adverbial phrase (marginally significant); (2) a BA construction is used in the following context; (3) the object NP has been mentioned in previous context; (4) the object NP is long. Again, the model indicated effects of object NP prominence (ObjMention_before) and structural parallelism (BA_after). However, contrary to the model of 放 *fàng*, the model of 拿 *ná* shows a positive effect of weight. A BA construction is more likely to be used when the object NP is **long**. This finding is apparently more expected given the previous literature (Yao and Liu 2010), although still no interaction of weight and information status is found.

Predictor	β	p
(Intercept)	-0.80	.021
AdvClause =T	1.10	.055
BA_after=T	0.61	.002
ObjMentioned_before =T	1.60	< .001
center(log(ObjLen))	0.32	.012

Table 4: Summary of fixed effects in the final model of 拿 *ná*.

Overall model accuracy is (669+125)/988 =

80.4%, compared to a baseline accuracy at (58+669)/988 = 73.6% (see Table 5. The improvement is less significant than the model of 放, probably due to a higher baseline prediction accuracy in 拿 *ná* sentences.

	Surface BA	Surface SVO
Predicted BA	125	58
Predicted SVO	136	669

Table 5: 拿 *ná* sentence counts by surface word order and predicted word order.

4.3 Discussion

In this study, we built two statistical models for predicting word order variation between BA and SVO constructions, one for the verb 放 *fàng* and the other 拿 *ná*. The two models exhibit both similarity and differences. First of all, both models show significant effects of object NP prominence. The more prominent the object is (definite, given, topic, etc), the more likely it is to use a BA construction. Structural parallelism is another common effect shown in both models. When BA construction has already been used in the context, it is more likely to used again.

The differences between the two models are obvious, too. While both models show significant effects of object NP weight, the directions of the effects are opposite of each other. The model of 放 *fàng* shows a negative effect of object weight on the use of BA construction, with shorter object NPs being more likely to be preposed before the verb (or in other words, longer object NPs are more likely to appear with SVO word order). The model of 拿 *ná*, on the other hand, features a positive effect of object weight, with longer object NPs being more likely to be preposed.

The co-existence of heavy NP shift in both directions is not unheard of. Yao and Liu (2010) reported in their study of the three-way Chinese dative variation that longer direct object NPs were more likely to be preposed before the verb, yet also more likely to appear at the end of the sentence after both the verb and the indirect object NP. Liu (2007) associated object weight and information status and claimed that if the object NP is given in the context, it tends to be preposed if it is longer whereas if the object NP is new, it tends to be preposed if it is shorter. Although the weight×givennes effect has not found direct evidence in either Yao and Liu (2010) or the current study, it remains to be checked whether the lack of the interaction effect is due to unbalanced datasets or the presence of confounding factors.

Last but not the least, the current study reveals significant cross-verb differences in the use of BA construction. Apart from the opposite weight effects as discussed above, the two models are also different in the presence/absence of other significant predictors and the magnitude of the effects. To our best knowledge, such verb-specific variation patterns have rarely been reported in the study of word order variation. An important takeaway message for future studies on Chinese BA-SVO variation is to be more aware of the vast cross-verb differences, which may hold a key to the perplexing nature of the variation phenomenon.

Acknowledgments

Research reported in this paper was supported by the Early Career Scheme of Hong Kong RGC (Grant No. 558913).

References

Bates, D., and M. Maechler. (2011). lme4: Linear mixed-effects models using S4 classes. R package version 0.999375-42. <http://CRAN.R-project.org/ package=lme4>.

Bresnan, Joan. (2007) Is syntactic knowledge probabilistic? Experiments with the English dative alternation. In Sam Featherston and Wolfgang Sternefeld (eds) *Roots: Linguistics in Search of its Evidential Base*, pp 77-96. Series: Studies in Generative Grammar. Berlin: Mouton de Gruyter.

Bresnan, Joan, Anna Cueni and Tatiana Nikitina and Harald Baayen. (2007) Predicting the dative alternation. In G. Boume et al. (eds) *Cognitive Foundations of Interpretation*, pp 69-94. Amsterdam: Royal Netherlands Academy of Science.

Bresnan, Joan and Marilyn Ford. (2010) Predicting syntax: Processing dative constructions in American and Australian varieties of English. *Language*, 86(1), 168-213.

Chen, Keh-jiann, Chu-Ren Huang, Li-ping Chang, and Hui-Li Hsu. (1996). Sinica Corpus: Design Methodology for Balanced Corpora. In B.-S. Park and J.B. Kim (eds) *Proceeding of the 11th Pacific Asia Conference on Language, Information and Computation.* Seoul:Kyung Hee University. pp.167-176.

Givón, Talmy. (1978) Definiteness and referentiality. In Joseph H. Greenberg (eds) Universals of Human Language, Vol. 4: Syntax, pp291-330. Stanford: Stanford University Press.

Hopper, Paul J. and Sandra Thompson. (1980) Transitivity in grammar and discourse. *Language*, 56, 251-299.

Li, Charles N. and Sandra A. Thompson. (1974) Historical change of word order: A case study in Chinese and its implications. In John Anderson and Charles Jones (eds) *Historical Linguistics*, pp199-217. Amsterdam: North-Holland.

Li, Charles N. and Sandra A. Thompson. (1975) The semantics function of word order: A case study in Mandarin. In Charles Li (eds) *Word Order and Word Order Change*, pp163-195. Austin: University of Texas press.

Li, Charles N. and Sandra A. Thompson. (1981) *Mandarin Chinese: A Functional Reference Grammar.* Berkeley: University of California Press.

Liu, Feng-hsi. (1999) Transitivity and structure preservation. In Michael Darnell et al. (eds) *Functionalism and Formalism in Linguistics II*, Case Studies, pp175-202. John Benjamins Publishers.

Liu, Feng-hsi. (2007) Word order variation and ba sentences in Chinese. *Studies in Language*, 31(3), 649 - 682.

R Development Core Team (2008). R: A language and environment for statistical computing. Vienna, Austria. ISBN: 3-900051-07-0. <http://www.R-project.org>.

Sun, Chaofen. (1995) Transitivity, the ba construction and its history. *Journal of Chinese Linguistics*, 23, 159-195.

Sun, Chaofen and Talmy Givón. (1985) On the so-called SOV word order in Mandarin Chinese: A quantified text study and its implications. *Language*, 61(2), 329 - 351.

Thompson, Sandra A. (1973) Transitivity and the ba construction in mandarin Chinese. *Journal of Chinese Linguistics*, 1, 208-221.

Tily, Harry, Susanne Gahl, Inbal Arnon, Neal Snider, Anubha Kothari and Joan Bresnan. (2009) Syntactic probabilities affect pronunciation variation in spontaneous speech. *Language and Cognition*, 1(2), 147-165.

Tsao, Feng-fu. (1987) A topic-comment approach to the ba construction. *Journal of Chinese Linguistics*, 15, 1-54.

Wolk, Christoph, Joan Bresnan, Anette Rosenbach and Benedikt Szmrecsányi. (2011) Dative and genitive variability in Late Modern English: Exploring cross-constructional variation and change. *Diachronica*, 30 (3), 382–419.

Xu, Liejiong. (1995) Definiteness effects on Chinese word order. *Cahiers de Linguistique-Asie Orientale*, 24(1), 29-48.

Yao, Yao and Feng-hsi Liu. (2010) A working report on statistically modeling dative variation in Mandarin Chinese. In *Proceedings of the 23rd International Conference on Computational Linguistics (COLING 2010).* Beijing, China.

"Guo1" and "Guo2" in Chinese Temporal System

QIU Zhuang, SU Qi*
School of Foreign Languages
Peking University, China
{1301213011,sukia}@pku.edu.cn

Abstract

This paper aims to investigate the subtle nuances of meaning of two Chinese particles "guo1" and "guo2" as well as their different functions in Chinese temporal system. Two technical terms, "tense" and "aspect", in traditional Chinese grammar are reconsidered in terms of the nature of these two concepts and the criteria to distinguish them. It is argued that in traditional Chinese grammar, "tense" and "aspect" are often mixed up by scholars, which has misled the study of "guo1" and "guo2". Contrast to the traditional theory, this paper argues that "guo1" is the marker of the terminative aspect, while "guo2" is the marker of the past tense. Moreover, based on the markedness theory, the semantic and functional differences between "guo1" and "guo2" can be regarded as different usage of the particle "guo" in the unmarked or the marked sense.

1. Introduction

Tense and aspect, which share certain similarity but significantly differ in nature, are crucial concepts in the temporal system of a language. Compared with English grammar, the temporal system of Chinese grammar has a short history and the concept of tense and aspect in Chinese have been confused with each other even by some renowned scholars. This has caused negative consequences in the study related to the grammaticalization of time. It has been widely accepted that three Chinese particles, "zhe" "le" and "guo", are aspect markers in Chinese. And "guo" can be subdivided into two semantic variants called "guo1" and "guo2", of which "guo1" has been regarded as expressing a sense of "completeness" and "guo2" has been regarded as the marker of the experiential aspect, which also means the completeness of an action. However, the traditional theory fails to answer questions like "what is the difference between 'guo1' and 'guo2' if they both mean 'completeness' ", "what is the relation between 'guo1' and 'guo2' " and "what is the nature of 'the experiential aspect' in Chinese". This paper attempts to provide answers to all these questions.

2. The concept of tense and aspect in Chinese temporal system.

The temporal system of English grammar which draws a clear distinction between tense and aspect has been established at the beginning of the twentieth century. Poutsma (1926) defines "tense"

* Corresponding author

Copyright 2014 by QIU Zhuang and SU Qi
28th Pacific Asia Conference on Language, Information and Computation pages 568–574

as the change of verb form in relation to the time during which the action takes place, while "aspect" refers to the property of the action itself, such as being durative or momentary and so on. Jakobson (1984) uses the concept of speech event and narrated event to distinguish tense from aspect. He claims that tense is a concept related to both speech event and narrated event. If the narrated event takes place before the speech event, then the speaker should use the past tense, while if the narrated event takes place after the speech event, the speaker should use the future tense. As to the concept of aspect, it concerns only with the narrated event itself, such as whether the event has been finished or not.

Compared with English grammar, the temporal system of Chinese has been established much later. Wang Li (1985) is one of the earliest linguists that have elaborated on the temporal system of Chinese. He argues that the grammaticalization of time has two levels. The first is the time when an action takes place and second is whether the action is finished or not with no reference to the time when it happens. He calls the second one "Qingmao". It seems that Wang Li has already drawn a distinction between tense and aspect, and the term "Qingmao" refers to aspect. He further proposes seven aspects in Chinese, which are "Putong Mao", "Jinxing Mao", "Wancheng Mao", "Jinguoqu Mao", "Kaishi Mao", "Jixu Mao" and "Duanshi Mao", and most of them have their counterparts in English grammar. [1] However, "Jinguoqu Mao" which belongs to the sphere of aspect in Wang's theory, refers to the action that has just happened. And this is exactly the function of post-preterite tense in English. Chen Ping (1988) establishes a temporal system with phase, tense and aspect, which is consistent with English temporal system. Gong Qianyan (1995) develops Chen's theory by further distinguishing eight aspects, and he regards Chinese particle "guo" as the marker of "the experiential aspect". However, so far as the definition is concerned, the experiential aspect in Gong's theory is the same as "Jinguoqu Mao" in Wang Li's theory, and both of them belong to the concept of tense rather than aspect. Moreover, the claim that "guo" is only the marker of experiential aspect fails to account for various usage of "guo" in terms of its place in Chinese temporal system.

3. The distinction between "guo1" and "guo2"

Lyu Shuxiang (2002) divides the usage of "guo" into three types, among which two of them are related to this study. He thinks "guo1" should always follow the verb, indicating that the action denoted by the verb has been finished. For example:

(1) Chi guo1 fan zai qu.
Eat finish food then go
"Go after you have finished your meal."

(2) Deng wo gandao nali, diyichang xi yijing yan guo1 le.
After I get to that place, the first play had already show finish
"After I got there, the first play had already been finished."

On the other hand, "guo2", indicates that the action denoted by the verb has happened in the past:

(3) Zheben xiaoshuo wo kan guo2.
This novel I read before
"I have read this novel before."

(4) Women tan guo2 zhege wenti.
We talk before this question
"We have talked about this question before."

Lyu further claims that one way to distinguish "guo1" from "guo2" is to insert "ceng jing" (which

[1] Based on Wang (1985)'s definition, "Jinxing Mao", "Wancheng Mao", "Kaishi Mao", "Jixu Mao" and "Duanshi Mao" correspond to "durative aspect", "perfective aspect". "ingressive aspect", "continuative aspect" and "momentaneous aspect" respectively in English grammar.

means "at some time in the past") before them. The construction "ceng jing + verb+guo2" is legitimate while "ceng jing + verb+guo1" is not grammatical:

(5) Zheben xiaoshuo wo cengjing kan guo2.
This novel I once read before
"I have read this novel before."

(6) Women cengjing tan guo2 zhege wenti.
We once talk before this question
"We have talked about this question before."

(7) *Cengjing chi guo1 fan zai qu.
Once eat finish food then go

(8) *Deng wo gandao nali, diyichang xi cengjing yan guo1 le.
After I get to that place, the first play once show finish

4. "Guo2" in Chinese temporal system

Contrast to Gong Qianyan (1995) who regards "guo2" as the marker of the experiential aspect, this paper argues that the function of "guo2" is more related to tense than aspect. Jakobson (1984) points out that tense is related to both speech event and narrated event, while aspect concerns only the narrated event itself. "Guo2" has the implication that the narrated event happens before the speech event thus should be regarded as a maker of the past tense.

On the other hand, "guo2" carries the implication of "completeness", which means the action referred to by "verb+guo2" has already been finished. However, "guo2" is semantically different from the perfective aspect marker "le". "Le" emphasizes the "realization" of an action, the change from one state to another, which is represented by Shi Yuzhi (1992) in the following diagram:

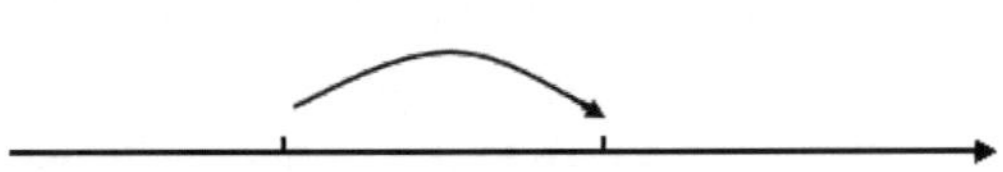

Figure 1. The meaning of "le"

In this diagram, "x" represents the starting point of the action while "a" is the end of the action. "Le" indicates the process from "x" to "a". As to the meaning of "guo2", it is argued that it should be represented as a dot in the diagram, rather than a segment:

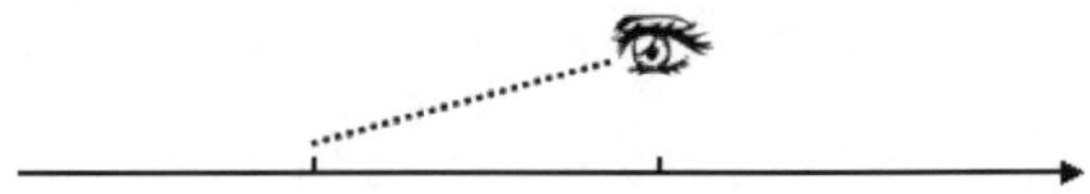

Figure 2. The meaning of "guo2"

In this diagram, "s" represents the time when the speech event takes place, while "x" and "a" respectively represent the starting point and end point of the denoted action. The speaker, at the "s" point, reflects an event that has happened before. Since "verb+guo2" represents an event as a whole rather than a process of realization, "x" and "a" coincide in the diagram. The subtle nuances of meaning of "le" and "guo2" are shown as follows:

(9) a. Ta he le liu ping pijiu.
He drink up six bottles beer
"He has drunk up six bottles of beer."
b. Ta he guo2 liu ping pijiu.
He drink before six bottles beer
"He has drunk six bottles of beer before"

(10) a. Xiao Wang chuipo le qiqiu.
Xiao Wang blow burst finish balloon
"Xiao Wang has burst the balloon when blowing it up"
b. Xiao Wang chuipo guo2 qiqiu.
Xiao Wang blow burst before balloon
"Xiao Wang has burst a balloon when blowing it up before."

(11) a. Bolichuang shang tie le chuanghua.
Glass windows on decorate finish papercuts
"Windows have been decorated by papercuts."
b. Bolichuang shang tie guo2 chuanghua.
Glass windows on decorate once papercuts
"Windows were once decorated by papercuts."

(12) a. Xiao Ming dang le banzhang.
Xiao Ming elect finish monitor of the class
"Xiao Ming has been elected monitor of the class."
b. Xiao Ming dang guo2 banzhang.
Xiao Ming elect once monitor of the class
"Xiao Ming was once elected monitor of the class."

The Chinese verbs in (9) and (10) denote actions. The construction "verb+le" represents the process of an action from the starting point to the end, and the ending point is the focus of attention. In (9a) the focus is on the fact that the sixth bottle is empty, while in (10a) the focus is on the burst of the balloon. Even though the focus is on the completeness of the action, the whole process of the action is within the meaning of "verb+le", thus the meaning of "le" is represented by a segment of line in *Figure 1*. By contrast, "guo2" does not denote the process of an action, but suggests that the action denoted by the verb happened in the past. That's why in the construction "verb+le", the process of the action can be modified, but not in the construction of "verb+guo2":

(13) a.Ta hua liangge xiaoshi he le liuping jiu.
He spend two hours drink finish six bottles of beer
"He has drunk up six bottles of beer using two hours."
b.*Ta hua liangge xiaoshi he guo2 liuping jiu.
He spend two hours drink before six bottles of beer.

(14) a. Xiao Wang fei le jiuniuerhuzhili chuipo le qiqiu.
Xiao Wang spend much effort blow burst finish balloon
"Xiao Wang has blown up and burst a balloon with lots of effort"
b. *Xiao Wang fei le jiuniuerhuzhili chuipo guo2 qiqiu.
Xiao Wang spend much effort blow burst before balloon

The Chinese verbs in (11) and (12) represent a state rather than an action, and in this case, "le" denotes the change from one state to another. For example, in (11a) "le" denotes the change of the window from "no decoration" to "being decorated by papercuts"; and in (12a) "le" denotes the change of the state from "an ordinary student" to "the monitor". By contrast, when following the verbs of state, "guo2" suggests that the state denoted by the verb existed in the past, with the implication that the state does not exist now. For example, (11b) carries the meaning that there are no papercuts on the window now; while (12b) has an implication that Xiao Ming is no longer the monitor now.

Moreover, "verb+guo2" does not specify the inner structure of the action or the state denoted by the verbs, but views the action or the state as a whole and indicates that the whole event happened in the past. This semantic feature accounts for some of the constraints on the usage of "guo2":

(15) a. Romeo ai Juliet.
Romeo love Juliet
"Romeo loves Juliet."
b.Romeo ai guo2 Juliet.
Romeo love before Juliet
"Romeo loved Juliet before."

(16) a.Guowang xiangxin wushi de hua.
The king believe wizard's word
"The king believes the wizard's word."
b.Guowang xiangxin guo2 wushi de hua.
The king believe before wizard's word
"The king believed the wizard's word before."

(17) a. Ta zhidao shiqing de zhenxiang.
He know thing of the truth
"He knows the truth of it."
b. *Ta zhidao guo2 shiqing de zhenxiang.
He know before thing of the truth

(18) a.Ta renshi maozhuxi de mishu.

He know Chairman Mao of secretary

"He knows Chairman Mao's secretary."

b.*Ta renshi guo2 maozhuxi de mishu.

He know before Chairman Mao of secretary

All of the Chinese verbs in (15) to (18) denote psychological states. When these verbs are followed by "guo2" it means the psychological states denoted by these verbs existed in the past, just like (15b) and (16b), with the implication that these psychological states no longer exist now. However, some verbs, such as "zhi dao" (which means "know") in Chinese, denote the psychological state that usually lasts forever, thus do not appear in the past tense. In this sense, the meaning of these verbs conflicts with the meaning of "guo2", thus these verbs do not collocate with "guo2", just like (17b) and (18b).

5. "Guo1" in Chinese temporal system

Compared with "guo2", the usage of "guo1" is not so complicated; however, there are also disagreements about it among Chinese linguists. First of all, in terms of the nature of "guo1", Lyu regards it as a particle, which is supported by Fang (2001), Chen and Li (2013). While Liu Yuehua (1983) argues that "guo1" functions as a complement and it is not a particle. This claim is supported by Gong (1995). It seems that Liu's opinion is more likely to be true since "guo1" can be followed by the particle "le", which indicates its function as something different from the particle:

(19) Chi guo1 (le) fan, tamen you jinyibu liaojie le qingkuang.

Eat up (complete) food they again further inquire situation

"After finishing their meal, they made a further inquiry."

(20) Xingli jiancha guo1 (le), mei wenti.

Luggage check finish (complete) no problem

"The luggage has already been checked, and there is no problem."

However, semantically, "guo1" does not specify the result of an action as those typical complements do. Comparing "da si" ("beat to death") and "da guo1" ("finish beating"), "ran hong" ("dye sth. red") and "ran guo1" ("finish dyeing"), one can feel that "guo1" only means that the action denoted by the verb has been finished, which is similar to the function of the particle "le". Thus it is argued that from a formal perspective, "guo1" is a compliment, but semantically it has the function of a particle. This paper places more emphasis on the position of "guo1" in the temporal system of Chinese grammar rather than the classification of "guo1" into certain word category.

In Chinese, "guo1" is not as frequently used as "guo2". According to the Corpus of Contemporary Chinese Function Words, the frequency of "guo2" is 352 while the frequency of "guo1" is 13. Some of the studies, such as Liu (1983) and Gong (1995), concern only the classification of "guo1" into certain word category with few remarks on its position in Chinese temporal system; while those who have studied "guo" in terms of the Chinese temporal system, such as Chen (1988) and Shi (1992), fail to distinguish "guo1" from "guo2".

It is argued that "guo1" is an aspect marker of Chinese, to be more specific, the marker of the terminative aspect. Based on the theory of Poutsma (1926), Mathesius (2008) and Trnka (1968), terminative aspect focuses on the final phase of an action. For example, the phrase "drink up", and the construction "finish+verb" both denote terminative aspect. Similarly, the construction "verb+guo1" in Chinese denotes terminative aspect, and this implies that this construction can be found in all of the three major tenses, the past tense, the present tense and the future tense:

(21) Zuotian ta chi guo1 fan cai zou.

Yesterday he eat finish food then go

"Yesterday, after finishing his meal, he went."

(22) Shiqing de jieguo zhiyou zuo guo1 le cai zhidao.
Thing of result only if do finish complete then know
"The result can only be known after you have finished doing it."

(23) Mingtian wo wen guo1 ta zai gaosu ni
Tomorrow I ask finish him then tell you
"After asking him about it tomorrow, I will tell you."

Sentences (21) to (23) are of the past tense, present tense and future tense respectively. And "guo1" appears in all of these sentences, which contrasts greatly with "guo2", since "guo2"only appears in the sentences denoting past events. On the other hand, "guo1" and "guo2" are similar in that both of them can be represented by a point, rather than a segment:

Figure 3. The meaning of "guo1"

In this diagram, "x" represents the starting point of the verbal action while "a" is the end of the action. "Guo1" denotes the point when the action is finished, rather than denoting the process of the action like "le" does. When "guo1" is followed by "le" and form the construction "verb+guo1+le", it represents the process of the action while the focus is on the end of the action. Moreover, since "verb+guo1" represents the end of an action, if this construction is followed by an adverbial adjunct denoting a period of time, it does not mean the time that the process of an action has lasted, but the time starting from the end of the action, for example:

(24) Chi guo1 fan (budao shi fenzhong) ta jiu zou le.
Eat finish food (less than ten minutes) he then go complete
"He went (less than ten minutes) after finishing his meal."

(25) Xinhaoqiang xiang guo1 (san miaozhong) zhihou, xuanshoumen cai chongchu paodao.
Signal pistol fire finish (three seconds) after contestants then run out track
"(Three seconds) after the sound of the starting pistol, the runners were all quick off the mark."

Moreover, it is argued that the relationship between "guo1" and "guo2" can be viewed from the perspective of the markedness theory. Jakobson (1984) illustrates the concept of markedness and argues that the difference between the marked category and the unmarked category is that the marked category announces the existence of certain character, while the unmarked category does not state whether this character exists or not, for example:

(26) a. Man shall not live by bread alone.
b. He is a man, not a woman.

"Man" in (26a) is the unmarked category since "man" means "human-beings" in a general sense and gives no information about the gender of the referred group. While "man" in (26b) is the marked category since "man" here refers to "male" which is more specific in meaning. Comrie (2005:112) claims that "the meaning of the unmarked category can encompass that of its marked counterpart", which is consistent with the fact that the meaning of "human beings" encompasses the meaning of both "male" and "female".

As to the relation between "guo1" and "guo2", it is argued that "guo1" denotes the completeness of the verbal action, and it can be found in the past, present and the future tense, while "guo2" only signifies the completeness of a past event. Thus "guo1" is the unmarked category, giving no specific information about the time when the verbal action takes place, while "guo2" is the marked category signifying the sense of "happened in the past".

6. Conclusion

In light of the above analysis, it can be found that there are both similarities and differences between "guo1" and "guo2" in terms of their semantic meaning and grammatical function. "Guo1" denotes the completeness of the verbal action and functions as a marker of the terminative aspect. Though "guo2" also has the implication of completeness, it is used in the case when the narrated event happens before the speech event, and thus it is the marker of the past tense. Based on the markedness theory, the differences between "guo1" and "guo2" can be regarded as the different usage of the particle "guo" in an unmarked or a marked sense. "Guo1" is the unmarked category giving no specific information about tense, while "guo2" is the marked category signifying the past tense.

Acknowledgments

This study is supported by National Natural Science Funds of China (61305089), Beijing Higher Education Young Elite Teacher Project (YETP0027).

References

Chen, Ping. 1988. On the structure of Chinese temporal system. *Zhongguo Yuwen*,6: 401-422.

Chen, Zhenyu & Li, Yuhu. 2013. EXPER guo2 and Repeatability, *Chinese Teaching in the World*,3: 331-345.

Comrie, Bernard. 2005. *Aspect*. Beijing: Peking University Press.

Fang, Yuqing. 2001. *A Practical Chinese Grammar*. Beijing: Peking University Press.

Gong, Qianyan. 1995. *On the phase, tense and aspect of Chinese*. Beijing: The Commercial Press.

Jakobson, Roman. 1984. *Russian and Slavic grammar: studies 1931-1981*. Berlin: Walter de Gruyter.

Liu, Yueyua et al. 1983. *A Practical Grammar of Modern Chinese*. Beijing: Foreign Language Teaching and Research Press.

Lyu, Shuxiang .2002. *A Lyu Shuxiang Anthology V: Eight Words in Modern Chinese*. Shenyang: Liaoning Education Press.

Mathesius,Vilém. 2008. *A Functional Analysis of Present Day English on A General Linguistic Basis*. Beijing: World Publishing Corporation.

Poutsma, Hendrik. 1926. *A grammar of late modern English (Vol. 2, No. 2)*. Groningen: P. Noordhoff

Shi, Yuzhi. 1992. On the Aspect of Modern Chinese. *Social Sciences in China*, 6: 183-201.

Trnka, Bohumil. 1968. *On the syntax of the English verb from Caxton to Dryden*. Kraus Reprint.

Wang, Li. 1985. *A Wang Li Anthology II: Modern Chinese Grammar*. Jinan: Shandong Education Press.

A Non-local Attachment Preference in the Production and Comprehension of Thai Relative Clauses

Teeranoot Siriwittayakorn
Department of Linguistics, Faculty of Arts,
Chulalongkorn University,
Phayathai Road, Pathumwan,
Bangkok, 10330, Thailand
steeranoot@gmail.com

Theeraporn Ratitamkul
Department of Linguistics, Faculty of Arts,
Chulalongkorn University,
Phayathai Road, Pathumwan,
Bangkok, 10330, Thailand
Theeraporn.R@chula.ac.th

Edson T. Miyamoto
University of Tsukuba, Graduate School of
Humanities and Social Sciences, Tsukuba,
Ibaraki, 305-8571, Japan
miyamoto@alum.mit.edu

Heeyoun Cho
College English Program, Faculty of Liberal
Education, Seoul National University,
Seoul, South Korea
heeyoun.cho@gmail.com

Abstract

In parsing, a phrase is more likely to be associated with an adjacent word than to a non-adjacent one. Instances of adjacency violation pose a challenge to researchers but also an opportunity to better understand how people process sentences and to improve parsing algorithms by, for example, suggesting new features that can be used in machine learning. We report corpus counts and reading-time data for Thai to investigate an adjacency violation that has been reported in other languages for ambiguous relative clauses that can be attached to either of two nouns, namely, the local noun (which is adjacent to the relative clause) or the non-local noun (which is farther from the relative clause). The results indicate that, unlike English, Thai violates adjacency by favoring non-local attachment even though the two languages share many grammatical features that have been linked to a local-attachment preference (e.g., rigid SVO word order). We re-interpret previous proposals to suggest that a language favors the non-local noun if it passes at least one of two tests. (1) Modifiers can intervene between noun and relative clause. (2) Adverbs can intervene between transitive verb and direct object.

1 Introduction

We investigated the role of *locality* (or *proximity)* in processing decisions by comparing two languages (Thai and English) that have evolved largely independently but share grammatical features that have been claimed to be crucial in sentence comprehension.

A preference to associate words locally has been reported at least since the 1970s (Kimball, 1973; Gibson, 1998; *inter alia*). For example, in (1), the underlined relative clause (RC) can be attached to the non-local noun (N1, *daughter*) or to the local noun (N2, *colonel*).

(1) The journalist interviewed the daughter of the colonel <u>who had the accident</u>.

English readers prefer the RC to modify N2, whereas N1 is preferred in the corresponding construction in Spanish (Cuetos and Mitchell, 1988). Various typological differences have been used to predict which languages violate locality by favoring N1 in such *complex NPs* (i.e., N1 of N2 RC).

(2) A language *L* favors N1 attachment if:

Copyright 2014 by Teeranoot Siriwittayakorn, Edson T. Miyamoto, Theeraporn Ratitamkul, and Heeyoun Cho
28th Pacific Asia Conference on Language, Information and Computation pages 575–584

a. L has no alternative construction for expressing the N1 interpretation (Frazier and Clifton, 1996);
b. L has flexible word order (Gibson et al., 1996);
c. L allows constituents (e.g., adverbs) to intervene between a verb and its direct object (Miyamoto, 1999);
d. L exhibits consistent use of relative pronouns (Hemforth et al., 2000);
e. L has pseudo-RCs (Grillo, 2012);
f. L allows constituents (e.g., adjectives) to intervene between the modified noun and the RC (schematically: *N adjective RC*, the *modifier-straddling hypothesis*, MSH, Cuetos and Mitchell, 1988).

All those competing proposals correctly predict that English does not violate locality as it favors N2. Thai is similar to English in a number of aspects. Word order is the same in the target construction (N1 of N2 RC) and a complementizer comparable to *that* (*thî:*) can be used as RC marker (there are two other RC markers, but *thî:* is the most frequent and has relatively few stylistic restrictions; Iwasaki and Ingkaphirom, 2009). The following properties are particularly relevant in the discussion on RC attachment.

(3)
a. Thai has at least two alternative unambiguous constructions to modify N1, namely, an RC-preposing construction (N1 RC of N2) and a compound-like structure (N1 N2 RC) resulting from the omission of the preposition.
b. Thai is a rigid SVO language, in particular, verb and direct object have to be adjacent.
c. The RC marker *thî:* has been claimed to be omissible in some environments (Iwasaki and Ingkaphirom, 2009; Kullavanijaya, 2010).
d. Pseudo relative clauses are not available in Thai.

The features in (3) together with the proposals in (2a-e) predict Thai to pattern with English in the comprehension of (1), thus resulting in a preference for N2 attachment.

In contrast, according to the MSH (see (2f)), if a language allows the sequence *N adjective RC*, the adjective can be generalized to other types of modifiers (e.g., *of N2*), hence weakening the adjacency bias and increasing the likelihood that the RC will skip the intervening modifier and attach to N1 (Cuetos and Mitchell, 1988; see the general discussion on some possible counter-examples). Unlike English, adjectives are postnominal in Thai and can intervene between the noun and the RC. This should lead Thai readers to favor N1 according to the MSH. Therefore, the goal of this paper is to test the MSH against the proposals in (2a-e), which predict Thai to be an N2-attachment language.

We report a corpus count and a self-paced reading experiment confirming the predictions of the MSH for *thî:*-marked RCs in Thai.

2 Corpus Count

A corpus count was conducted to determine production preferences in RC attachment in Thai taking the influence of context into consideration.

Since there are no plural markers or morphological agreement in Thai, ambiguity resolution is often based on plausibility. For this reason, surrounding context plays an important role in attachment. Although previous corpus counts on this topic have not included context as a factor, some studies have suggested that the matrix clause can favor N1 (e.g., by making the RC informative, Frazier 1990; increasing text coherence, Rohde et al., 2011; allowing for an alternative interpretation, see *pseudo RCs* in Grillo 2012; also Desmet et al., 2002b, on the matrix clause increasing the N1 preference in a norming questionnaire). Therefore, in order to measure the influence of the context surrounding the *complex NP*, tokens were classified according to whether information inside the complex NP was enough to determine attachment (*internally disambiguated*; e.g., *voice of men that was uttered)* or whether it was also necessary to consult the context surrounding the complex NP (*externally disambiguated*).

Moreover, it might be the case that together with context, other factors could affect attachment. One such a factor is the position of the *disambiguating context* (i.e., the information that indicates the attachment intended for the RC). Complex NPs are usually embedded in a larger context and the disambiguating context can come either before or after the complex NP. When the disambiguating context comes before the complex NP, N1 attachment might be favored in order to increase text coherence. However, N1 bias might be weaker when context comes after the NP.

Another possible factor in attachment is the syntactic position of the target NP (subject or object). If, for example, the context provided by the preceding clause, I_{n-1}, has already given sufficient information about the subject of clause I_n, further subject modification (i.e., N1) of the clause I_n, might be unnecessary. Although the same reasoning can be applied to an object NP, because a subject tends to be a discourse-old entity (see Mattausch, 2011 on related discussion), it is predicted that the plausibility for the preceding context to be related to a subject is higher than that of an object. Therefore, the rate of attaching an RC to N1, in the subject position might be lower than that in the object position.

In sum, instances of complex NP were classified according to the following three factors.

- point of disambiguation (internally or externally-disambiguated)
- syntactic position of the complex NP (subject or object position)
- for externally-disambiguated items, point of disambiguation was further classified according to the position of the disambiguating context (early or late; i.e., before or after the complex NP).

2.1 Method

Segments with *thî:* preceded by *khɔ̌:ŋ* "of" within a three-word window were extracted from the six writing genres of the Thai National Corpus (Aroonmanakun et al., 2009), namely fiction (which contains 7,469,530 words), newspaper (5,029,019 words), academic text (8,894,650 words), non-academic text (5,342,092 words), law (1,190,516 words) and miscellanea (4,000,160 words).

Out of 23,726 sequences found, 4,800 instances (800 instances per genre) were randomly selected and manually analyzed, and irrelevant cases discarded (e.g., if *thî:* was not used as an RC marker). From the 2,462 instances of *N1 of N2 RC* found, 356 instances (14.46%) were eliminated because the attachment site was not clear. Instances were also eliminated if the head nouns were not common nouns (481 instances, 19.54%, with proper names or pronouns, which are usually avoided in behavioral experiments) or were likely to attract the RC (308 instances, 12.51%; e.g., *khon* 'person' or *sìŋ* 'thing', see Wasow et al., 2011, for related discussion). The remaining 1,317 tokens were analyzed according to attachment.

Three native Thai speakers coded the sentences independently and disagreements (less than 5%) were settled after discussion.

2.2 Results

N1 attachments were more frequent than N2 attachments (χ^2 (1) = 42.3, p < .0001; see Table 1). The results held regardless of whether the complex NP was in subject or object position (subject position only: χ^2 (1) = 11.06, p < .001; object only: χ^2 (1) = 30.98, p < .0001).

To factor out the influence of the surrounding context, further analyses were conducted on the internally-disambiguated items. Attachments were more frequent to N1 than to N2 in all cases (overall: χ^2 (1) = 20.92, p < .0001; subject: χ^2 (1) = 6.8, p = .009; object: χ^2 (1) = 14.12, p < .001).

Analyses on externally-disambiguated items showed that when the disambiguating context came before the complex NP, the RC was more frequently attached to N1 than to N2 (χ^2 (1) = 51.58, p <.0001). The trend was the same when restricted to NPs in object position (χ^2 (1) = 47.26, p <.0001), and was marginally so for subject-position NPs (χ^2 (1) = 3.28, p = 0.07). Further analyses indicated such early contexts tended to favor N1. In the overall results (column *overall* in Table 1), the N1 bias went up

	Syntactic position		
Point of disambiguation:	Subject	Object	Overall
Internally-disambiguated	158 (58.09%)	518 (56.24%)	676 (56.67%)
Externally-disambiguated: early context	9 (81.82%)	74 (88.10%)	83 (87.37%)
Externally-disambiguated: late context	9 (81.82%)	9 (50.00%)	18 (62.07%)
Overall	176 (59.86%)	601 (58.75%)	777 (59.00%)

Table 1. Corpus frequency of N1 attachment according to point of disambiguation (internal or external), syntactic position (subject of object) and position of disambiguating context (early of late).

from 56.67% in the internally-disambiguated row to 87.37% in the row for externally-disambiguated items with early context (χ^2 (1) = 33.02, p <.0001). The trend was similar for the object-position NPs (from 56.24% to 88.10%, χ^2 (1) = 30.96, p <.0001), but it was not statistically reliable for subjects.

When context came after the complex NP, the frequencies of N1 and N2 attachments were not statistically different. There was only a marginal trend towards N1 attachment in subject position (χ^2 (1) = 3.28, p = 0.07).

Although there were few instances of N2 attachment among the externally-disambiguated tokens (overall: 23 tokens, subject: 4 tokens, object: 19 tokens), the results suggest that context can favor N2 attachment as well.

2.3 Discussion

There was a consistent preference for N1 attachment regardless of the different types of classifications used. Even after eliminating the influence of context, N1 attachment in both subject and object positions remains more frequent in Thai.

No previously-proposed grammatical factor except for the MSH (Cuetos & Mitchell, 1988) can explain the overall advantage for N1 attachment.

Some studies have suggested that animacy and concreteness can affect RC attachment (Desmet et al., 2002a; Desmet et al., 2006). However, more detailed analyses of the data suggest that they are not determining factors in Thai as there was a bias towards N1 attachment regardless of animacy and concreteness of the two nouns (see Appendix A).

3 Experiment

A reading-time experiment was conducted to investigate the on-line comprehension of RCs in Thai.

3.1 Method

Participants: Fifty-two native Thai speakers, undergraduate students at Chulalongkorn University, participated in the experiment for course credit. Since English is a compulsory subject in Thailand, the participants here and elsewhere in this paper are likely to have learnt it as a second language.

Stimuli: There were 112 test items divided into four types (28 items for each type) that varied according to the animacy of the nouns N1 and N2, that the RC could modify (only concrete nouns were used for N1 and N2). Although care was taken to control for various factors, items were excluded from the analyses because of a number of confounding factors (e.g., plausibility of the interpretations, frequency of the words in the RCs). Therefore, we will report results for a subset of 20 items in which both nouns are animate. Each item had two versions (i.e., N1-attachment and N2-attachment versions). See (4) for an example pair.

(4)

a. N1 attachment
khunphɔ̂: fà:k khɔ̌:ŋ hâj | khunkhru: khɔ̌:ŋ
father leave thing give| teacher of
lû:kcha:j | thî: |sɔ̌:n wíʔcha: pha:sǎ:thaj
son | that |teach subject Thai language
"The father left something for the teacher of his son that teaches Thai."

b. N2 attachment
khunphɔ̂: fà:k khɔ̌:ŋ hâj | khunkhru: khɔ̌:ŋ
father leave thing give| teacher of
lû:kcha:j | thî: | sɔ̀:ptòk wíʔcha: pha:sǎ:thaj
son | that |fail subject Thai language
"The father left something for the teacher of his son that failed a Thai exam."

Because Thai lacks agreement morphology, attachment was disambiguated based on plausibility (e.g., in (4b), a student is more likely to fail an exam compared to a teacher). To avoid possible differences related to extraction position, all RCs were subject extracted (see Grodner and Gibson, 2005, and references therein for a discussion on English).

Norming: The test items were disambiguated based on plausibility. Therefore, a questionnaire was conducted to ensure that the plausibility manipulations were effective. This type of supplementary questionnaire is commonly used to verify the items used in the main experiment. For example, to make sure that the two interpretations in (5a) are equally natural, the two sentences in (5b, c) are compared in a questionnaire (example adapted from Desmet et al., 2002b).

(5)

a. The police interrogate the advisor of the politician who speaks with a soft voice.

b. The assistant has a soft voice.

c. The politician has a soft voice.

Note that RCs are usually not used in (5b, c) since we are only interested in the plausibility of the interpretations (e.g., how natural it is for an assistant or a politician to have a soft voice; but see Desmet et al., 2002b, who used RCs instead, thus potentially confounding plausibility with attachment preference).

Because the matrix clause can affect RC attachment, it was included as a separate sentence (see Desmet et al., 2002b, for questionnaires with and without the matrix clause). For each item pair in the main study, four versions were created in a 2 by 2 design (noun: N1 or N2; plausibility: plausible or implausible). The examples in (6) are the four versions created for the item pair in (4).

(6)

a. N1-plausible
khunphɔ̂: fâ:k khɔ̌:ŋ hâj khunkhru: khɔ̌:ŋ
father leave thing give teacher of
lû:kcha:j | khunkhru sɔ̌:n wíʔcha: pha:sǎ:thaj
son | teacher teach subject Thai
"The father left something for the teacher of his son. The teacher teaches Thai."

b. N1-implausible
khunphɔ̂: fâ:k khɔ̌:ŋ hâj khunkhru: khɔ̌:ŋ
father leave thing give teacher of
lû:kcha:j | khunkhru sɔ̀:ptòk wíʔcha: pha:sǎ:thaj
son | teacher failed subject Thai
"The father left something for the teacher of his son. The teacher failed a Thai exam."

c. N2-plausible
khunphɔ̂: fâ:k khɔ̌:ŋ hâj khunkhru: khɔ̌:ŋ
father leave thing give teacher of
lû:kcha:j | lû:kcha:j sɔ̀:ptòk wíʔcha: pha:sǎ:thaj
son | son fail subject Thai
"The father left something for the teacher of his son. The son failed a Thai exam."

d. N2-implausible
khunphɔ̂: fâ:k khɔ̌:ŋ hâj khunkhru: khɔ̌:ŋ
father leave thing give teacher of
lû:kcha:j | lû:kcha:j sɔ̌:n wíʔcha: pha:sǎ:thaj
son | son teach subject Thai
"The father left something for the teacher of his son. The son teaches Thai."

As customary in Thai writing, spaces were used between sentences (indicated with vertical bars in (6)) but not between words.

By comparing (6a) and (6c) we can guarantee that the intended attachments were equally plausible. By comparing (6b) and (6d), we can determine whether the unintended interpretations were equally implausible and thus equally unlikely to interfere by competing with the intended interpretations. A new group of 76 native Thai students at Chulalongkorn University who did not participate in the main experiment rated sentences on a five-point scale (1 implausible, 5 plausible).

The results for the plausible attachments (mean 4.26; median 5) and for the implausible attachments (mean 1.91; median 1) suggest that the overall plausibility manipulation worked as planned for the 20 items reported in the main study.

More importantly, according to an ordinal logistic regression analysis (Agresti, 2002), there was no difference when attachment site (N1 or N2) was included as a factor as the two plausible conditions (6a) (mean 4.37, median 5) and (6c) (mean 4.15, median 5) were equally plausible, and the two implausible conditions (6b) (mean 2.04, median 1) and (6d) (mean 1.78, median 1) were equally implausible (all p's > .25).

Procedure: Each participant in the main experiment saw a list of 112 test items following a Latin Square design so that only one version from each pair was included. Test items were shown in random order interspersed with 195 fillers. Fillers included sentences with *thî:* not followed by an RC, *N1 of N2* sequences (not followed by an RC), a single noun followed by an RC, and a variety of unambiguous sentences with one or two clauses. To make sure that participants were reading carefully, half of the test items and two-fifth of the fillers (78 items) were followed by a comprehension question.

Test sentences were segmented into four regions as indicated by the vertical bars in (4) and shown using a non-cumulative self-paced reading presentation on E-Prime 2.0. Most sentences were too long to fit on a single line, therefore all items were presented with a line break after the second region (i.e., after *N1 of N2* sequence) (previous results indicate that a pause between N2 and the RC marker is not associated with an N1 preference, e.g., Clahsen and Felser, 2006). The test session was divided into three sub-sessions with optional breaks in-between and lasted for about an hour.

Analyses: For the first three regions, analyses are reported with length-residualized reading times (based on a linear regression including all test items and fillers; Ferreira and Clifton, 1986). Data points beyond four standard deviations from condition-region means were removed, affecting less than 1% of the test data (trends in the untrimmed results were similar to those with trimmed data).

Because the RCs (the critical region) differed in their words and plausibility biases, the reading times to the RC region were regressed against RC length, the judgments for the plausible and implausible conditions in the norming study, and the log-frequencies of words and bigrams obtained from the Thai National Corpus (Aroonmanakun et al., 2009). Residuals from this linear regression were trimmed in the same way as the whole data set (with less than 1% eliminated).

Reading times were analyzed with mixed-effects models using the lme4 package (Baayen et al., 2008, and references therein) on R (R Core Team, 2013). Wald chi-square was used to calculate p-values (function Anova in the package car; Fox and Weisberg, 2011). Pairwise comparisons with Tukey-adjusted p-values are reported (function lsmeans in the package lsmeans: Lenth, 2013).

3.2 Results

Comprehension accuracy of all test items and fillers was 96.70%. All participants scored over 88%, suggesting that they were paying attention during the experiment and therefore none of them was eliminated from further analyses. For the 20 animate-animate test items, response accuracy did not differ for the two types of attachment (N1: 96.54%; N2: 97.31%; mixed-model including random intercepts for subjects and items: $z < 1$).

Reading times: The mixed model included attachment as fixed factor and as random slope for participants and for items. To decrease correlation between the predictors in the model, a simple contrast-coding scheme was used for each categorical variable by comparing each level to the reference level and setting the intercept as the grand mean.

In region 1, N1 attachment was faster than N2 attachment ($p=.015$), but the difference was unexpected since attachment was not manipulated at this point, and it may have been caused by participants sometimes resting at the beginning of a new sentence. There were no differences in the next two regions (p's>.15). In the critical region (region 4), the RC was read faster when attached to N1 than to N2 (residualized reading times: χ^2 (1) = 4.166, p = .0412).

3.3 Discussion

The results showed that when the two nouns were animate, N1 attachment was preferred. However, this advantage for the non-local noun should be interpreted with caution for two reasons. First, although RC reading times were residualized against corpus frequencies, the corpus interface restricted the searches in a number of ways (e.g., some words were more likely to be prefixes; e.g., *khwa:m,* an adjective nominalizer).

Second, sentences were presented with a line break between N2 and the RC marker, potentially enhancing the perception of a pause, and decreasing the adjacency advantage for N2. Such an effect would be compatible with the *implicit prosody hypothesis* (Fodor, 1998; but see Clahsen and Felser, 2006; also, English readers prefer N2 attachment even with a break after N2, Felser et al., 2003).

The reading-time advantage for N1 is partially in line with the corpus counts. Only concrete nouns were used for N1 and N2 in the test items of the reading experiment. In the corpus, although N1 attachments were more frequent than N2 attachment overall, the advantage for N1 was not reliable when both nouns were concrete and animate (see Appendix A for the breakdown by animacy and concreteness) but perhaps a coarse-grained count is used (e.g., collapsing across different animacy and concreteness patterns; but see Desmet et al., 2006, on the need for fine-grained counts). Clearly, further results are needed to address this point in more detail.

4 General Discussion

Both production and comprehension data indicate that, unlike English, there is a preference for N1 attachment in Thai. The corpus study also suggested that N1 bias was present in both subject and object position, and context tended to favor N1 when it preceded the RC.

The modifier-straddling hypothesis (MSH; Cuetos & Mitchell, 1988) is the only grammatical factor that correctly predicts the N1-attachment preference for Thai observed in the corpus and in the animate-animate condition of the reading experiment. However, the MSH cannot explain the non-local preference reported for languages in which modifiers do not intervene between noun and RC (e.g., Dutch: Brysbaert and Mitchell, 1996; German: Hemforth et al., 2000).

One solution is to extend the notion of modifier in the MSH to include both adjectives and adverbs. Therefore, we propose a *generalized MSH* that includes a second factor namely adverb intervention, as mentioned in (2c).

(7) Generalized Modifier-Straddling Hypothesis (GMSH). A language favors N1 attachment if at least one of the following two triggers is set.

- Trigger 1. Modifiers (e.g., adjectives) can intervene between head noun and RC (Cuetos and Mitchell, 1988).
- Trigger 2. Adverbs can intervene between transitive verb and direct object (Miyamoto, 1999).

The first trigger is directly related to RCs. The second trigger is related to previous observations that (i) verb-object clusters tend to have a closer relation than verb-subject ones across a variety of typologically-distinct languages (Tomlin, 1986) and (ii) whether a language allows adverbs to intervene between verb and object has been associated with a number of word-order properties (Pollock, 1989).

According to the GMSH, there are roughly four types of languages. English is among the most restrictive and has neither trigger. Thai has only trigger 1. Dutch and German have the second but not the first. The most lenient languages such as Romance languages have both triggers. The last three types of languages should all favor N1 attachment. It is not clear whether the triggers necessarily entail gradient preferences (e.g., the N1 preference is stronger with both triggers than with just one), but this would be a natural prediction that could be pursued in the future. It is possible that the triggers are just tests, convenient ways of checking for properties (e.g. RC attachment) that cluster together.

Another question that needs to be addressed in the future is whether the GMSH affects attachment preferences directly by dictating parsing decisions during comprehension, or whether it affects attachment preference indirectly by dictating production processes (hence, frequency of use), which in turn affect expectation during comprehension as in *exposure-based accounts* (Desmet et al., 2006; Kamide, 2012; MacDonald and Christiansen, 2002; Mitchell et al., 1995; *inter alia*).

The GMSH can be further tested in a number of ways. It makes predictions about individual differences in that speakers who tend to accept the two triggers in (7) are more likely to attach RCs to N1 than to N2. It also suggests that the triggers can be incorporated as features in machine learning in order to better predict RC attachment in the target language.

4.1 Cross-linguistic Variation

A crucial theme in the research of RC attachment has been the observation that preferences vary across languages. However, the corpus count suggests that surrounding context can play a role in RC attachment and the bias is often but not exclusively to N1. Therefore, it is difficult to ascertain how much of the differences observed across various languages are cross-linguistic variations in the way native speakers parse RCs rather than differences in the contexts that were used in the previous studies. This is particularly true for corpus counts because it is unclear how context affected attachment in previous results.

But the observation may also apply to previous behavioral results. Although Desmet et al. (2002b and references therein) reported that surrounding context did not affect online processing, previous results may have been affected by subtle differences in the materials used. For example, although similar sentences were used in the original study comparing English and Spanish (Cuetos and Mitchell, 1988), closer inspection suggests that many English RCs used the simple past (*was*), whereas the Spanish translations used two forms (the preterit *estuvo* or the imperfect *estaba*). This may have caused the N1 preference in Spanish to look stronger than it actually is. The imperfect does not include the start or end points of the event and tends to be more natural when accompanied by a time reference (see Zagona, 2012, for relevant discussion). The matrix event can provide a time reference especially when the RC is attached to N1, which as an argument of the matrix verb makes the connection between the two events clearer.

5 Conclusion

We reported corpus and reading time data indicating that N1-attachment is favored in Thai. We proposed a generalized version of the MSH in which intervening constituents can increase the preference for associating an RC to a non-local head. The proposal can account for a range of cross-linguistic data. Cross-linguistic variation in RC attachment requires more careful studies given the possible influence of contexts used in previous results.

Acknowledgments

This work is a part of the first author's doctoral dissertation. It was supported by the Project on Language and Human Security in Thailand, within the Integrated Innovation Academic Centre (IIAC), Chulalongkorn University's Academic Development Plan (CU Centenary); and the Higher Education Research Promotion and National Research University Project of Thailand, Office of the Higher Education Commission under grant HS1153A.

References

Agresti, Alan. (2002). *Categorical Data Analysis* (2 ed.). New York, NY: Wiley.

Aroonmanakun, Wirote, Tansiri, Kachen, & Nittayanuparp, Pairit. (2009, 6-7 August). *Thai National Corpus: A progress report.* Paper presented at the 7th Workshop on Asian Language Resources, ACL-IJCNLP 2009, Suntec, Singapore.

Baayen, Rolf Harald, Davidson, Doug J., & Bates, Douglas M. (2008). Mixed-effects modeling with crossed random effects for subjects and items. *Journal of Memory and Language, 59*, 390–412.

Brysbaert, Marc, & Mitchell, Don C. (1996). Modifier Attachment in Sentence Parsing: Evidence from Dutch. *The Quarterly Journal of Experimental Psychology Section A, 49*(3), 664-695.

Clahsen, Harald, & Felser, Claudia. (2006). Continuity and shallow structures in languge processing. *Applied Psycholinguistics, 27*, 107-126. doi: 10.1017.S0142716406060206

Cuetos, Fernando, & Mitchell, Don C. (1988). Cross-linguistic differences in parsing: Restriction on the use of the Late Closure strategy in Spanish. *Cognition, 30*, 73-105.

Desmet, Timothy, De Baecke, Constantign, Drieghe, Denis, Brysbaert, Marc, & Vonk, Wietske. (2006). Relative clause attachment in Dutch: On-line comprehension corresponds to corpus frequencies when lexical variables are taken into account. *Language and Cognitve Processes, 21*(4), 453-485. doi: 10.1080/01690960400023485

Desmet, Timothy, Brysbaert, Marc, & De Baecke, Constantijn. (2002a). The correspondence between sentence production and corpus frequencies in modifier attachment. *Quarterly Journal of Experimental Psychology, 55A*(3), 879-896. doi: 10.1080/20724980143000604

Desmet, Timothy, De Baecke, Constantijn, & Brysbaert, Marc. (2002b). The influence of referential discourse context on modifier attachment in Dutch. *Memory & Cognition, 30*(1), 150-157.

Felser, Claudia, Roberts, Leah, Marinis, Theodore, & Gross, Rebecca. (2003). The processing of ambiguous sentences by first and second language learners of English. *Applied Psycholinguistics, 24*, 453-489.

Ferreira, Fernanda, & Jr., Charles Clifton. (1986). The independence of syntactic processing. *Journal of Memory and Language, 25*(3), 348–368.

Fodor, Janet Dean. (1998). Learning to parse? *journal of Psycholinguistic Research, 27*, 285-317.

Fox, John. & Weisberg, Sanford. (2011). *An R companion to applied regression* (2nd ed.). Thousand Oaks, CA: Sage.

Frazier, Lyn. (1990). Parsing modifiers: Special purpose routines in the human sentence processing mechanism. In D. A. Balota, G. B. F. d'Arcais & K. Rayner (Eds.), *Comprehension process in reading* (pp. 303-331). Hillsdale, NJ: Erlbaum.

Frazier, Lyn, & Clifton, Charles. (1996). *Construal.* Hong Kong: The MIT Press.

Gibson, Edward. (1998). Linguistic complexity: Locality of syntactic dependencies. *Cognition, 68*, 1-76.

Gibson, Edward, Schütze, Carson T., & Salomon, Ariel. (1996). The relationship between the frequency and the processing complexity of linguistic structure. *Journal of Psycholinguistic Research, 25*(1), 59-92.

Grillo, Nino. (2012). Local and Universal. In V. Bianchi & C. Chesi (Eds.), *Enjoy Linguistics. Papers offered to Luigi Rizzi on the occasion of his 60th birthday*: CISCL Press.

Grodner, Daniel J., & Gibson, Edward. (2005). Consequences of the Serial Nature of Linguistic Input for Sentential Complexity. *Cognitive Science, 29*, 261–291.

Hemforth, Barbara, Konieczny, Lars, & Scheepers, Christoph. (2000). Syntactic Attachment and Anaphor Resolution: The Two Sides of Relative Clause Attachment. In M. W. Crocker, M. Pickering & J. Charles Clifton (Eds.), *Architectures and Machanisms for Language Processing* (pp. 259-281). Cambridge, United Kingdom: Cambridge University Press.

Iwasaki, Shoichi, & Ingkaphirom, Preeya. (2009). *A reference grammar of Thai*. Cambridge: Cambridge University Press.

Kamide, Yuki. (2012). Learning individual talkers' structural preferences. *Cognition, 124*, 66-71. doi: 10.1016/j.cognition.2012.03.001

Kimball, John. (1973). Seven principles of surface structure parsing in natural language. *Cognition, 2*, 15-47.

Kullavanijaya, Pranee. (2010). อนุประโยคขยายนาม :คุณานุประโยคและอนุประโยคเติมเต็มนาม [Clauses modifying nouns: Relative clauses and complement clauses] .In A. Prasithrathsint (Ed.), *Controversial constructions in Thai grammar: Relative clause constructions, complement clause constructions, serial verb constructions, and passive constructions* (pp. 7-64). Bangkok: Chulalongkorn University Press.

Lenth, Russell. V. (2013). lsmeans: Least-squares means (1.10-2). R package.

MacDonald, Maryellen C., & Christiansen, Morten H. (2002). Reassessing working memory: A comment on Just & Carpenter (1992) and Waters & Caplan (1996). *Psychological Review, 109*, 35–54. doi: 10.1037//0033-295X.109.1.35

Mattausch, Jason. (2011). A note on the emergence of subject salience. In A. Benz & J. Mattausch (Eds.), *Bidirectional Optimality Theory* (Vol. 279, pp. 73–96): John Benjamins Publishing Company.

Mitchell, Don C., Cuetos, Fernando, Corley, Martin M. B., & Brysbaert, Marc. (1995). Exposure-based models of human parsing: Evidence for the use of coarse-grained (nonlexical) statistical records. *Journal of Psycholinguistic Research, 24*(6), 469-488. doi: 10.1007/BF02143162

Miyamoto, Edson T. (1999). *Relative clause processing in Brazilian Portuguese and Japanese* (Unpublished doctoral dissertation). Massachusetts Institute of Technology, Cambridge, MA.

Pollock, Jean-Yves. (1989). Verb Movement, Universal Grammar, and the Structure of IP. *Linguistic Inquiry, 20*(3), 365-424.

R Core Team (2013). R: A language and environment for statistical computing. Vienna, Austria: R foundation for statistical computing.

Rohde, Hannah, Levy, Roger, & Kehler, Andrew. (2011). Anticipating explanations in relative clause processing. *Cognition, 118*, 339-358. doi: 10.1016/j.cognition.2010.10.016

Tomlin, Russell S. (1986). *Basic Word Order: Functional Principles*. London: Croom Helm.

Wasow, Thomas, Jaeger, T. Florian, & Orr, David M. (2011). Lexical Variation in Relativizer Frequency. In H. J. Simon & H. Wiese (Eds.), *Expecting the unexpected: Exceptions in Grammar* (pp. 175-195). Germany: Mouton de Gruyter.

Zagona, Karen. (2012). Tense and aspect. In J. I. Hualde, A. Olarrea, & E. O'Rourke (Eds.), *The handbook of Hispanic linguistics* (pp. 355-372). Chichester, UK: Wiley Blackwell.

Appendix A.

See Tables 2 to 4 for the corpus frequencies according to animacy and concreteness.

		Types of N2				Total
		animate		inanimate		
		concrete (%)	abstract (%)	concrete (%)	abstract (%)	
animate	concrete	13 (54.17)	11 (47.83)*	7 (53.85)	0 (0.00)	31 (51.67)
	abstract	0 (0.00)	44 (95.65)*	1 (50.00)	1 (100.00)	46 (86.79)*
inanimate	concrete	54 (50.94)	25 (92.59)*	57 (52.78)	9 (56.25)	145 (56.42)*
	abstract	157 (59.70)*	107 (70.39)*	120 (46.33)	70 (46.98)	454 (55.16)*
Total		224 (56.42)*	187 (75.40)*	185 (48.43)	80 (48.19)	676 (56.67)*

Table 2. N1 attachments in internally-disambiguated sentences. (N1 bias in% each cell: *: p <% .05; +: p < .10 according to exact binomial texts).

		Types of N2				Total
		animate		inanimate		
		concrete (%)	abstract (%)	concrete (%)	abstract (%)	
animate	concrete	2 (40.00)	5 (50.00)	1 (33.33)	0 (0.00)	8 (44.44)
	abstract	0 (0.00)	6 (100.00)*	0 (0.00)	0 (0.00)	6 (75.00)
inanimate	concrete	17 (70.83)+	4 (80.00)	16 (55.17)	3 (60.00)	40 (63.49)*
	abstract	30 (68.18)*	20 (71.43)*	28 (44.44)	26 (54.17)	104 (56.83)+
Total		49 (66.22)*	35 (71.43)*	45 (46.88)	29 (54.72)	158 (58.09)*

Table 3. N1 attachments in subject position in internally-disambiguated sentences. (N1 bias in% each cell: *: p <% .05; +: p < .10 according to exact binomial texts).

		Types of N2				Total
		animate		inanimate		
		concrete (%)	abstract (%)	concrete (%)	abstract (%)	
animate	concrete	11 (57.89)	6 (46.15)	6 (60.00)	0 (0.00)	23 (54.76)
	abstract	0 (0.00)	38 (95.00)*	1 (100.00)	1 (100.00)	40 (88.89)*
inanimate	concrete	37 (45.12)	21 (95.45)*	41 (51.90)	6 (54.55)	105 (54.12)
	abstract	127 (58.00)*	87 (70.16)*	92 (46.94)	44 (43.56)	350 (54.69)*
Total		175 (54.18)	152 (76.38)*	140 (48.95)	51 (45.13)	518 (56.24)*

Table 4. N1 attachments in object position in internally-disambiguated sentences. (N1 bias in% each cell: *: p <% .05; +: p < .10 according to exact binomial texts).

Encoding Generalized Quantifiers in Dependency-based Compositional Semantics

Yubing Dong*
Department of Computer Science
University of Southern California
yubing.dong@usc.edu

Ran Tian
Graduate School of Information Sciences
Tohoku University
tianran@ecei.tohoku.ac.jp

Yusuke Miyao
National Institute of Informatics, Japan
yusuke@nii.ac.jp

Abstract

For textual entailment recognition systems, it is often important to correctly handle Generalized quantifiers (GQ). In this paper, we explore ways of encoding GQs in a recent framework of Dependency-based Compositional Semantics, especially aiming to correctly handle linguistic knowledge like hyponymy when GQs are involved. We use both the *selection operator* mechanism and a new *relation* extension to implement some major properties of GQs, reducing 69% errors of a previous system, and a further error analysis suggests extensions towards more powerful logical systems.

1 Introduction

Dependency-based Compositional Semantics (DCS) provides a formal yet intuitive way to model natural language semantics. It was initially proposed in Liang et al. (2011) as a relational database querying protocol, and later used for logical inference in Tian et al. (2014a). Although the DCS inference framework provided decent support for both quantifiers *all* (universal quantifier) and *no* (negated existential quantifier), attention is required for an RTE system to cope with generalized quantifiers (GQ), including "at most n", "at least n", "most", etc., which can affect the direction or even the existence of an entailment relation, as demonstrated in Examples 1 to 3.

*This work was conducted during an internship at the National Institute of Informatics, Japan.

Example 1. $P \Rightarrow H$ but $H \nRightarrow P$, where
P At most 5 students like noodles.
H At most 5 Japanese students like udon noodles.

Example 2. $P \Rightarrow H$ but $H \nRightarrow P$, where
P At least 5 Japanese students like udon noodles.
H At least 5 students like noodles.

Example 3. $P \nRightarrow H$ and $H \nRightarrow P$, where
P Most Japanese students like udon noodles.
H Most students like noodles.

In this paper, we explore ways of encoding GQs in a recent framework of Dependency-based Compositional Semantics (DCS) (Liang et al., 2013; Tian et al., 2014a), especially aiming to correctly handle linguistic knowledge like hyponymy when GQs are involved. We use *selection operators*, an extension mechanism described in Tian et al. (2014a), to implement a sub-type of GQs (Section 3.1). To deal with downward monotonicity of the predicate argument, we also propose a simple extension called "*relation*" to the framework (Section 3.2). This approach does not encode the exact semantics of every specific GQ, but instead captures some major properties that are both easily implementable with the current technology and useful in many cases.

As in Tian et al. (2014a), we empirically tested the extended system on the "Generalized Quantifiers" section of the FraCaS corpus (The Fracas Consortium et al., 1996), and reduced 69% of the previous errors. A further error analysis reveals some limitations of the current approach, suggesting extensions towards more powerful logical systems. We hope this research could make linguistic knowledge like

Copyright 2014 by Yubing Dong, Ran Tian, and Yusuke Miyao
28th Pacific Asia Conference on Language, Information and Computation pages 585–594

hyponymy a more effective resource for textual entailment tasks, and also shed some light on the handling of more complicated natural language inference phenomena. The extended system is publicly released at `https://github.com/tomtung/tifmo`.

2 Background

2.1 Properties of Generalized Quantifiers

In this paper, "*generalized quantifiers*" refers to quantity-denoting determiners such as *"few"*, *"most"*, *"at least 5"*, etc. They can bind with a property-denoting common noun phrase (e.g. *"students"*) to form a quantified noun phrase (e.g. *"few students"*), which can then bind with a predicate (e.g. *"like noodles"*) to form a sentence (e.g. *"few students like noodles"*). We regard the meanings of both the common noun phrase and the predicate as their *denotations*, i.e. let W be the universe containing all entities (a.k.a. the "world" set), then the meaning of "*students*" is regarded as a set **student** $\subseteq W$ containing all entities being students, and the meaning of "*(someone) likes noodles*" is regarded as a subset of W which contains all entities who like noodles. Thus, if we denote the power set of W as 2^W, then a GQ can be seen as a binary relation over 2^W, or in other words, a function F from $(A, B) \in 2^W \times 2^W$ to $F(A)(B) \in \mathbf{2} = \{0, 1\}$, in which the sets A and B are called *noun argument* and *predicate argument*, respectively.

Usually, the relation imposed by a GQ is based on the notion $|\cdot|$ of set cardinalities; for example, $AtMost[30\%](A)(B)$ represents the relation that $|A \cap B|/|A| \leq 30\%$. However, in practice it often requires a large amount of effort to introduce cardinalities into logical inference. Hence, in this paper we make a compromise by encoding properties of GQs that are most relevant to semantic relations like hyponymy and are useful for solving RTE problems. We mainly focus on three major properties, namely *interaction with universal and existential quantifications*, *conservativity*, and *monotonicity*.

Given a GQ, say F, one most basic semantic property is its interaction with universal and existential quantifications—whether $F(A)(B)$ is entailed by the noun argument being a subset of the predicate argument (for short, "*entailed by* $\forall$"), i.e. $A \subseteq B \Rightarrow F(A)(B)$, or whether it entails the two arguments having a non-empty intersection (for short, "*entails* $\exists$"), i.e. $F(A)(B) \Rightarrow A \cap B \neq \emptyset$. There are three cases:

$$A \subseteq B \Rightarrow F(A)(B) \Rightarrow A \cap B \neq \emptyset$$

as *"most"* in Example 4,

$$A \subseteq B \not\Rightarrow F(A)(B) \Rightarrow A \cap B \neq \emptyset$$

as *"a lot of"* in Example 5, and

$$A \subseteq B \not\Rightarrow F(A)(B) \not\Rightarrow A \cap B \neq \emptyset$$

as *"at most 5"* in Example 6.[1]

Example 4. $A \Rightarrow B \Rightarrow C$, where
A All students like noodles.
B Most students like noodles.
C There are students who like noodles.

Example 5. $A \not\Rightarrow B \Rightarrow C$, where
A All students like noodles.
B A lot of students like noodles.
C There are students who like noodles.

Example 6. $A \not\Rightarrow B \not\Rightarrow C$, where
A All students like noodles.
B At most 5 students like noodles.
C There are students who like noodles.

The *conservativity* property of GQs results from the "domain restraining" role of the noun argument, which effectively eliminates objects that do not have the noun property, so that we only need to consider which of the rest has the predicate property. For example:

Example 7. Few apples are toxic. $\Longleftrightarrow$ Few apples are toxic apples.

The intuition here is that to know whether *few apples* are *toxic*, it is sufficient to know which *apples* are *toxic*; those non-apple toxicants are irrelevant. We formally define the conservativity property as follows.

Definition 1 (Conservativity). A GQ F is *conservative* if for any $A, B \subseteq W$,

$$F(A)(B) \Longleftrightarrow F(A)(A \cap B).$$

[1] We have made a convenient and practical assumption here: for an English GQ denoted as $F(\cdot)(\cdot)$, $F(A)(B)$ presupposes $A \neq \emptyset$. Therefore we ignore the cases when $A \subseteq B \Rightarrow F(A)(B) \not\Rightarrow A \cap B \neq \emptyset$, because $A \neq \emptyset \wedge A \subseteq B \Rightarrow A \cap B \neq \emptyset$.

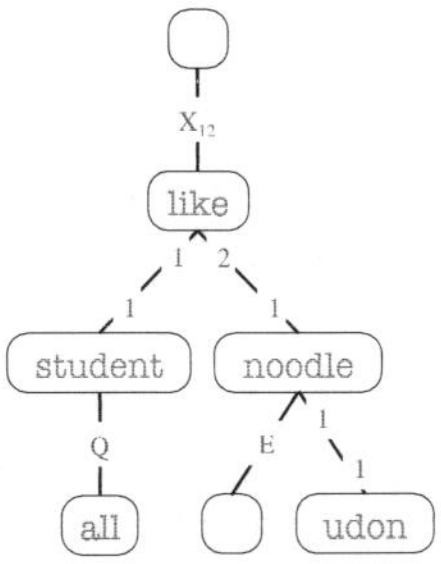

student

Tom
Kate
John
...

like

Mary	Teddy bear
John	kitsune udon
Mike	spaghetti
...	...

udon

kitsune udon
tempura udon
...

noodle

kitsune udon
spaghetti
...

Figure 1: A DCS tree of the sentence *"all students like udon noodles"*, with a given database.

Another important property that textual entailment could rely on is *monotonicity*.

Definition 2 (Monotonicity)**.** A GQ F is *upward-entailing* (resp. *downward-entailing*) in the noun argument if, for any $A, B \subseteq W$ and $A' \subseteq A$ (resp. $A' \supseteq A$),

$$F(A')(B) \Rightarrow F(A)(B).$$

F being *upward/downward-entailing* in the predicate argument can be defined in a similar manner.

For example, the GQ *"at most 5"* is downward-entailing in each argument as shown in Example 1; and the GQ *"at least 5"* is upward-entailing as shown in Example 2.

In Section 3, we will explore ways of encoding the properties discussed in this section in the DCS inference framework.

2.2 Dependency-based Compositional Semantics

DCS (Liang et al., 2013) was originally proposed as a natural language interface for querying concrete relational databases. The meanings of a natural language sentence in DCS are represented by a *DCS tree*, which is designed to be both semantically precise for execution on a database, and structurally straightforward for easy alignment to a syntactic dependency tree. For example, Figure 1 shows the DCS tree for the sentence "all students like udon noodles", with the corresponding tables in a given relational database.

When executed on databases, a DCS tree calculates *denotations* in a bottom-up manner. For example, the DCS tree in Figure 1 first takes the table `student`, and stores it at place "1"; then it calculates the intersection of entries in table `udon` and `noodle` to get the denotation of *"udon noodles"*, and stores the result at place "2". The execute marker "X_{12}" on the root edge imposes the wide reading of the quantifier *"all"*, and guides a calculation that first joins the result stored at place "2" with the second column of `like` table, producing the denotation of *"like udon noodles"*; then projects this denotation into the first column to get the denotation of *"subjects who like udon noodles"*; and finally checks if this is a superset of the denotation of *"students"* stored in place "1". The narrow reading of *"all"* (i.e. "there is a specific udon noodle liked by all students") can be produced by replacing the execute marker X_{12} with X_{21}, which will first assembles each entry x in the second column of the `like` table such that all students like x, then intersects the result with the denotation of *"udon noodles"*, and finally checks if the intersection is an empty set. For the precise calculation of a DCS tree and details of this "mark-execute" mechanism, please consult Liang et al. (2013).

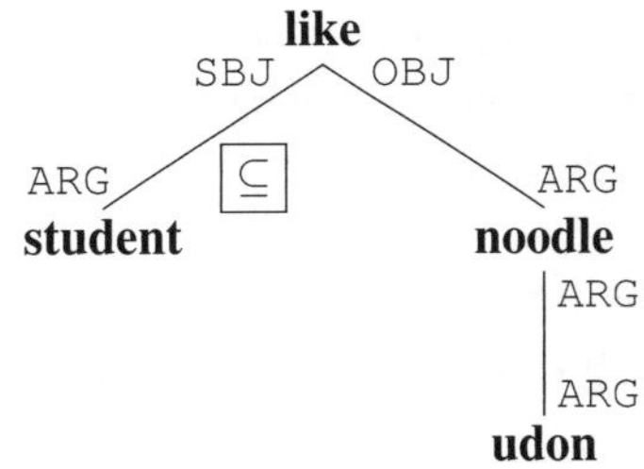

Figure 2: Adapted DCS tree for logical inference

In Tian et al. (2014a), the DCS framework was adapted to deal with open-domain textual inference. The idea is to use relational algebra operators (Codd, 1970) to formalize the calculation process used in DCS trees, so we can perform logical inference on this abstract level, without given a closed-domain relational database. For example, Figure 2 shows an adapted DCS tree representing the same sentence, *"all students like udon noodles"*; and it guides a calculation of the meaning parallel to the original DCS. Concretely, the *abstract denotation* of *"udon noodles"* is formulated as the following:

$$D_1 = \textbf{noodle} \cap \textbf{udon},$$

where **noodle** and **udon** are no longer given tables

in a relational database but abstract sets (treated as symbols) representing denotations of the words, and "$\cap$" is a relational algebra operator representing "intersection".

Similarly, the abstract denotation of *"like udon noodles"* is formulated by:

$$D_2 = \textbf{like} \cap (W_{\texttt{SBJ}} \times (D_1)_{\texttt{OBJ}}),$$

where W is the "world set" as mentioned in Section 2.1, and "$\times$" denotes the Cartesian product. Subscripts SBJ and OBJ are used to denote different dimensions.

Finally, the abstract denotation of *"subjects who like udon noodles"* is:

$$D_3 = \pi_{\texttt{SBJ}}(D_2),$$

where π is the projection operator. Here we use π_r to denote a projection into dimension r, whereas π^r denotes a projection to all dimensions other than r.

The adapted DCS tree in Figure 2 uses syntactic/semantic labels (SBJ, OBJ, etc.) instead of numbers in the original DCS tree to denote different dimensions (i.e. different columns in the tables of the relational database), because they provide database-independent explanations for these dimensions. In addition, the involved "mark-execute" mechanism for representing quantifier *"all"* (as illustrated by the Q, E and X_{12} markers in Figure 1) is simplified to a quantification marker "$\subseteq$" on the **student-like** edge (Figure 2), and explained as the division operator $q_{\subseteq}$ in relational algebra[2]:

$$q^r_{\subseteq}(R, C) = \{x |\ \emptyset \neq R \cap (\{x\} \times W_r) \subseteq \{x\} \times C_r\}$$

Therefore, the abstract denotations

$$\begin{aligned} D_4 &= q^{\texttt{SBJ}}_{\subseteq}\left(\pi^{\texttt{OBJ}}(D_2), \textbf{student}\right) \\ &= q^{\texttt{SBJ}}_{\subseteq}(D_3, \textbf{student}) \end{aligned}$$

and

$$D_5 = \pi^{\texttt{OBJ}}\left(q^{\texttt{SBJ}}_{\subseteq}(D_2, \textbf{student})\right),$$

correspond to the final results calculated by the original DCS tree according to the wide reading and narrow reading of *"all"*, respectively. For logical inference, instead of the database-dependent evaluations of such denotations, we mainly consider their *satisfiability*, i.e. whether D_4 (or D_5) $\neq \emptyset$. Here, by definition of the division operator, $D_4 \neq \emptyset \Leftrightarrow \textbf{student} \subseteq D_3$ and $D_5 \neq \emptyset \Leftrightarrow q^{\texttt{SBJ}}_{\subseteq}(D_2, \textbf{student}) \neq \emptyset \Leftrightarrow \exists x; \textbf{student}_{\texttt{SBJ}} \times \{x\}_{\texttt{OBJ}} \subseteq D_2$.

As we can see from the previous description, many intermediate or related denotations are produced during the processing of DCS trees. In Tian et al. (2014a), a special kind of auxiliary denotations is considered, which integrates the context information of an entire DCS tree, and is naturally linked to a single pairing of a syntactic/semantic label and a node in the DCS tree. Such a pair is called a *germ*, denoted by $(\textbf{like}, \texttt{SBJ})_{\mathcal{T}}$, $(\textbf{like}, \texttt{OBJ})_{\mathcal{T}}$, $(\textbf{noodle}, \texttt{ARG})_{\mathcal{T}}$, etc., where the subscript $\mathcal{T}$ is used to denote the whole DCS tree and emphasize the context awareness of the germ object. Abstract denotations linked to germs are closely related to the concept of *feasible values* defined in Liang et al. (2013). For example, if we consider the DCS tree $\mathcal{T}$ in Figure 2 and assume the wide reading of *"all"*, then the denotations linked to $(\textbf{like}, \texttt{OBJ})_{\mathcal{T}}$ and $(\textbf{noodle}, \texttt{ARG})_{\mathcal{T}}$ both equal to $\pi_{\texttt{OBJ}}(D_2) = \pi_{\texttt{OBJ}}(\textbf{like}) \cap D_1$, *"udon noodles that are liked by somebody"*; the denotation linked to $(\textbf{like}, \texttt{SBJ})_{\mathcal{T}}$ is D_3, *"subjects who like udon noodles"*; and the denotation linked to $(\textbf{student}, \texttt{ARG})_{\mathcal{T}}$ is **student**. The final result D_4 can then be seen as been calculated from the abstract denotations linked to germs $(\textbf{like}, \texttt{SBJ})_{\mathcal{T}}$ and $(\textbf{student}, \texttt{ARG})_{\mathcal{T}}$. Abstract denotations linked to germs are useful for encoding GQs in the DCS framework, as we describe in Section 3.2.

Another useful mechanism for implementing GQs is the *selection operator* s_f introduced in Tian et al. (2014a), which are marked on a DCS tree node and wrap an abstract denotation D to form a new abstract denotation $s_f(D)$ during the calculation process. Selection operators were introduced as an extension mechanism to represent the generalized selection operation in relational algebra, which selects a subset of specific properties from a given set; the axioms characterizing such properties can be user-defined. For example, in Tian et al. (2014a), selection operators are used to implement superlatives such as *"highest"*, so that $s_{\text{highest}}(\textbf{mountain})$ denotes the set of the highest mountains. Effectively, a selection operator s_f is a user-defined map from any

[2]When R and C have the same dimension, $q^r_{\subseteq}(R, C)$ is either the 0-dimension point set $\{*\}$ (if $R \subseteq C$) or (otherwise) $\emptyset$.

abstract denotation D to a new denotation $s_f(D)$. In Section 3.1 we will use this mechanism to encode GQs.

2.3 Related Work

GQs have been a topic of interest in study of logic since ancient time: Aristotle's syllogism could be seen as concerning the meanings and properties of four basic quantifiers, namely *"all"*, *"no"*, *"some"*, and *"not all"*. Gottlob Frege (Zalta, 2014), one of the founders of modern logic, in 1870s introduced $\forall$ and $\exists$, and formulated the notion of a quantifier as a second order relation. The idea of *generalized* quantifiers was introduced by Mostowski (1957) and generalized in Lindström (1966), forming the standard definition we use nowadays. Later, Barwise and Cooper (1981), following Montague (1973), showed the importance of GQs in the formal analysis of linguistic phenomena. By and large, these works cover the logical and linguistic background involved in this paper.

Although it has been recognized that it is important to encode GQs for solving textual entailment problems, this remains a big challenge. MacCartney et al. (2006), for example, tried to capture the use of GQs in feature vectors, but the capabilities of which are greatly limited without an inference engine. Even for systems that are backed by inference engines like in this paper, the focus still needs to be put on practical NLP rather than logic, linguistics, or semantic theory, and model complexity may need to be purposely traded for computation efficiency. For example, Lewis and Steedman (2013) used first-order logic for semantic representation, which is theoretically very expressive, but still unable to define GQs without some extensions (Barwise and Cooper, 1981) that are nontrivial especially for practical inference.

Some works made the compromise similar to ours: only encode the important properties of GQs rather than their perfect semantics. A notable recent work that focused on monotonicity is MacCartney and Manning (2008), in which the notion of monotonicity was generalized to support recursive determination of entailments of a compound expression from its constituents. To a large extent, this approach handled the interaction between multiple GQs in a single sentence. However, inference was based on a chain of shallow syntactic edit operations linking premise to hypothesis, which not only failed to include various inference patterns, but also was unreliable when there are multiple sentences in the premise, or when the premise is relatively long. The DCS inference framework, on the other hand, gracefully handles such cases in a uniform way, thanks to the more sophisticated inference engine. An empirical comparison is shown in Section 4.

The logical inference engine described in Tian et al. (2014a) treats abstract denotations as terms and represent meanings by atomic sentences, which is shown to be very efficient compared to first order logic provers (Tian et al., 2014b). The idea behind this is actually very similar to description logics (DL) (Baader et al., 2003); indeed, the $\mathcal{DLR}$ generalization of DLs towards n-ary relations (Calvanese et al., 1998) was proposed to deal with inference problems on database schemata expressed in relational models, which shares the same setting with the logical system proposed in Tian et al. (2014a). The $\mathcal{DLR}$ system includes intersections, Cartesian products of 1-dimensional sets and projections into 1-dimensional sets, as well as constructors not presented in Tian et al. (2014a)'s system such as complement, union, and qualified number restrictions. $\mathcal{DLR}$ is also shown to be reducible to the traditional DL (with binary relations) $\mathcal{ALCQI}$, for which many complete DL inference engines are available[3]. In comparison, Tian et al. (2014a)'s inference engine is not complete and lacks a thorough exploration from the theoretical side, e.g. on the decidability and complexity of the logical system, but it has a working natural language interface inherited from the DCS framework, and supports specific constructors tailored for textual inference, e.g. the division operator, which seems not easily encoded in $\mathcal{DLR}$. Description logics have been applied to natural language processing since the early days, but were used mostly for *semantic interpretation* (Brachman, 1985; Sowa, 1991; Knight and Luk, 1994), in which knowledge on syntactic, semantic, and pragmatic elements of natural language are encoded in DL to drive the process of converting utterances into deep and context-dependent logical

[3]`http://www.cs.man.ac.uk/~sattler/reasoners.html`

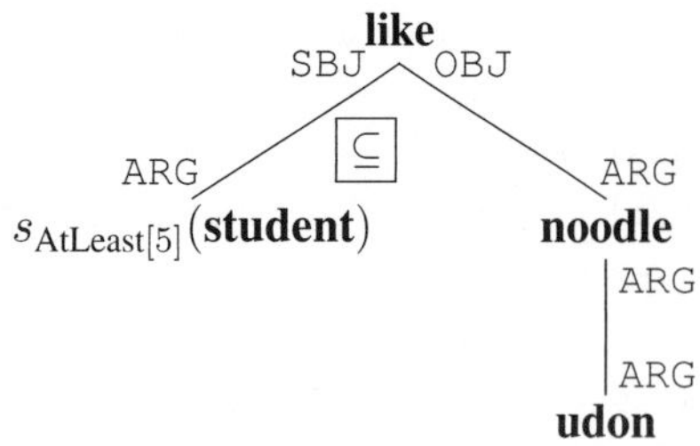

Figure 3: Encoding *"at least 5"* as selection

forms. Tian et al. (2014a)'s work on the other hand directly uses a DL-like logical system to represent semantics and perform textual inference, benefiting from the efficiency of DL logical inference. We explore ways of extending Tian et al. (2014a)'s system to deal with more advanced linguistic phenomena in this work, while trying to preserve its algebraic fashion to ensure efficiency, because we believe it is important to investigate to what extent the "natural" textual inference requires from a logical system. Some limitations of Tian et al. (2014a)'s framework has actually been revealed; for which we will discuss in Section 4.

3 Encoding Generalized Quantifiers

3.1 Encoding as Selections

Selections are used to encode GQs in the form of

$$F(A)(B) \equiv s_F(A) \subseteq B,$$

where s_F is the specific selection operator defined for the GQ F—that is, a selection operator s_F is always used together with a quantification marker "$\subseteq$", as exemplified in Figure 3. Note that $s_F(A)$ can be defined as any set related to A, not necessarily being its subset.

The basic requirement for encoding a GQ F in this way is that F should be upward-entailing in its predicate argument, because the form $s_F(A) \subseteq B$ implies such monotonicity. Entailment from universal quantification (Example 4)

$$A \subseteq B \Rightarrow s_F(A) \subseteq B$$

and conservativity

$$s_F(A) \subseteq (A \cap B) \Leftrightarrow s_F(A) \subseteq B$$

both hold if we add axiom:

$$s_F(A) \subseteq A$$

On the other hand, entailment to existential quantification (Example 5)

$$s_F(A) \subseteq B \Rightarrow A \cap B \neq \emptyset$$

can be implied from the custom axiom:

$$s_F(A) \cap A \neq \emptyset$$

The monotonicity in the noun argument can be implemented as well. If F is upward-entailing in the noun argument, we should add the axiom

$$A' \supseteq A \Rightarrow s_F(A') \subseteq s_F(A).$$

Note that the direction of $\subseteq$ is reversed because $s_F(A)$ serves as the *subset* in the form $F(A)(B) \equiv s_F(A) \subseteq B$. Similarly, downward-entailment in the noun argument can be achieved by the axiom

$$A' \subseteq A \Rightarrow s_F(A') \subseteq s_F(A).$$

A proof tree for Example 2 is shown in Figure 4, where D_3 is the denotation for *"subjects who like udon noodles"*, as defined in Section 2.2, and similarly $D'_3 = \pi_{\text{SBJ}}(\textbf{like} \cap (W_{\text{SBJ}} \times \textbf{noodle}_{\text{OBJ}}))$ for *"subjects who like noodles"*.

3.2 Encoding as Relations

As mentioned in Section 2.1, a GQ can be seen a binary relation over 2^W. From this point of view, we introduce a new extension called *relation* as a new type of statement into the framework. A relation r_f can be used to represent an arbitrary relation between two abstract denotations. A relation marker can be marked on a DCS tree edge to denote some relation between the child germ and the parent germ (Figure 5). In our implementation, the core inference engine keeps track of which term pairs are labeled with which relations: not only can it answer whether two terms have been claimed to have a certain relation, but also can it look up all terms that have a certain relation with a certain term. Similar to selections, we can also specify different sets of axioms for different relations—an axiom could be about either what a relation statement entails or what it is entailed by.

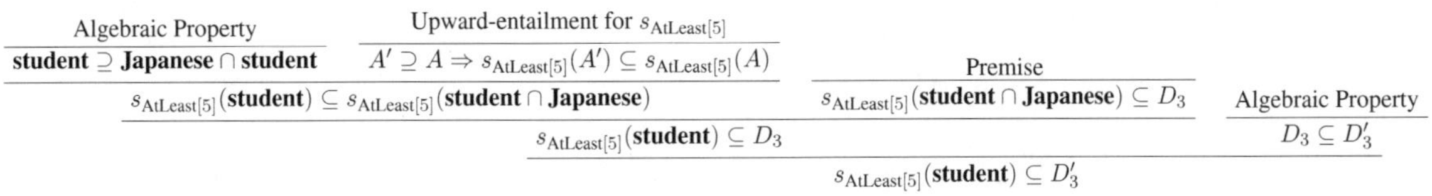

Figure 4: An example of proof with generalized quantifiers encoded as selections.

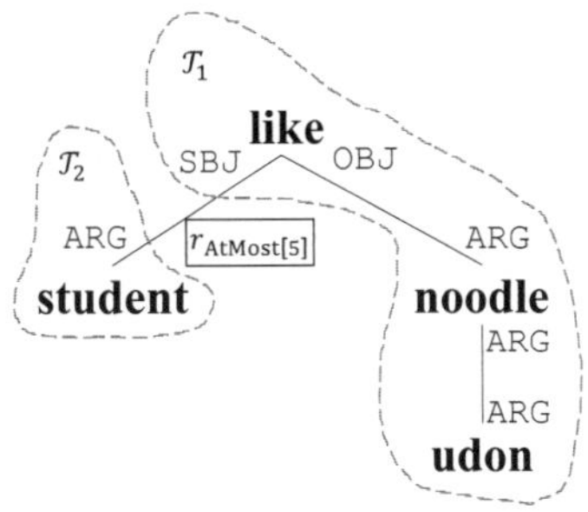

Figure 5: Encoding *"at most 5"* as relation

Intuitively, a GQ F can be represented by a relation r_F:

$$F(A)(B) \equiv r_F(A, B)$$

To enable the entailment from universal or to existential quantification, we simply add the axiom $A \subseteq B \Rightarrow r_F(A, B)$ or $r_F(A, B) \Rightarrow A \cap B \neq \emptyset$, respectively.

The axioms for monotonicity are also very intuitive. For GQs that are downward-entailing in both arguments (e.g. *"at most 5"* in Example 1), we put

$$r_f(A, B) \wedge A \supseteq A' \wedge B \supseteq B' \Rightarrow r_f(A', B').$$

Other kinds of monotonicity can be achieved in a similar way.

As for conservativity, we can simply implement

$$r_F(A, B) \Rightarrow r_F(A, A \cap B),$$

but the reverse

$$r_F(A, A \cap B) \Rightarrow r_F(A, B)$$

is a little tricky. This is because Tian et al. (2014a)'s inference engine is based on forward-chaining: it always tries to deduce *all* possible implications from given premises. This strategy is employed not only because of its efficiency, but also because it opens the possibility of adapting DCS for entailment generation (Androutsopoulos and Malakasiotis, 2010), in which case without any given hypotheses the system needs to actively explore what the premises entail. For example, from "few dinosaurs are pterosaurs", with the knowledge of GQ conservativity the system should figure out "few dinosaurs can fly" without being explicitly instructed to prove so. However, to implement $r_F(A, A \cap B) \Rightarrow r_F(A, B)$, the forward-chaining strategy would require the engine to find all Bs that satisfy $X = A \cap B$ whenever a relation $r_F(A, X)$ is claimed, in order to claim the relation $r_F(A, B)$. Though it is quite easy to check if $X = A \cap B$ for a given triple (X, A, B), issues arise when B is not given and we need to find all possibilities. It is generally impractical to enumerate all possible forms that a set X can be written as intersections; the number of possibilities easily explodes even for small-size problems[4]. Hence, we implement the rule $r_F(A, A \cap B) \Rightarrow r_F(A, B)$ as the following: if $r_F(A, X)$, *and* if $X \subseteq A$, then we take every $B \supseteq X$ and check if $X = A \cap B$. The necessary conditions $X \subseteq A$ and $B \supseteq X$ limit the search space at first. We would like to emphasize this detailed implementation issue here because formal semantics researchers are often not aware of such difficulties.

A shortcoming of the relation implementation is that, when processing DCS trees with relations, our extended system simply discards the edges marked as relations, then calculate the abstract denotations of germs in the resulting DCS forest, and finally use the denotations of corresponding germs as arguments of the relations to form statements. For example, in Figure 5, we calculate the denotations of germs $(\textbf{student}, \texttt{ARG})_{\mathcal{T}_2}$ and $(\textbf{like}, \texttt{SBJ})_{\mathcal{T}_1}$, which are **student** and D_3 (as defined in Section 2.2), respectively; then we form the statement $r_{\text{AtMost}[5]}(\textbf{student}, D_3)$ as the meaning of this sentence. This procedure implies that, relations in DCS trees are always explained as having the widest

[4]For example, $X = X \cap C$ for every $C \supseteq X$; even we only consider *minimal* intersections such that $X = A \cap B$ but $X \neq A$ and $X \neq B$, the possibilities could be exponential, e.g. consider $X = (A \cap B) \cap C = A \cap (B \cap C)$.

scope and hence we cannot deal with multiple relations in a single sentence. It causes errors when there are multiple GQs encoded as relations appear in the same sentence; we analyze this case in detail in Section 4.

4 Evaluation and Analysis

The FraCaS corpus (The Fracas Consortium et al., 1996)[5] was built in the mid 1990s by the FraCaS Consortium, which contains a set of hand-crafted entailment problems covering a wide range of semantic phenomena, organized in nine sections. The first section is titled "Generalized Quantifiers", and can serve as a good empirical test suite for RTE systems that handle general properties of GQs. This section contains 74 problems[6]; 44 of them have one premise sentence while the other 30 have multiple premises. The involved GQs and their properties are listed in Table 1.[7] Our implementation extends the TIFMO system publicly released with Tian et al. (2014a)[8]. Since we mainly focus on the performance of the DCS framework as formal semantics, on-the-fly knowledge and WordNet are not used. Major GQ properties can be implemented as composable and reusable units[9], so that each GQ can be created by simply composing the units that corresponds to the properties it has. This makes implementing new GQs very easy.

TIFMO uses the Stanford Parser[10] to obtain Stanford dependencies (de Marneffe et al., 2006) and POS tags, which are used to construct DCS trees based on a set of pre-defined rules. We extend those rules in order to recognize GQs in this step, and encode them under one of four settings, namely "Baseline", "Selection", "Relation", and "Selection+Relation". GQs are simply dropped in the "Baseline" setting. The "Selection" and "Relation" settings use the same DCS trees as in "Baseline", except for selection or relation markers on DCS trees to represent GQs. The "Selection" approach implements all GQs as selections (even for those are downward-entailing in the predicate argument), whereas "Relation" approach implements all GQs as relations. In the "Selection+Relation" setting, we use relations only for the GQs that are downward-entailing in the predicate argument (i.e. "few" and "at most n"), and implement the rest of the GQs as selections. We evaluate the system under each setting; the test results are shown in Table 2.

We compare our results with two previous textual inference systems, CCG-Dist (Lewis and Steedman, 2013) and NatLog (MacCartney and Manning, 2007; MacCartney and Manning, 2008), also shown

GQ	Entailed by ∀	Entails ∃	Monotonicity	
			Noun Arg.	Predicate Arg.
many	✓	✓	✗	↑
a lot of	✓	✓	✗	↑
few	✗	✓	↓	↓
a few	✓	✓	↑	↑
most	✓	✓	✗	↑
at most n	✗	✗	↓	↓
at least n	✗	✓	↑	↑

Table 1: Properties of GQs appear in FraCaS corpus, including the interaction with universal and existential quantifications, and the monotonicity in noun and predicate arguments, where "↑", "↓", and "✗" denote upward-entailing, downward-entailing, and non-monotone, respectively.

System		Accuracy		
		Single	Multi	Overall
NatLog	MacCartney07	84.1%	N/A	
	MacCartney08	**97.7%**		
CCG-Dist	Parser Syntax	70.5%	50.0%	62.2%
	Gold Syntax	88.6%	80.0%	85.1%
TIFMO	Baseline	79.5%	86.7%	82.4%
	Selection	90.9%	93.3%	91.9%
	Relation	88.6%	93.3%	90.5%
	Selection+Relation	93.2%	**96.7%**	**94.6%**

Table 2: Accuracies achieved on the first section of FraCaS corpus using different systems.

[5] We used the version converted to XML format by MacCartney and Manning (2007).

[6] 6 problems that do not have a defined solution are excluded.

[7] FraCaS dubiously interpreted "many" as denoting "a large proportion" rather than "a large absolute number", whereas "few" as denoting "a small absolute number" rather than "a small proportion". We also treat "a lot of" as a synonym of "many".

[8] `http://kmcs.nii.ac.jp/tifmo/`

[9] We implement GQ properties as stackable traits in Scala (Odersky et al., 2011), each consists of no more than a few dozen lines of code.

[10] `http://nlp.stanford.edu/software/lex-parser.shtml`

in Table 2. CCG-Dist uses rule-based conversion from CCG parses to first order logic formulas, and results are given using both parser syntax and gold syntax. The resulting accuracies are not very high, even for gold syntax, showing that implementing GQs is not an easily accomplishable task although first order logic is theoretically very expressive. NatLog is a system based on natural logic, which has almost perfect performance on single premise problems but faces difficulties dealing with premises of multiple sentences. In contrast, our extension of the TIFMO system achieves the best overall accuracy.

In each setting of our extension, almost all of the errors are related to the handling of GQs. The "Selection" approach cannot encode downward entailment in the predicate argument, as shown in Example 8; whereas the "Relation" approach fails to handle multiple GQs in a single sentence, as shown in Example 9.

Example 8. $P_1 \wedge P_2 \wedge P_3 \Rightarrow H$, where

P_1 Few committee members are from southern Europe.

P_2 All committee members are people.

P_3 All people who are from Portugal are from southern Europe.

H There are few committee members from Portugal.

Example 9. $P \not\Rightarrow H$, where

P At most ten commissioners spend a lot of time at home.

H At most ten commissioners spend time at home.

In Example 9, when both *"at most ten"* and *"a lot of"* are encoded as relations, both of them take the widest scope and the meaning of P is calculated as the conjunction of P_a *"at most ten commissioners spend (something) at home"*, and P_b *"(somebody) spend a lot of time at home"*. Then, P_a implies H since *"at most ten"* is downward-entailing in the predicate argument; the system produces a wrong answer. On the other hand, in the "Selection+Relation" setting, *"a lot of"* is encoded as selection and accompanied with the quantification marker "$\subseteq$", which can take a narrow scope and is explained as a division operator. Hence the calculated meaning of P becomes

$$r_{\text{AtMost[10]}}(\textbf{comm'r}, q_{\subseteq}^{\texttt{OBJ}}(D, s_{\text{ALotOf}}(\textbf{time})))$$

where D is the abstract denotation for *"spend at home"*

$$D = \textbf{spend} \cap (W_{\texttt{SBJ}} \times W_{\texttt{OBJ}} \times \textbf{home}_{\texttt{MOD}})$$

which is correct and solves this case. However, in general we need to further extend the notion of "relation" to handle different scopes, or at least we need something similar to the division operator but can be used to implement downward entailment in the predicate argument.

If we recall the definition of division operator $q_{\subseteq}$, it is natural to consider a similar operator as

$$q_{\supseteq}^{r}(R, C) = \{x \mid R \cap (\{x\} \times W_r) \supseteq \{x\} \times C_r\}.$$

Fortunately, $q_{\supseteq}$ can be defined algebraically as

$$q_{\supseteq}^{r}(R, C) = \pi^r(R) \setminus \pi^r(\bar{R} \cap (W^r \times C_r)),$$

where W^r denotes the Cartesian product of Ws on all dimensions other than r. This is implementable if we introduce complement $\bar{X}$ into Tian et al. (2014a)'s logical system. Operator "$q_{\supseteq}$" can be combined with selection operators to encode GQs that are downward-entailing in predicate argument, e.g. "at most ten". We may also be tempted to introduce free variables or higher order operators, especially when we begin to consider donkey anaphora (Heim, 1982) and other advanced inference phenomena. Such decisions should be made with caution because unguarded free variables easily lead to undecidability, as suggested by the research on description logics. However, further exploration on this topic should be a future direction but out of the scope of this work.

5 Conclusion

Encoding the semantics of a generalized quantifier is often crucial to correctly capturing the semantics of a sentence and making the right textual entailment. We have shown in this paper that major properties of GQs can be implemented in the DCS inference framework to correctly handle semantic relations like hyponymy. This tested and demonstrated the capabilities and potentials of the DCS framework, and suggested extensions towards more powerful logical systems for handling more sophisticated linguistic phenomena.

References

Ion Androutsopoulos and Prodromos Malakasiotis. 2010. A survey of paraphrasing and textual entailment methods. *J. Artif. Int. Res.*, 38(1):135–187, May.

Franz Baader, Diego Calvanese, Deborah L. McGuinness, Daniele Nardi, and Peter F. Patel-Schneider, editors. 2003. *The Description Logic Handbook: Theory, Implementation, and Applications*. Cambridge University Press, New York, NY, USA.

Jon Barwise and Robin Cooper. 1981. Generalized quantifiers and natural language. *Linguistics and Philosophy*, 4(2):159–219.

Ronald J. Brachman. 1985. On the epistemological status of semantic networks. In Ronald J. Brachman and Hector J. Levesque, editors, *Readings in Knowledge Representation*. Morgan Kaufmann.

Diego Calvanese, Giuseppe De Giacomo, and Maurizio Lenzerini. 1998. On the decidability of query containment under constraints. In *Proceedings of the 17th ACM SIGACT SIGMOD SIGART Symposium on Principles of Database Systems (PODS98)*.

Edgar F Codd. 1970. A relational model of data for large shared data banks. *Commun. ACM*, 13(6):377–387, June.

Marie-Catherine de Marneffe, Bill MacCartney, and Christopher D. Manning. 2006. Generating typed dependency parses from phrase structure parses. In *Proceedings of the 5th Language Resources and Evaluation Conference (LREC 2006)*, pages 449–454.

Irene Heim. 1982. *The semantics of definite and indefinite noun phrases*. Ph.D. thesis.

Kevin Knight and Steve K. Luk. 1994. Building a large-scale knowledge base for machine translation. In *Proceedings of AAAI '94*.

Mike Lewis and Mark Steedman. 2013. Combined distributional and logical semantics. *Transactions of the Association for Computational Linguistics*, 1:179–192.

Percy Liang, Michael Jordan, and Dan Klein. 2011. Learning Dependency-based Compositional Semantics. In *Proceedings of the 49th Annual Meeting of the Association for Computational Linguistics: Human Language Technologies*, pages 590–599, Stroudsburg, PA, USA. Association for Computational Linguistics.

Percy Liang, Michael I. Jordan, and Dan Klein. 2013. Learning dependency-based compositional semantics. *Computational Linguistics*, 39(2).

Per Lindström. 1966. First order predicate logic with generalized quantifiers. *Theoria*, 32(3):186–195.

Bill MacCartney and Christopher D. Manning. 2007. Natural logic for textual inference. In *Proceedings of the ACL-PASCAL Workshop on Textual Entailment and Paraphrasing*, pages 193–200. Association for Computational Linguistics.

Bill MacCartney and Christopher D. Manning. 2008. Modeling semantic containment and exclusion in natural language inference. In *Proceedings of the 22Nd International Conference on Computational Linguistics - Volume 1*, COLING '08, pages 521–528, Stroudsburg, PA, USA. Association for Computational Linguistics.

Bill MacCartney, Trond Grenager, Marie-Catherine de Marneffe, Daniel Cer, and Christopher D Manning. 2006. Learning to recognize features of valid textual entailments. In *Proceedings of the main conference on Human Language Technology Conference of the North American Chapter of the Association of Computational Linguistics*, pages 41–48. Association for Computational Linguistics.

Richard Montague. 1973. The proper treatment of quantification in ordinary english. In Patrick Suppes, Julius Moravcsik, and Jaakko Hintikka, editors, *Approaches to Natural Language*, volume 49, pages 221–242. Dordrecht.

Andrzej Mostowski. 1957. On a generalization of quantifiers. *Fundamenta mathematicae*, 44:12–36.

Martin Odersky, Lex Spoon, and Bill Venners. 2011. Traits as stackable modifications. In *Programming in Scala: A Comprehensive Step-by-Step Guide*, chapter 12.5, pages 267–271. Artima Inc, 2nd edition.

John F. Sowa, editor. 1991. *Principles of Semantic Networks: Explorations in the Representation of Knowledge*. Morgan Kaufmann.

The Fracas Consortium, Robin Cooper, Dick Crouch, Jan Van Eijck, Chris Fox, Josef Van Genabith, Jan Jaspars, Hans Kamp, David Milward, Manfred Pinkal, Massimo Poesio, Steve Pulman, Ted Briscoe, Holger Maier, and Karsten Konrad. 1996. Using the framework. *Fracas project LRE 62*, 51.

Ran Tian, Yusuke Miyao, and Takuya Matsuzaki. 2014a. Logical inference on dependency-based compositional semantics. In *Proceedings of Association for Computational Linguistics (ACL) 2014*.

Ran Tian, Yusuke Miyao, and Takuya Matsuzaki. 2014b. Efficient logical inference for semantic processing. In *Proceedings of the ACL 2014 Workshop on Semantic Parsing*.

Edward N. Zalta. 2014. Gottlob frege. In Edward N. Zalta, editor, *The Stanford Encyclopedia of Philosophy*. Spring 2014 edition.

On Common Ground, Context and Information Structure: The Case of Counter-Expectation in Thai

Upsorn Tawilapakul
Language Institute
Thammasat University
Bangkok, Thailand
u.tawilapakul@gmail.com

Abstract

This paper addresses the influences of common ground, context and information structure on the linguistic production and interpretation processes with a special reference to counter-expectation in Thai. It presents, first of all, a fresh view on the operation of the particle *lɛɛw45* as a marker of counter-expectation. It also indicates the association of the particle with focus and the influence of common ground and context, both of which control the use and interpretation of *lɛɛw45* as well as the conversation flow. Moreover, the unaccounted additional impact of numeral scalarity on the production of a counter-expectation has been detected. The paper applies the Question Under Discussion (QUD) technique in order to account for these phenomena.

1 Introduction

This introductory section addresses the re-appraisal of the role of the particle *lɛɛw45*. It also raises two problematic issues involving the impact of numeral scalarity and the association of *lɛɛw45* with focus.

1.1 The re-appraisal of the role of *lɛɛw45*

Lɛɛw45 has been regarded as a post-serial particle which acts either as a perfective aspect marker or a past time marker (Kanchanawan, 1978; Boonyapatipark, 1983). Also, Scovel (1970) proposes that it marks the completion of the event. Following these claims which are based hugely on the assumption that *lɛɛw45* plays its primary role in temporality, it can be concluded in (1) that the addition of *lɛɛw45* to the sentence generates perfectiveness, thereby asserting that the event *plaa33thɔɔŋ33 taay33* or *die (the goldfish)* happened before the time of utterance and satisfies the truth-condition *'the sentence is true if and only if there was a goldfish and it died at time t'* where *t* refers to the reference time.

(1) plaa33thɔɔŋ33 taay33 lɛɛw45
goldfish die LƐƐW45
'The goldfish died.'

Nonetheless, the perfectiveness as well as the completion of the above event can still be derived even when *lɛɛw45* is omitted. Findings from the data suggest that *lɛɛw45* actually implies an expectation about the issue under discussion based on the state of the issue prior to the reference time. It also suggests that the particle is used in order to denote a counter-expectation. This claim is supported by three pieces of evidence given in (2), (3) and (4) which present the co-occurrence of *lɛɛw45* with an achievement, an ongoing predicate and a state, respectively. They all indicate that the presence of *lɛɛw45* does not affect the derivation of the aspectual readings which are in fact derived through the aspectual nature of the predicates attached to *lɛɛw45*.

(2) fay33faa42 dap22 lɛɛw45
power go out LƐƐW45
'The power went out.'
→ Previously it was expected that the power would not go out.

Copyright 2014 by Upsorn Tawilapakul
28th Pacific Asia Conference on Language, Information and Computation pages 595–604

(3) maa45 kam33laŋ33 wiŋ42 lɛɛw45
horse PROG run LƐƐW45
'The horse is running now.'
→ Previously it was expected that the horse would not run.

(4) tɔɔn33nii45 baan42 sa22ʔaat22 lɛɛw45
now house be clean LƐƐW45
'The house is clean now.'
→ Previously it was expected that the house would not be clean

The appearance of *lɛɛw45* at the discourse level as shown in (5) also exhibits its function as a marker of counter-expectation.

(5) Context: Danai saw a beautiful vase at the pottery shop and wanted to buy it. However, he was running late for his class. He then decided to come back to buy the vase after work. Now he is at the pottery shop but does not see the beautiful vase he wants to buy. He then asks the shop assistant about it.

Danai: cɛɛ33kan33 bay33 nan45
vase CLASS DEM
pay33 nay24 khrup45
go where PART (POLITE.MAS)
'Where is that vase?'
SA: mii33 khon33 maa33 sʉʉ45
have person come buy
pay33 lɛɛw45 kha22
go PART PART (POLITE.FEM)
'A person has bought it.'
→ Previously it was expected to be available.

The utterance of the shop assistant marked by *lɛɛw45* implies the expectation about the vase, i.e. that the vase would be available, which was formed in accordance with the state of the vase prior to the reference time NOW. Secondly, it asserts the updated state of being unavailable of the vase at the reference time which counters the state of the vase present in the expectation. Now compare (5) to (6):

(6) Context: Danai saw that the shop assistant was busy with a customer. He wants to know what happened.

Danai: mʉa42kii45 mii33 ʔa22ray33
a moment ago have what
rʉʉ24 khrup45
QW PART (POLITE.MAS)
'What happened a moment ago?'
SA: mii33 khon33 maa33 sʉʉ45
have person come buy
cɛɛ33kan33 pay33
vase go
kha22
PART (POLITE.FEM)
'A person came to buy a vase.'

The broad question asked by Danai indicates that he does not acknowledge the existence of the vase. Or even if he does the shop assistant does not detect his expectation about the vase. Therefore, she does not add *lɛɛw45* to her utterance to overtly inform him that his expectation no longer holds.

The minimal pair of situations provided in (5) and (6) reveals that the presence of *lɛɛw45* gives two implications: 1) the existence of the issue under discussion; and 2) a particular expectation regarding the state of the issue under discussion and its validity prior and at the reference time. The semantics of *lɛɛw45* is summarised as shown in (7):

(7) $[[lɛɛw45]] = \exists y \exists x \forall t'<RT[(\text{expectation}\ (y)\ (t'): \sim p(x)) \wedge p(x)(RT)]$

In verse, when *lɛɛw45* appears it indicates that in all time intervals before the reference time $t'<RT$ someone y holds an expectation such that the issue under discussion x is in the state of $\sim p$ and at the reference time RT, x is in the state of p. These implications subsequently determine the conditions of use of *lɛɛw45*.

1.2 Two problematic issues detected in the production and interpretation processes

When *lɛɛw45* co-occurs with numbers, the production of a counter-expectation is not only controlled by the semantics of the particle but also by numeral scalarity. (8Bi) is an acceptable response to (8A) while (8Bii) is not.

(8) A: thuk45khraŋ45 da33nay33 kin33
every time Danai eat
yaa33 sɔɔŋ24 met45
medicine two CLASS
'Every time, Danai takes 2 tablets of paracetamol.'
B: (i) khraŋ45nii45 khaw24 kin33
this time he eat
pay33 saam24 met45 lɛɛw45
go three CLASS PART
'This time he has taken 3 tablets!'
(ii) khraŋ45nii45 khaw24 kin33
this time he eat
pay33 nʉŋ22 met45
go one CLASS
ʔeeŋ33/*lɛɛw45
only PART
'This time he has taken only 1 tablet!'

Basically, when *lɛɛw45* co-occurs with numbers, it urges a division of two sets—the set under expectation and the set countering expectation. In the situation in (8), *2* serves as the expected number which distinguishes the set under expectation *{0, 1, 2}* from the set countering expectation *{3, 4, ..}*. The former represents the state of *~p(t')* of the issue under discussion while the latter represents the state of *p(RT)* of the issue under discussion. The felicity of a sentence marked with *lɛɛw45* is determined by the existence of the entailment of the expected number in the state of *~p(t')* by the asserted number in the state of *p(RT)*. In (8Bi), the expected number *2* is reached and surpassed by the asserted number *3* which entails the expected number by default. On the contrary, in (8Bii) the expected number is not reached and thus not entailed by the asserted number. Thus, a counter-expectation is generated in (8Bi) but not in (8Bii).

Moreover, as shown in (9), the association of *lɛɛw45* with focus is detected. Given that the particle possibly associates either with the number or the subject NP, the sentence in (9A) can be interpreted in two ways which result with two possible responses in (9Bi) and (9Bii):

(9) A: da33nay33 kin33 kek45 pay33
Danai eat cake go
sip22 chin45 lɛɛw45
ten CLASS PART
'Danai has eaten 10 pieces of cake!'
B: (i) sip22 chin45!
ten CLASS
'10 pieces!'
(ii) da33naay33 ʔa22na45
Danai QW
'Danai?!'

The situation in (9) shows that a sentence with *lɛɛw45* does not always connote only one distinct counter-expectation. The expectation and what counters it are identified through the focused elements present in the antecedent and the postcedent. These foci call for the interpretation that complies with the appropriate common ground knowledge and context available on the addressee's side.

2 Common ground, context, information structure, and QUD

This section is aimed at, first of all, discussing the interactions among common ground, context and information structure. It is also aimed to introduce the mechanism of QUD and how it explains these interactions.

2.1 The interactions among common ground, context and information structure

Adopting Rooth's (1985, 1992) notion of focus, focus is a member of a set which contains all alternatives relevant to the issue under discussion. The set of alternatives is established from the substitutions for the variable standing at the focused position. Following this idea, the statement in (10) contains the *x* variable as shown in (11) and induces the set of alternatives as given in (12):

(10) Danai will buy a bottle of [red wine]$_F$.

(11) Danai will buy a bottle of *x*.

(12) {white wine, red wine, milk, gin, water, ...}

The variable *x* represents the focused element and refers to all plausible alternatives which include all bottled liquids that Danai will potentially buy.

In addition, according to Krifka (2007), in both the semantic and pragmatic uses of focus the focused element is required to match the appropriate common ground knowledge and context.

(13) A: What did the manager send to his daughter?
B: The manager sent [a POSTcard]$_F$ to his daughter.

(14) A: Who did the manager send a postcard to?
B: The manager sent a postcard to [his DAUGHter]$_F$.

The pragmatic use of focus as exemplified in (13) and (14) suggests that even though (13B) and (14B) share the same truth conditions, i.e. the sentence is true if and only if there is a definite manager that both A and B know and the manager sent a postcard to his daughter, the foci in the two sentences are assigned to the elements that correspond with the common ground and contexts, which, in these cases, suggested by the questions in (13A) and (14A). Such pragmatic use of focus illustrates the management of common ground in order to achieve a particular communicative purpose. It helps create the cognitive representation that the participants in the conversation rely on when the utterance is produced and interpreted. Assigning a focus to the element incompliant with the purpose of the speaker thus impedes the communication.

Regarding the semantic use of focus, different focus locations in a sentence with a focus-sensitive particle offer different truth conditions. A wrong assignment of focus results in the delivery of the information not supposed to be transferred to the addressee. The sentences in (15) and (16) present the association of the focus-sensitive particle *only* with focus:

(15) The manager only sent [a POSTcard]$_F$ to his daughter.

(16) The manager only sent a postcard to [his DAUGHter]$_F$.

The semantic exhaustivity of *only* is applied to two different focused elements resulting in different truth conditions as outlined in (17) and (18):

(17) (15) is true if and only if there is a definite manager who sent something to his daughter which was nothing else but a postcard.

(18) (16) is true if and only if there is a definite manager who sent a postcard to someone who was no one else but his daughter.

2.2 QUD and Information Structure

Roberts (1996) proposes that in each conversation, a conversational goal is set up based on the interaction between common ground and context. Common ground selects the contexts that represent the possible worlds in which the common ground information is true. The conversational goal requires a mutual commitment between the speaker and the addressee. It is accomplished through the setup move creating by the speaker and the payoff move determined by the addressee. A question represents the issue being discussed in the conversation and is thus referred to as a question under discussion.

QUD is developed by Roberts (1996, 2012) from the accounts of question proposed by Hamblin (1973), Groenendijk and Stockhof (1984) and von Stechow (1991). A question, according to Roberts (2012), designates a set of alternatives or *q-alternatives* which contains all alternatives that are eligible to be selected as the definitive answer to the question. The set of q-alternatives for a *wh*-question is established, as shown in the formality in (19), by abstracting the *wh*-phrase present in the *wh*-question and applying it to any entity that contains the properties identified in it.

(19) The *q-alternatives* corresponding to utterance of a clause α:
q-alt(α) = $\{p: \exists u^{i-1}, \ldots, u^{i-n} \in D[p = |\beta| (u^{i-1})\ldots(u^{i-n})]\}$
where α has the logical form $wh_{i-1}, \ldots, wh_{i-n} (\beta)$, with $\{wh_{i-1}, \ldots, wh_{i-n}\}$ the (possibly empty) set of *wh*-elements in α, and
where D is the domain of the model for the language, suitably sortally restricted,

(2012:10)

Concerning the congruence between a question and its set of q-alternatives, QUD relies on the influence of common ground as proposed in von Stechow's (1991) account of question. The content of a question corresponds to the common ground knowledge and thus determines the properties of all plausible alternatives.

In many cases achieving a particular communicative goal involves a stack of questions which includes both superquestions and subquestions stemmed in accordance with common ground and context. They are evaluated and ordered in accordance with the interlocutors' moves and context under the conditions as stated in (20) which generally require that the questions be answerable and not yet answered by the common ground knowledge. Also, they must be ordered in such a way that the complete answer to the lower ranked question is a partial answer to the higher ranked question. Accordingly, QUD, as shown in (21), functions in the way in which the relation among the superquestion and the subquestions is displayed.

(20) QUD, *the questions-under-discussion stack*, is a function from *M* (the moves in the discourse) to ordered subsets of $Q \cap Acc$ (the set of accepted setup and payoff moves in *M*) such that for all $m \in M$:
  i. For all $q \in Q \cap Acc$, $q \in$ QUD(m) *iff*
    1. $q < m$ (i.e. neither *m* nor any subsequent questions are included), and
    2. CG(m) fails to entail an answer to *q* and *q* has not been determined to be practically unanswerable.
  ii. QUD(m) is (totally) ordered by $<$.
  iii. For all $q, q' \in$ QUD(m), if $q < q'$, then the complete answer to q' contextually entails a partial answer to *q*.

(Roberts 2012:14-15)

(21)

QUD (1)	=	$\varnothing$
QUD(a)	=	$<1>$
QUD(a_i)	=	$<1, a>$
QUD(Ans(a_i))	=	$<1, a, a_i>$
QUD(a_{ii})	=	$<1, a>$
QUD(Ans(a_{ii})	=	$<1, a, a_{ii}>$
QUD(b)	=	$<1>$
QUD(b_i)	=	$<1, b>$
QUD(Ans(b_i))	=	$<1, b, b_i>$
QUD(b_{ii})	=	$<1, b>$
QUD(Ans(b_{ii}))	=	$<1, b, b_{ii}>$

(Roberts 2012:18)

In response to the question stack, the strategy of inquiry or the strategy to answer *q* is set up as demonstrated in (22). The pair of question and strategy $<q, S>$ prompts the setting of subinquiries to *q* or q' which leads to the function of the strategy of inquiry shown in (23). In summary, the strategy to answer 1 is to answer a by answering a_i and a_{ii} and to answer b by answering b_i and b_{ii}.

(22) The *strategy of inquiry* which aims at answering *q*, Start(q):
For any question $q \in Q \cap Acc$, Strat(q) is the ordered pair $<q, S>$, where *S* is the set such that:

If there are no $q' \in Q$ such that QUD(q') $= <...q>$, then $S = \varnothing$.
Otherwise, for all $q' \in Q$, QUD(q') $= <...q>$ iff Strat(q') $\in S$.

(Roberts 2012:18)

(23)

Strat(a_i)	=	$<a_i, \varnothing>$
Strat(a_{ii})	=	$<a_{ii}, \varnothing>$
Strat(a)	=	$<a, \{<a_i, \varnothing>, <a_{ii}, \varnothing>\}>$
Strat(b_i)	=	$<b_i, \varnothing>$
Strat(b_{ii})	=	$<b_{ii}, \varnothing>$
Strat(b)	=	$<b, \{<b_i, \varnothing>, <b_{ii}, \varnothing>\}>$
Strat(1)	=	$<1, \{<a, \{<a_i, \varnothing>, <a_{ii}, \varnothing>\}>, <b, \{<b_i, \varnothing>, <b_{ii}, \varnothing>\}>\}>$

(Roberts 2012:19)

Suppose there is a situation in which both Danai and Sunan acknowledge that Thani has recently acquired a cat. Sunan does not retain further information and only Danai has obtained it. She is aware of this fact and thus thinks Danai can be a good source of information. Her primary curiosity is about the appearance of the cat. The question she is going to ask, which become the goal of the conversation, is thus aimed at acquiring the information about the look of the cat. The dialogue between these two people takes place in the way as shown in (24):

(24) Sunan: What does the cat that Thani has recently bought look like?
Danai: It is a male Siamese cat.

In this case, the superquestion is multiplied to

subquestions which inquire about the specific features that make up the cat's overall appearance. These questions are listed in (25). Suppose each of the q-alternative sets for Subquestions a, b, c and d contains only two alternatives, the full question stack is created as shown in (26) and the full strategy of inquiry, in which the pairs of question and strategy for both the superquestion and the subquestions are ordered by the function <, is provided in (27):

(25) i) Does it have long fur?
ii) What colour is it?
iii) What is the colour of its eyes?
iv) Is it a male or a female?

(26) 1. What does the cat that Thani has recently bought look like?
a. What type of fur does it have?
a_i. Does it have long fur?
Ans(a_i) = No
a_{ii}. Does it have short fur?
Ans(a_{ii}) = Yes
b. What colour of fur does it have?
b_i. Does it have black fur?
Ans(b_i) = No
b_{ii}. Does it have brown fur?
Ans(b_{ii}) = Yes
c. What colour of eyes does it have?
c_i. Does it have blue eyes?
Ans(c_i) = Yes
c_{ii}. Does it have yellow eyes?
Ans(c_{ii}) = No
d. What gender is it?
d_i. Is it a male?
Ans(d_i) = Yes
d_{ii}. Is it a female?
Ans(d_{ii}) = No

(27) $\text{Strat}(1) = \langle 1, \{\langle a, \{\langle a_i, \varnothing\rangle, \langle a_{ii}, \varnothing\rangle\}\rangle, \langle b, \{\langle b_i, \varnothing\rangle, \langle b_{ii}, \varnothing\rangle\}, \langle c, \{\langle c_i, \varnothing\rangle, \langle c_{ii}, \varnothing\rangle\}\rangle, \langle d, \{\langle d_i, \varnothing\rangle, \langle d_{ii}, \varnothing\rangle\}\rangle\}\rangle$

3. Proposed account for the production and interpretation of *lɛɛw45*'s counter-expectation through QUD

This section will tackle the issues raised in Subsection 1.2 by applying the QUD technique. The section begins with the typical formation of denials through questions in Subsection 4.1. Subsection 4.2 addresses the formation of *lɛɛw45*'s counter-expectation through questions and accounts for the issue concerning numeral scalarity. Finally, Subsection 4.3 deals with the issue concerning common ground, context and information structure.

3.1 The Formation of Denials Through Questions

In general, a denial denotes an opposition against the proposition represented in the antecedent. It is not produced against a vague target but against a specific element which is deemed false. The target is signalled by means of focus assignment. This thus means that information structure also influences the production and interpretation processes. An example is given in (28):

(28) Danai: Thani's cat is a [Persian]$_F$ cat.
Sunan: It is not a [Persian]$_F$ cat. It is a [Siamese]$_F$ cat.

The above denial is targeted at the focused element *Persian*. The congruence of denial requires that the focused element in the postcedent be relevant to the focused element in the antecedent. In the case of (28), focus is assigned on the adjectival modifier *Persian* in both the antecedent and the first sentence of the postcedent. Besides, the second sentence of the postcedent provides the correct information through the adjectival modifier *Siamese* which receives focus.

Expressing an agreement or a disagreement is identical to answering a polar or yes/no question which is formed in accordance with common ground knowledge and context. Moreover, under QUD, the antecedent forms the setup move which induces either an agreement or a disagreement. In contrast, the postcedent represents the payoff move which requires the verifications for the existence of the definite NP, which represents the issue under discussion, and for the properties of the issue as depicted in the antecedent. Following this, Danai's statement in (28) is processed through the question stack shown in (29). Please note that this question stack mentions only two plausible alternatives for each subquestion.

(29) 1. Is it the case that Thani's cat is a Persian cat?
a. What kind of pet does Thani have?
a_i. Does Thani have a dog?
Ans(a_i) = No
a_{ii}. Does Thani have a cat?
Ans(a_{ii}) = Yes
b. What type of cat does Thani have?
b_i. Does Thani have a Persian cat?
Ans(b_i) = No
b_{ii}. Does Thani have a Siamese cat?
Ans(b_{ii}) = Yes

Sunan's reply suggests that the fact that Thani has a cat is the complete answer to question a and thus the existence of Thaini's cat, which is the issue under discussion, is confirmed. However, the result of the verification of the information concerning the type of the cat which is carried out through question b suggests a contrast between the assertion in the antecedent and Sunan's background knowledge. The answers to questions a and b encourage Sunan to express a denial and to provide the correct information.

3.2 The formation of *lɛɛw45*'s counter-expectation through questions

The formation of *lɛɛw45*'s counter-expectation can be carried out through questions. Consider (30):

(30) Danai: thaa33nii33 mii33 mɛɛw33
Thani have cat
sɔɔŋ24 tua33
two CLASS
'Thani has two cats.'
Sunan: tɛɛ22 tɔɔn33nii45 khaw24
but now he
mii33 saam24 tua33 lɛɛw45
have three CLASS PART
'But now he has three!'

In the case of *lɛɛw45*'s counter-expectation, similar to the case of denial, the setup move formed in the antecedent is aimed at asking either for an agreement or a disagreement while the payoff move calls for the verifications for the existence of the issue under discussion in the common ground and for the properties of the issue. Both verifications can be conducted through questions in (31) and (32):

(31) What kind of pet does Thani own?

(32) How many cats does Thani currently own?

However, *lɛɛw45*'s counter-expectations, unlike denials, are not made at this stage. The reason is, the semantics of *lɛɛw45* prompts a comparison between the states of the issue under discussion before and at the reference time. This comparison calls for two additional questions in (33) and (34). The questions are supposed to verify the existence of the expectation or the state of the issue under discussion prior to the reference time and, due to the presence of numbers, to check if the asserted number exceeds the expected number.

(33) How many cats did Thani previously own?

(34) What is the relation between the number of cats that Thani currently owns and the number of cats he previously owned?

The complete stack of questions and answers are compiled as shown in (35) while the strategy of inquiry is given in (36). Please note again that although each q-alternative set allows several alternatives, only two alternatives are mentioned:

(35) 1. Is it the case that Thani owns two cats?
a. What kind of pet does Thani own?
a_i. Does Thani own a dog?
Ans(a_i) = No
a_{ii}. Does Thani own a cat?
Ans(a_{ii}) = Yes
b. How many cats does Thani currently own?
b_i. Does Thani own two cats?
Ans(b_i) = No
b_{ii}. Does Thani own three cats?
Ans(b_{ii}) = Yes
c. How many cats did Thani previously own?
c_i. Did Thani own two cats?
Ans(ci) = Yes
c_{ii}. Did Thani own three cats?
Ans(cii) = No
d. What is the relation between the number of cats that Thani currently owns and the number of cats he

previously owned?

d_i. Is the former greater than the latter?
Ans(d_i) = Yes

d_{ii}. Is the former smaller than the latter?
Ans(d_{ii}) = No

(36) Strat(1) = $<1, \{<a, \{<a_i, \varnothing>, <a_{ii}, \varnothing>\}>, <b, \{<b_i, \varnothing>, <b_{ii}, \varnothing>\}, <c, \{<c_i, \varnothing>, <c_{ii}, \varnothing>\}>, <d, \{<d_i, \varnothing>, <d_{ii}, \varnothing>\}>\}>$

The answers to questions b and c indicate that Danai's statement in fact was true before the reference time and is false at the reference time NOW. Besides, they give rise to question d which leads to the division of the set under expectation *{0, 1, 2}* and the set countering expectation *{3, 4, ..}*. The answer to b suggests that the asserted number *3*, which represents *p(RT)*, exceeds and entails the expected number *2* present in *~p(t')* by default. *Lεεw45* is consequently used by Sunan in order to accomplish her payoff move, that is, to express a counter-expectation.

3.3 The problematic issue concerning context and information structure

(9A) contains the truth conditions *'the sentence is true if and only if there is a person called Danai and he has eaten ten pieces of cake'*. However, it can be interpreted in various ways due to the fact that focus is not overtly marked and thus can be assigned to any eligible element. The fixed location of *lεεw45* does not give any clue about the location of focus as intended by the speaker. Suppose there are two possible contexts which are compatible with the semantics of *lεεw45* and in which (9Bi) and (9Bii) are felicitous as given in (37):

(37) i) Danai eats less than 9 pieces of cake.

ii) Thani and Sutha eat more than 9 pieces of cake. Danai and Sunan eat less than 9 pieces.

The above contexts indicate two different foci and thus lead to two different variables as shown in (38).

(38) i) For the context in (37i):
Danai eats **less than 10** pieces of cake
Danai eats **x** pieces of cake

ii) For the context in (37ii):
Thani and Sutha eat more than 9 pieces of cake
x eats more than 9 pieces of cake

The interpretation processes of *lεεw45*'s counter-expectations under the two contexts above are carried out as follows. The context in (37i) hints that in the common ground of both interlocutors there exists the information on the number of cake that Danai normally eats. The number indicated in (37i) represents the expected number. It induces the division of the set under expectation *{1, 2, 3, 4, 5, 6, 7, 8, 9}* and the set countering expectation *{10, 11, 12, ...}*. After obtaining the new knowledge that this time Danai has eaten 10 pieces of cake, the speaker of (9A), guided by the common ground knowledge, is aware that the focus of (9A) must be assigned on the number of pieces of cake that Danai has eaten. Before uttering (9A) she has to verify the newly obtained information with the assistance from the question stack in (41). Note again that though the subquestions in this case actually involve more than two alternatives, only two alternatives are addressed.

(41) 1. Is it the case that Danai normally eats less than 10 pieces of cake?

a. What kind of dessert does Danai normally eat?

a_i. Does Danai normally eat cakes?
Ans(a_i) = Yes

a_{ii}. Does Danai normally eat fruit jelly?
Ans(a_{ii}) = No

b. How many pieces of cake does Danai normally eats?

b_i. Does Danai normally eat 9 pieces of cake?
Ans(b_i) = Yes

b_{ii}. Does Danai normally eat 10 pieces of cake?
Ans(b_{ii}) = No

c. How many pieces of cake has Danai eaten this time?

c_i. Has Danai eaten 9 pieces of cake?
Ans(c_i) = No

c_{ii}. Has Danai eaten 10 pieces of cake?
Ans(c_{ii}) = Yes

d. What is the relation between the number of cake Danai normally eats and the number of cake he has eaten this time?

d_i. Is the latter greater than the former?
Ans(d_i) = Yes

d_{ii}. Is the latter smaller than the former?
Ans(d_{ii}) = No

The new knowledge which suggests that Danai has eaten 10 pieces of cake provides answers to questions a and c. Danai does not eat less than 10 pieces of cake this time. The answer *10 pieces* to the question in c is then compared with the answer to b which represents the expected number. The answer to d suggests that the number asserted in (9A) is greater than the expected number. This contrast motivates the use of *lɛɛw45* in order to express a counter-expectation.

Regarding the interpretation process, the common ground information concerning the number of pieces of cake that Danai normally eats also facilitates the interpretation of *lɛɛw45*'s counter-expectation. Like in the production process, it directs the addressee to the question stack in (41) and enables her to identify the focus of (9A). At this stage the addressee recognises the association of the number of cake with *lɛɛw45* which suggests a counter-expectation. As (9Bi) shows, the addressee holds the same expectation concerning the number of cake that Danai normally eats. Moreover, she realises that the number of cake that Danai has eaten this time counters her expectation. Therefore, she expresses her surprise.

Regarding the context in (37ii), both interlocutors share the common ground information about the people who normally eat more than 9 pieces of cake and the people who normally eat less than 9 pieces of cake. They acknowledge that Thani and Sutha normally eat more than 9 pieces of cake while Danai and Thida normally eat less than 9 pieces of cake. Both of the interlocutors, or at least one of them, holds the expectation that only Thani and Sutha, not Danai and Sunan, will eat more than 9 pieces of cake. According to the common ground information, the people involved can be divided into the set under expectation which contains the people who normally eat more than 9 pieces of cake as shown in (42) and the set countering expectation which has the people who normally eat less than 9 pieces of cake as its members as shown in (43).

(42) {Thani, Sutha}

(43) {Danai, Sunan}

Suppose these four people are at the same cake party, the counter-expectation expressed in (9A) is thus bound to the question stack in (44):

(44) 1. Is it the case that Danai normally eats more than 9 pieces of cake?

a. What kind of dessert does Danai normally eat?

a_i. Does Danai normally eat cakes?
Ans(a_i) = Yes

a_{ii}. Does Danai normally eat fruit jelly?
Ans(a_{ii}) = No

b. Who normally eat more than 9 pieces of cake?

b_i. Does Thani normally eat more than 9 pieces of cake?
Ans(b_i) = Yes

b_{ii}. Does Danai normally eat more than 9 pieces of cake?
Ans(b_{ii}) = No

c. Who has eaten more than 9 pieces of cake this time?

c_i. Has Thani eaten more than 9 pieces of cake this time?
Ans(c_i) = No

c_{ii}. Has Danai eaten more than 9 pieces of cake this time?
Ans(c_{ii}) = Yes

d. What is the relation between the number of cake that Thani has eaten this time and the number of cake that Danai has eaten this time?

d_i. Is the latter greater than the former?
Ans(d_i) = Yes
d_{ii}. Is the latter smaller than the former?
Ans(d_{ii}) = No

According to the common ground information, Danai is not a member of the set under expectation but of the set countering the expectation. Therefore, the new information which says that Danai has eaten 10 pieces of cake opposes the expectation. That Danai is not the person who normally eats more than 9 pieces of cake, though it was valid previously, is invalid at the reference time. *Lɛɛw45* is thus added to denote the counter-expectation.

As for the interpretation by the addressee, the counter-expectation expressed by the speaker urges her, first of all, to identify the focus. She is able to do so with the help of common ground and context. Realising that *lɛɛw45* in this sentence associates with the focused subject NP *Danai*, she successfully derives the correct interpretation, that is, it is Danai who has eaten 10 pieces of cake, not Thani and Sutha as she previously expected. Surprised with the new information, she uttered (9Bii).

4 Conclusion

Following Robert's (1996, 2012) QUD mechanism, a counter-expectation generated by *lɛɛw45* is expressed in order to achieve the conversational goal, that is, to oppose the expectation regarding the state of the issue under discussion prevailing at the time before the reference time. It asserts that the expectation is no longer valid at the reference time and suggests that the updated information be added to the common ground. The production and interpretation of *lɛɛw45*'s counter-expectations are dependent upon the association of *lɛɛw45* with focus. Even though overt focus marking in Thai is optional, focus identification can be carried out with the help of the QUD technique. The formation of *lɛɛw45*'s counter-expectations is guided by the QUDs which reflect the common ground information while at the same time calling for the set of q-alternatives from which the focused element is selected. The QUDs validate the proposition that presents the expectation drawn from the state of the issue under discussion before the reference time. Moreover, they inquire for the information about the state of the issue at the reference time and check the relation between the two states. In the cases in which numbers appear, the two processes are also controlled by numeral scalarity which allows only the surplus of the asserted number over the expected number in the forward direction of the scale.

Acknowledgement

I would like to thank Malte Zimmermann and all colleagues at the SFB 632: Information Structure Project, University of Potsdam, Germany, for all precious exchanges of knowledge and ideas which hugely contribute to this study. I would also like to thank Eytan Zweig, Peter Sells and Martina Faller for their invaluable comments.

References

Tasanalai Boonyapatipark. 1983. A study of aspect in Thai. PhD Dissertation. School of Oriental and African Studies, University of London.

Jeroen Groenendijk and Martin Stokhof. 1984. Studies on the semantics of questions and the pragmatics of answers. Ph.D. Dissertation. University of Amsterdam.

Nittaya Kanchanawan. 1978. Expression for time in the Thai verb and its application to Thai-English machine translation. Ph.D. Dissertation. University of Texas at Austin.

Manfred Krifka. 2007. Basic notions of information structure. Interdisciplinary Studies of Information Structure 6, eds. by Caroline Féry, Gisbert Fanselow, and Manfred Krifka, 13-55. Potsdam: Universität Potsdam.

Craige Roberts. 1996/2012. Information structure in discourse: Towards an integrated formal theory of pragmatics. Semantics and Pragmatics 5(6):1–69. http://dx.doi.org/10.3765/sp.5.6.

Mats Rooth. 1985. Association with focus. Ph.D. Dissertation. University of Massachusetts at Amherst.

Mats Rooth. 1992. A theory of focus interpretation. Natural Language Semantics 1:75-116.

Thomas S. Scovel. 1970. A grammar of time in Thai. Ph.D. Dissertation. The University of Michigan.

Arnim von Stechow. 1989. Focusing and backgrounding operators. Arbeitspapier Nr. 6, Fachgruppe Sprachwissenschaft, Universität Konstanz.

Semantics and Pragmatics of Cantonese Polar Questions: an inquisitive approach

Yurie Hara
Department of Linguistics and Translation, City University of Hong Kong
83 Tat Chee Avenue Kowloon, Hong Kong SAR
y.hara@cityu.edu.hk

Abstract

This paper analyzes four kinds of Cantonese polar questions, HO2, ME1, AA4 and A-NOT-A questions in the framework of radical inquisitive semantics (Groenendijk & Roelofsen, 2010; Aher, 2012; Sano, 2014). HO2, ME1 and A-NOT-A questions have multi-dimensional semantics. In addition to their primary speech act of questioning, HO2 and ME1 interrogatives encode secondary assertive acts of positive and negative expectations, respectively, while A-NOT-A interrogatives conventionally encode lack of expectation, hence the neutral requirement. In contrast, AA4 interrogatives are semantically simplex question acts, thus they can be used in both biased and neutral contexts.

1 Introduction

Cantonese has a number of constructions that express a polar question as in (1) and (2). Examples in (1) are taken from Lam (2014b,a). All of them encode a polar question meaning but they also differ in terms of the context's bias/neutrality. (1-a), a so-called A-NOT-A question, can only be asked in a neutral context. (1-b) with a sentence-final particle HO2 is used when the speaker is biased toward the positive answer, while (1-c) with ME1 is asked when the speaker has a bias toward the negative answer.[1]

(1) a. zi3ming4 jau5 mou5 fu6ceot1
Jimmy have not.have devote
gwo3 si4gaan3 aa3?
ASP time PRT
'Has Jimmy spent time (on the project), or not?' (A-NOT-A Q)

b. zi3ming4 jau5 fu6ceot1 gwo3
Jimmy have devote ASP
si4gaan3 gaa3 ho2?
time PRT HO2
'Jimmy has spent time (on the project), hasn't he?' (HO2 Q)

c. zi3ming4 jau5 fu6ceot1 gwo3
Jimmy have devote ASP
si4gaan3 me1?
time ME
'Jimmy hasn't spent time (on the project), has he?' (ME1 Q)

In contrast, an AA4 question like (2), which is simply marked with a final question particle AA4 is not as restricted. It can be used in both neutral and biased contexts.[2]

(2) zi3ming4 jau5 fu6ceot1 gwo3 si4gaan3
Jimmy have devote ASP time
aa4?
AA4
'Has Jimmy spent time (on the project)?' (aa4 Q)

The goal of this paper is to provide a semantic analysis that derives each interpretation. Lam

[1] The numbers in Cantonese example sentences indicate lexical tones: 1 = high-level; 2 = medium rising; 3 = medium level; 4 = low falling; 5 = low rising; 6 = low level.

[2] There is also MAA3 particle, which is borrowed from Mandarin and somehow more formal (Matthews & Yip, 1994).

Copyright 2014 by Yurie Hara
28th Pacific Asia Conference on Language, Information and Computation pages 605–614

(2014a) argues that HO2 and ME1 questions are complex speech acts of questioning and asserting, while A-NOT-A questions are simple acts of questioning. Lam's (2014a) account of A-NOT-A questions fails to explain why they are more restricted than AA4 questions, which can be used in both biased and neutral contexts. Incidentally, Yuan & Hara (2013) claim that Mandarin A-NOT-A questions are also complex speech acts of questioning and asserting, where the content of the assertion is a tautology, 'p or not p'. Yuan & Hara (2013) argue that the assertion of 'p or not p' in effect indicates the ignorance of the speaker, hence the neutrality requirement. However, Yuan and Hara's analysis also poses a conceptual problem because in truth-conditional semantics, an assertion of 'p or not p' is equivalent to that of 'q or not q'. This paper thus offers a solution to this problem in the framework of inquisitive semantics (Groenendijk & Roelofsen, 2009). Contra Lam (2014a), the semantics of an A-NOT-A question is also multi-dimensional in that it has a question meaning as well as a secondary assertion meaning which indicates lack of 'anticipation of prior expectation-rejection shift'.

2 Lam (2014) on (non-)biased questions

Lam (2014a) analyzes the three interrogative constructions in (1) and proposes that an A-NOT-A question denote a simple speech act of questioning while ME1 and HO2 questions are complex speech acts of questioning and asserting.

Lam (2014a) provides convincing pieces of evidence supporting that A-NOT-A questions are neutral, HO2 questions have positive bias, and ME1 questions have negative bias.

First, only A-NOT-A questions can be used in neutral contexts as in (3). Examples (3)-(6) are adapted from Lam (2014a).

(3) Scenario: Jimmy is asked to take a seat in an interrogation room of a police station. A police officer asked for Jimmy's name and then says this.

a. nei5 hai6 m4 hai6 mei5gwok3 jan4?
   2SG COP NEG COP USA person
   'Are you American?' (A-NOT-A)

b. #nei5 hai6 mei5gwok3 jan4 ho2?
   2SG COP USA person HO2
   'You are American, right?' (HO2)

c. #nei5 hai6 mei5gwok3 jan4 me1?
   2SG COP USA person ME1
   'You aren't American, are you?' (ME1)

Second, A-NOT-A questions cannot be responded by 'You are right' (Asher & Reese, 2005).

(4) A: gam1 go3 ji6jyut6 jau5 mou5 jaa6gau2 hou6?
   this CL February have not.have twenty-nine number
   'Is there a 29th this February?'

   B: #nei5 aam1, nei5 aam1. jau5/mou5
   2SG right, 2SG right not.have/have
   'You are right, you are right. There is(n't).'

In contrast, to a HO2 question, the responder B can say 'You are right' to agree with the positive answer.

(5) A: gam1 go3 ji6jyut jau5 jaa6gau2 hou6 ho2?
   this CL February have twenty-nine number HO2
   'There is a 29th this February, isn't there?'

   B: nei5 aam1, nei5 aam1. ✓jau5/*mou5
   'You are right, you are right. There ✓is/*isn't.'

Similarly, to a ME1 question, the responder B can say 'You are right' to agree with the negative answer.

(6) A: gam1 go3 ji6jyut jau5 jaa6gau2 hou6 me1?
   this CL February have twenty-nine number ME1
   'There isn't a 29th this February, is there?'

   B: nei5 aam1, nei5 aam1. *jau5/✓mou5
   'You are right, you are right. There *is/✓isn't.'

Based on these data,[3] Lam (2014a) concludes that A-NOT-A questions are pure questions in that they are simple speech acts of questioning, thus can be used only when the context is neutral. On the other

[3]See Lam (2014a) for other arguments.

hand, HO2 questions are complex speech acts of questioning and assertion of p while ME1 questions are also complex speech acts of questioning and assertion of $\neg p$. Lam's analysis is summarized in Table 1.

Syntax	Observation	Analysis
A-NOT-A	neutral	QUEST(p)
HO2	p bias	QUEST(p)&ASSERT(p)
ME1	$\neg p$ bias	QUEST(p)&ASSERT($\neg p$)

Table 1: Lam's analysis of Cantonese polar questions

I agree with Lam (2014a) in that A-NOT-A questions are only used in neutral contexts, but contra Lam (2014a), I claim that A-NOT-A questions also have multi-dimensional semantics. To see this, let us compare A-NOT-A questions with another polar question, namely AA4 questions. First, AA4 questions are similar to A-NOT-A questions in that they are used in neutral contexts as in (7).

(7) Scenario: Jimmy is asked to take a seat in an interrogation room of a police station. A police officer asked for Jimmy's name and then says this.

nei5 hai6 mei5gwok3 jan4 aa4?
2SG COP USA person AA4

'Are you American?'

Also, just like A-NOT-A questions, AA4 questions cannot be responded by 'You're right', suggesting that AA4 questions are true questions without assertive contents.

(8) A: gam1 go3 ji6jyut6 jau5 jaa6gau2
this CL February have twenty-nine
hou6 aa4?
number AA4
'Is there a 29th this February?'
B: #nei5 aam1, nei5 aam1. jau5/mou5
'You are right, you are right. There is(n't).'

However, the parallel breaks down with respect to the following situation. In (9), A first asserted 'There is a 29th this February!' (p). Thus, when B responds, the context is biased toward p (see Gunlogson, 2003). In this biased context, an A-NOT-A question is odd while an AA4 question is good:

(9) A: gam1 go3 ji6jyut6 jau5 jaa6gau2 hou6 aa3!
'There is a 29th this February!'
B1:#zan1 hai2? gam1 go3 ji6jyut6 jau5 mou5 jaa6gau2 hou2?
'Really? Is there a 29th this February or not?'
B2: zan1 hai2? gam1 go3 ji6jyut jau5 jaa6gau2 hou6 aa4?
'Really? Is there a 29th this February?'

As summarized in Table 2, A-NOT-A questions can be used only in neutral contexts, while AA4 questions can be used in both neutral and biased contexts. In other words, an A-NOT-A question explicitly encodes its neutrality requirement in the semantics while an AA4 question simply performs a question act. Lam's (2014a) analysis fails to account for this contrast. Thus, this paper claims that A-NOT-A questions perform complex speech acts and AA4 questions perform simple question acts. The next section briefly reviews Yuan & Hara (2013) who make a similar claim for Mandarin polar questions.

Syntax	Neutral	Biased
A-NOT-A	OK	#
AA4	OK	OK ($\neg p$ bias)

Table 2: Difference among "neutral" questions

3 Yuan and Hara (2013) on Mandarin A-not-A questions

Yuan & Hara (2013) analyze Mandarin polar questions and argue that MA questions like (10) are simple questions while A-NOT-A questions like (11) perform questioning and asserting of ignorance at the same time. Mandarin data in this section are taken from Yuan & Hara (2013).

(10) Lin xihuan Wu ma?
Lin like Wu Q
'Does Lin like Wu?' (Mandarin MA Q)

(11) Lin xihuan bu xihuan Wu (ne)?
Lin like not like Wu NE
'Does Lin like or not like Wu?'
(Mandarin A-NOT-A Q)

Yuan and Hara's analysis is motivated by the following contrast. Just like Cantonese AA4 and A-NOT-A questions, MA questions can be used in both neutral and biased contexts, while A-NOT-A questions cannot be used in biased contexts:

(12) A: Lin xihuan Wu.
Lin like Wu
'Lin likes Wu.'
B: ✓Lin xihuan Wu ma? (MA Q)
#Lin xihuan bu xihuan Wu (ne)? (A-NOT-A Q)

According to Yuan & Hara (To appear), the Mandarin morpheme MA is a question operator. It takes a proposition p denoted by its sister TP and yield a context change potential (CCP; Heim (1982)), which adds a Hamblin (1958) set $\{p, \neg p\}$ created out of the proposition p onto the question under discussion (QUD) stack (Roberts, 1996).[4]

(13) $[\![\text{MA}]\!] = \lambda p.\lambda c.[\text{QUD}(c) + \{p, \neg p\}]$

Turning to Mandarin A-NOT-A questions Yuan & Hara (2013) follow Huang (1991) and propose that the surface structure of (11) is derived from a deep structure depicted in (14).

(14)

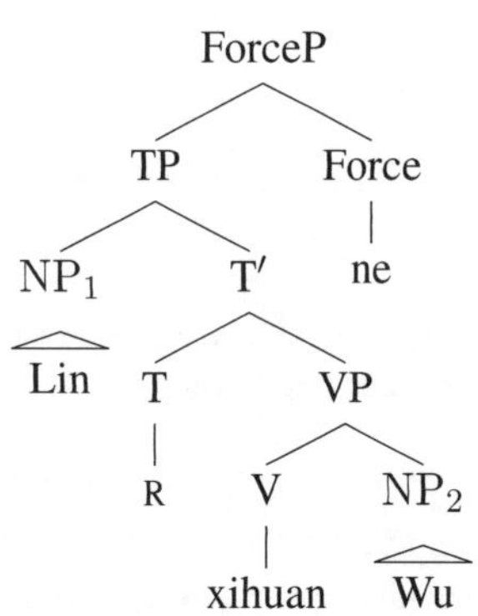

The reduplication feature R defined in (15) creates a Hamblin set; thus, the TP denotes a set of propositions as in (16).

(15) $[\![\text{R}]\!] = \lambda P.\lambda x.\{P(x), \neg P(x)\}$

(16) $[\![\text{TP}]\!] = [\![\text{R(like.Wu)(Lin)}]\!] = \{\text{p}, \neg\text{p}\}$
p ='Lin likes Wu'

[4]'+' is an update function. $\text{QUD}(c) + S$ is a stack that is exactly like $\text{QUD}(c)$ except that $\text{QUD}(c) + S$ has S as the topmost member of the stack.

The particle NE is another question operator which yield a multi-dimensional meaning as indicated by '×' in (17). On the one hand, it produces a question CCP, which adds the set of propositions S to the QUD stack. On the other hand, it outputs a single proposition by connecting each proposition in S with the disjunction '∨':

(17) $[\![\text{NE}]\!] = \lambda S.\lambda c.[\text{QUD}(c) + S]$
$\times\ \lambda S.(r_1 \vee r_2 \vee ... \vee r_{|S|}),$
$r_i \in S$ for all $1 < i \leqslant |S|$

Furthermore, Yuan & Hara (2013) show that A-NOT-A questions obligatorily end with the low boundary tone 'L%'. Adopting Bartels' (1997) analysis of English intonation, Yuan & Hara (2013) propose that the L% tone in a Mandarin A-NOT-A question is an intonational morpheme which is paratactically associated with the syntactic structure like (14). Semantically, it denotes an assertion, i.e., a CCP which adds a proposition to the Stalnakerian (1978) common ground (CG):[5]

(18) $[\![\text{L\%}]\!] = \lambda p.\text{ASSERT}(p) = \lambda p.\lambda c.[\text{CG}(c) + p]$

This morpheme is looking for a proposition as its argument. Now, among the two meanings generated by the structure in (14), the primary meaning is already a CCP of questioning; thus the morpheme *L%* can only attach to the secondary meaning, i.e., the disjunction $p \vee \neg p$. As a result, the whole A-NOT-A construction with the L% tone expresses a complex speech act, questioning and asserting. Yuan & Hara (2013) claim that this assertion of $p \vee \neg p$ is the source of the neutrality requirement of A-NOT-A questions. $p \vee \neg p$ is a tautology, thus asserting $p \vee \neg p$ is an uninformative act. Following Gricean principles, the questioner is indicating his or her ignorance towards the issue $p \vee \neg p$. When the context is biased, the speaker cannot be ignorant about the issue $p \vee \neg p$; thus an A-NOT-A question cannot be use in a biased context.

In short, a MA question is a simple act of questioning while an A-NOT-A question is a complex act of questioning and asserting, as summarized in Table 3. The neutrality meaning is reinforced by the asser-

[5]$\text{CG}(c) + p$ is a context that is exactly like $\text{CG}(c)$ except that $\text{CG}(c) + p$ has p.

tion component of the A-NOT-A question. The same explanation could be given to the contrast of Cantonese AA4 and A-NOT-A questions in (9). However, Yuan and Hara's implementation of the neutrality requirement faces a conceptual problem for both Mandarin and Cantonese. That is, in truth-conditional semantics, $p \vee \neg p$ is equivalent to $q \vee \neg q$ since they are both tautologies thus always true. Similarly, ASSERT($p \vee \neg p$) is equivalent to ASSERT($q \vee \neg q$), hence it cannot indicate the ignorance toward a particular issue $p \vee \neg p$. In order to solve this problem, this paper adopts another semantic framework, that is, inquisitive semantics.

Syntax	Observation	Analysis
A-NOT-A	anti-bias	QUEST(p)&ASSERT($p \vee \neg p$)
MA	neutral	QUEST(p)

Table 3: Yuan and Hara's analysis of Mandarin polar questions

4 Proposal: Inquisitive Semantics

In classical truth-conditional semantics, the meaning of a sentence is determined by its truth-condition:

(19) Truth-condition:
One knows the meaning of a sentence
iff
one knows under which circumstances the sentence is *true* and under which it is *false*. (Groenendijk & Roelofsen, 2013, 2)

In recent work by Groenendijk and his colleagues (Groenendijk & Roelofsen, 2009, among others),[6] it is argued that the truth-conditional semantics is not capable of analyzing interrogative sentences. In order to analyze both declarative and interrogative sentences, the new framework, inquisitive semantics, centers around support-conditions:

(20) Support-condition:
One knows the meaning of a sentence
iff
one knows which information states *support* the given sentence, and which don't. (Groenendijk & Roelofsen, 2013, 2)

[6]See https://sites.google.com/site/inquisitivesemantics/ for details.

Let us see the difference between the two frameworks with figures. Each figure represents an information state σ which contains only four possible worlds. In world 11, for instance, both p and q are true, in world 01, p is false but q is true, and so on. In truth-conditional semantics, both $p \vee \neg p$ and $q \vee \neg q$ are true in all four worlds. Thus, $p \vee \neg p$ and $q \vee \neg q$ cannot be distinguished from one another as noted above. In inquisitive, i.e., support-conditional, semantics, on the other hand, the two sentences are distinguished as follows: The information state depicted in Figure 1a supports $p \vee \neg p$, while the information state depicted in Figure 1b supports $q \vee \neg q$.

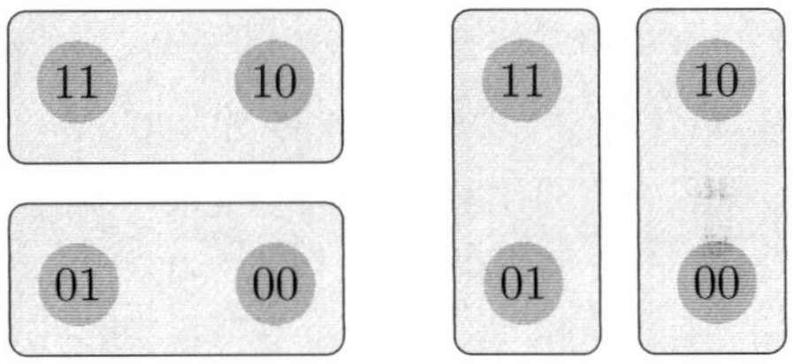

(a) $p \vee \neg p$ (b) $q \vee \neg q$

Figure 1: Support for disjunctive sentences

Another important feature of inquisitive semantics is that a polar question $?\varphi$ is defined in terms of disjunction:

(21) Questions and support:
A question $?\varphi = \varphi \vee \neg\varphi$ is supported in σ iff σ either supports φ or supports $\neg\varphi$.

4.1 Groendijk (2013) on Dutch biased questions

Groenendijk (2013) analyzes biased questions marked by a stressed particle *toch* in Dutch, which seem to have the same effect as Cantonese HO2 questions. Dutch examples in this section are taken from Groenendijk (2013).

Let us start with a declarative sentence with stressed TOCH as in (22). The sentence p-TOCH conveys a secondary meaning which indicates the speaker's *prior expectation* of $\neg p$:[7]

[7]Groenendijk (2013) calls this secondary meaning "conventional implicature". The current paper does not employ this term since at least for Cantonese data, the secondary meanings which arise from biased questions do not conform the properties of conventional implicatures in the sense of Potts (2005).

(22) Ad is TOCH in Amsterdam.
'Ad is in Amsterdam after all'
Secondary meaning: The speaker expected that Ad would not be in Amsterdam.

When TOCH is used in a question, p-TOCH?, as in (23), it gives rise to a *current* expectation of p 'Ad is in Amsterdam'.

(23) Ad is in Amsterdam, TOCH?
'Ad is in Amsterdam, right?'

The interpretation might be clearer with possible answers to (23). If the answer is 'yes', the prior expectation of p is confirmed. 'No' answers can be given either with or without TOCH. In (24-c), TOCH indicates that the *prior* expectation p is rejected.

(24) a. Ja, Ad is in Amsterdam.
b. Nee, Ad is niet in Amsterdam.
c. Nee, Ad is TOCH niet in Amsterdam.

As mentioned above, the interpretation of p-TOCH? is similar to that of a Cantonese HO2 question. The questioner is biased toward the positive answer p.

4.2 Radical Inquisitive Semantics

In analyzing TOCH sentences, Groenendijk (2013) employs a radical version of inquisitive semantics (Groenendijk & Roelofsen, 2010; Aher, 2012; Sano, 2014). In radical inquisitive semantics, the semantics of sentences are characterized by positive and negative semantic relations between sentences and information states, *support* and *reject*:[8]

(25) The atomic clause: ($|p|$ is the set of worlds where p is true)
support $\sigma \models^{+} p$ iff $\sigma \neq \emptyset$ and $\sigma \subseteq |p|$
reject $\sigma \models^{-} p$ iff $\sigma \neq \emptyset$ and $\sigma \cap |p| = \emptyset$

An information state σ is a set of possible worlds. A state σ supports an atomic sentence p just in case σ is consistent and p is true in all worlds in σ. In contrast, σ rejects p just in case σ is consistent and p is false in all worlds in σ.

As for negation, a state σ supports $\neg\varphi$ just in case it rejects φ, and it rejects $\neg\varphi$ just in case it supports φ.

(26) The clauses for negation:
a. $\sigma \models^{+} \neg\varphi$ iff $\sigma \models^{-} \varphi$
b. $\sigma \models^{-} \neg\varphi$ iff $\sigma \models^{+} \varphi$

Turning to conjunction, a state σ supports $\varphi \wedge \psi$ just in case it supports both φ and ψ , and it rejects $\varphi \wedge \psi$ just in case it rejects either φ or ψ .

(27) The clauses for conjunction:
a. $\sigma \models^{+} \varphi \wedge \psi$ iff $\sigma \models^{+} \varphi$ and $\sigma \models^{+} \psi$
b. $\sigma \models^{-} \varphi \wedge \psi$ iff $\sigma \models^{-} \varphi$ or $\sigma \models^{-} \psi$

Similarly, a state σ supports $\varphi \vee \psi$ just in case it supports either φ or ψ , and it rejects $\varphi \vee \psi$ just in case it rejects both φ and ψ.

(28) The clauses for disjunction:
a. $\sigma \models^{+} \varphi \vee \psi$ iff $\sigma \models^{+} \varphi$ or $\sigma \models^{+} \psi$
b. $\sigma \models^{-} \varphi \vee \psi$ iff $\sigma \models^{-} \varphi$ and $\sigma \models^{-} \psi$

In order to analyze TOCH, Groenendijk (2013) introduces a basic sentential operator, $(\neg)$. Thus, (29) translates as $(\neg)p$:

(29) Ad is TOCH in Amsterdam.
'Ad is in Amsterdam after all'

Recall that an interrogative sentence is defined as $?\varphi =_{\mathrm{def}} \varphi \vee \neg\varphi$. Now, an interrogative operator for TOCH? is defined as:

(30) $?_{(\neg)}\varphi =_{\mathrm{def}} \varphi \vee (\neg)\neg\varphi$

Consequently, (31) translates as $?_{(\neg)}p = p \vee (\neg)\neg p$.

(31) Ad is in Amsterdam, TOCH?
'Ad is in Amsterdam, right?'

As discussed in Section 4.1, sentences with TOCH give rise to prior/current expectations. Thus, in defining semantics for TOCH sentences, Groenendijk (2013) introduce two notions, 1) the expectations in an information state σ; and 2) the history of σ.

[8] Actually, Groenendijk (2013) uses a more recent version called suppositional inquisitive semantics (InqS) that includes the third semantic relation, *dismissing a supposition*, $\sigma \models^{\circ} p$ iff $\sigma = \emptyset$, which characterizes a denial of the antecedent of conditional sentences. For the purpose of the current paper, a (non-suppositional) radical inquisitive semantics suffices since we do not consider conditional sentences.

First, a model includes a function ϵ which takes any information state σ and yield an expectation state $\epsilon(\sigma) \subseteq \sigma$.

Second, in order to talk about different stages in the history of an information state, σ is now changed into a sequence of states. If σ is such a sequence, $\mathsf{length}(\sigma)$ returns the number of stages in σ. For $n < \mathsf{length}(\sigma)$, σ_n refers to the n-th stage in σ from the current stage σ_0. Thus, when σ_n is more recent than σ_m, $m > n$.

To define the semantics of $(\neg)\varphi$, Groenendijk (2013) introduces another semantic relation, *prior expectation-rejection shift*. It characterizes the changes of expectations through the stages. Initially, some proposition was expected but it became no longer expected at some later stage. At the most recent stage, the proposition is rejected.

(32) Prior expectation-rejection shift
Let $t < \mathsf{length}(\sigma)$.
$\sigma_t \models^{\bullet}_{\mathcal{M}} \varphi$ iff $\exists t' : \mathsf{length}(\sigma) > t' > t$ such that:

1.$\epsilon_{\mathcal{M}}(\sigma_{t'}) \models^{+}_{\mathcal{M}} \varphi$ and

2.$\forall t''$: if $t' > t'' > t$, then $\epsilon_{\mathcal{M}}(\sigma_{t''}) \not\models^{+}_{\mathcal{M}} \varphi$ and

3.$\sigma_{t+1} \models^{-}_{\mathcal{M}} \varphi$

Based on (32), semantics for TOCH sentences, i.e., $(\neg)\varphi$ is defined as follows:

(33) Semantics for TOCH

a. $\sigma_t \models^{+}_{\mathcal{M}} (\neg)\varphi$ iff
$\sigma_t \models^{+}_{\mathcal{M}} \varphi$ and $\sigma_t \models^{\bullet}_{\mathcal{M}} \neg\varphi$

b. $\sigma_t \models^{-}_{\mathcal{M}} (\neg)\varphi$ iff
$\sigma_t \models^{-}_{\mathcal{M}} \varphi$ and $\sigma_t \models^{\bullet}_{\mathcal{M}} \neg\varphi$

Let us see how the interpretations of (34) are derived. As its primary speech act, it asserts p ($\sigma_0 \models^{+}_{\mathcal{M}} p$). At the same time, as its secondary act, it indicates that $\neg p$ is a prior expectation, which is now rejected ($\sigma_0 \models^{\bullet}_{\mathcal{M}} \neg p$).

(34) Ad is TOCH in Amsterdam. $((\neg)p)$

That is, 'Ad would not be in Amsterdam' used to be expected, $\epsilon_{\mathcal{M}}(\sigma_2) \models^{+}_{\mathcal{M}} \neg p$, but at some point it stopped being expected, $\forall t''$: if $2 > t'' > 0$, $\epsilon_{\mathcal{M}}(\sigma_{t''}) \not\models^{+}_{\mathcal{M}} \neg p$. Finally, it is rejected, $\sigma_1 \models^{-}_{\mathcal{M}} \neg p$.

Let us turn to an interrogative TOCH?, namely $?_{(\neg)}\varphi$. Given that $?_{(\neg)}\varphi =_{\text{def}} \varphi \vee (\neg)\neg\varphi$, the semantics is derived as follows:

(35) Derived semantics for TOCH?

a. $\sigma_t \models^{+}_{\mathcal{M}} ?_{(\neg)}\varphi$
iff $\sigma_t \models^{+}_{\mathcal{M}} \varphi$, or
($\sigma_t \models^{+}_{\mathcal{M}} \neg\varphi$ and $\sigma_t \models^{\bullet}_{\mathcal{M}} \varphi$)

b. $\sigma_t \models^{-}_{\mathcal{M}} ?_{(\neg)}\varphi$ never

Thus, (36) asks $p \vee \neg p$, i.e., $\sigma_0 \models^{+}_{\mathcal{M}} p$ or $\sigma_0 \models^{+}_{\mathcal{M}} \neg p$, and at the same time, in case that the answer was negative, it anticipates a current expectation-rejection, $\sigma_0 \models^{\bullet}_{\mathcal{M}} p$.

(36) Ad is in Amsterdam, TOCH?
($?_{(\neg)}p = p \vee (\neg)\neg p$)

Thus, 'Ad is in Amsterdam' is currently expected, $\epsilon_{\mathcal{M}}(\sigma_2) \models^{+}_{\mathcal{M}} p$. But, there was some move in the conversation that made 'Ad is in Amsterdam' no longer expected, $\forall t''$: if $2 > t'' > 0$, then $\epsilon_{\mathcal{M}}(\sigma_{t''}) \not\models^{+}_{\mathcal{M}} p$.

If the answer to (36) is 'yes', there is no prior expectation-rejection shift. If the answer is 'no', 'Ad is in Amsterdam' is rejected, $\sigma_1 \models^{-}_{\mathcal{M}} p$:

(37) a. Ja, Ad is in Amsterdam.
b. Nee, Ad is niet in Amsterdam.
c. Nee, Ad is TOCH niet in Amsterdam.

In summary, a TOCH declarative, $(\neg)p$, conventionally encodes a rejection of prior expectation $\neg p$ as a secondary assertion. A TOCH? interrogative, $?_{(\neg)}p$, secondarily asserts the anticipation of a rejection of current expectation p.

Recall that a Cantonese HO2 question indicates a bias toward the positive answer. Thus, it can be analyzed analogously to the Dutch TOCH?.

4.3 Back to the Cantonese questions

Based on the data reported by Lam (2014a) and the novel data in (7)-(9) in Section 2, I propose that among the four kinds of the Cantonese questions, only an AA4 question denotes a simplex speech act of questioning, while A-NOT-A, HO2 and ME1 questions are multi-dimensional in that they perform question acts as well as secondary assertion acts.

I define the semantics of each questions which derives the correct interpretations in the framework of radical inquisitive semantics. First, let us take a HO2 question as it is identical to the Dutch TOCH? question, as in (38).

(38) Semantics of a HO2 question
$\sigma_t \models^+_{\mathcal{M}}$ HO2(φ) iff
$\sigma_t \models^+_{\mathcal{M}} \varphi$, or $(\sigma_t \models^+_{\mathcal{M}} \neg\varphi$ and $\sigma_t \models^{\bullet}_{\mathcal{M}} \varphi)$

Recall that HO2 questions cannot be used in neutral contexts (3-b) and the addressee can respond to a HO2 question by saying "You're right" to agree with the positive answer (5). Both facts are correctly predicted since HO2(p) semantically indicates that the questioner has an expectation toward p.

Similarly, a ME1 question indicates that the questioner has an expectation toward $\neg p$. Thus, it cannot be used in neutral contexts (3-c) ant can be responded with "You're right" to agree with the negative answer (6).

(39) Semantics of a ME1 question
$\sigma_t \models^+_{\mathcal{M}}$ ME1(φ) iff
$\sigma_t \models^+_{\mathcal{M}} \neg\varphi$, or $(\sigma_t \models^+_{\mathcal{M}} \varphi$ and $\sigma_t \models^{\bullet}_{\mathcal{M}} \neg\varphi)$

Now, let us turn to the two questions which appear to be "neutral". First, an AA4 question is defined as a simplex question as in (40).

(40) Semantics of an AA4 question
$\sigma_t \models^+_{\mathcal{M}}$ AA4(φ) iff $\sigma_t \models^+_{\mathcal{M}} \varphi$ or $\sigma_t \models^+_{\mathcal{M}} \neg\varphi$

Put another way, it does not encode any expectation within its semantics. Thus, it can be used in neutral contexts (7). At the same time, it can also be used in biased contexts (9), repeated here as (41).

(41) A: gam1 go3 ji6jyut6 jau5 jaa6gau2 hou6 aa3!
'There is a 29th this February!'
B: zan1 hai2? gam1 go3 ji6jyut jau5 jaa6gau2 hou6 aa4?
'Really? Is there a 29th this February?'

In this case, the bias or expectation meaning arises as a *pragmatic* effect. A asserted 'There is a 29th this February' $(= p)$. If B did not have any prior expectation, B should just accept p. Still, B asks a question $p \vee \neg p$. Hence, B is anticipating a rejection of his/her prior expectation $\neg p$. Furthermore, since it is a simple question, it cannot be responded by 'You are right', as we have seen in (8).

Finally, I agree with Lam (2014a) in that A-NOT-A questions are neutral questions, though contra Lam (2014a), I propose that A-NOT-A questions are complex speech acts. In other words, A-NOT-A questions are anti-bias questions. They semantically negate any anticipation of prior expectation-rejection shift toward p or $\neg p$.

(42) Semantics of an A-NOT-A question
$\sigma_t \models^+_{\mathcal{M}}$ A-NOT-A(φ) iff
$(\sigma_t \models^+_{\mathcal{M}} \varphi$ or $\sigma_t \models^+_{\mathcal{M}} \neg\varphi)$ and $\sigma_t \not\models^{\bullet}_{\mathcal{M}} \varphi \vee \neg\varphi$

Therefore, A-NOT-A questions can be of course used in neutral contexts (3-a). However, they cannot be used in biased contexts. Consider (43), which is a repetition of (9) followed by A's answer. As before, A asserted 'There is a 29th this February' p, but B still attempts to ask a question $p \vee \neg p$. This means that: 1) B had a prior expectation, $\epsilon_{\mathcal{M}}(\sigma_3) \models^+_{\mathcal{M}} p$; 2) A's first assertion indicates that p is no longer supported by the expectation state, $\epsilon_{\mathcal{M}}(\sigma_2) \not\models^+_{\mathcal{M}} p$; 3) A's answer indicates that p is rejected, $\sigma_1 \not\models^-_{\mathcal{M}} p$. Thus, $\sigma_1 \models^{\bullet}_{\mathcal{M}} p$. This contradicts the secondary component of the semantics of A-NOT-A question, $\sigma_1 \not\models^{\bullet}_{\mathcal{M}} p \vee \neg p$.

(43) A: gam1 go3 ji6jyut6 jau5 jaa6gau2 hou6 aa3!
'There is a 29th this February!'
B: #zan1 hai2? gam1 go3 ji6jyut6 jau5 mou5 jaa6gau2 hou2?
'Really? Is there a 29th this February or not?'
A: jau5.
'Yes.'

Note also that the conceptual problem that Yuan & Hara (2013) face does not arise here, since in inquisitive semantics, $p \vee \neg p$ is not a tautology. $\sigma_t \not\models^{\bullet}_{\mathcal{M}} p \vee \neg p$ is not equivalent to $\sigma_t \not\models^{\bullet}_{\mathcal{M}} q \vee \neg q$.

As summarized in Table 4, among the four Cantonese polar questions considered in this paper, only AA4 questions are simplex questions while HO2, ME1 and A-NOT-A questions have multi-dimensional semantics. The bias meaning that arises from an AA4 question is due to the pragmatic pressure. HO2 and ME1 questions semantically encode prior-expectations toward p and $\neg p$, respectively, as their secondary speech acts. Lastly, A-NOT-A questions encode the neutrality requirement in their semantics as lack of anticipation of prior expectation-rejection shift.

Syntax	Semantics
HO2	$\sigma_t \models^{+}_{\mathcal{M}} \varphi$, or ($\sigma_t \models^{+}_{\mathcal{M}} \neg\varphi$ and $\sigma_t \models^{\bullet}_{\mathcal{M}} \varphi$)
ME1	$\sigma_t \models^{+}_{\mathcal{M}} \neg\varphi$, or ($\sigma_t \models^{+}_{\mathcal{M}} \varphi$ and $\sigma_t \models^{\bullet}_{\mathcal{M}} \neg\varphi$)
AA4	$\sigma_t \models^{+}_{\mathcal{M}} \varphi$ or $\sigma_t \models^{+}_{\mathcal{M}} \neg\varphi$
A-NOT-A	($\sigma_t \models^{+}_{\mathcal{M}} \varphi$ or $\sigma_t \models^{+}_{\mathcal{M}} \neg\varphi$) and $\sigma_t \not\models^{\bullet}_{\mathcal{M}} \varphi \vee \neg\varphi$

Table 4: Inquisitive-semantics-based analysis of Cantonese polar questions

5 Conclusion

5.1 Summary

Cantonese has a variety of (non-)biased polar questions. HO2 and ME1 questions express a bias toward the positive and negative answers, respectively. In contrast, A-NOT-A and AA4 questions seem to be neutral questions. Thus, Lam (2014a) analyzes HO2 and ME1 questions as complex speech acts of questioning and asserting while A-NOT-A questions are simple acts of questioning. Lam's (2014a) account cannot explain the contrast between A-NOT-A and AA4 questions, A-NOT-A questions can only be used in neutral contexts while AA4 questions can be used in both neutral and biased contexts. Incidentally, Yuan & Hara (2013) claim that Mandarin A-NOT-A questions are also complex speech acts of questioning and asserting, where the content of the assertion is a tautology, 'p or not p'. Yuan & Hara (2013) argue that the assertion of 'p or not p' in effect indicates the ignorance of the speaker, hence the neutrality requirement. However, Yuan and Hara's analysis is also conceptually problematic. In truth-conditional semantics, an assertion of 'p or not p' is equivalent to that of 'q or not q'. This paper thus offers a solution to this problem in the framework of inquisitive semantics (Groenendijk & Roelofsen, 2009), where meaning of sentences are given based on support-conditions. Contra Lam (2014a), the semantics of an A-NOT-A question is also multi-dimensional in that it has a primary question meaning as well as a secondary assertion meaning which indicates lack of 'anticipation of prior expectation-rejection shift'. Therefore, A-NOT-A questions are anti-bias questions, thus cannot be used in biased contexts, while AA4 questions are simple questions which can be pragmatically rendered into biased questions in biased contexts.

5.2 Future direction

One important outstanding issue is the compositionality of the interpretations of these questions. In the current paper, semantics of each interrogative is stipulated at the level of the entire construction. Although Yuan and Hara's analysis of A-NOT-A questions has the conceptual problem in deriving the neutrality requirement, it has the nice compositional picture which derives the meaning from the syntactic structure and paratactic association of the L% tone with the construction. It appears to be fruitful to test whether a similar morphological analysis can be given to the Cantonese A-NOT-A construction.

Also, as mentioned in Footnote 8, radical inquisitive semantics is now evolved into suppositional inquisitive semantics which can handle conditional sentences. It would be interesting to see whether the new framework has any implication for the Cantonese conditional questions.

References

Aher, Martin. 2012. Free choice in deontic inquisitive semantics. In M. Aloni, V. Kimmelmann, F. Roelofsen, G.W. Sassoon, K. Schulz & M. Westera (eds.), *Logic, language and meaning, 18th Amsterdam Colloquium, Amsterdam*, 22–31. Lecture Notes in Computer Science.

Asher, Nicholas & Brian Reese. 2005. Negative bias in polar questions. In E. Maier, C. Bary & J. Huitink (eds.), *Proceedings of SuB9,*, 30–43.

Bartels, Christine. 1997. *Towards a compositional interpretation of English statement and question intonation*: University of Massachusetts dissertation.

Groenendijk, Jeroen. 2013. TOCH and TOCH? in dutch. Presented at the Questions in Discourse Workshop, December 2013, Amsterdam.

Groenendijk, Jeroen & Floris Roelofsen. 2009. Inquisitive semantics and pragmatics. Presented at the Workshop on Language, Communication, and Rational Agency at Stanford, May 2009.

Groenendijk, Jeroen & Floris Roelofsen. 2010. Radical inquisitive semantics. ILLC/Department of Philosophy University of Amsterdam.

Groenendijk, Jeroen & Floris Roelofsen. 2013. Suppositional inquisitive semantics. Workshop on Inquisitive Logic and Dependence Logic, ILLC, Amsterdam, June 17, 2013.

Gunlogson, Christine. 2003. *True to Form: Rising and Falling Declaratives as Questions in English.* New York: Routledge.

Hamblin, C.L. 1958. Questions. *Australasian Journal of Philosophy* 36. 159–168.

Heim, Irene. 1982. *The Semantics of Definite and Indefinite Noun Phrases*: University of Massachussets, Amherst dissertation. [Distributed by GLSA].

Huang, C.-T. James. 1991. Modularity and Chinese A-not-A questions. In Carol Georgopolous & Robert Ishihara (eds.), *Interdisciplinary Approaches to Language*, 305–22. Dordrecht: Kluwer.

Lam, Zoe Wai-Man. 2014a. A comlex forcep for speaker- and addressee-oriented discourse particles in cantonese. *Studies in Chinese Linguistics* 35(2). 61–80.

Lam, Zoe Wai-Man. 2014b. A unified account for biased and non-biased questions in Cantonese. Slides predented at WICL2 at University of Chicago, March 7 2014.

Matthews, Stephen & Virginia Yip. 1994. *Cantonese: a Comprehensive Grammar.* Routledge.

Potts, Christopher. 2005. *The Logic of Conventional Implicatures* Oxford Studies in Theoretical Linguistics. Oxford: Oxford University Press. [Revised 2003 UC Santa Cruz PhD thesis].

Roberts, Craige. 1996. Information structure: Towards an integrated formal theory of pragmatics. In Jae Hak Yoon & Andreas Kathol (eds.), *OSU Working Papers in Linguistics*, vol. 49, 91–136. Columbus, OH: The Ohio State University Department of Linguistics. Revised 1998.

Sano, Katsuhiko. 2014. An impossibility theorem in radical inquisitive semantics. Presented at Workshop on Relating Particles to Evidence and Inference, 14th July 2012, Goettingen, Germany. Current version, submitted for publication.

Stalnaker, Robert. 1978. Assertion. *Syntax and Semantics* 9. 315–332.

Yuan, Mengxi & Yurie Hara. 2013. Questioning and asserting at the same time: the L% tone in A-not-A questions. In Maria Aloni, Michael Franke & Floris Roelofsen (eds.), *Proceedings of the 19th Amsterdam Colloquium*, 265–272.

Yuan, Mengxi & Yurie Hara. To appear. The semantics of the two kinds of questions in Mandarin: A case study of discourse adverbs. In *NELS 44*, vol. 2, GLSA.

On the Argument Structures of the Transitive Verb *fan* 'annoy; be annoyed; bother to do': A study based on two comparable corpora

Jiajuan Xiong
CBS, The Hong Kong Polytechnic University;
jiajuanx@gmail.com

Chu-Ren Huang
CBS, The Hong Kong Polytechnic University
churen.huang@polyu.edu.hk

Abstract: This paper investigates the transitive uses of the verb *fan* 'annoy; be annoyed; bother to do', which exhibit both similarities and disparities between Beijing Mandarin and Taiwan Mandarin, as far as the data from Gigaword corpus, containing data from Mainland China (XIN) and Taiwan (CNA), are concerned. In terms of similarities, the causative (and agentive) use(s) of the transitive *fan* is/are shared by both Beijing Mandarin and Taiwan Mandarin. The disparity mainly lies in the mental use of *fan* 'be annoyed', which is not only unattested in the corpus of Taiwan Mandarin but also reported as weird by our informants. This mental use, on the other hand, is well attested in the corpus. In order to describe as well as explain the difference in uses between Beijing Mandarin and Taiwan Mandarin, we adopt the Theta System Theory (Reinhart 2002; Marelj 2004) to probe into the argument structures of the transitive verb *fan* and further pinpoint the fundamental syntactic difference between Beijing Mandarin and Taiwan Mandarin, that is, the absence or presence of the /+c feature in the argument structure. In particular, Taiwan Mandarin requires the obligatory presence of the /+c feature in the argument structure of *fan*, while Beijing Mandarin does not.

Keywords: transitive *fan*, corpus, Beijing Mandarin, Taiwan Mandarin, Theta System, /+c

1. Introduction: The intransitive *fan*

The verb *fan* in Chinese can function as an intransitive verb, meaning 'annoyed/ bothered' as well as 'annoying/bothersome'. These two uses are attested in both Beijing Mandarin and Taiwan Mandarin, as evidenced by the examples of (1)-(4) from the XIN and CNA, sub-corpora of Gigaword corpus.[1]

(1) Ta dang daxue jiaoshou de
he serve_as university professor DE
fuqin feidan bu guowen,
father not_only NEG meddle
fan'er yi kanjian ta jiu
instead whenever see he then
fan. (XIN)
be_annoyed
'His father, as a university professor, does not meddle with his business; instead, his father seems to be annoyed whenever he sees him.'

(2) Shoufeiyuan shengyingdi shuo, "nimen
cashier stiffly said you
zenme zheme **fan?**" (XIN)
how_can so annoying
'The cashier stiffly said that "How are you so annoying?"'

(3) Zuo taitai de jide
serve_as wife DE remember

[1] XIN and CNA refer to Beijing-based Xin Hua News Agency and Taiwan-based Central News Agency, respectively.

Copyright 2014 by Jiajuan Xiong and Chu-Ren Huang
28th Pacific Asia Conference on Language, Information and Computation pages 615–623

ziji shi taitai, buyao zhi
oneself be wife do_not only
tan qian qian qian,
talk_about money money money
zhangfu hui **fan**. (CNA)
husband will be_annoyed

'As a wife, one should remember your own role of being a wife and refrain from talking about money, money, money all the time. Otherwise, the husband would get annoyed.'

(4) Ni zenme name **fan**,
2SG how_can so annoying
name luosuo. (CNA)
so voluble
'How can you be so annoying and voluble?'

In addition to the intransitive uses, *fan* can be used transitively, which is noted as [A *fan* B] in this paper. Unlike intransitive *fan*, transitive *fan* exhibits syntactic differences between Beijing Mandarin and Taiwan Mandarin. The data of transitive *fan* will be presented in section 2.

2. Data Presentation: The transitive *fan*

The transitive *fan* is found to be syntactically different between Beijing Mandarin and Taiwan Mandarin, as far as the data from XIN and CNA are concerned. In Beijing Mandarin, [A *fan* B] can mean 'A annoys B' as well as 'A is annoyed by B', depending on the context. They are exemplified in (5) and (6), respectively.

(5) Qiye genju
enterprises according_to
shichang zishengzimie, buyong
market run_its_course need_not
zai **fan** zhengfu. (XIN)
again bother government
'Enterprises run their courses based on the market. There is no need to bother the government anymore.'

(6) Wo yixiang tong xiandaipai
I all_along with modernist
gegeburu, wo bijiao
incompatible I a_bit
fan tamen. (XIN)
feel_annoyed them
'I have never been able to get along well with the modernist school. I feel annoyed about them.'

The contrast between (5) and (6) seems to indicate that [A *fan* B] is bi-directional in the sense that A can be the Causer while B the Causee (as in 5), or the other way around (as in 6). However, the latter use of *fan*, as that in (6), is unattested in Taiwan Mandarin. Rather, in Taiwan Mandarin, [A *fan* B] is predominantly causative, in which A in is almost unambiguously interpreted as the Causer, as exemplified in (7).

(7) Wo jiang bu xunqiu lianren,
I will NEG seek reelection
nimen weihe haiyao **fan**
you why still annoy
wo? (CNA)
me
'I won't seek for reappointment. Why do you still annoy me?'

In addition to the above-exemplified [A *fan* B], there is another type of transitive *fan* attested in the CNA corpus, as presented in (8) and (9).

(8) Ta shuo, …, yici zhi **fan**
he said once only bother
yi jian shi, na jiushi
one CL issue that be
paidianying… (CNA)
make_film
'He said that he only bothers to do one thing at a time, that is, film-making.'

(9) Dui ta laishuo, lianqin
as_for she as_for play_the_piano
yi xiaoshi ta buhui
one hour she won't
fan xingzhengshiwu. (CNA)
bother administrative_services
'As for her, when she plays the piano, she won't bother to think about any administrative services.'

Albeit being transitive in (7)-(9), *fan* in (7) differs from that in (8) and (9) in that the former is causative while the latter is not. In addition, they seem to impose different restrictions of animacy on the object B. Specifically, [A *fan* B] in (7) requires B to be animate (in particular, Human) whereas [A *fan* B] in (8) and (9) features the inanimacy of B. This difference in animacy is by no means trivial. Being inanimate, the objects in (8) and (9) cannot be the ones that are annoyed. As the free translations suggest, they are the things that the subjects bother to conduct, in one way or another, depending on the context.

To complete the full picture, it should be mentioned that the transitive use of *fan* in (8) and (9) are not attested in the XIN corpus. In spite of the data gap, our Beijing Mandarin informants have no difficulty in understanding them. Therefore, they are still well-received in Beijing Mandarin.

Given the data collected above, we summarize the three attested transitive uses of *fan* in (10). Prior to our analysis in section 4, we label the two arguments of each transitive use intuitively. They will be refined in due course.

(10) [A *fan* B]:
a. causative: A → Causer
B→ Causee
b. mental: A → Experiencer
B→Causer
c. agentive: A → Agent,
B → Theme

These three types of transitive *fan* will be analyzed in detail in section 3.

3. Data Analysis: Tripartite use of transitive *fan*

3.1 Causative and mental *fan*: swap of arguments?

At first glance, the causative and the mental uses of *fan* are directionally opposite in the sense that they just swap their arguments. The evidence may come from the cases where the same transitive verb *fan* can give rise to two different interpretations at the same time. This usually occurs in the neutral context, as exemplified in (11).

(11) Zhangsan fan Lisi.
Zhangsan annoy/be_annoyed Lisi
'Zhangsan annoys Lisi.' or
'Zhangsan feels annoyed about Lisi.'

However, this analysis is more apparent than real. The first difference lies in the animacy condition of the Causer in these two cases. Causer in (10a) is basically [+HUMAN]. Even though the Causer *per se* does not take the animate form, it is most probably an organization and thus metonymically refers to people affiliated to that organization. This is exemplified in (12), in which *huaren shetuan* 'Chinese associations' and *huaren meiti* 'Chinese media' refer to people associated with these organizations through the mechanism of metonymy.

(12) Huaren shetuan yu
Chinese association and
huawen meiti yi zhaodao
Chinese media once find
jihui jiu yi **zhe ge**
chance then use this CL
wenti qu **fan** Guilianni. (CNA)
question go annoy Guilianni
'Once Chinese associations and Chinese media find a chance, they use this question to annoy Guilianni…'

Crucially, inanimate entities which cannot give rise to any metonymic interpretations fail to serve as subjects of the causative *fan*. Even though they occur, they can only be encoded as instruments, as exemplified by *zhege wenti* 'this question' in (12), as an adjunct. Similarly, the inanimate cause of the causative *fan*, i.e., *zhe zhong wuliao de wenti* 'this kind of stupid questions' in (13), occurs in the serial verb construction. On a par with that in (12), the inanimate noun phrase in (13) is also interpreted as an instrument.

(13) Xiwang meiti jizhe bie
hope media journalist NEG
na **zhe zhong wuliaode wenti**
use this CL stupid question
lai **fan** ta. (CNA)
come annoy him
'(We) hope that journalists in the media not bother him with this kind of stupid question.'

It should be further noted that the above mentioned inanimate entities can never function as the subject of the causative *fan* 'annoy'. This is illustrated by the unacceptability of (14) below:

(14) *Zhe ge wuliaode wenti
the CL stupid question
fan ta.
annoy him
Intended: 'This stupid question annoys him.'

On the other hand, in the case of the mental verb *fan* 'get annoyed', the Causer, in the form of a grammatical object, has no restrictions on its animacy. As exemplified in (15), the inanimate entity *dianhua* 'telephone', as the object, is the Causer for one's getting annoyed.

(15) Mei you dianhua pan
NEG have telephone long_for
dianhua, you le dianhua
telephone have PERF telephone
fan **dianhua**.
be_annoyed telephone
'When there were no telephones, people long for them; when there are telephones, people get annoyed because of them.'

The data exemplified above reveal that the semantic role Causer in the causative use of *fan* and that in the mental use of *fan* are crucially different, as the former must have the [+HUMAN] feature while the latter is not subject to any animacy restrictions.

Secondly, Causee and Experiencer, as the terms already suggest, are not the same. The Causee is the target of the "annoying" action while the Experiencer is the one who experiences the mental process of "being annoyed". Even though both of them are animate, they cannot be reduced to one argument, mainly because the Causee does not necessarily experience the mental process. As exemplified in (16), the noun phrase *ta fumu* 'his parents' is the Causee of the causative verb *fan*, as the target of "annoy". Crucially, this Causee might not undergo the mental process of "being annoyed", as evidenced by the continuous sentence in (16), in which the statement of "his parents' being annoyed" is negated. If Causee and Experiencer are identical, we would expect the sentence of (16) to be semantically anomalous. In actual fact, (16) is perfectly acceptable, indicating that Causee and Experiencer should be teased apart.

(16) Zhe ge xiaohai zai
this CL child PROG
fan ta fumu, dan ta fumu
annoy he parents but he parents
sihu bingbu
apparently by_no_means
fan ta.
be_annoyed him

'This child is annoying his parents. However, apparently, his parents are by no means annoyed by him.'

Having established the fact that the causative and the mental uses of *fan* are contrastive much beyond their opposite directionality, we proceed to the contrast between the mental and the agentive use of *fan*.

3.2 Mental and Agentive *fan*

The contrast between mental and agentive verbs can be teased apart through two tests. The first test is whether the verb can take degree adverbs. The second one is whether the verb can be embedded into volitional verbs like *qu* 'go; start' or *hui* 'will'. Prior to testing our target verb *fan*, let us first illustrate how these two tests work. We take the typical mental verb *xihuan* 'like' (as in 17a) and the typical agentive verb *yanjiu* 'study' (as in 17b) as examples. As illustrated in (18) and (19), it is the mental verb, instead of the agentive one, that can be modified by a degree adverb. On the other hand, it is the agentive verb, rather than the mental one, that can be embedded into a volitional verb.

(17) a. Wo xihuan yuyanxue. (*xihuan*: mental verb)
I like linguistics
'I like linguistics.'
b. Wo yanjiu yuyanxue. (*yanjiu*: agentive verb)
I study linguistics.
'I study linguistics.'

(18) a. Wo hen xihuan yuyanxue.
I very like linguistics
'I like linguistics very much.'
b. *Wo qu/hui xihuan yuyanxue.
I go/will like linguistics
*'I will go and like linguistics.'

(19) a. *Wo hen yanjiu yuyanxue.
I very study linguistics.
*'I study linguistics very much.'
b. Wo qu/hui yanjiu yuyanxue.
I very study linguistics.
'I will go and study linguistics.'

We apply the same tests to the verb *fan* in the XIN corpus and that in the CNA corpus. As shown in (20), the agentive verb *fan* is compatible with the degree adverb *bijiao* 'a bit'; while it cannot collocate with the volitional verb *qu* 'go'. That means, the verb *fan* in (20), a representative of Beijing Mandarin, behaves like a mental verb, on a par with *xihuan* 'like' in (17a).

(20) a. Wo yixiang tong xiandaipai gegeburu, wo bijiao **fan** tamen. (XIN)
I all_along with modernist incompatible I a_bit feel_annoyed them
'I have always been against the grain with the modernist school. I feel annoyed because of them.'
b. #Wo yixiang tong xiandaipai gegeburu, wo qu **fan** tamen. (XIN)
I all_along with modernist incompatible I go feel_annoyed them
#'I have always been against the grain with the modernist school. I go and feel annoyed about them.'
'I have always been against the grain with the modernist school. I go and annoy them.'[2]

Conversely, the agentive verb *fan* in Taiwan Mandarin, as illustrated in (21) and (22), rejects degree modification. However, it goes well with the volitional verbs *qu* 'go'

[2] (20b) is possible only when it is interpreted as a causative verb.

and/or *hui* 'will'. Therefore, the transitive verb *fan* in Taiwan Mandarin should be treated as a real agentive verb.

(21) a. #Ta shuo, …, yici zhi hen
he said once only very
fan yi jian shi, na
bother one CL thing that
jiushi paidianying…
be make_film
#'He said that he only bothers to do one thing at a time very much, that is, film-making.'

b. Ta shuo, …, yici zhi qu
he said once only go
fan yi jian shi, na
bother one CL issue that
jiushi paidianying…
be make_film
'He said that he goes and bothers to do one thing at a time very much, that is, film-making.'

(22) a. #Dui ta laishuo, lianqin
as_for she as_for play_the_piano
yi xiaoshi ta buhui
one hour she won't
hen **fan** xingzhengshiwu.
verybother administrative_services
#'As for her, when she plays the piano, she won't bother to do any administrative services very much.'

b. Dui ta laishuo, lianqin
as_for she as_for play_the_piano
yi xiaoshi ta
one hour she
buqu/ buhui **fan**
not_go/won't bother
xingzhengshiwu.
administrative_services
'As for her, when she plays the piano, she doesn't go or won't bother to do any administrative services.'

In what follows, we adopt the Theta System (Reinhart, 2002; Marelj 2004) to analyze the argument structures of the three types of transitive *fan*.

4. Our Proposal under the Theta System

According to the Theta System Theory (Reinhart 2002), lexical entries are coded concepts with formal features defining the theta relations of verb entries. Basically, there are two features, namely, /c (cause) and /m (sentience), to describe thematic arguments, and each of the two features can have either positive or negative value. Those feature clusters are somehow equivalent to the established semantic roles, as show in (23).

(23) a. [+c+m]: agent;
b. [+c-m]: instrument;
c. [-c+m]: experiencer;
d. [-c-m]: theme/patient
e. [+c]: cause;
f. [+m]: sentient;
g. [-m]: subject matter/source;
h. [-c]: goal/benefactor

In this study, we will use the feature clusters to describe the argument structures of different types of transitive *fan*, in order to work out the denominator as well as the minimal differing point of different uses of transitive *fan*.

Firstly, we analyze the causative use of *fan*. Recall that the subject of the causative *fan* 'annoy' obligatorily contains the semantic feature of [+HUMAN]. Moreover, an inanimate instrument can be licensed in this case, as exemplified in (11) and (12). Regarding this, the subject of the causative *fan* should be an Agent [+c+m], instead of a pure cause [+c], on the grounds that an Agent, instead of a Cause, can license an Instrument (Reinhart 2002). According to the analysis in Section 3, the object of the causative *fan* does not necessarily experience the mental process of "getting annoyed". Therefore, the object should be a

Recipient/Goal [-c] instead of an Experiencer [-c+m]. Although the object is, in most cases, animate, it is still [-c] in the sense that the feature /m is irrelevant. Given the analysis, the Theta grid of the causative *fan* is shown in (24) below:

(24) The Theta grid of the causative *fan*:
([+c+m], [-c], ([+c-m]))
(the Instrument is optional)

We now move to the mental use of *fan*, which is proven to be exclusive to Beijing Mandarin. Like the mental verbs *love* and *hate*, the mental verb *fan* has a sentient [+m] as its subject. It should be noted that a sentient [+m] is different from an Experiencer [-c+m] in that the former obligatorily merges externally while the latter, as a mixed feature cluster, can merge either internally or externally (Reinhart 2000; Marelj 2004). Since we have already demonstrated that the object of the verb *fan* cannot be an Experiencer (rather, it is a Recipient or Goal), the subject of the mental *fan* should be a Sentient. In terms of its object, it is a [-m], a Subject Matter or Source, which can actually give rise to causal paraphrase (Marelj 2004: 11), as illustrated in (25).

(25) a. Max worries about his health $_{[-m]}$.
(subject matter) (Marelj 2004: 9, 11)
b. His health caused Max to worry.

The same alternation is applicable to the mental verb *fan* as well, as (26a) and (26b) are truth-conditionally equivalent to each other.

(26) a. Wo bijiao **fan** tamen.
I a_bit feel_annoyed them
'I feel fairly annoyed about them.'
b. Tamen **rang** wo bijiao **fan**.
(causal paraphrase)
they cause me a_bit be_annoyed
'They made me feel fairly annoyed.'

In this connection, one thing is worth noting. That is, the [-m] role, as an under-specified role, cannot bear the ACC feature. In other words, the mental *fan* is not an accusative case assigner. This is actually borne out, as mental verb *fan* can take a full-fledged sentence, without incurring any case problems. One of the examples is cited in (27), in which a whole sentence serves as the object of *fan*.

(27) Luting fan **tamen wei**
Luting feel_annoyed them for
zhe dian shiqing zhenglun
this little thing dispute
lai zhenglun qu. (XIN)
come dispute go
'Luting got fed of their disputing over this little thing repeatedly.'

Given our analysis, the argument structure of the mental *fan* is shown in (28).

(28) The Theta grid of the mental *fan*:
([+m], [-m])

Before we proceed, let us linger a bit on the mental *fan*. Our informants, especially Taiwan Mandarin speakers, tend to paraphrase a sentence containing the mental *fan* into a bi-clausal sentence, as shown in (29a, b).

(29) a. Wo hen **fan** ta.
I very feel_annoyed him
'I feel annoyed about him.'
b. Wo juede ta hen **fan**.
I think he very annoying
'I think that he is quite annoying.'

Close examination shows that (29a) and (29b) are not semantically equivalent. The most obvious difference can be detected from the degree modification therein. The degree adverb *hen* 'very' in (29a) describes the degree of the Sentient's (i.e., *wo* 'I') "feeling annoyed", while the same adverb in

(29b) indicates the degree of "his being annoying".

Lastly, we deal with the agentive verb *fan*, which is attested in Taiwan Mandarin and acceptable to Beijing Mandarin speakers as well, as exemplified in (8) and (9). We analyze this *fan* as a typical agentive verb with an Agent [+c+m] and a Theme [-c-m], as shown in (30).

(30) <u>The Theta grid of the mental *fan*</u>:
   ([+c+m], [-c-m])

What is particular to the verb *fan* here is that it involves a coercion process, which introduces an action to the sentences. For example, *fan* in (8) can be interpreted as "bother to do", with the action of "doing" coerced; while *fan* in (9) can be understood as "bother to think about", even though the verbs of "doing" and "thinking" are not explicitly mentioned therein. Given this, the agentive *fan* is to a certain extent similar to the verb *start* in English. As illustrated in (31), the verb *start* is able to coerce different types of actions, such as reading and writing, into the sentence.

(31) He started a book. (coercion)
   a. He started **reading** a book.
   b. He started **writing** a book.

Having established the argument structures of the three types of transitive *fan*, we put them together in (32) so as to make a better comparison.

(32) <u>[A *fan* B]</u>:
   a. causative: ([+c+m], [-c], [+c-m])
   b. mental: ([+m], [-m]) → (missing in Taiwan Mandarin)
   c. agentive: ([+c+m], [-c-m])

The argument structures in (32) reveal that Beijing Mandarin and Taiwan Mandarin differ in the presence or absence of the [/+c] feature. Specifically, Taiwan Mandarin treats /+c as an indispensable feature of the transitive verb *fan*. Once this feature is missing, as in the case of (32b), the transitve *fan* will be filtered out. However, this condition does not apply to Beijing Mandarin. To sum up, the difference of transitive *fan* between Beijing Mandarin and Taiwan Mandarin is reduced to the /+c feature.

5. The Residue

Due to the required presence of the /+c feature in Taiwan Mandarin, the mental use of transitive *fan* is not attested, given that the subject of the mental *fan* is [+m]. There are, however, other attested transitive verbs to express the mental use of *fan*. As far as the corpus data are concerned, we find two general ways to express the equivalent meanings of the mental *fan*. Firstly, the verb takes the disyllabic form. The disyllabic verb may contain two synonymous components, such as *yanfan* 'get fed up with' in (33); alternatively, the disyllabic verb can be a resultative compound, such as *fantou* 'be deeply annoyed' in (34).

(33) Renmin yijing **yanfan**
   people already get_fed_up_with
   ta. (CNA)
   him
   'People have already been fed of him.'

(34) Yi ming bashiba sui de
   one CL eighty_eight year DE
   yeye, **fan-tou** le
   grandpa annoyed_thoroughly PERF
   shehuxian tengtong. (CNA)
   prostate pain
   'An eighty-eight-year-old grandpa was browned off by his prostate pain.'

Secondly, there are three occurrences of *fan-buguo* 'get annoyed so much that one cannot tolerate' in the CNA corpus. Crucially, *fan-buguo* is transitive, as evidenced by its occurrence in the *bei*-passive as in (35) and the presence of an object (i.e., *ta* 'he') between *fan* and *buguo* as in (36).

(35) You bushao muqin fanying
have many mother report
shi yinwei zhangfu bu
be because husband NEG
bangmang, jiashang **bei**
help plus BEI
xiaohai **fan-buguo**,
child get_annoyed_NEG_beyond
renbuzhu jiu dongshouda
cannot_help then lift_one's_hand_on
xiaohai. (CNA)
child
'Many mothers reported that they cannot help spanking children because their husbands do not help.'

(36) Maidanglao sihu **fan**
MacDonald seem get_annoyed
ta buguo... (CNA)
he NEG_beyond
'It seems that MacDonald cannot stand his consistent pestering ...'

As a matter of fact, the disyllabic uses of *yanfan* 'get fed up with' and *fantou* 'be deeply annoyed' are also attested in the XIN corpus. Therefore, they are not exclusive to Taiwan Mandarin. In other words, monosyllabic and disyllabic mental verbs are not in complementary distribution between Beijing Mandarin and Taiwan Mandarin.

What is consistently true is that the mental use of the monosyllabic transitive verb *fan* 'feel annoyed about' is commonly used in Beijing Mandarin whereas it is completely missing in Taiwan Mandarin, due to the required presence of /+c feature in the Theta grid of the transitive *fan* in Taiwan Mandarin.

Selected References:

Fillmore, C. J. and B. T. Atkins. 1992. Towards a frame-based lexicion: the case of RISK. In: A. Lehrer and E. Kittay (Hgg.): Frames, Fields, and Contrasts. Erlbaum, 75-102.

Marelj, M. 2004. *Middles and Argument Structure across Languages*. Utrecht: LOT.

Reinhart, T. 2000. The Theta System: Syntactic Realization of Verbal Concepts. *UiL-OT working Papers*. Utrecht: University of Utrecht.

Reinhart, T. 2002. The Theta System – An Overview. In W. Sternefeld (ed.), Theoretical Linguistics 28: 229-290 Berlin: Mouton.

Reinhart, T. , E. Reuland and T. Siloni. 2004. The Acc Case Parameter. Ms. UiL-OTS. University of Utrecht.

The Semantics of *khɨn3* and *loŋ1* in Thai Compared to *up* and *down* in English: A Corpus-Based Study

Junyawan Suwannarat
Department of Linguistics,
Faculty of Arts, Chulalongkorn University,
Phayathai Road, Pathumwan,
Bangkok, 10330, Thailand
junyawan.s@gmail.com

Theeraporn Ratitamkul
Department of Linguistics,
Faculty of Arts, Chulalongkorn University,
Phayathai Road, Pathumwan,
Bangkok, 10330, Thailand
Theeraporn.R@chula.ac.th

Abstract

This corpus-based study analyzes meanings of *khɨn3* 'ascend' and *loŋ1* 'descend' in Thai in comparison with *up* and *down* in English. Data came from three corpora: the Thai National Corpus (TNC) (Aroonmanakun et al., 2009), the British National Corpus (BNC), and the English-Thai Parallel Concordance (Aroonmanakun, 2009). Results of the analyses show that there are senses of the vertical spatial terms *khɨn3* and *loŋ1* in Thai that overlap with those of *up* and *down* in English. This reflects a universal image schema of vertical movement and similar semantic extension processes in the two languages. Data from the parallel corpus also reveal that the vertical spatial terms *khɨn3* and *loŋ1* do not always occur in the same contexts with *up* and *down*. But, when they do, the frequently shared meaning involves vertical movement, which is the basic sense of the terms. The use of corpora as a tool to study the semantics of vertical spatial terms in Thai and English makes it possible to obtain objective and naturalistic data as well as to observe frequency of various senses that are in use.

1 Introduction

Expressions of spatial directions are common in the world's languages. Given that spatial direction is a basic concept of humans (Langacker, 1987), spatial terms are expected to be of high frequency in language use. This study examines spatial terms for vertical directions in Thai and English. In particular, we focus on *khɨn3* 'ascend' and *loŋ1* 'descend' in Thai in comparison with *up* and *down* in English.

The words *khɨn3* 'ascend' and *loŋ1* 'descend' in Thai are high-frequency words whose fundamental meanings are about vertical movement of upward and downward directions, respectively. Similarly, the words *up* and *down* in English have the basic senses of vertical directions. Moreover, both *khɨn3* and *up* can be used to denote non-directional meanings (such as *man4 caj1* <u>*khɨn3*</u> 'be more confident' and *speed* <u>*up*</u>), and this is also true with the pair *loŋ1* and *down* (such as *sin3sut2* <u>*loŋ1*</u> 'end' and *close* <u>*down*</u>). However, while *khɨn3* and *loŋ1* occur as main verbs or subsidiary verbs in serial verb constructions in Thai, *up* and *down* rarely occur in verb slots in English; they usually appear as satellites accompanying verbs. It is therefore interesting to investigate to what extent these vertical spatial expressions, which belong to different grammatical categories, overlap in terms of senses.

To obtain objective, up to date and naturally occurring language data produced by various native speakers, this study utilized data from three corpora. The English data came from the British National Corpus (BNC), and the Thai data were drawn from the Thai National Corpus (TNC) (Aroonmanakun et al., 2009). A parallel corpus, the English-Thai Parallel Concordance

Copyright 2014 by Junyawan Suwannarat and Theeraporn Ratitamkul
28th Pacific Asia Conference on Language, Information and Computation pages 624–633

(Aroonmanakun, 2009), was also used to compare occurrences of *khɨn3* with *up*, and *loŋ1* with *down* in the same contexts. The aim of this paper is to analyze meanings of *khɨn3* and *loŋ1* in Thai, and *up* and *down* in English, as found in the corpora in order to compare senses of these vertical spatial terms used by native speakers of each language.

2 Previous studies

2.1 *Up* and *Down* in English

Tyler and Evans (2003) describe *up* and *down* in the framework of cognitive semantics. The image schema of *up* shows that a trajectory (TR) moves towards the top of a landmark (LM). To illustrate this, in *Jennifer climbed up the mountain*, where *Jennifer* is the TR and *mountain* is the LM, the TR moves upward to the top of the LM. On the contrary, the image schema of *down* displays movement of a TR towards the bottom of a LM. For example, in *The water went down the drain*, *water* is the TR while *drain* is the LM. The TR moves downward to the LM.

It is obvious that the meanings of *up* and *down* are not limited to vertical directions. The spatial image schemas mentioned earlier are also used to express non-spatial meanings by means of two main cognitive processes, namely **conceptual metaphor** and **metonymy**. These processes link different meanings of each directional word together (Kövecses, 2002). Lakoff and Johnson (1980) state that conceptual metaphor is a language phenomenon in which a speaker understands a particular concept through the use of another concept. For example, being in consciousness is associated with the concept of UP (as in *I'm up already*) whereas being in unconsciousness is connected to the concept of DOWN (*He fell asleep*). Lakoff and Johnson explain that humans sleep lying down and stand up when they awake. Therefore, the concept of DOWN is expanded to being unconscious, and the concept of UP to being conscious. Metonymy, on the other hand, refers to a process which uses a salient entity that is easy to understand as the referent point that links to a less salient entity (Langaker, 1999). Generally, a metonymy is the use of a salient phase or word instead of a non-salient one. As an instance, in *He picked up the phone*, manually picking a phone up is only a part of telephone answering procedures, but now 'picking up the phone' implies 'answering the phone' rather than just a part of the process (Seto, 1999). Through these cognitive processes, the original meanings involving vertical directions of *up* and *down* can be expanded.

Previous studies of *up* and *down* in English mostly concerned their metaphorical meanings (Lee, 2001; Otani, 2006; Hampe, 2006). The findings were usually consistent with Lakoff and Johnson (1980)'s proposal. According to Lakoff and Johnson, there are 10 conceptual metaphors of the concepts UP and DOWN in English, as illustrated in Table 1.

HAPPY IS UP	SAD IS DOWN
CONSCIOUS IS UP	UNCONSCIOUS IS DOWN
HEALTH IS UP	SICKNESS OR DEATH IS DOWN
HAVING CONTROL OR FORCE IS UP	BEING SUBJECT TO CONTROL OR FORCE IS DOWN
MORE IS UP	LESS IS DOWN
FORESEEABLE FUTURE IS UP	-
HIGH STATUS IS UP	LOW STATUS IS DOWN
GOOD IS UP	BAD IS DOWN
VIRTUE IS UP	DEPRAVITY IS DOWN
RATIONAL IS UP	EMOTIONAL IS DOWN

Table 1: Conceptual metaphors of UP and DOWN (Otani, 2006; adapted from Lakoff & Johnson, 1980)

Boroditsky (2001) did an experimental study to test whether English and Mandarin speakers thought about time differently. She found that Mandarin speakers commonly used vertical spatial terms *shàng* 'ascend' and *xià* 'descend' to talk about time (as in *shàng ge yuè* 'last month', *xià ge yuè* 'next month') while English speakers tended to think about time horizontally, e.g., *last (previous) month, next (following) month*. Later, Chun (2002) and Dong (2010) compared the meanings of *up* and *down* in English to *shàng* 'ascend' and *xià* 'descend' in Mandarin. The results showed that the conceptual metaphors of the words *shàng* 'ascend' and *xià* 'descend' in Mandarin were similar to those of *up* and *down* in English, except for time dimension. While a later time was expressed with UP and an earlier time with DOWN in English, Mandarin associates a later time with XIA and an earlier time with SHANG. This shows that senses of words denoting vertical directions differ across languages.

2.2 *khɨn3* 'ascend' and *loŋ1* 'descend' in Thai

Thai directional verbs *khɨn3* 'ascend', *loŋ1* 'descend', *khaw3* 'enter' and *ʔɔɔk2* 'exit' are categorized as non-deictic verbs (Zlatev and Yanglang, 2004). Previous studies on Thai directional verbs *khɨn3* and *loŋ1* focused on meanings and functions of these verbs (Panupong, 1977; Phanthumetha, 1982; Luksaneeyanawin, 1986; Thepkanjana, 1986; Saengchai, 1993; Thepkanjana and Uehara ,2008). The directional verbs *khɨn3* and *loŋ1* express basic meanings about directions with respect to vertical axis. They can function as main verbs and subsidiary verbs. As a main verb in (1) and a subsidiary verb in (2), *khɨn3* shows an upward direction. Examples (3) and (4) have *loŋ1* as a main verb and a subsidiary verb, respectively. *loŋ1* denotes the meaning of a downward direction. (Examples were taken from Saengchai (1993).)

(1) *lu:k3sa:w5 khɨn3 paj1 boʔn1*
daughter ascend go on
ba:n3 lɛ:w4
house perfective
'The daughter already went up the house.'

(2) *thuk4khon1 chuəj3 kan1 khon5*
everyone help each other carry
sam5pha:1raʔ4 khɨn3 ca:k2 phɛ:1
luggage up from raft
'Everyone helped each other carry luggage up from the raft.'

(3) *khun1ja:j1 loŋ1 ma:1 pə:t2*
grandma descend come open
praʔ2tu:1 haj3
door give
'Grandma came down to open the door (for someone).'

(4) *rɨə1bin1 kam1laŋ1 rɔn3 loŋ1*
airplane progressive hover down
khun1miŋ5
Kunming
'An airplane is hovering down to Kunming.'

Furthermore, *khɨn3* and *loŋ1* also appear in non-spatial situations to indicate, for example, change in quality or quantity (in (5) and (6)) and perfective aspect (in (7) and (8)).

(5) *khaʔ2na:t2 khɔ:ŋ huə5 caʔ2*
size of head modal
phɔ:ŋ1 to:1 khɨn3
swell big up
'Head size will swell up.'

(6) *phon5phaʔ2lit2 caʔ2 lot4*
product modal decrease
loŋ1 huəp3ha:p3
descend drastically
'Products will decrease drastically.'

(7) *ka:n1praʔ2kan1saŋ5khom1 riʔ4rə:m3*
social security start
khɨn3 thi:3 thaʔ4wi:p3 juʔ4ro:p2
ascend at continent Europe
'Social security started in Europe.'

(8) *pan1ha:5 thuk4 ja:ŋ2 juʔ4tiʔ2*
problem every classifier end
loŋ1
descend
'Every problem ended.'

A cross-linguistic comparison exists between subsidiary directional verbs *khɨn3* and *loŋ1* in Thai, and their equivalents *shàng* 'ascend' and *xià* 'descend' in Mandarin. Sae-Jia (1999) found that these directional verbs in Thai and Mandarin were similar regarding their meanings and usage. Nonetheless, there were contexts in which *khɨn3* and *loŋ1* were not used in Thai, when *shàng* and *xià* were used in Mandarin. However, it was not clear from Sae-Jia's work why *khɨn3* and *loŋ1*were absent in those contexts. To our knowledge, there has not been a study that examines the similarities and differences between *khɨn3* and *loŋ1*, and the English counterparts *up* and *down*.

The current study has two main parts. The first part analyzes and compares the meanings of *khɨn3* and *loŋ1* in Thai with *up* and *down* in English, by using the national corpora as the data resource. The second part compares the vertical spatial terms of each language in identical semantic contexts by using a parallel corpus as a tool.

3 Meaning comparison: *khɨn3* and *loŋ1* in the Thai corpus vs. *up* and *down* in the English corpus

The Thai data came from the largest Thai language corpus, the Thai National Corpus (TNC) (Aroonmanakun et al., 2009), which contains more than 31 million words of written samples from various genres including academic texts, non-academic texts, newspapers, fiction, law and music. The English data were taken from the British National Corpus (BNC), which contains 100 million words of written and spoken data from various sources, such as newspapers, journals, academic texts, fiction, letters and essays.

Five hundred samples of each of the vertical spatial terms were drawn from the corpora by setting *khɨn3*, *loŋ1*, *up* or *down* as the search input, resulting in 2,000 samples altogether. Each sample was analyzed for its underlying sense. It should be noted that the semantic analyses were inevitably influenced by the words with which the vertical spatial terms co-occurred. The analyses of *khɨn3* and *loŋ1* were cross-checked with a native speaker of Thai. In the same way, those of *up* and *down* were cross-checked with a native speaker of English.

For the Thai vertical directional verb *khɨn3*, it appears both as a main verb (N=85, 17%) and a subsidiary verb (N=415, 83%). We have found seven main senses of *khɨn3*, ranging from the most frequent to the least frequent. (Two of the senses, i.e. to show accomplishment and to show positive attitude, are observed only when *khɨn3* functions as a subsidiary verb.)

1. **Increase** (N=166, 33.2%)

(9) *man4caj1* *khɨn3*
confident ascend
'be more confident'

2. **Occur** (N=109, 21.8%)

(10) *hiw5* *khɨn3* *ma:1* *than1thi:1*
hungry ascend come suddenly
'become hungry suddenly'

3. **Show accomplishment** (N=100, 20%)

(11) *juʔ4* *khɨn3*
incite ascend
'have been incited'

4. **Move towards a higher position** (N=93, 18.6%)

(12) *lɔ:j1* *khɨn3* *ma:1*
float ascend come
'float up'

5. **Be subordinate to** (N=24, 4.8%)

(13) *ka:n1to:3tɔ:p2* *khɨn3* *ʔu:2*
reaction ascend stay
kap2 *siŋ2ra:w4*
with stimulus
'the reaction depends on the stimulus'

6. **Show positive attitude** (N=4, 0.8%)

(14) *thaj2ru:p3* *khɨn3*
take a photo ascend
'photogenic'

7. **Form a shape** (N=3, 0.6%)

(15) *khɨn3* *khro:ŋ1*
ascend format
'form a format'

The English vertical directional word *up* shows six main senses. While some of them are identical to the senses of *khɨn3*, the others are different.

1. **Show accomplishment** (N= 219, 43.8%)

(16) *Syl was eating them all up*

2. **Move towards a higher position** (N=160, 32%)

(17) *slide your hands up*

3. Increase (N=46, 9.2%)

(18) *Rib Transfer Carriage really speed up my knitting*

4. Be in a higher position (N= 41, 8.2%)

(19) *They're in a bag up the chimney*

5. Occur (N=30, 6%)

(20) *The crossbows came up again*

6. Be subordinate to (N=4, 0.8%)

(21) *it is up to each mother to decide to work or not*

Comparing the meanings of the Thai verb *khɨn3* with those of *up* in English, the analysis shows that there are five senses that overlap, which are **to increase**, **to occur**, **to show accomplishment**, **to move towards a higher position**, and **to be subordinate to**. However, *khɨn3* is different from *up* in that the meanings of showing positive attitude and forming a shape are used only in Thai while being in a higher position is seen only in English.

With regard to frequency of occurrence, the most common meanings found for *khɨn3* are to increase (33.2%), to occur (21.8%), to show accomplishment (20%), and to move towards a higher position (18.6%) whereas those found for *up* are to show accomplishment (43.8%) and to move towards a higher position (32%). The other meanings occur less than 10% of the time. It can be further observed that two overlapping senses of *khɨn3* and *up*, i.e. to move towards a higher position and to show accomplishment, are among those of high frequency in both languages.

The findings correspond with Lakoff and Johnson (1980). The vertical spatial terms *khɨn3* in Thai and *up* in English imply an increase, as suggested by the conceptual metaphor MORE IS UP. Moreover, the conceptual metaphor GOOD IS UP can be perceived in the use of *khɨn3* to express positive attitude in Thai.

For the Thai vertical spatial verb *loŋ1*, it also appears both as a main verb (N=166, 33.2%) and a subsidiary verb (N=334, 66.8%). There are six main senses, ranging from the most frequent to the least frequent. (Two of the senses, i.e. to show accomplishment and to increase in negative quality, are observed only when *loŋ1* functions as a subsidiary verb.)

1. Move towards a lower position (N=203, 40.6%)

(22) *də:n1* *loŋ1* *paj1*
walk descend go
'walk down'

2. Decrease (N=110, 22%)

(23) *ra:1kha:1* *thɔ:ŋ1* *loŋ1*
price gold descend
'gold price decreased'

3. Write or list something (N=99, 19.8%)

(24) *loŋ1* *ban1chi:1*
descend account
'post an account'

4. Show accomplishment (N=57, 11.4%)

(25) *sin3sut2* *loŋ1*
end descend
'end'

5. Increase in negative quality (N=20, 4%)

(26) *ʔɔ:n2ʔɛ:1* *loŋ1*
weak descend
'weaker'

6. Participate (N=11, 2.2%)

(27) *loŋ1* *khɛŋ5khan1*
descend competition
'participate in a competition'

The analysis of *down* in English also reveals six main senses as shown in the following listed by order of frequency.

1. **Move towards a lower position** (N=242, 48.4%)

(28) *They laughed, and skied happily <u>down</u> the white snow*

2. **Be in a lower position** (N=100, 20%)

(29) *Will you see her from <u>down</u> there?*

3. **Show accomplishment** (N=90, 18%)

(30) *you've passed your second test, so it's two <u>down</u> and four more to go*

4. **Decrease** (N=40, 8%)

(31) *Can you turn the heating <u>down</u>?*

5. **Write or list something** (N=19, 3.8%)

(32) *they're putting it <u>down</u> in the paper*

6. **Feel unhappy** (N= 9, 1.8%)

(33) *I went <u>down</u> so hard when I didn't get that job*

When we compare the senses of *loŋ1* above with those of *down*, there are four senses that overlap, namely **to move towards a lower position**, **to decrease**, **to write or list something**, and **to show accomplishment**. Nevertheless, *loŋ1* is different from *down* in that it can denote the meanings of an increase in negative quality and participation. Besides, the meaning of feeling unhappy can be found only with the English *down*.

In terms of frequency, the most frequent meaning of *loŋ1* that appears in the samples is to move towards a lower position (40.6%), and the same is true for *down* (48.4%). The other common meanings of *loŋ1* are to decrease (22%), to write or list something (19.8%), and to show accomplishment (11.4%) while those of *down* are to be in a lower place (20%) and to show accomplishment (18%). The other meanings are less than 10%. Hence, the highly frequent meanings shared by *loŋ1* and *down* are to move towards a lower position and to show accomplishment.

The analysis of *loŋ1* and *down* is also consistent with Lakoff and Johnson (1980). The vertical spatial terms showing downward directions in both Thai and English indicate a decrease, conforming to LESS IS DOWN. The Thai verb *loŋ1* is also used to show an increase in negative quality, which follows the conceptual metaphor BAD IS DOWN. Lastly, as suggested by the conceptual metaphor SAD IS DOWN, *down* in English involves unhappy feeling.

To sum up, the meaning comparison reveals that the Thai vertical spatial terms *khɨn3* and *loŋ1*, and the English *up* and *down*, have partly overlapping senses. One of the frequently observed meanings in both languages is movement towards a higher or lower position, which is the basic sense of the vertical spatial terms. The shared sense of vertical movement probably results from a universal image schema of spatial directions. Moreover, the overlapping senses of these terms could also come from the similar cognitive processes of conceptual metaphor and metonymy in Thai and English. As for those senses that do not overlap, they could possibly disclose differences in terms of linguistic structures as well as cultural experience.

4 Context of occurrence: *khɨn3 – up* and *loŋ1 – down* in the parallel corpus

The purpose of the second part of the study is to investigate to what extent the pairs *khɨn3 – up* and *loŋ1 – down* occur in the same contexts. In order to do so, we utilized an English-Thai parallel corpus. According to Glottopedia (2009), a parallel corpus is a corpus built up from an original document in a language and its translated version in another language. This type of corpus is useful for a cross-linguistic study. Data in this study came from the English-Thai Parallel Concordance (Aroonmanakun, 2009), which contains up to 66,402 data pairs from various English to Thai translation works, such as translated fiction and translation students' term papers.

To begin with, we drew 100 data pairs from the concordance by setting the Thai directional verb *khɨn3* as the search input only. The search input in English was left unspecified. The same procedure was executed for *loŋ1*. This brought about 200 samples with *khɨn3* and *loŋ1* as the search input.

We then examined whether the English vertical directional words *up* and *down* also appeared in the same contexts in the English original texts. The results show that 42 instances (42%) of *khɨn3* occur in the same context with *up*. For *loŋ1*, there are only 36 instances (36%) where *loŋ1* and *down* match. Figure 1 displays the percentage of co-occurrence between *khɨn3* and *up*, and between *loŋ1* and *down*.

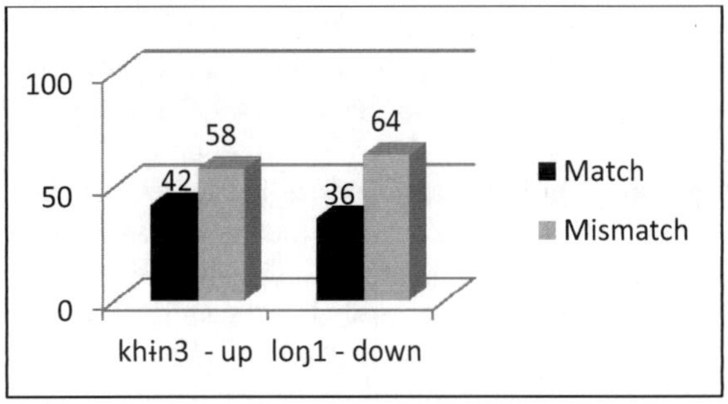

Figure 1: Percentage of co-occurrence between *khɨn3* and *up*, and between *loŋ1* and *down*

The main reason why more than half of the Thai vertical directional verbs do not appear in the same context as the English directional terms has to do with structural differences between Thai and English. To illustrate this, certain English verbs such as *rise*, *fall*, and *drop* contain an implied sense of vertical movement so the directional words *up* and *down* are not indispensable. Directional verbs in Thai, on the other hand, frequently occur as part of serial verbs to convey directional senses. The following examples were taken from the corpus.

(34) **Thai**:
khwa:m1gro:t2 *phuəj1phuŋ3*
angry rise abruptly
khɨn3 *ma:1* *lɛʔ4* *jut2*
ascend come and stop
thi:3 *huə5caj1* *thə:1*
at heart you

English:
And an angry feeling rose in her and stopped around her heart.

(35) **Thai**:
na:3rot4 *rə:m3* *phuŋ3* *tam2* *loŋ1*
front of car begin dart low descend

English:
The nose of the car dropped.

Moreover, while English has specific morphemes to express the comparative degree, Thai relies on the word *khɨn3* and *loŋ1*. Examples are seen in (36) and (37).

(36) **Thai**:
du:1 *khun1* *saʔ2baj1* *khɨn3*
watch you good ascend
yɛ4 *chiaw1*
much indeed

English:
You're much better.

(37) **Thai**:
rot4jon1hɔʔ2 *khɔ:j3khɔ:j3*
flying car slowly
lɔ:j1 *tam2* *loŋ1* *ma:1*
float low descend come

English:
Lower and lower went the flying car.

Another reason for the mismatch between the Thai and English directional words in the same contexts is that some of the Thai directional verbs occur as part of idioms and fixed phases. It is then not surprising that the word *up* or *down* are absent in these contexts. Following are some examples.

(38) **Thai**:
loŋ1 *mɨə1*
descend hand

English:
start to do something

(39) ***Thai:***
khɨn3 *ŋən1*
ascend money

English:
cash (check)

Next, to look closely at the contexts in which both the Thai and English vertical spatial expressions occur, we set *khɨn3* and *loŋ1* as the search input in Thai, and at the same time set *up* and *down* as the search input in English. Two hundred data pairs (100 pairs for *khɨn3 – up* and 100 pairs for *loŋ1 – down*) were gathered from the concordance. Figure 2 shows the percentage of senses of *khɨn3 – up* and *loŋ1 – down* that occur in the same contexts. When *khɨn3* is used in Thai and *up* in English, the directional terms express one of the three senses, namely to move towards a higher position (81%), to occur (12%), and to increase (7%). Examples are seen in (40). For *loŋ1* and *down*, when they co-occur, they share only two senses: to move towards a lower position (98%) and to decrease (2%). Examples are shown in (41).

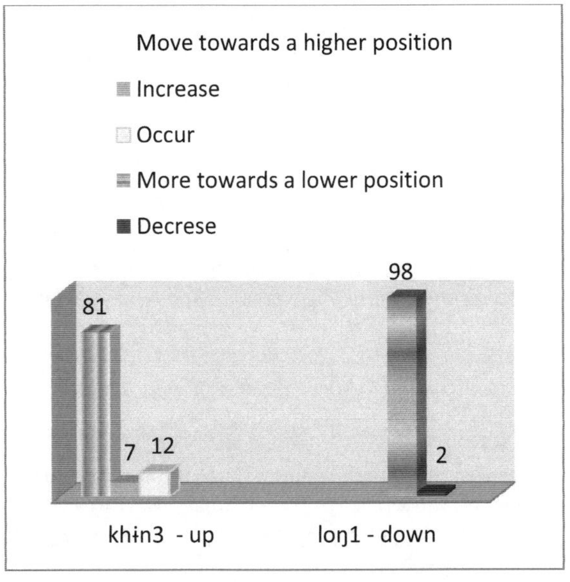

Figure 2: Percentage of senses of *khɨn3 - up* and *loŋ1 - down* that occur in the same contexts

(40) **Thai**:
bak4bi:k2 *luk4* <u>*khɨn3*</u> *ji:n1*
Buckbeak rise ascend stand
English:
Buckbeak stood up.

(41) **Thai**:
khaw5 *kom3* <u>*loŋ1*</u> *mɔ:ŋ1* *tha:1rok4*
he bent descend look baby
English:
He bent down to take a look at the baby.

To summarize, the analysis of the pairs *khɨn3 – up* and *loŋ1 – down* in the English-Thai Parallel Concordance shows that when the contexts are held constant, less than half of instances of *khɨn3* and *loŋ1* in Thai correspond with instances of *up* and *down* in English. The mismatch is accounted for in light of structural differences between the two languages as well the fact that the Thai directional words sometimes appear in formulaic expressions. As for instances in which *khɨn3 – up* and *loŋ1 – down* are used in the same contexts, three semantic dimensions are involved, that is, movement towards a higher or lower position, a change in quantity, and occurrence. The majority of the contexts where *khɨn3* is chosen as a translation of *up*, and *loŋ1* is chosen as a translation of *down*, have the sense of upward or downward movement. This agrees with the fact that vertical directions are the basic meanings shared by these directional terms.

5 Conclusion

In an attempt to study the semantics of vertical spatial terms in Thai in comparison with English, this work draws upon samples from corpora in order to obtain objective and naturalistic data. Meaning analyses of *khɨn3* and *loŋ1* in the Thai National Corpus, and *up* and *down* in the British National Corpus, show that there are overlapping senses in the pairs *khɨn3 – up* and *loŋ1 – down.* The senses involving movement towards a higher or lower position and accomplishment are frequently found in both languages. This reflects a universal image schema of vertical movement as well as similar processes of meaning expansion in Thai and English. Furthermore, the use of data from the parallel corpus, the English-Thai Parallel Concordance, allows us to examine the vertical spatial terms *khɨn3 – up* and *loŋ1 – down* in identical context. We have discovered that instances of *khɨn3* and *loŋ1* in Thai do not necessarily co-occur with their counterparts *up* and *down* in English. The mismatch can be explained in terms of disparate linguistic structures in the two languages. Investigating which senses are shared when *khɨn3* appears in the same contexts with *up* and *loŋ1* with *down*, we have found that these terms mostly co-occur when they denote vertical movement. It should be noted this work is an unprecedented study that make use of a parallel corpus to explore vertical spatial expressions in Thai and English. Obviously, the parallel corpus enables us to make a clear and tangible cross-linguistic comparison.

The study of *khɨn3* and *loŋ1* in Thai along with *up* and *down* in English is a contribution to the body of work on vertical spatial terms across languages. Our future direction is to increase the number of samples used. In addition, since this work concerns mainly with the semantics of the vertical spatial terms, it will be helpful to include syntactic analyses in the future work.

Acknowledgments

This work is a part of the first author's doctoral dissertation. It was partly supported by a grant from the Higher Education Research Promotion and National Research University Project of Thailand, Office of the Higher Education Commission (HS1153A).

References

Aroonmanakun, Wirote, Tansiri, Kachen, & Nittayanuparp, Pairit. (2009). *Thai National Corpus: A progress report*. Paper presented at the 7th Workshop on Asian Language Resources, ACL-IJCNLP 2009, Suntec, Singapore.

Aroonmanakun, Wirote. (2009). English-Thai Parallel Concordance. Retrieved 20 June 2014 http://ling.arts.chula.ac.th/ParaConc/index.html

Boroditsky, Lera. (2001). Does Language Shape Thought?: Mandarin and English Speakers' Conceptions of Time. *Cognitive Psychology 43*, 1–22.

Chun, Lan. (2002). A Cognitive Approach to Up/Down Metaphors in English and Shang/Xia Metaphors in Chinese. In Bengt Altenberg & Sylviane Granger (Eds.), *Lexis in Contrast. Corpus-based approaches* (pp. 161-184). Philadelphia, PA, USA: John Benjamins.

Corpus, British National. (2007). [bnc] British National Corpus Retrieved 20 June 2014, from http://www.natcorp.ox.ac.uk/

Dong, XuXiang. (2010). *A Cognitive Study on Spatial Metaphors in English and Chinese*. Master degree thesis, Chongqing Normal University.

Glottopedia. (2009, 18 July 2014). Parallel corpus Retrieved 22 July 2014, from http://www.glottopedia.org/index.php/Parallel_corpus

Hampe, Beate. (2006). When the Down is not Bad, and Up not Good enough: A usage-based Assessment of the Plus-Minus Parameter in Image-Schema Theory *Cognitive Linguistics 16* (4), 810-112.

Kövecses, Zoltán. (2002). *Metaphor: A Practical Introduction*. New York: Oxford University Press.

Lakoff, George, & Johnson, Mark. (1980). *Metaphors We Live By*. Chicago: University of Chicago Press.

Langacker, Ronald W. (1987). *Foundations of Cognitive Grammar*. Stanford: Stanford University Press.

Langacker, Ronald W. (1999). *Grammar and Conceptualization*. New York: Mouto de Gruyter.

Lee, David. (2001). Extension from Spatial Meanings. *Cognitive Linguistics: An Introduction* (pp. 30-51). New York: Oxford University Press.

Luksaneeyanawin, Sudaporn. (1986). The Meaning of the Word `khvn2' (up) and `long0' (down) in Thai: The Theory of Opposition (pp. 13-23). Bangkok: Text Press Service.

Otani, Naoki. (2006). The Conceptual Basis of the Particles Up and Down in English: Asymmetrics in the Vertical Axis. *Papers in Linguistic Science, 12*, 95-115.

Panupong, Vichin. (1981). *The Structure of Thai: Grammatical System* Bangkok: Ramkhamhaeng Press.

Phanthumetha, Nawawan. (1982). *Thai Grammar*. Bangkok: Chula Press.

Sae-Jia, Hathai. (1999). *A Comparison of the Directional Complements "Shang" "Xia" in Mandarin Chinese and Their Thai Equivalents*. Master degree thesis, Chulalongkorn University.

Saengchai, Sopawan. (1993). *Subsidiary Verbs /khin3/ "ASCEND" and /loŋ1/ "DESCEND" in Thai*. Master degree thesis, Chulalongkorn University.

Seto, Ken-ichi. (1999). Distinguishing Metonymy from Synecdoche. In Klaus-Uwe Panther & Günter Radden (Eds.), *Metonymy in Language and Thought* (pp. 77-120). Amsterdam/Philadelphia: John Benjamins.

Thepkanjana, Kingkarn, & Uehara, Satoshi. (2008). Directional Verb as Success Markers in Thai: Another Grammaticalization Path. In Anthoy V. N. Diller, Jarold A. Edmondson & Yogxian Luo. (Eds.), *The Tai-Kadai Languages*. New York: Routledge.

Thepkanjana, Kingkarn. (1986). *Serial Verb Constructions in Thai*. PhD Dissertation, University of Michigan.

Tyler, Andrea, & Evans, Vyvyan. (2003). *The Semantics of English Preposition: Spatial Scenes Embodied Meaning and Cognition*. New York: Cambridge University Press.

Zlatev, Jordan, & Yangklang, Peerapat. (2004). A Third Way of Travel: The Place of Thai in Motion-Event Typology. In Sven Strömqvist & Ludo Verhoeven (Eds.), *Relating Events in Narrative: Topological and Contextual Perspectives* (pp. 159-190). Mahwah, NJ: LEA Publishers.

Constructions: a new unit of analysis for corpus-based discourse analysis

Samia Touileb
Information Science and Media Studies
University of Bergen
N-5020 Bergen
Norway
samia.touileb@gmail.com

Andrew Salway
Uni Research Computing
Thormøhlensgt. 55
N-5008 Bergen
Norway
andrew.salway@uni.no

Abstract

We propose and assess the novel idea of using automatically induced constructions as a unit of analysis for corpus-based discourse analysis. Automated techniques are needed in order to elucidate important characteristics of corpora for social science research into topics, framing and argument structures. Compared with current techniques (keywords, n-grams, and collocations), constructions capture more linguistic patterning, including some grammatical phenomena. Recent advances in natural language processing mean that it is now feasible to automatically induce some constructions from large unannotated corpora. In order to assess how well constructions characterise the content of a corpus and how well they elucidate interesting aspects of different discourses, we analysed a corpus of climate change blogs. The utility of constructions for corpus-based discourse analysis was compared qualitatively with keywords, n-grams and collocations. We found that the unusually frequent constructions gave interesting and different insights into the content of the discourses and enabled better comparison of sub-corpora.

1 Introduction

In recent years, with the increasing availability of online text data and computing power, there has been a rapid increase in interest in corpus-based discourse analysis, particularly among social science researchers. Within social science, discourse analysis is concerned with how societally important issues and opinions are expressed through language, e.g. in news and social media. The scale of the data sets means that automated techniques are essential, at least to give researchers an overview of the content in a corpus and to elucidate interesting aspects for further investigation.

The aim of this paper is to assess the novel idea of using automatically induced constructions for corpus-based discourse analysis. Section 2 provides some background about corpus-based discourse analysis and discusses some limitations of the automated techniques that are commonly used. It also describes what constructions are and how some constructions can be induced automatically by taking advantage of recent developments in natural language processing. Then in Section 3 we report our investigation into the use of constructions for corpus-based discourse analysis. This compared the utility of unusually frequent constructions with current techniques, based on how they gave insights into the content of a large corpus of climate change blogs, and how they elucidated interesting phenomena for further investigation. Section 4 summarises our conclusions and contributions, and outlines future work.

2 Background

In this section we review the use of automated text analysis techniques for corpus-based discourse analysis, and explain why we propose constructions as a new unit of analysis (section 2.1). Then we explain how the state-of-the-art in grammar

Copyright 2014 by Samia Touileb and Andrew Salway
28th Pacific Asia Conference on Language, Information and Computation pages 634–643

induction means that it is now possible to automatically induce some constructions from unannotated corpora (section 2.2).

2.1 Corpus-based discourse analysis

In the social sciences, the term discourse is used to refer to how ideas and opinions are formed, influenced and expressed through language (Baker, 2006). Researchers study discourses in order to explain the effect of language use on social, political, legal and environmental issues, among many others. An often-cited and simple example is how the difference between referring to an individual as a "freedom fighter" or a "terrorist" effects a reader's perception and opinions.

Corpus-based approaches take advantage of automated techniques in order to analyse large-scale discourses such as those in corpora of news and social media (e.g. Fløttum et al, 2014; Kim, 2014; Jaworska and Krishnamurthy, 2012; Grundman and Krishnamurthy, 2010). The techniques can reveal interesting phenomena within the corpus that would not be apparent to a researcher who read the material (Baker, 2006); often there is too much material for a researcher to read anyway. That said, automated analyses alone are not normally sufficient: they must be complemented with manual inspections of the texts and consideration of their contexts.

For many social science researchers, an important part of discourse analysis is the characterisation of how issues are framed. To frame an issue is to "select some aspects of a perceived reality and make them more salient in a communicating text" (Entman, 1993). Framing is also defined as "a central organizing idea or story line that provides meaning to an unfolding strip of events" (Gamson and Modigliani, 1989).

Framing analysis necessarily involves text analysis in order to identify salient formulations (frames) and to uncover how issues are represented differently by participants in discourses. In a recent paper, Touri and Koteyko (2014) provide an extensive review of methods for framing analysis and describe ways in which corpus linguistic techniques can be applied, with a focus on keywords and concordances. A keyword list helps to identify words that indicate what perspective is being taken on an issue; cf. the "freedom fighter/terrorist" example. Then, concordances which show instances of words and their co-texts can be read in order to understand more about the ways in which words are being used as parts of frames.

Another recent paper shows how collocation data can be used to analyse how issues are represented in the media (McEnery et al., 2013). Statistically significant collocations around words that refer to an issue of interest are interpreted, for example, as giving a positive or negative tone.

There is also the potential for automated techniques to contribute to investigations in other areas of social science research by identifying some of the linguistic patterns that are used to build discourses. For example, the ability to characterise and compare dominant topics, and the ways in which they are expressed, is relevant for investigating: agenda setting – what issues get more attention in the media, e.g. (Grundman and Krishnamurthy, 2010); polarisation – how different social groups form increasingly divergent opinions, e.g. (Elgesem et al., 2014), (Adamic and Glance, 2005); and argument structures – the ways in which writers try to persuade others, e.g. (Koteyko et al., 2013).

In general, keywords and n-grams can be seen as highlighting salient ideas and opinions in discourses. Collocations characterise language use around keywords and can be seen as giving insights into the meanings typically associated with issues. However, as noted previously, these techniques can only be a starting point for a researcher. The lack of information about the co-text around keywords and n-grams restricts the extent to which they can be interpreted without the close reading of concordances. Increasingly, corpora of interest to social scientists are too large for close reading of all the relevant concordances, so we see a need for techniques to condense information about co-texts.

Collocation data already provides some information about a keyword's co-text, i.e. it shows the words that have a statistically significant association with the keyword. However, collocation data is typically presented as a large grid of statistics for one keyword. It seems to us that it would be desirable to have a simpler picture that is more intuitive to interpret.

Furthermore, by prioritising lexical elements, the use of keywords, n-grams and collocations may fail to elucidate relevant grammatical phenomena. As noted by Baker (2006), unusually frequent grammatical phenomena (as well as words and phrases), can also reveal the non-obvious meanings of a discourse. It seems to us that they are particularly important for framing and argumentation analysis.

All these observations lead us to propose constructions as a new unit of analysis for corpus-based discourse analysis, to complement existing techniques. A construction is defined as a form-meaning pair (Goldberg, 2009). The form of a construction can be any combination of morphemes, words, phrases, idioms, local grammatical templates and word classes, as well as general linguistic structures. Thus, we see constructions as a convenient way to conceptualise language for the purposes of corpus-based discourse analysis. Firstly, they encompass a wide variety of linguistic forms. Secondly, these forms are thought of as mapping directly to meaning which is the ultimate object of study in discourse analysis. In particular, constructions that capture local grammatical templates and word classes may be particularly useful.

Our idea is that a researcher can start an investigation by looking at a set of salient constructions, perhaps alongside keywords, n-grams and collocations, in order to get deeper insights into the distinctive characteristics of a particular discourse. In the following sub-section we discuss how it is possible to induce some salient constructions automatically from an unannotated corpus.

2.2 The automatic induction of constructions

Developments in natural language processing have led to the automatic induction of grammatical structures from unannotated corpora, e.g. the ADIOS algorithm (Solan et al., 2005); see D'Ulizia et al. (2011) for a review of the field of grammatical inference.

ADIOS (Automatic DIstillation of Structure) is an unsupervised algorithm that discovers hierarchical structures in sequential data, e.g. words in sentences. It identifies the most significant patterns (horizontal sequences) and equivalence classes (vertical groups) within the context of patterns, using statistical information. Each sentence is loaded onto a directed pseudograph with one vertex for each vocabulary item: this means that partially aligned sentences share sub-paths across the graph. In each iteration, the most significant pattern is identified with a statistical criterion that favours frequent sequences that occur in a variety of contexts. Then, the algorithm looks for possible equivalence classes within the context of the pattern, i.e. it identifies positions in the pattern that could be filled by different items and forms an equivalence class with those items. At the end of the iteration, the new pattern and equivalence class become vocabulary items in the graph, so that they can become part of further patterns and equivalence classes, and hence hierarchical structures are formed.

From our point of view, ADIOS has three particularly good features. Firstly, it is unsupervised which means that it should be portable across different languages and domains. Secondly, since equivalence classes only exist in the specified contexts of patterns, the structures induced by ADIOS will generate less overgeneralization than methods assigning global categories to each unit of a sentence, i.e. it gives a better description of local grammatical features. Thirdly, induced patterns may encapsulate units occurring in positions far apart from each other.

The ADIOS algorithm, like some others, builds on the insights of Zellig Harris who argued that grammatical structures can be induced through a distributional analysis of the surface forms of languages (Harris, 1954). He also showed how linguistic structures that are identified in this way map to important information structures, especially in domain-specific corpora (Harris, 1988).

This second point motivated work to modify and apply the ADIOS algorithm for text mining purposes, i.e. to extract salient information structures from an unannotated corpus (Salway and Touileb, 2014). The learning regime of ADIOS was modified in order to focus the algorithm on text snippets around key terms of interest, rather than processing all sentences. This change was influenced by the theory of local grammars (Gross, 1997), i.e. the idea that language is best described with word classes that are specific to local contexts. Another modification targeted the most frequent and meaningful structures. To do this, after each iteration, instances of the most frequent patterns were replaced with common identifiers in the input file so that patterning around them was more explicit in subsequent iterations.

Following this method, 671 patterns were induced from a corpus of climate change blogs by Salway and Touileb (2014); see section 3.1 for a description of this corpus. Table 1 shows some examples of the patterns generated by the automatic process. The patterns and the equivalence classes that they contain are bracketed. The elements of patterns are separated by white space and the elements of equivalence classes are separated by '|'.

Pattern 1 in the table captures a simple word sequence which is a domain term – "fossil fuels". Pattern 2, with the equivalence class "(carbon|(greenhouse gas)|co2)", captures three near-equivalent domain terms – "carbon emissions", etc. Pattern 3 does something similar to capture two interchangeable phrases that are common in the corpus; note, in this pattern there is overgeneralization due to the equivalence class "(of|for)". Pattern 4 shows some grammatical structure being captured with three verbs – "(combat|minimize|tackle)" – that appeared in the same context in the corpus. Patterns 5 and 6 capture both grammatical structure and some near-synonyms.

1. (fossil fuels)
2. ((carbon|(greenhouse gas)|co2) emissions)
3. ((consequences|impacts) ((of|for) climate change))
4. ((to (combat|minimize|tackle)) climate change)
5. (((due to)|(caused by)) ((climate change)|(global warming)))
6. (((((global|some|sophisticated|complex|the) climate models)|climate models) (project|suggest|predict)) that)
7. ((of global warming) (was|are|is))
8. (in (order|(the (atmosphere|recessions))))

Table 1. Examples of the patterns induced from a corpus of climate change blogs (Salway and Touileb, 2014).

Given Goldberg's definition of a construction, cf. section 2.1, it seems reasonable to refer to patterns 1-5 as constructions. Of course, that is not to say that the induction process captures all kinds of constructions. Rather, it seems to capture mainly terms, phrases and local grammatical templates. We previously noted the need for techniques to condense information about keywords' co-texts, in order to reduce the need for reading large quantities of concordance lines. It may be argued that patterns 3-5 are doing a useful job in condensing some of the co-texts around "climate change".

It should be noted that some patterns are incomplete constructions, e.g. "7. ((of global warming) (was|are|is))", and others are not constructions at all because they mix grammatical structures and contain equivalence classes that are semantically incoherent, e.g. "8. (in (order|(the (atmosphere|recessions))))".

Since we have no automatic way to separate patterns that are constructions from those that are not constructions, we can only use the complete set of patterns for corpus-based discourse analysis, cf. section 3.2. As will be seen in section 3.3, the presence of patterns that are not constructions does not have an adverse effect on results. For convenience, from this point forward, we refer to the set of patterns as a set of constructions, whilst noting that it contains some non-constructions.

3 Assessing the use of constructions for corpus-based discourse analysis

The investigation focussed on two main questions. (1) Do unusually frequent constructions reflect the distinctive content of a (sub-) corpus? (2) If so, do they suggest interesting lines of further investigation for discourse analysis?

In order to answer these questions, we analysed constructions in a corpus of climate change blogs. Specifically, we identified unusually frequent constructions in three major blogs (which can be considered as sub-corpora), and qualitatively evaluated the utility of these constructions for corpus-based discourse analysis. We then compared their utility with keywords, n-grams and collocations.

Section 3.1 describes the climate change corpus and the three blogs analysed. Section 3.2 describes how unusually frequent constructions were identified. Section 3.3 discusses how these constructions give insights into the content of each blog and how they suggest further lines of investigation for corpus-based discourse analysis. Section 3.4 compares the insights gained from the constructions with what can be learnt from keywords, n-grams and collocations for the same blogs. Section 3.5 discusses the findings with respect to the two questions stated above.

3.1 Corpus

The NTAP corpus comprises about 3000 English language blogs (1.4 million blog posts) related to climate change issues (Salway et. al, 2013). This corpus is interesting for discourse analysis because climate change is a complex and contested issue with diverse sub-topics, perspectives and opinions. It may be hypothesised that the discourses around climate change are polarized (sceptics and acceptors), framed in different ways (e.g. science, politics, national and local issues), and contain a variety of argumentation structures used to support different positions.

As an example of social media, blogs represent both an opportunity and challenge for corpus-based discourse analysis. They may reflect a greater variety of perspectives and opinions than traditional media. However, the large volume of material and the greater variety of language use mean that new unsupervised automated techniques are required.

For assessing the utility of unusually frequent constructions, we focussed our analysis on three major blogs that we already knew something about (Elgesem et al., 2014). The blog *wattsupwiththat.com* (4996 posts; 3.5m words) is one of the most central blogs in the sceptical blog community and is concerned with climate science issues. The blog *itsgettinghotinhere.org* (1343 posts; 0.8m words) is a central blog in the accepters community and discusses both climate science and climate politics. The third blog, *chimalaya.org* (3782 posts; 3.1m words) has many links to the other two blogs, and is concerned with climate politics issues for the Himalaya region.

3.2 Unusually frequent constructions

We took the set of constructions extracted by Salway and Touileb (2014), as described in section 2.2; recall, this set includes some patterns that are not constructions but we refer to it as a set of constructions for convenience. It was decided that constructions with frequency less than 50 in the whole corpus were unlikely to be unusually frequent in any single blog and so they were removed. Then we counted the frequency for each remaining construction (381 constructions) in each of the three blogs. This was straightforward because each construction is described as a regular expression.

In order to identify the unusually frequent constructions in each blog relative to the other two blogs, we used the RRF statistic – ratio of relative frequencies (Edmundson and Wyllys, 1961). This is a simple measure that reflects how much more (or less) something appears in corpus A compared to corpus B, whilst factoring in the sizes of the corpora. The RRF for a unit is computed as:

$$RRF_U = {}^{RF_{UA}}/_{RF_{UB}}$$

RF_{UA}: Relative frequency of unit U in corpus A.
RF_{UB}: Relative frequency of unit U in corpus B.

Where:

$$RF_U = {}^{F_U}/_N$$

F_U: Frequency of unit U in the corpus.
N: Total number of words (tokens) in the corpus.

Note, there can be an issue with division by zero in the RRF equation when F_U is zero in corpus B. However this situation did not arise in the current analysis.

For each of the three blogs we ranked the 381 constructions according to their RRF values, where corpus B was the union of the other two blogs. The RRF statistic can give misleading results for low frequency values: it is "easier" for a low-frequency item to get a high RRF value. With this in mind, a frequency threshold was applied to the ranked lists of constructions. After testing various thresholds, it was decided to use a frequency threshold equal to 0.001% of the size of each blog. Thus constructions only appear in the ranked RRF lists if they have frequencies greater than: *chimalaya* (30), *itsgettinghotinhere* (8), *wattsupwiththat* (34). These thresholds mean that we can be more confident that the ranked constructions for a blog are reflective of that blog's content in general, rather than just a few blog posts within it.

3.3 Results

Table 2 presents the top 10 constructions ranked by RRF values for the three blogs *chimalaya*, *itsgettinghotinhere* and *wattsupwiththat*. These are the most unusually frequent constructions that we assume will reveal some of each blog's distinctive characteristics. Each construction is presented with an ID (for ease of reference), and using brackets and '|'s as described in section 2.2. For each construction the table gives its total frequency, and then a breakdown of the frequencies of its various forms. For example, C2 (C for *chimalaya*) occurs 1172 times in total – 1061 times as "developing countries" and 111 times as "poor countries".

We envisage a social science researcher using ranked lists of constructions as a starting point to investigate the discourses in one or more (sub-) corpora. Thus, the constructions should provide a convenient overview of the content and draw attention to potentially interesting phenomena, like topics, framing and argument structures. In the following sub-sections we discuss how the constructions in Table 2 could be used for these purposes.

3.3.1 Constructions elucidating topics?

Many of the constructions in Table 2 do indeed reflect what we already know about the content of the blogs: *chimalaya* – climate politics, Himalaya region; *itsgettinghotinhere* – climate science, climate politics; *wattsupwiththat* – sceptical views of climate science. Furthermore, many of the constructions give a finer-grained view on how the distinctive topics are expressed in each blog.

For example, constructions C1, C3, C5 and C9 all indicate that *chimalaya* focusses on the impacts/effects of climate change, rather than its causes. Constructions C3 and C9 include both "causes" and "effects" but from the frequencies of the different forms it is apparent that this blog is much more concerned with the effects. The blog's interests in addressing climate change are highlighted by constructions C7 and C8, with frequent mentions of meetings in C4. Its focus on the kinds of countries that comprise the Himalaya region is indicated by C2.

Itsgettinghotinhere's constructions I5, I6 and I9 all highlight its concern with taking action to address climate change issues, although perhaps cotexts for I5 and I9 should be checked to confirm this. Constructions I1, I4, I7 and I8 are terms that suggest a focus on discussing the link between climate change and energy production. Various ways to express the idea of "cap and trade schemes" as part of a solution to climate change are captured by I2, and partially by the incomplete construction I3.

Constructions W3 and W10 indicate that *wattsupwiththat* discusses the role of humans in causing global warming, although none of the constructions indicate this blog's sceptical viewpoint, except perhaps the form "no global warming" in W10. The partial constructions W4 and W8 suggest an interest in climate models, but further investigation would be needed to see what is being said about them. Compared with the other two blogs, we get a less clear picture of this blog's distinctive content.

3.3.2 Constructions related to frames?

As discussed in section 2.1, framing analysis has benefited from automated techniques such as keywords and collocations. However, we noted the potential for constructions to elucidate richer linguistic patterning that could be related to how different perspectives are represented in corpora. Here we give some examples of how constructions highlight framing phenomena that would not be so apparent using current techniques.

It could be argued that the construction "C2 ((developing|poor) countries)" suggests that in *chimalaya* the climate issue is framed from the perspective of developing countries and their particular concerns. We note though that, in this case, there is a fuzzy boundary between this notion of framing and the notion of topic. A clearer framing interpretation is the strong preference for the form "developing countries" (f=1061) compared with "poor countries" (f=111) which indicates a choice to frame these countries in a positive way.

Another interesting construction that is unusualy frequent in this blog is "C8 (to (combat|minimize|tackle)) climate change)". The construction itself suggests two different framings on how the climate issue can be addressed. Firstly, there is a rather dispassionate and diplomatic approach – indicated by the form "to minimize climate change". Secondly, there is a more passionate and confrontational position which is expressed with stronger words – "to combat|tackle climate change". The frequencies of these forms within *chimalaya* make it clear that this blog is firmly taking the second position (f=1 vs f=129); this is further supported by C7. Perhaps collocation data would show "combat" and "tackle" as being associated with "climate change" in this blog: however, the grammatical structure captured by C8 also elucidates the contrast with "minimize".

The construction W3, which is unusually frequent in *wattsupwiththat*, highlights a difference in framing between saying "man made global warming" and "anthropogenic global warming". Whilst these terms have the same meaning, the latter has a more scientific connotation. The preference for the form "anthropogenic global warming" in this blog strikes us as interesting, because in another analysis we have seen a general preference for "man made global warming" in sceptical blogs. This prompted us to look at the concordances for

chimalaya.org

C1. (impact ((of|for) climate change)): 284 - *impact of climate change (284)*

C2. ((developing|poor) countries): 1172 - *developing countries(1061), poor countries (111)*

C3. (the (causes|effects) | (consequences|impacts) ((of|for) climate change))): 460 - *the impacts of climate change (224), the effects of climate change (203) , the consequences of climate change (29), the causes of climate change (4)*

C4. (climate change (talks|meeting|summit| conference)): 131 - *climate change conference (55), climate change talks (47), climate change summit (21)*

C5. ((consequences|impacts) ((of|for) climate change)): 478 - *impacts of climate change (416), consequences of climate change (62)*

C6. (\d+ per cent): ***695*** - *\d+ per cent (695)*

C7. (tackling climate change): 47 - *tackling climate change (47)*

C8. ((to (combat|minimize|tackle)) climate change): 130 - *to tackle climate change (72), to combat climate change (57), to minimize climate change (1)*

C9. ((causes|effects) ((of|for) climate change)): 357 - *effects of climate change (345), causes of climate change (12)*

C10. (to climate change): 1289 - *to climate change (1289)*

itsgettinghotinhere.org

I1. (global warming pollution): 23 - *global warming pollution (23)*

I2. (a (cap and) ((trade|trading|cap and trade) (scheme|system|program|approach))): 13 - *a cap and trade system (8), a cap and trade program (4), a cap and trade scheme (1)*

I3. (cap and): 92 - *cap and (92)*

I4. (clean air): 33 - *clean air (33)*

I5. (to (stem|stop)): 266 - *to stop (263), to stem (3)*

I6. (action (on climate change)): 36 - *action on climate change (36)*

I7. (power plants): 133 - *power plants (133)*

I8. (fossil fuels): 213 - *fossil fuels (213)*

I9. (to regulate): 29 - *to regulate (29)*

I10. (a (pilot|national|possible|nationwide|broad based)): 108 - *a national (97), a nationwide (6), a possible (3), a pilot (2)*

wattsupwiththat.com

W1. (the carbon tax): 37 - *the carbon tax (37)*

W2. ((global warming|((and|to) global warming)) (has|can|will)): 71 - *global warming has (32), global warming will (27), global warming can (8), and global warming has (2), to global warming will (2)*

W3. ((man made|anthropogenic) global warming): 69 - *anthropogenic global warming (61), man made global warming (8)*

W4. ((analysing|in|on|by) climate models): 45 - *in climate models (24), by climate models (15), on climate models (6)*

W5. (global warming (is|was)): 226 - *global warming is (200), global warming was (26)*

W6. ((to|between|by|about) \d+): 4382 - *to \d+ (1985), about \d+ (1363), by \d+ (659), between \d+ (375)*

W7. ((would|will) be): 3239 - *will be (1873), would be (1366)*

W8. ((global|some|sophisticated|complex|the) climate models): 126 - *the climate models (92), global climate models (25), some climate models (4), complex climate models (4), sophisticated climate models (1)*

W9. ((who|he) (was|are|is)): 915 - *he was (248), who are (203), he is (189), who is (169), who was (106)*

W10. ((a|no) (((man made|anthropogenic) global warming)|global warming)): 40 - *a global warming (22), no global warming (18)*

Table 2. Top 10 constructions ranked by RRF for three blogs. Each construction is given with ID, its total frequency, and the frequencies of its different forms.

"anthropogenic global warming" within *wattsupwiththat*. We saw that it was typically used to frame the issue in scientific terms, but then to comment on the views of climate scientists in negative and sarcastic ways.

3.3.3 Constructions related to argument structures?

The construction "W7 ((would|will) be)" struck us as interesting because it contains only grammatical words. Since these words are usually very frequent and part of general language, it is particularly interesting when they have a high RRF. By looking at the frequencies of the two forms of W7 in the three blogs, we see that its high RRF is mainly due to a relatively high use of the form "would be". In the other two blogs the frequency of "would be" is less than 45% of the frequency of "will be", but in *wattsupwiththat* it is 73%, Table 3.

Blog	"will be"	"would be"
wattsupwiththat	1873	1366
chimalaya	2122	891
itsgettinghotinhere	564	250

Table 3. Frequencies of the forms of W7.

From a preliminary analysis of the concordances of "would be" in *wattsupwiththat*, we got the impression that it is being used as part of argumentation structures in a scientific style of language; for example, statements of hypotheses like "if X then Y would happen". This could perhaps be a starting point for investigating the degree to which climate issues are discussed in a scientific style across the blogosphere.

Another example of a construction that relates to argument structures was found just outside of the top 10: this was "((you|we) (can|should))" which was 15th in the ranking for *itsgettinghotinhere*. The frequencies of its four forms were: "we can" (f=302), "you can" (f=196), "we should" (f=84), "you should" (f=8). The preference for "we" versus "you" suggests that the writers are trying to be inclusive of their readers, and are urging for collective action against climate change. This perhaps contrasts with the third person style of scientific writing in other blogs.

The even stronger preference for "can" versus "should" suggests that the writers are trying to maintain an encouraging and positive tone, and to avoid alienating people by not telling them directly what to do. Of course, all these observations would have to be supported by more analyses, but it seems that the constructions did highlight interesting aspects of the discourses.

3.4 Comparison with current techniques

In order to make a qualitative comparison between the use of constructions and current techniques, we generated keyword, n-gram and collocation data from the same three blogs. Of course, there are multiple ways to implement these techniques so a comprehensive comparison is not possible here. We have tried to follow typical implementations of the techniques and believe that our general observations would hold regardless of implementation details. We recognise the need for more extensive and quantitative evaluation in future work, but this was beyond the scope of the current paper.

3.4.1 Keywords and key n-grams

We generated a list of 20 keywords and 20 key n-grams for each blog, using a frequency threshold and the RRF statistic to rank them, cf. section 3.2. Some of *chimalaya's* keywords and n-grams reflect the fact that it is broadly about climate and the Himalaya region, e.g. "Kashmir", "Nepalese", "Bhutanese", "Punjab", "GEF" (Global Environment Facility), "in the Himalayan region", "mountain ecosystem", "climate related issues". There are also indications of its interest in development, e.g. "ADB" (Asian Development Bank), "knowledge sharing", "capacity building".

Similarly, some keywords and key n-grams point broadly to the topics of the other two blogs: *itsgettinghotinhere* – "BP" (British Petroleum), "RBC" (Royal Bank of Canada), "clean energy economy", "action network"; *wattsupwiththat* – "OHC" (Ocean Heat Content), "ASOS" (Automated Surface Observing Stations), "MMTS" (Maximum/Minimum Temperature System), "linear trend", "data sets", "climate audit".

It might be possible to use some of the keywords and n-grams as the starting point for framing analysis, cf. the method described by Touri and Koteyko (2014). However this would entail extensive reading of concordance lines. On a separate point, as far as we can see, none of the keywords and n-grams suggest distinctive argument structures.

3.4.2 Collocations

We generated a list of the top 10 collocates of the word "climate" in each blog, using a span of +/- 5 words, and ranking on mutual information (Baker, 2006); again the 0.001% frequency threshold was applied.

In all three blogs there was an unsurprising association between "climate" and "change". More specifically, in *chimalaya* the words most strongly associated with "climate" included "intergovernmental" and "panel" which point to the term "Intergovernmental Panel on Climate Change". Other strongly associated words point to the blog's interest in addressing climate change, e.g. "combat", "combating", "adapting", "mitigating". Likewise, collocates of "climate" in the other two blogs also reflected something about their foci: *itsgettinghotinhere* – "causes", "effects", "impact", "addressing"; *wattsupwiththat* – "denier", "impacts", "panel", "framework", "intergovernmental".

3.5 Discussion

The results from this investigation suggest that a list of unusually frequent constructions reflects some of the distinctive content of a (sub-) corpus. Further, and in answer to our second question, there were examples of constructions that revealed linguistic patterning that would be of interest for further analysis into topics, framing and argumentation structures.

With regards to topic analysis, the constructions are useful because, unlike keywords, they capture terms and phrases which could enable finer-grained topic classification and text retrieval. Terms and phrases will be present in n-gram lists but these lists are typically very long and noisy. A further apparent advantage of constructions is that they group together alternative ways to refer to the same concept.

For the analysis of framing and argumentation structures, the fact that some constructions explicate local grammatical structures gives an advantage over current techniques. For example, the construction "(to (combat|minimize|tackle)) climate change)" highlights a potential framing choice more explicitly than the equivalent keyword or collocation data. The words "combat", "minimize" and "tackle" could appear as keywords and collocates, but the researcher would have to then analyse large numbers of concordance lines to establish that they were part of frames.

It was also seen that some constructions comprising only grammatical words highlighted linguistic patterning that was relevant for the analysis of argument structures, i.e. "((would|will) be)" and "((you|we) (can|should))". The grammatical structures in these constructions would certainly not be apparent with current techniques, and indeed it is unlikely that the individual words would even be noticed in lists of keywords and collocates because they are so frequent in general language.

4 Concluding remarks

This paper has proposed and assessed the novel idea of using constructions as a unit of analysis for corpus-based discourse analysis. We envisage researchers consulting lists of unusually frequent constructions as a first step in data-driven investigations, i.e. in order to get an overview of the content of large corpora, and to identify interesting phenomena for more detailed analysis. The use of constructions is appealing because, unlike current techniques, they capture both lexical and grammatical patterning.

Building on recent work in natural language processing it was possible to automatically identify unusually frequent constructions within a large corpus of climate change blogs. We showed how lists of unusually frequent constructions highlighted a variety of linguistic phenomena relating to topic, framing and argumentation structures. These phenomena would all be interesting for corpus-based discourse analysis and would not be so apparent to researchers using keywords, n-grams, collocations and concordances.

Whilst we only looked at constructions within one corpus, there is good reason to believe that the approach would be broadly applicable because the induction process is unsupervised. That said, because the induction process exploits partially overlapping word sequences around key terms, we expect that it will be most effective on large corpora with relatively constrained language use. In other words, it will work best with corpora that consist of a single domain and a single text genre.

In order for this approach to be integrated into social science research methods, it will be important to understand more about how the induction process works. Although we can observe the interesting constructions that it gives, as yet we know little about what it misses and why. See Salway and Touileb (2014) for more about related ongoing work. This must include a more rigorous, and ideally automated, separation of induced patterns into constructions and non-constructions.

Acknowledgments

We thank Zach Solan for providing an implementation of the ADIOS algorithm, Knut Hofland and Lubos Steskal for creating the NTAP blog corpus, and Dag Elgesem for his helpful comments. This research was supported by a grant from The Research Council of Norway's VERDIKT program.

References

Lada Adamic and Natalie Glance. 2005. The Political Blogosphere and the 2004 U.S. Election: Divided They Blog. *Procs. of the 3rd International Workshop on Link discovery - LinkKDD*, 36–43.

Paul Baker. 2006. *Using corpora in discourse analysis*. 2006 London: Continuum.

Arianna D'Ulizia, Fernando Ferri and Patrizia Grifoni. 2011. A survey of grammatical inference methods for natural language learning. *Artificial Intelligence Review,* 36(1):1-27.

Harold P. Edmundson and Ronald Eugene Wyllys. 1961. Automatic Abstracting and Indexing - Survey and Recommendations. *Communications of the Association for Computer Machinery*, 4(5).

Dag Elgesem, Lubos Steskal and Nicholas Diakopoulos. 2014. The structure and content of the discourse on climate change in the blogosphere: the big picture. To appear in: *Environmental Communication. Special issue on climate change communication on the Internet.*

Robert Entman. 1993. Towards clarification of a fractured paradigm. *Journal of Communication*, 43(4):51-58.

Kjersti Fløttum, Øyvind Gjerstad, Anje Müller Gjesdal, Nelya Koteyko and Andrew Salway. 2014. Representations of the FUTURE in English language blogs on climate change. To appear in: *Global Environmental Change.*

William A. Gamson and Andre Modigliani. 1989. Media discourse and public opinion on nuclear power: a constructionist approach. *American Journal of Sociology*, 95(1):1-37.

Adele Goldberg. 2009. The nature of generalization in language. *Cognitive Linguistics*, 20(1):93–127.

Maurice Gross. 1997. The Construction of Local Grammars. In: E. Roche and Y. Schabes (eds.), Finite-State *Language Processing. The MIT Press, Cambridge MA*, 329-354.

Reiner Grundmann and Ramesh Krishnamurthy. 2010. The Discourse of Climate Change: A Corpus-based Approach. *Critical Approaches to Discourse Analysis Across Disciplines*, 4(2):125-146.

Zellig Harris. 1954. Distributional structure. *Word*, 10:(2/3).146-162.

Zellig Harris. 1988. *Language and Information*. Columbia University Press, New York.

Sylvia Jaworska and Ramesh Krishnamurthy. 2012. On the F word: A corpus-based analysis of the media representation of feminism in British and German press discourse, 1990–2009. *Discourse & Society*, 23(4):401-431.

Kyung Hye Kim. 2014. Examining US news media discourses about North Korea: A corpus-based critical discourse analysis. *Discourse & Society*, 25(2):221-244.

Nelya Koteyko, Rusi Jaspal and Brigitte Nerlich. 2013. Climate change and 'climategate' in online reader comments: A mixed methods study. *The Geographical Journal*, 179(1):74–86.

Tony McEnery, Amanda Potts and Richard Xiao. 2013. Is there a reputational benefit to hosting the Olympics and Paralympics? *Procs. Corpus Linguistics 2013,* Lancaster University.

Andrew Salway, Knut Hofland and Samia Touileb. 2013. Applying Corpus Techniques to Climate Change Blogs. *Procs. Corpus Linguistics 2013,* Lancaster University.

Andrew Salway and Samia Touileb. 2014. Applying grammar induction to text mining. *Procs. 52nd ACL Conference* (short papers), 712-717.

Zach Solan, David Horn, Eytan Ruppin and Shimon Edelman. 2005. Unsupervised learning of natural languages. *Procs. of the National Academy of Sciences,* 102(33):11629–11634.

Maria Touri and Nelya Koteyko. 2014. Using corpus linguistic software in the extraction of news frames: towards a dynamic process of frame analysis in journalistic texts. *International Journal of Social Research Methodology*, Published online 3 July2014. DOI:10.1080/13645579.2014.929878.

Noun Paraphrasing Based on a Variety of Contexts

Tomoyuki Kajiwara
Department of Electrical Engineering
Nagaoka University of Technology
Nagaoka City, Niigata, Japan
kajiwara@jnlp.org

Kazuhide Yamamoto
Department of Electrical Engineering
Nagaoka University of Technology
Nagaoka City, Niigata, Japan
yamamoto@jnlp.org

Abstract

We paraphrase nouns along the contexts of sentence input on the basis of a variety of contexts obtained from a large-scale corpus. The proposed method only uses the number of types of context, not word frequency or co-occurrence frequency features. This method is based on the notion that paraphrase candidates appear more commonly with target words in the same context. The results of our experiment demonstrate that the approach can produce more appropriate paraphrases than approaches based on co-occurrence frequency and pointwise mutual information.

1 Introduction

Although extensive and various forms of text data are easily available in the present age, in order for readers to gather information effectively, they need technology that overcomes any differences in their linguistic competence. For example, technology that buries the difference in the linguistic competence of foreign language learners, children, the elderly, and disabled persons is useful (Inui and Fujita, 2004). We present our research on paraphrasing to control language at the elementary school level in order to simplify texts for children. We believe that vocabulary simplification for children can be realized by paraphrasing text according to Basic Vocabulary to Learn (BVL) (Kai and Matsukawa, 2002) . BVL is a collection of words selected on the basis on a lexical analysis of elementary school textbooks. It contains 5,404 words that can help children write expressively.

As previous work indicated, there are lexical paraphrases that define statements from a Japanese dictionary (Kajiwara et al., 2013). The definition statements from the Japanese dictionary explain a given headword in several easy words. Therefore, lexical simplification and paraphrasing that conserves a particular meaning are expected by paraphrasing the headword with the words in the definitions. However, definition statements are short sentences that consist of several words. Consequently, there are few paraphrase candidates, and natural paraphrasing is difficult even if we use certain dictionaries together. In addition, the definition statement as a whole is equivalent to the headword; there is no guarantee that any individual word extracted from the definition statement can paraphrase the headword.

We propose lexical paraphrasing based on a variety of contexts obtained from a large corpus without depending on existing lexical resources from such a background. The proposed method is not dependent on language, thus it can perform lexical paraphrases using a corpus of arbitrary languages. In this paper we examine and report on Japanese nouns.

2 Related Works

As paraphrase acquisition from a corpus, a study with a parallel corpus and comparable corpus has been performed. Barzilay and McKeown paraphrase text using plural English translations made from the same document (Barzilay and McKeown, 2001). In addition, Shinyama and Sekine paraphrase using plural newspaper articles that report the same event (Shinyama and Sekine, 2003). In a text sim-

Copyright 2014 by Tomoyuki Kajiwara and Kazuhide Yamamoto
28th Pacific Asia Conference on Language, Information and Computation pages 644–649

plification task, Coster and Kauchak create a parallel corpus that matches English Wikipedia and Simple English Wikipedia, and they perform text simplification using the framework of statistical machine translation (Coster and Kauchak, 2011). However, the technique of using these parallel corpora and comparable corpora is problematic in terms of the accuracy of alignment of corresponding expressions and quantity of the corpora that can be used. For example, for Japanese, there is no large-scale parallel corpus in which simplification is possible for use in the framework of statistical machine translation. In this paper, we generate paraphrases using only a single-language corpus so as not to come under these influences.

In their research with paraphrasing based on the similarity of the context obtained from a non-parallel corpus, Marton et al. propose a method for paraphrasing unknown words to improve machine translation systems (Marton et al., 2009). They select candidate words with a context common to the subject. Moreover, they calculate cosine similarities of their feature vectors based on the co-occurrence frequency of subjects. Bhagat and Ravichandran extract paraphrases from a massive, 25-billion word corpus (Bhagat and Ravichandran, 2008). They regard English word 5-gram as one phrase, and they generate feature vectors using pointwise mutual information (PMI) scores. They then select the best phrase-paraphrase pairs based on their cosine similarity.

Our proposed method is different from these methods in that it does not use co-occurrence frequency or word frequency of conventional features. We focus on the variety of context. Assuming that successful paraphrases have context that is common with their subject, we select paraphrases based only on the number of types of context.

3 Proposed Method

In this paper, noun paraphrasing is achieved based on the variety of contexts extracted from a large corpus. According to Harris's Distributional Hypothesis (Harris, 1954), first, the nouns used in a context similar to the input sentence are extracted from the corpus. Then, the context similarity for each extracted noun and the noun in the input sentence is calculated utilizing the case-frame dictionary. An abstract of the proposed method is illustrated in Figure 1.

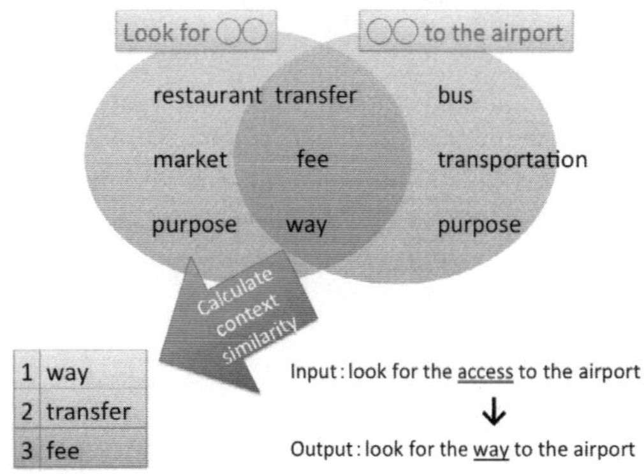

Figure 1: Noun paraphrasing in the proposed method.

3.1 Extraction of Paraphrase Candidates

In this method, we hypothetically define the pre-phrase and post-phrase of the target noun as the context; nouns used in a similar context are extracted from the corpus.

First, the input sentence is divided into two different contexts: *pre*-context and *post*-context. Then, the input sentence is searched through each corpus. The common nouns found at the end (tail) of the pre-context and at the start (head) of the post-context are extracted.

For example, when the phrase look for the access to the airport is given as an input sentence and the word access is the paraphrase target word, the pre-context is look for X and the post-context is X to the airport. Both contexts are searched through the corpus for any phrases that have the exact same phrases next to the X for any other nouns, and the replaceable nouns for X are extracted. In the example shown in Figure 1, the pre-context and post-context have the words *transfer*, *fee*, and *way* in common.

3.2 Selection of Paraphrase Candidates

This paper forms two hypotheses and defines Equation (1) to obtain high values for similar context nouns to paraphrase a given target word.

$$sim(n_t, n_c) = com(n_t, n_c) * \log(\frac{N}{var(n_c)}) \tag{1}$$

$$cooccurrence(w_i, w_j) = \sum_{s_n \in S} freq_n(w_i, w_j) \tag{2}$$

$$pmi(w_i, w_j) = \log(\frac{cooccurrence(w_i, w_j) \sum_{s_n \in S} \sum_{w_m \in s_n} freq_n(w_m)}{\sum_{s_n \in S} freq_n(w_i) \sum_{s_n \in S} freq_n(w_j)}) \tag{3}$$

$$cos(\vec{u}, \vec{v}) = \frac{\vec{u} \cdot \vec{v}}{|\vec{u}||\vec{v}|} \tag{4}$$

1. When the paraphrased target word and the paraphrase candidate have the maximum possible number of common contexts, the paraphrasability increases.

2. When the paraphrase candidates have several different contexts, the paraphrasability decreases.

In the Equation (1), n_t is the paraphrase target noun, n_c is the paraphrase candidate noun, $com(n_t, n_c)$ is the number of types of common contexts, N is the sum of the number of contexts, and $var(n_c)$ is the unique number of contexts in which n_c is used. For the first term, if the number of different common contexts is large, the value also becomes larger. For the latter term, the fewer the number of contexts for the paraphrase candidate, the larger its value becomes. Hence, a high $sim(n_t, n_c)$ indicates that two contexts are similar.

According to the distribution hypothesis, the word of the similar meaning is used in the similar context. The first term of the Equation (1) expresses that context is similar so that there is much common context. However, the word used in many contexts, such as *boss* and *start*, cannot be said to be that the context resembles the paraphrase target noun even if $com(n_t, n_c)$ are large. Therefore we filter it in the latter term of the Equation (1) and lower score of the paraphrase candidate noun used in much context.

4 Experiment

4.1 Experimental Object

To test our proposed method, we conducted an experiment using the Web Japanese N-gram (Kudo and Kazawa, 2007). The Web Japanese N-gram includes the word N (1 to 7)-grams parsed by the Japanese language morphological analyzer MeCab (Kudo et al., 2004). Each N-gram appears more than 20 times in 20 billion sentences in Web text. We considered that the longest 7-gram data is a sentence and used all 570,204,252 sentences. In addition, we selected 1,365,705 sentences where the head was a noun and the tail was the original form of a verb. In the experiment we used most-frequent 200 sentences as a target. Also, nouns at the beginning of sentences are excluded. In addition, we used MeCab to determine the parts of speech.

4.2 Experimental Procedure

We calculated distributional similarity using the Kyoto University case frame (KCF) (Kawahara and Kurohashi, 2009) data on the extracted nouns. KCF is the predicate and noun pair that has a case relationship, and it is built automatically (Kawahara and Kurohashi, 2005) from 1.6 billion Web texts. In the experiment, we used all 34,059 predicates and 824,639 nouns. In addition, we assumed that these predicates are contexts and calculated their distributional similarity using Equation (1).

4.3 Evaluation

To evaluate the proposed method, we compared it with related paraphrasing methods based on distributional similarity. We selected nouns included in the top 10 similarities from 200 input sentences; in addition, we extracted the paraphrasing target as described in Section 4.1 using our proposed method, the method by Marton et al. (2009), and the method by Bhagat and Ravichandran (2008). Three evaluators selected one noun each to paraphrase with a paraphrasing target in an input sentence.

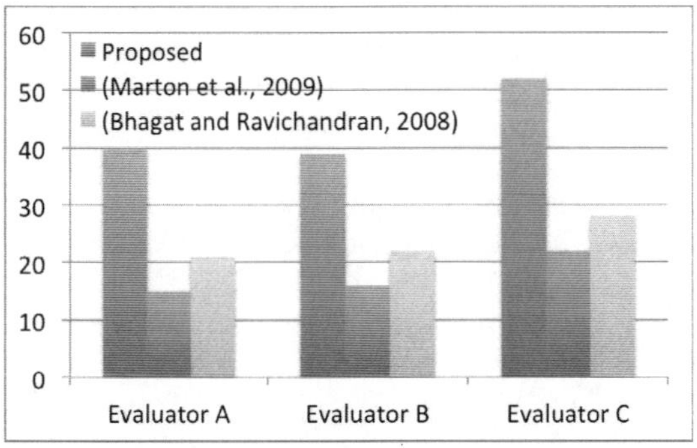

Figure 2: Number of paraphrasable nouns to first place of similarity.

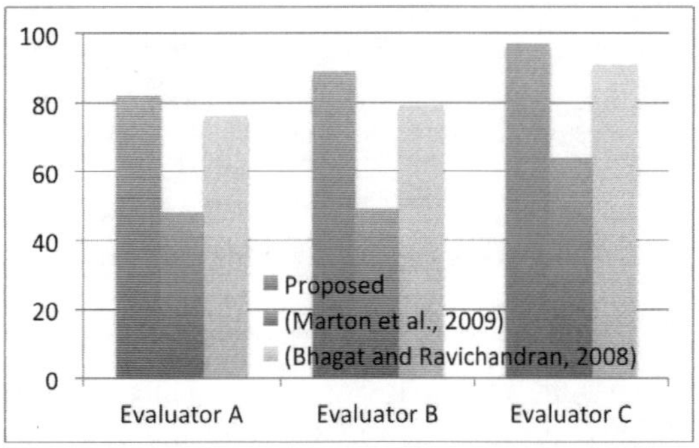

Figure 3: Number of paraphrasable nouns to the 10th place of similarity.

Marton et al. (2009) produce a feature vector by co-occurrence frequency with a noun and the context, and they calculate vector similarity by cosine. On the other hand, Bhagat and Ravichandran (2008) produce a feature vector by PMI with a noun and the context and calculates vector similarity by cosine. Both methods define nouns and verbs in dependency relationships to the context and produce feature vectors using Web Japanese N-gram. We define the co-occurrence frequency in Equation (2), PMI in Equation (3), and cosine similarity in Equation (4).

In the equations, $s_n \in S$, $w_m \in s_n$, $w_m \in W$, S is the set of sentences, W is the set of words, $freq_n(w_m)$ is the appearance frequency of word w_m in sentence n, $freq_n(w_i, w_j)$ is the co-occurrence frequency of word w_i and w_j in sentence n and $\vec{u}$ and $\vec{v}$ are the feature vectors.

5 Experiment Results

Figure 2 and Figure 3 show the evaluation results of the experiment described in Section 4, with a paraphrase of 200 sentences. The Fleiss's Kappa coefficient of three evaluators is 0.61. Thus, the agreement degree between raters is high enough.

Figure 2 shows the number of nouns evaluated as the possible paraphrase for each method.

On one hand, (Marton et al., 2009) applied the idea that the frequently co-occurring context is the important context. On the other hand, (Bhagat and Ravichandran, 2008) argued that the biasedly co-occurring context is important. Therefore, (Marton et al., 2009)'s method depends solely on high frequency words, whereas (Bhagat and Ravichandran, 2008)'s method relies on low frequency words. Hence, for (Marton et al., 2009)'s method, the word thing is suggested as the paraphrase candidate for 100 combinations out of 200 combinations. For (Bhagat and Ravichandran, 2008), the counter words, which are words that describe the number of items, are suggested as paraphrase candidates a significant number of times.

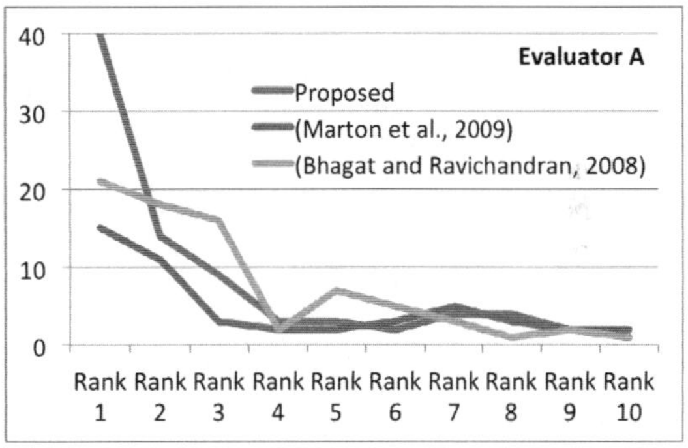

Figure 4: Relationships by order of similarity and number of paraphrasable nouns.

The proposed method does not rely on the frequency of the context; therefore, such an effect is disregarded as possible, and as a result, our method obtains high scores.

Figure 3 shows the number of nouns evaluated as possible candidates for paraphrases for the top 10 nouns of similarity. When observing the top 10 nouns, the results of (Bhagat and Ravichandran, 2008)'s method are close to the results of the proposed method. Figure 4 shows the rankings of similarities and the relationship of the number of possi-

Table 1: English translation of paraphrases generated by the proposed method.

Owner's [recognition → permission] is required.
Proceeding the [subject → problem] as important matter.
Generous [fee → price] is offered.
National agriculture's [advance → growth] is obstructed.
Education's [expansion → strengthening] are the examples.

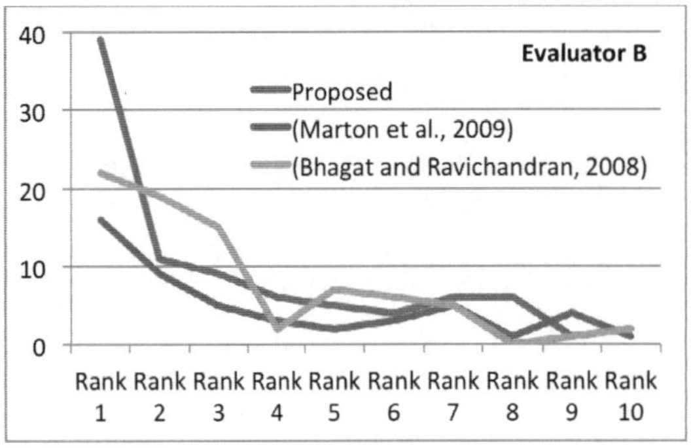

Figure 5: Relationships by order of similarity and number of paraphrasable nouns.

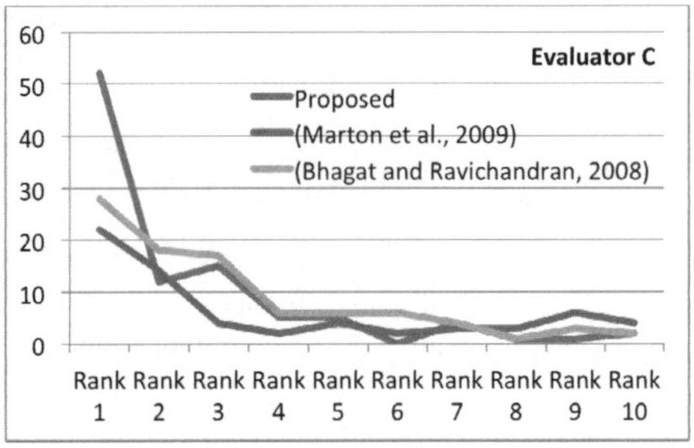

Figure 6: Relationships by order of similarity and number of paraphrasable nouns.

ble paraphrase candidates. Although Figure 4 shows the results for Evaluator A, the tendency is the same as for Evaluator B (Figure 5) and Evaluator C (Figure 6). In the results of the proposed method, there is a significant gap in the numbers of first-ranked and second-ranked nouns. However, in the results of (Bhagat and Ravichandran, 2008)'s method, the gap is insignificant. This is because the proposed method strictly applies the paraphrase process to nouns that are exactly in the context in which they are used in the input sentence. Because (Bhagat and Ravichandran, 2008)'s method does not consider the context of the input sentence, the quality is not always guaranteed to obtain the possible best score.

For instance, given an input sentence such as *assign a maximum [penalty] of $*, the paraphrase process for *[penalty]* in both (Marton et al., 2009) and (Bhagat and Ravichandran, 2008) grants *imprisonment* the highest score. On the other hand, the proposed method shows *paying penalty* with the best score, followed by correctional fine; *imprisonment* does not even appear as a candidate.

For the input sentence, *reduce the [burdens] on the back*, in the case of paraphrasing *[burdens]*, (Bhagat and Ravichandran, 2008)'s method suggests *cost*, *expenses*, and *actual cost*, all of which are money-related; any words listed within the top 10 are not appropriate paraphrase candidates.

Meanwhile, the proposed method suggests *loads*, *stress*, *damage*, *exhaustion*, *tense*, *impact*, etc., all of which are considerably appropriate for paraphrasing. Table 1 presents a list of successful examples.

6 Conclusion and Future Work

In this paper, we showed the effectiveness of the method of paraphrasing a noun along the context of a given input sentence based on the variety of contexts obtained from a large-scale corpus. Our proposed method can paraphrase nouns depending on the context of the input sentence, and we can obtain the appropriate paraphrase independently of the appearance frequency and co-occurrence frequency of the word. This is because we select a noun that shares more contexts with the paraphrasing target in the paraphrase.

This paper discussed the validity of paraphrases using a different statistics value from frequency called the number of types of the context. Our goal is to simplify vocabulary by paraphrasing, and it considers the restriction to plain vocabularies, such as the Basic Vocabulary to Learn, to maintain the accuracy and comprehensibility of lexical paraphrasing.

References

Regina Barzilay and Kathleen R. McKeown. 2001. Extracting Paraphrases from a Parallel Corpus. In *Proceedings of the 39th Annual Meeting of the Association for Computational Linguistics (ACL 2001)*, pages 50–57.

Rahul Bhagat and Deepak Ravichandran. 2008. Large Scale Acquisition of Paraphrases for Learning Surface Patterns. In *Proceedings of the 46th Annual Meeting of the Association for Computational Linguistics (ACL 2008)*, pages 674–682.

William Coster and David Kauchak. 2011. Simple Wikipedia: A New Simplification Task. In *Proceedings of the 49th Annual Meeting of the Association for Computational Linguistics (ACL 2011)*, pages 665–669.

Zellig S. Harris. 1954. Distributional Structure. *Word*, 10(23):146–162.

Kentaro Inui and Atsushi Fujita. 2004. A Survey on Paraphrase Generation and Recognition. *Journal of Natural Language Processing*, 11(5):151–198.

Mutsuro Kai and Toshihiro Matsukawa. 2002. Method of Vocabulary Teaching: Vocabulary Table version. Mitsumura Tosho Publishing Co., Ltd.

Tomoyuki Kajiwara, Hiroshi Matsumoto and Kazuhide Yamamoto. 2013. Selecting Proper Lexical Paraphrase for Children. In *Proceedings of the Twenty-Fifth Conference on Computational Linguistics and Speech Processing (ROCLING 2013)*, pages 59–73.

Daisuke Kawahara and Sadao Kurohashi. 2005. Gradual Fertilization of Case Frames. *Journal of Natural Language Processing*, 12(2):109–131.

Daisuke Kawahara and Sadao Kurohashi. 2009. Kyoto University' s Case Frame Data ver 1.0. Gengo Shigen Kyokai.

Taku Kudo and Hideto Kazawa. 2007. Web Japanese N-gram Version 1. Gengo Shigen Kyokai.

Taku Kudo, Kaoru Yamamoto and Yuji Matsumoto. 2004. Applying Conditional Random Fields to Japanese Morphological Analysis. In *Proceedings of the Conference on Empirical Methods in Natural Language Processing (EMNLP 2004)*

Yuval Marton, Chris Callison-Burch and Philip Resnik. 2009. Improved Statistical Machine Translation Using Monolingually-Derived Paraphrases. In *Proceedings of the 2009 Conference on Empirical Methods in Natural Language Processing (EMNLP 2009)*, pages 381–390.

Yusuke Shinyama and Satoshi Sekine. 2003. Paraphrase Acquisition for Information Extraction. In *Proceedings of the 2nd International Workshop on Paraphrasing: Paraphrase Acquisition and Applications (IWP 2003)*, pages 65–71.

Sentential Paraphrase Generation for Agglutinative Languages Using SVM with a String Kernel

Hancheol Park[1], Gahgene Gweon[1], Ho-Jin Choi[2], Jeong Heo[3], Pum-Mo Ryu[3]
[1]Department of Knowledge Service Engineering, KAIST
[2]Department of Computer Science, KAIST
[3]Knowledge Mining Research Team, ETRI
{hancheol.park, ggweon, hojinc}@kaist.ac.kr
{jeonghur, pmryu}@etri.re.kr

Abstract

Paraphrase generation is widely used for various natural language processing (NLP) applications such as question answering, multi-document summarization, and machine translation. In this study, we identify the problems occurring in the process of applying existing probabilistic model-based methods to agglutinative languages, and provide solutions by reflecting the inherent characteristics of agglutinative languages. More specifically, we propose and evaluate a sentential paraphrase generation (SPG) method for the Korean language using Support Vector Machines (SVM) with a string kernel. The quality of generated paraphrases is evaluated using three criteria: (1) meaning preservation, (2) grammaticality, and (3) equivalence. Our experiment shows that the proposed method outperformed a probabilistic model-based method by 12%, 16%, and 17%, respectively, with respect to the three criteria.

1 Introduction

Paraphrase generation (PG) is a useful technique in various natural language processing (NLP) applications, where it expands natural language expressions. In question answering systems, PG can be utilized to generate semantically equivalent questions. It can solve word mismatch problems when searching for answers (Lin and Pantel, 2001; Riezler et al., 2007). For multi-document summarization, it also helps to generate a summary sentence by identifying repeated information among semantically similar sentences (McKeown et al., 2002). In addition, for machine translation, paraphrasing can mitigate the scarcity of training data by expanding the reference translations (Callison-Burch, 2006).

In this study, we focus on a paraphrase generation approach, namely, sentential paraphrase generation (SPG), which takes a whole sentence as an input and generates a paraphrased output sentence that has the same meaning. Figure 1 shows an overview of the SPG process in general.

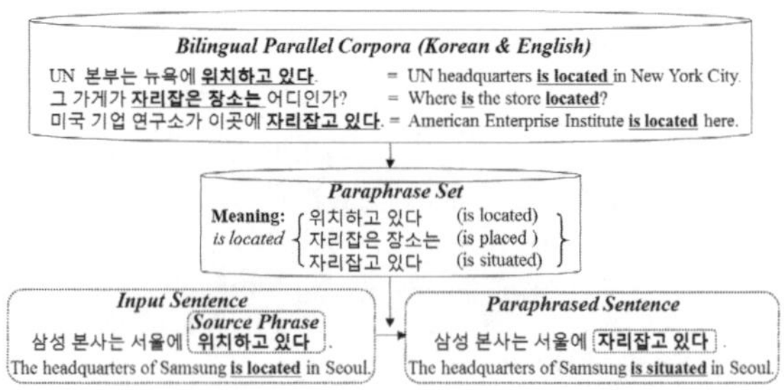

Figure 1: Example of the SPG process.

For example, let us assume that we would like to generate a paraphrased sentence using bilingual parallel corpora for a Korean input sentence "삼성본사는 서울에 위치하고 있다 (The headquarters of Samsung is located in Seoul)." For simplicity, in the examples used in this paper, we assume that an input sentence has only one source phrase to be substituted/ paraphrased. In our sample sentence, the source phrase is "위치하고 있다 (is located)." Currently, popular methods for SPG use phrase-based statistical machine

Copyright 2014 by Hancheol Park, Gahgene Gweon, Ho-Jin Choi, Jeong Heo, and Pum-Mo Ryu
28th Pacific Asia Conference on Language, Information and Computation pages 650–657

translation (PBSMT) techniques (Bannard and Callison-Burch, 2005; Callison-Burch, 2008; Zhao et al., 2009; Wubben et al., 2010) with phrase-based paraphrase sets extracted from bilingual or monolingual parallel corpora. Such methods based on PBSMT use probabilistic-based models (e.g., a paraphrase model (PM) and a language model (LM)) to select the best phrase for substitution from a paraphrase set, which contains phrases that share the same meaning, to produce a paraphrased sentence. Probabilistic-based methods improve the system as the size of the corpora increases with increased frequency of the phrases. However, these methods tend to encounter two problems when applied to agglutinative languages (e.g., Korean, Japanese, and Turkish), which are morphologically rich languages.

The first problem is that it is very difficult to obtain a reliable probability distribution in agglutinative languages. Isolating (e.g., Chinese) and inflectional (e.g., Latin and German) languages employ fewer lexical variants to represent diverse grammatical functions or categories, whereas in agglutinative languages this process leads to an enormous number of possible inflected variants of a word. This is because a word is formed by combining at least one root, which represents a meaning, with various function or bound morphemes (e.g., postpositional particles and affixes). Furthermore, agglutinative languages suffer from the problem of resource scarcity (Wang et al., 2013). This problem becomes even more severe when obtaining an appropriate probability distribution for each variant, because the frequency of each phrase in a paraphrase set is less than in other languages, given the same quantity of corpora. In this study, therefore, we propose to use Support Vector Machines (SVM) for classification, which select the best paraphrase without employing probability information.

The second problem in using previously proposed probabilistic-based methods with agglutinative languages is that these methods lead to lower grammaticality because these methods do not consider the internal structure of a source phrase and the internal structures of dependent words of the source phrase. These methods take into account only the surface form distribution. It is very difficult to identify grammatically correct candidates in the paraphrase sets. This problem appears to be much more severe in agglutinative languages than in isolating or inflectional languages.

For this reason, in this study, we propose to utilize the similarity of syntactic categories, grammatical categories, and contextual information between the source phrase and its candidate paraphrases, when selecting the best paraphrase.

In this paper, we propose a novel SPG method that deals with the two problems mentioned above, for the Korean language, which is an agglutinative language. In the remainder of this paper, we review background literatures for our method on paraphrase generation in section 2; describe our proposed method in section 3, explain the experimental settings and results in section 4, and conclude in section 5.

2 Background

2.1 Probabilistic Model-Based Paraphrase

An SPG process begins with paraphrase phrases extraction from monolingual or bilingual parallel corpora. In this section, we review a popular paraphrasing method introduced by Bannard and Callison-Burch (2005). Since this is one of the very first studies to be conducted using bilingual parallel corpora and is a fundamental method in research on paraphrasing with bilingual parallel corpora, we used it as the baseline for our comparative experiment in this paper.

The method assumes that phrases that share commonly aligned foreign phrases are likely to be paraphrases of each other. For example, English phrases e_1 and e_2 that share commonly aligned foreign phrases f can be regarded as paraphrases of each other and their "*paraphrase probability*" is expressed as follows:

$$p(e_2|e_1) = \sum_f p(e_2|f)\, p(f|e_1)$$

Given a source phrase e_1 in a new input sentence, the best paraphrase $\hat{e_2}$ is chosen from candidate phrases e_2 as expressed in equation below:

$$\hat{e_2} = argmax_{e_2:\, e_2 \neq e_1}\, p(e_2|e_1)$$
$$p(w_{-2}\, w_{-1}\, e_2\, w_{+1}\, w_{+2})$$

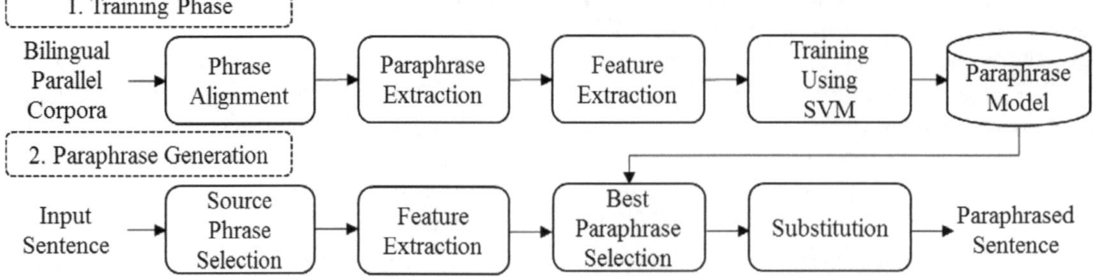

Figure 2: Overview of the proposed SPG method.

Since we use a trigram LM to decide how acceptable each e_2 is for a given input, w_{-2} and w_{-1} are the two words preceding e_2, and w_{+1} and w_{+2} are the two words following e_2. The phrase e_1 is substituted with the best paraphrase $\hat{e_2}$, which has the highest probability.

2.2 Classification Using SVM with a String Kernel

In this study, we propose an SPG method using SVM, instead of using the probabilistic-based model, which is used in the approach described in section 2.1.

An SVM is a linear classifier that finds a linear hyper-plane that separates positive and negative instances of labeled samples with the largest margin. This classifier is designed to reduce the generalization error rate, which is the ratio of incorrectly predicted classes to the novel inputs, because it is less overfitted to the training data set than other methods (Kozareva and Montoyo, 2006). With reference to sparseness of each lexical variant in agglutinative languages, it is also more tolerant than probabilistic-based models because it does not largely depend on the frequency of instances.

For problems that are not linearly separable, SVM uses a kernel function that implicitly transforms a non-linear problem into a higher-dimension space and makes the problem into a linearly separable one. A kernel is a similarity function between a pair of instances. In particular, since string kernels are useful in terms of measuring the similarity of non-fixed size feature vectors (e.g., text documents, the dependency tree of a sentence, and syntax trees) (Erkan et al., 2007), we used a string kernel given that the features that consider the morphological structures of words are variable in length. More specifically, we use the edit distance kernel function (Erkan et al., 2007) as follows:

$$K(\boldsymbol{x}_i, \boldsymbol{x}_j) = \exp(-\gamma \text{ edit\_distance}(\boldsymbol{x}_i, \boldsymbol{x}_j))$$

Here, *edit_distance* is defined as the Levenshtein distance between string $\boldsymbol{x}_i$ and $\boldsymbol{x}_j$. i.e., the minimum number of edits (deletions, insertions, or substitutions at the word level) required to transform one string into another. One of the advantages of using this kernel is that it takes into account the order of the strings in the structured data (e.g., a dependency path tree) as opposed to other string kernels (e.g., cosine similarity kernel) which consider only the common terms when measuring similarity.

In our study, the class for SVM is each phrase in a paraphrase set, which contains a source phrase. In addition, the SPG used in our study can be regarded as a multiclass classification problem. Thus, to solve this problem with a binary classifier, we adopted a "one-against-one" approach (Chang and Lin, 2011). This approach constructs $k(k-1)/2$ classifiers, where k is the number of classes, with a training data set from two classes. A new data point is allocated to the class with the most votes during each binary classification.

3 Paraphrase Generation Using SVM with a String Kernel

This section describes our proposed SPG method, which uses an SVM with a string kernel. Figure 2 shows an overview of this method.

3.1 Training Phase

In the training phase, phrase alignment is first conducted manually using training sentences, which is composed of bilingual parallel corpora of the Korean and English languages, as shown in Figure 1. Phrase alignment can be automatically conducted using the GIZA++ toolkit (Och and Ney, 2003) and phrase alignment heuristics (Koehn et al., 2003). However, in this study, we evaluate the performance of our generation method independently from the quality of automatic word or phrase alignment algorithms. Therefore, we conduct manual alignment, which is much more accurate than automatic alignment. In addition, applying these alignment tools to the Korean language is not appropriate because they only obtain a few correct results.

We align Korean phrases that range from unigrams to trigrams with English. For example, "뉴욕에 위치하고 있다 = is located in New York City" in the bilingual parallel corpora shown in Figure 1 can be aligned as follows:

- 뉴욕에 (unigram)

  = in New York City

- 뉴욕에 위치하고 (bigram)

  = located in New York City

- 뉴욕에 위치하고 있다 (trigram)

  = is located in New York City

With these aligned phrases, we extract paraphrase sets by grouping phrases that have common foreign phrases (i.e., English) because they are likely to have the same meaning (e.g., is located = 위치하고 있다, 자리잡은 장소는, 자리잡고 있다 in Figure 1).

Next, for feature extraction, three types of features are generated for the training phrases in paraphrase sets, referring to the sentences that the phrases are originally contained in: syntactic categories (SC), grammatical categories (GC), and contextual information (CI). For each type of feature, characteristics of the training phrase as well as the dependent words that precede and follow the training phrase in a Korean training sentence are extracted.

These three features help enhance the paraphrasing method using the agglutinative languages. Using the SC and GC features helps maintain the grammaticality of the source phrase. However, given the high variation in postpositional particles or affixes in agglutinative languages, there is a low probability of matching the SC and GC features in the source and training phrases. Therefore, by considering the SC and GC features of the dependent words in addition to the features of the source phrase, our method considers the context of the source phrase in terms of grammaticality to find the best candidate for paraphrasing. The CI features have a similar purpose in that they consider the context of the word sense of neighboring words.

- **Syntactic Categories (SC):** This feature helps to select a phrase with an acceptable syntactic type based on the structure of a given sentence. Morphological analysis is conducted for three phrases: the training phrase as well as the two dependent words preceding and following the training phrase. Based on the result of the morphological analysis, features are extracted such as phrase type (e.g., noun phrase (NP), verb phrase (VP)), case (e.g., subject (SBJ), and object (OBJ)), and tags of morphemes (e.g., pronoun (np) and case particle (jc)) for the three phrases.

- **Grammatical Categories (GC):** This feature helps to select a phrase that preserves the grammatical categories of a source phrase. Grammatical categories are extracted for the training phrase as well as the dependent words preceding and following the training phrase. They are extracted by considering the affixes of each phrase or word. Sample features for GC include the sentence type (e.g., interrogative sentence (INT), declarative sentence (DEC)), voice (e.g., passive (PAS), active (ACT)), and tense (past (PAST), present (PRES), and future (FUTU)). This feature is labeled as "N/A" if a corresponding feature does not exist.

- **Contextual Information (CI):** This feature helps to select a phrase that has the same word sense as a source phrase. Contextual information is extracted by taking the roots for the preceding and following dependent words.

The features are represented as a string instead of a numerical feature vector since a string kernel is used. Finally, phrases in a paraphrase set with identical meanings and corresponding features are

Method	Sentences
TS	[이것은][1] [무엇으로][2] [이용되는가][3]? (What is this utilized for?)
Baseline	[그것은][1] [어떤][2] [사용했던][3]? (That used as what?)
SKBPG	[그것은][1] [어떤 것으로][2] [사용되었는가][3]? (What was that used as?)
TS	우리 [나라에서][1] [최고로][2] 긴 다리는 [길이가 얼마인가][3]? (What is the length of the longest bridge in our country)
Baseline	우리 [국가에서][1] [많이][2] 긴 다리는 [얼마인가][3]? (How much is the very long bridge in our country?)
SKBPG	우리 [국가의][1] [가장][2] 긴 다리는 [얼마나 긴가][3]? (How long is the longest bridge of our country?)
TS	루이 암스트롱은 [몇 년도에][1] [출생하였는가][2]? (What year was Louis Armstrong born?)
Baseline	루이 암스트롱은 [시기는][1] [태어났는가][2]? (Timeline was Louis Armstrong was born?)
SKBPG	루이 암스트롱은 [어느 년도에][1] [태어났는가][2]? (In what year was Louis Armstrong born?)

Table 1: Examples of test sentences (TS) and paraphrased sentences obtained using each method (Baseline and SKBPG). In the examples of sentences, the same superscript numbers indicate the source in a TS and the paraphrased phrase selected from each method.

trained together using the SVM to generate a paraphrase model. This model is used in the paraphrase generation phase, as described in section 3.2. Figure 3 illustrates the three types of features used in our model for one sentence from the bilingual parallel corpora example shown in Figure 1.

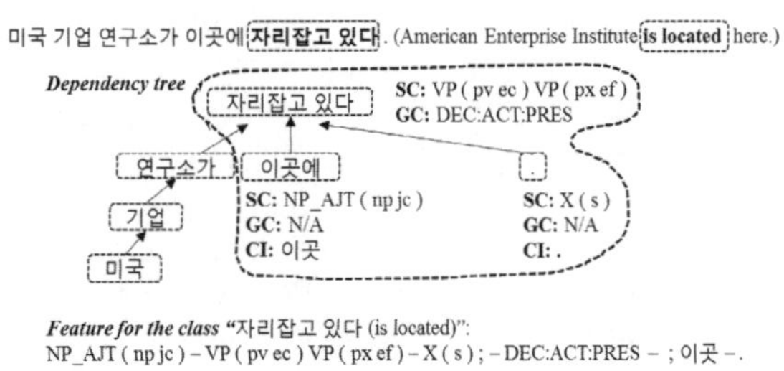

Figure 3: Sample sentence with the three types of features extracted.

3.2 Paraphrase Generation

In the paraphrase generation step, a source phrase in the input sentence is replaced by a candidate phrase in its corresponding paraphrase set, and as a result, a paraphrased sentence is produced. This step starts by locating a source phrase in an input sentence. For the input sentence "삼성 본사는 서울에 위치하고 있다. (The headquarters of Samsung is located in Seoul.)," as shown in Figure 1, our method first selects a source phrase. If multiple candidates appear, one with the maximum length of words is selected. If both phrases, "위치하고 있다 (is located)" and "위치하고 (located)" are possible candidates, for instance, the longer phrase "위치하고 있다 (is located)" will be selected. Next, dependent words preceding and following the source phrase are used together with the source phrase to obtain the three types of features described in section 3.1. Next, the SVM classifier is used to identify the best phrase in the paraphrase set for the source phrase that was built during the training phase.

Finally, the source phrase is substituted with the selected best paraphrase. Although in this example, we assumed the input sentence to have only one source phrase for simplicity, in our actual implementation the paraphrase generation process was repeated for multiple source phrases in the input sentence as shown in Table 1.

4 Evaluation

We evaluated our proposed method by comparing it with the popular method proposed by Bannard and Callison-Burch (2005). This baseline[1] method was implemented by using probabilistic models and is described in section 2.1. Our proposed method, string kernel-based paraphrase generation (SKBPG), was implemented by using the edit distance string kernel, which is described in section 2.2.

4.1 Experimental Resources

In order to generate paraphrase sets, we used 998 randomly selected English sentences from the Text REtrievial Conference (TREC) question answering track (2003-2007)[2] and their translations (Korean words: 5,286, English words: 7,474). The question answering track was selected so that we could apply our method to a question answering system.

For the test sentences, 100 quiz sentences from Korean TV quiz shows (e.g., Golden Bell Challenge!) were selected. The sentences had to contain at least one possible source phrase with multiple candidates in its corresponding paraphrase set. Table 1 shows examples of the test sentences and the paraphrased sentences obtained using each method.

For the baseline method, we used 52,732 Korean sentences (Korean words: 322,306) in KAIST language resources (Choi, 2001) for training trigram LMs, in addition to the questions from TREC. This additional resource was included to make probability distribution in LM stable by expanding size of corpus. The LM probability was acquired using the IRSTLM toolkit (Federico and Cettolo, 2007), and conditional probability in LM was calculated by applying modified Kneser-Ney smoothing.

For the SKBPG method, we used ETRI linguistics analyzer (Lee and Jang, 2011) for dependency parsing and morphological analysis. For the SVM, we used LIBSVM-string (Guo-Xun Yuan, 2010; Chang and Lin, 2011), which supports the edit distance kernel option and multiclass classification based on the one-against-one approach, as described in section 2.2. The parameter of edit distance kernel (γ) was 0.1.

[1] We were not able to obtain Bannard and Callison-Burch's implementation, so we implemented it ourselves.

[2] These resources are available at http://trec.nist.gov/data/qa.html.

4.2 Evaluation Metrics

The Korean paraphrase pairs that we generated were evaluated by two native Korean speakers according to the following three criteria:

- **Meaning Preservation (MP):** Does a generated paraphrase preserve the meaning of the source phrase?
- **Grammaticality (G):** Is the generated paraphrase grammatical?
- **Equivalence (E):** Are the paraphrased pairs equivalent?

We used two types of scales as shown in Table 2. These criteria were adopted from previous research (Callison-Burch, 2008; Fujita et al., 2012).

Criterion	**5-point**	**Binary scale**
MP	(1: worst 5: best)	(true: MP > 3, false: otherwise)
G	(1: worst 5: best)	(true: G > 4, false: otherwise)
E	N/A	(true: MP > 3 & G > 4, false: otherwise)

Table 2: Two types of scales used by the three evaluation criteria.

In terms of the inter-annotator agreement using Kappa, K = .412 for the 5-point scale, which is considered as "Moderate." For the binary scale, K = .612, which is regarded as "Substantial" (Landis and Koch, 1977; Carletta, 1996).

4.3 Results and Discussion

In the section, we summarize the results of our manual evaluation, which show that our method outperformed the baseline method, as shown in Table 3 and Table 4.

	MP	**G**
Baseline	M = 3.28 SD = 1.29	M = 3.54 SD = 1.23
SKBPG	**M = 3.62** **SD = 1.32**	**M = 3.97** **SD = 1.20**

Table 3: Results of the manual evaluation using the 5-point scale (M: mean, SD: standard deviation).

	MP	G	E
Baseline	.57	.42	.36
SKBPG	**.69**	**.58**	**.53**

Table 4: Results of the manual evaluation using the binary scale.

For the manual evaluation using the 5-point scale, an independent-samples t-test showed that SKBPG significantly outperformed the baseline for both meaning preservation (t(398) = 2.564, p = .011) and grammaticality (t(398) = 3.501, p = .001). The evaluation using the binary scale also showed that SKBPG outperformed the baseline by 12%, 16%, and 17% for the three criteria of meaning preservation, grammaticality, and equivalence, respectively.

Interestingly, even though more resources were used in the baseline method for training the LM (52,732 Korean sentences), it did not outperform SKBPG. This suggests that our method is more efficient in terms of using fewer resources with less amount of data storage space. One plausible reason for such efficiency is that given that agglutinative languages have a large number of variants of lexicons for a root, it is difficult to account for most of the variations. Since the baseline method uses probabilistic models that utilize the frequency of each variation, much more data is needed. Another potential reason for the efficiency is that the word order for agglutinative languages is not critical for maintaining grammaticality. As opposed to isolating languages in which the word order determines grammatical functions, agglutinative languages use the postpositional particles or affixes of a root in a word to determine grammatical functions. Therefore, rather than using a LM that calculates the probability of contiguous words sequences, utilizing dependency grammar between words, as in SKBPG, can be more efficient.

5 Conclusion

In this study, we proposed a novel paraphrasing method, which considers the inherent characteristics of agglutinative languages by using an SVM with a string kernel.

Our evaluation of the generated paraphrases showed that the proposed method outperformed the probabilistic model-based method by 12%, 16%, and 17%, with respect to meaning preservation, grammaticality, and equivalence even with fewer resources than in the baseline method.

A limitation of this study is that the data set was aligned manually for paraphrase extraction between the two languages and due to this reason our data set size was relatively small with 1515 paraphrase sets. This limitation led to several problems in our evaluation. Sometimes, there were no appropriate grammatically correct candidates in the paraphrase sets for a certain input sentence. This also led to reduced coverage of paraphrases.

In addition, our method does not consider many semantic features such as semantic roles and named entities. This point suggests that our method is fragile in meaning preservation of the source sentence as the data size increases.

Therefore, we plan to work on automatic paraphrase extraction method tailored to agglutinative languages in order to increase the size of our data set. We also expect to expand the feature set by considering additional semantic features for our future work.

Acknowledgments

This work was supported by the IT R&D program of MSIP/IITP [10044577, Development of Knowledge Evolutionary WiseQA Platform Technology for Human Knowledge Augmented Services].

References

Atsushi Fujita, Pierre Isabelle, and Roland Kuhn. 2012. Enlarging Paraphrase Collections through Generalization and Instantiation. In *Proceedings of EMNLP*, pages 631-642.

Changki Lee and Myung-Gil Jang. 2011. Large-Margin Training of Dependency Parsers Using Pegasos Algorithm. *ETRI Journal*, 32(3):486-489.

Chih-Chung Chang and Chih-Jen Lin. 2011. LIBSVM: A Library for Support Vector Machines. *ACM Transactions on Intelligent Systems and Technology*, 2(3): 1-27, http://www.csie.ntu.edu.tw/~cjlin/libsvm.

Chris Callison-Burch. 2008. Syntactic constraints on paraphrases extracted from parallel corpora. In *Proceedings of EMNLP*, pages 196-205.

Chris Callison-Burch, Philipp Koehn, and Miles Osborne. 2006. Improved Statistical Machine

Translation Using Paraphrases. In *Proceedings of HLT-NAACL*, pages 17-24.

Colin Bannard and Chris Callison-Burch. 2005. Paraphrasing with Bilingual Parallel Corpora. In *Proceedings of ACL*, pages 597-604.

Dekang Lin and Patrick Pantel. 2001. Discovery of Inference Rules for Question Answering. *Natural Language Engineering*, 7(4):343-360.

Franz Josef Och and Hermann Ney. 2003. A Systematic Comparison of Various Statistical Alignment Models. *Computational Linguistics*, 29(1):19-51.

Guo-Xun Yan. 2010. LIBSVM-String: An Extension to LIBSVM for Classifying String Data. http://www.csie.ntu.edu.tw/~cjlin/libsvmtools/#libsvm_for_string_data.

Günes Erkan, Arzucan Özgür, and Dragomir R. Radev. 2007. Semi-Supervised Classification for Extracting Protein Interaction Sentences Using Dependency Parsing. In *Proceedings of EMNLP-CoNLL,* pages 228-237.

J. Richard Landis, Gary G. Koch. 1977. The Measurement of Observer Agreement for Categorical Data. *Biometrics,* 33(1):159-174.

Jean Carletta. 1996. Assessing Agreement on Classification Tasks: The Kappa Statistic. *Computational Linguistics*, 22(2):249-254.

Kathlenn R. McKeown, Regina Barzilay, David Evans, Vasileios Hatzivassiloglou, Judith L. Klavans, Ani Nenkova, Carl Sable, Barry Schiffman, and Sergey Sigelman. 2002. Tracking and Summarizing News on a Daily Basis with Columbia's Newsblaster. In *Proceedings of HLT.* pages 280-285.

Key-Sun Choi. 2001. KAIST language resources v.2001. Result of Core Software Project from Ministry of Science and Technology, Korea (http://kibs.kaist.ac.kr).

Marcello Federico, and Mauro Cettolo. 2007. Efficient Handling of N-gram Language Models for Statistical Machine Translation. In *Proceedings of Second Workshop on StatMT*, pages 88-95.

Philipp Koehn, Franz josef Och, and Daniel Marcu. 2003. Statistical Phrase-Based Translation. In *Proceedings of HLT-NAACL*, pages 48-54.

Sander Wubben, Antal van den Bosch, and Emiel Krahmer. 2010. Paraphrase Generation as Monolingual Translation: Data and Evaluation. In *Proceedings of INLG*, pages 203-207.

Shiqi Zhao, Xiang Lan, Ting Liu, and Sheng Li. 2009. Application-Driven Statistical Paraphrase Generation. In *Proceedings of ACL-AFNLP*, pages 834-842.

Stefan Riezler, Alexander Vasserman, Ioannis Tsochantaridis, Vibhu Mittal, and Yi Liu. 2007. Statistical Machine Translation for Query Expansion in Answer Retrieval. In *Proceedings of ACL*, pages 464-471.

Zhiyang Wang, Yajuan Lü, Meng Sun, and Qun Liu. 2013. Stem Translation with Affix-Based Rule Selection for Agglutinative Languages. In *Proceedings of ACL*, pages 364-369.

Zornitsa Kozareva and Andrés Montoyo. 2006. Paraphrase Identification on the Basis of Supervised Machine Learning Techniques. In *Proceedings of International Conference on NLP*, pages 524-533.

K-repeating Substrings: a String-Algorithmic Approach to Privacy-Preserving Publishing of Textual Data

Yusuke Matsubara and **Kôiti Hasida**
Social ICT Research Center, School of Information Science and Technology,
The University of Tokyo
7-3-1 Hongo, Bunkyo-ku, Tokyo, Japan
matsubara@sict.i.u-tokyo.ac.jp,
hasida.koiti@i.u-tokyo.ac.jp

Abstract

De-identifying textual data is an important task for publishing and sharing the data among researchers while protecting privacy of individuals referenced therein. While supervised learning approaches are successfully applied to the task in the clinical domain, existing methods are hard to transfer to different domains and languages because they require a considerable cost and time for preparation of linguistic resources. This paper presents an efficient unsupervised algorithm to detect all substrings occurring less than k times in the input string, based on the assumption that such rare sequences are likely to contain sensitive information such as names of people and rare diseases that may identify individuals. The proposed algorithm works in asymptotically and empirically linear time against the input size when k is a constant. Empirical evaluation on the *i2b2* (Informatics for Integrating Biology and Bedside) dataset shows the effectiveness of the algorithm in comparison to baselines that use simple word frequencies.

1 Introduction

The increasing amount of electronically available and searcheable texts poses an increasing need for privacy protection. Adversaries may extract previously unconnected information about a person by aggregating different data sources. IDs such as social security numbers in the United States are obvious means to aggregate data sources, but full names, residential addresses, and other attributes about individuals and their combinations may also work as pseudo identifiers from which one may be able to identify persons, or to raise the probability of successful identification (Sweeney, 2002)(Fung et al., 2010). While researchers and service providers wish to publish and share such textual data with the community to help facilitate further research, it is costly to do so while preserving utility of non-sensitive part of the data.

In response to the demand for efficient and accurate automatic methods to help removing sensitive material from textual data, the last decade has seen progress in automatic anonymization and de-identification of text (Liu, 2012; Fung et al., 2010; Uzuner et al., 2007). For example, health care industry puts efforts in utilizing electronic health record data that is accumulated daily while ensuring patients' privacy (Kushida et al., 2012; Meystre et al., 2010). Nevertheless, two major problems remain unaddressed: 1) How to reduce human labor to prepare resources for automatic methods, including pattern-matching rules and training data for supervised-learning systems. 2) How to increase utility of published text by requiring less preprocessing of the input text.

Our work explores aplicability of string algorithms into privacy-preserving publishing of textual data that reduce resource requirements. We propose using new variations of maximum repeats algorithms to unsupervisedly suggest spans to be hidden. We argue that our approach brings new assets to previous studies in text anonymization by requiring less linguistic resources and preprocessing; these points will be discussed in more detail in Section 3.

Contributions of this paper are as follows.

Copyright 2014 by Yusuke Matsubara and Ko^iti Hasida
28th Pacific Asia Conference on Language, Information and Computation pages 658–667

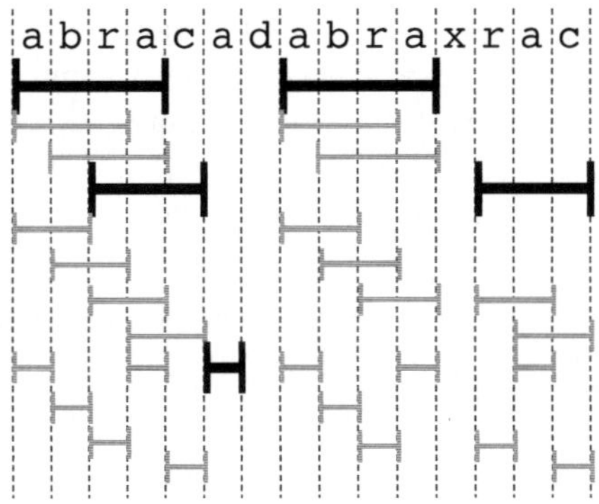

Figure 1: The repeats and maximum repeats (=2-repeating substrings) in the string "abracadabraxrac". Maximum repeats are indicated as intervals with thicker black lines. Non-maximum repeats are in thinner gray lines. Note that every non-maximum repeats is subsumed by at least one maximum repeat.

- We formalize the notion of k-repeating substrings (Section 4).
- We present a natural and simple generalization to algorithms for finding maximum repeats, allowing arbitrary choice of the frequency threshold k, and provide theoretical guarantees to the computational complexity. (Section 5)
- We present an efficient algorithm to cover a given string with its k-repeating substrings, ensuring every continuous substring in it has k or more occurrences. (Section 5)
- We show effectiveness and scalability of the proposed algorithm by providing empirical performance analyses of the new algorithms, and release our software implementation. (Sections 6)

2 Approach

Our hypothesis in this paper is that sensitive information is more likely to reside in texts with lower frequency than in those with higher frequency, because if a piece of information is frequently mentioned, it is likely to be already known to the public. Given statistics of a corpus that is large enough to represent a (sub-)language, we assume that phrases with a larger number of occurrences are more likely to express common knowledge rather than private information.

We explore computationally practical ways to implement algorithms to test the hypothesis above. We give a formal definition of k-repeating substrings in Section 7, based on the hypothesis above. It will be followed by an efficient algorithm, described in Section 5, to compute k-repeating substrings, as illustrated in Figure 1, utilizing devices of algorithms on strings.

It is important to note that the concept of k-repeating substrings itself is not intended to yield a theoretical guarantee of anonymity. Rather, our approach is expected to capture statistical tendencies and our assumptions are justified by the experimental evaluation using a real-world dataset, described in Section 6.

We anticipate further research on how to combine strengths and complement weaknesses of our work and other approaches including pattern-based ones and supervised ones. One of the strengths of our approach is that it is resource-free and assumption-free; it works on a unprocessed string and require no external knowledge sources. We anticipate this method to be used as an informed baseline before building a full stack anonymization system. On the other hand, our approach may be prone to false positives, because rare sequences do not necessarily express private information, especially when the given source of the text statistics is small.

One may think that it is sufficient to simply enumerate frequent-enough words or N-grams and use them as a whitelist to avoid suppressing their occurrences. However, such approaches have limitations, because multiple common words may form a rare and identifying sequence when combined. For example, an address line such as *Pine street* may serve as an informative clue to identify a specific location, while each of constituents of the expression is a common word that is unlikely to be suppressed by simple word frequency threshold. Simple segmentation by space may not capture subword structure that is found in highly-inflected languages (such as German and Arabic) and agglutinative languages (such as Chinese and Japanese). On the other hand, N-grams, regardless of how large N is, it still can have only fixed-length sequences as units. Our method proposed in this paper addressed these problems by automatically choosing appropriate length of substrings under a certain condition defined in Section 7, without having to rely on linguistic resources.

3 Related work

To put our work in context, we give a brief overview of studies on privacy-preserving text publishing [1], describing some of their shortcomings. For more comprehensive surveys, we refer readers to (Liu, 2012), (Uzuner et al., 2007) and (Kushida et al., 2012).

Local methods Text de-identification has been intensively studied in the context of protected health information (PHI) in medical informatics (Meystre et al., 2010; Kushida et al., 2012). Most of them use "local" context by matching with predefined patterns or features with weights learned from training data by a supervised learning algorithm. In the first *i2b2* challenge (Uzuner et al., 2007), it has been shown that machine learning methods utilizing PHI-annotated texts by human are effective, while use of lexical resources such as lists of names and UMLS (Unified Medical Language System) Meta thesaurus (Aronson, 2001) play a key role to boosting up the performance. While the state-of-the-art de-identification methods provide high accuracy (F-measure=0.98) that almost matches average human performance (Uzuner et al., 2007), they require a high cost for data preparation. Top systems of the first *i2b2* (Uzuner et al., 2007) challenge requires various resources: texts in the same domain with gold-standard annotations, manually curated patterns and rules, and lexical resources of terms in the domain (Meystre et al., 2010).

Global methods Another line of research has applied the idea of k-anonymity (Sweeney, 2002), originated in the study of anonymizing structured data, into textual data which is inherently unstructured. We call here them "global", because, unlike local methods described above, they rely on statistics extracted from a data collection to find documents with rare combination of features. Such rare combination could work as pseudo identifiers that help adversaries to identify the individuals a given document describes. Most of the existing methods of k-anonymity for texts and strings assume strings as inseparable values or assume bag-of-words representations (Aggarwal and Yu, 2007; Chakaravarthy et al., 2008; Jiang et al., 2009; Anandan et al., 2012) as surveyed in (Liu, 2012). While these methods inherit theoretical strengths of k-anonymization, they do not fit well with free-form text, especially when no thesaurus is assumed to be available.

3.1 Maximum repeats

In string algorithms, finding maximum repeats has been a focus of attention, in part for its practical applications including DNA sequencing in bioinformatics. Ilie and Smyth (2011) showed a simple liner-time algorithm to compute maximal substrings that occur at least twice in the given string, utilizing suffix arrays (Manber and Myers, 1993; Nong et al., 2011) and longest common prefix arrays. In Section 5 we show that how our method generalizes their MAXREPEATS algorithm, while maintaining the time complexity linear when k is constant.

We consider this generalization of maximum repeats as a key contribution to make this approach applicable to a wider range of textual data including free-text natural language. This is because noises ubiquitously found in natural-language text collections, including duplicates and near-duplicates, limit usefulness of the definition of repeats as substrings with two or more occurrences. It is natural to consider different thresholds for web-scale document collections and for a collection containing less than a hundred authors. Our generalized algorithm provides a way to tune the threshold frequency k to be better adjusted to the nature of the datasets in concern.

4 Definitions

In this section, we give formal definitions and notations to notions that we use throughout the paper.

Let $T \in \Sigma^n$ denote the input substring where n the length of T. Let $\star \notin \Sigma$ is the suppression symbol. The character at the i-th position in T is denoted by T_i. A substring of T starting from i and ending at j is denoted by $T_{i...j}$ (note that the indexes

[1] We include studies on privacy-preserving data publishing related to text, text sanitization, and text de-identification here, and do not discuss slight differences among them, if any.

are both inclusive). We call f an *suppression function* on Σ and $\star$ when $f : \Sigma^n \to (\Sigma \cup \{\star\})^n$ fulfills $(f(T))_i = T_i$ or $\star$. Regions on a string T are denoted by pairs of integers $r = (i, j)$. i and j are called the beginning and end of the region r, denoted by $r.left$ and $r.right$.

We say that a string T fulfills ***substring k-anonymity*** when every substring of T that does not contain the suppression symbol $\star$, occurs at least $(k-1)$ times elsewhere in the string, allowing overlaps. For example, when $T =$ `abracadabra` and $f_1(T) =$`abra⋆a⋆abra`, $f_1(T)$ is a 2-anonymized string of T because all substrings with no "$\star$" in it, i.e., `abra` and `a`, occur twice or more in T. This is formally defined as follows.

Definition 4.1. *Let f an suppression function on Σ and $\star$. Let $S(T')$ an a set of substrings of T' such that $S(T') \triangleq \{(T')_{i\dots j} \mid 0 \le i \le j < n, \forall c \in T'_{i\dots j} c \ne \star\}$. A string $f(T) \in (\Sigma \cup \star)^n$ or is a **k-anonymized string** of $T \in \Sigma^n$, or fulfills **substring k-anonymity**, if $\forall s \in S(f(T))$ has at least k occurrences in T.*

In what follows, we refer to strings that fulfill the above definition of substring k-anonymity as *k-anonymized strings*. If for $\forall T \in \Sigma^n$ $f(T)$ is a k-anonymized string, we call f a *k-anonymity suppression function* or *k-anonymizer function*. We say that a substring S' of an anonymized string $S \in (\Sigma \cup \{\star\})^n$ is *continuous* when $S' \in \Sigma^n$.

5 Method

In this section we introduce a method for realizing the suppression function using k-repeating substrings defined in Section 4. In order to make it practical, our objective is to have an algorithm with following properties: it is an efficient ans scalable algorithm, which always transforms the input string into a k-anonymized string (i.e., no continuous substring will occur less than k times therein), suppressing only a reasonably small number of characters.

These properties are proven in the later part of this section, and empirically evaluated in Section 6.

We divide the problem of finding substring k-anonymity suppression into two steps. We first identify all parts of the input string T that have k or more occurrences in T, and then fill the original strings with these repeats so that no pair of repeats neighbors each other. More specifically, the two components are: (1) finding *generalized maximum repeats* that occurs at least k times in the input string, and (2) translating generalized maximum repeats into a set of regions on the input string that need to be suppressed.

Table 1: Example of the suffix array and longest common prefix array of $T =$ `abracadabra$`

i	SA_i	LCP_i	$T_{SA_i \dots n}$
0	11	0	`$`
1	10	0	`a$`
2	7	1	`abra$`
3	0	4	`abracadabra$`
4	3	1	`acadabra$`
5	5	1	`adabra$`
6	8	0	`bra$`
7	1	3	`bracadabra$`
8	4	0	`cadabra$`
9	6	0	`dabra$`
10	9	0	`ra$`
11	2	2	`racadabra$`

5.1 Generalized maximum repeats

We define generalized maximum repeats of the string T and the threshold k as a set of repeating substrings that have at least k occurrences in T, allowing overlaps. Once these repeats are identified in the string, it is straightforward to derive a greedy algorithm for finding suppression that ensures substring k-anonymity by a greedy algorithm, as we will describe in Section 5.2.

Our algorithm for generalized maximum repeats is inspired by the *maximum-repeats* algorithm proposed by Ilie and Smyth (2011) and contains it as a special case where $k = 2$. We start by briefly revisiting their method and then we describe how to generalize it for general k's.

Ilie and Smyth (2011) use longest common prefix (LCP) arrays to identify *maximum repeating substrings* (or *maximum repeats* for short). In their definition, a substring is a repeat when it occurs elsewhere in the enclosing string, and a maximum repeating substring is a repeat with the property that extending the substring by one character, either towards the beginning or the end, makes it a unique substring that occurs exactly once (i.e., not a repeat any more). Their algorithm achieves linear-time complexity, based on the fact that suffix arrays and LCP arrays can be constructed in $O(n)$ time. We show that by introducing *generalized common prefix arrays* we can induce a generalized algorithm to extract substring regions that occur at least k times.

Let us first recall properties of LCPs in relation to repeats. LCPs are defined on lexicographically sorted suffixes of the string in concern (Crochemore et al., 2007). LCP_i is defined as the length of the maximum common prefix of two lexicographically neighboring suffixes $T_{SA_{i-1}..n}$ and $T_{SA_i..n}$, where T is the string in concern and SA is the suffix array of T. When using LCPs for finding repeats, an important property to be utilized is that LCP arrays represent substrings that repeats twice or more in the given string (or corpus). Let us see how it works by the example shown in Table 1. The entries with $LCP_i = 0$ do not contain any repeats in prefixes of their corresponding suffixes. The entries with $LCP_i > 0$ corresponds to repeats, which may or may not be textitmaximum; non-maximum repeats are entirely contained by at least one larger repeat, and may be considered redundant. For example, in Table 1, the entry at $i = 2$ implies a repeat $T_{10...10}$ = $T_{7...7}$ = a, and the entry at $i = 2$ a repeat $T_{7...10}$ = $T_{0...3}$ = abra. Only $T_{7...10}$ is maximum among the substrings $T_{7...7}$ and $T_{7...10}$.

We define generalized LCP array $GLCP_i$ of $T \in \Sigma^n$ and k as the lengths of common prefixes of $(T_{SA_{i-1}...n}, T_{SA_{i-2}...n}, \ldots T_{SA_{i-k+1}...n})$. Intuitively, just like $LCP_i > 0$ corresponds to existence of a repeat (with at least 2 occurrences), an entry with $GLCP_i > 0$ indicates the substring of T starting at SA_i with length $GLCP_i$ has length k or more occurrences in T.

We present Algorithm 1 for finding generalized maximum repeats of T and k. The main objective of this algorithm is to obtain spans on T that are maximum repeats as an integer array, mr, where $\mathsf{mr}_j = i$ denotes a maximum repeat when $i >= 0$.

First, suffix arrays and longest common prefix (LCP) are constructed at Line 1. Note that the construction of suffix arrays requires $O(n)$ time and space. Likewise, LCP arrays can be constructed in linear time and space. For their details, we refer readers to (Nong et al., 2011) and (Kasai et al., 2001). In the experiments, we use a publicly-available implementation *jsuffixarrays*[2].

Algorithm 1: Finding generalized maximum repeats of T and k

input : A string $T \in \Sigma^n$, an integer k
output: A set of substring regions

1 mr $\leftarrow$ size-n array filled with -1's ;
2 glcp $\leftarrow$ size-n array filled with -1's ;
3 sa $\leftarrow$ suffix array of T ;
4 lcp $\leftarrow$ longest common prefixes of T ;
5 **for** $i \leftarrow 0$ **to** n **do**
6 | $\mathsf{glcp}_i \leftarrow min(\mathsf{lcp}_{i-k+1}, \ldots, \mathsf{lcp}_i)$
7 **end**
// For each of glcp_i, update the corresponding entry in mr
8 **for** $i \leftarrow 0$ **to** n **do**
9 | $\mathsf{G} \leftarrow max(\mathsf{glcp}_{i-k+2}, \ldots, \mathsf{glcp}_{i+2})$
| **if** $\mathsf{G} \geq 1 \wedge \mathsf{sa}_i < \mathsf{mr}_{\mathsf{sa}_i+\mathsf{G}-1}$ **then**
10 | | $\mathsf{mr}_{\mathsf{sa}_i+\mathsf{G}-1} \leftarrow \mathsf{sa}_i$
11 | **end**
12 **end**
13 **return** $\{(i, j) \mid 0 \leq j < n \wedge i = \mathsf{mr}_j\}$

At Line 5 we create the generalized longest common prefix array of T and k, mr. This array indicates existence of substrings that occur at least k times by taking the minimum of k consecutive values on longest common prefixes. An value mr_j of mr, when it is non-negative, indicates a repeat beginning at mr_j and (inclusively) ending at i.

At Line 8, for each generalized common prefix, entries of mr are overwritten when the newly found repeat is longer than the corresponding span the entry stores.

At Line 13, we collect maximum repeats as spans from non-negative values of mr.

Sketch of proof. It is trivial to show the result of Algorithm 1 contains substrings that ocurrs k times or more. We show that they are maximum by contradiction. Assume a span $T[i \ldots j]$ in the result of Algorithm 1 is not a maximum k-repeat. Then $T[i-1 \ldots j]$ or $T[i \ldots j+1]$ must be a k-repeat.

[2] *jsuffixarrays* is a Java library written by Dawid Weiss and available at `http://labs.carrotsearch.com/jsuffixarrays.html`.

If the former, there exists n where $MR[i] > n$ and $LCP[n] \geq k$. As some point in iteration, $MR[i]$ becomes n. Because $MR[i]$ monotonically increases, when the algorithm terminates, $MR[i] \geq n$. The same can be derived similarly for he latter case. This is a contradiction. [3] □

5.1.1 Analysis

The time complexity of Algorithm 1 is given by:

Theorem 5.1. *Algorithm 1 is $O(kn)$ in time, where k is the minimum frequency of the maximum repeats in the output, and n is the size of the input string.*

Sketch of proof. Construction of suffix arrays and longest common prefix arrays takes $O(n)$ time (Nong et al., 2011; Kasai et al., 2001). The loop starting from Line 5 is $O(kn)$, because it iterates over size-n array and each iteration takes $O(k)$ time for finding the minimum among the k elements. Similarly, the loop starting from Line 8 is $O(kn)$ for there are n iterations and each iteration takes $O(k)$ for the max operation. By summing these up, the Algorithm 1 is $O(kn)$ in time. □

Note that, in practice, we can usually assume that k is a small constant. According to our experiments, typically preferred values of k are less than 10. Yet we expect that the larger the corpus size is, the larger the optimal value of k slowly becomes.

5.2 Translating maximum repeats into suppression

As seen in Figure 1, maximum repeats may overlap with each other. In Algorithm 2, we present a greedy algorithm translate a set of regions on T into a set of non-overlapping suppressed regions, conforming the substring k-anonymity we defined in Section 4.

Assuming that hash maps and hash sets work in $O(1)$ time for each operation, we have the following time complexity of Algorithm 2:

Algorithm 2: Greedy algorithm for turning repeats into suppression

input : A set of regions S
output: A set of positions in T

1 map $\leftarrow$ a hash map from integer to a hash set of pairs of integers ;
2 regions $\leftarrow$ an empty list of integers;
3 flags $\leftarrow$ a all-false Boolean array ;
4 add $\forall$r $\in S$ to map$_{r.right-r.left}$
5 regions $\leftarrow$ map.$values$
6 **foreach** $(s, e) \in$ regions **do**
7   **if** ($s == 0 \lor$ flags$_{s-1}$ = false) $\land$ flags$_{e+1}$ = false **then**
8   **for** $i \leftarrow$s to e **do**
9   flags$_i \leftarrow$ true
10   **end**
11   **end**
12 **end**
13 **return** $\{i \mid 0 \leq i < n \land$ flags$_i$ = true$\}$

Theorem 5.2. *When $max(\{r.right - r.left \mid r \in S\})$ is $O(1)$, Algorithm 2 is $O(|S|)$ in time.*

Sketch of proof. In Algorithm 2, every operation on the hash map and list takes $O(1)$ in time. Line 4-5 takes $O(|S|)$ and $O(1)$ operations. Line 6-12 takes $O(|S| + 1) = O(|S|)$ operations as per assumption. Summing these up, Algorithm 2 is $O(|S|)$ in time. □

We end this subsection by noting that the condition in Theorem 5.2 often holds in natural language in practice. For example, in a preliminary experiment we obtained 63 regions for a 3 mega-byte string in Japanese. In fact, unless one deals with strings that are hardly found in natural language, such as de Bruijn strings(Crochemore et al., 2007) [4] as inputs, it is reasonable to think each repeat occupies only a small region of the parent string, making $r.right - r.left$ small.

5.3 Covering with k-repeating substrings

By simply sequentially combining Algorithm 1 and 2, we induce a k-anonymization method as Algo-

[3] To empirically evaluate the correctness of the Algorithm 3, we naively enumerate all continuous substrings in the processed string and count their frequencies in the original string. When, due to its quadratic time complexity, exhaustive trial is unrealistic (for example, when the input size is larger than tens of megabytes), we perform the test for a randomly selected sample of continuous substrings. We performed the test above against samples are taken from MED in Section 6, varying sizes between 1% and 10%, all of whose results passed the condition of the substring k-anonymity.

[4] Ilie and Smyth (2011) mention de Bruijn strings as strings with highest possible numbers of maximum repeats.

rithm 3. A length threshold l for repeats may be set to filter out too-short repeats. The default value of l is 1, which allows repeats of all lengths. It works also as a parameter to prefer whether scattered suppression (lower l) or continuous suppression (higher l).

Algorithm 3: Algorithm for covering with k-repeating substrings based on generalized longest common prefixes

input : A string $T \in \Sigma^n$, a frequency threshold $k \geq 2$, a lower-bound l for the length of repeats

output: A string retaining its k-repeating substrings only

```
def findMaximumRepeats (T, k):
    yield to Algorithm 1
def findCovering (R):
    yield to Algorithm 2
mr ← {r | r ⊂ findMaximumRepeats(T, k) ∧ r.right − r.left + 1 ≥ l} ;
indexes ←findCovering (mr) ;
return {S_i | if 0 ≤ i < n∧ (if i ∈ indexes then T_i else ⋆)}
```

Two theorems 5.1 and 5.2 imply that our anonymization method of covering with k-repeating substrings, which simply calls Algorithm 1 and then feeds its result to 2, is $O(kn)$. When k is considered constant, it is $O(n)$ in time. In order to derive this conclusion, we suffice it to note that the size of the input to Algorithm 2, which is the output of Algorithm 1, is $O(n)$ where n is the size of the input string, because the size of the array MR in Algorithm 1 is n.

6 Experiments

We empirically evaluate the efficiency and scalability of the proposed method, described in Section 5.

6.1 Materials

We use following materials and implementation for the experiments.

Corpora Table 2 summarizes statistics of the corpora we used for the following experiments. In addition to a de-identification dataset, our primary target, we add corpora of Japanese, a language without word boundary in its orthography, and corpora of differing sizes for comparison and scalability evaluation. DEID is a part of the datasets used in the *i2b2* shared task of text de-identification (Uzuner et al., 2007), containing diagnostic reports written in English. The portion of the *i2b2* dataset we evaluate on is taken from its training set, and consists of 388 records. The remaining 283 of the training set were used to find the optimal parameter values of the length lower-bound l (described in Section 5.3) and percentage R (described in Section 6.2). MED refers to a corpora composed of 50,000 English abstracts, extracted from the publicly-available MEDLINE abstracts [5] containing abstracts of research paper in the biomedical domain in English. WKT refers to an approximately 38% sample an XML dump of a publicly-available multilingual dictionary, containing 31,894 entries [6]. All corpora were preprocessed to remove XML tags expressing meta information.

Table 2: Statistics of the corpora used to evaluate the k-repeating substrings method based on generalized longest common prefixes (the proposed method). Sizes are in characters. E: English. J: Japanese.

Name	Size	Content type
DEID	1,283,481	diagnostic reports (E)
MED	7,192,989	research papers (E)
WKT	45,838,626	dictionary (J)

Implementation We implemented our method using Scala in 714 lines excluding comments and blank lines. We used*jsuffixarrays*[2], a suffix array and longest common prefixes library, and a standard Java virtual machine [7]. As soon as this work is published, we will provide our implementation as a Java library, publicly available through our website[8][9]. We ran the

[5]The MEDLINE abstracts are available at `http://mbr.nlm.nih.gov/`.

[6]We used the dump of its Japanese edition with current versions only, available at `http://dumps.wikimedia.org/jawiktionary/20130202/`.

[7]We used Java Standard Edition Runtime Environment 1.6.0_22, Java HotSpot 64-Bit Server VM.

[8]`http://www.yusuke.matsubara.name`

[9]`http://github.com/whym/growthring`

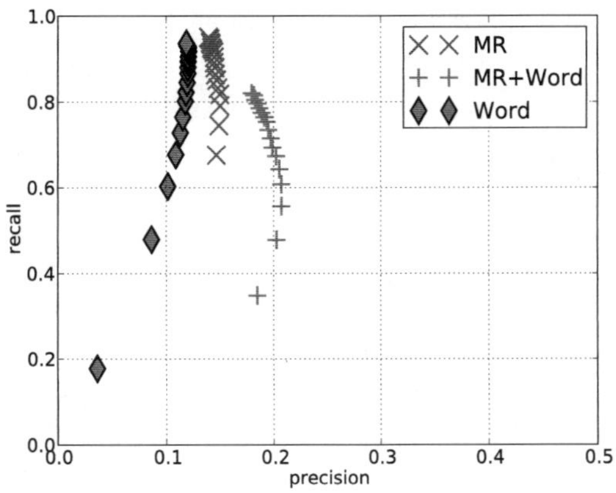

Figure 2: Recall-Precision curves of the proposed generalized maximum repeats algorithm ("MR"), the baseline word-based method ("Word"), and their hybrid ("MR+Word") against the *i2b2* dataset DEID described in Table 2. Each plot point corresponds to different k ranging from 2 to 18. Parameters were chosen with a development set were $l = 6$ and $R = 0.2$ (See Sections 5.3 and 6.2 for their definitions).

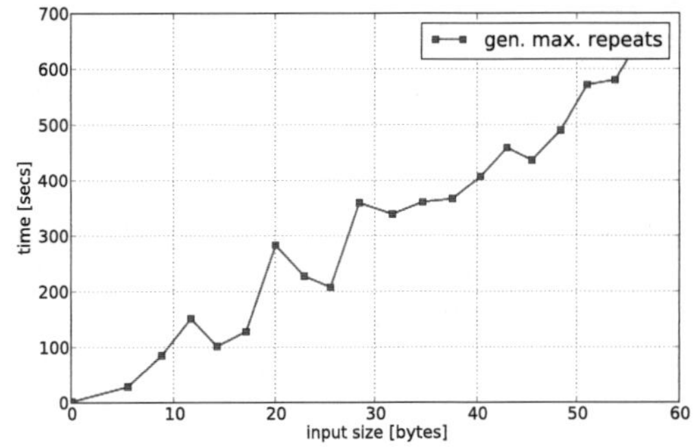

Figure 3: Computational time of the proposed method (gen. max. repeats) for covering with k-repeating substrings against the input size where $k = 4$. (WKT in Table 2)

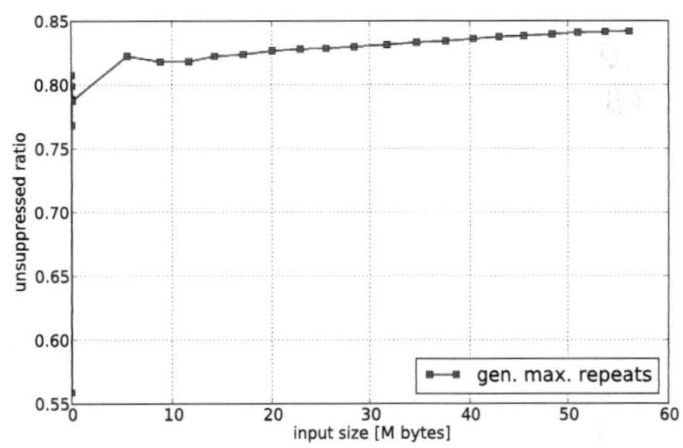

Figure 4: Ratio of the number of positions unsuppressed by the proposed method (gen. max. repeats) to cover the input string with its k-repeating substrings where $k = 4$, against the input length. (WKT in Table 2)

program on Java 1.6.0_22 on Linux 2.6.26-2-amd64. All experiments were performed on a computer with Intel Xeon E5410 2.33 G Hz (2×4 cores) CPU and 24GB memory.

6.2 Evaluation metrics

Precision-Recall We use token-based precision-recall against the de-identification dataset of *i2b2* (Uzuner et al., 2007) to measure the utility of the algorithms. We take tokens labeled as "PHI" (protected health information) in the *i2b2* dataset as positive examples, and the others negative examples. To decide whether a partially suppressed token by an algorithm should be protected or not, we introduce a parameter R ($0\% \leq R \leq 100\%$) and interpret tokens with more than R % of its component characters suppressed as protected (or positive) tokens in the system's output. We also introduce a set of white-space characters and other symbols which are to be unsuppressed regardless of the judgement by the algorithm. This is necessary in order to ensure that all token boundaries are kept consistent to allow comparison, and to ensure that most obvious tokens with only one character are caught. The set is composed of 16 characters including space, new line character, tab, parentheses, etc.

Time To evaluate the scalability, we measure the wall-clock time elapsed while running the program.

Unsuppressed ratio We measure the ratio of unsuppressed positions on the input string T against the length $n = |T|$. Larger values are preferred because it preserves a larger part of the text, offering better readability and usefulness of the published text.

6.3 Results

Figure 2 shows precision-recall curves of the methods against the DEID dataset, with plot points obtained by varying the threshold value of k of repeats, ranging from 2 to 18. The proposed method gave higher precisions with a similar level of recall. Moreover, a hybrid method "MR+Word", which we will discuss in Section 7, provides an alternative inclined towards even better precision with a slight drop in recall.

We measured the running time varying the input from less than 1% to 100% of the corpora. Figure 3 shows the running time for samples with different sizes taken from the corpus WKT. It is reasonable to say the running time is linear to the input size. The fluctuations found in the elapsed times are considered to be due to locality in the repetitiveness of the text, and fluctuations in IO responses of the computer.

Figure 4 shows how much portion of the input string survives after covering with k-repeating substrings where $k = 4$. Notice, except for the initial fluctuations for the inputs of less than 10 mega bytes, that the ratio consistently raises along the increase of the input. This is natural because, having k fixed, the larger the original string is, the more substrings may have frequencies higher than or equal to k.

7 Discussions and future work

Here we discuss the theoretical and empirical results given in Sections 5 and 6, and describe possible improvements of the proposed method.

7.1 Effectiveness

We consider that precision and recall shown in Figure 2 are a promising indication that our approach using generalized maximum repeats provides a basic unsupervised baseline and complementary information that might be unavailable with existing approaches. Higher precision values combined with similar recall values of the proposed method against the word-based baseline mean that the proposed method gives a less noisy hint to indicate regions with information that should be suppressed.

It was unsurprising to see that the performance of the unsupervised methods discussed so far is not close to that of supervised methods which score at more than 90% in F-measure as reported in (Meystre et al., 2010). We argue again that our goal is to find a promising unsupervised way to augment existing supervised methods, and that our results support our hypothesis that covering with k-repeating substrings yields a useful result, when no word boundary or morphological boundary is assumed.

A manual inspection of the results revealed that the proposed maximum repeats algorithm not only outperformed the word-based baseline, but also it produced a suppression pattern that was significantly different from the baseline. To demonstrate this, we implemented a simple hybrid method of the two; the hybrid method is a simple consensus of the word-based baseline and the maximum repeats method. Its results shown in Figure 2 demonstrates that this re-examination step yields better precision scores, by a considerable margin, that were unattainable by any of the two.

7.2 Document-aware anonymity

Natural language data may have informal structure with units such as documents where repeats inside of a unit may be ignored in the context of anonymization, because those occurrences are may not independent; without a notion of document it is hard to properly treat cases where a patient name is repeatedly mentioned in one document which describes the patient itself, but does not occur elsewhere in a document collection. One way to incorporate document boundaries in our framework may be employing ideas of pseudo characters for document boundaries from (Yamamoto and Church, 2001).

7.3 Computational efficiency

We consider the computational time of the proposed method is satisfactorily small both in theory (Theorems 5.1 and 5.2), and in practice (Figure 3) up to the scale of 60 megabytes. We also note that our Scala implementation is not fully optimized, allowing a room for further software optimization for speedup.

Nevertheless, for massive text data, which may be larger than the typical RAM size, our method may still need to introduce a way to reduce the memory footprint. Although we believe that the space complexity of the proposed algorithm is $O(n)$ as well, it is still demanding of space in practice, because it stores all the arrays on memory. Following other work dealing with massive data using suffix arrays, solutions to memory constraints may include distributed processing (Kulla and Sanders, 2007), external memory algorithms (Bingmann et al., 2012) and succinct data structures.

8 Conclusion

In this paper, we have introduced the problem of covering a string with its k-repeating substrings, and given efficient algorithm to solve it. Based on the hypothesis that rare substrings are likely to contain sensitive information, we have applied it to the task of text de-identification. Analyses on its computational complexity and empirical evaluations using real-world data have shown that the method may augment traditional ones for privacy-preserving publishing of textual data.

Acknowledgments

We thank Prof. Eiji Aramaki for his inspiring suggestions. We thank anonymous reviewers for their valuable comments.

References

Charu C. Aggarwal and Philip S. Yu. 2007. On privacy-preservation of text and sparse binary data with sketches. In *Proceedings of SIAM International Conference on Data Mining (SDM07)*.

Balamurugan Anandan, Chris Clifton, Wei Jiang, Mummoorthy Murugesan, Pedro Pastrana-Camacho, and Luo Si. 2012. t-plausibility: Generalizing words to desensitize text. *Trans. Data Privacy*, 5(3):505–534, December.

Alan R Aronson. 2001. Effective mapping of biomedical text to the umls metathesaurus: the metamap program. In *Proceedings of the AMIA Symposium*, page 17. American Medical Informatics Association.

Timo Bingmann, Johannes Fischer, and Vitaly Osipov. 2012. Inducing suffix and lcp arrays in external memory. In *Proceedings of Meeting on Algorithm Engineering and Experiments (ALENEX)*.

Venkatesan T. Chakaravarthy, Himanshu Gupta, Prasan Roy, and Mukesh K. Mohania. 2008. Efficient techniques for document sanitization. In *Proceedings of the 17th ACM conference on Information and knowledge management*, CIKM '08, pages 843–852, New York, NY, USA. ACM.

Maxime Crochemore, Christophe Hancart, and Thierry Lecroq. 2007. *Algorithms on Strings*. Cambridge University Press.

Benjamin Fung, Ke Wang, Rui Chen, and Philip S Yu. 2010. Privacy-preserving data publishing: A survey of recent developments. *ACM Computing Surveys (CSUR)*, 42(4):14.

Lucian Ilie and W. F Smyth. 2011. Minimum unique substrings and maximum repeats. *Fundamenta Informaticae*, 110(1–4):183–195.

Wei Jiang, Mummoorthy Murugesan, Chris Clifton, and Luo Si. 2009. t-plausibility: Semantic preserving text sanitization. In *Computational Science and Engineering, 2009. CSE'09. International Conference on*, volume 3, pages 68–75. IEEE.

Toru Kasai, Gunho Lee, Hiroki Arimura, Setsuo Arikawa, and Kunsoo Park. 2001. Linear-time longest-common-prefix computation in suffix arrays and its applications. In *Proceedings of the 12th Annual Symposium on Combinatorial Pattern Matching*, number 2089 in Lecture Notes in Computer Science, pages 181–192.

Fabian Kulla and Peter Sanders. 2007. Scalable parallel suffix array construction. *Parallel Computing*, 33(9):605–612.

Clete A Kushida, Deborah A Nichols, Rik Jadrnicek, Ric Miller, James K Walsh, and Kara Griffin. 2012. Strategies for de-identification and anonymization of electronic health record data for use in multicenter research studies. *Medical Care*, 50:S82–S101.

Junqiang Liu. 2012. Privacy preserving disclosing of unstructured data. *Journal of Information and Computational Science*, 9(1):75–83.

Udi Manber and Gene Myers. 1993. Suffix arrays: a new method for on-line string searches. *SIAM Journal on Computing*, 22(5):935–948.

Stephane M Meystre, Forrest J Friedlin, Brett R South, Shuying Shen, and Matthew H Samore. 2010. Automatic de-identification of textual documents in the electronic health record: a review of recent research. *BMC Medical Research Methodology*, 10(70).

Ge Nong, Sen Zhang, and Wai Hong Chan. 2011. Two efficient algorithms for linear suffix array construction. *IEEE Transactions on Computers*, 60(10):1471–1484.

Latanya Sweeney. 2002. k-anonymity: A model for protecting privacy. *International Journal of Uncertainty, Fuzziness and Knowledge-Based Systems*, 10(05):557–570.

Özlem Uzuner, Yuan Luo, and Peter Szolovits. 2007. Evaluating the state-of-the-art in automatic de-identification. *Journal of American Medical Informatics Association*, 14(5):550–563.

Mikio Yamamoto and Kenneth W Church. 2001. Using suffix arrays to compute term frequency and document frequency for all substrings in a corpus. *Computational Linguistics*, 27(1):1–30.